LAW OF ENVIRONMENTAL AND TOXIC TORTS

CASES, MATERIALS AND PROBLEMS

Third Edition

By

M. Stuart Madden
Distinguished Professor of Law
Pace University School of Law

Gerald W. Boston
Late Professor of Law
Thomas M. Cooley Law School

AMERICAN CASEBOOK SERIES®

Mat #40300892

American Casebook Series and West Group are trademarks registered in the U.S. Patent and Trademark Office.

COPYRIGHT © 1994 WEST PUBLISHING CO.
© West, a Thomson business, 2001
© 2005 Thomson/West
        610 Opperman Drive
        P.O. Box 64526
        St. Paul, MN 55164–0526
        1–800–328–9352

Printed in the United States of America

ISBN 0–314–15607–0

 TEXT IS PRINTED ON 10% POST CONSUMER RECYCLED PAPER

Dedication

———

For my sons, Chris and Mike.

*

Appreciation

    The author extends his gratitude to research assistants Maryam T. Afif and Michael Stalzer for their invaluable contributions to the preparation of this Third Edition.

*

Introduction to Third Edition

Nearly five years have passed since the publication of this volume's Second Edition, and the growth and dynamism of environmental and toxic tort law continue apace with that of other areas of tort law. The ghost at the feast of modern tort law is and will for some time continue to be state and federal "Tort Reform". Opinions will be varied as to whether as modified by "reform" tort law as litigated in the United States comes closer to, or departs further from, providing substantial justice.

Chapter 1 includes a new and concise scholarly contribution that gives an effective overview of the field, including its relation to statutory environmental law. The volume as a whole presents new decisional material in a broad range of important subject matters, that include: (1) nuisance, trespass and strict liability claims associated with substances ranging from gasoline to stray electricity; (2) residential realtor and home seller duties to disclose environmental contaminants such as lead paint; (3) the regulatory particularity necessary for the invocation of the negligence per se doctrine; (4) the intentional tort exception to the workers' compensation bar as applicable to a geologist assigned to a hazardous waste site; (5) the leavening of the *Daubert* gate-keeping rubric for admissible evidence of disease causation in instances of a strong temporal relation between the exposure and the harm; (6) a relaxed standard for emotional distress damages in one state's class action certification for a strict liability, nuisance and trespass claim for environmental harm; (7) punitive damages in an environmental contamination litigation that has not attracted the attention of the Supreme Court, and is, for that reason, as or more instructive doctrinally than the cases that have; and (8) as a breath of fresh air, a Fed. R. Civ. Proc. 23(b)(3) class action certification in a casino second-hand-smoke litigation.

Regarding style matters, the casebook adopts certain conveniences in furtherance of brevity and readability. When material has been deleted, either ellipses or asterisks mark it, as aesthetics dictate. Deleted authority within a decision is marked similarly, or by the notation [Cc].

I hope that law teachers and students alike find these decisions, materials and problems a provocative and effective learning experience. I welcome any comments at   .

M. STUART MADDEN

White Plains, New York
May 2005

*

Summary of Contents

―――――――――

*

Table of Contents

Table of Cases

The principal cases are in bold type. Cases cited or discussed in the text are in roman type. References are to pages. Cases cited in principal cases and within other quoted materials are not included.

*

Table of Statutes and Regulations

LAW OF ENVIRONMENTAL AND TOXIC TORTS

CASES, MATERIALS AND PROBLEMS

Third Edition

*

Chapter One

OVERVIEW: CONFLICTING PERSPECTIVES ON THE ADEQUACY OF THE TORT SYSTEM

A. GENERALLY

As a modern legal term, "tort," derived from the Latin term for "twisted," is a civil, non-contractual wrong for which an injured person may seek a "remedy" in the form of money damages. A tort is a *civil* wrong in the sense that the injured party's remedy is a civil suit brought by a private party for compensatory damages, as distinct from a suit brought by the government for civil or criminal monetary penalties.

Environmental and toxic torts comprise harms to persons, to property, or to the environment due to the toxicity of a product, a substance, or a process.[1] Unlike the injuries to persons or property that are conventional to many other torts, the injurious consequences of the toxic harm, be it personal injury or property damage, may be latent, and thus evade detection for a period of time, even years. Indeed, a disease resulting from an exposure or multiple exposures to toxins may not be diagnosable for decades.

Tort law is the cluster of doctrines imposing civil liability, usually in the form of money damages, upon persons or businesses whose substandard conduct causes personal physical or emotional injury to others, or damage to their property.[2] In addition to, or instead of, money damages

---

1. E.g., Westley v. Ecolab, Inc., 2004 WL 1068805 (E.D. Pa. 2004) (allegation of chemical burns received from use of defendant's floor-cleaning compound); Cutlip v. Norfolk S. Corp., 2003 Ohio 1862, ___ N.E.2d ___ (Ohio Ct. App. 2003) (employee locomotive engineer allegation that he contracted asthma from inhalation of diesel fumes); E.I. du Pont de Nemours and Company, Inc. v. C.R. Robinson, 923 S.W.2d 549 (Tex.1995) (action against fungicide manufacturer for damage to orchard).

2. An popular definition of tort law as comprising liability for civil, non-contractual, non-statutory harm is, today, somewhat misleading. For example, the remedy for breach of the implied warranty of merchantability, UCC 2–314, providing money damages for toxic harm is by its terms, contractual. But when employed as a sepa-

the environmental tort plaintiff may seek equitable relief in the form of an injunction or order in abatement.

Moreover, modern environmental and toxic tort law is substantially interwoven with provisions of state and federal statutes pertaining to subjects such as burdens of proof, liability, and comparative fault. By way of illustration: (1) a business' failure to comply with a standard of care established by a labeling regulation might, under state law, be deemed negligence *per se*; or (2) a state or federal environmental statute may vest in individuals or businesses the right to pursue private cost recovery lawsuits against a polluter.

1. TORT GOALS AND THEIR APPLICATION

It is accepted generally that the goals of tort law are these: (1) assignment of responsibility, in money damages or equitable relief, to those responsible for creating a risk that produces harm; (2) requiring businesses that employ processes or sell products to "internalize" the total cost of their activities, including liability (most frequently third-party insurance) costs; (3) effectuating corrective justice and fairness by requiring the compensation of persons for personal injury or property damage caused by another's tortious conduct; (4) deterrence of further unreasonably hazardous conduct by the responsible party and others engaged in similar pursuits; and (5) reduction of avoidable accident costs, through the encouragement of safer discharge of existing practices, and promotion of innovation, such as changes in processes, transportation, disposal, design, formulation, packaging, or labeling that will reduce or eliminate unreasonable hazards.

In an environmental or toxic tort suit, plaintiff most frequently sues the putative tortfeasor for compensatory damages, *i.e.*, a monetary award calculated to remedy the harm defendant has caused, compensating the injured party for the loss or harm suffered. When the toxic harm is to property, or to an ongoing business, compensatory damages can be assessed on the basis of lost profits, typically down-time, and related economic loss. In these instances compensatory damages may come close to placing the injured party in the economic position he would have enjoyed but for defendant's conduct, fulfilling a restorative objective.

Where, on the other hand, the harm suffered by defendant's wrongdoing is personal physical injury, emotional harm, disease, or death, these losses cannot be entirely compensated for. Money damages cannot restore the plaintiff to his pre-tort condition, and it would be uncommon that a prevailing plaintiff would have made an *ex ante* agreement to sustain an injury or disease in return for an award of money damages.

rate count in a multi-count complaint, the proof required (showing that a substance is "unfit for its ordinary purpose" as opposed to in a "defective condition") and the remedies available (money damages for past, current and sometimes even prospective harm, as well as orders of abatement and remediation, or an injunction), the application of this implied warranty strongly resembles that of a plaintiff's count alleging one or more environmental torts.

Nonetheless, a judge's or a jury's finding of liability and the award of money damages in a toxic tort claim provides the best recompense available through the American legal system.

There are, of course, variations on these themes. Statutes may confer a specialized standing status upon a plaintiff so that a noncompensatory but remedial "citizen suit" claim may be brought to force compliance with state or federal environmental statutes. In addition, when defendant's injurious conduct is of a continuing nature, a court may enjoin further similar conduct. A defendant failing to comply with the requirements of such an injunction or order in abatement may be held in contempt of court and may also be subject to money penalties.

In addition to compensatory damages, punitive damages may be awarded upon plaintiff's showing that defendant's conduct was of such an aggravated and reprehensible nature as to warrant financial punishment in addition to the burden of compensating plaintiff for the injury sustained. See generally, TXO Production Corp. v. Alliance Resources Corp., 509 U.S. 443, 113 S.Ct. 2711, 125 L.Ed.2d 366 (1993). Punitive damages are not intended to compensate plaintiff for the harm suffered, but rather to punish a particularly blameworthy defendant who has acted in knowing or reckless disregard of the interests of plaintiff, and to serve to deter that defendant, and others, from engaging in future similar risk-elevating or hazardous conduct.

2. TYPICAL ENVIRONMENTAL OR TOXIC TORT CLAIMS

The harm associated with a toxic or environmental tort will include injury to both person and property. It may take the form of contamination of groundwater by inappropriate waste disposal,[3] or the administration of residential or agricultural pesticides.[4] The toxic tort harm may arise from a worker's exposure to hazardous chemicals in the workplace, such as by inhalation of respirable carcinogens.[5] An injury may be personal, physical injury to a worker, a patient, a product user or consumer, or a bystander. A person's physical injury may range from nausea to neurological damage or death. See generally, Shorter v. Champion Home Builders Co., 776 F.Supp. 333 (N.D.Ohio 1991) (claim against homebuilders asserting injurious exposure to formaldehyde vapors, and

3. See, e.g., Redland Soccer Club, Inc. v. Department of Army of U.S., 548 Pa. 178, 696 A.2d 137 (Pa. 1997) (held: medical monitoring relief available under Pennsylvania law for claims arising from toxic wastes deposited in landfill later converted to a soccer field).

4. See, e.g., Coffin v. Orkin Exterminating Co., Inc., 20 F.Supp.2d 107 (D.Me.1998) (suit against exterminator arising out of application of pesticides in office building).

5. For discussion of illustrative claims, see Brent M. Rosenthal, Toxic Torts and Mass Torts (Texas), 56 SMU L. Rev. 2053

(2003). For a discussion of the insurance coverage issues raised by such claims, see Belt Painting Corp. v. TIG Ins. Co., 100 N.Y.2d 377, 763 N.Y.S.2d 790, 795 N.E.2d 15 (N.Y. 2003) (insurance coverage issues raised by worker's claim that he was sickened by vapors and fumes in the course of his work as a paint stripper for the insured's business); Continental Casualty Co. v. Rapid–American Corp., 80 N.Y.2d 640, 593 N.Y.S.2d 966, 609 N.E.2d 506 (1993) (evaluating insurer's duty to defend actions for personal injuries sustained through exposure to asbestos).

alleging diverse personal injuries, including lethargy, headaches and emotional harm). On particular facts, the complainant may be able to recover expenses for the future medical monitoring or surveillance of his physical condition or disease progression, or for the emotional distress associated with his illness.

Various health procedures may give rise to toxic tort claims, with such claims ranging from harmful radiological exposure to x-rays, to treatment with potentially toxic medical devices or implants, or to employment of dental surgery products containing paraformaldehyde that plaintiff alleges have leached into his blood system.[6]

As in any tort litigation, the claimant must prove causation. Expert evidence of causation is an invariable necessity, and at the trial stage requires determination of whether the experts' methodology is reliable and helpful to the jury in weighing a fact in issue–irrespective of whether the trial judge assigns credibility to the expert's conclusion. See Daubert v. Merrell Dow Pharmaceuticals, Inc., 509 U.S. 579, 113 S.Ct. 2786, 125 L.Ed.2d 469 (1993) (proposed causation testimony of plaintiff's experts in Bendectin litigation). See also General Electric Company v. Joiner, 522 U.S. 136, 118 S.Ct. 512, 139 L.Ed.2d 508 (1997) (standard of review of district court's order to exclude scientific evidence); Allison v. McGhan Med. Corp., 184 F.3d 1300 (11th Cir.1999) (affirming trial court's exclusion of breast implant litigant's causation experts).

Toxic tort liability and pharmaceutical products liability often converge, and this is particularly true in long latency disease claims in which the plaintiff is unable to identify his exposure to a particular manufacturer's product, substance, or pharmaceutical. Some courts have permitted the tortfeasor identification problem to be resolved on a theory of "market-share" liability or modifications thereof. Plaintiffs have sought to apply market-share liability to toxic products other than pharmaceuticals, such as HIV-contaminated anti-coagulant blood products, lead paint pigments and asbestos. Accordingly, the casebook does explore drug products liability suits bearing on these and similar subjects.

B. SPECIAL CHARACTERISTICS OF ENVIRONMENTAL TORT CLAIMS

1. GENERALLY

The environmental or toxic tort claimant frequently phrases a complaint in terms of multiple theories of recovery. For example, in the

---

6. See, in turn, Faya v. Almaraz, 329 Md. 435, 620 A.2d 327 (1993) (plaintiff seeking recovery for fear of contracting AIDS following treatment by surgeon infected with the virus; held: trial court erred in dismissing claims) and Doe v. Noe, 303 Ill.App.3d 139, 236 Ill.Dec. 461, 707 N.E.2d 588 (Ill. Ct. App. 1998) (dismissing similar claim on the basis of failure to show actual exposure). See also Ellingwood v. Stevens, 564 So.2d 932 (Ala.1990) (claim of inade-quate shielding of patient's spinal cord during radiation therapy); Spitzfaden v. Dow Corning Corp., 619 So.2d 795 (La.App.1993) (silicone breast implant litigation), reversed for trial court irregularities in class action certification in 833 So.2d 512 (La. Ct. App. 2002); Koslowski v. Sanchez, 576 So.2d 470(La.1991), modified on other grounds, Russo v. Vasquez, 648 So.2d 879 (La. 1995) (root canal filler use of N–2 paste containing 6.5% paraformaldehyde).

well-water contamination suit of Merry v. Westinghouse Electric Corp., 684 F.Supp. 852 (M.D.Pa.1988), plaintiffs brought suit under theories of negligence, strict liability for abnormally dangerous activities, trespass and nuisance. Even in a modern personal injury action claiming a manufacturer of asbestos products failed to provide adequate warnings, a court may turn to the common law negligence standard to find the applicable duty. E.g., Graham v. Pittsburgh Corning Corp., 593 A.2d 567, 568 (Del.Super.1990) ("Delaware law measures the duties owed in terms of reasonableness. One's duty is to act reasonably, as a reasonably prudent [person] (or entity) would.").

2. LONG LATENCY PERIODS

Environmental or toxic torts often involve injury or damage that remains undiscovered for years after the exposure or contamination. A shipyard worker's exposure to respirable asbestos fibers may result in asbestos-related disease only years later. An electroplating plant's contamination of its property, surrounding property, or subterranean aquifers may only be discovered years thereafter when a successor owner of the property wishes to sell it. The Gulf War veteran or the agricultural worker exposed to a chemical may only be diagnosed with neurological disease or other illness many years later.

Lengthy disease etiology can compound the plaintiff's burden in proving causation. If long latency is a characteristic of the illness the plaintiff claims was caused by the defendant's toxin, the plaintiff may find that the passage of years makes it difficult to identify, much less to prove, which product or process he was exposed to. Indeed, for products ranging from DES to asbestos, many of the companies that previously produced the product may no longer be in business, complicating the location of business records. If the disease progression is a lengthy one, the defendant will often claim that any exposure to its product was incidental, and that the more likely cause of the plaintiff's illness was exposure to other products or processes, including "personal vice" exposures such as alcohol of tobacco. Along similar lines, the defendant may seek to prove that the plaintiff's disease is the result of "background" risks, such as the exposure to low level carcinogens, that are unfortunately frequent in today's life, in industrial cities or otherwise. Additionally, long latency periods create difficult statutes of limitation and repose problems not implicated in ordinary accident or property damage litigation.

3. PROOF OF CAUSATION

In claims for environmental or toxic harm, plaintiff must demonstrate that defendant's activity or product was a proximate cause of the resulting personal injury or damage to property. Proximate cause means that the challenged act (1) was a substantial contributing factor in bringing about the injury (or a "but for" cause), that is, it was at least "a" cause in fact of the harm; and (2) that the relationship between defendant's act and the harm is not so remote or attenuated as to suggest that the harm was not foreseeable, rendering it unfair or unreasonable to hold defendant responsible.

Due to the imperfect knowledge of disease etiology, the majority of toxic tort claims pose distinctive problems in the proof of proximate cause. In addition, the lapse of time often makes it quite difficult for plaintiff to identify the particular substance involved, and the specific actor who was responsible. Years after exposure to respirable asbestos, a pipe fitter may be unable to identify the particular manufacturer of asbestos products he was exposed to. Even where a particular manufacturer's asbestos products, or chemical solvents, or pesticide can be identified, the passage of time may hinder plaintiff's demonstration of the times, circumstances and degree of exposure suffered.

4. ROLE OF EXPERT SCIENTIFIC OR MEDICAL TESTIMONY

As suggested, proof of causation in an environmental or toxic tort claim is often more difficult than proof in many conventional personal injury claims. Where, for example, the disease suffered by a toxic tort litigant is cancer of the liver, the plaintiff must demonstrate by a preponderance of the evidence that the toxic exposure was at least a substantial factor in the plaintiff's contracting of the illness, *i.e.,* that the disease was not simply liver cancer attributable to the "background" risk of the disease, or by other third-party exposures, or by the plaintiff's own lifestyle choices.

Because lay jurors cannot, on the basis of common knowledge, resolve the causal inquiry, plaintiff must introduce expert scientific or medical evidence that defendant's product or process was a but-for cause or a substantial contributing factor in plaintiff's injury or loss. This evidence is ordinarily described as having two components: (1) general causation; and (2) specific causation. To prove "general causation", an epidemiologist, toxicologist or other qualified risk statistician will testify that the toxic environment, product or process to which the plaintiff has been exposed is capable of causing the illness that the plaintiff now suffers. This proof of "general causation" is sometimes described as proof that the toxin "could" cause the plaintiff's illness. It is not necessary that the expert be familiar with the circumstances of the particular plaintiff, as such a premise can be the basis for a hypothetical question. As a consequence, the "basis" of an expert's evidence as to "general causation" may be studies and other scholarly, clinical or diagnostic work of others in the field.

As suggested, in some contexts, vigorous scientific debate exists as to whether the toxic substance is capable, under any circumstances, of causing the type of injury or disease that plaintiff suffers. Defendant may offer evidence that the injury or disease was caused by (1) exposure to the product of another producer; (2) exposure to a different product or substance altogether, such as alcohol or tobacco products, for which defendant should bear no responsibility; or that (3) the disease or injury is simply a background case occurring generally in the population, and for which no known cause has been identified.

For proof of "specific" or "particular" causation, the plaintiff must adduce expert evidence that his illness in particular was caused by the toxic exposure. It follows that this expert must base his opinion in part upon the specifics of the plaintiff's illness and exposures. The evidence will often be given by the plaintiff's treating physician, but it is not necessary, and the testimony of an expert toxicologist has, for example, been permitted to prove specific causation.

While the burden of proof in a tort suit follows the "preponderance of the evidence" standard, this is not the language used by physicians or allied professionals. Accordingly, in most jurisdictions the plaintiff's expert offering testimony as to "specific causation" is required to testify that "to a reasonable degree of medical certainty" the individual plaintiff's illness was caused by exposure to the individual toxin or toxins. The language "reasonable degree of medical certainty" is a phrase of art, and expert causation testimony that has departed from this stock attestation has been found to fall short of proving a plaintiff's burden of showing "specific causation".

The defendant, in turn, will ordinarily counter with experts of its own choosing who have reached conflicting conclusions as to the toxic potential of the substance involved, or who seek to discredit the diagnostic or statistical bases upon which plaintiff's witnesses relied. Accordingly, most toxic tort claims involve complicated, laborious, and expensive litigation preparation.

Additionally, defendant might argue that plaintiff's exposure to the substance was too remote (*i.e.*, plaintiff was employed at a work station far removed from the location of the toxic substance); or that the form of the toxin was such as to make exposure to it non-harmful (*i.e.*, the asbestos-containing pipe fittings in question were resin-bonded, minimizing the release of friable asbestos fibers). On all of these issues, both plaintiff and defendant will need to produce expert witnesses to support their claims or defenses.

5. RELATIONSHIP OF ENVIRONMENTAL TORT LAW TO STATUTORY ENVIRONMENTAL LAW

Manufacturers of a wide array of potentially toxic products are subject to government licensing, regulation, enforcement, and penalties. A person's act, or failure to act, regarding a toxic substance may violate such an environmental or occupational health statute or regulation. Many regulatory environmental claims involving toxic substances are brought by the federal government, claiming that defendant's conduct violated a statute or a regulation.[7] In addition, numerous state environmental statutes provide mechanisms for imposing penalties or remediation requirements upon those responsible for environmental harms.[8] This body of law, *i.e.*, public regulation of environmental or toxic harms to persons, property, or the environment, is described as "environmental law."

Most environmental suits brought pursuant to statute by a public body are called "enforcement" or "penalty" actions, in which the agency might seek civil or criminal monetary penalties. When the government prevails in a penalty or an enforcement action, any moneys recovered devolve to the government's general fund, or to special funds created by the government.

6. RECURRING THEMES IN ENVIRONMENTAL TORTS

Whenever the tort system has been faced with new classes of litigation that raise potentially unique and special problems distinguishable from the traditional tort case, *i.e.*, the automobile or other sporadic accident case, commentators and courts ask whether tort liability rules should be adjusted to accommodate such cases. The overarching question might be phrased: Can the tort system adequately accommodate society's call for providing compensation to individuals suffering from environmental harms consistent with the other objectives of tort law, such as deterrence, economic efficiency, and fairness?

The following article by Kenneth S. Abraham offers an overview of coming attractions. When the student has read this commentary, he or

---

7. A partial list of the sprawling number of statutes that pertain to toxic wrongdoing at the federal level would include the Federal Insecticide, Fungicide and Rodenticide Act ("FIFRA"), 7 U.S.C.A. § 136 et seq.; The Toxic Substances Control Act ("TSCA"), 15 U.S.C.A. § 2601 et seq.; The Surface Mining Control and Reclamation Act ("SMRCA"), 30 U.S.C.A. § 1201 et seq.; The National Environmental Policy Act ("NEPA"), 42 U.S.C.A. § 4321 et seq.; The Solid Waste Disposal Act ("SWDA"), 42 U.S.C.A. § 6093 et seq.; The Comprehensive Environmental Response, Compensation, and Liability Act ("CERCLA"), 42 U.S.C.A. § 9601 et seq.; The Occupational Safety and Health Act ("OSHA"), 29 U.S.C.A. § 651 et seq.; The Federal Water Pollution Control Act ("FWPCA") (Clean Water Act), 33 U.S.C.A. § 1251 et seq.; and The Clean Air Act ("CAA"), 42 U.S.C.A. § 7401 et seq.

8. E.g., Massachusetts Water Quality Standards, codified at Mass. Regs. Code 314, § 4.01 et seq. (2004); Michigan Natural Resources and Environmental Protection Act, Mich. Comp. Laws § 324.301 et seq.; California Hazardous Substance Account Act, West's Ann.Cal. Health & Safety Codes § 25300–04.

she may begin preliminarily to arrive at individual conclusions as to the adequacy and efficiency of the tort system's mechanisms for responding to environmental torts.

THE RELATION BETWEEN CIVIL LIABILITY AND ENVIRONMENTAL REGULATION: AN ANALYTICAL OVERVIEW[9]

Kenneth S. Abraham
41 Washburn L.J. 379 (2002)

I. THE COMMON CHARACTERISTICS OF ENVIRONMENTAL TORTS

The very notion of an "environmental tort" is somewhat indeterminate, since the category has no particular doctrinal significance. Nonetheless, four characteristics of what might be called "environmental torts" are worth noting. Taken together, these characteristics tend to render environmental torts at least arguably distinctive. These characteristics are 1) the long-latency of many environmental harms; 2) the frequent difficulty of pinpointing the party or parties responsible for causing these harms; 3) the corresponding difficulty of pinpointing the particular individuals who have suffered injury caused by harmful environmental exposure; and 4) the fact that a public regulatory regime typically has already also addressed the activity that is the subject of the private suit.

A. Long Latency of Harm

Although some environmental harms are open and obvious from the moment they occur, many occur slowly and out of sight, only to manifest themselves many years after the event that set the harm in motion. For example, certain diseases have long latency periods—i.e., periods between the time of exposure to a pollutant or contaminant and the time when a disease resulting from that exposure either occurs or becomes detectable. In contrast, some environmental harms may begin to occur immediately or soon after the release of a substance into the environment. Many of these harms are not detected or detectable, however, until many years have passed. For instance, hazardous waste may seep into groundwater and begin to migrate offsite shortly after it is deposited, but the resulting contamination of drinking water may not be discovered until much later.

The long-latent character of many environmental harms has far-reaching factual and legal implications for lawsuits seeking damages for these harms. As a factual matter, reconstructing a chain of events that occurred decades ago is likely to be far more difficult and time consuming than proving what occurred more recently. Therefore, the burden of evidentiary production shouldered by plaintiffs in environmental tort actions typically is far more onerous than in conventional cases. In addition, because the facts developed are likely to be more sparse the more distantly in the past an event occurred, decisions by the trier of fact are likely to be less well informed in such cases. Since ordinarily the burden of persuasion rests on the plaintiff, the sparsity of the factual record may also work against plaintiffs.

The legal rules governing tort actions are in effect constitutive of these factual considerations. Traditionally the plaintiff bears the burdens of production and persuasion on each element of a tort claim. Proof by a preponderance of the evidence of negligence (or in appropriate cases the requisites of strict liability), causation, and both past and future damages is therefore required. Yet because of the long latency of most of the harms at issue in environmental tort cases, evidence of exactly what the defendant or defendants did may be uncertain; scientific and medical proof of a causal connection between the defendant's conduct, whatever it was, and the plaintiff's injury may make it difficult to adduce; and because the harm at issue is often still in process, proof of future damages is likely to be necessary. Yet that is always a somewhat speculative venture.

In fact, the other common characteristics of environmental torts are each at least partly related to the uncertainties that result from the long latency of many environmental harms. Modification of the legal rules governing environmental torts—both actual and proposed—are in effect a reaction to these uncertainties.

B. The Indeterminate Defendant

As in any tort action, to prevail in an environmental tort action the plaintiff must prove, among other things, that the defendant is responsible for the harm at issue. But the source of a substance that is an environmental pollutant or contaminant is not always readily identifiable, especially if the substance was released into the environment in the distant past. Moreover, sometimes there are multiple sources. Even when all potential sources can be identified, it may be difficult or impossible to determine the proportion of each source's responsibility for the total harm that has occurred.

The cluster of issues associated with source identification is often termed the problem of the indeterminate defendant. As I will explain below, several legal doctrines have developed in response to this problem, and there have been a number of proposals for additional—and sometimes quite fundamental—changes in legal doctrine to deal with the problem of the indeterminate defendant.

C. The Indeterminate Plaintiff

Just as it is sometimes difficult to identify the party responsible for environmental injury, it may also be difficult to determine the party or parties who have been harmed by exposure to environmental pollutants or contaminants. This is the problem of the indeterminate plaintiff.

The genesis of this problem is the fact that many diseases have multiple possible causes. For most diseases there is a "background rate" at which the population contracts the disease. For example, even if exposure to a substance is known to cause a particular form of cancer in a given percentage of those exposed, some portion of the exposed population that contracts this form of cancer would have contracted the disease even absent exposure—i.e., these individuals would have figured in the background rate. Thus, an affirmative answer to the question whether exposure to a substance could have caused a particular disease in a particular plaintiff does not answer whether exposure did in fact cause the disease in that plaintiff.

This problem of the indeterminate plaintiff is often exacerbated by two factors. First, even when there is medical and scientific data on the disease-causing properties of certain substances, that data may not be sufficient to permit inferences as to the precise probability of a causal connection between exposure and harm. Yet the conventional rules governing proof of causation require at least enough precision to support a factual finding that an exposure for which the defendant is responsible was more probably than not the cause of harm suffered by the plaintiff. Second, even when data is sufficient to permit an inference as to causal probability, the only permissible inference may be that the probability that the defendant is responsible for any given plaintiff's harm is less than fifty percent. Yet under conventional rules governing proof of causation, a defendant cannot be held liable, despite the fact that it very probably caused the harm suffered by a discrete subset of all plaintiffs, absent proof regarding the particular plaintiffs whose harm was more probably than not caused by that defendant.

D. The Intersection of Public Law and Civil Liability

Public law potentially plays a role in any tort action. Statutes and regulations governing health and safety abound. These sources of public law sometimes specify the role that proof of compliance or violation is to play in tort actions; common law rules governing these issues have long dictated the role to be played by such proof in the absence of statutory specification regarding this issue.

Statutes and regulations governing activities that pose the risk of environmental harm, however, are particularly dense. At the federal level, extraordinarily detailed statutes and implementing regulations address a wide variety of environmental risks. Less visible but often equally detailed and important environmental health and safety standards exist at the state level as well. For this reason, the intersection between public law and civil liability is of particular significance in tort actions involving environmental harm. Far from being the exception, the pre-existing applicability of a public law regime to the activity that is the subject of an environmental tort action is likely to be the norm.

II. THEORIES OF LIABILITY AND REMEDIAL ALTERNATIVES

A rich array of causes of action is potentially available in cases involving environmental harm. In addition, the field has spawned a series of innovative remedial alternatives, actual and proposed, to deal with the problems of the indeterminate defendant and indeterminate plaintiff.

A. Theories of Liability

Virtually the full arsenal of tort law causes of action for physical harm is potentially available in environmental tort actions. In addition, statutory causes of action for the cost of environmental remediation are often available under federal and state law.

1. Trespass and Nuisance

These torts protect the rights of possession and peaceful enjoyment of land, respectively. Recovery in trespass is available for actual physical invasions of property. In contrast, nuisance actions traditionally remedy the kinds of non-possessory interferences typical of pollution. Nuisances are usually actionable for both personal injury and property damage.

The touchstone of liability in nuisance is the existence of an "unreasonable" interference with the interest of the plaintiff or plaintiffs. This should not be confused, however, with unreasonable conduct. A nuisance may be actionable on the ground that it is intentional, negligent, or satisfies the requirement of a strict liability cause of action. Rather, a nuisance constitutes an unreasonable interference when, under all the circumstances, the interference is substantial. Traditionally the courts "balance the equities"—taking into account the locational setting, the burden on the plaintiff, and the history of land uses in the area, among other things—in making the unreasonableness determination. Thus, air pollution in an industrialized neighborhood is less likely to constitute a nuisance than in a rural area where there has never before been any manufacturing.

2. Negligence

A cause of action for negligence—unreasonably risking foreseeable injury or damage—is of course potentially available in cases involving environmental harm. The principal hurdle that plaintiffs in such cases must overcome is the requirement that foreseeability be proved. When long-latent harm materializes many years after allegedly negligent conduct has occurred, the plaintiff must prove that, at the time the conduct occurred, the defendant knew or should have known of the risk that its conduct could cause harm. In some cases this is feasible; in others, however, it is only after the harm in question has materialized that the causal connection between that harm and the defendant's conduct becomes understood. For example, the potential for certain hazardous substances to migrate through dense soil and into groundwater is much better understood today than it was fifty years ago. Similarly, the connection between exposure to comparatively small doses of toxic substances and certain diseases may become recognized only after a sufficient number of people have been exposed over a long enough period of time to afford a statistically significant sample on which to base epidemiological studies.

Whereas the foreseeability requirement is a disadvantage for plaintiffs in a negligence case, the negligence per se doctrine is an advantage to plaintiffs. In most jurisdictions, the unexcused violation of an applicable statute or administrative regulation is negligence as a matter of law. When violation results in the same kind of harm to the same class of persons whom the statute or regulation is designed to protect, then the cause of action is complete. Foreseeability (or unforeseeability) may still play a role under the rubric of proximate cause, however, when the harm that occurs does not satisfy these requirements. Violation of a statute designed to protect against the risk of poisoning, for example, does necessarily mean that a party is liable when the substance unforeseeably causes a different kind of harm, such as a chronic disease. Moreover, as I will discuss below in Part III, some statutes are not silent about their role in tort litigation, but actually specify that role.

3. *Strict Liability*

In addition to negligence, strict liability may be imposed for injury or damage caused by "abnormally dangerous" activities. Although the requirements of this cause of action vary a bit across jurisdictions, in general the activity must pose significant foreseeable risk that cannot be eliminated even when reasonable care is exercised in the conduct of the activity. In many jurisdictions the activity must also not be a matter of common usage; in other jurisdictions a kind of sliding scale takes the degree to which the activity is a matter of common usage into account, but does not require absolutely that the activity not be a matter of common usage. * * *

4. *CERCLA Cost Recovery*

The Comprehensive Environmental Response, Compensation, and Liability Act of 1980 ("CERCLA"), sometimes known as the "Superfund" Act, creates a regime designed to accomplish the remediation of sites containing hazardous waste that pose a threat to health or the environment. Many states have enacted their own very similar "mini-Superfund" statutes applying to sites that fall outside the scope of the federal regime.

CERCLA imposes retroactive, strict, and joint and several liability for the cost of cleanup at sites to which the statute applies, on past and present owners of such a site, on parties who transported material to a site, and on parties who generated material deposited at a site. Since it is generally the federal government or a state government that has incurred these costs, these entities are the typical plaintiffs in a CERCLA or state-based cost recovery action against these "responsible parties." On occasion, however, other parties have incurred such costs and are entitled to private cost recovery. The joint-and-several liability provisions of the statutes also may result in private contribution actions brought by parties claiming that have been held liable for a disproportionate share of the cost of cleanup. Finally, CERCLA also provides for the imposition of liability on responsible parties for damage to natural resources resulting from exposure to hazardous substances at a site.

Although these statutory regimes do not impose liability for personal injury, it is common for private tort actions to parallel CERCLA and state cleanup actions, and to base their claims at least in part on the same core facts as these actions. Indeed, frequently it is the discovery of offsite drinking water contamination or personal injury that prompts the initiation of federal or state cleanup action.

5. *Dealing with the Indeterminate Defendant*

Cutting across the available causes of action is the problem of the indeterminate defendant. Whether a claim is based on nuisance, negligence, or strict liability, a separate element of each cause of action traditionally is that the defendant be proved by a preponderance of the evidence to have caused harm to the plaintiff. But because many environmental harms are the result of contributions by multiple parties, there often can be no recovery under traditional rules because of the difficulty of proving which party caused what damage.

Certain alternatives to this hard-edged rule developed mainly in products liability law, however, may find application in the environmental field as well. First, the doctrine of "alternative liability" may apply when two defendants have each breached a duty to the plaintiff but the particular defendant whose actions caused the harm in question cannot be identified. Second, when there was concert of action by a universe of defendants, each whose actions caused harm to one or more of the plaintiffs, the burden of disproving causation may be shifted to the defendants. Third, when each defendant marketed a product identical in relevant respects, but each plaintiff harmed cannot be matched up with any particular defendant's product, market-share liability may be imposed. Fourth, if a reliable proxy for causal contribution is available, then liability for damages in proportion to the amount of each defendant's contribution to the total harm suffered may be imposed. For example, where responsibility for the cost of environmental cleanup is at issue and the different pollutants pose roughly the same dangers and involve similar degrees of difficulty in remediation, then CERCLA liability can be imposed in proportion to the volume of pollutants for which each individual defendant was responsible.

This last general approach holds out the most hope for plaintiffs seeking damages for personal injuries resulting from environmental exposure. Imposing proportional liability could enable plaintiffs to circumvent the otherwise often-insurmountable hurdle of proving causation by a preponderance of the evidence. But there is considerable distance between a theoretically plausible venue of recovery and a practical rule of law. First, if proportional recovery is available in cases where the preponderance-of-the-evidence rule cannot be satisfied, consistency would seem to require that there also be proportional recovery—i.e., less than full compensation—even in cases where the rule is satisfied. That would of course work a fundamental change in the conduct of tort suits and in tort law, since it would mean that most plaintiffs would recover less than their full amount of damages. Second, even setting the consistency objection aside, we are probably a long way from being systematically able to quantify causal probabilities with the degree of precision that would be necessary to make a system of proportional liability feasible.

B. Remedial Alternatives

The imposition of civil liability is generally understood to serve two main functions: corrective justice and deterrence. Although liability for monetary damages is the remedy most frequently used to serve these functions, occasionally injunctive relief is also employed to do so. Nowhere have the characteristics of environmental torts produced more innovative and radical proposals for, as well as actual, doctrinal change than in the area of remedies.

1. Injunctive Relief

The principal common law setting in which injunctions are regularly issued involves nuisance. The traditional rule was that a successful nuisance plaintiff is entitled to damages for past losses and an injunction directing the defendant to abate the nuisance to prevent any future losses. That rule has eroded somewhat in recent times, at least in part because of judicial recognition of the role that environmental regulation plays in controlling activities that create large-scale nuisances. As a consequence, plaintiffs are sometimes limited to the damages remedy for future losses.

CERCLA also contains an injunctive remedy that operates in tandem with its cost-recovery provisions. Instead of undertaking cleanup itself and seeking subsequent cost recovery, the Environmental Protection Agency ("EPA") is entitled under the statute to issue administrative orders directing responsible parties to conduct cleanup; alternatively, the EPA may seek a judicially-issued injunction ordering cleanup. In contrast to the injunctive relief that is available in nuisance—which is the only means of obtaining nuisance abatement—the injunctive remedies under CERCLA are simply substitutes for government-conducted cleanup. Injunctions in effect order responsible parties to fund cleanups at the front end, whereas government-conducted cleanups followed by cost recovery result in responsible party funding at the back end.

Many of the other federal environmental-protection statutes also make provision for the issuance of injunctions in cases where there is imminent and substantial danger to health or the environment. But these provisions more closely resemble targeted regulation than the imposition of civil liability, and are therefore appropriately understood as part of the regulatory arsenal.

2. Conventional Damages and the Problem of Inchoate Loss

Liability for damages is the only remedy available in the overwhelming majority of environmental tort actions. Under traditional rules, the plaintiff is entitled to both out-of-pocket, or "special" damages, and pain-and-suffering, or "general" damages. A single recovery is awarded for both past and future special and general damages that the plaintiff proves by a preponderance of the evidence he or she has suffered, or will suffer in the future.

This is utterly familiar and unremarkable. Although predicting long-term future loss may sometimes be a more speculative enterprise than is acknowledged, recovery for such loss is available only if the plaintiff has suffered some past or present compensable personal injury or property damage. In this situation the plaintiff will already be recovering an award; the future-loss issue merely involves the magnitude of the award, not recovery vel non.

The discovery that potentially harmful environmental exposures have occurred, however, sometimes is made a considerable period of time before any physical harm whatsoever resulting from exposure will manifest itself. Individuals may learn that they have been exposed to carcinogenic substances, for example, decades before any cancer caused by the exposure develops and is manifested. And as noted above, even at that time identifying the responsible defendant and proving causation is sometimes difficult.

As a consequence, significant aspects of both corrective justice and deterrence may sometimes be sacrificed. From the standpoint of corrective justice, fear of suffering injury or disease in the future, while not a tangible physical loss, is of course a real loss that has been imposed on the victim by the party responsible for creating this fear. Similarly, medical monitoring necessitated by a hazardous exposure involves real costs, even if the monitoring never reveals any injury or disease. In part for this reason, some courts have relaxed the traditional restrictions on recovery for these forms of loss in the absence of tangible physical harm, and permitted such recovery under limited circumstances.

From the standpoint of deterrence there also is potential concern. A party whose conduct imposes the risk of harm on others but who does not bear full liability for the harm ultimately caused by that conduct is suboptimally deterred. Yet it is in the environmental tort setting that problems involving long-latency disease, indeterminate plaintiffs, and indeterminate defendants create the greatest obstacles to the imposition of full liability for harm caused. Potential defendants are therefore inadequately deterred, and an excessive level of risk is created.

This kind of predicament is of course precisely what gives rise to the public regulation of environmental risk. But in the face of what they consider the inadequacies of regulation, some scholars have proposed recognition of a cause of action for tortious creation of risk. A number of these proposals leave the contours of such a cause of action to be worked out, while others are richly detailed. Their overall common purpose, however, is to promote internalization of the costs of risky activity, and thereby to achieve more nearly optimal deterrence.

Such a cause of action would of course be concerned exclusively with future loss. Therefore, it would of necessity involve some form of proportional liability linked to the probability that the risk in question would materialize in harm. Some of the difficulties that would be associated with this approach parallel those discussed above in connection with proportional liability for actual harm. In most cases, sufficiently precise data on causal probabilities is unlikely to be available; and to the extent that such data is available, imposing proportional liability is inconsistent with awarding full recovery in cases where a causal connection is proved by a preponderance of the evidence but not to a moral certainty.

Other difficulties would arise from the fact that compensation would be paid in advance, and ordinarily far in advance, of the actual occurrence of harm. The result would be that comparatively large numbers of claimants would receive compensation, but probably for a comparatively small percentage of the damages that could be recoverable for actually-occurring harm. Such payments could be understood in two ways: 1) as largely unnecessary for the vast majority of claimants but insufficient for the unfortunate minority; or 2) as a way of funding premiums for insurance purchased by all potential claimants. The trouble with the first conception is obvious; and the trouble with the second conception is that the insurance in question is only partially available, at best. A solution to this problem would be to impose liability for risk at the time of its creation, but to award compensation only at the time when harm actually occurred. David Rosenberg, one of the leading proponents of the approach has thus called for what amount to "insurance fund judgments" in connection with liability for risk-creation. But this proposal entails its own not inconsiderable difficulties.

In short, the imposition of liability for risk alone is both politically implausible and subject to serious challenge on pragmatic grounds. In my view the proposals for doing so are most usefully viewed as heuristic devices. By taking these proposals seriously as an intellectual matter, we can better understand both how the tort system can be reformed to deal more effectively with environmental torts, and the points at which even a reformed system would run up against its own limits in attempting to solve problems in this field.

III. The Intersections of Civil Liability and Regulation

The intersection of liability and regulation takes place in both domains. Civil liability plays a role in regulation, and regulation plays a role—in fact, a variety of quite different roles—in civil liability. We thus have a mixed system in two senses: we address environmental risk through both liability and regulation, and each approach plays a role in the other.

A. Civil Liability in the Regulatory Process

Civil liability plays no formal role in the promulgation or enforcement of environmental statutes and regulations. But this is far from saying that civil liability is irrelevant to these processes. In fact, developments in the civil liability arena sometimes trigger regulation. The investigatory incentives of attorneys representing plaintiffs in civil litigation may lead them to produce data and uncover facts that legislatures and administrative agencies would be very unlikely to develop on their own. Armed with this information, legislatures and agencies may then be prompted to conduct their own independent investigations and promulgate regulatory standards applicable to the activity that is the subject of the prior civil litigation.

Moreover, despite the extensiveness of environmental health and safety regulation at both the federal and state levels, newly-recognized risks may materialize in harm that does not fall within any pre-defined regulatory jurisdiction. As Robert Rabin has pointed out, at important points in their history there was no regulatory agency charged with responsibility for monitoring the health effects of asbestos or tobacco. So the availability of civil liability may in fact sometimes be a catalyst for regulation.

B. The Role of Regulation in Civil Liability

In contrast to the non-formal role played by civil liability in regulation, regulation often plays a prominent and formal role in civil liability. In fact, there are four different roles that are played by regulation, depending on the legal setting and the statutory framework that applies: 1) regulation may pre-empt liability; 2) compliance with regulatory standards may be a defense to liability; 3) violation of regulatory standards may constitute negligence per se; or 4) violation or compliance may be merely evidentiary on the issue of liability.

1. Pre-emption

Under the Supremacy Clause of the U.S. Constitution, [U.S. Const. art. VI, cl. 2], Congress has the power to pre-empt state tort actions pertaining to any activity that the Congress may regulate. Similarly, state legislatures have virtually unlimited authority, subject only to each state's own constitution, to overturn the common law. This authority undoubtedly comprehends pre-empting tort liability. Consequently, whether regulation of an activity by statute pre-empts civil liability for injury or damage caused by that activity is predominantly a question of statutory interpretation.

It turns out that at both the federal and state levels, however, the courts have developed rules of interpretation holding that there is in effect a presumption against pre-emption. As the U.S. Supreme Court described its approach in one of the more recent cases addressing the issue, "because the States are independent sovereigns in our federal system, we have long presumed that Congress does not cavalierly pre-empt state-law causes of action." This is a presumption against what might be called vertical pre-emption—whether a federal regulatory scheme pre-empts state tort law. A similar rule regarding horizontal pre-emption—whether a state's regulatory scheme pre-empts state common law—also pertains. Thus, in the absence of something approaching express language evidencing legislative intent to pre-empt, civil liability operates in tandem with environmental regulation.

Nevertheless, certain federal and state environmental regulatory regimes have been interpreted to pre-empt civil liability. Significantly, such rulings apply not only to civil liability for violation of these statutes, but also to causes of action alleging that there is liability notwithstanding compliance with the statutory requirements. Thus, pre-emption simply takes civil liability out of play. Penalties or sanctions for violation are to be found within the regulatory regime only; there are no externally available penalties or sanctions, whether or not there is compliance.

2. *Regulatory Compliance as a Defense*

The regulatory compliance defense contrasts with pre-emption in two respects. First, whereas pre-emption is by definition a product of statutory purpose, a regulatory compliance defense may arise by virtue of statutory purpose or common law decision. Second, the regulatory compliance defense obviously does not preclude the imposition of liability for injury or damage resulting from violation of a statute or regulation. The defense applies only when there has been compliance. When liability has been pre-empted by statute, however, even claims for injury or damage resulting from violation of the statute are precluded. The operative difference between pre-emption and the regulatory compliance defense, then, involves the difference between remedies for violation of a statute or regulation. The regulatory compliance defense permits imposition of civil liability for harm caused by a statutory or regulatory violation, but pre-emption does not. The former creates a safe harbor only; but the latter wholly occupies the field and completely displaces civil liability.

Although there has been considerable academic and policy debate about the regulatory compliance defense, the defense has been infrequently prescribed by statute and rarely invoked by the courts. The inference that probably should be drawn from this state of affairs is that the middle ground between full pre-emption and unconstrained civil liability that is potentially occupied by a regulatory compliance defense is in fact almost always empty. Either regulation of a particular matter or activity is sufficiently definitive to pre-empt the simultaneous operation of civil liability altogether, or regulatory requirements are considered minimum standards of conduct only, leaving full room for the parallel operation of civil liability when more than the regulatory minimum amount of safety is expected.

3. *Regulatory Violation as Negligence Per Se*

The conventional and majority rule is that the unexcused violation of a health or safety statute or regulation is negligent "per se"—that is, negligent as a matter of law. This is a matter of common law doctrine, not statutory interpretation. Statutes sometimes expressly specify that violation gives rise to civil liability for resulting harm. But the negligence per se doctrine does not hold that there is an implied statutory cause of action even when a statute is silent on the issue. Rather, violation of statutory and regulatory standards constitutes negligence as a matter of law because it is negligent to violate a statute or regulation. Absent a legally cognizable excuse that for practical purposes renders a statutory or regulatory standard inapplicable, reasonable prudence requires compliance with these standards. Therefore, the trier of fact in a negligence case is not free to weigh the violation as part of an assessment of the conduct in question. As the classic case on the issue puts it, unexcused violation "is negligence itself."

* * *

4. Compliance and Violation as Evidence Only

In the absence of pre-emption or a regulatory compliance defense, all jurisdictions hold that evidence of compliance with a statute or regulation is admissible, but not dispositive on the negligence issue. A party whose conduct has complied with an applicable statute or regulation is entitled to have this fact considered by the trier of fact assessing that conduct. But the trier of fact is free to conclude that it was negligent to fail to take more care than was required by the statute or regulation. This rule is simply the logical corollary of statutes that do not pre-empt common law actions or create a regulatory compliance defense. What is not pre-empted or made a defense is the potential for liability notwithstanding compliance.

On the other hand, in cases where there has been violation, a minority of jurisdictions reject the negligence per se doctrine, and hold that violation is treated the same way as compliance. The jury may consider violation of a statute or regulation in making its negligence determination, but is free to find that the conduct at issue was reasonable notwithstanding violation.

* * *

IV. The Virtues and Vices of a Mixed System

It should be obvious from the foregoing discussion that we have a mixed system of civil liability and environmental regulation. We actually employ a number of different combinations of these two regimes, depending on the setting. In a few settings, environmental statutes wholly pre-empt civil liability. Occasionally, in a few other settings, civil liability is only partially displaced, through a regulatory compliance defense. But in the vast majority of settings, we quite literally mix regimes, by preserving potential civil liability not only when there has been violation of an environmental statute or regulation, but even when there has been compliance.

Some of the virtues and vices of this approach have long been recognized, while others have not. By retaining the possibility of full pre-emption or of employing a regulatory compliance defense, the system provides for those rare endeavors that require an extraordinary degree of predictability to their liability exposure. Without such predictability, desirable investment in the endeavor may be undermined. The needs of the nuclear energy industry several decades ago are perhaps a prime example of this phenomenon, although the problem was solved at that time with a partial rather than full pre-emption of civil liability. One weakness of this rationale is that it may prove too much. If in fact an endeavor requires this degree of insulation from the threat of civil liability to be workable, the risks the endeavor poses may not be worth taking. Another weakness is that, even if the rationale is tenable when immunity is provided to an endeavor, that immunity is likely to have a tendency to become politically difficult to modify even after the conditions warranting it have changed.

In addition, the regulatory compliance defense may be appropriate where a regulatory regime is so pervasive and exacting that threatening actors with civil liability for harm that occurs even in the face of compliance with regulatory standards is unduly harsh. The principal focus of proponents of this rationale has been the federal regulation of pharmaceuticals by the Food and Drug Administration, whose standards are widely recognized as being among the most stringent in the world of health and safety regulation. Here the two downsides are political influence and the unknown. The greater the impartiality and degree of expertise of a regulatory agency, the stronger the justification for a regulatory compliance defense in the domain of its jurisdiction. Impartiality, however, is not only an ideal; it is a dynamic phenomenon to which legal doctrine is unsuited to make quick reactions. An agency whose impartiality warrants deference from the civil liability system at one point in time may not remain immune to political influence over time. Equally to the point, even an impartial agency can act only on the basis of what is known when it acts. In contrast, the threat of civil liability notwithstanding compliance with an agency's dictates can create the incentive for discovery of information by both regulated actors and injured parties that would not exist in the absence of this threat.

The result is that although pre-emption and the regulatory compliance defense remain as theoretically available approaches, in point of fact the dominant approach is a mix of regulation and civil liability in which regulatory compliance is not an automatic defense. Regulatory standards are for the most part only minimums. Compliance does not insulate an actor from liability for harm suffered by those a standard seeks to protect, though violation almost automatically results in the imposition of liability for such harm. The system has in effect hedged its bets.

Like all hedges, this one protects against downside risk: if regulation fails to control a risk that should be controlled, civil liability is potentially available to do so. Thus, risks that slip through the regulatory net for reasons of politics, inexpertise, chance, or lack of jurisdiction may be picked up nonetheless in the civil liability system. Conversely, as I noted at the outset, regulation is much better equipped to deal with certain types of risks than is civil liability, and environmental risks are foremost among these. When it is difficult to pinpoint causation yet harm may be significant if it occurs, the great strength of regulation is that it can address risk ex ante and require a margin of safety that the threat of civil liability over the long term is much less likely to achieve.

The protection against downside risk that is accomplished by our mixed system, however, comes at the cost of potential overkill. What amounts to double regulation may take place, with a dual set of requirements that, while not inconsistent, nevertheless may seem to send two messages. Instead of hearing what our mixed system nominally says, "Be at least as safe as the regulations require, but consider whether you ought to do more," regulated actors may actually hear the system say, "The government tells you one thing, but juries are free to second-guess the government and tell you something else." To the extent that there is an element of randomness in this arrangement, the threat of liability under these circumstances acts as a kind of "uncertainty tax" that is simply a cost of doing business in a mixed system of liability and regulation.

There is a good deal to criticize about this arrangement, since its disadvantages are obvious. But one infrequently-noticed advantage is worth underscoring. The great strength of our mixed system is that it leaves room for the economically venturesome. Actors in a system of regulation so pervasive that it required no civil liability to back it up would tend to resemble a public utility, with a guaranteed rate of return but a ceiling on profitability. Many of the risks such actors would be permitted to take or be prohibited from taking would be uniform; the returns on investment in the businesses of these actors would therefore tend to converge. In contrast, under regimes with less ex ante regulation and a greater but uncertain threat of ex post civil liability, there will be more room for divergence in risk taking, and in all probability more actual divergence. Returns on investment will vary, depending on the degree of historical risk taking by an enterprise and its success in predicting which risks will materialize in harm. Different businesses will show different rates of profitability, in part based on their fortunes in the civil liability system. The availability of civil liability will have enabled us to avoid the uniformity that would result from highly rigorous regulation. Ironically, then, our system of economic liberties may thus depend to a greater extent than might be thought on a thriving system of civil liability.

Therefore, when we look at what the tort system has done to asbestos defendants and others similarly situated, we ought to recognize that this is only half the story. The same legal system that made it possible to impose these liabilities also has made it possible for other enterprises to take risks that did not materialize in harm. These enterprises have instead made significant contributions to the productivity of our economy and the well-being of their employees and shareholders. It may be that particular features of the civil liability system are in need of reform—perhaps even radical reform. I am on record as favoring a number of these reforms. An argument for preserving a mixed system of civil liability and environmental regulation is not an argument for preserving the excesses of the civil liability system. But neither is it an argument for a pure system of one or the other. Without the downside of civil liability, it would not have an upside.

Chapter Two

TRESPASS ACTIONS

A. GENERAL PRINCIPLES OF TRESPASS

1. THE INTENT REQUIREMENT

Trespass is classified as one of the "intentional" torts in most casebooks, but in reality could just as logically be classified as a strict liability tort. At common law, the intent element was satisfied by an entry upon the land of another, by a person or thing, as a consequence of a volitional act, regardless of the absence of any "intent" to make an unpermitted entry upon the land of another. Thus, the intent to commit a "trespass" is not necessary. In other words, the defendant need not have intended to invade plaintiff's interest in the exclusive possession of land; it was sufficient that such an invasion actually resulted from a volitional act. Moreover, the risk of mistake was borne entirely by the defendant—an honest and reasonable belief that the defendant was on his own property was not on another's property, or that its actions and the invasions were authorized by the plaintiff, was not a defense, and neither intent nor negligence by the defendant was an essential element in terms of the fault requirement. The rationale for the strictness of these rules was that a trespass action was a legal means for a lawful possessor to maintain the integrity of his ownership.

As leading commentators have summarized, an intentional trespass occurs in "situations where the defendant intended to be where he was but did not intend the harmful consequences of his action. The point is that the defendant intended the intrusion." Prosser & Keeton on Torts 73 (5th ed. 1984). Therefore, it becomes clear that "one who innocently enters upon someone else's property without intending to trespass and under the mistaken belief that he or she is entitled or authorized to enter is nevertheless a trespasser." Baltimore Gas and Elec. Co. v. Flippo, 112 Md.App. 75, 684 A.2d 456, 460 (Md.App.1996), aff'd, 348 Md. 680, 705 A.2d 1144 (Md. 1998).

While liability for trespass does not depend on a defendant's specific intent to invade unlawfully the property of another, "[w]hat is required, however, is volition, i.e., a conscious intent to do the act that constitutes the entry upon someone else's real or personal property. An involuntary entry onto another's property is not a trespass." Baltimore Gas and Elec. Co. v. Flippo, 684 A.2d at 461. As formulated in a well-known New York decision: "While the trespasser, to be liable, need not intend or expect the damaging consequences of his intrusion, he must intend the act which amounts to or produces the unlawful invasion, and the intrusion must at least be the immediate or inevitable consequence of what he willfully does, or which he does so negligently as to amount to willfulness." Phillips v. Sun Oil Co., 307 N.Y. 328, 121 N.E.2d 249, 250–51 (N.Y. 1954).

Restatement (Second) of Torts § 158 (1964) preserves this concept of strictness for intentional trespass. Thus, to satisfy the "intent" requirement of the prima facie case in trespass, plaintiff need only prove that defendant intended the act that resulted in the trespass, i.e., that defendant's act was volitional, and done with knowledge to a substantial certainty that the act would result in introduction of the substance onto plaintiff's property. As comment i to § 158 makes manifest:

> In order that there may be a trespass under the rule stated in this Section, it is not necessary that the foreign matter should be thrown directly and immediately upon the other's land. It is enough that an act is done with knowledge that it will to a substantial certainty result in the entry of the foreign matter.

This statement from the Restatement captures the essential issue in environmental tort cases relying on an intentional trespass theory.

Some of the cases presented below, such as Martin v. Amoco Oil Co., 679 N.E.2d 139 (Ind.App.1997) and United Proteins, Inc. v. Farmland Industries, 259 Kan. 725, 915 P.2d 80 (Kan. 1996) develop the principles of intentional trespass in some detail. Gradually over the centuries the law came to distinguish between intentional entries upon the land of another (entering another's land with knowledge that it is another's land), and unintentional entries. For *unintentional* entries, modern liability in trespass typically turns on whether the entry is reckless, negligent, or the result of abnormally dangerous activity. Later in this Chapter liability for negligent trespass is considered.

For *intentional* invasions of the land of another, the law of torts still retains most of its strict and inflexible character, except that today a host of privileges may apply to release the defendant from any liability. The Restatement (Second) of Torts recognizes twenty nonconsensual privileges. See Restatement (Second) of Torts §§ 191–211. These privileges embrace such justifications as private necessity (a limited privilege), public necessity (a broad privilege), entry to abate a private nuisance, entry to execute civil process, etc. The most important characteristic of the privileges is that they are very specific and narrow in identifying the factual circumstances which give rise to the privilege to commit what would otherwise constitute an actionable trespass. See Prosser and Keeton on Torts 67–84 (5th ed. 1984); 1 Harper, James & Gray, The Law of Torts §§ 1.11–1.28, 1.22 (3d ed. 1996). However, as is discussed in Chapter 12 on defenses, in an appropriate case a plaintiff may be found to have consented to the entry.

2. POSSESSORY INTEREST

To maintain an action in trespass, plaintiff must have a contemporaneous legal interest in possession of the property. The consequences of failure to show such a possessory interest was shown in Davey Compressor Co. v. City of Delray Beach, 613 So.2d 60 (Fla.App.1993), a city's suit in trespass and other claims for toxic contamination beneath its water well field. In that suit, the evidence showed that Delray supplied its citizens with water as permitted by a consumptive use permit issued by the South Florida Water Management District, which permit was to expire in 1997. From 1981 to 1987, Davey disposed of toxic solvents, used to clean air compressors, onto the ground behind its operating facility. Delray discovered the presence of these solvents in the groundwater, and won a judgment of over $3 million in past damages, and $5.6 million in future damages. On appeal, the Florida appeals court upheld the award of past damages, but reversed the award of future damages on the grounds that damages awarded for dates following 1997 were in error, stating: "Since appellant failed to establish its legal interest in the groundwater beneath its well field beyond the expiration date of its water consumptive use permit, appellee cannot recover future damages after the expiration date of its permit."

The Ohio Supreme Court considered a different dimension of this issue in Chance v. BP Chemicals, Inc., 77 Ohio St.3d 17, 670 N.E.2d 985 (Ohio 1996), where a chemical refiner had applied "deepwell" injection technology for the disposal of refining byproducts nearly 2900 feet below the earth's surface. Plaintiffs maintained that the injected substances had migrated laterally beneath their properties. Defendant argued that the injectate had dispensed into native brine waters, and that such waters were waters of the state and exclusively regulated by the state so that the plaintiffs had no possessory interest in the waters. The court held:

> To the extent that appellee [defendant] appears to be arguing that the way the injectate disperses into the native brine serves to insulate appellee from all liability in all circumstances, we reject appellee's contention. The native brine exists naturally in the porous sandstone into which the injecting is done. The injectate displaces and mixes with the brine in the injection zone. Appellants [plaintiffs] have a property interest in the rock into which the injectate is placed, albeit a potentially limited one, depending on whether appellants' ownership rights are absolute. If appellee's act of placing the injectate into the rock interferes with appellants' reasonable and foreseeable use of their properties, appellee could be liable regardless of the way the injectate mixes with the native brine.

> Our analysis above concerning the native brine illustrates that appellants do not enjoy absolute ownership of waters of the state

below their properties, and therefore underscores that their subsurface ownership rights are limited. 670 N.E.2d at 992.

3. EXTENT OF INVASION: ARE ACTUAL DAMAGES NECESSARY?

Trespass protects a plaintiff's interest in the surface land itself, the earth or other material beneath the surface, and "the air space above it." Restatement (Second) of Torts § 158 comment i. At common law, plaintiff did not have to suffer substantial harm to sue, since many actions were instituted primarily to vindicate an ownership interest, and at least nominal damages were recoverable for any material intrusion. Today, in many jurisdictions the availability of a remedy in trespass may turn upon the seriousness of the contamination of plaintiff's land or of the environment. Where there is an actual invasion, and where the interference is substantial, defendant may be liable in trespass; where the pollution or contamination is of a lesser or a transitory nature, courts in many jurisdictions find the claim to be in nuisance alone. In National Telephone Co–op. Ass'n v. Exxon Corp., 38 F.Supp.2d 1, 15 (D.D.C.1998), a case involving claims that leakage of gasoline constituted a trespass, the court stated:

> Courts pragmatically modified this common-law principle as an increasing number of trespass claims were brought based on invisible, microscopic invasions of toxins or contaminants. In response, the courts fashioned a rule that required a plaintiff to prove actual harm to the property in order to prevail on a claim for trespass based on invisible particulate deposits. Thus, the tort of trespass, when based on the invasion of gases or microscopic particles, has assumed similar dimensions of nuisance law by requiring an actual showing of harm or interference with land.

See, also, Maddy v. Vulcan Materials Co., 737 F.Supp. 1528, 1540 (D.Kan.1990) ("Only if the indirect and intangible invasions causes substantial damage to the plaintiff's property, thereby infringing [upon] his exclusive possessory interest in the property, will an action for trespass lie."); accord, Leaf River Forest Products, Inc. v. Simmons, 697 So.2d 1083, 1085–86 (Miss.1996).

The recent authority also makes clear that the common law distinction between direct and indirect invasions is no longer legally significant, at least in environmental tort cases. Thus, the invasion of plaintiff's property need not be direct, if plaintiff can prove that an intentional act of defendant resulted in the harm. Thus, the causal intervention of natural conditions, such as deterioration, wind, or rain, in initiating or exacerbating the trespass will not absolve defendant of liability.[1] It was

---

1. Comment i to Restatement (Second) of Torts § 158 gives this example: "[O]ne who piles sand so close to his boundary that by force of gravity alone it slides down on to his neighbor's land, or who builds an embankment that during ordinary rainfalls the dirt is washed from it upon adjacent lands, becomes a trespasser on the other's land."

so held in one action where plaintiff claimed that defendant's dumping of asphalt waste on land contiguous to plaintiff's fish pond eventually resulted in the pollution of the pond. Rushing v. Hooper–McDonald, Inc., 293 Ala. 56, 300 So.2d 94 (Ala.1974) ("This court holds that it is not necessary that the asphalt or foreign matter be thrown or dumped directly and immediately upon the plaintiff's land but that it is sufficient if the act is done so that it will to a substantial certainty result in the entry of the asphalt or foreign matter onto the real property that the plaintiff possesses.")

The party prevailing in a trespass action may recover all damages that are the natural and proximate consequence of the trespass. See, e.g., Kelly v. Para–Chem Southern, Inc., 311 S.C. 223, 428 S.E.2d 703 (S.C.1993), in which the trespass and nuisance claims of Kelly, the owner of a 330 acre tract contiguous to Para–Chem's property, recovered $14,000 for groundwater contamination. Chapter 5 on remedies considers in detail the damages recoverable in nuisance and trespass actions.

The decision in Chance v. BP Chemicals, 77 Ohio St.3d 17, 670 N.E.2d 985 (Ohio 1996), quoted above, also posed the separate question of whether a trespass to subterranean rock strata by the deepwell injectate required plaintiffs to prove actual damages as an element of the claim. The court ruled they had such a burden:

> Appellants [plaintiffs] in essence argue that through its rulings, the trial court mistakenly imposed a requirement that they prove "actual" damages as an element of their trespass claim. Appellants argue that damages can be presumed in every case of trespass, and given that the bifurcation order left damages to be quantified at a future time, the trial court erred in requiring proof of any damages at all, much less of "actual" ones. We do not accept appellants' argument in this regard in the specific circumstances of this case, but find that some type of physical damages or interference with use must be shown in an indirect invasion situation such as this. Even assuming that the injectate had laterally migrated to be in an offending concentration under some of the appellants' properties, we find that some type of physical damages or interference with use must have been demonstrated for appellants to recover for a trespass.

> Additionally, appellants in essence argue that even if the trial court was correct in requiring them to prove "actual" damages as an element of their trespass claim, the trial court erred by unduly restricting what type of damages they were required to demonstrate. For example, appellants argue that the trial court should have allowed appellants to present evidence that environmental stigma associated with the deepwells had a negative effect on appellants' property values due to the public perception that there may have been injectate under appellants' properties and that the injectate may be dangerous. We find that the trial court did not abuse its

discretion in the circumstances of this case in foreclosing appellants from presenting evidence of speculative stigma damages. Therefore, the trial court was correct in requiring appellants to prove some physical damages or interference with use proximately caused by the deepwells as part of their trespass claim in the circumstances of this case, thus placing on appellants the burden of establishing that the injectate interfered with the reasonable and foreseeable use of their properties. 670 N.E.2d at 993.

What is the justification for demanding proof of actual harm in *Chance*? If plaintiffs had sought to extract natural gas from beneath their land which was interfered with by the injectate, would that suffice?

4. RELATIONSHIP TO NUISANCE

The claim in trespass may be readily confused with that in private nuisance. As explained by a leading authority, "[t]he distinction which is now accepted is that trespass is an invasion of the plaintiff's interest in the exclusive possession of his land, while nuisance is an interference with his use and enjoyment of it." Prosser and Keeton on Torts 622 (5th ed. 1984). In most jurisdictions, invasions of plaintiff's property that amount to trespass may also, if they interfere with plaintiff's use and enjoyment of the property, be actionable in nuisance. In such circumstances, "plaintiff may have his choice" of a claim in trespass or in nuisance, "or may proceed upon both." Mangini v. Aerojet–General Corp., 230 Cal.App.3d 1125, 281 Cal.Rptr. 827 (1991), appeal after remand, 26 Cal.App.4th 760, 31 Cal.Rptr.2d 696 (1994), superseded, 35 Cal.Rptr.2d 269, 883 P.2d 387, appeal after remand, 12 Cal.4th 1087, 51 Cal.Rptr.2d 272, 912 P.2d 1220 (1996) (quoting Restatement (Second) of Torts § 821D, comment e) (plaintiff's land contamination claim in nuisance, trespass, and other common law causes of action). See, e.g., Wilson v. Amoco Corp., 33 F.Supp.2d 969 (D.Wyo.1998) (in property owners' claims against operators of a railyard and dry cleaning facility for release of hazardous substances that contaminated their properties, the court denied defendants' motions for summary judgment on claims of trespass, nuisance and negligence).

A claim in trespass requires that plaintiff demonstrate that defendant's pollutant or contaminant have settled on or infiltrated plaintiff's property. The *invasory* (physical interference) requirement of trespass can be satisfied even by contamination by PCBs or by radiation not visible to the naked eye. See Nieman v. NLO, Inc., 108 F.3d 1546 (6th Cir.1997) (discharge of uranium and radiation from nuclear processing facility into the air, groundwater, and aquifer constitutes trespass).

5.   CONTINUING TRESPASS

a.   *The Basic Idea*

A polluter's failure to remove a pollutant or a contaminant from plaintiff's land may represent a "continuing" tort. Plaintiff may frame a claim in *continuing* trespass,[2] which, upon sufficient evidence, "confers on the possessor of the land an option to maintain a succession of actions based on a theory of continuing trespass, or to treat the continuation of the thing on the land as an aggravation of the original trespass." Restatement (Second) of Torts § 899, comment d. The key distinction between a continuing and a permanent trespass is that if a trespass can be discontinued or abated at any time, it is considered a continuing one, and the plaintiff "is permitted to bring successive actions as damages accrue until abatement takes place." Capogeannis v. Superior Court, 12 Cal.App.4th 668, 15 Cal.Rptr.2d 796, 800 (1993). In contrast, where the trespass is deemed permanent or unabatable, the land possessor can maintain only one action for the damage sustained and may encounter a statutes of limitation problem if the invasion preceded the prescribed period. The significance of the designation "continuing trespass" is primarily that of relieving some of the strictures of limitations periods within which the possessor would have to bring a toxic tort claim.[3]

b.   *Continuing Damages or Injury; Abatability*

But the authorities are split on *what* needs to be "continuing." The majority of courts rule that it is the *damages* or injury that must be continuing, as opposed to the tortious *conduct*. Thus, in Nieman v. NLO, Inc., 108 F.3d 1546 (6th Cir.1997) plaintiffs alleged that a massive leak of uranium and radiation from defendant's facility occurred on December 10, 1984. Defendant ended its operations in 1985. Suit was filed in 1994. The Sixth Circuit Court of Appeals, applying Ohio law, rejected defendant's argument that continued ownership and control of the plant was a prerequisite to a continuing trespass claim because the cause of action demands continuing wrongful conduct, not just continuing damages caused by the original conduct. After surveying Ohio authority on the issue which titled against defendant's position, the court quoted the Restatement (Second) of Torts:

> The definition of "continuing trespass" in the Restatement (Second) of Torts also supports Nieman's view:
>
> > A trespass may be committed by the continued presence on the land of a structure, chattel, or other thing which the actor has tortiously placed there, whether or not the actor has the ability to

2. "The actor's failure to remove from land in the possession of another a thing he has tortiously * * * placed on the land constitutes a continuing trespass for the entire time which the thing is on the land[.]"

Restatement (Second) of Torts § 899, comment d.

3. Restatement (Second) of Torts § 161, comment b. In Chapter 12 we consider this issue in detail.

remove it. Restatement (Second) of Torts § 161(1) (1965). Likewise, the comments to this section focus on the actor's failure to remove from another's land the thing which the actor has tortiously placed there:

> The actor's failure to remove from land in the possession of another a structure, chattel or other thing which he has tortiously ... placed on the land constitutes a continuing trespass for the entire time during which the thing is wrongfully on the land and ... confers on the possessor of the land an option to maintain a succession of actions based on the theory of continuing trespass or to treat the continuance of the thing on the land as an aggravation of the original trespass.

* * *

Similarly, § 899 of the Restatement (Second) of Torts supports the view that proof of continuing harm suffices to establish a continuing trespass:

* * *

Thus, under the Restatement, a claim for continuing trespass is not defeated where the defendant's last affirmative act of wrongdoing precedes the filing of the complaint by a period longer than the statute of limitations.

* * *

Thus, Ohio law does not support appellees' contention that because they have not managed the FMPC since 1985 they cannot be liable for a continuing trespass action filed in 1994. We hold only that, under Ohio law, a claim for continuing trespass may be supported by proof of continuing damages and need not be based on allegations of continuing conduct. 108 F.3d at 1557,1559

In Mangini v. Aerojet–General Corp., 12 Cal.4th 1087, 51 Cal. Rptr.2d 272, 912 P.2d 1220 (Cal. 1996), a property owner's suit against a former lessee arising from contamination due to the dumping and burning of "toxic solid fuel components, amounting to several million pounds, including, to adopt Aerojet's characterization, 'quantities of waste sludge consisting of highly explosive rocket propellants containing a cleaning solvent' known as trichloroethylene (or TCE) that is toxic to human and animal life[,]" the California Supreme Court wrote that "[T]he crucial test of the permanency of a trespass or a nuisance is whether the trespass or nuisance can be discontinued or abated (citation)." On the evidence before it, the court concluded:

> We accept as general proposition that something less than total decontamination may suffice to show abatability. However, there is no evidence in this case of what that might be. Thus plaintiffs did not submit evidence of cleanup levels acceptable to or ordered by the regulatory agencies for this property. * * *

Plaintiff[s] failed to show abatability at any level.

The Maine Supreme Judicial Court weighed in on the side of continuing damage and an abatability test in Jacques v. Pioneer Plastics, Inc., 676 A.2d 504 (Me.1996), noting that "the subject of our inquiry is not the dumping itself [hazardous materials at a former lagoon dump site partially situated on plaintiff's property] but instead the hazardous material that remains on the plaintiffs' land." The court cited a state Department of Environmental Protection compliance order that required the defendant's preparation of a remediation feasibility study that would include at least the option of the removal of all wastes and contaminated soils from the site, creating a factual issue on the continuing nature of the trespass.

In Hoery v. United States, 64 P.3d 214 (Colo. 2003), the Colorado Supreme Court, sitting en banc, held that as applied to environmental trespass or nuisance claims alike, the defendant's conduct may constitute a continuing tort irrespective of whether (1) the defendant has terminated or continued the challenged conduct; or (2)) the contamination is abatable or unabatable. A trespass or a nuisance would be considered to be continuing if either the presence or the migration of the unwelcomed substance on the complainant's property was unalleviated.

ROBERT N. HOERY v. UNITED STATES

Supreme Court of Colorado, En Banc, 2003.
64 P.3d 214.

Justice BENDER delivered the Opinion of the Court.

I. INTRODUCTION

In this case, we agreed to answer two certified questions from the United States Court of Appeals for the Tenth Circuit regarding continuing trespass and nuisance under Colorado law. Pursuant to C.A.R. 21.1, the Tenth Circuit certified the following state law questions pertinent to an appeal pending in that court:

(1) Does the continued migration of toxic chemicals from defendant's property to plaintiff's property, allegedly caused by chemical releases by the defendant, constitute continuing trespass and/or nuisance under Colorado law?

(2) Does the ongoing presence of those toxic chemicals on plaintiff's property constitute continuing trespass and/or nuisance under Colorado law? We answer both questions in the affirmative.

The plaintiff, Robert Hoery, brought suit under the Federal Tort Claims Act against the defendant, the United States, asserting claims for, among other things, continuing trespass and nuisance. Hoery claimed that the United States negligently released toxic chemicals from Lowry Air Force Base into the ground which contaminated his nearby residential property. The United States District Court dismissed the case, concluding that Hoery failed to state a claim for continuing trespass or nuisance under either federal or Colorado law. On appeal, the Tenth Circuit determined that there was no controlling Colorado precedent to determine whether Hoery stated a claim for continuing trespass and nuisance under Colorado law and thus certified the questions to this court for our resolution.

Upon considering our precedent and other jurisdictions that have considered these questions, we hold that the alleged migration and ongoing presence of toxic chemicals on Hoery's property each constitutes a continuing trespass and nuisance under Colorado law. The alleged tortious conduct of the United States includes its failure to abate and to remove the toxic chemicals it placed beneath Hoery's property. In addition, we hold that this tortuous conduct is not limited to the initial release of those chemicals from Lowry.

Thus, we answer both certified questions in the affirmative and return this case back to the Tenth Circuit for further proceedings.

II. FACTS AND PROCEEDINGS

We rely on the Tenth Circuit's rendition of a substantial portion of the underlying facts of this case, which we accept as true for our purposes here.

Robert Hoery and his wife bought a residence in the East Montclair neighborhood of Denver, Colorado in 1993. The property has a groundwater well in the backyard to irrigate the lawn and vegetable garden. Hoery's well is located seven blocks north of Lowry Air Force Base.

The United States operated Lowry as an active military base between the 1940s and September 1994. During that time period, the United States disposed of trichloroethylene ("TCE") and other toxic chemicals at Lowry. These releases created plumes of toxic pollution underneath property extending several miles north of Lowry, including the area underneath Hoery's property in the Montclair neighborhood. In 1997, the United States tested Hoery's irrigation well and found it was contaminated with TCE.

Although the United States stopped all operations at Lowry related to the use of TCE in 1994, the toxic plume continues to migrate underneath the Montclair neighborhood. TCE remains on Hoery's property and enters his groundwater and soil on a daily basis, unabated by the United States. [Hoery's expert, a hydrogeologist, testified in his affidavit that based upon the information available in November 1999, the contamination was not permanent and there were remediation strategies that could restore Hoery's property. The United States did not address this factual issue.]

Hoery brought suit under the Federal Tort Claims Act ("FTCA") in 1998 against the United States asserting claims for, among other things, continuing trespass and nuisance and sought unspecified damages. See 28 U.S.C. §§ 2671–80. Hoery alleged that the United States negligently released the TCE and caused contamination of his property, including groundwater, soil, and a well.

The District Court granted the United States's motion to dismiss all of Hoery's claims for lack of subject matter jurisdiction under Fed. R.Civ.P. 12(b)(1). The District Court held that Hoery presented permanent tort claims that were time-barred. Federal law governs when a cause of action under the FTCA accrues. [Cc] For permanent torts, the claim accrues the later of when the injury first occurs or when the plaintiff learned or should have learned of his injury and its cause. See, e.g., Kronisch v. United States, 150 F.3d 112, 121 (2d Cir.1998); [Cc]. For continuing torts, however, federal law provides that the claim continues to accrue as long as the tortious conduct continues. In this event, plaintiff's recovery is limited to the statute of limitations period dating back from when plaintiff's complaint was filed. United States v. Hess, 194 F.3d 1164, 1177 & n. 12 (10th Cir.1999).

Because a two-year statute of limitations applies to FTCA claims, see 28 U.S.C. § 2401(b), the District Court held that Hoery's 1998 claims were untimely because Hoery knew or should have known his property might be contaminated by TCE from Lowry as of 1995. Hoery did not appeal that ruling.

In addition to the ruling construing federal statutes, the District Court further held that its ruling was consistent with Colorado law. Under the FTCA, the United States is liable "in the same manner and to the same extent as a private individual under like circumstances," 28 U.S.C. § 2674, and "in accordance with the law of the place where the act or omission occurred." 28 U.S.C. § 1346(b). Because the acts alleged here occurred in Colorado, our precedent controls as to whether the allegations constitute a continuing trespass and nuisance.

The Court reasoned that the only "wrongful act" alleged by Hoery was the actual release of toxic chemicals by the United States, and that no continuing tort had been alleged because this act had ended in September 1994 when the United States stopped operating Lowry. Citing two of Colorado's "irrigation ditch cases," see Middelkamp v. Bessemer Irrigating Ditch Co., 46 Colo. 102, 103 P. 280 (1909) and Hickman v. North Sterling Irrigation Dist., 748 P.2d 1349 (Colo.App.1987), the District Court concluded that the nuisance and trespass was limited to the actual release of TCE by the United States and not the continued migration or ongoing presence of pollution on Hoery's property. Hoery appealed this ruling.

On appeal, Hoery argued that the migration and presence of toxic chemicals on his property were in themselves wrongful acts for which the United States was responsible and constituted continuing torts under our decision in Wright v. Ulrich, 40 Colo. 437, 91 P. 43 (1907). In the alternative, the United States asserted that Mr. Hoery's claims were permanent torts under our irrigation ditch cases and time-barred under the FTCA's statute of limitations. The Tenth Circuit, after reviewing these Colorado cases, determined that none of them indicated how we would rule on whether Hoery alleged continuing trespass and nuisance claims, and suspended the proceedings pending our response to the certified questions presented here.

III. ANALYSIS

As background to our discussion of the certified questions, we briefly describe the underlying torts of trespass and nuisance and the distinctions between "continuing" and "permanent" torts under Colorado law.

A. Trespass and Nuisance

The elements for the tort of trespass are a physical intrusion upon the property of another without the proper permission from the person legally entitled to possession of that property. Public Serv. Co. of Colorado v. Van Wyk, 27 P.3d 377, 389 (Colo.2001); Gerrity Oil & Gas Corp. v. Magness, 946 P.2d 913, 933 (Colo.1997). The intrusion can occur when an actor intentionally enters land possessed by someone else, or when an actor causes something else to enter the land. For instance, an "actor, without himself entering the land, may invade another's interest in its exclusive possession by . . . placing a thing either on or beneath the surface of the land." Restatement (Second) of Torts §§ 158(a) cmt. i, 159(1) (1965). A landowner who sets in motion a force which, in the usual course of events, will damage property of another is guilty of a trespass on such property. Miller v. Carnation Co., 33 Colo.App. 62, 68, 516 P.2d 661, 664 (1973) (citing Fairview Farms, Inc. v. Reynolds Metals Co., 176 F.Supp. 178, 188 (D.Or. 1959)); see also Restatement (Second) of Torts § 158(a) cmt. i ("It is enough that an act is done with knowledge that it will to a substantial certainty result in the entry of the foreign matter.").

Another type of property invasion is a nuisance. [Cc] A claim for nuisance is predicated upon a substantial invasion of an individual's interest in the use and enjoyment of his property. Public Serv. Co. of Colorado, 27 P.3d at 391. Liability for nuisance may rest upon any one of three types of conduct: an intentional invasion of a person's interest; a negligent invasion of a person's interest; or, conduct so dangerous to life or property and so abnormal or out-of-place in its surroundings as to fall within the principles of strict liability. Id.; [Cc]. Like a trespass, conduct constituting a nuisance can include indirect or physical conditions created by defendant that cause harm. Restatement (Second) of Torts § 834 cmt. b.

B. Continuing and Permanent Torts

Having delineated the elements of the underlying torts of trespass and nuisance, we must determine what makes them "continuing" or "permanent." The typical trespass or nuisance is complete when it is committed; the cause of action accrues, and the statute of limitations beings to run at that time. But in cases, for example, when the defendant erects a structure or places something on or underneath the plaintiff's land, the defendant's invasion continues if he fails to stop the invasion and to remove the harmful condition. In such a case, there is a continuing tort so long as the offending object remains and continues to cause the plaintiff harm. See W. Page Keeton et al., Prosser and Keeton on The Law of Torts § 13 (5th ed.1984).

In the context of trespass, an actor's failure to remove a thing tortiously placed on another's land is considered a "continuing trespass" for the entire time during which the thing is wrongfully on the land. Restatement (Second) of Torts § 161 cmt. b. Until the thing tortiously placed on the land, or underneath the land, is removed, then liability for trespass remains. See 75 Amer. Jur.2d Trespass § 26 (2002).

The same is true for nuisance. If the defendant causes the creation of a physical condition that is of itself harmful, even after the activity that created it has ceased, a person who carried on the activity that created the condition is subject to continuing liability for the physical condition. Restatement (Second) of Torts § 834 cmt. e.

For continuing intrusions—either by way of trespass or nuisance—each repetition or continuance amounts to another wrong, giving rise to a new cause of action. See Fowler V. Harper et al., The Law of Torts § 1.7 (3d ed.1996). The practical significance of the continuing tort concept is that for statute of limitation purposes, the claim does not begin to accrue until the tortious conduct has ceased. Id.

We recognized claims for continuing torts in Wright, 40 Colo. 437, 91 P. 43. In Wright, the plaintiff's house was adjacent to the defendant's slaughterhouse. We held that the harmful noises and stenches emanating from the slaughterhouse to the plaintiff's property constituted a continuing nuisance. We reasoned that the defendant was liable until the "nuisance was abated and the cause of damage removed." 40 Colo. at 440, 91 P. at 44 (citing Consol. Home Supply Ditch Co. v. Hamlin, 6 Colo.App. 341, 40 P. 582 (1894)). The plaintiff's claim was not barred by the statute of limitations because "the continuing of a trespass or nuisance from day to day is considered in law a several trespass on each day." Id. In other words, for statute of limitations purposes, a claim would only accrue once the defendant abated the nuisance and removed the cause of damage.

Since Wright, Colorado courts have applied the concept of continuing trespass to various factual contexts; however, these cases reflect little additional analysis. See Steiger v. Burroughs, 878 P.2d 131, 136 (Colo. App.1994) (defendant's house remaining on plaintiff's property constituted continuing trespass); Cobai v. Young, 679 P.2d 121, 123–24 (Colo. App.1984) (snow sliding from defendant's roof to plaintiff's house constituted continuing trespass); Docheff v. City of Broomfield, 623 P.2d 69, 71 (Colo.App.1980) (defendant's storm drainage system flooding plaintiff's adjacent property constituted continuing trespass). Notably, we have also held a defendant liable for continuing nuisance for discharging pollution into a creek used by farmers downstream to irrigate land and crops. See Wilmore v. Chain O'Mines, Inc., 96 Colo. 319, 327, 44 P.2d 1024, 1028 (1935).

Although continuing trespass and nuisance remain viable concepts in Colorado under Wright and its progeny, not every trespass or nuisance that continues is necessarily regarded as one. Harper et al., The Law of Torts § 1.7. Colorado courts have embraced the concept of "permanent trespass and nuisance" to distinguish those unique factual situations—primarily in the context of irrigation ditches and railway lines—where the trespass or nuisance would and should continue indefinitely. [Cc].

In Middelkamp v. Bessemer Irrigating Ditch Co., 46 Colo. 102, 103 P. 280 (1909), the defendant built an irrigation ditch in loose, porous soil. As a result of the loose soil, water seeped through the bottom and sides of the ditch, causing flooding damage to plaintiff's adjacent properties. [Cc] We found that the irrigation ditch, as a permanent improvement, was distinguishable from the abatable nuisance we analyzed in Wright (house adjacent to cattle slaughterhouse). We reasoned that irrigation ditches were intended to be permanent structures and seep by necessity. [Cc]. Because the irrigation ditches were permanent, the seepage would continue indefinitely absent extraordinary measures. [Cc] Other jurisdictions have attempted to clarify the distinctions between continuing and permanent torts by focusing either on the "cause" of the harm, see Breiggar Prop., L.C. v. H.E. Davis & Sons, Inc., 52 P.3d 1133, 1135 (Utah 2002) (looking solely at the act constituting trespass, not the harm resulting from the act), or the "harm" resulting from that cause. See Wood v. Amer. Aggregates Corp., 67 Ohio App.3d 41, 585 N.E.2d 970, 973 (1990) (focusing on continuing damages, not conduct). We do not find these classifications helpful to our analysis, particularly in the context of this case where it is difficult to determine whether the toxic pollution plume is the cause of Hoery's alleged harm or the harm itself.

* * *

Even if the seepage was abatable, we declined to require it for defendants who lawfully constructed irrigation ditches because they represented a class of enterprises "so vital to the future development of our state." [Cc].; see also Ft. Lyon Canal Co. v. Bennett, 61 Colo. 111, 123, 156 P. 604, 609 (1916) (declining to find that seepage from an irrigation ditch constituted a continuing nuisance because maintenance of the siphon was a "laudable occupation authorized by the laws and statutes of the state."). The practical impact of the Middelkamp decision was that an action to recover for present and future damages would accrue when the lands were first visibly affected. 46 Colo. at 112, 103 P. at 283.

* * *

In sum, Colorado law recognizes the concepts of continuing trespass and nuisance for those property invasions where a defendant fails to stop or remove continuing, harmful physical conditions that are wrongfully placed on a plaintiff's land. The only exception is a factual situation—such as an irrigation ditch or a railway line—where the property invasion will and should continue indefinitely because defendants, with lawful authority, constructed a socially beneficial structure intended to be permanent.

C. Whether the Ongoing Presence and Continued Migration of Toxic Chemicals Each Constitutes a Continuing Trespass and Nuisance Under Colorado Law

Having reviewed our cases regarding continuing and permanent torts, we turn to the certified questions before us. Specifically, we must determine whether the continuing migration and ongoing presence of toxic pollution on a plaintiff's property constitutes a continuing trespass and/or nuisance, even though the condition causing that pollution has ceased.

Hoery contends that he asserted continuing trespass and nuisance claims under Wright because the United States remains liable for any harmful conditions it causes as long as those conditions continue to exist and cause injury. Under his theory, the migration of toxic chemicals and their continued presence on his property are still wrongful acts by the United States, which should be responsible until it stops the migration and removes the toxic chemicals.

In response, the United States argues that the claims alleged here cannot be continuing because any "wrongful conduct" that may have constituted a trespass or nuisance ceased in 1994, when the United States stopped operating Lowry as a military base. Because the tortious acts have stopped, the United States claims, the continued migration and ongoing presence of toxic chemicals on Hoery's property represent the damage caused by that tortious activity, but not the activity itself. In other words, the continued migration and ongoing presence of chemicals represent property damage caused by past acts. Therefore, the United States claims there is no continuing trespass and nuisance.

In support of its argument, the United States claims that our irrigation ditch cases hold that upon cessation of the negligent or wrongful act that caused the seepage, the claim accrues upon the discovery of the alleged property damage. In essence, the United States argues that we should extend our permanent tort concept to the facts alleged here.

Technically speaking, this is an issue of first impression in Colorado. Although we have recognized the concepts of continuing and permanent torts, we have not addressed an environmental contamination case where the contamination remains and continues to migrate daily onto a plaintiff's property, but where the cause of the contamination has ceased .

While we have not addressed this issue, other jurisdictions have. A number of jurisdictions have determined that the cessation of the condition causing the contamination is not material. These jurisdictions have held that even if the condition causing the contamination has ceased, provided the contamination remains on the plaintiff's land, or continues to migrate onto the plaintiff's land, the defendant remains liable for a continuing tort. See Nieman v. NLO Inc., 108 F.3d 1546, 1559 (6th Cir.1997) (nuclear processing facility stopped operating but uranium contamination remained on plaintiff's property); Arcade Water Dist. v. United States, 940 F.2d 1265, 1266 (9th Cir.1991) (laundry facility closed but contamination continued to leach into plaintiff's well); In re ASARCO/Vashon–Maury Island Litig., No. COO–695Z, 2001 U.S. Dist. LEXIS 7154, at *11–13 (W.D.Wash. May 23, 2001) (smokestack no longer operational but contaminated soil remained on plaintiff's property); Taygeta Corp. v. Varian Assoc. Inc., 436 Mass. 217, 763 N.E.2d 1053, 1065 (Mass.2002) (although defendant stopped dumping hazardous material years earlier, the remaining presence of the hazardous material on plaintiff's property was an ongoing source of groundwater contamination that continued to flow unabated onto the site); Kulpa v. Stewart's Ice Cream, 144 A.D.2d 205, 534 N.Y.S.2d 518, 520 (N.Y. App. Div. 1988) (contamination remained in plaintiff's well, even though underground gasoline storage tanks were drained and stopped leaking years earlier).

Arcade is particularly instructive because the facts are analogous to this case. In Arcade, the United States operated an army laundry facility from 1941 until 1973. During that time period, the laundry discharged waste residues into the ground. A domestic-use water well, operated by the Arcade Water District, was located approximately 2,000 feet from the laundry. facility. Arcade, 940 F.2d at 1266. Although the United States closed the laundry facility in 1973, subsequent testing of Arcade's well revealed that it was contaminated and that ground contamination from the laundry continued to leach into Arcade's well. In 1984, Arcade filed a FTCA suit against the United States, alleging that the release of laundry wastes constituted a continuing nuisance. The District Court dismissed the complaint as time-barred.

On appeal the Ninth Circuit reversed, holding that it was not material that the laundry facility was no longer operational. In determining under California law whether the nuisance was continuing, the Ninth Circuit reasoned that the most salient allegation was that contamination continued to leach into Arcade's well. Id. at 1268. That court concluded that because Arcade presented an engineer's affidavit stating that he could not say the contamination was permanent, it could not hold as a matter of law that the nuisance was permanent. Thus, the court held that Arcade alleged a set of facts which constituted a continuing nuisance.

We find the analysis in Arcade and other cases that have considered this issue persuasive and consistent with Wright and our continuing tort concept. Therefore, we agree with Hoery that the ongoing presence and continued migration of toxic chemicals originally emanating from Lowry constitute a continuing trespass and nuisance and decline to extend the permanent tort concept of the irrigation ditch cases to the facts alleged here.

For purposes of answering the certified questions before us, no dispute exists about whether the United States released TCE into the ground and by doing so, invaded Hoery's property. The property invasion constituted a trespass because the toxic pollution released by the United States physically intruded upon Hoery's property without his permission. See Public Serv. Co. of Colorado, 27 P.3d at 389. It also constituted a nuisance because the toxic pollution released by the United States substantially invaded Hoery's interest in the use and enjoyment of his property. See id. at 391.

We also hold that these property invasions by way of trespass and nuisance are continuing. The allegations in this case support such a finding on two grounds. First, TCE pollution remains on Hoery's property. The failure of the United States to remove the pollution from Hoery's property which it wrongfully placed there constitutes a continuing property invasion for the entire time the contamination remains. Wright, 40 Colo. at 440, 91 P. at 44; Restatement (Second) of Torts §§ 161 cmt. b, 834 cmt. e; Nieman, 108 F.3d at 1559; ASARCO, 2001 U.S. Dist. LEXIS 7154 at *11–13; Kulpa, 534 N.Y.S.2d at 520. Second, the toxic pollution continues to migrate onto his property on a daily basis. The failure of the United States to stop the toxic pollution plume that it created from entering Hoery's property also constitutes a continuing property invasion. [Cc]

Pursuant to the fundamental principles of tort law, the United States's failure to act, or its omissions, can be the basis for tortious conduct. As the Restatement explains, "The word 'actor' is used merely for convenience, and is used not only in its primary sense of denoting one who acts, but also as denoting one who deliberately or inadvertently fails to act." Restatement (Second) of Torts § 3 cmt. a; § 158 cmt. l ("A trespass on land may be by a failure of the actor to leave the land of which the other is in possession."); Graham v. Beverage, 211 W.Va. 466, 566 S.E.2d 603, 614 (2002) ("[W]e hereby hold that where a tort involves a continuing or repeated injury, the cause of action accrues at and the statute of limitations begins to run from the date of the last injury or when the tortious overt acts or omissions cease.")

These continuing property invasions are not dependent upon whether the United States still releases TCE into the ground. We decline to hold, as urged by the United States, that its wrongful conduct has ceased and that the contamination of Hoery's property represents only the product of that prior conduct. Taygeta, 763 N.E.2d at 1058, 1065 (rejecting the trial court's finding that the ongoing contamination was only a product of the previously terminated tortious conduct of dumping hazardous wastes and thus not itself a continuing nuisance); ASARCO, 2001 U.S. Dist. LEXIS 7154 at *13 (rejecting defendant's argument that although contamination remained in plaintiff's soil, its tortious conduct ceased years earlier when it stopped operating its smokestack). The daily migration and presence of those chemicals on Hoery's property constitute the continuing torts of trespass and nuisance in this case. While these continuing property invasions remain, it is immaterial whether the United States continues to release toxic pollutants from Lowry.

* * *

We also note that the continued contamination does not benefit the development of our state. In contrast to our policy supporting our holding that the seepage from irrigation ditches constituted a permanent property invasion, there exists no sound public policy supporting the classification of contamination from the release of toxic chemicals as a permanent property invasion. One basis for classifying a property invasion as permanent is whether public policy favors the continuation of the invasion. See Dan B. Dobbs, Law of Torts § 57 (2000). Irrigation ditches or railway lines are permanent improvements that help develop the state and should be encouraged. This rationale comports with the underlying principles of tort law. See Denver Publ'g Co. v. Bueno, 54 P.3d 893, 897–98 (Colo.2002) ("Torts are designed to encourage socially beneficial conduct and deter wrongful conduct."); Restatement (Second) of Torts § 901(c). Although plaintiffs still suffered a property invasion in such cases, we limited their recovery to one action for all present and future damages.

Here, we find that public policy favors the discontinuance of both the continuing migration and the ongoing presence of toxic chemicals into Hoery's property and irrigation well. Under Colorado law, a tortfeasor's liability for continuing trespass and nuisance creates a new cause of action each day the property invasion continues. Hence, the alleged tortfeasor has an incentive to stop the property invasion and remove the cause of damage.

V. CONCLUSION

For the reasons stated above, we answer both certified questions in the affirmative and return this case back to the Tenth Circuit for further proceedings.

[The dissenting opinion of Justice Kourlis, joined by Justice Coats, is omitted].

c. *Continuing Tortious Conduct*

The dissenting opinion in *Nieman* above at p. 29, made a conflicting interpretation of Ohio authorities and cited 54 C.J. S. Limitations of Actions § 177 (1987), a section entitled "Continuing or Repeated Injury in General," which states that "[a] 'continuing tort' is one inflicted over a period of time; it involves a wrongful conduct that is repeated until desisted, and each day creates a separate cause of action. A continuing tort sufficient to toll a statute of limitations is occasioned by continual unlawful acts, not by continual ill effects from an original violation, and for there to be a continuing tort there must be a continuing duty." Further, the dissenter presented Ohio authority suggesting that a continuing trespass is "wrongful conduct which can be reasonably physically abated," and that the plaintiffs' had failed aver that removal of radioactive byproducts from their property would be "realistically feasible." 108 F.3d at 1565 (Krupansky, J., dissenting).

In Carpenter v. Texaco, Inc., 419 Mass. 581, 646 N.E.2d 398 (Mass. 1995), the Carpenters owned land near a gasoline service station formerly owned by Texaco. The Carpenters became aware in 1982 that gasoline from an underground storage tank was leaking onto their property, and argued that the continued presence of gasoline on their property amounted to a continuing trespass and nuisance. Finding that after 1984 there was "no continuing release of gasoline from the gasoline station property, nor seepage of gasoline onto the plaintiff's property," summary judgment was affirmed because there was no evidence that any seepage has occurred within the three-year statute of limitations period prior to the commencement of the suit. The *Carpenter* court found that a continuing nuisance or trespass must be based on "recurring tortious or unlawful conduct, and is not established by the continuation of harm caused by previous but terminated tortious or unlawful conduct."

d. Who's Right?

Are there reasons to treat environmental contamination differently than, say, an encroaching building? Consider this statement of the Maine Supreme Judicial Court in *Jacques*:

> The defendants argue that even if abatability is the rule in Maine, public policy supports not applying that rule to environmental contamination cases. We see no reason why our long-standing rule of what constitutes a continuing nuisance or trespass should contain an exception for environmental waste. Our rule without such an exception encourages abatement by the responsible party, an important public policy consideration. In contrast, if we were to exclude from this test environmental contamination cases the effect would be to grant defendants the equivalent of an easement, thereby reducing significantly the chances that the hazardous materials would be cleaned up. 676 A.2d at 508.

6. CAUSATION

Of course, trespass is no different than any other tort in that the plaintiff must establish that it was the defendant's substance that entered in the land, that is, that the defendant caused the trespass. For example, in Anglado v. Leaf River Forest Products, Inc., 716 So.2d 543 (Miss.1998), the Supreme Court of Mississippi held that plaintiffs in a toxic tort suit failed to produce evidence that the dioxins and other chemicals their properties were exposed to came from a nearby pulp mill. The pulp mill presented uncontradicted evidence that the dioxins and other chemicals present on the tested properties were inconsistent with the chemical fingerprint of the effluent from their pulp mill, and that therefore the offending chemicals were not discharged by the mill. In addition, the mill presented evidence that dioxin is produced by many natural and artificial sources. Further, the plaintiffs produced no evidence that the mill was the source of any dioxin. Therefore, summary judgment for the mill was held proper.

As the following excerpts from Parks Hiway Enterprises, LLC v. CEM Leasing, Inc., 995 P.2d 657 (Alaska 2000) make clear, the questions of the defendant's control over the invading material and causation are intertwined:

* * *

I. INTRODUCTION

After Parks Hiway's groundwater was contaminated by fuel leaking from an adjacent service station, it sued the station's fuel supplier, Petroleum Sales. The superior court granted summary judgment to Petroleum Sales, finding its relationship to the contamination too remote to impose statutory or common law liability. Parks Hiway now appeals the court's dismissal of its various claims. Because we agree with the superior court's findings, we affirm.

II. FACTS AND PROCEEDINGS

Phillip and Genevieve Carboy have owned and operated the Gold Hill Service Station in Fairbanks since 1981. Throughout the Carboys' ownership, Gold Hill maintained up to three underground storage tanks on its property to hold gasoline. Although the Carboys checked their tanks periodically for leaks, they failed to comply with regulations requiring tank operators to report the tanks' registration numbers, proof of financial responsibility, and proof of testing to the state.

From 1981 until 1994, Petroleum Sales, Inc., supplied petroleum products to Gold Hill. When Gold Hill required additional fuel, Phillip Carboy would telephone Petroleum Sales and place an order. Petroleum Sales would then deliver the product to Gold Hill and directly fill the appropriate tanks. Carboy did not instruct Petroleum Sales' delivery personnel on how to fill the tanks during this process.

Gold Hill and Petroleum Sales are independent, separately owned, unaffiliated companies. Petroleum Sales did not oversee, manage, or operate the Gold Hill station and did not construct, install, maintain, or test the station's tanks. Moreover, Gold Hill never asked or authorized Petroleum Sales to perform any such work.

Parks Hiway Enterprises, LLC, owned the parcel adjacent to the Gold Hill station. In 1994 the Alaska Department of Environmental Conservation (the Department) determined that benzene had contaminated the groundwater under Parks Hiway's property. The Department identified Gold Hill as a probable source of the pollution. Gold Hill promptly removed its tanks, after which investigators discovered that the soil and groundwater surrounding the tank area were heavily contaminated with petroleum components. The rate of leakage was estimated at approximately one to two quarts per month over a twenty-year period.

Parks Hiway subsequently ceased drawing drinking water from its well. Parks Hiway suffered economic loss as a result of this action.

Parks Hiway sued the Carboys in 1995 and settled with them in 1996. In 1997 Parks Hiway filed an amended complaint naming Petroleum Sales as a defendant. Parks Hiway's amended complaint also named as defendants CEM Leasing, Inc., James E. Weymiller, Steven C. Winquist, and Phillip M. Tannehill. We refer to these defendants collectively as "Petroleum Sales." The complaint alleged that Petroleum Sales was responsible for the soil and groundwater contamination of Parks Hiway's property, and it asserted claims under strict liability, nuisance, trespass, and negligence theories.

Petroleum Sales moved for summary judgment in March 1997. The superior court granted Petroleum Sales' motion on December 16, 1997. Parks Hiway subsequently moved both for reconsideration and to file an amended complaint. The superior court agreed to reconsider its ruling. But in its January 23, 1998, order granting final judgment to Petroleum Sales, the court ultimately denied both of Parks Hiway's motions.

Parks Hiway appeals the superior court's grant of summary judgment to Petroleum Sales, the denial of its motion to submit an amended complaint, and the court's refusal to strike two affidavits Petroleum Sales submitted during the summary judgment proceedings.

III. DISCUSSION

* * *

C. The Superior Court Did Not Err by Rejecting Parks Hiway's Trespass Theory of Liability.

Trespass is an unauthorized intrusion or invasion of another's land, [Cc] including subsurface areas. [Cc] Trespass liability may result from an actor's intentional, negligent, or ultrahazardous conduct. [Cc] The superior court rejected Parks Hiway's attempt to hold Petroleum Sales liable for common law trespass, ruling that Petroleum Sales did not own or control the fuel when it contaminated the groundwater beneath Parks Hiway's property. Parks Hiway challenges this ruling, arguing that ownership of the invading substance is irrelevant for purposes of trespass liability where the actor "sets in motion" the release of the substance.

This court has not addressed the issue of whether a supplier of a substance is liable for trespass when, after delivery to the buyer, the substance escapes and invades neighboring land. Parks Hiway cites no authority explicitly recognizing a cause of action against the supplier under such circumstances. [Cc] Several cases have held that courts do not impose trespass liability on sellers for injuries caused by their product after it has left the ownership and possession of the sellers. [Cc] The courts in City of Bloomington v. Westinghouse Electric Corp., [Cc] Jordan v. Southern Wood Piedmont Co., [Cc] Town of Hooksett v. W.R. Grace & Co., [Cc] and City of Manchester v. National Gypsum Co. [Cc] accordingly refused to hold suppliers liable for trespass under facts roughly analogous to the present case.

The general consensus thus suggests that ownership or control of the intruding instrumentality is dispositive of an actor's trespass liability. Because its ownership and control over the fuel terminated upon the product's transfer into Gold Hill's tanks, Petroleum Sales bears no trespass liability for the fuel's subsequent migration.

Moreover, "a trespass action will exist if there is a direct causal relation between the conduct of the actor and the intrusion of foreign matter upon the possessor's land." [Cc] Actors therefore assume liability only when they "set[ ] in motion a force which, in the usual course of events, will damage property of another." [Cc] As a supplier of gasoline to Gold Hill, Petroleum Sales merely performed a delivery function which, "in the usual course of events," would not contaminate neighboring property. The direct causal connection required to establish trespass is thus absent from the present case. We accordingly reject Parks Hiway's trespass argument.

* * *

B.   JUDICIAL APPLICATIONS OF TRESPASS

MARTIN v. AMOCO OIL COMPANY

Court of Appeals of Indiana, 1997.
679 N.E.2d 139, aff'd in part, rev'd
in part on other grounds 696 N.E.2d 383
(Ind. 1998).

GARRARD, JUDGE.

James Martin, et. al. (collectively "Class Plaintiffs"), Amoco Oil Company ("Amoco"), and Joseph and Dorthea Zrnchik, et. al. (collectively "Intervenors") appeal various facets of a class action involving the alleged underground migration of oil from Amoco's Whiting, Indiana refinery to Class Plaintiffs' and Intervenors' property.

FACTS

This bitterly contested and often vexatious appeal began its journey to this court on February 1, 1991, when Robert O'Drobinak and Eugene Burkat filed suit against Amoco in Hammond, Indiana on behalf of themselves and the 500 residents of Whiting, Indiana who had received notice from Amoco of the possible underground migration of oil onto their properties. The complaint, as finally amended, alleged negligence, negligence per se, nuisance, strict liability, negligent/intentional infliction of emotional distress, and intentional trespass on the part of Amoco

The jury returned a verdict of not liable on all counts. [The trial judge] entered final judgment on this verdict on December 14, 1993 * * * On August 1, 1994, the Judge entered his order on the various motions to correct error. This order granted judgment on the evidence on the intentional trespass claim against Amoco. The Judge then proceeded to hold that the class representatives had failed to prove any compensatory damages and awarded each of the named class representatives nominal damages in the amount of one dollar. In all other respects, the Judge affirmed the verdict of the jury.

* * *

Amoco's Claim

Amoco claims that the trial court erred when it granted Class Plaintiffs' motion to correct error and entered judgment on the evidence finding Amoco liable for intentional trespass. More specifically, Amoco claims that the trial court applied the incorrect intent standard for proving intentional trespass. In its order on the motion to correct error, the trial court stated that Amoco's intent to refine oil in Whiting was sufficient to fulfill the intent element of the intentional trespass claim. Amoco claims that the mere intent to refine oil is not sufficient to satisfy this requirement. We agree. Because we find the issue of intent to be dispositive, we need not discuss the sufficiency of the evidence of trespass.

In its order granting judgment on the evidence, the trial court found that the simple intent to refine oil at Whiting was sufficient to support the finding of intentional trespass. Amoco claims that it must have intended that the oil migrate under the Class Plaintiffs' land, while Class Plaintiffs' argue, quite naturally, that the trial court was correct. Both parties rely on Hawke v. Maus, 141 Ind.App. 126, 226 N.E.2d 713 (1967) to support their contentions. Hawke involved an intentional trespass claim against the driver of a delivery truck which struck the plaintiff's tree. From the facts of the case, it was clear that the truck driver did not intend the trespass. The main issue before the court of appeals was whether the trespass was the result of a volitional act by the driver or whether the driver was forced into the tree by the third party. Quoting the Restatement (Second) of Torts § 164 cmt. a, p. 296 (1965), the court stated, " '[t]he intention which is required to make the actor liable under the rule stated in this Section is an intention to enter upon the particular piece of land in question, irrespective of whether the actor knows or should know that he is not entitled to enter.' " 226 N.E.2d at 715. The court went on to state that " '[a]lthough it is not necessary that the trespasser intend to commit a trespass or even that he know that his act will constitute a trespass, it is required for trespass that there be an intentional act and an intent to do the very act which results in the trespass.' " Id. at 716 (quoting 87 C.J.S. TRESPASS § 5, p. 960). Neither these statements nor subsequent case law do much to clarify what intent is necessary for intentional trespass.

Though it is not binding authority, we find persuasive the definition of intent the Washington Supreme Court used in Bradley v. American Smelting and Refining, 104 Wash.2d 677, 709 P.2d 782 (1985). Bradley dealt with an intentional trespass claim against a smelting plant for hazardous airborne emissions that landed on the plaintiff's land. The defendant knew that airborne emissions from its plant were landing on the plaintiff's property and those around it, but could not prevent the emissions absent discontinuing operations at the plant. Much like in Hawke, the court relied heavily on the Restatement (Second) of Torts in defining the requisite intent but focused on § 158 rather than § 164. Quoting from sec. 8(A) (1965), the court stated that " '[t]he word "intent" is used ... to denote that the actor desires to cause consequences of his act, or that he believes that the consequences are substantially certain to result from it.' " Id. 709 P.2d at 785. The court further stated that " '[i]ntent is not, however, limited to consequences which are desired. If the actor knows that the consequences are certain, or substantially certain, to result from his act, and still goes ahead, he is treated by the law as if he had in fact desired to produce the result.' " Id. (quoting Restatement (Second) of Torts § 8A cmt. b, p. 15 (1965)).

We believe that the definition of intent espoused in Bradley correctly describes the intent discussed by the court in Hawke. We hold that Amoco must have intentionally committed an act that it knew or was substantially certain would result in the migration of oil onto the Class Plaintiffs' property for it to fulfill the intent element of intentional trespass. Absent some evidence of knowledge of the certain or substantially certain migration, mere intent to refine the oil was not sufficient.

Even though Class Plaintiffs requested a new trial, the trial court granted judgment on the evidence, so it is the judgment on the evidence standard of review to which we now turn. In considering a motion for judgment on the evidence after a jury verdict, the trial court must look only to the evidence and reasonable inferences therefrom favorable to the nonmoving party.

To uphold the trial court's judgment on the evidence in this case, the evidence must point unerringly to the conclusion that Amoco knew or was substantially certain that oil would migrate onto the Class Plaintiffs' property if Amoco operated its Whiting refinery. Though the testimony is conflicting, it does not point unerringly to this conclusion. Amoco presented evidence that it employed various devices to prevent any migration of oil off its property and that it believed that these devices were effective. Amoco also presented evidence that it met all federal safety requirements and all standards set by the Indiana Department of Environmental Management. Though Class Plaintiffs claim that this evidence should be discounted, it is not the province of this court to weight the evidence. We hold that the evidence does not point unerringly to a conclusion opposite that of the jury verdict and, therefore, the trial court erred by granting judgment on the evidence on the intentional trespass claim.

Because Class Plaintiffs did not challenge the underlying jury verdict on the intentional trespass claim, we now remand this issue to the trial court and order the trial court to reinstate the jury verdict.

Notes and Questions

1. *A Seminal Decision.* The opinion in *Martin* quotes from the leading decision in Bradley v. American Smelting and Refining Co., 104 Wash.2d 677, 709 P.2d 782 (Wash. 1985) in which the Washington Supreme Court answered a series of questions certified to it by a federal district court. In addition to resolving the question of what constitutes the requisite intent for trespass, the court determined that the "intentional deposit of microscopic particulates, undetectable by the human senses, upon a person's property gives rise to a cause of action for trespassory invasion of the person's right to exclusive possession of property as well as a claim of nuisance." After tracing the history of the tort and the "non-sensical barrier" of requiring a direct and immediate and tangible invasion, it observed:

> Atmospheric or hydrologic systems assure that pollutants deposited in one place will end up somewhere else, with no less assurance of causation than the blaster who watches the debris rise from its property and settle on his neighbor's land. Trespassory consequences today may be no less "direct" even if the mechanism of delivery is viewed as more complex.

* * *

> ["]Under the modern theory of trespass, the law presently allows an action to be maintained in trespass for invasions that, at one time, were considered indirect and, hence, only a nuisance. In order to recover in trespass for this type of invasion [i.e., the asphalt piled in such a way as to run onto plaintiff's property, or the pollution emitting from a defendant's smoke stack, such as in the present case], a plaintiff must show 1) an invasion affecting an interest in the exclusive possession of his property; 2) an intentional doing of the act which results in the invasion; 3) reasonable foreseeability that the act done could result in an invasion of plaintiff's possessory interest; and 4) substantial damages to the *res*.["] quoting Borland v. Sanders Lead Co., 369 So.2d 523, 529 (Ala.1979).

Consistent with this position, the *Bradley* court held:

> No useful purpose would be served by sanctioning actions in trespass by every landowner within a hundred miles of a manufacturing plant. Manufacturers would be harassed and the litigious few would cause the escalation of costs to the detriment of the many. The elements that we have adopted for an action in trespass from Borland require that a plaintiff has suffered actual and substantial damages. Since this is an element of the action, the plaintiff who cannot show that actual and substantial damages have been suffered should be subject to dismissal of his cause upon a motion for summary judgment. 709 P.2d at 789.

2. *Bradley* is important because the court makes several significant changes in the rules usually governing trespass actions. First, it *lowers* the physical invasion requirement by recognizing that increased scientific knowledge enables courts to find, as "physical" intrusions, invasions which were previously not observable and, accordingly, not legally cognizable. Indeed, as

the court correctly points out, scientific understanding allows us to demonstrate that most interferences are "physical" in the sense that energy, unleashed by a defendant, produces a movement of molecules across land boundaries, in the form of tiny particles, or even noise and light. Second, and closely related, it abolishes the historical distinction between direct and indirect invasions of the landowner's interest. Third, the court *increases* the harm requirement by necessitating that the plaintiffs show that the invasion produced substantial harm to their property. Why is this third requirement so important?

3. *More Battles Over Intent.* This question of intent addressed in Martin v. Amoco and *Bradley* is often pivotal in environmental trespass actions. In United Proteins, Inc. v. Farmland Industries, Inc., 259 Kan. 725, 915 P.2d 80 (Kan. 1996), in which chemicals from a fertilizer manufacturer's plant (hexavalent chromium) had been released, contaminating the aquifer under plaintiff's property, the Kansas Supreme Court reversed the trial court's finding of an intentional trespass, and held that that plaintiff failed to satisfy the Restatement (Second) of Torts requirement that defendant be shown to have known that the chemicals were substantially certain to enter plaintiff's property.

In seeming contrast to *United Proteins* is Scribner v. Summers, 84 F.3d 554 (2d Cir.1996) (applying New York law). Defendant operated a steel-treating facility on a site bordering plaintiffs' property. The facility used furnaces that leave a sludge residue containing barium chloride. Defendant periodically took the furnaces outside the building and washed them down. Residue flowed into a drainage ditch that ran downhill to an area adjacent to plaintiffs' property. In 1986 barium was declared a hazardous waste by New York environmental authorities. In the early 1990's plaintiffs discovered that their property was contaminated with defendant's barium. They brought suit for damages alleging that defendant "trespassed on their property because of the migration or leaching of barium particles across" the property line. The trial court found no trespass because "[t]here is no evidence [that defendant] intended the water used in [the] cleaning process to enter plaintiffs' land." On appeal, *held*, reversed. Citing Phillips v. Sun Oil Co., 307 N.Y. 328, 121 N.E.2d 249 (N.Y. 1954), the court said:

> In determining whether [defendant] had the requisite intent for trespass under New York law, * * * the appropriate standard is whether [defendant]: (i) "intended the act which amounts to or produces the unlawful invasion," and (ii) "had good reason to know or expect that subterranean and other conditions were such that there would be passage [of the contaminated water] from defendant's to plaintiff's land." Phillips, 307 N.Y. at 331.

The court concluded:

> Defendant concedes, "in the process of removing and breaking up the worn out furnaces, small amounts of barium salts escaped onto the pavement. These barium particles were carried by moving water into a swale on Jasco's land, but near the boundary with plaintiffs." Further, the parties agree that the Scribners' property was located downhill from Jasco's property.

Under Phillips, Jasco intended the acts which caused the invasion of the Scribners' property. "[T]he contamination [on the Scribners' property] was caused over time by the business operations and activities at the Jasco site. And, on these facts, we find that Jasco 'had good reason to know or expect' that barium particles would pass from the pavement where the furnaces were washed and demolished, into the swale, and onto the Scribners' property, which was located at a lower elevation level." We therefore conclude that Jasco is liable in trespass for the damage caused to the Scribners' property. 84 F.3d at 557–58.

Is the New York standard of "good reason to know or expect" that the contaminates would reach plaintiffs' property a relaxation of the Restatement standard of intent?

4. *Air versus Surface versus Subsurface Pollution*. The foregoing authorities imply that the nature of the pollution-causing activity is extremely relevant. Thus, with air pollution it is difficult for a defendant to deny that it knew that air-borne particles would be taken downwind and be deposited to the property of others, as *Bradley* exemplifies. Similarly, *Scribner* shows that for surface liquid pollution it is equally difficult for a defendant to deny knowledge that adjacent properties downhill from its operations would be contaminated.

But with subsurface and groundwater contamination the science of movement is complex, the effects not visible to the ordinary observer, and hence defendant may not possess the requisite knowledge as *Martin* and *United Proteins* both illustrate. However, as is described in the next section, such cases may support a claim for *negligent* trespass.

On the question of intent, see also Ducham v. Tuma, 265 Mont. 436, 877 P.2d 1002, 1005 (Mont.1994) (intent proven when overflow from defendant's trout pond was dispersed via a swale to cross-plaintiff's property); Seal v. Naches–Selah Irrigation District, 51 Wash.App. 1, 751 P.2d 873, 874 (Wash. App.1988) (intent not proven for seepage from irrigation canal into plaintiff's property where defendant showed its efforts to alleviate seepage problems).

5. *What's Not A Physical Invasion*. If the traditional distinction between tangible and intangible invasions has been abolished by *Bradley* and *Martin*, what about odors as constituting a trespass? In Brown v. County Commissioners of Scioto County, 87 Ohio App.3d 704, 622 N.E.2d 1153 (Ohio App. 1993), the court considered plaintiffs' allegations that the odors emanating from the sewage treatment plant operated by defendants had been so bad that the "germs and bacteria emitted [had] rotted the ears off of two rabbits that the Browns owned." They further established that the plant had been cited for violations of EPA's standards on bacteria content in its effluent which in turn caused the emission of noxious odors; that its equipment had malfunctioned further exacerbating the odors; and that their home had suffered $25,000 in diminished value. After noting the liberalized trend in trespass cases, the appeals court observed that trespass nevertheless requires at least some interference with the right to the exclusive possession of property. It concluded:

* * *

There is no summary judgment evidence of the polluting substance, i.e., noxious odors, depositing particulate matter on appellant's real property or causing physical damage to it. We are persuaded that under either the traditional or modern views, since appellant has failed to adduce summary judgment evidence of physical damage to her real property, appellees were entitled to summary judgment on appellant's trespass claim.

Therefore, despite the relaxation in the nature of invasions that will satisfy the requirements of trespass, it remains the law that an actual physical invasion is demanded. See Leaf River Forest Products, Inc. v. Simmons, 697 So.2d 1083, 1085 (Miss.1996).

6. *Stray Electricity and Electro–Magnetic Fields as Invasions.* Fletcher v. Conoco Pipe Line Co., 129 F.Supp.2d 1255 (W.D. Mo. 2001) arose out of "stray electricity" escaping from the cathodic process used by a natural gas pipeline company as part of its fuel transportation apparatus. The court's treatment of the plaintiff's trespass claim follows.

* * *

C. Counts VI & XVI—Trespass

Defendant argues that, as a matter of law, the presence of "stray electricity" on Plaintiffs' properties cannot constitute a physical interference sufficient to provide the basis for a trespass claim. Plaintiffs assert that Defendant's "stray electricity" is a tangible phenomenon that invades their lands and causes palpable damage.

In Missouri, trespass is described as a direct physical interference with the property of another. See Maryland Heights Leasing, Inc. v. Mallinckrodt, Inc., 706 S.W.2d 218, 225 (Mo.Ct.App.1985) (citing Looney v. Hindman, 649 S.W.2d 207, 212 (Mo.1983)). Liability for trespass also may arise where entry is made with consent but the scope of the consent is exceeded. See Griesenauer v. Emsco Corp., 399 S.W.2d 147, 151 (Mo.Ct.App.1965). Missouri courts do not appear to have addressed the question of whether electrical emissions can constitute a physical interference with land sufficient to support a trespass claim.

Plaintiffs cite to Dabb v. NYNEX Corp., 262 A.D.2d 1079, 691 N.Y.S.2d 840 (N.Y.App.Div.1999) as support for the proposition that other courts have allowed trespass claims in "stray electricity" cases. The Court agrees with Defendant that Plaintiffs' citation is misleading in that the opinion does not directly address the validity of a trespass claim based on the presence of electricity.

The Court observes that when presented with this issue, the California Supreme Court concluded that homeowners could not assert a trespass claim against an electric utility for allegedly emitting electromagnetic radiation onto their property. See San Diego Gas & Electric Co. v. Superior Court, 13 Cal.4th 893, 55 Cal.Rptr.2d 724, 920 P.2d 669, 696 (1996). The court reasoned that recovery in trespass actions is generally "predicated upon the deposit of particulate matter upon the plaintiffs' property or on actual physical damage thereto" and because the electric and magnetic fields from the defendant's powerlines "are wholly intangible phenomena" that cause no physical damage to property, an action in trespass could not lie. Id.

In Maryland Heights Leasing, Inc. v. Mallinckrodt, Inc., the Eastern District of Missouri dealt with the analogous issue of whether radioactive emissions can constitute a physical interference with property. 706 S.W.2d at 225. The Court declared that for an "interference to constitute a trespass, appellants must prove the intrusion interfered with their actual possession, their right of exclusive possession, in order to distinguish between trespass and nuisance, an interference with the mere use and enjoyment." Id. at 225–226. To further demonstrate the distinction between trespass and nuisance, the court stated:

> The classic cases of the barking dog, the neighboring bawdy house, noise, smoke, fumes, or obnoxious odors generally invoke the doctrine of the law of nuisance. These intrusions do not typically result in any actionable damage to the res; the injury caused by such acts usually results in a diminution of the use value of the property causally related to the harmful conduct made the basis of the claim ... but, if, as a result of the defendant's operations, [a] ... substance is deposited upon the plaintiff's property, thus interfering with his exclusive possessory interest by causing substantial damage to the res, then the plaintiff may seek his remedy in trespass.

Id. at 225 (quoting Borland v. Sanders Lead, Co., 369 So.2d 523, 529–30 (Ala.1979)). Concluding that radioactive emissions may constitute a trespass, the court found that the 'physical invasion' alleged by appellants, broadly construed, permitted the inference that radioactive material had been deposited on appellants' property.

The Court finds that, based upon the rationale in Maryland Heights Leasing, Inc., Plaintiffs have alleged a "physical invasion" sufficient to support a claim of trespass. The present case is distinguishable from San Diego Gas & Electric Co. because Plaintiffs have alleged actual physical damage to their property. Plaintiffs claim, inter alia, that the escaping electricity "has a deleterious affect on electric motors and any electric appliance, including light bulbs" and "causes accelerated corrosion of metal structures ... such as well casings and fence posts." The Court concludes that Plaintiffs' allegations, as pleaded, state a claim for trespass. Therefore, Defendant's Motion to Dismiss Counts VI and XVI is DENIED.

As regards electric and magnetic fields, or EMFs, San Diego Gas & Electric Co. v. Covalt, 13 Cal.4th 893, 55 Cal.Rptr.2d 724, 920 P.2d 669 (Cal. 1996), was an action brought by homeowners against a utility, alleging that electric and magnetic fields (EMF) emitted from nearby electric power lines constituted a trespass, summarized the boundaries of the tort, quoting in part from its decision in Wilson v. Interlake Steel Co., 32 Cal.3d 229, 185 Cal.Rptr. 280, 649 P.2d 922 (Cal. 1982):

> [T]he court [in Wilson] reasoned that "Noise alone," without damage to the property, will not support a tort action for trespass. Recovery allowed in prior trespass actions predicated upon noise, gas emissions, or vibration intrusions has, in each instance, been predicated upon the deposit of particulate matter upon the plaintiffs' property or on actual physical damage thereto. All intangible intrusions, such as noise, odor, or light alone, are dealt with as nuisance cases, not trespass. Succinctly

stated, the rule is that actionable trespass may not be predicated upon non-damaging noise, odor, or light intrusion; * * * First, electric and magnetic fields arising from powerlines are wholly intangible phenomena within the meaning of Wilson. Indeed, unlike noise, odors, or light, they cannot be directly perceived by the senses. Instead, electric and magnetic fields are more akin to television and radio waves: as we explained in our background discussion, such fields are an extremely low frequency, non-ionizing form of electromagnetic energy.

Second, plaintiffs do not allege, as they are required to do under Wilson, that the electric and magnetic fields at issue in this case caused any physical damage to their property. Nor can they so allege, given the low frequency and consequent low energy of such fields. Plaintiffs do allege that the fields in question made their property "unsafe and uninhabitable." But property is "unsafe and uninhabitable" only to the extent that it creates a risk of personal harm to its occupants, which is manifestly different from damage to the property itself. 920 P.2d at 695.

7. See also Padilla v. Lawrence, 101 N.M. 556, 685 P.2d 964 (N.M. Ct. App.1984) (odor, dust and flies caused by manure processing plant did not constitute trespass where there was no proof of matter settling on and damaging property); Nissan Motor Corp. v. Maryland Shipbuilding and Drydock Co., 544 F.Supp. 1104 (D.Md.1982), affirmed 742 F.2d 1449 (4th Cir.1984) (smoke and soot that landed on new cars constituted neither trespass nor nuisance, since there was no interference with automobile company's exclusive possession, and "normal" occupants would not be substantially annoyed or disturbed). But see Maryland Heights Leasing, Inc. v. Mallinckrodt, Inc., 706 S.W.2d 218 (Mo.App.1985) (complaint alleged cause of action for nuisance and trespass arising out of damage to property caused by low-level radiation emission).

8. *Trespass as a Taking.*

A federal district court in an unusual ruling held that defendant chemical company may have "taken" its neighbors property in violation of the federal and Louisiana constitutions when hazardous waste from its governmentally-permitted underground injection wells migrated off site.

In Mongrue v. Monsanto Co., 1999 WL 219774 (E.D.La.1999) the plaintiffs claimed the state-permitted contamination violated the takings clause of the Fifth Amendment to the U.S. Constitution, which prohibits taking private property "for public use, without just compensation." Provisions of the Fifth Amendment apply to state actions through the 14th Amendment. The Louisiana Constitution contains a more specific provision: "Property shall not be taken or damaged by the state * * * except for public purposes and with just compensation paid * * * Property shall not be taken or damaged by any private entity authorized by law to expropriate, except for a public and necessary purpose and with just compensation paid."

The state and Monsanto knew that the waste would eventually spread under the plaintiff's land, plaintiffs alleged. When a company applies for a hazardous waste injection well permit, it is required to project where the waste will extend for 10,000 years The Plaintiffs claimed: "Monsanto's projections showed the waste would encroach on [plaintiffs'] land as early as 2007."

A permanent, physical intrusion on to the plaintiff's property, even if minor, is a taking, the court said, citing *Loretto v. Teleprompter Manhattan CATV Corp.* (458 U.S. 419, 102 S.Ct. 3164, 73 L.Ed.2d 868 (1982)), which involved compensation for installation of cable television equipment in New York apartment buildings. *Loretto* held that a "permanent physical occupation authorized by state law is a taking without regard to whether the State, or instead a party authorized by the State" is the actor. Further, compensation is required regardless of whether the defendant's occupation is lawful, the court noted. The district court also rejected Monsanto's argument that an action authorized by the state could not be an unlawful trespass.

9.   For a general treatment of the particulate matter issue, see Annotation, 2 A.L.R. 4th 1054 (1980). See also Robert L. Glicksman, A guide to Kansas Common Law Actions Against Industrial Pollution Sources, 33 U. Kan. L. Rev. 621 (1985); Warren J. Hurwitz, Environmental Health: An Analysis of Available and Proposed Remedies for Victims of Toxic Waste Contamination, 7 Am. J. L. & Med. 61 (1981); Putt & Bolla, Invasion of Radioactive Particulates as a Common Law Trespass–An Overview, 3 Urb. L. Rev. 206 (1980); Comment, Remedies for Intangible Intrusions: The Distinction Between Trespass and Nuisance Actions Against Lawfully Zoned Businesses in California, 17 U.C. Davis L. Rev. 389 (1983).

Note on Negligent Trespass

1.   The majority of environmental trespass actions are of the intentional variety exemplified by *Martin v. Amoco Oil Co.*, *United Proteins v. Farmland*, and *Bradley v. American Smelting*. But unintentional trespass based on negligent conduct is also actionable. In Lever Brothers Co. v. Langdoc, 655 N.E.2d 577 (Ind.App.1995) a tenant of an apartment building located next to a manufacturing plant brought a trespass claim seeking to recover for property damage caused by the plant's discharge of an 8,000 gallon slug of blended oil into the public sewer system, resulting in a fatty, greasy substance seeping up from the tenant's basement drain. The appeals court's analysis of the negligent trespass claim, affirming the jury's verdict for the tenant, follows:

> Lever Brothers contends that the trial court erred in determining that it was liable for negligent trespass. An action for trespass requires the plaintiff to prove that he was in possession of the land and that the defendant entered the land without right. Moreover, it is a general rule of tort law that:

> > One who recklessly or negligently, or as a result of an abnormally dangerous activity, enters land in the possession of another or causes a thing or third person so to enter is subject to liability to the possessor if, but only if, his presence or the presence of the thing or the third person upon the land causes harm to the land, to the possessor, or a thing or a third person in whose security the possessor has a legally protected interest.

> Restatement (Second) of Torts § 165 (1965).

> While no Indiana case has examined whether the entry of noxious material onto one's property causing harm constitutes a trespass, other

jurisdictions have determined that a trespass action will exist if there is a direct causal relation between the conduct of the actor and the intrusion of foreign matter upon the possessor's land causing harm.

* * *

Here, Langdoc suffered property damage as a result of a fatty, greasy substance which seeped from her basement drain which was caused by Lever Brothers' discharge of prohibited materials into a public sewer system. Applying § 165 of the Restatement (Second), we determine that Lever Brothers' actions prompted foreign matter to enter property possessed by Langdoc causing her property damage; this constitutes a negligent trespass. Accordingly, we conclude that the trial court did not err when it held Lever Brothers liable for negligent trespass. 655 N.E.2d at 581–82.

Restatement (Second) of Tort § 165, quoted in *Lever Brothers*, clearly authorizes a negligent trespass action so long as the plaintiff sustains some actual harm to person or property. The negligence in *Lever Brothers* was predicated on a violation of an ordinance prohibiting the discharge of the substances which produced the harm, thus creating a negligence per se basis of liability.

In the *United Proteins* decision quoted earlier, that found no evidence of intent, the Kansas Supreme Court implied that a negligent trespass claim would have been viable but for the statutes of limitation which had barred any claim based on strict liability or negligence.

2.   Other environmental tort actions have applied a negligent trespass theory. See, e.g., Scottish Guarantee Ins. Co., Ltd. v. Dwyer, 19 F.3d 307, 311 (7th Cir.1994) (plaintiffs had cause of action for negligent trespass for personal injuries and property damage arising from defendant's toxic chemicals, released during a fire, which seeped into plaintiffs' soil contaminating their water wells). In Fortier v. Flambeau Plastics Co., 164 Wis.2d 639, 476 N.W.2d 593 (Wis.App.1991), the Court of Appeals of Wisconsin addressed a case with facts similar to *Lever Brothers*. There, three chemical companies deposited toxic chemicals into a city landfill, contrary to municipal ordinances, and the chemicals seeped or leached from the landfill to the plaintiffs' nearby properties contaminating their water wells. Adopting Restatement (Second) of Torts § 165, the court determined that chemical compounds intruded on the plaintiffs' property causing personal injury and property damage, and thus, the plaintiffs' had a cause of action for negligent trespass.

See also McDowell v. State of Alaska, 957 P.2d 965 (Alaska 1998), in which property owners brought negligence and strict liability claims against service station owners and the state for injuries to real property caused by petroleum contamination. For purposes of applying the statute of limitations (six years for trespass; two years for negligence), the Alaska Supreme Court opted for the trespass statute of limitations because the plaintiffs allegation of an invasion of their interest in exclusive possession and the nature of their injury "sound[ed] in trespass." "Our conclusion that the McDowells' claims sound in trespass is consistent with the results reached in other cases, which have held that negligent contamination of real property is an injury to land in the nature of trespass." 957 P.2d at 968.

Chapter Three

NUISANCE: THE COMPREHENSIVE ENVIRONMENTAL TORT THEORY

A. NUISANCE: AN INTRODUCTION

Nuisance is a broad and often misunderstood term that is employed to describe a diversity of harms. More than any other tort cause of action, a claim that defendant's actions constitute a nuisance is at the core of environmental torts. To begin, a nuisance may be either "public" or "private". As explained by the Colorado Supreme Court in Hoery v. United States, 64 P.3d 214 (Colo. 2003) (en banc), a suit brought by a landowner claiming the toxic contamination of his property, including his well water, arising from the nearby disposal of trichloroethylene ("TCE") and other toxic chemicals: "A private nuisance is distinguishable from a public nuisance. A private nuisance is a tort against land and the plaintiff's actions must always be founded upon his interest in the land. A public or common nuisance covers the invasion of public rights, that is, rights common to all members of the public. See Restatement (Second) of Torts § 821B, 821D."

Professor William H. Rodgers, Jr., Environmental Law § 2.1 at 112–113, 114–115 (2d ed. West 1994), summarizes the significance of nuisance doctrines in environmental litigation:

> To a surprising degree, the legal history of the environment has been written by nuisance law. There is no common law doctrine that approaches nuisance in comprehensiveness or detail as a regulator of land use and of technological abuse. Nuisance actions reach pollution of all physical media—air, water, land, groundwater—by a wide variety of means. Nuisance actions have challenged virtually every major industrial and municipal activity that today is the subject of comprehensive environmental regulation—the operation of land fills, incinerators, sewage treatment plants, activities at chemical plants, aluminum, lead and copper smelters, oil refineries, pulp mills, rending plants, quarries and mines, textile mills and a

host of other manufacturing activities. Nuisance litigation has influenced energy policy at all stages—fuel exploration, transportation, siting of facilities, fuel combustion, waste disposal and reclamation. Nuisance theory and case law is the common law backbone of modern environmental and energy law.

* * *

Nuisance lawsuits have brought under scrutiny * * * pollution from a coal-burning power plant, sewage treatment plant, a lead smelter, a nitric acid plant, concrete plant, feed lot, grain storage facility, airport, the town dump, and a variety of other sources. More recently, nuisance law has been invoked against an unauthorized dump, a hazardous waste disposal site, a sanitary landfill, a waste treatment lagoon, other sewage treatment works, a carpet dye plant, and a mine that was the source of acid drainage (citations omitted).

There exists confusion as to what the word "nuisance" describes: Is it the nature of the defendant's conduct or defendant's activity? Or is it the nature of the invasion that the plaintiff has experienced? When we describe something as a nuisance are we expressing the legal conclusion that it is an activity for which the actor is liable? Can a nuisance exist without liability?

While many decisions characterize the doctrine inexactly, the term "nuisance" is best understood as the *result* of the activity of an actor which interferes with a landowner's, or an occupant's, right of quiet or profitable enjoyment of property. Activity satisfying this description creates a nuisance whether or not liability attaches. Thus "for a nuisance to exist there must be harm to another or the invasion of an interest, but there need not be liability for it * * *. [N]uisance does not signify any particular kind of conduct on the part of the defendant. Instead the word has reference to two particular kinds of harm—the invasion of two kinds of interests," public nuisance and private nuisance. Restatement (Second) of Torts § 821A, comment b.

B. PUBLIC NUISANCE

1. INTRODUCTION

A public nuisance is an *"unreasonable* interference with a right common to the general public." Restatement (Second) of Torts § 821B. The origins of the public nuisance doctrines are found in interferences or infringements of the rights of the British Crown, which were applied to any action that produced an inconvenience or some kind of harm to members of the public. A public nuisance was regarded as a crime, and it came to be defined as "any act not warranted by law, or omission to discharge a legal duty, which obstructs or causes inconvenience or damage to the public in the exercise of rights common to all Her Majesty's subjects." Stephen, General View of the Criminal Law of England 105 (1890).

Restatement (Second) of Torts § 821B comment b points out the earmarks of common law public nuisances:

> b. *Common law public nuisances*. At common law public nuisance came to cover a large, miscellaneous and diversified group of minor criminal offenses, all of which involved some interference with the interests of the community at large—interests that were recognized as rights of the general public entitled to protection. Thus public nuisances included interference with the public health, as in the case of keeping diseased animals or the maintenance of a pond breeding malarial mosquitoes; with the public safety, as in the case of the storage of explosives in the midst of a city or the shooting of fireworks in the public streets; with the public morals, as in the case of houses of prostitution or indecent exhibitions; with the public peace, as by loud and disturbing noises; with the public comfort, as in the case of widely disseminated bad odors, dust and smoke; with the public convenience, as by the obstruction of a public highway or a navigable stream; and with a wide variety of other miscellaneous public rights of a similar kind. In each of these instances, the interference with the public right was so unreasonable that it was held to constitute a criminal offense. For the same reason it also constituted a tort.

The material below shows that there are three primary questions posed in the assertion of a public nuisance theory of liability in environmental litigation: (1) has the defendant interfered with a public, as opposed to a solely private, right; (2) was the interference unreasonable; and (3) if a plaintiff is seeking a monetary remedy, did the plaintiff sustain the kind of unique or special injury that differentiates his harm from that suffered by the general public.

2. UNREASONABLENESS OF THE INTERFERENCE

Restatement (Second) of Torts § 821B(2) sets out three criteria for deciding if the interference with the public right is "unreasonable":

> (2) Circumstances that may sustain a holding that an interference with a public right is unreasonable include the following:
>
> (a) Whether the conduct involves a significant interference with the public health, the public safety, the public peace, the public comfort or the public convenience, *or*
>
> (b) whether the conduct is proscribed by a statute, ordinance or administrative regulation, *or*
>
> (c) whether the conduct is of a continuing nature or has produced a permanent or long-lasting effect, and, as the actor knows or has reason to know, has a significant effect upon the public right.

Because these three standards are listed in the disjunctive, the presence of any one of them may be sufficient to support a finding of an unreasonable interference with the public right. It is important that only subsection (c) requires, or even assigns relevance to, what the defendant *knew* or should have known about the extent of the interference. Under subsections (a) and (b) any significant interference with public health or safety or comfort or convenience or statutory breach produces a finding of a public nuisance, without any evidence of the defendant's awareness of the impact its conduct or activity is having upon such public rights. In other words, the liability is strict.

Today many states have statutes which declare that certain conduct—such as polluting the public waters of the state—constitutes a public nuisance for which the actor is liable for a penalty to the state. E.g., Ariz. Rev. Stat. § 36–601(A)(1998), describing specific "conditions" that constitute "public nuisances dangerous to the public health[.]" Or.Rev.Stat. § 196.855 (1991) ("The removal of material from the bed or banks or filling any of the waters of this state without a permit" or contrary to a permit "issued under ORS 196.825 * * * is a public nuisance."); Or.Rev.Stat. § 468b.025 (1991) (polluting state waters or violating the parameters of a waste discharge permit is a public nuisance).

Representative of a public nuisance claim predicated on violation of a statute is Akzo Coatings of America, Inc. v. American Renovating, 842 F.Supp. 267 (E.D.Mich.1993), where plaintiffs brought an action under CERCLA to recover their share of response costs incurred by them in connection with a consent decree entered into with the United States that obligated them to pay $10 million toward the clean up of an industrial waste site. The court denied defendants' motion for summary judgment:

> Congress did not intend for CERCLA[1] to preempt state law remedies, such as nuisance.

> * * *

> Plaintiffs' count VII is based on public nuisance, for the role defendants played in transporting or arranging for the disposal of hazardous wastes at the site. The pecuniary damages resulting from the alleged nuisance include government oversight costs and any past and future costs to abate the nuisance. Plaintiffs are stating an alternative theory for reimbursement of costs they incurred with respect to the site. Because private costs were not covered by the consent decree entered by defendant, summary judgment will not be granted as to plaintiffs' public nuisance claim.

> * * *

> Defendants * * * argue that plaintiffs have failed to state a valid cause of action for nuisance. Plaintiffs must allege a statutory violation and show that they sustained damages distinct and different from the injury suffered by the public generally. Here, plaintiffs

---

1. Chapter 10 considers liability under the Comprehensive Environmental Re- sponse, Liability and Compensation Act, 42 U.S.C. § 9601 et seq (West 1999).

do allege a statutory violation by defendants, specifically that they arranged for the disposal or treatment of hazardous wastes at the site [in violation of CERCLA]. Plaintiffs also suffered pecuniary damages not faced by the public generally in that they continue to pay [one defendant's] alleged share of response costs to remediate the site. Plaintiffs have thus stated a cause of action for public nuisance, and defendants' Motion for Summary Judgment is denied. 842 F.Supp. at 273.

With the growing array of comprehensive environmental regulations at the federal and state level the statutory basis for public nuisance liability is an increasingly important tool for redressing environmental torts. There is a clear analogy to the doctrine of negligence as a matter of law, under which a legislative act is taken as laying down a specific rule of conduct that substitutes for the general standard of what a reasonable prudent person would do in like circumstances. § 821B, comment e. One commentator captured the affinity between statutory law and public nuisance in these words: "As New Age environmental problems are identified and grappled with, public nuisance can be looked to as a remedy itself or as a supplement to statutory remedies. Nuisance can fill the inevitable interstices of an ever expanding regulatory system. Long-lived and adaptable, public nuisance is the common-law equivalent of a species blessed with opposable thumbs." James A. Sevinsky, Public Nuisance: A Common–Law Remedy Among the Statutes, 5 Nat. Resources & Env't 29 (1990).

3.   WHAT IS A "PUBLIC RIGHT?"

What is a "public right" which the doctrine of public nuisance seeks to protect? The public right is one "common to all members of the general public," such as the right of all members of the public to fish in a navigable stream in the state without interference in the form of pollution that kills the fish. It is not necessary that all members of the public be adversely affected by the nuisance "so long as the nuisance will interfere with those who come in contact with it in the exercise of a public right or it otherwise affects the interests of the community at large." Restatement (Second) of Torts § 821B comment g. Moreover, the sometimes close relationship between public and private nuisances can be observed in situations where the nuisance affects a large number of persons in the use and enjoyment of their land, which effect often accompanies some interference with a public right.[2] Thus, if a defendant's activity interferes with the private interests of a substantial number of individuals, it is quite likely that it will also interfere with a public right. This is often true in the air and water pollution cases, where the private interests and public interests are closely aligned.

2. Prosser and Keeton state that whether there is an interference with a "public right" is seldom a problem in the litigated cases. Prosser and Keeton on Torts § 90 (5th ed. 1984).

Nevertheless, some decisions hold that creation of a private nuisance to many persons does not for that reason alone constitute a public nuisance. In County of York v. Tracy, 5 Neb.App. 240, 558 N.W.2d 815 (Neb.App.1996) the court rejected the plaintiffs' public nuisance theory on the following logic:

> The question before us is whether Tracy's operation of his refuse and recycling business constitutes a public nuisance and not whether it constitutes a private nuisance to several persons.
>
> In an apparent effort to show a public nuisance, the County called as a witness an adjoining landowner who testified that material from Tracy's property had blown onto his property, possibly contaminating ground water. A previous and the current York County zoning administrator both testified the County received several complaints about the manner in which Tracy was operating his business on the property. This evidence does not establish a public nuisance under the definition of "public nuisance" * * *
>
> In determining whether Tracy's business operation constitutes a public nuisance, we find no evidence in the record which causes us to conclude that the operation of Tracy's business rises to the level of public nuisance. While material blowing onto a neighbor's property might create a cause of action for a private nuisance, this question is not before us. The neighbor also testified he had concerns about the ground water. The neighbor's concerns are not evidence or proof that Tracy's business operation has contaminated the ground water. Furthermore, the County offered no evidence or proof that the ground water was in any way contaminated. [T]he water department manager for the Upper Big Blue Natural Resources District, testified that the only pollution in a nearby recharge lake was from pesticide as a result of runoff from cropland. Tracy's business cannot be found to constitute a public nuisance absent evidence or proof that the environment has been adversely impacted or that the public, as opposed to the immediate neighborhood, was in some way damaged. 558 N.W.2d at 824.

This point is clarified by Restatement (Second) of Torts § 821B comment g ("[t]he pollution of a stream that merely deprives fifty or a hundred lower riparian owners of the use of the water for purposes connected with their land does not for that reason alone become a public nuisance. If, however, the pollution prevents the use of a public bathing beach or kills the fish in a navigable stream and so deprives all members of the community of the right to fish, it becomes a public nuisance.")

Public nuisance theory is also employed in disputes between competing governmental entities. In Keeney v. Town of Old Saybrook, 239 Conn. 786, 686 A.2d 991 (Conn. 1997), the Commissioner of Environmental Protection of Connecticut sued a municipality for injunctive relief and penalties for violating abatement orders. The evidence showed that:

> Old Saybrook has failed to implement the appropriate programs to inspect area septic systems, monitor contamination of area

groundwater and surface waters, regulate the pumping of septic systems through a permit system, effect maintenance of septic systems by residential property owners through an enforcement system, and has failed to report its compliance with these orders to the commissioner. Furthermore, Old Saybrook has failed to build a regional wastewater treatment facility without challenging the adequacy of the financial contributions to be made by neighboring towns or the scientific validity of the engineering study that had found that failing septic systems were polluting the Connecticut River in a manner that could be remedied best by the construction of such a regional wastewater treatment facility. 686 A.2d at 992.

The court applied a standard that required proof of intentional conduct to support a public nuisance, which was amply supported by the record:

> The trial court found that Old Saybrook had acted intentionally by failing to abate the public nuisance of pollution in the town. It found specifically that "Old Saybrook intentionally created the public nuisance because it knew that the public nuisance was resulting or substantially certain to result from its conduct. . . . " The court further found that Old Saybrook's "conduct continued after it knew by the issuance of [department of environmental protection] orders and by the conclusions of its own engineering reports that failing septic systems within the town were creating the public nuisance by causing pollution." Id. at 993.

The court cited § 825 of the Restatement (Second) of Torts which defines an "intentional invasion" of the public right as knowing "that [the invasion] is resulting or is substantially certain to result" from defendant's conduct. Therefore, although § 821(B) calls for a strict basis of liability, a court can opt for the more demanding intent standard, which it felt was justified by the presence of a municipal defendant.

NASHUA CORPORATION v. NORTON COMPANY

United States District Court, Northern District of New York, 1997.
1997 WL 204904.

POOLER, DISTRICT JUDGE.

Plaintiff Nashua Corporation ("Nashua") purchased a pressure-sensitive tape manufacturing facility (the "facility") from defendant Norton Corporation ("Norton"). In this lawsuit, Nashua alleges that Norton contaminated the soil and groundwater under the facility through massive leaks of hazardous chemicals. Nashua seeks to recover damages both for its remediation costs and—under a nuisance theory—for any diminution in property value remaining after remediation. Norton seeks to limit Nashua's damages to the lesser of remediation costs or diminution in value.

BACKGROUND

Norton sold its facility to Nashua in 1974. During the time Norton owned the facility, solvents including Toluene and Tolusol allegedly leaked from underground pipes that Norton had installed into the ground. The leaks purportedly caused complaints from neighbors and "certain" deaths prior to the sale. Nashua claims that Norton did not disclose the leaks and resulting contamination. Long after the sale, in August 1988, Nashua allegedly discovered liquid chemicals in the soil in the vicinity of the subsurface piping.

In addition, between 1974 and 1990, Norton leased back a portion of the facility—the Beartex Premises—from Nashua. Nashua claims that in July 1989, Nashua discovered Norton employees releasing unknown quantities of solvent and/or other hazardous chemicals from the Beartex Premises to the portion of the facility Nashua operated (the "Nashua Plant").

In August 1989, the United States Environmental Protection Agency ("EPA") and the New York State Department of Environmental Conservation ("DEC") investigated storm sewer contamination on and in the vicinity of the Nashua Plant. On August 31, 1989, EPA issued notices to Nashua and Norton informing them of potential liability under the Comprehensive Environmental Response, Compensation and Liability Act ("CERCLA"), 42 U.S.C. § 9601 et seq. After an initial report from a consultant retained jointly by Nashua and Norton, Nashua performed further investigation on its own. Nashua then demanded that Norton indemnify it for the cost of investigation and future response costs.

Because Norton refused Nashua's demand, Nashua commenced this action on December 14, 1990. The original complaint contained causes of action pursuant to CERCLA and the Declaratory Judgment Act and also alleged that Norton had created a public and private nuisance under New York law. As damages on its nuisance cause of action, Nashua sought recovery for the cost of cleaning up the site as well as compensation for the diminished value of the facility after cleanup.

Norton answered, asserting in a counterclaim and affirmative defense that Nashua assumed all of Norton's liabilities, including CERCLA liabilities, in the contract of sale for the facility. Norton also brought a third party action against its insurer, Liberty Mutual Insurance Company.

* * *

On June 19, 1995, Norton moved for partial summary judgment.
* * *

Discussion

Nashua seeks recovery under theories of both private and public nuisance * * * The public nuisance claim fails, Norton posits, because (1) Nashua did not allege sufficient harm to the public and (2) Nashua did not allege special harm.

* * *

I turn now to Nashua's public nuisance claim. A public nuisance is an offense against the State and is generally prosecuted by the State. Copart Ind., Inc. v. Consolidated Edison Co., 41 N.Y.2d 564, 568, 362 N.E.2d 968 (1977). The tort "consists of conduct or omissions which offend, interfere with or cause damage to the public in the exercise of rights common to all in a manner such as to offend public morals, interfere with use by the public of a public place or endanger or injure the property, health, safety or comfort of a considerable number of persons." A private party "may maintain an action [for public nuisance] when he suffers special damage" from the nuisance. Norton contends that Nashua has shown neither conduct that injures the public generally nor special damages peculiar to Nashua.

In New York "the release or threat of release of hazardous waste into the environment unreasonably infringes upon a public right and thus is a public nuisance as a matter of New York law." State of New York v. Shore Realty Corp., 759 F.2d 1032, 1051 (2d Cir.1985). Nashua clearly alleged in its amended complaint that Norton released hazardous waste into the environment. Nevertheless, Norton argues that Nashua has failed to allege damage to the public within the meaning of Copart and Shore because Nashua's own engineering study shows that contamination was limited to the facility. Norton's argument fails both legally and factually. In Shore, the court held that public nuisance did not require a showing of "actual, as opposed to threatened, harm." Id. Moreover, although the bulk of Nashua's expert's report discusses contamination at the Facility, the expert also states "residue of the leakage from the underground transfer pipes will persist in the subsurface environment of the Nashua facility and the surrounding areas." Williams Aff., Dkt. No. 132, Ex. A at 9. Further, the report indicates that the spill will contaminate groundwater "for a long time." Id. If proven, Norton's releases of toxic chemicals into the subsurface environment constitute a public nuisance.

Moreover, Nashua's response costs constitute special harm giving Nashua standing to assert a public nuisance claim. Therefore, * * * Nashua can maintain a public nuisance claim with respect to the hazardous chemicals at the Facility as well as those on the Beartex premises.

Under Norton's analysis, however, the determination that Nashua can maintain nuisance claims represents no more than a Pyrrhic victory. Norton argues that (1) Nashua can recover only response costs—a form of damage identical to that requested on Nashua's CERCLA * * * claim—on its public nuisance claim and (2) any recovery for property damage is limited to the lesser of diminished property value or cost of remediation.

I consider first whether Nashua's public nuisance claim is limited to response costs. Norton argues that nuisance actions are classically actions to abate a nuisance and therefore Nashua's remedy must be limited to the cost of remediation. * * * In general, a non-governmental plaintiff is entitled to recover pecuniary damages in a public nuisance action if it demonstrates "a private and peculiar injury." The damage suffered "must be 'of a different kind from that suffered by other persons exercising the same public right * * * '" [quoting Restatement (Second) of Torts § 821C comment b]. Nashua may demonstrate special damages by showing that its property value has been diminished by Norton's actions. If during the second phase of the trial, Nashua can demonstrate that it suffered diminishment of its property value in a manner unlike the general public, it can recover for that diminishment.

* * *

Notes and Questions

1. As Nashua Corporation v. Norton Company explains, a private party may bring a claim in public nuisance when (1) the defendant's conduct creates and unreasonable interference with a public right; and (2) in addition to the harm suffered by members of the general community, the plaintiff has suffered a "special injury", which is to say, a harm that is qualitatively distinct from the harm suffered more broadly by the public. The "special injury" rule is treated in detail in the section to follow.

2. *More On The "Public Rights."* What was the "public right" with which Norton allegedly unreasonably interfered? If the affidavit quoted by the court asserted only contamination of the facility's "subsurface environment" would that have been sufficient? What is the relevance of the quotation from the *Shore Realty* opinion that refers to "threatened harm"? What harm was threatened here? If groundwater contamination creates a public nuisance, won't most ground contamination situations qualify for the tort? Was *Nashua* based on § 821B's statutory violation clause or substantial interference with public health or safety clause? A number of cases have found that a release or threatened release of hazardous substances into the environment (air or surface waters, or groundwater) constitutes a public nuisance. See State of New York v. Shore Realty Corp., 759 F.2d 1032, 1051 (2d Cir.1985); U.S. v. Hooker Chemical & Plastics Corp., 118 F.R.D. 321 (W.D.N.Y.1987); Westwood Pharmaceuticals v. National Fuel Gas Distr. Corp., 737 F.Supp. 1272, 1281 (W.D.N.Y.1990); Scheufler v. General Host Corp., 895 F.Supp. 1513, 1514 (D.Kan.1995); But not all courts agree. See, e.g., Briggs & Stratton Corp. v. Concrete Sales & Services, 29 F.Supp.2d 1372 (M.D.Ga.1998) (violation of Resource Conservation and Recovery Act for dumping activities not sufficient for public nuisance; with the court continuing: "Unlike a claim for public nuisance, however, the ability to pursue and the standing to maintain a citizen suit under RCRA held a citizen suit does not require [plaintiff] to demonstrate either actual harm to the public or that all persons coming within the sphere of the release of hazardous substances were damaged by the release.").

3. *Of Strict Liability and Agency Principles.* In a leading New York decision, State of New York v. Schenectady Chemicals, Inc., 117 Misc.2d 960, 459 N.Y.S.2d 971 (Sup. Ct. 1983), aff'd, 103 A.D.2d 33, 479 N.Y.S.2d 1010 (App. Div. 1984), the court found a public nuisance:

The court must decide if the State, either by statute or common law, can maintain an action to compel a chemical company to pay the costs of cleaning up a dump site so as to prevent pollution of surface and ground water when the dumping took place between 15 to 30 years ago at a site owned by an independent contractor hired by the chemical company to dispose of the waste material.

* * *

During the 1950's until the mid–1960's the defendant disposed of its chemical wastes by way of contract with Dewey Loeffel, one of Mr. Loeffel's corporations. Mr. Loeffel made pickups at the defendant's manufacturing plants and disposed of the material by dumping directly into lagoons at the Loeffel site, and in some instances by burying the wastes. It is alleged that with knowledge of the danger of environmental contamination if its wastes were not properly disposed, and knowing of Loeffel's methods, Schenectady Chemicals: (1) hired an incompetent independent contractor to dispose of the wastes; and (2) failed to fully advise Loeffel of the dangerous nature of the waste material and recommend proper disposal methods.

It is alleged that the Loeffel site is approximately 13 acres of low-lying swamp land located in a residential-agricultural area in Rensselaer County with surface soil consisting mainly of gravel and sand. The ground water beneath the site is part of an aquifer which serves as the sole source of water for thousands of area residents and domestic animals.

The complaint alleges that over the years the chemical wastes have migrated into the surrounding air, surface and ground water contaminating at least one area drinking well and so polluting, or threatening to pollute, the area surface and ground water as to constitute an unreasonable threat to the public well-being and a continuing public nuisance. As a result, the Department of Environmental Conservation (DEC) developed a plan to prevent further migration of chemical wastes from the site, and General Electric and Bendix have agreed to pay 82.2% of the costs thereof. Defendant's refusal to pay its portion of the clean-up costs give rise to this suit.

* * *

"[W]ith reference to a public nuisance, it is not necessary to show acts of negligence" (42 NY Jur, Nuisances, § 16, p 462), although such a showing is not prohibited. One who creates a nuisance through an inherently dangerous activity or use of an unreasonably dangerous product is absolutely liable for resulting damages, [r]egardless of fault, and despite adhering to the highest standard of care[.]

* * *

Even a non-landowner can be liable for taking part in the creation of a nuisance upon the property of another. * * * The common law is not static. Society has repeatedly been confronted with new inventions and products that, through foreseen and unforeseen events, have imposed dangers upon society (explosives are an example) . . . The modern chemical industry, and the problems engendered through the disposal of its by-products, is, to a large extent, a creature of the twentieth century. Since the Second World War hundreds of previously unknown chemicals have been created. The wastes produced have been dumped, sometimes openly and sometimes surreptitiously, at thousands of sites across the country. Belatedly it has been discovered that the waste products are polluting the air and water and pose a consequent threat to all life forms.

It is significant that the defendant in *Schenectady Chemicals* was *not* the owner of the waste disposal site, but rather was one of three generators of the hazardous waste. On certain facts liability, under public nuisance law may attach not only to the party responsible for releasing the chemicals into the groundwater, but also to the source generator of the waste. Agency law principles are sufficient to regard the site operator or owner as the agent of the defendant, regardless of whether the site operator is an independent contractor.

In its affirmance, the Appellate Division wrote:

The issue of whether Loeffel acted as defendant's agent or as an independent contractor in disposing of the wastes presents a question of fact not to be resolved at this stage of the proceedings. Even the assumption that Loeffel acted as an independent contractor does not insulate defendant from liability, for an employer may be responsible for the actions of an independent contractor in creating a public nuisance. Particularly is this so where the work involved is inherently dangerous, as may reasonably be deemed the case where the disposal of hazardous wastes are involved and the employer has failed to take proper precautions in selecting a competent party with whom to contract. 479 N.Y.S.2d 1010, 1014 (App. Div. 1984).

4. PRIVATE ACTION FOR PUBLIC NUISANCE—THE SPECIAL INJURY RULE

The opinion in *Nashua* introduced the principle of special injury application of which is often critical to the outcome of public nuisance actions seeking money damages. Historically the common law has been slow to recognize the right of a private person to maintain an action for a public nuisance. Until 1536 private actions for public nuisance were disallowed on the grounds that "only the King, and certainly no common person" could have a remedy because of a crime. See William Prosser, Private Actions for Public Nuisance, 52 Va.L.Rev. 997, 1005 (1966). In that year a court allowed a private tort action for a public nuisance in a case where the defendant blocked the King's highway and impeded the plaintiff's access "to his close." In the court's language: "Where one man has greater hurt or inconvenience than any other man had * * * then he who had more displeasure or hurt, etc. can have an action to recover his damages that he had by reason of his special hurt." Anonymous, Y.B. 27 Hen. 8 of. 26, pl. 10 (1536). This is the origin of the modern special injury rule, which provides that a private plaintiff can maintain a suit for a public nuisance only if he can demonstrate a particular, unique damage different from that suffered by the public generally.

At common law, three reasons were offered to justify this special injury requirement: (1) that only the sovereign should maintain actions for harm suffered by the public; (2) that courts should protect defendants from a multitude of actions by private parties and from the potential of harassment; and (3) the courts did not wish to be burdened with many suits for trivial damages.

Restatement (Second) of Torts § 821c addresses the question of *standing*—that is, who can maintain an action, as a consequence of sustaining the type of injury necessary to confer on that person the right to sue:

§ 821C. Who Can Recover for Public Nuisance

(1) In order to recover damages in an individual action for a public nuisance, one must have suffered harm of a kind different from that suffered by other members of the public exercising the right common to the general public that was the subject of interference.

(2) In order to maintain a proceeding to enjoin or abate a public nuisance, one must

    (a) have the right to recover damages, as indicated in Subsection (1), or

    (b) have authority as a public official or public agency to represent the state or a political subdivision in the matter, or

    (c) have standing to sue as a representative of the general public, as a citizen in a citizen's action or as a member of a class in a class action.

Thus, under the Restatement (Second), a private plaintiff who maintains an action for *damages* must still satisfy the special injury requirement. In contrast, a private plaintiff seeking to enjoin or abate a public nuisance is conferred the necessary standing either if acting as a public official or, more importantly, if suing as a representative of the general public, as a citizen in a citizen's action, or as a member in a class action.

What justifications are there for retaining the special injury rule at all? Why should standing requirements in equitable actions seeking injunctive relief be more liberal than standing in private suits for damages?

What have the courts done to the special injury rule in environmental tort actions for damages in the last twenty years? The decisions below all involve some aspect of the special injury rule, but not all of them specifically label it as such, nor do all of the cases necessarily involve public nuisance actions. Closely related to the special injury requirement in public nuisance actions is the requirement of the economic loss doctrine, which provides generally that parties suffering purely economic losses occasioned by the defendant's negligent conduct (e.g., the defendant negligently interferes with contractual relations or prospective economic advantage) cannot maintain a tort action for such losses, unless the party has also sustained physical harm to person or property, or damage to a proprietary interest, or is otherwise entitled to recover on the basis of a separate tort (e.g., fraud). For the definitive analyses of the economic loss doctrine, see East River Steamship Corp. v. Transamerica Delaval, Inc., 476 U.S. 858, 106 S.Ct. 2295, 90 L.Ed.2d 865 (1986) (holding that under maritime tort law a ship charterer that suffered economic losses because of a defect in the turbines manufactured by defendant could not recover such losses on a products liability or negligence theory). See also Robert L. Rabin, Tort Recovery for Negligently Inflicted Economic Loss: A Reassessment, 37 Stan.L.Rev. 1513 (1985); Gary T. Schwartz, Economic Loss in American Tort Law: The Examples of J'Aire and Products Liability, 23 San Diego L.Rev. 37 (1986).

The decision that follows demonstrates the continued vitality of the special injury rule in perhaps the most infamous environmental catastrophe in our history.

IN RE THE EXXON VALDEZ; ALASKA NATIVE CLASS v. EXXON CORP.

United States Court of Appeals, Ninth Circuit, 1997.
104 F.3d 1196.

SCHWARZER, SENIOR DISTRICT JUDGE:

This is one of the numerous actions arising out of the 1989 grounding of the EXXON VALDEZ in Prince William Sound, Alaska, and the resulting massive oil spill. The action, which named Exxon Corporation and others as defendants (collectively referred to as "Exxon"), was originally filed in Alaska state court and was later removed. The complaint alleged a number of claims on behalf of a class of Alaska Natives ("the Class"); the Class consists of:

> all Alaska Natives and Native organizations including but not limited to, individuals, Native villages, incorporated and unincorporated Native entities and associations and tribal entities, who engage in, rely upon, promote or preserve, wholly or in part, a subsistence way of life. . . .

The class definition was later modified to exclude all Native villages and government entities, thereby limiting the claim to 3,455 individual Alaska Natives. The "subsistence way of life" allegedly harmed by the spill is:

> dependent upon the preservation of uncontaminated natural resources, marine life and wildlife, and reflects a personal, economic, psychological, social, cultural, communal and religious form of daily living. The complaint alleges injury to the "subsistence way of life," archaeological sites and artifacts . . . natural resources and property

upon which [plaintiffs] depend and/or which are part of their natural habitat and lives. [Complaint at 40].

Exxon moved for summary judgment on all of the noneconomic claims asserted by the Class for injury to culture or to the subsistence way of life. The Class acknowledged that the motion was for judgment on the noneconomic claims but argued that its members were entitled to recover noneconomic damages under general maritime law, the Alaska Environmental Conservation Act (Alaska Stat. § 46.03.822), and the common law of Alaska. In a thorough and well-considered opinion, the court granted the motion for summary judgment on the Class claims for noneconomic injury. Subsequently, at the request of the parties, the court issued an order directing entry of final judgment pursuant to Fed.R.Civ.P. 54(b). The order recites that the Class presented two claims, one for cultural damage and the other for harvest damage. The Class claims for harvest damage were settled, and the court consequently determined that there was no just reason for delay in the entry of final judgment as to all "subsistence lifestyle" cultural damage claims.

* * *

DISCUSSION

The principal contention of the Class is that it has stated a public nuisance claim for noneconomic damage under federal maritime law. The district court rejected the claim on the ground that "a private litigant cannot recover damages for a public nuisance unless he or she can show a special injury different in kind from that suffered by the general public." (citing Oppen v. Aetna Ins., 485 F.2d 252, 259 (9th Cir.1973), cert. denied, 414 U.S. 1162, 94 S.Ct. 925, 39 L.Ed.2d 116 (1974)). The district court therefore held that "[t]he Alaska Natives' non-economic subsistence claims are not 'of a kind different from [those] suffered by other members of the public exercising the right common to the general public that was the subject of interference.' " Id. at 5–6 (quoting Restatement (Second) of Torts, § 821C(1), cmt. b).

The Class does not dispute the applicability of the Restatement rule but argues that the court erred in failing to recognize that the Alaska Natives suffered special injury different in kind from that suffered by the general public. The authorities on which it relies, however, all involve economic damage suffered as a result of a public nuisance. See, e.g., Hampton v. North Carolina Pulp Co., 223 N.C. 535, 27 S.E.2d 538, 545 (1943) (damage to commercial fishing interests); Union Oil Co. v. Oppen, 501 F.2d 558, 570 (9th Cir.1974) (same); Holcomb Constr. Co. v. Armstrong, 590 F.2d 811 (9th Cir.1979) (interference with contract); Oppen v. Aetna, 485 F.2d 252, 260 (9th Cir.1973) (same), cert. denied, 414 U.S. 1162, 94 S.Ct. 925, 39 L.Ed.2d 116 (1974).

There is no dispute concerning the Alaska Natives' right to recover economic damage flowing from loss of fishing resources. In a separate order, the district court held that the Alaska Natives who fished for subsistence were entitled to the benefit of the exception for special injury. The parties then settled [those] claims, with the Class receiving compensation for the commercial value of harvest damages. The settlement agreement reserved the "cultural damage claims" of the Class, and only those claims are at issue here.

The determinative issue is whether cultural damage—damage to the Class members' "subsistence way of life"—may cause compensable injury. The Class asserts that its claims "comport with established principles of tort recovery" but cites no authority and does not dispute Exxon's assertion that no reported decision supports such a claim. Instead, the Class attempts to infuse an economic character into its claims by arguing that Class members suffered "economically measurable damages" beyond the commercial injury. The Class asserts that its cultural injury has a "pervasive economic foundation" and is based on "economic injuries from disruption of Native subsistence activities." The spill allegedly harmed "an integrated system of communal subsistence . . . inextricably bound up not only with the harvesting of natural resources damaged by the spill but also with the exchange, sharing and processing of those resources as the foundation of an established economic, social and religious structure." These arguments miss the mark, however, for all economic claims were resolved in the settlement, and the district court's judgment is specifically limited to noneconomic claims.

Admittedly, the oil spill affected the communal life of Alaska Natives, but whatever injury they suffered (other than the harvest loss), though potentially different in degree than that suffered by other Alaskans, was not different in kind. We agree with the district court that the right to lead subsistence lifestyles is not limited to Alaska Natives. See Alaska Const. art. VIII, §§ 3, 15 & 17; Gilbert v. State Dept. of Fish & Game, 803 P.2d 391, 399 (Alaska 1990); McDowell v. State, 785 P.2d 1, 11–12 (Alaska 1989). While the oil spill may have affected Alaska Natives more severely than other members of the public, "the right to obtain and share wild food, enjoy uncontaminated nature, and cultivate traditional, cultural, spiritual, and psychological benefits in pristine natural surroundings" is shared by all Alaskans. The Class therefore has failed to prove any "special injury" to support a public nuisance action. Restatement (Second) of Torts § 821c, cmt. b.

In light of the foregoing disposition of this appeal, * * * there is no need to address Alaska statutory and common law, inasmuch as the Class has pointed to no provision or precedent that would permit recovery for cultural damage claims. The Class concedes that Alaska public nuisance law applies the Restatement criteria, and the Restatement standard explicitly precludes the Class claim. Indeed, the strict liability provisions of the Alaska Act only permit recovery for loss of "benefit measurable in economic terms." Alaska Stat. § 46.03.826(2).

The judgment is AFFIRMED.

Notes and Questions

1. *Settlement of Economic Injury Claims.* The court in *Exxon* relates that Exxon settled the Native Alaskans' claims for commercial injury. Why? Restatement (Second) of Torts § 821C comment h, provides, in part:

> h. *Pecuniary loss.* Pecuniary loss to the plaintiff resulting from the public nuisance is normally a different kind of harm from that suffered by the general public. A contractor who loses the benefits of a particular contract or is put to an additional expense in performing it because of the obstruction of a public highway preventing him from transporting materials to the place of performance, can recover for the public nuisance. The same is true when it can be shown with reasonable certainty that an established business has lost profits, as when the obstruction of the highway prevents a common carrier from operating buses over it or access to the plaintiff's place of business is made so inconvenient that customers do not come to it.

* * *

2. *Compensable and Non-compensable Pecuniary Losses: The Maritime Cases.* Not all pecuniary losses, however, satisfy the special injury rule. Consider the leading decision in State of Louisiana ex rel. Guste v. M/V Testbank, 752 F.2d 1019 (5th Cir.1985). In *Testbank*, the M/V SEA DANIEL, an inbound bulk carrier, and the M/V TESTBANK, an outbound container ship collided in the Mississippi River Gulf outlet. At impact, a white haze enveloped the ships until carried away by prevailing winds. Many of the containers aboard TESTBANK were damaged or lost overboard. The white haze proved to be hydrobromic acid and the contents of the containers which went overboard proved to be approximately twelve tons of pentachlorophenol, PCP, assertedly the largest such spill in the United States history. The collision caused the U.S. Coast Guard to quarantine the area for 17 days, producing substantial economic losses to numerous claimants. These suits presented claims of, among others, shipping interests, marina and boat rental operators, wholesale and retail seafood enterprises not actually engaged in fishing, seafood restaurants, tackle and bait shops, and recreational fishermen. The Fifth Circuit held that summary judgment was properly granted to defendant shipowner against all claimants who suffered purely economic losses, except those of commercial oystermen, shrimpers, crabbers and fishermen who made commercial use of the embargoed waters. As to the first cluster of claimants, the court applied the economic loss doctrine to rule that negligent interference with contractual or economic relations is not actionable barring some physical injury to property or person. The court relied on the venerable Supreme Court decision in *Robins Dry Dock v. Flint*, 275 U.S. 303, 48 S.Ct. 134, 72 L.Ed. 290 (1927). Second, the court held that the public nuisance doctrine could not be used as a device to circumvent application of the economic loss rule:

> Plaintiffs argue alternatively that their claims of economic losses are cognizable in maritime tort because the pollution from the collision constituted a public nuisance, and violated the Rivers and

Harbors Appropriation Act of 1899 and Louisiana law. We look to each in turn.

Plaintiffs seek to avoid the *Robins* rule by characterizing their claims as damages caused by a public nuisance. They suggest that when a defendant unreasonably interferes with public rights by obstructing navigation or negligently polluting a waterway he creates a public nuisance for which recovery is available to all who have sustained "particular damages." As defined at common law such damages are those which are substantially greater than the presumed-at-law damages suffered by the general public as a result of the nuisance. See generally Restatement (Second) of Torts §§ 821B, 821C (1977); Prosser, Private Action For Public Nuisance, 52 Va.L.Rev. 997 (1966). Characterizing the problem as one of public nuisance, however, does not immediately solve the problems with plaintiffs' damage claims for pure economic losses.
* * *

The problem in public nuisance theory of determining when private damages are sufficiently distinct from those suffered by the general public so as to justify recovery is as difficult, if not more so, as determining which foreseeable damages are too remote to justify recovery in negligence. In each case it is a matter of degree, and in each case lines must be drawn. With economic losses such as the ones claimed here the problem is to determine who among an entire community that has been commercially affected by an accident has sustained a pecuniary loss so great as to justify distinguishing his losses from similar losses suffered by others. Given the difficulty of this task, we see no jurisprudential advantage in permitting the use of nuisance theory to skirt the *Robins* rule. 752 F.2d at 1030.

3. See also Burgess v. M/V Tamano, 370 F.Supp. 247 (D.Me.1973), aff'd, 559 F.2d 1200 (1st Cir.1977), where plaintiffs brought a class action seeking damages from an oil spill off the coast of Maine. The federal trial court denied motions to dismiss the claims of the commercial clam diggers and commercial fishermen, but granted the motions as to the owners of motels, trailer parks, campgrounds, restaurants, and grocery stores in the beach area which was affected by the spill. The court stated:

Since the fishermen and clam diggers have no individual property rights with respect to the waters and marine life allegedly harmed by the oil spill, their right to recover in the present action depends upon whether they may maintain private actions for damages based upon the alleged tortious invasion of public rights which are held by the State of Maine in trust for the common benefit of all the people. As to this issue, the longstanding rule of law is that a private individual can recover in tort for invasion of a public right only if he has suffered damage particular to him—that is, damage different in kind rather than simply in degree from that sustained by the public generally.

* * *

The commercial fishermen and clam diggers in the present cases clearly have a special interest, quite apart from that of the public generally, to take fish and harvest clams from the coastal waters of the

State of Maine. The injury of which they complain has resulted from defendants' alleged interference with *their* direct exercise of the public right to fish and dig clams. It would be an incongruous result for the Court to say that a man engaged in commercial fishing or clamming, and dependent thereon for his livelihood, who may have had his business destroyed by the tortious act of another, should be denied any right to recover for his pecuniary loss on the ground that his injury is no different in kind from that sustained by the general public.

The court, however, rejected the claims of those suffering *indirect* injury:

> Unlike the commercial fishermen and clam diggers, the Old Orchard Beach businessmen do not assert any interference with *their* direct exercise of the public right. They complain only of loss of customers *indirectly resulting* from alleged pollution of the coastal waters and beaches in which they do not have a property interest. Although in some instances their damage may be greater in degree, the injury of which they complain, which is *derivative* from that of the public at large, is common to all businesses and residents of the Old Orchard Beach area. In such circumstances, the line is drawn and the courts have consistently denied recovery. (emphasis in original).

Is *Burgess* consistent with *Testbank*? See also Pruitt v. Allied Chemical Corp., 523 F.Supp. 975 (E.D.Va.1981) (reaching the same conclusion as *Testbank* where the chemical Kepone had damaged marine life in Chesapeake Bay and allowing commercial users of the water to recover but not those suffering indirect economic loss). Accord, Connerty v. Metropolitan District Commission, 398 Mass. 140, 495 N.E.2d 840 (1986) (holding that a licensed master clam digger could maintain an action on his own behalf and on behalf of other licensed clam diggers for damages to his business caused by the discharge of raw sewage into the harbor by the Metropolitan District Commission. The case was ultimately dismissed on governmental immunity grounds).

4. *More on Exxon Valdez.* Interestingly, the federal district court in Alaska had several years earlier rejected the claims of inland area businesses such as boat charterers, taxidermists, fishing lodges, sport fishermen, photographers, kayakers, and fish processors. In re Exxon Valdez, 767 F.Supp. 1509 (D.Alaska 1991). Agreeing with a dissenting opinion in Louisiana ex rel. Guste v. M/V Testbank, the *Exxon Valdez* court stated: "As the dissent points out, the exception to Robbins Dry Dock is arbitrary. It offers no guidance in distinguishing which of the plaintiffs targeted by Alyeska's motion might fit within its protection." In certifying an interlocutory appeal to the Ninth Circuit, the court questioned the continued wisdom of maintaining the arbitrary line separating fishermen from other inland businesses, a concept recognized by the Ninth Circuit in an earlier decision, Union Oil v. Oppen, 501 F.2d 558 (9th Cir.1974).

> [T]his court does not understand how, as a matter of principle, the rule * * * can have application for all claimants who suffer economic loss as a result of a marine tort except commercial fishermen. If the court of appeals were to have second thoughts about its decision in Oppen * * * the implications of such a change of direction in this case would be of monumental proportions. The court assumes without know-

ing that there are thousands of commercial fishermen's claims involved in this litigation. Even if Oppen remains the law of the Ninth Circuit, this court * * * and, since it is bound to follow federal admiralty law as well, the Superior Court for the State of Alaska urgently needs to know whether and to what extent the rule of Robins Dry Dock will apply to the economic claims of those who are not commercial fishermen. 767 F.Supp. at 1518.

The issue, however, was not appealed. The Ninth Circuit opinion in *Exxon Valdez (Native Alaskans)* case appears to reaffirm the rule.

Given the criticism, what commends the special injury rule and *Robins Dry Dock* rule to the judiciary?

5. Many state statutes have codified the special injury requirement in public nuisance actions maintained by private parties. See, e.g., West's Ann.Cal. Civil Code § 3493 (1993) ("A private person may maintain an action for public nuisance, if it is specifically injurious to himself but not otherwise."). See also, e.g., Alaska Stat. 9.45.230 (private nuisance section extended to public nuisances); Official Ga. Code Ann. § 72–103. Compare the language employed in Alabama: "Nuisances are either public or private. A public nuisance is one which damages all persons which come within the sphere of its operations * * *. Generally a public nuisance gives no right of action to an individual." "If a public nuisance causes a special damage to an individual in which the public does not participate, such special damage gives a right of action." Ala. Code § 6–5–121; § 6–5–123 (1999); Mich. Comp. Laws Ann. § 600.380 (1998).

5. A NOTE ON ECONOMIC PRINCIPLES

Much has been written in recent years regarding the need for tort law to embrace economic efficiency goals in allocating risks of loss among parties. Three individuals have been most influential in bringing about more interest in examining economic considerations in determining legal liability. See Guido Calabresi, The Costs of Accidents: A Legal and Economic Analysis (1970); Ronald H. Coase, The Problem of Social Cost, 3 J.Law & Econ. 1 (1960); Richard A. Posner, Economic Analysis of Law (5th ed. 1998). Calabresi has argued that the risks of loss ought to be placed on the party with the lowest avoidance costs so that the aggregate sum of accident costs and avoidance costs are minimized.

Calabresi and Melamed, in a leading article, summarize their view of economic considerations which should be applied in fashioning rules in which the transaction costs are especially high:

(1) that economic efficiency standing alone would dictate that set of entitlements which favors knowledgeable choices between social benefits and the social costs of obtaining them, and between social costs and the social costs of avoiding them; (2) that this implies, in the absence of certainty as to whether a benefit is worth its costs to society, that the cost should be put on the party or activity best located to make such a cost-benefit analysis; (3) that in particular contexts like accidents or pollution this suggests putting costs on the

party or activity which can most cheaply avoid them; (4) that in the absence of certainty as to who that party or activity is, the costs should be put on the party or activity which can with the lowest transaction costs act in the market to correct an error in entitlements by inducing the party who can avoid social costs most cheaply to do so; and (5) that since we are in an area where by hypothesis markets do not work perfectly—there are transaction costs—a decision will often have to be made on whether market transactions or collective fiat is most likely to bring us closer to the Pareto optimal result the "perfect" market would reach.

Guido Calabresi and A. Douglas Melamed, Property Rules, Liability Rules, and Inalienability, 85 Harv.L.Rev. 1089, 1096–97 (1972). See also Richard A. Posner, A Theory of Negligence, 1 J.Legal Stud. 29, 39–40 (1972). An excellent discussion of the economic principles that may be applied in determining liability in cases such as *Testbank* is contained in Union Oil Co. v. Oppen, 501 F.2d 558, 570 (9th Cir.1974), discussed in *Exxon Valdez*. In *Oppen*, the court allowed commercial fishermen to recover for losses caused by defendant's oil spill off the coast of California, but did not reach the question of whether others suffering economic losses could recover:

> [O]ur holding * * * does not open the door to claims that may be asserted by those, other than commercial fishermen, whose economic or personal affairs were discommoded by the oil spill * * *. Nothing said in this opinion is intended to suggest * * * that every decline in the general commercial activity of every business in the * * * area following the [spill] constitutes a legally cognizable injury for which the defendants may be responsible.

The Ninth Circuit also concluded that, as between it and the commercial users of the fish in the ocean, the oil company was the least cost avoider:

> The same conclusion is reached when the issue before us is approached from the standpoint of economics. Recently a number of scholars have suggested that liability for losses occasioned by torts should be apportioned in a manner that will best contribute to the achievement of an optimum allocation of resources. This optimum, in theory, would be that which would be achieved by a perfect market system. In determining whether the cost of an accident should be borne by the injured party or be shifted, in whole or in part, this approach requires the court to fix the identity of the party who can avoid the costs most cheaply. Once fixed, this determination then controls liability.

> It turns out, however, that fixing the identity of the best or cheapest cost-avoider is more difficult than might be imagined. In order to facilitate this determination, Calabresi suggests several helpful guidelines. The first of these would require a rough calculation designed to exclude as potential cost-avoiders those groups/activities which could avoid accident costs only at an extremely high expense. While not easy to apply in any concrete sense, this guide-

line does suggest that the imposition of oil spill costs directly upon such groups as the consumers of staple groceries is not a sensible solution. Under this guideline, potential liability becomes resolved into a choice between, on an ultimate level, the consumers of fish and those products derived from the defendant's total operations.

* * *

[Calabresi's final guideline] unmistakably points to the defendants as the best cost-avoider. Under this guideline, the loss should be allocated to that party who can best correct any error in allocation, if such there be, by acquiring the activity to which the party has been made liable. The capacity "to buy out" the plaintiffs if the burden is too great is, in essence, the real focus of Calabresi's approach. On this basis there is no contest—the defendant's capacity is superior.

For a fascinating account of Calabresi's principles applied to air pollution torts, see Frank Michaelman, Pollution as a Tort: A Non–Accidental Perspective on Calabresi's Costs, 80 Yale L.J. 647 (1971). See also, William M. Landes and Richard A. Posner, The Economic Structure of Tort Law 29–53 (1987); Richard A. Posner, Economic Analysis of Law, 5–9, 42–48, 56–57 (3d ed. 1986); Jeffrey G. Murphy and Jules L. Coleman, The Philosophy of Law 228–34 (1984); A. Mitchell Polinsky, An Introduction to Law and Economics 11–24 (1983).

6. PHYSICAL HARM AS CONSTITUTING SPECIAL INJURY

The courts generally hold that when a plaintiff has suffered demonstrable physical harm the special injury rule is satisfied. Restatement (Second) of Torts § 821C, comment d, explicitly provides that personal injuries are inherently "of a kind different from that suffered by other members of the public."

1. *A Civil Action.* In Anderson v. W.R. Grace & Co., 628 F.Supp. 1219 (D.Mass.1986), the case made famous by Jonathan Haar's book and the Movie "A Civil Action", the court considered defendants' alleged contamination of the groundwater in certain areas of Woburn, Massachusetts with chemicals that were capable of causing serious injuries. The plaintiffs consisted of 33 persons: five administrators of estates of children who died of leukemia allegedly caused by those chemicals; 16 persons who were family members of the decedents seeking to recover for emotional distress; five persons still living but suffering from leukemia; and others living who alleged a variety of physical illnesses or damage to their bodies' systems. This decision is discussed in Chapter 5 (dealing with compensable harms in environmental tort cases), but for current purposes the court denied defendants' motion to dismiss the damages claims but granted the motion as to the claim for injunctive relief. On the special injury requirement it stated:

The alleged contamination of the groundwater in East Woburn falls into the category of public nuisances. * * *

* * *

Defendants argue that plaintiffs as private persons, have no standing to bring an action based on the public nuisance of a restriction on use of Woburn's groundwater. The general rule is that the private injury sustained where a common right is impaired is "merged in the common nuisance and injury to all citizens, and the right is to be vindicated [through suit by a public official]." But when a plaintiff has sustained "special or peculiar damage", he or she may maintain an individual action. Injuries to a person's health are by their nature "special and peculiar" and cannot properly be said to be common or public. Restatement (Second) of Torts § 821C, comment d. As plaintiffs allege that they have suffered a variety of illnesses as a result of exposure to the contaminated water, they have standing to maintain this nuisance action.

2. See also Wood v. Picillo, 443 A.2d 1244 (R.I.1982), allowing an action for public and private nuisance on behalf of individuals living near a "chemical nightmare" who had suffered physical effects from their exposure to the chemicals; Burns v. Jaquays Mining Corp., 156 Ariz. 375, 752 P.2d 28 (App. 1987), holding, *inter alia*, that plaintiffs who suffered exposure to asbestos tailings which came from the defendants' asbestos mill were entitled to recover on a public or private nuisance theory for discomfort, inconvenience, annoyance and property damage.

3. *Harm to Land.* Harm to real property or chattels will also suffice to satisfy the special injury rule. In Prescott v. Leaf River Forest Products, Inc., 740 So.2d 301 (Miss.1999), the Mississippi Supreme Court sustained public nuisance claims where the plaintiff group "offered evidence that the Mill effluent was discoloring the River and staining the sandbars, which is sufficient to infer a significant interference with the public's enjoyment of the Leaf River." As to special injury, the court reasoned:

Interference with the condition of land is sufficient to constitute harm different than that suffered by the public at large. During the hearing on the Leaf River Defendant's motion for summary judgment, counsel for the Plaintiff Group described the photographs depicting the stains on the sandbars, stating "The west side of the river here is Dan Dornan's who is a plaintiff of ours; the east side is Jackie and Margaret's property * * * [T]his looks like, to me, looks like motor oil."

* * *

That black water is on their sandbars and staining them, just as those pictures say. This was sufficient evidence of an individualized harm, so as to forestall the dismissal of the public nuisance claim on motion for summary judgment.

See Graham Oil Co. v. BP Oil Co., 885 F.Supp. 716 (W.D.Pa.1994) (held: special injury satisfied where plaintiff alleged "that it is uniquely affected by * * * contamination of its property and that any present or future commercial use of its property will be affected by the contamination. Specifically, * * * that contamination has diminished the value of the Leased Premises, caused [it] to lose the use of the Leased Premises, and disrupted [its] contractual relationships.").

4. It has also been held that the state may maintain an action for damages resulting from a public nuisance which causes environmental harm to natural resources. See, e.g., State ex rel. Dresser Industries v. Ruddy, 592 S.W.2d 789 (Mo.1980), for an excellent discussion of the special injury rule in the context of state actions. The potential availability of the public nuisance remedy for damage to natural resources grows in significance. See the natural resource damage provisions of the Comprehensive Environmental Response, Compensation and Liability Act, 42 U.S.C.A. §§ 9601(16), 9607(f), 9613(g); see also Ohio v. United States Dept. of Interior, 880 F.2d 432 (D.C.Cir.1989).

7. EQUITABLE ACTIONS FOR PUBLIC NUISANCE

As noted above, the Restatement (Second) of Torts dropped the special injury requirement entirely for equitable actions. See § 821C, comment j. For a thorough discussion, see Shay Scott, Combining Environmental Citizen Suits & Other Private Theories of Recovery, 8 J.Envtl.L. & Litig. 369 (1994).

a. Private Attorneys General

In Miotke v. City of Spokane, 101 Wash.2d 307, 678 P.2d 803 (1984), owners of waterfront property and the Lake Spokane Environmental Association sued the City of Spokane and the Washington State Department of Ecology for declaratory, equitable, and monetary relief after the city discharged raw sewage into the Spokane River. The discharge fouled the waters of the river and adjoining Lake Long with fecal matter, solids, toilet paper, prophylactics, and slime; discolored the water; and filled the air with rancid, noxious, and repulsive odors. The trial court enjoined further discharge of raw sewage and awarded the plaintiffs damages, attorneys' fees, and costs. On appeal, the Washington Supreme Court upheld the plaintiffs' right to bring a public nuisance action because they had suffered nausea, headaches, nervousness, and insomnia. Finding that the plaintiffs had incurred considerable expense to effectuate an important public policy that benefitted a large class of people, the court characterized the plaintiffs as common law private attorneys general and upheld the award of the attorneys' fees incurred in seeking the injunction.

Under the test applied in *Miotke*, plaintiffs have standing to sue if they allege exposure to an unpleasant condition and resulting physical symptoms, which may be relatively minor and temporary. The arguable triviality of the personal injuries was counterbalanced by the public interest in preventing the defendants' actions, even where the defendants were public entities. Were you surprised by the award to plaintiffs of attorneys' fees?

b. Citizen Suits

Many federal environmental laws contain citizen suit provisions which authorize "any citizen" to sue "any person" violating the statutory standards. If the plaintiff prevails in the citizen suit the typical remedy is preventative or affirmative injunctive relief, with the court authorized to award costs, attorneys' fees and expert witness fees. See, e.g., Clean Air Act, 42 U.S.C. §§ 7401–7642 (West 1999) (§ 7604 authorizes citizen suits); Clean Water Act, 33 U.S.C. §§ 1251–1387 (West 1999) (§ 1365 authorizes citizen suits); Comprehensive Environmental Response, Compensation and Liability Act, 42 U.S.C. §§ 9601–9675 (West 1999) (§ 9659 authorizes citizen suits). Citizen suit plaintiffs may add state-law claims for public nuisance which the federal court may entertain under pendant or supplement jurisdiction. See Shay Scott, Combining Environmental Citizen Suits and other Private Theories of Recovery, 8 J. Envtl L. & Litig. 369 (1993) (thorough discussion of these issues).

For a substantial discussion of the operation of the citizen suits provision of the Clean Water Act, see American Canoe Assoc. v. District of Columbia Water and Sewer Authority, 306 F.Supp.2d 30 (D.D.C. 2004), set forth at Chapter 6 A. 2.

c. Class Actions

The Hawaii Supreme Court adopted the position recognized by the Restatement (Second), and explicitly rejected the special injury rule in a class action suit brought to enforce public rights-of-way along once public trails to a beach. See Akau v. Olohana Corp., 65 Hawaii 383, 652 P.2d 1130 (1982), in which the court found that the trend in the law had turned "away from focusing on whether the injury is shared by the public to whether the plaintiff was in fact injured[,]" and held that a member of the public without special injury has standing to sue to enforce the rights of the public if he can show injury-in-fact and satisfy the court that the concerns of a multiplicity of suits will be satisfied "by any means."

d. Associational Standing

The right of a citizen group to seek equitable relief for a public nuisance was specifically recognized in Leo v. General Electric Co., 145 A.D.2d 291, 538 N.Y.S.2d 844 (App. Div. 1989), where associations of fishermen sued defendant for polluting the Hudson River. The New York Appellate Court held that the representative associations had standing to maintain the action for public nuisance because they were "peculiarly aggrieved," after the state banned the sale of fish obtained from the River. The court noted that authorities made it "clear that the plaintiff associations are proper parties to this action. Since the plaintiff associations seek, inter alia, some form of prospective relief, it can reasonably be supposed that, if ultimately granted, it will inure to the benefit of the members actually injured." Here, because the association's members also sustained special injury, they could recover damages.

C. PRIVATE NUISANCE

1. GENERALLY

A claim for private nuisance "is predicated upon a substantial invasion of an individual's interest in the use and enjoyment of his property. Liability for nuisance may rest upon any one of three types of conduct: an intentional invasion of a person's interest; a negligent invasion of a person's interest; or, conduct so dangerous to life or property and so abnormal or out-of-place in its surroundings as to fall within the principles of strict liability. Like a trespass, conduct constituting a nuisance can include indirect or physical conditions created by defendant that cause harm. Restatement (Second) of Torts § 834 cmt. b." Hoery v. United States, 64 P.3d 214 (Colo. 2003) (en banc) (citations omitted).

The Restatement (Second) defines private nuisance as a "nontrespassory invasion of another's interest in the private use and enjoyment of land." Restatement (Second) of Torts § 821D. The ownership or rightful possession of land carries with it not only the right to exclude other persons and things from gaining entry onto the land, but embraces the right to use and enjoy the land free from significant interferences caused by those outside of the land. The interests protected by the tort of private nuisance are broad and imprecise.[4] Although, in one court's words, "[t]here are countless ways to interfere with the use and enjoyment of land[,] including interference with the physical condition of the land itself, disturbance in the comfort or conveniences of the occupant including his peace of mind, and threat of future injury that is a present menace and interference with enjoyment[,] [t]he essence of private nuisance is the protection of a property owner's or occupier's reasonable comfort[.]" Adkins v. Thomas Solvent Co., 440 Mich. 293, 487 N.W.2d 715, 720 (1992). *Adkins* is set forth below.

Some low level airborne pollution may not altogether prevent an occupant from using his property, but may, nevertheless, interfere with his enjoyment of it, as might a variety of intrusions by odor. It is

---

4. "It comprehends not only the interests that a person may have in the actual present use of land for residential, agricultural, commercial, industrial, and other purposes, but also his interests in having the present use value of the land unimpaired by changes in its physical condition.

* * * 'Interest in use and enjoyment' also comprehends the pleasure, comfort and enjoyment that a person normally derives from the occupancy of land. * * * ." Restatement (Second) of Torts § 821D, comment b.

accepted generally that "smoke, offensive odors, noise or vibrations" that "materially interfere" with the possessor's "ordinary comfort" may constitute a nuisance. E.g., Baldwin v. McClendon, 292 Ala. 43, 288 So.2d 761 (1974) (hog parlor proximate to plaintiff's land); Brown v. County Commissioners of Scioto County, 87 Ohio App.3d 704, 622 N.E.2d 1153 (Ohio App. 1993) (held: complaint regarding odors emanating from sewage treatment plant stated a claim in qualified private and public nuisance).

A toxic nuisance might take a wide range of forms. The pollution of a residence's well water would interfere with both a resident's use *and* enjoyment of a property. Illustrative is a federal district court opinion in Wilson v. Amoco Corp., 33 F.Supp.2d 969 (D.Wyo.1998) which considered private nuisance claims brought by property owners (along with claims under the Clean Water Act, 33 U.S.C.A. § 1311 and the Resource Conservation and Recovery Act, 42 U.S.C. § 6922) against operators of a railroad yard and dry cleaning facility for discharge of hazardous substances. The court denied summary judgment motions on the nuisance claims finding that the following could constitute interference with use or enjoyment: (1) indoor air tests of some plaintiffs' home indicating presence of PCE (perchloroethylene) affected enjoyment; (2) refusal because of PCE-contaminated groundwater to use the well on the property to water the plaintiff's garden and lawn interferes with use; (3) crawl space of one plaintiff's home emits constant odor, interfering with enjoyment; (4) plaintiff denied bank loan because of contamination interferes with use; (5) poor health of trees and gardens because of contamination interferes with use and enjoyment.

2. RESTATEMENT'S FORMULATION

The Restatement (Second) of Torts §§ 821D to 828 contain the governing principles. The Restatement rejects the arcane and incomprehensible distinctions followed in some jurisdictions between so-called nuisances *per se* and nuisance *per accidens*.[5]

a. *Standing: Who Can Sue for Private Nuisance*

What kind of interest must a plaintiff have in order to have standing to maintain a private nuisance action? The general rule is that the plaintiff must have either an ownership or possessory interest to bring a

---

5. A nuisance *per se* would be any act that constitutes a nuisance "at all times and under any circumstances," such as, for example, the permanent or chronic contamination of plaintiff's property. Vickridge 1st and 2nd Addition Homeowners Ass'n v. Catholic Diocese, 212 Kan. 348, 510 P.2d 1296 (1973). Nuisance *per accidens*, on the other hand, requires the fact finder's evaluation of whether, under all the surrounding circumstances defendant's action substan-tially interferes with plaintiff's comfortable enjoyment. Successful nuisance claims *per accidens* have gained orders in abatement or damages for invasions by particulate matter such as limestone dust. E.g., Crushed Stone Co. v. Moore, 369 P.2d 811 (Okla.1962) (the injury claimed by plaintiff included, inter alia, aggravation of allergies and worsening of one resident's nervous condition).

private nuisance action. Thus, in Arnoldt v. Ashland Oil, Inc., 186 W.Va. 394, 412 S.E.2d 795 (1991), the court held that adult children and non-owners residing with relatives did not have standing because they lacked the requisite ownership or possessory interest. Nevertheless, while nuisance law is designed to protect interests in land "any interest sufficient to be dignified as a property right will support the action." Prosser & Keeton on Torts 621 (5th ed. 1984). In contrast to *Arnoldt*, one court has recognized the standing of a minor child of a tenant to maintain a private nuisance action. Gesswin v. Beckwith, 35 Conn.Sup. 89, 397 A.2d 121 (1978); see also William H. Rodgers, Jr., Environmental Law: Air and Water § 2.4 at 42 (1986). The Restatement indicates that family members have standing because "occupancy is a sufficient interest in itself to permit recovery." § 821E. See Bowers v. Westvaco, 244 Va. 139, 419 S.E.2d 661 (Va. 1992) (children of owner are "occupants" with standing to sue for private nuisance). If a property interest is essential for a private nuisance, how might a student in a school or a worker in a factory who is affected by a nuisance circumvent the standing limitation?

b. *Requirement of Significant Harm*

The universal rule, memorialized in the Restatement § 821F only allows a plaintiff to recover damages on a private nuisance theory if she suffers "significant harm," which is defined as harm: "of a kind that would be suffered by a normal person in the community or by property in normal condition and used for a normal purpose." This statement recognizes a "live and let live" principle that precludes recovery for slight inconveniences and petty annoyances. On the other hand, when the invasion involves a detrimental change in the physical condition of land, there is seldom any doubt as to the significance of the harm.

In San Diego Gas & Electric Co. v. Covalt, 13 Cal.4th 893, 55 Cal.Rptr.2d 724, 920 P.2d 669 (1996), a homeowner's action alleging that electric and magnetic fields emitted from electric power lines constituted a private nuisance, the California Supreme Court expressed the rationale for the significant harm requirement:

> This requirement flows from the law's recognition that "Life in organized society and especially in populous communities involves an unavoidable clash of individual interests. Practically all human activities unless carried on in a wilderness interfere to some extent with others or involve some risk of interference, and these interferences range from mere trifling annoyances to serious harms. It is an obvious truth that each individual in a community must put up with a certain amount of annoyance, inconvenience and interference and must take a certain amount of risk in order that all may get on together. The very existence of organized society depends upon the principle of 'give and take, live and let live,' and therefore the law of torts does not attempt to impose liability or shift the loss in every case in which one person's conduct has some detrimental effect on another. Liability for damages is imposed in those cases in which the

harm or risk to one is greater than he ought to be required to bear under the circumstances, at least without compensation." (Rest. 2d Torts, § 822, com. g.)

The Restatement (Second) recognizes the same requirement as the need for proof of "significant harm" which it variously defines as "harm of importance" and a "real and appreciable invasion of the plaintiff's interests" and an invasion that is "definitely offensive, seriously annoying or intolerable." The degree of harm is to be judged by an objective standard, i.e., what effect would the invasion have on persons of normal health and sensibilities living in the same community? "If normal persons in that locality would not be substantially annoyed or disturbed by the situation, then the invasion is not a significant one, even though the idiosyncracies of the particular plaintiff may make it unendurable to him." (Rest. 2d Torts, § 821F, com. d, p. 106) This is, of course a question of fact that turns on the circumstances of each case. 920 P.2d at 696.

See also Harper, James & Gray, The Law of Torts § 1.23 (3d ed. 1996) (Plaintiff must suffer "substantial actual damage"); In re Burbank Environmental Litigation, 42 F.Supp.2d 976 (C.D.Cal.1998) (deposits of dust and debris on plaintiffs' property due to airplane manufacturer's demolition of its plant and remediation of contamination, which covered furniture and houses, caused pets to die and paint to peel, constituted significant harm for private nuisance).

c. *General Liability Rules*

§ 822. **General Rule**

One is subject to liability for a private nuisance if, but only if, his conduct is a legal cause of an invasion of another's interest in the private use and enjoyment of land, and the invasion is either

> (a) intentional and unreasonable, or

> (b) unintentional and otherwise actionable under the rules controlling liability for negligent or reckless conduct, or for abnormally dangerous conditions or activities.

The general rule clarifies that an invasion of a person's interest in the private use and enjoyment of land by any type of liability-forming conduct is a private nuisance. The invasion that subjects a person to liability may be either intentional or unintentional. A person is subject to liability for an intentional invasion when his conduct is unreasonable under the circumstances of the particular case, and he is subject to liability for an unintentional invasion when his conduct is negligent, reckless, or abnormally dangerous.

Therefore, liability for private nuisance depends upon the presence of some type of tortious conduct. Most invasions are intentional, as will be explained below, but negligence too can form the basis of liability. The failure to recognize that private nuisance has reference to the nature of the interest invaded, and not to the type of conduct that subjects the defendant to liability has led to confusion. Thus, negligence can be a basis of liability, but negligence liability is not necessary for private nuisance.

d. What Constitutes An "Intentional" Invasion?

Alternative definitions of an "intentional invasion" of another's interest in land are recognized in Restatement (Second) of Torts § 825:

> An invasion of another's interest in the use and enjoyment of land or an interference with the public right, is intentional if the actor (a) acts for the purpose of causing it, or (b) knows that it is resulting or is substantially certain to result from this conduct.

The Restatement, at § 825 comments c and d, elaborates:

> c. Meaning of "intentional invasion." To be "intentional," an invasion of another's interest in the use and enjoyment of land, or of the public right, need not be inspired by malice or ill will on the actor's part toward the other. An invasion so inspired is intentional, but so is an invasion that the actor knowingly causes in the pursuit of a laudable enterprise without any desire to cause harm. It is the knowledge that the actor has at the time he acts or fails to act that determines whether the invasion resulting from his conduct is intentional or unintentional. It is not enough to make an invasion intentional that the actor realizes or should realize that his conduct involves a serious risk or likelihood of causing the invasion. He must either act for the purpose of causing it or know that it is resulting or is substantially certain to result from his conduct * * *

> d. Continuing or recurrent invasions. Most of the litigation over private nuisances involves situations in which there are continuing or recurrent invasions resulting from continuing or recurrent conduct; and the same is true of many public nuisances. In these cases the first invasion resulting from the actor's conduct may be either intentional or unintentional; but when the conduct is continued after the actor knows that the invasion is resulting from it, further invasions are intentional.

The Restatement's characterization of intent has been adopted in numerous jurisdictions. See, e.g., United Proteins, Inc. v. Farmland Industries, Inc., 259 Kan. 725, 915 P.2d 80 (Kan. 1996); Hall v. Phillips, 231 Neb. 269, 436 N.W.2d 139 (Neb. 1989); Morgan v. Quailbrook Condominium Co., 704 P.2d 573 (Utah 1985); Copart Industries, Inc. v. Consolidated Edison Co. of New York, 41 N.Y.2d 564, 394 N.Y.S.2d 169, 362 N.E.2d 968 (N.Y. 1977); Frady v. Portland General Electric Co., 55 Or.App. 344, 637 P.2d 1345, 1348 (Or.App.1981). The *United Proteins* decision below develops the principle of intent.

While the intent requirement for private nuisance does not require that the actor have subjectively desired the outcome of his actions, the plaintiff must at least show that the defendant had actual or constructive control over the agency claimed to have deprived the plaintiff of his right to quiet enjoyment of the property. This point is well made by the Alaska Supreme Court in Parks Hiway Enterprises, LLC v. CEM Leasing, Inc., 995 P.2d 657 (Alaska 2000), a gasoline contamination claim that included a separate count against the fuel suppliers to the subject service stations:

* * *

E.   *THE SUPERIOR COURT DID NOT ERR BY REFUSING TO HOLD PETROLEUM SALES LIABLE FOR PRIVATE NUISANCE.*

Private nuisance liability results from an intentional and unreasonable interference with another's use and enjoyment of his or her own property. [Cc] Unintentional conduct may also warrant nuisance liability if negligent, reckless, or abnormally dangerous. [Cc] To incur liability, an actor's conduct must be a substantial factor in causing the nuisance. [Cc]

The superior court rejected Parks Hiway's private nuisance theory, reasoning that "[o]ne who has no control over property at the time of the nuisance cannot be held liable therefor." Echoing the court, Petroleum Sales accurately cites numerous cases that have refused to extend nuisance liability to hazardous material vendors uninvolved in the operation of the facility from which the pollution eventually migrated. [Cc] These courts agree that "liability for damage caused by a nuisance turns on whether the defendants were in control over the instrumentality alleged to constitute the nuisance." [Cc] Moreover, at least one court has noted the absence of cases holding manufacturers liable for nuisance claims arising from the use of their products after sale. [Cc] The Restatement likewise couches its nuisance liability rule in terms of "the possessor of [the] land" from which the nuisance emanates. [Restatement (Second) of Torts § 839 (1965)]

Against this apparent judicial consensus, Parks Hiway cites Shockley v. Hoechst Celanese Corp. [793 F.Supp. 670 (D.S.C.1992), rev'd in part on other grounds, 996 F.2d 1212 (4th Cir.1993)] and Northridge Co. v. W.R. Grace & Co., [205 Wis.2d 267, 556 N.W.2d 345 (Wis. Ct. App.1996)]. Shockley involved a manufacturer who "knowingly delivered rusty, aging, and leaking barrels of hazardous chemicals" to a waste disposal site operated by another entity. [Cc] Because the condition causing the nuisance, i.e., the leaking barrels, existed when the manufacturer delivered them to the property from which the contamination ultimately emanated, the court concluded that the manufacturer had satisfied the Restatement's "substantial factor" test. [Cc] The present case is distinguishable from Shockley because here the fuel delivered was not defective, whereas the barrels in Shockley were. Northridge involved a suit for private nuisance against an asbestos manufacturer whose product was installed in a shopping mall. [Cc] The Wisconsin appellate court affirmed the manufacturer's nuisance liability, reasoning that "one who has erected a nuisance will be responsible for its continuance, even after he has parted with the title and the possession." [Cc]

Northridge is distinguishable from the present case because there is no evidence that Petroleum Sales had any reason to know that a nuisance would result from filling Gold Hill's tanks. Moreover, Petroleum Sales did not "erect a nuisance" by delivering gasoline to Gold Hill's leaking tanks; the defective tanks, rather than the fuel migrating from them, constituted the nuisance. Petroleum Sales did not control either Gold Hill's tanks or the fuel when the contamination of Parks Hiway's groundwater occurred. It was therefore not a substantial factor in creating the alleged nuisance and should bear no liability.

* * *

e. *What Is Unreasonableness?*

Because the Restatement refers to an intentional and "unreasonable" invasion of another's interest in use and enjoyment of land, the meaning of "unreasonable" becomes critical. The Restatement (Second) of Torts § 826 provides:

§ 826. Unreasonableness of Intentional Invasion

An intentional invasion of another's interest in the use and enjoyment of land is unreasonable if:

(a) the gravity of the harm outweighs the utility of the actor's conduct, or

(b) the harm caused by the conduct is serious and the financial burden of compensating for this and similar harm to others would not make the continuation of the conduct not feasible.

It is significant that subsections (a) and (b) are in the disjunctive—either will suffice. Subsection (a) is a balancing of the actual harm (not the risk of harm as in a negligence case) against the "utility of the actor's conduct."

Subsection (b), however, creates an alternative basis for liability in cases seeking *damages only*. In such cases, the harm must be "serious" and the "financial burden of compensating" the plaintiff (and others similarly situated) must not require that the defendant cease its operations. The careful weighing process between utility and harm applicable to injunction suits gives way to a rule that allows compensatory damages to be awarded, even if the utility of the activity exceeds the harm, so long as the damages are not so great as to become, for practical purposes, an injunction of sorts, shutting down the activity. The objective of the action for damages is not to stop the activity, but rather to require the activity to bear the costs of compensating for the harm it causes to others. Comment f to § 826 states:

It may sometimes be reasonable to operate an important activity if payment is made for the harm it is causing, but unreasonable to continue it without paying. The process of weighing the gravity of the harm against the utility of the conduct assesses the social value of the actor's activity in general. * * * The process of comparing the general utility of the activity with the harm suffered as a result is adequate if the suit is for an injunction prohibiting the activity. But it may sometimes be incomplete and therefore inappropriate when the suit is for compensation for the harm imposed. The action for damages does not seek to stop the activity; it seeks instead to place on the activity the cost of compensating for the harm it causes. The financial burden of this cost is therefore a significant factor in determining whether the conduct of causing the harm without paying for it is unreasonable. * * *

With the prevalence of insurance coverage held by large corporate entities for business-related losses caused to others, the financial burden concern of § 826(b) rarely comes into play. Its application is described further in subsection 5. to follow.

In San Diego Gas & Electric Co. v. Covalt, 13 Cal.4th 893, 55 Cal.Rptr.2d 724, 920 P.2d 669, 696–97 (Cal. 1996) the California Supreme Court captured the principle of unreasonableness in holding that EMF emissions from electric power lines did not create an unreasonable invasion with plaintiffs' use and enjoyment, which is to say, that a "substantial" interference is not definitionally synonymous with an "unreasonable" interference:

The second additional requirement for nuisance is superficially similar but analytically distinct: "The interference with the protected interest must not only be substantial, but it must also be unreasonable," i.e., it must be "of such a nature, duration or amount as to constitute unreasonable interference with the use and enjoyment of the land." The primary test for determining whether the invasion is unreasonable is whether the gravity of the harm outweighs the social utility of the defendant's conduct taking a number of factors into account. Again the standard is objective: the question is not whether the particular plaintiff found the invasion unreasonable, but "whether reasonable persons generally, looking at the whole situation impartially and objectively, would consider it unreasonable." And again this is a question of fact: "Fundamentally, the unreasonableness of intentional invasions is a problem of relative values to be determined by the trier of fact in each case in the light of all the circumstances of that case." With these principles in mind we turn to the case at bar.

* * *

Plaintiffs now contend the EMF fields impaired their use and enjoyment of the property simply because they assertedly feared that the fields would cause them physical harm. We need not and do not decide here whether a fear of future harm will support a cause of action for private nuisance. * * * Even if we assume arguendo that plaintiffs could amend their complaint to allege such a fear, an award of damages on that basis would interfere with the policy of the [public utility commission] on power line electric and magnetic fields. As we have seen, in order to award such damages on a nuisance theory the trier of fact would be required to find that reasonable persons viewing the matter objectively (1) would experience a substantial fear that the fields cause physical harm and (2) would deem the invasion so serious that it outweighs the social utility of SDG & E's conduct. Such findings, however, would be inconsistent with the [Commission's] conclusion reached after consulting with [Department of Health Services], studying the reports of advisory groups and experts, and holding evidentiary hearings, that the available evidence does not support a reasonable belief that 60 Hz electric and magnetic fields present a substantial risk of physical harm, and that unless and until the evidence supports such a belief regulated utilities need take no action to reduce field levels from existing power lines.

Should the balancing process dominate whenever the defendant is a public utility or performs other essential functions? Why treat San Diego Gas & Electric different from an ordinary corporate polluter? What is the significance that a government agency found the potential harm to be not unreasonable? In later sections of this chapter and in Chapter 6 we examine the effect to be given to governmental permits or other authorization.

Thus, § 826(b) attempts to provide a mechanism for enabling injured private landowners to recover damages whenever the invasion is intentional and serious. The principle here at work is that a business operated for economic gain should internalize the costs of its operations—the harm that it produces is part of the costs of doing business, to be passed along to those to whom it sells or provides services. Some courts, as illustrated by the *San Diego Gas* decision, insist on allowing a utility and harm weighing test to be outcome determinative even in cases of a clear and substantial invasion, where the plaintiff is seeking only damages, and where there is no risk that paying such damages would impair the defendant's ability to continue its operations. The decision in Carpenter v. Double R Cattle Company later in this chapter manifests this approach.

The dispute over the reasonableness of a defendant's activities can take many forms. For example, in Benjamin v. Nelstad Materials Corp., 214 A.D.2d 632, 625 N.Y.S.2d 281 (App. Div. 1995), a New York decision, the majority and dissenting opinions, after each quoting § 822 of the Restatement, disagreed over whether the record supported the trial court's finding that defendant had taken reasonable steps to avoid causing harm to plaintiff landowners. The majority, after pointing out that what constitutes reasonable use of one's property depends on the circumstances, stated:

The record supports [the trial court's] determination that the corporate defendant presently uses the best and most modern equipment and has eliminated most of the noise, dust, and bright lights emanating from the plant. Although not conclusive, weight must also be given to the plaintiffs' awareness of the existence of the cement plant on the subject premises prior to purchasing their respective homes.

The dissent painted quite a different picture of the defendants' initiatives to minimize the harm:

[N]otwithstanding the trial court's and this court's finding to the contrary, no evidence at all was adduced by the defendants regarding their adoption of "the best and most modern equipment" to decrease the extraordinary noise and dust pollution generated by their enterprise, except for the [defendant's] self-serving testimony that he knew of no other procedures or machinery that he could install to diminish his company's pernicious side-effects. Surely the fact that the defendants complied with the requirements of the City of New Rochelle, before it would sanction their continued expansion, that they put mufflers on their unmuffled vehicles and cease beaming their brilliant security lights into the residential community (which actions the defendants had initiated to punish neighbors who had complained about their operations) hardly qualifies as good faith efforts at remediation, let alone installation of the best and most modern equipment.

In the area of remediation, the defendant['s officer] admitted at the trial that great quantities of white dust are produced in the cement-making process, and that he had recently purchased a new filtering machine to better control the problem, although for unexplained reasons he had not yet installed it. Pictures of these dust clouds were admitted into evidence, and the plaintiffs testified to observing the dust as it drifted from the defendants' plant onto their property and into their houses and yards. 625 N.Y.S.2d at 282–83 (citations omitted).

f. The Weighing Process

(i) Gravity of the Harm

When the weighing process called for under § 826(a) is applied, the Restatement sets forth the factors which the trier of fact is to consider.

As expressed in the Restatement, § 827:

Gravity of Harm—Factors Involved

In determining the gravity of the harm from an intentional invasion of another's interest in the use and enjoyment of land, the following factors are important:

(a) The extent of the harm involved;

(b) the character of the harm involved;

(c) the social value that the law attaches to the type of use or enjoyment invaded;

(d) the suitability of the particular use or enjoyment invaded to the character of the locality; and

(e) the burden on the person harmed of avoiding the harm.

A few points are noteworthy. Under subsection (a) the degree of the invasion *and* its duration are both relevant. Even minor interferences if extended indefinitely may produce significant harm. The character of the harm under subsection (b) is obviously important: does it consist of damage to land or buildings or to crops, or is it a personal annoyance or discomfort? Does it raise serious personal safety and health concerns (e.g., carcinogenic chemical wastes)?

The factor in subsection (d) is sometimes referred to as the "locality rule." Comment g to Restatement (Second) of Torts § 827 notes that the harm to a residential plaintiff in a residential area will be considered more serious than the harm to a resident whose home is located in a predominantly business or commercial community, not because the harm is less in some objective sense, but because public policy demands that the character of the uses in the area be assigned some weight in the process. For example, zoning ordinances can be relevant in examining this factor. Finally, as subsection (e) recognizes, the plaintiff may easily be able to minimize the effect of the invasion by shutting the windows or taking other simple steps.

(ii) Utility of Defendant's Conduct

The Restatement describes the factors controlling the utility analysis in § 828:

§ 828. Utility of Conduct—Factors Involved

In determining the utility of conduct that causes an intentional invasion of another's interest in the use and enjoyment of land, the following factors are important:

(a) the social value that the law attaches to the primary purpose of the conduct;

(b) the suitability of the conduct to the character of the locality; and

(c) the impracticality of preventing or avoiding the invasion.

Subsection (a) addresses the usual understanding of the term and requires no special attention beyond that paid to it in the cases below. Subsections (b) and (c) raise the same points as found in assessing the gravity of the harm, asking as to the defendant's activity: how locationally appropriate is the activity and could the defendant have done anything reasonably feasible to reduce or eliminate the invasion?

(iii) Other Considerations on Unreasonableness

In addition to the factors in Restatement §§ 827 and 828, the Restatement recognizes that certain kinds of invasions will be regarded as unreasonable. The invasion of the plaintiff's interest will be found to be unreasonable where the defendant's conduct is malicious or indecent (§ 829); where the resulting invasion could have been avoided by the defendant relatively easily ("without undue hardship") (§ 830); where the plaintiff's use of his land is, and the defendant's conduct is not, suited to the locality in which the invasion occurred (§ 841); or where the harm resulting is "severe" and greater than the plaintiff should be required to bear without compensation (§ 829A).

3. NATURE OF THE INTEREST INTERFERED WITH

The particular use to which a property is put and the sensitivities of the persons using the property may be factors in evaluating if defendant's conduct constitutes an unreasonable interference that rises to the level of a private nuisance. For example, if a morning sulphurous smell enveloped the premises of a nursery school playground, or a retirement residence, the occupants of either could argue plausibly that the odor interfered substantially with their use of the properties for those purposes. If, on the other hand, the odor affected only adjoining properties engaged in smelting operations, any interference with either use or enjoyment might be too insubstantial to warrant a remedy in private nuisance.

As was pointed out in Chapter 2, the interests protected by private nuisance doctrine are distinguishable from trespass, but the two torts may overlap. An invasion of one's possessory interest in land is often accompanied by some interference with the use and enjoyment of land, which is especially likely to occur if the trespass produces actual harm to the land. One factor which distinguishes trespass from private nuisance is that the nuisance action may be maintained only if there is "significant harm," a harm of importance, involving more than a slight inconvenience or petty annoyance. See generally, Page Keeton, Trespass, Nuisance and Strict Liability, 59 Colum.L.Rev. 457 (1959).

Will the plaintiff's apprehension that the defendant's operation will impair the value of property support a claim of private nuisance? Herein of so-called "stigma" damages:

ADKINS v. THOMAS SOLVENT COMPANY

Supreme Court of Michigan, 1992.
440 Mich. 293, 487 N.W.2d 715.

Boyle, J.

The question before us is whether a claim for relief may be maintained by plaintiffs who claim the right to damages in nuisance for property depreciation caused by environmental contamination of ground water despite testimony by both plaintiffs' and defendants' experts that their properties were not and would never be subject to ground water contamination emanating from the defendants' property. The trial court dismissed these plaintiffs' claims on the basis that it found no support for recovery in Michigan law. The Court of Appeals reversed the decision of the trial court, rejecting its conclusion that the facts presented no cognizable claim for nuisance.

[We reverse, for we] are persuaded that the boundaries of a traditional nuisance claim should not be relaxed to permit recovery on these facts. Compensation for a decline in property value caused by unfounded perception of underground contamination is inextricably entwined with complex policy questions regarding environmental protection that are more suitably resolved through the legislative process.

* * *

I

In 1984, the plaintiffs sued the Thomas Solvent Company in the Calhoun Circuit Court for damages and injunctive relief from injuries allegedly resulting from the improper handling of chemicals and industrial waste. Claiming that the Thomas Solvent Company's and other defendants' improper handling and storage of toxic chemicals and industrial waste had contaminated the ground water, the plaintiffs brought claims sounding in negligence, continuing nuisance, continuing trespass, strict liability, and ultrahazardous activities.

* * *

[The plaintiffs complained of contaminants emanating from two sites owned or operated by the Thomas Solvent defendants.] As discovery continued, it became clear that contaminants allegedly discharged into the ground water by the defendants never reached these plaintiffs' property. The plaintiffs' expert * * * testified that no contaminants from the Thomas Solvent facilities had any effect on the properties of these plaintiffs.

[In responding to defendants' motion to dismiss, plaintiffs] conceded that no contaminants ever reached these twenty-two plaintiffs' property, but urged the court to impose liability on the defendants for any loss in property values due to public concern about the contaminants in the general area. Concluding that any damages that these plaintiffs suffered resulted from unfounded public perception that their ground water was contaminated, the trial court dismissed their claims. * * *

* * *

III

* * * [T]he gist of a private nuisance action is an interference with the occupation or use of land or an interference with servitudes relating to land. There are countless ways to interfere with the use and enjoyment of land including interference with the physical condition of the land itself, disturbance in the comfort or conveniences of the occupant including his peace of mind, and threat of future injury that is a present menace and interference with enjoyment. * * * The pollution of ground water may constitute a public or private nuisance. 4 Restatement Torts, 2d, § 832, p. 142.

According to the Restatement, an actor is subject to liability for private nuisance for a nontrespassory invasion of another's interest in the private use and enjoyment of land if (a) the other has property rights and privileges in respect to the use or enjoyment interfered with, (b) the invasion results in significant harm, (c) the actor's conduct is the legal cause of the invasion, and (d) the invasion is either (i) intentional and unreasonable, or (ii) unintentional and otherwise actionable under the rules governing liability for negligent, reckless, or ultrahazardous conduct. 4 Restatement Torts, 2d, §§ 821D–F, 822, pp. 100–115.

Prosser & Keeton's enumeration of the requirements to recover on a private nuisance theory is similar. They set forth the following requirements: "(1) The defendant acted with the intent of interfering with the use and enjoyment of the land by those entitled to the use; (2) There was some interference with the use and enjoyment of the land of the kind intended, although the amount and extent of that interference may not have been anticipated or intended; (3) The interference that resulted and the physical harm, if any, from that interference proved to be substantial. * * * The substantial interference requirement is to satisfy the need for a showing that the land is reduced in value because of the defendant's conduct; (4) The interference that came about under such circumstances was of such a nature, duration or amount as to constitute unreasonable interference with the use and enjoyment of the land. This does not mean that the defendant's conduct must be unreasonable. It only means that the interference must be unreasonable and this requires elaboration." Prosser & Keeton, supra, pp. 622–623.

* * * In this case, the Court considers whether property depreciation based on unfounded fears falls within the boundaries of an action for private nuisance in Michigan. The plaintiffs alleged that the defendants' improper handling and storage of toxic chemicals and hazardous waste contaminated underground water in the area, thus supporting their recovery of money damages for nuisance. * * *

The Court of Appeals focused upon the lack of any physical intrusion onto plaintiffs' land, stressing that an interference with the use and enjoyment of land need not involve a physical or tangible intrusion. We do not disagree with this rule of law. Nevertheless, we conclude that the trial court properly found that the plaintiffs failed to trace any significant interference with the use and enjoyment of land to an action of the defendants.

The crux of the plaintiffs' complaint is that publicity concerning the contamination of ground water in the area (although concededly not their ground water) caused diminution in the value of the plaintiffs' property. This theory cannot form the basis for recovery because negative publicity resulting in unfounded fear about dangers in the vicinity of the property does not constitute a significant interference with the use and enjoyment of land.

* * *

The doctrine of nuisance traditionally encompassed geographic, temporal, and proprietary aspects. In geographic terms, nuisance arose when occupants of neighboring land had a dispute, typically over the proper use of the defendant's land. * * *

In temporal terms, nuisance normally required some degree of permanence. If the asserted interference was "temporary and evanescent," there was no actionable nuisance. This requirement is normally subsumed in the question whether the interference with the use and enjoyment of property is substantial. * * *

As the doctrine of trespass was gradually transmuted into the action upon the case for nuisance, the requirement that the injury involve entry onto the complainant's land was eliminated. To limit the broader action on the case for nuisance, courts added the requirement that a litigant seeking to recover for nuisance must show a legally cognizable injury, requiring proof of a significant interference with the use and enjoyment of land. * * * Stated otherwise, while nuisance may be predicated on conduct of a defendant that causes mental annoyance, it will not amount to a substantial injury unless the annoyance is significant and the interference is unreasonable in the sense that it would be unreasonable to permit the defendant to cause such an amount of harm without paying for it.

Nuisance on the case thus involved the common law's attempt to ensure accommodation between conflicting uses of adjoining property. * * * Because the doctrine sought to acknowledge the right of both the property owner to carry out a particular use and the neighbor whose property or use and enjoyment of property might be injured by the use, de minimus annoyances were not actionable. Only for a substantial interference with the use and enjoyment of property would an action lie. As a part of this scheme, courts frequently concluded that diminution in property values alone constitutes damnum absque injuria.

The reasoning in Gunther v. E.I. Du Pont De Nemours & Co., 157 F.Supp. 25 (N.D.W.Va., 1957), app. dismissed 255 F.2d 710 (4th Cir. 1958), exemplifies this reluctance to find a nuisance for mere diminution of property value on the basis of unfounded beliefs or fear of injury. In *Gunther,* the plaintiffs unsuccessfully sought damages and injunctive relief for claimed injuries to their property and person from test explosions conducted by the defendant in the vicinity of their property. The court refused to find nuisance, reasoning: "The Court believes it a fair inference from the evidence that the Gunthers' enjoyment of their property was lessened because they believed that the test blasting had injured them. If such belief is unfounded, what is left other than depreciation in value? Mere diminution of the value of property because of the use to which adjoining or nearby premises is devoted, if unaccompanied with other ill results, is damnum absque injuria—a loss without an injury, in the legal sense."

That same reasoning applies to this case. Plaintiffs have stipulated the dismissal of all claims except those predicated upon an alleged depreciation in the market value of the property because of the unfounded fears of purchasers. The fact, as the dissent recognizes, that plaintiffs make no claim for relief arising out of their own fears, illustrates the point that defendants' activities have not interfered with their use and enjoyment of property.

This Court has held that property depreciation alone is insufficient to constitute a nuisance. Although there is early authority to the contrary involving circumstances largely subsumed in zoning regulations, most recently this Court has held that a cause of action for nuisance may not be based on unfounded fears. Smith v. Western Wayne Co. Conservation Ass'n., 380 Mich. 526, 543, 158 N.W.2d 463 (1968). In *Smith*, the plaintiffs sought to have a gun range declared a nuisance, contending that it created fear of injuries, thus decreasing their property values. Adopting the trial court's opinion that "no real or actual danger" existed from the use of the gun range, the Court further held that, even assuming a decrease in property values, this was not "in itself sufficient to constitute a nuisance."

Just as the development of nuisance on the case responded to the limitations of trespass by recognizing a cause of action when there was damage, but not injury amounting to use, the modern formulation of nuisance in fact, acknowledges changing conditions by declining to recognize a cause of action where damage and injury are both predicated on unfounded fear of third parties that depreciates property values. The rationale may be expressed by observing that reasonable minds cannot differ that diminished property value based on unfounded fear is not a substantial interference in and of itself. Thus, in rejecting a claim that tort liability could be based on the creation of fear that depreciates property values, one federal district court observed that the theory was based on "a public reaction which is conjectural, transitory and ephemeral."

This response also corresponds with the historical premise underlying tort liability for nuisance in fact, i.e., that when some significant interference with the use and enjoyment of land causes the property value loss, courts of law accommodate conflicting interests by recognizing claims designed to shift the loss. However, on the present state of the record, plaintiffs do not contend that the condition created by the defendant causes them fear or anxiety. Thus, not only have these plaintiffs not alleged significant interference with their use and enjoyment of property, they do not here posit any interference at all.

Plaintiffs correctly observe that property depreciation is a traditional element of damages in a nuisance action. See, e.g., Prosser, supra, pp. 637–640. We are not persuaded, however, and the dissent has not cited authority to the contrary, that an allegation of property depreciation alone sets forth a cognizable claim in private nuisance of significant interference with the use and enjoyment of a person's property. Diminution in property values caused by negative publicity is, on these facts, damnum absque injuria—a loss without an injury in the legal sense. * * *

* * *

We are thus unpersuaded by the dissent's attempt to avoid the stipulation of the parties by referring throughout the opinion to facts and counts that are not before us. * * * Unlike the dissent, we proceed on the assumption the parties presented to us. We do not know why counsel chose not to assert claims of personal discomfort or annoyance as he did with regard to other plaintiffs, or to appeal from the trial court's order denying leave to amend. These were probably strategy decisions based on his clients' responses in discovery. We are entitled to assume that counsel's present posture is motivated by legitimate interest in securing an appellate court decision that diminution in value is recoverable without a showing of substantial interference with use or enjoyment of property. * * * So viewed, the structuring of this lawsuit involves not a hypertechnical issue, but an issue of considerable significance to these plaintiffs, to litigants similarly situated, and to the jurisprudence.

In short, we do not agree with the dissent's suggestion that wholly unfounded fears of third parties regarding the conduct of a lawful business satisfy the requirement for a legally cognizable injury as long as property values decline. Indeed, we would think it not only "odd," but anachronistic that a claim of nuisance in fact could be based on unfounded fears regarding persons with AIDS moving into a neighborhood, the establishment of otherwise lawful group homes for the disabled, or unrelated persons living together, merely because the fears experienced by third parties would cause a decline in property values.

When appropriate, we have not hesitated to examine common-law doctrines in view of changes in society's mores, institutions, and problems, and to alter those doctrines where necessary. * * *

This case does not present that situation. * * *

The plaintiffs concede that a ground water divide prevented the migration of contaminated water to their property. Nevertheless, the plaintiffs seek to recover for damages because the defendants allegedly contaminated property in the general area. * * *

If any property owner in the vicinity of the numerous hazardous waste sites that have been identified[37] can advance a claim seeking damages when unfounded public fears of exposure cause property depre-

---

37. Seventy-seven Michigan hazardous waste sites are on the National Priorities List. 56 Fed.Reg. 5606–5627 (February 22, 1991). In addition, the Department of Natural Resources, pursuant to the Environmental Response Act, 1982 P.A. 307, M.C.L. § 299.601 et seq.; M.S.A. § 13.32(1) et seq., has identified approximately 2,837 sites of environmental contamination throughout the state. Department of Natural Resources, Michigan Sites of Environmental Contamination, Act 307 (March, 1991), p. 9.

ciation, the ultimate effect might be a reordering of a polluter's resources for the benefit of persons who have suffered no cognizable harm
at the expense of those claimants who have been subjected to a substantial and unreasonable interference in the use and enjoyment of property.
Thus, while we acknowledge that the line drawn today is not necessarily
dictated by the spectral permutations of nuisance jurisprudence, if the
line is to be drawn elsewhere, the significant interests involved appear to
be within the realm of those more appropriate for resolution by the
Legislature.

Notes and Questions

1. Why did the majority consider the fears of third parties "unfounded?" Was its conclusion based solely on the hydrogeological fact that contamination from defendants' operations could not reach plaintiffs' property?
What rationales did the majority offer to support its conclusion? Was a
concern for unlimited or disproportionate liability among the reasons offered? Did the dissent's test of requiring "a condition tortiously created or
maintained by the defendant on *neighboring* property" address the widespread liability issue?

2. In Chapter 5 we consider the question of what damages are recoverable once liability for a private nuisance is found to exist. In that context we
examine stigma damages which represent a diminution in the value of the
property *after* the contamination has been removed. But the issue in *Adkins*
is not one of recoverable damages—it is the threshold issue of whether there
is any actionable nuisance at all.

3. *The Debate Over the Substantiality of the Interference: Is Intrusion
Necessary? Adkins* sheds light on an issue that has engendered considerable
division among the cases: how much does it take to satisfy the requirement
for a substantial interference? For example, is actual contamination of the
property necessary? *Adkins*, in dicta, said no: ("The Court of Appeals
focused on the lack of any physical intrusion onto plaintiffs' land, stressing
that an interference with the use and enjoyment of land need not involve a
physical tangible intrusion. We do not disagree with this rule of law.")
Exxon Corporation v. Yarema, 69 Md.App. 124, 516 A.2d 990, 1001 (1986)
("Exxon argues that * * * a plaintiff may not recover in tort when there is
no tangible or physical impact on plaintiff's property. We conclude that there
is no such rule of law.") cert. denied, 309 Md. 47, 522 A.2d 392 (1987).

However, in Adams v. Star Enterprise, 51 F.3d 417 (4th Cir.1995), the
Fourth Circuit held that a plaintiff may not recover damages in nuisance for
environmental contamination which is not physically perceptible from the
plaintiff's property. *Adams* involved an oil spill which occurred at defendants' distribution facility. Petroleum products from the spill leached into
the groundwater and surface waters and formed an underground plume.
Plaintiffs, a group of homeowners, brought an action for damages alleging
fear of future contamination and diminution in property values arising from
the fears of the buying public. As in *Adkins*, there was no evidence of
groundwater contamination of plaintiffs' properties, oil odors or any other
material interference. The District Court dismissed the nuisance cause of

action on the ground that there was no showing of actual intrusion into the plaintiffs' use and enjoyment of their lands. The Fourth Circuit characterized the issue before it as whether the property owners may recover for the diminution in the value of their property and their reasonable fear of negative health effects resulting from the proximity of their property to an environmental hazard such as an underground oil spill. In construing Virginia law, the Fourth Circuit affirmed the district court's dismissal. Although the Fourth Circuit begins its analysis by focusing on the lack of any interference with the landowners' use or enjoyment of their land as a result of the oil spill, the court holds that future plaintiffs may not recover for any activity or condition complained of that is not "physically perceptible" from the plaintiffs' property.

But the District Court for the district of the Virgin Islands rejected *Adams* in In re Tutu Wells Contamination Litigation, 909 F.Supp. 991 (D.V.I.1995). In *Tutu* the court set forth the facts:

> The Esso Defendants argued that the Plaintiff's property which is the subject of the current litigation has not actually been contaminated as a result of the any alleged contamination of the Turpentine Run Aquifer by the Esso Defendants. In fact, the Esso Defendants claim that the expert reports in this case show that the Harthman property is unlikely to become contaminated barring the occurrence of extraordinary circumstances. Based on these assertions, the Esso Defendants argue that this court should grant summary judgment in their favor because the Plaintiffs will be unable to show that they have suffered any harm as a result of any contamination of the aquifer because their property has not been and will not become contaminated as a result of any such contamination. In response, the Plaintiffs assert that they have been harmed by the contamination of the aquifer in two ways: (1) they have been prohibited from engaging in the business of selling well water which they would have pumped from their land and (2) they have suffered a diminished market value in their land.

The District Court rejected the notion that the Plaintiffs must prove that they have suffered a physical harm—that is, the harm the defendants cause must be physical, either bodily injury or property damage, or at least involve intrusion onto plaintiffs' land. The court interpreted the "Restatement as requir[ing] the Plaintiffs to make two fundamental showings: (1) the existence of a nuisance and (2) significant harm as a result of that nuisance." It continued:

> To the extent that the Esso Defendants argue that a party interferes with another's use and enjoyment of his land only where that party causes a physical harm to the other's property. The Restatement does not contemplate that an actionable interference occurs only where there has been a physical invasion of one's land.

> * * *

> [T]he Esso Defendants have not cited and the court has been unable to locate any authority for the proposition that "significant" harm extends only to physical invasion or harm.

> * * *

[I]n this case, the landowners may be prohibited from pumping water from their land because of contamination of a nearby connected water supply. Not only would it work an injustice to deny any relief to such plaintiffs, but such denials of relief under the physically perceptible standard [of *Adams*] would lead to underdeterrence of environmental contamination which may or may not otherwise be the subject of governmental laws and regulations. 909 F.Supp. at 995, 998.

4. *More Mixed Authority.* Despite the statement in *Tutu* that *Adams* stands alone in demanding an actual intrusion, other authorities offer support. In Berry v. Armstrong Rubber Co., 989 F.2d 822 (5th Cir.1993), cert. denied, 510 U.S. 1117, 114 S.Ct. 1067, 127 L.Ed.2d 386 (1994), plaintiff property owners brought an action for damages due to the dumping of hazardous wastes which allegedly occurred from 1937 to 1970. Plaintiffs alleged that the hazardous wastes contaminated their land and groundwater. Their common-law nuisance claims were dismissed because there was no showing that their land or water was contaminated. Plaintiffs' expert testimony indicated that "it was more probable than not" that plaintiffs' land was contaminated, but the expert opinions were not based upon tests of water or soil samples from plaintiffs' property but rather from other locations. There was also testimony from a realtor regarding the negative stigma resulting from the public perception that plaintiffs' properties were contaminated. The court held that in order to support a cause of action in nuisance, plaintiffs needed to present evidence of an "invasion" of their property which they had not done.

Accord, McGinnis v. Tennessee Gas Pipeline Co. 25 F.3d 1049 (6th Cir.1994) (there must be expert testimony on more than just a risk of contamination to prevail in nuisance action); Nalley v. General Electric Co., 165 Misc.2d 803, 630 N.Y.S.2d 452, 457 (N.Y.Sup.Ct.1995).

> In the case at bar, there is no evidence that the land or water of the plaintiffs who are subject to this motion is contaminated by toxic substances. While there is some evidence of the migration of hazardous wastes from the Loeffel site to surrounding lands, the evidence is not probative of injury to plaintiffs' properties. Nor is there a competent evidentiary showing of an imminent threat of contamination to any of these properties, or even a showing of a high likelihood of future contamination. Without specific evidentiary support, it is mere speculation as to whether or when plaintiffs' property will ever be affected by the migration of wastes from the Loeffel site. In the Court's view, it was incumbent upon the plaintiffs to produce competent and convincing proof, through qualified experts, demonstrating the immediate effects of property contamination and/or, at the very least, a reasonable probability and expectation of contamination in the future.

The *Nalley* court, however, does sustain claims for odors and fumes that may have been emitted from the waste site, that caused eye irritations. But don't odors physically "intrude?" Yes, in the sense of molecules reaching plaintiffs' properties from their source.

Why is this issue of intrusion so critical in environmental contamination cases? Remember that trespass absolutely demands some physical intrusion; should nuisance law make a similar demand? Why are many courts so reluctant to allow those neighboring on waste sites to sue for nuisance in the absence of actual intrusion or demonstrable effects on use (e.g., inability to pump water from an aquifer)? Why do odors qualify as an interference, but contamination of nearby properties do not? For a decision allowing one neighbor to recover for nuisance for methane gas escaping from a former landfill based largely on evidence of the gas' presence on property across the street, see Hammond v. City of Warner Robins, 224 Ga.App. 684, 482 S.E.2d 422 (Ga.App.1997); see dissenting opinion (Beasley, J.) rejecting the majority's analysis as misunderstanding the law of nuisance (482 S.E.2d at 431–432).

4. BASIS OF LIABILITY

The Restatement provisions explained above permit liability based on intentional, negligent, reckless or abnormally dangerous conduct. Most decisions, however, rest on intentional nuisances, which is considered in the next case.

UNITED PROTEINS, INC. v. FARMLAND INDUSTRIES, INC.

Supreme Court of Kansas, 1996.
259 Kan. 725, 915 P.2d 80.

LARSON, JUSTICE:

This case arises from the contamination of the Ogallala aquifer under plaintiff United Proteins, Inc.'s (UPI) pet food plant by hexavalent chromium released by defendant Farmland Industries, Inc. (Farmland). UPI sought damages for holding costs it allegedly incurred due to its inability to sell the plant on theories of trespass and intentional private nuisance after its strict liability and negligence theories were dismissed as barred by the statute of repose. The trial court found Farmland liable but awarded only nominal damages. Both parties appeal. Although there is merit to UPI's contention that the trial court improperly computed damages, we agree with Farmland's arguments that UPI has failed to prove essential elements under both trespass or intentional private nuisance. Farmland is entitled to judgment as a matter of law.

FACTS

UPI owns an 85–acre tract with a 10–acre pet food plant development outside of Dodge City, Kansas. UPI initially acquired an interest in the Dodge City property in August 1989. It acquired full ownership of the plant upon exercising a purchase option by paying off industrial revenue bonds in 1993.

Farmland owns and operates a fertilizer plant adjacent to UPI's property in which it used hexavalent chromium as a corrosion inhibitor in the cooling water system prior to June 1982. At some point while that system was in operation, approximately 1,200 gallons of hexavalent chromium was released, contaminating the Ogallala aquifer under Farmland's property. This hazardous substance leached into the groundwater under UPI's property in concentrations in excess of regulatory limits. UPI knew of this contamination at the time it acquired the property.

In June 1982, Farmland notified the Kansas Department of Health and Environment of the contamination and began a remediation program by drilling approximately 91 monitoring and recovery wells on and around Farmland's property, including 15 wells on UPI's property. The remediation program consists of recovery of the water in the aquifer through the above-described wells and then treating the water and returning it to the aquifer. This "pump and treat" program will eventually reduce the chromium contamination to within regulatory limits.

UPI has plugged its wells to the Ogallala aquifer and now draws water from the deeper Dakota aquifer. Although this reduced the amount of available water and the efficiency of the pet food plant, UPI discontinued pet food operations for reasons totally unrelated to the contamination of the aquifer and began efforts to sell the plant in early 1991. It had been unable to do so at the time of trial in August 1994, although it sold similar facilities in other parts of the country with no contamination in 3 to 15 months.

On August 27, 1993, UPI commenced the present action. UPI initially asserted claims under the theories of intentional nuisance, strict liability, intentional trespass, and negligence. In June 1994, upon Farmland's motion for summary judgment, the trial court dismissed the strict liability and negligence claims as barred by the statute of repose. The trial court refused Farmland's request for judgment on the remaining nuisance and trespass claims but limited recovery to that available because of the defendant's activity within the limitations period under those two theories. UPI contended it suffered $373,500 in damages because it was unable to sell the plant.

In a trial to the court only UPI presented evidence. UPI's real estate appraisal expert opined that a property like the UPI Dodge City plant would ordinarily be expected to sell within one year but had not sold in this instance because it was contaminated. The trial court ruled that Farmland was liable under the theories argued by UPI, but that the exclusive measure of damages was the decreased rental market value of the UPI plant. The court found UPI presented insufficient evidence of such damages and awarded nominal damages of $1.

UPI appeals the trial court's determination that only damages measured by the reduced rental value of the property could be recovered. Farmland cross-appeals the determination that it was liable under either a trespass or intentional nuisance theory.

Because we reverse the trial court's ruling that Farmland was liable under either the trespass or the nuisance theory and rule that judgment is to be entered in favor of Farmland and against UPI, we need not consider UPI's appeal and will limit ourselves only to the contentions of Farmland's cross-appeal.

Did the trial court apply the wrong legal standard to determine Farmland had the intent to trespass?

It is essential to first realize and understand that while this might have been a relatively simple case of negligence or strict liability, neither of those theories were available because of UPI's delay in filing. With those two potentially winning theories lost by UPI's untimeliness, UPI was left in the unenviable position of pursuing theories which alleged Farmland had engaged in some tortious conduct within the limitations period. Continuing trespass was one such possible theory. Although the original trespass was outside the limitations period, if UPI could prove that Farmland permitted the contamination to remain on UPI's property within the limitations period and that the original intrusion was tortious, there might be culpable conduct on which recovery could be based. See Restatement (Second) of Torts § 161 (1963); Prosser and Keeton, Law of Torts § 13, p. 83 (5th ed. 1984).

On the trespass claim, Farmland argues the trial court used a legally improper standard to determine whether its conduct was intentional. The trial court held as a conclusion of law: "In the case of continuing trespass, the intent requirement may be satisfied by knowledge, either actual or inferred, that the substance was reaching the land of another." As we will hereafter show, this is not the complete test under Kansas law.

"The concept of trespass should be used, if at all, only where defendant intends to have the foreign matter intrude upon the land, or where defendant's 'act is done with knowledge that it will to a substantial certainty result in the entry of foreign matter.'" 1 Harper, James & Gray, The Law of Torts § 1:7, p. 1:30 (3d ed. 1996). Liability for a continuing trespass is premised on the original intrusion being trespassory. Harper, James & Gray § 1:7, p. 1:30. Thus, if the original intrusion is not trespassory, mere knowledge that a substance reached the land of another is insufficient to establish a continuing trespass.

Consequently, the question becomes whether Farmland's mere knowledge that the substance reached UPI's land would satisfy UPI's burden to prove the original intrusion was intentional. UPI pled trespass as an intentional tort and asserted neither that Farmland was negligent nor that Farmland was engaged in an abnormally dangerous activity. We therefore start with the proposition provided by Restatement (Second) of Torts § 166 (1963): "Except where the actor is engaged in an abnormally dangerous activity, an unintentional and non-negligent . . . causing a thing . . . to enter the land, does not subject the actor to liability to the possessor, even though the entry causes harm." Consistent with this rule, Kansas has recognized intent is an element of a claim for non-negligent intrusion upon the land of another. Riddle Quarries, Inc. v. Thompson, 177 Kan. 307, 311, 279 P.2d 266 (1955); 75 Am.Jur.2d, Trespass § 25 ("A trespass to real property is characterized as an intentional tort."). Although in its historical development through the common law at certain times trespass has encompassed unintentional and non-negligent acts, Kansas follows the modern and near universal view that it is an intentional tort. See Prosser and Keeton, Law of Torts § 13, pp. 67–68 (5th ed. 1984).

Restatement (Second) of Torts § 164, Comment a (1963), explains the nature of the intent required: "In order to be liable for trespass [for an intentional intrusion] it is necessary only that the actor intentionally be upon any part of the land in question." Am.Jur.2d, Trespass § 29, relying on Restatement (Second) of Torts § 163, Comments b & c (1963), summarizes the intent required for actionable intentional trespass: "[T]he intention required to make the actor liable for trespass is an intention to enter upon the particular piece of land in question, irrespective of whether the actor knows or should know that he is not entitled to enter. In order [that] an actor may intentionally enter a particular piece of land, it is not necessary that he act for the purpose of entering; it is enough that he knows that his conduct will result in such an entry, inevitably or to a substantial certainty. Further, the doing of an act which will almost certainly result in the entry of foreign matter upon another's land, such as the operation of a cement plant which continuously deposits dust and other substances onto a neighboring property, suffices for an intentional trespass to land, regardless of the lack of an intent to harm."

Thus, as with other intentional torts, UPI had to show either the misconduct, in this case entry, was purposeful, or that it was substantially certain to occur. In addition, it must also have been shown that Farmland intended the act which constituted the invasion of UPI's rights. The legal standard employed by the trial court fails to reflect the full scope of Farmland's intent, which UPI was required to prove.

* * *

Our case is similar to Moulton v. Groveton Papers Co., 112 N.H. 50, 54, 289 A.2d 68 (1972), in which the court rejected a claim that where the failure of defendant's dam damaged the plaintiff's land, an action for trespass could be supported through the plaintiff's "constructive intent." The court found this was an impermissible attempt to impose absolute liability.

Testimony before the trial court provided absolutely no basis to conclude the discharge of hexavalent chromium was either purposeful or substantially certain to occur. UPI presented no evidence whatsoever as to the cause or circumstances of the discharge. Thus, UPI failed to meet its burden of proof.

In sum, the trial court applied the wrong legal standard to determine whether UPI met its burden of proof on the element of intent on the trespass claim. Even if the correct legal standard had been applied, UPI could not have prevailed. Therefore, we are compelled to reverse the judgment of the trial court on UPI's trespass theory, and this case need not be remanded to the trial court for any further determinations on this issue.

Does the record support a presumption that the trial court found the nuisance created by Farmland was intentional?

On the nuisance claim, Farmland argues the trial court found it liable without making any specific finding that the nuisance was intentional. Farmland suggests this presents a question of law for our review, considering whether liability can be imposed without a finding that the conduct was intentional. * * *

In its reply brief, Farmland clarifies that it does not take issue with any of the trial court's factual findings but only with the legal conclusion that intent may be established by "knowledge, either actual or inferred, that the substance was reaching the land of another." The trial court used this reasoning only as to the trespass claim. Consequently, our scope of review over the nuisance claim is to determine whether substantial competent evidence establishes intent.

We note that the trial court found: "Having contaminated the aquifer with a hazardous substance, Farmland is unquestionably obligated to make good any temporary losses incurred by UPI as a result." This could be read to imply that the trial court relied on a strict liability theory rather than the intentional nuisance theory pled by UPI. The parties have not interpreted this statement in this way and we choose not to either.

Remember again that because its claim was dismissed on summary judgment prior to trial, UPI could not rely on a theory of strict liability for an abnormally dangerous activity. This is not a Rylands v. Fletcher case [3 H.L. 330 (1868)]. * * *

Although a nuisance action can also be based on strict liability or negligence, UPI explicitly set out in its petition that it sought relief on a theory of intentional nuisance. Under the rule synthesized in the Restatement (Second) of Torts § 825(a) and 825(b) (1965), intentional nuisance requires the actor act with the purpose of causing the nuisance, or know that it is resulting or substantially certain to result from his or her conduct. Comment c to Restatement (Second) of Torts § 825 provides: "It is not enough to make an invasion intentional that the actor realizes or should realize that his conduct involves a serious risk or likelihood of causing an invasion. He must either act for the purpose of causing it or know that it is resulting or is substantially certain to result from his conduct."

Sandifer Motors, Inc. v. City of Roeland Park, 6 Kan.App.2d 308, Syl. P 11, 628 P.2d 239, rev. denied 230 Kan. 819 (1981), states the nature of the intent required in Kansas: "To create an 'intentional' nuisance, it is not enough to intend to create a condition causing harm; the defendant must either specifically intend to damage the plaintiff or act in such a way as to make it 'substantially certain' that damage will follow."

Williams v. Amoco Production Co., 241 Kan. 102, 734 P.2d 1113 (1987), controls this issue. In Williams, the plaintiff argued the trial court should have given an instruction on private nuisance. Plaintiff's action claimed damages for natural gas leaking from the defendant's wells into the aquifer and contaminating irrigation water. This court noted that the intent to interfere with the use and enjoyment of the land by one entitled to that use is an element of such a private nuisance claim. It concluded: "There is no evidence in this case that Amoco intended for natural gas to leak from its wells into the aquifer and eventually into appellees' irrigation water. Nor is there any evidence that Amoco intended this condition to continue once discovered. Accordingly, one of the elements necessary to recover on a nuisance theory was not established. We hold the trial court did not err in failing to instruct on nuisance." 241 Kan. at 118, 734 P.2d 1113.

In this case, the pollution which migrated into the water table under UPI's property was the result of a release of chromium from Farmland's plant. There is no showing Farmland intended this leak into the aquifer and eventually under UPI's land. There is no showing Farmland intended this release to continue after it was clear that it had damaged the aquifer under the UPI's land. There was no showing the discharge was the result of any intentional act of Farmland. There was no showing of either purpose to cause an invasion or the substantial certainty of such invasion required to support an intentional private nuisance action. A review of the record does not support the presumption that the trial court found all necessary facts. From the record, it is clear that a finding of intent, required by the law of intentional private nuisance, is not supported by substantial competent evidence. The trial court must be reversed.

In both the trespass and nuisance claims, UPI essentially attempts to expand the scope of strict liability beyond that outlined in the Restatement (Second) of Torts §§ 519 and 520 and adopted by this court. Having failed in its initial strict liability claim because of the statute of repose, UPI will not be permitted to create new causes of action for absolute continuing liability through traditionally intentional torts by eviscerating the element of intent.

* * *

Reversed.

Notes and Questions

1. *The Role of Intent.* The rule enunciated in *United Proteins* demanding proof of purposive or knowledge-based intent clearly comports with what the Restatement (Second) of Torts § 825 demands. In a case such as *United Proteins* how would a plaintiff set about to prove an intentional nuisance? Is it ever possible in situations involving underground leaks?

Recall that the comment to § 825 quoted earlier pointed out that where the invasions are recurrent or continuing, intent may be found:

"In these cases the first invasion resulting from the actor's conduct may be either intentional or unintentional; but when the conduct is continued after the actor knows that the invasion is resulting from it, further invasions are intentional.''

In Morgan v. Quailbrook Condominium Company, 704 P.2d 573 (Utah 1985) the court applied precisely that reasoning to find an intentional nuisance with a surface water discharge:

> In the present case, Quailbrook claimed to have reasonably relied on its engineers for the initial design and construction work, and no substantial evidence appears to support a finding to the contrary. Had the invasion occurred only once, this reliance would have insulated Quailbrook from a finding of the requisite intent. However, several witnesses testified that on numerous occasions plaintiffs complained to Quailbrook personnel about the change in the surface water discharge. Therefore, there is substantial evidence that after Quailbrook learned of the invasion resulting from its work, it failed to take corrective action and the invasion continued. If Quailbrook knew the consequences of its work and failed to alter its surface drainage system, then under the Restatement, the jury was justified in finding that Quailbrook had the requisite mental state for an intentional tort. The jury then only needed to find that the invasion was unreasonable, which it did.

2. *How About Strict Liability?* The Restatement (Second) of Torts § 822 makes clear that tortious conduct is necessary—intent, negligence, or abnormally dangerous activity. But not all jurisdictions agree. For example, in Washington Suburban Sanitary Comm. v. CAE–Link Corp., 330 Md. 115, 622 A.2d 745 (Md. 1993), Maryland's highest court rejected the Restatement standards: ''[Defendant] provides no reasoned basis for our discarding the strict liability standard what has a pedigree of long standing in this state.'' What rationales might support strict liability (apart from the doctrine of abnormally dangerous activities considered in Chapter 4)?

3. *Effect of Compliance With Government Standards.* What if the activity engaged in by defendant satisfies applicable government standards or environmental laws or regulations? Chapter 6 examines the issue of preemption, but apart from that question can defendant assert compliance as a defense?

For example, in Bowers v. Westvaco Corp., 244 Va. 139, 419 S.E.2d 661 (Va. 1992), a trucking staging facility argued that ''when the Board of Supervisors, after reviewing a particular activity and imposing conditions designed to minimize its effect on neighbors, has rezoned a property to accommodate that activity, the court may not superimpose its judgment by declaring the activity a nuisance.''

The Virginia Supreme Court rejected that proposition:

> [T]he location of a business enterprise, or the zoning classification of the property on which the business is located, cannot immunize the business from a nuisance action. It is generally held that the location of an industry in an industrial area and its importance to the wealth and prosperity of the community do not give to it rights superior to the primary or natural rights of those who live nearby. We hold that the trial court did not err by finding that the acts of the defendants constituted a private nuisance. The court properly considered the zoning

classification of the property as an important factor in determining whether the business is so conducted as to constitute a nuisance. 419 S.E.2d at 665, 666.

Note, however, that compliance with zoning was deemed "an important factor" in resolving the nuisance question. This factor is explicitly recognized in the Restatement §§ 826 and 827 which inquire into the locational appropriateness of defendant's activity.

In Layton v. Yankee Caithness Joint Venture, 774 F.Supp. 576 (D.Nev. 1991) plaintiff homeowners contended that the operation of a geothermal power plant was a nuisance because of emissions of hydrogen sulfide. Although rejecting the nuisance claim, the court also ruled that defendant's compliance with all EPA and county standards for emission of hydrogen sulfides, including ambient air standards "does not prevent this court from finding that the YCJV plant is a nuisance. However, proof of compliance with all applicable state and county regulations is persuasive, although not dispositive evidence of the reasonableness of YCJV's use of its property." *Id.* at 579, n.1.

Compare Tiegs v. Boise Cascade Corp., 83 Wash.App. 411, 420, 922 P.2d 115, 120 (1996) (affirming $2.5 million verdict in favor of potato farmers whose crops were damaged by irrigation groundwater contaminated by chemicals from a paper mill's wastewater lagoon; court believes that compliance with an NPDES permit would be a legalized nuisance but says: "If Boise wanted to rely upon its NPDES permit as proof that its conduct relative to its wastewater treatment operation was legal, then it also had the burden of showing that it complied with the permit.").

Similar statements abound in the decisional law. See, e.g., Union Oil Co. v. Heinsohn, 43 F.3d 500, 504 (10th Cir.1994) (facts that gas processing plants operated by oil company, which held oil and gas lease respecting property were approved by reviews by state environmental agency in applications for permits and that permits had been granted in accordance with Oklahoma statutes did not preclude liability of company to property surface owners for nuisance under Oklahoma law; licensing was not in itself enough to avoid liability); see also Borland v. Sanders Lead Co., 369 So.2d 523 (Ala.1979), in which the court held that compliance with the Alabama Air Pollution Control Act did not shield a lead company from nuisance liability for damages caused by pollutants, i.e., lead particulates and sulfoxide deposits, emitting from its smelter and settling onto plaintiffs' adjacent property, making it unsuitable for raising cattle or growing crops.

But the decisions also make it clear that compliance with zoning and other use regulations may suggest that defendant's use is compatible with the character of the area and neighboring uses, and hence is not an unreasonable use. See, e.g., Karpiak v. Russo, 450 Pa.Super. 471, 676 A.2d 270 (Pa.Super.1996).

4. *What of Court Orders?* But what about compliance with federal court orders mandating that defendant Sanitary Commission construct and operate a sewage sludge composting facility? The Maryland Court of Appeals in Washington Suburban Sanitary Comm. v. CAE–Link Corp., 330 Md. 115, 622 A.2d 745 (Md.1993) held that the operator of a sewage sludge composting facility could be strictly liable for a nuisance as a result of its operation

of the facility built in response to federal court orders; although the federal district court had ordered the operator to build the facility in a particular county, the court did not select the site, which was selected by the county for which the operator provided water and sewage service, and the court did not mandate how, as opposed to when, construction would proceed. It also found no preemption under the Clean Water Act, 33 U.S.C. § 1365(e).

In Chapter 6, the flip-side issue of what effect should be given to a statutory or regulatory violation is considered.

5. *Causation.* As with all torts, in nuisance, too, plaintiff must offer evidence to support the finding that it was defendant's activity that caused the invasion of plaintiff's interest in use and enjoyment. Moreover, proof of causation may demand the testimony of experts whenever the connection to plaintiffs' injuries are beyond the knowledge of the ordinary lay person. Thus, in Layton v. Yankee Caithness Joint Venture, 774 F.Supp. 576 (D.Nev.1991) the court dismissed nuisance claims alleging headaches, bloody noses, dizziness, sore throats and irritated eyes resulting from the operation of a geothermal power plant which emitted hydrogen sulfide fumes because of the absence of expert testimony on causation:

> Headaches, nosebleeds, dizziness and eye irritation may have many causes. Analyzing the toxic effects of exposure to hydrogen sulfide, and diagnosing the cause of headaches, nosebleeds, dizziness and eye irritation are beyond the common knowledge of the lay person. Therefore, expert testimony is required to prove a causal relationship between the hydrogen sulfide from the YCJV plant and the physical injuries suffered by Plaintiffs. The unrefuted evidence in this case shows the absence of causation between the emission from the plant and Plaintiffs' complaints of physical injuries. Defendants' motion for summary judgment on the physical injury claims is GRANTED.

See also Nichols v. Mid–Continent Pipe Line Co., 933 P.2d 272 (Okla. 1996) (no error to admit evidence of physical conditions suffered by plaintiffs from ingestion of hydrocarbons where medically established nexus is supported in the record).

In Chapter 8, we consider causation in some detail. The point here is to remind the student that nothing contained in the nuisance and trespass doctrines implies that proof of causation is excused. See also Cavallo v. Star Enterprise, 892 F.Supp. 756, 757 (E.D.Va.1995), aff'd in part, rev'd in part 100 F.3d 1150 (4th Cir.1996) (a tough-minded *Daubert* "gatekeeper" grant of summary judgment for defendant, in which court barred the court the use of two experts who linked a variety of respiratory and allergic problems to a single 5 to 30 minute exposure to a 61 mg/m3 concentration of aviation jet fuel that was spilled at a terminal when plaintiff was walking across a parking lot after dining at a Chinese restaurant The court answered in the negative the question of whether the "opinions of two experts that Plaintiff's exposure to AvJet caused her various chronic respiratory illnesses are admissible where no study or published literature links AvJet vapors to Plaintiff's claimed illnesses and where the experts fail to establish why studies showing a correlation between exposure to other chemicals and much less significant illnesses support their proffered conclusions in this case," citing In re Paoli Railroad Yard PCB Litigation, 35 F.3d 717 (3d Cir.1994), cert. denied 513 U.S. 1190, 115 S.Ct. 1253, 131 L.Ed.2d 134 (1995) and Developments in the Law—Confronting the New Challenges of Scientific Evidence, 108 Harv. L. Rev. 1481 (1995)).

6. *Prejudice Related to Evidence of Leakage at Distant Sites Outweighs Probative Value.* In Walter v. Pantry Inc., 173 F.3d 427 (4th Cir.1999), the Fourth Circuit Court of Appeals ruled that it was appropriate to exclude certain evidence of leaking underground storage tanks at distant sites as highly prejudicial. While evidence of the other sites' leaks may have been relevant to intent (focusing on punitive damages), the court ruled that the Federal Rules of Evidence allow a trial judge to exclude evidence if the prejudicial impact outweighs its probative value. The plaintiff had purchased commercial property in South Carolina for the purpose of building a car wash. The property was next to a convenience store and gas station owned by the defendant. The plaintiff sued the company for the release of gasoline onto the adjacent property and for the failure to clean up the soil and groundwater. The trial court had ruled that the evidence of releases at other sites did not establish the cause of the specific release or the party responsible for causing the release that resulted in contamination of the adjacent property.

7. *Continuing Nuisance.* The trespass chapter contained a collection of authorities on the distinction between continuing trespass [or nuisance] and permanent ones. Those authorities are equally applicable to nuisance actions. See, e.g., Mangini v. Aerojet–General Corp., 12 Cal.4th 1087, 51 Cal.Rptr.2d 272, 912 P.2d 1220 (1996) (California Supreme Court held that the lack of evidence that hazardous waste contamination was reasonably "abatable" at a reasonable cost precluded a continuing nuisance or trespass claim and, thus, precluded an award of damages for $132 million to property owners for nuisance or trespass claims brought on a theory of continuing nuisance after three-year statute of limitations applicable to permanent nuisances had expired; property owners had admitted the absence of evidence showing extent of contamination and cost of remediation).

Compare Hoery v. United States, 64 P.3d 214 (Colo. 2003), in which the Colorado Supreme Court held, on certified question, that toxic chemicals released by a nearby Air Force base that migrated to the land of a nearby homeowner constituted a continuing nuisance or trespass for statute of limitations purposes.

5. HARM VERSUS UTILITY BALANCING

Restatement (Second) of Torts § 826, explored earlier in this chapter, calls for balancing only when an injunction is sought; for damages-only actions § 826(b) only requires that the harm be "serious" and the defendant can afford to pay compensation without ceasing operations. But the following opinion demonstrates that not all courts have adopted the Restatement's approach.

CARPENTER v. THE DOUBLE R CATTLE COMPANY, INC.

Supreme Court of Idaho, 1985.
108 Idaho 602, 701 P.2d 222.

BAKES, J.

Plaintiffs appealed a district court judgment based upon a court and jury finding that defendant's feedlot did not constitute a nuisance. The Court of Appeals reversed[.] [W]e vacate the decision of the Court of Appeals and affirm the judgment of the district court.

Plaintiff appellants are homeowners who live near a cattle feedlot owned and operated by respondents. Appellants filed a complaint in March, 1978, alleging that the feedlot had been expanded in 1977 to accommodate the feeding of approximately 9,000 cattle. Appellants further alleged that "the spread and accumulation of manure, pollution of river and ground water, odor, insect infestation, increased concentration of birds, * * * dust and noise" allegedly caused by the feedlot constituted a nuisance. After a trial on the merits a jury found that the feedlot did not constitute a nuisance. The trial court then also made findings and conclusions that the feedlot did not constitute a nuisance.

Appellants assigned as error the jury instructions which instructed the jury that in the determination of whether a nuisance exists consideration should be given to such factors as community interest, utility of conduct, business standards and practices, gravity of harm caused, and the circumstances surrounding the parties' movement to their locations. * * *

The case was assigned to the Court of Appeals which reversed and remanded for a new trial. The basis for this reversal was that the trial court did not give a jury instruction based upon subsection (b) of Section 826 of the Restatement (Second) of Torts. That subsection allows for a finding of a nuisance even though the gravity of harm is outweighed by the utility of the conduct if the harm is "serious" and the payment of damages is "feasible" without forcing the business to discontinue.

This Court granted defendant's petition for review. We hold that the instructions which the trial court gave were not erroneous, being consistent with our prior case law and other persuasive authority. We further hold that the trial court did not err in not giving an instruction based on subsection (b) of Section 826 of the Second Restatement, which does not represent the law in the State of Idaho, as pointed out in Part III. Accordingly, the decision of the Court of Appeals is vacated, and the judgment of the district court is affirmed.

* * *

THE LAW OF NUISANCE

The Court of Appeals adopted subsection (b) of Section 826 of the Restatement (Second), that a defendant can be held liable for a nuisance regardless of the utility of the conduct if the harm is "serious" and the payment of damages is "feasible" without jeopardizing the continuance of the conduct. We disagree that this is the law in Idaho.

* * *

The Court of Appeals, without being requested by appellant, adopted the new subsection (b) of Section 826 of the Second Restatement partially because of language in Koseris [v. J.R. Simplot Co., 82 Idaho 263, 352 P.2d 235 (1960) (action for injunction only)], which reads:

"We are constrained to hold that the trial court erred in sustaining objections to those offers of proof [evidence of utility of conduct], since they were relevant as bearing upon the issue whether respondents, in seeking injunctive relief, were pursuing the proper remedy; nevertheless, on the theory of damages which respondents had waived, the ruling was correct."

The last phrase of the quote, relied on by the Court of Appeals, is clearly dictum, since the question of utility of conduct in a nuisance action for damages was not at issue in Koseris. It is very doubtful that this Court's dictum in Koseris was intended to make such a substantial change in the nuisance law. When the isolated statement of dictum was made in 1960, there was no persuasive authority for such a proposition. Indeed, no citation of authority was given. The three cases from other jurisdictions which the Court of Appeals relied on for authority did not exist until 1970. See Boomer v. Atlantic Cement Co., 257 N.E.2d 870 (N.Y.1970); Jost v. Dairyland Power Coop., 45 Wis.2d 164, 172 N.W.2d 647 (Wis.1970). The third case from Oregon, Furrer v. Talent Irr. Dist., 466 P.2d 605 (Or.1970), was not even a nuisance case. Rather, it was an action in "negligence." The Second Restatement, which proposed the change in the law by adding subsection (b) to Section 826, was also not in existence until 1970. Therefore, we greatly discount this Court's dictum in the 1960 Koseris opinion as authority for such a substantial change in the nuisance law. The case of McNichols v. J.R. Simplot Co., 74 Idaho 321, 262 P.2d 1012 (1953) should be viewed as the law in Idaho that in a nuisance action seeking damages the interests of the community, which would include the utility of the conduct, should be considered in the determination of the existence of a nuisance. The trial court's instructions in the present case were entirely consistent with McNichols. A plethora of other modern cases are in accord.

The State of Idaho is sparsely populated and its economy depends largely upon the benefits of agriculture, lumber, mining and industrial development. To eliminate the utility of conduct and other factors listed by the trial court from the criteria to be considered in determining whether a nuisance exists, as the appellant has argued throughout this appeal, would place an unreasonable burden upon these industries. * * * Accordingly, the judgment of the district court is affirmed and the Court of Appeals decision is set aside.

DONALDSON, C.J., and SHEPARD, J., concur.

BISTLINE, J., dissenting.

* * *

I applaud the efforts of the Court of Appeals to modernize the law of nuisance in this state. I am not in the least persuaded to join the majority with its narrow view of nuisance law as expressed in the majority opinion.

The majority today continues to adhere to ideas on the law of nuisance that should have gone out with the use of buffalo chips as fuel. We have before us today homeowners complaining of a nearby feedlot— not a small operation, but rather a feedlot which accommodates 9,000 cattle. The homeowners advanced the theory that after the expansion of the feedlot in 1977, the odor, manure, dust, insect infestation and increased concentration of birds which accompanied all of the foregoing, constituted a nuisance. If the odoriferous quagmire created by 9,000 head of cattle is not a nuisance, it is difficult for me to imagine what is. However, the real question for us today is the legal basis on which a finding of nuisance can be made.

[The majority reasons that] the correct rule of law for Idaho [is that] in a nuisance action seeking damages, the interests of the community, which includes the utility of the conduct, should be considered in determining the existence of a nuisance. I find nothing immediately wrong with this statement of the law and agree wholeheartedly that the interests of the community should be considered in determining the existence of a nuisance. However, where this primitive rule of law fails is in recognizing that in our society, while it may be desirable to have a serious nuisance continue because the utility of the operation causing the nuisance is great, at the same time, those directly impacted by the serious nuisance deserve some compensation for the invasion they suffer as a result of the continuation of the nuisance. This is exactly what the more progressive provisions of § 826(b) of the Restatement (Second) of Torts addresses. * * *

* * *

Notes and Questions

1. What do you suppose is the principal rationale for the majority's refusal to apply Restatement (Second) of Torts § 826(b)? Do you agree or disagree with the dissent's argument (not quoted above) that by refusing to award damages the court is subsidizing the prices of meat (or other products or services) because defendant is not internalizing all the real costs of doing business?

2. Is the court totally rejecting corrective justice principles? One of the often-stated purposes of tort law liability rules is to deter risk-creating conduct by imposing liability on those who create the risks. Does the majority's opinion subvert or advance the deterrence objective of tort law?

3. The majority's position is perhaps one of the most extreme in refusing to award damages where plaintiffs have actually suffered substan-

tial harm and where there was no showing that imposing damages on the defendant would have necessitated that it cease operations. Reconsider this decision after Chapter 5.

4. What is the consequence of the majority's holding on future cases involving an alleged private nuisance producing substantial harm to private parties? Can a private party *ever* prevail in an action for damages in Idaho if the defendant's business operation is important to the community?

We know the answer to that question. In Payne v. Skaar, 127 Idaho 341, 900 P.2d 1352 (Idaho 1995), the Idaho Supreme Court, in a case involving remarkably similar facts (a feed lot processing up to 5,000 head of cattle), affirmed the issuance of an injunction substantially curtailing the defendant's operation, but not totally shutting it down, without (1) ever even citing the *Carpenter* opinion, (2) ever citing § 826 of the Restatement, or (3) ever discussing or alluding to the value of defendant's activity to the community. What might explain such an about-face? In addition, the court held that the Idaho Right-to-Farm statute (Idaho Code § 22–4501) was inapplicable because defendant was expanding its operations, although the Act makes no reference to that as a precondition to its application. In Chapter 12 we examine Right-to-Farm laws, which purport to immunize agricultural operations from nuisance actions by neighboring residents, if certain conditions are satisfied.

5. Where the harm to plaintiff's land is substantial, many courts have declined to permit the defendant to exculpate itself by showing that the value of its conduct outweighed the gravity of any harm to the plaintiff. See, e.g., Jost v. Dairyland Power Cooperative, 45 Wis.2d 164, 172 N.W.2d 647 (1969) (sulphur dioxide emissions from power company smokestack). Some courts have adopted a "comparative injury," or utilitarian analysis. For example, in Crushed Stone v. Moore, 369 P.2d 811 (Okl.1962), the court described the process, which it nevertheless rejected: "While we recognize that in proper cases, especially involving businesses upon which the public's interest, or necessity, depends, the matter of 'comparative injury' should be given prominent consideration, this court is among those holding that where damages in an action at law will not give plaintiffs an adequate remedy against a business operated in such a way that it has become a nuisance, and such operation causes plaintiffs substantial and irremediable injury, they are entitled, as a matter of right, to have same abated, by injunction, * * * notwithstanding the comparative benefits conferred thereby or the comparative injury resulting therefrom." Chapter 5 contains a fuller consideration of the balancing of the equities involved in injunctive proceedings. Decisions such as *Crushed Stone*, however, are directed more to the question of an appropriate remedy, and less to the question resolved in *Carpenter* of whether an actionable nuisance exists at all.

6. NOTE ON ANTICIPATORY NUISANCE AND INJUNCTIONS

Chapter 5 considers injunctive relief as integral to an analysis of toxic tort remedies. In the environmental-regulatory era that commenced with passage of major federal statutes in 1970 (the National Environmental Policy Act, the Clean Air Act), the issuance of injunctions and abatement orders barring or remediating of some polluting activities have largely been undertaken at the initiative of federal or state governments or agencies, not private parties. Relatively few common-law based nuisance decisions result in the issuance of an injunction that orders an on-going business to cease operations. There are a few exceptions, however, as is shown below.

Closely related is the doctrine of anticipatory or prospective nuisance. An Alabama Supreme Court opinion in Parker v. Ashford, 661 So.2d 213, 217–18 (Ala.1995) summarizes the principles:

> If it is impossible, before the construction of a project has been completed and the project is operating, for a court to ascertain whether it will or will not constitute a nuisance, or if reasonable doubt exists as to the probable effect of the proposed project, then a court will not intervene until the project is completed and can be tested by actual use. That is, if from the facts it appears that the injury or harm alleged by the persons seeking an injunction is uncertain or speculative; that the use of the project is only possibly productive of injury; or that the public benefit to be served by the project may outweigh the inconvenience caused to the plaintiffs, then the court must refuse the injunction and await the completion and operation of the project to determine whether the project is a nuisance. However, [w]here the consequences of a nuisance about to be erected or commenced will be irreparable in damages and such consequences are not merely possible but to a reasonable degree certain, a court may interfere to arrest a nuisance before it is completed. For the court not to interfere would be to ignore the location [of the proposed project] and the court's common knowledge of the inevitable consequences to follow upon the conduct of the business which [the] defendant proposes to carry on, however well conducted. An activity that is lawful in its nature and that is not a nuisance in one locality may be or become a nuisance when erected and maintained in certain other localities, depending on the particular location of the activity and the way it is managed or operated.

We now turn to an opinion illustrative of the anticipatory nuisance doctrine in the context of a proposed landfill. The opinion is also included to point out some of the scientific principles involved in environmental tort litigation.

SHARP v. 251st STREET LANDFILL, INC.

Supreme Court of Oklahoma, 1996.
925 P.2d 546.

(SHARP II)

LAVENDER, JUSTICE.

This is the second time this matter has been before us. In the first appeal we affirmed the decision of the trial court to grant a temporary injunction prohibiting construction and operation of a landfill at a location in Okmulgee County. Sharp v. 251st Street Landfill, Inc., 810 P.2d 1270 (Okla.1991), overruled on other grounds DuLaney v. Oklahoma State Department of Health, 868 P.2d 676 (Okla.1993) (Sharp I). The claim for injunctive relief was brought by appellees—either adjacent or nearby landowners—to enjoin construction and operation of the landfill based on an anticipatory nuisance theory which in turn was anchored on the asserted probability ground and/or surface water sources used by them would likely be polluted by operation of the landfill. (footnote omitted).

After the matter returned to the trial court following the first appeal, appellant, 251st Street Landfill, Inc., made certain changes to its proposed landfill design, which included a leachate[2] collection system and a geomembrane—i.e., plastic—liner, modifications geared toward providing additional protection against the probability of water pollution. The Oklahoma Department of Environmental Quality (DEQ) (footnote omitted) determined the modifications complied with certain proposed new rules of DEQ concerning solid waste landfills, which determination essentially acted as DEQ's authorization to go forward with construction and operation of the landfill at the designated location. The matter then proceeded to trial. Following trial a decree permanently enjoining construction and operation at the proposed site was entered by the trial court. An appeal by appellant followed and we have retained the matter in this Court.

Two general issues are posed for our review: 1) whether reversible error occurred in the admittance and consideration of testimony from an engineer as expert testimony for appellees and, 2) whether the trial court erred in granting the permanent injunction because his decision was clearly against the weight of the evidence? We hold no reversible error occurred in either acceptance of the expert testimony or in granting the permanent injunction. The decision to permanently enjoin construction and operation of the landfill at the proposed location is, therefore, affirmed.

I. STANDARD OF REVIEW.

The rules governing appellate review in regard to injunctive relief are well settled. The award of a permanent injunction is a matter of equitable concern. Jackson v. Williams, 714 P.2d 1017, 1020 (Okla.1985). Granting or denying injunctive relief is generally within the sound discretion of the trial court and a judgment issuing or refusing to issue an injunction will not be disturbed on appeal unless the lower court has abused its discretion or the decision is clearly against the weight of the evidence. * * * If the facts and law warrant, however, this Court will affirm the judgment or order of the trial court if the correct ultimate conclusion was reached.

---

2. Leachate is a contaminate that usually comes from solid waste sites as surface water infiltrates into compacted refuse. It is a quantity of liquid that has percolated through a solid and leached out some of its constituents. Leachate may contain various pollutants depending on the makeup of the refuse disposed of at a particular site.

We must also keep in mind the following principles in our review. An injunction is an extraordinary remedy that should not be lightly granted. Entitlement to injunctive relief must be established in the trial court by clear and convincing evidence and the nature of the complained of injury must not be nominal, theoretical or speculative. There must be a reasonable probability that the injury sought to be prevented will be done if no injunction is issued—a mere fear or apprehension of injury will not be sufficient. Further, the decision of DEQ to grant a permit to appellant to construct and operate the landfill at the proposed site comes with a presumption DEQ has properly carried out its duties and responsibilities under the Oklahoma Solid Waste Management Act, 27A O.S.Supp.1995, § 2–10–101 et seq., as amended. Sharp I, 810 P.2d at 1276. However, if it is adequately shown the decision of an administrative agency is inconsistent with legislative intent a court is not bound by such decision and may grant injunctive relief to effectuate the legislative design, assuming, of course, the plaintiff shows entitlement to injunctive relief under traditional equitable principles. Sharp I, 810 P.2d at 1275–1276.

* * *

II. ADMITTANCE AND CONSIDERATION OF EXPERT TESTIMONY.

Appellant claims the trial court erred in admitting and considering part of the expert opinion testimony of Richard N. DeVries. It is argued his testimony concerning landfill design should have been disregarded primarily because of the assertion he lacks knowledge and experience to give an expert opinion on landfill design and he was not qualified to express an opinion on the adequacy of the environmental protection systems embodied in the proposed landfill design. We disagree. * * *

Our interpretation of the record is that no abuse of discretion occurred by the trial court's acceptance of the qualifications of Dr. DeVries to give expert opinions in this matter on landfills, landfill design, the potentiality of ground and surface water pollution and generally the adequacy of the environmental protection systems associated with this particular proposed landfill. In our view, he was qualified by virtue of a mixture or combination of the five factors. Clearly, his education and training provide him with the ability to express expert opinion concerning the hydrology of the site and surrounding area. The evidence also shows he has experience in the area of potential pollution of water sources and the causes thereof. As to landfills and landfill design particularly, this record shows he has acquired knowledge and skill in these areas, some of it by study and some by actual experience. His disqualification in these areas is not warranted simply because he has not actually designed a landfill exactly like the one proposed. Therefore, we conclude the decisions of the trial court to accept the qualifications of Dr. DeVries as an expert in the areas specified above and, obviously, to rely on those opinions in reaching a decision to enjoin the proposed landfill, did not constitute an abuse of discretion nor do they provide any basis for reversal.

III. Entitlement to Permanent Injunction.

When it is clearly made to appear by the evidence that a business cannot be conducted in any manner at the place where situated without constituting a substantial injury to adjoining or nearby property owners a permanent injunction absolutely prohibiting operation of such business at the particular location is appropriate. Further, when a neighboring landowner is confronted with a nuisance and threatened with a complete loss of their water supply, they do not have to wait the actual infliction of such loss, but have a right to apply to a court for injunctive relief. Baker v. Ellis, 292 P.2d 1037, 1039 (Okla.1956); See also McPherson v. First Presbyterian Church, 120 Okla. 40, 248 P. 561, 566 (1926) (harm suffered must be irreparable in damages and the evidence must be clear and convincing that there is a reasonable probability of injury, not just a mere apprehension). We have also recently recognized that the use and control of fresh water is a matter of publici juris and of immediate local, national and international concern. DuLaney v. Oklahoma State Department of Health, supra, 868 P.2d at 684. "No commodity affects and concerns the citizens of Oklahoma more than fresh groundwater." Id.

In our opinion, if the trial court determined the new or modified safety measures proposed by appellant for the landfill were inadequate to protect against probable pollution of appellees' water sources by operation of the landfill at its proposed location, an appropriate remedy would be a permanent injunction. Sharp I, 810 P.2d at 1281–1282. Although the trial court's order granting a permanent injunction was made without specific findings, we must assume the trial court concluded that the additional proposed safety measures are inadequate and that operation of the landfill cannot be conducted at the particular location without the reasonable probability of polluting appellees' water sources.[7] We do not find this conclusion clearly against the weight of the evidence.

7. In appellant's first proposition contained in its Brief in Chief submitted in this appeal it is contended the injunction must be reversed because the trial court absolutely prohibited construction and operation of the landfill, rather than limiting the injunction to the aspects he found objectionable. Appellant asserts absolute prohibition was not warranted because the evidence did not show it was impossible to construct and operate the landfill without pollution of appellees' property. Appellant also apparently contends the trial court somehow erred by failing to follow our opinion in Sharp I, supra, note 1, because he failed to determine if other measures would provide adequate protection for appellees' water sources. As we noted in the text, we must assume the trial court found the new or modified safety features proposed would not be adequate and that operation of the landfill cannot be conducted at the proposed site without the reasonable probability of pollution of appellees' water sources. We do not believe the trial court had to go further. Appellant's argument here is essentially based on the theory the design features presently proposed are adequate. That some other non-specified feature or method of protection might exist in the abstract, in our view, does not provide a basis to reverse the trial court's injunction. See Kenyon v. Edmundson, 80 Okla. 3, 193 P. 739, 742 (1920) (when owner of business has been given opportunity to show a business can be operated at a particular location in such a manner so as not to create a nuisance and the owner fails to so show, it is not error for trial court to enjoin continuation of business at the location). We add that although some evidence was presented that redundant (i.e. more than one) liner and/or leachate collection systems might provide additional protection to the water sources in the area, as we understand the opinion of Dr. DeVries, it is that given current technology in the field of landfill design—coupled with the hydrology at the proposed site and in

As we noted in Sharp I, the decision of DEQ to authorize construction and operation of the proposed landfill comes to us with a presumption DEQ has adequately carried out its duties and responsibilities under, and has effectuated the purposes behind, the Oklahoma Solid Waste Management Act. 810 P.2d at 1276. Two of these general purposes are protecting the public health, safety and welfare and the environment of this State. 27A O.S.Supp.1995, § 2–10–102. However, as we further recognized in Sharp I, if it is adequately shown the permitting of a landfill at a particular location does not effectuate the legislative purposes and a plaintiff shows entitlement to relief under traditional equitable principles, an injunction against operation of a landfill is an appropriate remedy. In our view, the decision of DEQ to authorize this landfill was at odds with the legislative purposes behind the Oklahoma Solid Waste Management Act and it was not error for the trial court to have concluded appellees were entitled to the remedy of an injunction.

The landfill site is the West ½ of Section 10, Township 15 North, Range 12 East, Okmulgee County, Oklahoma. About 90 of the 320 acres of the proposed site will be used as cells for the disposal of refuse. The landfill was originally permitted under Oklahoma Department of Health regulations as a Type I–B facility, which was generally defined as a metropolitan sanitary landfill serving populations of 30,000 or more which does not accept hazardous waste. The majority of waste to be deposited at the proposed landfill will be domestic waste. However, evidence was presented at the temporary injunction hearing and the subsequent trial that domestic waste contains a certain amount of toxic or hazardous household waste. Although screening of the waste will apparently occur, we believe a reasonable conclusion is that a certain amount of toxic materials will find their way into the landfill.

U.S. Highway 75 is a half mile east of the site. Directly north of the site is 251st Street. At least some of the appellees have artesian wells on their property.[9] The wells are used for domestic purposes, livestock and agricultural purposes. Further, Eagle Creek, a creek running through the landfill site (but apparently not through the cells where waste is to be deposited) also runs through the land of some of the appellees. The creek is used by these appellees either for recreational purposes or watering livestock.

When the matter was initially here in Sharp I, it was proposed that the cells where waste was to be deposited were to be lined with a three foot thick clay liner, the then minimum standard required by Oklahoma

the area—a landfill cannot be built and operated at the site without posing the reasonable probability the water sources of some of appellees will be polluted by such operation.

9. An artesian well is made by boring into the earth until water is reached which from internal pressure flows up like a fountain. WEBSTER'S NEW COLLEGIATE DICTIONARY 63 (1979). Testimony at the temporary injunction hearing indicated it was a well drilled into the earth's strata until a confined aquifer is encountered and the water confined therein rises above the confining layer. As we noted in Sharp I, a confined aquifer consists of a permeable zone of the earth's strata containing water which is bounded above and below by strata of low permeability.

Department of Health regulations. Subsequent to Sharp I appellant modified its design to comply with the "technical" requirements of proposed new DEQ regulations—Municipal Solid Waste Landfill Regulations—and in August 1993 DEQ apparently determined the design modifications were in compliance with the proposed new rules. These DEQ regulations were eventually adopted and became effective in October of 1993. The current rules can be found at Oklahoma Administrative Code (OAC) Title 252, Chapter 510. Refer to 13 Okla.Reg. 1977 et seq. (1996) for the most recent modifications to these rules.

Generally, the design characteristics of the proposed landfill are as follows. First, a compacted clay liner at least 3 feet thick will be placed on a soil base a minimum of two feet above the highest recorded groundwater (i.e. water table) level. A geomembrane liner (some type of flexible, plastic sheeting, designed to be apparently impermeable) will be placed on top of the clay liner. Above the geomembrane liner will be a geotextile liner, a heavy cloth designed to protect the geomembrane liner from puncture. Above these liners will be a leachate collection system, a system of perforated pipes and pumps designed to collect any leachate that might flow through the landfill. On top of the leachate collection system will be a granular drainage blanket comprised of at least one foot of gravel large enough so as not to clog the pipes, but porous enough for the leachate to flow through to the pipes. Finally, the granular drainage blanket will be protected by another foot of additional protective cover, either soil, or clay, or an additional granular blanket. Compacted trash will be placed on top of this, and each day's trash will be covered with one-half foot of soil to prevent loose trash from blowing.

The plans also call for monitoring wells around the perimeter of the landfill which are to act as detection devices should any leachate escape the protective devices specified in the above paragraph. The landfill is also to have a system of trenches and berms which will be designed to protect against the possibility of leakage or runoff into Eagle Creek.

Appellees identify two primary mechanisms for potential pollution of their properties—contamination of the confined, artesian aquifer under the site and contamination of Eagle Creek. To support their case principal reliance was placed on the testimony and opinions of Dr. DeVries, although documentary evidence was also relied on.

First off, there was evidence in the record that showed the site of the proposed landfill overlies a major regional aquifer—the Wewoka Formation or Aquifer. It was Dr. DeVries' opinion that appellees' artesian wells were tapping into the same confined or artesian aquifer as that under the landfill. It was also his view that given the hydrology in the area that the potential existed for pollution of this aquifer. He further expressed the opinion the direction of groundwater flow for this confined aquifer was to the northeast, i.e., from the landfill site toward the artesian wells of appellees.

Furthermore, although the artesian aquifer was in a confined state apparently at least a minimum of sixty (60) feet below the proposed landfill site, Dr. DeVries testified, and other evidence corroborated the fact, that the piezometric or potentiometric surface of the artesian aquifer was actually above ground level at the proposed landfill site. What this means is that because the artesian aquifer is in such a confined—and, thus, pressurized state—it has the potential to rise above the ground when punctured. Thus, a well drilled into this aquifer would flow above the ground like a fountain. Dr. DeVries believed this high piezometric surface of the confined aquifer held the potential for water from the confined aquifer coming up under the liner of the landfill and/or blowing a hole in the landfill's liner system, which he indicated had been detailed in the literature to have previously occurred.

It was also Dr. DeVries' opinion that the water table in the area under the site was a high one, i.e. at certain places under the proposed landfill site it was relatively close to the surface of the ground. His view was because of this state it would be necessary to artificially raise by the use of fill material the surface of the ground at certain places of the landfill to maintain an adequate minimum distance between the protective layer(s) of the landfill and the water table. He was of the view that because man cannot compact soil as well as nature, settlement of the fill material would occur, which held out the possibility of the sub-base cracking which in turn could cause cracks in the liner system of the landfill—i.e. a potential conduit for pollution. Although there is some dispute over the direction of flow of the water table or unconfined aquifer under the site, Dr. DeVries' opinion was and other evidence appeared to show that, at least, in part it flows north and east, which is toward appellees.[11] Dr. DeVries also held the view that both the confined and unconfined aquifers contributed flow to Eagle Creek.

In addition, certain evidence showed that Eagle Creek, which runs through the site and the land of some of the appellees, generally flows in the direction from the site toward these appellees, i.e. in a northeasterly direction. Evidence also showed that the one hundred (100) year flood plain or boundary was as close as twenty-five (25) to thirty-five (35) feet from the area where trash would be deposited at the landfill site. Dr. DeVries also testified that the drainage area for Eagle Creek includes both the landfill site and the properties of appellees. He also indicated that the landfill site is near the high point of the drainage area and that anything that drains off the site—any pollutant or contaminant—would go downstream toward the lands of appellees.

In view of the matters specified above and other evidence presented, the opinion of Dr. DeVries was essentially that the proposed site for this landfill was not suitable because of the hydrology in the area, and given the state of current technology an environmentally safe landfill could not be built at the site. His view was generally that water resources under,

11. Sharp I, supra, note 1, previously defined an unconfined aquifer. 810 P.2d at 1279 n. 13. Unlike a confined aquifer it is not bounded above and below by relatively impermeable layers and, consequently, the water confined therein is not in a pressurized state. Water from a well drilled into such an aquifer will not rise above the aquifer. An unconfined aquifer is commonly referred to as the water table.

in and around the site made the location especially non-conducive to a safe and environmentally sound waste disposal facility. In essence it was his opinion the design of the landfill, including the protective devices to be installed therein, would not be sufficient to protect against pollution of the water resources in the area, but instead a high probability existed that leachate would escape and contaminate the water resources. His ultimate opinion was that there was a very high probability downstream property owners—i.e., at least some of appellees—would suffer both ground and surface water pollution from operation of the landfill. He also noted that it was very difficult to completely remediate such pollution once it occurs, in either the groundwater or surface water systems.[12]

As would be expected, appellant countered the opinions of Dr. DeVries with experts of its own. These experts gave opinions that the protective devices to be installed at the landfill were adequate to protect the water systems in the area and, essentially, there was a negligible possibility of pollution. Evidence was also presented that the landfill would be constructed and operated in compliance with DEQ regulations. There was also evidence presented that at least some of Dr. DeVries' views concerning the hydrology or hydrogeology[13] in the area were incorrect, e.g., the view was presented that the direction of the water flow or movement of the confined aquifer(s) under the landfill site was to the northwest, which would be away from the property of appellees which generally lies north and east of the landfill site.

As pointed out in Sharp I, the trial court was not required to credit the testimony of the experts presented by appellant over the testimony of appellees' expert. In our view, sufficient evidence was presented to overcome any favorable presumption to be accorded to the decision of DEQ in permitting or authorizing the involved landfill. Based on our review of the record, the decision to permanently enjoin construction and operation of the solid waste disposal facility at its proposed location comported with applicable law and such decision cannot be said to have been clearly against the weight of the evidence. Thus, in this particular case, given the demonstrated sensitivity of the water resources in the area, and the probability operation of the proposed landfill would pollute the water resources of at least some of the appellees, we believe no reversible error occurred by the grant of a permanent injunction.

* * *

12. We recognized in Sharp I, supra, note 1, that the difficulty, complexity and costliness of remedying groundwater contamination was well documented and that once seriously contaminated groundwater is often rendered unusable and cleaning it up is often unsuccessful. 810 P.2d at 1279 n. 15.

13. As we noted in Sharp I, supra, note 1 [810 P.2d at 1279 n. 12], hydrogeology is a part of geology that studies the relations of water on or below the surface of the earth.

Notes and Questions

1. Several things especially stand out in the *Sharp* opinion: first, is the minimal citation of supporting authority on the law of nuisance. Once the court refers to plaintiffs' anticipatory nuisance theory and the standard of review for injunctions, the opinion is fact-driven, not law-driven. Barely is there any reference to balancing of the gravity of harm against the utility of defendant's operation. Second is the court's giving such short-shrift to the Oklahoma DEQ's authorization which it finds "inconsistent with the legislative intent" underlying the Oklahoma Solid Waste Management Act. Shouldn't the court grant more deference to the administrative agency charged with enforcement of the SWMA? Third, the extensive discussion of the landfill design is noteworthy. While this coursebook is not for a science course, attempting to map out the description of the area and the design of landfill may be useful.

2. The opinion in *Sharp II* refers to earlier opinions in the same case. In Sharp v. 251st Street Landfill, Inc., 810 P.2d 1270 (Okla.1991) (Sharp I), the court affirmed issuance of a preliminary injunction against construction of the landfill as then designed. It was in response to that proceeding that defendant, with approval of the Oklahoma DEQ made modifications to the landfill design that, of course, proved to be unavailing. Much of the opinion in *Sharp I* addresses the question of whether the Oklahoma Solid Waste Management Act preempted common-law, tort-based, injunctive actions, the court holding that it did not. We consider the preemption issue in Chapter 6.

3. In The Village of Wilsonville v. SCA Services, Inc., 86 Ill.2d 1, 55 Ill.Dec. 499, 426 N.E.2d 824 (1981) the Illinois Supreme Court affirmed an injunction sought by a small community (joined in by the state's Attorney General) against a newly built state-of-the-art hazardous waste facility, located above abandoned coal mine shafts. A snippet of the court's reasoning, which first held that the evidence supported finding an existing and prospective public and private nuisance, is as follows:

> Reasonableness is the standard by which the court should fashion its relief in ordinary nuisance cases, and reasonableness is also the appropriate standard for relief from environmental nuisance. Ordinarily a permanent injunction will not lie unless (1) either the polluter seriously and imminently threatens the public health or (2) he causes non-health injuries that are substantial and the business cannot be operated to avoid the injuries apprehended. Thus the particular situation facts of each pollution nuisance case will determine whether a permanent injunction should be issued.

> This case is readily distinguishable [from Harrison v. Indiana Auto Shredders, 528 F.2d 1107 (7th Cir.1975)] for the reason that the gist of this case is that the defendant is engaged in an extremely hazardous undertaking at an unsuitable location, which seriously and imminently poses a threat to the public health. We are acutely aware that the service provided by the defendant is a valuable and necessary one. We also know that it is preferable to have chemical-waste-disposal sites than to have illegal dumping in rivers, streams, and deserted areas. But a site such as defendant's, if it is to do the job it is intended to do, must be located in a secure place, where it will pose no threat to health or life, now, or in the future. This site was intended to be a permanent disposal

site for the deposit of extremely hazardous chemical-waste materials. Yet this site is located above an abandoned tunneled mine where subsidence is occurring several years ahead of when it was anticipated. Also, the permeability-coefficient samples taken by defendant's experts, though not conclusive alone, indicate that the soil is more permeable at the site than expected. Moreover, the spillage, odors, and dust caused by the presence of the disposal site indicate why it was inadvisable to locate the site so near the plaintiff village.

Therefore, we conclude that in fashioning relief in this case the trial court did balance relative hardship to be caused to the plaintiffs and defendant, and did fashion reasonable relief when it ordered the exhumation of all material from the site and the reclamation of the surrounding area. The instant site is akin to Mr. Justice Sutherland's observation that "Nuisance may be merely a right thing in a wrong place—like a pig in the parlor instead of the barnyard." Village of Euclid v. Ambler Realty Co., 272 U.S. 365, 388, 47 S.Ct. 114, 118, 71 L.Ed. 303 (1926).

4. The plaintiff in *Wilsonville* was a village. What if the plaintiffs consisted of several residents of the village suing solely on a theory of private nuisance: would the outcome (issuance of a permanent injunction) have been different? The *Sharp* opinion suggests not, because only private citizens, without any governmental backing, succeeded in securing a permanent injunction. Would the court's analysis of the reasonableness of the invasion have been different? Would private persons suing on a public nuisance theory have to satisfy the special injury requirement? Could they have done so in *Sharp* or *Wilsonville*? Would it depend on the kind of relief sought— injunctive or damages?

5. To dispel the impression that the outcomes in *Sharp* and *Wilsonville* are a recent phenomenon, consider the early nuisance decision of the Michigan Supreme Court in People v. Detroit White Lead Works, 82 Mich. 471, 46 N.W. 735 (1890), where the defendant corporation demonstrated both that it conducted its operations "in a careful and prudent manner," and that when it had begun its business, "the lands in the vicinity of its work were open commons." Whenever such a "business becomes a nuisance," the Court stated, "it must give way to the rights of the public, and the owners thereof must either devise some means to avoid the nuisance, or must remove or cease the business."

6. Are *Sharp* and *Wilsonville* really zoning cases masquerading as nuisance cases? See the discussion of the relationship between zoning laws and nuisance doctrine in 4 William H. Rodgers, Jr., Environmental Law: Hazardous Wastes and Substances § 7.30 (1992). Rodgers points out that in waste-disposal nuisance cases the decisions reflect more a pattern of strict liability than nuisance balancing. § 7.30 at 408. As we saw in *Sharp*, that is precisely what the court did.

Problem

Magnum Computer Inc. (Magnum) is a manufacturer of computer hardware. Immediately adjacent and hydrogeologically upgradient to Magnum is a paint and thinner supplier, Thinner Corp. (Thinner). Recently, consumers have returned a large quantity of computer parts manufactured by Magnum, complaining that the parts are defective.

Magnum, which is located in a rural area, uses water from an on-site well in its manufacturing process. While investigating the cause of the defective products, Magnum's quality control personnel discover that the defects are caused by a reaction between a material used in manufacturing the parts and certain toxic chemicals found in the water supplied by Magnum's well. Although Thinner denies any responsibility for the chemicals' presence in the groundwater below Magnum's plant, the toxic chemicals in the water are those that Thinner regularly sells to its customers.

Magnum's attorney is considering a suit against Thinner for costs of removing the toxic contamination from Magnum's property, the economic damages suffered by the company, and for degradation of the groundwater. Magnum, however, is unable to find any direct evidence of spills or careless handling of chemicals by Thinner. It will therefore have difficulty proving that Thinner caused the release of toxic chemicals which seeped into the soil and eventually into the groundwater, or that the Thinner-created contaminant plume subsequently migrated into the groundwater below Magnum's facility.

As Magnum's attorney what evidentiary approach might be considered to overcome the proof problems? What theory of liability is most promising?

7.   NOTE ON NEGLIGENT CONDUCT

Section 822, quoted above, allows for liability when the invasion is the result of negligent or reckless or abnormally dangerous conduct. The latter is considered in Chapter Four as an independent basis of liability. Negligence claims can arise in two legal contexts: first, as the basis for finding a private nuisance; and, second, as a free-standing basis of liability. The decisions do not always distinguish between the two.

Recall that in the United Proteins v. Farmland Industries decision reproduced earlier in the Chapter, the court stated that a negligence theory was precluded by the statute of limitations, but noted that "this might have been a relatively simple case of negligence[.]"

As in all negligence cases, the defendant must create unreasonable risks of harm. The unreasonableness of the risk of harm is determined by the same risk versus utility analysis undertaken in other negligence cases. Note that it is the *risk* of harm that is weighed, not the harm that actually materialized. The same utility considerations discussed above apply to these cases. Restatement (Second) of Torts § 291 essentially incorporates Learned Hand's test of negligence from United States v. Carroll Towing Co., 159 F.2d 169 (2d Cir.1947), by defining the unreasonableness of the actor's conduct by whether the magnitude of the risks created outweighs the utility of the act, where utility includes the extent of the chance that the interest being advanced by the defendant's conduct can be advanced by a less dangerous course of conduct.

In nuisance actions, as in trespass, the negligence-based cases often involve underground leakage, as from underground petroleum storage tanks. Illustrative of such cases is Bargmann v. Soll Oil Co., 253 Neb. 1018, 574 N.W.2d 478 (Neb. 1998) where residents who suffered damage to their properties as a result of petroleum contamination, brought claims for negligence and private nuisance. There was evidence that a plume of contamination ran from Derald Bargmann's service station operation to the plaintiffs' homes, which was joined by a second plume of contamination originating at the Soll Oil operation.

The court's analysis of the negligence claim is as follows:

In September 1994, the Nebraska Department of Environmental Quality hired Terracon Environmental to assess and remedy the contamination problem and to pinpoint the source of the contamination. Stephen K. Bunting, a Terracon employee, is of the view that Derald Bargmann's operation is the source of the contamination under the Terry Bargmann and Tonjes residences and that both Derald Bargmann's operation and the Soll interests' operation are the sources of contamination under the Lutjen residence. Bunting found no other areas of possible sources for the groundwater contamination.

Bunting investigated some underground gasoline storage tanks which had been removed from the Soll interests' property and discovered that they were corroded and had holes and pitting in them. Terracon tested soil samples from the excavation area, and the results showed no significant impact.

* * *

The plaintiffs argue in their briefs that Derald Bargmann was negligent in not investigating the possibility of contamination after he discovered that one of his tanks was leaking. They also urge that the Soll interests were negligent in not investigating the possible contamination in the soil underneath its excavated underground tanks.

The evidence establishes that after a routine inventory check revealed a leak in one of his tanks, Derald Bargmann did not check for any possible contamination. However, it is uncontroverted that the soil surrounding this tank showed no signs of contamination and that there were no visible leaks or holes in the tank. The evidence also establishes that the underground tanks the Soll interests excavated were corroded and that some product had leaked into the soil. But not only is there no evidence as to when the corrosion developed, it is uncontroverted that the company the Soll interests hired to analyze the soil underneath the excavated tanks never told the Soll interests of any problems.

More importantly, the plaintiffs failed to present any evidence as to the standard of care owed by one in the business of storing and selling petroleum products. One who undertakes to render services

in the practice of a trade is required to exercise the skill and
knowledge normally possessed by members of that trade in good
standing in similar communities.

* * *

Because with respect to Derald Bargmann the record lacks any
evidence as to the applicable standard of care and because there is
no evidence regarding what specific acts of negligence by him caused
the contamination, the district court was correct in finding that as a
matter of law the record failed to establish that he breached any
duty.

* * *

However, with respect to the Soll interests, the situation is
otherwise. In that regard, there is evidence that the Soll interests'
failure to close the holes resulting from the removal of the underground tanks contributed to the contamination. Thus, the district
court was incorrect in finding that as a matter of law the record
failed to establish that the Soll interests breached any duty. 574
N.W.2d at 484–85.

Negligence is an important complementary theory to nuisance for
another reason: suppose plaintiffs assert a claim against the haulers or
transporters of hazardous waste, that was deposited at a landfill, and
subsequently caused harm to plaintiffs properties. A New Jersey Superi-
or Court held that while a nuisance theory is inappropriate because of
defendant-haulers lack of connection to the landfill, a negligence theory
was viable. Kenney v. Scientific, Inc., 204 N.J.Super. 228, 497 A.2d 1310
(N.J. Super. 1985). The court reasoned:

It appears that some generators left the choice of the landfill
entirely to the hauler, whereas other generators chose the landfill
themselves. A hauler who selects a landfill which he knows or
reasonably has reason to know to be hazardous should be held
accountable in negligence. Similarly, if a hauler who does not
himself select the landfill knows or reasonably has reason to know
that the site selected by the generator is dangerous or has become
dangerous, his making deliveries under such circumstances may be
considered to be negligence. As in the case of the generators,
although the haulers may show governmental approval as a factor in
determining negligent choice of a landfill, such approval will not in
itself determine the issue.

See also Fortier v. Flambeau Plastics Co., 164 Wis.2d 639, 476
N.W.2d 593, 607 (Wis.App.1991) ("It is undisputed that chemical compounds containing VOCs seeped from the landfill into plaintiffs' well
water. Chemicals seeping or percolating through groundwater can constitute an invasion. We have already concluded that the companies are not
entitled to dismissal of the plaintiffs' claim based on common law
negligence. Because under sec. 822(b) a negligent invasion may be the
basis of liability under a private nuisance theory, the companies have not

shown that they are entitled to summary judgment dismissing the plaintiffs claims for private nuisance.'').

Wilson v. Amoco Corp., 33 F.Supp.2d 969 (D.Wyo.1998) (defendant railyard and dry cleaning facility owed a duty to conduct their operations so as not to release contaminants from their facilities that would migrate and impact plaintiffs' properties; it is not necessary for plaintiff to prove that precise injuries could be foreseen; and it was jury question on proximate causation where evidence showed up to 17 potential sources for the PCE plume).

Problem

The following facts appeared in the November 23, 1992 edition of the National Law Journal, p. 1, under the caption "Toxic Refuge."

The story highlights several families that had moved from New York City to Haverstraw, a sleepy town about 50 miles north, in New York State, and purchased "affordable" middle class homes in a development known as Warren Court. The Warren Court homes cost $161,000, with only a 5% down payment and below-market interest rates offered by the development's manager, the Pension Fund of Carpenters' Union 964. One Warren Court family, the Riveras, had been experiencing a persistent smell of rotten eggs around their home. In January 1992 they discovered the source when the sewer line collapsed beneath their home. When Haverstraw village workers dug into the earth they discovered decomposing gypsum wallboard and an overpowering wave of fumes.

It seems that the homes in Warren Court were built on an industrial landfill consisting of 10,000 cubic yards of gypsum board. Gypsum board, which is not considered hazardous waste, when buried and deprived of oxygen and surrounded by dampness, surrenders to a bacteria that acts upon the harmless material to produce hydrogen sulfide gas. In the late 1960s and 1970s, U.S. Gypsum Company had arranged with village officials to bury its scrap wallboard. The village had been happy to oblige because Haverstraw, once known as "Bricktown," had large unstable underground areas that remained from the clay mining era of the early Twentieth Century. Indeed, the ground was so unstable that in 1906 twenty Haverstraw residents were buried alive when their shanties collapsed into a mine. To reclaim this area, village officials began using the scrap wallboard provided by U.S. Gypsum as clean fill material at many mining sites. By the early 1970s, area residents had discovered that the buried gypsum yielded that terrible rotten egg odor created by hydrogen sulfide gas.

In 1985, the village, which owned the mining areas, rezoned one fill site to residential use. Anchorage Construction Co. ("Anchorage") planned to build twenty-one affordable homes on the site. Anchorage obtained financing from the Carpenters' Pension Fund. However, as construction costs escalated because of the soft ground which made foundations unstable, thereby requiring extra materials and labor, the Pension Fund took over ownership of the project.

The Riveras and others have learned that all state, county, and local permits and environmental audits had been complied with. They also have learned that "high levels" of hydrogen sulfide can be "poisonous."

The village refuses to accept responsibility other than to revoke occupancy permits for the nine unsold homes. The county refuses to permit evacuation of the twelve occupied homes because the gas poses no acute health hazard to the residents. The Pension Fund recommends "neutralizing" the odor, but offers no other relief. The State of New York's Department of Environmental Conservation can't help, because the dumping of wallboard occurred before state law prohibited such disposal. The EPA has agreed to "study" the problem but holds out little opportunity for relief.

Several homeowners, including the Riveras, have filed suit against the Pension Fund, Anchorage, the village, the county, the State of New York, and U.S. Gypsum. What theories of liability may be promising? Drawing on the materials in Chapters 2 and 3 on trespass, negligence, and public and private nuisance describe plaintiffs' claims and defendants' likely responses.

Chapter Four

STRICT LIABILITY FOR ABNORMALLY DANGEROUS ACTIVITIES AND OTHER THEORIES

A. EVOLUTION OF THE STRICT LIABILITY DOCTRINE

1. GENESIS: RYLANDS v. FLETCHER

An important theory of tort liability in the arsenal of environmental torts is strict liability attaching to injury caused by conducting activities regarded as "abnormally dangerous" or "ultrahazardous." As noted above under the discussions of private nuisance, one type of a defendant's conduct that gives rise to liability under § 822 is engaging in abnormally dangerous activity. Whether the liability of a defendant engaged in abnormally dangerous activity is treated as a private nuisance under § 822, or as a separate strict liability tort under §§ 519 and 520 of the Restatement (Second) of Torts, both theories are dependent upon establishing the basis for strict liability arising from abnormally dangerous activities.

The common law doctrine of strict liability for abnormally dangerous activities has taken on heightened significance since the advent of the nation's struggle to clean up the consequences of the disposal of hazardous wastes. As you read this chapter, ask yourself how fairly or efficiently this doctrine, which originated in 1866, can be applied to distribute the costs of remediating land and groundwater from the adverse effects of disposal of hazardous wastes and chemicals. What advantages does the doctrine offer that nuisance or trespass does not? What is the primary impediment to more widespread use of the doctrine? Who can be held liable under this doctrine? Will it include previous owners, operators, or generators of the waste or chemicals? What kinds of activities are properly denominated "abnormally dangerous"? Must a defendant know that its activities are highly dangerous? What role should the doctrine of caveat emptor play in strict liability cases?

The seminal decision is Rylands v. Fletcher, 1 L.R.-Exch. 265 (1866), which involved the flooding of the plaintiff's coal mine by water from the defendant's reservoir which had burst through tunneling. Although the contractors who built the reservoir for defendant were possibly negligent, Judge Blackburn of the Exchequer Chamber, predicated liability on a different theory:

> The question of law therefore arises, what is the obligation which the law casts on a person who, like the defendants, lawfully brings on his land something which, though harmless whilst it remains there, will naturally do mischief if it escape out of his land.

> * * *

> We think that the true rule of law is, that the person who for his own purposes brings on his lands and collects and keeps there anything likely to do mischief if it escapes, must keep it in at his peril, and, if he does not do so, is prima facie answerable for all the damage which is the natural consequence of its escape. * * * [I]t seems but reasonable and just that the neighbour, who has brought something on his own property which was not naturally there, harmless to others so long as it is confined to his own property, but which he knows to be mischievous if it gets on his neighbour's, should be obliged to make good the damage which ensues if he does not succeed in confining it to his own property.

The House of Lords, hearing the case as Rylands v. Fletcher, 3 H.L. 330 (1868), affirmed the judgment of the Exchequer Chamber, thus endorsing a strict liability theory. Lord Cairns quoted approvingly the above language of Justice Blackburn but added an alternative gloss of his own; he explained:

> "On the other hand if the Defendants, not stopping at the natural use of their close, had desired to use it for any purpose which I may term a non-natural use, for the purpose of introducing into the close that which in its natural condition was not in or upon it, for the purpose of introducing water either above or below ground in quantities and in a manner not the result of any work or operation on or under the land, and if in consequence of their doing so, or in consequence of any imperfection in the mode of their doing so, the water came to escape and to pass off into the close of the Plaintiff, then it appears to me that that which the Defendants were doing they were doing at their own peril; and, if in the course of their doing it, the evil arose to which I have referred, the evil, namely, of the escape of the water and its passing away to the close of the Plaintiff and injuring the Plaintiff, then for the consequence of that, in my opinion, the Defendants would be liable * * *"

3 H.L. at 339.

Thus, liability would turn on whether defendant's use of land was a "natural use of their close," meaning "any purpose for which it might in the ordinary course of the enjoyment of land be used," as opposed to a "non-natural use." 3 H.L. at 339–40 (1968).

Thus, while Judge Blackburn premised strict liability on any non-natural use of the land, by which he meant any use by the defendant of its land by bringing onto it some "mischief" which by nature was not present, Lord Cairns defined non-natural in a narrower way, by limiting the concept to activities which are *abnormal*, not ordinary, uses of the land, considering the character and general uses of the surrounding land. What might have caused Lord Cairns to adopt a narrower test of strict liability? For an early analysis of the *Rylands* decision, see Francis H. Bohlen, The Rule in Rylands v. Fletcher, 59 U. Pa. L. Rev. 298 (1911); A.W.B. Simpson, Legal Liability for Bursting Reservoirs: The Historical Context of Rylands v. Fletcher, 13 J. Legal Studies 209 (1984); Fleming, The Law of Torts, Ch. 16 (8th ed. 1992).

2. AMERICAN RECOGNITION AND THE FIRST RESTATE-MENT

In early American decisions the rule of *Rylands* was rejected by courts which regarded it as holding a defendant absolutely liable whenever anything under its control escapes and produces damage without regard to its locational appropriateness or its dangerousness. For example, in the 1873 decision in Losee v. Buchanan, 51 N.Y. 476, a boiler exploded in defendant's factory, damaging plaintiff's adjacent property. The court refused to impose liability in the absence of negligence:

> We must have factories, machinery, dams, canals and railroads. They are demanded by the manifold wants of mankind, and lay at the basis of all our civilization. [The victim of an accident] receives his compensation * * * by the general good, in which he shares, and the right which he has to place the same things upon his lands.

At about the same time, American courts were generally invoking strict liability on behalf of those injured by explosives—a position that antedated *Rylands* and was accepted as valid in *Losee*. See, e.g., Hay v. Cohoes Co., 2 N.Y. 159 (1849); Carman v. Steubenville & Ind. R.R., 4 Ohio St. 399 (1854); see, also Comment, The Rylands v. Fletcher Doctrine in America: Abnormally Dangerous, Ultrahazardous or Absolute Nuisance, 1978 Ariz. St. L. J. 99.

However, after an inhospitable beginning, courts began to adopt the narrower rule that the majority of states have embraced in some form, essentially extending it to embrace liability for activities "out of place, the abnormally dangerous condition or activity which is not a 'natural' one where it is." Prosser & Keeton on Torts § 78 at 549, 551 (5th ed. 1984). The First Restatement of Torts, published in 1934, accepted the principle of *Rylands*, but specifically limited it to "ultrahazardous activity" of the defendant, which was defined as one which "necessarily involves a risk of serious harm to the person, land or chattels of others which cannot be eliminated by the exercise of the utmost care," and "is not a matter of common usage." Restatement of Torts §§ 519 and 520.

Clearly what the First Restatement sought to capture, and the Reporter, Francis Bohlen himself had advocated in an article cited above, was a burgeoning principle of enterprise liability. He relied primarily on a couple of decisions to support strict liability for ultrahazardous activity.

In 1924 the Minnesota Supreme Court in Bridgeman–Russell v. City of Duluth, 158 Minn. 509, 197 N.W. 971 (Minn. 1924), extended the *Rylands* strict liability rule beyond reservoirs to the escape of water from the principal main leading from a reservoir. The court wrote that "[i]n such a case, even though negligence is absent, natural justice would seem to demand that the enterprise, or what is really the same thing, the whole community benefitted by the enterprise, should stand the loss rather than the individual." This language suggests a broad theory of enterprise liability–that strict liability properly applies to business enterprises that benefit from hazardous activities and can spread losses among the whole community.

So too the California Supreme Court in Green v. General Petroleum Corp., 205 Cal. 328, 270 P. 952, 955 (Cal. 1928), extended strict liability beyond blasting and explosives to the nonnegligent operations of an oil company when an oil well had "blown out," casting debris on plaintiff's property. The court declined to endorse *Rylands* openly but fashioned a broad principle of strict liability:

> Where one, in the conduct and maintenance of an enterprise lawful and proper in itself, deliberately does an act under known conditions, and, with knowledge that injury may result to another, proceeds, and injury is done to the other as the direct and proximate consequence of the act, however carefully done, the one who does the act and causes the injury should, in all fairness, be required to compensate the other for the injury done.

> * * *

> In our judgment, no other legal construction can be placed upon the operations of the appellant in this case than that, by its deliberate act of boring its well, it undertook the burden and responsibility of controlling and confining whatever force or power it uncovered. Any other construction would permit one owner, under like circumstances, to use the land of another for his own purpose and benefit, without making compensation for such use. We do not conceive that to be the law.

Finally, in Exner v. Sherman Power Construction Co., 54 F.2d 510, 514 (2d Cir.1931), Judge Augustus Hand extended strict liability beyond blasting to the storage of explosives, and beyond damage caused by debris cast on the land of another to damage caused by the concussion. Again, the early stirrings of an enterprise liability theory appear in the court's opinion. The court stated that the extent to which one is liable for injuries to another absent negligence "involves an adjustment of conflicting interests." Then the court held:

> When, as here the defendant, though without fault, has engaged in the perilous activity of storing large quantities of a dangerous explosive for use in his business, we think there is no justification for relieving it of liability, and that the owner of the business, rather than a third person who has no relation to the explosion, other than that of injury, should bear the loss.

The First Restatement, relying heavily on these three opinions, manifestly goes beyond the rule of *Rylands*, and focuses primarily on three considerations: (1) the dangerousness of the activity; (2) the impossibility of eliminating the danger with all possible care; and (3) whether the activity is a matter of common usage. Thus, the essence of the First Restatement was to impose strict liability on those activities, however socially desirable, that created in the community an abnormal risk of a serious nature. See, Comment, Absolute Liability for Ultrahazardous Activities: An Appraisal of the [First] Restatement Doctrine, 37 Cal. L. Rev. 269 (1949).

3.   THE RESTATEMENT (SECOND) OF TORTS

But the Restatement (Second) was to find itself the object of strong criticism from one whose opinion mattered a good deal. Writing in 1953, William Prosser leveled these criticisms at the First Restatement's formulation:

> This [Restatement] goes beyond the English rule in ignoring the place where the activity is carried on and its surroundings, and falls short of it in the insistence on extreme danger and the impossibility of eliminating it with all possible care. This shift of emphasis to the nature of the activity itself rather than its relation to is surroundings is not reflected in the American cases, which have laid quite as much stress as the English ones upon the place where the thing is done.

Prosser, *The Principle of Rylands v. Fletcher,* in Selected Topics in the Law of Torts 158 (1953).

As the Reporter for the Restatement (Second) of Torts, Prosser would have an opportunity to rectify these deficiencies. Commencing in 1958 as the Reporter, Prosser proposed to the American Law Institute a modified version of strict liability, which was ultimately published in 1977, several years after his death. The Second Restatement changed the prior label of "ultrahazardous activity" and replaced it with "abnormally dangerous activity."

In May, 1964, the Institute membership considered §§ 519 and 520 which were approved. Proceedings of the ALI, May 23, 1964 (at 449–465). As to § 520, Prosser explained that he had initially sought to draw the Section as a set of requirements with the "primary test" the "inappropriateness of the activity to the place where it is carried on." However, the Advisers had convinced him that because nuclear fission is dangerous regardless of where it is undertaken, a locational test could not be an absolute requirement in every case. Therefore, he opted for a set of six factors which are to be considered with the core idea being that the activity must be "substantially dangerous," "not slightly dangerous," or represent an "abnormal danger," "not usually encounter[ed]." *Id.* at 456.

Prosser repeated that he believed the multi-factor approach was "unsatisfactory" and that he did "not like this section" because of its indefiniteness, but he and the Council "felt helpless as to doing anything to improve it." *Id.* at 457. For a review of this history, see, Gerald W. Boston, Strict Liability for Abnormally Dangerous Activity: The Negligence Barrier, 36 San Diego L. Rev. 597 (1999).

B.   RESTATEMENT (SECOND) OF TORTS STANDARD OF LIABILITY

When the Restatement (Second) was published in 1976, it changed the prior label of "ultrahazardous activity" and replaced it with "abnormally dangerous activity." Sections 519 and 520, reproduced below, set forth the governing standards:

§ 519. General Principle

(1) One who carries on an abnormally dangerous activity is subject to liability for harm to the person, land or chattels of another resulting from the activity, although he has exercised the utmost care to prevent the harm.

(2) This strict liability is limited to the kind of harm, the possibility of which makes the activity abnormally dangerous.

§ 520. Abnormally Dangerous Activities

In determining whether an activity is abnormally dangerous, the following factors are to be considered:

(a) existence of a high degree of risk of some harm to the person, land or chattels of others;

(b) likelihood that the harm that results from it will be great;

(c) inability to eliminate the risk by the exercise of reasonable care;

(d) extent to which the activity is not a matter of common usage;

(e) inappropriateness of the activity to the place where it is carried on; and

(f) extent to which its value to the community is outweighed by its dangerous attributes.

1. RELATIONSHIP TO NEGLIGENCE AND BALANCING

The Restatement (Second) formulation distinguishes "ordinary" industrial and commercial enterprises, to which strict liability will not be extended, from those that are "abnormally," unusually, or atypically dangerous. The Restatement (Second)'s six factors can be grouped into two categories: subsections (a) through (c) characterize the abnormally dangerous nature of the activity, which depends on a high degree of risk, the potential of producing significant harm, and the inability to eliminate that risk even by the exercise of great care. Subsections (d) through (f), in contrast, characterize the positive side of the activity, by focusing on its commonness, locational appropriateness, and value to the community. So viewed, the analysis of whether an activity is to be subjected to strict liability, as opposed a negligence test, involves a balancing of these six considerations. That balancing, of course, begins to take on the very trappings of the risk-versus-utility calculus, which is the core of negligence theory. Thus, the strict liability label disguises latent similarities to negligence. For example, drawing on Judge Learned Hand's formula for breach of duty as whether $PL > B$, under § 520, the product of the PL is very high, but the B is virtually infinite because no amount of care is capable of eliminating the risk of harm created by the activity. Therefore, if the B is extremely high liability under negligence principles would be precluded, thereby creating a rationale for imposing strict liability.

This weighing or balancing process that is contemplated by the application of the six "factors" is explained in the comment to § 520 as follows: "In determining whether the danger is abnormal, the factors listed in Clauses (a) to (f) of this Section are all to be considered, and are all of importance. *Any one of them is not necessarily sufficient* of itself in a particular case, and ordinarily several of them will be required for strict liability. On the other hand, it is not necessary that each of them be present, especially if others weigh heavily. Because of the interplay of these various factors, it is not possible to reduce abnormally dangerous activities to any definition. The essential question is whether the risk created is so unusual, either because of its magnitude or because of the circumstances surrounding it, as to justify the imposition of strict liability for the harm that results from it, even though it is carried on with all reasonable care. In other words, are *its dangers and inappropriateness for the locality so great* that, despite any usefulness it may have for the community, it should be required as a matter of law to pay for any harm it causes, *without the need of a finding of negligence.*" (emphasis added.)

2. RELATIONSHIP TO NUISANCE

How do the theories of nuisance and strict liability relate? Prosser & Keeton point out that there is a close identity between the concept of "absolute nuisance" and strict liability:

Actually even the jurisdictions which reject Rylands v. Fletcher by name have accepted and applied the principle of the case under the cloak of various other theories. Most frequently, in all of the American courts, the same strict liability is imposed upon defendants under the name of nuisance. The "absolute nuisances" for which strict liability is found without intent to do harm or negligence fall into categories already familiar. They include * * * explosives or inflammable liquids stored in quantity in thickly settled communities or in dangerous proximity to valuable property; blasting; * * * oil wells or abnormal mining operations; the accumulation of sewage; * * * and in addition such things as smoke, dust, bad odors, noxious gases and the like from industrial enterprises, all obviously closely related to the cases following Rylands v. Fletcher. There has been general recognition in these nuisance cases that the relation of the activity to its surroundings is the controlling factor; * * * The "non-natural use" becomes an "unreasonable use."

* * *

There is in fact probably no case applying Rylands v. Fletcher which is not duplicated in all essential respects by some American decision which proceeds on the theory of nuisance; and it is quite evident that under that name the principle is in reality universally accepted.

Id. at 552–553. The Restatement (Second) of Torts in comment *c* to § 520 also recognizes this close relationship between absolute nuisances and strict liability, in stating that strict liability is "applied by many courts under the name of absolute nuisance." For an excellent analysis of the relationship between trespass, nuisance and strict liability, see Page Keeton, Restating Strict Liability and Nuisance, 48 Vanderbilt L. Rev. 595 (1995).

3. HIGH RISKS OF HARM

Comment *g* of § 520, "Risk of harm," explains clauses (a) and (b) of § 520. It speaks of a "high degree of risk of serious harm;" but Prosser points out that in determining if a given activity imposes a major risk, it may be "necessary to take into account the place where the activity is conducted." The comments to § 520 also evidence an intent that the sections interplay so that a small probability of great harm could yield a finding of abnormally dangerous (i.e., Three Mile Island) or, alternatively, a higher probability of significant, but lesser, harm (i.e., fireworks display). There is no question that many of the decisions actually applying the doctrine involve highly dangerous activities pursuant to the formula, such as the use of explosives, impounding billions of gallons of phosphate slime, or disposal of hazardous substances containing mercury into a sensitive estuary.

Thus, although § 520(a) and (b) involve "factors," the fact remains that the doctrine of § 520 has only been applied to activities that are "abnormally" dangerous, clearly connoting a level of risk not normal or that is unusual.

A Florida court in Cities Service Co. v. Florida, 312 So.2d 799, 803 (Fla.Dist.Ct.App. 1975), in holding that the impoundment of billions of gallons of phosphate slime as incidental to mining phosphate rock behind earthen dams was abnormally dangerous focused on the magnitude of the danger, discounting the other factors:

> In the final analysis, we are impressed by the *magnitude of the activity and the attendant risk of enormous damage*. The impounding of billions of gallons of phosphatic slimes behind earthen walls which are subject to breaking even with the exercise of the best of care strikes us as being both "ultrahazardous" and "abnormally dangerous," as the case may be.

> This is not clear water which is being impounded. Here Cities Service introduced water into its mining operation which when combined with phosphatic wastes produced a phosphatic slime which had a high potential for damages to the environment. If a break occurred, it was to be expected that extensive damage would be visited upon property many miles away. In this case, the damage, in fact, extended almost to the mouth of the Peace river, which is far beyond the phosphate mining area described in the Cities Service affidavit. We conclude that the Cities Service slime reservoir constituted a non-natural use of the land such as to invoke the doctrine of strict liability.

In this decision it is the magnitude of the risk that compelled the court to apply strict liability—it dwarfed the other factors.

In contrast, the Fifth Circuit concluded that storage of anhydrous ammonia was not abnormally dangerous because it is poisonous only in large concentrations, so the likelihood that storage would lead to great harm is "small," thereby not fulfilling factors (a) and (b). Sprankle v. Bower Ammonia & Chemical Co., 824 F.2d 409 (5th Cir.1987).

In some decisions courts have looked to evidence in the record in the form of government reports to support the conclusion that the activity falls within clauses (a) and (b). The New Jersey Supreme Court in State, DEP v. Ventron, 94 N.J. 473, 468 A.2d 150, 160 (N.J. 1983), in addressing the dangerousness of disposal of mercury-laden wastes cited reports to the U.S. Congress, as well as law review articles which recognized that disposal of toxic wastes could cause substantial environmental harms. Based on these authorities, the Court concluded that "mercury and other toxic wastes are abnormally dangerous and the disposal of them, past and present, is an abnormally dangerous activity."

A Wisconsin appeals court looked to letters in the record from the state environmental protection agency to support its finding that the placement of volatile organic compounds (VOCs) in a municipal landfill created a likelihood of great harm. Fortier v. Flambeau Plastics Co., 164 Wis.2d 639, 476 N.W.2d 593 (Wis.Ct.App.1991).

4. THE NEGLIGENCE BARRIER AND SECTION 520(c)

Many commentators have anticipated or advocated that the rule of strict liability of §§ 519 and 520 would become a major tort law tool in confronting environmental harms. See, e.g., Nolan & Ursin, The Revitalization of Hazardous Activity Strict Liability, 65 N.C.L. Rev. 257 (1987) (the title notwithstanding, there has been little revitalization); Ehrenzwieg, Negligence without Fault, 54 Cal. L. Rev. 1422 (1966); Jones, Strict Liability for Hazardous Enterprise, 92 Colum. L. Rev. 1765 (1992); King, A Goals–Oriented Approach to Strict Tort Liability for Abnormally Dangerous Activities, 48 Baylor L. Rev. 341 (1996). But see, Gertsfeld, Should Enterprise Liability Replace the Rule of Strict Liability for Abnormally Dangerous Activities?, 45 UCLA L. Rev. 611 (1998).

Any expectation of an enlivened resort to "abnormally dangerous activity" liability has not been borne out by the ensuing decisional law. To identify one or more principal reasons for this, the researcher need only note the significant discussion the courts have dedicated to the question posed by § 520 (b), i.e., whether the risk can be eliminated by the exercise of reasonable care. The following federal trial court decision, applying the law of Missouri, details its application of this evaluation to a claim arising from the low-level escape of electricity, or "stray electricity", from the cathodic protection appurtenant to the defendant's pipeline.

FLETCHER v. CONOCO PIPE LINE

United States District Court, W.D. Missouri, 2001.
129 F.Supp.2d 1255.

ORDER

WHIPPLE, District Judge.

Pursuant to Federal Rule of Civil Procedure 12(b)(6), Defendant Conoco Pipe Line Company ("Defendant") moves the Court to dismiss Counts IV, V, VI, VII, VIII, XIV, XV, XVI, XVIII, XIX, XXI, and XXII of Plaintiff Dallas Fletcher, Katherine Fletcher, Clyde Kent and Dorothy Kent's ("Plaintiffs") Third Amended Complaint. Alternatively, Defendant moves the Court to strike Counts VII, VIII, XIX, and XXII as duplicative pursuant to Federal Rule of Civil Procedure 12(f). Plaintiffs filed Suggestions in Opposition to Defendant's Motion to Dismiss and Defendant filed a Reply, addressing Plaintiffs' arguments. Having carefully considered the parties' arguments, the Court holds that Defendant's 12(b)(6) Motion to Dismiss is GRANTED IN PART and DENIED IN PART. In addition, the Court GRANTS Defendant's Motion to Strike Counts VII, VIII, XIX and XXII pursuant to Federal Rule of Civil Procedure 12(f).

I. Standard of Review

[The court's discussions of the Motion to Dismiss standard of Fed. R. Civ. Proc. 12(b)(6) and the Motion to Strike standard of Fed. R. Civ. Proc. 12(f) are omitted]

II. Factual Background

[This Factual Background is derived from the allegations in the Plaintiffs' complaint. In ruling on a Motion to Dismiss, these allegations are taken as true.]

Defendant owns and operates underground pipelines that transport oil, crude petroleum, and petroleum products. In the 1930's, Defendant's predecessor in interest, the Ajax Pipeline Company ("Ajax"), obtained what the Plaintiffs characterize as "pipeline permits" from the former owners of Plaintiffs' properties. The "pipeline permits" granted Ajax a right of way to lay, construct, maintain, operate, alter, repair, remove, change the size of, and replace two lines of pipe for the transportation of oil, crude petroleum and petroleum products. The pipelines at issue begin near Ponca City, Oklahoma, run across, on or near the Plaintiffs' properties, and terminate in Wood River, Illinois.

Defendant's pipelines have cathodic protection as mandated by federal regulations that require protection of all underground steel pipes. See 49 C.F.R. § 195.242. Cathodic protection entails passing a low-voltage electrical current along the metal pipeline to protect against corrosion. Plaintiffs assert that the electricity designed to provide cathodic protection has escaped from the pipeline, traveling up to and beyond a distance of thirty feet, and thereby exceeding the scope of the "pipeline permits." The essence of Plaintiffs' claim is that this "stray electricity" is traveling onto and contaminating their land. According to Plaintiffs, representatives of Defendant have made inspections and done testing on the pipeline that should have caused them to conclude that this "stray electricity" was escaping, yet they allegedly failed to prevent the escapage or warn Plaintiffs of possible danger. Plaintiffs assert that the stray voltage contamination has caused them to suffer personal injury, loss of consortium, loss of enjoyment of life, lost profits, and property damage. In particular, Plaintiffs describe how the "stray electricity" has negatively affected livestock, made their electric bill erratic, shortened the life expectancy of motors, appliances, and light bulbs, and accelerated the corrosion of metal structures, such as well casings and fence posts. Plaintiffs seek to impose liability on Defendant for this "stray electricity" pursuant to a number of theories, including, inter alia, nuisance, negligence, strict liability, breach of contract, trespass, loss of consortium, nuisance, inverse condemnation, and ejectment.

III. Discussion

A. Counts IV & XIV Strict Liability

Defendant argues that Plaintiffs' strict liability claims must fail because neither the operation of the pipeline nor the use of cathodic protection are abnormally dangerous activities that warrant the imposition of strict liability. Plaintiffs disagree and assert that the operation of petroleum pipelines charged with electricity is an abnormally dangerous activity that has the potential to cause widespread death and destruction. Missouri courts have not addressed the issue of whether strict liability applies to the operation of cathodically-protected petroleum pipelines. The Court concludes that the doctrine of strict liability does not apply because neither the operation of a petroleum pipeline nor the use of cathodic protection are abnormally dangerous activities, as a matter of law.

The doctrine of strict liability arose from an English case, Rylands v. Fletcher, 1 L.R.-Ex. 265 (Ex. Ch. 1866), aff'd, 3 L.R.-E & I.App. 330 (H.L.1868). Rylands established the premise that if a person brings something on his land which, if it escapes, is likely to do great damage, that person is prima facie liable for all the harm naturally occurring if there is an escape. [Cc] This theory of strict liability, as it was first articulated in Rylands, has been very narrowly applied by Missouri courts. See Bennett v. Mallinckrodt, Inc., 698 S.W.2d 854, 868 (Mo.App. 1985) (noting how Missouri courts have historically rejected claims based upon strict liability and required plaintiffs to bring negligence, nuisance or trespass actions instead). Missouri law dictates that a person is strictly liable "when he damages another by a thing or activity unduly dangerous and inappropriate to the place where it is maintained, in the light of the character of that place and its surroundings." Clay v. Missouri Highway and Transp. Comm'n, 951 S.W.2d 617, 623 (Mo.App. 1997) (citations omitted). While Missouri courts are generally reluctant to extend the use of strict liability as a theory for relief, activities such as blasting and nuclear operations have been deemed sufficiently dangerous to warrant the imposition of strict liability. See Donnell v. Vigus Quarries, Inc., 526 S.W.2d 314, 316 (Mo.Ct.App.1975) (holding that the theory of strict liability applies to blasting); Bennett, 698 S.W.2d at 867 (stating that strict liability should apply to claims based on radiation damage because use of nuclear material is uncommon and poses great danger).

The Restatement (Second) of Torts similarly embraces a narrow application of Rylands. See Clay, 951 S.W.2d at 623 (citing Bennett, 698 S.W.2d at 867). According to the Restatement, strict liability dictates that "[o]ne who carries on abnormally dangerous activity is subject to liability for harm to the person, land or chattels of another resulting from the activity, although he has exercised the utmost care to prevent the harm." Restatement (Second) of Torts § 519(1). In ascertaining whether an activity should be deemed "abnormally dangerous," the Restatement directs courts to assess the following factors:

[A recitation of (Restatement (Second) of Torts § 520(a)-(f)) is omitted.]

* * *

Missouri courts appear to have adopted the Restatement's definition of strict liability—they apply the Restatement's list of factors to determine whether the risks of a perilous activity outweigh the benefits, to the extent that strict liability should apply. * * *

The only factor Plaintiffs discuss is factor (b), the likelihood that the harm that results from the activity will be great. Plaintiffs state that the potential for petroleum pipelines charged with electricity to "cause widespread death, destruction or damage to other persons or their property is axiomatic." Plaintiffs fail, however, to offer any support for this assertion; they neither cite to any cases nor reference any news articles. While the Court is willingly to concede that petroleum spills have the potential to cause tremendous property and environmental damage, the Court fails to see the potential for "widespread death and destruction" in the general operation of cathodically-protected petroleum pipelines. Perhaps it is the Court's limited imagination, but no scenarios come to mind. Moreover, a survey of federal case law fails to uncover any such cataclysmic events.

For many courts, the analysis of whether an activity is abnormally dangerous revolves around factor (c), whether the activity can be made safe through the exercise of reasonable care. See, e.g., Toledo v. Van Waters & Rogers, Inc., 92 F.Supp.2d 44, 56 (D.R.I.2000) (finding that transporting chemicals cannot be considered an ultrahazardous activity "because it can be, and has been, performed safely when the parties involved exercise reasonable care"); Chaveriat, 1994 WL 583598, at *5 (stating that the third Restatement factor—the extent to which reasonable care can reduce the risk of harm—merits primary attention). The inquiry should be: "how likely is this type of accident if the actor uses due care?" See Chaveriat, 1994 WL 583598, at *5. As one court explained, "if an activity can be performed safely with ordinary care, negligence serves both as an adequate remedy for injury and a sufficient deterrent to carelessness" and the imposition of strict liability is unnecessary. Id.

For example, due to uncontrollable factors like wind and terrain, blasting remains an unpredictable and risky activity regardless of what precautions are taken. See M.W. Worley Constr. Co., Inc. v. Hungerford Inc., 215 Va. 377, 210 S.E.2d 161, 163 (1974). Conversely, unlike blasting, the operation and cathodic protection of a petroleum pipeline is a routine and easily regulated activity. As one court observed in the analogous context of underground gasoline storage tanks:

> Maintained, monitored, and used with due care, [they] present virtually no risk of injury from seepage of their contents. They are not abnormally dangerous. Sound tanks, timely replacement of impaired tanks, modern corrosion control techniques, and adequate testing for leakage can eliminate all but a tolerably small amount of risk.

See Arlington Forest Assocs. v. Exxon Corp., 774 F.Supp. 387, 390 (E.D.Va.1991).

* * *

Finally, the Court finds it significant that Plaintiffs fail to cite a single case applying strict liability to petroleum pipeline operations. On the other hand, the Court notes that several courts have rejected the contention that the operation of a petroleum pipeline is an abnormally dangerous activity. See Melso, 576 A.2d at 1004 (citing Cities Serv. Pipe Line Co. v. United States, 742 F.2d 626 (Fed.Cir.1984)). Additionally, in regard to the cathodic protection of the pipeline, the Court observes that Missouri courts have declined to impose strict liability on the activities of electrical generating corporations. See Mrad v. Missouri Edison Co., 649 S.W.2d 936, 941 (Mo.Ct.App.1983).

For the foregoing reasons, the Court finds that, as a matter of law, the operation of a cathodically-protected petroleum pipeline is not an abnormally dangerous activity. The Court anticipates that, if presented with the issue, the Missouri Supreme Court would likely hold that the narrow doctrine of Rylands should not be expanded to impose strict liability on petroleum pipeline operations. Accordingly, the Court holds that Plaintiffs fail to state a claim for strict liability as a matter of law and DISMISSES Counts IV & XIV.

B.   Counts V & XV—Breach of Contract

[The discussion of the Plaintiffs' Breach of Contract claim is omitted]

* * *

D.   Counts XVIII & XXI—Ejectment

[The Court's discussion of the Plaintiffs' claim in ejectment is omitted]

E.   Counts XIX & XXII—Permanent Injunction

Defendant argues that because a permanent injunction is a remedy and not a cause of action, Plaintiffs failed to state a claim for which relief can be granted. See Fed.R.Civ.P. 12(b)(6). In the alternative, Defendant asserts that Counts XIX & XXII should be stricken as redundant because, elsewhere in their Complaint, Plaintiffs request injunctive relief for the majority of their claims.

The Court agrees that there is no "injunctive" cause of action under Missouri or federal law. Instead, Plaintiffs must allege some wrongful conduct on the part of Defendant for which their requested injunction is an appropriate remedy. See Reuben H. Donnelley Corp. v. Mark I Mkgt. Corp., 893 F.Supp. 285, 293–94 (S.D.N.Y.1995). Reading Plaintiffs' Complaint broadly, as we must under Federal Rule of Civil Procedure 8(f), the wrongful conduct on which Plaintiffs primarily base their plea for injunctive relief appears to be Defendant's refusal to desist from allowing "stray electricity" to invade Plaintiffs' properties. Plaintiffs claim that they will suffer irreparable harm if Defendant is allowed to "continue to apply cathodic protection to the pipeline in the area of Plaintiffs' property at such a level as to cause or allow electricity to stray off of the pipeline and out of [Defendant's] easement." The Court concludes that Plaintiffs' "Permanent Injunction" causes of action are in fact reiterations of Plaintiffs' Trespass claims, within which Plaintiffs already request injunctive relief. See Sudul, 868 F.Supp. at 61 (holding that a claim was redundant within the meaning of Rule 12(f) where it essentially duplicated another claim). Accordingly, the Court DISMISSES Plaintiffs' "Permanent Injunction" claims (Counts XIX and XXII) as redundant pursuant to Federal Rule of Civil Procedure 12(f).

F.   Counts VII & VIII—Personal Injury

Defendant contends that Plaintiffs' "Personal Injury" causes of action, like Plaintiffs' "Permanent Injunction" claims, are not distinct causes of action recognized by Missouri courts. Alternatively, Defendant asserts that Plaintiffs' "Personal Injury" counts are merely reiterations of Plaintiffs' other negligence claims. Plaintiffs argue that Counts VII and VIII are capable of standing separate and apart from the other counts in their Complaint, but the Court notes that Plaintiffs fail to explain how this is so.

In Counts VII and VIII, entitled "Personal Injury," Plaintiffs allege that Defendant was "negligent and careless in allowing said electricity to escape from the prescribed pipeline permits" and that "as a direct and proximate result of the negligence and carelessness of Defendant," Plaintiffs suffered injury. These allegations are nearly identical to the allegations pleaded by Plaintiffs in Counts II, III, and XII, entitled "Negligence," "Negligence—Res Ipsa Loquitor," and "Specific Negligence," respectively. In each of these counts, Plaintiffs similarly assert that as a direct and proximate result of the negligent acts and omissions of the Defendant, they have continued to suffer damages. The Court agrees with Defendant that Plaintiffs' "Personal Injury" causes of action (Counts VII and VIII) are duplicative of Plaintiffs' other claims and must be DISMISSED pursuant to Federal Rule of Civil Procedure 12(f). See Dethmers Mfg. Co., Inc., 23 F.Supp.2d at 1009 (concluding that a claim that merely recasts the same elements under the guise of a different theory may be stricken as redundant pursuant to Rule 12(f)).

IV.   CONCLUSION

For the foregoing reasons, the Court hereby:

GRANTS Defendant's Federal Rule of Civil Procedure 12(b)(6) Motion to Dismiss as to Plaintiffs' Strict Liability claims (Counts IV & XIV), Breach of Contract claims (Counts V and XV), and Ejectment claims (Counts XVIII and XXI);

GRANTS Defendant's Federal Rule of Civil Procedure 12(f) Motion to Strike Plaintiffs' Personal Injury claims (Counts VII and VIII), and Permanent Injunction claims (Counts XIX and XXII); and

DENIES Defendant's Motion to Dismiss Plaintiffs' Trespass claims (Counts VI and XVI). IT IS SO ORDERED.

By far the most pervasive reason for the limited use of strict tort liability to environmental tort actions is that plaintiffs cannot satisfy the burden imposed by § 520(c) of demonstrating that the risks of the activity are ones which cannot be eliminated or reduced to acceptable levels by exercising reasonable care.

Perhaps the most exhaustive treatment of factor (c) of § 520 and the interplay between negligence and strict liability is Judge Richard Posner's opinion in the case that follows:

INDIANA HARBOR BELT RAILROAD COMPANY v. AMERICAN CYANAMID COMPANY

United States Court of Appeals, Seventh Circuit, 1990.
916 F.2d 1174.

POSNER, CIRCUIT JUDGE.

American Cyanamid Company, the defendant in this diversity tort suit governed by Illinois law, is a major manufacturer of chemicals, including acrylonitrile, a chemical used in large quantities in making acrylic fibers, plastics, dyes, pharmaceutical chemicals, and other intermediate and final goods. On January 2, 1979, at its manufacturing plant in Louisiana, Cyanamid loaded 20,000 gallons of liquid acrylonitrile into a railroad tank car that it had leased from the North American Car Corporation. The next day, a train of the Missouri Pacific Railroad picked up the car at Cyanamid's siding. The car's ultimate destination was a Cyanamid plant in New Jersey served by Conrail rather than by Missouri Pacific. The Missouri Pacific train carried the car north to the Blue Island railroad yard of Indiana Harbor Belt Railroad, the plaintiff in this case, a small switching line that has a contract with Conrail to switch cars from other lines to Conrail, in this case for travel east. The Blue Island yard is in the Village of Riverdale, which is just south of Chicago and part of the Chicago metropolitan area.

The car arrived in the Blue Island yard on the morning of January 9, 1979. Several hours after it arrived, employees of the switching line noticed fluid gushing from the bottom outlet of the car. The lid on the outlet was broken. After two hours, the line's supervisor of equipment was able to stop the leak by closing a shut-off valve controlled from the top of the car. No one was sure at the time just how much of the contents of the car had leaked, but it was feared that all 20,000 gallons had, and since acrylonitrile is flammable at a temperature of 30° Fahrenheit or above, highly toxic, and possibly carcinogenic, the local authorities ordered the homes near the yard evacuated. The Illinois Department of Environmental Protection ordered the switching line to take decontamination measures that cost the line $981,022.75, which it sought to recover by this suit.

[After some procedural tangles, the district judge granted plaintiff summary judgment on its strict liability claim and dismissed plaintiff's negligence claim. Defendant appealed and plaintiff cross-appealed.]

The question whether the shipper of a hazardous chemical by rail should be strictly liable for the consequences of a spill or other accident to the shipment en route is a novel one in Illinois.* * *

The parties agree * * * that the Supreme Court of Illinois would treat as authoritative the provisions of the Restatement governing abnormally dangerous activities. The key provision is section 520, which sets forth six factors to be considered in deciding whether an activity is abnormally dangerous and the actor therefore strictly liable.

The roots of section 520 are in nineteenth-century cases. The most famous one is Rylands v. Fletcher, 1 Ex. 265, aff'd, L.R. 3 H.L. 300 (1868), but a more illuminating one in the present context is Guille v. Swan, 19 Johns. (N.Y.) 381 (1822). A man took off in a hot-air balloon and landed, without intending to, in a vegetable garden in New York City. A crowd that had been anxiously watching his involuntary descent trampled the vegetables in their endeavor to rescue him when he landed. The owner of the garden sued the balloonist for the resulting damage, and won. Yet the balloonist had not been careless. In the then state of ballooning it was impossible to make a pinpoint landing.

Guille is a paradigmatic case for strict liability. (a) The risk (probability) of harm was great, and (b) the harm that would ensue if the risk materialized could be, although luckily was not, great (the balloonist could have crashed into the crowd rather than into the vegetables). The confluence of these two factors established the urgency of seeking to prevent such accidents. (c) Yet such accidents could not be prevented by the exercise of due care; the technology of care in ballooning was insufficiently developed. (d) The activity was not a matter of common usage, so there was no presumption that it was a highly valuable activity despite its unavoidable riskiness. (e) The activity was inappropriate to the place in which it took place—densely populated New York City. The risk of serious harm to others (other than the balloonist himself, that is) could have been reduced by shifting the activity to the sparsely inhabited areas that surrounded the city in those days. (f) Reinforcing (d), the value to the community of the activity of recreational ballooning did not appear to be great enough to offset its unavoidable risks.

These are, of course, the six factors in section 520. They are related to each other in that each is a different facet of a common quest for a proper legal regime to govern accidents that negligence liability cannot adequately control. The interrelations might be more perspicuous if the six factors were reordered. One might for example start with (c), inability to eliminate the risk of accident by the exercise of due care. The baseline common law regime of tort liability is negligence. When it is a workable regime, because the hazards of an activity can be avoided by being careful (which is to say, nonnegligent), there is no need to switch to strict liability. Sometimes, however, a particular type of accident cannot be prevented by taking care but can be avoided, or its consequences minimized, by shifting the activity in which the accident occurs to another locale, where the risk or harm of an accident will be less (e), or by reducing the scale of the activity in order to minimize the number of accidents caused by it (f). By making the actor strictly liable—by denying him in other words an excuse based on his inability to avoid accidents by being more careful—we give him an incentive, missing in a negligence regime, to experiment with methods of preventing accidents that involve not greater exertions of care, assumed to be futile, but instead relocating, changing, or reducing (perhaps to the vanishing point) the activity giving rise to the accident. The greater the risk of an accident (a) and the costs of an accident if one occurs (b), the more we want the actor to consider the possibility of making accident-reducing activity changes; the stronger, therefore, is the case for strict liability. Finally, if an activity is extremely common (d), like driving an automobile, it is unlikely either that its hazards are perceived as great or that there is no technology of care available to minimize them; so the case for strict liability is weakened.

The largest class of cases in which strict liability has been imposed under the standard codified in the Second Restatement of Torts involves the use of dynamite and other explosives for demolition in residential or urban areas. Explosives are dangerous even when handled carefully, and we therefore want blasters to choose the location of the activity with care and also to explore the feasibility of using safer substitutes (such as a wrecking ball), as well as to be careful in the blasting itself. Blasting is not a commonplace activity like driving a car, or so superior to substitute methods of demolition that the imposition of liability is unlikely to have any effect except to raise the activity's costs.

Against this background we turn to the particulars of acrylonitrile. Acrylonitrile is one of a large number of chemicals that are hazardous in the sense of being flammable, toxic, or both; acrylonitrile is both, as are many others. A table in the record, contains a list of the 125 hazardous materials that are shipped in highest volume on the nation's railroads. Acrylonitrile is the fifty-third most hazardous on the list. * * * The plaintiff's lawyer acknowledged at argument that the logic of the district court's opinion dictated strict liability for all 52 materials that rank higher than acrylonitrile on the list, and quite possibly for the 72 that rank lower as well, since all are hazardous if spilled in quantity while being shipped by rail. Every shipper of any of these materials would therefore be strictly liable for the consequences of a spill or other accident that occurred while the material was being shipped through a metropolitan area. The plaintiff's lawyer further acknowledged the irrelevance, on her view of the case, of the fact that Cyanamid had leased and filled the car that spilled the acrylonitrile; all she thought important is that Cyanamid introduced the product into the stream of commerce that happened to pass through the Chicago metropolitan area. Her concession may have been incautious. One might want to distinguish between the shipper who merely places his goods on his loading dock to be picked up by the carrier and the shipper who, as in this case, participates actively in the transportation. But the concession is illustrative of the potential scope of the district court's decision.

* * * [W]e * * * apply section 520 to the acrylonitrile problem from the ground up. To begin with, we have been given no reason, * * * or any other, for believing that a negligence regime is not perfectly adequate to remedy and deter, at reasonable cost, the accidental spillage of acrylonitrile from rail cars. Acrylonitrile could explode and destroy evidence, but of course did not here. * * * More important, although

acrylonitrile is flammable even at relatively low temperatures, and toxic, it is not so corrosive or otherwise destructive that it will eat through or otherwise damage or weaken a tank car's valves although they are maintained with due (which essentially means, with average) care. No one suggests, therefore, that the leak in this case was caused by the inherent properties of acrylonitrile. It was caused by carelessness— whether that of the North American Car Corporation in failing to maintain or inspect the car properly, or that of Cyanamid in failing to maintain or inspect it, or that of the Missouri Pacific when it had custody of the car, or that of the switching line itself in failing to notice the ruptured lid, or some combination of these possible failures of care. Accidents that are due to a lack of care can be prevented by taking care; and when a lack of care can * * * be shown in court, such accidents are adequately deterred by the threat of liability for negligence.

* * * For all that appears from the record of the case or any other sources of information that we have found, if a tank car is carefully maintained the danger of a spill of acrylonitrile is negligible. If this is right, there is no compelling reason to move to a regime of strict liability, especially one that might embrace all other hazardous materials shipped by rail as well. * * * If the vast majority of chemical spills by railroads are preventable by due care, the imposition of strict liability should cause only a slight, not as [amici] argue a substantial, rise in liability insurance rates, because the incremental liability should be slight. The amici have momentarily lost sight of the fact that the feasibility of avoiding accidents simply by being careful is an argument against strict liability.

* * *

The district judge and the plaintiff's lawyer make much of the fact that the spill occurred in a densely inhabited metropolitan area. Only 4,000 gallons spilled; what if all 20,000 had done so? Isn't the risk that this might happen even if everybody were careful sufficient to warrant giving the shipper an incentive to explore alternative routes? Strict liability would supply that incentive. But this argument overlooks the fact that, like other transportation networks, the railroad network is a hub-and-spoke system. And the hubs are in metropolitan areas. Chicago is one of the nation's largest railroad hubs. In 1983, the latest year for which we have figures, Chicago's railroad yards handled the third highest volume of hazardous-material shipments in the nation. East St. Louis, which is also in Illinois, handled the second highest volume. With most hazardous chemicals (by volume of shipments) being at least as hazardous as acrylonitrile, it is unlikely—and certainly not demonstrated by the plaintiff—that they can be rerouted around all the metropolitan areas in the country, except at prohibitive cost. Even if it were feasible to reroute them one would hardly expect shippers, as distinct from carriers, to be the firms best situated to do the rerouting. Granted, the usual view is that common carriers are not subject to strict liability for the carriage of materials that make the transportation of them abnormally dangerous, because a common carrier cannot refuse service to a shipper of a lawful commodity. Restatement, supra, § 521. Two courts, however, have rejected the common carrier exception. National Steel Service Center, Inc. v. Gibbons, 319 N.W.2d 269 (Ia.1982); Chavez v. Southern Pacific Transportation Co., 413 F.Supp. 1203, 1213–14 (E.D.Cal.1976). If it were rejected in Illinois, this would weaken still further the case for imposing strict liability on shippers whose goods pass through the densely inhabited portions of the state.

The difference between shipper and carrier points to a deep flaw in the plaintiff's case. Unlike *Guille* * * * and unlike the storage cases, beginning with *Rylands* itself, here it is not the actors—that is, the transporters of acrylonitrile and other chemicals—but the manufacturers, who are sought to be held strictly liable. A shipper can in the bill of lading designate the route of his shipment if he likes, 49 U.S.C. § 11710(a)(1), but is it realistic to suppose that shippers will become students of railroading in order to lay out the safest route by which to ship their goods? Anyway, rerouting is no panacea. Often it will increase the length of the journey, or compel the use of poorer track, or both. When this happens, the probability of an accident is increased, even if the consequences of an accident if one occurs are reduced; so the expected accident cost, being the product of the probability of an accident and the harm if the accident occurs, may rise. It is easy to see how the accident in this case might have been prevented at reasonable cost by greater care on the part of those who handled the tank car of acrylonitrile. It is difficult to see how it might have been prevented at reasonable cost by a change in the activity of transporting the chemical. This is therefore not an apt case for strict liability.

In emphasizing the flammability and toxicity of acrylonitrile rather than the hazards of transporting it, as in failing to distinguish between the active and the passive shipper, the plaintiff overlooks the fact that ultrahazardousness or abnormal dangerousness is, in the contemplation of the law at least, a property not of substances, but of activities: not of acrylonitrile, but of the transportation of acrylonitrile by rail through populated areas.

The relevant activity is transportation, not manufacturing and shipping. This essential distinction the plaintiff ignores. But even if * * * [defendant] is treated as a transporter and not merely a shipper, it has not shown that the transportation of acrylonitrile in bulk by rail through populated areas is so hazardous an activity, even when due care is exercised, that the law should seek to create—perhaps quixotically—incentives to relocate the activity to nonpopulated areas, or to reduce the scale of the activity, or to switch to transporting acrylonitrile by road rather than by rail. * * * It is no more realistic to propose to reroute the shipment of all hazardous materials around Chicago than it is to propose the relocation of homes adjacent to the Blue Island switching yard to more distant suburbs. It may be less realistic.

The briefs hew closely to the Restatement, whose approach to the issue of strict liability is mainly allocative rather than distributive. By this we mean that the emphasis is on picking a liability regime (negligence or strict liability) that will control the particular class of accidents in question most effectively, rather than on finding the deepest pocket and placing liability there. At argument, however, the plaintiff's lawyer invoked distributive considerations by pointing out that Cyanamid is a huge firm and the Indiana Harbor Belt Railroad a fifty-mile-long switching line that almost went broke in the winter of 1979, when the accident occurred. Well, so what? A corporation is not a living person but a set of contracts the terms of which determine who will bear the brunt of liability. Tracing the incidence of a cost is a complex undertaking which the plaintiff sensibly has made no effort to assume, since its legal relevance would be dubious. We add only that however small the plaintiff may be, it has mighty parents: it is a jointly owned subsidiary of Conrail and the Soo line.

The case for strict liability has not been made. Not in this suit in any event. * * *

The defendant concedes that if the strict liability count is thrown out, the negligence count must be reinstated, as requested by the cross-appeal. * * *

Notes and Questions

1. *Proof of Negligence.* What do you think of Judge Posner's rationale? Central to his analysis is the apprehension that applying strict liability here would imply that all manufacturers and shippers of hazardous chemicals would be liable whenever later events in the distribution of the product resulted in injury. How important is this fact? Judge Posner also emphasized that if the risks can be eliminated by due care there is no occasion to apply strict liability. The plaintiff's negligence count in *Harbor Belt* was permitted to proceed to trial, so the plaintiff was not left without a theory of liability. Could the plaintiff prove negligence on these facts? Assume that a bystander had been injured by the escape of the chemical.

2. *More on the Negligence Barrier.* The Wisconsin Supreme Court in Grube v. Daun, 213 Wis.2d 533, 570 N.W.2d 851, 857 (Wis. 1997), with somewhat briefer analysis, in holding that contamination from underground storage tanks was not subject to strict liability, declared:

> USTs, while admittedly disfavored under today's environmental laws, are not inherently dangerous. Absent negligence or application of an outside force, use of USTs does not create a high degree of risk of harm to the person, land or chattels of another. Moreover, those risks that do exist *can be minimized by the exercise of reasonable care* by the owner or possessor of the tank. * * *

> If an activity can be performed safely with ordinary care, negligence serves both as an adequate remedy for injury and a sufficient deterrent to carelessness. Strict liability is reserved for selected uncommon and

extraordinarily dangerous activities for which negligence is an inadequate deterrent or remedy.

The New York Court of Appeals in Doundoulakis v. City of Hempstead, 42 N.Y.2d 440, 398 N.Y.S.2d 401, 368 N.E.2d 24, 27 (N.Y. 1977), in a case involving damage to plaintiffs' properties from a hydraulic landfill project which created a 70–acre lake, concluded that the record contained insufficient evidence for making the determination of whether the city's activity was abnormally dangerous. In criticizing the absence of record evidence and the lower courts' conclusions that strict liability did apply to the landfill method used by defendant, it commented:

> There is little if any information, for example, of the degree to which hydraulic landfilling poses a risk of damage to neighboring properties. Nor is there data on the gravity of any such danger, or the extent to which the danger can be eliminated by reasonable care. Basic to the inquiry, but not to be found in the record, are the availability and relative cost, economic and otherwise, of alternative methods of landfilling.

What is significant is that the New York court held that the record must contain substantial evidence regarding alternative methods of landfilling as a predicate to deciding if due care could have avoided the risks of harm and, therefore, as a precondition to finding the activity abnormally dangerous.

The New Hampshire Supreme Court, in Bagley v. Controlled Environment Corp., 127 N.H. 556, 503 A.2d 823, 826 (N.H. 1986), in an opinion by Judge Souter (now U.S. Supreme Court Justice) involving the release of hazardous chemicals from defendant's property that contaminated plaintiff's soil and groundwater, explained the critical role of proving the unavailability of negligence:

> Good arguments could have been made for the existence of abnormal danger in the operation of the amusement ride in *Siciliano*, the maintenance of the high voltage power line in *Wood* and, probably, the maintenance of the dam in *Moulton*. We nonetheless refused to extend strict liability to cover the claims of the plaintiffs in each of those cases, and we held in effect that the abnormally dangerous nature of the activity could be addressed adequately *either in determining the precaution that reasonable care would demand, or in requiring conformance to statutory mandates.*

> We follow those cases today and decline to impose strict liability *in the absence of any demonstration that the requirement to prove legal fault acts as a practical barrier to otherwise meritorious claims.* With respect to the dumping of the waste products and leakage of gasoline in this case, *there is no apparent impossibility of proving negligence.*

This language couldn't be clearer: Plaintiff must demonstrate that negligence represents an evidentiary impossibility.

3. *Expert Testimony on Due Care Sinks Strict Liability.* In some cases plaintiff's own expert may undermine the strict liability claim by testifying that due care on defendant's part would have prevented the injury. In a personal injury action, plaintiff alleged that he was injured when one of defendant's drivers pumped sulfuric acid into the wrong tank in a waste

treatment facility, leading to a severe chemical reaction that released toxic gas. A California appeals court in Edwards v. Post Transportation Co., 228 Cal.App.3d 980, 279 Cal.Rptr. 231, 234 (Cal.Ct.App.1991), in affirming the trial court's refusal to submit the strict liability issue to the jury, resoundingly declared the pre-eminence of clause (c) of § 520, after having found that clauses (a) and (b) were satisfied in this case:

> Plaintiff loses his case, however, with the application of factor (c). The issue posed by factor (c) is whether the risk involved in an admittedly dangerous activity can be eliminated through the exercise of reasonable care. The same experts who testified to the dangerous attributes of the acid were in agreement that the actual risk of harm to people could be eliminated by the use of proper handling procedures. One plaintiff's expert, a civil engineer and "sanitarian," agreed that "If * * * sulfuric acid is handled in a proper fashion, it is no danger." Since sulfuric acid is governmentally classified as a hazardous material, its transporters must be specially classified or registered. It appears, however, that such regulation, including special training, is designed to and does eliminate the special risk related to handling the acid. The fact that the material "requires special handling" and one must "be careful with it," as plaintiff's expert testified, leads to the logical conclusion that risk can be eliminated through care.
>
> This conclusion undermines the argument that the use of sulfuric acid should lead to strict liability. *The theory of imposition of strict liability for ultrahazardous activity is that the danger cannot be eliminated through the use of care.* Since the activity is in some sense beneficial, useful or necessary to society, the actor is not deemed negligent simply for engaging in it. Damage resulting to others, however, is taxed to the actor because he is the person who most logically should bear the cost. Where the activity is dangerous only if insufficient care is exercised, ordinary rules of fault are sufficient for allocation of the risk. There is no need for liability without proof of fault, because definitionally if there is damage it will have resulted from negligence and will be compensable.

Accord, Erbrich Products Co. v. Wills, 509 N.E.2d 850 (Ind.Ct.App.1987) (due care by manufacturer of household liquid bleach could have prevented the escape of raw chlorine gas used in the plant, where even plaintiff's counsel admitted on oral argument that "but for the malfunctioning of Erbrich's fans within their plant which blew chlorine gas outside" the plaintiffs' injuries would not have occurred). For a collection of the decisions addressing this issue, see, Gerald W. Boston, Strict Liability for Abnormally Dangerous Activity: The Negligence Barrier, 37 San Diego L. Rev. 597 (1999).

5. SOME CONTRARY VOICES

There are a handful of decisions, unmistakably a minority, that eschew any reliance on § 520(c). A decision that exemplifies this practice is T & E Industries, Inc. v. Safety Light Corp., 123 N.J. 371, 587 A.2d 1249 (N.J. 1991), where the New Jersey Supreme Court held that the disposal of radium tailings in the early Twentieth Century on property later purchased by plaintiff was an abnormally dangerous activity. The court focused not on the Restatement factors but on the issue of foreseeability and knowledge, that is, whether an actor can be strictly liable even though at the time of the activity the dangers it posed to others were not known. The court inferred constructive knowledge of the dangers by defendant. In its only possible reliance on clause (c), it stated that "one cannot safely dispose of radium by dumping it onto the vacant portions of an urban lot."

See also Klein v. Pyrodyne Corp., 117 Wash.2d 1, 810 P.2d 917, 920 (Wash. 1991) (en banc), in which the court held that setting off public fireworks displays is an abnormally dangerous activity justifying imposition of strict liability; the activity entails existence of a high degree of risk of some harm to person, land, or chattels of others, the likelihood that harm that results from it will be great; there is an inability to eliminate the risk by the exercise of reasonable care, and the activity is not of common usage. It stated: "Furthermore, no matter how much care pyrotechnicians exercise, they cannot entirely eliminate the high risk inherent in setting off powerful explosives such as fireworks near crowds."

6. DEFINING THE "ACTIVITY" THAT MAY BE ABNORMALLY DANGEROUS

a. *Activities, not Substances*

In resolving whether strict liability may apply, how the court defines what constitutes the "activity" is critical. Recall that Judge Posner went to great lengths to explain that the relevant "activity" was the shipment of hazardous chemicals by rail.

A couple of Pennsylvania decisions also make the point that defining the activity is crucial to the disposition under § 520. In Smith v. Weaver, 445 Pa.Super. 461, 665 A.2d 1215 (Pa.Super.1995), the court rejected plaintiff's argument that a leaking underground storage tank was abnormally dangerous, by stressing the definition of the activity:

> The buyers would urge us to consider not whether underground tanks are abnormally dangerous, but rather whether underground storage tanks which are *leaking a hazardous substance,* are abnormally dangerous. By so phrasing the issue the buyers are seeking to have us view the *results of the activity,* instead of the activity itself. Although a dangerous condition may have later developed, or harm may have occurred, the proper focus is on the activity itself, the storage of potentially hazardous substances in an underground tank.

This analysis is performed antecedent to applying the factors of § 520, but it dictates the outcome. The court easily finds that gasoline and other petroleum products can be stored and dispensed safely with reasonable care. In another case, Diffenderfer v. Staner, 722 A.2d 1103 (Pa.Super.1998), the court considered whether the storage in a barn of Thimet, a highly toxic pesticide, which ended up tainting cow feed and killing several dairy cows, was an abnormally dangerous activity. The court reversed the trial court for submitting the issue to the jury because the "instruction focused the strict liability claim on the leaking of the pesticide, not on its storage." The court, looking to the Restatement factors, pointed out that storing pesticides in a barn does not constitute a high degree of risk to others, and, based on expert testimony at the trial, concluded that "the risk of storing Thimet can be eliminated with the exercise of reasonable care."

The Rhode Island Supreme Court in Splendorio v. Bilray Demolition Co., 682 A.2d 461, 466 (R.I.1996), applied similar reasoning in holding that an engineering firm that undertook an asbestos remediation project as part of a building demolition that released asbestos fibers onto plaintiff's property was not engaged in an abnormally dangerous activity. The court emphasized that strict liability applied only to activities, not to dangerous materials—that is, "defendant's activity as a whole" is to be analyzed: "[I]f the rule were otherwise, virtually any commercial activity involving substances which are dangerous in the abstract automatically would be deemed as abnormally dangerous. This result would be intolerable."

A federal district court in an underground storage tank case undertook a considerable discussion of this issue. In Arlington Forest Assoc. v. Exxon Corp., 774 F.Supp. 387 (E.D.Va.1991), the court criticized plaintiff for characterizing the relevant activity as the leaking of moribund underground tanks, rather than the "normal and nondefective condition of underground tanks." The court explained why plaintiff's particularized approach was objectionable since it would "enable plaintiffs to invoke strict liability for all negligently-conducted activity." It continued: "Any plaintiff in a negligence action should simply characterize the offending behavior as incapable of being safely performed even with due care, thus bringing it within the scope of strict liability. For example, the activity of 'driving a car' can be made sufficiently safe by exercise of reasonable care. But 'driving a car at an excessive rate of speed' cannot be made safe except by ceasing to drive too fast. Clearly this approach would extend the reaches of strict liability far beyond the bounds of the law and of common sense. The Court does not doubt that the injury inflicted in this case stems from the presence of moribund storage tanks; however, this fact properly relates to the issue of negligence." Id. at 392–93. How would you approach this issue? Do you agree with the rulings in these cases?

b. Contrary Approaches

Two New Jersey Supreme Court opinions which are often cited as showing the potential reach of the Restatement doctrine both couched the description of the relevant activity in terms that assured compliance with § 520(c). In State, Department of Environmental Protection v. Ventron, 94 N.J. 473, 468 A.2d 150 (N.J. 1983), the court overruled a century-old decision, and adopted the doctrine of Rylands v. Fletcher. *Ventron* involved mercury pollution from a processing plant from which mercury-laden effluent had escaped and reached a creek that flowed into a tidal estuary. The court adopted a sweeping proposition that "a land owner is strictly liable to others for harm caused by toxic wastes that are stored on his property and flow onto the property of others." After tracing the history of *Rylands* in New Jersey, it adopted the Restatement (Second) formulation which it believed incorporated the standard of *Rylands*. As to clause (c), the entire analysis consisted of this statement: "With respect to the ability to eliminate the risks involved in disposing of hazardous wastes by the exercise of reasonable care, no safe way exists to *dispose of mercury by simply dumping it onto land or into water*." Id. at 160. By characterizing the activity and focusing on the end result—"dumping it onto land or into water," the court could easily find that due care at that point in the sequence of events could not possibly prevent harm from occurring. Thus, *Ventron* demonstrates at the other end of the definitional process—with a particularized description *after* the result of the activity takes place—how the activity can be characterized is outcome determinative.

The New Jersey Supreme Court used the same post hoc characterization in T & E Industries v. Safety Light Corp., 123 N.J. 371, 587 A.2d 1249 (N.J. 1991), in a case involving disposal of radium tailings. The court never really purported to undertake a factor-by-factor analysis under § 520; instead, it simply concluded:

> Furthermore, although the risks involved in the processing and disposal of radium might be curtailed, *one cannot safely dispose of radium by dumping it onto the vacant portions of an urban lot*. Because of the extraordinarily-hazardous nature of radium, the processing and disposal of that substance is particularly inappropriate in an urban setting. We conclude that despite the usefulness of radium, defendant's processing, handling, and disposal of that substance under the facts of this case constituted an abnormally-dangerous activity.

Regardless of these New Jersey decisions, it is evident that many courts describe the "activity" in its benign, pre-injury-causing condition, and as a consequence conclude that reasonable care could have prevented the risk of harm. In both *Ventron* and *T & E Industries* if the activity is viewed as management of mercury or radium in the manufacturing processes, then the exercise of reasonable care could have avoided the dumping of mercury or the disposal of radium tailings. The court is probably correct in its conclusion that once radium or mercury is dumped into the soil or groundwater reasonable care can't eliminate the high degree of risk—but is that not the proper characterization of the activity? See, also, Albahary v. City and Town of Bristol, 963 F.Supp. 150, 155 (D.Conn.1997). ("Because hazardous materials are an instrumentality capable of producing harm, and because the circumstances and conditions of its disposal into a municipal landfill, irrespective of a lawful purpose or due care, involve a substantial risk of probable injury to the person or property of others, the Court concludes that disposal of hazardous and toxic wastes at a landfill may constitute an abnormally dangerous or ultrahazardous activity sufficient to maintain a cause of action for strict liability.'')

7. EFFECT OF GOVERNMENT REGULATIONS

a. *Regulations As Implying that Due Care Is the Test*

In many recent cases, especially in the environmental field, the activity under consideration has been the subject of government regulations that prescribe how the activity is to be safely undertaken. This fact can influence the § 520 analysis in at least two ways. Some decisions have stated or implied that such regulations strongly support the inference that due care can produce reasonable safety, so that the activity is not abnormally dangerous. Thus, a federal district court in Schwartzman v. General Electric Co., 848 F.Supp. 942 (D.N.M.1993), in analyzing the disposal of hazardous substances at a superfund site, concluded that "although hazardous material and petroleum products may present a substantial degree of risk when mishandled, * * * [these] risks can be eliminated through the exercise of reasonable care." As its rationale it offered this: "Indeed, the premise of many environmental laws (RCRA; Toxic Substances Control Act, 15 U.S.C. §§ 2601 et seq.; Federal Insecticide, Fungicide, and Rodenticide Act, 7 U.S.C. §§ 136 et seq.) is that proper handling and disposal of these materials minimizes or eliminates the risk of their use."

In Arlington Forest, 774 F.Supp. 387 (E.D.Va.1991), a holding quoted earlier involving leaking underground storage tanks, the court observed what is obvious, that "advances in technology and safety standards continue to enhance safety," thereby demonstrating that negligence is the proper standard.

A Connecticut Superior Court in Sanchez v. General Urban Corp., 1997 WL 78176 (Conn.Super.Ct.1997), refused to apply strict liability to premises containing lead-based paint largely because of the extensive regulations governing the abatement of such painted surfaces. Although the plaintiffs argued that the regulatory scheme demonstrated the unavoidable risk of harm to minor children, the court rejected that position:

> The "regulations * * * demonstrate that the dangers associated with lead-based paint can be avoided, so long as landlords comply with the statutory and regulatory schemes governing lead-based paint." Thus, since the landlord, in the exercise of reasonable care, is able to eliminate the risk of lead-based paint through inspection and abatement of defective surfaces, the doctrine of abnormally dangerous activity is inapplicable.

Accord, Cadena v. Chicago Fireworks Manuf. Co., 297 Ill.App.3d 945, 232 Ill.Dec. 60, 697 N.E.2d 802, 814–15 (Ill.Ct.App.1998) (extensive regulation of fireworks supports finding that reasonable care would prevent harm.)

But some opinions have latched on to regulatory schemes as supporting the inference that the activity is one of extreme danger. For example, the New Jersey Supreme Court in State Department of Environmental Protection v. Ventron, 94 N.J. 473, 468 A.2d 150 (N.J. 1983), and the Utah Supreme Court in Branch v. Western Petroleum Inc., 657 P.2d 267 (Utah 1982), cited extensive regulations as supporting, not undermining, the application of § 520. In *Ventron,* the court suggested that the state's policy represented by a strict liability Spill Compensation Control Act, bolstered the arguments respecting the dangers of disposing of mercury. And in *Branch*, Utah's laws protecting surface and subterranean waters from oil pollution was supportive of a finding of abnormally dangerous activity.

b. Negligence Per Se

A second way in which regulatory systems can influence whether a court applies the doctrine of § 519 and § 520 is finding that noncompliance with the regulations constitutes negligence per se, a kind of "strict liability." Illustrative of this phenomenon is Bagley v. Controlled Environment Corp., 127 N.H. 556, 503 A.2d 823 (N.H. 1986), in which, as quoted earlier, the court rejected strict liability because there was no showing of the impossibility of proving negligence. However, Souter, J., found that plaintiff's case was saved by a violation of New Hampshire's waste disposal laws. Indeed, he used the statutory violation as a justification for *not* applying strict liability. He continues:

> While we therefore affirm the dismissal of the count in strict liability, it does not follow that the dangers of hazardous wastes will have no particular recognition in the law of the State, because we do hold that the plaintiff has stated a cause of action predicated on a statutory violation. It is well established law in this State that a causal violation of a statutory standard of conduct constitutes legal fault in the same manner as does the causal violation of a common-law standard of due care, that is, causal negligence. In both instances liability is imposed because of the existence of legal fault, that is, a departure from a required standard of conduct.

Id. at 826.

In other words, § 519 and § 520 must be read to incorporate *any* basis for a negligence action, including those predicated on negligence per se. This makes sense only if plaintiff can prove that no form of negligence is available, thereby warranting reliance on strict liability. After all, who needs § 520 and its complex set of factors if a claimant can sustain a cause of action for true "strict liability," that is, negligence per se.

The Connecticut Supreme Court, in Gore v. People's Savings Bank, 235 Conn. 360, 665 A.2d 1341 (Conn. 1995), employed similar reasoning in an action brought by minor children against a landlord for alleged poisoning from lead-based paints. The court held that a statute providing that the presence of paint containing lead in excess of federally pre-scribed standards, or the presence of certain flaking or peeling paint constituting a "health hazard," renders the premises uninhabitable and imposes a duty, the violation of which constitutes negligence per se.

The important topic of negligence per se is further taken up in Chapter 6.

8. ROLE OF COMMON USAGE AND LOCATIONAL APPROPRI-ATENESS

a. *The Restatement Explanation*

As to matters of common usage, the comments to subsection (d) of Restatement (Second) of Torts § 520 define such activities as those engaged in "by the great mass of mankind or by many people in the community." Comment *i*. To illustrate, the comment states that the use of automobiles is a common usage, whereas the use of explosives, the operation of oil wells, and blasting activities, while of significant social utility, are carried on only by a few persons and are therefore not common usage. What about oil well operations in certain areas of Alaska or Texas? Might they be so prevalent as to constitute a "common usage"?

Section 520(e) requires the court to assess the activity's appropriate-ness to the place where it is carried on in deciding whether it is *abnormally* dangerous. As explained in comment *j*: If the place is one inappropriate to the particular activity, and other factors are present, the danger created may be regarded as an abnormal one.

Even a magazine of high explosives, capable of destroying everything within a distance of half a mile, does not necessarily create an abnormal danger if it is located in the midst of a desert area, far from human habitation and all property of any considerable value. The same is true of a large storage tank filled with some highly inflammable liquid such as gasoline. Blasting, even with powerful high explosives, is not abnor-mally dangerous if it is done on an uninhabited mountainside, so far from anything of considerable value likely to be harmed that the risk if it does exist is not a serious one. On the other hand, the same magazine of explosives, the huge storage tank full of gasoline or the blasting opera-tions all become abnormally dangerous if they are carried on in the midst of a city. * * * In other words, the fact that the activity is inappropriate to the place where it is carried on is a factor of importance in determining whether the danger is an abnormal one. This is some-times expressed, particularly in the English cases, by saying there is strict liability for a "non-natural" use of the defendant's land.

b. *Exploration for Fuel, and its Transportation and Storage: Common Usage? Appropriate Locations?*

Clauses (d) and (e) of § 520 have also served to circumscribe the scope of liability, but have not had nearly the kind of effect that the rule of § 520(c) has produced. As we saw earlier Prosser was extremely anxious to reincorporate the non-natural user principle of *Rylands* into the black letter rule, and did so in § 520(e). He also retained the common usage test that Bohlen had formulated.

In Fletcher v. Conoco Pipe Line Co., 129 F.Supp.2d 1255 (W.D. Mo. 2001), the fuel pipeline-stray electricity litigation discussed above, the court was clear in its determination that transmission of natural gas and petroleum products was not so unusual as to be not a matter of common usage:

> The Court also finds that factors (d) and (f) weigh heavily against the application of strict liability. Factor (d) directs courts to consider the extent to which the activity is or is not a matter of common usage. Factor (f) examines the extent to which the value of the activity outweighs the potential danger. Various courts have observed that the transmission of natural gas and petroleum products by pipeline is a common activity in our highly-industrialized society. See Melso v. Sun Pipe Line Co., 394 Pa.Super. 578, 576 A.2d 999, 1003 (1990); New Meadows Holding Co. by Raugust v. Washington Water Power Co., 102 Wash.2d 495, 687 P.2d 212, 216 (1984) (holding that the transmission of natural gas is a matter of common usage and noting that roughly 720,900 miles of distribution pipelines crisscross communities nationwide). There is also general agreement that the transportation of petroleum products is a highly beneficial activity necessary for civilization as we know it. See Chaveriat, 1994 WL 583598, at *6.

A sampling of decisions place the primary reliance on the location of the activity, but as a general rule common usage and locational settings are not outcome determinative. In Yommer v. McKenzie, 255 Md. 220, 257 A.2d 138, 140 (Md. 1969), Maryland's highest court ruled that a service station's placement of underground storage tanks in proximity to residential water wells passed muster under the definition of § 520. The court concluded:

> The fifth and perhaps most crucial factor under the Institute's guidelines as applied to this case is the appropriateness of the activity in the particular place where it is being carried on. No one would deny that gasoline stations as a rule do not present any particular danger to the community. However, when the operation of such activity involves the placing of a large tank adjacent to a well from which a family must draw its water for drinking, bathing and laundry, at least that aspect of the activity is inappropriate to the locale, even when equated to the value of the activity.

See also Tutu Wells Contamination Litigation, 846 F.Supp. 1243 (D.V.I.1993) "It may well be, as Defendants contend, that operation and ownership of service stations is a matter of common usage and that it is not unusual today to find service stations in residential areas. But where, as here, the risk of seepage is contamination of the area's precious and limited water supply, locating the storage tanks above the aquifer created an abnormally dangerous and inappropriate use of the land." Id. at 1269.

Some decisions involving underground storage tanks decided subsequent to *Yommer* have held that reasonable precautions could have prevented their leakage, thereby nullifying strict liability. See, e.g., Arlington Forest Assoc. v. Exxon Corp., 774 F.Supp. 387, 391 (E.D.Va. 1991); Hudson v. Peavey Oil Co., 279 Or. 3, 566 P.2d 175, 178 (Or.1977); Smith v. Weaver, 445 Pa.Super. 461, 665 A.2d 1215, 1219–20 (Pa.Super.1995); Walker Drug Co. v. La Sal Oil Co., 902 P.2d 1229, 1233 (Utah 1995); Grube v. Daun, 213 Wis.2d 533, 570 N.W.2d 851, 856–57 (Wis. 1997). Unlike archetypical abnormally dangerous activities such as blasting, there is no evidence to suggest "that the risk of seepage [from USTs] cannot be eliminated by the exercise of reasonable care, or that the harm to be anticipated from the underground seepage of gasoline is 'grave'." *Hudson*, 566 P.2d at 178; see also *Smith*, 665 A.2d at 1220 ("Gasoline and other petroleum products can be stored and dispensed safely with reasonable care."); *Walker Drug Co.*, 902 P.2d at 1233 ("[W]e are not convinced that the risk cannot be eliminated by the exercise of reasonable care,"); *Grube*, 570 N.W.2d at 857 ("Absent negligence or application of an outside force, use of a UST does not create a high degree of risk of harm to the person, land or chattels of another. Moreover those risks that do exist can be minimized by the exercise of reasonable care by the owner or possessor of the tank."). Perhaps because reasonable care will typically guard against any harm that USTs may inflict, "the storage of [gasoline] in tanks is a common use and is valuable to a modern society." *Smith*, 665 A.2d at 1220; see also *Walker Drug Co.*, 902 P.2d at 1233 ("[T]he operation of a gas station is common, appropriate, and of significant value to the community."); *Arlington Forest*, 774 F.Supp. at 391 (holding that gasoline stations fulfill essential transportation needs in modern society).

c. *Other Applications of Factors (d) and (e)*

A Pennsylvania court has held that the storage of a highly toxic pesticide was a matter of common usage, and hence was not an abnormally dangerous activity, because of testimony that 4 million of the 36 million acres of U.S. farmland treated with any pesticide, were treated with the pesticide Thimet. Diffenderfer v. Staner, 722 A.2d 1103, 1108 (Pa.Super.1998). The Kansas Supreme Court, in turn, held that the drilling and operation of natural gas wells is not abnormally dangerous because the operation of wells in "the Hugoton Gas Field is a matter of common usage and is an appropriate activity for the place it is carried on–i.e., it does not constitute a non-natural use of the land." Williams v. Amoco Production Co., 241 Kan. 102, 734 P.2d 1113, 1123 (Kan. 1987).

In contrast, the Alaska Supreme Court held that storage of 80,000 pounds of explosives in a suburban area was locationally inappropriate, despite the fact that storage took place on land designated for that purpose by the United States government, because the population of the area had grown since the designation. Yukon Equipment, Inc. v. Fireman's Fund Insurance Co., 585 P.2d 1206, 1210 (Alaska 1978). But a New Mexico Court of Appeals rejected that view, holding that the storage of explosives, as opposed to blasting, was not inappropriately located although placed near electrical boxes. Otero v. Burgess, 84 N.M. 575, 505 P.2d 1251 (N.M.Ct.App.1973).

You saw earlier that some courts (particularly in New Jersey) have held that disposal of hazardous wastes constituted an abnormally dangerous activity, placing emphasis on the dangerousness of waste disposal and that it was not common usage nor in a proper place. See, e.g., State, DEP v. Ventron, 94 N.J. 473, 468 A.2d 150 (N.J. 1983); T & E Industries v. Safety Light Corp., 123 N.J. 371, 587 A.2d 1249 (N.J. 1991). But a Wisconsin appeals court, focusing on the degree of knowledge of the dangers posed by disposal of hazardous materials at a landfill, concluded that "depositing compounds containing VOCs at the landfill was a matter of common usage." Indeed, when the defendants continued to deposit such materials after regulations made it unlawful to do so, it was still deemed "part of a common usage;" however, because the landfill license did not permit such disposal "the companies' use of the landfill was inappropriate to the place it was carried on." Fortier v. Flambeau Plastics Company, 164 Wis.2d 639, 476 N.W.2d 593, 600 (Wis.Ct.App. 1991).

And finally, how about the impoundment of millions of gallons of phosphate slime behind earthen walls in connection with the mining of phosphate rock? The earthen walls break—even with the best of care—causing extensive damage to property located miles away. The Florida court upholds strict liability because of the magnitude of the activity and its attendant risk of enormous damage, despite accepting defendant's contention that the activity was a suitable use of the land. Cities Service Co. v. State of Florida, 312 So.2d 799, 801 (Fla.Ct.App.1975).

All of this points in one direction: Liability does not rise or fall on common usage or locational suitability; the cases are all over the map on these factors.

9. VALUE TO THE COMMUNITY

The cases are mixed in their recognition of this factor of § 520. Judge Posner in *Indiana Harbor Belt* makes virtually no mention of clause (f) and one is left with the impression that perhaps he too regards it as superfluous to the analysis.

Few cases discuss this issue in any depth, and the "value" which the activity provides is more a matter of judicial notice than an evidentiary record. For example, the Pennsylvania Superior Court simply summarily declared that gasoline service stations are "valuable to modern society," a statement that seems nothing more than a truism. Smith v. Weaver, 445 Pa.Super. 461, 665 A.2d 1215, 1220 (Pa.Super.1995) (finding underground storage tanks not abnormally dangerous activity); See Walker Drug Co. v. La Sal Oil Co., 902 P.2d 1229, 1233 (Utah 1995) (gas station "of significant value to the community"); Grube v. Daun, 213 Wis.2d 533, 570 N.W.2d 851, 857 (Wis. 1997) ("at the time the allegedly hazardous activity took place, the value to the community of having USTs was believed to outweigh any danger from their use."). Another Pennsylvania decision was equally unenlightening, declaring that the community value of a reservoir outweighed its dangerous attributes. Albig v. Municipal Authority of Westmoreland County, 348 Pa.Super. 505, 502 A.2d 658 (1985). See also Cadena v. Chicago Fireworks Manufacturing Co., 297 Ill.App.3d 945, 232 Ill.Dec. 60, 697 N.E.2d 802, 815 (Ill.Ct.App.1998) ("value of fireworks displays to the community does * * * outweigh their dangerous attributes," with no explanation). The Rhode Island Supreme Court similarly concluded, in a case involving the release of asbestos fibers as part of a building demolition and clean up project:

> Finally, and perhaps most importantly, the value to the community of Certified's activities far outweighed its dangerous attributes. Cleanup operations serve the valuable and essential social function of reducing the danger of potentially harmful substances such as asbestos. Therefore, public policy, as well as the other factors listed in Restatement (Second) of Torts § 520, support our conclusion that Certified could not on the facts present in this case be held strictly liable for its activities.

Splendorio v. Bilray Demolition Co., 682 A.2d 461, 466 (R.I.1996) (citation omitted).

Accord, Ganton Technologies, Inc. v. Quadion Corp., 834 F.Supp. 1018, 1020 (N.D.Ill. E.D. 1993) (clean up of PCB's from an industrial site is not an abnormally dangerous activity that warrants the application of strict liability because of its importance to the community).

Finally, a Wisconsin court, in considering contamination of water wells emanating from a landfill at which defendants had deposited VOCs, which after 1969 violated regulatory standards, concluded that the activity was not abnormally dangerous because "the fact remains * * * that after 1969 the value to the community of the use of the landfill for VOC waste continued as before to outweigh its dangerous attributes." Fortier v. Flambeau Plastics Company, 164 Wis.2d 639, 476 N.W.2d 593, 608 (Wis.Ct.App.1991).

Many decisions suggest that factor (f) will just be ignored or given short shrift. For example, in Green v. Ensign–Bickford Company, 25 Conn.App. 479, 595 A.2d 1383 (Conn. Ct. App. 1991), in a case involving damage resulting from an explosives manufacturer's experimentation with a highly explosive chemical, the court did hold that it was an ultrahazardous activity. It concluded that "the record is devoid of facts to satisfy this [factor]" and since "all six factors do not need to be satisfied," it could find the activity abnormally dangerous.

The New Jersey Supreme Court in State, DEP v. Ventron, 94 N.J. 473, 468 A.2d 150, 160 (N.J. 1983), made only a cursory and oblique reference to § 520(f), commenting that:

> We recognize that one engaged in the disposing of toxic waste may be performing an activity that is of some use to society. Nonetheless, the unavoidable risk of harm that is inherent in it requires that it be carried on at his peril, rather than at the expense of the innocent person who suffers harms as a result of it.

This too is full of truisms, and perhaps the court is really saying that whatever community value may be associated with dumping mercury-laden wastes into a waterway, it is irrelevant to the court's commitment to enterprise liability for dangerous activities. That interpretation finds support in T & E Industries v. Safety Light Corp., 123 N.J. 371, 587 A.2d 1249 (N.J. 1991), where the same court referenced the lack of common usage and locational appropriateness in the dumping of radium tailings, but never cited § 520(f) nor discussed value to the community, but instead described, at some length, the principle of enterprise responsibility. It is quite clear that whatever value to the community might have been assigned to defendant's activities, that factor would not have influenced the court's holding one iota. See, also, In re Tutu Wells Contamination Litigation, 846 F.Supp. 1243, 1270 (D.V.I.1993) (the court concluded that "the community's interest in a clean water supply far outweighs the benefits of the service station to the community.").

10. QUESTION OF LAW: WHO DOES THE BALANCING?

a. *Function of the Court*

Whether the activity is an abnormally dangerous one is to be determined by the Court, upon consideration of all the factors listed in this section, and the weight given to each that it merits upon the facts in evidence. In this it differs from questions of negligence. * * * The standard of the hypothetical reasonable [person] is essentially a jury standard, in which the Court interferes only in the clearest cases. * * * The imposition of strict liability, on the other hand, involves a characterization of the defendant's activity or enterprise itself, and a decision as to whether he is free to conduct it at all without becoming subject to liability for the harm that ensues even though he has used all reasonable care. This calls for a decision of the Court; and it is no part of the province of the jury to decide whether an industrial enterprise upon which the community's prosperity might depend is located in the wrong place or whether such an activity as blasting is to be permitted without liability in the center of a large city.

Restatement (Second) of Torts § 520 comment i.

One advantage of the abnormally dangerous doctrine is that it enables the parties to secure a determination of whether it applies at the summary judgment stage of the case. Is the Restatement correct that the balancing under § 520 strict liability is fundamentally different from that involved in negligence? What were the likely motivations for making the finding of whether an activity is abnormally dangerous a function for the court?

Despite the widespread adoption of strict liability Restatement formulation of §§ 519 and 520, some jurisdictions continue to reject the notion of a separate theory of strict liability for abnormally dangerous activities. See, e.g., Doddy v. OXY, USA, Inc., 101 F.3d 448 (5th Cir. 1996) (concluding that the Texas Supreme Court has rejected the doctrine and would not in any event apply it to the escape of toxic chemicals from oil and gas wells); Nevada didn't recognize the doctrine until 1993. See, Valentine v. Pioneer Chlor Alkali Co., 109 Nev. 1107, 864 P.2d 295 (Nev. 1993).

At the other end of the spectrum a few courts apply the strict liability doctrine, but in the form expressed in Rylands v. Fletcher, without the Restatement's elaborate balancing process. For example, in Evans v. Mutual Mining Co., 199 W.Va. 526, 485 S.E.2d 695 (W.Va. 1997), the West Virginia Supreme Court of Appeals ruled, after quoting *Rylands*, that a mining company was strictly liable for damages suffered by owners of homes when a sediment pond maintained by the company broke, sending water, mud and debris down a mountain onto their properties.

b. Inconsistent Findings: Disposal of Hazardous Waste

You might be surprised to learn that the courts that have considered whether the disposal of hazardous wastes and chemicals is an abnormally dangerous activity are hopelessly inconsistent. Decisions cited earlier in this chapter revealed that the activity of placing underground storage tanks in connection with gasoline service stations is not abnormally dangerous. But how about a business that intentionally disposes of waste on its property that migrates to other properties and causes harm to water wells and the occupants? Here too no firm rule can be drawn.

A federal district court in Connecticut noted that the courts' rulings in that state were not uniform. In Albahary v. City of Bristol, 963 F.Supp. 150 (D.Conn.1997), it held that the operation of a landfill that accepted hazardous materials did qualify for strict liability, thereby distinguishing those decisions involving other kinds of businesses for whom the disposal of waste was incidental and not the purpose of the operation:

> A critical difference between the factual posture of Barnes and those of *Arawana Mills, Nielsen,* and *Stop and Shop* is that the former dealt with direct disposal of hazardous contaminants into

soil, resulting from the purposeful business activity of running a landfill. The latter cases address storage of such contaminants in connection with the operation of other businesses, which presents a different legal and factual problem. * * * [One court reasoned] that although a substance may be dangerous if dumped on the soil or fatal if swallowed or inhaled, it does not necessarily follow that when the substance is reasonably handled and safely stored as part of the industrial or business activity in which it is used, the use or storage of the substances should be defined as an ultrahazardous activity. In short, not all hazardous materials are highly corrosive and are therefore incapable of being stored safely.

A landfill that accepts hazardous materials for purpose of disposal stands on a different footing than a machine shop whose purpose is to repair engines, and whose storage and use of hazardous materials is incidental to that repair business. Indeed, as the court concluded in *Barnes*, disposal of hazardous and toxic wastes at a municipal landfill involves a high degree of risk of harm to property and persons, which unlike storage and use of hazardous materials, cannot be eliminated by the exercise of reasonable care.

Here, plaintiffs allege that: The Defendant has caused and allowed the disposal of hazardous wastes and substances in the Bristol landfill in a manner that has resulted in the pollution and contamination of the soil, ground, and water beneath the Norton land with volatile organic compounds and other substances. The Defendant's activities in operating and managing the Bristol landfill includes [sic] operating it as an open dump, as defined by federal law; allowing the discharge in the landfill of hazardous wastes and substances; and operating the landfill without a liner, which allows the migration of a leachate plume from the landfill onto adjacent, privately owned property.

Compl. ¶ 4, 963 F.Supp. at 154–156.

See Barnes v. General Electric Co., 1995 WL 447904 (Conn. Super.1995) (landfill disposal–strict liability applies); Arawana Mills Co. v. United Technologies, 795 F.Supp. 1238 (D.Conn.1992) (machine shop handled, stored and released hazardous chemicals into soil–no strict liability); Nielsen v. Sioux Tools, Inc., 870 F.Supp. 435 (D.Conn.1994) (machine shop and distribution center deposited hazardous substances into a leaking underground storage tank).

What do you think of this distinction? Is it viable? Take the six factors from § 520 and assess each one in the landfill context versus the machine shop context. Which factors seem to weigh more heavily toward strict liability for landfills?

How about the generators of waste that is deposited at a landfill and escapes to cause harm? In Fortier v. Flambeau Plastics Co., 164 Wis.2d 639, 476 N.W.2d 593 (Wis.Ct.App.1991), the court, in an exhaustive analysis of the six factors, concluded that strict liability did not apply.

c. *Sale of Product Does Not Qualify*

What if plaintiffs sustained personal injuries and property damage from contamination that emanated from a battery recycling facility that contained hazardous lead deposits. Can these plaintiffs pursue a strict liability claim against the businesses that sold batteries to the facility operator? The Alabama Supreme Court in S.B. Thompson v. Mindis Metals, Inc., 692 So.2d 805, 806–807 (Ala.1997) held no:

> Thompson argues that this Court should expand the common law doctrine of strict liability to encompass the sale of batteries to the recycling facility. In Harper v. Regency Development Co., 399 So.2d 248, 253 (Ala.1981), this Court held that "[strict] liability for an abnormally dangerous activity arises out of the intrinsic danger of the ultrahazardous activity itself and the risk of harm it creates to those in the vicinity." (emphasis added) (citing Restatement (Second) of Torts, § 519, cmt. *d* (1977)). For example, the use of high explosives near a populated area is an ultrahazardous activity because reasonable care cannot eliminate the danger inherent in that activity. In contrast, the sale of firearms in and of itself has been held not to constitute an ultrahazardous activity. See Hammond v. Colt Indus. Oper. Corp., 565 A.2d 558, 562–63 (Del.Super.1989) (refusing to apply strict liability concept in the Restatement of Torts to sale of firearms because the sale of the products, as opposed to their use, is not abnormally dangerous). The sale of whole batteries is even less hazardous than the sale of firearms, and it certainly is not an ultrahazardous activity. The lead contamination alleged by Thompson did not result from the sale of the batteries. Instead, it came from the operations conducted by the recycling facility. Consequently, this claim is without merit.

Accord, City of Bloomington v. Westinghouse Electric Corp., 891 F.2d 611, 615 (7th Cir.1989) (held: sale by chemical company of PCBs to electrical equipment manufacturers for use as insulating material not subject to strict liability, when one of its customers used the PCBs in its plant and deposited waste containing PCBs at landfills):

> Here the harm to the City's sewage and landfill was not caused by any abnormally dangerous activity of Monsanto but by the buyer's failure to safeguard its waste. In denying liability for an ultrahazardous activity here, the district court pointed out that Monsanto did not control the PCBs contained in Westinghouse's waste. This accords with the Restatement view because the Restatement confines strict liability to "[o]ne who carries on an abnormally dangerous activity." Restatement § 519(1). Here that definition would include Westinghouse but not Monsanto.

d. Operation of Uranium Metals Production Plant Does Qualify

In Crawford v. National Lead Co., 784 F.Supp. 439, 442–443 (S.D.Ohio 1989), the court held that defendant's operation of a federally-owned uranium metals production plant that emitted uranium and other harmful materials was subject to strict liability. After quoting §§ 519 and 520, it continued:

> We have little difficulty in concluding that the operation of the FMPC is an abnormally dangerous activity. The comments to the factors (a), (b), and (c), section 520, listed above, note that these factors are satisfied by activities involving atomic energy, and we agree with the reasoning of the American Law Institute as expressed in these comments. The production of uranium is clearly not a matter of common usage, as it is not "customarily carried on by the great mass of mankind or by many people in the community." Restatement (Second) of Torts § 510, Comment on Clause (d). The production of uranium metals at the FMPC is inappropriate to the place where it is carried on, because the government and defendants recognized when the plant was built that some hazardous materials would seep into property, springs, rivers, and wells owned or utilized by the neighboring public, and such production is clearly within the meaning of "non-natural use" as described in Rylands v. Fletcher. Finally, there is no indication that the FMPC's value to the Fernald community is greater than the danger it represents. Accordingly, we have no doubt that Ohio courts would consider the production of uranium at the FMPC an abnormally dangerous activity.

11. KNOWLEDGE OF THE DANGER OR FORESEEABILITY OF HARM AS A PREREQUISITE TO STRICT LIABILITY

T&E INDUSTRIES v. SAFETY LIGHT CORPORATION

Supreme Court of New Jersey, 1991.
123 N.J. 371, 587 A.2d 1249.

[In this portion of the opinion the court addresses whether the depositing of radium tailings constituted an abnormally dangerous activity. The court quotes the six factors from Restatement (Second) of Torts § 520 and then continues its analysis:]

B

We focus now on the elements of the abnormally-dangerous-activity doctrine. That doctrine is premised on the principle that "one who carries on an abnormally dangerous activity is subject to liability for harm to the person, land or chattels of another resulting from the activity, although he has exercised the utmost care to prevent the harm." Restatement (Second) of Torts § 519. The Restatement sets forth six factors that a court should consider in determining whether an activity is "abnormally dangerous." [Restatement (Second) of Torts, supra, § 520.]

* * * Because of the interplay of [those] factors, it is not possible to reduce abnormally dangerous activities to any definition. Thus, a court must make the determination about the abnormally-dangerous character of an activity one case at a time. The Appellate Division failed to observe that mandate in this case and consequently gave Ventron too broad a reading in concluding that "the processing of radium and the disposal of its waste product is an abnormally dangerous activity as a matter of law."

Defendant does not dispute that liability can be imposed on enterprises who engage in abnormally-dangerous activities that harm others; but it contends that such liability is contingent on proof that the enterpriser knew or should have known of the "abnormally dangerous character of the activity." According to defendant, absent such knowledge the enterpriser "is in no position to make the cost-benefit calculations that will enable him to spread the risk and engage in the optimal level of activity." Defendant argues that absent such an opportunity, the policy basis for imposing strict liability on those who engage in abnormally-dangerous activities, namely, cost spreading, cannot be realized.

Defendant adds that knowledge, or the ability to acquire such knowledge, must be assessed as of the time the enterpriser engaged in the activity, not at a later time—that is, if the risk of harm from the activity was scientifically unknowable at that time, an enterpriser should not be held liable. Defendant also insists that the inquiry must focus on the enterpriser's ability to learn of the risks inherent in the precise activity that causes harm, not merely of the hazards inherent in the business in general. Thus, defendant stresses that strict liability should be imposed in this case only if USRC knew in 1926 of the specific dangers inherent in the discarded tailings, not simply of those associated with the processing and handling of radium.

Defendant's argument poses an interesting question concerning the availability of a state-of-the-art defense—that is, the risk of the activity was scientifically unknowable at the time—to a strict-liability claim for abnormally-dangerous activities. It is a question we need not resolve here, however, because state-of-the-art becomes an issue only if we agree that knowledge is a prerequisite for strict-liability claims and if we accept defendant's narrow view of the "knowledge" inquiry.

* * *

[R]equirements such as "knowledge" and "foreseeability" smack of negligence and may be inappropriate in the realm of strict liability.

We need not, however, determine whether knowledge is a requirement in the context of a strict-liability claim predicated on an abnormally-dangerous activity. Even if the law imposes such a requirement, we are convinced, for the reasons set forth more fully below, that defendant should have known about the risks of its activity, and that its constructive knowledge would fully satisfy any such requirement.

C

That brings us to the question of whether defendant's activity was such as to fall within the meaning of "abnormally-dangerous activity." As indicated above, our opinion in [State DEP v. Ventron, 468 A.2d 150 (N.J.1983)] instructs that in making such a determination a court must consider the factors set forth in the Restatement of Torts. As in Ventron, we apply those factors to the circumstances in this case.

Radium has always been and continues to be an extraordinarily-dangerous substance. Although radium processing has never been a common activity, the injudicious handling, processing, and disposal of radium has for decades caused concern; it has long been suspected of posing a serious threat to the health of those who are exposed to it. The harm that can result from excess radium exposure, namely, cancer, is undoubtedly great. In light of those suspicions and the magnitude of the harm, it is not surprising that in the 1930s and 1940s experts concluded that radon exposure should be limited. Wisely, the government now regulates such exposure.

Furthermore, although the risks involved in the processing and disposal of radium might be curtailed, one cannot safely dispose of radium by dumping it onto the vacant portions of an urban lot. Because of the extraordinarily-hazardous nature of radium, the processing and disposal of that substance is particularly inappropriate in an urban setting. We conclude that despite the usefulness of radium, defendant's processing, handling, and disposal of that substance under the facts of this case constituted an abnormally-dangerous activity. * * * Because plaintiff vacated the premises in response to the health concerns posed by the radium-contaminated site and because the danger to health is "the kind of harm, the possibility of which [made defendant's] activity abnormally dangerous," defendant is strictly liable for the resulting harm. Restatement of Torts, supra, § 519. Defendant's asserted lack of knowledge cannot relieve it of that liability.

Recall that defendant argues that the knowledge required is of the precise dangers associated with the disposal of the tailings, not merely those inherent in the processing and handling of radium. Defendant has not, however, cited any authority that supports such a narrow inquiry, nor do we believe that the focus should be that narrow.

Here defendant knew that it was processing radium, a substance concededly fraught with hazardous potential. It knew that its employees who handled radium should wear protective clothing; it knew that some employees who had ingested radium had developed cancer; and prior to the sale of the property, it knew that the inhalation of radon could cause lung cancer. Despite that wealth of knowledge concerning the harmful effects of radium exposure, defendant contends that it could not have known that disposal of the radium-saturated by-products behind the plant would produce a hazard. That contention appears to rest on the idea that somehow the radium's potential for harm miraculously disappeared once the material had been deposited in a vacant corner of an urban lot, or at the least that one might reasonably reach that conclusion—a proposition that we do not accept.

Surely someone engaged in a business as riddled with hazards as defendant's demonstrably was should realize the potential for harm in every aspect of that dangerous business. If knowledge be a requirement, defendant knew enough about the abnormally-dangerous character of radium processing to be charged with knowledge of the dangers of disposal.

* * *

Notes and Questions

1.　A question raised but not resolved by the principal case is whether defendant's knowledge or appreciation of the danger should be a prerequisite to strict liability. What is your opinion? In Chapter 7, we explore that issue as it relates to toxic products where the courts have generally held that a party may defend on the ground that a risk was not scientifically knowable. This defense is sometimes referred to inexactly as the state-of-the-art defense, but is more accurately described as the state-of-knowledge defense. If the state of knowledge is relevant in abnormally dangerous activity cases, should it be plaintiff's burden to establish that the defendant had knowledge of its abnormally dangerous character? Should it be sufficient that reasonable persons in defendant's shoes would have known? Or should any knowledge within the relevant technical, industrial, or scientific communities be sufficient for liability? How should society's ever-increasing understanding of environmental dangers be accounted for in strict liability cases? Rather than place the burden of proof on plaintiff, should it be considered as an affirmative defense where the defendant bears the burden of pleading and proof on the issue?

2.　On the facts in *T & E Industries*, did defendant really have knowledge of the dangerousness of buried *tailings*, as opposed to the dangers associated with use of radium by its employees? Does knowledge of the latter necessarily imply knowledge of the former? Does it matter that other firms similarly situated as USRC in the 1920s and 1930s also buried their tailings? On this point, see Fortier v. Flambeau Plastics Co., 164 Wis.2d 639, 476 N.W.2d 593 (Wis.Ct.App.1991), where the court held that defendant generators of hazardous waste did not engage in abnormally dangerous activity by depositing such wastes in city-owned landfills because it was a matter of common usage, engaged in by households, municipalities, and private industry, and was entirely lawful when done. Moreover, it concluded that the value to the community of such practices outweighed the dangers, as then perceived, that it created. How might these points bear on the state of knowledge issue?

3.　Few cases actually address this issue. See, Perez v. Southern Pacific Transp. Co., 180 Ariz. 187, 883 P.2d 424 (Ariz.Ct.App.1993) (hindsight test rejected in favor of foreseeability test). The most authoritative of all sources as to the meaning of Rylands v. Fletcher, the English House of Lords, issued an extremely important opinion in 1994 in Cambridge Water Co. v. Eastern Counties Leather Plc, [1994] 2 A.C. 264 (H.L.), 2 W.L.R. 53. Eastern Counties Leather Plc (ECL) had regularly spilled organochlorines, a solvent used in its tanning process, at its tannery prior to 1976. The organochlorines had polluted the groundwater beneath the tannery and had migrated to a borehole at Sawston Mill, a distance of 1.3 miles. Cambridge Water Company (CWC), a public water supply company, had purchased the borehole in 1976, having tested the water extracted from it to ensure that the water was suitable for public supply purposes by the standards that then applied. But, in 1980, the Council of the European Community issued a directive imposing stricter limits on the amount of organochlorines permitted in drinking water. In accordance with the directive, the Department of the Environment issued a circular in 1982 prohibiting water that exceeded the limits from being used for public supply purposes after 1985. The Sawston Mill borehole was closed in October 1983 when it was learned that water extracted from it exceeded the permitted limits. The loss of the Sawston Mill borehole meant that, in order to meet its supply needs, CWC had to develop a new source of water at a cost of nearly £1 million (roughly $2.8 million).

CWC, with the aid of the British Geological Survey, traced the source of the organochlorines to ECL and, possibly, another tannery in the area. CWC subsequently sued ECL and the other tannery for damages under causes of action based on nuisance, negligence, and the ruling in Rylands v. Fletcher. The judge at first instance, Mr. Justice Ian Kennedy, held that although ECL had polluted the groundwater extracted by CWC from its borehole at Sawston Mill, ECL was not liable to CWC in nuisance or in negligence, because both causes of action required the defendant to foresee the consequences of its actions, and a reasonable tannery supervisor could not have foreseen that the pollution of the Sawston Mill borehole would be a consequence of the spillage. The judge also held that ECL was not liable under the ruling in Rylands v. Fletcher. The judge considered that this rule, which imposes strict liability for the natural consequences of the escape of a substance *"likely to do mischief"* which had been brought onto, or accumulated on, land, was subject to an exception for a "natural" use of land. The judge took the view that the tannery was situated in an "industrial village" and that the use of organochlorines to clean pelts in 20th century England was a natural use of the land.

The court of appeal reversed, holding that CWC was entitled to extract water from beneath its land as a "natural right" and was entitled to receive the water in its natural state, unpolluted by the organochlorines used in the tannery process. In the view of the court of appeal, CWC did not have to prove that ECL foresaw or should have foreseen the consequence of spilling the organochlorines and allowing them to escape from its land.

The House of Lords held that ECL was not liable to CWC because ECL could not reasonably have foreseen, at the time it used organochlorines in its tanning process, that the spillage of organochlorines would lead to any environmental hazard or damage at CWC's borehole. The House of Lords also rejected any argument that, from a later date, ECL should be liable for the continuing escape of organochlorines from the pools of chemical still in existence at the base of the aquifer beneath the tannery's premises because the organochlorines had "passed beyond the control of ECL" and "had become irretrievably lost in the ground below."

The House of Lords further held that, although the natural or ordinary use of land remains an exception to the rule in Rylands v. Fletcher, the storage of substantial quantities of chemicals on industrial premises such as a tannery was "an almost classic case of non-natural use." Thus, if CWC had been able to prove that ECL knew or should reasonably have known that the escape of the organochlorines could pollute groundwater and render it unfit for public supply purposes, ECL would have been liable to CWC for damages.

Returning to the question of whether foreseeability was a requirement of nuisance liability, Lord Goff concluded that it was. A defendant was not liable in nuisance or negligence for damage of a type that he could not reasonably foresee [citing the second *Wagon Mound* case Overseas Tankship Ltd. v. Miller Steamship Co. (The Wagon Mound) (No. 2), 1 A.C. 617 (1967)]. Lord Goff reasoned:

> [T]he development of the law of negligence in the past 60 years points strongly towards a requirement that such foreseeability should be a prerequisite of liability in damages for nuisance, as it is of liability in negligence. For if a plaintiff is in ordinary circumstances only able to claim damages in respect of personal injuries where he can prove such foreseeability on the part of the defendant, it is difficult to see why, in common justice, he should be in a stronger position to claim damages for interference with the enjoyment of his land where the defendant was unable to foresee such damage.

2 A.C. at 300

Against this background Lord Goff turned to the defendant's contention that a similar foreseeability rule applied to liability under the rule in Rylands v. Fletcher. In the portion of his judgment expressing the "rule," Blackburn J. spoke of keeping on land "anything *likely* to do mischief if it escapes," liability to "answer for the natural *and anticipated* consequences" of its escape, and a person who has brought something onto his property "which he *knows* to be mischievous if it gets on his neighbour's." Knowledge, or at least foreseeability, of the risk was thus a prerequisite for liability. Furthermore, "the historical connection [of *Rylands*] with the law of nuisance must now be regarded as pointing towards the conclusion that foreseeability of damage is a prerequisite of the recovery of damages" under the rule in Rylands v. Fletcher. As recovery of damages in private nuisance depended on foreseeability by the defendant of the relevant type of damage, it would appear logical to extend the same requirement to liability under Rylands v. Fletcher. *Id.* at 304.

Further, Goff noted that as a general rule, it was more appropriate for strict liability in respect of high risk operations to be imposed by Parliament than by the courts. If such liability was imposed by statute, the relevant activities could be identified and precise criteria for the incidence and scope of liability could be established. "[T]hose concerned can know where they stand."

It was of particular relevance that the present case was concerned with environmental pollution.

The protection and preservation of the environment is now perceived as being of crucial importance to the future of mankind; and public bodies, both national and international, are taking significant steps towards the establishment of legislation which will promote the protection of the environment, and make the polluter pay for damage to the environment for which he is responsible. * * * But is does not follow from these developments that a common law principle, such as the rule in Rylands v. Fletcher, should be developed or rendered more strict to provide for liability in respect of such pollution. On the contrary, given that so much well-informed and carefully structured legislation is now being put in place for this purpose, there is less need for the courts to develop a common law principle to achieve the same end, and indeed it may well be undesirable that they should do so.

2 A.C. at 305.

Notes and Questions

1.   One authority summarizes the significance of the Cambridge Water Co. ruling as follows:

First, liability for contamination of underground water extracted by a plaintiff is governed by the law of nuisance and the rule in Rylands v. Fletcher. There is no special rule for such cases that makes liability more strict than under nuisance and Rylands v. Fletcher or that dispenses with a requirement that the damage be reasonably foreseeable.

Second, it is a prerequisite to damages liability in nuisance, as in negligence, that the harm be of a kind that is reasonably foreseeable. A defendant is not liable to a damages claim for harm of a type that was not reasonably foreseeable to the defendant.

Third, the rule in Rylands v. Fletcher properly is viewed as an extension of the law of nuisance to cases of isolated escape. It is not a distinctly different form of strict liability and it did not establish or lead to a general rule of strict liability for ultrahazardous activities.

Fourth, Rylands v. Fletcher liability is subject to the requirement of foreseeability of damage. A defendant is not liable to a damages claim under the rule in Rylands v. Fletcher for harm of a type that the defendant could not reasonably foresee.

Fifth, a defendant's knowledge that a substance may do harm if it escapes, acquired after the substance has passed beyond the defendant's control, is not the foreseeability required for liability. Foreseeability of a type of damage before a harmful substance escapes from the defendant's land does not satisfy the foreseeability requirement when the substance has already gone beyond the defendant's control, as when it is below the surface of the land and irretrievable.

Sixth, the natural use "exception" to Rylands v. Fletcher liability has come to mean ordinary use of land, but a use of land is not natural by virtue of its being common in the defendant's industry. Neither is it within the exception to liability by virtue of the benefit the community derives from the use of land, including industrial employment in an "industrial village." The storage of substantial quantities of chemicals on industrial premises, in an "industrial village" and elsewhere, is a non-natural use of land.

Kutner, The End of Rylands v. Fletcher? Cambridge Water Co. v. Eastern Counties Leather Plc., 31 Torts & Ins. L. J. 73, 88 (1995).

2. Notice how Lord Goff relied on legislative developments in the environmental field as a reason for *not* extending the rule in *Rylands* to reach unforeseeable consequences. What should be the role of federal and state environmental regulation in influencing the common-law tort rules?

3. For some academic literature on these topics, see Beggs, As Time Goes By: The Effect of Knowledge and the Passage of Time on the Abnormally Dangerous Activity Doctrine, 21 Hofstra L. Rev. 205 (1992).

C. RATIONALES FOR IMPOSING STRICT LIABILITY

1. INTERNALIZATION OF ALL COSTS: THE ENTERPRISE MODEL

As several of the quotations included earlier illustrate, one rationale for the imposition of strict liability is that profit-motivated enterprises should pay for all of the losses their activities generate, including so-called "externalities," such as damage from pollution which are external to the enterprise's operations, by incorporating them into the costs of doing business. This rationale states that if an enterprise engages in an activity that is highly dangerous, however socially valuable, and unavoidably exposes others to those risks, then the enterprise should internalize the risk of loss just as product sellers do under § 402A, through adjustments of the price and reallocation of the loss among all consumers of the enterprise's services. The argument has both fairness and efficiency aspects. It is fair to require firms to internalize costs and redistribute losses among all users of the services and not expect innocent persons to bear those losses. It promotes efficiency, the argument continues, for by increasing the costs and prices of those services, it will deter their consumption. For an opinion that contains an eloquent description of this rationale, see Atlas Chemical Indus., Inc. v. Anderson, 514 S.W.2d 309, 315–16 (Tex.Civ.Ct.App.1974), aff'd in part, rev'd in part 524 S.W.2d 681 (Tex.1975), where the court stated:

> We further believe the public policy of this State to be that however laudable an industry may be, its owners or managers are still subject to the rule that its industry or its property cannot be so used as to inflict injury to the property of its neighbors. * * * The costs of injuries resulting from pollution must be internalized by industry as a cost of production and borne by consumers or shareholders, or both, and not by the injured individual.

Will firms invest more heavily in safety or preventative technology under a strict liability theory than under negligence? Why or why not?

What does Judge Posner in *Indiana Harbor Belt* say about the incentives created by imposing strict liability? Are there justifications for treating product manufacturers differently from those engaged in abnormally dangerous activities in terms of internalizing losses created by their activities? Does strict products liability under Restatement (Second) of Torts § 402A achieve similar fairness and efficiency objectives?

2. CALABRESI'S MODEL

A second rationale for imposing strict liability derives from the economics of strict liability, which Guido Calabresi first expressed in his classic work, The Costs of Accidents: A Legal and Economic Analysis 26 (1970). Dean Calabresi (who is now a United States Circuit Court Judge) advocates liability rules that are most likely "to reduce the sum of accident costs and the costs of avoiding accidents":

> This cost, or loss, reduction goal can be divided into three subgoals. The first is reduction of the number and severity of accidents. The second cost reduction subgoal is concerned with * * * reducing societal costs resulting from accidents * * *. The third subgoal * * * involves reducing the costs of administering our treatment of accidents.

Among the criteria that he suggests for determining outcomes in particular cases is to allocate losses to those who can most cheaply reduce the risks of accidents, the so-called "cheapest cost avoider." Calabresi defines the notion of the cheapest cost avoider as the party who can best assess the costs and benefits of the action which caused the harm and can remediate those risks, where appropriate, most effectively and efficiently. This strict liability test does not require a court to evaluate a party's actual or projected costs of avoiding an accident. Instead, the court merely has to choose the party that was in the best position to make that decision. This judicial approach requires no financial acumen per se, just an insight into who had the knowledge and expertise to have made the decision. "[T]he strict liability test would simply require a decision as to whether the injurer or the victim was in the better position both to judge whether the avoidance costs would exceed foreseeable accident costs and to act on that judgment." See Guido Calabresi and Jon T. Hirschoff, Toward a Test for Strict Liability in Tort, 81 Yale L.J. 1055, 1060 (1972).

For example, will it cost less to abate the emissions from the defendant's plant or to install air conditioners on homes of plaintiffs' who are suffering from those emissions? Calabresi would argue that the plant's managers would likely be in the better position to weigh the costs of harm occurring to homeowners and the costs of installing preventative technology, and hence to know which strategy produces lower overall costs. If this weighing is undeterminable or inconclusive, Calabresi then turns to the party that can best correct any error in its entitlements (the best "briber") by purchasing the other parties' interests. Thus, the defendant might occupy the better position to acquire adjoining properties, and therefore, reach an efficient solution. For an opinion applying the "cheapest cost avoider" principle, see Union Oil Co. v. Oppen, 501 F.2d 558, 570 (9th Cir.1974), involving an oil spill.

Under Calabresi's analysis, in most cases involving abnormally dangerous activities the enterprise engaging in the activity would represent the cheaper cost avoider. What problems do you see in this rationale for strict liability?

3. NON–RECIPROCAL RISKS MODEL

A third rationale for imposing strict liability is advanced by Professor George Fletcher, in Fairness and Utility in Tort Theory, 85 Harv. L. Rev. 537 (1972). He rejects the search for lowest cost avoiders in favor of a search for a rights-based, corrective justice rationale. Professor Fletcher advances a test of fairness that revolves around reciprocal and non-reciprocal risks. Under this paradigm of reciprocity, if the defendant and plaintiff exposed each other to similar degrees of risk (created reciprocal risks), then no strict liability ought to apply. An example of reciprocal risks are those posed by two automobiles converging on a two-lane highway. Even if one vehicle is being operated without due care, as an abstract proposition, each of the two vehicles creates an equivalent or reciprocal risk to the other.

In contrast, if defendant's uncommon activity exposes the plaintiff to a unilateral, non-reciprocal risk, courts should hold the defendant strictly liable:

> Expressing the standard of strict liability as unexcused, non-reciprocal risk-taking provides an account not only of the *Rylands* * * * decision, but of strict liability in general. It is apparent, for example, that the uncommon, ultrahazardous activities pinpointed by the Restatement are readily subsumed under the rationale of non-reciprocal risk-taking. If uncommon activities are those with few participants, they are likely to be activities generating non-reciprocal risks. Similarly dangerous activities like blasting, fumigating, and crop dusting stand out as distinct, non-reciprocal risks in the community. They represent threats of harm that exceed the level of risk to which all members of the community contribute in roughly equal shares. * * * [A]ccording to the paradigm of reciprocity, the interests of the individual require us to grant compensation whenever this disproportionate distribution of risk injures someone subject to more than his fair share of risk.

George P. Fletcher, Fairness and Utility in Tort Theory, 85 Harv. L. Rev. 537, 547, 551 (1972).

Calabresi criticizes Fletcher's theory of reciprocity as a mere surrogate for which party can better evaluate the costs and benefits of the activity. Do you agree? Are the pollution cases we have examined up to this point all examples of non-reciprocal risks?

4. EPSTEIN'S CORRECTIVE JUSTICE MODEL

Yet another rationale for strict liability is offered by Professor Epstein, who, like Fletcher, rejects an efficiency or utilitarian approach, preferring a concept of fairness. Richard Epstein, A Theory of Strict Liability, 2 J. Legal Stud. 151 (1973). He states that the objective is to develop a normative theory of torts that takes into account common sense notions of individual responsibility and causation. The core of Epstein's position is that individuals possess entitlements to personal bodily integrity (ownership), just as they possess title to land or chattels, that entitle the individual to be free from invasions that cause harm or damage to those interests. He asserts that the concept of causation should be dominant because "it is dominant in the language that people * * * use to describe conduct and to determine responsibility." Id. at 164. While causation may not be necessary to "the development of some theory of tort if the goal of the system is the minimization of the costs of accidents," it is vital to tort law if the system is to "respond to ordinary views on individual blame and accountability." Epstein argues that causation, as in the phrase "A caused harm to B," plays the central role in cases of force (battery), fright (assault), compulsion (false imprisonment), and various instances where A's conduct has created a condition dangerous to B.

In discussing dangerous conditions as a source of harm to others, Epstein contends that a defendant's responsibility depends on a showing that he created the dangerous condition and that the condition "resulted in" (i.e., caused) harm to another. Id. at 177. But once the causation is shown, he argues that affirmative defenses and justifications must be narrowly applied because the focus should be on what the defendant *did*.

As you saw in Chapter 3, Epstein has also spoken of the dominance of corrective justice in nuisance cases and the limited role occupied by utilitarian constraints. Are the two propositions wholly consistent?

5. POSNER'S REDUCTION IN LEVELS OF ACTIVITY MODEL

Recall that Judge Richard Posner raises the proposition in Indiana Harbor Belt Railroad v. American Cyanamid Co., 916 F.2d 1174 (7th Cir.1990) that one purpose of imposing strict liability for high-risk activities is to reduce the frequency with which actors choose to engage in such activities or to alter the location in which they do so. This reduction in activity levels is not explicitly referenced in the Restatement, but represents an incentive that may be created by strict liability.

Take a typical pollution case: a manufacturing facility has disposed of hazardous materials that have permeated the soil, reached a water source, and contaminated plaintiffs' residential wells. If strict liability is applied, what incentives does it create? Will such actors be more likely to avoid disposals of hazardous substances? Will they be more likely to dispose of them at alternative locations away from water sources? What costs will such actors weigh in making decisions about disposal activities? What alternatives might such actors possess? How about hiring a third party to transport wastes to a government-certified facility? See Posner, Economic Analysis of Law, 192–197 (5th ed. 1998).

D. THE RELATIONSHIP BETWEEN STATUTORY AND COMMON–LAW STRICT LIABILITIES

Up to now we have concentrated on common-law tort strict liability, which as we have seen, has yielded only a modicum of success in the field of environmental torts. In Chapter 10 we consider one critically important federal tort environmental statute–the Comprehensive Environmental Response Compensation and Liability Act, 42 U.S.C. § 9601, et seq. Many states have enacted a plethora of environmental statutes, some of which are tort-like and apply a no-fault basis of liability. The following decision applies one such statute in which the court relies heavily on common-law tort principles as an interpretative guide.

HAGEN v. TEXACO REFINING AND MARKETING, INC.

Supreme Court of Iowa, 1995.
526 N.W.2d 531.

TERNUS, JUSTICE.

This case requires that we consider the scope and meaning of the cost recovery enforcement provisions of Iowa Code chapter 455G (1993). We granted permission to the Intervener, The Iowa Comprehensive Petroleum Underground Tank Fund Board, to bring this interlocutory appeal from the district court's ruling on the Board's motion for partial summary judgment. The district court held (1) factual issues existed which were material to whether defendants, Texaco Refining and Marketing, Inc., Seneca Corporation, and J & R Drilling Services, Inc., were liable for the release of petroleum from an underground storage tank, and (2) the owners of the underground storage tank could be assigned a percentage of fault in this cost recovery action. We affirm the district court's denial of partial summary judgment as to Texaco and reverse the district court's ruling on the other issues.

I. BACKGROUND FACTS.

In the fall of 1985, plaintiffs, Dean R. Hagen and Nancy K. Hagen, purchased a retail service station from Texaco. The purchase agreement required Texaco to install monitoring wells on the property. Texaco contracted with Seneca to install these monitoring wells. Seneca then subcontracted with J & R to drill the wells. Seneca was responsible for locating the exact place where J & R would drill.

The record shows that one Friday in the fall of 1985, a Seneca employee went to the Hagens' service station and placed "manways," (twelve-inch-diameter metal rings), on the ground where the wells were to be drilled. Three days later, on Monday, the cement contractor, Nelson Construction, poured cement at the station, encasing the manways in concrete. About one month later J & R drilled the monitoring wells at the locations designated by the manways.

Seneca did not check the location of the manways on Monday to be sure they had not been moved over the weekend nor did it have anyone present when the concrete was poured. Although the monitoring wells were not drilled until a month later, Seneca did not check the placement of the manways before J & R drilled.

It is undisputed that J & R pierced an underground storage tank when it drilled one of the monitoring wells. Unfortunately, the Hagens did not discover the hole in the tank for three weeks. During these three weeks, the Hagens filled the tank several times. It is estimated that 2300 gallons of petroleum escaped from the tank through the hole.

II. PROCEDURAL HISTORY.

In August of 1990, the Hagens applied for remedial benefits under Iowa's underground storage tank financial assistance program. See Iowa Code § 455G.9 (1993). The Board allowed the claim and expended money for corrective action taken at the site. The Hagens incurred expenses not covered by the program by virtue of the minimum copayments required of owners under chapter 455G. See id. § 455G.9(4).

The Hagens sued Texaco, Seneca and J & R alleging the defendants were negligent and seeking damages for the contamination and cleanup of the Hagens' property. Each defendant cross-claimed against the other defendants for contribution or indemnity. In addition, Seneca alleged that the Hagens were contributorily negligent.

The district court allowed the Board to intervene. The Board sought to recover from the defendants the moneys it had spent on corrective action. See id. § 455G.13.

After pursuing discovery, the Board filed a motion for partial summary judgment. It claimed that the undisputed facts showed that all defendants were strictly liable as a matter of law for the release of petroleum from the tank. See id. § 455G.13(7) (the standard of liability under section 455G.13 is "strict liability").

* * *

In the order from which the Board appeals, the district court denied the Board's motion for partial summary judgment and ruled that a factual dispute existed as to whether the defendants were liable for the release.

* * *

IV. STATUTORY FRAMEWORK.

In 1989 the Iowa legislature enacted a comprehensive law relating to petroleum underground storage tanks. 1989 Iowa Acts ch. 131. The act established the Iowa Comprehensive Petroleum Underground Storage Tank Fund which is administered by the Intervener Board. Iowa Code §§ 455G.3–.4 (1993). Revenue for the fund includes bonds issued by the Board, various taxes and fees, insurance premiums and recoveries from persons liable for petroleum releases. Id. § 455G.8.

Moneys in the fund are used in part for a "remedial program." Id. § 455G.9. This program provides assistance to eligible owners and operators of underground storage tanks for corrective action to clean up existing petroleum contamination.[2] Id. The release involved here qualified for the fund's remedial program.

Although moneys for the cleanup were available from the fund, a minimum copayment schedule applied to the Hagens as the owners of the tank. They were required to pay eighteen percent of the first $80,000 for the cost of corrective action and thirty-five percent of the cost above that figure. The fund was obligated to pay the balance of the costs of corrective action up to one million dollars.

Chapter 455G contains detailed provisions for the fund's recovery of moneys spent on corrective action. In general, these provisions require the Board to recover the cost of corrective action from an owner, an operator or any other potentially responsible party. In addition, the Board may recover reasonable attorney fees and costs of litigation.

The statute defines a "potentially responsible party" as "a person who may be responsible or liable for a release for which the fund has made payments for corrective action. * * *" Id. § 455G.2(15). The statute specifically provides that the "standard of liability for a release of petroleum * * * is strict liability." Id. § 455G.13(7).

The interpretation of these cost recovery provisions is the heart of this case.

V.   Positions of the Parties With Respect to Defendants' Liability.

The Board sought partial summary judgment on the basis that the defendants were strictly liable as a matter of law because they were potentially responsible parties "liable for the release" under section 455G.13. The defendants acknowledge that their conduct is judged under strict liability standards, but claim that summary judgment is inappropriate.

Texaco claims that it cannot be a potentially responsible party because it exercised no control over the installation of the monitoring wells. Seneca argues that when the record is viewed most favorably to the parties against whom summary judgment is sought, one can only conclude that Seneca's involvement in the release was limited to two

---

2. "Corrective action" includes any action taken to minimize, eliminate or clean up a release of petroleum. Iowa Code § 455G.2(6) (1993). It does not include "third-party liability"—property damage or bodily injury sustained by third parties. Id.

§ 455G.2(6), (20). "Owner or operator" means the owner or operator of the tank at the time a covered release is reported or the application for fund benefits is submitted. Id. § 455G.9(9).

actions. First, Seneca hired J & R to drill the wells. Second, Seneca identified the spot, albeit not the spot used, for the drilling. Seneca contends this conduct does not provide an adequate basis for a finding of causation.

Finally, J & R claims that factual disputes prevent the court from ruling as a matter of law that it is liable for the release. J & R asserts that these factual disputes control whether its conduct was a proximate cause of the release. The factual disputes upon which J & R relies include (1) whether the Hagens refilled the tank when they knew or should have known that the tank had been pierced, and (2) who placed the manway in the location where the well was drilled. J & R argues that either the action of the Hagens or of the person placing the manway is the sole proximate cause of the release.

VI. STANDARD OF LIABILITY.

As we previously noted, the statute defines a "potentially responsible party" as "a person who may be responsible or liable for a release." Iowa Code § 455G.2(15) (1993). The standard of liability is strict liability. Id. § 455G.13(7). Thus, this case requires us to decide whether any of the defendants are strictly liable for the release of petroleum from the Hagens' tank as a matter of law. That, in turn, requires us to determine what the legislature meant by the term "strict liability."

The statute does not define the term "strict liability" nor does it set out the elements the Board must prove to recover under this standard from potentially responsible parties. Therefore, we must resort to principles of statutory construction. One relevant principle of statutory construction is that the legislature is presumed to know the meaning given to a particular term by the courts unless the context shows otherwise. Therefore, we will examine how we have defined this term in our case law.

A. Liability without fault. Our court has used the term "strict liability" in different ways. We have frequently used this term to refer to liability imposed by statute. E.g., Gail v. Clark, 410 N.W.2d 662, 667 (Iowa 1987) (interpreting Iowa Code section 123.92 (1985)—the dram shop statute); Wenndt v. Latare, 200 N.W.2d 862, 869 (Iowa 1972) (interpreting Iowa Code section 188.3 (1971)—the animal trespass statute). In Wenndt, we characterized the strict liability of section 188.3 as lying "in principle between liability based on negligence and absolute liability." Wenndt, 200 N.W.2d at 869. We noted that it applies in the absence of fault but is not absolute liability because the statute provides for a defense.

We have also used the term "strict liability" as a label for some common-law tort theories. * * * [One] common-law tort theory to which we apply this label is the liability standard adopted in abnormally dangerous activities cases. E.g., National Steel Serv. Ctr., Inc. v. Gibbons, 319 N.W.2d 269, 270 (Iowa 1982); see Restatement (Second) of Torts § 519 (1977) (applying strict liability to one involved in abnormally dangerous activities) [hereinafter "Restatement"]. But see Davis v. L & W Constr. Co., 176 N.W.2d 223, 224–25 (Iowa 1970) (liability for ultrahazardous activity is more appropriately termed "liability without fault" rather than "strict liability").

Although we have given the term "strict liability" a variety of meanings depending upon the context in which it is used, we have consistently defined it as liability without fault when referring to statutory causes of action. We assume the legislature was aware of this meaning when it used this term in section 455G.13. Therefore, we conclude that the term "strict liability" in section 455G.13 must refer to liability without fault. Used in this fashion, strict liability means liability that exists even in the absence of negligence or intent to harm.

B. Proximate cause. Although we have concluded that the strict liability standard eliminates questions of negligence or intent to harm, we must still identify exactly what the Board must prove to establish that a potentially responsible party is in fact liable. In common-law strict liability cases, we have consistently required that the defendant's actions be a proximate cause of the plaintiff's damages. E.g., National Steel Serv. Ctr., Inc., 319 N.W.2d at 270 (person who engages in ultrahazardous activity is liable for the consequences proximately resulting from the activity); Haumersen v. Ford Motor Co., 257 N.W.2d 7, 15 (Iowa 1977) (ordinary tort rules of causation apply in strict products liability cases).

We presume the legislature understood when it used the term "strict liability" that we have traditionally included a causation component in this theory of liability. Therefore, we conclude that in order for the Board to establish the responsibility or liability of a potentially responsible party, the Board must prove that the actions of that party were a proximate cause of the release of petroleum for which the Board expended cleanup funds.

Proximate cause includes both cause in fact and legal causation. Cause in fact requires that a particular action in fact cause certain consequences to occur. This requirement is met upon proof that a defendant's conduct was a substantial factor in producing the damages and the damages would not have occurred except for the defendant's conduct.

"Legal causation presents a question of whether the policy of the law will extend responsibility to those consequences which have in fact been produced." Dunlavey v. Economy Fire & Casualty Co., 526 N.W.2d 845, 853 (Iowa 1995). Because legal causation is based on policy, a nebulous and undefined concept, we use criteria adapted to particular problem areas to evaluate this aspect of causation. One set of criteria relevant to this case is that for intervening, superseding cause.

We have held that a defendant's conduct is not a legal cause of a plaintiff's harm if it is superseded by later independent forces or conduct. The court must find that "the later-occurring event is such as to break the chain of causal events between the actor's [conduct] and the plaintiff's injury." Kelly v. Sinclair Oil Corp., 476 N.W.2d 341, 349 (Iowa 1991).

Although the standard for legal causation is a question of law, proximate cause is a question of fact for the jury. Spaur v. Owens–Corning Fiberglas Corp., 510 N.W.2d 854, 858 (Iowa 1994) (proximate cause is ordinarily a question for the jury); Haumersen, 257 N.W.2d at 15 (whether conduct was an intervening, superseding cause is for the jury unless undisputed facts leave no room for a reasonable difference of opinion). Consequently, in our review of the court's denial of the Board's motion for partial summary judgment, we must decide whether the undisputed material facts show that the actions of the defendants were a proximate cause of the release of petroleum from the Hagens' underground storage tank as a matter of law.

VII. LIABILITY OF DEFENDANTS.

There are * * * factual disputes. The parties disagree on whether someone moved the manway after its initial placement by Seneca and before J & R drilled the well. There is also a dispute concerning whether the Hagens filled the tank when they should have known the tank was leaking. In this regard there is some conflict about whether petroleum was released immediately upon the tank being punctured or only upon the tank being filled by the Hagens. Because we view the record in the light most favorable to the defendants, we assume for purposes of our analysis that someone moved the manway after it was correctly placed by Seneca, that the Hagens were negligent in putting petroleum in the tank after the monitoring wells had been drilled, and that no petroleum escaped from the tank until the Hagens filled it after the drilling.

A. Texaco. We first note that the Board does not rely on Texaco's own actions to impose liability on Texaco. * * *

The Board's argument is that Texaco is vicariously liable for the conduct of its independent contractor, Seneca. See Restatement § 427A (one who employs an independent contractor to do work involving an abnormally dangerous activity is liable to the same extent as the contractor for physical harm to others). The Board claims that digging a monitoring well near an underground storage tank is an abnormally dangerous activity. * * * However, we disagree with the Board that drilling a monitoring well at a retail service station is an abnormally dangerous activity.

Factors to be considered in deciding whether an activity is abnormally dangerous include the existence of a high risk of harm, the likelihood that such harm will be great, an inability to eliminate the risks of the activity by the exercise of reasonable care, the extent to which the activity is uncommon, whether the activity is inappropriate in the place where it is conducted, and the extent to which the activity's value to the community outweighs its dangerous attributes. Maguire v. Pabst Brewing Co., 387 N.W.2d 565, 568 (Iowa 1986) (citing Restatement § 520). We observed in Maguire that the legal principles imposing liability for abnormally dangerous activities are "aimed at risks which are not eliminated by the exercise of all reasonable precautions." We concluded that the claim stated in that case did not provide a basis for the recovery of damages as a matter of law.

We reach a similar conclusion here. Monitoring wells can be installed safely if reasonable care is taken. Moreover, drilling monitoring wells is not an unusual activity around underground storage tanks and, therefore the activity was not conducted in an inappropriate place. We conclude that the rules concerning abnormally dangerous activities do not apply to the drilling of monitoring wells under the circumstances of this case. Therefore, the vicarious liability rule of section 427A does not apply. * * *

B. Seneca. Seneca claims that its actions in hiring J & R and in identifying the location of the wells were not a proximate cause of the release. The Board responds that Seneca's employment of J & R makes it liable under the vicarious liability rule for abnormally dangerous activities. It further argues that Seneca's performance of its responsibility to locate the wells makes it strictly liable.

We agree with Seneca that its employment of J & R does not make it vicariously liable for the same reasons that Texaco is not liable for the actions of Seneca. The rule of vicarious liability for abnormally dangerous activities does not apply.

However, we disagree with Seneca that its conduct in marking the location for the drilling was not a proximate cause of the release. * * *

Seneca's obligation was to inform J & R of the correct location to drill the monitoring wells. It failed to do so. Whether this failure is attributable to negligence by Seneca or the conduct of some unknown person in moving the manway is irrelevant because Seneca is strictly liable to the Board. Clearly the location of the manways was a cause in fact of the release. Because Seneca was responsible for identifying the drilling sites for J & R, Seneca's conduct, whether in the form of action or inaction, was a cause in fact of the release as a matter of law.

Therefore, we must address an additional argument made by both Seneca and J & R. They claim that the conduct of the Hagens in refilling the tank with petroleum even though they should have known the tank had been punctured was an intervening superseding cause of the release. We conclude * * * the conduct of the Hagens is not a superseding cause of the release for several reasons.

First, an intervening act may relieve a defendant of liability only if the intervening act was not reasonably foreseeable. No reasonable mind could conclude that putting petroleum in an underground petroleum storage tank was not reasonably foreseeable. The occurrence of this event was one of the underlying premises of installing the monitoring wells in the first place—there would be no leakage of petroleum to detect unless petroleum was put in the tank.

The only aspect of the Hagens' conduct which makes their action even arguably unforeseeable was the allegedly negligent manner in which the Hagens acted. However, the fact that the Hagens may have been negligent in refilling the tank does not necessarily make their conduct unforeseeable. An intervening act is not a superseding cause merely because it is negligent if "a reasonable [person] knowing the situation existing when the act of the third person was done would not regard it as highly extraordinary that the third person had so acted." Restatement § 447(b).

The defendants claim that the Hagens should have been alerted to the hole in their tank because a check on the amount of petroleum in the tank after the drilling showed an increase of 209 gallons over what had been there before the drilling even though no petroleum had been added. (The parties theorize that rock and dirt fell into the tank through the hole, causing the petroleum level in the tank to rise.) However, we think as a matter of law it is not "extraordinary" for a tank owner to refill a tank under these circumstances. Surely a reasonable person would not consider it extraordinary that the owners failed to recognize that an increased level of petroleum in the tank suggested the existence of a hole because one would ordinarily expect leakage from the hole and consequently a lower level of petroleum in the tank. Therefore, the allegedly negligent nature of the Hagens' conduct is not sufficient to make their otherwise foreseeable action a superseding cause of the release.

Second, what the defendants are really arguing is that the Hagens should have discovered the condition created by the defendants and corrected that condition before it caused harm. However, the failure of a third person to prevent harm to another threatened by the original tortfeasor's conduct is not a superseding cause. Restatement § 452(1).

The third and final reason that the Hagens' conduct is not a superseding cause of the release is that the Hagens' conduct caused the same harm as that risked by Seneca's and J & R's initial conduct. Section 442B states this rule:

> Where the negligent conduct of the actor creates or increases the risk of a particular harm and is a substantial factor in causing that harm, the fact that the harm is brought about through the intervention of another force does not relieve the actor of liability, except where the harm is intentionally caused by a third person and is not within the scope of the risk created by the actor's conduct.

Applying this rule to the facts of this case, if the conduct of Seneca and J & R created the risk of a release of petroleum from the underground tank, the fact that the release occurred through the act of the Hagens in refilling the tank does not relieve Seneca and J & R from liability unless the release was intentionally caused by the Hagens. The defendants make no claim that the Hagens intentionally caused the release of petroleum from the underground storage tank. Therefore, this rule applies and prevents the Hagens' action from being a superseding cause.

Viewing the facts in the light most favorable to the defendants, we conclude * * * Seneca's conduct is, as a matter of law, a proximate cause of the release of petroleum from the Hagens' tank and Seneca is liable as a matter of law. The district court erred in failing to grant the Board partial summary judgment on this issue.

C.   J & R Drilling. The undisputed facts show that J & R drilled the well that punctured the underground tank. They also establish that this puncture allowed the escape of petroleum from the tank. Despite the actions of others before or after the puncture of the tank, J & R's conduct was, as a matter of law, a cause in fact of the release. * * * We also conclude that someone's act in moving the manway is not a superseding cause. The altered location of the manway occurred before J & R's action in puncturing the tank. It cannot be a superseding cause of the release because it was not an intervening cause. Therefore, this factual dispute does not affect whether J & R is liable for the release.

Since J & R's conduct was a proximate cause of the release, it is liable as a matter of law. The district court erred in refusing to grant the Board partial summary judgment on the issue of J & R's liability.

Notes and Questions

1.   The *Hagen* opinion relied on the common-law tort theory of abnormally dangerous activities as a guide in interpreting the meaning of the statutory language "strict liability." Which liability is more "strict"? The statutory standard or Restatement §§ 519 and 520? The answer of course is obvious and demonstrates dramatically why liability under the Restatement is barely "strict" in comparison to true strict liability. For an analysis of a statute similar to that analyzed in *Hagen*, see New Jersey Dept. of Environmental Protection v. Alden Leeds, Inc., 153 N.J. 272, 708 A.2d 1161 (N.J. 1998) (although Air Pollution Control Act was silent, court holds that APCA imposes strict liability by looking to statute's goals). Some states have enacted statutes that explicitly incorporate the language of the Restatement. For example, Rhode Island's Low Level Radioactive Waste Act, R.I. Gen. Laws. § 23–19.9–10(d) (1998), provides, in part:

> (d) It shall be the responsibility of each regional facility's operator or custodial agency to take all necessary steps to clean up, stabilize and restore the facility and surrounding areas whenever there has been damage to the facility or surrounding areas which may cause or contribute to a hazard to the public health or the environment. Any person who carries on an abnormally dangerous activity involving the management of low-level waste shall be subject to strict liability for harm to the person, land or property of another resulting from the activity. This strict liability shall be limited to the kind of harm, the possibility of which makes the activity abnormally dangerous.

2.   *Super Strict Statutes.* Some statutes go beyond just strict liability, and dispense with a causation requirement. For example, the Pennsylvania Storage Tank and Spill Prevention Act, Pa. Stat. Ann. tit. 35 § 6021.1311(a), says that the owner or operator of a UST:

> shall be liable, without proof of fault, negligence or causation, for all damages, contamination or pollution within 2,500 feet of the perimeter

of the site of a storage tank containing or which contained a regulated substance of the type which caused the damage, contamination or pollution.

Moreover, evidence that an underground petroleum storage tank does not leak is not the clear and convincing evidence necessary to rebut a statutory presumption imposing strict liability for contamination from an underground storage tank, a federal district court in Pennsylvania found, denying a defendant's summary judgment motion. W.N. Stevenson Co. v. Oslou Corp., 1999 WL 96005 (E.D. Pa. 1999).

3. *Vicarious Liability.* The court in *Hagen* rejected the argument made by the Board that Texaco should be vicariously liable for the acts of the independent contractor, Seneca, because it retained Seneca to engage in abnormally dangerous activity–drilling the monitoring well. The court accepted the principle of Restatement (Second) of Torts § 427A that employment of an independent contractor to engage in such activities is a basis for vicarious liability.

As *Hagen* illustrates, principals and employers can be held liable for the highly risky activities of their agents. Under the Restatement § 427A, the party who employs an independent contractor to perform abnormally dangerous activities will be subject to the same liability as the contractor. The rationale for doing so is not solely to find a solvent defendant, but to assure that the employer does not intentionally retain judgment-proof contractors to perform dangerous tasks knowing that the contractors are unable to pay for the costs of injuries and that the employers are not legally obligated to do so. See Anderson v. Marathon Petroleum Co., 801 F.2d 936 (7th Cir.1986), where Judge Posner articulates this rationale. Additionally, as Judge Posner points out, one of the policy objectives identified earlier—that of creating incentives to reduce the frequency or level of the activity—is frustrated if the employer can ignore the accident costs created by the activity by having someone else perform it.

4. In contrast to *Hagen*, see Shell Oil Co. v. Meyer, 705 N.E.2d 962 (Ind. 1998), where the Supreme Court of Indiana held that Shell Oil Company was liable as an operator of stations with leaking underground storage tanks under Indiana law. The court reversed a lower court's holding that the oil companies were automatically responsible by virtue of their power to influence the activities of the stations, absent some direct contractual authority. The oil companies would be liable for the actions of their independent contractors under principals of common law because the operation of the tanks, including filling, measuring and dispensing fuel, was an inherently hazardous activity. The court stated:

> As a general matter, under the common law a principal is not liable for damages resulting from an independent contractor's wrongful acts or omissions. Under accepted tort doctrines however, an independent contractor may create liability for a principal under some circumstances. * * * A second analogous doctrine is that one who employs an independent contractor to perform work that is abnormally dangerous or is likely to include trespass or nuisance is subject to liability to the same extent as the contractor for physical harm to others. Id. §§ 427A & 427B

* * *

Work is intrinsically dangerous if the risk of injury involved cannot be eliminated or significantly reduced by taking proper precautions. Filling a tank that is known to have the potential to leak and, if it does, to contaminate others' water supplies has elements that are strongly reminiscent of these doctrines. Indeed, the trial court found that underground storage tanks leak despite any known precautions. Contaminant finding its way onto the property of the Landowners has elements of both a trespass and a nuisance and, in addition, is abnormally dangerous. Accordingly, we conclude that in the context of operating a UST, a principal is liable under the Act for an independent contractor's actions to the same extent that common law liability exists for the contractor's actions.

705 N.E.2d at 978.

5.   The New Jersey Supreme Court, one of the most aggressive courts in applying the strict liability doctrine, however, refused to find Texaco liable for the actions of a service station operator. In Bahrle v. Exxon Corp., 145 N.J. 144, 678 A.2d 225 (N.J. 1996), the court reasoned as follows:

Plaintiffs claim that Texaco is vicariously liable for the discharge from Rule's service station [Rule is the owner-operator of the service station] of petroleum products into the groundwater. * * * The issue of Texaco's alleged liability for conduct of an inherently or abnormally dangerous activity requires * * * discussion.

Ordinarily, an employer that hires an independent contractor is not liable for the negligent acts of the contractor in the performance of the contract. * * * [A]n employer is strictly liable for harm resulting from the performance by an independent contractor of abnormally dangerous work.

* * *

The employer's liability stems from a non-delegable duty to exercise reasonable care when performing the inherently or abnormally dangerous activity, a duty that the employer can not discharge by hiring an independent contractor.

* * *

Essential to the application of these rules, however, is the existence of an independent contractor relationship.

* * *

Plaintiffs' claim against Texaco fails for the basic reason that they have failed to prove that Texaco hired Rule as an independent contractor. Except for the three-to six-month period during the early 1970s when Texaco supplied Rule with gasoline, Rule had no direct relationship with Texaco. Rule dealt exclusively with Kalsch–Forte [a petroleum products distributor]. A contractual relationship existed between Rule and Kalsch–Forte, not between Rule and Texaco. Indeed, the jury found that Kalsch–Forte, not Texaco, owned the tanks. Neither Kalsch–Forte nor Texaco exercised control over the operation of the service station. Rule simply purchased Texaco products from Kalsch–Forte.

The record is devoid of information about the relationship between Kalsch–Forte and Texaco. Nothing supports plaintiffs' allegations that Texaco hired Rule as an independent contractor to sell Texaco products. Hence, we need not consider whether Rule's operation of the service station was either an inherently or abnormally dangerous activity, or whether Rule created a nuisance at the station. * * *

Plaintiffs also urge us to "fashion a common law basis of recovery against major oil companies when defunct suppliers and uninsured gasoline service station owners cause [surface and ground water] contamination." In effect, they invite us to constitute major oil companies as insurers of due care at all service stations, regardless of the relationship between the oil company and the service station operator or the degree of control exercised by the oil company over the operations at individual stations. We decline the invitation. Nothing in the record justifies the imposition of liability on oil companies for harms caused by conduct over which they have no reasonable means of influence or control. Adequate statutory and common-law remedies exist for parties who suffer injury from the discharge of petroleum products into surface and ground water.

678 A.2d at 230–231.

Why might the New Jersey Supreme Court have refused to create a special rule making oil companies vicariously liable for contamination at any service station dispensing that brand of petroleum products? Is it simply an issue of their inability to control the operation of the facility? If such liability did exist, what incentives might that create for oil companies? See, Oshinskie, Tanks for Nothing: Oil Company Liability for Discharges of Gasoline from Underground Storage Tanks Divested to Station Owners, 18 Va. Envtl. Law. J. 1 (1999) (advancing a variety of legal theories for holding the oil company liable, including fraudulent concealment and products liability); Using the Abnormally Dangerous Activity Doctrine to Hold Principals Vicariously Liable for the Acts of Manufacturers, 21 B.C. Envtl. Aff. L. Rev. 587 (1994).

6. *Liability of Lessors.* How about the liability of lessors for the injury-causing activities of lessees? Here the cases show little uniformity. The Restatement (Second) of Torts § 379A provides that a lessor is not responsible for injuries inflicted by a lessee upon persons outside the land unless the lessor had knowledge, at the time of the making of the lease, that the lessee's activities would "unavoidably involve * * * unreasonable risk." Thus, a lessor is liable for harm inflicted by the lessee's blasting operations if, at the time of making of the lease, the lessor knew or had reason to know that "such blasting [would] involve an unreasonable risk of physical harm to those outside of the land." Comment *b*. The Restatement formulation seems to be limited to negligence, but some of the cases go further. In Salazar v. Webb, 44 Colo.App. 429, 618 P.2d 706 (Colo.Ct.App.1980), plaintiffs were injured by a methane gas explosion on land owned by defendant and leased to another for a sanitary landfill. The court held that the lessor was liable if the accident was a natural consequence of a dangerous activity of the lessee.

A more restrictive approach was employed in Peterick v. State, 22 Wash.App. 163, 589 P.2d 250 (Wash.Ct.App.1977), in which employees in an explosives plant were killed in an explosion. Despite the hazardous nature of the lessee's activity, the court rejected a suit against the owner-lessor of the land on which the plant was located. Even though the owner had a right to inspect the plant and to require compliance with safety regulations, it did not have day-to-day control of the plant and was held not to be responsible for the actions of the lessee.

For example, consider the scope of lessor liability in State v. Monarch Chemicals, Inc., 111 Misc.2d 343, 443 N.Y.S.2d 967 (Sup. Ct. 1981), modified, 90 A.D.2d 907, 456 N.Y.S.2d 867 (App. Div. 1982), a public nuisance action against persons storing toxic chemicals, some of which had escaped and polluted public water supplies. Knowles, the lessor of the premises, sought to be dismissed from the action. He alleged that, when he had leased the site, it had consisted of a vacant lot and a warehouse; that the lessee thereafter had installed the chemical storage tanks which led to the pollution in issue; that he, Knowles, had no knowledge as to the contents of the tanks; and that "at no time prior to the making of the lease did he know that [the lessee] would be handling or storing toxic chemicals on the site." 443 N.Y.S.2d at 969. The court ruled that Knowles had a responsibility to act reasonably after the lessee took possession, taking account of "the existence of a duty to repair, the right to re-enter, and the landlord's overall involvement in the tenancy." The court found a triable issue as to whether Knowles had knowledge of the toxic chemicals and sufficient power to control the use of the premises. For this reason, it refused to dismiss the action against Knowles.

See also Russell–Stanley Corp. v. Plant Indus., 250 N.J.Super. 478, 595 A.2d 534 (N.J. Super. Ct. Ch. Div. 1991) (involving a site polluted by a tenant). The Russell–Stanley court observed that the lessor actively administered the leasehold through inspections, and held that there was a triable issue as to whether the lessor was liable for clean-up costs. It followed a prior statutory case holding that "a lessor of a site was liable for the costs of cleaning up a tenant's toxic wastes." *Id.* at 544–46.

7. *Causation.* The *Hagen* opinion contained a discussion revealing that the doctrine of strict liability does not, by itself, abrogate the traditional rules of cause-in-fact and legal cause that control in negligence actions. Note that the court relied on the Restatement (Second) of Torts rules for cause-in-fact (but for and substantial factor causation) and for legal cause. For a discussion of the substantial factor test see, Wagner v. Anzon, Inc., 453 Pa.Super. 619, 684 A.2d 570 (Pa.Super.1996), in which the court approves a jury instruction that explains the test as meaning that defendant's tortious conduct does not have to be the sole cause of plaintiff's harm.

In Chapter 8 we consider the special problems of cause-in-fact created by exposure to hazardous substances. The important point here is for the student to realize that "strict" liability does not mean "absolute" in the sense that a plaintiff is excused from pleading and proving a physical and scientific connection between the activity that is abnormally dangerous and the harm suffered. As we saw in nuisance and trespass cases it is not necessarily obvious that a polluting activity engaged in a mile away from plaintiff's property can be connected to the harm. In the blasting and explosives cases, cause and effect are usually evident, but in contamination situations the relationships are much more problematic and usually demand expert testimony on groundwater hydrology and geology before a fact finder can draw the causal inference.

8. *Scope of the Abnormal Risk.* Section 519 of the Restatement (Second) makes it clear that liability extends only to damages that are "within the scope of the abnormal risk that is the basis of the liability." Comment *e.* Thus, the enterprise is not liable for every harm that may result from carrying on the activity. For example, in a jurisdiction where crop-dusting by small aircraft has been found to represent an abnormally dangerous activity, the risk to be avoided within the meaning of the doctrine is the erroneous, in content or in target, application of pesticides or herbicides. A mishap of such a nature would be within the contemplation of the abnormally dangerous activities remedy, while an accident involving the crash of the aircraft would not.

Or suppose that an invitee on defendant's premises was exposed to hazardous substances that had leaked from holding tanks. Defendant would argue that strict liability is inapplicable because the abnormal risk of the activity would relate to environmental contamination and not to ordinary premises liability, which should be governed by negligence principles.

While review of the decisional law reveals that § 519(2) surfaces infrequently as an impediment to recovery, consider the following excerpt of a decision of the Alaska Supreme Court in Parks Hiway Enterprises, LLC v. CEM Leasing, Inc., et al., 995 P.2d 657 (Alaska 2000), in which the court distinguished between the potential application of strict liability in a fuel burning or explosion case and a claim that might arise from environmental contamination:

* * ** *

D. *The Superior Court Did Not Err by Rejecting Parks Hiway's Attempt to Hold Petroleum Sales Strictly Liable Under the Common Law Doctrine of Ultrahazardous Activity.*

Strict liability attaches to actors engaged in ultrahazardous activities. [Cc] An activity is ultrahazardous if it "(a) necessarily involves a risk of serious harm ... which cannot be eliminated by the exercise of the utmost care, and (b) is not a matter of common usage." [Cc] "What facts are necessary to make an activity ultrahazardous ... is a matter for the judgment of the court" rather than the jury. [Cc] In Matomco Oil Co. v. Arctic Mechanical, Inc., we suggested that hauling gasoline as freight represents an ultrahazardous activity for which strict liability would apply. [Cc]

The superior court, however, ruled that although transporting gasoline is an "ultrahazardous activity," strict liability would attach only to harm arising "from the risk which, being incapable of elimination by utmost care, makes the activity ultrahazardous." Reasoning that transporting fuel was deemed ultrahazardous due solely to gasoline's inherent volatility, the superior court refused to extend strict liability to harm falling outside the scope of the risk of explosion. The court thus rejected Parks Hiway's attempt to hold Petroleum Sales strictly liable for environmental damage resulting from the fuel's delivery. We agree with the superior court's reasoning. [Cc]

On appeal, Parks Hiway refines its argument to assert that transporting gasoline to defective tanks should constitute an "ultrahazardous" activity warranting strict liability. Parks Hiway relies upon City of Northglenn v. Chevron U.S.A., Inc., [519 F.Supp. 515, 515–16 (D.Colo.1981)] and Yommer v. McKenzie, [255 Md. 220, 257 A.2d 138, 140–42 (App.1969)] ... which held operators of large underground gasoline storage facilities strictly liable for the contamination of neighboring property. But the persuasive value of Northglenn and Yommer to the present case remains extremely limited, as both opinions involved facility owners rather than suppliers or transporters of gasoline.

In the analogous case of City of Bloomington v. Westinghouse Electric Corp., the court refused to hold a seller of products containing toxic components strictly liable where the contamination occurred after the buyer's purchase. [Cc] Emphasizing that even strict liability contains a causation element, the court reasoned that "the harm ... was not caused by any abnormally dangerous activity of [the seller] but by the buyer's failure to safeguard its waste." [Cc] The Bloomington court was thus "unwilling to extend the doctrine of strict liability for an abnormally dangerous activity to the party whose activity did not cause the injury." [Cc]

We agree with Bloomington and refuse to hold Petroleum Sales strictly liable for contamination occurring after it delivered its product to Gold Hill. As in that case, Parks Hiway's injury resulted from Gold Hill's failure to properly maintain its tanks rather than Petroleum Sales' delivery of the fuel.

Notes and Questions

1. The intervening actions of third parties—be they innocent, negligent, or reckless—will not defeat liability. See Restatement (Second) of Torts § 522. For example, in Old Island Fumigation Inc. v. Barbee, 604 So.2d 1246 (Fla.Ct.App.1992), it was immaterial that architects and contractors were negligent in building a fire wall that permitted defendant's fumigation gas to enter a building adjacent to the one it was spraying, since the fumigation was an abnormally dangerous activity.

2. In *Hagen* any negligence by the owners in filling the underground tank was regarded as foreseeable as a matter of law; so too negligent placement of the manway or its relocation was deemed to be within the foreseeable risks of the drilling process. Why do you think the Iowa Supreme Court was reluctant to carve out an area of superseding causes? Do you think it was influenced by the "strict liability" of the statute?

3. What kind of intervening causes are most likely to appear in abnormally dangerous activity cases? What about unforeseeable forces of nature? How about unpreventable acts of third persons (e.g., midnight dumpers)? Interestingly, these two are precisely the kinds of intervening events that are expressly recognized as defenses under the Clean Water Act,

33 U.S.C. § 1321(f) (1997) and CERCLA, 42 U.S.C. § 9607 (1998), both of which are strict liability regimes.

Professor Jones is critical of infusing legal causation tests into strict liability:

> But a substantial number of cases, along with the federal statutes imposing strict liability for water pollution and hazardous waste disposal, allow defenses for acts of God or acts of unrelated third parties. Recognition of these defenses triggers further inquiries into whether the force of nature was unforeseeable, or whether the act of the third party could have been prevented by the exercise of reasonable care.
>
> This mode of proceeding has been defended as a means of overcoming difficulties confronted by plaintiffs in establishing negligence when negligence is probable but not easily proved. Under this regime, culpability is presumed from the fact of the accident, but the defendant can seek to rebut the presumption by demonstrating the intervention of an unforeseeable force of nature or an unpreventable act of a third party. Issue is then joined on the question of foreseeability or feasible prevention, injecting a negligence issue into a supposedly strict liability case. Accordingly, this practice raises many of the same difficulties of proof as an ordinary negligence case whenever the plaintiff is less knowledgeable than the defendant–a fairly common phenomenon. More importantly, this approach reduces the efficacy of strict liability in providing incentives for defendants to adopt all cost-effective precautions and to limit the level of their activities whenever social benefits are less than social burdens.

92 Colum. L. Rev. 1754–55 (citations omitted).

With whom do you agree? Should strict liability incorporate negligence-derived legal causation principles? What might be the consequences of excluding such defenses?

4. Another aspect of causation and risk relates to the plaintiff's own sensitivity to injury. In that regard, see:

§ 524. A Plaintiff's Abnormally Sensitive Activity

There is no strict liability for harm caused by an abnormally dangerous activity if the harm would not have resulted but for the abnormally sensitive character of the plaintiff's activity.

Do § 524 and § 519(2) always lead to the same results? See Great Lakes Dredging and Dock Co. v. Sea Gull Operating Corp., 460 So.2d 510 (Fla.Ct. App.1984).

E. APPLICATION OF NUISANCE, TRESPASS, NEGLIGENCE, AND STRICT LIABILITY TO VERTICAL RELATIONSHIPS

In the past few years, one of the battlegrounds which courts have addressed is whether a purchaser or lessee of real property can sue a former owner, lessee or lessor of the same property on a theory of private nuisance, trespass, negligence or strict liability to recover for damages flowing from contamination of the property. In other words, in these cases the relationship between the parties is not that of horizontal, concurrent owners or occupiers of land, but rather vertical relationships between successors in interest. The following opinion is one of many that has ruled that nuisance, negligence, and strict liability theories cannot be used by current property owners to sue prior owners for contamination on the property.

ROSENBLATT v. EXXON COMPANY, U.S.A.

Court of Appeals of Maryland, 1994.
335 Md. 58, 642 A.2d 180.

MURPHY, CHIEF JUDGE.

This case involves the question whether, under Maryland law, a subsequent occupier of commercial property has a cause of action in strict liability, negligence, trespass, or nuisance, for economic losses sustained, against a former occupant whose activities during its occupancy allegedly caused the property to become contaminated by toxic chemicals.

I

In July 1986, Thomas Rosenblatt leased a parcel of real property located in Prince George's County, Maryland, from its owner, Earl Wenger. The lease agreement contained the language that Rosenblatt was accepting the property "as is." Rosenblatt planned to open and operate a "Grease–N–Go" automotive quick lubrication business on the property. Rosenblatt's rental payments were contingent upon his obtaining a special exception to permit the operation of the business and a building permit for construction.

The previous tenant, Exxon Company, U.S.A., had leased the property from 1951 to 1985, and had subleased the property during that period to various independent dealers for use as a gasoline station. In 1951, Exxon had installed gasoline storage tanks on the property; the tanks remained on the property until 1985, when Exxon's lease was terminated.

In preparing for the construction of his "Grease–N–Go" facility, Rosenblatt hired ATEC Environmental Consultants (ATEC) to perform a geotechnical study of the property to identify potential construction problems. In ATEC's initial report, dated January 30, 1987, it noted the presence of a "very strong" hydrocarbon odor in soil and groundwater samples, and it recommended that a separate environmental study be performed to determine whether hydrocarbon contamination was present.

In May 1988, the special exception was granted, and in October 1988, Rosenblatt began paying rent on the property. In January 1989, Rosenblatt notified Exxon of the possible contamination. * * * Rosenblatt thereafter requested that ATEC complete an environmental assessment of the property. In March 1989, ATEC conducted a study and found extensive petroleum contamination of the soil and groundwater on the property, specifically benzene, a known carcinogen, and other toxic substances.

As a result of this discovery, the Maryland Department of the Environment was notified, conducted an investigation, and issued a Notice of Violation, advising that the contamination constituted a violation of Maryland law, and requiring Exxon to perform a hydrogeological study of the property. Exxon commenced its study in May 1989, and thereafter undertook a remediation of the property. The State's Hazardous and Solid Waste Management Administration informed Rosenblatt and Wenger that construction efforts could continue but would have to be coordinated with Exxon's remediation efforts.

In January 1990, Rosenblatt filed suit against Exxon in the Circuit Court for Prince George's County, seeking economic damages, including expenses incurred as a result of the contamination and lost future profits from his planned business. His complaint included counts of negligence, strict liability, trespass, nuisance, and other counts not here at issue. [I]n March 1990, Rosenblatt was informed by the bank to which he had applied for financing that it would not finance the "Grease–N–Go" project, in part because of the environmental condition of the property. Without this financing, Rosenblatt was unable to start his business.

* * *

On July 13, 1993, the [circuit] court granted the motions [for summary judgment], stating that Maryland law does not provide tenants of commercial property with a cause of action based upon negligence, strict liability, trespass or nuisance against previous tenants of the property. The court stated that these tort claims were available only to occupants of neighboring land or others to whom a duty was owed by the defendant.

Rosenblatt appealed to the Court of Special Appeals. We granted certiorari prior to review by the intermediate appellate court to consider the issues presented in this appeal.

II

Rosenblatt argues that an occupier of land should have a cause of action in strict liability against a prior occupier whose abnormally dangerous activity contaminated the land. He acknowledges that this principle has heretofore been applied in Maryland to actions by occupants of neighboring land, rather than subsequent occupiers of the same land. He argues, however, that the policies underlying the strict liability principles support their extension to the instant case. He observes that courts in two other jurisdictions have held that subsequent occupiers may sue under a theory of strict liability and urges that Maryland join those jurisdictions.

Rosenblatt contends that the transport, storage and dispensing of gasoline constitute abnormally dangerous activities. He urges that Exxon, as an enterprise engaging in such activities, should bear the risk of harm resulting therefrom. Exxon's liability, he asserts, should not be limited to adjacent property owners. He suggests that although Exxon and Rosenblatt were not neighbors geographically, they were "neighbors in time." He urges that it "makes no sense" to allow a geographic neighbor of the affected property to maintain a strict liability cause of action, but not to allow one who subsequently comes into possession of the contaminated property to do so. He suggests that a restriction on the doctrine of strict liability to claims involving neighboring landholders would serve to exonerate tenants who have contaminated a property and then moved on.

He argues further that a cause of action in negligence should also be available to the subsequent occupier of contaminated land. He says that a subsequent occupier of contaminated land is owed a tort duty by a prior occupier because it is foreseeable that contamination from the activities of a prior occupant will harm subsequent occupants. Because Exxon was a lessee, he contends that it was foreseeable to the company that a subsequent lessee would be harmed by Exxon's failure to exercise care in the conduct of its business. Moreover, he suggests that Exxon, because it is in the business of producing, handling, storing and marketing petroleum products, should be held to a high degree of care in conducting its business. He maintains that Exxon was aware of the risk of petroleum products leaking from underground storage tanks and was also aware that measures could be taken to reduce the risk of leakage. Thus, he concludes, it owed a duty to Rosenblatt to prevent such harm.

Rosenblatt asserts that a subsequent possessor of land may also bring a claim of trespass against a prior occupant of the same land. He maintains that when a prior occupant creates a condition on land that interferes with the subsequent occupant's interest and exclusive possession of the land, there is a trespass. * * * He claims that when property changes hands, but the presence of contamination placed there by the former occupant continues so that it invades a new possessor's interest, a continuing trespass has occurred. * * *

Moreover, Rosenblatt contends that a subsequent occupant of contaminated land has a cause of action in nuisance against a prior occupant whose contamination of the property interferes with the subsequent occupant's interest in the private use and enjoyment of the property. He argues that the nuisance doctrine is not limited to interference with an adjacent landowner's use of land, but should be extended to an occupant of land previously occupied by the one who created the damage.

Exxon and the independent operators (collectively Exxon) aver that causes of action traditionally available only to geographical neighbors should not be extended to subsequent occupants of property. Exxon argues that, unlike a contemporary occupier of land, a subsequent occupant can avoid harm simply by investigating prior to occupying the land.

III

We here determine whether the trial court was legally correct in concluding that Exxon was entitled to judgment as a matter of law on Rosenblatt's strict liability, negligence, trespass and nuisance claims.

A

THE STRICT LIABILITY CLAIM

We have long recognized the doctrine of strict liability, derived from the rule of Rylands v. Fletcher. See Baltimore Breweries' Co. v. Ranstead, 78 Md. 501, 28 A. 273, 27 L.R.A. 294 (1894); Susquehanna Fertilizer Co. v. Malone, 73 Md. 268, 20 A. 900, 25 Am.St.Rep. 595 (1890). The rule enunciated in *Rylands* provided that "the person who, for his own purposes, brings in his lands and collects and keeps there anything likely to do mischief if it escapes must keep it in at his peril; and if he does not do so, is prima facie answerable for all the damage which is the natural consequence of its escape." Fletcher v. Rylands, L.R. 1 Ex. 265, 279 (1866). *Rylands* involved damage to the plaintiff's coal mine resulting from the escape of water from the defendant's reservoir.

We adopted the modern version of the strict liability doctrine in Yommer v. McKenzie, 255 Md. 220, 257 A.2d 138 (1969). We therein adopted the definition set forth in § 519 of the Restatement (Second) of Torts (1965). * * *

In Yommer, an owner of residential property brought a claim against the owners of a gasoline station immediately adjacent to the residential property after gasoline leaked into the property owner's well. We there held that the doctrine of strict liability applied because, while "the operation of a gasoline station [did] not of itself involve 'a high degree of risk of some harm to the person, land or chattels of others,' the placing of a large underground gasoline tank in close proximity to the appellees' residence and well * * * involve[d] such a risk, since it [was] not a matter of common usage." 255 Md. at 224–25, 257 A.2d 138. We stated that the most crucial factor in determining whether an activity was abnormally dangerous was the "appropriateness of the activity" to the place in which it was carried on. Id. at 225, 257 A.2d 138. We noted that the distinction between "natural" and "non-natural" uses served to limit the application of the rule, a limitation that was necessary to avoid unduly burdening landowners. [I]n Toy v. Atlantic Gulf & Pacific Co., 176 Md. 197, 212–13, 4 A.2d 757 (1939), we declined to extend the abnormally dangerous activity doctrine to situations in which the alleged tortfeasor was not the owner or occupier of land. Id. at 213, 4 A.2d 757. In that case, the defendant was a contractor who was dredging a canal and disposing of dredged material on government land which was adjacent to the plaintiffs' land. The plaintiffs brought suit when an embankment, constructed by the government to confine the excavated material, collapsed, causing a large mass of earth to obstruct a channel which provided plaintiffs access to their land by boat. We stated that because the defendant had no right of ownership or control of the site, its liability was limited to negligence, and could not be enlarged, under the circumstances, to a liability without fault. Id. at 213–14, 4 A.2d 757.

We similarly limited the doctrine in Kelley v. R.G. Industries, Inc., 304 Md. 124, 497 A.2d 1143 (1985), holding that it was not applicable to hold the manufacturer or marketer of a handgun liable to a person injured by the handgun during the course of a crime.

* * *

Thus, we have applied the doctrine only to claims by an occupier of land harmed by an activity abnormally dangerous in relation to the area, which is carried on by a contemporaneous occupier of neighboring land.

We are here asked to expand the application of this doctrine to claims by subsequent occupants of the land on which the dangerous activity took place. Rosenblatt relies primarily upon cases from two jurisdictions where recovery was allowed under a strict liability theory to subsequent occupiers of property contaminated by a previous occupant.

In T & E Industries v. Safety Light Corp., 123 N.J. 371, 587 A.2d 1249 (1991), the New Jersey Supreme Court held that a subsequent occupier of property could maintain an action for strict liability against its predecessor who dumped radium on a portion of the property. The property had changed hands several times before T & E leased and eventually purchased the land. The court focused upon the dangerousness and inappropriateness of the activity, stating that those who, for their own benefit, introduce an extraordinary risk of harm to the community should bear the risk. 587 A.2d at 1257. The court concluded that this policy consideration justified the broadening of the doctrine's application beyond the claims of adjacent landowners. Id. Similarly, in Prospect Industries Corp. v. Singer Co., 238 N.J.Super. 394, 569 A.2d 908 (1989), the Superior Court granted summary judgment on the plaintiff's strict liability count against the prior owner, whose equipment had leaked toxic wastes, causing the property to become contaminated. The court held that this leakage constituted an abnormally dangerous activity for which the prior owner should be held responsible. 569 A.2d at 911. Both of these New Jersey courts held that the fact that the purchasers agreed to take the property "as is" did not affect the sellers' strict liability because there was no evidence that the purchasers were aware of the contamination when they entered into the contracts, and a party ignorant of the presence of an abnormally dangerous condition could not be held to have assumed the risk posed by the condition. 587 A.2d at 1259; 569 A.2d at 912.

In Hanlin Group v. Intern. Minerals & Chemical Corp., 759 F.Supp. 925 (D.Me.1990), the court held that a strict liability claim could be asserted against a prior owner who engaged in abnormally dangerous activities, namely, the disposal of hazardous chemicals, including mercury and carbon tetrachloride, on the property. The Hanlin court reasoned that it was not necessary for the plaintiff to prove negligence where the activity carried out by the defendant was an abnormally dangerous activity. Id. at 933. The court distinguished the disposal of hazardous chemicals from other activities, such as blasting, which were "not only lawful but useful, usual and probably necessary" and were a reasonable use of property, thus requiring a showing of negligence for liability to be imposed upon the defendant. Id.

The above cases involved claims by purchasers against prior owners of the affected property. Rosenblatt urges that we apply the reasoning of these cases to hold Exxon strictly liable for the gasoline contamination of the land which he leased.

We are unwilling to extend the doctrine of strict liability to the claim presented in this case. We have taken care to limit the application of this doctrine because of the heavy burden it places upon a user of land. Our cases have limited the class of abnormally dangerous activities to those activities which would be abnormally dangerous in relation to the area where they occur. Moreover, we have limited the doctrine with regard to the class of actors to which it applies: we have required that the one engaging in the relevant activity have ownership or control over the land. See *Toy*, supra, 176 Md. at 213–14, 4 A.2d 757. And, finally, we have required that the act have a relation to the occupation or ownership of land. See *Kelley*, supra, 304 Md. at 133, 497 A.2d 1143.

By these limitations we have delineated narrow circumstances in which the imposition of an additional burden on the occupier of land is justified. When an owner or occupier of land engages in activities which are related to such ownership and occupation and which are abnormally dangerous in relation to the particular site, we place upon the actor the burden of bearing the risk of any harm to neighbors which arises from the activity, notwithstanding the absence of fault on the part of the actor. This burden is justified when weighing the rights of the actor, who benefits from the activity, against those of the occupants of neighboring land, who do not benefit and have no way of avoiding the harm to their property that may result from a dangerous activity on adjacent land. Subsequent users, however, are able to avoid the harm completely by inspecting the property prior to purchasing or leasing it. Thus, it is not unreasonable to expect subsequent users to bear the risk of such harm.[7] We think, however, that it would be unreasonable to hold the prior user liable to remote purchasers or lessees of commercial property who fail to inspect adequately before taking possession of the property.

Additionally, the extension of this doctrine is inconsistent with the principles set forth in the Restatement, upon which Maryland's strict liability principles are based. Section 519 of the Restatement makes clear that the harm for which the actor conducting the abnormally dangerous

---

7. Moreover, the common law rule of caveat emptor, although legislatively abrogated in the context of residential property, is still applicable in Maryland with regard to the sale of commercial property.

activity will be held liable is harm to the person or property of another. It would be illogical to interpret this language to hold the actor strictly liable for harm to the actor's own property in those cases in which, at some time thereafter, the property changes hands. Other courts have similarly held. See Wellesley Hills Realty Trust v. Mobil Oil Corp., 747 F.Supp. 93 (D.Mass.1990) (Plaintiff failed to state a claim for strict liability for gasoline contamination of property by a prior owner because harm was not to property of another as required by the doctrine); Futura Realty v. Lone Star Bldg. Centers, 578 So.2d 363 (Fla.App. 3 Dist.1991) (same; rejecting the analysis of T & E Industries).

We note also that Rosenblatt alleges no personal injury or property damage resulting from the contamination; his only claimed losses are economic in nature. The doctrine of strict liability, by its express language and traditional application, is aimed at protecting against harm to person or property which arises from the dangerous activity. It is not designed to protect against economic losses resulting from failed business opportunities. Therefore, we will not extend the doctrine's application to a claim for economic loss by a lessee of commercial property against a prior lessee for gasoline contamination to the property leased.

B

The Negligence Claim

* * *

The existence of a legally cognizable duty owed by the defendant to the plaintiff or a class of persons of which the plaintiff is a member is essential to a cause of action for negligence. Erie Ins. Co. v. Chops, 322 Md. 79, 84, 585 A.2d 232 (1991). Thus, even if Rosenblatt can show that Exxon caused the property now leased by him to be contaminated and that he has suffered an injury resulting from the contamination, he cannot state a cause of action in negligence unless he first shows that Exxon owed a duty to him to avoid that injury. The question whether Exxon owed a duty to Rosenblatt is an issue of law, to be determined by the court. See Prosser and Keeton, Law of Torts, § 45 at 320 (5th ed. 1984).

It is well settled that an occupier of land owes certain duties with regard to the safety of individuals who come onto the land, the extent of the duty being dependent upon the status of the visitor, i.e. as an invitee or licensee. Similarly, the occupier of land owes a duty to occupants of neighboring land to use care when conducting activities on the land so as to avoid causing harm to the neighboring land. See Toy, supra, 176 Md. at 208–09, 4 A.2d 757. We have not heretofore extended the duty of the occupier of land to the avoidance of harm to one's own land that may cause injury or loss to a subsequent occupier of the same land.

In determining the existence of a duty owed to a plaintiff, we have applied a "foreseeability of harm" test, which is based upon the recognition that duty must be limited to avoid liability for unreasonably remote consequences. Inherent also in the concept of duty is the concept of a relationship between the parties out of which the duty arises. See Prosser and Keeton, supra, § 53 at 356. But, ultimately, the determination of whether a duty should be imposed is made by weighing the various policy considerations and reaching a conclusion that the plaintiff's interests are, or are not, entitled to legal protection against the conduct of the defendant. Id. at 357–58.

In this situation, we conclude that they are not. There exists no relationship between the parties which would have made it foreseeable that an act or failure to act by Exxon would result in harm to Rosenblatt. Moreover, we are unwilling to impose upon a lessee of commercial property a duty to remote successor lessees for losses resulting from a condition on the property that could have been discovered with reasonable diligence prior to occupancy and thus could have been avoided. * * * A lessee of commercial property * * * is expected to make basic inquiry and inspection of the property prior to entering into a lease. When Rosenblatt entered into the lease, he was aware that the property had been used for a gas station. Thus, he knew or should have known that gasoline contamination was possible. He could have required that the property be tested for contamination; he could have negotiated express warranties in the lease. He was in a position to avoid completely the harm he now alleges.

Because there was no duty owed to Rosenblatt, we conclude that Exxon was entitled to judgment on the negligence count as a matter of law; hence, summary judgment was correctly entered.

The Trespass Claim

We have recognized that a trespass occurs when there is interference in the exclusive possession of the land of another, * * * but we have never recognized a trespass where the thing which intrudes actually entered the land during the "trespasser's" possession and the plaintiff took possession of the land subsequent to the "intrusion."

Rosenblatt relies upon § 161 of the Restatement (Second) of Torts (1965) to support his position that Exxon committed a trespass when it allegedly caused the property to be contaminated during its occupancy and the contamination continued into Rosenblatt's occupancy of the land. Section 161 provides that: "A trespass may be committed by the continued presence on the land of a structure, chattel, or other thing which the actor has tortiously placed there."

Section 161 does not support Rosenblatt's position. It explicitly provides that a trespass involves the tortious placing of something on the land and implicitly provides that the affected land is the land of another. Section 158 further supports this interpretation. It states that "one is subject to liability to another for trespass ... if he intentionally enters *land in the possession of the other*, or causes a thing or a third person to do so, or remains on the land, or fails to remove from the land a thing which he is under a duty to remove." (emphasis added). Exxon did not cause the contamination to occur during Rosenblatt's occupancy; the introduction of the contamination could only have occurred prior to its relinquishing possession of the land. Additionally, Exxon owed Rosenblatt no duty to remove the contamination.

Rosenblatt cites no authority, nor do we find any, to support the position he asserts. At least two courts have explicitly rejected similar claims, see Wilson Auto Enterprises v. Mobil Oil Corp., 778 F.Supp. 101 (D.R.I.1991) (company's release of oil on own land could not constitute trespass upon subsequent occupier); Wellesley Hills, supra, 747 F.Supp. at 99 (same), and we think that theirs is the better interpretation. We conclude, therefore, that the trial court did not err in granting Exxon's motion for summary judgment.

THE NUISANCE CLAIM

Rosenblatt cites no legal authority for his claim that the law provides a cause of action in nuisance to a subsequent occupant of land against a prior occupant for activities conducted on the land during the prior occupancy. Nor does our review of the authorities reveal any support for this position.

We have considered the application of the theory of nuisance with regard to the rights of the community at large, in a situation involving a public nuisance, see Tadjer v. Montgomery County, 300 Md. 539, 479 A.2d 1321 (1984), and the rights of adjoining property owners, in the context of a private nuisance, see WSSC v. CAE–Link Corp., 330 Md. 115, 622 A.2d 745, cert. denied, 510 U.S. 907, 114 S.Ct. 288, 126 L.Ed.2d 238 (1993).

Section 821D of the Restatement (Second) of Torts (1965) defines a private nuisance as "a nontrespassory invasion of another's interest in the private use and enjoyment of land." In this regard, we have held that "where a trade or business as carried on interferes with the reasonable and comfortable enjoyment *by another of his property*, a wrong is done to a *neighboring owner* for which an action lies * * *." Meadowbrook Swimming Club v. Albert, 173 Md. 641, 645, 197 A. 146 (1938) (emphasis added).

We have not previously considered a nuisance claim by a subsequent occupier of property. Courts which have considered such claims have rejected them on the basis that a cause of action for private nuisance requires an interference with a neighbor's use and enjoyment of the land. See Philadelphia Electric Co. v. Hercules, Inc., 762 F.2d 303, 313–15 (3d Cir.), cert. denied, 474 U.S. 980, 106 S.Ct. 384, 88 L.Ed.2d 337 (1985); Mayor and Council v. Klockner & Klockner, 811 F.Supp. 1039, 1057–58 (D.N.J.1993); Berry v. Armstrong Rubber Co., 780 F.Supp. 1097, 1103 (S.D.Miss.1991), aff'd, 989 F.2d 822 (5th Cir.1993); Wilson Auto, supra, 778 F.Supp. at 106; Hanlin, supra, 759 F.Supp. at 935; Wellesley Hills, supra, 747 F.Supp. at 98–99. We are in agreement with these authorities. We conclude, therefore, that the instant case does not present a cause of action for nuisance, and the trial court was correct in granting summary judgment on this count.

Notes and Questions

1. Do you agree with the court's conclusion that subsequent owners do not have standing to sue a prior owner for engaging in an abnormally dangerous activity? What language in § 519 most supports that holding? What policy reasons does the court offer to sustain its holding? Is the court relying solely on the caveat emptor doctrine which it stated continues to apply to the sale of commercial, as opposed to residential, property?

2. *Majority Agrees with Rosenblatt.* As the authorities cited in *Rosenblatt* indicated, most courts have arrived at the same conclusion refusing to allow abnormally dangerous activity claims against predecessors in the chain of title or use. For example, in Wellesley Hills Realty Trust v. Mobil Oil Corp., 747 F.Supp. 93, 102 (D.Mass.1990), the court refused to extend liability for abnormally dangerous activities to subsequent owners, finding such liability inconsistent with the focus in § 519 and in *Rylands* on harm to the property of another. The court found that it would be "nonsensical to even formulate a rule that an actor is strictly liable for harm inflicted on his or her own property or person." Accord, 325–343 E. 56th Street Corp. v. Mobil Oil Corp., 906 F.Supp. 669, 677–78 (D.D.C.1995); 55 Motor Ave. Co. v. Liberty Indus. Finishing Corp., 885 F.Supp. 410, 423 (E.D.N.Y.1994); Hydro–Manufacturing, Inc. v. Kayser–Roth Corp., 640 A.2d 950, 955 (R.I.1994); Futura Realty v. Lone Star Bldg. Centers, 578 So.2d 363 (Fla.App.1991), review denied, 591 So.2d 181 (Fla.1991).

In Andritz Sprout–Bauer, Inc. v. Beazer East, Inc., 12 F.Supp.2d 391, 420 (M.D.Pa.1998), the court surveyed all of the authorities and found that New Jersey "appears to be unique in recognizing a cause of action in strict liability assertable by subsequent owners." The *Andritz* court refused to follow the New Jersey approach, instead sticking with the *Rosenblatt* analysis:

> However, the courts rejecting application of the doctrine looked to the language of section 519 and to its origins in English common law. That analysis is, we are persuaded, the proper one. It is plain from the language of section 519 that its scope was not intended to extend to successors-in-title. On that basis, we decline to extend it to the claims asserted here.

3. *The New Jersey Rule.* In T & E Industries v. Safety Light Corp., 123 N.J. 371, 587 A.2d 1249 (N.J. 1991), the Supreme Court of New Jersey held that the current owner can assert a cause of action in strict liability for abnormally dangerous activities against a predecessor in title who disposed of radium on the premises. The court focused on the dangers posed by defendants' alleged conduct and on the inappropriateness of the activity, concluding that those who, to gain some advantage or benefit for themselves, introduce or create an extraordinary risk of harm to the community should, as a matter of policy, bear the risk their acts create to those who acquire title after them. These considerations, the court concluded, justify extending strict liability to successors in title who suffer or are required to redress the consequences of harm caused by the activities of prior owners. The court rejected the contention that by agreeing to purchase the property "as is,"

the purchaser waived any right to bring a strict liability claim, since there was no evidence that the purchaser was aware of the contamination when they agreed to purchase the premises. A party ignorant of the presence of an abnormally dangerous condition could not reasonably be held to have assumed the risk, the courts held.

The court in *T & E* reasoned as follows:

The rule [of strict liability] reflects a policy determination that such "enterprise[s] should bear the costs of accidents attributable to highly dangerous [or unusual activities]." Because some conditions and activities can be so hazardous and of "such relative infrequent occurrence," the risk of loss is justifiably allocated as a cost of business to the enterpriser who engages in such conduct. Although the law will tolerate the hazardous activity, the enterpriser must pay its way.

The rule recognizes an additional policy consideration: such enterprises are in "a better position to administer the unusual risk by passing it onto the public." Because of that opportunity, the enterprise can better bear the loss.

Neither policy rests on notions of property rights. Rather, the first serves to induce certain businesses to "internalize" the external costs of business, while the second seeks to shift a seemingly-inevitable loss onto the party deemed best able to shoulder it. Because the former owner of the property whose activities caused the hazard might have been in the best position to bear or spread the loss, liability for the harm caused by abnormally-dangerous activities does not necessarily cease with the transfer of property.

* * *

The same rationale is just as, if not more, persuasive when a seller who has engaged in an abnormally-dangerous activity and disposed of the by-products of that activity onto the property markets the land. With knowledge of its activity and of its use of the land, the seller is in a better position to prevent future problems arising from its use of the property. And again, allowing a buyer to recover would place liability on the party responsible for creating the hazardous condition and marketing the contaminated land. Moreover, in many respects that rationale echoes the underlying policy of the abnormally-dangerous-activity doctrine: certain enterprises should bear the costs attributable to their activities.

Id. at 387–389.

––––––––

Which rationale is more persuasive? The *Rosenblatt* court's reasoning or that of *T & E Industries*? Is there a rationale for allowing vertical actions in cases involving abnormally dangerous activity but not in nuisance or trespass cases? What two rationales did the court in *T & E* offer for extending liability of the remote seller? Do those policy objectives, which are relied upon in products liability cases, have the same force in vertical real property cases? What may have motivated the court to jettison caveat emptor in *this* case? In hazardous waste cases generally? Why are "as is" contracts insufficient to create an assumption of the risk by the buyer? How can defendant corporation shift the liability imposed on it in 1991 for activities of its corporate predecessor undertaken in the 1920s?

4. *No Liability to Successors for Private Nuisance.* The leading decision holding that subsequent owners do not have standing to sue a prior owner on a private nuisance theory is Philadelphia Electric Co. v. Hercules, Inc., 762 F.2d 303 (3d Cir.1985), cited in *Rosenblatt*. The court's opinion, authored by Judge Leon Higginbotham, reasoned as follows:

> The parties have cited no case from Pennsylvania or any other jurisdiction, and we have found none, that permits a purchaser of real property to recover from the seller on a private nuisance theory for conditions existing on the very land transferred, and thereby to circumvent limitations on vendor liability inherent in the rule of caveat emptor. In a somewhat analogous circumstance, courts have not permitted tenants to circumvent traditional limitations on the liability of lessors by the expedient of casting their cause of action for defective conditions existing on premises (over which they have assumed control) as one for private nuisance.

> * * *

> Similarly, under the doctrine of caveat emptor Hercules [the remote vendor] owed only a limited duty to Gould and, in turn, to PECO [the buyer]. PECO concedes that this duty was not violated. PECO cannot recover in private nuisance for the violation of a duty Hercules may have owed to others–namely, its neighbors.

> We believe that this result is consonant with the historical role of private nuisance law as a means of efficiently resolving conflicts between neighboring, contemporaneous land uses. All of the very useful and sophisticated economic analyses of private nuisance remedies published in recent years proceed on the basis that the goal of nuisance law is to achieve efficient and equitable solutions to problems created by discordant land uses. In this light nuisance law can be seen as a complement to zoning regulations, * * * and not as an additional type of consumer protection for purchasers of realty. Neighbors, unlike the purchasers of the land upon which a nuisance exists, have no opportunity to protect themselves through inspection and negotiation. The record shows that PECO acted as a sophisticated and responsible purchaser–inquiring into the past use of the Chester site, and inspecting it carefully. We find it inconceivable that the price it offered Gould did not reflect the possibility of environmental risks, even if the exact condition giving rise to this suit was not discovered.

> Where, as here, the rule of caveat emptor applies, allowing a vendee a cause of action for private nuisance for conditions existing on the land transferred–where there has been no fraudulent concealment–would in effect negate the market's allocations of resources and risks, and subject vendors who may have originally sold their land at appropriately discounted prices to unbargained-for liability to remote vendees. Such an extension of common law doctrine is particularly hazardous in an area,

such as environmental pollution, where Congress and the state legislatures are actively seeking to achieve a socially acceptable definition of rights and liabilities. We conclude that PECO did not have a cause of action against Hercules sounding in private nuisance.

Id. at 313–316.

5.   Do you agree with Judge Higginbotham's analysis? Insofar as private nuisance is relied upon, he accurately portrays the state of the law; that is, the decisions had uniformly disallowed subsequent owners to sue predecessors in title for the costs of remediating the property from the consequences of the predecessor's activities, so long as fraud or misrepresentation in the sale is not shown. See also Diffenderfer v. Staner, 722 A.2d 1103 (Pa.Super.1998) ("precluding private nuisance claims by subsequent owners or tenants for conditions existing on the very land transferred is sound public policy."); Amland Properties Corp. v. Aluminum Co. of America, 711 F.Supp. 784, 807–08 (D.N.J.1989) (no vertical actions on a nuisance theory); Allied Corp. v. Frola, 730 F.Supp. 626, 634 (D.N.J.1990); 55 Motor Ave. Co. v. Liberty Indus. Finishing Corp., 885 F.Supp. 410, 421 (E.D.N.Y.1994) (finding that courts "have consistently rejected the efforts of property owners who discover contamination on their properties to maintain private nuisance claims against the former owners or lessees"); Rosenblatt v. Exxon, 335 Md. 58, 642 A.2d 180, 189 (1994) ("Courts which have considered such claims have rejected them on the basis that a cause of action for private nuisance requires an interference with a neighbor's use and enjoyment of the land."). However, two California appellate cases, Mangini v. Aerojet–General Corp., 281 Cal.Rptr. 827, 230 Cal.App.3d 1125 (1991) superseded 12 Cal.4th 1087, 51 Cal.Rptr.2d 272, 912 P.2d 1220 (1996), and Capogeannis v. Superior Court, 12 Cal.App.4th 668, 15 Cal.Rptr.2d 796 (1993), have broken this rule and authorized vertical actions on a private nuisance theory.

6.   In Mangini v. Aerojet–General Corp., property owners sued parties who had leased the land from prior owners and contaminated it with hazardous wastes during the leasehold. According to plaintiffs, defendant had leased the property for ten years pursuant to a lease that required the tenant to surrender the premises in "as good a state and condition as when received by lessee, reasonable use and wear thereof consistent with the business engaged in by lessee * * * excepted"; and that defendant had burned or deposited and failed to remove millions of pounds of waste rocket fuel materials and other hazardous substances. Plaintiffs alleged nine different theories, including public and private nuisance, negligence per se (for violating the state health code and water code), trespass, and strict liability for abnormally dangerous activities. The Court of Appeals reversed the trial court's dismissal of these claims, holding the *Philadelphia Electric* and other general authorities on the law of nuisance "do not correctly reflect California law." It continued:

In particular, defendant fails to recognize that California nuisance law is a creature of statute. The California nuisance statutes have been construed, according to their broad terms, to allow an owner of property to sue for damages caused by a nuisance created *on* the owner's property. Under California law, it is not necessary that a nuisance have its origin in neighboring property.

Id. at 834, 230 Cal.App.3d at 1134.

It noted that under California statutes, "an action may be brought by any person whose property is injuriously affected, or whose personal enjoyment is lessened by a nuisance." West's Ann. Cal. Code Civil Procedure § 731. Nuisance is defined in Cal. Civil Code § 3479 (West 1998). Moreover, it also held that it was not necessary that defendant have a possessory interest in the property at the time suit was filed. It acknowledged that consent could be a defense if defendant's use of the property was authorized by the lease, but found the provisions of the lease "patently ambiguous with respect to whether [it] authorized hazardous waste disposal during the term of the lease" and imposed an obligation upon defendant to clean up any hazard before vacating the premises.

7. *Public Nuisance.* Should the principle of caveat emptor that bars private nuisance claims between those in the chain of title apply with equal force to public nuisance claims? At least one case holds "no." In Westwood Pharmaceuticals, Inc. v. National Fuel Gas Dist. Corp., 737 F.Supp. 1272 (W.D.N.Y.1990), aff'd, 964 F.2d 85 (2d Cir.1992), a purchaser of a gas manufacturing facility site was permitted to maintain a public nuisance action to recover the costs of remediating the property against a former operator of the facility. The court distinguished the *Hercules* case on the grounds that New York's law of standing in public nuisance cases was broader than Pennsylvania's, that defendant's release of hazardous substances at the site was a public nuisance, and that plaintiff's incurrence of response costs constituted special injury. However, consistent with *Hercules*, it rejected plaintiff's private nuisance claim as barred by the doctrine of caveat emptor. Also allowing a public nuisance claim by the purchaser against a former owner is Interstate Power Co. v. Kansas City Power & Light Co., 909 F.Supp. 1224 (N.D.Iowa 1991).

8. *Negligence. Rosenblatt* also held that a former owner or tenant of the property owes no duty to a subsequent owner to protect it from contamination on the property. What was the court's primary rationale for so holding? Why doesn't foreseeability of harm operate as a sufficient test in cases such as *Rosenblatt*? If owners and occupiers of land owed a duty to successors-in-title, what disincentives does that create for buyers?

The most exhaustive analysis of negligence liability is set forth in Hydro–Manufacturing, Inc. v. Kayser–Roth Corp., 640 A.2d 950 (R.I.1994), where a property owner sued a prior owner for extensive contamination which the state environmental agency had ordered to be remediated. In holding that the extension of a common-law duty from prior owners is not warranted, the court offered these reasons: (1) the buyer's ability to inspect the property; (2) a cause of action for misrepresentation exists if the seller is untruthful; (3) buyer can negotiate a price to reflect the actual economic value of the land; (4) or get a warranty or indemnity clause from the seller; (5) the buyer has a cause of action under CERCLA and possibly state environmental law.

9. *Trespass.* Finally *Rosenblatt* rejected the argument that a prior owner could be liable on a trespass theory to a subsequent owner. Plaintiff's trespass theory is that the releases and discharges of hazardous substances by the defendants and the presence of these substances in the soil and

groundwater of the property constitute a "continuing trespass," and that the plaintiffs never authorized the invasion of their property with hazardous substances. In support of this claim, plaintiffs rely on Section 161(1) of the Restatement (Second) of Torts which provides in pertinent part "[a] trespass may be committed by the continued presence on the land of a * * * thing which the actor has tortiously placed there, whether or not the actor has the ability to remove it."

The principal case supporting this position is a decision of a California intermediate appellate court, Newhall Land and Farming Co. v. Superior Court of Fresno County, 19 Cal.App.4th 334, 23 Cal.Rptr.2d 377 (1993). In *Newhall* the court concluded that the owner of property was liable to the property's subsequent owner for continuing trespass since the first owner during its occupancy had placed contaminants in the soil which remained on the property. The court concluded that the first owner had "tortiously" placed the contaminants in the soil in the first instance since in so doing he created a public nuisance and the continued presence of the contaminants constituted a continuing trespass.

The overwhelming majority of courts have rejected this theory. For example in 55 Motor Avenue Co. v. Liberty Industrial Finishing Corp., 885 F.Supp. 410, 424 (E.D.N.Y.1994), the court reasoned as follows:

> An actionable trespass must involve a wrongful or unjustifiable entry upon the land of another. * * * Although New York Courts have not addressed a trespass claim on facts similar to the instant case, this Court does not believe that New York courts would follow the California precedent and eliminate the basic element of a trespass claim, namely, the invasion of the property of another. The majority of jurisdictions to address claims of continuing trespass where a current owner of property seeks damages for contamination from a former owner or lessee have rejected these claims for failure to allege the basic element of intrusion upon the land of another, since in each case the contamination occurred prior to plaintiffs' ownership and while the defendants were lawful occupants of the premises.

In one sense trespass is the weakest of theories: How can one "trespass" on one's own property?

Problem

From 1977 to 1987, Chemco, Inc. manufactured chlorine using the mercury cell process at its facility on the edge of a riverside industrial park in Newburg, New Union. Louise River bisects Newburg with the industrial park upriver about two miles from the center of town. The manufacturing process produced a waste in the form of a wet, mercury-contaminated sludge.

From 1977 to 1980, prior to the introduction of its state-of-the-art waste handling and disposal process, Chemco placed the sludge into concrete lined basins. The sludge was allowed to settle in the basins, which were separate from the facility's waste water treatment system. During those three years, following the settling process, Chemco separated reusable brine at the top of the basins from the heavy sludge which sank to the bottom of the basins: Mr. David Doubilet managed the Chemco facility throughout 1977–1987.

In 1987, Chemco sold the chlorine facility to Pinatubo Chemical Co. (PCC). PCC retained David Doubilet as plant manager and, under his supervision, made further improvements to its waste handling and disposal process.

In 1992, following an unusual number of neurological disorders and other health problems in the neighborhood, two hundred area residents abutting the industrial park brought a class action against PCC and twenty other manufacturing facilities located in the park, and each of their plant managers. The complaint demanded $100 million in compensatory damages for personal injuries and diminution of property values as a result of chemical contamination of their groundwater, and $200 million in punitive damages for knowing concealment of the contamination. Plaintiffs' class action relied on theories of trespass, public and private nuisance, negligence, and strict liability for abnormally dangerous activities. In their complaint, plaintiffs' alleged that pre-suit hydrogeological studies revealed that traces of mercury threatened the groundwater and were present in the wells of several class members.

After plaintiffs' complaint was filed, Mr. Doubilet informs his counsel (separate from counsel representing PCC), that he is aware of facts that would be prejudicial to both himself and PCC. On three or four different occasions that he can't recall exactly, before Chemco sold the facility to PCC, he observed one of Chemco's officers overseeing several other employees drain the concrete basins into an outflow which flowed through its primary industrial sewer into the Louise River. Doubilet states that he also saw liquid contents at the bottom of the basins seeping into the ground.

Mr. Doubilet tells his lawyer that he does not know whether that drainage or seepage reached the groundwater table eight feet beneath the basins and about three hundred yards to the north of the nearest residential well, but his "guess" is that the mercury-contaminated liquid probably did, or probably will, spill or leak into the groundwater. The facility never has had a permit to dispose of hazardous waste on the ground or into the groundwater, and never has disclosed to any regulatory authority any nonpermitted disposal of hazardous waste. While acknowledging that he is no expert in hydrogeology, he recalls once being advised by the New Union Department of Natural Resources, at the time the industrial park was obtaining the necessary permits, that the area had experienced problems with water wells because the groundwater moved very rapidly through the kind of soil prevalent in that area. Moreover, he recalls being told that anything reaching the Louise River had the potential of contaminating water supplies in the area.

At all times since 1977, federal and New Union laws have prohibited the disposal by any person of hazardous waste (including mercury-contaminated sludge) into the environment (including the groundwater) without a permit. New Union environmental protection statutes, like the federal law, define disposal to mean "the discharge, deposit, injection, dumping, spilling, leaking or placing" of hazardous wastes and defines persons to include "any individual, corporation or other entity who knows or should know of a disposal of hazardous waste." Any violation of these federal and state laws carries civil penalties of $25,000 per day, and constitutes a felony.

Part A

You are counsel for PCC. Among the tasks you need to accomplish is to evaluate plaintiffs' legal theories. You would like to move to dismiss at least a few of the counts based on nuisance, public and private, and trespass, as early in the case as possible. *Assuming* that traces of mercury are found in plaintiffs' wells and in groundwater samples and also assuming that those traces could have (but not necessarily did) originated at PCC's facility, evaluate the public and private nuisance and trespass claims.

Part B

Assume you are counsel for Mr. Doubilet. Your objective is to get your client out of this mess without exposing him to criminal or civil liabilities. Counsel for the class has noticed Doubilet's deposition. Doubilet has shared with you all of the information described above. How do you advise your client to respond to the inevitable questions that will be directed at him regarding his knowledge and participation in the potentially damaging events?

Part C

You are one of the class counsel and have interviewed at least ten residents of the area near the Riverside Industrial Park. Two of your clients were formerly employed by Chemco, but lost their jobs when the plant was sold to PCC. One formerly worked for the cost control manager and he recalls on at least two occasions that the manager had instructed him (and a few others) to drain the contents of the basins into the outflow because they were getting too full. As Chairperson of the Class Coordinating Committee, you know that this newly discovered information is potentially explosive. One threshold question you must resolve is whether to recommend amending the complaint to name Chemco as a defendant. Discuss the strategic concerns relating to instituting suit against Chemco based on the same nuisance and trespass theories and strict liability.

Part D

Assume PCC cleans up the contamination on the property following an EPA or state order to do so. Can PCC sue Chemco on a theory of trespass, nuisance, or strict liability to recover the costs of cleanup?

Alternatively, assume that PCC entered into a settlement agreement with other defendants to pay the class a total of $20 million. If PCC's portion of the settlement is $1 million, can it sue Chemco for recovery of that amount? What tort theories will it rely upon? What other factors might bear upon its ability to recover from Chemco?

For some academic literature on this topic, see, Albert G. Besser, Caveat Emptor–Where Have You Gone?, 4 Hofstra Prop. L. J. 203 (1992); Jim C. Chen & Kyle E. McSlarrow, Application of the Abnormally Dangerous Activities Doctrine to Environmental Cleanups, 47 Bus. Law. 1031 (1992); (Comment, Hazardous Waste: Liability of Predecessors in Title, 29 San Diego L. Rev. 93 (1992)). Christine M. Beggs, As Time Goes By: The Effect of

Knowledge and the Passage of Time on the Abnormally Dangerous Activity Doctrine, 21 Hofstra L. Rev. 205 (1992).

F. MISREPRESENTATION AS A BASIS OF LIABILITY

If none of the theories of liability heretofore considered can support suits by a current owner against a former owner or user of the property, is the owner left without a remedy? Not necessarily. Caveat emptor can be trumped by the tort of fraud or misrepresentation. If the seller affirmatively represents that there is no contamination on the property a statement known to be false, the buyer can maintain an action for fraudulent misrepresentation after the contamination is discovered and causes damage. See, Restatement (Second) of Torts § 523 (1977).

So too, if the seller takes affirmative steps to conceal the presence of contamination or prevent the buyer from ascertaining the true state of affairs, liability can attach for fraudulent concealment. See Restatement (Second) of Torts § 523.

1. LIABILITY FOR NON–DISCLOSURE

But what if the seller does neither, but merely remains silent while possessing knowledge of such a dangerous condition on the property? Assume also that the buyer never asks a question as to which such a disclosure would be responsive. And how about going one step further, the seller possesses knowledge of the existence of a former landfill near to the property? What are the seller's obligations to disclose to the buyer this kind of "negative" information? The next opinion considers these important questions.

STRAWN v. CANUSO

Supreme Court of New Jersey, 1995.
140 N.J. 43, 657 A.2d 420.

O'HERN, J.

The issue in this case is whether a builder-developer of new homes and the brokers marketing those homes have a duty to disclose to prospective buyers that the homes have been constructed near an abandoned hazardous-waste dump. The Appellate Division held that such a duty exists. We agree and affirm the judgment of the Appellate Division primarily for the reasons stated in its opinion.

I

The case concerns the claims of more than 150 families seeking damages because the new homes that they bought in Voorhees Township, New Jersey, were constructed near a hazardous-waste dump site, known as the Buzby Landfill. The complaint named as defendants John

B. Canuso, Sr., and John B. Canuso, Jr., and their companies: Canetic Corporation and Canuso Management Corporation. Fox & Lazo Inc. (Fox & Lazo), the brokerage firm that was the selling agent for the development, was also named as a codefendant.

Plaintiffs base their claims on common-law principles of fraud and negligent misrepresentation, and the New Jersey Consumer Fraud Act, N.J.S.A. 56:8–1 to–66. [Plaintiffs] purchased their homes between 1984 and 1987.

The Buzby Landfill consists of two tracts of property, a nineteen-acre portion owned by RCA and a contiguous thirty-seven-acre parcel now owned by Voorhees Township. Those two tracts were the site of a landfill from 1966 to 1978. Although the Buzby Landfill was not licensed to receive liquid-industrial or chemical wastes, large amounts of hazardous materials and chemicals were dumped there. The landfill was also plagued by fires.

Toxic wastes dumped in the Buzby Landfill began to escape because it had no liner or cap. Tests done by the New Jersey Department of Environmental Protection and Energy (DEPE) revealed that leachate was seeping from the landfill into a downstream lake. The DEPE estimated that half of the landfill material was submerged in ground water, thereby contaminating the ground water with hazardous substances. Additional tests indicated the presence of hazardous waste in ground water, in marsh sediments taken from the landfill, and in lakes southeast of the landfill.

RCA installed a system at the landfill to vent excessive levels of methane gas at the site. DEPE's site manager discovered gas leaks in that venting system. Those leaks released contaminants, including benzene and other volatile organic compounds. In 1986, methane gases, which naturally accumulate in landfills, emanated from the dump site. Reports of the federal Environmental Protection Agency (EPA) confirm that residents' complaints about odors and associated physical symptoms are consistent with expected reactions to exposure to gases from the landfill. EPA recommended that the site be considered for a Superfund cleanup.

Plaintiffs allege that the developers knew of the Buzby Landfill before they considered the site for residential development. Plaintiffs contend that although defendants were specifically aware of the existence and hazards of the landfill, they did not disclose those facts to plaintiffs when they bought their homes. A 1980 EPA report warned: "The proposed housing development on land adjacent to the site has all the potential of developing into a future Love Canal if construction is permitted." A copy of the EPA report was in the Canuso defendants' files. Those defendants also met with a DEPE employee to discuss the prospects of building homes near the landfill. (Later reports of regulatory agencies tempered those earlier reports, one of which described any risk as "indeterminate.") * * *

In addition, one of Fox & Lazo's marketing directors urged his firm and the individual Canuso defendants to disclose the existence of the Buzby Landfill to home buyers. Each refused that request and instead followed a policy of nondisclosure. That policy continued even after early purchasers complained about odors. Defendants' representatives were instructed never to disclose the existence of the Buzby Landfill, even when asked about such conditions. Later, some prospective home buyers, having independently learned about the Buzby Landfill, refused to convert their initial non-binding deposits into enforceable agreements of sale.

John Canuso, Jr., who personally supervised the sales force, instructed his sales manager to ascertain what information DEPE was providing to people who asked about the landfill. The sales manager spoke with a DEPE representative, who again warned defendants of the problems of building a large development near the landfill. The sales manager repeated in a memorandum the warnings given to her by the DEPE employee and placed the memorandum with related papers in a "hazardous waste" file that the Canuso defendants maintained. John Canuso, Jr., discussed this memorandum with his father, John Canuso, Sr., who refused to disclose to home buyers the proximity of the landfill.

On defendants' motions for summary judgment against the individual plaintiffs, the trial court ruled that "there is no duty that the owner of lands owe[s] to a prospective purchaser to disclose to that prospective purchaser the conditions of somebody else's property," but added that if the sellers made a statement concerning someone else's property they could be liable for their affirmative misrepresentations. The trial judge granted summary judgment dismissing all of the claims of seven plaintiff-families. (The nineteen other plaintiff-families who asserted that affirmative misrepresentations had been made to them were granted jury trials on common-law fraud and Consumer Fraud Act claims.)

The seven plaintiff-families sought leave to appeal to the Appellate Division. After granting leave to appeal, the Appellate Division held that the builders and brokers of the new multi-home development had a duty to disclose to potential buyers the existence of a nearby, closed landfill.

Only gradually has the law of real property assimilated other principles of law. One commentator observed that "the law offers more protection to a person buying a dog leash than it does to the purchaser of a house." John H. Scheid, Jr., Note, Mandatory Disclosure Law: A Statute for Illinois, 27 J.Marshall L.Rev. 155, 160 (1993) (citing Paul G. Haskell, The Case for an Implied Warranty of Quality in Sales of Real Property, 53 Geo.L.J. 633 (1965)). For years, "[c]ourts continued to cling to the notion that a seller had no duty whatsoever to disclose anything to the buyer."

* * *

[I]n the field of real property, the doctrine of caveat emptor survived into the first half of the twentieth century. Generally speaking, "the principle of caveat emptor dictates that in the absence of express agreement, a seller is not liable to the buyer or others for the condition of the land existing at the time of transfer." T & E Indus., Inc. v. Safety Light Corp., 123 N.J. 371, 387, 587 A.2d 1249 (1991) (citing Restatement (Second) of Torts § 352 comment *a* (1977)).

III

Whatever its origins or purposes, "the rule of caveat emptor has not retained its original vitality. With time, and in differing contexts, we have on many occasions questioned the justification for the rule." *T & E Indus., Inc.*, supra, 123 N.J. at 388, 587 A.2d 1249.

Exceptions to the broad immunity of caveat emptor inevitably developed in the sale of land. In Schipper v. Levitt & Sons, Inc., 44 N.J. 70, 207 A.2d 314 (1965), the Court held that a builder-developer of real estate gave an implied warranty that the structure it built would be properly constructed—a warranty of its habitability.

In McDonald v. Mianecki, 79 N.J. 275, 298, 398 A.2d 1283 (1979), the Court extended the principles of Schipper to a small-scale builder of new homes and held that an implied warranty of habitability included a potable water supply. The Court used the occasion to note that the doctrine of caveat emptor "as applied to new houses is an anachronism patently out of harmony with modern home buying practices."

Finally, in Weintraub v. Krobatsch, 64 N.J. 445, 455–56, 317 A.2d 68 (1974), the Court ruled that a seller of real estate had an obligation to disclose the existence of roach infestation unknown to the buyers. The Court noted that in certain circumstances " 'silence may be fraudulent.' " Id. at 449, 317 A.2d 68. Further, "relief may be granted to one contractual party where the other suppresses facts," that he or she "under the circumstances, is bound in conscience and duty to disclose to the other party, and in respect to which he cannot, innocently, be silent."

IV

Other jurisdictions have limited the doctrine of caveat emptor. In California, when the seller knows of facts materially affecting the value or desirability of property and the seller also knows that such facts are not known to, or within the reach of the diligent attention and observation of the buyer, the seller is subject to a duty to disclose those facts to the buyer. Lingsch v. Savage, 213 Cal.App.2d 729, 29 Cal.Rptr. 201, 209 (1963); see also Easton v. Strassburger, 152 Cal.App.3d 90, 199 Cal.Rptr. 383 (1984) (imposing duty on broker to inspect property listed for sale to determine whether settlement or erosion problems are likely to occur and to disclose such information to prospective purchasers).

One author has noted:

California and Colorado courts have taken the lead in imposing on sellers affirmative obligations to disclose matters materially affecting the value of the property. This information disclosure obligation applies broadly and includes defects in construction and soil conditions as well as matters wholly external to the property that appreciably affect its value.

* * *

Sellers generally need disclose only matters of which they have some degree of personal knowledge. Thus, the complicated issue of a seller's knowledge remains a major matter of dispute. Sellers, moreover, need only disclose matters not reasonably ascertainable by the buyer, a limit that denies relief to buyers who should have known the relevant information. Under some formulations of the duty the seller must also know or suspect that the buyer is acting in ignorance. Different jurisdictions limit relief in other ways. Wisconsin, for example, only imposes disclosure duties on professional sellers.

[Eric T. Freyfogle, Real Estate Sales and the New Implied Warranty of Lawful Use, 71 Cornell L.Rev. 1, 25–28 (1985) (footnotes omitted).]

We need not debate the outer limits of the duty to disclose. As of 1988, the courts of only California, New Mexico, and Utah had "advanced the law of real estate beyond fraud to simple negligence by establishing an affirmative duty to buyers to investigate the property for material defects." Sarah Waldstein, A Toxic Nightmare on Elm Street: Negligence and the Real Estate Broker's Duty in Selling Previously Contaminated Residential Property, 15 B.C.Envtl.Aff.L.Rev. 547, 551 (1988). Several jurisdictions have responded to such developments with statutory amendments. California and Illinois have adopted mandatory disclosure laws. Cal.Civ.Code §§ 1102 to 1102.15; Ill.Ann.Stat. ch. 765, para. 77/1 to /99. * * *

V

In the absence of such legislation or other regulatory requirements affecting real estate brokers, the question is whether our common-law precedent would require disclosure of off-site conditions that materially affect the value of property. By its favorable citation of California precedent, *Weintraub*, supra, 64 N.J. at 454–55, 317 A.2d 68, establishes that a seller of real estate or a broker representing the seller would be liable for nondisclosure of on-site defective conditions if those conditions were known to them and unknown and not readily observable by the buyer. Such conditions, for example, would include radon contamination and a polluted water supply. Whether and to what extent we should extend this duty to off-site conditions depends on an assessment of the various policies that have shaped the development of our law in this area.

As noted, the principal factors shaping the duty to disclose have been the difference in bargaining power between the professional seller of residential real estate and the purchaser of such housing, *McDonald*, supra, 79 N.J. at 289–90, 398 A.2d 1283; Schipper, supra, 44 N.J. at 91–92, 207 A.2d 314, and the difference in access to information between the seller and the buyer, *Weintraub*, supra, 64 N.J. at 455–56, 317 A.2d 68. Those principles guide our decision in this case.

The first factor causes us to limit our holding to professional sellers of residential housing (persons engaged in the business of building or developing residential housing) and the brokers representing them. Neither the reseller of residential real estate nor the seller of commercial property has that same advantage in the bargaining process. Regarding the second factor, professional sellers of residential housing and their brokers enjoy markedly superior access to information. Hence, we believe that it is reasonable to extend to such professionals a similar duty to disclose off-site conditions that materially affect the value or desirability of the property.

In addition, we note that the policies of New Jersey's Consumer Fraud Act apply to commercial sellers of real estate and brokers engaged in such transactions. "[T]he [Consumer Fraud] Act was intended as a response only to the public harm resulting from ' * * * unconscionable practices engaged in by professional sellers seeking mass distribution of many types of consumer goods,' and not to the isolated sale of a single family residence by its owner." DiBernardo v. Mosley, 206 N.J.Super. 371, 376, 502 A.2d 1166 (App.Div.) Real estate brokers, agents, and salespersons representing professional sellers of real estate are subject to the provisions of the Consumer Fraud Act.

Practices prohibited by the Consumer Fraud Act include affirmative acts and acts of omission. Consumer fraud consisting of affirmative acts does not require a showing of intent. To hold a defendant liable for an act of omission, however, requires a finding that defendant acted "knowingly." Chattin v. Cape May Greene, Inc., 243 N.J.Super. 590, 598–99, 581 A.2d 91 (App.Div.1990), aff'd o.b., 124 N.J. 520, 591 A.2d 943 (1991). The Consumer Fraud Act states that "the omission of any material fact with intent that others rely upon such * * * omission, in connection with the sale * * * of * * * real estate" is an "unlawful practice." N.J.S.A. 56:8–2. A "material fact" is not confined to conditions on the premises. Defendants, however, would have us limit their liability to nondisclosures violative of Restatement (Second) of Torts § 551 (1977). That is, the conduct must be the equivalent of "swindling" or "shocking to the ethical sense of the community." Restatement (Second) of Torts § 551(2)(e) comment 1 (1977). When conduct rises to that level, a purchaser may recover treble damages for any ascertainable loss, plus reasonable attorney's fees under the Consumer Fraud Act. Cox v. Sears Roebuck & Co., 138 N.J. 2, 24, 647 A.2d 454 (1994).

Short of that showing of unconscionability, a purchaser may establish a common-law claim by showing that the seller's or the broker's nondisclosure of material facts induced the purchaser to buy.

The silence of the Fox & Lazo representatives and the Canuso Management Corporation's principals and employees "created a mistaken impression on the part of the purchaser." Defendants used sales-promotion brochures, newspaper advertisements, and a fact sheet to sell the homes in the development. That material portrayed the development as located in a peaceful, bucolic setting with an abundance of fresh air and clean lake waters. Although the literature mentioned how far the property was from malls, country clubs, and train stations, "neither the brochures, the newspaper advertisements nor any sales personnel mentioned that a landfill [was] located within half a mile of some of the homes."

The fact that no affirmative misrepresentation of a material fact has been made does not bar relief. The suppression of truth, the withholding of the truth when it should be disclosed, is equivalent to the expression of falsehood. The question under those circumstances is whether the failure to volunteer disclosure of certain facts amounts to fraudulent concealment, or, more specifically, whether the defendant is bound in conscience and duty to recognize that the facts so concealed are significant and material and are facts in respect to which he [or she] cannot innocently be silent. Where the circumstances warrant the conclusion that [the seller] is so bound and has such a duty, equity will provide relief.

Is the nearby presence of a toxic-waste dump a condition that materially affects the value of property? Surely, Lois Gibbs would have wanted to know that the home she was buying in Niagara Falls, New York, was within one-quarter mile of the abandoned Love Canal site. See Lois M. Gibbs, Love Canal: My Story (1982) (recounting residents' political struggle concerning leaking toxic-chemical dump near their homes). In the case of on-site conditions, courts have imposed affirmative obligations on sellers to disclose information materially affecting the value of property. There is no logical reason why a certain class of sellers and brokers should not disclose off-site matters that materially affect the value of property.

We know that the physical effects of abandoned dump sites are not limited to the confines of the dump. For example, in Ayers v. Township of Jackson, 106 N.J. 557, 525 A.2d 287 (1987), toxic pollutants from a landfill contaminated the water supply of residents of nearby homes. In Citizens for Equity v. New Jersey Department of Environmental Protection, 126 N.J. 391, 599 A.2d 507 (1991), we invalidated a regulation of the New Jersey Department of Environmental Protection that prohibited an award of value-diminution damages to owners of property located more than one-half mile from the landfill area. Implicit in that regulation was the recognition that even without physical intrusion a landfill may cause diminution in the fair market value of real property located nearby. We agreed with the Appellate Division's determination that regulation contravened the Sanitary Landfill Facility Closure and Contingency Fund Act, specifically N.J.S.A. 13:1E–106, which makes the fund liable for all damages proximately resulting from operations or closure of any sanitary landfill. 126 N.J. at 393, 599 A.2d 507.

In short, our precedent and policy offer reliable evidence that the value of property may be materially affected by adjacent or nearby landfills. Professional sellers in southern New Jersey could not help but have been aware of the potential effects of such conditions. * * *

In December 1983, the Real Estate Commission wrote to the Camden County Board of Realtors, stating that "[b]ecause of the potential effects on health, and because of its impact on the value of property, location of property near a hazardous waste site is a bit of information that should be supplied to potential buyers. Difficulties in selling such property should be disclosed to potential sellers." In addition, N.J.A.C. 11:5–1.23(b) requires that a broker "make reasonable effort to ascertain all pertinent information concerning every property for which he accepts an agency * * *. The licensee shall reveal all information material to any transaction to his client or principal and when appropriate to any other party." Although not dispositive of the issues in this case, those sources certainly suggest that professional sellers should have been aware of some changing duty requiring them to be more forthcoming with respect to conditions affecting the value of property.

The duty that we recognize is not unlimited. We do not hold that sellers and brokers have a duty to investigate or disclose transient social conditions in the community that arguably affect the value of property. In the absence of a purchaser communicating specific needs, builders and brokers should not be held to decide whether the changing nature of a neighborhood, the presence of a group home, or the existence of a school in decline are facts material to the transaction. Rather, we root in the land the duty to disclose off-site conditions that are material to the transaction. That duty is consistent with the development of our law and supported by statutory policy.

We hold that a builder-developer of residential real estate or a broker representing it is not only liable to a purchaser for affirmative and intentional misrepresentation, but is also liable for nondisclosure of off-site physical conditions known to it and unknown and not readily observable by the buyer if the existence of those conditions is of sufficient materiality to affect the habitability, use, or enjoyment of the property and, therefore, render the property substantially less desirable or valuable to the objectively reasonable buyer. Whether a matter not disclosed by such a builder or broker is of such materiality, and unknown and unobservable by the buyer, will depend on the facts of each case.

We realize that there is considerable debate regarding the nature and extent of the hazard imposed by the Buzby Landfill. For example, defendants note that the Buzby Landfill has never been on the Superfund list or the New Jersey Priority List, both of which delineate toxic landfill sites; that much of the information on which plaintiffs rely postdates their purchase of the property; that Fox & Lazo was involved in only a portion of the sales (those between 1985 and 1986); and that some of the plaintiffs have already sold their homes at a profit. Those and other facets of the case will bear on its final resolution.

Ultimately, a jury will decide whether the presence of a landfill is a factor that materially affects the value of property; whether the presence of a landfill was known by defendants and not known or readily observable by plaintiffs; and whether the presence of a landfill has indeed affected the value of plaintiffs' property. Location is the universal benchmark of the value and desirability of property. Over time the market value of the property will reflect the presence of the landfill. Professional builders and their brokers have a level of sophistication that most home buyers lack. That sophistication enables them better to assess the marketability of properties near conditions such as a landfill, a planned superhighway, or an office complex approved for construction. With that superior knowledge, such sellers have a duty to disclose to home buyers the location of off-site physical conditions that an objectively reasonable and informed buyer would deem material to the transaction, in the sense that the conditions substantially affect the value or desirability of the property.

Notes and Questions

1. *Fraud.* The elements of fraud are straightforward:

a. A false representation made by the defendant. In the ordinary case, this representation must be one of fact.

b. Knowledge or belief on the part of the defendant that the representation is false—or, what is regarded as equivalent, that he has not a sufficient basis of information to make it. This element often is given the technical name of "scienter."

c. An intention to induce the plaintiff to act or to refrain from action in reliance upon the misrepresentation.

d. Justifiable reliance upon the representation on the part of the plaintiff, in taking action or refraining from it.

e. Damage to the plaintiff, resulting from such reliance.

See Prosser & Keeton, Law of Torts § 105.

2. *Concealment.* In addition to positive misrepresentations, an action for fraud may be predicated on active concealment of the truth; that is, words or acts which create a false impression covering up the truth, as by placing defective sheets of aluminum between many good sheets and making it difficult for the buyer to examine any but the top and bottom sheets, constitutes a fraudulent concealment. Prosser & Keeton, Law of Torts § 106. The Restatement (Second) of Torts § 550 expresses the concealment principle as follows:

> One party to a transaction who by concealment or other action intentionally prevents the other from acquiring material information is subject to the same liability to the other, for pecuniary loss as though he had stated the nonexistence of the matter that the other was thus prevented from discovering.

3. *Nondisclosure.* In contrast to concealment, the Restatement and commentators have struggled with the issue of how to treat pure or tacit

nondisclosures, where the defendant has not actively made any assertion nor prevented the plaintiff from acquiring the truth by concealment, but is nevertheless aware that the plaintiff is operating under a misapprehension respecting the true state of affairs. That, of course, is the *Strawn* case. Although the general rule may still be that "pure" nondisclosure is not actionable as fraud, the rule is riddled with exceptions that create a duty to make full or truthful disclosure of the material facts to another. Among the exceptions are:

> a.   Where the defendant stands in a fiduciary relation or position of trust to the plaintiff.

> b.   Where the defendant has made a partial or ambiguous statement that will be misleading absent full disclosure.

> c.   Where the defendant acquires new information that renders previously furnished statements misleading.

In addition, the Restatement (Second) of Torts adds another, more amorphous standard, that creates a duty to disclose "facts basic to the transaction if he knows the other is about to enter it under a mistake as to them and that the other, because of the relationship between them, the customs of the trade, or other objective circumstances, could reasonably expect a disclosure of those facts." § 551. The court in *Strawn* did not rely on this Restatement provision in arriving at the duty to disclose it created.

4.   *The Limits of the Duty to Disclose.* What limitations did the court in *Strawn* place on this newly-recognized duty to disclose off-site conditions? On whom did the court place the duty to disclose? All sellers of real property? Commercial sellers? Brokers?

5.   *Brokers and Codes of Ethics.* One frequently overlooked area to support a buyer's action consists of the professional codes of conduct of the potential defendants. Courts have recognized that the Code of Ethics of the National Association of Realtors may also impose a duty upon real estate salespersons. Menzel v. Morse, 362 N.W.2d 465, 469 (Iowa 1985); Easton v. Strassburger, 152 Cal.App.3d 90, 101–02, 199 Cal.Rptr. 383 (1984). See Neveroski v. Blair, 141 N.J.Super. 365, 375, 358 A.2d 473 (App.Div.1976) (broker may be liable to purchaser for failure to disclose material facts affecting the desirability and value of property).

6.   *What Information Must Be Disclosed? Role of Justifiable Reliance.* An Ohio court in an environmental tort case summarized the justifiable reliance test as follows:

> Reliance is justified if the representation does not appear unreasonable on its face and if, under the circumstances, there is no apparent reason to doubt the veracity of the representation. Crown Property Dev., Inc. v. Omega Oil Co., 113 Ohio App.3d 647, 681 N.E.2d 1343, 1349 (Ohio Ct. App. 1996).

In addition to the scienter requirement actionable fraud also requires justifiable reliance by the plaintiff. Thus, the plaintiff must actually rely on the misrepresentation in acting as he or she did, and the reliance must be justifiable. Restatement (Second) of Torts § 537. The idea is that if the misrepresentation was not relied upon by the plaintiff there is no basis for liability. The issue of the justifiability of the reliance turns primarily on the materiality or significance of the facts misrepresented:

(1) Reliance upon a fraudulent misrepresentation is not justifiable unless the matter misrepresented is material.

(2) The matter is material if

(a) a reasonable [person] would attach importance to its existence or nonexistence in determining his choice of action in the transaction in question; or

(b) the maker of the representation knows or has reason to know that its recipient regards or is likely to regard the matter as important in determining his choice of action, although a reasonable [person] would not so regard it.

Restatement (Second) of Torts § 538.

Prosser & Keeton on Torts § 110 at 766–67 expresses the importance of materiality as follows:

The party deceived must not only be justified in his belief that the representation is true, but he must also be justified in taking action on that basis. This usually is expressed by saying that the fact represented must be a material one. There are misstatements which are so trivial, or so far unrelated to anything of real importance in the transaction, that the plaintiff will not be heard to say that they substantially affected his decision. Necessarily the test must be an objective one, and it cannot be stated in the form of any definite rule, but must depend upon the circumstances of the transaction itself. The most cogent reason for the requirement of materiality is that of promoting stability in commercial transactions.

Was the information not disclosed in *Strawn* "material"? Would a reasonable buyer, objectively assessed, attach importance to the existence of a closed landfill in the neighborhood? In what way was the information potentially material?

Was the buyer's reliance on nondisclosure justifiable? Was this the kind of information that is not reasonably ascertainable by the buyer? How might a buyer go about obtaining information respecting environmental risks? If you represented buyers of residential property, how would you advise your clients?

The court gives as other examples of material information that would require disclosure, i.e., radon contamination and a polluted water supply. What other examples can you think of?

Some cases fail for lack of justifiable reliance. In Crown Property Development, Inc. v. Omega Oil Co., 113 Ohio App.3d 647, 681 N.E.2d 1343 (Ohio Ct. App. 1996), a prospective purchaser sued the vendor for fraud and negligent misrepresentation, arguing that seller had orally agreed to grant it a right of first refusal to acquire the property during the time that remediation was ongoing pursuant to an Ohio governmental order. The court, however, held that reliance on such an oral representation was not justifiable because the buyer knew that remediation was an ongoing process and prior extensions or modifications had all been in writing.

7. *Off-Site Conditions. Strawn* is not the first decision to impose a duty to disclose off-site conditions. See, e.g., O'Leary v. Industrial Park Corp., 14 Conn.App. 425, 542 A.2d 333 (1988) (seller liable for fraudulent misrepresentation based on failure to disclose existence of a well 1700 feet from site of real estate); Powell v. Wold, 88 N.C.App. 61, 362 S.E.2d 796 (1987) (home buyers stated claims against broker for both fraud and negligent misrepresentation for failing to disclose plans to build major highway extension near home being sold, where buyers had asked broker if there was any factor that would adversely affect the value of the property and his response mentioned one factor but not this, even though the broker knew or should have known of this project and its substantial adverse impact on property value); McRae v. Bolstad, 32 Wash.App. 173, 646 P.2d 771 (1982), aff'd, 101 Wash.2d 161, 676 P.2d 496 (1984). See Feist v. Roesler, 86 S.W.2d 787 (Tex. Ct. Civ. App. 1935) (buyer of property liable for fraudulent nondisclosure that affected value of land).

8. *Causation.* What if the seller offers evidence that the buyer would have consummated the transaction even if it was aware of the information? In other words, must the absence of the disclosure be a cause-in-fact of the deal? Florida courts have noted that "a fact is material when if the representation had not been made, the contract or transaction would not have been entered into. Conversely, a representation is not material when it appears that the contract or transaction would have been entered into notwithstanding it." Morris v. Ingraffia, 154 Fla. 432, 18 So.2d 1, 3 (1944).

Who should have the burden of proof on this issue? Won't the buyer invariably offer self-serving testimony that she would not have gone through with the transaction if she had been informed of the nondisclosed information? If materiality is judged by an objective standard, does that not mean causation also should be objectively assessed?

9. *Commercial Property.* Is the court fashioning a rule of disclosure between a commercial seller and commercial buyer? If not, why not? What are the major policy justifications the court offers for its disclosure duty? Would those policy reasons apply with equal force if the owner of an industrial facility declined to disclose past disposal practices to a buyer of all its assets? How can commercial enterprises best protect themselves from environmental liabilities? In Chapter 10 we consider in some detail the rules governing a current owner's claim against past owners and operators of the property to recover clean-up costs under CERCLA. But such suits are incredibly expensive and protracted, and may not represent the best alternative for the current owner of the property. Chapter 10 also includes material on contractual indemnification, which may permit a disgruntled buyer to pursue a simpler contractual remedy in lieu of tort or statutory remedies. On this topic, see, Fraud and the Duty to Disclose Off–Site Land Conditions: Actual Knowledge Versus Seller Status, 24 B.C. Envtl. Aff. L. Rev. 897 (1997).

2. FAILURE TO PROVIDE DISCLOSURE MANDATED BY LAW

Disclosure of property contamination may be required by state or federal law. Whether the buyer should be permitted to avoid the sale, or to prevail in an action for money damages, is the subject of the following decision. The facts involved the seller's failure to either provide to the buyer a "negative" that the property was not contaminated, or an affirmation to the state environmental department that the property was contaminated but that the seller would undertake its remediation. Prior to its sale as a warehouse, the property had been used as a gasoline service station.

EDWARD A. VISCONTI, JR. v. PEPPER PARTNERS LIMITED PARTNERSHIP

Appellate Court of Connecticut, 2003.
77 Conn.App. 675, 825 A.2d 210.

OPINION BY: PETERS

OPINION:

When there is a sale of real property that may be environmentally contaminated, the Hazardous Waste Transfer Act (Transfer Act), General Statutes § 22a–134 et seq., requires a transferor either to provide to a transferee a negative declaration to indicate that the property poses no environmental threat or to certify to the department of environmental protection that remediation measures will be undertaken. In this case, the contract for the sale of the property provided that the transferee would take the risk of environmental contamination and bear the cost of whatever remediation might be necessary. The principal issue is whether these express provisions should be set aside because they resulted from fraudulent misrepresentation or nondisclosure. Concluding that the plaintiff transferee had failed to allege sufficient facts to demonstrate fraudulent misconduct, the trial court granted a motion for summary judgment filed by the defendant transferors. We affirm the judgment of the trial court.

The plaintiff, Edward A. Visconti, Jr., n1 filed a twelve count complaint seeking damages and injunctive relief from the defendants, Pepper Partners Limited Partnership (Pepper Partners), Ernest A. Wiehl, Jr. (Ernest Wiehl), Richard V. Wiehl and Consumer Petroleum of Connecticut, Inc. Only four of these counts are before us on this appeal. These counts allege fraud (count one), fraudulent nondisclosure (count two), negligent misrepresentation (count seven) and breach of duty to remediate (count eleven). The plaintiff claimed that he was entitled to monetary and injunctive relief and to a declaratory judgment requiring the defendants to remediate all environmental contamination on the property and to reimburse him for the reasonable costs that he had incurred for the containment, removal or mitigation of such environmental contamination.

* * *

Defendants denied the material allegations in the plaintiff's complaint and filed a number of special defenses. The most significant of these special defenses asserted that the plaintiff's claims were barred by the terms of the contract of sale of the property and by applicable statutes of limitation. The defendants also filed a counterclaim based on an indemnity provision in the contract of sale.

[The trial court] the court granted the [defendants'] motion for summary judgment.

The record and the court's memorandum of decision set out the relevant undisputed facts. On February 9, 1996, the plaintiff bought property located at 199–211 Naugatuck Avenue, Milford, from the defendant Pepper Partners by quitclaim deed. At that time, the property was vacant but, as the plaintiff knew, a gasoline station and an automobile repair shop previously had been located there. The plaintiff had worked at the gasoline station at an earlier time.

In 1988, as a result of an order of abatement issued by the city of Milford, Ernest Wiehl had three underground gasoline tanks and one waste oil storage tank removed from the property. At the same time, he had the contaminated soil in the vicinity of the tanks removed and replaced by clean fill. In 1989, Ernest Wiehl quitclaimed his ownership in the property to Pepper Partners. The property lay idle until the plaintiff purchased it in 1996.

In 1995, observing that the property was for sale, the plaintiff visited the site in the company of a real estate agent representing Ernest Wiehl. The agent told the plaintiff, and Ernest Wiehl subsequently confirmed, that the underground tanks had been removed and that the authorities were satisfied. The plaintiff observed the difference in the soil where the tanks had been removed and new fill had been brought in.

In his deposition, the plaintiff acknowledged that, after the site visit, he assumed that the soil around the tank area was contaminated. None of the defendants ever told him that the soil was environmentally clean. None of the defendants ever told him not to have the soil tested to discover whether it was contaminated.

Later in 1995, the plaintiff and Pepper Partners entered into negotiations for the conveyance of the property to the plaintiff. Throughout, the plaintiff was represented by counsel of his choice. Under the terms of the contract of sale that the plaintiff executed in January, 1996, the plaintiff agreed to purchase the property for a down payment of $5000 and to execute a mortgage note to Pepper Partners for $200,000. At the closing on February 9, 1996, the plaintiff made the down payment and executed the mortgage and the note. He has not made any further payments since that time.

The contract of sale specifically addressed the environmental concerns raised by the hazardous waste generated by the use of the property as a gas station and an automobile repair shop in the 1980s. The contract provided that the plaintiff, at his own expense, would "make such inspections of the Premises (including without limitation a Phase I environmental site assessment)" as the plaintiff deemed appropriate. The contract advised the plaintiff that the property might fall within the definition of a hazardous waste "establishment" that would require environmental remediation. It placed on the plaintiff the burden of executing the requisite environmental certifications, of paying the accompanying filing fees and of taking responsibility for any needed environmental testing and cleanup.

* * *

Prior to the closing, Pepper Partners reminded the plaintiff of his environmental obligations. Pepper Partners indicated its willingness to postpone the closing until the plaintiff had undertaken an environmental study of the property and to release the plaintiff from the contract of sale in the event that the study dissuaded the plaintiff from proceeding further. Pepper Partners insisted, however, that it would not convey the property without the plaintiff's signing and filing of the required Transfer Act forms. To this end, Pepper Partners provided the necessary forms to the plaintiff, stating therein the environmental history of the property's prior use as an automobile repair shop. In the contract of sale, the plaintiff acknowledged that Pepper Partners had made no representations about the environmental condition of the property except to inform the plaintiff that the property might be an environmental "establishment" because of its prior use as a service station.

The plaintiff declined to perform a preclosing environmental examination of the property and signed and filed the Transfer Act forms, without additions or deletions, as they had been prepared by Pepper Partners. [Cc] On February 5, 1996, the plaintiff advised Pepper Partners that he was anxious to close the sale as early as possible. The closing took place on February 9, 1996. [Cc]

The trial court granted the motion of the defendants for summary judgment on all counts of the plaintiff's complaint. It concluded, in relevant part, that the plaintiff, in count one, had not alleged material facts to sustain his claim of fraud because, even if Ernest Wiehl had been untruthful in representing that the 1988 cleanup had satisfied the relevant authorities, the plaintiff had not relied on that representation to establish that the property was not contaminated. It further held that count two, alleging fraudulent nondisclosure, was untenable in light of the provisions in the contract of sale that assigned the risk of environmental hazards to the plaintiff. It determined that the plaintiff could not succeed in count seven, alleging negligent misrepresentation, for the same reason that it could not succeed on the fraud count. Finally, the court held that the statute of limitations barred the plaintiff's statutory claim in count eleven to recover for environmental damage. In this appeal, the plaintiff challenges the validity of each of these conclusions.

We review the granting of a motion for summary judgment according to a well-established standard. * * * In deciding whether the trial court properly determined that there was no genuine issue of material fact, we review the evidence in the light most favorable to the "nonmoving party." [Cc] (Citation omitted; internal quotation marks omitted.) * * *

I. Negligent or Fraudulent Misrepresentation

The plaintiff's claims for negligent misrepresentation (count seven) and fraud (count one) focus on the statement made to the plaintiff by Ernest Wiehl, which informed the plaintiff that, after the 1988 removal of underground tanks from the property that the plaintiff subsequently purchased, "the authorities were satisfied." The trial court held that this statement "might equal" a false representation.

The plaintiff emphasizes the importance of a false representation to a claim of negligent misrepresentation. Proving a false representation is, however, only one part of a claim of actionable misrepresentation. To prevail, the plaintiff also was required to show that he reasonably relied on that misrepresentation. "One who, in the course of his business, profession or employment . . . supplies false information for the guidance of others in their business transactions, is subject to liability for pecuniary loss caused to them by their justifiable reliance upon the information, if he fails to exercise reasonable care or competence in obtaining or communicating the information." (emphasis added; internal quotation marks omitted.) Williams Ford, Inc. v. Hartford Courant Co., 232 Conn. 559, 575, 657 A.2d 212 (1995); * * * 3 Restatement (Second) Torts § 552, pp. 126–27 (1977).

The requirement of reliance applies also to an action for fraud. "The essential elements of an action in common law fraud . . . are that: (1) a false representation was made as a statement of fact; (2) it was untrue and known to be untrue by the party making it; (3) it was made to induce the other party to act upon it; and (4) the other party did so act upon that false representation to his injury." (Emphasis added; internal quotation marks omitted.) Suffield Development Associates Ltd. Partnership v. National Loan Investors, L.P., 260 Conn. 766, 777, 802 A.2d 44 (2002)[.]

To prevail, therefore, the plaintiff must have alleged sufficient facts to demonstrate his reliance on the statement made by Ernest Wiehl. He has failed to do so. In his deposition, he acknowledged his independent knowledge of continued soil contamination, derived from his observation of differences in the color of the soil at the site of the removal of the storage tanks. In the contract of sale, he acknowledged that the property might be an environmental "establishment" and undertook to investigate and disclose the environmental condition of the property. In the mortgage, he again acknowledged that he had assumed the responsibility for remediating any environmental hazards that the property might contain. In light of these specific assertions of assumption of risk, the trial court properly found no probative value in the plaintiff's bare statements that he had relied on Wiehl's representation.

II. Fraudulent Nondisclosure

The plaintiff's claim of fraudulent nondisclosure, in count two of his complaint, arises out of the fact that, in 1989, when the property was transferred to Pepper Partners, the defendants did not comply with the reporting provisions of the Transfer Act. That failure came to light on May 22, 2000, when the department of environmental protection issued a notice of violation to Ernest Wiehl. The notice informed him that "contamination existed on this parcel prior to the transfer" because of the former use of the property as an auto body repair shop.

The plaintiff maintains that the defendants' failure to comply with the Transfer Act in 1989 was, in effect, an assertion that the property contained nothing that would give rise to any environmental concern. Had the defendants made the proper filings, they would have had to undertake the required environmental cleanup. Instead, he argues, having failed to comply with the Transfer Act, they fraudulently transferred contaminated property to him.

The plaintiff does not dispute the fact that, in the contract of sale of the property to him, he expressly undertook to take whatever steps for remediation the property might require. He recognizes that in Holly Hill Holdings v. Lowman, 226 Conn. 748, 628 A.2d 1298 (1993), our Supreme Court held that contractual provisions may preclude "a private right of action ... based on a transferor's noncompliance with pretransfer disclosure regulations." In that case, as in this one, the transferee "had actual knowledge of the existing underground gasoline storage tanks ... that were associated with the service station." Further, as in this case, the transferor had not given the transferee or the department of environmental protection the written notification contemplated by the applicable environmental statute. Id .. * * *

Section 22a–449 (d)–1 (f) (1) of the Regulations of Connecticut State Agencies provides: "No owner or operator shall transfer ownership, possession or control of any new or existing facility without full disclosure to the transferee of the status of the facility with respect to compliance with these regulations at least fifteen (15) days prior to the transfer. Such disclosure shall include an up-to-date copy of the information submitted to the commissioner pursuant to subsection (d)."

The plaintiff would have us distinguish this case from Holly Hill Holdings on the ground that he was unaware of the environmental hazards posed by the property. That argument is untenable. His deposition discloses that he knew the soil near the removed tanks to be contaminated even after removal of the tanks themselves.

The unassailable fact is that, in the contract of sale, the plaintiff assumed the risk that the property might have environmental problems when he purchased it. He had the opportunity to investigate possible environmental hazards before the transfer of the property but chose not to make the relevant inquiries. We agree with the trial court that, under these circumstances, the defendants had no duty to make any further disclosures to the plaintiff. See * * *; 3 Restatement (Second), supra, § 551 (2) (e), comment (j), p. 123.

III. VIOLATION OF GENERAL STATUTES § 22A–16

In his final claim before this court, the plaintiff claims that he is entitled to a remedy under General Statutes § 22a–16, n11 which authorizes "any person" to bring an action "for the protection of the public trust in the air, water and other natural resources of the state from unreasonable pollution, impairment or destruction. . . . " Tracking the language of the statute, the plaintiff, in count eleven of his complaint, alleged that the defendants' actions in causing the environmental contamination of his property "unreasonably polluted, impaired, or destroyed the public trust in the water and/or natural resources of the state of Connecticut."

In one of their special defenses, the defendants asserted that this claim was barred by the statute of limitations contained in General Statutes § 52–577. That statute requires an action "founded upon a tort" to be brought "within three years from the date of the act or omission complained of." The plaintiff does not dispute the applicability of this statute in this case. The trial court agreed with the defendants that the plaintiff's statutory claim was time barred. * * * The plaintiff's argument on appeal focuses on the fact that the defendants continued to own the polluted property after it had been vacated. According to the plaintiff, the defendants had a continuing duty to remediate the pollution caused by the former use of the property as a gasoline station and an automobile repair shop. The department of environmental protection apparently takes the same view. In May, 2000, the department notified Pepper Partners that the partnership should have complied with the requirements of the Transfer Act in 1989, when it acquired the property from Ernest Wiehl. The notice advised Pepper Partners to file the requisite environmental condition assessment form and a property transfer program—form III within thirty days.

According to the plaintiff, Pepper Partners' failure to comply with their continuing duty to remediate the environmental pollution on their property was a continuing breach of duty that was actionable until his purchase of the property in 1998. This argument raises a question of first impression.

The defendants argue, as the trial court held, that the plaintiff's analysis is flawed because, under § 52–577, the clock starts running on the date of the act or omission of which the plaintiff complains. [Cc]The plaintiff has not challenged that proposition.

The question that must yet be answered, however, is whether a failure to remediate pollution of which the defendants were aware is an "omission" that continues to be actionable as long as it continues to exist. The defendants maintain that § 22a–16 authorizes the plaintiff's pursuit of an environmental cause of action for negligent contamination only if that contamination was caused by their treatment, storage or disposal of hazardous waste, waste oil or petroleum or chemical liquids. As the defendants note, the plaintiff's complaint is so phrased. Once the property became vacant, the defendants did not cause further pollution. In other words, the plaintiff's failure to charge them with an "omission" of their continuous duty to remediate the pollution and his concomitant failure to invoke an argument of omission in response to the motion for summary judgment now bars him from any recovery under § 22a–16.

This procedural argument, standing alone, might not be persuasive. It is buttressed, however, by the text of § 22a–16.

The plaintiff cites Starr v. Commissioner of Environmental Protection, 627 A.2d 1296 (1993), and Starr v. Commissioner of Environmental Protection, 675 A.2d 430 (1996). Those cases involved the question whether an innocent landowner bore liability for "maintaining" preexisting environmental contamination by failing to undertake remedial measures. Until the legislature created an innocent landowner defense, the Supreme Court construed the applicable statute, General Statutes § 22a–432, to impose continuing liability for maintaining a condition that reasonably could be expected to create a source of pollution.

The Starr cases are, however, distinguishable because the governing statute, § 22a–432, expressly imposed liability on a property owner who maintained a contaminated condition on his property. Section 22a–16 has no comparable language. We decline to engraft language on § 22a–16 that it does not contain. See Spears v. Garcia, 263 Conn. 22, 32, 818 A.2d 37 (2003)[.]

We conclude, therefore, that the trial court properly granted the defendants' motion for summary judgment with respect to the plaintiff's statutory claim under § 22a–16. It might be troublesome that the statute of limitations had run on this claim even before the plaintiff purchased the property if the plaintiff had not unequivocally assumed all environmental risks by the terms of the contract of sale to which he subscribed.

The judgment is affirmed.

In this opinion the other judges concurred.

3. NEGLIGENT MISREPRESENTATION

What if the seller simply fails to exercise reasonable care in providing information on environmental risks to a buyer? Is negligence alone a sufficient basis for liability? The following opinion demonstrates the reach of negligence and negligent misrepresentation.

BINETTE v. DYER LIBRARY ASSOCIATION

Supreme Judicial Court of Maine, 1996.
688 A.2d 898.

RUDMAN, JUSTICE.

David and Karen Binette appeal from the summary judgments entered in the Superior Court in favor of the Dyer Library Association, Clifford Purvis, and Vacationland Realty on the Binettes' claims of negligent misrepresentation and violation of the Maine Unfair Trade Practices Act (UTPA), 5 M.R.S.A. §§ 205–A to 214 (1989 & Supp.1995).

The Binettes argue (1) that the Dyer Library Association, Purvis, and Vacationland Realty breached a duty of reasonable care by omitting to tell them of the existence of a 3000–gallon underground oil tank on property owned by the library association and sold to the Binettes, (2) that the defense of charitable immunity, 14 M.R.S.A. § 158–A (Supp. 1995), is not available to Purvis on their claim for negligent misrepresentation, and (3) that the defendants' failure to disclose the existence of the tank to them prior to the sale constitutes an unfair and deceptive act in violation of section 207 of the UTPA. We affirm in part and vacate in part the summary judgments entered in favor of the defendants.

The Dyer Library Association, a charitable corporation, operates a library and a museum in Saco. In 1987 the library association acquired a residential property in Saco on the death of Joseph Deering. The Deering property harbored a 3000–gallon underground heating oil storage tank registered by Deering with the Department of Environmental Protection. The library association listed the property for sale with Vacationland Realty, a partnership in which Clifford Purvis and another were partners. In addition to being a licensed real estate broker, Purvis was a trustee and officer of the Dyer Library Association. In July 1988 David and Karen Binette bought the Deering property for $351,000. The library association paid a sales commission of $8,775 to Vacationland Realty.

The Binettes contend that they learned of the existence of the oil tank only after the closing, when their first oil delivery was made. They contend they were forced to have the tank removed because it was corroded and allowed oil to leak into the ground and water to leak into their fuel oil, contaminating their property and destroying their heating system.

In 1994 the Binettes filed a three-count complaint against the Dyer Library Association, Vacationland Realty, and Clifford Purvis for fraud, negligent misrepresentation, and violation of the UTPA. The Binettes later voluntarily dismissed their claims for fraud. The court granted a motion for summary judgments filed by defendants Purvis and Vacationland Realty pursuant to M.R.Civ.P. 56. * * * This appeal followed.

I

We consider one by one the Binettes' claims against the three defendants for negligent misrepresentation. * * *

II

We consider next whether the court erred in granting the Dyer Library Association's motion for a summary judgment on the Binettes' claim for negligent misrepresentation.

Maine has adopted section 552 of the Restatement (Second) of Torts as the appropriate standard for "negligent misrepresentation claims." Bowers v. Allied Inv. Corp., 822 F.Supp. 835, 839 (D.Me.1993) (citing

Diversified Foods, Inc. v. First Nat'l Bank of Boston, 605 A.2d 609, 615 (Me.1992)). The Restatement (Second) provides:

> One who, in the course of his business, profession or employment, or in any other transaction in which he has a pecuniary interest, supplies false information, for the guidance of others in their business transactions, is subject to liability for pecuniary loss caused to them by their justifiable reliance upon the information if he fails to exercise reasonable care or competence in obtaining or communicating the information.

Restatement (Second) of Torts § 552(1) (1977). The entry of a summary judgment in favor of the defendant library association is improper if the record establishes prima facie evidence that the Dyer Library Association (1) in a transaction in which the association had a pecuniary interest (2) supplied false information for the guidance of the Binettes (3) without exercising reasonable care or competence and that (4) the Binettes justifiably relied on that false information in their purchase of the Deering property.

A Transaction of Pecuniary Interest

The Dyer Library Association does not dispute that the transaction here was one in which the association had a pecuniary interest.

Supplying False Information

Before we can assess whether prima facie evidence on the record establishes that the Dyer Library Association supplied false information to the Binettes, we must determine as a matter of law what may constitute the supplying of false information. The Dyer Library Association said nothing to the Binettes concerning the underground oil tank. The library association argues that liability for negligent misrepresentation requires the affirmative supplying of false information. We disagree.

We have adopted for purposes of fraudulent misrepresentation the doctrine that an omission by silence may constitute the supplying of false information. Horner v. Flynn, 334 A.2d 194, 203 (Me.1975), overruled on other grounds by Taylor v. Comm'r of Mental Health & Mental Retardation, 481 A.2d 139 (Me.1984). We now hold for purposes of negligent misrepresentation that, although not every failure to disclose constitutes a misrepresentation, silence rises to the level of supplying false information when such failure to disclose constitutes the breach of a statutory duty.

Pursuant to 38 M.R.S.A. § 563(6) (1989), which became effective September 27, 1987, the owner of real estate on which an underground oil tank is located must file written notice of the existence of the tank prior to the sale or transfer of that real estate. Section 563(6) is a safety statute. 38 M.R.S.A. § 561 (1989 & Supp.1995). Buyers of real estate on which an underground oil tank is located are vulnerable to the dangers of an oil leak on the property and are among those the statute is intended to protect.

Section 563(6) does not limit the disclosure requirement to those sellers who know of an underground storage tank on their property. The statute's disclosure requirement, rather, is absolute. Section 563(6) mandates that when an underground oil tank exists on property for sale the seller of that property may not remain silent.

A Duty of Reasonable Care

Because the evidence establishes that the Dyer Library Association owed the Binettes an absolute statutory duty to disclose the existence of the underground oil tank, the library association's silence regarding the tank constitutes supplying false information as a matter of law. Although Maine does not recognize the doctrine of negligence per se, violation of a safety statute constitutes evidence of a breach of a duty of reasonable care owed to those the statute is designed to protect. The Dyer Library Association's failure to disclose the tank, a violation of section 563(6), is evidence of a breach by the library association of a duty of reasonable care owed to the Binettes, and can be considered by a factfinder along with other evidence relevant to the "reasonable care" element of the tort of misrepresentation.

Justifiable Reliance

David Binette testified he believed the property he bought from the Dyer Library Association would have been maintained by the well known Deering family with "the best" heating system. He testified he bought the property in the belief that the heating system was "perfect." The record, therefore, includes evidence that the Binettes bought the Deering property in reliance on the library association's failure to disclose otherwise.

The Binettes' testimony, viewed in the light most favorable to them, establishes prima facie evidence that the Binettes did not know of the underground tank prior to the sale and furthermore that its existence was not obvious. When, as here, the defendant is under a duty to disclose, a plaintiff need not investigate the truth of the defendant's silence in order to be held to have relied justifiably on that silence. Given the existence at the time of the sale of a statute requiring the Dyer Library Association to inform the Binettes of an underground oil storage tank that was neither known to the Binettes nor obvious, the Binettes may be held to have relied justifiably on the library association's silence in concluding there was no underground oil storage tank on the Deering property, let alone a leaking one, and in buying the property based on that belief.

Summary Judgment Improper

The affidavits, depositions, and testimony on the record, viewed in the light most favorable to the Binettes, establish as a matter of law that the Dyer Library Association, in a transaction in which the association had a pecuniary interest, supplied false information. There remain, however, genuine issues of material fact as to whether the library association's breach of its statutory duty was without the exercise of reasonable care or competence and whether the Binettes reliance was justifiable. The court erred in granting a summary judgment to the Dyer Library Association on the Binettes' claim for negligent misrepresentation.

III

We complete our triad review of the summary judgments entered on the Binettes' claims for negligent misrepresentation by considering the summary judgment entered in favor of Vacationland Realty.

"A trial court is free to consider company or state regulations among the factors to be weighed in deciding whether a legal duty existed." Trusiani v. Cumberland & York Distribs., Inc., 538 A.2d 258, 262 (Me.1988). Regulations promulgated by the Real Estate Commission of the Department of Professional and Financial Regulation pursuant to 32 M.R.S.A. § 13065 (1988) and in effect at the time of the July 1988 sale of the Deering property required a licensed listing broker to inform himself of hazardous materials on property for sale, expressly including underground storage tanks, and to convey information pertinent to such hazardous materials in writing to the buyer prior to or during preparation of an offer. Me. Dep't of Professional and Financial Regulations Reg. 330.19 (Feb. 1, 1988).

As with other rules promulgated pursuant to subchapter II of chapter 113 of Title 32, Reg. 330.19 is a judicially enforceable standard of care intended to serve the interests of the public as well as the real estate industry. 32 M.R.S.A. §§ 13065, 13068 (1988). By its own terms Reg. 330.19 is a safety regulation whose purpose is to protect real estate customers.

The relevant real estate regulations create no absolute duty of disclosure for brokers akin to that imposed on property owners by statute. That statute deals only with information that owners of property must give to prospective buyers. * * *

Although the real estate regulations applicable to a broker also describe information that the broker must impart to the prospective buyer, they do not do so in the absolute terms of the statute. Instead, the regulations create a duty to disclose material defects of which a licensee has knowledge or should have had knowledge given the exercise of reasonable care, and establish the licensee's obligations to inquire of the property owner as to any hazardous materials on or in the real estate, including underground storage tanks, and to convey in writing to the buyer what is learned or the fact that the information is unavailable. Me. Dep't of Prof. and Fin.Reg. 330.14, 330.19 (Feb. 1, 1988).

Thus, the real estate regulations prescribe a process of interaction between the broker, the owner, and the buyer intended to keep buyers informed about hazardous materials that are or might be on the property. In this instance, the jury should decide whether Vacationland Realty and Purvis exercised reasonable care in light of these regulatory requirements. Put most simply, the owners of the property were responsible for the misrepresentation about the presence of the underground oil tank. Arguably, the brokers could have prevented that misrepresentation if they had performed as the regulations require. This is the familiar negligence inquiry, not an inquiry about negligent misrepresentation.

We vacate the summary judgment in favor of Vacationland Realty on plaintiffs claim of negligent misrepresentation and direct the court to allow the plaintiffs to amend their complaint to recast the negligent misrepresentation claims against Vacationland Realty and Purvis as claims of negligence.

Notes and Questions

1. Question of Duty. If Maine had not enacted a statutory duty on sellers to disclose the existence of underground storage tanks, would the court have recognized a common-law duty in negligence as the New Jersey Supreme Court did in *Strawn* based on fraud? Recall that duty is a question of law and a court can determine under what circumstances one party has an obligation to use reasonable care for the protection of another.

In *Rosenblatt* the Maryland Court of Appeals refused to create a duty running from a remote seller to a buyer. Is that holding consistent with the holding in *Binette*? What is the crucial difference between the two cases? Is it the degree of remoteness in the relationship between plaintiff and defendant? Does the court in *Binette* place any reliance on privity of contract? In *Rosenblatt,* if the law of Maryland had a statute similar to Maine's, would the outcome have differed? Does the fact that plaintiff is a noncommercial buyer have any significance?

2. Broker Liability. Note that Vacationland Realty may face liability for simple negligence, *not* negligent misrepresentation or nondisclosure. What is it that the broker should have done? How can a broker best assure that the seller discloses to it information respecting hazardous materials? If the broker is found liable on remand, does it have an indemnity or contribution claim against the Library Association? Does the broker have an obligation to inspect the property for the presence of hazardous chemicals? Some jurisdictions have chosen to regulate brokers' responsibilities for environmental matters by statute. See, e.g., Cal. Civil Code §§ 1102–1102.15 (West 1998); Ill. Ann. Stat., Ch. 765, ¶ ¶ 77/1 to 77/99 (1998).

3. Unfair Deceptive Trade Practices. In *Binette*, the court also considered a claim under the Maine Unfair Trade & Practices Act, 5 M.R.S.A. § 207. Coverage of these statutes is beyond our purview. But the prudent lawyer, where a defendant is engaged in a trade or business, must investigate the availability of such a statutory remedy.

4. Notification Statutes. The reporting statute in *Binette* is not unusual. Many jurisdictions have enacted statutes requiring that industrial facilities report the release of contaminants into the environment. See, e.g., New Jersey Air Pollution Control Act, N.J.S.A. 26:2C–1 to 25.2 (requiring that DEP be notified "immediately" of release of air pollutants); see, New Jersey Department of Envt. Protection v. Alden Leeds, Inc., 153 N.J. 272, 708 A.2d

1161 (N.J. 1998) (notification of fire caused by release of chemicals within 18 minutes satisfied "immediately" test); California Hazardous Substance Account Act, Cal. Health & Safety Code § 25363 (West 1998). (Pursuant to California's Hazardous Substances Account Act), the property owner should immediately report the findings of contamination to both the appropriate regional office and the state headquarters of the Department of Toxic Substances Control, a unit of the California Environmental Protection Agency.

A Note on Some Other Potentially Liable Parties

We have for the most part focused on the liability of property owners and property sellers. Certainly these are the most frequent targets of environmental tort suits. But occasionally, as in the *Hagen* case reproduced earlier, the net of liability can reach contractors and consultants. But there may be impediments to such claims.

1. *Consultants.* Consider the case of Bronstein v. GZA GeoEnvironmental, Inc., 140 N.H. 253, 665 A.2d 369 (N.H. 1995), in which the purchasers of property sued an environmental firm hired by the seller to conduct an environmental survey of the property, on which hazardous waste was subsequently discovered. The court's analysis in finding that defendant owed no duty to the plaintiffs is as follows:

> The second question presented by this interlocutory appeal is whether based on the facts appearing in the record below, GZA owed a duty in tort to the purchasers of the property, the BFM plaintiffs. GZA was hired by plaintiff Stephen Bronstein to prepare an environmental assessment of the property. GZA never dealt directly with the BFM plaintiffs. The BFM plaintiffs, however, argue that GZA owed them a duty of care because it was reasonable that they would rely on GZA's environmental assessment of the property.

> A duty of care arises if harm is a sufficiently probable consequence of an act that a careful person would avoid. See Chiuchiolo v. New England Wholesale Tailors, 84 N.H. 329, 332, 150 A. 540, 542 (1930) (duty of care arises "when the probable chances of injury are great enough to lead the ordinary [person] in the defendant's place to take measures to lessen or avoid the chances"). "Duty and foreseeability are inextricably bound together. The risk reasonably to be perceived defines the duty to be obeyed." Corso v. Merrill, 119 N.H. 647, 651, 406 A.2d 300, 303 (1979) (quotation omitted). GZA's duty, therefore, "is measured by the scope of the risk [that its] negligent conduct foreseeably entails." Id. (quotation omitted).

> The BFM plaintiffs argue that GZA owed them a duty of care because GZA was in the business of providing information for the guidance of others. The plaintiffs rely on § 552 of the Restatement (Second) of Torts:

> (1) One who, in the course of his business * * * supplies false information for the guidance of others in their business transactions, is subject to liability for pecuniary loss caused to them by their justifiable

reliance upon the information, if he fails to exercise reasonable care * * * in obtaining or communicating the information.

(2) Except as stated in Subsection (3), the liability stated in Subsection (1) is limited to loss suffered

(a) by the person or one of a limited group of persons for whose benefit and guidance he intends to supply the information or knows that the recipient intends to supply it; and

(b) through reliance upon it in a transaction that he intends the information to influence or knows that the recipient so intends or in a substantially similar transaction.

Restatement (Second) of Torts § 552, at 126–27 (1977). Under the terms of the agreement between GZA and Bronstein, the report was prepared "for the exclusive use of [Bronstein]." Bronstein could convey the report to its lender and title insurer, but further dissemination to other parties was forbidden "except for the specific purpose, and to the specific parties alluded to above, without the prior written consent of GZA."

The report itself contained a similar limitation. It is clear, therefore, from the language in the agreement that GZA only intended to benefit Bronstein. While GZA knew that the report would be furnished to the lender, it was not reasonably foreseeable that Bronstein would furnish the information to the BFM plaintiffs, or that the BFM plaintiffs would rely on the report. GZA therefore owed no duty of care to the BFM plaintiffs. Corso, 119 N.H. at 651, 406 A.2d at 303 (individual is liable "only to those who are foreseeably endangered [and] only with respect to those risks or hazards whose likelihood made the conduct unreasonably dangerous" (quotation omitted)).

The BFM plaintiffs argue that because GZA knew that Bronstein would transmit the report to its lender, it was reasonably foreseeable that the lender would transmit the report to other buyers. We disagree. The report itself contained the limitation on dissemination. The lender, therefore, was aware of the limitations. Additionally, it would not be reasonably foreseeable that information supplied to a lender by a potential purchaser would be transmitted by that lender to other purchasers.

We therefore affirm the trial court's * * * grant of summary judgment based on the absence of a duty owed by GZA to the BFM plaintiffs. 665 A.2d at 371–72.

Bronstein reminds the student of the principle from the basic torts course that negligence duties arise out of the relationship between the parties. Essentially here plaintiffs and defendants were strangers–no contractual privity existed between them, nor any "foreseeable" reliance by plaintiffs on defendants' work product. As to liability of remediation contractors see, Lemmon, The Developing Doctrine of Rylands v. Fletcher: Hazardous Waste Remediation Contractors Beware, 42 Loy. L. Rev. 287 (1996).

2. *Attorneys.* What if an attorney for one party to a transaction negligently prepares and delivers to the vendor inaccurate reports respecting percolation tests performed on the property which report the prospective buyer relies on in making the purchase? Can the buyer non-client sue the attorney for negligence? In Petrillo v. Bachenberg, 139 N.J. 472, 655 A.2d

1354 (N.J. 1995), the New Jersey Supreme Court held that the attorney owed a duty to the buyer and should have foreseen use of the report in any attempted sale of the property and that a prospective purchaser would rely on the report in deciding whether to buy the property. Some of the court's reasoning is as follows:

> As a claim against an attorney for negligence resulting in economic loss, Petrillo's claim against Herrigel is essentially one for economic negligence. Formerly, the doctrine of privity limited such claims by non-clients against attorneys and other professionals. Jay M. Feinman, Economic Negligence: Liability of Professionals and Businesses to Third Parties for Economic Loss 29 (1995). More recently, other doctrines have replaced privity as a means of limiting a professional's duty to a non-client.

* * *

> Whether an attorney owes a duty to a non-client third party depends on balancing the attorney's duty to represent clients vigorously, Rules of Professional Conduct, Rule 1.3 (1993), with the duty not to provide misleading information on which third parties foreseeably will rely, Rules of Professional Conduct, Rule 4.1 (1993). See also Restatement of the Law Governing Lawyers § 73 comment b (Tentative Draft No. 7, 1994) (discussing rationale for imposing duty to non-clients).

* * *

> The New York Court of Appeals has likewise held that an attorney may owe a duty to specific non-clients who rely on the attorney's representations. See Prudential Insurance Co. of America v. Dewey, Balantine, Bushby, Palmer & Wood, 80 N.Y.2d 377, 590 N.Y.S.2d 831, 605 N.E.2d 318 (1992). In Prudential, a lender sued a borrower's attorney for negligently preparing an opinion letter that was provided to the lender as a condition to a debt restructuring. An attorney could be liable to a non-client for negligent misrepresentation, the court conceded, if the nature of the relationship between the attorney and the non-client was "so close as to approach that of privity." 605 N.E.2d at 320. The court stated the criteria for finding a duty:

> (1) an awareness by the maker of the statement that it is to be used for a particular purpose; (2) reliance by a known party on the statement in furtherance of that purpose; and (3) some conduct by the maker of the statement linking it to the relying party and evincing its understanding of that reliance. 605 N.E.2d at 321–22.

> Thus, when courts relax the privity requirement, they typically limit a lawyer's duty to situations in which the lawyer intended or should have foreseen that the third party would rely on the lawyer's work. For example, a lawyer reasonably should foresee that third parties will rely on an opinion letter issued in connection with a securities offering.

* * *

> Likewise, in Century 21 Deep South Properties, Ltd. v. Corson, 612 So.2d 359 (Miss.1992), a buyer of real property sued alleging negligence

of the attorney for the seller, who had conducted a title search on which the buyer had detrimentally relied. The Mississippi Supreme Court held that "an attorney performing title work will be liable to reasonably foreseeable persons who, for a proper business purpose, detrimentally rely on the attorney's work." Id. at 374.

Similarly, section 73 of the proposed Restatement of the Law Governing Lawyers, supra, pertaining to "duty to certain non-clients," provides:

For the purposes of liability[,] * * * a lawyer owes a duty to use care * * *:

* * *

(2) To a non-client when and to the extent that the lawyer or (with the lawyer's acquiescence) the lawyer's client invites the non-client to rely on the lawyer's opinion or provision of other legal services, the non-client so relies, and the non-client is not, under applicable law, too remote from the lawyer to be entitled to protection. * * *

We also recognize that attorneys may owe a duty of care to non-clients when the attorneys know, or should know, that non-clients will rely on the attorneys representations and the non-clients are not too remote from the attorneys to be entitled to protection. The Restatement's requirement that the lawyer invite or acquiesce in the non-client's reliance comports with our formulation that the lawyer know, or should know, of that reliance. No matter how expressed, the point is to cabin the lawyer's duty, so the resulting obligation is fair to both lawyers and the public.

After also quoting § 552 of the Restatement, it turned to the facts of the case:

Here, Herrigel [the attorney] did not prepare an opinion letter. * * * [W]e infer that Herrigel extracted information from existing percolation-test reports, created the composite report, and delivered the report to a real estate broker. Our initial inquiry, as with an opinion letter or comparable document, is to ascertain the purpose of the report.

Although Herrigel may have intended that the composite report would demonstrate only that the property had passed two percolation tests, his subjective intent may not define the objective meaning of the report. The roles and relationships of the parties color our assessment. In making that assessment, we cannot ignore the fact that Herrigel is an attorney who, in connection with his client's efforts to sell the property, provided the report to a real estate broker. We infer that when he delivered the report to Bachenberg, Herrigel knew, or should have known, that Bachenberg might deliver it to a prospective purchaser, such as Petrillo. Herrigel did nothing to restrict a prospective purchaser's foreseeable use of the report. In neither the report, a covering letter, nor a disclaimer did Herrigel even hint that the report was anything but complete and accurate.

Significantly, Herrigel's involvement continued after he delivered the report to Bachenberg. After Bachenberg purchased the property,

Herrigel acted as his lawyer and negotiated the terms of the contract for the sale of commercial property to Petrillo. Although compiling an engineering report to help a client sell real estate may not be part of a lawyer's stock-in-trade, representing the seller of real estate is a traditional legal service. By representing Bachenberg on the sale to Petrillo, Herrigel confirmed the continuity of his involvement as a lawyer. On these facts, Herrigel's continuing involvement permits the inference that the objective purpose of the report was to induce a prospective purchaser to buy the property. His involvement supports the further inference that Herrigel knew that Bachenberg intended to use the report for that purpose.

Furthermore, a purchaser reading the composite report reasonably could conclude that the property had passed two of seven, not two of thirty, percolation tests. Based on that conclusion, a purchaser reasonably could decide to sign a purchase contract, although the purchaser would not have signed the contract if he or she had seen the complete set of percolation reports. So viewed, Herrigel should have foreseen that Petrillo would rely on the total number of percolation tests in deciding whether to sign the purchase contract. In sum, a jury reasonably could infer that the composite report misrepresented material facts.

By providing the composite report to Bachenberg and subsequently representing him in the sale, Herrigel assumed a duty to Petrillo to provide reliable information regarding the percolation tests. Herrigel controlled the risk that the composite report would mislead a purchaser. Fairness suggests that he should bear the risk of loss resulting from the delivery of a misleading report. We further conclude that Herrigel should have foreseen that a prospective purchaser would rely on the composite report in deciding whether to sign the contract and proceed with engineering and site work.

655 A.2d at 1358–1361.

Notes and Questions

1. How does the court in *Petrillo* reach a different conclusion than the court in *Bronstein?* In other words, assuming the legal rules do not differ, what factual differences are critical between the two cases?

2. Does the concept of a lawyer's duty to a non-client shock you? The issue seems to have first arisen in cases involving the negligent preparation of a will, where a potential beneficiary sues the attorney. See, Stephen Gillers, Regulation of Lawyers 656–64 (3d ed. 1992) (discussing duty to non-clients); Geoffrey C. Hazard, Jr. & W. William Hodes, The Law of Lawyering § 1.1:203, § 2.3:102 (2d ed. 1990) (same). *Petrillo* appears to be the first case where an attorney is held liable in the environmental tort context.

3. *Advising Lawyers.* Assume you are the senior partner of a law firm, and are terrorized by the *Petrillo* opinion. You want to issue a memorandum to your colleagues advising them on steps they must take to avoid the liability that the attorney in *Petrillo* faced. Precisely what steps can attorneys reasonably take to prevent liability to non-clients?

What did GZA do in *Bronstein*? What kind of disclaimer can a lawyer make? Of what importance is the fact that the report contained no "legal" advice? In fact the tests of the property yielded only two successful percolation tests out of 30 conducted, whereas the composite report indicated that two out of 7 were successful.

4. Dissenting Opinion. The dissenting opinion in *Petrillo* raises the specter of defensive lawyering, more expensive insurance rates, and making lawyers "guarantors of the accuracy of surveys and other similar experts' reports that they merely transmit." 655 A.2d at 1366. Is this last concern valid? Does the majority hold the lawyer liable for the experts' reports? Or is the court merely holding the lawyer responsible for misrepresenting the contents of the reports?

5. Malpractice. A federal district in New York denied a law firm's motion for summary judgment in a legal malpractice case alleging that it failed to ferret out the existence of contamination in connection with a client's purchase of business property. Keywell Corp. v. Piper & Marbury, L.L.P., 1999 WL 66700 (W.D.N.Y. 1999). Defendant Piper & Marbury L.L.P. failed to show that its former client, Keywell Corp., would have purchased the Frewsburg, N.Y., manufacturing plant under the same terms had it known of the contamination. It therefore rejected Piper's motion that it was entitled to summary judgment because, even if its representation were negligent, which Piper denies, Keywell suffered no damages. As a result, Keywell may proceed with its claims that Piper was negligent in failing to provide information to the environmental auditor it hired and in failing to authorize further environmental testing that would have uncovered extensive contamination at the plant, which Keywell purchased in 1987 from Vac Air Inc.

Piper hired a contractor, Conestoga–Rogers & Associates, to perform the environmental assessment. The law firm was supposed to supply CRA with relevant documents and arrange a meeting with a Vac Air representative to discuss the site's history. Piper arranged for CRA to talk with Anthony Boscarino, who assured CRA's representative that there had been no onsite disposal of hazardous wastes. "As it evolved, Boscarino was lying," the court said. Vac Air had, during the 1960s and 1970s, disposed of trichloroethylene directly onto the ground and in drums it buried onsite.

6. The Oregon Supreme Court said that a jury may determine whether an attorney followed his client's instructions to limit underground storage tank/environmental liabilities without hearing expert testimony in a malpractice suit. Larry J. Vandermay, et al. v. Paul D. Clayton, 984 P.2d 272, 328 Or. 646 (Or.1999). Vandermay filed a malpractice suit against their former attorney seeking more than $550,000 for failing to thoroughly explain an environmental indemnification provision in an agreement of sale of his oil company. Vandermay had signed the agreement believing he would only be responsible for $5,000 in cleanup costs, but the indemnification provision left him open to whatever liability was available under the law.

Chapter Five

REMEDIES AND COMPENSABLE INTERESTS

Determining that a defendant should be subject to liability under a theory of trespass, nuisance, negligence, strict liability or misrepresentation for an environmental tort does not end the inquiry. One of the most troublesome and ancient issues in environmental litigation is the court's determination of the appropriate remedy. This Chapter considers (1) the distinctions between injunctive remedies and damages; and (2) where damages may be appropriate, the types of harms for which they are awardable.

A. INJUNCTIONS: THE COMPARATIVE INJURY CALCULUS

Many of the cases considered in Chapters 2, 3 and 4 have discussed the question of what remedies are appropriate in environmental tort cases. The debate over the appropriate remedies in nuisance suits is not new, and the decisions reveal that the corrective justice view has been in conflict with the utilitarian view for at least a century. Should a plaintiff who has suffered and will continue to suffer substantial harm from a nuisance caused by the defendant's business operations be entitled to injunctive relief to abate the nuisance, when the consequence may be to adversely affect defendant's investment and socially useful operations or shut down such operations entirely? In this section we review briefly three decisions, all nearly ninety years old, which could easily arise today. Each involves paradigmatic claims in nuisance, the staple of environmental torts.

1. First, let us consider two opinions, often cited or quoted, that reflect a strong sense of corrective justice or fairness principles. One early case is Whalen v. Union Bag & Paper Co., 208 N.Y. 1, 101 N.E. 805 (1913), where the plaintiff was the owner of a 255–acre farm located along a stream. The defendant's pulp mill, a few miles up the stream, represented a $1 million investment and employed 400 to 500 persons.

The mill discharged into the stream large quantities of a liquid effluent containing sulphuric acid, lime, sulphur and waste material, such as pulp, resins, sawdust, and fiber. At the trial court, the plaintiff secured damages of $312 per year, and an injunction. The decision was reversed by the intermediate appellate court. The New York Court of Appeals reinstated the injunction:

> The setting aside of the injunction was apparently induced by a consideration of the great loss likely to be inflicted on the defendant by the granting of the injunction as compared with the small injury done to the plaintiff's land by that portion of the pollution which was regarded as attributable to the defendant. Such a balancing of injuries cannot be justified by the circumstances of this case. * * *

> One of the troublesome phases of this kind of litigation is the difficulty of deciding when an injunction shall issue in a case where the evidence clearly establishes an unlawful invasion of a plaintiff's rights, but his actual injury from the continuance of the alleged wrong will be small as compared with the great loss which will be caused by the issuance of the injunction. * * * Even as reduced at the Appellate Division, the damages to the plaintiff's farm amount to $100 a year. It can hardly be said that this injury is unsubstantial, even if we should leave out of consideration the peculiarly noxious character of the pollution of which the plaintiff complains. The waste from the defendant's mill is very destructive, both to vegetable and animal life, and tends to deprive the waters with which it is mixed of their purifying qualities. It should be borne in mind also that there is no claim on the part of the defendant that the nuisance may become less injurious in the future. Although the damage to the plaintiff may be slight as compared with the defendant's expense of abating the condition, that is not a good reason for refusing an injunction. Neither courts of equity nor law can be guided by such a rule, for if followed to its logical conclusion it would deprive the poor litigant of his little property by giving it to those already rich. * * *

Id. at 5, 101 N.E. at 806.

2. A similar position was taken in McCleery v. Highland Boy Gold Mining Co., 140 Fed. 951 (C.C.D.Utah 1904), in which the plaintiffs were owners of farms located near defendant's mine and smelter, which employed 450 workers. The fumes from defendant's operations containing sulfur dioxide were injurious to the plaintiffs' crops and animals. In discussing whether to grant the injunction, the court stated:

> The title of the complainants to their respective farms is admitted. The substantial invasion of their rights to some extent and the purpose to continue this invasion is also admitted. * * * The substantial contention of the defendant is that it is engaged in a business of such extent and involving such a large capital that the value of the plaintiffs' rights sought to be protected is relatively small, and that therefore an injunction, destroying the defendant's

business, would inflict a much greater injury on it than it would confer benefit upon the plaintiffs. Under such circumstances, it is asserted, courts of equity refuse to protect legal rights by injunction and remit the injured party to the partial relief to be obtained in actions at law. * * *

I am unable to accede to this statement of the law. If correct, the property of the poor is held by uncertain tenure, and the constitutional provisions forbidding the taking of property for private use would be of no avail. As a substitute it would be declared that private property is held on the condition that it may be taken by any person who can make a more profitable use of it, provided that such person shall be answerable in damage to the former owner for his injury. * * * Public policy, I think, is more concerned in the protection of individual rights than in the profits to inure to individuals by the invasion of those rights.

Id. at 952.

* * *

The federal appeals court, nevertheless, refused an abatement order on the ground that plaintiffs had delayed seeking an injunction until two or three years after the damage had commenced, during which time the defendant had made substantial additional investments in its operation. Permanent damages were, however, awarded. *Whalen* and *McCleery* continue to be relied upon as articulating the rationale for granting an injunction regardless of the comparative "injuries" of the parties. If "damage to the plaintiff [is] slight as compared with defendant's expense of abating the condition," (per *Whalen,*) what other actions might defendant take? In Chapter 3 we saw that Restatement §§ 822 and 826 (and comments thereto) imply that a "balancing of the equities" is appropriate in injunction cases, but not necessary when damages are sought, so long as the defendant can afford to pay damages without ceasing its operations. Are these cases necessarily inconsistent with that position?

3. Contrary to *McCleery* and *Whalen*, is the decision in Madison v. Ducktown Sulphur, Copper & Iron Co., 113 Tenn. 331, 83 S.W. 658 (1904), where the Tennessee Supreme Court surveyed virtually all of the arguments, pro and con, for granting or denying an injunction. Here the plaintiffs were farmers who suffered crop damage, timber damage, and ill health, who sought to enjoin defendants' copper mining operations using an open air roasting process that produced large volumes of sulfurous smoke. Since roasting was the only known method of ore reduction, an abatement order would terminate their operations, employing 2500 and representing one-half the tax assessment for the county.

The lower court granted the injunction, but the state high court held for the defendants. While recognizing that defendants' operations clearly created a nuisance, it also recognized that the availability of injunctive relief is discretionary and relied upon two principles of equity that compelled denial of the injunction. First, undue delay in seeking an injunction—or laches—was found to be a bar to equitable relief because plaintiffs had waited for ten years before instituting suit. The court developed the second ground for denying the injunction as follows:

> In order to protect by the injunction several small tracts of land, aggregating in value less than $1,000, we are asked to destroy other property worth nearly $2,000,000, and wreck two great mining and manufacturing enterprises, that are engaged in work of very great importance, not only to their owners, but to the state, and to the whole country as well, to depopulate a large town, and deprive thousands of working people of their homes and livelihood, and scatter them broadcast. The result would be practically a confiscation of the property of the defendants for the benefit of the complainants—an appropriation without compensation. The defendants cannot reduce their ores in a manner different from that they are now employing, and there is no more remote place to which they can remove. The decree asked for would deprive them of all of their rights. * * * [I]n case[s] of conflicting rights, where neither party can enjoy his own without in some measure restricting the liberty of the other in the use of property, the law must make the best arrangement it can between the contending parties, with a view to preserving to each one the largest measure of liberty possible under the circumstances. * * *

Id. at 667.

Notes and Questions

1. What "rights" of the defendant is the court referring to? Is the court totally rejecting corrective justice or only insofar as an injunction is concerned? Does an award of damages sufficiently protect the rights of the plaintiffs? Do injunction proceedings necessarily require a balancing process that weighs utilitarian considerations? As these decisions illustrate, the courts often struggle with the propriety of granting injunctive relief where the effect may be to curtail or eliminate the defendant's operations. Injunctions in environmental tort cases can be a powerful remedy and the only remedy that is capable of assuring that the harm will be abated or will not be repeated. Recall that in Sharp v. 251 Street Landfill, 925 P.2d 546 (Okla. 1996), in Chapter 3, the Oklahoma Supreme Court enjoined the operation of defendant's hazardous waste site. The cases quoted above demonstrate that these issues are not of recent origin, but that in varying degrees the nature of operations have changed.

2. *Injunction: A Cause of Action or a Remedy?* It is accepted generally that a claim for an injunction is prayer for relief, and not a separate cause of action. This conclusion was reached in Fletcher v. Conoco Pipe Line Co., 129 F.Supp.2d 1255 (W.D. Mo. 2001), a "stray electricity" negligence, trespass, and strict liability injury suit. Explaining its reasons for striking certain of the plaintiffs' claims pursuant to Fed. R. Civ. Proc. 12(f), the court wrote:

* * *

E. Counts XIX & XXII—Permanent Injunction

Defendant argues that because a permanent injunction is a remedy and not a cause of action, Plaintiffs failed to state a claim for which relief can be granted. See Fed.R.Civ.P. 12(b)(6). In the alternative, Defendant asserts that Counts XIX & XXII should be stricken as redundant because, elsewhere in their Complaint, Plaintiffs request injunctive relief for the majority of their claims.

F. Counts VII & VIII—Personal Injury

Defendant contends that Plaintiffs' "Personal Injury" causes of action, like Plaintiffs' "Permanent Injunction" claims, are not distinct causes of action recognized by Missouri courts. Alternatively, Defendant asserts that Plaintiffs' "Personal Injury" counts are merely reiterations of Plaintiffs' other negligence claims. Plaintiffs argue that Counts VII and VIII are capable of standing separate and apart from the other counts in their Complaint, but the Court notes that Plaintiffs fail to explain how this is so.

In Counts VII and VIII, entitled "Personal Injury," Plaintiffs allege that Defendant was "negligent and careless in allowing said electricity to escape from the prescribed pipeline permits" and that "as a direct and proximate result of the negligence and carelessness of Defendant," Plaintiffs suffered injury. These allegations are nearly identical to the allegations pleaded by Plaintiffs in Counts II, III, and XII, entitled "Negligence," "Negligence—Res Ipsa Loquitor," and "Specific Negligence," respectively. In each of these counts, Plaintiffs similarly assert that as a direct and proximate result of the negligent acts and omissions of the Defendant, they have continued to suffer damages. The Court agrees with Defendant that Plaintiffs' "Personal Injury" causes of action (Counts VII and VIII) are duplicative of Plaintiffs' other claims and must be DISMISSED[.] * * *

B. STANDARDS FOR GRANTING INJUNCTIONS: BALANCING THE EQUITIES

An injunction may be "prohibitory," forbidding a defendant from acting in a certain manner; or "mandatory," requiring the defendant to undertake some affirmative action to ameliorate an existing or prospective harm. See generally Dan B. Dobbs, Law of Remedies § 2.9 (2d ed. 1993); reconsider also the discussion of injunctive remedies in *Sharp*, discussed in Chapter 3.

Because injunctions are a form of equitable relief and courts possess wide-ranging discretion in determining whether to issue such relief, they vary widely in their terms and application. Restatement (Second) of Torts § 936 sets forth the factors that are relevant when an injunction is sought:

(1) The appropriateness of the remedy of injunction against a tort depends upon a comparative appraisal of all of the factors in the case, including the following primary factors:

(a) the nature of the interest to be protected,

(b) the relative adequacy to the plaintiff of injunction and of other remedies,

(c) any unreasonable delay by the plaintiff in bringing suit,

(d) any related misconduct on the part of the plaintiff,

(e) the relative hardship likely to result to defendant if an injunction is granted and to plaintiff if it is denied,

(f) the interests of third persons and of the public, and

(g) the practicability of framing and enforcing the order of judgment.

These factors usually compel the court to engage in some type of balancing process in deciding whether to issue injunctive relief and the precise nature and terms of the order granting the relief. Section 941 specifically addresses subsection (e), the balancing of the relative hardships which flow if the relief sought is granted or denied, and points out the difficult choices which courts face in making the determination of whether to grant injunctive relief. It provides that courts have at least three possible solutions: (1) holding that there is no actionable nuisance and that the plaintiff must simply bear the harm as a consequence of living in an industrial society; (2) holding that there is a nuisance for purposes of a damage action, but refusing the injunction—that is, the plaintiff must bear the harm, but will receive compensation; and (3) holding that the plaintiff is to be relieved from the harm by an injunction. Restatement (Second) of Torts § 941, comment *c*.

The following material from the influential work of Professor Dobbs surveys the law respecting the balancing process that occurs in environmental nuisance cases:

Dan B. Dobbs, Law of Remedies § 5.7(2)*

Balancing Hardships and Equities

Threshold, rights, and remedies types of balancing. The discretion in equity to deny, limit or shape relief is reflected in the flexible process of balancing hardships and equities. Relief is limited or expanded in accord with that balance. Balancing occurs in several distinct ways. There is some "threshold balancing," as it has been called, to determine whether the plaintiff has standing in equity in the light of unclean hands, estoppel, laches or the like. Another kind of balancing occurs on the substantive issues themselves in some cases. Nuisance cases, for example, are largely a matter of degree, so a discretionary kind of weighing of relative hardships is almost always involved in such cases. A third level of balancing occurs when the court, having found a nuisance or statutory violation to exist, must determine whether to use a damages remedy or an injunctive

* 765–70 (2d ed. 1993) (footnotes omitted).

remedy. And finally, a similar balancing or discretion is invoked at a fourth stage when the court fixes the exact scope and commands of the injunction issued.

Rights-balancing. In determining whether the defendant's activity is a nuisance at all, courts traditionally balanced the benefits derived from that activity with the harm it caused. A balance of harms, costs, utilities and hardships suggests, for example, that a very valuable industry which is causing annoyance to neighbors might not be a nuisance at all in the light of the relative utilities. In such a case there are no remedial issues at all because there are no rights to be redressed.

The "modern" view taken by the Restatement would hold that some conditions constitute a nuisance even if the nuisance is the result of a socially useful activity. In this view, a balancing of utilities, costs or hardships would be important, but only on the choice of remedies, not on the initial question whether a nuisance existed. The two approaches are quite different, but both recognize that a balancing of utilities or hardships on the remedies issue is distinct from a balancing of utilities on the question whether a nuisance exists at all. The main concern of this text is the balance of utilities or hardships in determining the appropriate remedy and in determining its scope.

Remedies balancing generally. When a nuisance is found to exist, either on the balance of utilities or otherwise, it is still important to balance or re-balance the relative costs and hardships in determining the appropriate remedy. At the remedies stage of the claim, courts routinely reconsider the balance to determine whether an injunction should be granted or whether the plaintiff should be limited to some other remedy such as damages.

Specifically, courts consider the public benefit derived from the defendant's operations, the public benefits that might result from a grant of the injunction, the relative hardships or the economic costs the parties would be likely to suffer if the nuisance is or is not enjoined, and the equities between the parties such as laches, bad faith or misconduct. This new balancing of public and private benefits and harms may lead the court to deny an injunction and leave the plaintiff to a damages remedy on the ground that an injunction would do more harm than good.

* * *

Hardships and economic waste. Courts also take into account the relative hardships of the parties. The hardship that may be worked upon the defendant if the injunction goes is compared to the hardship that may be wreaked upon the plaintiff if it does not. The plaintiff's hardship in nuisance cases is often expressed as an intangible impairment of enjoyment of the quality of living on the property; but this impairment, if substantial, will be reflected in diminished property values as well. In any event, if sufficiently proven, the hardship may outweigh the tangible economic losses the defendant will suffer if its business is enjoined.

The hardship attributed to the defendant is often more frankly economic, and courts often mention the investment that would be lost if the injunction goes. This calls, however, for a practical judgment. If there are reasonable alternatives available to the defendant that will accomplish his goals without causing a nuisance, the supposed hardship counts for little. The same point can be recognized in decisions that grant an injunction against a full-scale operation by the defendant but leave it open to him to operate in ways that cause less harm.

* * *

Public interests against the injunction. A public interest in favor of the defendant and against the injunctive remedy is sometimes found in the fact that the defendant's nuisance is a business or factory that employs individuals and brings economic well-being to the community. Much of what goes under the name of hardship is economic cost. Economic costs, though they do not directly harm the whole community, may do so indirectly. If an injunction closing or limiting the operation of the defendant's business will cause the loss of an investment, courts weigh this factor against the injunction, or at least against it in its broadest and most destructive form.

Public interests favoring the injunction. On the other hand, there may be a public interest in terminating a nuisance causing environmental pollution, even if that nuisance is caused by a conduct that otherwise contributes to the public weal. Poisoning the water supply of a town could hardly be justified even by the most important of industries. Much serious environmental pollution will generate strong public interest reasons in support of an injunction. In less obvious cases, public interest balancing may be controversial and is likely to involve at least some element of political or social decision-making outside the traditional judicial role.

However, the political or social balancing may have been done before trial by the legislature itself. When the defendant's conduct violates a statute, it is possible that the legislature has already weighed the competing interests and has reflected its judgment in the statute. In such a case the court may be willing to discount its own assessment of public interests and issue the injunction authorized by statute.

The judicial decision which is most often cited or relied upon in these disputes over remedies in environmental tort cases is *Boomer v. Atlantic Cement Company* entered by the Court of Appeals of New York, that state's highest court.

BOOMER v. ATLANTIC CEMENT COMPANY, INC.

Court of Appeals of New York, 1970.
26 N.Y.2d 219, 309 N.Y.S.2d 312, 257 N.E.2d 870.

BERGAN, J.

Defendant operates a large cement plant near Albany. These are actions for injunction and damages by neighboring land owners alleging injury to property from dirt, smoke and vibration emanating from the plant. A nuisance has been found after trial, temporary damages have been allowed; but an injunction has been denied.

* * *

But there is now before the court private litigation in which individual property owners have sought specific relief from a single plant operation. The threshold question raised by the division of view on this appeal is whether the court should resolve the litigation between the parties now before it as equitably as seems possible; or whether, seeking promotion of the general public welfare, it should channel private litigation into broad public objectives.

A court performs its essential function when it decides the rights of parties before it. Its decision of private controversies may sometimes greatly affect public issues. Large questions of law are often resolved by the manner in which private litigation is decided. But this is normally an incident to the court's main function to settle controversy. It is a rare exercise of judicial power to use a decision in private litigation as a purposeful mechanism to achieve direct public objectives greatly beyond the rights and interests before the court.

Effective control of air pollution is a problem presently far from solution even with the full public and financial powers of government. In large measure adequate technical procedures are yet to be developed and some that appear possible may be economically impracticable.

It seems apparent that the amelioration of air pollution will depend on technical research in great depth; on a carefully balanced consideration of the economic impact of close regulation; and of the actual effect on public health. It is likely to require massive public expenditure and to demand more than any local community can accomplish and to depend on regional and interstate controls.

A court should not try to do this on its own as a by-product of private litigation, and it seems manifest that the judicial establishment is neither equipped in the limited nature of any judgment it can pronounce nor prepared to lay down and implement an effective policy for the elimination of air pollution. This is an area beyond the circumference of one private lawsuit. It is a direct responsibility for government and should not thus be undertaken as an incident to solving a dispute between property owners and a single cement plant—one of many—in the Hudson River valley.

The cement making operations of defendant have been found by the court at Special Term to have damaged the nearby properties of plaintiffs in these two actions. That court, as it has been noted, accordingly found defendant maintained a nuisance and this has been affirmed at the Appellate Division. The total damage to plaintiffs' properties is, however, relatively small in comparison with the value of defendant's operation and with the consequences of the injunction which plaintiffs seek.

The ground for the denial of injunction, notwithstanding the finding both that there is a nuisance and that plaintiffs have been damaged substantially, is the large disparity in economic consequences of the nuisance and of the injunction. This theory cannot, however, be sustained without overruling a doctrine which has been consistently reaffirmed in several leading cases in this court and which has never been disavowed here, namely that where a nuisance has been found and where there has been any substantial damage shown by the party complaining an injunction will be granted.

The rule in New York has been that such a nuisance will be enjoined although marked disparity be shown in economic consequence between the effect of the injunction and the effect of the nuisance.

The problem of disparity in economic consequence was sharply in focus in Whalen v. Union Bag & Paper Co. (208 N.Y. 1). A pulp mill entailing an investment of more than a million dollars polluted a stream in which plaintiff, who owned a farm, was "a lower riparian owner". The economic loss to plaintiff from this pollution was small. This court, reversing the Appellate Division, reinstated the injunction granted by the Special Term against the argument of the mill owner that in view of "the slight advantage to plaintiff and the great loss that will be inflicted on defendant" an injunction should not be granted. "Such a balancing of injuries cannot be justified by the circumstances of this case." He continued: "Although the damage to the plaintiff may be slight as compared with the defendant's expense of abating the condition, that is not a good reason for refusing an injunction."

* * * This states a rule that had been followed in this court with marked consistency.

* * * Thus if, within Whalen v. Union Bag & Paper Co. which authoritatively states the rule in New York, the damage to plaintiffs in these present cases from defendant's cement plant is "not unsubstantial," an injunction should follow.

Although the court at Special Term and the Appellate Division held that injunction should be denied, it was found that plaintiffs had been damaged in various specific amounts up to the time of the trial and damages to the respective plaintiffs were awarded for those amounts. The effect of this was, injunction having been denied, plaintiffs could maintain successive actions at law for damages thereafter as further damage was incurred.

* * *

This result at Special Term and at the Appellate Division is a departure from a rule that has become settled; but to follow the rule literally in these cases would be to close down the plant at once. This court is fully agreed to avoid that immediately drastic remedy; the difference in view is how best to avoid it.[6]

One alternative is to grant the injunction but postpone its effect to a specified future date to give opportunity for technical advances to permit defendant to eliminate the nuisance; another is to grant the injunction conditioned on the payment of permanent damages to plaintiffs which would compensate them for the total economic loss to their property present and future caused by defendant's operations. For reasons which will be developed the court chooses the latter alternative.

If the injunction were to be granted unless within a short period— e.g., 18 months—the nuisance be abated by improved methods, there would be no assurance that any significant technical improvement would occur.

The parties could settle this private litigation at any time if defendant paid enough money and the imminent threat of closing the plant would build up the pressure on defendant. If there were no improved techniques found, there would inevitably be applications to the court at Special Term for extensions of time to perform on showing of good faith efforts to find such techniques.

Moreover, techniques to eliminate dust and other annoying by-products of cement making are unlikely to be developed by any research the defendant can undertake within any short period, but will depend on the total resources of the cement industry Nationwide and throughout the world. The problem is universal wherever cement is made.

For obvious reasons the rate of the research is beyond control of defendant. If at the end of 18 months the whole industry has not found a technical solution a court would be hard put to close down this one cement plant if due regard be given to equitable principles.

On the other hand, to grant the injunction unless defendant pays plaintiffs such permanent damages as may be fixed by the court seems to do justice between the contending parties. All of the attributions of economic loss to the properties on which plaintiffs' complaints are based will have been redressed.

The nuisance complained of by these plaintiffs may have other public or private consequences, but these particular parties are the only ones who have sought remedies and the judgment proposed will fully

---

6. Respondent's investment in the plant is in excess of $45,000,000. There are over 300 people employed there.

redress them. The limitation of relief granted is a limitation only within the four corners of these actions and does not foreclose public health or other public agencies from seeking proper relief in a proper court.

It seems reasonable to think that the risk of being required to pay permanent damages to injured property owners by cement plant owners would itself be a reasonably effective spur to research for improved techniques to minimize nuisance.

The power of the court to condition on equitable grounds the continuance of an injunction on the payment of permanent damages seems undoubted.

The damage base here suggested is consistent with the general rule in those nuisance cases where damages are allowed. "Where a nuisance is of such a permanent and unabatable character that a single recovery can be had, including the whole damage past and future resulting therefrom, there can be but one recovery" (66 C.J.S., Nuisances § 140, p. 947). * * *

The present cases and the remedy here proposed are in a number of other respects rather similar to Northern Indiana Public Serv. Co. v. Vesey (210 Ind. 338) decided by the Supreme Court of Indiana. The gases, odors, ammonia and smoke from the Northern Indiana company's gas plant damaged the nearby Vesey greenhouse operation. An injunction and damages were sought, but an injunction was denied and the relief granted was limited to permanent damages "present, past, and future."

Denial of injunction was grounded on a public interest in the operation of the gas plant and on the court's conclusion "that less injury would be occasioned by requiring the appellant [Public Service] to pay the appellee [Vesey] all damages suffered by it * * * than by enjoining the operation of the gas plant; and that the maintenance and operation of the gas plant should not be enjoined."

The Indiana Supreme Court opinion continued: "When the trial court refused injunctive relief to the appellee upon the ground of public interest in the continuance of the gas plant, it properly retained jurisdiction of the case and awarded full compensation to the appellee. This is upon the general equitable principle that equity will give full relief in one action and prevent a multiplicity of suits."

It was held that in this type of continuing and recurrent nuisance permanent damages were appropriate. See also City of Amarillo v. Ware (120 Tex. 456) where recurring overflows from a system of storm sewers were treated as the kind of nuisance for which permanent depreciation of value of affected property would be recoverable.

* * *

Thus it seems fair to both sides to grant permanent damages to plaintiffs which will terminate this private litigation. The theory of damage is the "servitude on land" of plaintiffs imposed by defendant's nuisance.

The judgment, by allowance of permanent damages imposing a servitude on land, which is the basis of the actions, would preclude future recovery by plaintiffs or their grantees.

This should be placed beyond debate by a provision of the judgment that the payment by defendant and the acceptance by plaintiffs of permanent damages found by the court shall be in compensation for a servitude on the land.

Although the Trial Term has found permanent damages as a possible basis of settlement of the litigation, on remission the court should be entirely free to re-examine this subject. It may again find the permanent damage already found; or make new findings.

The orders should be reversed, without costs, and the cases remitted to Supreme Court, Albany County to grant an injunction which shall be vacated upon payment by defendant of such amounts of permanent damage to the respective plaintiffs as shall for this purpose be determined by the court.

[The dissent by JASEN, J. is omitted.]

Notes and Questions

1.   Do you agree with the majority? Does the majority's approach create for polluters the power to condemn and appropriate a neighbor's property by paying permanent damages? Did the court overrule *Whalen*? The dissenting opinion labels the effect of the majority's holding as creating an "inverse condemnation" by a private party? Do you agree? For a discussion of *Boomer*, see Comment, Involuntary Sale Damages in Permanent Nuisance Cases: A Bigger Bang From Boomer, 14 B.C. Envtl. Aff. L. Rev. 61 (1986).

2.   What do you think of the court's statement that "[f]or obvious reasons the rate of the research is beyond control of defendant"? Consider the comment of the New Jersey Supreme Court in the asbestos products liability personal injury suit Beshada v. Johns–Manville Products Corp., 90 N.J. 191, 447 A.2d 539 (N.J.1982): "[T]he level of investment in safety research by manufacturers is one determinant of the state-of-the-art at any given time. Fairness suggests that manufacturers not be excused from liability because their prior inadequate investment in safety rendered the hazards of their product unknowable." Are the situations comparable? Are product and nuisance cases, or the role of federal statutory programs, sufficiently different to explain the distinction?

3.   The court is visibly concerned with the fact that its role is to adjudicate the dispute before it between two private parties, yet a full resolution of the problem the case presents would require the involvement of numerous public and private groups not before it, such as the legislature, industry groups, and other experts and affected parties. Do you agree that a court of general jurisdiction should be concerned that the factual and policy record before it does not permit it to resolve systemic issues?

4. The opinion claims that courts are poorly equipped to reach a just solution to the problem of airborne pollution from an industrial enterprise because they lack all of the information needed to devise and implement such a solution. Keeping in mind modern liberal discovery rules and the capacity of federal courts, and many state courts, to appoint their own experts, can you make the opposite argument?

5. Should a comparative injury calculus be the primary determinant in these cases? In what kinds of cases will it be most appropriate to adopt this test as the primary consideration? What if the plaintiff was a representative of a class action of all residences within two miles downwind of the plant? Would the court reach a different conclusion? What might be the consequences of awarding permanent damages to hundreds of residents?

6. In a subsequent decision, the New York Court of Appeals described and distinguished *Boomer* as a case where "no zoning violation, or for that matter, the violation of any other statute, was involved" and, hence, an injunction would issue against an asphalt plant constructed and operated contrary to local zoning ordinances. Little Joseph Realty, Inc. v. Town of Babylon, 41 N.Y.2d 738, 395 N.Y.S.2d 428, 363 N.E.2d 1163 (1977). Is that an appropriate and viable basis for distinguishing *Boomer*?

7. *The Rarity of Boomer.* In the thirty years since *Boomer* was decided, very few cases have explicitly addressed the questions here presented: injunctive relief versus permanent damages and solving major pollution problems by damages alone between private litigants versus injunctions and technological limitations related hereto.

One explanation for why *Boomer* stands almost alone could be that within months after the decision, President Nixon signed the Clean Air Act Amendments of 1970 which achieved precisely the kind of public response that the court in *Boomer* acknowledged it could not achieve. Clean Air Act, 42 U.S.C. §§ 7401 et. seq. Those amendments established a comprehensive program for cleaner air, including national ambient air quality standards that address pervasive pollution that endangers public health and safety and established technological milestones that each industry, i.e., the cement industry, would have to achieve by specific deadlines. An elaborate rule-making process is created that authorizes the EPA to issue implementing regulations on the relevant technology, with ever-increasing forcing provisions. Recall that this process was precisely what the court in *Boomer* stated it was ill-equipped to do.

Congress didn't stop with cleaner air goals. In 1972 it enacted the Federal Water Pollution Control Act, 33 U.S.C. §§ 1251–1387. [Referred to by practitioners as the Clean Water Act—CWA] The CWA required EPA to fix nationwide effluent standards on an industry-by-industry basis, based on the capabilities of pollution control technologies and their costs to regulated industries.

The decade of the 1970's also saw the passage of the Resource Conservation and Recovery Act—RCRA, 42 U.S.C. §§ 6901 et seq. (sometimes referred to as The Solid Waste Disposal Act). RCRA is designed to provide "cradle to grave" controls by imposing management requirements on generators and transporters of hazardous wastes and upon owners and operators of treatment, storage, and disposal facilities. Next came the Safe Drinking

Water Act in 1977, 42 U.S.C. §§ 300f et seq., and the Comprehensive Environmental Response, Compensation and Liability Act—CERCLA in 1980, 42 U.S.C. §§ 9601 et seq., which we consider in Chapter 10.

Once the regulatory environmental era was ushered in, responsibility for seeking injunctive relief from courts or issuing administrative orders compelling some kind of pollution control transferred from private litigants to the federal EPA and state counterparts, and in some cases environmental groups via citizen suit provisions.

A court today does not engage in the *Boomer* type debate because courts have been largely ousted of jurisdiction to create new or different standards from those issued by Congress or the EPA.

8. *Modern Injunctions*. But the foregoing discussion does not mean that courts never issue injunctions to abate nuisances or trespasses. In Chapter 3, recall the section on anticipatory nuisances and injunctive relief. In some decisions, courts simply decline to issue injunctive relief because the requirements for irreparable injury or the balancing of the equities point against it. See, e.g., Kernen v. Homestead Development Co., 232 Mich.App. 503, 591 N.W.2d 369 (Mich.Ct.App.1998) (riparian landowners were not entitled to injunction prohibiting adjoining riparian owner from discharging treated wastewater into wetland on its property, which flowed into wetland on landowners' property, where, other than general claims that value of their property would decrease and that they had right of exclusive possession, landowners presented no evidence of specific irreparable harm). Escobar v. Continental Baking Co., 33 Mass.App.Ct. 104, 596 N.E.2d 394 (Mass. Ct.App.1992) (balance of equities weighed against issuing injunctions against nighttime operation of defendant's facility, where relocating the plant would cost $1.7 million and plaintiff's harm was insubstantial).

In contrast, see the Nebraska Supreme Court ruling in Goeke v. National Farms, Inc., 245 Neb. 262, 512 N.W.2d 626, 632 (Neb. 1994), involving the operation of a swine raising facility constituted a nuisance:

> We have not found that this court has ever attempted to define substantial interference in the context of a suit to enjoin or abate a nuisance. We have repeatedly stated that to justify the abatement of a claimed nuisance, the annoyance must be such as to cause actual physical discomfort to one of ordinary sensibilities. There is a presumption, in the absence of evidence to the contrary, that a plaintiff in an action for abatement of a nuisance has ordinary sensibilities. * * *

> The [defendants] produced no evidence that any of the plaintiffs were not of ordinary sensibilities, and all of the plaintiffs testified that the odors emanating from the [defendants'] waste-treatment operation had caused them to suffer actual physical discomfort. By their testimony, the plaintiffs established that they suffered damages as a proximate result of the nuisance caused by the [defendants'] waste treatment operation. We, therefore, affirm the district court's granting an injunction prohibiting the [defendants] from producing offensive odors and ordering the [defendants] to abate the odors produced by their waste-treatment system or cease operating their facility.

So, too, in Hulshof v. Noranda Aluminum, Inc., 835 S.W.2d 411 (Mo.Ct. App.1992), the Missouri Appellate Court concluded that sufficient evidence supported an injunction preventing an aluminum plant from continuing to discharge industrial waste waters and storm water into a drainage ditch which flowed onto plaintiff's farm despite the jury's failure to award damages, since evidence also sustained a finding that substantial future harm was threatened by the plant's discharges.

However, the fact that a defendant's activity constituted a public nuisance because it violated a city ordinance will not justify, in and of itself, granting a private party an injunction. See, Smicklas v. Spitz, 846 P.2d 362 (Okla.1992). Finally, in Ritchhart v. Gleason, 109 Ohio App.3d 652, 672 N.E.2d 1064 (Ohio Ct.App.1996), the court held that the grant of a permanent injunction, prohibiting the discharge of waste water treatment effluent into neighboring property owners' private ditch, was supported by evidence that the waste water treatment plant was designed to discharge 26,000 gallons of treated sewage per day, that the effluent would cause minimal erosion of the ditch and sewage constituents would settle on property, that landowners would be harmed by damage that trespass would cause, and that landowners had no adequate remedy at law as damages to the ditch would be difficult to measure.

For an interesting account of the post-*Boomer* era, see Dobris, Boomer Twenty Years Later, 54 Alb. L. Rev. 171 (1990). For an insightful analysis into the damages versus injunction versus no remedy debate, see Richard Epstein, Protecting Property Rights With Legal Remedies, 32 Val. U. L. Rev. 833 (1998).

9.   While there are many law review articles dealing with the questions raised by these cases, several are especially interesting: John A. Humbach, Evolving Thresholds of Nuisance and the Takings Clause, 18 Colum. J. Envtl. Law 1 (1993); A. Mitchell Polinsky, Resolving Nuisance Disputes: The Simple Economics of Injunctive and Damage Remedies, 32 Stan. L. Rev. 1075 (1980); Robert C. Ellickson, Alternatives to Zoning: Covenants, Nuisance Rules and Fines as Land Use Controls, 40 U. Chi. L. Rev. 681 (1973); Edward Rabin, Nuisance Law: Rethinking Fundamental Assumptions, 63 Va. L. Rev. 1299 (1977); Comment, Internalizing Externalities: Nuisance Law and Economic Efficiency, 53 N.Y.U. L. Rev. 219 (1978); Guido Calabresi & A. Douglas Melamed, Property Rules, Liability Rules and Inalienability: One View of the Cathedral, 85 Harv. L. Rev. 1089 (1972).

C. DAMAGES FOR INJURY TO REAL PROPERTY

1. HARM TO THE PHYSICAL CONDITION OF LAND

a. *The General Rules*

Nuisance, trespass, negligence and strict liability cases often involve some harm to the plaintiff's interests in real property, and in most of the cases considered in Chapters 2, 3 and 4, plaintiffs sustained such damage. The Restatement (Second) of Torts in § 929 states the governing principles for the awarding of damages for harm to real property:

§ 929. Harm to Land From Past Invasions

(1) If one is entitled to a judgment from harm to land resulting from a past invasion and not amounting to a total destruction of value, the damages include compensation for

(a) the difference between the value of the land before the harm and the value after the harm, or at his election in an appropriate case, the cost of restoration that has been or may be reasonably incurred,

(b) the loss of use of the land, and

(c) discomfort and annoyance to him as an occupant.

As a general rule, tort compensation principles endeavor to place the injured party, as best they can, in its pre-tort position—that is, a restorative objective. Therefore, in the ordinary case the general rule permits the plaintiff to recover the difference in the property's value before and after the defendant's tortious acts. Often in nuisance and trespass cases the defendant's acts have permanently adversely affected the value of the land as by pollution, flooding, groundwater contamination, and the like, and the plaintiff is able to establish, usually by introduction of expert testimony, that the price a reasonable purchaser would offer for the land has diminished as a consequence of the resultant harm. However, § 929(1)(a) does not declare that diminution in value is the exclusive remedy; rather, in appropriate cases the plaintiff may be entitled to the costs of restoring the land to its pre-tort condition, § 929 comment *b* thereto states:

b. *Restoration.* Even in the absence of value arising from personal use, the reasonable cost of replacing the land in its original position is ordinarily allowable as the measure of recovery. Thus if a ditch is wrongfully dug upon the land of another, the other normally is entitled to damages measured by the expense of filling the ditch, if he wishes it filled. If, however, the cost of replacing the land in its original condition is disproportionate to the diminution in the value of the land caused by the trespass, unless there is a reason personal to the owner for restoring the original condition, damages are measured only by the difference between the value of the land before and after the harm. This would be true, for example, if in trying the effect of explosives, a person were to create large pits upon the comparatively worthless land of another.

On the other hand, if a building such as a homestead is used for a purpose personal to the owner, the damages ordinarily include an amount for repairs, even though this might be greater than the entire value of the building.

As the quotations from the Restatement comments, controversy may arise where the plaintiff elects to recover the costs of restoration, but such costs exceed the diminution in value to the property. In Board of County Commissioners v. Slovek, 723 P.2d 1309 (Colo.1986), a case involving the county's negligence in allowing river water to enter a gravel pit on its property, overflow from that pit, and inundate much of plaintiffs' property, the Colorado Supreme Court summarized the essential principles and struck the following balance:

In Zwick v. Simpson, 193 Colo. 36, 572 P.2d 133 (Colo. 1977), a trespass action, we were confronted with an issue concerning the appropriate measure of damages for injury to real property, and we concluded as follows: As the court of appeals noted, market value before and after the injury is ordinarily a rule applied to measure damages to real property. Since the goal of the law of compensatory damages is reimbursement of the plaintiff for the actual loss suffered, there may, of course, be instances in which repair or restoration cost may be a more appropriate measure such as (1) where the property has no market value, or (2) where repairs have already been made, or (3) where the property is a recently acquired private residence and the plaintiff's interest is in having the property restored, repair costs will more effectively return him to the position he was in prior to the injury. The county argues that our discussion in *Zwick* concerning the exceptions to the "ordinary rule" was dicta, and that when squarely considered we should conclude that any measure of damages other than diminution of market value is inappropriate. We do not agree that damages in the present case must be limited to diminution of market value.

The measure of damages for injury to real property "is not invariable." [I]n justifying the deviation from the market value standard, a Restatement comment relies on such factors as the nature of the owner's use of the property—in particular, whether the owner uses the property as a personal residence, whether the owner has some personal reason for having the property in its original condition, or both—and the nature of the injury—in particular, whether the injury is reparable and at what cost. Restatement (Second) of Torts § 929 comment *b*. These factors, to varying extents, have also been considered of significance by other commentators and by courts that have considered the issue.

* * *

We agree that the factors enumerated in Restatement (Second) of Torts § 929 comment *b* are important in determining whether a case is appropriate for application of "cost of restoration" rather than "diminution of market value" as the measure of damages for tortious injury to land. We conclude, however, that the considerations governing what is an "appropriate case" for departure from the market value standard are not susceptible to reduction to a set list and that no formula can be devised that will produce litmus-test certainty and yet retain the flexibility to produce fair results in all cases.

* * *

We prefer to leave the selection of the appropriate measure of damages in each case to the discretion of the trial court, informed by the considerations previously discussed. The trial court must take as its principal guidance the goal of reimbursement of the plaintiff for losses actually suffered, but must be vigilant not to award damages that exceed the goal of compensation and inflict punishment on the defendant or encourage economically wasteful remedial expenditures by the plaintiff.

The county contends that if this court allows the cost of restoration to be considered a proper measure of damages, fairness demands that we place a cap on the recovery of such costs. The county argues that repair costs should not exceed the diminution of the value of the property, or, at least, should not exceed the pre-tort value of the property.

We have no difficulty in rejecting the first limit offered. It is precisely because the reduction in market value is not in many instances an adequate measure of the loss suffered—that is, it is not an amount that most closely approximates what is required to return the property owner to the pre-tort position—that courts allow plaintiffs to recover the costs of restoration in appropriate circumstances. To limit the recovery to an amount that does not exceed the diminution of market value undermines the purpose for allowing the alternative measure of damages.

Although a more compelling case can be made for restricting the award of costs to the pre-tort value of the land—on the theory that defendants should not have to pay more than they would pay for irreparable total damage—we decline to adopt this as an invariable limit either. If the damage is reparable, and the costs, although greater than original value, are not wholly unreasonable in relation to that value, and if the evidence demonstrates that payment of market value likely will not adequately compensate the property owner for some personal or other special reason, we conclude that the selection of the cost of restoration as the proper measure of damages would be within the limits of a trial court's discretion.

Obviously, to the extent that a property owner is allowed to recover costs of restoration that are greater than the diminution in market value, there is the possibility that the owner will receive a monetary windfall by choosing not to restore the property and by selling it instead, profiting to the extent that restoration costs recovered exceed the diminution of market value. The problem is no different, except in degree, if restoration costs are allowed in an amount exceeding the pre-tort value of the property. These possibilities suggest the need for careful evaluation by the trial court to assure that any damages allowed in excess of either of these two measures are truly and reasonably necessary to achieve the cardinal objective of making the plaintiff whole.

* * *

Has the court adequately addressed the "windfall" problem? Should a "personal or special reason" ever justify recovering more for restoration costs than the pre-tort value of the land? Will the restoration affect the value of the land? Should the plaintiff "capture" that gain?

The flexible approach adopted in *Slovek* finds support in other modern decisions. See, e.g., Reeser v. Weaver Brothers, Inc., 78 Ohio App.3d 681, 605 N.E.2d 1271 (1992) (pollution of lake and killing of fish as a result of defendant's negligence and nuisance); and Heninger v. Dunn, 101 Cal.App.3d 858, 162 Cal.Rptr. 104 (1980) (bulldozing a road that destroyed 225 trees and much undergrowth at the ill advice of counsel that defendant had an easement on plaintiff's land to cut the road).

b. *Environmental Damages: Restoration Versus Diminution and the Role of Stigma Damages*

IN RE PAOLI RAILROAD YARD PCB LITIGATION

United States Court of Appeals, Third Circuit, 1994.
35 F.3d 717, aff'd 113 F.3d 444 (1997).

BECKER, CIRCUIT JUDGE.

The plaintiffs in this toxic tort case have lived for many years in the vicinity of the Paoli Railyard, a railcar maintenance facility at which polychlorinated biphenyls (PCBs) were used in profusion for over a quarter century. They have sued to recover damages * * * for property damage against the corporations that have maintained the railyard and that sold the PCBs.

* * *

[] We will reverse the grant of summary judgment on plaintiffs' claim with respect to diminution in property value. Based on an extrapolation from existing Pennsylvania case law, we predict that where (1) the defendants have caused some physical harm to plaintiffs' property; (2) repair of this damage will not restore the value of the property to its prior level; and (3) there is at least some ongoing risk to the plaintiffs' land, Pennsylvania would allow plaintiffs to recover damages for the diminution of their property value. On the present record, there remains a genuine issue of material fact on the permanency of damage issue.

* * *

Beginning in the 1950s, if not before, PCBs were used at the Paoli Railroad Yard (the "Yard") as a fire-resistant insulating fluid in railroad car transformers. PCBs gradually accumulated in the Yard and leaked off the Yard into groundwater and ultimately into the soil of nearby residences. * * * Several studies from 1979–1986 documented high levels of PCBs in the Yard and in nearby water and land. The National Institute for Occupational Safety and Health (NIOSH) identifies the site as containing the worst PCB contamination it has ever encountered during a health inspection.

In 1986, the United States sued SEPTA, Conrail and Amtrak under the Comprehensive Environmental Response Compensation and Liability Act (CERCLA), 42 U.S.C. § 9601, to compel the cleanup of the Yard. After the entry of five consent decrees, which primarily required the control of leakage from the Yard, EPA adopted a final plan, the Record of Decision, in July of 1992. This plan requires extensive excavation and treatment of soils both at the Yard and on nearby residential property and streams, and erosion controls at the Yard.

The plaintiffs in this action consist of individuals who lived near the Yard in areas identified by EPA and by the railroad defendants' contractor, Groundwater Technologies, Inc., as having experienced the most severe run-off from the Yard. The plaintiffs have adduced evidence of significant levels of PCBs in the soil at their homes. Many of the plaintiffs played in the soil at their homes while growing up, gardened in it, and ate vegetables grown from it. Many also regularly traversed the Yard on foot as a short cut to their destinations.

In 1986, thirty eight plaintiffs brought suit in the District Court for the Eastern District of Pennsylvania. * * * [S]ome of the plaintiffs have brought claims for the decrease in value to their property caused by the presence of PCBs on the land.

* * *

In November of 1988 the district court * * * granted summary judgment in favor of the defendants on these claims * * * The court held that Pennsylvania law only allows recovery for diminution of a property's market value if there has been permanent damage to the property; and the court found that plaintiffs could not prove such permanent damage in light of EPA's proposed cleanup plan.

The plaintiffs challenge the district court's subject matter jurisdiction, all of its admissibility decisions, its legal conclusions regarding diminution of a property's market value, and the court's grant of summary judgment. We will reverse * * * its grant of summary judgment on the plaintiffs' claims for * * * diminution in property value.

* * *

[Discussion of jurisdiction issue omitted].

* * *

Plaintiffs * * * argue that it is reasonable to conclude that * * * furans and dioxins leaked from the Yard onto plaintiffs' soil, because a worker spread waste transformer fluids from the drums directly on the parking lot, and that some of these fluids, if they followed normal water run off patterns, would have entered plaintiffs' yards. Dr. Kopstein buttressed the plaintiffs' argument. He explained that "fires at the yard would had to have produced furans and dioxins;" as a result, he "concluded that * * * there was an ongoing and continuous release of PCBs and most likely to a reasonable—within a reasonable degree of scientific certainty furans and dioxins, into the neighborhood during that 35–year period."

The district court found that, although dioxins and furans were measured in the Yard, they were measured in quantities below the Center for Disease Control's ("CDC") level of concern. Because soil in the Yard was the only sample of any sort tested for dioxins and furans, the district court found the soil readings in the Yard to be basically conclusive of the fact that dioxins and furans were not present in sufficient quantities to injure.

* * *

In EPA's Risk Assessment for the Paoli PCB Superfund site, it concluded that PCB levels in residential soils must be reduced to two parts per million to reduce cancer risks to acceptable levels (EPA has set acceptable risk at 1 in 100,000, although EPA's point of departure for risk assessments is 1 in 1,000,000). As was mentioned above, EPA's March 1992 "Proposed Plan Paoli Railyard Superfund Site" concludes that there are presently extensive PCBs in residential soils in Paoli which create an "incremental cancer risk for children and adults in the residential area near the Rail Yard with lifetime exposure to residential soils * * * in the range of $1 \times 10-4$ to $1 \times 10-5$."

* * *

The district court found that [] EPA already ha[d] a plan under which it can and will remove the alleged contamination to plaintiffs' property. The court found that the plaintiffs had not submitted any evidence to indicate that EPA's remedy would not be effectuated or would be inadequate with regard to real property or groundwater contamination. The court concluded that absent permanent physical damage, plaintiffs had no claim. Any decrease in market value caused by the stigma associated with living near the railyard was not, in its view, compensable under Pennsylvania law. The court held that harm to the property (repair costs) rather than diminution of value is the proper measure of damages where the harm is temporary and remediable (citing Kirkbride v. Lisbon Contractors, 385 Pa.Super. 292, 560 A.2d 809, 812 (1989)); and Rabe v. Shoenberger Coal Co., 213 Pa. 252, 62 A. 854 (Pa.1906)). The court stated that only if the damages are permanent is the proper measure of damages the diminution in value (citing Ridgeway Court, Inc. v. Landon Courts, Inc., 295 Pa.Super. 493, 442 A.2d 246, 248 (1981), and that Pennsylvania law presumes that damage is temporary and remediable and justifies a finding to the contrary only if the harm is "unequivocally beyond repair." (citing Kirkbride, 560 A.2d at 812–13).

Here, according to the district court, the damage to the property was repairable.

Plaintiffs respond that even under the rule cited by the district court, the proper measure of damages is diminution in market value because there was in fact permanent damage to plaintiffs' property. First, EPA itself estimates that its cleanup will lower cancer risk only to 1 in 100,000, which is ten times higher than its normal remedial goal of lowering risk to 1 in 1,000,000.

Second, Dr. Kopstein indicated that the EPA plan will not be effective in eliminating groundwater contamination, exposure through the air, and the continuing release of sediments from the Yard.

However, the district court found that Dr. Kopstein did not assert that a human health hazard would remain. He only stated that he could not calculate the levels of exposure levels from groundwater, air and sediment runoffs that would remain after the cleanup. The court added that Dr. Kopstein's testimony had only been offered for the purpose of establishing plaintiffs' "opportunities for exposure" to PCBs and thus could not establish a continuing health hazard. It noted that EPA's reduction of PCB levels to 2 ppm ensures that these levels are less than those the FDA allows in food packaging material, poultry and animal feed. See 21 C.F.R. § 109.30.

Despite Pennsylvania's presumption that damage is not permanent, we think the district court's decision to grant summary judgment was incorrect. As we see it, the EPA's own normal practice of cleaning up property to the point where the risk is 1 in 1,000,000 creates a genuine issue of material fact as to whether a cancer risk of 1 in 100,000 constitutes permanent damage; the tension with the FDA standards is for the jury to resolve. Moreover, the clear import of Dr. Kopstein's testimony, giving every inference to the nonmoving party, is that a human health hazard will remain after the EPA cleanup. In testifying to "opportunities for exposure," Dr. Kopstein could certainly testify that exposure on plaintiffs' properties was likely to continue to be high.

Plaintiffs also presented evidence to demonstrate permanent damage in a second way. While the requirement of permanent damage to property seems on its face to require permanent physical damage, plaintiffs convincingly argue that the stigma associated with the prior presence of PCBs on their land constitutes permanent, irremediable damage to property under Pennsylvania case law such that they can recover for the diminution of value of their land. They cite Willsey v. Kansas City Power & Light Co., 6 Kan.App.2d 599, 631 P.2d 268, 273–75 (1981), which states that in eleven of twenty six jurisdictions to consider the issue, loss of market value is recoverable when the government takes part of an owner's property and places electric power lines on it even if the market's fear of the power lines is unreasonable, see e.g., United States ex rel. Tenn. Valley Auth. v. Easement and Right of Way, 405 F.2d 305, 309 (6th Cir.1968) ("[I]n final analysis, we are only concerned with market value. Although these studies may show objectively the complete safety of these structures, we are not convinced that certain segments of the buying public may not remain apprehensive of these high voltage lines"), and that in another nine jurisdictions, the rule is that diminution of market value is compensable so long as it has some reasonable basis, see, e.g., Kentucky Hydro Electric Co. v. Woodard, 216 Ky. 618, 287 S.W. 985 (1926) ("If he cannot sell his property at as good a figure with this line on it as he could without it by reason of reasonable fears, not speculative but founded on experience and entertained by those who wish to buy, has he not been damaged in this regard?").

Plaintiffs submit that Pennsylvania has essentially adopted one of these two positions and that it applies to tort cases as well as takings cases. In Appeal of Giesler, 154 Pa.[Commw.] 48, 622 A.2d 408, 411–12 (1993), decided after the district court decision in this case, the court held in a takings case that just compensation for land taken by the government to run an electric power line included full diminution of market value of the remaining land. The court quoted United States v. Easement and Right of Way, 249 F.Supp. 747, 750 (W.D.Ky.1966) which held that, "[a]pprehension of injuries to person or property by the presence of power lines on the property may be taken into consideration insofar as the line affects the market value of the land. In the opinion of the Court, the apprehension of such danger constitutes an element of damage." 622 A.2d at 411–12. The court made this determination even though evidence on the health effects of electric lines was speculative. Wade v. S.J. Groves & Sons Co., 283 Pa.Super. 464, 424 A.2d 902, 912 (1981), also supports the proposition that a reduction in market value is recoverable even absent permanent physical damage to the plaintiffs' property. *Wade* involved the negligent modification by plaintiff's neighbor of a natural gully on that neighbor's land which changed the drainage patterns on that land and caused flooding on plaintiff's land. The damage was repairable and the Wades were able to reduce to negligible levels any significant risk of future damage by undertaking a variety of flood control measures. See id. 424 A.2d at 911. Nonetheless, there was a permanent change in the flood plain of the neighbor's land, a slight ongoing risk of renewed flooding, and a significant diminution in the value of the Wades' land. Despite the fact that the actual permanent change was to the neighbor's land, the court allowed compensation for the diminution in market value to the plaintiff's property that would remain after repairs were made. See id. 424 A.2d at 911–12.

Defendants assert that *Wade* and *Giesler* do not support plaintiffs' proposition, and that plaintiffs' citation to the law of other jurisdictions is irrelevant and contradicted by the law of other jurisdictions. See, e.g., Adams v. Star Enter., 1994 WL 172266 at *3, 851 F.Supp. 770 (E.D.Va. 1994) (holding that stigma damages based on unfounded fear about dangers in the vicinity of property are unavailable in a nuisance action). Defendants submit that the presence of the electric lines in *Giesler* and the change in the flood plain in *Wade* were permanent whereas the PCBs here are, presumably, not present permanently. However, the permanent physical changes in *Wade* and *Giesler* were to neighboring land; there was no permanent physical change to plaintiffs' land. Defendants respond that the changes to neighboring land posed a continuing risk of damage to plaintiffs' land. But it is not clear why this continuing risk constitutes permanent physical damage to any greater extent than the continuing stigma of living on property which once contained significant amounts of PCBs.

Moreover, defendants are incorrect that the changes to neighboring land in Giesler posed a continuing risk to plaintiffs' land.

The *Giesler* court assumed that the electric lines caused no actual physical risk of any sort to plaintiffs' land. This means that the only ongoing damage to the property in *Giesler* was the diminution in value caused by the stigma of living near electric lines which is comparable to the stigma of living on property which once contained significant quantities of PCBs.[61] And, in any case, there is some ongoing risk to plaintiffs here based on the admittedly small quantities of PCBs left on the land.[62]

Even if the facts of *Wade* and *Giesler* are somewhat distinguishable from the facts here, the principles articulated in *Wade* essentially eliminate the possibility that an injury to land must be physical for it to be considered permanent. After citing the traditional Pennsylvania rule that diminution in market value is only recoverable if damage is permanent, the court stated that the term permanent injury was meant to apply whenever repair costs would, for some reason, be an inappropriate measure of damages. See *Wade*, 424 A.2d at 912. And an appropriate measure of damages is generally defined as what is necessary to compensate fully the plaintiff. See id. at 911–12.

This approach is normally consistent with the view that, when physical damage is temporary, only repair costs are recoverable, because in a perfectly functioning market, fully repaired property will return to its former value. Thus, an award of repair costs will be fully compensatory. And it makes sense to award repair costs rather than the equivalent diminution of value absent repair, because it is easier to measure repair costs. Hence, normally, it is only when property cannot be repaired that courts must award damages for diminution of value in order to fully compensate plaintiffs. However, the market sometimes fails and repair costs are not fully compensatory. In such cases, according to the principles of the *Wade* court, plaintiffs should be compensated for their

---

61. It is possible to argue that the taking of property to install the electric lines in *Giesler* was permanent—thus, there was a permanent change to some of the Gieslers' land. However, the Gieslers could have been fully compensated for the permanent loss of this land without being compensated for the diminution in value of their remaining land—land which was not physically damaged. Moreover, in *Wade*, there was no taking of plaintiffs' land nor any permanent damage to plaintiffs' land.

62. Defendants also attempt to distinguish *Giesler* on the basis that it was a

takings case not a tort case. However, In re Larsen, 532 Pa. 326, 616 A.2d 529 (1992), cert. denied, 510 U.S. 815, 114 S.Ct. 65, 126 L.Ed.2d 34 (1993), held that compensation in a tort case is generally at least as great as in a takings case. In a tort case, unlike a takings case, the goal is to compensate the plaintiff "for all injuries proximately caused by the defendant's action" including property lost and incidental injuries not recognized in eminent domain actions. See *Larsen*, 616 A.2d at 599–600. Indeed, *Wade* was a tort case.

remaining loss. Absent such an approach, plaintiffs are permanently deprived of significant value without any compensation. See id.

Although post-*Wade* cases, including Pennsylvania Supreme Court cases, continue to cite the traditional Pennsylvania rule without discussing *Wade's* interpretation of that rule, see, e.g., *Kirkbride,* 560 A.2d at 813 (holding that "where an injury is reparable, the damage is the cost of repair or restoration") (citing Lobozzo v. Adam Eidemiller, Inc., 437 Pa. 360, 263 A.2d 432 (1970)), none have rejected Wade's interpretation of that rule.[63] We hope that the Pennsylvania courts will provide further guidance on this issue. For now, although *Wade* and *Giesler* are not decisions of the Pennsylvania Supreme Court, they are well reasoned decisions, and we think that at least where (1) defendants have caused some (temporary) physical damage to plaintiffs' property; (2) plaintiffs demonstrate that repair of this damage will not restore the value of the property to its prior level; and (3) plaintiffs show that there is some ongoing risk to their land, plaintiffs can make out a claim for diminution of value of their property without showing permanent physical damage to the land.[64] Thus, we will reverse the district court's grant of summary judgment on the plaintiffs' property damage claims.

We think that these concerns are overstated. The rule we have articulated only allows recovery when there has been some initial physical damage to plaintiffs' land. Cf. Berry v. Armstrong Rubber Co., 989 F.2d 822 (5th Cir.1993), cert. denied, 510 U.S. 1117, 114 S.Ct. 1067, 127 L.Ed.2d 386. Subnom. Cooper v. Armstrong Rubber Co. 1994 (holding that Mississippi law only allows recovery for a decrease in property value caused by stigma where there has been some physical harm to the property). This rules out recovery in cases such as the establishment of a group home for the disabled; moreover, recovery in such cases might well be barred as against public policy. Any risk of an avalanche of litigation with every market fluctuation will be prevented by the need of plaintiffs to establish causation and to prove that the stigma associated with their

---

63. Defendants' citations to the contrary are inapposite. Hughes v. Emerald Mines Corp., 303 Pa.Super. 426, 450 A.2d 1, 8 (1982) reversed an award of loss-in-market-value damages for the pollution of the plaintiffs' wells because restoration of those wells was possible. But the plaintiffs did not present any evidence in that case that a diminution in market value would remain even after restoration of the wells.

64. Defendants' amicus, the American Insurance Association, cites cases from several jurisdictions where plaintiffs who lived near contaminated sites or nuclear power plants were denied recovery for diminution in property value. In Adkins v. Thomas Solvent Co., 440 Mich. 293, 487 N.W.2d 715 (1992) for example, the Michigan Supreme Court held that allowing recovery in such cases might permit recovery for "unfounded fears regarding persons with AIDS moving into a neighborhood, the establishment of otherwise lawful group homes for the disabled, or unrelated persons living together, merely because the fears experienced by third parties would cause a decline in property values." Id. 487 N.W.2d at 726. The amicus also argues that allowing a tort for diminution in value would allow thousands of insubstantial and peripheral claims, would often grant recoveries for routine fluctuations in market prices thus generating windfalls, and would increase insurance costs, reduce the availability of insurance, and reduce the availability of funds to compensate those who were actually injured. See Kenneth S. Abraham, Environmental Liability and the Limits of Insurance, 88 Colum. L.Rev. 942, 972–74 (1988).

land will remain in place after any physical damage to their land has been repaired.

Notes and Questions

1. *Full Recovery Goal:* Putting aside stigma damages for the moment, Professor Dobbs also considers whether in environmental damage cases the costs of restoration should be the appropriate measure. Dan B. Dobbs, Law of Remedies § 5.2(5) (2d ed. 1993):

> In this situation, damages should not usually be limited to the diminished market value of the land. Instead, the landowner should be permitted to recover full restoration costs and all consequential damages that are properly established, at least if he can give the court assurance that repair, restoration or cleanup will actually take place. Such a scenario gives the landowner no windfall and it entails no waste. Because costs of the pollution affect others, or the public at large, the diminished value of the plaintiff's land is no guide to the actual costs imposed by the pollution. Cost or repair or cleanup are thus appropriate, even if they exceed the diminished value of the land. As indicated below, this result is supported by analogy to environmental laws, even if those laws do not apply to the particular case.

What is the principal rationale for abandoning the common law damage rules in cases of environmental harm? What if a defendant could establish that the contamination created no threats of injury to anyone other than the plaintiff? Professor Dobbs also discusses CERCLA, and by analogy argues that environmental statutes, which deal with harms to land that produce harm to the public or those outside the land, are relevant authority in crafting private remedies. Id., § 5.2(5) at 725–30. See also, e.g., Terra–Products, Inc. v. Kraft General Foods, Inc., 653 N.E.2d 89 (Ind.Ct.App.1995) ("We agree with the trial court that in light of the often exorbitant costs of remediation, the traditional common law economic waste analysis is inadequate when measuring damages to land from environmental contamination. Land subject to hazardous waste or PCB contamination is required to be remediated virtually without regard to cost. PCB contamination, therefore, will generally be considered a temporary injury capable of being remediated or 'repaired.' ")

2. *Permanent versus Temporary Classification*: This classification is relevant because historically, if injury to land is permanent, the owner is entitled to diminution in value, but not if the damage is regarded as temporary. But deciding how to classify an injury to real property from chemical pollution is extremely difficult. Instructive is the analysis in Mel Foster Co. Properties v. American Oil Co., 427 N.W.2d 171 (Iowa 1988). In *Mel Foster* the Supreme Court of Iowa held nuisance actions for land contaminated by chemical pollutants should be classified as permanent nuisances so as to entitle the landowner to diminution in market value damages.

In *Mel Foster* a property owner's land was contaminated by gasoline which had leaked from an underground gasoline tank on an adjacent property owned by U–Haul and from a distribution line from a nearby gasoline station owned by Amoco. U–Haul and Amoco immediately took steps to clean up the gasoline leaks. The trial court ruled the nuisance was temporary and the landowner could bring successive suits to recover damages for lost rents until the nuisance was fully abated.

On appeal, the Supreme Court of Iowa acknowledged:

Underground gasoline contamination does not fit neatly into a category as either a temporary or permanent nuisance. Case law concerning temporary nuisances often deals with the type of interference with the use of property which is abated when the cause of the nuisance has abated. [citations.] These cases, which address an interference with the use of property but do not encompass injury to the property itself, are not instructive in dealing with chemical pollution to real estate which will remain in the soil for an indefinite period of time. * * *

Chemical contamination of land, such a the gasoline on Foster's property, encompasses aspects of both a temporary and permanent nuisance. This injury is temporary in the sense that the cause of the pollution has been discovered and abated, and the harmful chemicals in the ground will eventually dissipate. This nuisance is permanent in the sense that it constitutes damage to the ground itself and will continue for an indefinite but significant period of time. An attempt to classify chemical pollution as a permanent or temporary nuisance is further complicated by the presence of rapidly changing scientific technology. Scientific knowledge enables society to successfully clean up pollution once thought to be permanent; it also reveals hidden dangers in chemicals once thought to be safe. * * *

When a nuisance results in contamination of property for an indefinite period of time, the proper measure of damages is the diminution of the market value of the property. This measure of damages is proper even when the source of the contamination has been abated [in this case tanks and distribution lines removed]. Permanent damages may be awarded even if the nuisance is classified as temporary. * * *

The award of permanent damages based on the reduction of market value provides that the plaintiff's remedies stemming from this particular incident will be addressed in one legal action. Successive actions to recover temporary damages stemming from one incident, such as the action currently filed by Foster, are contrary to the goal of efficient legal remedies. * * *

"We conclude the proper measure of damages in this nuisance case is the difference between the market value of Foster's property immediately before contamination and the market value of that property after the contamination." * * *

427 N.W.2d at 174–176.

The *Mel Foster* approach has found other supporters. See, e.g., Santa Fe Partnership v. ARCO Products Co., 46 Cal.App.4th 967, 54 Cal.Rptr.2d 214, (Cal.Ct.App.1996) ("the decision in *Mel Foster* makes a very strong argument for classifying injuries to land from contamination by toxic or hazardous materials as permanent nuisances.")

3. *Stigma Damages*: The debate over the propriety of stigma damages for post-cleanup remaining diminution has generated considerable judicial and law review commentary. The Utah Supreme Court in Walker Drug Co. v. La Sal Oil Co., 972 P.2d 1238 (Utah 1998), an oil contamination case, citing *Paoli*, adopted the doctrine, explaining it in simple terms:

> Stigma damages are a facet of permanent damages, and recovery for stigma damages is compensation for a property's diminished market value in the absence of "permanent 'physical' " harm. This Court has not assessed the availability of stigma damages in any prior case.

> A majority of courts from other jurisdictions, however, allows recovery when a defendant's trespass or nuisance has caused some temporary physical injury to the property but, despite the temporary injury's remediation, the property's market value remains depressed.

> Thus, stigma damages compensate for loss to the property's market value resulting from the long-term negative perception of the property in excess of any recovery obtained for the temporary injury itself. Were this residual loss due to stigma not compensated, the plaintiff's property would be permanently deprived of significant value without compensation.

> We find the majority position convincing. Stigma damages are therefore recoverable in Utah when a plaintiff demonstrates that (1) defendants caused some temporary physical injury to plaintiff's land and (2) repair of this temporary injury will not return the value of the property to its prior level because of a lingering negative public perception.

972 P.2d at 1246–47.

In *Walker Drug*, the court reversed the trial court for excluding plaintiffs' witness who testified that during the statute of limitations period (1990 to 1993), the public perception regarding the effect of environmental contamination on property values "changed dramatically." The court continued, at 1247:

> In particular, she testified from her experience that buyers were much more sophisticated after 1990 about environmental contamination. They asked detailed questions about possible contamination and gave contamination more consideration in assessing value, whereas during the 1980s contamination was viewed as relatively unimportant. She also referred to regulatory changes occurring after 1990 that increased the effect of environmental contamination on property values. It was not until 1993 that real estate agents were required to disclose to prospective buyers land conditions that affected a property's environmental purity.

> While [the real estate agent] did not testify about changes in public perception relating specifically to the Drugstore Property after 1990, it can clearly be inferred from her testimony that a potential buyer after March 1, 1990, would have viewed the contaminated property much more cautiously than would a buyer before then. This is true notwithstanding the undisputed fact, recognized by [the real estate agent] that overall contamination levels on the Drugstore Property had decreased

since 1990. Because the Drugstore Property was not for sale during the relevant time period, no witness would likely have been able to testify, with the degree of specificity that the trial court apparently required, about the stigma attributed to the property by potential buyers.

What would you require as a sufficient testimonial basis for allowing a jury to award stigma damages? Don't forget all plaintiffs must prove causation, that the nuisance or trespass is the cause-in-fact of the diminution in value from public perceptions.

Many decisions have applied the *Paoli* analysis and adopted its three-part test. See, e.g., Terra–Products, Inc. v. Kraft General Foods, Inc., 653 N.E.2d 89 (Ind.Ct.App.1995) (landowner seeks recovery from PCB contamination to land); Santa Fe Partnership v. ARCO Products Co., 46 Cal.App.4th 967, 54 Cal.Rptr.2d 214 (Cal.Ct.App.1996) (property owners seeks damages for petroleum contamination of property); Scribner v. Summers, 138 F.3d 471 (2d Cir.1998) (New York law, by implication) (landowners filed action against neighboring business for barium contamination of property); Bisson v. Eck, 40 Mass.App.Ct. 942, 667 N.E.2d 276 (Mass.Ct.App. 1996) (present owner of real property seeks recovery against prior owner to recover cleanup costs and for diminution in value of land). Compare McKay v. United States, 703 F.2d 464 (10th Cir.1983) (Colo. Law) (allegations of substantial contamination of land by plutonium, americium and uranium).

4. *The Necessity of Physical Harm*: The cases awarding stigma damages appear to be nearly uniform in demanding some actual physical injury to the property as a precondition to recovery. Thus, just living near to a hazardous waste site is an insufficient basis even though a plaintiff's property value may be adversely affected. See, e.g., Chance v. BP Chem., Inc., 77 Ohio St.3d 17, 670 N.E.2d 985 (Ohio 1996) (property owners seeks to recover for damages caused by lateral migration of injectate used by defendant to dispose of refining byproducts by deepwell injection); Santa Fe Partnership v. ARCO Products Co., 46 Cal.App.4th 967, 54 Cal.Rptr.2d 214 (Cal.App.1996) (stating "courts have uniformly rejected claims for stigma damages absent evidence the plaintiff's own property suffered physical injury from the contamination.")

In the absence of physical harm, how might a plaintiff go about proving her loss? What reasons support limiting the availability of this remedy?

Consider this comment in Schlichter, Stigma Damages In Environmental Contamination Cases: A Possible Windfall for Plaintiffs? 34 Houston L. Rev. 1125, 1156 (1997):

> Probably the most compelling collateral effect argument against the award of stigma damages is that "[s]tigma damages clearly present the potential to [increase] fraudulent claims and to [increase] the cost of remediation, cleanup and other [arguably] stigmatizing, but necessary, social activities." The consequence of such awards would be the courts "opening the judicial system to tenuous claims that would not have clear boundaries or stopping points." Furthermore, "[a]llowing this form of damages has the potential to dis-serve the public interest and to reward only those claiming temporary inconvenience and loss, rather than true permanent loss." The true goal of damage awards is to compensate a plaintiff for losses incurred at the hands of a defendant, which is not

accomplished by the award of damages for other than "true permanent loss."

5. *Literature.* The issue of stigma damages and all other damages in environmental contamination cases has produced much literature. See, e.g., Andrew N. Davis & Santo Longo, Stigma Damages in Environmental Cases: Developing Issues and Implications for Industrial and Commercial Real Estate Transactions, 25 Envtl. L. Rep. 10,345 (1995); Timothy J. Muldowney & Kendall W. Harrison, Stigma Damages: Property Damage and the Fear of Risk, 62 Def. Couns. J. 525, 526 (1995); L. Neal Ellis, Jr., & Charles D. Case, Toxic Tort and Hazardous Substance Litigation § 6–5(a) (1995); Jean Johnson, Environmental Stigma Damages: Speculative Damages in Environmental Tort Cases, 15 UCLA J. Envtl. L. 185 (1997); William Stack & Terri Jacobson, Diminution in Property Value Arising From Stigma of Environmental Contamination: A Phantom Injury in Search of Actual Damages, 11 Envtl. Claims J. 21 (1999); Anthony Roisman & Gary Masson, Nuisance and Stigma Damages: Eliminating the Confusion, 26 Envtl. L. Rep. 10070 (1996).

2. LOSS OF USE OR ENJOYMENT

In many environmental tort cases—whether predicated on nuisance, trespass, negligence or strict liability theories—the plaintiff has sustained some economic loss because of the inability or diminished ability to make use of the land damaged by pollution or other invasion. In addition to diminished market value (if the land itself is harmed) and the costs of repairs or abatement (to abate the nuisance or trespass and prevent future injury), the loss of rental or use values is an appropriate measure of the damages, covering the rental value of the property for the period that the nuisance has been or will be in existence. Dan B. Dobbs, Law of Remedies § 5.6(2) (2d ed. 1993). For an excellent discussion see Davey Compressor Co. v. City of Delray Beach, 613 So.2d 60 (Fla.Ct.App. 1993) which illustrates application of this measure of damages.

Decisions have awarded loss of rental or use value resulting from a nuisance or trespass. See, e.g., Miller v. Cudahy Co., 592 F.Supp. 976 (D.Kan.1984), aff'd, 858 F.2d 1449 (10th Cir.1988); Coty v. Ramsey Associates, Inc., 149 Vt. 451, 546 A.2d 196 (1988); National Steel Corp. v. Great Lakes Towing Co., 574 F.2d 339 (6th Cir.1978). For a discussion on the upper limits on recovery of loss of use value, see Dan B. Dobbs, Law of Remedies § 5.6(2), at 755–57.

3. PERSONAL DISCOMFORT AND ANNOYANCE

Restatement (Second) of Torts § 929 also provides that in addition to damages for diminished value, restoration costs and loss of use, a plaintiff may be entitled to recover for the personal discomfort, annoyance and even for personal injury attributable to the nuisance. See § 929 comment *e.* An extreme example of this type of damage is the following description in Filisko v. Bridgeport Hydraulic Co., 176 Conn. 33, 404 A.2d 889, 893–94 (1978), where polluted water from the defendant's refuse dump ran onto plaintiffs' land and into their pond, causing them

* * * annoyance, discomfort and inconvenience * * * during eight years of continuous pollution to their property. They lost completely the enjoyable uses for which they built the pond. They were subjected to the sight of "big globs of brown-yellow gooey stuff" oozing onto their property, and to the constant odor of "rotten eggs" that was at times so powerful they had difficulty sleeping.

See also Branch v. Western Petroleum, Inc., 657 P.2d 267, 278 (Utah 1982) (recovery for mental suffering, discomfort and annoyance for pollution of culinary water wells from percolation of oil well formation waters).

For an example of personal injury, see Lentz v. Mason, 32 F.Supp.2d 733 (D.N.J.1999) (plaintiff entitled to recover for asthma attacks caused by disposal of toxic materials on property).

HAWKINS v. SCITUATE OIL CO., INC.

Supreme Court of Rhode Island, 1999.
723 A.2d 771.

FLANDERS, JUSTICE.

When a tortfeasor's negligence deprives a family of the use and enjoyment of their home, is the family entitled to recover damages for their resulting inconvenience, discomfort, and annoyance? We answer this question in the affirmative, reverse the Superior Court's contrary ruling, and remand this case for a trial on damages.

FACTS AND TRAVEL

On a fateful day in October 1993, a delivery man working for defendant, Scituate Oil Co., Inc. (defendant or Scituate Oil), drove his truck up to plaintiffs' Glocester residence and mistakenly pumped 100 gallons of home heating oil down the wrong pipe. The oil flooded their unfinished basement and finished their home's habitability. While workmen attempted to resuscitate their house from this oily deluge, the Hawkins family had to relocate to new quarters. Because they could not afford more salubrious accommodations, they scrunched themselves into a small, rented trailer on their property. The family hunkered down there for more than sixteen months until they were able to construct and move into a new house on the same property.

In September 1996, the parties reached a partial settlement of the Hawkins' claims against Scituate Oil. This settlement, however, related only to the actual damages plaintiffs sustained to their real and personal property. Even though it included reimbursement for their out-of-pocket costs and their expenditures relating to consultants, rental of a trailer, and their other, spill-related disbursements, the settlement specifically preserved the Hawkins' remaining claims for a damages trial.

At the conclusion of plaintiffs' case, the trial justice granted defendant's motion for judgment as a matter of law and dismissed plaintiffs' complaint. In doing so, he relied upon the lack of expert medical testimony to buttress plaintiffs' damage claims for the alleged inconvenience, discomfort, and annoyance they suffered as a result of their oleaginous eviction. The Hawkins appealed from this judgment.

For the reasons set forth below, we hold that the trial justice committed reversible error when he granted defendant's motion for judgment as a matter of law. In our opinion, he should not have done so because he thereby prevented the jury from awarding damages to the Hawkins family for the inconvenience, discomfort, and annoyance they suffered after Scituate Oil's tragic misdump left their home uninhabitable. * * *

ANALYSIS

This Court has allowed occupants of real property to recover consequential and compensatory damages resulting from a tortious interference with their possessory interest in such property. See Harris v. Town of Lincoln, 668 A.2d 321 (R.I.1995) (affirming a damages award of $400 per month to compensate for the diminution in the plaintiffs' use and enjoyment of their property caused by the defendant's tortious conduct); Vogel v. McAuliffe, 18 R.I. 791, 31 A. 1 (1895) (awarding damages to the plaintiff tenant for his "trouble" and inconvenience caused by the defendant's destruction of and refusal to replace the leased premises' furnace). Such a damages award may properly include compensation to the occupants for annoyance, mental suffering, and anxiety proximately caused by any interference with or diminution of their enjoyment of the property.

The great weight of authority in other jurisdictions also allows occupants of real property to recover damages for the inconvenience and aggravation caused by a tortfeasor's interference with or deprivation of their use and enjoyment of their property. See, e.g., Board of County Commissioners of Weld v. Slovek, 723 P.2d 1309 (Colo.1986) (recognizing that the plaintiffs may recover personal-injury damages for discomfort, annoyance, and sickness caused by the defendant's negligent maintenance of a breach in a river bank that resulted in water damage to their property); Evans v. Mutual Mining, 199 W.Va. 526, 485 S.E.2d 695 (W.Va.1997) (considering annoyance and inconvenience in measuring damages for the loss of use of real property due to the defendant's negligence); Piorkowski v. Liberty Mutual Insurance Co., 68 Wis.2d 455, 228 N.W.2d 695 (Wis.1975) (allowing the plaintiffs to recover damages for their inconvenience after the defendant contractor negligently cut off the well-water supply to their household for six months). See generally Restatement (Second) Torts, § 929 at 544 (1979), which states, in pertinent part:

> "(1) If one is entitled to a judgment for harm to land resulting from a past invasion and not amounting to a total destruction of value, the damages include compensation for * * *
>
> (c) discomfort and annoyance to him as an occupant."

Comment e to this section elaborates on this point:

Discomfort and other bodily and mental harms. Discomfort and annoyance to an occupant of the land and to the members of the household are distinct grounds of compensation for which in ordinary cases the person in possession is allowed to recover in addition to the harm to his proprietary interests. He is also allowed to recover for his own serious sickness or other substantial bodily harm but is not allowed to recover for serious harm to other members of the household, except so far as he maintains an action as a spouse or parent * * *. [Restatement (Second) Torts, § 929 cmt. *e*, at 546–47.]

The necessity for proving some interference with or deprivation of a possessory interest in the property in question as a condition precedent to obtaining damages for any resulting inconvenience, discomfort, or annoyance distinguishes this type of case from those alleging a mere intentional or negligent infliction of emotional distress. See, e.g., Swerdlick v. Koch, 721 A.2d 849, 862–64 (R.I.1998); see also, e.g., Vallinoto v. DiSandro, 688 A.2d 830, 838–40 (R.I.1997); Clift v. Narragansett Television L.P., 688 A.2d 805, 812–14 (R.I.1996); Reilly v. United States, 547 A.2d 894 (R.I.1988). In the above-cited cases, the plaintiffs failed to allege or establish any tortious interference with or deprivation of their use or enjoyment of any possessory interest in real property. In such circumstances, to safeguard against bogus or exaggerated emotional-damage claims, we have held that plaintiffs seeking to recover a monetary award for the tortious infliction of emotional distress must establish, among other elements, that they experienced physical symptoms of their alleged emotional distress, and that expert medical testimony supports the existence of a causal relationship between the putative wrongful conduct and their injuries. See Vallinoto, 688 A.2d at 838–40; Clift, 688 A.2d at 812–13; Reilly v. United States, 547 A.2d 894 (R.I. 1988). In property-loss cases like this one, however, where a tortfeasor's wrongdoing has interfered with the plaintiff's rightful occupancy of his or her premises, it is unnecessary to mandate evidence of physical symptomatology plus medical-causation expertise before allowing such plaintiffs to recover damages for their resulting discomfort and annoyance. Because property-loss victims like the Hawkins typically will experience inconvenience, discomfort, and annoyance following such a tangible deprivation as occurred in this case—albeit no corporeal symptoms or medical expertise corroborates such a loss—we have no need to insist upon the heightened levels of proof that we would otherwise require in establishing pure emotional-distress claims. In sum, in cases like this one involving a physical interference with or a loss of a possessory interest in real property, the prevention of trumped-up or specious-damage demands for alleged intangible personal injuries is of less an evidentiary concern than it is in the context of cases alleging a mere intentional or negligent infliction of emotional distress.

Accordingly, with respect to the Hawkins' negligence-based damage claims seeking to recover for the inconvenience, discomfort, and annoyance they experienced after the defendant's negligent oil spill flushed them from their home, the trial justice erred in granting Scituate Oil's motion for judgment as a matter of law.

On any retrial, the court shall allow the Hawkins to introduce evidence concerning—and to recover damages for—any inconvenience, discomfort, or annoyance that they experienced in connection with having to abandon their oil-befouled home and with having to take up residence elsewhere. Moreover, the court shall allow the Hawkins to recover for such injuries irrespective of whether they can point to any physical symptoms of their distress or whether they can proffer any medical expertise to support such claims. They also shall be allowed to recover compensatory damages for any other losses not covered by the settlement that they can prove were attributable to Scituate Oil.

Notes and Questions

1. A leading decision on discomfort and annoyance damages, often called "quality of life" damages, is Ayers v. Township of Jackson, 106 N.J. 557, 525 A.2d 287 (N.J. 1987). The litigation involved claims by over 150 plaintiffs for damages sustained because plaintiffs' well water was contaminated by toxic pollutants leaching into the aquifer from a landfill operated by Jackson Township. The jury found that the township had created a nuisance and awarded over $5 million for deterioration in the quality of their lives. The issue was whether such damages were precluded under the State Torts Claims Act (N.J.S.A. 59:9–2(d)) which barred claims for "pain and suffering" against the township.

A substantial number of the plaintiffs gave testimony with respect to damages, describing in detail the impairment of their quality of life during the period that they were without running water, and the emotional distress they suffered.

The court's opinion in important part, continues:

In November 1978, the residents of the Legler area of Jackson Township were advised by the local Board of Health not to drink their well water, and to limit washing and bathing to avoid prolonged exposure to the water. This warning was issued by the Board after tests disclosed that a number of wells in the Legler area of the township were contaminated by toxic chemicals. Initially, the township provided water to the affected residents in water tanks that were transported by tank trucks to various locations in the neighborhood. Plaintiffs brought their own containers, filled them with water from the tanks, and transported the water to their homes.

This water supply system was soon discontinued and replaced by a home delivery system. Residents in need of water tied a white cloth on their mailbox and received a 40 gallon barrel containing a plastic liner filled with water. The filled barrels weighed in excess of 100 pounds and were dropped off, as needed, on the properties of the Legler area residents.

The trial court charged the jury that plaintiffs' claim for "quality of life" damages encompassed "inconveniences, aggravating, and unnecessary expenditure of time and effort related to the use of the water hauled to their homes, as well as to other disruption in their lives, including disharmony in the family unit." The aggregate jury verdict on this claim was $5,396,940. This represented an average award of slightly over $16,000 for each plaintiff; thus, a family unit consisting of four plaintiffs received an average award of approximately $64,000.

The Tort Claims Act's provision against recovery of damages for "pain and suffering resulting from any injury" is intended to apply to the intangible, subjective feelings of discomfort that are associated with personal injuries. It was not intended to bar claims for inconvenience associated with the invasion of a property interest. Although the disruption of plaintiffs' water supply is an "injury" under the Act, N.J.S.A. 59:1–3, the interest invaded here, the right to obtain potable running water from plaintiffs' own wells, is qualitatively different from "pain and suffering" related to a personal injury.

As the Appellate Division acknowledged, plaintiffs' claim for quality of life damages is derived from the law of nuisance. It has long been recognized that damages for inconvenience, annoyance, and discomfort are recoverable in a nuisance action [citing, Restatement (Second) of Torts § 929].

As such, damages for inconvenience, discomfort, and annoyance constitute "distinct grounds of compensation for which in ordinary cases the person in possession is entitled to recover in addition to the harm to his proprietary interests." Restatement (Second) of Torts § 929 comment e (1977).

Accordingly, we conclude that the quality of life damages represent compensation for losses associated with damage to property, and agree with the Appellate Division that they do not constitute pain and suffering under the Tort Claims Act. We therefore sustain the judgment for quality of life damages.

2. How does "discomfort and annoyance" differ from emotional distress? The court in *Ayers* emphasizes that these quality of life damages are based on objective life-style evidence, not subjective "feelings" evidence. Does the court in *Hawkins* explain or even recognize this distinction? Might the *Ayers* court's distinction be based on the need to avoid the bar of the tort claims act for "pain and suffering"? In fact, in *Ayers* the court reversed a separate award for emotional distress precisely because it did come within the "pain and suffering" exclusion of the Act.

3. *Fear As Discomfort*. A leading case on fear manifested as emotional distress, but sought to be recovered as discomfort and annoyance, is the Tenth Circuit Court of Appeals' decision in Boughton v. Cotter Corp., 65 F.3d 823, 834–35 (10th Cir.1995). Applying Colorado law, the court refused to permit 580 residents who had alleged exposure of their persons and property to hazardous emissions from a uranium mill to recover for their fears of contracting cancer as part of their nuisance and trespass claims. The court affirmed the district court's exclusion of evidence of unfounded fears as constituting annoyance and discomfort. Plaintiffs relied on a comment to § 821F of the Restatement (Second) of Torts to show that fears, even if illogical or unfounded, can establish a basis for damages in a nuisance case.

The Court of Appeals pointed out that the comment dealt with whether a nuisance had caused significant harm so as to be actionable, and did not relate to what constitutes compensable annoyance or discomfort. Expressing its concern that plaintiffs' theory could lead to fraudulent or speculative claims, it concluded: "In our judgment the potential for fraudulent or speculative claims could only be effectively limited in a nuisance or trespass case such as this by a rule requiring evidence substantiating that the fears of disease, resulting from the contamination of land, are reasonable and have a sound foundation in medical, scientific or statistical evidence."

D. DAMAGES TO PERSONS AND PRESENT LIABILITY FOR PROSPECTIVE HARM

1. INTRODUCTION: THE ISSUES IDENTIFIED

The diseases and illnesses that form the basis of damage claims in many environmental tort actions develop over long periods, derive from extended periods of exposure to toxic substances, and typically are ones for which the disease processes are not fully understood by medical science, and therefore, pose special problems of proof. Understandably, plaintiffs assert claims for future harms that have not yet, and possibly never will, manifest themselves; or when the disease process is in an early stage and its progression is highly speculative. These claims of prospective harms consist of four kinds:

(1) The plaintiff is suffering an *existing* physical injury that may worsen or develop into or be related to more serious consequences, such as asbestosis and its relation, if any, to lung cancer;

(2) The plaintiff is not suffering any existing injury or disease, but because of the exposure to the toxic substance is at an increased risk of developing a particular disease, often cancer, in the future;

(3) The plaintiff, because of his or her enhanced susceptibility to contracting such a disease, suffers present emotional distress, usually in the form of fear or anxiety about the prospective harm, sometimes accompanied by physical manifestations and sometimes not; and

(4) The plaintiff, again because of the enhanced risk of future serious disease or physical injury, incurs or should incur present and future medical expenses in the nature of surveillance and monitoring costs to ascertain the presence or development of the disease.

2. JUDICIAL TREATMENT OF MEDICAL MONITORING AND EMOTIONAL DISTRESS

METRO-NORTH COMMUTER RAILROAD COMPANY v. BUCKLEY

Supreme Court of the United States, 1997.
521 U.S. 424, 117 S.Ct. 2113, 138 L.Ed.2d 560.

JUSTICE BREYER delivered the opinion of the Court.

The basic question in this case is whether a railroad worker negligently exposed to a carcinogen (here, asbestos) but without symptoms of any disease can recover under the Federal Employers' Liability Act (FELA), * * * 45 U.S.C. § 51 et seq., for negligently inflicted emotional distress. We conclude that the worker before us here cannot recover unless, and until, he manifests symptoms of a disease. We also consider a related claim for medical monitoring costs, and we hold, for reasons set out below, that the respondent in this case has not shown that he is legally entitled to recover those costs.

I

[Respondent, Michael Buckley, a pipefitter for Metro–North, a railroad was exposed to asbestos one hour per day for three years (1985–1988). Upon attending an "asbestos awareness" class in 1987 he began having fear of developing cancer. Since 1989, he has received periodic medical checkups for asbestosis and cancer, but the tests have revealed no such evidence.]

Buckley sued Metro–North under the FELA, a statute that permits a railroad worker to recover for an "injury * * * resulting * * * from" his employer's "negligence." 45 U.S.C. § 51. He sought damages for his emotional distress and to cover the cost of future medical check-ups. His employer conceded negligence, but it did not concede that Buckley had actually suffered emotional distress, and it argued that the FELA did not permit a worker like Buckley, who had suffered no physical harm, to recover for injuries of either sort. After hearing Buckley's case, the District Court dismissed the action. The court found that Buckley did not "offer sufficient evidence to allow a jury to find that he suffered a real emotional injury."

Buckley appealed, and the Second Circuit reversed. 79 F.3d 1337 (1996). Buckley's evidence, it said, showed that his contact with the insulation dust (containing asbestos) was "massive, lengthy, and tangible," id., at 1345, and that the contact "would cause fear in a reasonable person." id., at 1344. Under these circumstances, the court held, the contact was what this Court in *Gottshall* had called a "physical impact"—a "physical impact" that, when present, permits a FELA plaintiff to recover for accompanying emotional distress. The Second Circuit also found in certain of Buckley's workplace statements sufficient expression of worry to permit sending his emotional distress claim to a jury. Finally, the court held that Buckley could recover for the costs of medical check-ups because the FELA permits recovery of all reasonably incurred extra medical monitoring costs whenever a "reasonable physician would prescribe * * * a monitoring regime different than the one that would have been prescribed in the absence of" a particular negligently caused exposure to a toxic substance. Id. at 1347 (internal quotation marks omitted).

We granted certiorari to review the Second Circuit's holdings in light of *Gottshall*.

II

The critical question before us in respect to Buckley's "emotional distress" claim is whether the physical contact with insulation dust that accompanied his emotional distress amounts to a "physical impact" as this Court used that term in *Gottshall*. In *Gottshall*, an emotional distress case, the Court interpreted the word "injury" in § 1, FELA a provision that makes "[e]very common carrier by railroad * * * liable in damages to any person suffering injury while * * * employed" by the carrier if the "injury" results from carrier "negligence." 45 U.S.C. § 51. * * * The Court stated that "common-law principles," where not rejected in the text of the statute, "are entitled to great weight" in interpreting the Act, and that those principles "play a significant role" in determining whether, or when, an employee can recover damages for "negligent infliction of emotional distress."

The Court also set forth several more specific legal propositions. It recognized that the common law of torts does not permit recovery for negligently inflicted emotional distress unless the distress falls within certain specific categories that amount to recovery-permitting exceptions. The law, for example, does permit recovery for emotional distress where that distress accompanies a physical injury; Restatement (Second) of Torts § 924(a) (1977), and it often permits recovery for distress suffered by a close relative who witnesses the physical injury of a negligence victim. The Court then held that FELA § 1, mirroring the law of many States, sometimes permitted recovery "for damages for negligent infliction of emotional distress," and, in particular, it does so where a plaintiff seeking such damages satisfies the common law's "zone of danger" test. It defined that test by stating that the law permits "recovery for emotional injury" by "those plaintiffs who sustain a physical impact as a result of a defendant's negligent conduct, or who are placed in immediate risk of physical harm by that conduct." *Gottshall* at 547–548, 114 S.Ct. at 2406.

The case before us, as we have said, focuses on the italicized words "*physical impact*." The Second Circuit interpreted those words as including a simple physical contact with a substance that might cause a disease at a future time, so long as the contact was of a kind that would "cause fear in a reasonable person." 79 F.3d, at 1344. In our view, however, the "physical impact" to which *Gottshall* referred does not include a simple physical contact with a substance that might cause a disease at a substantially later time—where that substance, or related circumstance, threatens no harm other than that disease-related risk.

First, *Gottshall* cited many state cases in support of its adoption of the "zone of danger" test quoted above. And in each case where recovery for emotional distress was permitted, the case involved a threatened physical contact that caused, or might have caused, immediate traumatic harm. [Extensive citations omitted.]

Second, *Gottshall's* language, read in light of this precedent, seems similarly limited. * * *

Taken together, language and cited precedent indicate that the words "physical impact" do not encompass every form of "physical contact." And, in particular, they do not include a contact that amounts to no more than an exposure—an exposure, such as that before us, to a substance that poses some future risk of disease and which contact causes emotional distress only because the worker learns that he may become ill after a substantial period of time.

Third, common-law precedent does not favor the plaintiff. Common law courts do permit a plaintiff who suffers from a disease to recover for related negligently caused emotional distress, and some courts permit a plaintiff who exhibits a physical symptom of exposure to recover, see, e.g., Herber v. Johns–Manville Corp., 785 F.2d 79, 85 (C.A.3 1986); Mauro v. Owens–Corning Fiberglas Corp., 225 N.J.Super. 196, 542 A.2d 16 (App.Div.1988). But with only a few exceptions, common law courts have denied recovery to those who, like Buckley, are disease and symptom free. [Extensive citations omitted.] See, Potter v. Firestone Tire & Rubber Co., 6 Cal.4th 965, 863 P.2d 795 (1993) (no recovery for fear of cancer unless plaintiff is "more likely than not" to develop cancer).

Fourth, the general policy reasons to which *Gottshall* referred—in its explanation of why common law courts have restricted recovery for emotional harm to cases falling within rather narrowly defined categories—militate against an expansive definition of "physical impact" here. Those reasons include: (a) special "difficult[y] for judges and juries" in separating valid, important claims from those that are invalid or "trivial," * * * (b) a threat of "unlimited and unpredictable liability," and (c) the "potential for a flood" of comparatively unimportant, or "trivial," claims. * * *

To separate meritorious and important claims from invalid or trivial claims does not seem easier here than in other cases in which a plaintiff might seek recovery for typical negligently caused emotional distress. The facts before us illustrate the problem. The District Court, when concluding that Buckley had failed to present "sufficient evidence to allow a jury to find * * * a real emotional injury," pointed out that, apart from Buckley's own testimony, there was virtually no evidence of distress. Indeed, Buckley continued to work with insulating material "even though * * * he could have transferred" elsewhere, he "continued to smoke cigarettes" despite doctors' warnings, and his doctor did not refer him "either to a psychologist or to a social worker." The Court of

Appeals reversed because it found certain objective corroborating evidence, namely "workers' complaints to supervisors and investigative bodies." 79 F.3d, at 1346. Both kinds of "objective" evidence—the confirming and disconfirming evidence—seem only indirectly related to the question at issue, the existence and seriousness of Buckley's claimed emotional distress. Yet, given the difficulty of separating valid from invalid emotional injury claims, the evidence before us may typify the kind of evidence to which parties and the courts would have to look.[65]

* * *

More important, the physical contact at issue here—a simple (though extensive) contact with a carcinogenic substance—does not seem to offer much help in separating valid from invalid emotional distress claims. That is because contacts, even extensive contacts, with serious carcinogens are common. They may occur without causing serious emotional distress, but sometimes they do cause distress, and reasonably so, for cancer is both an unusually threatening and unusually frightening disease. * * * The relevant problem, however, remains one of evaluating a claimed emotional reaction to an increased risk of dying. An external circumstance—exposure—makes some emotional distress more likely. But how can one determine from the external circumstance of exposure whether, or when, a claimed strong emotional reaction to an increased mortality risk (say from 23% to 28%) is reasonable and genuine, rather than overstated—particularly when the relevant statistics themselves are controversial and uncertain (as is usually the case), and particularly since neither those exposed nor judges or juries are experts in statistics? The evaluation problem seems a serious one.

* * *

We cannot find in *Gottshall's* language, cited precedent, other common law-precedent, or related concerns of policy, a legal basis for adopting the emotional-distress recovery rule adopted by the Court of Appeals.

* * *

This argument, however, while important, overlooks the fact that the common law in this area does not examine the genuineness of emotional harm case by case. Rather, it has developed recovery-permitting categories the contours of which more distantly reflect this, and other, abstract general policy concerns. The point of such categorization is to deny courts the authority to undertake a case by case examination. The common law permits emotional-distress recovery for that category of

65. The Court in *Gottshall* made a similar point:

"[T]esting for the 'genuineness' of an injury alone * * * would be bound to lead to haphazard results. Judges would be forced to make highly subjective determinations concerning the authenticity of claims for emotional injury, which are far less susceptible to objective medical proof than are their physical counterparts. To the extent the genuineness test could limit potential liability, it could do so only inconsistently." *Gottshall*, supra, at 552, 114 S.Ct. at 2409.

plaintiffs who suffer from a disease (or exhibit a physical symptom), for example, thereby finding a special effort to evaluate emotional symptoms warranted in that category of cases—perhaps from a desire to make a physically injured victim whole or because the parties are likely to be in court in any event. In other cases, however, falling outside the special recovery-permitting categories, it has reached a different conclusion. The relevant question here concerns the validity of a rule that seeks to redefine such a category. It would not be easy to redefine "physical impact" in terms of a rule that turned on, say, the "massive, lengthy, [or] tangible" nature of a contact that amounted to an exposure, whether to contaminated water, or to germ-laden air, or to carcinogen-containing substances, such as insulation dust containing asbestos. But, in any event, for the reasons we have stated, supra, we cannot find that the common law has done so.

Finally, Buckley argues that the "humanitarian" nature of the FELA warrants a holding in his favor. * * * But just as courts must interpret that law to take proper account of the harms suffered by a sympathetic individual plaintiff, so they must consider the general impact, on workers as well as employers, of the general liability rules they would thereby create. Here the relevant question concerns not simply recovery in an individual case, but the consequences and effects of a rule of law that would permit that recovery. And if the common law concludes that a legal rule permitting recovery here, from a tort law perspective, and despite benefits in some individual cases, would on balance cause more harm than good, and if we find that judgment reasonable, we cannot find that conclusion inconsistent with the FELA's humanitarian purpose.

* * *

III

Buckley also sought recovery for a different kind of "injury," namely the economic cost of the extra medical check-ups that he expects to incur as a result of his exposure to asbestos-laden insulation dust. * * * We agreed to decide whether the court correctly found that the FELA permitted a plaintiff without symptoms or disease to recover this economic loss.

The parties do not dispute—and we assume—that an exposed plaintiff can recover related reasonable medical monitoring costs if and when he develops symptoms. As the Second Circuit pointed out, a plaintiff injured through negligence can recover related reasonable medical expenses as an element of damages. * * * No one has argued that any different principle would apply in the case of a plaintiff whose "injury" consists of a disease, a symptom, or those sorts of emotional distress that fall within the FELA's definition of "injury." Much of the Second Circuit's opinion suggests it intended only to apply this basic principle of the law of damages. * * *

Other portions of the Second Circuit's opinion, however, indicate that it may have rested this portion of its decision upon a broader ground, namely that medical monitoring costs themselves represent a separate negligently caused economic "injury," 45 U.S.C. § 51, for which a negligently exposed FELA plaintiff (including a plaintiff without disease or symptoms) may recover to the extent that the medical monitoring costs that a reasonable physician would prescribe for the plaintiff exceed the medical monitoring costs that "would have been prescribed in the absence of [the] exposure." 79 F.3d, at 1347 (citation omitted). This portion of the opinion, when viewed in light of Buckley's straightforward claim for an "amount of money" sufficient to "compensate" him for "future medical monitoring expenses," suggests the existence of an ordinary, but separate, tort law cause of action permitting (as tort law ordinarily permits) the recovery of medical cost damages in the form of a lump sum, and irrespective of insurance, Restatement (Second) of Torts § 920A(2) (1977). As so characterized, the Second Circuit's holding, in our view, went beyond the bounds of currently "evolving common law."

Guided by the parties' briefs, we have canvassed the state-law cases that have considered whether the negligent causation of this kind of harm (i.e., causing a plaintiff, through negligent exposure to a toxic substance, to incur medical monitoring costs) by itself constitutes a sufficient basis for a tort recovery. We have found no other FELA decisions. We have put to the side several cases that involve special recovery-permitting circumstances, such as the presence of a traumatic physical impact, or the presence of a physical symptom, which for reasons explained in Part II are important but beside the point here. * * *

We find it sufficient to note, for present purposes, that the cases authorizing recovery for medical monitoring in the absence of physical injury do not endorse a full-blown, traditional tort law cause of action for lump-sum damages—of the sort that the Court of Appeals seems to have endorsed here. Rather, those courts, while recognizing that medical monitoring costs can amount to a harm that justifies a tort remedy, have suggested, or imposed, special limitations on that remedy. Compare *Ayers*, supra, at 608, 525 A.2d, at 314 (recommending in future cases creation of "a court-supervised fund to administer medical-surveillance payments"); *Hansen*, supra, at 982 (suggesting insurance mechanism or court-supervised fund as proper remedy); *Potter*, supra, 1010, n. 28, 25 Cal.Rptr.2d, at 580, n. 28, 863 P.2d, at 825, n. 28 (suggesting that a lump-sum damages award would be inappropriate); *Burns*, supra, 381, 752 P.2d, at 34 (holding that lump-sum damages are not appropriate) with, e.g., Honeycutt v. Walden, 294 Ark. 440, 743 S.W.2d 809 (1988) (damages award for future medical expenses made necessary by physical injury are awarded as lump-sum payment). We believe that the note of caution, the limitations, and the expressed uneasiness with a traditional lump-sum damages remedy are important, for they suggest a judicial recognition of some of the policy concerns that have been pointed out to us here—concerns of a sort that *Gottshall* identified.

Since, for example, the particular, say cancer-related, costs at issue are the extra monitoring costs, over and above those otherwise recommended, their identification will sometimes pose special "difficult[ies] for judges and juries." *Gottshall*, 512 U.S. at 557, 114 S.Ct. at 2411. Those difficulties in part can reflect uncertainty among medical professionals about just which tests are most usefully administered and when. * * * And in part those difficulties can reflect the fact that scientists will not always see a medical need to provide systematic scientific answers to the relevant legal question, namely whether an exposure calls for extra monitoring. * * * Buckley's sole expert, then, was equivocal about the need for extra monitoring, and the defense had not yet put on its case.

Moreover, tens of millions of individuals may have suffered exposure to substances that might justify some form of substance-exposure-related medical monitoring * * * and that fact, along with uncertainty as to the amount of liability, could threaten both a "flood" of less important cases (potentially absorbing resources better left available to those more seriously harmed, and the systemic harms that can accompany "unlimited and unpredictable liability") (say, for example, vast testing liability adversely affecting the allocation of scarce medical resources). * * *

Finally, a traditional, full-blown ordinary tort liability rule would ignore the presence of existing alternative sources of payment, thereby leaving a court uncertain about how much of the potentially large recoveries would pay for otherwise unavailable medical testing and how much would accrue to plaintiffs for whom employers or other sources (say, insurance now or in the future) might provide monitoring in any event. Cf. 29 CFR § 1910.1001(*l*) (1996) (requiring employers to provide medical monitoring for workers exposed to asbestos). The Occupational Safety and Health Administration regulations (which the dissent cites) help to demonstrate why the Second Circuit erred: where state and federal regulations already provide the relief that a plaintiff seeks, creating a full-blown tort remedy could entail systemic costs without corresponding benefits. Nor could an employer necessarily protect itself by offering monitoring, for that is not part of the rule of law that the dissent would endorse—a rule that, if traditional, would, as we have noted, allow recovery irrespective of the presence of a "collateral source" of payment.

We do not deny important competing considerations—of a kind that may have led some courts to provide a form of liability. Buckley argues, for example, that it is inequitable to place the economic burden of such care on the negligently exposed plaintiff rather than on the negligent defendant.... He points out that providing preventive care to individuals who would otherwise go without can help to mitigate potentially serious future health effects of diseases by detecting them in early stages; again, whether or not this is such a situation, we may assume that such situations occur. And he adds that, despite scientific uncertainties, the difficulty of separating justified from unjustified claims may be less serious than where emotional distress is the harm at issue. * * *

We do not deny that the dissent paints a sympathetic picture of Buckley and his co-workers; this picture has force because Buckley is sympathetic and he has suffered wrong at the hands of a negligent employer. But we are more troubled than is the dissent by the potential systemic effects of creating a new, full-blown, tort law cause of action—for example, the effects upon interests of other potential plaintiffs who are not before the court and who depend on a tort system that can distinguish between reliable and serious claims on the one hand, and unreliable and relatively trivial claims on the other. * * *

We have not tried to balance these, or other, competing considerations here. We point them out to help explain why we consider the limitations and cautions to be important—and integral—parts of the state-court decisions that permit asymptomatic plaintiffs a separate tort claim for medical monitoring costs. That being so, we do not find sufficient support in the common law for the unqualified rule of lump-sum damages recovery that is, at least arguably, before us here. And given the mix of competing general policy considerations, plaintiff's policy-based arguments do not convince us that the FELA contains a tort liability rule of that unqualified kind.

IV

For the reasons stated, we reverse the determination of the Second Circuit, and we remand the case for further proceedings consistent with this opinion.

It is so ordered.

3. NOTE ON POST–EXPOSURE, PRE–SYMPTOM MEDICAL SURVEILLANCE DAMAGES

a. *Supporting Authority*

Justice Ginsburg with whom Justice Stevens joins concurred in the judgment in part and dissented in part. They concurred with respect to Buckley's distress claim because of a lack of objective evidence of severe emotional distress. Justice Ginsberg wrote in part:

Buckley's extensive contact with asbestos particles * * * constituted "physical impact" as that was used in *Gotshall.*

Concerning medical monitoring, the Court of Appeals ruled that Buckley stated a triable claim for monitoring expenses made "necessary because of his exposure to asbestos," expenses essential "to ensure early detection and cure of any asbestos-related disease he develops." 79 F.3d at 1347. I would not disturb that ruling. * * *

"[A medical monitoring] action has been increasingly recognized by state courts as necessary given the latent nature of many diseases caused by exposure to hazardous materials and the traditional common law tort doctrine requirement that an injury be manifest."

If I comprehend the Court's enigmatic decision correctly, Buckley may replead a claim for relief and recover for medical monitoring, but he must receive that relief in a form other than a lump sum. Unaccountably, the Court resists the straightforward statement that would enlighten courts in this and similar cases: A claim for medical monitoring is cognizable under FELA; it is a claim entirely in step with "evolving common law." I therefore dissent from the Court's judgment to the extent it relates to medical monitoring.

Id. at 444–456, 114 S.Ct. at 2124–2130.

Justice Ginsburg may have the better of the argument that the clear trend is toward recognizing a remedy of medical monitoring in toxic exposure litigation. Decisions discussed throughout this chapter recognizing the remedy and establishing specific elements to make out a claim include: Bower v. Westinghouse Electric Corp., 206 W.Va. 133, 522 S.E.2d 424 (W.Va.1999); Friends for All Children, Inc. v. Lockheed Aircraft Corp., 746 F.2d 816, 824–825 (D.C.Cir.1984); Ayers v. Jackson, 106 N.J. 557, 525 A.2d 287 (1987); Hansen v. Mountain Fuel Supply Co., 858 P.2d 970 (Utah 1993); Potter v. Firestone Tire & Rubber Co., 6 Cal.4th 965, 25 Cal.Rptr.2d 550, 863 P.2d 795 (1993); Burns v. Jaquays Mining Corp., 156 Ariz. 375, 752 P.2d 28 (Ct. App. 1987); Redland Soccer Club v. Department of Army, 548 Pa. 178, 696 A.2d 137 (Pa. 1997); Bourgeois v. A.P. Green Industries, Inc., 716 So.2d 355 (La.1998).

As in quality of life damages examined earlier, a seminal opinion is that of the New Jersey Supreme Court in Ayers v. Township of Jackson, 106 N.J. 557, 525 A.2d 287 (N.J. 1987). In *Ayers* the court concluded that: "the cost of medical surveillance is a compensable item of damages where the proofs demonstrate, through reliable expert testimony predicated upon: (1) the significance and extent of exposure to chemicals; (2) the toxicity of the chemicals; (3) the seriousness of the diseases for which individuals are at risk; (4) the relative increase in the chance of onset of disease in those exposed; and (5) the value of early diagnosis that such surveillance to monitor the effect of exposure to toxic chemicals is reasonable and necessary. Plaintiff must reasonably show that medical monitoring/surveillance is required because the exposure caused a distinctive increased risk of future injury and would require a course of medical monitoring independent of any other that the plaintiff would otherwise have to undergo."

The court in *Ayers* offered these supporting rationales:

Compensation for reasonable and necessary medical expenses is consistent with well-accepted legal principles. See C. McCormick, Handbook on the Law of Damages § 90 at 323–27 (1935). It is also consistent with the important public health interest in fostering access to medical testing for individuals whose exposure to toxic chemicals creates an enhanced risk of disease. The value of early diagnosis and treatment for cancer patients is well-documented. * * * An application of tort law that allows post-injury, pre-symptom recovery in toxic tort litigation for reasonable medical surveillance costs is manifestly consistent with the public interest in early detection and treatment of the disease.

Recognition of pre-symptom claims for medical surveillance serve other important public interests. The difficulty of proving causation, where the disease is manifested years after exposure, has caused many commentators to suggest that tort law has no capacity to deter polluters, because the costs of proper disposal are often viewed by polluters as exceeding the risk of tort liability. However, permitting recovery for reasonable pre-symptom, medical-surveillance expenses subjects polluters to significant liability when proof of the causal connection between the tortuous conduct and the plaintiffs' exposure to chemicals is likely to be most readily available. The availability of a substantial remedy before the consequences of the plaintiffs' exposure are manifest may also have the beneficial effect of preventing or mitigating serious future illnesses and thus reduce the overall costs to the responsible parties.

Other considerations compel recognition of a pre-symptom medical surveillance claim. It is inequitable for an individual, wrongfully exposed to dangerous toxic chemicals but unable to prove that disease is likely, to have to pay his own expenses when medical intervention is clearly reasonable and necessary.

* * *

What reasoning do you find more persuasive? What did Justice Breyer in *Buckley* say with respect to these matters?

Despite strong supporting authority for the suitability of the medical monitoring remedy for common law tort claims, *Buckley,* as the Supreme Court's holding reached under partial principles of FELA, stands as a potentially strong contrary voice. By way of example, after the Louisiana Supreme Court created the medical monitoring remedy in Bourgeois v. A.P. Green Indus., Inc., 716 So.2d 355 (La.1998), the Louisiana legislature prohibited damages for costs for future medical treatment, surveillance, or procedures of any kind unless those services are directly related to a manifest present physical or mental injury or disease. House Bill 1784 (June 21, 1999).

b. *Evolution of the Elements of the Remedy*

1. The *Paoli* Opinion. Next to *Ayers*, the leading opinion, which was quoted by Justice Ginsburg, is that of the Third Circuit's in In re Paoli Railroad Yard PCB Litigation, 916 F.2d 829 (3d Cir.1990) cert. denied, 499 U.S. 961, 111 S.Ct. 1584, 113 L.Ed.2d 649 (1991) (Paoli I). The Third Circuit concluded that the plaintiff would have to prove to a "reasonable degree of medical certainty" that (1) Plaintiff was significantly exposed to a proven hazardous substance through the negligent actions of defendant; (2) As a proximate result of exposure, plaintiff suffers an increased risk of contracting a serious latent disease; (3) That

increased risk makes periodic diagnostic medical examinations reasonably necessary; and (4) Monitoring and testing procedures exist which make the early detection and treatment of the disease possible and beneficial.

Four years after the decision in *Paoli I* the Third Circuit refined this test in *Paoli* II, 35 F.3d 717 (3d Cir.1994), cert. denied, 513 U.S. 1190, 115 S.Ct. 1253, 131 L.Ed.2d 134 (1995). The court held that in addition to the elements of the *Paoli I* test, a plaintiff had to show that "a reasonable physician would prescribe for her or him a monitoring regime different than the one that would have been prescribed in the absence of that particular exposure." The court explained that "special medical monitoring" was a necessary element of the claim "because under this cause of action, a plaintiff may recover only if the defendant's wrongful acts increased the plaintiff's incremental risk of incurring the harm produced by the toxic substance enough to warrant a change in the medical monitoring that otherwise would be prescribed for the plaintiff." 35 F.3d at 788.

In yet another Third Circuit decision, Redland Soccer Club, Inc. v. Department of the Army, 55 F.3d 827 (3d Cir.1995), cert. denied, 516 U.S. 1071, 116 S.Ct. 772, 133 L.Ed.2d 725 (1996), the court explained why this additional element of "special" monitoring is essential:

> *Paoli II's* requirement of "special" medical monitoring implicitly recognizes the longstanding requirement in all tort cases other than those based on the old "intentional" common law torts for various forms of trespass that a plaintiff must prove an injury before he may recover anything from a defendant. Otherwise, a polluter would become a health care insurer for medical procedures routinely needed to guard persons against some of the ordinary vicissitudes of life. It would convert toxic torts into a form of specialized health insurance. Imposition of liability on this basis seems to go beyond current tort theories of negligence or strict liability by requiring a polluter to pay for medical procedures that the general population should receive. Thus, *Paoli II* requires plaintiffs to show not only that their exposure to toxic substances is greater than normal background levels, but that the increased risk of injury from such exposure warrants medical monitoring against future illness beyond that which is recommended for everyone.

55 F.3d at 846 n.8.

c. *Other Courts' Variations*

In 1993 the Utah Supreme Court in an asbestos exposure case, like *Buckley,* developed a somewhat more demanding set of requirements. In Hansen v. Mountain Fuel Supply Co., 858 P.2d 970 (Utah 1993) the court required that a plaintiff prove these eight elements:

(1) exposure; (2) to a toxic substance; (3) which exposure was caused by the defendant's negligence; (4) resulting in an increased

risk; (5) of a serious disease, illness, or injury; (6) for which a medical test for early detection exists; (7) and for which early detection is beneficial, meaning that a treatment exists which can alter the course of illness; (8) and which test has been prescribed by a qualified physician according to contemporary scientific principles.

The plaintiff must also establish that "the test is shown by expert testimony to be one a reasonable physician in the area of specialty would order of a patient similarly situated, *i.e.,* facing a similar risk of the same serious illness from the same cause."

In 1997 the Pennsylvania Supreme Court joined the list of state supreme courts adopting a medical monitoring remedy. In Redland Soccer Club v. Department of the Army, 548 Pa. 178, 696 A.2d 137 (Pa. 1997), an environmental exposure case, the court stated that the Third Circuit opinions in *Paoli I, Paoli II,* and *Redland* provided a "persuasive approach to defining the elements of the cause of action for medical monitoring." Nevertheless, it formulated its own standards which it actually drew more closely from the *Hansen* decision of the Utah Supreme Court:

> Accordingly, we hold that a plaintiff must prove the following elements to prevail on a common law claim for medical monitoring: (1) exposure greater than normal background levels; (2) to a proven hazardous substance; (3) caused by the defendant's negligence; (4) as a proximate result of the exposure, plaintiff has a significantly increased risk of contracting a serious latent disease; (5) a monitoring procedure exists that makes the early detection of the disease possible; (6) the prescribed monitoring regime is different from that normally recommended in the absence of the exposure; and (7) the prescribed monitoring regime is reasonably necessary according to contemporary scientific principles.

In 1993 the California Supreme Court adopted the *Ayers* factors virtually verbatim. See Potter v. Firestone Tire & Rubber Co., 6 Cal.4th 965, 25 Cal.Rptr.2d 550, 863 P.2d 795 (1993).

In 1998, the Louisiana Supreme Court in Bourgeois v. A.P. Green Indus., Inc., 716 So.2d 355, 359–61 (1998) set forth the elements of the remedy as follows: 1) significant exposure to a proven hazardous substance; 2) as a proximate result of this exposure, plaintiff suffers a significantly increased risk of contracting a serious latent disease; 3) plaintiff's risk of contracting a serious latent disease is greater than a) the risk of contracting the same disease had he or she not been exposed and b) the chances of members of the public at large of developing the disease; 4) a monitoring procedure exists that makes the early detection of the disease possible; 5) the monitoring procedure has been prescribed by a qualified physician and is reasonably necessary according to contemporary scientific principle; 6) the prescribed monitoring regime is different from that normally recommended in the absence of exposure; and 7) there is some demonstrated clinical value in the early detection and diagnosis of the disease.

Here the Chief Justice concurred with the majority opinion, but disagreed with requiring all seven elements. In his view "if a plaintiff has satisfied the first six stated elements, he is entitled to recover medical monitoring expenses, notwithstanding the fact that the early detection of the disease would not cure or ameliorate the consequence of the illness." He disagreed with the majority's conclusion that "[u]nless such treatment is available, then there is nothing for plaintiff to gain for a hastened diagnosis. * * * If [p]laintiff is able to take advantage of medical monitoring and the monitoring detects no evidence of the disease, then, at least for the time being, the plaintiff can receive the comfort of peace of mind." Id. at 363. As noted earlier, this approach was later modified by the Louisiana legislature.

Finally in Bower v. Westinghouse Electric Corp., 206 W.Va.133, 522 S.E.2d 424 (W.Va.1999) the court adopted the *Paoli* test but refused to require a plaintiff to prove that treatment currently exists for the disease at issue. Armed with these lists of elements, determine for yourself, assuming you would recognize the remedy at all, what you would require for a plaintiff to recover.

How would you handle a case where the plaintiff was a long-time smoker and had tuberculosis exposure before exposure to defendant's substances? In other words, how are pre-existing conditions and exposures to be treated? See, Gutierrez v. Cassiar Mining Corporation, 64 Cal.App.4th 148, 75 Cal.Rptr.2d 132 (1998) (Court held that defendant's liability for medical monitoring costs was limited to monitoring which was in addition to or different from that already required because of plaintiff's preexisting lung conditions; and improper exclusion of instruction so limiting defendant's liability for medical monitoring was prejudicial error.)

d. The Form of the Remedy: Lump Sum Award or Court Supervised Fund

1. Returning to *Buckley*. Why might the distinction between lump-sum payments and trust funds have been so important to Justice Breyer's analysis? Are Justice Breyer's policy considerations legitimate? Every day judges and juries sift through evidence about future damage claims and make reasonable, if not precisely accurate, decisions about what those expenses are likely to be. See *Buckley*, 117 S.Ct. at 2128 (Justice Ginsberg dissenting in part). No empirical evidence or rationale is offered to support the suggestion that lump-sum claims would result in a "flood" of litigation. Justice Ginsberg describes this fear as "overblown." Id. Justice Breyer's concern about over-compensating medical monitoring plaintiffs could apply to many personal injury plaintiffs whose damage claims are founded on expenses covered by insurance or some other third party.

2. One explanation for the concern about lump-sum damage awards is strictly economic in nature: cash payments today for bills to be

incurred in the future will attract more plaintiffs and plaintiffs' attorneys than will the creation of court-supervised funds that simply pay expenses as they arise. The form of relief requested has a dramatic impact on the financial incentive to pursue such claims. This explanation is not explicitly offered in *Buckley*, but it appears, however, to lurk just beneath the surface of Justice Breyer's words.

3. There is no question that most courts that have considered the issue expressly opt for the court-supervised fund rather than the traditional lump-sum award that so concerned Justice Breyer. See, e.g. Potter v. Firestone, 6 Cal.4th 965, 25 Cal.Rptr.2d 550, 863 P.2d 795 (Cal. 1993); Hansen v. Mountain Fuel Supply Co., 858 P.2d 970 (Utah 1993); Redland Soccer Club v. Department of Army, 548 Pa. 178, 696 A.2d 137 (Pa. 1997); All holding that a court supervised fund to pay medical monitoring claims as they accrue, rather than the lump-sum verdict may be more appropriate in environmental toxic tort cases. But see, Bower v. Westinghouse Electric Corp., 206 W.Va.133, 522 S.E.2d 424 (W.Va.1999) (court declined to stipulate that medical monitoring costs can only be administered through a court supervised fund). What explains this strong judicial preference for the court supervised equitable fund approach over the traditional compensatory damages approach? How do plaintiffs benefit? How do defendants benefit? What about plaintiffs' lawyers who receive a contingent fee award?

4. Could a state court applying federal maritime law recognize a medical monitoring remedy after *Buckley*? If so, what shape would the remedy take? In Dragon v. Cooper/T. Smith Stevedoring Co., 726 So.2d 1006 (La.Ct.App.1999) the court concluded that *Buckley* did not rule out medical monitoring in all federal law cases so long as it was not a lump-sum remedy. The court found that "[t]he holding of the Supreme Court in *Buckley* speaks directly to a cause of action for a lump-sum award for medical monitoring * * *. [I]t was unable to conclude that the holding precludes a claim under FELA for all types of medical monitoring claims * * *. [T]he Supreme Court was careful to point out that its holding did not include the extent to which the federal legislation may accommodate medical cost recovery rules more finely tailored that the one considered therein".

The court concluded "[t]here is no applicable contrary federal legislation that would prevent the application of the tort claim recognized under Louisiana law. The Louisiana law may be applied as a supplement to the general maritime law, except to any claim for lump-sum damages." Do you agree with the court's interpretation of *Buckley*?

5. For a thorough discussion of the legal versus equitable remedy distinction in the context of whether to certify a class action seeking medical monitoring, see Barnes v. American Tobacco Co., 161 F.3d 127, 131 (3d Cir.1998). "The dispositive factor that must be assessed to determine whether a medical monitoring claim may be certified is what type of relief plaintiff seeks. If plaintiff seeks relief that is a disguised request for compensatory damages, then the medical monitoring claim

can only be characterized as a claim for monetary damages. If plaintiffs seek the establishment of a court-supervised medical monitoring program through which the class members will receive periodic medical examinations, then plaintiffs' medical monitoring claims can be properly characterized as a claim seeking injunctive relief."

e. *Medical Monitoring Under CERCLA*

Plaintiffs in a substantial number of cases have sought to recover medical monitoring costs under the Comprehensive Environmental Response Compensation and Liability Act, 42 U.S.C. § 9601 et seq., which allows private parties to recover "the necessary costs of response," which are the costs associated with remediation and removal of contamination at various sites around the nation. See Chapter 10 which addresses the CERCLA liability scheme and private actions. Courts have rejected plaintiffs' contentions in this regard. Price v. United States Navy, 39 F.3d 1011 (9th Cir.1994) (homeowner seeks recovery of response cost from the Dept. of Navy); Daigle v. Shell Oil Co., 972 F.2d 1527 (10th Cir.1992) (residents brought suit alleging damage by airborne pollutants during cleanup of site). Accord, Durfey v. DuPont De Nemours & Co., 59 F.3d 121 (9th Cir.1995) (class action against operating contractors of plutonium production facility); Hanford Downwinders Coalition v. Dowdle, 71 F.3d 1469 (9th Cir.1995) (citizen group brought action to begin medical monitoring of those exposed to radiation from nuclear reservation.)

An exhaustive consideration of the issue is found in Werlein v. United States, 746 F.Supp. 887, 903–04 (D.Minn.1990), which held that medical surveillance costs are not recoverable under CERCLA because the Act expressly created mechanisms for the Agency of Toxic Substances and Disease Registry to conduct health effects studies to determine the health impact of exposure to toxic chemicals in a community, including providing medical care and testing to exposed individuals but, in the sections dealing with response costs available to private litigants, deleted medical monitoring provisions.

f. *Generalized Scientific Studies to Determine Increased Risk*

A series of lawsuits instituted by residents of Colorado living near the Rocky Flats Nuclear Weapons Plant owned by Rockwell International and Dow Chemical sought generalized medical surveillance relief. See Cook v. Rockwell International Corp., 755 F.Supp. 1468, 1477–78 (D.Colo.1991). The plaintiffs sought to have defendants pay the cost to perform population-based epidemiological studies to determine *if* they were at increased risk for contracting disease. The court rejected that request:

> Even assuming that the Colorado Supreme Court would recognize a tort claim for individualized medical monitoring, I do not

believe that the Colorado Supreme Court would recognize as cognizable plaintiffs' claim for generalized scientific studies.

A medical monitoring claim compensates a plaintiff for diagnostic treatment, a tangible and quantifiable item of damage caused by a defendant's tortious conduct. Such relief is akin to future medical expenses. The claim does not compensate a plaintiff for testing others to determine the odds that a particular person might contract a disease. * * *

Plaintiffs have cited no authority for their common law claims to recover the costs of generalized scientific studies. I discern no basis for such a claim. Thus, I hold that the scientific studies requested by plaintiffs here are not recoverable under a medical monitoring cause of action. * * *

On the other hand, the court did retain plaintiffs' request for a fund that would be used to pool the data derived from the medical tests of the exposed plaintiffs:

Assuming, as I must at this juncture, that pooling the results of these diagnostic medical examinations is reasonably necessary to detect the onset of disease, I conclude that this relief is cognizable in a medical monitoring cause of action. Pooling the examination results is a reasonable complement to normal diagnostic testing that furthers the objective behind the tort–to assure the early diagnosis of a latent disease.

See Barth v. Firestone Tire & Rubber Co., 661 F.Supp. 193 (N.D.Cal.1987) (authorizing injunctive relief to establish a medical monitoring fund to pay for medical monitoring and to establish an information-sharing mechanism; to gather and forward to treating physicians information relating to the diagnosis and treatment of diseases which may result from plaintiffs' exposure to toxins); Werlein v. United States, 746 F.Supp. 887, 895 (D.Minn.1990) ("In a case where a number of persons are exposed to a toxin about which little is known, and it is necessary to gather and share information regarding diagnosis and treatment through screening, the court would consider framing a medical monitoring and information-sharing program as injunctive relief.")

g. *Literature*

Much has been written about medical monitoring as a remedy. While early articles were largely laudatory, later articles raise issues such as those that troubled Justice Breyer in *Buckley*. See, e.g. George W.C. McCarter, Medical Sue–Veillance: A History and Critique of the Medical Monitoring Remedy in Toxic Tort Litigation, 45 Rutgers L. Rev. 227, 234–35 (1993); Medical Monitoring in Toxic Tort Cases: Another Windfall for Texas Plaintiffs?, 33 Hous. L. Rev. 473, 483 (1996).

For a thorough consideration of the period payment alternative, see Amy B. Blumenberg, Medical Monitoring Funds: The Periodic Payment of Future Medical Surveillance Expenses in Toxic Exposure Litigation, 43 Hastings L.J. 661 (1992); see also Roger C. Henderson, Designing a Responsible Periodic–Payment System for Tort Awards: Arizona Enacts a Prototype, 32 Ariz. L. Rev. 21, 25 (1990). See also Kara McCall, Medical Monitoring Plaintiffs and Subsequent Claims for Disease, 66 U. Chicago L. Rev. 969 (1999) (arguing that after a plaintiff gets a medical monitoring reward, that fact should not preclude a claim for personal injury if it later develops, under claim preclusion doctrine); Matthew Hamrick, Theories of Injury and Recovery for Post–Exposure Pre–Symptom Plaintiffs: Supreme Court Takes a Critical Look, 29 Cumb. L. Rev. 401 (1999). Professor Andrew Klein, Rethinking Medical Monitoring, 64 Brook L. Rev. 1, 3 (1998), suggests the following rule:

> The Supreme Court's *Buckley* decision places the "tort" of medical monitoring at a crossroad, marking an important juncture at which to examine the competing interests to which the Court refers. This Article begins this examination by briefly sketching the doctrinal development of medical monitoring. In so doing, the Article challenges the assumption that it is appropriate to construe the leading cases as creating a unique cause of action. Instead, the Article argues that medical monitoring simply describes a potential remedy in established tort actions. From that baseline, the Article asserts that courts ordinarily should award medical monitoring damages to a PE/PS plaintiff only when toxic exposure has more than doubled that plaintiff's risk of disease–that is, when the plaintiff can prove that if she later contracts the disease, the defendant's conduct was more likely than not the cause. In most other cases, the Article concludes, the tort system is simply the wrong place for plaintiffs to seek recovery.

What do you think of Professor Klein's method to limit the availability of the remedy? Consider the following problem.

Problem

Assume that a community of 10,000 people had been subjected to a contaminated water supply similar to the plaintiffs in *Ayers*. Also assume that the plaintiffs' medical experts testified that the exposure had increased their risk of a particular disease threefold. For example, if the pre-exposure risk of contracting the disease was 10 in 10,000, the post-exposure risk (based on epidemiological studies) was that 30 of the 10,000 would develop the disease. On the basis of this record could any specific plaintiff in a population of 10,000 recover on an enhanced risk claim? Would it fulfill *Ayers'* demand for a "quantified" enhanced risk? What is troubling about doing so? Could the 10,000, as part of a class action, recover medical monitoring expenses? Does it fulfill the criteria in *Ayers*, assuming the disease is serious and one for which early diagnosis is beneficial? Would it be relevant that monitoring would require expensive scanning and laboratory tests?

h. Proving Medical Monitoring Damages

Assume you represent a plaintiff in a case that seems to qualify for medical monitoring. What evidence do you gather? What experts do you retain? Consider the following:

To prove that monitoring damages are reasonable and necessary, the attorney should ask: (1) does the plaintiff need monitoring? (2) If so, what is the monitoring protocol? and (3) What is the estimated cost?

The attorney will need the following information:

- vital statistics on each plaintiff,
- health history,
- medical records,
- physical examination,
- tests (blood, urine, X-rays), and
- exposure data.

Experts are also necessary. A toxicologist studies the exposure information, including the substance to which the plaintiff was exposed, the concentrations involved, the duration of the exposure and the toxicity (carcinogenic and non-carcinogenic) of each substance. Based on this information, the toxicologist then determines whether the plaintiff is at risk for developing a disease from the exposure.

The toxicologist reviews current scientific data to determine the nature and extent of the human health hazards associated with exposure to each toxin. Combinations of toxin exposures may produce additive or synergistic toxicity, and combination of toxins may produce disease where each toxin alone may be harmless.

A physician specializing in occupational and environmental medicine first determines the current health status of the plaintiff by reviewing past health records, taking a thorough history, performing a detailed physical examination, and ordering laboratory tests. The physician reviews the information supplied by the toxicologist and decides whether medical monitoring is reasonable and necessary after considering the elements of the remedy outlined above.

Once the need for medical monitoring has been determined, the physician designs a surveillance protocol, which will differ according to the specifics of the toxin, the exposure, and the person. Generally, however, it should include the following:

Baseline examination. This is to determine the person's current state of health with special consideration of those organ systems potentially affected by the toxic exposure. The examination should include a thorough history, physical examination, and laboratory tests to evaluate the current state of health of the organ systems.

Periodic re-examination. This is to determine whether damage has occurred to the organ systems. The reexamination procedure should include repeat histories, physical examinations, and laboratory tests. The frequency of the various repeat examinations may not all be the same.

Once the protocol is designed, a cost estimator will determine the dollar value by finding the current cost for the baseline physical examination and estimating the costs for proposed future tests and examinations, taking into account the rising costs of medical care. This expert may be a medical economist, a hospital administrator, a health maintenance organization manager, or a practicing physician.

This material is drawn from Donnelly Hadden, Steven Huff, Thomas Colbert, Proving Medical Monitoring Damages, TRIAL 44–45 (July 1995).

4. JUDICIAL TREATMENT OF FEAR OF FUTURE DISEASE AND EMOTIONAL DISTRESS

ISABEL v. VELSICOL CHEMICAL CO.

United States District Court, Western District of Tennessee, 2004.
327 F.Supp.2d 915.

DONALD, District Judge.

Before the Court is the motion of Velsicol Chemical Corporation

("Defendant") for partial dismissal of the class action complaint of Mildred Isabel, Charles and Evalina Black, and Elizabeth Gate ("Plaintiffs"). Specifically, Defendant requests dismissal of Plaintiffs' claims for 1) strict liability, 2) damages based on emotional distress, 3) attorney fees, and 4) punitive damages.... For the following reasons, the Court grants in part Defendant's motion to dismiss the claim for attorney fees and denies in part Defendant's motion to dismiss the claims for strict liability, emotional distress damages, and punitive damages.

I. FACTUAL BACKGROUND

Plaintiffs are owners of real property located in Memphis, Tennessee. Defendant is an Illinois corporation. Plaintiffs bring this lawsuit on behalf of: The named plaintiffs and all similarly situated Tennessee property owners that either own or lease real property located directly along the banks of the area commonly known as "Cypress creek" in North Memphis, Shelby County, Tennessee whose land has been affected by the presence of elevated levels of Dieldrin in their soil.

Defendant owns a manufacturing plant in Memphis, Tennessee. In the mid-to-late 1940s, Defendant discovered and began to produce a chemical called Aldrin. Aldrin turns into a chemical called Dieldrin after a certain time.

Defendant began discharging Aldrin/Dieldrin along with wastewater downstream into Cypress Creek, where the chemicals collected in the soils at the creek's bottom and along its banks. Aldrin and Dieldrin are hydrophobic, and both, but especially Dieldrin, do not dissolve easily in water. Therefore, Dieldrin remains in the soil for an extremely long period of time.

Dieldrin is known to pose serious long-term health risks and has been linked to cancer, Parkinson's disease, birth defects, and other health problems. Any amount of Dieldrin above normal levels in the soil can potentially cause long-term health problems to those exposed, and the detection of any above-normal level requires removal of the Dieldrin or evacuation of the premises.

In or about May 2002, Defendant tested various property owners' soils. From those tests, Defendant learned that the properties along the banks of the Cypress Creek contained elevated levels of Dieldrin. Plaintiffs and the other class members own residential property located along the banks of Cypress Creek downstream from Defendant's manufacturing plant.

On or about March 24, 2004, Defendant began informing certain class members that their property contained heightened levels of Dieldrin in the soil. In those letters, Defendant admitted that the compounds got into the creek sediments from wastewater discharges from its manufacturing plant.

The real property of Plaintiffs and the class members has been rendered worthless in its present form as a result of Defendant's discharge of the dangerous chemicals, and Plaintiffs allege that they and the class members have suffered monetary damages. Plaintiffs and the class members now fear for their personal health and well-being, and for the health and well-being of their family members and those who come in contact with their property. Plaintiffs and the class members also fear that the value of their property will be diminished.

II. Procedural Background

Plaintiffs filed this class action complaint on April 1, 2004, in the Chancery Court of Tennessee for the Thirtieth Judicial District[.] Plaintiffs alleged state law claims of trespass, nuisance, negligence, and strict liability. Plaintiffs requested compensatory damages for the class members based on the diminution in the value of their property and on their emotional distress in general and specifically over their diminished property values and concerns for their personal health. Plaintiffs also requested punitive damages of up to $1,000,000,000.00. Plaintiffs requested a declaration that Defendant's acts rendered their property worthless and uninhabitable. Finally, Plaintiffs requested attorney fees, costs, pre-and post-judgment interest, and any such further relief that the Court may deem just and proper.

Defendant removed to this Court based on diversity of citizenship[.] ... [In] this motion for partial dismissal[,] Defendant argues that 1) Plaintiffs alleged no basis for strict liability based on either strict products liability or participation in an ultrahazardous activity; 2) Plaintiffs did not allege actual exposure to Aldrin/Dieldrin, and therefore Plaintiffs have no claim for emotional distress damages based on health concerns; 3) Plaintiffs did not allege a contractual or statutory basis for attorney fees; and 4) Plaintiffs alleged no facts supporting a claim for punitive damages.

* * *

III. Rule 12(B)(6) Standard

... [A Motion to Dismiss under Rule 12(b)(6)] tests only whether the plaintiff has pleaded a cognizable claim ..... Even if the plaintiff's chances of success are remote or unlikely, a motion to dismiss should be denied.... In reviewing the complaint, the court must accept as true all factual allegations in the complaint and construe them in the light most favorable to the plaintiff .....

IV. Analysis

A. Strict Liability

In Tennessee, a defendant engaged in an ultrahazardous activity is held strictly liable for injuries caused to the person or property of another by the defendant's participation in the activity. Tennessee courts have traditionally classified ultrahazardous activities as "those presenting an abnormally dangerous risk of injury to persons or their property, including the carrying out of blasting operations, [or] the storage of explosives or harmful chemicals[.]" The application of strict liability for ultrahazardous activities appears to be rather limited in Tennessee, as it is in other jurisdictions.... But see Sterling v. Velsicol Chem. Corp., 647 F.Supp. 303, 315–16 (W.D.Tenn.1986) (holding that, under facts presented, defendant's creation, location, operation, and closure of toxic chemical dump was abnormally dangerous and ultrahazardous activity), rev'd in part on other grounds, 855 F.2d 1188 (6th Cir.1988).

The allegations in this case are that Defendant discharged into a creek, which bordered residential property, the chemicals Aldrin/Dieldrin, which pose "serious long-term health risks," such as cancer, Parkinson's disease, and birth defects; that the discharges were substantial enough to cause elevated levels of Dieldrin in the soil along the banks of the creek; and that any level of Dieldrin above normal in the soil requires removal of the chemical or evacuation of the premises. The Court cannot say that this activity as alleged is not ultrahazardous as a matter of law. For example, that the chemicals went into a creek bordering residential property indicates that the location may not have been appropriate for the activity of eliminating dangerous chemicals. The allegations also show that harm from the activity may be great, by causing serious long-term health problems.... [F]or purposes of this Rule 12(b)(6) motion, the allegations are sufficient to state a claim for strict liability based on an ultrahazardous activity.....

B. Emotional Distress Damages

Defendant argues that Plaintiffs have not stated a claim for emotional distress damages based on their alleged concerns for their health because they did not allege actual exposure to the chemicals. Plaintiffs respond that they alleged that the soil of their and the class members' property is contaminated with the chemicals, and that it is a logical inference that they came into contact with the soil on their property, thus putting them into contact with the chemicals. What Plaintiffs must show to receive emotional distress damages on this basis is shown by the Tennessee Supreme Court's decision in Laxton v. Orkin Exterminating Company, Incorporated, 639 S.W.2d 431 (Tenn.1982). In Laxton, the defendant negligently contaminated the plaintiffs' water supply with chlordane, a dangerous, potentially carcinogenic chemical, while spraying for insects. The evidence at trial indicated that the plaintiffs drank the contaminated water, but medical examinations revealed that no physical damage had been done to them. Also, the mental anxiety of the plaintiffs did not manifest itself in any physical way.

After a jury verdict for the plaintiffs, the Court of Appeals affirmed the judgment for property damages and out-of-pocket expenses, but reversed the judgment for damages based on mental anguish. On appeal, the Tennessee Supreme Court concluded that the plaintiffs could still recover for their emotional distress damages based on their fear for the health and welfare of themselves and their children, despite the fact that the traditional requirements of the physical injury or manifestation rule had not been met.

In our opinion, in addition to cases where it has previously been allowed, recovery for the negligent infliction of mental anguish should be allowed in cases where, as a result of a defendant's negligence, a plaintiff has ingested an indefinite amount of a harmful substance. In such cases the finder of fact may conclude that the plaintiff has sustained sufficient physical injury to support an award for mental anguish even if subsequent medical diagnosis fails to reveal any other physical injury. The period of mental anguish, of course, would be confined to the time between discovery of the ingestion and the negative medical diagnosis or other information that puts to rest the fear of injury. Cf.Carroll v. Sisters of Saint Francis Health Servs., Inc., 868 S.W.2d 585 (Tenn.1993) (holding that, to recover damages for negligent infliction of emotional distress based on fear of contracting AIDS, plaintiff must allege actual exposure to HIV). In other words, the de minimus "physical injury" of ingesting the contaminated water sufficiently satisfied the physical injury or manifestation rule so as to justify the award of emotional distress damages.

* * *

Plaintiffs in this case specifically allege damages based on the diminished value of their real property and on their emotional distress based on fears over their health. [U]nder Laxton, it appears that emotional distress damages may not be "parasitic" upon property damages alone, because the plaintiffs in Laxton suffered property damage based on diminished value, but the Court still required them to prove some de minimus "physical injury," specifically, ingestion. Laxton, 639 S.W.2d at

431, 434. Thus, it appears that Plaintiffs here must also prove some sort of "physical injury," even though they also alleged property damage.

It is taken as true for this motion that the soil on Plaintiffs' and the other class members' property was contaminated with Aldrin/Dieldrin. Plaintiffs argue that, since the contaminated soil was on their real property, they necessarily came into contact with it, thus providing the required allegation of actual exposure. The Court finds this to be a logical inference. Plaintiffs obviously need not allege that they ingested the contaminated soil; unlike in a contaminated drinking water case, the Court could not realistically require ingestion. Contact appears to satisfy the exposure requirement under the circumstances, and logic dictates that Plaintiffs came into contact with the soil on their property. Plaintiffs, of course, will have to prove exposure should this case proceed to trial[.] ... Accordingly, the Court denies Defendant's motion to dismiss Plaintiffs' claim for such emotional distress damages.

C. Attorney Fees

Under the American rule, "attorney's fees may not be awarded to the prevailing party absent statutory authorization or an agreement between the parties so providing." John Kohl & Co. P.C. v. Dearborn & Ewing, 977 S.W.2d 528, 534 (Tenn.1998) ... The American rule is firmly established in the courts of Tennessee.... Defendant argues that Plaintiffs fail to state a claim for attorney fees because they do not allege any statutory or contractual right for such an award. The Court agrees that any such allegation is absent from the complaint, and, indeed, Plaintiffs do not contest this point. Accordingly, the Court grants Defendant's motion to dismiss Plaintiffs' claim for attorney fees.

D. Punitive Damages

Under Tennessee law, a court may award punitive damages if the plaintiff proves by clear and convincing evidence that the defendant acted either intentionally, fraudulently, maliciously, or recklessly. Hodges v. S.C. Toof & Co., 833 S.W.2d 896, 901 (Tenn.1992). A person acts intentionally when it is the person's conscious objective or desire to engage in the conduct or cause the result. A person acts fraudulently when (1) the person intentionally misrepresents an existing, material fact or produces a false impression, in order to mislead another or to obtain an undue advantage, and (2) another is injured because of reasonable reliance upon that representation. A person acts maliciously when the person is motivated by ill will, hatred, or personal spite. A person acts recklessly when the person is aware of, but consciously disregards, a substantial and unjustifiable risk of such a nature that its disregard constitutes a gross deviation from the standard of care that an ordinary person would exercise under all the circumstances....

Defendant contends that Plaintiffs have not pled any facts indicating that Defendant's alleged tortious conduct was intentional, fraudulent, malicious, or reckless. Plaintiffs respond that the complaint at least raises the issue of intentional conduct and that the facts alleged show recklessness.

Taking the allegations in the complaint as true, the Court finds that Plaintiffs alleged facts sufficient to show at least recklessness supporting an award for punitive damages. Plaintiffs alleged the following facts: that Defendant discovered and produced Aldrin/Dieldrin, that Defendant admits discharging Aldrin/Dieldrin with wastewater into Cypress Creek, which borders residential property, and that Aldrin/Dieldrin is known to pose serious long-term health risks to humans. From the fact that Defendant was the discoverer and producer of Aldrin/Dieldrin, the Court may legitimately infer that Defendant knew of the serious long-term health risks that the chemicals posed. The allegations that Defendant discharged into a creek bordering residential property chemicals known to pose serious long-term health risks to humans are sufficient to allege recklessness under the standard set forth in Hodges. As such, the complaint alleges facts sufficient to support an award of punitive damages . . . . .

V. CONCLUSION

Plaintiffs' complaint fails to state a claim for attorney fees because it does not allege a contractual or statutory right to them. Accordingly, the Court GRANTS in part Defendant's motion to dismiss the claim for attorney fees. Plaintiffs' complaint does state a claim for strict liability based on ultrahazardous activity, emotional distress damages based on fear over health, and punitive damages based on at least recklessness. Accordingly, the Court DENIES in part Defendant's motion to dismiss the claims for strict liability, emotional distress damages, and punitive damages.

a. *Sterling v. Velsicol Chemical*

A leading decision on the compensability of emotional distress in the form of fear of future disease (usually cancer) is Sterling v. Velsicol Chemical Corp., 855 F.2d 1188 (6th Cir.1988), a class action bright by five representative plaintiffs who lived on property near defendant's landfill where defendant had deposited 300,000 55–gallon steel drums containing extremely hazardous chemical wastes and hundreds of fiberboard cartons containing hazardous dry chemical wastes. Extensive studies revealed that before making its deposits defendant never conducted any hydrogeological studies to assess soil composition under the site, or the directional flow of water, or the location of the local aquifer, nor drilled any monitoring wells. Initial U.S. and state governmental investigations in 1967 indicated that chlorinated hydrocarbons had migrated down into the subsoil but had not reached the aquifer; however, a later study, prompted by residents' complaints of well water contamination, revealed that the aquifer was indeed "highly contaminated" and the groundwater directional flow was toward the residential wells.

A jury awarded the five plaintiffs amounts ranging from $50,000 to $250,000 for the fear and distress of the increased risk of developing cancer. The Court of Appeals rejected defendant's challenge of these awards:

Mental distress, which results from fear that an already existent injury will lead to the future onset of an as yet unrealized disease, constitutes an element of recovery only where such distress is either foreseeable or is a natural consequence of, or reasonably expected to flow from, the present injury. See Payton v. Abbott Labs, 386 Mass. 540, 437 N.E.2d 171 (1982) * * *. However damages for mental distress generally are not recoverable where the connection between the anxiety and the existing injury is either too remote or tenuous. * * * While there must be a reasonable connection between the injured plaintiff's mental anguish and the prediction of a future disease, the central focus of a court's inquiry in such a case is not on the underlying odds that the future disease will in fact materialize. To this extent, mental anguish resulting from the chance that an existing injury will lead to the materialization of a future disease may be an element of recovery even though the underlying future prospect for susceptibility to a future disease is not, in and of itself, compensable inasmuch as it is not sufficiently likely to occur. In the context of certain types of injuries and exposures to certain chemicals, cancerphobia has been one basis of claims for mental anguish damages.

Sterling at 1194.

After citing a Tennessee Supreme Court opinion in Laxton v. Orkin Exterminating Co., 639 S.W.2d 431 (Tenn.1982), which had allowed plaintiffs who had ingested substantial quantities of water contaminated with chlordane and heptachlor (both carcinogens) contained in termite spray to recover for emotional distress, the court in *Sterling* concluded:

> In the instant case, the plaintiffs' fear clearly constitutes a present injury. Each plaintiff produced evidence that they personally suffered from a reasonable fear of contracting cancer or some other disease in the future as a result of ingesting Velsicol's chemicals. Consistent with the extensive line of authority in both Tennessee and other jurisdictions, we cannot say that the district court erred in awarding the five representative plaintiffs damages for their reasonable fear of increased risk of cancer and other diseases.

Sterling at 1206.

The Court of Appeals did, however, reduce the size of the awards ranging from $27,000 to $72,000, using as the controlling factor the time period during which each had actually consumed the tainted water.

Notes and Questions

1.   The *Sterling* court rejects as compensable damage the increased risk of cancer and other diseases. It states: "Where the basis for awarding damages is the potential risk of susceptibility to future disease, the predicted future disease *must be medically reasonably certain* to follow from the existing present injury." For this reason, the "mere increased risk of future disease or condition" that might result from an existing condition is not compensable.

2. In treating the plaintiffs' claims for fear of future illness, the court in *Sterling* characterized it as "merely a specific type of mental anguish" which is compensable "only where such distress is either foreseeable or is a natural consequence of or reasonably expected to flow from, the present injury. * * * [T]he central focus of a court's inquiry in such a case is not on the underlying odds that the future disease will in fact materialize." What do you think of the court's formulation of the test of liability? Should the plaintiffs' entitlement to emotional distress damages deriving from the future risk of cancer and the claim of increased future risk of cancer be tied together? How would a court judge the reasonableness of the distress without reference to the magnitude of the risk of the disease? Should "fear" be distinguished from "danger"?

b.   A Civil Action

A leading case on standards for emotional distress claims is Anderson v. W.R. Grace & Co., 628 F.Supp. 1219 (D.Mass.1986) (made famous in the book and movie A Civil Action), where the district court considered claims of plaintiffs who consumed water from wells contaminated in Woburn, Massachusetts by chemicals from defendants' operations, including trichloroethylene and tetrachloroethylene which are known carcinogens. The case included wrongful death claims on behalf of decedents' who died of leukemia allegedly caused by exposure to the chemicals. Other family members asserted claims for emotional distress caused by witnessing the deaths of these children, claims of leukemia of individuals who were in remission, and other physical ailments and emotional distress claims.

The defendant contended that those plaintiffs who did not suffer from leukemia should be barred from recovering emotional distress damages because they sustained no physical harm. The court found that some plaintiffs had alleged sufficient physical harm, and objective symptomology, to satisfy the Massachusetts rule that:

> [I]n order for * * * plaintiffs to recover for negligently inflicted emotional distress, [they] must allege and prove [they] suffered physical harm as a result of the conduct which caused the emotional distress. We answer, further, that a plaintiff's physical harm must either cause or be caused by the emotional distress alleged, and that the physical harm must be manifested by objective symptomatology and substantiated by expert medical testimony.

However, the court rejected those claims of emotional distress deriving solely from the defendants' conduct in contributing to the groundwater pollution—"anxiety, fear, depression, anger, hopelessness, and distress"—where these emotional conditions were not directly caused by physical harm that they had allegedly suffered. On the other hand, "elements of plaintiffs' emotional distress [which] stem from the physical harm to their immune systems allegedly caused by defendants' conduct are compensable."

The court also rejected the bystander emotional distress claims asserted by family members who witnessed the deaths from leukemia of five minor children on the grounds that only distress associated with witnessing a dramatic, traumatic shock would be actionable, not that associated with a prolonged illness.

What problems do you foresee courts will experience in applying tort rules, such as those governing emotional distress claims, that were developed in accident and sudden injury cases and applying them to claims in prolonged illness and exposure cases? Should there be separate standards for such cases? What might they consist of?

The material below may seem lengthy and detailed. The reason is that claims for emotional distress are so frequent in toxic tort litigation, as was illustrated in *Buckley* and *Sterling*, that any practitioner must master the jurisdiction governing principles; also as you know from your basic torts course, more than one test has emerged to govern recovery for emotional distress and courts have especially struggled in the field of environmental torts.

c. *Physical Harm, Impact or Related Requirements*

In toxic tort cases such as *Sterling* and *Anderson* (A Civil Action), individuals exposed to hazardous chemicals may develop an understandable fear or dread of developing cancer in the future. The physical injury rule, however, often functions as a bar.

1. *Restatement Rule*: A majority of jurisdictions continue to preserve the requirement that to be compensable, the emotional distress must cause or be caused by some bodily injury. The Restatement (Second) of Torts §§ 313 and 436 require bodily harm as an essential condition to an action for negligently caused emotional distress, and make no provision for a different rule in environmental tort cases.

See also Restatement (Second) of Torts § 436A, which sets forth what is still the rule adhered to by the majority of American courts: "If the actor's conduct is negligent as creating an unreasonable risk of causing either bodily harm or emotional disturbance to another, and it results in such emotional disturbance alone, without bodily harm or other compensable damage, the actor is not liable for such emotional disturbance."

2. *Bodily Harm Test*: Similar to the opinion in *Buckley* that demanded a substantial impact or actual symptom of disease, many decisions adopt a comparable standard. Most of these decisions, like *Buckley* have arisen in the asbestos or other products liability context. These cases have usually demanded substantial bodily harm as a precondition to recovery.

The Pennsylvania Supreme Court in Simmons v. Pacor, Inc., 543 Pa. 664, 674 A.2d 232 (Pa. 1996) illustrates the point. In *Simmons* two plaintiffs exposed to asbestos products had developed pleural thickening and were at a greater risk of developing asbestosis and mesothelioma, a rare but lethal form of lung cancer. In their products liability actions their experts' testimony established that neither of the plaintiffs had any functional impairment as a result of their exposure. The Supreme Court, concluding that "non-impairing, asymptomatic pleural thickening was not compensable as a matter of law," rejected plaintiffs' claims. Turning to the plaintiffs' claims for recovery of mental anguish caused by an increased fear of cancer, it summarily rejected them:

> Notwithstanding the fact that Appellants' fear presently exists, we hold that because asymptomatic pleural thickening is not a sufficient physical injury, the resultant emotional distress damages are likewise not recoverable. It is the general rule of this Commonwealth that there can be no recovery of damages for injuries resulting from fright or nervous shock or mental or emotional disturbances or distress unless they are accompanied by physical injury or physical impact. We decline to adopt the view that the pleural thickening establishes a sufficient "impact" to warrant recovery for mental anguish.

674 A.2d at 238.

Accord, Burns v. Jaquays Min. Corp., 156 Ariz. 375, 752 P.2d 28 (Ariz.Ct.App.1987), rev. dismissed, 162 Ariz. 186, 781 P.2d 1373 (1989) ("There can be no claim for damages for the fear of contracting asbestos-related diseases in the future without the manifestation of a bodily injury. The psychosomatic injuries diagnosed by Dr. Gray consist of headaches, acid indigestion, weeping, muscle spasms, depression and insomnia. There is no evidence that these were other than transitory physical phenomena. They were not linked to any specific plaintiff, and they are not the type of bodily harm which would sustain a cause of action for emotional distress."), 752 P.2d at 31–32 (citing Restatement (Second) of Torts § 436A comment c).

Accord, In re Hawaii Federal Asbestos Cases, 734 F.Supp. 1563 (D.Haw.1990) (workers must show some underlying compensable harm, which requires some function functional impairment due to asbestos exposure).

What rationales support a test that requires proof of bodily harm?

An experience in Texas illustrates the resiliency of the bodily harm rule. A lower Texas court had held in Carter v. Temple–Inland Forest Products Corp., 943 S.W.2d 221, 223 (Tex. Ct. App. 1997):

> Consequently, it is well established a plaintiff may recover for mental anguish based upon fear of cancer even though the evidence shows the plaintiff does not have, and in reasonable medical probability, will not have cancer, so long as there has been exposure to the causative agent and the fear is reasonable.

The evidence showed that plaintiffs' probability of developing cancer was from 1.0% to .0002%, which the court held was sufficient to make the reasonableness of their fear a jury question.

However, the Texas Supreme Court reversed, 993 S.W.2d 88 (Tex. 1999), drawing support from the U.S. Supreme Court in *Buckley*, holding that a person who is placed in peril because of the negligence of another and escapes injury may not recover damages just because he has been placed in a perilous position. The court added that "mere fright" is not enough to award damages. "Absent physical injury, the common law has not allowed recovery for negligent infliction of emotional distress except in certain specific, limited instances," the court said. "Plaintiff's claims in this case do not fall within any of the categories in which recovery has been allowed," the court ruled. "Moreover, a landowner's tortious breach of his duty to invitee—like Temple–Inland's negligently exposing Carter and Wilson to asbestos—is not a wrong for which mental anguish is compensable absent physical injury. This is true whether the landowner's duty arises from the common law or from the federal regulation invoked by Carter and Wilson in their pleadings."

As to the fear of future disease it noted that "if bodily injury is at most latent and any eventual consequences uncertain, as when a person's exposure to asbestos has not produced disease, then the case for recovery is much weaker." After citing the same policy reasons identified in *Buckley* it concluded:

> The question is not, of course, whether Carter and Wilson have themselves suffered genuine distress over their own exposure. We assume they have, and that their anxiety is reasonable. The question, rather, is whether this type of claim-for-fear of an increased risk of developing an asbestos-related disease when no disease is presently manifest—should be permitted, regardless of any individual plaintiff's circumstances, when the effort in determining the genuineness of each claim and assuring appropriate recovery is beset with the difficulties we have described. We conclude that no such action should be recognized.

Id. at 93.

3. *Impact Test*: *Buckley,* of course, is now a classic impact rule case. Although the impact rule has largely been discarded in most jurisdictions as an exclusive test in favor of a zone of danger or bystander rule, that doesn't preclude its functioning as an *additional* basis of liability for emotional distress.

A Florida opinion considered the relationship between the impact rule and "fear of" claims in Eagle–Picher Industries v. Cox, 481 So.2d 517 (Fla.Ct.App.1985), the court finding that asbestos fibers in the lungs fulfilled the impact rule and thereby relieved plaintiff of having to prove any physical manifestation of the distress itself. It ruled that "fear of" claims, however, presented difficulties of burdening the court system and manufacturers, and held that plaintiff had to prove some asbestos-related injury, such as asbestosis "since plaintiffs with asbestosis may have a well-founded greater reason to fear contracting cancer than those who do not have asbestosis." Thus, in *Cox,* the physical injury that supported the emotional distress claim was not that caused by the distress, nor, in all likelihood, the cause of the distress, but simply some physical harm caused by the asbestos exposure that implied that plaintiff's distress was genuine and reasonable. See Adams v. Star Enterprise, 51 F.3d 417 (4th Cir.1995) (applying Virginia law) (in environmental exposure case, court held that plaintiffs alleging fear of significant health risks from exposure to fumes and vapors could not recover).

4. *Environmental Exposure Cases*: In environmental exposure cases (as distinguished from products cases) courts have struggled to determine whether exposure to the chemicals is a sufficient basis standing alone to support a "fear of" claim.

For example, the Mississippi Supreme Court considered a case where nearby residents and a former employee brought a toxic tort action against a chemical manufacturing facility. Plaintiff's claims were limited to emotional distress and fear of contracting a future illness due to defendant's alleged release of chemicals from its facility. The court ruled that Mississippi law does not recognize a cause of action for fear of possibly contracting a disease at some point in the future. Plaintiffs failed to provide substantial evidence of exposure and medical evidence showing they would contract a future illness. Therefore, the trial court grant of summary judgment was proper. Brewton v. Reichhold Chemicals, Inc., 707 So.2d 618 (Miss.1998).

Recall that in *Sterling*, the court looked to Laxton v. Orkin, 639 S.W.2d 431 (Tenn.1982), where the plaintiffs brought suit seeking damages for mental anguish, personal injury and property damage as a result of Orkin's negligence in contaminating the plaintiffs' household water supply with the toxic chemical chlordane. A verdict was rendered in favor of the plaintiffs and each claimant was awarded damages for "injury, mental pain and suffering (mental anguish)" as a result of their drinking the contaminated water. The Supreme Court of Tennessee, affirming the judgment, analogized the case to those involving contaminated food products, stating that:

> [r]ecovery of damages resulting from the ingestion of deleterious food or beverages also has been permitted in numerous cases in this state, though physical injury, if any, was slight. * * * In many of them, * * * recovery was permitted with a minimum showing of physical injury; where this did occur, full recovery has been allowed for the fright, shock, or other "mental" aspect of the claim.

Id. at 433–34.

Upholding the trial court's characterization of this case as a "technical physical injury," the court reasoned that recovery for negligent infliction of emotional distress should be allowed where "as a result of a defendant's negligence, a plaintiff has ingested an indefinite amount of a harmful substance." Whether the ingestion was sufficient to support recovery without a diagnosable physical injury was, according to the court, a question of fact for the jury.

Ironbound Health Rights Advisory Comm. v. Diamond Shamrock Chemicals Co., 243 N.J.Super. 170, 578 A.2d 1248 (1990) (exposure of neighborhood residents to dioxin and other toxic chemicals manufactured at a nearby plant did not give rise to a claim for emotional distress damages absent showing of some physical injury, despite residents' fear that they might some day become seriously ill from previous inhalation and absorption of dioxin; concerns, although understandable, were not compensable where there was no claim of serious mental illness); accord, Ball v. Joy Technologies, Inc., 958 F.2d 36 (4th Cir.1991) (employees exposed to PCBs, dioxins, TCE, and furans could not recover for emotional distress because exposure itself did not constitute a physical injury under Virginia and West Virginia law: "The mere exposure of the plaintiffs to toxic chemicals does not provide the requisite physical injury to entitle the plaintiffs to recover for their emotional distress."); The Wyoming Supreme Court also declined to recognize an emotional distress claim against a county that condemned plaintiffs' property because of methane and hydrogen sulfide gases from a nearby coal mine. Miller v. Campbell County, 854 P.2d 71 (Wyo.1993).

The New York rule is interesting as described in Abusio v. Consolidated Edison Co., 238 A.D.2d 454, 656 N.Y.S.2d 371, 372 (N.Y.App.Div. 1997):

> The Supreme Court properly set aside the jury verdict awarding damages for emotional distress and/or future medical monitoring costs. Under the prevailing case law, in order to maintain a cause of action for fear of developing cancer or for future medical monitoring costs following exposure to a toxic substance like polychlorinated biphenyls (hereinafter PCBs), a plaintiff must establish both that he or she was in fact exposed to the disease-causing agent and that there is a "rational basis" for his or her fear of contracting the disease. This "rational basis" has been construed to mean the clinically demonstrable presence of PCBs in the plaintiff's body, or some indication of PCB-induced disease i.e., some physical manifestation of PCB contamination. * * *

Accord, Dangler v. Town of Whitestown, 241 A.D.2d 290, 672 N.Y.S.2d 188 (1998). Thus, the foregoing cases are nearly uniform in refusing to allow fear-based emotional damages based solely on exposure to a toxic chemical.

In 2 American Law Institute, Enterprise Responsibility for Personal Injury 380 (1991), the Reporters' Study concluded:

> We do not advocate compensating individuals who are stricken by "cancerphobia." Although some courts have been willing to reimburse individuals for the pain, discomfort, fear, anxiety, annoyance, and emotional distress suffered as a result of exposure to potentially hazardous vapors, this type of reimbursement is highly variable and introduces great uncertainty into hazardous substance litigation. It contrasts sharply with medical monitoring damages, which must be based on expert testimony, perhaps with input from court-appointed

experts or science panels regarding the presence of an increased risk of disease. Consequently, we do not advocate reimbursement for emotional damages or for increased risk per se.

Do you agree with the Reporters' conclusions? Is the concern for "variability" and "uncertainty" legitimate? What kind of variability is being referred to?

d. *California Standard of Reasonableness and Probability of Disease*

The California Supreme Court opinion in Potter v. Firestone Tire & Rubber Co., 6 Cal.4th 965, 25 Cal.Rptr.2d 550, 863 P.2d 795, 816 (Cal. 1993), an environmental exposure case, is one of the most quoted in the country. Plaintiffs sued alleging claims based on negligence and nuisance, including negligent infliction of emotional distress. They sought recovery for fear of disease, medical monitoring, alleging that they were subjected to prolonged exposure to certain carcinogens including benzene and vinyl chloride, resulting from defendant's waste disposal practices at a nearby landfill. Although plaintiffs testified to a variety of physical symptoms, the court held that there was an inadequate factual record to determine whether such "impairment to the immune response system or cellular damage constitutes a physical injury for which parasitic damages for emotional distress ought to be available." The court nonetheless concluded that there is no present physical injury requirement to recover fear of cancer damages. However, the court set forth an exacting standard for recovery of damages for fear of cancer in negligence actions where no present physical injury has been established, requiring that plaintiff prove that it is more likely than not that cancer will develop in the future as a result of the toxic exposure:

> Unless an express exception to this general rule is recognized in the absence of a present physical injury or illness, damages for fear of cancer may be recovered only if the plaintiff pleads and proves that (1) as a result of the defendant's negligent breach of a duty owed to the plaintiff, the plaintiff is exposed to a toxic substance which threatens cancer; and (2) the plaintiff's fear stems from a knowledge, corroborated by reliable medical or scientific opinion, that it is more likely than not that the plaintiff will develop the cancer in the future due to the exposure.

The court, however, did not stop at its "greater than 50 percent" standard, but offered an alternative test. The court crafted an exception to the general rule when a defendant has engaged in conduct that amounts to "oppression, fraud, or malice," as defined in California Civil Code § 3294 (the state's punitive damages statute) and plaintiff's fear is supported by expert testimony that the risk of cancer is "significant."

What do you think of the California approach? How likely is it that a plaintiff will be able to establish this standard?

e.   *Choosing From Among the Alternatives*

Which standard for "fear of" claims do you find most appropriate? What about a simple reasonableness test where the jury could weigh all the evidence, including evidence of the quantum of the increased risk? Consider this statement, in Hagerty v. L & L Marine Services, Inc., 788 F.2d 315 (5th Cir.1986), where the court recognized a claim for fear of future illness where a seaman had been drenched with toxic chemicals and rejected reliance on the physical manifestation requirement:

> With or without physical injury or impact, a plaintiff is entitled to recover damages for serious mental distress arising from fear of developing cancer where his fear is reasonable and causally related to the defendant's negligence. The circumstances surrounding the fear-inducing occurrence may themselves supply sufficient indicia of genuineness. It is for the jury to decide questions such as the existence, severity and reasonableness of the fear.

Id. at 318.

Why have so many courts refused to accept this standard in environmental exposure cases? What reasons did Justice Breyer offer in *Buckley*? What reasons support the California bright line rule of greater than a fifty percent chance?

1.   *Statutory Limits on Non-economic Damages.* Many jurisdictions have enacted caps on the size of awards for emotional distress or pain and suffering that would govern "fear of" claims. Alaska Stat. 09.17.010 (1980); Cal. Civil Code § 3333.2 (1997); Md. Code Cts & Jud. Proc. § 11–108(a) (1994).

2.   *Literature*: Unsurprisingly, much has been written on this topic of emotional distress and "fear of" claims. See, e.g., Kenneth Miller, Toxic Torts and Emotional Distress: The Case For an Independent Cause of Action for Fear of Future Harm, 40 Ariz. L. Rev. 681 (1998); Scott D. Marrs, Mind over Body: Trends Regarding the Physical Injury Requirement in Negligent Infliction of Emotional Distress and 'Fear of Disease' Cases, 28 Tort & Ins. L. J. 1 (1992); Paige Freeman Rosato, Combating Fear of Future Injury and Medical Monitoring Claims, 61 Def. Couns. J. 554, 562 (1994); Irresponsible Use and Disposal of Toxic Substances: The Case for Legislative Recognition of Increased Risk Causes of Action, 49 Vand. L. Rev. 789, 803 (1996); Paul R. Lees–Haley & Eric H. Marcus, Litigating Cancerphobia and Toxic Allergy Claims, 57 Def. Couns. J. 377 (1990); Janet Smith, Increasing Fear of Future Injury Claims: Where Speculation Carries the Day, 64 Def. Couns. J. 547 (1997); Jason Yearort, Fear of Future Harm in Toxic Tort Litigation: The Appropriate Measure of Damages, 22 Am. J. Trial Advoc. 639 (1999).

f. Increased Risk Alone Not Compensable

1. Ayers v. Township of Jackson, 106 N.J. 557, 579, 525 A.2d 287 (N.J.1989). As the court in *Sterling* states, the increased risk of future disease, say a 10% increased risk of cancer from the environmental exposure, is not, standing alone, compensable. *Ayers* is a leading case which also denied recovery for enhanced risk as a separate compensable item of damages. Some of the New Jersey Supreme Court's discussion of and rationales for not recognizing such a claim follow:

> Our evaluation of the enhanced risk and medical surveillance claims requires that we focus on a critical issue in the management of toxic tort litigation: at what stage in the evolution of a toxic injury should tort law intercede by requiring the responsible party to pay damages?

> * * *

> The enhanced risk claim seeks a damage award, not because of any expenditure of funds, but because plaintiffs contend that the unquantified injury to their health and life expectancy should be presently compensable, even though no evidence of disease is manifest. Defendant does not dispute the causal relationship between the plaintiffs' exposure to toxic chemicals and the plaintiffs' increased risk of diseases, but contends that the probability that plaintiffs will actually become ill from their exposure to chemicals is too remote to warrant compensation under principles of tort law.

> Our disposition of this difficult and important issue requires that we choose between two alternatives, each having a potential for imposing unfair and undesirable consequences on the affected interests. A holding that recognizes a cause of action for unquantified enhanced risk claims exposes the tort system, and the public it serves, to the task of litigating vast numbers of claims for compensation based on threats of injuries that may never occur. It imposes on judges and juries the burden of assessing damages for the risk of potential disease, without clear guidelines to determine what level of compensation may be appropriate. It would undoubtedly increase already escalating insurance rates. It is clear that the recognition of an "enhanced risk" cause of action, particularly when the risk is unquantified, would generate substantial litigation that would be difficult to manage and resolve.

The court's argument that allowing enhanced risk claims will under compensate those who later do develop cancer and overcompensate those who do not is frequently relied upon in these types of cases. How persuasive is it? The court holds that it will not recognize a cause of action for *unquantified* enhanced risk of disease. How much and how certain must quantification be before it would be compensable under this standard? Would a five percent chance be sufficient? Or would the court require a "reasonable medical certainty," "more probably than not," or similar degree of quantification that exceeds 50%? Would a 30% risk be sufficient if the expert stated that she was 90% certain of her opinion?

2. *Prevailing Rule*: The general rule today is that the increased risk of developing a future disease, such as cancer, as a consequence of exposure to toxic chemicals is not compensable unless the plaintiff can establish that the probability of the future disease is greater than 50%. In Wilson v. Johns–Manville Sales Corp., 684 F.2d 111, 119 (D.C.Cir. 1982), the D.C. Circuit Court of Appeals offered this statement of the rule:

> The traditional American rule * * * is that recovery of damages based on future consequences may be had only if such consequences are "reasonably certain." Recovery of damages for speculative or conjectural consequences is not permitted. To meet the "reasonably certain" standard, courts have generally required plaintiffs to prove that it is more likely than not (a greater than 50% chance) that the projected consequence will occur. If such proof is made, the alleged future effect may be treated as certain to happen and the injured party may be awarded full compensation for it; if the proof does not establish a greater than 50% chance, the injured party's award must be limited to damages for harm already manifest.

Other recent decisions have essentially arrived at the same conclusion as the courts in *Ayers* and *Sterling* and denied the claim for an increased risk unless the plaintiff offers compelling expert testimony about the substantiality of the increased likelihood of contracting cancer.

Among toxic tort cases rejecting liability for damages based on enhanced risk is Anderson v. W.R. Grace & Co., 628 F.Supp. 1219 (D.Mass.1986). That case * * * involved defendants' alleged chemical contamination of the groundwater in areas of Woburn, Massachusetts. Plaintiffs alleged that two wells supplying water to the City of Woburn drew upon the contaminated water, and that exposure to the contaminated water caused five deaths and severe personal injuries among plaintiffs. Among the claims for personal injuries dismissed before trial were plaintiff's claims for damages based on enhanced risk. Relying on the Massachusetts rule regarding prospective damages, the *Anderson* court reasoned that "recovery depends on establishing a 'reasonable probability' that the harm will occur." Id. at 1231 (citing Restatement (Second) of Torts § 912 comment *e*). The *Anderson* court held that the plaintiffs failed to satisfy this threshold standard. They had not quantified their alleged enhanced risk: "Nothing in the present record indicates the magnitude of the increased risk or the diseases which plaintiffs may suffer." Id.

Accord, Hagerty v. L & L Marine Servs., 788 F.2d 315 (5th Cir.1986) ("[A] plaintiff can recover [damages for enhanced risk] only where he can show that the toxic exposure more probably than not will lead to cancer." The complaint does not allege that "plaintiff will probably develop cancer in the future."); Stites v. Sundstrand Heat Transfer, Inc., 660 F.Supp. 1516 (W.D.Mich.1987). But see, Werlein v. United States,

746 F.Supp. 887 (D.Minn.1990) (court refuses to dismiss increased risk claim because it finds plaintiffs suffer a present injury in the form of "chromosome breakage" and that such subcellular injuries can support the increased risk claim).

The New Jersey Supreme Court revisited the increased risk issue a few years after and reaffirmed its holding in Mauro v. Raymark Industries, Inc., 116 N.J. 126, 561 A.2d 257 (1989). There it rejected a plaintiff's claim of enhanced risk of cancer attributable to working with asbestos, where the experts testified that there was a "high probability" that the plaintiff had an increased risk of contracting cancer in his lifetime, but they were unable to testify that it was probable that the plaintiff would contract cancer. The opinion contains a thorough discussion of the policy considerations for and against recognizing the enhanced risk claim, and a dissenting opinion that would have permitted the enhanced risk claim, as representing a more efficient use of judicial resources and as more attuned to achieving an optimal level of deterrence.

Problem

Plaintiffs, Mr. and Mrs. Embry and their two children lived from 1963 to 1986 in a residential neighborhood of Unionville, a moderate size city. Unionville's residential area abutted an area zoned for light manufacturing. The defendant, Pester–Cide, Inc., a company that has manufactured various types of pesticides (DDT from 1960 until 1975, and chlordane and heptachlor from 1960 until 1980), is located across the street from the plaintiffs' house, a distance of about 800 feet. The plaintiffs allege that pesticides from the defendant's facility drifted across the street and settled in the soil, and also in the dust in their attic where they are found at concentrations in excess of normal "background" levels. The plaintiffs maintain that they have suffered headaches, watery eyes, and asthma due to this continuous exposure during the time defendant's plant was in active production, during which period plaintiffs could also distinctly smell strong odors from the plant. Now, because of their toxic exposures and their demonstrated earlier vulnerability to these poisons, plaintiffs allege further that they live in constant fear of contracting cancer and other serious illnesses.

Plaintiffs demand that defendant Pester–Cide, Inc. pay the costs of monitoring their health to minimize long term effects of exposure to defendant's pesticides by early detection and surveillance. Plaintiffs' plan to offer expert testimony from Dr. Alan Levin concerning the need for medical monitoring, and the damage to plaintiffs' immune systems resulting from alterations to cells in their immune system, which currently leaves them vulnerable to predictable, as well as unpredictable, health problems ranging from allergies to cancer.

You are an associate at the law firm of Grab & Greed that represents Pester–Cide on a number of matters. The partner in charge is concerned that plaintiffs' claims for medical monitoring might fare better than their claims for (1) fear of contracting cancer; and (2) the actual physical symptoms experienced during the plant's operations, as the statute of limitations may have run on any claims for injuries sustained while the plant was actively producing pesticides. The partner acknowledges that she is no expert in toxic tort nuances, but his impression is that some jurisdictions recognizing a claim for medical monitoring have adopted watered-down standards of causality and established elements of the claim that can too easily be satisfied. She asks you to analyze the decisional law in neighboring jurisdictions, since no decided case in Columbia has addressed the question.

Describe for the partner what "medical monitoring" is in terms of a cause of action, a claim for relief, a remedy, or however it may be characterized in legal terms. Analyze the relevant decisional law, and provide the partner with an assessment of what evidence plaintiffs must offer to make out a "claim" for medical monitoring. What underlying causes of action will, or must, plaintiffs assert? How will plaintiffs' claims for emotional distress fare, assuming no statute of limitation problems?

5. PUNITIVE DAMAGES

Awards of punitive damages are increasing in frequency in environmental tort cases. The court in *Sterling* sustains the basis for punitive awards (although it remands for reconsideration of the appropriate amount treating the class as a whole) which are predicated on the defendant's conduct in continuing to dispose of hazardous waste after being warned by governmental officials that it posed a material risk of harm to the community. The court reverses, however, awards of punitive damages based on the defendant's conduct in the trial of the case, specifically the defendant's asserting an assumption of the risk defense and asserting that the government agencies were partially responsible for plaintiffs' damages. This certainly seems to be the proper conclusion; a party should not be at risk for punitive damages just because it raises an unpopular or even inflammatory defense. The proper remedy for raising frivolous claims or defenses is the imposition of sanctions under Federal Rule 11 of the Federal Rules of Civil Procedure. For a discussion of Rule 11, see Cooter & Gell v. Hartmarx Corp., 496 U.S. 384, 110 S.Ct. 2447, 110 L.Ed.2d 359 (1990).

In Oros v. Hull & Assoc., Inc., 302 F.Supp.2d 839, 849 (N.D. Ohio 2004), an employee's suit alleging that his employer intentionally caused him to be exposed to be exposed to toxic waste during his employment, the federal trial court set forth Ohio's "actual malice" standard for the award of punitive damages in this way:

> Punitive damages are designed not to compensate an injured plaintiff, but to punish an offending party and set him up "as an example to others that they might be deterred from similar conduct." Preston v. Murty, 32 Ohio St.3d 334, 335, 512 N.E.2d 1174 (1987) [Cc] The party seeking punitive damages, therefore, must show more than mere negligence: he must establish that the offending party acted with "actual malice." [Cc]

> The Ohio Supreme Court has explained that actual malice is: "(1) that state of mind under which a person's conduct is characterized

by hatred, ill will or a spirit of revenge, or (2) a conscious disregard for the rights and safety of other persons that has a great probability of causing substantial harm. In the latter case, before submitting the issue of punitive damages to the jury, a trial court must review the evidence to determine if reasonable minds can differ as to whether the party was aware his or her act had a great probability of causing substantial harm. Furthermore, the court must determine that sufficient evidence is presented revealing that the party consciously disregarded the injured party's rights or safety." [Cc]

a.   *Constitutional and Other Limitations*

The Due Process Clause of the Fourteenth Amendment places substantive limits on the amount of punitive damages a court may award. In line with the Constitution, the Supreme Court of the United States has held that an award of punitive damages must not be greatly excessive that it would shock the judicial conscience. If it does an appellate court may hold the award arbitrary and a violation of the due process clause after conducting an inquiry of the state interests that the punitive award is designed to serve.

The case below exemplifies the steps that are necessary in evaluating an excessive punitive damage award.

JOHANSEN v. COMBUSTION ENGINEERING, INC.

United States Court of Appeals, Eleventh Circuit, 1999.
170 F.3d 1320.

HILL, SENIOR CIRCUIT JUDGE:

Property owners brought a nuisance and trespass action against the present owner of a former mining site, Combustion Engineering, Inc. ("CE"), alleging that acidic water had escaped from the site, damaging streams that run through their properties. The jury awarded the owners an aggregate of $47,000 in compensatory damages and $45 million in punitive damages which the district court reduced to $4.35 million. All parties have appealed.

I.

In the 1920's, a company named Tiffany's mined a site in Lincoln County, Georgia for rutile, a substance used for polishing diamonds. At some point thereafter, Aluminum Silicates, Inc. began mining the site for kyanite, a mineral used to make heat-resistant products. In the mid–1960's, CE purchased the site and began mining kyanite. It conducted these mining operations until 1984, when it sold the property to Pasco Mining Company ("Pasco"). Pasco operated the mine site until November 1, 1986, at which time Pasco defaulted on its obligations and the facility and all environmental responsibilities for the property reverted to CE pursuant to the parties' 1984 contract. CE never resumed mining operations.

At the time the mining originally began, Graves Mountain was essentially a big, solid rock. The mine operator would remove, crush, and process the rock in order to extract the kyanite. After the removal of the kyanite, the remaining crushed rock, or "tailings," would be deposited into containment areas, known as "tailings ponds." One of the minerals in the tailings was pyrite. When rainwater falls on pyrite that has been exposed to oxygen, a chemical reaction takes place that renders the water more acidic. Periodically, acidic water from the mining site seeped into streams that flowed through CE's property affecting their quality as they ran through the properties downstream.

In August of 1991, several individuals who owned a total of sixteen tracts downstream from the mine site sued CE claiming damages for trespass and nuisance. Several other property owners filed suit in May of 1992, and the two suits were consolidated. Property owners' claim was that the streams looked and smelled bad, that the streams no longer contained fish, and that cows would not drink from the streams. They did not allege any personal injuries, risk to human health, diminution in property value, damage to crops or animals, or any other economic loss.[2]

The case was tried to a jury in a two-phase trial in which issues relating to punitive damages were decided separately from liability for the underlying torts and compensatory damages. The jury was instructed that the relevant time frame for damages purposes was the four-year period prior to the commencement of the property owners' suit.

In the first phase of the trial, the jury returned a total of thirteen verdicts for compensatory damages in favor of the various property owners in an aggregate amount of $47,000. The thirteen verdicts ranged from $1000 to $10,000. The jury also awarded property owners litigation costs in the amount of $227,000.

In the punitive damages phase of the trial, property owners were required as a matter of Georgia law to prove by clear and convincing evidence that CE's actions "showed willful misconduct, malice, fraud, wantonness, oppression, or that entire want of care which would raise the presumption of conscious indifference to consequences." O.C.G.A. § 51–12–5(b). To recover more than $250,000 each, property owners were required to demonstrate, again by clear and convincing evidence, that CE acted "with the specific intent to cause harm." Id. at § 51–12–5.1(f).

The jury awarded $3 million in punitive damages to each of the fifteen property owners who owned the sixteen parcels of land at issue, for a total of $45 million.

The district court found this amount "shocking," which if allowed to stand would "give[ ] the system a black eye." The court entered an order granting CE's motion for a new trial unless property owners agreed to

2. Few of these individuals live on their property. Some do not use their property at all, and several others have been to their property (or the streams on it) only rarely if at all over the past several years. The plaintiffs who do use their property, do so for raising cattle, storing junked cars, hunting, timbering, or growing hay.

remit all punitive damages over $15 million. Property owners agreed to do so and the court entered separate judgments totaling $15 million in punitive damages. * * *

We affirmed those judgments without opinion. Johansen v. Combustion Engineering, Inc., 67 F.3d 314 (11th Cir.1995).

CE petitioned the Supreme Court for certiorari, contending that the punitive damage award was still excessive. The Supreme Court, based on its ruling in BMW of North America, Inc. v. Gore, 517 U.S. 559, 116 S.Ct. 1589, 134 L.Ed.2d 809 (1996) * * * that the Constitution does not permit "excessive" punitive damage awards, granted CE's petition, vacated this court's judgment, and remanded the case to us for further consideration in light of *BMW*.

We remanded the case to the district court. The district court reexamined the punitive award under *BMW*, and concluded that the Constitution would permit punitive damages in an amount no more than 100 times each plaintiff's compensatory award. Therefore, he ordered the entry of judgment for each of the remaining plaintiffs in an amount equal to the jury's compensatory award plus 100 times that amount as punitive damages. This resulted in an aggregate punitive damage award of $4.35 million. The district court did not afford property owners the opportunity to elect a new trial.

CE appealed, arguing that even $4.35 million in punitive damages is unconstitutionally excessive on the facts of this case. * * *

Property owners cross-appealed arguing that the district court erred in holding that the $15 million punitive damages award was unconstitutionally excessive. They seek restitution of the district court's remittitur of $15 million which they accepted in lieu of a new trial. * * *

Finally, property owners claim that the district court committed constitutional error when it reduced the jury's punitive damage verdicts to $4.35 million and unilaterally entered judgments totaling that amount. * * *

II.

A federal court has no general authority to reduce the amount of a jury's verdict. * * *

A district court may, however, order a new trial. * * * Therefore, when a court finds that a jury's award of damages is excessive, it may grant the defendant a new trial. Gasperini v. Center for Humanities, Inc., 518 U.S. 415, 433, 116 S.Ct. 2211, 135 L.Ed.2d 659 (1996).

A federal court's power to "order" a remittitur grew out of this authority to grant a new trial. A court which believes the jury's verdict is excessive may order a new trial unless the plaintiff agrees to remit a portion of the jury's award. * * *

The Seventh Amendment requires, however, that the plaintiff be given the option of a new trial in lieu of remitting a portion of the jury's award. * * * If the plaintiff does not consent to the remittitur, the court has no alternative but to order a new trial.

In this case, however, that did not happen. This reduction was neither consented to nor rejected in favor of a new trial. Rather, the district court entered reduced judgments totaling $4.35 million in punitive damages, without seeking property owners' consent nor affording them the option of electing a new trial. * * *

In sum, we have for review an "order of remittitur" which has neither been consented to nor rejected by property owners. * * *

In TXO Production Corp. v. Alliance Resources Corp., 509 U.S. 443, 454, 113 S.Ct. 2711, 125 L.Ed.2d 366 (1993), the Supreme Court held that the due process clause prohibits a state from imposing a "grossly excessive" punishment on a tortfeasor. Three years later, in *BMW*, the Court reversed a punitive damage award because it was unconstitutionally excessive. The Court held that the Constitution provides an upper limit on punitive damage awards so that a person has "fair notice not only of the conduct that will subject him to punishment but also of the severity of the penalty that a State may impose." Id. at 574, 116 S.Ct. 1589.

No one would dispute that the court, not the jury, has the responsibility for determining this constitutional limit. Courts decide questions of law, not juries. The real issue, therefore, is whether the court may enter judgment for a constitutionally reduced award without plaintiff's consent. So put, the question answers itself. Plaintiff's consent is irrelevant if the Constitution requires the reduction.

A constitutionally reduced verdict, therefore, is really not a remittitur at all. A remittitur is a substitution of the court's judgment for that of the jury regarding the appropriate award of damages. The court orders a remittitur when it believes the jury's award is unreasonable on the facts. A constitutional reduction, on the other hand, is a determination that the law does not permit the award. Unlike a remittitur, which is discretionary with the court and which we review for an abuse of discretion, *Gasperini,* 518 U.S. at 435, 116 S.Ct. 2211, a court has a mandatory duty to correct an unconstitutionally excessive verdict so that it conforms to the requirements of the due process clause. *BMW,* 517 U.S. at 585, 116 S.Ct. 1589.

We conclude that, upon determination of the constitutional limit on a particular award, the district court may enter a judgment for that amount as a matter of law. * * * Thus, a court proceeds under Rule 50, not Rule 59, in the entry of judgment for a constitutionally reduced award and the Seventh Amendment is not implicated in this legal exercise. * * *

In this case, the district court held that the $15 million punitive damage award was unconstitutionally excessive and entered judgments totaling $4.35 million. * * * Accordingly, we hold that the district court correctly entered judgments in this case and that these judgments are properly before us for review.

IV.

Next, we consider whether the district court correctly determined the punitive damages permitted by the Constitution in this case. Unless its award is at this constitutional "upper limit," it must be vacated.

1. THE CONSTITUTIONAL ANALYSIS

In *BMW*, the Supreme Court held that punitive damages may be so excessive as to be unconstitutional. The Court outlined a two-step process for determining when this has occurred. The first step is to marshal the facts which will inform our ultimate judgment regarding the constitutionality of the punitive damage award. Then, based upon these constitutionally relevant facts, we draw a legal conclusion as to whether the punitive damages awarded in the case are excessive.

The first step, then, is to identify the constitutionally relevant facts. The Supreme Court has instructed that punitive damages must be based upon conduct in a single state—the state where the tortious conduct occurred—and reflect a legitimate state interest in punishing and deterring that conduct. The Constitution also requires that the defendant had fair notice that its conduct could result in punitive damages and in the severity of the potential damages. *BMW* establishes three "guideposts" for determining whether the defendant had fair notice:

    1) the degree of reprehensibility of the defendant's conduct;

    2) the ratio of punitive damages to the actual harm inflicted on plaintiffs; and

    3) the comparison between punitive damages and potential civil or criminal penalties for defendant's conduct. Id. at 575, 116 S.Ct. 1589.

The district court in this case found that the conduct punished did occur in a single state and that this state—Georgia—has expressed a strong interest in deterring environmental pollution and in protecting the rights of property owners "to have water flow upon [their] land in its natural state free from adulteration." The court further found that:

    1) "it is absolutely clear * * * that the degree of reprehensibility [of CE's conduct] is not very severe;"

    2) the ratio of the punitive ($15 million) to the actual damages ($47,000) was 320:1; and

    3) the ratio of the $15 million award to the administrative penalty imposed upon CE ($10,000) was 1500:1.

The district court concluded that an award of $15 million was "grossly disproportionate" to both the actual damages and the administrative penalty. Since CE's conduct was "not very severe," the district court held that CE had no notice that such a disproportional amount might be awarded and, therefore, the punitive damage award was unconstitutionally excessive. The court reduced the punitive damages awarded to $4.35 million, the maximum it believed the Constitution permits in this case. * * *

2. THE STANDARD OF REVIEW

Although the Seventh Amendment limits appellate review of state-law remittiturs to an abuse of discretion standard, *Gasperini*, 518 U.S. at 435, 116 S.Ct. 2211, *BMW* makes clear that there is a constitutional limit on a punitive damage award beyond which neither the jury nor the court has any discretion to venture. The abuse of discretion standard is inapplicable where no discretion may be exercised.

The ultimate question whether a punitive damage award is constitutionally excessive is, of course, a legal issue. We review questions of law de novo. Therefore, whenever an award of punitive damages is asserted to have entered that "zone of arbitrariness that violates the Due Process Clause of the Fourteenth Amendment," *BMW*, 517 U.S. at 568, 116 S.Ct. 1589, we review the award de novo under federal constitutional standards. * * *

Review of a punitive damage award for constitutional error, therefore, requires first that we identify the state's interest in deterring the relevant conduct and the strength of that interest. Next, we review the district court's findings regarding the three *BMW* guideposts. To the extent that these are findings of fact, we review them for clear error. Finally, we determine de novo whether the punitive damage award is constitutionally excessive when measured by these guideposts.

In performing the latter assessment, the essential legal issue is whether the relevant facts of this case, as indicated by the various *BMW* factors, constitutionally support the punitive damage award, i.e., do these facts indicate that CE had adequate notice that its conduct might subject it to this punitive damage award. We will measure the adequacy of this notice by the degree of reprehensibility of CE's conduct, and the disparities between the actual damage it caused and the other available sanctions and the punitive damages that were ultimately awarded. In determining whether these disparities are constitutionally excessive, we will be informed by the strength of the state's interest in deterring CE's conduct.

V.

First, we find no error in the district court's findings that the conduct punished here occurred in a single state and that the Georgia statutes express a strong interest in deterring environmental pollution. This interest would support a substantial punitive award. To determine the maximum punitive award permitted by the Constitution in this case, we turn now to the district court's findings on the notice CE had regarding its potential liability.

1. REPREHENSIBILITY OF CE'S CONDUCT

The most important indicum of the reasonableness of a punitive damages award may be the degree of reprehensibility of the defendant's conduct. *BMW*, 517 U.S. at 575, 116 S.Ct. 1589. The relevant conduct of CE in this case involves only the four years preceding the filing of the property owners' complaint in August of 1992. The evidence was that, during that time, the mining site was not operated by CE. CE reacquired the property in 1986 from Pasco, but never resumed mining operations.

During the four years at issue, the district court found that CE put into effect a land reclamation plan, which was approved by the Georgia Environmental Protection Division, and which was designed to restore the property and prevent the problem of acidic rain water entering the streams flowing through its property. CE also cooperated with the Environmental Protection Division. Although its efforts were not entirely successful, the district court concluded that CE's "most egregious conduct was the failure to do more to prevent the acidic water problem."

The district court concluded that the degree of CE's reprehensibility was not great. Given the "developing" science of land reclamation which characterized the late 1980's, and CE's significant efforts in that regard, the district court held that there was not evidence in this case of "that high degree of culpability that warrants a substantial punitive damages award." *BMW*, 517 U.S. at 580, 116 S.Ct. 1589.

Although, under Georgia law, the jury must have found "specific intent to cause harm" to award punitive damages of this amount, the district court found that there was no direct evidence of such intent. The court concluded that the jury must have determined that CE's conduct exhibited a want of care rising to the level of conscious or deliberate indifference to the consequences of its actions. Specific intent to cause harm may properly be inferred from deliberate indifference, but the court concluded that CE's "deliberate indifference" did not constitute severe "reprehensibility" under *BMW*.

Furthermore, the district court found that none of the "aggravating factors associated with particularly reprehensible conduct," *BMW*, 517 U.S. at 576, 116 S.Ct. 1589, was present in this case. The district court found that:

> The evidence does not suggest that [CE] affirmatively engaged in prohibited conduct of any kind after it reacquired the property. It did not commit illegal acts, knowing or suspecting that the acts were illegal. In fact, [CE] responded to any criticisms or penalties levied against it by the Environmental Protection Division in a positive, more aggressive manner. Hence, there is no evidence that [CE] is a recidivist that continually repeats certain misconduct.

As there was ample evidence to support the district court's view of the evidence, we hold that its finding that CE's conduct was not highly reprehensible is not clearly erroneous.

2.   RATIO OF ACTUAL TO PUNITIVE DAMAGES

Punitive damages must bear a "reasonable relationship" to actual damages. *BMW*, 517 U.S. at 580, 116 S.Ct. 1589 (collecting cases). If the ratio of actual to punitive damages is too great, it is an indication that the defendant did not have adequate notice that its conduct might subject it to an award of this size. Id. at 574, 116 S.Ct. 1589 ("Elementary notions of fairness enshrined in our constitutional jurisprudence dictate that a person receive fair notice not only of the conduct that will subject him to punishment but also of the severity of the penalty that a State may impose.").

In this case, property owners were awarded an aggregate of $47,000 in actual damages. The aggregate $15 million punitive award, therefore, was almost 320 times the amount of actual damage. The district court concluded such a ratio was constitutionally excessive because it approached the 500:1 ratio found "breathtaking" by the Court in *BMW*. 517 U.S. at 583, 116 S.Ct. 1589. The district court's reduction to an aggregate of $4.35 million represents a ratio of 100:1.

3.   CIVIL OR CRIMINAL SANCTIONS FOR THE MISCONDUCT

There may also be a lack of adequate notice if the difference between the civil or criminal penalties that were or could have been imposed and the punitive damage award is too great. *BMW*, 517 U.S. at 584, 116 S.Ct. 1589. In this case, Georgia law provides for civil fines of up to $100,000 per day for pollution of its streams. O.C.G.A. §§ 12–5–20—12–5–53. The statute is administered by the Georgia Environmental Protection Division. The only fine it actually imposed on CE for the conduct at issue in this case was $10,000.

The district court selected the $10,000 actual fine imposed as the most relevant "other sanction" for comparison with the punitive damage award as required by *BMW's* third guidepost. We agree.

Whether a defendant had constitutionally adequate notice that his conduct might result in a particular damage award depends in large part upon the available civil and criminal penalties the state provides for such conduct. In *BMW*, the Court clearly stated that "a reviewing court engaged in determining whether an award of punitive damages is excessive should 'accord substantial deference' to legislative judgments concerning appropriate sanctions for the conduct at issue." 517 U.S. at 583, 116 S.Ct. 1589 (citations omitted).

If a statute provides for a range of penalties depending on the severity of the violation, however, it cannot be presumed that the defendant had notice that the state's interest in the specific conduct at issue in the case is represented by the maximum fine provided by the statute. On the contrary, the extent of the defendant's statutory notice is related to the degree of reprehensibility of his conduct. For example, if the defendant had emptied a bottle of soda pop into a Georgia stream, it cannot reasonably be said that he was on notice he could be fined $100,000. Similarly, constitutionally adequate notice of potential punitive damage liability in a particular case depends upon whether this defendant had reason to believe that his specific conduct could result in a particular damage award.

The district court found that the degree of reprehensibility of CE's conduct was not severe. Furthermore, Georgia fined CE's conduct an amount far below the maximum permitted under its statute. The record reveals no indication that the $10,000 fine did not represent the strength of Georgia's interest in CE's conduct. Under these circumstances, the most relevant comparison under the third *BMW* guidepost is between the actual fine imposed and the punitive damage award. Where the state has actually imposed a penalty for the conduct at issue, the district court may choose to look to that penalty as an indication of the "legislative judgment" as to the "appropriate sanctions for the conduct at issue." *BMW*, 517 U.S. at 583, 116 S.Ct. 1589.

The remitted punitive award of $15 million was 1500 times the amount of the $10,000 Georgia fine. The district court concluded that $15 million was "grossly disproportionate to the penalties that [CE] has suffered or has come to expect" and "would not comport with the fair notice requirements of the Constitution." The court's reduction of the punitive damages to $4.35 million represents an award 400 times greater than the actual civil sanction.

In sum, the district court found CE's conduct not very reprehensible, with no aggravating factors present. It found the $15 million punitive damage award to be 1500 times the administrative sanction imposed and 320 times the actual damages found by the jury. The district court reduced the $15 million to an aggregate of $4.35 million, thereby reducing the relevant ratios to 400:1 and 100:1. We consider now whether the district court erred in holding that $4.35 million is the maximum amount of punitive damages the Constitution permits in this case.

VI.

A punitive damage award may not be "grossly out of proportion to the severity of the offense." *BMW*, 517 U.S. at 576, 116 S.Ct. 1589. We agree with the district court that the initial disparities in the relevant ratios were genuinely "shocking," and that $15 million in punitive damages was grossly excessive.

The reduction to $4.35 million also produced ratios which were gross enough to "raise a suspicious judicial eyebrow." Id. (quoting TXO Production Corp. v. Alliance Resources Corp., 509 U.S. 443 482, 113 S.Ct. 2711, 125 L.Ed.2d 366 (1993)). There is, however, no "mathematical bright line between the constitutionally acceptable and the constitutionally unacceptable that would fit every case." Id. (quoting Pacific Mut. Life Ins. Co. v. Haslip, 499 U.S. 1, 18, 111 S.Ct. 1032, 113 L.Ed.2d 1 (1991)). In examining the ratio between the actual damages and the punitive award in a given case, a "general concern of reasonableness * * * properly enter[s] into the constitutional calculus." Id.

The Supreme Court recognized in *BMW* that there would be times when a substantial disparity between actual damages and the punitive award would be expected and, therefore, not constitutionally excessive. * * *

This is such a case. The actual damages awarded were relatively small; yet the state's interest in deterring the conduct—environmental pollution—is strong. In order to achieve this goal, ratios higher than might otherwise be acceptable are justified. * * *

Furthermore, in promoting deterrence, the economic wealth of a tortfeasor may be considered. TXO Production Corp. v. Alliance Resources Corp., 509 U.S. 443, 462 n. 28, 113 S.Ct. 2711, 125 L.Ed.2d 366 (1993). A bigger award is needed to "attract the * * * attention" of a large corporation. CE is a large and extremely wealthy international corporation. It is not unlikely that having to pay $4.35 million in punitive damages would not make the company newsletter.[3] It should, however, attract the attention of whomever is in charge of the corporation's daily decisions regarding environmental protection, and would, no doubt, bear heavily upon regional or local managers where failures to regard consequences would be expected to subject their employer to loss. The $4.35 million award is not so large, however, as to "implicate[ ] the federal interest in preventing individual States from imposing undue burdens on interstate commerce." *BMW*, 517 U.S. at 585, 116 S.Ct. 1589.

We conclude therefore, that substantial punitive damages are warranted for deterrence and, since the actual damages are quite small, must be somewhat disproportional to the actual damage award. The ratio of the district court's reduced award of $4.35 million to the administrative fine of $10,000 is significant, but the Georgia statutes provided fair notice to CE that it might be subject to a substantial penalty for pollution of the streams running though its property. The 100:1 ratio of the punitive to the actual damages is at the upper limits of the Constitution, but is justified by the need to deter this and other large organizations from a "pollute and pay" environmental policy. Under the circumstances of this case, then, $4.35 million in punitive damages is not so disproportional as to offend the "[e]lementary notions of fairness enshrined in our constitutional jurisprudence." *BMW*, 517 U.S. at 574, 116 S.Ct. 1589.

We hold, therefore, that $15 million was a constitutionally excessive punitive damage award in this case, and the district court correctly

---

3. Such a ratio might not be a direct deterrence to stockholders; it may not attract the attention of the board of directors. But it is not the act or omission of stockholders or directors that pollutes. The decision-maker on the scene whose conduct subjects the company to $4.5 million in damages is acutely aware that this loss affects the year-end reports of the department or division within which he works. An award sufficient to attract the attention of the department head in charge of the local decision-maker can be instrumental in deterring local disregard of the rights of others. In that sense, vast international corporations are made up of many smaller enterprises and deterrence of the small may be sufficient.

reduced it to $4.35 million, the maximum the Constitution permits in this case.

Notes and Questions

1. *Reprehensibility of Defendant's Conduct*: There is no question that the egregiousness of what the defendant did is the primary of the three "guideposts." How would you evaluate CE's conduct in this case? Very reprehensible? Moderately? Slightly? Not at all? Presumably, reasonable minds (such as those of students) could disagree over this question. What alteration in the facts might cause you to make a higher award? What if the defendant made deliberately false statements to government officials or plaintiffs? What if it engaged in a concealment or cover-up of its activities or of relevant evidence? What if it deposited the "tailings" in the containment area desiring that rain would carry acid away to plaintiffs' property, out of some motive for revenge? Is CE a case of "intentional" dumping or releasing contaminants, or a case of negligence or inadvertence only?

Did CE possess knowledge or awareness that its activities were producing harm to the streams or invading plaintiffs' rights to the beneficial use of their land? How relevant is it that, as noted in footnote 2, plaintiffs did not live on the property? In *BMW* the court stated that the highest reprehensibility would be assigned to conduct that violated safety and personal injury interests. Did CE knowingly violate a Georgia environmental statute?

Is this a case where defendant failed to investigate whether its activities were producing harm to others and is charged with the knowledge that such an investigation would reveal?

2. *Statutory Conduct Standard*: Recall that under the Georgia punitive damages statutes, the jury had to find, before any punitive damages could be awarded, that CE's actions showed willful misconduct, malice, fraud, wantonness, oppression, or that entire want of care which would raise the presumption of "conscious indifference to consequences." O.C.G.A. § 51–12–5.1(b). Which word or phrase in the statute best describes CE's actions? Might it be "conscious indifference"?

However, for the jury to award punitive damages above $250,000 per plaintiff it had to also find by clear and convincing evidence that CE acted "with the specific intent to cause harm." What evidence supported such a finding? The award of $4.35 million converts to roughly a bit over $250,000 per plaintiff.

The Georgia statutory language is common. Most jurisdictions have adopted a dual standard for the award of punitive damages: (1) malice, spite, intent to harm; or (2) recklessness, conscious indifference, flagrant disregard. See Gerald W. Boston, Punitive Damages in Tort Law, ch. 2 (1996).

3. *Alternatives Available to Defendant*: Did CE have available to it the means or methods by which to reduce or eliminate or abate the risk or harm from its activities? What relevance should be assigned to the fact that CE was engaging in reclamation efforts and cooperating with government agencies?

4. *Exxon Valdez*: A federal district court issued 12 rulings upholding $5 billion in punitive damages and $289 million in compensatory damages against Exxon Corp., denying the company's requests for a new trial, and upholding other pretrial rulings in litigation involving the 1989 oil spill from the Exxon Valdez into Prince William Sound, Alaska. The court upheld the jury's determination that Exxon was liable for the acts of the ship's captain based on the finding that he acted in a managerial capacity and that the act of leaving the bridge was within the scope of his employment. The court upheld its instruction to the jury that it could award punitive damages for conduct that manifests "reckless disregard for the rights of others." The court properly instructed the jury to use the "preponderance of the evidence" standard for awarding such damages, rather than the "clear and convincing evidence" standard. The court held that the awards were neither grossly excessive nor a violation of due process. Also, there was substantial evidence to allow a reasonable jury to find that Exxon's conduct was reckless. The district court in Alaska said that Exxon was found to have acted recklessly and that evidence showed it knew transporting oil could be catastrophic. "The evidence also established that Captain Hazelwood suffered from an alcohol abuse problem" and was drunk at the time, the judge said.

The jury could have found that Exxon, with knowledge of the risks, placed a relapsed alcoholic in charge, Judge Holland said, adding that Exxon inadequately monitored the captain and caused crew fatigue by work schedules. "The evidence established that with relatively small expense * * * Exxon could have insured that its * * * crews were rested and not captained by relapsed alcohol abusers."

The court stated that, "Exxon has not established that the only possible conclusion is that neither Exxon nor Hazelwood acted recklessly." The court continued stating that the verdict "was supported by substantial evidence." *In re Exxon Valdez*, 1995 WL 527989, 1995 WL 527988 (D.Alaska 1995).

5. The Supreme Court has also waded in on the question of whether federal appeals court review of trial court punitive damage awards should be conducted on a deferential abuse of discretion standard or be subjected to the more rigorous de novo review. This and associated developments are discussed in the following excerpt from M. Stuart Madden, Renegade Conduct and Punitive Damages in Tort, 53 S.C.L. Rev. 1175 (2002):

> Cooper Industries, Inc. v. Leatherman Tool Group., Inc., 532 U.S. 424 (2001) involved two manufacturers of multifunction hand tools, both seeking to improve the venerable Swiss army knife. Leatherman's tool enjoyed the dominant market position at the time Cooper undertook to introduce its new product. In the course of promoting its new product, but before commencing its actual production and sale, Cooper used in its advertising materials photographs of a modification of the Leatherman product. Leatherman filed trade-dress infringement, unfair competition, and false advertising claims under the Lanham Act, 15 U.S.C. § 1125(a), and common law claims of unfair competition. The jury awarded $50,000 in actual damages and entered a $4.5 million punitive damage verdict as well. The trial court rejected Cooper's post-trial claims that the punitive damage award was "grossly excessive,"

and the Ninth Circuit Court of Appeals affirmed the punitive damages award, finding that the trial court had not "abuse[d] its discretion in declining to reduce the amount."

The Supreme Court granted certiorari on the single issue of whether the appellate court's application of an "abuse of discretion" standard in its review was proper, as contrasted with review on a de novo basis. Reversing and remanding, the Court held that in matters of appellate review of punitive damage awards, federal appeals courts should employ de novo review. In so doing, the Court principally focused on three considerations: (1) the departure of punitive damage awards from ordinary "findings of fact" associated with awards of compensatory damages; (2) the respective capacities of the trial and appellate courts to apply the indicia established in BMW of North America, Inc. v. Gore.; and (3) the virtues of appellate court de novo review in the achievement of a semblance of uniformity and predictability in allowable exemplary damage awards.

1. *Exemplary Awards Differ From Compensatory Damage Findings of Fact*

The Seventh Amendment's Re-examination Clause "controls the allocation of authority to review verdicts", Gasperini v. Ctr. for Humanities, Inc., 518 U.S. 415, 432 (1996), and provides that "no fact tried by jury, shall be otherwise re-examined in any Court of the United States, than according to the rules of the common law." It has been accepted generally that the Re-examination Clause is not violated by appellate review applying a deferential "clearly erroneous" standard. Cooper Indus., Inc., 532 U.S. at 437–40. Central to the Court's analysis in Cooper was its conclusion that punitive damage awards differ from ordinary jury findings of fact, and therefore may be subject to appellate review without the constraints of the Re-examination Clause. In the Court's words, "[u]nlike the measure of actual damages suffered, which presents a question of historical or predictive fact, ... the level of punitive damages is not really a 'fact' 'tried' by the jury." Rather, in the Court's view, awards of exemplary damages are "expression[s] of ... moral condemnation" intended to "punish reprehensible conduct and to deter its future occurrence."

2. *Respective Trial and Appellate Court Capacity*

While the "Jury Trial" and Re-examination Clauses make essential obeisances to the trial court's superior position in evaluating what proof is to be admitted into evidence and whether sufficient support exists for conventional findings of fact, the Court's conclusion which vantage point—that of the trial court or that of the appellate court—was superior for that awards of exemplary damages do not constitute conventional findings of fact invited it to consider application of the Gore factors. If the appeals courts were better able to apply the Gore factors, such a conclusion would bolster the argument that the "clearly erroneous" standard of review would be less warranted, and hence more support for de novo review by the appeals court.

Taking the Gore factors seriatim, the Court conceded that as to the first Gore factor requiring consideration of the degree of reprehensibility of the defendant's conduct, the trial courts "have a somewhat superior vantage over courts of appeals," but added "that the advantage exists primarily with respect to issues turning on witness credibility and demeanor."

As to the second Gore factor, relating to "the disparity between the harm (or potential harm) suffered by the plaintiff and the punitive damage award," the Court determined that "[t]rial courts and appellate courts seem equally capable of analyzing the second factor." Lastly, the third factor's call for consideration of "the difference between the punitive damages awarded by the jury and the civil penalties authorized or imposed in comparable cases" called, in the Court's view, "for a broad legal comparison ... more suited to the expertise of appellate courts." Taken in the aggregate, the majority concluded that "[c]onsiderations of institutional competence therefore fail to tip the balance in favor of [the] deferential [clearly erroneous standard of] review."

3. *The Value of Uniformity and Predictability*

The Court also highlighted the objectives of bringing uniformity and predictability to review of exemplary damage awards. It stated that "[i]ndependent review is therefore necessary if appellate courts are to maintain control of, and to clarify, the legal principles." Quoting Justice Breyer's concurrence in Gore, the Court emphasized that "[r]equiring the application of law, rather than a decisionmaker's caprice, does more than simply provide citizens notice of what actions might subject them to punishment; it also helps to assure the uniform treatment of similarly situated persons that is the essence of law itself."

4. *Justice Ginsberg's Dissent*

The gravamen of Justice Ginsberg's dissent was that the majority erred in finding that awards of punitive damages were not "findings of fact" within the reach of the Re-examination Clause. Adopting the majority's language that a telling characteristic of findings of fact is their character as "historical or predictive fact," Justice Ginsberg conceded that exemplary awards involved a panoply of considerations. However, she continued by urging that while punitive awards differed from compensatory awards in the cluster of considerations that make up the jury verdict, the difference was a matter of degree and not of kind. "[T]here can be no question that a jury's verdict on punitive damages is fundamentally dependent on determinations we characterize as factfindings," she wrote, using as examples "the extent of harm or potential harm caused by the defendant's misconduct, whether the defendant acted in good faith, whether the misconduct was an individual instance or part of a broader pattern, [and] whether the defendant behaved negligently, recklessly, or maliciously."

Justice Ginsburg asserted that the inexact relation between an award of punitive damages and a compensatory damage award should not vitiate the underlying reality that each is tethered to jury findings of fact. Using noneconomic damages (usually pain and suffering) as a basis for comparison, Justice Ginsberg suggested that "[o]ne million dollars' worth of pain and suffering does not exist as a 'fact' in the world any more or less than one million dollars' worth of moral outrage. Both derive their meaning from a set of underlying facts as determined by a jury. If one set of quantification is properly regarded as factfinding, it seems to me that the other should be so regarded as well."

5. *What Will Be The Impact of Cooper?*

In anticipatory humility, the Cooper majority concurred with the dissent in admitting that the redefined appellate role of de novo review "will affect the result of the Gore analysis in only a relatively small number of cases[,]" and thus there is reason to surmise that the impact of Cooper will not materially change the quantity of punitive damage awards handed down by juries, nor the quantum of the individual awards. Federal trial court judges now have years of experience in applying the Gore factors, and there has been no indication that they have failed to execute the Supreme Court's charge in that decision as faithfully as they must any other instruction from the Court, including the gratuitously minimized trial court capacity to evaluate "the difference between the punitive damages awarded by the jury and the civil penalties authorized or imposed in comparable cases."

It is delicious, nonetheless, to speculate whether the trial bar will develop special interrogatories for jurors in exemplary award cases in an effort to provide a fact-based underpinning that could move a court to conclude that the award of exemplary damages was indeed a conclusion based upon "historic or predictive fact," and thus akin to conventional compensatory damage awards suited to "clearly erroneous," rather than de novo, review.

CONCLUSION

An irony of punitive damages is that the tort remedy intended as a prophylaxis for conduct so aggravated as to require extraordinary, noncompensatory measures for its containment will itself continue to prompt vigorous state and constitutional law restraints—a modern genie in the bottle. While abolishing punitive damages altogether remains an option to state legislatures, most states will almost certainly continue to preserve exemplary awards for truly outrageous conduct as a necessary instrument in correcting the under-deterrence of ordinary compensatory damages. At the same time, states can be expected to experiment with various forms of limitations, or develop new ones, to ameliorate the claimed overdeterrence risks of broad jury discretion in the entry of such awards.

The Due Process and Excessive Fines Clauses importantly frame the boundaries of permissible awards in terms that hearken to conventional fairness goals of remedies for avoidable accidents. The Haslip, TXO, Gore, and Cooper decisions establish the Supreme Court's position that while constitutionally lawful, important substantive restrictions and mechanisms for the consistent application of those restrictions are necessary dimensions of the continued application of exemplary awards. In essence, the Supreme Court has imposed a constitutional requirement that punitive damage awards will only pass constitutional muster after successful passage through several fairness checkpoints.

   In tort law's lengthy development of governing liability for causing injurious and avoidable accidents, it has been a truism that common law causes of actions and remedies have developed by accretion, with new remedies or limitations advanced upon the presentation of new facts, developing societal expectations, or both. At the same time, state legislatures have not balked at the task of sculpting or placing limitations upon such judicially-created remedies. In no area of tort law is the influence of state legislative and United States constitutional collaboration more focused than in the law of exemplary damages. In a petrie dish in which the these creative and restrictive agents alike have been introduced, each modifying, retarding, or enhancing the other, will be witnessed the continuing evolution of our modern law of punitive damages.

Chapter Six

ENVIRONMENTAL STATUTORY REGULATION AND THE COMMON LAW: PREEMPTION AND IMPLIED RIGHTS

A. GENERAL PRINCIPLES OF FEDERAL PRECLUSION AND ENHANCEMENT OF PRIVATE RIGHTS

1. INTRODUCTION

The law of nuisance, negligence, and strict liability for abnormally dangerous activities is affected today by numerous state and federal environmental statutes, along with volumes of regulations affecting the quality of the air, the purity of the water, control of toxic substances, and disposal of hazardous wastes.

At common law and early in this century, the private rights of action available primarily under nuisance, public or private, trespass, and negligence stood as the sole remedies for environmental or toxic harm. With the adoption of statutory and regulatory schemes, the question arises as to how those statutes and regulations affect the rights and remedies of private parties to maintain tort actions.

There are significant differences between the structure and workings of the common law tort system and the structure and operation of the statutory environmental schemes. Choosing one example, the law of nuisance is thought of as a body of private law, subject to enforcement by private individuals, among others. Environmental regulation, on the other hand, is regarded as public law, with enforcement vested principally in public officials. The law of nuisance consists of general, broad and abstract principles of unreasonable interferences, applicable to any activity. The regulatory structure, in contrast, is highly particularized, detailed and expected to govern well-defined kinds of activity. In nuisance, plaintiff's rights are exclusively determined by courts of general jurisdiction. To be contrasted, the regulatory structure is drafted, enforced and adjudicated within regulatory agencies and under the supervision of officials commanding technical expertise in particular, and often quite specialized, areas of regulation.

While these two systems—one private and one public—can and do operate independently and concurrently, the practical pressure for some level of coordination between the two systems is powerful. The interrelationship between the two is the topic of this Chapter.

2. REGULATION AS ENHANCING COMMON LAW RIGHTS

A statute or regulation may function offensively in private litigation. The private litigant may seek to utilize the statutory mandates by pleading and proving a defendant's violations in the private lawsuit seeking common law remedies of damages or abatement. Alternatively, where the private litigant focuses on obtaining redress for "public" wrongs, she functions as a "private attorney general," supplementing the regulatory machinery in securing compliance.

In addition, the statute and accompanying regulations may themselves expressly provide for citizen actions against violators. Many environmental statutes do so, more often authorizing private actions for equitable relief, as distinct from actions for damages. But even where the legislature is silent about citizen suits, courts may still permit private enforcement actions by one of two means. First, courts may find that a private right of action is implied in the statutory scheme. An implied right to sue is said to turn on whether the would-be plaintiff is one of a class specially benefitted by the statute, and requires an analysis of legislative intent, underlying purposes of the statute, and the likely contribution of private enforcers to fulfillment of the statutory objectives.

Second, courts may view highly specific regulatory standards as an apt way of crystallizing broad common law principles, as in the doctrine of negligence per se. In the latter setting, the private suit retains its common law character, but statutory standards operate within it, in terms of proof or presumptions, to govern or guide decisions. One salient difference is that an implied right under a federal statute gives rise to a federal claim, while suits at common law under negligence per se or related principles are normally matters for state courts or federal courts sitting in diversity jurisdiction.

Citizen suit provisions, a dramatically progressive phenomenon introduced earlier at Chapter 3 B. 7. c, may have jurisdictional prerequisites, including notice and standing provisions, that can operate as "traps for the unwary," as that phrase was used in Greenman v. Yuba Power Products, 59 Cal.2d 57, 27 Cal.Rptr. 697, 377 P.2d 897 (Cal. 1962). The following decision pertaining to, inter alia, citizen suite notice provisions under the Clean Water Act, is revealing:

AMERICAN CANOE ASSOC. v. DISTRICT OF COLUMBIA WATER AND SEWER AUTHORITY

United States District Court for the District of Columbia, 2004.
306 F.Supp.2d 30.

OPINION BY: Henry H Kennedy, Jr.

MEMORANDUM OPINION

This action is brought under the citizen suit provision, 33 U.S.C. § 1365, of the Federal Water Pollution Control Act ("Clean Water Act" or "CWA"), 33 U.S.C. §§ 1251–1387. Plaintiffs American Canoe Association, Inc., Potomac Conservancy, Inc., and Canoe Cruisers Association of Greater Washington, Inc. (collectively "plaintiffs") charge that the District of Columbia Water and Sewer Authority ("WASA"), an independent authority of the District of Columbia government, has violated the terms and conditions of a permit, National Pollutant Discharge Elimination System ("NPDES") permit number DC0021199 ("Permit"), issued to WASA by the [EPA] to operate the Potomac Interceptor Sewer and Upper Potomac Interceptor Relief Sewer. Alleging that these permit violations have resulted in the emission of hydrogen sulfide from the sewers, plaintiffs seek injunctive and other relief. Before the court are the parties' cross-motions for summary judgment [Cc] Upon consideration of the motions, the respective oppositions thereto, and the record of this case, the court concludes that defendant's motion for summary judgment must be granted and plaintiffs' motion for summary judgment must be denied.

I. BACKGROUND

A. Clean Water Act

In passing the Federal Water Pollution Control Act, 33 U.S.C. §§ 1251–1387, Congress established a comprehensive regulatory scheme to control the discharge of waste and pollutants into the nation's navigable waters. The Act's objective is to "restore and maintain the chemical, physical, and biological integrity of the Nation's waters." 33 U.S.C. § 1251. The CWA makes unlawful any pollutant discharges into navigable waters, except as authorized by other provisions of the CWA, 33 U.S.C. §§ 1311(a), 1342, and requires the promulgation of effluent limitations which set the maximum allowable quantities, rates and concentrations of different pollutants that may be discharged into waters. 33 U.S.C. § 1362(11). The EPA enforces the CWA through the National Pollutant Discharge Elimination System, under which the EPA has the discretion to issue permits, or delegate that power to states, for the discharge of otherwise prohibited effluents, after a public hearing and subject to conditions set by the EPA. 33 U.S.C. § 1342(a)(1).

While the EPA and states generally enforce NPDES permit terms, private citizens may also enforce the CWA: "Any citizen may commence a civil action on his own behalf ... against any person ... who is alleged to be in violation of ... an effluent standard or limitation under this chapter...." 33 U.S.C. § 1365(a). The CWA defines "citizen" as "a person or persons having an interest which is or may be adversely affected." 33 U.S.C. § 1365(g). Further, under the citizen suit provision, "effluent standard or limitation" includes "a permit or condition thereof issued under section 1342 [of the NPDES permiting regime]." 33 U.S.C. § 1365(f)(6).

B. Factual Background

WASA operates the Blue Plains Sewage Treatment Plant ("Blue Plains"), Potomac Interceptor Sewer ("PI"), and Upper Potomac Interceptor Relief Sewer ("UPI"), which together carry sewage from the District of Columbia and Loudoun, Montgomery, and Fairfax Counties, to Blue Plains for treatment. There are approximately 34 vents installed along the PI and UPI sewer mains. The EPA issued a NPDES permit to WASA on January 22, 1997 to operate the Blue Plains sewage collection system and related sewer interceptors and overflows. See [DES Permit No. DC0021189, Jan. 22, 1997) ("1997 Permit")]. Section II.B.1 of the permit ("M&O Clause") requires WASA to:

> properly operate, inspect and maintain all facilities and systems of treatment and control (and related appurtenances including sewers, intercepting chambers, interceptors, combined sewer overflows, pumping stations and emergency bypasses) which are installed or used by the permittee to achieve compliance with the conditions of this permit.

Id. at 9.

Plaintiffs claim that WASA has violated, and continues to violate, its 1997 Permit and, therefore, puts it in violation of 33 U.S.C. § 1342, which constitutes the NPDES program. More specifically, plaintiffs allege violation of the 1997 Permit's M&O Clause because WASA has failed to fulfill its obligation to the National Park Service ("Park Service" or "NPS") to install "odor controlled carbon filters" on vents located on Park Service property. Compl. P 18. [For general want of] "any sort of filtration system or other means of controlling hydrogen sulfide emissions," WASA is in violation of its permit. Furthermore, plaintiffs contend that the PI and UPI vents have emitted and continue to emit, intermittently, hydrogen sulfide, which directly and adversely affects the "health, economic, recreational, aesthetic and environmental interests" of plaintiffs and their members. [Id.]

On August 6, 1999, plaintiffs wrote WASA, the EPA, and other local and federal authorities to provide notice of the alleged violations and of plaintiffs' intent to pursue a citizen suit in federal district court. See Compl. at Ex. 1 (Bookbinder Ltr. to Williams, Linton & Johnson, Aug. 6, 1999). Shortly thereafter, on October 22, 1999, plaintiffs filed the present suit seeking a declaratory judgment that WASA has violated and continues to violate its permit and the CWA, an injunction against further violations, an order requiring WASA to conduct monitoring of the PI and UPI sewer vents, appropriate civil penalties, and attorneys' and expert witnesses' fees.

In December 1999, WASA filed a motion to dismiss on the grounds that (1) plaintiffs had no Article III standing to bring a suit, [Cc]; (2) plaintiffs failed to state a claim for which relief can be granted, [Cc]; and (3) the statute of limitations barred plaintiffs' action. [Cc] In its November 19, 2000 order, this court denied WASA's motions to dismiss. ["Nov. 2000 Order"] After engaging in discovery, the parties filed the cross-motions for summary judgment presently before the court.

II. ANALYSIS

A. Legal Standards

[The court's description of the standards for granting summary, and that of the effect of a previous motion to dismiss, are omitted.]

B. Jurisdiction

Jurisdiction is a threshold matter without which this court has no authority to decide other potentially dispositive issues in this case. [Cc] Therefore, before considering the parties' cross-motions for summary judgment on the merits, the court must consider the two jurisdictional issues raised by WASA-notice and standing. The notice argument did not appear in WASA's motion to dismiss. The standing argument was denied in the court's previous order, see Nov. 2000 Order at 3–9, but the issue merits further discussion because WASA introduces new evidence and cites new cases decided after the court's order.

1. Notice

The CWA's citizen suit provision requires that a plaintiff provide notice to alleged violators of the Act and provide them 60 days to respond before bringing suit. 33 U.S.C. § 1365(b). Federal regulations require that the notice letter include certain items, including inter alia, "sufficient information to permit the recipient to identify the specific requirement alleged to have been violated" and "the date or dates of such violation." 40 C.F.R. § 135.12(a). Strict compliance with this provision is a mandatory jurisdictional prerequisite for a citizen suit. Nat'l Parks Conservation Ass'n, Inc. v. Tenn. Valley Auth., 175 F.Supp.2d 1071, 1077 (E.D. Tenn. 2001). WASA claims that plaintiffs provided defective notice before bringing the present suit. Specifically, WASA alleges that plaintiffs notice letter failed to provide specific information on (1) the dates of alleged violations and (2) pollutants discharged unlawfully. These arguments are without merit.

WASA alleges that plaintiffs fail to identify precise dates on which odors were emitted from the PI. Plaintiffs notice letter alleged that WASA "has and continues to violate" its NPDES permit by failing to maintain vents and vent filters on the Potomac Interceptor. See [Bookbinder Ltr. to Williams, Linton & Johnson, Aug. 6, 1999]. Reference to ongoing violations is sufficiently specific notice. See Natural Resources

Def. Council, Inc. v. Southwest Marine, Inc., 236 F.3d 985, 996 (9th Cir.2000) (holding that allegation of ongoing wrongdoing, a failure "to prepare and implement plans that were required by ... permit," provided defendant sufficient notice of specific date under 40 C.F.R. § 135.3(a)). WASA cites one case in which a notice letter containing allegations of repeated, if intermittent, emissions was deemed insufficient warning for the purposes of a regulation analogous to 40 C.F.R. § 135.12(a). See [Nat'l Parks Conservation Ass'n, 175 F.Supp.2d at 1077 (analyzing similar regulation, 40 C.F.R. § 54.3(b), promulgated pursuant to the Clean Air Act)]. That case, however, is distinguishable. While the hydrogen sulfide odor emanating from the PI's vents is intermittent, plaintiffs' notice letter alleged an ongoing, and likely future, failure to properly maintain carbon filters on vents. Def.'s App. at 1288 (alleging past and continuing failure to properly operate and maintain vents on the PI and UPI). The plaintiffs in National Parks Conservation Association, by contrast, alleged no such ongoing, current failure to act but, instead, alleged discrete, past emissions violations without identifying dates, though exact dates were critical to determining whether Clean Air Act violations had occurred at all. See 175 F.Supp.2d at 1076 (noting allegations of over 6,000 discrete violations of an air-opacity requirement of the Clean Air Act without the identifying particular dates, while the relevant permit excused such violations under certain factual situations and allowed unexcused violations 2% of the time). Plaintiffs' letter, therefore, provided WASA sufficient notice of the specific dates of violation.

Second, WASA argues that plaintiffs' letter failed to provide notice of the effluents WASA allegedly discharged in violation of its permit. Plaintiffs, according to the relevant regulation, must identify "the specific requirement alleged to have been violated." 40 C.F.R. § 135.12(a). See also 40 C.F.R. § 135.3(a) (requiring notice letter from plaintiff to include "sufficient information to permit the recipient to identify the specific standard, limitation, or order alleged to have been violated"). Nothing in § 135.12(a) requires a plaintiff's notice letter to identify specific effluents or pollutants when the complaint does not allege violations of effluent limitations. Yet WASA cites Catskill Mountains v. City of New York, 273 F.3d 481 (2d Cir.2001), out of context by claiming that it holds that all notice letters must identify specific effluents. [Cc] Rather, the case merely indicates that if a plaintiff alleges effluent limitation violations, her notice letter must identify particular effluents. [Cc] * * * Catskill Mountains says nothing about how specific notice must be when a citizen suit is brought to stop violations of non-effluent portions of a NPDES permit. [Cc] In this case, plaintiffs' notice letter clearly identified the harm they suffered, Def.'s App. at 1288 (alleging emission of hydrogen sulfide) and the specific permit provision they believe WASA violated. Id. at 1287–88 (alleging violation of the M&O clause, citing specifically to 1997 Permit at 19).

WASA claims that plaintiffs' letter did not indicate "what would constitute compliance," but neither § 135.12(a) nor case law requires that a notice letter identify a technical solution to the violation. A notice letter need not tell an alleged violator "what would constitute compliance." See Def.'s Mot. For Summ. J. at 56. Rather, § 135.12(a) merely gives alleged CWA violators the opportunity to "identify its own violations and bring itself into compliance voluntarily, thus making a costly lawsuit unnecessary." Catskill Mountains, 273 F.3d at 488. Plaintiffs' letter sufficed to give WASA proper notice and the opportunity to "bring itself into compliance" as required by federal regulations.

2. Standing

In its motion for summary judgment, WASA raises arguments which are variations on a theme it presented in its motion to dismiss-that plaintiffs have no standing to sue under the Clean Water Act because their claim is unrelated to the purposes of the Act, which regulates water quality. See Def.'s Mot. To Dismiss at 9 ("The disconnect between air emissions and waters protected by the Clean Water Act prevents [plaintiffs] from suing under the Clean Water Act ... because ... a complaint about odor is simply not a Clean Water Act case. . . ."); id. at 10–11 ("To be actionable, plaintiffs' allegations must implicate the purpose of the NPDES program, which is to regulate discharges of pollutants into national waters."). In the present iteration of this "zone of interests" argument, WASA provides factual materials and new cases to support its argument. Instead of explicitly raising standing as a jurisdictional issue, however, WASA requests summary judgment on the merits. Specifically, WASA argues that (1) the EPA has no authority or intent to regulate odor, Def.'s Mot. For Summ. J. at 33; (2) nuisance actions are not cognizable under the CWA, id. at 52; (3) an implied odor requirement would violate the Due Process Clause, id. at 38–44; and (4) the 1997 NPDES Permit does not require odor control.

* * *

The court previously denied WASA's motion to dismiss and held that plaintiffs had Article III standing under the CWA, 33 U.S.C. § 1365(f), to challenge any conditions of an NPDES permit, whether or not they state effluent limitations. See Nov. 2000 Order at 6–9. In finding plaintiffs' claims to be inside the zone of interests protected by the Clean Water Act, the court's previous order was based on two rationales, neither of which WASA directly challenges in its current summary judgment motion. First, it is well-established that whether a claim is within the zone of interests protected by a statute is to be evaluated "not by reference to the overall purpose of the Act in question, ... but by reference to the particular provision of law upon which the plaintiff relies." Bennett v. Spear, 520 U.S. 154, 175–76 (1997)[.] That the Act's overall purpose is to regulate water quality is irrelevant. What matters is that a plaintiff identifies a "particular provision of law" within the Act. Id.

Second, the court found that plaintiffs had standing because they alleged violation of a specific provision of the CWA. Nov. 2000 Order at 7. Plaintiffs invoked 33 U.S.C. § 1365(a)(1) and § 1342, and a plain reading of these statutes together indicates that a citizen may sue for any violation of an NPDES permit. See id. 7–8 & n.4. Further, the court found, id., that a body of persuasive authority supported this reading of the statutes. See Friends of the Earth, Inc. v. Gaston Copper Recycling Corp., 204 F.3d 149, 152 (4th Cir.2000) (en banc) (finding that 33 U.S.C. § 1365(f) allows citizen suits for "any term or condition of an approved [NPDES] permit"); Northwest Envtl. Advocates v. City of Portland, 56 F.3d 979, 986 (9th Cir.1995) ("The plain language of [§ 1365] authorizes citizens to enforce all permit conditions"); [Cc].

While WASA does not challenge these cases, WASA challenges the court's finding on several other grounds. WASA asks the court to reconsider its previous decision to decline to follow Citizens Coordinating Comm. on Friendship Heights, Inc. v. Washington Metro. Transit Auth., 247 U.S. App. D.C. 15, 765 F.2d 1169 (D.C. Cir. 1985) ("Friendship Heights"). See Nov. 2000 Order at 8–9 (evaluating and distinguishing inapposite Friendship Heights case). WASA argues that Friendship Heights controls, and that the factual distinction made in the previous order was erroneous. Id. ("The Friendship Heights plaintiff did allege the same type of [CWA] violation as Canoeists allege here. The Court should recognize that the claims in both cases are commonlaw tort claims ... dressed in sheep's clothing of a [CWA] citizen suit."). This court held that plaintiffs in the present action had clearly alleged a violation of an "effluent standard or limitation"—namely the M&O Clause of the 1997 Permit. See Nov. 2000 Order at 9.

The court's previous decision on this issue stands, though the court's analysis of Friendship Heights merits some elaboration. Simply put, Bennett supercedes Friendship Heights—at least as WASA understands the latter case. In Friendship Heights, the D.C. Circuit, in finding that the court had no jurisdiction to consider a claim involving the seepage of diesel fuel into a mall's basement, made reference to the general purpose of the CWA. See Friendship Heights, 765 F.2d at 1173 ("The Clean Water Act, however, was enacted not to create a federal tort of subterranean trespass but to protect navigable rivers and streams from pollution...."). However, Bennett bars precisely the sort of reasoning Friendship Heights applied in excluding the diesel fuel claims from the CWA's zone of interests. 520 U.S. at 175–76. In Bennett, the Supreme Court simply reaffirmed a well-established doctrine-that a plaintiff's suit need not "vindicate the overall purpose" of a statutory regime so long as her interest is protected by "the specific provision which they alleged had been violated." Id. at 176. Whether or not it cites Friendship Heights, WASA cannot prevail on its argument that the CWA provides standing only for claims directly involving the pollution of navigable waters. See [citing Friendship Heights, 765 F.2d at 1173], as support for the statement that "only discharges to navigable waters may be permitted under NPDES program."). [Cc] As a result, the court finds no reason to disturb its previous order.

WASA also cites new case law which, WASA claims, limits the CWA's jurisdictional reach. See Solid Waste Agency v. United States Army Corps of Eng'rs, 531 U.S. 159 (2001)). WASA argues that Solid Waste indicates that CWA jurisdiction "extends only to discharges interacting with navigable waters." Def.'s Mot. for Summ. J. at 35. However, Solid Waste did not purport to reinterpret the general scope of the CWA. Rather, the Court found that a rule promulgated by the Army Corps specifically exceeded the scope of 33 U.S.C. § 1344(a). [Cc] The Court rejected the Army Corps' regulation after an exegesis of the text and legislative background of § 1344(a) in particular. Solid Waste did not reject the Army Corps' rule because it failed to serve the CWA's general purpose. See 531 U.S. at 167–72 . Solid Waste simply does not support WASA's standing argument because it did not purport to limit the zone-of-interests protected by CWA provisions other than § 1344(a). [Cc] To apply Solid Waste, as WASA understands it, to the present case would be to contradict Bennett, 520 U.S. at 175–76 (requiring zone of interests arguments to be made by "by reference to the particular provision of law upon which the plaintiff relies"), which Solid Waste did not purport to supercede or overrule. [Cc] Indeed, it is difficult to see how Solid Waste can be applied to limit the general scope of the CWA when courts have, apparently, had difficulty applying the case to what it purportedly limited—rules promulgated under § 1344(a). See, e.g., FD & P Enters. v. United States Army Corps of Eng'rs, 239 F.Supp.2d 509, 513 (D.N.J. 2003) ("In the wake of Solid Waste, courts have struggled with evaluating the jurisdictional reach of [§ 1344(a)].").

Clearly, plaintiffs brought suit to stop the emission of odors. This fact alone does not bar plaintiffs' claim so long as they allege violation of a specific CWA or NPDES permit provision. Neither the CWA nor case law requires a direct connection between the violation of an NPDES permit provision and a plaintiff's injury. Indeed, Courts are not at liberty to write their own rules of evidence for environmental standing by crediting only direct evidence of impairment. Such elevated evidentiary hurdles are in no way mandated by Article III. Nor are they permitted by the Federal Rules of Evidence or the text of the Clean Water Act. It is in fact difficult to see how one can move from the [§ 1365(g), the citizen suit provision] standard of "an interest which is or may be adversely affected" to a standard of direct scientific proof of an observable negative impact on a waterway. Friends of the Earth, 204 F.3d at 149 (Wilkinson, C.J., writing for en banc court). So long as plaintiffs allege a violation of a specific provision of the CWA, they have standing to sue.

C. Statute of Limitations

WASA asserts, as it did in its motion to dismiss, that plaintiffs' claim is barred by the general five-year statute of limitations in 28 U.S.C. § 2462. Specifically, WASA claims that the limitations period begins to run at the moment of violation. See 3M v. Browner, 17 F.3d 1453, 1461 (D.C. Cir. 1994)). WASA provides that any "moment of violation," if one existed, occurred prior to 1987 when all carbon filters were removed. See Def.'s Mot. for Summ J. at 59[.] These arguments both ignore the law of the case and misunderstand 3M.

WASA raises essentially the same statute of limitations argument in its summary judgment motion as in its motion to dismiss. [Cc] The court found this argument meritless when it denied WASA's motion to dismiss: "It is patently clear that plaintiffs allege an ongoing continuous violation of WASA's permit." [See] L.E.A.D. Group of Berks v. Exide Corp., 1999 WL 124473, at *3–4, *19–20 (E.D. Pa. Feb. 19, 1999) and United States v. Reaves, 923 F.Supp. 1530, 1533 (M.D. Fla. 1996) as authority that five-year statute of limitations period does not run when defendant's (CWA violation is ongoing). WASA cites a number of "new" factual materials in its motion for summary judgment. [Cc] These sources support assertions WASA made in its motion to dismiss-that it had "abandoned proper maintenance of the alleged carbon filters several decades ago," that the statute of limitations began to run more than five years ago, and that the present action is therefore "barred." Def.'s Mot. to Dismiss at 24.

However, these essentially undisputed facts are immaterial to the law established by the court's previous order, which recognized that plaintiffs alleged ongoing violations of an NPDES permit. Nov. 2000 Order at 3 n.1. Furthermore, as plaintiffs argue, * * * 3M does not bar entirely an action brought to stop ongoing violations which began more than five years before the complaint was filed. Rather, 3M holds that § 2462 does not permit the collection of civil penalties for violations that took place more than five years before the action commenced. 17 F.3d at 1454–55. In 3M, the EPA filed suit in 1988 alleging repeated violations of the Toxic Substances Control Act, 15 U.S.C. §§ 2601–2629, from 1980 to 1986. Id. The D.C. Circuit precluded EPA from recovering civil penalties for violations between 1980 and 1983, five years before EPA instituted its lawsuit. See id. at 1463 ("EPA may not assess civil penalties against 3M for any violations . . . allegedly committed by the company more than five years before EPA commenced its proceeding"). Otherwise, 3M did not bar as untimely suits, by citizens or EPA, to stop alleged ongoing violations of an environmental statute. Id.

The 3M case does bar plaintiffs from recovering civil penalties for CWA violations WASA committed before 1994, five years before the commencement of the present action. But 3M does not bar the present suit as untimely. The court therefore denies WASA summary judgment on its statute of limitations argument.

D.   Interpretation of NPDES Permit Provision

Plaintiffs satisfied the zone of interests standing requirement by bringing suit under a particular CWA provision and alleging that WASA violated a specific NPDES permit provision. Plaintiffs were not required to show that the permit provision which they sought to enforce directly advanced the Act's general purpose of limiting effluents introduced into the nation's waterways. There is, however, a difference between alleging an injury sufficient to maintain standing, as a matter of jurisdiction, and providing enough evidence to prevail on summary judgment. See Piney Run Preservation Ass'n v. County Comm'rs of Carroll County, Maryland, 268 F.3d 255, 263–64, 270–71 (4th Cir.2001) (finding that while plaintiff association properly demonstrated standing, by tracing injury to defendant's actions, it failed to demonstrate that defendant's NPDES permit prohibited the alleged activity); [Cc]

In order to prevail on summary judgment, plaintiffs must demonstrate that there is no genuine issue of fact regarding their claim. FED. R. CIV. P. 56. In this case, they must demonstrate that WASA had an obligation, under the M&O Clause of the 1997 Permit, to operate and maintain carbon filters. See Compl. PP 18, 22. Plaintiffs must also show that WASA failed to comply with this obligation. Id. P 22. The court must deny plaintiff's summary judgment motion and must grant WASA's summary judgment motion. There is no genuine issue of material fact with regard to the claim that the 1997 Permit itself created an obligation to operate or maintain carbon filters; plaintiffs provide no materials to support this assertion, and all other evidence tend to contradict the assertion.

The interpretation of a NPDES permit provision is a question of law for the courts to decide. Natural Resources Def. Council, Inc. v. Texaco Refining & Mktg., Inc., 20 F.Supp.2d 700, 710 (D. Del. 1998). Indeed, another circuit found it "manifestly erroneous" to allow a jury to decide the meaning of an NPDES permit. United States v. Weitzenhoff, 35 F.3d 1275, 1286–87 (9th Cir.1993). Furthermore, courts must analyze a provision of a NPDES permit in the same manner it would review a contract or another legal document. Piney Run, 268 F.3d at 269; Northwest Envtl. Advocates, 56 F.3d at 983. That is, if a NPDES permit provision is unambiguous, that language controls. See Piney Run, 268 F.3d at 269; Northwest Envtl. Advocates, 56 F.3d at 982–83. But if the permit provision is ambiguous, the court may examine extrinsic evidence to uncover the provision's meaning. See Piney Run, 268 F.3d at 270; Northwest Envtl. Advocates, 56 F.3d at 982; Texaco, 20 F.Supp.2d at 709.

1. Express Text

The specific issue, at this point in the analysis, is whether the M&O Clause is ambiguous. If its meaning is clear upon an examination of its explicit terms, the provision is unambiguous. See Potomac Elec. Power Co. v. Mirant Corp, 251 F.Supp.2d 144, 148 (D.D.C. 2003). However, if its provisions are "reasonably or fairly susceptible of different constructions or interpretations," it is ambiguous. Id. The parties' cross-motions for summary judgment imply two different questions of ambiguity-first, in support of plaintiffs, does the M&O Clause unambiguously require WASA to maintain carbon filters? And, second, in support of WASA's argument, does the clause unambiguously excuse WASA from the same? Because the answer to both questions is no, the court finds the M&O Clause ambiguous.

The M&O Clause is a boilerplate provision lifted entirely from 40 C.F.R. § 122.41(e). Compare 1997 Permit at 19 with 40 C.F.R. § 122.41(e). It does not once mention carbon filters, hydrogen sulfide or anything of the sort. The M&O Clause cannot be read to expressly or unambiguously require the maintenance of filters on vents or odor control when it does not even mention them. See 1997 Permit at 19. Plaintiffs essentially concede this. Pls.' Cross–Mot. for Summ. J. at 35 ("Plaintiffs do not, and have never, claimed that the Permit contains express limits on hydrogen sulfide or odor.") (emphasis added). On the other hand, the M&O Clause does not expressly or unambiguously excuse WASA from maintaining carbon filters. The clause requires proper maintenance, operation and inspection of those "systems of treatment and control . . . which are installed or used by the permittee to achieve compliance with conditions of this permit." Id. Clearly, the permit requires WASA to properly maintain equipment used to comply with express permit provisions, e.g., effluent limitations. However, what remains unclear is whether "conditions of this permit" requires proper maintenance of equipment used to comply with implied permit provisions. The word "conditions" is not synonymous with "express terms" or "written terms"; its meaning is rather broader, something more akin to a general obligation, express or implied. See, e.g., WEBSTER'S NINTH NEW COLLEGIATE DICTIONARY (9th ed. 1985) (explaining "condition," in the first definition listed, to be "a premise upon which the fulfillment of an agreement depends"). Because the word "conditions" is susceptible to two reasonable readings-encompassing both express and implied obligations-the M&O Clause cannot be read to exclude the possibility that WASA was obligated to maintain equipment used to comply with implied permit provisions. Therefore, the court finds the M&O Clause ambiguous. As a result, the court may refer to extrinsic evidence in order to interpret the M&O Clause. See Piney Run, 268 F.3d at 270; Northwest Envtl. Advocates, 56 F.3d at 982.

It is troubling, though not dispositive, that plaintiffs concede that the M&O Clause does not explicitly require WASA to install carbon filters or control odor. In successful citizen suits brought to enforce non-effluent limitations, the prevailing plaintiffs seemed always able to identify violations of explicit permit provisions. See Friends of the Earth, 204 F.3d at 153, 157 (allowing suit to enforce express effluent limitations on discharge of cadmium, copper, iron, lead and zinc); Northwest Envtl. Advocates, 56 F.3d at 979, 986 (upholding enforcement of a NPDES permit that was "clear on its face in permitting [combined sewer overflow] events under specified conditions")[.] [Cc] At least one court indicated its reluctance to enforce specific, though implied, conditions through the general, but explicit, terms of a NPDES permit. See Piney Run, 268 F.3d at 271 (finding that neither the express terms, nor extrinsic evidence interpreting such terms, of a NPDES permit supported a reading that prohibited heat discharges). Persuasive authority, therefore, seems to require courts to examine extrinsic evidence in interpreting NPDES terms [Cc] while discouraging them from being eager to enforce implied obligations in permits

2.   Extrinsic Evidence

When the express terms of a legal document are ambiguous, extrinsic evidence may be used to interpret it. Specifically, extrinsic evidence is used to "determine the circumstances surrounding the making of the contract so as to ascertain what a reasonable person in the position of the parties would have thought the words meant." Potomac Elec., 251 F.Supp.2d at 150. Therefore, both objective and subjective (the intentions of the parties) evidence can be relevant. Id. at 148 (applying the "objective law of contracts whereby the written language embodying the terms of an agreement will govern ... , irrespective of the intent of the parties at the time they entered the contract, unless the written language is not susceptible of a clear and definite understanding. ...") [I]d at 149 ("The court should look to the intent of the parties entering into the agreement."). Relevant forms of extrinsic evidence include circumstances before, during, and surrounding the making of the contract, customary practices the parties had reason to know about, and the course of conduct of the parties. Id. at 150.

Plaintiffs' claim depends almost completely on extrinsic evidence, since the 1997 Permit says nothing specific-that is, nothing at all-about WASA's obligation to operate and maintain carbon filters. See generally 1997 Permit; Pls.' Cross–Mot. for Summ. J. at 35 (acknowledging that 1997 Permit contained no express limits on hydrogen sulfide or odor control requirements). The evidence upon which plaintiffs relies does show WASA's obligation, but only vis-a-vis the Park Service, to operate and maintain carbon filters; they fail to show that such obligations were enforceable, or were connected in any way to, the 1997 Permit. Other pieces of extrinsic evidence support the conclusion that none of the parties (EPA, Park Service, WASA) involved in executing relevant legal documents (1997 Permit, Park Service permits) intended the filter obligations in the Park Service permits to be enforced through 1997 Permit or CWA. The court analyzes, first, evidence that the Park Service obligated WASA to maintain carbon filters, and, second, the evidence that those obligations were enforceable through the 1997 Permit.

First, plaintiffs arguments hint that certain Park Service (not NPDES) permits requiring carbon filters are critical to proving their claim, for they create WASA's legal obligation in the first place. Plaintiffs claim that WASA's predecessor "needed NPS permission to construct, operate and maintain [the District of Columbia-based] portions of the system." [Cc] Further, plaintiffs maintain that "as a necessary precondition to the construction and operation of portions of the Potomac Interceptor, the Park Service required WASA to install and maintain carbon filters on all vents ... located on U.S. Government Property." [Cc] As a result, plaintiffs conclude that "an odor-control system on the PI vents was a necessary condition for the construction of PI [and] remains a necessary condition for its operation," and that WASA's predecessor acquiesced to these requirements. Pls.' Cross–Mot. for Summ. J. at 35. In other words, this is the "implied condition" which plaintiffs claim to be enforceable through the M&O Clause. The 1997 Permit requires WASA to properly maintain all equipment used to comply with "conditions of the permit," 1997 Permit at 19, and plaintiffs allege that one "necessary precondition" to the permit is odor control via carbon filter.

Indeed, the Park Service permits do show that WASA had duty to install filters. In 1962, the Park Service clearly required some form of odor management-either ventilation of odors off of Park lands or filtering of hydrogen sulfide-when it first allowed WASA's predecessor to construct the PI and UPI on federal lands. See Horne Ltr. to Bd. of Commissioners, Gov't of Dist. of Columbia at 1, 3 (Apr. 12, 1962) (requiring WASA predecessor to abide by all terms in the permit "as long as this facility is in place" and requiring, inter alia, that "all vent structures shall either be located off United States property or shall provide for odor controlled carbon filters."); [Cc] * * * Further, in 1999, the Park Service reminded WASA of its duty to maintain carbon filters just before plaintiffs initiated the present action:

> The permit issued to your agency on April 12, 1962, states in paragraph 16, "All vent structures shall either be located off United States property or shall provide for odor controlled carbon filters." The strong odor that is present seems to indicate that the carbon filters have failed and maintenance is required. Please arrange to correct this problem as soon as possible.

[See] (Faris Ltr. to Marcotte, Aug. 24, 1999). In response, WASA's General Manager Michael Marcotte neither confirmed nor denied having an obligation to maintain the filters, but rather reported that WASA would "review their condition and odors associated with the operation of the sewer" and would "advise you of our specific action plans as they are developed." [See] (Marcotte Ltr. to Faris, Sept. 10, 1999). In between 1962 and 1999, the Park Service reminded, at least once, WASA of the issue of carbon filters. NPS complained of a "continual discharge of sewer gas" and noted that the under the 1962 and 1966 permit actions, charcoal filters "were and still are required." [See] (Stanton Ltr. to White, Jun. 13, 1984)[.] [Cc]

* * *

Whether the Park Service obligated WASA to install carbon filters requires no further scrutiny. An examination of the Park Service permits does, however, highlight the comparative dearth of evidence to support the next logical step in plaintiffs' argument. Because plaintiffs bring suit under the CWA to enforce an NPDES permit provision, they must demonstrate not only that WASA has an obligation to operate and maintain filters, but also that that obligation is enforceable through the 1997 Permit. Plaintiffs fail to present any evidence on this second, critical point. No evidence even suggests that these obligations were enforceable through the 1997 Permit, or that the Park Service or EPA had any such intention. Without this critical link, the court must deny plaintiffs' summary judgment motion and grant WASA's motion.

Neither party identifies materials that indicate that the EPA, Park Service or WASA intended or believed that the Park Service permit requirements were enforceable through the 1997 Permit specifically. Nothing in the record suggests that the 1997 Permit incorporated by reference the Park Service requirements. See generally 1997 Permit. Certainly, as plaintiffs concede, nothing in the M&O clause refers to maintenance of equipment to fulfill Park Service obligations. See id. at 19. Indeed, the 1997 Permit mentions the National Park Service only once. The permit requires WASA to submit a quarterly report to the Park Service, amongst other "users of the sanitary system and local government officials and the general public," in order to inform them of "the extent of actual compliance with permit requirements and conditions; additionally the permittee shall include in this report information the efficacy of all (on and off site) operations utilized in the disposal of sludge from the Blue Plains WWTP." See 1997 Permit at 31. Under the 1997 Permit, WASA's only obligation vis-a-vis the Park Service is to provide compliance reports. In addition, no Park Service documents on the record suggest that the Park Service intended or believed its permits to be enforceable through the 1997 Permit. Indeed, the Park Service documents fail to mention the EPA, Clean Water Act, or 1997 Permit even once. [Cc] Finally, plaintiffs agree that they are not enforcing the Park Service permit itself. See Def.'s App. at 929–31. As a result, the court concludes there is no evidence, objective or subjective (i.e., regarding the intentions of the EPA or the Park Service) that the filter maintenance requirement was specifically enforceable through the 1997 Permit.

As a more general matter, it seems that the EPA did not intend to allow enforcement of conditions external to a NPDES permit through the permit itself. Neither did EPA apparently intend to require odor control.

General EPA guidance documents indicate that the boilerplate M&O Clause, included in all NPDES permits, does not generally enforce conditions external to a NPDES permit. The most direct evidence of this is EPA's manual on NPDES permits. See Def.'s App. at 1017–25 (U.S. EPA NPDES Permit Writers' Manual (1996)) ("NPDES Manual"). The manual advises permitting authorities, explaining the meaning of and reasons for different permit provisions. Id. at 1021–22 (NPDES Manual at 176–68). In a section on boilerplate clauses, the EPA explains the M&O Clause, lifted verbatim from 40 C.F.R. § 122.41(e), this way:

> Proper Operation and Maintenance ... The permittee must properly operate and maintain all equipment and treatment systems used by the permittee for compliance with the terms of the permit. The permittee must provide appropriate laboratory controls and quality assurance procedures. Backup systems are required when needed to

ensure compliance. However, each main line unit treatment process must be operated at a minimum.

[See] NPDES Manual at 168 (emphasis added). This guidance document, somewhat more explicitly than the M&O Clause itself, only requires permittees to maintain equipment in order to comply with other express permit provisions. Compare 1997 Permit at 19 (requiring maintenance of systems used for "compliance with conditions of the permit."). Put another way, the manual interprets the boilerplate M&O clause not to require maintenance of equipment used to comply with implied permit conditions. The EPA NPDES manual can hardly be said to provide extensive guidance, but it is the only evidence presented by the parties that helps interpret the M&O Clause, and it supports WASA's reading of the maintenance provision.

In addition, other guidance documents indicate that the EPA generally abstains from regulating odor. One indicates that the best, and only extant, means of regulating odor is the state common law of nuisance:

> Efforts to establish quantified acceptability or annoyance threshold levels for any particular odorant [sic] are fraught with subjective evaluations. Subjective reactions to odor differ between individuals and between communities. Indeed, this factor is a major reason for the view that nuisance law is an appropriate mechanism for addressing odor problems. Despite all of its substantive, procedural, and evidentiary shortcomings, the nuisance approach is the only odor regulation strategy now in use that is tied directly to the basic criterion of an unreasonable interference with public or private rights.

[See] Regulatory Options for the Control of Odors, EPA Doc. 450 5–80–003, at 14 (1980). That is, EPA does not purport to regulate odor through either the CWA or Clean Air Act. See id. A different EPA guidance manual document-both thorough and thoroughly technical-on hydrogen sulfide odor and corrosion in sewer systems provides no indication that the CWA, or EPA generally, requires odor control technology. [See] Design Manual: Odor and Corrosion Control in Sanitary Sewerage Systems and Treatment Plants, EPA Doc. EPA/625/1–85/018 (1985). Rather, the EPA seems to acknowledge the need for wastewater authorities to balance competing factors-on the one hand, "wastewater is known to the public for its potential to create odor nuisance" but, on the other, hydrogen sulfide can "corrode various materials used in sewer and treatment plant construction." [See] Design Manual at 1) (emphasis added). The manual also assumes that state law, not federal law or the EPA, operates to require odor control. See id. Put together, these guidance documents indicate that the EPA did not intend, in drafting the 1997 Permit and M&O Clause, to obligate WASA to install and maintain filters or control odor.

After exhausting the possibilities, the court finds, as a matter of law, there is no connection between the M&O Clause, or any other 1997 Permit provision, and the Park Service requirement that WASA maintain carbon filters. As plaintiffs present it, the Park Service requirement is, legally, an obligation in the air, detached from the very NPDES permit which plaintiffs claim to enforce. The court concludes that WASA had no obligation under its NPDES permit to operate or maintain carbon filters. The court need not reach WASA's other arguments in support of summary judgment.

Plaintiffs are wrong if they mean to suggest that the carbon filters must be maintained and operated, under the M&O Clause, simply because they are "integral "parts of the design of the PI and UPI. Nothing suggests that the absence of filters on vents would collapse the PI or UPI, or otherwise cause WASA to violate the effluent limitations in its permit. Clearly, it is not in the strict structural or engineering sense that plaintiffs mean "integral."

Rather, whether or not equipment is "integral" is a legal matter not dictated by project design but rather obligations imposed by permit. The carbon filters are "integral" only to the extent that the Park Service requires them. The court has already established that obligations imposed by Park Service permits can not be enforced through the 1997 Permit. There is no reason, independent of the Park Service permits, that the carbon filters are necessary to the operation of the PI and UPI.

CONCLUSION

Plaintiffs fail to demonstrate a connection between any obligations imposed by the Park Service and the NPDES permit provision through which they sought indicate their claim. Plaintiffs sued under the CWA and must, therefore, identify a legal obligation specifically under the CWA which WASA failed to uphold. The boilerplate maintenance provision requires reference to another, explicit NPDES permit provision. By failing to connect the dots, as it were, plaintiffs cannot maintain an action under the CWA.

Plaintiffs' argument is troubling because the principle underlying it would expand the CWA beyond recognition, such that it would be hard to distinguish actions properly brought under the Act and actions conveniently brought through it. Plaintiffs argue that it is absurd to think that their argument would, as WASA suggests, validate actions to quell the noise from a wastewater facility, or actions to remove or paint over unsightly pipes in the view of area residents. [Cc]. But, if the court correctly understands plaintiffs' argument, these actions would be enforceable under the CWA had the Park Service required noise control or aesthetically pleasing pipes as conditions for the construction of the PI and UPI. In this case, plaintiffs' attempt to enforce obligations not contained in the CWA or WASA's NPDES permit and conceded to be unrelated to the general purposes of the CWA.

The CWA is already generous to the extent that it allows the EPA and affected citizens to bring suit for violations of any NPDES permit violations even though the permit provisions themselves may not be strictly related to limiting water pollution. Bennett, amongst other cases, allows this. See 520 U.S. at 175–76.

Perhaps it would not be possible to advance the primary objectives of a statutory regime (e.g., controlling water pollution) without enforcement of mundane administrative or maintenance requirements, such as contained in the M&O Clause. But to allow the enforcement of legal obligations not actually contained in a permit would be to open the floodgates, as it were. At some point, the CWA, like any federal statutory regime, must have boundaries. Whether or not a principled line, separating proper CWA actions from non-CWA actions, can be cleanly drawn, in this case, plaintiffs' claim falls on the wrong side of the line. The CWA citizen suit provision, by way of WASA's 1997 Permit, is the wrong mechanism to enforce WASA's obligation to maintain carbon filters.

ORDER

For the reasons set forth in the court's Memorandum Opinion docketed this same day, it is this 2nd day of March, 2004, hereby ORDERED that Judgment is entered in favor of Defendant.

Note

For a survey and analysis of alternatives concerning private enforcement, see Richard B. Stewart and Cass R. Sunstein, Public Programs and Private Rights, 95 Harv. L. Rev. 1195 (1982). See also, Middlesex County Sewerage Authority v. National Sea Clammers Assoc., 453 U.S. 1, 101 S.Ct. 2615, 69 L.Ed.2d 435 (1981), (Stevens, J., on the implied-rights doctrine in the Supreme Court) (portions are reproduced below).

3. REGULATION AS PRECLUDING COMMON LAW RIGHTS

The regulatory scheme may serve defensively as a *shield* against private suits. Instead of recognizing regulatory norms and nuisance principles as complementary bodies of law variously enforced, courts may regard the two as competitive and incompatible, and conclude that systematic regulation within a circumscribed area requires the displacement of nuisance and other common law remedies. When that is true, the common law remedies are precluded from imposing more stringent controls than those prescribed by the regulatory apparatus. The defendant will contend that its compliance with the regulatory scheme should constitute a complete defense, and if the public agency could not secure relief because it is in compliance, then the private party should be disabled from doing so.

Again, the matter may be settled by express legislative provision. A statute may declare that it means to occupy a given field completely and so preclude common law actions. Conversely, the statute may contain a "saving clause"—common in environmental legislation—preserving non-statutory remedies. But when the legislature is silent about the continuing vitality of the common law, courts may still hold against it under the judicial doctrine of "preemption." Whether a regulatory statute displaces or preempts other law turns on an analysis of legislative intent, the need for uniform or coordinated prescription, and the appropriateness of the subject matter for dual or multiple legal controls. In a federal system, the question is further complicated by the existence of both "vertical" and "horizontal" preemption, each with its distinctive characteristics and effects. Preemption is considered horizontal when it preempts so-called "federal common law" within a given subject matter. Preemption is called vertical when, pursuant to the Supremacy Clause, it preempts state statutes, regulations, or decisional law.

We will consider below decisions of the Supreme Court that (1) grapple with the question of federal preemption and the proper accommodation between federal and state law and common law rights and remedies; and (2) that consider the presence or absence of implied rights of action. Included is the 1992 Supreme Court decision Cipollone v. Liggett Group, Inc., which defines the judicial doctrine of preemption in the context of the 1965 and 1969 federal cigarette labeling acts. As will be seen, the impact of *Cipollone* transcends its smoking subject matter, and affects preemption doctrine under environmental statutes such as the Federal Insecticide, Fungicide and Rodenticide Act ("FIFRA").

4. SUPREME COURT DECISIONS PRECLUDING COMMON LAW RIGHTS

MILWAUKEE v. ILLINOIS

Supreme Court of the United States, 1981.
451 U.S. 304, 101 S.Ct. 1784, 68 L.Ed.2d 114.

* * *

JUSTICE REHNQUIST delivered the opinion of the Court.

When this litigation was first before us we recognized the existence of a federal "common law" which could give rise to a claim for abatement of a nuisance caused by interstate water pollution. Illinois v. Milwaukee, 406 U.S. 91 (1972). Subsequent to our decision, Congress enacted the Federal Water Pollution Control Act Amendments of 1972. We granted certiorari to consider the effect of this legislation on the previously recognized cause of action.

I

Petitioners, the City of Milwaukee, the Sewerage Commission of the City of Milwaukee, and the Metropolitan Sewerage Commission of the County of Milwaukee, are municipal corporations organized under the laws of Wisconsin. Together they construct, operate, and maintain sewer facilities serving Milwaukee County. * * * On occasion, particularly after a spell of wet weather, overflows occur in the system which result in the discharge of sewage directly into Lake Michigan or tributaries leading into Lake Michigan. The overflows occur at discrete discharge points throughout the system.

Respondent Illinois complains that these discharges, as well as the inadequate treatment of sewage at the two treatment plants, constitute a threat to the health of its citizens. Pathogens, disease-causing viruses and bacteria, are allegedly discharged into the lake with the overflows and inadequately treated sewage and then transported by lake currents to Illinois waters. * * *

* * *

On May 19, 1972, Illinois filed a complaint in the United States District Court for the Northern District of Illinois, seeking abatement, under federal common law, of the public nuisance petitioners were allegedly creating by their discharges.

Five months later Congress * * * passed the Federal Water Pollution Control Act Amendments of 1972, * * * Petitioners did not fully comply with the requirements of the permits and, as contemplated by the Act, § 402 (b)(7), 33 U.S.C. § 1342 (b)(7), see Wis. Stat. Ann. § 147.29 (West 1974), the state agency brought an enforcement action in state court. On May 25, 1977, the state court entered a judgment requiring discharges from the treatment plants to meet the effluent limitations set forth in the permits and establishing a detailed timetable for the completion of planning and additional construction to control sewage overflows.

* * * [T]he District Court rendered a decision finding that respondents had proved the existence of a nuisance under federal common law, both in the discharge of inadequately treated sewage from petitioners' plants and in the discharge of untreated sewage from sewer overflows. The court ordered petitioners to eliminate all overflows and to achieve specified effluent limitations on treated sewage. * * *

On appeal, the Court of Appeals for the Seventh Circuit affirmed in part and reversed in part. * * *

II

Federal courts, unlike state courts, are not general common-law courts and do not possess a general power to develop and apply their own rules of decision. Erie R. Co. v. Tompkins, 304 U.S. 64, 78 (1938). The enactment of a federal rule in an area of national concern, and the decision whether to displace state law in doing so, is generally made not by the federal judiciary, purposefully insulated from democratic pressures, but by the people through their elected representatives in Congress. * * *

When Congress has not spoken to a particular issue, * * * and when there exists a "significant conflict between some federal policy or interest and the use of state law," the Court has found it necessary, in a "few and restricted" instances, to develop federal common law. Nothing in this process suggests that courts are better suited to develop national policy in areas governed by federal common law than they are in other areas, or that the usual and important concerns of an appropriate division of functions between the Congress and the federal judiciary are inapplicable. * * *

* * *

III

We conclude that, at least so far as concerns the claims of respondents, Congress has not left the formulation of appropriate federal standards to the courts through application of often vague and indeterminate nuisance concepts and maxims of equity jurisprudence, but rather has occupied the field through the establishment of a comprehensive regulatory program supervised by an expert administrative agency. The 1972 Amendments to the Federal Water Pollution Control Act * * * were viewed by Congress as a "total restructuring" and "complete rewriting" of the existing water pollution legislation considered in that case.

* * * Congress' intent in enacting the Amendments was clearly to establish an all-encompassing program of water pollution regulation. * * * The establishment of such a self-consciously comprehensive program by Congress, which certainly did not exist when Illinois v. Milwaukee was decided, strongly suggests that there is no room for courts to attempt to improve on that program with federal common law.[14]

Turning to the particular claims involved in this case, the action of Congress in supplanting the federal common law is perhaps clearest when the question of effluent limitations for discharges from the two treatment plants is considered. The duly issued permits under which the city Commission discharges treated sewage from the Jones Island and South Shore treatment plants incorporate * * * the specific effluent limitations established by EPA regulations pursuant to § 301 of the Act[.] There is thus no question that the problem of effluent limitations has been thoroughly addressed through the administrative scheme established by Congress, as contemplated by Congress. This being so there is no basis for a federal court to impose more stringent limitations than those imposed under the regulatory regime by reference to federal common law, as the District Court did in this case. * * *

Federal courts lack authority to impose more stringent effluent limitations under federal common law than those imposed by the agency charged by Congress with administering this comprehensive scheme.

The overflows do not present a different case. They are point source discharges and, under the Act, are prohibited unless subject to a duly issued permit. As with the discharge of treated sewage, the overflows, through the permit procedure of the Act, are referred to expert adminis-

---

14. This conclusion is not undermined by Congress' decision to permit States to establish more stringent standards, see § 510, 33 U.S.C. § 1370. While Congress recognized a role for the States, the comprehensive nature of its action suggests that it was the exclusive source of federal law. * * *

trative agencies for control. All three of the permits issued to petitioners explicitly address the problem of overflows. * * *

* * *

It is quite clear from the foregoing that the state agency duly authorized by the EPA to issue discharge permits under the Act has addressed the problem of overflows from petitioners' sewer system. The agency imposed the conditions it considered best suited to further the goals of the Act, and provided for detailed progress reports so that it could continually monitor the situation. Enforcement action considered appropriate by the state agency was brought, as contemplated by the Act, again specifically addressed to the overflow problem. There is no "interstice" here to be filled by federal common law: overflows are covered by the Act and have been addressed by the regulatory regime established by the Act. Although a federal court may disagree with the regulatory approach taken by the agency with responsibility for issuing permits under the Act, such disagreement alone is no basis for the creation of federal common law.

* * *

The invocation of federal common law by the District Court and the Court of Appeals in the face of congressional legislation supplanting it is peculiarly inappropriate in areas as complex as water pollution control. * * * Not only are the technical problems difficult—doubtless the reason Congress vested authority to administer the Act in administrative agencies possessing the necessary expertise—but the general area is particularly unsuited to the approach inevitable under a regime of federal common law. Congress criticized past approaches to water pollution control as being "sporadic" and "ad hoc," S. Rep. No. 92–414, p. 95 (1971), 2 Leg. Hist. 1511, apt characterizations of any judicial approach applying federal common law[.]

It is also significant that Congress addressed in the 1972 Amendments one of the major concerns underlying the recognition of federal common law in Illinois v. Milwaukee. We were concerned in that case that Illinois did not have any forum in which to protect its interests unless federal common law were created. In the 1972 Amendments Congress provided ample opportunity for a State affected by decisions of a neighboring State's permit-granting agency to seek redress. Under § 402 (b)(3), a state permit-granting agency must ensure that any State whose waters may be affected by the issuance of a permit receives notice of the permit application and the opportunity to participate in a public hearing. Wisconsin law accordingly guarantees such notice and hearing[.] Respondents received notice of each of the permits involved here, and public hearings were held, but they did not participate in them in any way. Section 402 (b)(5) provides that state permit-granting agencies must ensure that affected States have an opportunity to submit written recommendations concerning the permit applications to the issuing State and the EPA, and both the affected State and the EPA must receive notice and a statement of reasons if any part of the recommendations of the affected State are not accepted. Again respondents did not avail themselves of this statutory opportunity. * * * Under § 402 (d)(4) of the Act, the EPA itself may issue permits if a stalemate between an issuing and objecting State develops. The basic grievance of respondents is that the permits issued to petitioners pursuant to the Act do not impose stringent enough controls on petitioners' discharges. The statutory scheme established by Congress provides a forum for the pursuit of such claims before expert agencies by means of the permit-granting process. It would be quite inconsistent with this scheme if federal courts were in effect to "write their own ticket" under the guise of federal common law after permits have already been issued and permittees have been planning and operating in reliance on them.

* * *

We therefore conclude that no federal common-law remedy was available to respondents in this case. The judgment of the Court of Appeals is therefore vacated, and the case is remanded for proceedings consistent with this opinion.

The dissenting opinion of JUSTICE BLACKMUN, with whom JUSTICE MARSHALL and JUSTICE STEVENS join, is omitted.

Notes and Questions

1. One of the criteria applied in these types of cases is to determine if the federal statutory scheme left any "gaps" or "interstices" that must be filled by application of federal common law. Should the courts be aggressive or cautious in finding the need to exercise interstitial law-making to occupy such gaps? Does the Supreme Court seem to endorse one approach over the other?

2. Under the approach followed in *Milwaukee*, the process of deciding whether the court should find horizontal preemption or displacement requires two steps. First, whether the common law claim being asserted is within the regulatory field occupied by the federal statute; and second, whether the regulatory authorities within that broad field have attempted to address the specific subject of the common law claim. The problem is, of course, that the answers to these two questions are usually not clear, especially to the second question, which often is influenced by the existence or perception of inconsistencies between the federal regulatory scheme and the common law remedies sought.

3. The Court seems to place some significance on the State of Illinois' nonparticipation in the Wisconsin permit process, participation of a type explicitly authorized by the Act. Why do you suppose Illinois chose not to participate in the Wisconsin regulatory proceeding?

4. What is the source of the federal common law of interstate pollution control? Why is there a need for such a common law? Is there a need for such a law after the 1972 Amendments to the Federal Water Pollution Control Act? Does the federal common law of interstate pollution control

always disappear when Congress gets active in the area? Is it necessary that the federal statute explicitly "preempt" federal common law? Or is it sufficient that it merely addresses the same subject matter? Is it simply a matter of Congressional intent? Or is it a matter of legal analysis?

5. A municipal sewage treatment plant in State A discharges untreated wastes, which foul the beaches of State B. State B brings a *state* nuisance action against the relevant city in State A. Does *Milwaukee II* bar this suit? Cf. Scott v. City of Hammond, 530 F.Supp. 288 (N.D.Ill.1981) rev'd in part, aff'd in part, 741 F.2d 992 (7th Cir.1984). If the suit is not barred, which state's law applies? May State B constitutionally apply its own law? See International Paper Co. v. Ouellette, 479 U.S. 481, 107 S.Ct. 805, 93 L.Ed.2d 883 (1987) (reproduced below); Note, *Milwaukee II*: The Abatement of Federal Common Law Actions for Interstate Pollution, 1982 Utah L.Rev. 401, 416. See also Note, *City of Milwaukee v. Illinois*: The Demise of the Federal Common Law of Water Pollution, 1982 Wis.L.Rev. 627.

6. The denial of an implied private right of action is consistent with the Supreme Court's policy of restricting the availability of such actions. See California v. Sierra Club, 451 U.S. 287, 101 S.Ct. 1775, 68 L.Ed.2d 101 (1981), decided the same day as *Milwaukee*. In that case the plaintiffs claimed that they had an implied private right of action to enjoin violations of section 10 of the Rivers and Harbors Act. The Supreme Court found no Congressional intent to allow a private remedy for violations of the Act and refused to imply the existence of such a remedy.

7. Would any obstacle exist to the application of the law of the state of discharge in order to recover damages, particularly when the harm is accompanied by a violation of state and/or federal permitting requirements? This, of course, assumes that such a state remedy exists and that it applies to harm caused to interests outside the state.

Even if the statutory or common law of the state in which the pollution originates offers some possibility of relief, would a *state* court within that state be an ideal forum to press such a claim by "foreign" interests? How could subject matter jurisdiction exist in federal court?

If suit is brought in state or federal court in the plaintiff's home state, additional problems of obtaining *in personam* jurisdiction might arise. Even under a state long-arm statute, there would be a question of whether a discharger had sufficient minimum contacts within the state where the harm occurred. Would a county or city sewerage authority be likely to have the requisite contacts in the affected state? If the state long-arm statute considers a tort to be sufficient contact, where did the tort occur? Where the pollution was discharged or where it caused the harm?

8. Courts can also conclude that the defendant's compliance with the federal regulatory requirements should preclude its liability under federal common law rules, and this seems especially compelling where the regulatory provisions are technical and the defendant's actions have received express approval by the regulatory agency. In New England Legal Foundation v. Costle, 666 F.2d 30 (2d Cir.1981), the Second Circuit considered whether the plaintiff, a legal foundation, could maintain an action against the Long Island Lighting Company (LILCO), a public utility, and the EPA based on violations of the Clean Air Act and federal common law nuisance. The

complaint alleged that LILCO maintained a common law nuisance by burning oil containing 2.8% sulphur at its power plant, which was authorized by the EPA. The Court held that "EPA's approval of LILCO's use of high sulphur fuel precludes [plaintiff] from maintaining a common law nuisance action against LILCO." Relying on the Supreme Court's decision in *Milwaukee II*, the court found that the granting of approval by the EPA must bar a private action:

> Courts traditionally have been reluctant to enjoin as a public nuisance activities which have been considered and specifically authorized by the government. The exercise of such restraint is especially appropriate here where the conduct sought to be enjoined implicates the technically complex area of environmental law and where Congress has vested administrative authority in a federal agency presumably having significant technical expertise. In doing so, Congress has indicated that regulation may be better achieved through a comprehensive statutory approach than through ad hoc common law remedies. The federal courts of course must bow to that expression of congressional intent. *City of Milwaukee*[.] To proceed otherwise by fashioning federal equitable remedies to proscribe the very conduct that the EPA, acting in its regulatory capacity pursuant to its statutory mandate, has specifically approved, as the district court below held, would be both counter-productive and beyond the proper scope of the judicial function.

See, e.g., Twitty v. North Carolina, 527 F.Supp. 778 (E.D.N.C.1981), where property owners brought suit for damages and injunctive relief against the state for storing PCBs in a landfill and the EPA for authorizing the storage under the Toxic Substances Control Act. The court dismissed plaintiffs' claims:

> There is no contention by the plaintiffs that the Toxic Substances Control Act is unconstitutional or that the regulations promulgated thereunder contravene or exceed the authority delegated. This being true, the plaintiff's first [nuisance] and third [violation of a county ordinance] causes of action must fail because courts will not enjoin as a nuisance an action authorized by valid legislative authority and because the Act preempts any local ordinances.

9. In Middlesex County Sewage Authority v. National Sea Clammers Assoc., 453 U.S. 1, 101 S.Ct. 2615, 69 L.Ed.2d 435 (1981), the Supreme Court again visited the issues of damages remedies under either federal common law or under the provisions of two Acts—the Federal Water Pollution Control Act (FWPCA), 33 U.S.C.A. § 1251 et seq., and the Marine Protection, Research, and Sanctuaries Act of 1972 (MPRSA), 33 U.S.C.A. § 1401 et seq. Justice Powell delivered the opinion of the Court:

> * * * We granted [the petitions for certiorari], limiting review to three questions: (i) whether FWPCA and MPRSA imply a private right of action independent of their citizen-suit provisions, (ii) whether all federal common-law nuisance actions concerning ocean pollution now are pre-empted by the legislative scheme contained in the FWPCA and the MPRSA, and (iii) if not, whether a private citizen has standing to sue for damages under the federal common law of nuisance. We hold that there is no implied right of action under these statutes and that the

federal common law of nuisance has been fully pre-empted in the area of ocean pollution.

II

A

It is unnecessary to discuss at length the principles set out in recent decisions concerning the recurring question whether Congress intended to create a private right of action under a federal statute without saying so explicitly. The key to the inquiry is the intent of the Legislature. Texas Industries, Inc. v. Radcliff Materials, Inc., 451 U.S. 630, 639 (1981)[.] We look first, of course, to the statutory language, particularly to the provisions made therein for enforcement and relief. Then we review the legislative history and other traditional aids of statutory interpretation to determine congressional intent.

These Acts contain unusually elaborate enforcement provisions, conferring authority to sue for this purpose both on government officials and private citizens. * * *

These enforcement mechanisms * * * are supplemented by the express citizen-suit provisions in § 505 (a) of the FWPCA, 33 U.S.C. § 1365 (a), and § 105 (g) of the MPRSA, 33 U.S.C. § 1415 (g). These citizen-suit provisions authorize private persons to sue for injunctions to enforce these statutes. Plaintiffs invoking these provisions first must comply with specified procedures—which respondents here ignored—including in most cases 60 days' prior notice to potential defendants.

In view of these elaborate enforcement provisions it cannot be assumed that Congress intended to authorize by implication additional judicial remedies for private citizens suing under MPRSA and FWPCA. * * * In the absence of strong indicia of a contrary congressional intent, we are compelled to conclude that Congress provided precisely the remedies it considered appropriate.

* * *

* * * [Moreover], it is clear that the citizen-suit provisions apply only to persons who can claim some sort of injury and there is, therefore, no reason to infer the existence of a separate right of action for "injured" plaintiffs. * * *

* * *

[T]he structure of the Acts and their legislative history both lead us to conclude that Congress intended that private remedies in addition to those expressly provided should not be implied. Where, as here, Congress has made clear that implied private actions are not contemplated, the courts are not authorized to ignore this legislative judgment.

* * *

III

The remaining two issues on which we granted certiorari relate to respondents' federal claims based on the federal common law of nuisance. * * * The Court has now held that the federal common law of nuisance in the area of water pollution is entirely pre-empted by the more comprehensive scope of the FWPCA, which was completely revised soon after the decision in Illinois v. Milwaukee. See Milwaukee v. Illinois, 451 U.S. 304 (1981).

This decision disposes entirely of respondents' federal common-law claims, since there is no reason to suppose that the pre-emptive effect of the FWPCA is any less when pollution of coastal waters is at issue. To the extent that this litigation involves ocean waters not covered by the FWPCA, and regulated under the MPRSA, we see no cause for different treatment of the pre-emption question. The regulatory scheme of the MPRSA is no less comprehensive, with respect to ocean dumping, than are analogous provisions of the FWPCA.

We therefore must dismiss the federal common-law claims because their underlying legal basis is now pre-empted by statute. As discussed above, we also dismiss the claims under the MPRSA and the FWPCA because respondents lack a right of action under those statutes. We vacate the judgment below with respect to these two claims, and remand for further proceedings.

It is so ordered.

The dissenting opinion of Justice Stevens, with whom Justice Blackmun joined, concurring in the judgment in part, is omitted.

10. Should the court have distinguished *Sea Clammers* from *Milwaukee II* ? The standard for finding preemption of federal common law which the Court used in *Milwaukee* was whether Congress had spoken directly and comprehensively to the subject matter. While Congress had spoken to the subject of water pollution control, it had not addressed compensation for harm caused by water pollution; nowhere does the Act provide for private damages. Isn't this exactly the type of statutory interstice that federal common law is intended to fill? See United States v. Little Lake Misere Land Co., 412 U.S. 580, 593, 93 S.Ct. 2389, 37 L.Ed.2d 187 (1973), where the Court stated: "The inevitable incompleteness presented by all legislation means that interstitial federal law making is a basic responsibility of the federal courts." In that case, the Court also cited the following language with approval:

> At the very least, effective Constitutionalism requires recognition of power in the federal courts to declare, as a matter of common law or "judicial legislation," rules which may be necessary to fill in interstitially or otherwise effectuate the statutory patterns enacted in the large by Congress. In other words, it must mean recognition of federal judiciary competence to declare the governing law in an area comprising issues substantially related to an established program of government operation.

11. In a situation similar to *Sea Clammers*, where damages were sought and permits were violated, would a court be fulfilling its proper role in awarding damages? William H. Rodgers, Jr., Environmental Law § 2.12 at 47 (1984 Supp.) criticizes the *Sea Clammers* decision because the court

seems to find the field occupied and the common law displaced without any detailed analysis, and notes:

"*Milwaukee v. Illinois* itself requires that the subject of the preempted right be taken up in the administrative process, thus requiring that the common law remedy be displaced and driven out, not merely intimidated into retreat by a potential entry."

12. *Maritime Torts*. The plaintiffs in *Sea Clammers* also asserted a claim based on federal maritime tort. The Circuit Court held that this constituted a valid claim, 616 F.2d 1222, 1236 (3d Cir.1980), but the Supreme Court did not review this issue.

Maritime tort is a part of the body of admiralty law which came to the United States from England along with the concepts of common law and equity. The Constitution has been construed to have incorporated this admiralty law as it then existed as the law of the United States, subject to the power of Congress to alter. Federal courts have exclusive jurisdiction over maritime torts. To invoke that jurisdiction, a plaintiff must show that the tort occurred in a maritime locality (most courts hold that "navigable" waters are sufficient), and that there exists a significant relationship between the tort and a traditional maritime activity (injury to the fishing industry generally meets this requirement). After establishing jurisdiction, a plaintiff must then prove that a tort occurred which caused injury to the plaintiff.

Does the Clean Water Act preempt the field of maritime tort with respect to injuries caused by water pollution?

13. Many federal statutes contain explicit citizen suit provisions. See, e.g., Toxic Substances Control Act, § 20(c)(3), 15 U.S.C.A. § 2619(c)(3); Solid Waste Disposal Act § 7002(f), 42 U.S.C.A. § 6972(f); Surface Mining Control and Reclamation Act of 1977 § 520(e), 30 U.S.C.A. § 1270(e); Clean Air Act § 304(e); 42 U.S.C.A. § 7604(e); Deepwater Port Act § 16(e), 33 U.S.C.A. § 1515(e); Marine Protection, Research and Sanctuaries Act § 105(g)(5), 33 U.S.C.A. § 1515(e).

14. William H. Rodgers, Jr., Environmental Law § 2.12 at 45–46 (1984 Supp.), points out that the trend set in *Milwaukee* and *Sea Clammers* has been generally followed in later decisions:

A comparison of the case law before and after *Milwaukee v. Illinois* shows a sharp responsivity to Supreme Court trend-setting. After the decision, courts have embraced the displacement position—by finding a retroactive pre-emption of claims extant before the federal laws were enacted, by turning back the United States' attempts to supplement prescribed remedies, by declining to attach significance to the scaled-down regulatory features of the Clean Air Act and other laws, and even by finding state remedies preempted by the federal choice to have no remedy.

INTERNATIONAL PAPER CO. v. OUELLETTE

Supreme Court of the United States, 1987.
479 U.S. 481, 107 S.Ct. 805, 93 L.Ed.2d 883.

JUSTICE POWELL delivered the opinion of the Court.

This case involves the pre-emptive scope of the Clean Water Act, [33 U.S.C. § 1251 et seq.] (CWA or Act). The question presented is whether the Act pre-empts a common-law nuisance suit filed in a Vermont court under Vermont law, when the source of the alleged injury is located in New York.

I

Lake Champlain forms part of the border between the States of New York and Vermont. Petitioner International Paper Company (IPC) operates a pulp and paper mill on the New York side of the lake. In the course of its business, IPC discharges a variety of effluents into the lake through a diffusion pipe. The pipe runs from the mill through the water toward Vermont, ending a short distance before the state boundary line that divides the lake.

Respondents are a group of property owners who reside or lease land on the Vermont shore. In 1978 the owners filed a class action suit against IPC, claiming, inter alia, that the discharge of effluents constituted a "continuing nuisance" under Vermont common law. Respondents alleged that the pollutants made the water "foul, unhealthy, smelly, and ... unfit for recreational use," thereby diminishing the value of their property. The owners asked for $20 million in compensatory damages, $100 million in punitive damages, and injunctive relief that would require IPC to restructure part of its water treatment system. The action was filed in State Superior Court, and then later removed to Federal District Court for the District of Vermont.

IPC moved for summary judgment and judgment on the pleadings, claiming that the CWA pre-empted respondents' state-law suit. * * *

* * * [The District Court] acknowledged that federal law normally governs interstate water pollution. It found, however, that two sections of the CWA explicitly preserve state-law rights of action. First, § 510 of the Act provides: "Except as expressly provided ... , nothing in this chapter shall ... be construed as impairing or in any manner affecting any right or jurisdiction of the States with respect to the waters (including boundary waters) of such States."

In addition, § 505(e) states: "Nothing in this section shall restrict any right which any person (or class of persons) may have under any statute or common law to seek enforcement of any effluent standard or limitation or to seek any other relief...."

The District Court held that these two provisions (together, "the saving clause") made it clear that federal law did not pre-empt entirely the rights of States to control pollution. * * *

The District Court * * * held that a state action to redress interstate water pollution could be maintained under the law of the State in which the injury occurred. * * *

* * * [T]he Court of Appeals for the Second Circuit affirmed[.] We granted certiorari to resolve the circuit conflict on this important issue of federal pre-emption. We now affirm the denial of IPC's motion to dismiss, but reverse the decision below to the extent it permits the application of Vermont law to this litigation. We hold that when a court considers a state-law claim concerning interstate water pollution that is subject to the CWA, the court must apply the law of the State in which the point source is located.

II

A brief review of the regulatory framework is necessary to set the stage for this case. Until fairly recently, federal common law governed the use and misuse of interstate water. * * *

We had occasion to address this issue in the first of two Supreme Court cases involving the dispute between Illinois and Milwaukee. * * * [Milwaukee I] held that these cases should be resolved by reference to federal common law; the implicit corollary of this ruling was that state common law was preempted. * * *

Congress thereafter adopted comprehensive amendments to the Act. We considered the impact of the new legislation when Illinois and Milwaukee returned to the Court several years later. Milwaukee v. Illinois, 451 U.S. 304 (1981) (Milwaukee II). There the Court noted that the amendments were a " 'complete rewriting' " of the statute considered in Milwaukee I, and that they were " 'the most comprehensive and far reaching' " provisions that Congress ever had passed in this area. Consequently, the Court held that federal legislation now occupied the field, pre-empting all federal common law. The Court left open the question of whether injured parties still had a cause of action under state law. * * *

One of the primary features of the 1972 amendments is the establishment of the National Pollutant Discharge Elimination System (NPDES), a federal permit program designed to regulate the discharge of polluting effluents. * * *

The amendments also recognize that the States should have a significant role in protecting their own natural resources. 33 U.S.C. § 1251(b). * * * Even if the Federal Government administers the permit program, the source State may require discharge limitations more stringent than those required by the Federal Government. See 40 CFR § 122.1(f) (1986). Before the Federal Government may issue an NPDES permit, the Administrator must obtain certification from the source State that the proposed discharge complies with the State's technology-based standards and water-quality-based standards. 33 U.S.C. § 1341(a)(1). The CWA therefore establishes a regulatory "partnership" between the Federal Government and the source State.

While source States have a strong voice in regulating their own pollution, the CWA contemplates a much lesser role for States that share an interstate waterway with the source (the affected States). Even though it may be harmed by the discharges, an affected State only has an advisory role in regulating pollution that originates beyond its borders. Before a federal permit may be issued, each affected State is given notice and the opportunity to object to the proposed standards at a public hearing. An affected State has similar rights to be consulted before the source State issues its own permit; the source State must send notification, and must consider the objections and recommendations submitted by other States before taking action. Significantly, however, an affected State does not have the authority to block the issuance of the permit if it is dissatisfied with the proposed standards. An affected State's only recourse is to apply to the EPA Administrator, who then has the discretion to disapprove the permit if he concludes that the discharges will have an undue impact on interstate waters. Also, an affected State may not establish a separate permit system to regulate an out-of-state source. Thus the Act makes it clear that affected States occupy a subordinate position to source States in the federal regulatory program.

At one point IPC was operating under a federal NPDES permit. A draft of the permit was submitted to Vermont as an affected State, and Vermont as well as other interested parties objected to the proposed discharge standards. Thereafter, New York obtained permitting authority under 33 U.S.C. § 1342(b) and it now administers the permit.

III

With this regulatory framework in mind, we turn to the question presented: whether the Act pre-empts Vermont common law to the extent that law may impose liability on a New York point source.

* * *

A

As we noted in Milwaukee II, Congress intended the 1972 Act amendments to "establish an all-encompassing program of water pollution regulation." 451 U.S., at 318. * * * The Act applies to all point sources and virtually all bodies of water, and it sets forth the procedures for obtaining a permit in great detail. The CWA also provides its own remedies, including civil and criminal fines for permit violations, and "citizen suits" that allow individuals (including those from affected States) to sue for injunctions to enforce the statute. In light of this pervasive regulation and the fact that the control of interstate pollution is primarily a matter of federal law, it is clear that the only state suits that remain available are those specifically preserved by the Act.

Although Congress intended to dominate the field of pollution regulation, the saving clause negates the inference that Congress "left no room" for state causes of action. Respondents read the language of the saving clause broadly to preserve both a State's right to regulate its waters, 33 U.S.C. § 1370, and an injured party's right to seek relief under "any statute or common law," § 1365(e). They claim that this language and selected portions of the legislative history compel the inference that Congress intended to preserve the right to bring suit under the law of any affected State. We cannot accept this reading of the Act.

To begin with, the plain language of the provisions on which respondents rely by no means compels the result they seek. Section 505(e) merely says that "[n]othing in this section," i.e., the citizen-suit provisions, shall affect an injured party's right to seek relief under state law; it does not purport to preclude pre-emption of state law by other provisions of the Act. Section 510, moreover, preserves the authority of a State "with respect to the waters (including boundary waters) of such Stat[e]." This language arguably limits the effect of the clause to discharges flowing directly into a State's own waters, i.e., discharges from within the State. The savings clause then, does not preclude pre-emption of the law of an affected State.

Given that the Act itself does not speak directly to the issue, the Court must be guided by the goals and policies of the Act in determining whether it in fact pre-empts an action based on the law of an affected State. After examining the CWA as a whole, its purposes and its history, we are convinced that if affected States were allowed to impose separate discharge standards on a single point source, the inevitable result would be a serious interference with the achievement of the "full purposes and objectives of Congress." Because we do not believe Congress intended to undermine this carefully drawn statute through a general saving clause, we conclude that the CWA precludes a court from applying the law of an affected State against an out-of-state source.

* * *

B

In determining whether Vermont nuisance law "stands as an obstacle" to the full implementation of the CWA, it is not enough to say that the ultimate goal of both federal and state law is to eliminate water pollution. A state law also is preempted if it interferes with the methods by which the federal statute was designed to reach this goal. In this case the application of Vermont law against IPC would allow respondents to circumvent the NPDES permit system, thereby upsetting the balance of public and private interests so carefully addressed by the Act.

By establishing a permit system for effluent discharges, Congress implicitly has recognized that the goal of the CWA—elimination of water pollution—cannot be achieved immediately, and that it cannot be realized without incurring costs. The EPA Administrator issues permits according to established effluent standards and water quality standards, that in turn are based upon available technology, 33 U.S.C. § 1314, and competing public and industrial uses, § 1312(a). The Administrator must consider the impact of the discharges on the waterway, the types of effluents, and the schedule for compliance, each of which may vary widely among sources. If a State elects to impose its own standards, it also must consider the technological feasibility of more stringent controls. Given the nature of these complex decisions, it is not surprising that the Act limits the right to administer the permit system to the EPA and the source States.

An interpretation of the saving clause that preserved actions brought under an affected State's law would disrupt this balance of interests. If a New York source were liable for violations of Vermont law, that law could effectively override both the permit requirements and the policy choices made by the source State. The affected State's nuisance laws would subject the point source to the threat of legal and equitable penalties if the permit standards were less stringent than those imposed by the affected State. Such penalties would compel the source to adopt different control standards and a different compliance schedule from those approved by the EPA, even though the affected State had not engaged in the same weighing of the costs and benefits. This case illustrates the problems with such a rule. If the Vermont court ruled that respondents were entitled to the full amount of damages and injunctive relief sought in the complaint, at a minimum IPC would have to change its methods of doing business and controlling pollution to avoid the threat of ongoing liability. In suits such as this, an affected-state court also could require the source to cease operations by ordering immediate abatement. Critically, these liabilities would attach even though the source had complied fully with its state and federal permit obligations. The inevitable result of such suits would be that Vermont and other States could do indirectly what they could not do directly— regulate the conduct of out-of-state sources.

Application of an affected State's law to an out-of-state source also would undermine the important goals of efficiency and predictability in the permit system. The history of the 1972 amendments shows that Congress intended to establish "clear and identifiable" discharge standards. See S. Rep. No. 92–414, p. 81 (1971), 2 Leg. Hist. 1499. As noted above, under the reading of the saving clause proposed by respondents, a source would be subject to a variety of common-law rules established by the different States along the interstate waterways. These nuisance standards often are "vague" and "indeterminate." The application of numerous States' laws would only exacerbate the vagueness and resulting uncertainty. The Court of Appeals in Milwaukee III identified the problem with such an irrational system of regulation: "For a number of different states to have independent and plenary regulatory authority over a single discharge would lead to chaotic confrontation between sovereign states. Dischargers would be forced to meet not only the statutory limitations of all states potentially affected by their discharges but also the common law standards developed through case law of those states. It would be virtually impossible to predict the standard for a lawful discharge into an interstate body of water. Any permit issued under the Act would be rendered meaningless." [Illinois v. Milwaukee,

731 F.2d 403, 414 (7th Cir.1984), cert. denied 469 U.S. 1196, 105 S.Ct. 979, 83 L.Ed.2d 981 (1985)].

It is unlikely—to say the least—that Congress intended to establish such a chaotic regulatory structure.

Nothing in the Act gives each affected State this power to regulate discharges. The CWA carefully defines the role of both the source and affected States, and specifically provides for a process whereby their interests will be considered and balanced by the source State and the EPA. This delineation of authority represents Congress' considered judgment as to the best method of serving the public interest and reconciling the often competing concerns of those affected by the pollution. It would be extraordinary for Congress, after devising an elaborate permit system that sets clear standards, to tolerate common-law suits that have the potential to undermine this regulatory structure.

C

Our conclusion that Vermont nuisance law is inapplicable to a New York point source does not leave respondents without a remedy. The CWA precludes only those suits that may require standards of effluent control that are incompatible with those established by the procedures set forth in the Act. The saving clause specifically preserves other state actions, and therefore nothing in the Act bars aggrieved individuals from bringing a nuisance claim pursuant to the law of the source State. By its terms the CWA allows States such as New York to impose higher standards on their own point sources, and in Milwaukee II we recognized that this authority may include the right to impose higher common-law as well as higher statutory restrictions. 451 U.S., at 328 (suggesting that "States may adopt more stringent limitations ... through state nuisance law, and apply them to in-state dischargers"); see also Committee for Jones Falls Sewage System v. Train, 539 F.2d 1006, 1009, and n. 9 [4th Cir.1976] (CWA preserves common-law suits filed in source State).

An action brought against IPC under New York nuisance law would not frustrate the goals of the CWA as would a suit governed by Vermont law. First, application of the source State's law does not disturb the balance among federal, source-state, and affected-state interests. Because the Act specifically allows source States to impose stricter standards, the imposition of source-state law does not disrupt the regulatory partnership established by the permit system. Second, the restriction of suits to those brought under source-state nuisance law prevents a source from being subject to an indeterminate number of potential regulations. Although New York nuisance law may impose separate standards and thus create some tension with the permit system, a source only is required to look to a single additional authority, whose rules should be relatively predictable. Moreover, States can be expected to take into account their own nuisance laws in setting permit requirements.[20]

---

20. Although we conclude that New York law generally controls this suit, we note that the pre-emptive scope of the CWA necessarily includes all laws that are incon-

IPC asks the Court to go one step further and hold that all state-law suits also must be brought in source-state courts. As petitioner cites little authority or justification for this position, we find no basis for holding that Vermont is an improper forum. Simply because a cause of action is pre-empted does not mean that judicial jurisdiction over the claim is affected as well; the Act pre-empts laws, not courts. In the absence of statutory authority to the contrary, the rule is settled that a district court sitting in diversity is competent to apply the law of a foreign State.

IV

The District Court correctly denied IPC's motion for summary judgment and judgment on the pleadings. Nothing in the Act prevents a court sitting in an affected State from hearing a common-law nuisance suit, provided that jurisdiction otherwise is proper. Both the District Court and the Court of Appeals erred, however, in concluding that Vermont law governs this litigation. * * *

The decision of the Court of Appeals is affirmed in part and reversed in part. The case is remanded for further proceedings consistent with this opinion.

The Opinion of JUSTICE BRENNAN, with whom JUSTICE MARSHALL and JUSTICE BLACKMUN join, concurring in part and dissenting in part, is omitted. The Opinion of JUSTICE STEVENS, with whom JUSTICE BLACKMUN joins, concurring in part and dissenting in part, is omitted.

Notes and Questions

1. Under the Court's holding a federal court sitting in Vermont may apply New York common law to a New York point without being barred by the preemption of the Clean Water Act, but that the same court cannot apply Vermont common law to the same activity because it is barred by the preemptive effect of the Clean Water Act. Did you follow the Court's rationale for distinguishing between these two situations? In other words, the Court is finding partial vertical federal preemption, where the state of the source and state of the law are different, e.g., interstate; but no vertical preemption where the state of the source and state of the law are the same, e.g., intrastate.

2. After the Supreme Court's decision, International Paper Co. moved for the trial court to dismiss the plaintiffs' state common law nuisance

sistent with the "full purposes and objectives of Congress." See Hillsborough County v. Automated Medical Laboratories, Inc., 471 U.S. 707, 713 (1985). We therefore do not agree with the dissent that Vermont nuisance law still may apply if the New York choice-of-law doctrine dictates such a result. As we have discussed, supra, the application of affected-state law would frustrate the carefully prescribed CWA regula-tory system. This interference would occur, of course, whether affected-state law applies as an original matter, or whether it applies pursuant to the source State's choice-of-law principles. Therefore if, and to the extent, the law of a source State requires the application of affected-state substantive law on this particular issue, it would be pre-empt-ed as well.

claims for the interstate *air* pollution from the mill. Applying the Supreme Court's reasoning on the water claims, the trial court held that plaintiffs' nuisance claim for air pollution was not preempted by the Clean Air Act, insofar as it was based on New York law. Ouellette v. International Paper Co., 666 F.Supp. 58 (D.Vt.1987).

We now turn to further examples of vertical preemption, an analysis that requires evaluation of the relationship between federal statutory law and state common law remedies.

CIPOLLONE v. LIGGETT GROUP

Supreme Court of the United States, 1992.
505 U.S. 504, 112 S.Ct. 2608, 120 L.Ed.2d 407.

JUSTICE STEVENS delivered the opinion of the Court, except as to Parts V and VI.

"WARNING: THE SURGEON GENERAL HAS DETERMINED THAT CIGARETTE SMOKING IS DANGEROUS TO YOUR HEALTH." A federal statute enacted in 1969 requires that warning (or a variation thereof) to appear in a conspicuous place on every package of cigarettes sold in the United States.[1] The questions presented to us by this case are whether that statute, or its 1965 predecessor which required a less alarming label, pre-empted petitioner's common law claims against respondent cigarette manufacturers.

Petitioner is the son of Rose Cipollone, who began smoking in 1942 and who died of lung cancer in 1984. He claims that respondents are responsible for Rose Cipollone's death because they breached express warranties contained in their advertising, because they failed to warn consumers about the hazards of smoking, because they fraudulently misrepresented those hazards to consumers, and because they conspired to deprive the public of medical and scientific information about smoking. The [Third Circuit] Court of Appeals held that petitioner's state law claims were pre-empted by federal statutes, and other courts have agreed with that analysis. The highest courts of the states of Minnesota and New Jersey, however, have held that the federal statutes did not pre-empt similar common law claims. Because of the manifest importance of the issue, we granted certiorari to resolve the conflict[.] We now reverse in part and affirm in part.

I

* * *

Petitioner's third amended complaint alleges several different bases of recovery, relying on theories of strict liability, negligence, express warranty, and intentional tort. These claims, all based on New Jersey

---

1. Public Health Cigarette Smoking Act of 1969, Pub. L. 91–222, 84 Stat. 87, as amended, 15 U.S.C. §§ 1331–1340. In 1984, Congress amended the statute to require four more explicit warnings, used on a ro-

tating basis. See Comprehensive Smoking Education Act, Pub. L. 98–474, 98 Stat. 2201. Because petitioner's claims arose before 1984, neither party relies on this later Act.

Law, divided into five categories. The "design defect claims" allege that respondents' cigarettes were defective because respondents failed to use a safer alternative design for their products and because the social value of their product was outweighed by the dangers it created [Count 2]. The "failure to warn claims" allege both that the product was "defective as a result of [respondents'] failure to provide adequate warnings of the health consequences of cigarette smoking" [Count 3], and that respondents "were negligent in the manner [that] they tested, researched, sold, promoted, and advertised" their cigarettes [Count 4]. The "express warranty claims" allege that respondents had "expressly warranted that smoking the cigarettes which they manufactured and sold did not present any significant health consequences" [Count 7]. The "fraudulent misrepresentation claims" allege that respondents had wilfully "through their advertising, attempted to neutralize the [federally mandated] warning" labels [Count 6], and that they had possessed, but had "ignored and failed to act upon" medical and scientific data indicating that "cigarettes were hazardous to the health of consumers" [Count 8]. Finally, the conspiracy to defraud claims "allege that respondents conspired to deprive the public of such medical and scientific data" [Count 8].

* * *

* * * We granted the petition for certiorari to consider the pre-emptive effect of the federal statutes.

II

* * *

In 1964, the [Surgeon General's Advisory Committee] issued its Report, which stated as its central conclusion: "Cigarette smoking is a health hazard of sufficient importance in the United States to warrant appropriate remedial action." U.S. Dept. of Health, Education, and Welfare, U.S. Surgeon General's Advisory Committee, Smoking and Health 33 (1964). Relying in part on that report, the Federal Trade Commission (FTC), which had long regulated unfair and deceptive advertising practices in the cigarette industry, promulgated a new trade regulation rule. That rule, which was to take effect January 1, 1965, established that it would be a violation of the Federal Trade Commission Act to "fail to disclose, clearly and prominently, in all advertising and on every pack, box, carton, or container [of cigarettes] that cigarette smoking is dangerous to health and may cause death from cancer and other diseases." 29 Fed. Reg. 8325 (1964). Several States also moved to regulate the advertising and labeling of cigarettes. Upon a congressional request, the FTC postponed enforcement of its new regulation for six months. In July 1965, Congress enacted the Federal Cigarette Labeling and Advertising Act.[8] The 1965 Act effectively adopted half of the FTC'S Regulation: The Act mandated warnings on cigarette packages (§ 5(A)),

---

8. [15 U.S.C.A. §§ 1331–1340].

but barred the requirement of such warnings in cigarette advertising (§ 5(B)).

Section 2 of the Act declares the Statute's two purposes: (1) adequately informing the public that cigarette smoking may be hazardous to health, and (2) protecting the national economy from the burden imposed by diverse, nonuniform and confusing cigarette labeling and advertising regulations. In furtherance of the first purpose, § 4 of the Act made it unlawful to sell or distribute any cigarettes in the United States unless the package bore a conspicuous label stating: "CAUTION: CIGARETTE SMOKING MAY BE HAZARDOUS TO YOUR HEALTH." In furtherance of the second purpose, § 5, captioned "Preemption," provided in part:

> "(a) No statement relating to smoking and health, other than the statement required by section 4 of this Act, shall be required on any cigarette package.

> (b) No statement relating to smoking and health shall be required in the advertising of any cigarettes the packages of which are labeled in conformity with the provisions of this Act."

Although the Act took effect January 1, 1966, § 10 of the Act provided that its provisions affecting the regulation of advertising would terminate on July 1, 1969.

As that termination date approached, federal authorities prepared to issue further regulations on cigarette advertising. The FTC announced the reinstitution of its 1964 proceedings concerning a warning requirement for cigarette advertisements. The Federal Communications Commission (FCC) announced that it would consider "a proposed rule which would ban the broadcast of cigarette commercials by radio and television stations." State authorities also prepared to take actions regulating cigarette advertisements.

It was in this context that Congress enacted the Public Health Cigarette Smoking Act of 1969,[12] which amended the 1965 Act in several ways. First, the 1969 Act strengthened the warning label, in part by requiring a statement that cigarette smoking "is dangerous" rather than that it "may be hazardous." Second, the 1969 Act banned cigarette advertising in "any medium of electronic communication subject to [FCC] jurisdiction." Third, and related, the 1969 Act modified the preemption provision by replacing the original § 5(b) with a provision that reads: "(b) No requirement or prohibition based on smoking and health shall be imposed under State law with respect to the advertising or promotion of any cigarettes the packages of which are labeled in conformity with the provisions of this Act." Although the Act also directed the FTC not to "take any action before July 1, 1971, with respect to its pending trade regulation rule proceeding relating to cigarette advertising", the narrowing of the pre-emption provision to prohibit only restrictions "imposed under State law" cleared the way for the FTC to extend

---

12. [15 U.S.C.A. §§ 1331–1340].

the warning-label requirement to print advertisements for cigarettes. The FTC did so in 1972.

III

Article VI of the Constitution provides that the laws of the United States "shall be the supreme Law of the Land; ... any Thing in the Constitution or Laws of any state to the Contrary notwithstanding." Art. VI, cl. 2. Thus, since our decision in McCulloch v. Maryland, 4 Wheat. 316, 427 (1819), it has been settled that state law that conflicts with federal law is "without effect." Maryland v. Louisiana, 451 U.S. 725, 746 (1981). Consideration of issues arising under the Supremacy Clause "start[s] with the assumption that the historic police powers of the States [are] not to be superseded by ... Federal Act unless that [is] the clear and manifest purpose of Congress." Accordingly, " '[t]he purpose of Congress is the ultimate touchstone' " of pre-emption analysis.

Congress' intent may be "explicitly stated in the statute's language or implicitly contained in its structure and purpose." In the absence of an express congressional command, state law is pre-empted if that law actually conflicts with federal law, or if federal law so thoroughly occupies a legislative field " 'as to make reasonable the inference that Congress left no room for the States to supplement it.' "

* * *

In our opinion, the pre-emptive scope of the 1965 Act and the 1969 Act is governed entirely by the express language in § 5 of each Act. When Congress has considered the issue of pre-emption and has included in the enacted legislation a provision explicitly addressing that issue, and when that provision provides a "reliable indicium of congressional intent with respect to state authority," Malone v. White Motor Corp., 435 U.S., at 505, "there is no need to infer congressional intent to pre-empt state laws from the substantive provisions" of the legislation. California Federal Savings & Loan Assn. v. Guerra, 479 U.S. 272, 282 (1987) (opinion of Marshall, J.). Such reasoning is a variant of the familiar principle of *expressio unius est exclusio alterius*: Congress' enactment of a provision defining the pre-emptive reach of a statute implies that matters beyond that reach are not pre-empted. In this case, the other provisions of the 1965 and 1969 Acts offer no cause to look beyond § 5 of each Act. Therefore, we need only identify the domain expressly pre-empted by each of those sections. As the 1965 and 1969 provisions differ substantially, we consider each in turn.

IV

In the 1965 pre-emption provision regarding advertising (§ 5(b)), Congress spoke precisely and narrowly: "No statement relating to smoking and health shall be required in the advertising of [properly labeled] cigarettes." Section 5(a) used the same phrase ("No statement relating to smoking and health") with regard to cigarette labeling. As § 5(a) made clear, that phrase referred to the sort of warning provided for in

§ 4, which set forth verbatim the warning Congress determined to be appropriate. Thus, on their face, these provisions merely prohibited state and federal rule-making bodies from mandating particular cautionary statements on cigarette labels (§ 5(a)) or in cigarette advertisements (§ 5(b)).

Beyond the precise words of these provisions, this reading is appropriate for several reasons. First, as discussed above, we must construe these provisions in light of the presumption against the pre-emption of state police power regulations. This presumption reinforces the appropriateness of a narrow reading of § 5. Second, the warning required in § 4 does not by its own effect foreclose additional obligations imposed under state law. That Congress requires a particular warning label does not automatically pre-empt a regulatory field. Third, there is no general, inherent conflict between federal pre-emption of state warning requirements and the continued vitality of state common law damages actions. For example, in the Comprehensive Smokeless Tobacco Health Education Act of 1986,[14] Congress expressly pre-empted State or local imposition of a "statement relating to the use of smokeless tobacco products and health" but, at the same time, preserved state law damages actions based on those products. See 15 U.S.C. § 4406. All of these considerations indicate that § 5 is best read as having superseded only positive enactments by legislatures or administrative agencies that mandate particular warning labels.

This reading comports with the 1965 Act's statement of purpose, which expressed an intent to avoid "diverse, nonuniform, and confusing labeling and advertising *regulations* with respect to any relationship between smoking and health." Read against the backdrop of regulatory activity undertaken by state legislatures and federal agencies in response to the Surgeon General's report, the term "regulation" most naturally refers to positive enactments by those bodies, not to common law damages actions.

The regulatory context of the 1965 Act also supports such a reading. As noted above, a warning requirement promulgated by the FTC and other requirements under consideration by the States were the catalyst for passage of the 1965 Act. These regulatory actions animated the passage of § 5, which reflected Congress' efforts to prevent "a multiplicity of State and local regulations pertaining to labeling of cigarette packages," H.R. Rep. No. 89–449, 89th Cong., 1st Sess., 4 (1965), and to "pre-empt [all] Federal, State, and local authorities from requiring any statement ... relating to smoking and health in the advertising of cigarettes." Id., at 5 (emphasis supplied).

For these reasons, we conclude that § 5 of the 1965 Act only pre-empted state and federal rulemaking bodies from mandating particular cautionary statements and did not pre-empt state law damages actions.

14. [15 U.S.C.A. §§ 4401–4408].

V

Compared to its predecessor in the 1965 Act, the plain language of the pre-emption provision in the 1969 Act is much broader. First, the later Act bars not simply "statements" but rather "requirement[s] or prohibitions . . . imposed under State law." Second, the later Act reaches beyond statements "in the advertising" to obligations "with respect to the advertising or promotion" of cigarettes.

Notwithstanding these substantial differences in language, both petitioner and respondents contend that the 1969 Act did not materially alter the pre-emptive scope of federal law. Their primary support for this contention is a sentence in a Committee Report which states that the 1969 amendment "clarified" the 1965 version of § 5(b). S. Rep. No. 91–566, p. 12 (1969). We reject the parties' reading as incompatible with the language and origins of the amendments. As we noted in another context, "[i]nferences from legislative history cannot rest on so slender a reed. Moreover, the views of a subsequent Congress form a hazardous basis for inferring the intent of an earlier one." The 1969 Act worked substantial changes in the law: rewriting the label warning, banning broadcast advertising, and allowing the FTC to regulate print advertising. In the context of such revisions and in light of the substantial changes in wording, we cannot accept the parties' claim that the 1969 Act did not alter the reach of § 5(b).

Petitioner next contends that § 5(b), however broadened by the 1969 Act, does not pre-empt *common law* actions. He offers two theories for limiting the reach of the amended § 5(b). First, he argues that common law damages actions do not impose "requirement[s] or prohibition[s]" and that Congress intended only to trump "state statute[s], injunction[s], or executive pronouncement[s]." We disagree; such an analysis is at odds both with the plain words of the 1969 Act and with the general understanding of common law damages actions. The phrase "[n]o requirement or prohibition" sweeps broadly and suggests no distinction between positive enactments and common law; to the contrary, those words easily encompass obligations that take the form of common law rules. As we noted in another context, "[state] regulation can be as effectively exerted through an award of damages as through some form of preventive relief. The obligation to pay compensation can be, indeed is designed to be, a potent method of governing conduct and controlling policy."

Although portions of the legislative history of the 1969 Act suggest that Congress was primarily concerned with positive enactments by States and localities, see S. Rep. No. 91–566, p. 12, the language of the Act plainly reaches beyond such enactments. "We must give effect to this plain language unless there is good reason to believe Congress intended the language to have some more restrictive meaning." In this case there is no "good reason to believe" that Congress meant less than what it said; indeed, in light of the narrowness of the 1965 Act, there is "good reason to believe" that Congress meant precisely what it said in amending that Act.

Moreover, common law damages actions of the sort raised by petitioner are premised on the existence of a legal duty and it is difficult to say that such actions do not impose "requirements or prohibitions." See W. Prosser, Law of Torts 4 (4th ed. 1971); Black's Law Dictionary 1489 (6th ed. 1990) (defining "tort" as "always [involving] a violation of some duty owing to plaintiff"). It is in this way that the 1969 version of § 5(b) differs from its predecessor: Whereas the common law would not normally require a vendor to use any specific *statement* on its packages or in its advertisements, it is the essence of the common law to enforce duties that are either affirmative *requirements* or negative prohibitions. We therefore reject petitioner's argument that the phrase "requirement or prohibition" limits the 1969 Act's pre-emptive scope to positive enactments by legislatures and agencies.

Petitioner's second argument for excluding common law rules from the reach of § 5(b) hinges on the phrase "imposed under State law." This argument fails as well. At least since Erie R. v. Tompkins, 304 U.S. 64 (1938), we have recognized the phrase "state law" to include common law as well as statutes and regulations. Indeed just last Term, the Court stated that the phrase "all other law, including State and municipal law" "does not admit of [a] distinction ... between positive enactments and common-law rules of liability." Although the presumption against pre-emption might give good reason to construe the phrase "state law" in a pre-emption provision more narrowly than an identical phrase in another context, in this case such a construction is not appropriate. As explained above, the 1965 version of § 5 was precise and narrow on its face; the obviously broader language of the 1969 version extended that section's pre-emptive reach. Moreover, while the version of the 1969 Act passed by the Senate pre-empted "any State *statute or regulation* with respect to ... advertising or promotion," S. Rep. No. 91–566, p. 16, the Conference Committee replaced this language with State *law* with respect to "advertising or promotion." In such a situation, § 5(b)'s pre-emption of "state law" cannot fairly be limited to positive enactments.

That the pre-emptive scope of § 5(b) cannot be limited to positive enactments does not mean that that section pre-empts all common law claims. For example, as respondents concede, § 5(b) does not generally pre-empt "state-law obligations to avoid marketing cigarettes with manufacturing defects or to use a demonstrably safer alternative design for cigarettes." For purposes of § 5(b), the common law is not of a piece.

Nor does the statute indicate that any familiar subdivision of common law claims is or is not pre-empted. We therefore cannot follow petitioner's passing suggestion that § 5(b) pre-empts liability for omissions but not for acts, or that § 5(b) pre-empts liability for unintentional torts but not for intentional torts. Instead we must fairly but—in light of the strong presumption against pre-emption—narrowly construe the precise language of § 5(b) and we must look to each of petitioner's common law claims to determine whether it is in fact pre-empted. The central inquiry in each case is straightforward: we ask whether the legal duty that is the predicate of the common law damages action constitutes a "requirement or prohibition based on smoking and health . . . imposed under State law with respect to . . . advertising or promotion," giving that clause a fair but narrow reading. As discussed below, each phrase within that clause limits the universe of common law claims pre-empted by the statute.

We consider each category of damages actions in turn. In doing so, we express no opinion on whether these actions are viable claims as a matter of state law; we assume *arguendo* that they are.

FAILURE TO WARN

To establish liability for a failure to warn, petitioner must show that "a warning is necessary to make a product . . . reasonably safe, suitable and fit for its intended use," that respondents failed to provide such a warning, and that that failure was a proximate cause of petitioner's injury. In this case, petitioner offered two closely related theories concerning the failure to warn: first, that respondents "were negligent in the manner [that] they tested, researched, sold, promoted, and advertised" their cigarettes; and second, that respondents failed to provide "adequate warnings of the health consequences of cigarette smoking." App. 85–86.

Petitioner's claims are pre-empted to the extent that they rely on a state law "requirement or prohibition . . . with respect to . . . advertising or promotion." Thus, insofar as claims under either failure to warn theory require a showing that respondents' post–1969 advertising or promotions should have included additional, or more clearly stated, warnings, those claims are pre-empted. The Act does not, however, pre-empt petitioner's claims that rely solely on respondents' testing or research practices or other actions unrelated to advertising or promotion.

BREACH OF EXPRESS WARRANTY

Petitioner's claim for breach of an express warranty arises under N.J. Stat. Ann. § 12A:2–313(1)(a) (West 1991), which provides:

"Any affirmation of fact or promise made by the seller to the buyer which relates to the goods and becomes part of the basis of the bargain creates an express warranty that the goods shall conform to the affirmation or promise."

Petitioner's evidence of an express warranty consists largely of statements made in respondents' advertising. Applying the Court of Appeals' ruling that Congress pre-empted damage[s] actions . . . that challenge . . . the propriety of a party's actions with respect to the "advertising and promotion of cigarettes," the District Court ruled that this claim "inevitably brings into question [respondents'] advertising and promotional activities, and is therefore pre-empted" after 1965. As demonstrated above, however, the 1969 Act does not sweep so broadly: the appropriate inquiry is not whether a claim challenges the "propriety" of advertising and promotion, but whether the claim would require the imposition under state law of a requirement or prohibition based on smoking and health with respect to advertising or promotion.

A manufacturer's liability for breach of an express warranty derives from, and is measured by, the terms of that warranty. Accordingly, the "requirements" imposed by [an] express warranty claim are not "imposed under State law," but rather imposed *by the warrantor.*[23] If, for example, a manufacturer expressly promised to pay a smoker's medical bills if she contracted emphysema, the duty to honor that promise could not fairly be said to be "imposed under state law," but rather is best understood as undertaken by the manufacturer itself. While the general duty not to breach warranties arises under state law, the particular "requirement . . . based on smoking and health . . . with respect to the advertising or promotion [of] cigarettes" in an express warranty claim arises from the manufacturer's statements in its advertisements. In short, a common law remedy for a contractual commitment voluntarily undertaken should not be regarded as a "requirement . . . *imposed under State law* "within the meaning of § 5(b).

That the terms of the warranty may have been set forth in advertisements rather than in separate documents is irrelevant to the preemption issue (though possibly not to the state law issue of whether the alleged warranty is valid and enforceable) because although the breach of warranty claim is made "with respect to advertising" it does not rest on a duty imposed under state law. Accordingly, to the extent that petitioner has a viable claim for breach of express warranties made by respondents, that claim is not pre-empted by the 1969 Act.

Fraudulent Misrepresentation

Petitioner alleges two theories of fraudulent misrepresentation. First, petitioner alleges that respondents, through their advertising, neutralized the effect of federally mandated warning labels. Such a claim is predicated on a state-law prohibition against statements in advertising and promotional materials that tend to minimize the health hazards associated with smoking. Such a *prohibition*, however, is merely the converse of a state law *requirement* that warnings be included in advertising and promotional materials. Section 5(b) of the 1969 Act pre-empts both requirements and prohibitions; it therefore supersedes petitioner's first fraudulent misrepresentation theory.

Regulators have long recognized the relationship between prohibitions on advertising that downplays the dangers of smoking and require-

---

23. Thus it is that express warranty claims are said to sound in contract rather than in tort. Compare Black's Law Dictionary 1489 (6th ed. 1990) (defining "tort": "There must always be a violation of some duty . . . and generally such duty must arise by operation of law and not by mere agreement of the parties") with id., at 322 (defining "contract": "An agreement between two . . . persons which creates an obligation").

ments for warnings in advertisements. For example, the FTC, in promulgating its initial trade regulation rule in 1964, criticized advertising that "associated cigarette smoking with such positive attributes as contentment, glamour, romance, youth, happiness . . . at the same time suggesting that smoking is an activity at least consistent with physical health and well-being." The Commission concluded:

"To avoid giving a false impression that smoking [is] innocuous, the cigarette manufacturer who represents the alleged pleasures or satisfactions of cigarette smoking in his advertising must also disclose the serious risks to life that smoking involves." 29 Fed. Reg., at 8356.

Long-standing regulations of the Food and Drug Administration express a similar understanding of the relationship between required warnings and advertising that "negates or disclaims" those warnings: "A hazardous substance shall not be deemed to have met [federal labeling] requirements if there appears in or on the label . . . statements, designs, or other graphic material that in any manner negates or disclaims [the required warning]." 21 CFR § 191.102 (1965). In this light it seems quite clear that petitioner's first theory of fraudulent misrepresentation is inextricably related to petitioner's first failure to warn theory, a theory that we have already concluded is largely pre-empted by § 5(b).

Petitioner's second theory, as construed by the District Court, alleges intentional fraud and misrepresentation both by "false representation of a material fact [and by] conceal[ment of] a material fact." The predicate of this claim is a state law duty not to make false statements of material fact or to conceal such facts. Our pre-emption analysis requires us to determine whether such a duty is the sort of requirement or prohibition proscribed by § 5(b).

Section 5(b) pre-empts only the imposition of state law obligations "with respect to the advertising or promotion" of cigarettes. Petitioner's claims that respondents concealed material facts are therefore not pre-empted insofar as those claims rely on a state law duty to disclose such facts through channels of communication other than advertising or promotion. Thus, for example, if state law obliged respondents to disclose material facts about smoking and health to an administrative agency, § 5(b) would not pre-empt a state law claim based on a failure to fulfill that obligation.

Moreover, petitioner's fraudulent misrepresentation claims that do arise with respect to advertising and promotions (most notably claims based on allegedly false statements of material fact made in advertisements) are not pre-empted by § 5(b). Such claims are not predicated on a "duty based on smoking and health" but rather on a more general obligation—the duty not to deceive. This understanding of fraud by intentional misstatement is appropriate for several reasons. First, in the 1969 Act, Congress offered no sign that it wished to insulate cigarette manufacturers from longstanding rules governing fraud. To the contrary, both the 1965 and the 1969 Acts explicitly reserved the FTC's authority to identify and punish deceptive advertising practices—an authority that the FTC had long exercised and continues to exercise. See § 5(c) of the 1965 Act; § 7(b) of the 1969 Act[.] This indicates that Congress intended the phrase "relating to smoking and health" (which was essentially unchanged by the 1969 Act) to be construed narrowly, so as not to proscribe the regulation of deceptive advertising.

Moreover, this reading of "based on smoking and health" is wholly consistent with the purposes of the 1969 Act. State law prohibitions on false statements of material fact do not create "diverse, nonuniform, and confusing" standards. Unlike state law obligations concerning the warning necessary to render a product "reasonably safe", state law proscriptions on intentional fraud rely only on a single, uniform standard: falsity. Thus, we conclude that the phrase "based on smoking and health" fairly but narrowly construed does not encompass the more general duty not to make fraudulent statements. Accordingly, petitioner's claim based on allegedly fraudulent statements made in respondents' advertisements are not pre-empted by § 5(b) of the 1969 Act.

CONSPIRACY TO MISREPRESENT OR CONCEAL MATERIAL FACTS

Petitioner's final claim alleges a conspiracy among respondents to misrepresent or conceal material facts concerning the health hazards of smoking. The predicate duty underlying this claim is a duty not to conspire to commit fraud. For the reasons stated in our analysis of petitioner's intentional fraud claim, this duty is not pre-empted by § 5(b) for it is not a prohibition "based on smoking and health" as that phrase is properly construed. Accordingly, we conclude that the 1969 Act does not pre-empt petitioner's conspiracy claim.

VI

To summarize our holding: The 1965 Act did not pre-empt state law damages actions; the 1969 Act pre-empts petitioner's claims based on a failure to warn and the neutralization of federally mandated warnings to the extent that those claims rely on omissions or inclusions in respondents' advertising or promotions; the 1969 Act does not pre-empt petitioner's claims based on express warranty, intentional fraud and misrepresentation, or conspiracy.

The judgment of the Court of Appeals is accordingly reversed in part and affirmed in part, and the case is remanded for further proceedings consistent with this opinion.

It is so ordered.

The concurrences and partial concurrences by JUSTICES BLACKMUN, SCALIA, KENNEDY and SOUTER are omitted.

Notes and Questions

1. Justice Steven's opinion commanded a plurality of four Justices. Three Justices, Blackmun, Kennedy and Souter, would have found that no

tort actions were preempted by either the 1965 or 1969 Acts. Two Justices, Scalia and Thomas, would have found all claims preempted. According to the Supreme Court in *Cipollone*, in determining if the field is occupied and the common law preempted, should the courts consider whether, in Professor Roger's words, "the field is occupied by remote sentinel only or must it be seized, tilled and harvested"? William H. Rogers, Jr., Environmental Law, § 2.12 at 46.

2. If preemption is express, not implied, as held by the plurality, what is the logic for construing the language narrowly? Do the same considerations against broad construction of an implied preemption apply with equal force to expressly preempted fields?

3. *Preemption Under FIFRA.* A plaintiff's state law tort claim against the manufacturer of a pesticide for inadequate warning may be preempted by the Federal Insecticide, Fungicide and Rodenticide Act (FIFRA). This act, which is codified at 7 U.S.C.A. § 136, is designed to provide a comprehensive system for the regulation and labeling of pesticides. The EPA is responsible for its enforcement; a pesticide that is duly registered with the EPA must be accompanied by a label that contains EPA-approved warnings that its product is adequate to protect health and environment. 7 U.S.C.A. § 136(q)(1)(G). Moreover, a label cannot contain language that is not approved by the EPA. 40 C.F.R. § 156.10(a)(1).

Following *Cipollone*, the question arises as to the effect of that decision's preemption analysis upon environmental or toxic tort suits involving pesticides, fungicides and rodenticides. Consider the observations of Professor Richard C. Ausness, The Impact of the *Cipollone* case on Federal Preemption Law, 15 J. Prod. & Tox. Liab. 1, 21–22 (1993):

[FIFRA] gives the EPA the power to oversee most aspects of pesticide development, manufacture, sale, and use. Although the states are given authority to regulate pesticide use to the extent that their activities do not conflict with FIFRA, the EPA retains exclusive control over pesticide labeling. Numerous persons have brought suit against pesticide manufacturers, claiming that EPA-approved warning labels were inadequate. As might be expected, pesticide manufacturers have argued that FIFRA preempts such claims.

[Prior to *Cipollone*,] courts have ruled in favor of the pesticide manufacturers, but a considerable minority have refused to preempt failure to warn claims. Virtually all courts have rejected express preemption and occupation of the field theories, electing instead to approach the preemption issue in terms of an actual conflict analysis. As in other preemption areas, most of [the pre-*Cipollone*] cases have turned on whether common-law claims are considered to be a form of regulation.

Applying the *Cipollone* Court's preemption analysis to FIFRA, one would start with the statute's preemption provision. This provision does not expressly preempt common-law claims; rather, it prohibits state law "requirements" inconsistent with federal safety standards. FIFRA's legislative history is also silent on the question of whether Congress intended to preempt state law failure to warn claims. Nevertheless, the Court, if it chose, could argue that FIFRA expressly preempts failure to warn claims because they rely on a state requirement with respect to labeling that differs from the requirement imposed by the EPA.

Do you agree with Professor Ausness' prediction? Consider the following opinion in Shaw v. Dow Brands, Inc.

SHAW v. DOW BRANDS, INC.

United States Court of Appeals, Seventh Circuit, 1993.
994 F.2d 364.

CUMMINGS, J.

Billy Joe Shaw claims his lungs were permanently damaged when, on August 12, 1990, he tried to clean his bathroom. Shaw mixed something called "X–14 Instant Mildew Stain Remover" with Dow Bathroom Cleaner, a product manufactured by defendant. Though he opened the windows, set the ceiling fan swirling and let the air conditioner blow, Shaw was twice overcome by the fumes. When an hour later he found it hard to breathe, Shaw went to a doctor and eventually was put in the hospital to treat a lung condition known as Bronchiolitis Obliterans, allegedly caused by exposure to toxic fumes.

Shaw sued a series of companies[.] * * * Shaw filed his suit in Massac County, Illinois; Dow Brands had it removed to federal court in the Southern District of Illinois. The district judge decided that Shaw's state law strict liability and negligence claims for failure to warn were pre-empted by the Federal Insecticide, Fungicide and Rodenticide Act, more commonly and easily referred to as FIFRA, 7 U.S.C. § 136 et seq. Based on a recent Supreme Court decision, we affirm the district court's pre-emption finding. * * *

* * *

[W]e must decide whether federal pre-emption of an area of regulation also prohibits state common law tort actions. The district judge found that because of FIFRA, the federal law in question, Shaw could not bring a damages action claiming that the label on Dow Bathroom Cleaner was defective because Congress alone may regulate the labels and warnings on such products. FIFRA, enacted in 1947, was originally intended as a licensing and labeling statute for pesticides. Amendments in 1972 strengthened the law, and it became a comprehensive regulation of the sale and use of pesticides and other chemicals including such products as bathroom cleaners. Wisconsin Public Intervenor v. Mortier, 111 S.Ct. 2476 (1991).

* * * Whether a federal statute pre-empts state law turns on congressional intent. That intent may be explicit in the statute itself, Jones v. Rath Packing Co., 430 U.S. 519, 525 [1977]; in this case it is, at least as far as labeling and packaging are concerned. The Act says flatly: "Such State shall not impose or continue in effect any requirements for labeling or packaging in addition to or different from those required under this subchapter." 7 U.S.C. § 136v(b). The Supreme Court recently

noted the absolutist nature of FIFRA's pre-emption in the labeling and packaging context even as it held that FIFRA does not pre-empt generalized state regulation of pesticides. Mortier, 111 S.Ct. at 2486. Since the parties do not dispute that Congress has exclusive jurisdiction in labeling and packaging, the only question is: how exclusive is exclusive? Shaw maintains that there is still room for common law tort actions for defective labels.

Shaw's argument is appealing because, unlike federal regulations which firms are required to follow, common law duties may be simply ignored by defendants. See, e.g., Ferebee v. Chevron Chemical Co., 736 F.2d 1529, 1540–1541 (D.C.Cir.), cert. denied, 469 U.S. 1062 (1984) (despite pre-emption under FIFRA, state may decide that manufacturer should bear the risk for compensating losses). Indeed, they are smart to do so if the cost of compensating victims is less than the cost of altering the behavior that gives rise to the suit. On the other hand, damages actions, just like regulatory mandates, cause companies to modify their economic decisions. It would be silly to pretend that federal lawmakers, seeking to occupy a whole field of regulation, wouldn't also be concerned about the distorting effects of tort actions.

In any event, Shaw's argument about common law actions evaporated last summer when the Supreme Court decided Cipollone v. Liggett Group, Inc., 112 S.Ct. 2608 (1992). That opinion held that sweeping congressional efforts to pre-empt state regulation also bar state damages claims. Although the Court said that "there is no general, inherent conflict between federal pre-emption of state warning requirements and the continued vitality of state common law damages actions," it also held that a broad statement in a federal law prohibiting state regulation does, in fact, wipe away common law attempts to impose liability on top of the federal regulation.

The federal laws at issue in Cipollone were the Federal Cigarette Labeling and Advertising Act ("1965 Cigarette Act") and the Public Health Cigarette Smoking Act of 1969 ("1969 Cigarette Act"), 15 U.S.C. §§ 1331–1340. These laws are responsible for, among other things, the surgeon general's warnings that grace the sides of cigarette packages. The pre-emption provision in the 1965 Cigarette Act was quite narrow and said, "No statement relating to smoking and health shall be required in the advertising of [properly labeled] cigarettes." Congress' emphasis on the words "statement" and "advertising" led the Court to conclude that the 1965 Cigarette Act only pre-empted state and federal rules that might require additional warnings, but not state law damages actions. The 1969 Cigarette Act, however, was much broader; it barred not merely "statements" but any "requirement[s] or prohibition[s] * * * imposed under State law." This language, the Court held, signalled legislative intent to ban common law tort actions along with direct state regulation. As Justice Stevens wrote:

> The phrase "[n]o requirement or prohibition" sweeps broadly and suggests no distinction between positive enactments and common

law; to the contrary, those words easily encompass obligations that take the form of common law rules. As we noted in another context, "[state] regulation" can be as effectively exerted through an award of damages as through some form of preventive relief. The obligation to pay compensation can be, indeed is designed to be, a potent method of governing conduct and controlling policy.

In order to succeed in the wake of Cipollone, then, Shaw would have to show that FIFRA's pre-emption language is less sweeping than the language of the 1969 Cigarette Act. Yet we can discern no significant distinction at all—FIFRA says that "[s]uch State shall not impose * * * any requirements for labeling or packaging in addition to or different from those required * * *," while the cigarette law says "[n]o require-ment[s] or prohibition[s] * * * imposed under State law" shall be permitted. Both seem equally emphatic: "[n]o requirements or prohibi-tions" is just another way of saying a "[s]tate shall not impose * * * any requirements." Not even the most dedicated hair-splitter could distin-guish these statements. If common law actions cannot survive under the 1969 cigarette law, then common law actions for labeling and packaging defects cannot survive under FIFRA. The Tenth Circuit recently held the same thing. Arkansas–Platte & Gulf Partnership v. Van Waters & Rogers, Inc., 981 F.2d 1177, 1179 (10th Cir.1993) ("We believe also the prohibition of 'any' requirement is the functional equivalent of 'no' requirement. We see no difference between the operative effect of the two acts"). Because Cipollone destroyed whatever argument Shaw might have had about pre-emption, we are compelled to affirm the district court decision that FIFRA bars this action.

The Dissent by SHADUR, S.D.J., is omitted.

Notes and Questions

1. A further discussion of issues of preemption as it relates to products liability is contained in Chapter 7. See generally Richard C. Ausness, The Impact of *Cipollone* on Federal Preemption Law, 15 J. Prod. & Tox. Liab. 1 (1993); Valle Simms Dutcher, The Malboro Man Meets the Orkin Man: The Effect of Cipollone v. Liggett Group, Inc. on Federal Preemption by the Federal Insecticide, Fungicide and Rodenticide Act of Failure to Warn Claims Brought Under State Tort Law, 15 J. Prod. & Tox. Liab. 29 (1993).

2. In the above article, Dutcher writes:

[After] *Cipollone*, several causes of action relating to failure to warn remain open to plaintiffs [alleging toxic harm caused by products regulated under FIFRA]. First, the Court did not address the issue of whether a manufacturer's failure to submit an adequate label in compli-ance with federal standards could be held negligence per se. Further, the Court stated that claims based on defendant's negligent testing proce-dures were not preempted under the 1969 Cigarette Act. Therefore, it could be argued that a pesticide manufacturer is negligent when the label it submits to EPA is inadequate due to insufficient testing. Additionally, the *Cipollone* Court held that breach of warranty actions are not preempted by federal law[.] [Because pesticide manufacturers] submit a label as part of the application for registration under FIFRA, it could be argued that such a submission represents an implied warranty that the product is fit for foreseeable uses in the marketplace.

On the basis of Dutcher's observations, how would you craft additional arguments for Shaw's claim against Dow Brands?

B. STATE JUDICIAL CONSIDERATIONS OF PREEMPTION: A COMPLEMENTARY APPROACH

1.   In State of Missouri ex rel. Dresser Indus. v. Ruddy, 592 S.W.2d 789 (Mo.1980), the defendant, Dresser, conducted a barite mining operation, which used settling basins with holding ponds which collected waste from the mining activity. A "dam" in the settling basin ruptured, thus polluting the streams, and ultimately a major river, for a period of 200 days. The Missouri Clean Water Commissioner and Department of Natural Resources brought a two-count action, one alleging a violation of clean water law and the other alleging public nuisance, seeking compensatory and punitive damages. Dresser argued that (1) the State could not maintain an action on a nuisance theory, and (2) the Clean Water Act preempted the field, thereby displacing common law nuisance. The court held that the government could maintain a public nuisance action for damages or injunctive relief. A statute provided that "pollution of the waters of this State constitutes a menace ... and creates a public nuisance.... " The court found inapplicable authorities declaring that a public entity was barred from recovering damages for the harm to the protectable public interests. On the preemption question the Missouri Supreme Court wrote:

> Did enactment of the Clean Water Law, Chapter 204, pre-empt the field of water pollution "public nuisance" law in Missouri? We have concluded that it did not. Section 204.131, heretofore quoted, in part declares that the Act does not alter or abridge "any right of action" now existing. In so providing, it is apparent that the General Assembly intended to *expand* rather than restrict available remedies. In accordance with the prescriptions of the Federal Water Pollution Control Act, 33 U.S.C. §§ 1251, et seq., § 1253 (1976), the Clean Water Commission was created under the Department of Natural Resources in 1972. §§ 204.021, 204.136, RSMo Supp. 1975. Eminent among its duties is the development of "comprehensive plans and programs for the prevention, control and abatement of new or existing pollution of the waters of the state." § 204.026.2 * * * [T]he statutory scheme envisions a comprehensive remedial approach to water pollution problems, but preservation of common law remedies is consistent therewith—simply because preservation thereof strengthens and makes cumulative the powers of those charged with taking corrective measures.... Because of the provisions of § 204.131, nothing could be gained by an effort to analyze

cases holding otherwise, and we hold that enactment of Chapter 204 did not proscribe common-law nuisance actions for pollution of streams and waterways on behalf of the state or private individuals.

2. It is significant that the last sentence preserves the common law nuisance actions for both public and private parties. Was it critical that the Missouri Clean Water Act contained a savings clause that explicitly preserved "any right of action" now existing? What would have been the outcome if the statute had been silent about the preservation of state common law rights?

In the area of state horizontal preemption (whether a state's regulatory scheme preempts a state's common law) the cases reflect the presumption *against* preemption, and the courts do not usually find a preclusive effect in the absence of explicit legislative intent or an irreconcilable conflict between the statutory objectives and the common law rights.

3. In Marshall v. Consumers Power Co., 65 Mich.App. 237, 237 N.W.2d 266 (1975) a state appellate court considered a vertical preemption question. The plaintiff brought action in state court claiming that defendant's proposed nuclear power plant would constitute a nuisance (a) because its cooling system would create dangerous and annoying "fog and icing" in the vicinity of the plant and (b) because of "the possibility of nuclear accident." The Federal Atomic Energy Commission (AEC) [Now the Nuclear Regulatory Commission] after lengthy hearings had issued a permit authorizing construction of the plant, and a federal appeal from that action was pending. The trial court dismissed plaintiff's nuisance suit on the ground that the federal scheme for regulating atomic energy "preempted the field." But the appellate court disagreed. Federal regulation "preempts state action concerning radiological, but not non-radiological matters." Thus state courts may hear plaintiff's complaint about "effects of steam, fog and icing" and may issue a remedy "founded on common law nuisance theory." The Michigan Court explained:

> First, the parties, the rights adjudicated, the interests alleged, and the basic nature of the forum are so different in a state court from what they are in AEC administrative hearings that an adjudication by one should not always prevent the other from deciding a similar question. * * *

> * * * A state court must make a case-by-case determination based on a number of factors. * * * In each case, of course, the court is a neutral arbiter. In each case, the only concern is the adjudication of a state common law right.

> The AEC, on the other hand, cannot be accurately termed neutral. The agency was established to fulfill the often conflicting goals of both regulating and promoting nuclear energy. * * * The tendency of regulatory agencies to be 'captured' by those whom they regulate is well known. In the agency balancing process, state and local interests will be but one factor, and they will have to compete

against concerns vital to national and international policy. Commentators have opined that, in AEC determinations, such Federal concerns as the promotion of nuclear power and the national need for more sources of energy will get greater precedence than such local concerns as icing or fogging.

* * *

Second, without recourse to a state court, * * * a private citizen would be forced to raise the state interest by appealing the AEC ruling. * * * [R]eviewing courts will defer to an agency determination so long as, upon an examination of the whole record, there is substantial evidence upon which the agency could reasonably base its decision. Judicial deference to AEC expertise may make this review a narrow one.

Were you surprised by the court's distinction between "radiological" and "non radiological" matters? Is that a viable and meaningful distinction upon which to circumvent the strong preemption in the nuclear regulatory field?

4. Consider Silkwood v. Kerr–McGee, 464 U.S. 238, 104 S.Ct. 615, 78 L.Ed.2d 443 (1984), where the Supreme Court ruled that the federal statutory scheme did bar the states from regulating the safety aspects of nuclear development and of hazardous nuclear materials, but nevertheless, found ample evidence in the legislative history of the Price–Anderson Act that Congress did not intend to forbid states from providing tort remedies for injuries caused by nuclear radiation. As a result, "[s]tate law remedies, in whatever form they might take, [are] available to those injured by nuclear accidents." Consequently, the mere fact that the federal government has occupied the field of safety does not foreclose state remedies for radiation injuries. Rather, the test for determining preemption in the nuclear energy field is:

> [1] whether there is an irreconcilable conflict between the federal and state standards or [2] whether the imposition of a state standard in a damages action would frustrate the objectives of the federal law. See also, Bennett v. Mallinckrodt, Inc., 698 S.W.2d 854 (Mo.App.1985) (no preemption of state law claim for damages from injuries at radiopharmaceutical processing plant).

5. In some cases the courts find that the federal and state regulatory schemes are not only not irreconcilable, but rather complementary, and apply the statutory objectives and the defendant's breach thereof to support a common law nuisance action. In Miotke v. City of Spokane, 101 Wash.2d 307, 678 P.2d 803 (1984), private owners of waterfront property sued the City of Spokane for injunctive and monetary relief for discharging raw sewage into the river. The Washington Supreme Court stated that the fundamental issue was whether "any cause of action lies against governmental units for injuries allegedly caused by their actions taken in violation of various environmental laws." The court found that discharging raw sewage into the Spokane River in violation of a waste

disposal permit to be a wrongful act which gives rise to a public nuisance action. After the court summarizes the harm suffered by the plaintiffs as a result of defendants' bypassing the ordinary treatment process in order to expedite construction of a new treatment facility, the court concluded that defendant's failure to secure a permit for the bypass was a violation of state and federal water pollution laws.

The court then addressed the question of the availability of a private action based on those violations, since the statutes contained no provisions authorizing a *private* party to sue for damages. The court considered the state statutes which generally recognize a nuisance cause of action and concluded that a nuisance action could be maintained:

> The October 1975 bypass constituted a nuisance under the statutory definitions. It was a wrongful act (RCW 7.48.120) because it was conducted in violation of a waste disposal permit and RCW 90.48. The bypass therefore does not fall within the protection of [the state law] which insulates acts performed under express statutory authority from actions for nuisance. Moreover, the trial court concluded that the bypass "denied Plaintiffs the full use and enjoyment of their lake front properties and lifestyle." There is ample support for this conclusion in the record. This is equivalent to a finding that the bypass "essentially interfere[d] with the comfortable enjoyment of the life and property" of plaintiffs [in violation of the state's nuisance law].

> The bypass, therefore, constituted a nuisance for which an action in damages may be maintained[.] The bypass affected the rights of all members of the community living along the shores of Long Lake. It therefore comprised a public nuisance[.]

> The plaintiffs are entitled to bring an action for this public nuisance because they can show it is "specially injurious" to themselves. RCW 7.48.210. As residents of properties along the waterfront, plaintiffs suffered as a result of the bypass injuries considerably greater than those suffered by the general public.

6. Miotke is important precedent for the proposition that private parties can maintain a private and public nuisance action for violation of the state and federal water pollution laws. The court did not dispense with the special injury requirement for public nuisance actions brought by private parties because it found the nuisance "specially injurious" to plaintiffs. It is also significant that plaintiffs recovered attorneys fees of $88,000 because of the public interest vindicated by their suit. In that sense plaintiffs acted as private attorneys general vindicating a public right that was violated by a public entity.

7. See also, Concerned Citizens of Bridesburg v. City of Philadelphia, 643 F.Supp. 713 (E.D.Pa.1986), affirmed, 843 F.2d 679 (3d Cir. 1988), allowing residents to maintain an action under the citizens' suit provisions of state law against the city for "malodors" emanating from a sewage disposal plant, contrary to the Pennsylvania Air Pollution Control Act and the Philadelphia Air Management Code. The court found

that private common law rights were "additional and cumulative remedies to abate pollution of the air," consistent with the statutory scheme. The court allowed an injunction even though plaintiffs had failed to notify the Attorney General as required under the state law; it also disallowed an award of attorneys' fees.

C. NEGLIGENCE PER SE

In some instances a plaintiff may contend that the defendant's violation of a regulatory standard can be utilized to support a private right of action for damages. The contention is that the regulatory standard represents a standard of conduct or standard of care that should be applicable to civil tort cases even though the legislature or administrative agency was silent about the standard's possible application to such civil litigation. The doctrine that incorporates this offensive use of violations of regulatory standards is negligence per se—that is, the defendant's breach of the regulatory requirement is treated as a breach of the standard of conduct that is inferred by the court from the regulatory standard. Where the requisites of the negligence per se doctrine are met, the statute or regulation creates the standard of conduct (or care) that the actor must achieve; the violation of the statute or regulation constitutes the breach of the standard of conduct (or care), and is therefore regarded as conclusive proof of negligence.

In matters of environmental or toxic torts, plaintiffs frequently argue that the breach of the regulatory standard should constitute negligence per se and provide a cause of action, independent of any cause of action for nuisance, strict liability or trespass. An overarching requirement is that the regulatory standard that the plaintiff urges is applicable pertain precisely to the same risk, the same protected class, and the same harm as actually occurred, which is to say, the conventional requirements for application of negligence per se. Per the holding in Nunez v. J.L. Sims Co., Inc., 2003 WL 21473328 (Ohio App. 1st Dist. 2003), the regulatory standard must also be clear as to the specific duty imposed, the person upon whom the duty is imposed, and the absolute nature of the duty, as distinct from leaving "to the trier of fact a determination from all of the facts and circumstances of each particular case whether the alleged violator acted as a reasonably prudent person would have." Nunez was a multi-count tort claim brought by a house purchaser against the seller, the realtor and others in which there was evidence that one or more defendants had failed to comply with regulations regarding lead paint disclosure:

* * *

The Nunezes alleged negligence per se by Carney, Rakstang, Re/Max, and Associates in counts 24 and 25. In their complaint, they cited to the "Federal Residential Lead–Based Paint Hazard Reduction Act (40 C.F.R. Section 745.113 et seq.)" that imposed specific duties upon the sellers who "breached these specific safety requirements contained in the regulations and this constitutes negligence per se."

The Ohio Supreme Court has distinguished rulemaking from lawmaking in the application of negligence per se, stating that strict compliance with a multitude of rules put forth by administrative agencies would be virtually impossible and would open the floodgates to litigation. [Cc] Even if a negligence-per-se analysis was applicable in this case, the violations claimed by the Nunezes would not have survived scrutiny as a matter of law. We note that the Ohio Supreme Court has distinguished negligence per se from negligence as follows: "Where there exists a legislative enactment commanding or prohibiting for the safety of others the doing of a specific act and there is a violation of such enactment solely by one whose duty it is to obey it, such violation constitutes negligence per se; but where there exists a legislative enactment expressing for the safety of others, in general or abstract terms, a rule of conduct, negligence per se has no application and liability must be determined by the application of the test of due care as exercised by a reasonably prudent person under the circumstances of the case." [Cc] The Ohio Supreme Court has rejected a claim of negligence per se for the violation of a state statute that imposed no fixed and absolute duty that was the same under all circumstances, but rather left to the trier of fact a determination from all of the facts and circumstances of each particular case whether the alleged violator acted as a reasonably prudent person would have and that left the determination whether a violation had occurred to the consideration of more than a single issue of fact. [Cc]

In this case, more than a single issue of fact had to be considered before a determination could be made whether the regulations in Section 745.107 et seq., Title 40, C.F.R., issued pursuant to the Residential Lead–Based Paint Hazard Reduction Act of 1992, had been violated. Among other things, the conduct at issue required a determination by a trier of fact whether any person had "knowingly" violated the duties imposed for the disclosure of lead-based-paint hazards; whether some other equivalent pamphlet approved by the EPA for use in one's state was given to the potential buyer if the EPA document identified in the regulations was not; whether the potential buyer waived his opportunity to conduct a risk assessment or inspection; and whether the waiver was properly documented. Clearly the consideration of more than just one fact, the commission or omission of a specific act prohibited or required, would have been required. [Cc] In light of this, we cannot hold that the Nunezes' claimed regulatory violations, even if identical to violations of the federal statute, could have provided a basis for the application of negligence per se. Because negligence per se had no application in this case, the trial court did not err in granting summary judgment on these claims.

Notes

As both Nunez and the following article demonstrate, some regulatory standards are appropriate for use in civil litigation as a standard of care, and others are not. It is for the court, not the jury, to decide in individual cases the propriety of applying the regulatory standard to tort cases.

SHEILA BUSH, CAN YOU GET THERE FROM HERE? NONCOMPLIANCE WITH ENVIRONMENTAL REGULATION AS NEGLIGENCE PER SE IN TORT CASES

25 Idaho L.R. 469 (1988–1989).

* * *

[B] THE REQUIREMENT OF A CLEAR STANDARD

The first requirement for application of the negligence per se doctrine is that the statute, ordinance or regulation clearly define the required standard of conduct. If the regulation is clear, a reasonable person presumably can determine and meet the standard of conduct. Despite a well-developed and often well-deserved reputation for unabashed complexity, environmental regulations appear fairly clear in some instances.

An environmental regulation that imposes a specific numerical standard appears definite on its face. For example, the primary and secondary NAAQS for ozone under the Clean Air Act is "0.12 part per million (230 ug/m3)" measured by a designated reference method; "the standard is attained when the expected number of days per calendar year with maximum hourly average concentrations above 0.12 part per million (235 ug/m3) is equal to or less than one," as determined by a designated method. If a facility caused a monitoring device to register 0.44 ppm for three days in 1988 under the designated reference method, then it clearly failed to comply with the regulation. In a tort suit, the plaintiff's counsel could argue that the company's conduct fell below the standard established by law or the protection of others against unreasonable risk of harm, i.e., that the company was negligent per se.

However, this superficial analysis of clarity fails to account for the way standards actually are set. For example, in setting the ozone standard, the EPA considered the available scientific information on the effects of ozone on human health and the environment. EPA then exercised its judgment, allowing a margin of safety, and established the number (0.12 ppm) for the standard. Although the numerical standard is certainly clear, the data on which it is based did not lead inexorably to that conclusion. The number was chosen based only on the scientific evidence available at the time it was set, and the agency's best judgment. A violation of the standard therefore may not necessarily signal unreasonable behavior in terms of health or environmental risk.

A violation of a standard later determined scientifically infirm offers the most extreme illustration of this proposition. In fact, the EPA has withdrawn and modified standards based on a better understanding of the scientific evidence. State environmental agencies, lacking the resources of the EPA, often are forced to set standards or regulations based on skimpy records of scientific evidence. * * *

* * *

Many environmental regulations, although complex, apparently meet the clarity requirement of the negligence per se doctrine. However, other factors may militate against using the standard of conduct contained in an environmental regulation. Since a numerical standard is based solely on available scientific evidence and agency judgment, non-compliance with a standard may not necessarily result in unreasonable behavior in terms of health or environmental risk. In addition, the agency may promulgate regulations inconsistent with the enabling statute. The difficulty environmental regulations present in meeting the clarity requirement is echoed in the applicability requirements.

C.   CLASS OF PERSONS PROTECTED

* * *

Historically, the negligence per se doctrine has recognized that courts should adopt as the standard of conduct only the requirements of statutes and regulations intended to protect a particular class of individuals, and not the interests of the state or the public at large. * * *

A hypothetical scenario illustrates the issue in the environmental context. A plaintiff who has lived for many years beneath the stack of a smelter now brings suit alleging injury to health caused by exposure to lead and to fine particles. The plaintiff argues that the smelter periodically violated the national ambient standards for lead and particulate matter under the Clean Air Act, and thus was negligent per se. But are the standards 'applicable?' The courts have already agreed that Congress' 'paramount consideration' in enacting the Clean Air Act was protection of public health. While the plaintiff argues that he is a member of the class intended to be protected, the defendant smelter argues that the standards promulgated under the Clean Air Act are not appropriate targets for negligence per se because they are intended to protect the public at large, not a particular class.

When the plaintiff offers an environmental statute or regulation to establish the standard of conduct in a tort case, this issue likely will recur because the purpose Congress advanced in the statutes was protection of the public at large. * * *

D.   TYPE OF RISK COVERED

* * *

When an environmental regulation imposes a numerical standard calculated to protect human health and environment, a plaintiff alleging injury to health or property caused by non-compliance with the standard appears to state exactly the harm the regulation was intended to prevent. Because of the different levels of proof required, the courts should hesitate to elevate the regulation to a standard of conduct, whereby the violation of such standard would establish negligence. A plaintiff in a tort case must prove the defendant's breach of duty by a preponderance of the evidence based on adjudicative facts. By contrast, an administrative agency considers legislative facts and exercises its judgment to adopt a regulation setting a numerical standard based on the scientific evidence presented, and incorporating a margin of safety. Unlike the tort case, the 'evidence' in a rulemaking proceeding need not demonstrate the conclusion reached by a preponderance of the evidence.

* * *

Permitting regulations raise equally difficult issues. Traditionally, courts found that the only purpose of a statute imposing an automobile registration requirement was to raise revenue, so the driver of an unlicensed car was not liable to those with whom he collided if he was otherwise exercising proper care. Although resembling a registration requirement, a permit requirement accomplishes more than mere registration because it translates statutory and regulatory requirements into specific obligations for an individual facility.

A key provision of any permitting regulatory scheme is the requirement to obtain a permit in certain instances. For example, a person who discharges a pollutant from a point source into the waters of the United States must obtain an NPDES permit. If a company fails to get a permit when required, and an individual alleges injury from exposure to the unpermitted effluent discharged, courts will have to determine whether failure to obtain a required permit causes harm the regulation was designed to prevent. The court can either allow the plaintiff to establish negligence per se based on the company's failure to get a permit, or allow proof regarding the reasonableness of the company's conduct, or both.

The Fourth Circuit [has] determined * * * that failure to obtain a permit does not constitute negligence per se.[83] Schlitz Brewing Company had violated a city ordinance that required every user of industrial sewers to obtain a discharge permit. The ordinance also limited a user's discharge to wastes containing 2,500 ppm biochemical oxygen demand (BOD) or less, and imposed surcharges for BOD pound loadings caused by concentrations above 300 ppm. Until April of 1971, Schlitz operated without a permit and paid BOD surcharges since its effluent contained more than 2,500 ppm BOD. Land owners along the Yadkin River alleged that the brewery overloaded the city sewage treatment plant, causing it to pollute the river, kill unprecedented numbers of fish, and damage their riverfront property.

The court found that Schlitz's failure to obtain a permit until May, 1971 did not provide the plaintiffs with grounds for recovery. The Fourth Circuit reasoned that the required permit did not protect ripari-

83. Springer v. Joseph Schlitz Brewing Co., 510 F.2d 468 (4th Cir.1975).

an land owners, but was only an instrument of the city's enforcement program. The absence of a permit, and the failure to comply with the permitting ordinance, did not pollute the river. A logical corollary follows from the court's reasoning: If a company has acted reasonably in controlling pollution, then its failure to obtain a permit should not constitute negligence per se; conversely, if a company has acted unreasonably, the company is indeed negligent, but the failure to obtain a permit is independent of the negligence.

[T]he Supreme Court of New Hampshire reached the opposite result in Bagley v. Controlled Environment Corp.[90] The plaintiff alleged that the defendant dumped oil, grease, and other waste materials on its property that contaminated the plaintiff's nearby land and groundwater, and caused her personal injury. The plaintiff alleged generally that the defendant had violated the New Hampshire statutes governing hazardous wastes. One statute required that any person operating a 'hazardous waste facility,' defined as a location where hazardous waste is disposed, obtain a permit. The court noted that the plaintiff's pleading was unclear regarding whether the violation alleged was the failure to obtain a permit, the failure to abide by the terms of a permit, or the failure to conform to the substantive requirements of the statute and regulations.

The court held that both the failure to obtain a permit and the failure to comply with permit terms stated a cause of action based on statutory noncompliance. It reasoned that the legislature regarded the permit process as the essential opportunity to develop detailed substantive standards for a specific facility, so that failure to submit to the permit process could preclude the derivation of standards adequate to protect the public against the dangers posed by hazardous wastes. Given the function of the permitting process, the court reasoned that permit conditions should be accorded the same status as standards contained in a statute or rule.

* * *

IV. WHERE TO GO WHEN YOU CAN'T GET THERE FROM HERE

Noncompliance with environmental regulations does not lead neatly to negligence per se. The folk wisdom "you can't get there from here" perhaps more accurately describes the relationship. Negligence per se grew up in an era when statutes and regulations more likely reflected a societal consensus on the standard of conduct required in particular situations. Environmental regulations more often reflect an imperfect judgment based on uncertain scientific evidence locked at a point in time already past. * * *

* * *

One possible solution may lie in the treatment accorded statutory and regulatory noncompliance originally rejected by courts in favor of the negligence per se doctrine. The negligence per se doctrine deems

90. 503 A.2d 823 (N.H.1986).

negligence to be conclusively shown once the breach of an applicable statute has been proven, and requires the court to so direct the jury. Courts have treated a violation of a statute or regulation differently under the doctrines of negligence per se with excuse, prima facie case of negligence, and mere evidence of negligence, as well as negligence per se. * * *

The negligence per se with excuse doctrine represents an incremental shift away from the conclusiveness of the strict negligence per se theory by allowing the court to excuse reasonable departures from the regulatory standard. Once the plaintiff has proven noncompliance within an environmental regulation, the burden of proof shifts to the defendant to show sufficient evidence to excuse or justify defeating the presumption. So long as a court maintains flexibility in accepting evidence of excuse, this doctrine appears to provide the defendant with an opportunity to address the noncompliance issue while still providing the plaintiff a hopscotch over the proof of duty and breach.

The prima facie case of negligence theory presents an option one more step removed from negligence per se. The plaintiff's evidence of noncompliance with an environmental regulation under this theory is sufficient to withstand a motion to dismiss. Demonstration of noncompliance with an environmental regulation assures the plaintiff that the jury will consider the case, but the defendant is equally assured of the opportunity to present relevant evidence in rebuttal. * * *

The final option of treating noncompliance with an environmental regulation as "mere evidence of negligence" may be most appropriate. Jurisdictions that treat noncompliance as mere evidence of negligence attach less significance to noncompliance with a statute or regulation. The "mere evidence" theory does not shift the burden of proof to the defendant nor give greater weight to evidence of a violation than to any other type of evidence. The rationale for this theory is that the statutes and regulations only represent "the collective opinion or judgment of the community in the matter." Since environmental regulations represent only the agency's collective judgment on uncertain science, the reasoning behind the theory applies. Courts therefore should consider foregoing the negligence per se doctrine in favor of the mere evidence negligence treatment.

* * *

Notes and Questions

1. In Bagley v. Controlled Environment Corp., 127 N.H. 556, 503 A.2d 823 (1986), discussed in the Bush article, the plaintiff's suit also contained a count asserting strict liability for abnormally dangerous activities under Restatement (Second) of Torts §§ 519 and 520. The New Hampshire Supreme Court, in an opinion by Judge (now U.S. Supreme Court Justice) Souter, rejected the Rylands v. Fletcher doctrine on the ground that in most situations where plaintiffs seek to rely on the doctrine, they can usually

establish the defendant's failure to exercise reasonable care, and therefore, prove a negligence cause of action. Do you agree with this conclusion?

The court's consideration of the negligence per se doctrine based on the statutory violation is instructive. The court employs the expression "causal violation" rather than negligence per se, but the analysis is identical:

Souter, J., delivered the opinion of the court.

* * *

While we * * * affirm the dismissal of the count in strict liability, it does not follow that the dangers of hazardous waste will have no particular recognition in the law of the State, because we do hold that the plaintiff has stated a cause of action predicated on a statutory violation. "It is well established law in this State that a causal violation of a statutory standard of conduct constitutes legal fault in the same manner as does the causal violation of a common law standard of due care, that is, causal negligence. In both instances liability is imposed because of the existence of legal fault, that is, a departure from a required standard of conduct." Moulton v. Groveton Papers Co., 112 N.H. 50, 52, 289 A.2d 68, 71 (1972)[.] A causal violation, as that term is used here, is a violation resulting in the damage that the statute was apparently intended to guard against.

* * *

Insofar as the count pleads a violation of RSA chapter 147–A (Supp. 1983), however, it rests on firmer footing. RSA 147–A:4, I (Supp. 1983) requires, inter alia, that any person "operating" a "hazardous waste facility" obtain a permit. An "operator" is "any person who ... operates, or otherwise directs or controls activities at a facility." RSA 147–A:2, XI (Supp. 1983). A "facility" is "a location at which hazardous waste is subjected to ... disposal." RSA 147–A:2, IV (Supp. 1983). "Waste" includes "spent, discarded or abandoned material." RSA 147–A:2, XVIII (Supp. 1983). "Hazardous waste" includes a "liquid ... [w]hich, because of either quantity, concentration, or physical, chemical, or infectious characteristics may ... [p]ose a present or potential threat to human health or the environment when improperly ... disposed of." RSA 147–A:2, VII(a)(2) (Supp. 1983). Such an operator is obligated to conform to the standards set forth in RSA chapter 147–A (Supp. 1983) and in any rules adopted by the office of waste management, and to obey the terms and conditions of any permit issued to him. See RSA 147–A:9,:14, I,:16,:17, I (Supp. 1983).

Turning to the plaintiff's pleadings, the declaration charges that the defendant was an operator of a facility in the sense, at the least, that it disposed of a liquid that was hazardous waste by virtue of its threat to health. It is likewise clear that the declaration charges the defendant with causing contamination and injury by means of disposal of such waste.

The only further allegation necessary to state a claim for causal violation of the statute is the allegation of the violation itself. Although the declaration expressly charges a violation, it does so without specifying whether the violation consisted of a failure to obtain a permit, failure to abide by the terms of a permit or failure to conform to the substantive requirements of the statute or of agency rules. While the courts and parties can reasonably demand more specific pleading than this, under our traditional practice the remedy for undue generality at this stage of a case is normally an order requiring a more definite statement rather than an order of dismissal. We will, therefore, consider the three possible specifications mentioned above, to determine whether the express allegation of one or more of them would complete the statement of a cause of action and withstand a motion to dismiss.

Under the traditional rule, a claim that the defendant had violated a substantive standard imposed by statute or rule would, of course, state a cause of action. Moulton holds that a violation of a statutory "standard of conduct" is equivalent to a violation of the common law duty of care."

It does not, however, follow from our holding in Moulton that the plaintiff would state a claim by alleging only that the defendant's causal violation of the statute consisted of a failure to obtain a necessary permit or a violation of its terms. We nonetheless hold that an allegation of either would be sufficient to state a cause of action. Two considerations lead us to this conclusion. The first is that the permit process itself will be the source of substantive standards. The statute and the rules do not purport to specify all of the circumstances in which the various sorts of hazardous waste should or should not be disposed, and it appears that the legislature regarded the permit process as an essential opportunity for developing standards necessary to protect against the dangers posed by hazardous waste. See, e.g., RSA 147–A:5, I(b) (Supp. 1983) (permits shall be issued only to those with financial responsibility to ensure that "appropriate" measures will be taken to prevent damage to public health and safety and to the environment); N.H. Admin. Rules. The object of the permit process, therefore, is not merely to ensure that an operator will comply with the appropriate statutory or regulatory standards, but to provide the opportunity to devise detailed substantive disposal standards appropriate for the specific case, in light of the statutory objectives.

It follows that the conditions imposed by terms of such a permit should be accorded the same status as substantive standards contained in a statute or rule. It also follows that a failure to comply with, or refusal to submit to, the permit process could preclude the derivation of substantive standards adequate to protect the public. Therefore, such a failure or refusal should itself be treated as causal and as sufficient to establish liability.

The second consideration that supports our holding that the allegation of the causal violation of a permit or of the requirement to obtain a permit states a private cause of action rests by analogy on the provision for a public cause of action found in RSA chapter 147–A. RSA 147–A:9 (Supp. 1983) provides, inter alia, that an operator who disposes of hazardous waste "in violation of RSA 147–A or rules adopted or permits issued under RSA 147–A" shall be "strictly liable" for costs of containment, cleanup and removal of hazardous wastes, and that the attorney general may institute an action to recover these costs.

This is a provision for damages, not a provision for penalty, which is dealt with separately. See RSA 147–A:14,:16,:17 (Supp. 1983). The quoted language makes it clear that such public civil liability for damages is not limited to cases involving violations of substantive statutory or regulatory standards; the statute is explicit in providing that violation of a permit's terms may give rise to a public action for damages, and the further reference to "violation of RSA 147–A" can only mean that disposal without any permit may also be the basis of public liability. (We note in passing that this statute's reference to strict liability is not technically correct; liability is not imposed merely because the operator caused damage, but because he either failed to obtain, or to abide by the terms of, a permit.) Thus, the legislature has evidently assumed that the permit process itself lessens the risk of harm from the disposal of hazardous waste and has therefore provided that disposal without a permit is sufficient to establish legal fault for purposes of an action for damages.

If such a cause of action is appropriate to compensate the general public for the cost of cleanup that it would otherwise bear in the interest of public health and safety, a similar cause of action is appropriate to compensate a private or property-owning plaintiff for the acute damage and injury that can result from unlicensed disposal. Since such a plaintiff, unlike the general public, can suffer personal injury and harm to property, the private right of action should provide compensation for these elements of damage in addition to recoupment of money actually expended on cleanup and containment.

* * *

What did you think of the court's analysis?

2. What are your views regarding the broad question of whether it is appropriate to apply environmental regulations and their breach to tort litigation? The Bush article suggests that the question can only be answered by undertaking a careful analysis of the precise standard, the purpose it was designed to accomplish, the class of persons it was intended to protect, and the harm it was intended to prevent. Further, the article concluded that even in those cases where the regulatory violation should constitute negligence, that the evidentiary effect afforded to that violation should not be conclusive proof of negligence, but rather some lesser level, such as presumptive evidence or merely some evidence of negligence. Do you agree?

Problem

Congress enacted the Alcoholic Beverage Labeling Act of 1988, 102 Stat. 4518, containing the following provisions:

> Section 204.(a) On and after the expiration of the 12–month period following the date of enactment of this title, it shall be unlawful for any person to manufacture, import or bottle for sale or distribution in the United States any alcoholic beverage unless the container of such beverage bears the following statement:

> > **GOVERNMENT WARNING:** (1) According to the Surgeon General, women should not drink alcoholic beverages during pregnancy

because of the risk of birth defects. (2) Consumption of alcoholic beverages impairs your ability to drive a car or operate machinery, and may cause health problems.

Section 205. No statement relating to alcoholic beverages and health, other than the statement required by section 204 of this title, shall be required under state law to be placed on any container of an alcoholic beverage, or on any box, carton, or other package, irrespective of the material from which made, that contains such a container.

What impact will this statute have on tort suits brought under § 402A for failure to warn for actions that accrue after its enactment? Address the impact which the decision in Cipollone v. Liggett Group might have on such actions. Will the courts experience the same pre-and post-enactment problems that have been so determinative in cigarette litigation? Describe other causes of action that might survive enactment of the Alcoholic Beverage Labeling Act.

Chapter Seven

TOXIC PRODUCTS, PROCESSES AND SERVICES

A. INTRODUCTION: SOME GENERAL PRINCIPLES

Up to now we have considered liability for environmental harm where the plaintiff and defendant usually stood in a horizontal relationship, typically concurrent adjoining landowners or landowners within the same geographical area, and where the defendant's activity resulted in an invasion of the plaintiff's use and enjoyment of land. Liability was premised on trespass, nuisance, negligence, negligence per se, or strict liability for abnormally dangerous activities. We now turn to vertical relationships between a manufacturer, product seller or service provider, and consumers or users of a product or service down the chain of distribution.

Products liability is best understood by introducing the four major theories of liability: negligence, warranty, strict liability in tort, and misrepresentation.

The factual situations accounting for practically all products liability claims for toxic or environmental injury involve (1) defective design or formulation; (2) the failure to give adequate warnings or instructions for safe use; (3) breach of express or implied warranties; or (4) the failure to truthfully represent a material quality of a product, i.e., safety or performance. The meanings the courts have given to these terms and phrases are described below.

At the outset, it is essential to understand that a single seller dereliction, such as, for example, failure to provide adequate instructions for the application of a herbicide, may give rise to an injured party's cause of action under several legal theories. For example, if presented with facts suggesting a manufacturer's responsibility for a failure to provide information adequate for the safe use of a toxic product, one will necessarily examine the viability of plaintiff's cause of action in each of the available legal theories: negligence, warranty, strict liability in tort, and misrepresentation (including, upon occasion, fraud).

1. NEGLIGENCE

The law of negligence is primarily concerned with the provision of reparations to persons suffering personal injury or property loss due to a failure of others to act with due care under the circumstances. The premises of negligence liability are that (a) the theory is devoted to the protection of persons and property from unreasonable risk of harm; and (b) the actor's liability in tort is limited by concepts of reasonable foreseeability.

From the above, we can state a rule for negligence liability for the sale of an unreasonably dangerous product: A product seller is liable in negligence if he acts or fails to act in such a way as to create an unreasonable risk of harm or loss to the user of a product, or to another who might foreseeably be injured thereby. As in all torts, for plaintiff to prevail in negligence there must be harm to the plaintiff's person or property, and proximate cause between the actor's conduct and the harm suffered.

To locate the line between the reasonable risk and the unreasonable one, most courts use the formulation of Judge Learned Hand, or a comparable risk-benefit model. The Hand formulation states that an actor's conduct creates an unreasonable risk of harm where the burden of taking measures to avoid the harm would be less than the multiple of the likelihood that the harm will occur times the magnitude of the harm should it occur. In formula $(B<(P)(L))$, the actor will be considered negligent when B is less than $(P)(L)$, that is, B (Burden of precautions) is less than P (likelihood, in terms of percentage Probability) times L (magnitude of Loss should the harm occur at all). United States v. Carroll Towing Co., 159 F.2d 169 (2d Cir.1947).

The plaintiff's negligence cause of action in products liability involving toxic harm will be available principally in claims for defective formulation and for failure to provide adequate warnings or instructions. In each instance, a cost benefit analysis will support part or all of the requisite negligence analysis.

2. BREACH OF WARRANTY

There are three primary ways in which the seller may breach its warranty to the purchaser. There may be the breach of an express warranty, the breach of the implied warranty of merchantability, and the breach of the implied warranty of fitness for a particular purpose. In a given factual setting, it is possible for a product to breach one, two, or even all of these warranties.

a. Express Warranty

The express warranty is made when the seller makes a material representation as to the product's composition, durability, performance, or safety. The express warranty may be made by any means of communication, from spoken comment, to leaflets, to product wrappers, to advertisements.

Not every statement from a seller to a buyer creates an express warranty. Where the seller's assurance of qualities in the product pertain to matters equally understandable and observable to the purchaser, the seller's statement will ordinarily not be described as material, and instead is "puffing", which does not create an express warranty.

Prior to the Uniform Commercial Code, to preserve a claim in express warranty the buyer might be required to show that she relied specifically upon the express warranty of the seller. The comments of UCC § 2–313 now provide that the buyer's reliance upon an express warranty will be presumed unless the lack of reliance is proved by the seller. This liberalization of the historical reliance requirement is relevant to the buyer who after the injury or loss may only imperfectly recall (1) the assurances the seller made orally; or (2) which of the seller's written assurances the buyer actually read prior to the mishap. The UCC creates a presumption that the buyer relied upon the seller's warranty in deciding to purchase the product, and the presumption will only be defeated by the seller's affirmative proof to the contrary. For a thorough discussion of the theory of express warranty in the context of tobacco litigation, see Cipollone v. Liggett Group, Inc., 893 F.2d 541 (3d Cir. 1990), reversed on other grounds 505 U.S. 504, 112 S.Ct. 2608, 120 L.Ed.2d 407 (1992).

b. Implied Warranty of Merchantability

The implied warranty of merchantability, UCC § 2–314, provides that any seller impliedly warrants that the product sold is fit for its ordinary purposes. This warranty, as its name suggests, conveys with the sale of the product irrespective of the seller's statements or comments. The separate issues of the seller's disclaimer of this and other warranties, or limitation of the remedies available under warranty, are described below.

The threshold issue raised by the implied warranty of merchantability is what is the ordinary purpose of a product. Ordinary purpose is distinguishable from the manufacturer's intended purpose for the product; witness the common use of rubbing alcohol as a cleaning solvent or nail polish remover. Most courts would characterize such use of rubbing alcohol as ordinary, even though admittedly not the use intended by the seller. However, an aerosol tick bomb would not ordinarily be used in a kennel from which the dogs had not first been removed, and injury to animals associated with the latter use would not be redressable in implied warranty of merchantability.

c. Implied Warranty of Fitness for a Particular Purpose

The implied warranty of fitness for a particular purpose, UCC § 2–315, contemplates the buyer's explicit or implicit request that a seller having specialized knowledge of the nature and usage of her products recommend a product suitable for the buyer's goal or project. Where the seller knows of the purchaser's special need, and where the buyer completes the purchase in reliance upon the seller's knowledge and expertise, there arises an implied warranty of fitness for a particular purpose.

The value of this warranty is in providing a remedy to a buyer who has purchased and used an otherwise merchantable product (e.g., house-paint) in a specialized way (to paint a confined area in a home that cannot be effectively ventilated), and has suffered product disappointment, personal injury or property loss resulting from the seller's erroneous advice. Unlike the implied warranty of merchantability, requiring no buyer reliance, and the express warranty, in which there is a rebuttable presumption of reliance, under UCC § 2–315 the buyer must plead and prove reliance upon the seller's knowledge and expertise.

d. Proper Plaintiffs to a Warranty Claim

In warranty, the proper plaintiffs are decided by reference to which Alternative to UCC § 2–318 a jurisdiction has selected. The authors of the UCC gave the states three options: Alternative A, the most restrictive, confines the class of plaintiffs along the lines of the common law privity requirement, including members of the buyer's household and guests therein. Alternatives B and C are progressively more liberal in availing the warranty remedy to nonpurchasing users of products and to unrelated bystanders.

In addition to the buyer's cause of action, UCC § 2–318 Alternative A permits a cause of action to "any natural person who is in the family or household of his buyer, or who is a guest in his home, ... " The use of the phrase "natural person" precludes a cause of action to a business or corporation. Alternative B similarly confines the cause of action to natural persons, but extends the class of parties plaintiff to the limits of reasonable foreseeability, i.e., to all natural persons "who may be reasonably expected to use, consume, or be affected by the goods." Alternative C describes a class of permissible plaintiffs coextensive with the liberal class of plaintiffs recognized in the tort remedies of negligence and strict liability. Under Alternative C, plaintiffs are not limited to natural persons, and therefore organizations and businesses may bring an action in warranty. The language of reasonable foreseeability is identical to that of Alternative B.

e. *Warranty Disclaimers and Limitations*

One of the most significant distinctions between products liability remedies in tort and in warranty is that the UCC explicitly grants the seller the ability to disclaim or limit the remedies available to the purchaser. The most straightforward rationale for permitting disclaimers in warranty and not in tort is that the warranty remedies, arising in contract, are said to represent the mutual assent of the buying and selling parties. These parties, given fair and reciprocal disclosure of the terms of the sale, are free to create a contract with any terms not so hidden or oppressive as to be unconscionable in enforcement. A principal goal of tort remedies, on the other hand, is reparations for parties suffering injury or loss caused by the substandard conduct of others. Tort policy generally, and the remedy of strict tort liability specifically, discourages permitting an actor to disclaim or limit damages for injuries caused by his injurious actions.

Where the seller has given an express warranty, a disclaimer of that warranty will not be allowed, as it would be inherently misleading and unfair to permit the seller to give the buyer a remedy with one hand (potential recompense for breach of express warranty) and take that remedy away, by disclaimer, with the other hand.

The seller may, however, disclaim the implied warranty of merchantability or fitness for a particular purpose. UCC § 2–316 provides that the implied warranty of merchantability may be effectively disclaimed if the disclaimer mentions merchantability and is conspicuous. The implied warranty of fitness for a particular purpose, in turn, may be disclaimed where the disclaiming language is "by a writing and conspicuous." The decisions are in substantial agreement that disclaiming language will be considered conspicuous where it is on the face of the controlling document, where it is distinctively displayed by positioning, background, border, type or color, and where the typeface of the disclaimer is at least as large or larger than that used in the balance of the document. 1 Madden & Owen on Products Liability § 4:15 (2000).

Under all circumstances, UCC § 2–316 states that implied warranties may be excluded "by expressions like 'as is', 'with all faults' or other language which in ordinary understanding calls the buyer's attention to the exclusion of warranties and makes plain that there is no implied warranty[.]"

Pursuant to UCC § 2–719, a seller may limit remedies available under a warranty, such as, for example, limiting the buyer's remedies to return of the goods and repayment of the purchase price or repair. Courts will sustain such limitations unless they operate to deprive the buyer of the remedy's essential purpose, i.e., to receive a fit product or a return of purchase money. In addition, while UCC § 2–719(3) countenances limitation or exclusion of consequential damages, it adds that where the alleged product flaw results in personal injury, limitation of consequential damages for warranties of consumer goods is "prima facie unconscionable."

3. STRICT LIABILITY IN TORT

The limitations inherent in the remedies of negligence and warranty liability encouraged creation of a products liability tort remedy that would alleviate some of the privity and evidentiary burdens placed upon plaintiffs. In negligence the most obvious obstacle to plaintiff's recovery was, and is, the requirement that plaintiff identify and prove that point in the process of manufacture or sale that the seller's conduct fell below the requisite due care under the circumstances. Such proof typically requires plaintiff to not only amass a familiarity with often very complex manufacturing processes, but to be prepared as well to rebut the defendant's claims that its practices, conforming with the actions of other producers in the same industry, did represent due care. In warranty, distinct but equally imposing obstacles to the plaintiff's recovery take the form of the requirement of timely notice to the seller, privity barriers that vary from state to state, and the seller's ability to limit warranty remedies or disclaim warranties altogether.

In 1963 the California Supreme Court in Greenman v. Yuba Power Products, Inc., 59 Cal.2d 57, 27 Cal.Rptr. 697, 377 P.2d 897 (1963) announced a remedy of tort liability without the necessity of proving negligence, that is, strict liability in tort, stating: "A manufacturer is strictly liable in tort when an article he places on the market, knowing that it is to be used without inspection for defects, proves to have a defect that causes injury to a human being."

Prompted by the decision in *Greenman* and the urgings of other courts, in 1965 the American Law Institute (ALI) published Restatement (Second) of Torts § 402A, proposing strict liability in tort for any person "who sells a product in a defective condition unreasonably dangerous to the user or consumer or his property." Since its publication a majority of jurisdictions have adopted § 402A or variations thereon.

The essential distinction between the remedies in negligence and those under § 402A is that in strict liability the focus is on the condition of the product, while in negligence the primary inquiry pertains to the conduct of the seller. In strict liability, liability will be imposed for the sale of a defective, unreasonably dangerous product irrespective of how cautious, circumspect, or reckless the seller has been. Strict liability is liability without regard to fault or negligence for the sale of an unreasonably dangerous product.

As in warranty (except UCC § 2–315), under § 402A the defendant must be a seller of such products in the ordinary course. A growing number of courts have extended the strict liability cause of action to businesses whose position in the stream of commerce resembles that of a product seller in terms of expertise and ability to detect and correct hazards. Thus, many decisions impose strict liability upon product lessors and bailors.

Concerning the language "defective condition unreasonably dangerous", most jurisdictions require that the product be in both a defective condition and unreasonably dangerous. Those courts reason that as tort law is primarily concerned with the creation of remedies for conduct and conditions that create an unreasonable risk of injury, a product that is merely defective, but creates no hazard or danger to persons or to other property, is the proper concern of warranty law, but not tort. In a minority of jurisdictions, however, including California, courts have decided that the language "unreasonably dangerous" hints too strongly of a negligence analysis, and induces juries to adopt a higher burden of proof than the language "defective condition." Courts or legislatures in these latter jurisdictions have removed the "unreasonably dangerous" criterion from plaintiff's prima facie case.

Comment i to § 402A states a "consumer expectation" standard for what represents an unreasonably dangerous condition, and provides that evaluation of what is unreasonably dangerous should be had by reference to whether the article sold is "dangerous to an extent beyond that which would be contemplated by the ordinary consumer who purchases it, with the ordinary knowledge common to the community as to its characteristics." More specialized risk/utility evaluations for what constitutes a design defect have been adopted by many courts.

4. MISREPRESENTATION

The remedy of strict liability for misrepresentation, stated in Restatement (Second) of Torts § 402B, was created to afford a tort remedy to one injured in person due to reliance on the product seller's misrepresentation of a material fact. In ways similar to the plaintiff's cause of action in breach of express warranty, § 402B nonetheless differs from warranty in its retention of the requirement that plaintiff prove actual, subjective reliance upon the seller's representations. The section differs from § 402A in that the § 402B misrepresentation remedy does not require that the product be dangerously defective. Under § 402B even the sale of a merchantable product may create a cause of action if the seller's blandishments as to the product's performance or other material qualities, such as safety, are false, and the user is injured in reliance thereon.

A leading case creating the model for the authors of § 402B was Baxter v. Ford Motor Co., 168 Wash. 456, 12 P.2d 409 (1932), affirmed 168 Wash. 456, 15 P.2d 1118 (1932). The Washington Supreme Court therein suggested that where a product's defect was such that "[a]n ordinary person would be unable to discover [it] by the usual and customary examination," liability for misrepresentation without the need to show negligence is appropriate, because placing the product on the market in a condition that does not conform with the advertising or labeling representations in effect breaches the warranty that an article placed in commerce be "safe for the purposes for which the consumer would ordinarily use it."

The plaintiff proceeding under § 402B must show that there has been justifiable reliance upon the misrepresentation, and that personal physical injury resulted. Comment j thereto states that the remedy will not be available "where the misrepresentation is not known [to the buyer], or there is [buyer] indifference to it, and it does not influence the purchase or subsequent conduct."

While the range of products that may be implicated in toxic products suits is unlimited, most litigation has involved workplace injuries from chemical exposures, such as asbestos or Agent Orange, from the consumption of prescription drugs, such as DES and Bendectin, or from the use of tobacco products.

These toxic product cases differ from typical products liability cases in three respects. First, the plaintiffs are seeking compensation for chronic injuries or diseases caused by toxic substances contained in the products, rather than compensation for traumatic injuries involved in sporadic accident cases. The kinds of harms experienced in these cases are different—cancer, birth defects, asbestosis, asthma—rather than the broken bones more typical of products cases. Second, these toxic product claims usually involve long latency periods, and frequently also long periods of exposure to the toxic substance before there exists any objective manifestation of the injury or disease. Asbestos, cigarette and DES-related injuries all illustrate this phenomenon. Third, the number of persons who can suffer harm as a result of exposure to a generic product may be measured in hundreds or thousands, producing a comparable number of individual lawsuits, class actions or multidistrict mass tort proceedings.

5. RESTATEMENT (SECOND) OF TORTS § 402A: STRICT LIABILITY AND NEW APPROACHES

Let us turn to Restatement (Second) of Torts § 402A:

§ 402A. Special Liability of Seller of Product for Physical Harm to User or Consumer

(1) One who sells any product in a defective condition unreasonably dangerous to the user or consumer or to his property is subject to liability for physical harm thereby caused to the ultimate user or consumer, or to his property, if

    (a) the seller is engaged in the business of selling such a product, and

    (b) it is expected to and does reach the user or consumer without substantial change in the condition in which it is sold.

(2) The rule stated in Subsection (1) applies although

    (a) the seller has exercised all possible care in the preparation and sale of his product, and

    (b) the user or consumer has not bought the product from or entered into any contractual relation with the seller.

If success is measured solely in terms of adoption by courts in various jurisdictions, Restatement (Second) of Torts § 402A proved the most successful Restatement provision of that learned institution. In the decades following its adoption, however, its simple devotion to the concept of an actionable product flaw as being a product in a "defective condition unreasonably dangerous to the user and consumer" proved at once too elastic and too rigid for predictable resolution of products liability claims. An emerging consensus of courts and scholars noted that irrespective of whether a claim was brought in "strict" tort, negligence, or implied warranty, the gravaman of practically all claims was that the product at issue contained a manufacturing defect, a design defect, or was defective for want of adequate warnings or instructions.

Accordingly, the Restatement (Third) of Torts: Products Liability, also often named the Products Liability Restatement, put aside the doctrinal categories of and within tort and warranty, and classified defective products according to their functional flaw, i.e., a manufacturing flaw, a design flaw, or a failure to provide adequate warnings or instructions. Products Liability Restatement § 1 provides:

Liability of Commercial Seller or Distributor for Harm Caused by Defective Products

One engaged in the business of selling or otherwise distributing products who sells or distributes a defective product is subject to liability for harm to persons or property caused by the defect.

Section 2 continues, defining the categories of actionable defects:

Categories of Product Defect

A product is defective when, at the time of sale or initial distribution, it contains a manufacturing defect, is defective in design, or is defective because of inadequate warnings. A product:

    (a) contains a manufacturing defect when the product departs from its intended design even though all possible care was exercised in the preparation and marketing of the product;

    (b) is defective in design when the foreseeable risks of harm posed by the product could have been reduced or eliminated by the adoption of a reasonable alternative design by the seller or other distributor, or a predecessor in the commercial chain of distribution, and the omission of the alternative design renders the product no reasonably safe;

    (c) is defective because of inadequate warnings or instructions when the foreseeable risks of harm posed by the product could have been reduced or avoided by the provision of reasonable instructions or warnings by the seller or other distributor, or a predecessor in the commercial chain of distribution, and the omission of the warnings renders the product not reasonably safe.

A toxic or an otherwise environmentally harmful product may contain a design defect even if it is produced as intended but its formulation is such as to pose an unreasonable risk of harm, and there exists a technologically feasible and commercially practicable alternative to it. Thus, for example, one can hypothesize a bathroom cleanser that contains a level of acid substantially in excess of that necessary to accomplish ordinary cleaning objectives, and which, due to its concentration, renders the product so caustic as to make even momentary dermal exposure painfully injurious.

Even more frequent, however, will be a claim that a product created an avoidably high risk of harm because it lacked warnings as to its non-obvious risks or it lacked instructions appropriate to permit persons to use it in a reasonably safe way. Products Liability Restatement § 2(c) comment i suggests considerations that will be appropriate in evaluating claims of informational defects. The student will not err in sensing that the comment i language conveys strong overtones of a negligence evaluation. The comment reads in pertinent part:

> In evaluating the adequacy of product warnings and instructions, courts must be sensitive to many factors. It is impossible to identify anything approaching a perfect level of detail that should be communicated in products disclosures. For example, educated or experienced product users and consumers may benefit from the inclusion more information about the full spectrum of product risks, whereas less-educated or unskilled users may benefit from more concise warnings and instructions stressing only the most crucial risks and safe handling practices. In some contexts, products intended for special categories of users, such as children, may require more vivid and unambiguous warnings. In some cases, excessive detail may detract from the ability of typical users and consumers to focus on the important aspects of the warnings, whereas in others reasonably full disclosure will be necessary to enable informed, efficient choices by product users. Product warnings and instructions can rarely communicate all potentially relevant information, and the ability of a plaintiff to imagine a hypothetically better warning in the aftermath of an accident does not establish that the warning actually accompanying the product was inadequate. No easy guideline exists for courts to adopt in assessing the adequacy of products warnings and instructions. In making their assessments, courts must focus on various factors, such as content and comprehensibility, intensity of expression, and the characteristics of expected user groups.

The prominence of warnings and other informational issues in toxic products litigation warrants these additional observations: The duty of a manufacturer to provide warnings can be understood and justified on grounds of reducing accident costs. See Guido Calabresi, The Costs of

Accidents: A Legal and Economic Analysis 26 (1970). Warnings and related product information enhance safety by enabling the user to avoid dangers related to product use which can be averted or reduced when the user is informed of the hazards. Second, warnings promote individual autonomy by informing the user of the risks involved and enabling the individual to make an informed choice of whether to encounter unavoidable risks.

A claim of warning or other informational deficiency may be the only theory available to a plaintiff, in that theories of defective design or formulation usually require the plaintiff to establish an alternative safer design that would have averted or lessened the danger. As the risks of many toxic substances, such as asbestos, prescription drugs and tobacco, are inherent to the formulation of the product and cannot usually be designed out in any meaningful way, the plaintiff's only viable claim may be to assert that the manufacturer did not provide adequate warnings or instructions regarding the risks of harm associated with the use of the product. For differing views on the scope and nature of the obligation to warn consumers and users, compare Aaron Twerski, et al., The Use and Abuse of Warnings in Products Liability—Design Defect Litigation Comes of Age, 61 Cornell L.Rev. 495 (1976), with M. Stuart Madden, The Duty to Warn in Products Liability: Contours and Criticism, 89 W.Va. L. Rev. 221 (1987).

B. TOXIC PRODUCT CLAIMS BY TYPE

1. ASBESTOS

a. *Liability Standards and Defenses*

Judge Alpert of the Court of Special Appeals of Maryland captured in colorful terms the history of asbestos litigation in Eagle–Picher Industries, Inc. v. Balbos, 84 Md.App. 10, 578 A.2d 228, 231 (1990), modified 326 Md. 179, 604 A.2d 445 (1992):

> In this, the last decade of the 20th Century, our judicial system faces an apocalypse in the guise of asbestos cases. As did the "Apocalyptic beast," asbestos rose up "as from the depths of the sea," after having lain dormant for decades, to plague our industries initially and our judicial system consequentially, spreading cancer and asbestosis to thousands of workers along the way.

> This 10–week case is just one of more than 8,000 asbestos cases that have been filed in Maryland since 1980. Although estimates vary, it has been reported that there are as many as 50,000 asbestos cases pending nationally. Quite apart from the sheer magnitude in numbers, asbestos litigation presents features that, unfortunately, are common to complex litigation. Most of the cases are of the multi-litigant variety, averaging as many as twenty defendants. When the multitude of cross-claims between those defendants are factored in, the complex metamorphosizes into the maxi-complex. Thus, it seems

quite possible that our dockets shall be visited with asbestos litigation well into the next century, each case presenting its unique yet similar tragic scenario.

Against that vivid backdrop we examine the history of asbestos litigation.

BOREL v. FIBREBOARD PAPER PRODUCTS CORPORATION

United States Court of Appeals, Fifth Circuit, 1973.
493 F.2d 1076, cert. denied 419 U.S. 869, 95 S.Ct. 127, 42 L.Ed.2d 107 (1974).

WISDOM, C.J.:

This product liability case involves the scope of an asbestos manufacturer's duty to warn industrial insulation workers of dangers associated with the use of asbestos.

* * * [Clarence] Borel allege[s] that he had contracted the diseases of asbestosis and mesothelioma as a result of his exposure to the defendants' products over a thirty-three year period beginning in 1936 and ending in 1969. The jury returned a verdict in favor of Borel on the basis of strict liability. We affirm.

I.

* * * Borel's employment necessarily exposed him to heavy concentrations of asbestos dust generated by insulation materials. In his pretrial deposition, Borel testified that at the end of a day working with insulation material containing asbestos his clothes were usually so dusty he could "just barely pick them up without shaking them." * * *

Borel said that [although] he had known for years that inhaling asbestos dust "was bad for me"[,] * * * he never realized that it could cause any serious or terminal illness. * * *

[Borel testified that respirators] were not furnished during his early work years. Although respirators were later made available on some jobs, insulation workers usually were not required to wear them and had to make a special request if they wanted one. Borel stated that he and other insulation workers found that the respirators furnished them were uncomfortable, could not be worn in hot weather, and—"you can't breathe with the respirator." * * *

* * *

[In January 1969, Borel was diagnosed with pulmonary asbestosis. In a 1970] surgery, the examining doctors determined that Borel had a form of lung cancer known as mesothelioma, which had been caused by asbestosis. As a result of these diseases, Borel later died before the district case reached the trial stage.

* * *

At issue in this case is the extent of the defendants' knowledge of the dangers associated with insulation products containing asbestos. We pause, therefore, to summarize the evidence relevant to this question.

Asbestosis has been recognized as a disease for well over fifty years. The first reported cases of asbestosis were among asbestos textile workers. In 1924, Cooke in England discovered a case of asbestosis in a person who had spent twenty years weaving asbestos textile products. * * *

* * *

Throughout the 1950's and 1960's, further studies and medical reports on asbestosis were published. In 1965, I. J. Selikoff and his colleagues published a study entitled "The Occurrence of Asbestosis Among Insulation Workers in the United States." The authors examined 1,522 members of an insulation workers union in the New York–New Jersey metropolitan area. Evidence of pulmonary asbestosis was found in almost half the men examined. Among those with more than forty years experience, abnormalities were found in over ninety percent. The authors concluded that "asbestosis and its complications are significant hazards among insulation workers". Other studies have since confirmed these findings.

* * *

The plaintiff introduced evidence tending to establish that the defendant manufacturers either were, or should have been, fully aware of the many articles and studies on asbestosis. The evidence also indicated, however, that during Borel's working career no manufacturer ever warned contractors or insulation workers, including Borel, of the dangers associated with inhaling asbestos dust[.] * * *

* * *

II.

* * *

Here, the plaintiff alleged that the defendants' product was unreasonably dangerous because of the failure to give adequate warnings of the known or knowable dangers involved. As explained in comment j to [Restatement (Second) of Torts] section 402A, a seller has a responsibility to inform users and consumers of dangers which the seller either knows or should know at the time the product is sold. The requirement that the danger be reasonably foreseeable, or scientifically discoverable, is an important limitation of the seller's liability. * * * [A] seller is under a duty to warn of only those dangers that are reasonably foreseeable. The requirement of foreseeability coincides with the standard of due care in negligence cases in that a seller must exercise reasonable care and foresight to discover a danger in his product and to warn users and consumers of that danger. * * *

* * *

[I]n cases such as the instant case, the manufacturer is held to the knowledge and skill of an expert. This is relevant in determining (1) whether the manufacturer knew or should have known the danger, and (2) whether the manufacturer was negligent in failing to communicate this superior knowledge to the user or consumer of its product. The manufacturer's status as expert means that at a minimum he must keep abreast of scientific knowledge, discoveries, and advances and is presumed to know what is imparted thereby. But even more importantly, a manufacturer has a duty to test and inspect his product. The extent of research and experiment must be commensurate with the dangers involved. A product must not be made available to the public without disclosure of those dangers that the application of reasonable foresight would reveal. Nor may a manufacturer rely unquestioningly on others to sound the hue and cry concerning a danger in its product. Rather, each manufacturer must bear the burden of showing that its own conduct was proportionate to the scope of its duty.

* * *

[T]he defendants contend that the district court erred in refusing to instruct the jury that a product cannot be unreasonably dangerous if it conforms to the reasonable expectations of the industrial purchasers, here, the insulation contractors. The defendants assert, in effect, that it is the responsibility of the insulation contractors, not the manufacturers, to warn insulation workers of the risk of harm. We reject this argument. We agree with the Restatement: a seller may be liable to the ultimate consumer or user for failure to give adequate warnings. The seller's warning must be reasonably calculated to reach such persons and the presence of an intermediate party will not by itself relieve the seller of this duty. * * *

[We conclude] that the trial court did not err in instructing the jury on strict liability.

* * *

III.

* * *

[The defendants] challenge the jury's finding that their products were unreasonably dangerous for failure to give warnings. * * * They attempt to circumvent this finding by arguing, disingenuously, that the danger was obvious. For present purposes, it is sufficient to note that Borel testified that he did not know that inhaling asbestos dust could cause serious illness until his doctors advised him in 1969 that he had asbestosis. Furthermore, we cannot say that, as a matter of law, the danger was sufficiently obvious to asbestos installation workers to relieve the defendants of the duty to warn.

The jury found that the unreasonably dangerous condition of the defendants' product was the proximate cause of Borel's injury. This necessarily included a finding that, had adequate warnings been provided, Borel would have chosen to avoid the danger. * * *

* * *

IV.

* * *

* * * Under the law of torts, a person has long been liable for the foreseeable harm caused by his own negligence. This principle applies to the manufacture of products as it does to almost every other area of human endeavor. It implies a duty to warn of foreseeable dangers associated with those products. This duty to warn extends to all users and consumers, including the common worker in the shop or in the field. Where the law has imposed a duty, courts stand ready in proper cases to enforce the rights so created. Here, there was a duty to speak, but the defendants remained silent. The district court's judgment does no more than hold the defendants liable for the foreseeable consequences of their own inaction.

For the reasons stated, the decision of the district court is

Affirmed.

Notes and Questions

1. *Borel* is a leading decision in articulating the basis of liability for asbestos producers on a failure to warn theory. The informational defects in this case relate largely to informed choice, and only secondarily to risk reduction. As the court states elsewhere in its opinion, "the rationale for this rule [requiring disclosure of the risks] is that the user or consumer is entitled to make his own choice as to whether the product's utility or benefits justify exposing himself to the risk of harm." Will employees in the workplace, once informed of the risks, usually make the choice of exposure? See Chapter 9, discussing obligations created by the Occupational Safety and Health Act of 1970, which requires, among other things, that employers provide employees with information regarding the risks of exposure for toxic chemicals.

2. In many toxic tort cases, including asbestos cases, courts have adopted the so-called "heeding presumption." This presumption affects plaintiff's burden of showing that the absence of an adequate warning was a proximate cause of his or her harm by creating a presumption that had an adequate warning been given, plaintiff would have read and heeded it. Cf., Restatement (Second) of Torts § 402A comment j ("Where a warning is given, the seller may reasonably assume that it will be read and heeded[.]"). In Theer v. Philip Carey Co., 133 N.J. 610, 628 A.2d 724 (1993), an action bought on behalf of a deceased asbestos fitter, the New Jersey Supreme Court explained the rationale for the "heeding presumption": "[T]he heeding presumption in failure-to-warn cases serves to ease an injured plaintiff's burden of proof. That objective is especially important because 'in a failure to warn' case, establishing that the absence of a warning was a substantial

factor in the harm alleged to have resulted from exposure to the product is 'particularly difficult.' In particular, the heeding presumption serves to eliminate conjecture about whether a given plaintiff would have heeded a hypothetical warning, and discourages determinations that are based on extraneous, speculative considerations and unreliable or self serving evidence."

3. *Borel* is also important because it elaborates the extent of the manufacturer's obligation to become aware of risks inherent in its products: The manufacturer must keep itself informed of the medical and scientific knowledge generally available as well as undertake its own research regarding the dangers that may be associated with the use of its products. The manufacturer will be held to the standard of an expert in the field. It is critical to understand that the duty recognized in *Borel* pertains only to risks that are, in fact, known or knowable. According to the court, and to most courts considering the question, strict liability under comment j of § 402A does not hold a manufacturer strictly liable for failure to warn of risks that are unknown or unknowable.

4. In the Preliminary Draft of the Restatement (Third) of Torts: Products Liability, Reporters Henderson and Twerski propose a conforming position with this comment: "[B]ecause risks of harm arising from the foreseeable consumption of toxics and prescription drugs are sometimes unknowable at the time of sale, it would be inappropriate to attribute knowledge of risks to the seller as a matter of law."

5. *Special Problems of Unknown Risks.* An alternative phrasing of the "unknown and unknowable risk" issue raised in *Borel* is sometimes stated as the availability of the "state of the art" defense to a toxic tort defendant, i.e., can a manufacturer defend a charge that it failed to warn of a danger by demonstrating that its knowledge and warnings were "state-of-the-art" at the time the product was distributed? The counter argument was best stated in another asbestos personal injury suit, as the following excerpted discussion from Beshada v. Johns–Manville Products Corp., 90 N.J. 191, 447 A.2d 539 (1982) (Pashman, J.) reveals:

> [The most important inquiry] is whether imposition of liability for failure to warn of dangers which were undiscoverable at the time of manufacture will advance the goals and policies sought to be achieved by our strict liability rules. We believe that it will.
>
> *Risk Spreading.* One of the most important arguments generally advanced for imposing strict liability is that the manufacturers and distributors of defective products can best allocate the costs of the injuries resulting from it. The premise is that the price of a product should reflect all of its costs, including the cost of injuries caused by the product. This can best be accomplished by imposing liability on the manufacturer and distributors. Those persons can insure against liability and incorporate the cost of the insurance in the price of the product. In this way, the costs of the product will be borne by those who profit from it[.] * * *
>
> Defendants argue that this policy is not forwarded by imposition of liability for unknowable hazards. Since such hazards by definition are not predicted, the price of the hazardous product will not be adjusted to reflect the costs of the injuries it will produce. Rather, defendants state,

the cost "will be borne by the public at large and reflected in a general, across the board increase in premiums to compensate for unanticipated risks." There is some truth in this assertion, but it is not a bad result.

* * * [S]preading the costs of injuries among all those who produce, distribute and purchase manufactured products is far preferable to imposing it on the innocent victims who suffer illnesses and disability from defective products. * * *

Finally, contrary to defendants' assertion, this rule will not cause the price and production level of manufactured products to diverge from the so-called economically efficient level. Rather, the rule will force the price of any particular product to reflect the cost of insuring against the possibility that the product will turn out to be defective.

Accident Avoidance. * * * Defendants urge that this argument has no force as to hazards which by definition were undiscoverable. Defendants have treated the level of technological knowledge at a given time as an independent variable not affected by defendants' conduct. But this view ignores the important role of industry in product safety research. The "state-of-the-art" at a given time is partly determined by how much industry invests in safety research. By imposing on manufacturers the costs of failure to discover hazards, we create an incentive for them to invest more actively in safety research.

Fact finding process. The analysis thus far has assumed that it is possible to define what constitutes "undiscoverable" knowledge and that it will be reasonably possible to determine what knowledge was technologically discoverable at a given time. * * *

Scientific knowability, as we understand it, refers not to what in fact was known at the time, but to what could have been known at the time. In other words, even if no scientist had actually formed the belief that asbestos was dangerous, the hazards would be deemed "knowable" if a scientist could have formed that belief by applying research or performing tests that were available at the time. Proof of what could have been known will inevitably be complicated, costly, confusing and time-consuming. * * * We doubt that juries will be capable of even understanding the concept of scientific knowability, much less be able to resolve such a complex issue. * * *

* * *

In addition, discussion of state-of-the-art could easily confuse juries into believing that blameworthiness is at issue. * * *

What do you think of the court's conclusion that strict liability means that the ability of the manufacturer to know of the danger posed by the product is irrelevant? Should manufacturers of products be held liable for unknown or unknowable risks that materialize? Should only manufacturers of very dangerous products (i.e., asbestos) be held to such as standard? How should such product categories be determined? By a hindsight test of what harm has actually occurred?

6. Not long after its decision in *Beshada* rejecting the state-of-the-art defense in failure to warn cases, the New Jersey Supreme Court considered

the same issue in the context of prescription drugs. In Feldman v. Lederle Laboratories, 97 N.J. 429, 479 A.2d 374 (1984), cert. denied 505 U.S. 1219, 112 S.Ct. 3027, 120 L.Ed.2d 898 (1992), the court concluded that strict liability would apply to prescription drugs, and then considered whether *Beshada* or a state of the art defense should apply, and stated:

> [A]s to warnings, generally conduct should be measured by knowledge at the time the manufacturer distributed the product. Did the defendant know, or should he have known, of the danger, given the scientific, technological, and other information available when the product was distributed; or, in other words, did he have actual or constructive knowledge of the danger? * * *

> * * *

> This test does not conflict with the assumption made in strict liability design defect and warning cases that the defendant knew of the dangerous propensity of the product, if the knowledge that is assumed is reasonably knowable in the sense of actual or constructive knowledge. A warning that a product may have an unknowable danger warns one of nothing. * * *

> * * *

> * * * The rationale of Beshada is not applicable to this case. We do not overrule Beshada, but restrict Beshada to the circumstances giving rise to its holding. * * *

7.   With reference to *Beshada*, compare the following statements by two commentators. Allen Schwartz, Products Liability, Corporate Structure and Bankruptcy: Toxic Substances and the Remote Risk Relationship, 14 J. Legal Stud. 689, 736 (1985):

> Courts should not impose remote risks on firms. A remote risk is a risk whose full extent a cost-justified research program would not reveal. To impose such risks is unfair, for it makes firms responsible for what they would not prevent. Also, firms have incentives to pursue inefficient strategies, such as liquidating when their going concern value exceeds their liquidation value, just to avoid the surprising liability that a remote risk imposition creates.

Joseph Page, Generic Product Risks: The Case Against Comment k and For Strict Liability, 58 N.Y.U.L.Rev. 853, 891 (1983):

> Both the satisfaction of justifiable expectations on the part of product victims and the achievement of modest advances in safety justify the application of strict liability to harm from unknowable generic hazards.

8. *Beshada* was challenged on constitutional equal protection grounds—that is, that the New Jersey Supreme Court had created an irrational classification between asbestos and nonasbestos manufacturers, denying the state of the art defense only to the former. The *Feldman–Beshada* distinction was upheld narrowly in In re Asbestos Litigation, 829 F.2d 1233 (3d Cir.1987), cert. denied 485 U.S. 1029, 108 S.Ct. 1586, 99 L.Ed.2d 901 (1988). Consider the following statement by Judge Weiss:

In refining and narrowing the § 402A theory, *Beshada* eliminates one more defense to the liability of asbestos defendants. * * * [We cannot] conclude that the state court's position is irrational. The concepts of risk-spreading and compensation for victims by manufacturers of unreasonably dangerous products are cornerstones of § 402A, and they may be consistently applied to asbestos as well as to other products.

Although not in itself a determinative factor in the elimination of a substantive defense, the desirability of simplifying the fact-finding process and thus making it easier for victims to recover has been recognized by the law. Workers' compensation programs and no-fault auto insurance plans share that common goal. * * *

Administrative convenience standing alone is not an adequate ground for the elimination of a substantive defense. However, we cannot help but be conscious of the extraordinary size of the asbestos personal injury litigation. * * * [T]his unprecedented phenomenon in American tort law requires states be given some leeway in devising their own solutions.

9. The symbiosis between worker's compensation claims and the often-later-filed personal injury suits always requires counsel's attention. For example, the issue of when plaintiff's cause of action accrues for limitations purposes was raised in the context of a silicosis claim in Martinez v. Humble Sand and Gravel, 860 S.W.2d 467 (Tex.App.1993), a suit brought by a sandblaster. The Texas appellate court held that the plaintiff's products liability claim accrued on the date that he filed a workers' compensation claim with the Industrial Accident Board, alleging that he had contracted silicosis as a result of his employment. In Chapter 9 we consider the relationship between the workers compensation system and tort law, and in Chapter 12 the special statutes of limitation concerns are addressed.

10. In toxic torts litigation, as in products liability litigation generally, plaintiff often seeks to introduce evidence that following the injurious exposure or contamination, defendant undertook remedial measures that would permit the inference that defendant's pre-curative conduct was negligent. Federal Rule of Evidence 407 precludes introduction of post-incident remedial measures to show negligence or culpable conduct, on the logic that such evidence is (1) only minimally probative of the care defendant exercised before the mishap; (2) quite prejudicial to defendant; and (3) admission of such evidence would chill the motivation of manufacturers and others to improve their products or processes. See generally M. Stuart Madden, The Admissibility of Post–Incident Remedial Measures, 5. J. Prod. Liab. 1 (1982). In the environmental tort context, consider In re Joint Eastern Dist. and Southern Dist. Asbestos Litigation, 995 F.2d 343 (2d Cir.1993), where the Second Circuit found reversible error in the trial court's admission of evidence that the manufacturer of encapsulated asbestos valve packing placed warnings on its product some time after the last exposure claimed by plaintiff.

11. *Insurance: Liability and Unknowable Risks.* Asbestos liability litigation presents two important issues involving liability insurance. First, can manufacturers adequately insure against risks that are unknown at the time the products are distributed? Second, as of what time does the plaintiff's

"bodily injury" (the insured-against event) occur for purposes of determining which of several insurance policies covers the liability in question?

Regarding the first of these issues, a number of commentators have argued that manufacturers cannot, by hypothesis, insure against risks no one knows exist. As a consequence, when liability is later imposed strictly, based on hindsight, all they can do is charge the losses against earnings or capital, or go out of business. Either way, inefficiencies result. See generally, Patricia M. Danzon, Tort Reform and the Role of Government in Private Insurance Markets, 13 J. Legal Stud. 517 (1984). Of course, this answer begs the question of whether efficiency ought to be an overriding consideration. For the argument that fairness reasons do not support hindsight-based strict liability, see generally, James A. Henderson, Jr., Coping with the Time Dimension in Products Liability, 69 Calif. L.Rev. 919 (1981).

As to the issue of which liability policy should cover a risk that took 20 or 30 years (from first distribution to full manifestation of plaintiff's injury) to materialize, courts have disagreed. See discussion of insurance issues in Chapter 11.

b.   *Punitive Damages in Asbestos Litigation*

While *Borel* and the early asbestos cases involved only requests for compensatory damages, it wasn't long before plaintiffs began to request and recover punitive damages. The following decision in Fischer v. Johns–Manville Corp., 103 N.J. 643, 512 A.2d 466 (1986) summarizes the tests for punitive liability that apply in the majority of jurisdictions and the evidence critical to satisfying those tests in the asbestos context.

FISCHER v. JOHNS–MANVILLE CORPORATION

Supreme Court of New Jersey, 1986.
103 N.J. 643, 512 A.2d 466.

CLIFFORD, J.

Plaintiff James Fischer and Geneva Fischer, his wife, brought suit against multiple defendants seeking to recover damages for lung diseases suffered by James Fischer as a result of his exposure to asbestos. The complaint sought compensatory and punitive damages from defendants-suppliers of asbestos under negligence, breach of warranty, and strict products liability theories. Plaintiffs elected to press at trial only the strict liability cause of action for compensatory damages, while at the same time they sought punitive damages. * * *

The case was tried to a jury. At the close of trial, the jury awarded compensatory damages of $86,000 to James Fischer and $5,000 to Geneva Fischer. The jury found Johns–Manville eighty percent liable and Bell twenty percent liable. The jury also awarded James Fischer $300,000 in punitive damages, of which $240,000 was assessed against Johns–Manville and $60,000 against Bell. Both defendants appealed and the Appellate Division affirmed in its entirety the judgment of the trial court.

* * *

* * * Johns–Manville's petition urges that the Appellate Division's determination runs counter to decisions by New Jersey federal district courts and thus requires clarification. As well it repeats the arguments made below, that (1) punitive damages "cannot conceptually flow" from a claim based on strict liability for failure to warn, (2) punitive damages "serve no purpose" in asbestos mass litigation, and (3) the record does not support a finding of punitive damages against Johns–Manville. [We affirm].

I

* * *

* * * [P]laintiffs' punitive damage claim hinged on their contention that "defendants knew of these hazards as early as the 1930's and had made a conscious business decision to withhold this information from the public." * * *

The Appellate Division summarized the evidence in support of those allegations as follows[:]

Johns–Manville, in its answers to interrogatories, which were read to the jury, admitted that

> [t]he corporation became aware of the relationship between asbestos and the disease known as asbestosis among workers involved in mining, milling and manufacturing operations and exposed to high levels of virtually 100% raw asbestos fibers over long periods of time by the early 1930s. The corporation has followed and become aware of the general state of the medical art relative to asbestos and its relationship to disease processes, if any.

In response to plaintiffs' requests for admissions, also read to the jury, it admitted that in the early 1940's it knew that asbestos "was dangerous to the health" of those industrial workers who were exposed to excessive amounts of the material. Plaintiffs, moreover, produced as a witness Dr. Daniel C. Braun, president of the Industrial Health Foundation, a research organization which develops, accumulates and disseminates information about occupational diseases. Dr. Braun testified that Johns–Manville has been a member of the Foundation since 1936. He also testified that since 1937 the Foundation has sent to its members a monthly digest of articles appearing in scientific journals which relate to occupational disease. Relevant portions of the digests, which were admitted into evidence, included references to eleven scientific articles published between 1936 and 1941 documenting the grave pulmonary hazards of exposure to asbestos and discussing measures which could be taken to protect workers. * * *

In December of that year high-level representatives of Johns–Manville met with officials of Raybestos–Manhattan, another major asbestos supplier, to discuss steps which the industry as a whole might take to reduce employee risk. It appears, however, that Johns–Manville never did arrange for or participate in any industry-wide meetings on the subject. The minutes of that 1933 meeting also confirm the participants' view that at least for the time being "our past policy of keeping this matter confidential is to be pursued."

Perhaps most damning of all is the so-called Sumner Simpson correspondence of 1935 and 1941. Simpson was president of Raybestos. In October 1935, he received a letter from a Miss Rossiter, editor of the trade periodical Asbestos, suggesting that despite Simpson's earlier requests, made "for certain obvious reasons," that articles relating to asbestosis not be published, perhaps the time had come to print a positive article about industry efforts to reduce the risk in order "to combat some of the rather undesirable publicity given to it [asbestosis] in current newspapers." Simpson thereupon sent a copy of the letter to Johns–Manville's secretary, Vandiver Brown, expressing his opinion that "the less said about asbestos, the better off we are." Brown's reply stated in part: "I quite agree with you that our interests are best served by having asbestosis receive the minimum of publicity." * * *

* * *

* * * On this appeal Johns–Manville's position, succinctly stated, is that the punitive damages award against it is legally impermissible, ill-advised as a matter of public policy in litigation of this nature, and factually unwarranted.

II

The "legally impermissible" argument rests on an asserted theoretical inconsistency between strict liability and punitive damages, which would preclude punitive damage claims when liability for compensatory damages is founded on strict products liability doctrine, if not in all situations at least in asbestos, strict liability lawsuits. We hold that there is no per se legal bar to pursuing a strict liability, failure-to-warn claim and a punitive damage claim in the same case. * * *

* * *

The type of conduct that will warrant an award of punitive damages has been described in various ways. The conduct must be "wantonly reckless or malicious. There must be an intentional wrongdoing in the sense of an 'evil-minded act' or an act accompanied by a wanton and willful disregard of the rights of another." * * *

As should now be apparent, the proofs needed to establish a prima facie case of failure-to-warn, strict products liability differ markedly from the proofs that will support an award of punitive damages. Despite their differences—one going to the theory of liability, the other bearing on the form and extent of relief—they are not mutually exclusive nor even incompatible. There is no reason they cannot be litigated together. * * *

* * *

III

* * *

[One] concern created by the time gap between exposure and litigation is that the corporate personnel who made the decisions at the time of the exposure are no longer with the defendant company, possibly no longer alive. From this fact it is argued that punitive damages are inappropriate because they will not punish the true wrongdoers. But as many courts have observed, this contention ignores the nature of a corporation as a separate legal entity. Although the responsible management personnel may escape punishment, the corporation itself will not. * * * We are reminded that a primary goal of punitive damages is general deterrence—that is, the deterrence of others from engaging in similar conduct. That purpose is, of course, well served regardless of changes in personnel within the offending corporation.

A related argument, which similarly ignores the legal nature of corporations, is that punitive damages unfairly punish innocent shareholders. This argument has been rejected repeatedly. It is the corporation, not the individual shareholders, that is recognized as an ongoing legal entity engaged in manufacturing and distributing products. True, payment of punitive damages claims will deplete corporate assets, which will possibly produce a reduction in net worth and thereby result in a reduction in the value of individual shares. But the same is true of compensatory damages. * * * [W]e would not consider it harmful were shareholders to be encouraged by decisions such as this to give close scrutiny to corporate practices in making investment decisions.

* * *

Defendant argues that the amount of compensatory damages assessed and to be assessed is so great that it will effectively serve the functions of punitive damages—that is, defendants are more than sufficiently punished and deterred. We are not at all satisfied, however, that compensatory damages effectively serve the same functions as punitive damages, even when they amount to staggering sums. Compensatory damages are often foreseeable as to amount, within certain limits difficult to reduce to a formula but nonetheless familiar to the liability insurance industry. * * * The risk and amount of such damages can, and in some cases will, be reflected in the cost of a product, in which event the product will be marketed in its dangerous condition.

Without punitive damages a manufacturer who is aware of a dangerous feature of its product but nevertheless knowingly chooses to market it in that condition, willfully concealing from the public information regarding the dangers of the product, would be far better off than an innocent manufacturer who markets a product later discovered to be dangerous—this, because both will be subjected to the same compensatory damages, but the innocent manufacturer, unable to anticipate those damages, will not have incorporated the cost of those damages into the cost of the product. All else being equal, the law should not place the innocent manufacturer in a worse position than that of a knowing wrongdoer. Punitive damages tend to meet this need.

Defendant argues further that the cumulative effect of punitive damages in mass-tort litigation is "potentially catastrophic." The Johns–Manville bankruptcy is offered as proof of this effect. We fail to see the distinction, in the case of Johns–Manville, between the effect of compensatory damages and that of punitive damages. The amount of punitive damages and the determination that they would cause insolvency that could be avoided in their absence are so speculative as to foreclose any sound basis for judicial decision. * * *

* * *

At the state court level we are powerless to implement solutions to the nationwide problems created by asbestos exposure and litigation arising from that exposure. That does not mean, however, that we cannot institute some controls over runaway punitive damages. * * * [T]here should be some limits placed on the total punishment exacted from a culpable defendant. We conclude that a reasonable imposition of those limits would permit a defendant to introduce evidence of other punitive damage awards already assessed against and paid by it, as well as evidence of its own financial status and the effect a punitive award would have. * * *

We realize that defendants may be reluctant to alert juries to the fact that other courts or juries have assessed punitive damages for conduct similar to that being considered by the jury in a given case. * * * The willingness to accept that risk is a matter of strategy for defendant and its counsel, no different from other strategy choices facing trial lawyers every day.

When evidence of other punitive awards is introduced, trial courts should instruct juries to consider whether the defendant has been sufficiently punished, keeping in mind that punitive damages are meant to punish and deter defendants for the benefit of society, not to compensate individual plaintiffs.

* * *

IV

Defendant argues that even if punitive damages are allowed in strict products liability, mass tort actions, they should not have been assessed against Johns–Manville in this action. We disagree. We hold that punitive damages are available in failure-to-warn, strict products liability actions when a manufacturer is (1) aware of or culpably indifferent to an unnecessary risk of injury, and (2) refuses to take steps to reduce that danger to an acceptable level. This standard can be met by a showing of "a deliberate act or omission with knowledge of a high degree of probability of harm and reckless indifference to consequences." * * *

* * *

Notes and Questions

1. A significant number of decisions have affirmed or authorized awards of punitive damages in asbestos litigation. See Thiry v. Armstrong World Industries, 661 P.2d 515 (Okl.1983) (answering certified questions); Jackson v. Johns–Manville Sales Corp., 781 F.2d 394 (5th Cir.1986) (*Jackson III*), cert. denied 478 U.S. 1022, 106 S.Ct. 3339, 92 L.Ed.2d 743 (1986); Dykes v. Raymark Industries, Inc., 801 F.2d 810 (6th Cir.1986), cert. denied 481 U.S. 1038, 107 S.Ct. 1975, 95 L.Ed.2d 815 (1987); Racich v. Celotex Corp., 887 F.2d 393 (2d Cir.1989); Glasscock v. Armstrong Cork Co., 946 F.2d 1085 (5th Cir.1991), cert. denied 503 U.S. 1011, 112 S.Ct. 1778, 118 L.Ed.2d 435 (1992); Owens–Illinois, Inc. v. Armstrong, 87 Md.App. 699, 591 A.2d 544 (1991), modified on other grounds 326 Md. 107, 604 A.2d 47 (1992), cert. denied 506 U.S. 871, 113 S.Ct. 204, 121 L.Ed.2d 145 (1992). But see Martin v. Johns–Manville Corp., 508 Pa. 154, 494 A.2d 1088 (1985); MCIC v. Zenobia, 86 Md.App. 456, 587 A.2d 531 (1991) (vacating one award, affirming one award), reversed 325 Md. 420, 601 A.2d 633 (1992).

2. Decisions such as *Fischer* that reject policy arguments made against the imposition of multiple punitive awards are legion. Defendants have pressed the argument that multiple awards violated constitutional due process, i.e., the cumulative effect of multiple awards could become so burdensome on a defendant as to constitute a violation of substantive due process protections against grossly excessive punishments. In 1989 one United States District Court ruled that repetitive awards of punitive damages for the same conduct violates a defendant's due process rights. In Juzwin v. Amtorg Trading Corp., 705 F.Supp. 1053 (D.N.J.1989), vacated 718 F.Supp. 1233 (D.N.J.1989), Judge Sarokin wrote:

> subjecting defendants to the possibility of multiple awards of punitive damages for the single course of conduct alleged in this action would deprive defendants of the fundamental fairness required by the Due Process Clause.

After acknowledging the due process problems, Judge Sarokin called for appropriate legislation to address this issue and to set meaningful standards and guidelines. This legislation would include:

> (1) determining initially whether punitive damages should be allowed in mass tort cases, and if so; (2) establish standards for their imposition and for the amounts to be awarded; (3) determine if maximum limits should be imposed and whether they should be fixed by amount or some formula based upon the net worth of the defendant; (4) provide procedures for dealing with successive claims; and (5) determine who shall be entitled to receive and participate in those awards.

In the subsequent vacating opinion, Judge Sarokin expressed concern about the fairness of retroactively applying its ruling "to those adversely affected by this ruling and the court's inability to effectuate its ruling prospectively absent uniformity either through legislation or a Supreme Court determination." The court held that to bar a subsequent claim for punitive damages, the following must be established as having taken place during the first proceeding:

1. A full and complete hearing must be held, after adequate time has elapsed to investigate and discover the full scope and consequences of such conduct and during which all relevant evidence is presented regarding the conduct of the defendant against whom the claim is made;

2. Adequate representation is afforded to the plaintiff, with an opportunity for plaintiffs similarly situated and their counsel to cooperate and contribute towards the presentation of the punitive damages claim, including presentation of the past and probable future consequences of the defendant's wrongful conduct;

3. An appropriate instruction to the jury that their award will be the one and only award of punitive damages to be rendered against the company for its wrongful conduct;

4. Such other conditions as will assure a full, fair and complete presentation of all the relevant evidence in support of and in opposition to the claim. 718 F.Supp. 1233 (D.N.J.1989).

In Leonen v. Johns–Manville Corp., 717 F.Supp. 272 (D.N.J.1989), another New Jersey District Court judge reached a contrary conclusion respecting the due process issues inhering in multiple awards.

3. Subsequent to *Juzwin* and *Leonen,* numerous appellate courts have rejected defendants' due process arguments. See, e.g., Racich v. Celotex Corp., 887 F.2d 393 (2d Cir.1989); Simpson v. Pittsburgh Corning Corp., 901 F.2d 277 (2d Cir.1990), cert. denied 497 U.S. 1057, 111 S.Ct. 27, 111 L.Ed.2d 840 (1990); King v. Armstrong World Industries, 906 F.2d 1022 (5th Cir. 1990), cert. denied 500 U.S. 942, 111 S.Ct. 2236, 114 L.Ed.2d 478 (1991); Glasscock v. Armstrong Cork Co., 946 F.2d 1085 (5th Cir.1991), cert. denied 503 U.S. 1011, 112 S.Ct. 1778, 118 L.Ed.2d 435 (1992). In Chapter 5 the general due process limitations on punitive damages, both procedural and substantive, were considered. The Supreme Court has not addressed the question of what constitutional constraints, if any, exist on multiple awards arising from a product line or course of conduct.

4. In Dunn v. HOVIC, 1 F.3d 1371 (3d Cir.1993) (en banc), the Third Circuit ruled 8 to 5, that repeated impositions of punitive damages on mass tort defendants is not by itself so unreasonable as to violate substantive due process.

In *Dunn* a jury awarded plaintiff $500,000 in compensatory damages and $25 million in punitive damages against Owens–Corning Fiberglas Corp. The trial court remitted the latter award to $2 million. A panel of the Third Circuit affirmed, but remitted the punitives to $1 million. Owens–Corning sought en banc review to consider its constitutional argument that repetitive impositions of punitive damages arising out of the same course of conduct violated substantive due process. Writing for a majority, Chief Judge Sloviter noted that in Pacific Mutual Life Insurance Co. v. Haslip, 499 U.S. 1, 111 S.Ct. 1032, 113 L.Ed.2d 1 (1991), the Supreme Court approved appellate review of punitive awards to determine if a particular award is greater than is reasonably necessary to punish and deter. After stating that en banc review was justified because of the importance of the question, the court observed that the vast majority of federal and state courts that have addressed the issue have declined to strike punitive awards solely because they constituted repetitive punishments for the same conduct. It commented: "Those courts, and this court, have recognized the arbitrariness of imposing caps on such damages in only one jurisdiction, when what is required is a national, uniform solution to the problem."

Moreover, the court noted that the Supreme Court decision in TXO Production Corp. v. Alliance Resources Corp., 509 U.S. 443, 113 S.Ct. 2711, 125 L.Ed.2d 366 (1993), held only that the enormous award in that case posed no substantive due process violation, and made no reference to the possible impact of repetitive awards. Judge Sloviter continued:

"We would be intrepid indeed were we to use this case to iterate a blanket policy judgment against punitive damages in asbestos cases in light of the Supreme Court's studied silence on the issue."

Nevertheless, the Third Circuit held that a further remittitur was appropriate because the district court gave insufficient consideration to the effect of successive punitive awards in asbestos litigation:

"This factor, above all, leads us to conclude that the maximum amount of punitive damages that could reasonably have been awarded in this case is $1 million."

Judge Joseph Weis dissented from the en banc opinion, and stated that in the unique context of asbestos litigation "punitive awards are not needed for retribution and deterrence. Actually there is little conduct to deter because few asbestos-containing products are still manufactured in the United States." Noting that Owens–Corning stopped manufacturing Kaylo in November 1972 and no longer produces any asbestos-containing products so that there was no conduct to deter in the future, Judge Weis continued: "The avalanche of compensatory claims against asbestos manufacturers has surely served as more of a punishment and deterrent than individual punitive assessments," concluding: "There is no compelling reason why injured but fully compensated plaintiffs should receive punitive awards."

Like the majority, Judge Weis acknowledged the need for a national solution, but the immediate need was to "stop the hemorrhaging so as to protect future claimants." He stated that courts should not await congressional or state legislative action, when the courts created the problem. "It is judicial paralysis, not activism, that is the problem ... " Finally, Weis stressed that the available resources of asbestos manufacturers will be exhausted before all deserving claimants are compensated; compensation should rank first, then administrative costs, and far down the list, "if not at the very bottom" should come punitive awards.

Who has the better of the constitutional argument? Are there nonconstitutional grounds for refusing to allow repetitive awards of punitive damages? Should asbestos cases have different substantive rules governing punitive damages? What about the concern that future claimants may be denied compensatory damages if punitive damages exhaust defendants' assets?

How might a defendant set out to establish the proposition that resources will be inadequate to compensate future claimants?

2. ALCOHOL

1.   Can a manufacturer or distributor of alcohol be liable when a consumer suffers a physical disability or disease from the consumption of moderate quantities of the beverage? A new genre of failure to warn cases is emerging from injuries attributable to moderate use of alcohol, in circumstances where the risks of consumption are not so obvious: pregnant women whose consumption produces fetal injuries and adults whose long-term consumption results in serious conditions, even death.

In Hon v. Stroh Brewery Co., 835 F.2d 510 (3d Cir.1987), we see an early appellate ruling to consider this informational defect claim. *Hon* was a wrongful death action brought by the surviving spouse, whose husband died at age 26 from pancreatitis, allegedly from his consumption of alcohol. Mr. Hon drank Old Milwaukee Beer and Old Milwaukee Light, two to three cans a night, an average of four nights a week. Plaintiff's expert in an affidavit expressed these opinions: (1) the understanding shared by members of the public is that excessive and prolonged use of alcoholic beverages is likely to result in disease, principally of the liver; (2) Mr. Hon's case was not within the risk thus appreciated by the public because (a) his use was prolonged but not excessive and (b) his disease was of the pancreas; and (3) the public's understanding is "archaic" because medical science has now established that either excessive or prolonged, even though moderate, use of alcohol may result in disease of many kinds, including pancreatic disease.

The court then considered the application of Restatement (Second) of Torts § 402A:

"In applying [Restatement (Second) of Torts § 402A], the Supreme Court of Pennsylvania has held that the trial judge must decide a threshold issue as a matter of law: taking the allegations of the complaint to be true, would the social policy considerations underlying strict liability justify recovery under § 402A in this case." The court must thus balance the product's social utility against its unavoidable risks to determine whether the condition of the product could be labeled "unreasonably dangerous" and the risk of loss placed on the manufacturer. Only if the court decides that strict liability would be appropriate does the case go to the jury for a determination regarding the truth of the plaintiff's allegations. * * *

* * *

As one would expect, a manufacturer whose products will enter Pennsylvania may assume that users or consumers will possess the common knowledge of the community. It must therefore warn only of latent risks. If the product's risks "w[ere] known or should have been known to the user, liability cannot be imposed upon the manufacturer merely because the manufacturer allegedly has failed to warn of that propensity." [See also] Restatement (Second) of Torts § 402A comment i ("The article sold must be dangerous to an extent beyond that which would be contemplated by the ordinary knowledge common to the community as its characteristics.'').

* * *

Although the district court in this case did not expressly undertake [a] threshold social policy analysis[,] * * * it did suggest that allowing strict liability in this case "could impose an impractical burden on manufacturers of alcoholic beverages to devise warnings suitable for the particular tolerance of each consumer," 665 F.Supp. at 1146. Mrs. Hon does not take issue with this suggestion. Rather, she insists that a general warning of the risk of moderate consumption would suffice, for example, "Alcohol can have adverse effects on your health even when consumed in moderate amounts." If Stroh shows that it is not feasible for it to give an effective warning of the hazard that led to Mr. Hon's death, this case might present a more substantial social policy issue than the typical warning case[.] We do not resolve that issue here because the district court did not fully address it and because we believe the issue would benefit from a more complete development of the record.

The remaining issue under the analysis taught in the Pennsylvania cases is whether, given the common knowledge of the community with respect to the hazards of alcohol consumption, a warning was an "element necessary to make [Stroh's beer] safe for its intended use," namely human consumption. This issue is for the jury unless the record created in response to Stroh's motion for summary judgment reveals no factual basis for an affirmative answer to this crucial question. * * *

The district court granted summary judgment to Stroh because it concluded "as a matter of law that [Mr. Hon] knew or should have known that the amount of beer that he consumed was potentially lethal." 665 F.Supp. at 1146. It erred in reaching this conclusion. On the record before the district court, a trier of fact could properly find that while the amount of beer consumed by Mr. Hon was potentially lethal, that fact was known neither to him nor to the consuming public. For this reason, we conclude that there is a material dispute of fact as to whether Stroh's beer without a warning is safe for its intended purpose and, accordingly, that summary judgment was inappropriate.

Dr. Marks' and Dr. Plotnick's affidavits provide evidence tending to show that beer in the quantity and manner Mr. Hon consumed it can have fatal consequences. Nothing in the record suggests that Mr. Hon was aware of this fact, however. Moreover, Dr. Plotnick's affidavit tends to show that the general public is unaware that consumption at this level and in this manner can have any serious adverse effects. There is no evidence in the record that the public appreciates any hazard that may be associated with this kind of consumption.

In addition, we conclude that the story boards of Stroh's commercials provide additional evidence from which a jury could conclude that the general public is unaware of the hazard that allegedly led to Mr. Hon's death. If a jury finds that Stroh's marketing of its product has effectively taught the consuming public that consumption of beer on the order of eight to twelve cans of beer per week can be a part of the "good life" and is properly associated with healthy, robust activities, this conclusion would be an important consideration for the jury in determining whether an express warning was necessary to make Old Milwaukee beer safe for its intended purpose. Cf., Baldino v. Castagna, [505 Pa. 239, 478 A.2d 807, 810 (1984)] (jury may consider whether a manufacturer has nullified warning that has been given by its promotion of the product); Incollingo v. Ewing, [444 Pa. 263, 282 A.2d 206, 220 (1971)] ("Action designed to stimulate the use of a potentially dangerous product must be considered in testing the adequacy of a warning as to when and how the product should not be used...."). Based on this evidence we believe there is a material dispute of fact as to whether the sale of Stroh's beer products with no warning was safe for its intended purpose.

Stroh's primary argument in response to the evidence presented by Mrs. Hon is that under comment j of § 402A, all that is required to preclude liability is that the consumption of alcohol be "prolonged."[5] * * * [Comment j] specifically cites alcohol as an example, states that no warning is needed for products that are made dangerous only "when consumed in excessive quantity, or over a long period of time, *when the danger, or potentiality of danger is generally known and recognized.*" Restatement § 402A comment j (emphasis added).

Stroh interprets comment j to mean that "the dangers of the prolonged consumption of alcohol are well known to the public." But comment j does not say that whenever alcohol is consumed over a long period of time the dangers are necessarily generally known. Rather, it says that when the danger is generally known, no warning is required. * * *[6]

* * *

5. Comment j states in relevant part:

"j. Directions or warning. In order to prevent the product from being [in a defective condition] unreasonably dangerous [to the user or consumer], the seller may be required to give directions or warning, on the container, as to its use. The seller may reasonably assume that those with common allergies, as for example to eggs or strawberries, will be aware of them, and he is not required to warn against them. Where, however, the product contains an ingredient to which a substantial number of the population are allergic, and the ingredient is one whose danger is not generally known, or if known is one which the consumer would reasonably not expect to find in the product, the seller is required to give warning against it, if he has knowledge, or by the application of reasonable, developed human skill and foresight should have knowledge, of the presence of the ingredient and the danger. Likewise in the case of poison-

ous drugs, or those unduly dangerous for other reasons, warning as to use may be required."

"But a seller is not required to warn with respect to products, or ingredients in them, which are only dangerous, or potentially so, when consumed in excessive quantity, or over a long period of time, when the danger, or potentially of danger, is generally known and recognized. Again the dangers of alcoholic beverages are an example, as are also those of foods containing such substances as saturated fats, which may over a period of time have a deleterious effect upon the human heart."

6. In pertinent part, comment i states:

"Many products cannot possibly be made entirely safe for all consumption, and any food or drug necessarily involves some risk of harm, if only from over consumption.... The article sold must be dangerous to an

With one possible exception, all of the cases cited by Stroh presented records from which a trier of fact could conclude only that the consumer of the alcoholic beverages knew or should have known that his or her consumption created a substantial risk of bodily injury. Accordingly, these cases are entirely consistent with Mrs. Hon's theory of liability. * * *

It is true, as Stroh stresses, that Mrs. Hon cites no case holding a brewer strictly liable for a failure to warn. We find this fact neither surprising nor at odds with our analysis, however. So far as we have been able to ascertain, there is no case in which the plaintiff allegedly consumed beer in the quantity and manner reflected in this record. The fact that such a case has not been litigated is explainable on either of two grounds. It may be, as Mrs. Hon contends, that consumers are unaware of the risk created by the consumption of beer in this manner. On the other hand, it may be, as Stroh's answer indicates it will attempt to prove, that Mr. Hon's quantity and manner of beer consumption poses no significant risk of bodily injury. In this context, the absence of authority for Mrs. Hon's position provides no persuasive reason to depart from the analysis suggested by the Pennsylvania authorities we have discussed above.

III.

We will vacate the summary judgment granted to Stroh and remand the case to the district court for further proceedings consistent with this opinion.

Notes and Questions

1. What if the record shows that Mr. Hon would not have heeded such a warning as Mrs. Hon argues should have been given?

2. Congress enacted the Alcoholic Beverage Labeling Act of 1988, 27 U.S.C.A. § 201 et seq., which contains the following provisions:

Section 204.(a) On and after the expiration of the 12–month period following the date of enactment of this title, it shall be unlawful for any person to manufacture, import or bottle for sale or distribution in the United States any alcoholic beverage unless the container of such beverage bears the following statement:

GOVERNMENT WARNING: (1) According to the Surgeon General, women should not drink alcoholic beverages during pregnancy because of the risk of birth defects. (2) Consumption of alcoholic beverages

extent beyond that which would be contemplated by the ordinary consumer who purchases it, with the ordinary knowledge common to the community as its characteristics. Good whiskey is not unreasonably dangerous merely because it will make some people drunk, and is especially dangerous to alcoholics. . . ."

Restatement (Second) of Torts § 402A comment i. Thus, although like comment j, comment i cites alcohol as an example, the exception to liability applies only because the dangers of intoxication and alcoholism are within the contemplation of the ordinary consumer.

impairs your ability to drive a car or operate machinery, and may cause health problems.

Section 205. No statement relating to alcoholic beverages and health, other than the statement required by section 204 of this title, shall be required under state law to be placed on any container of an alcoholic beverage, or on any box, carton, or other package, irrespective of the material from which made, that contains such a container.

What impact should this statute have on suits brought for actions that accrue after its enactment? Will the courts experience the same pre and post-enactment problems that have been so determinative in cigarette litigation?

3.   The Texas Court of Appeals held in McGuire v. Joseph E. Seagram & Sons, Inc., 790 S.W.2d 842 (Tex.App.1990), reversed 814 S.W.2d 385 (Tex.1991) that alcohol manufacturers, distributors and their trade association have a duty to warn consumers of some of the dangers of alcohol; and that under strict liability when the manufacturer knows or should know of the potential danger to consumers because of the nature of the product and its likelihood of prolonged use, the manufacturer is duty-bound to provide warnings of such dangers. The Texas Supreme Court reversed, 814 S.W.2d 385 (Tex.1991), holding that manufacturers of alcoholic beverages have no duty to warn of the dangers of developing alcoholism from prolonged consumption of their products. This conclusion is consistent with those of many other courts that have held as a matter of law that distilled spirits and other alcoholic beverages are not more dangerous to personal health than would be expected by the ordinary adult consumer.

4.   The vitality of a "consumer expectations" approach to evaluating a "defect" in toxic product claims would be affected by its probable abandonment in the expected new Products Liability Restatement. The Preliminary Draft of a Restatement (Third) of Torts: Products Liability, introduced earlier, emphasizes that the classical "consumer expectations" test "is explicitly abandoned as an independent test for determining defect." In its words, the test for design defect properly employs "a risk-utility balancing to determine defectiveness in the context of design." How would you phrase Stroh's risk-utility argument for the acceptable safety of its products? How might a plaintiff argue the case?

The Reporters' proposed liability standards reject the "open and obvious" or "patent danger" rule as a total bar to a design defect claim, and state that "the obviousness of the danger is one factor among many to consider as to whether a product design meets risk-utility norms." In contrast, however, the Reporters state that there is no duty to warn about obvious dangers. Explaining the compatibility between a rule that obviousness is no automatic bar to a design defect claim, and one that preserves obviousness as an exculpatory factor relating to informational obligations, Professors Henderson and Twerski cite their own earlier commentary to this effect:

"[T]he argument for abandoning the patent danger rule in warning cases, simply because the rule has been abandoned in design cases, makes no sense. In the design case, the obviousness of the danger does not necessarily preclude the possibility that an alternative design could reduce the risk cost-effectively. By contrast, assuming that some risks are patently obvious, the obviousness of a product-related risk invariably serves the same function as a warning that the risk is present. Thus nothing is to be gained by adding a warning of the danger already telegraphed by the product itself."

Henderson & Twerski, Doctrinal Collapse in Products Liability: The Empty Shell of Failure to Warn, 65 N.Y.U.L. Rev. 265, 282 (1990).

3. PRESCRIPTION PHARMACEUTICALS, BIOLOGICAL PRODUCTS AND MEDICAL DEVICES

A third and principal class of products that may produce exposure to toxic substances is prescription products. Within this general grouping are prescription pharmaceuticals, blood and other biological products, and medical devices. Widely reported personal injury litigation within these categories has involved products ranging from DES, to Bendectin, to contaminated blood or blood derivatives, to silicone breast implants. One similarity between and among most of these categories is the hotly contested issue of causation, a question that is addressed separately in Chapter 8. The second similarity is that each of these products is available only though prescription. The implications of being a prescription product are twofold. The first is that a seller ordinarily discharges its duty to provide adequate warnings, instructions and other information by making that information available to the health provider, most often a physician. The second is that the strict products liability evaluation under Restatement (Second) of Torts § 402A is governed by comment k thereto. The significance of the latter is the subject of the following decision of the California Supreme Court.

a. *Pharmaceuticals and comment k*

BROWN v. SUPERIOR COURT

Supreme Court of California, 1988.
44 Cal.3d 1049, 245 Cal.Rptr. 412, 751 P.2d 470.

Mosk, J.

In current litigation several significant issues have arisen relating to the liability of manufacturers of prescription drugs for injuries caused by their products. Our first and broadest inquiry is whether such a manufacturer may be held strictly liable for a product that is defective in design. * * *

A number of plaintiffs filed actions in the San Francisco Superior Court against numerous drug manufacturers which allegedly produced DES, a substance plaintiffs claimed was used by their mothers to prevent miscarriage. They alleged that the drug was defective and they were injured in utero when their mothers ingested it. * * *

The trial court * * * determined that defendants could not be held strictly liable for the alleged defect in DES but only for their failure to warn of known or knowable side effects of the drug.

* * *

[The Court of Appeal affirmed.] We granted review to examine the conclusions of the Court of Appeal and its potential conflict with Kearl v. Lederle Laboratories [218 Cal.Rptr. 453 (1985)], on the issue of strict liability of a drug manufacturer for a defect in the design of a prescription drug.

I. STRICT LIABILITY

* * *

B. *Strict Liability and Prescription Drugs*

* * *

[Restatement (Second) of Torts § 402A comment k] provides that the producer of a properly manufactured prescription drug may be held liable for injuries caused by the product only if it was not accompanied by a warning of dangers that the manufacturer knew or should have known about. It declares:

> k. Unavoidably unsafe products. There are some products which, in the present state of human knowledge, are quite incapable of being made safe for their intended and ordinary use. These are especially common in the field of drugs. An outstanding example is the vaccine for the Pasteur treatment of rabies, which not uncommonly leads to very serious and damaging consequences when it is injected. Since the disease itself invariably leads to a dreadful death, both the marketing and use of the vaccine are fully justified, notwithstanding the unavoidable high degree of risk which they involve. Such a product, properly prepared, and accompanied by proper directions and warning, is not defective, nor is it unreasonably dangerous. The same is true of many other drugs, vaccines, and the like, many of which for this very reason cannot legally be sold except to physicians, or under the prescription of a physician. It is also true in particular of many new or experimental drugs as to which, because of lack of time and opportunity for sufficient medical experience, there can be no assurance of safety, or perhaps even of purity of ingredients, but such experience as there is justifies the marketing and use of the drug notwithstanding a medically recognizable risk. The seller of such products, again with the qualification that they are properly prepared and marketed, and proper warning is given, where the situation calls for it, is not to be held to strict liability for unfortunate consequences attending their use, merely because he has undertaken to supply the public with an apparently useful and desirable product, attended with a known but apparently reasonable risk.

Comment k has been analyzed and criticized by numerous commentators. While there is some disagreement as to its scope and meaning, there is a general consensus that, although it purports to explain the strict liability doctrine, in fact the principle it states is based on negligence. * * *

Comment k has been adopted in the overwhelming majority of jurisdictions that have considered the matter.

* * *

* * * Most cases have embraced the rule of comment k without detailed analysis of its language. A few, notably Kearl v. Lederle Laboratories, supra, 172 Cal.App.3d 812 (hereafter *Kearl*), have conditioned application of the exemption stated therein on a finding that the drug involved is in fact 'unavoidably dangerous,' reasoning that the comment was intended to exempt only such drugs from strict liability. (Accord, Toner v. Lederle Laboratories (1987) 112 Idaho 328 [732 P.2d 297, 303–309]; see also Feldman v. Lederle Laboratories (1984) 97 N.J. 429 [479 A.2d 374, 382–383] [involving allegations of a failure to warn, but stating that "whether a drug is unavoidably unsafe should be decided on a case-by-case basis."].) * * *

We appear, then, to have three distinct choices: (1) to hold that the manufacturer of a prescription drug is strictly liable for a defect in its product because it was defectively designed, as that term is defined in Barker [v. Lull Engineering Co., 573 P.2d 443 (Cal.1978)], or because of a failure to warn of its dangerous propensities even though such dangers were neither known nor scientifically knowable at the time of distribution; (2) to determine that liability attaches only if a manufacturer fails to warn of dangerous propensities of which it was or should have been aware, in conformity with comment k; or (3) to decide, * * * that strict liability for design defects should apply to prescription drugs unless the particular drug which caused the injury is found to be "unavoidably dangerous."

We shall conclude that (1) a drug manufacturer's liability for a defectively designed drug should not be measured by the standards of strict liability; (2) because of the public interest in the development, availability, and reasonable price of drugs, the appropriate test for determining responsibility is the test stated in comment k; and (3) for these same reasons of policy, we disapprove the holding of Kearl that only those prescription drugs found to be "unavoidably dangerous" should be measured by the comment k standard and that strict liability should apply to drugs that do not meet that description.

1. *Design Defect*

[Barker] set forth two alternative tests to measure a design defect: first, whether the product performed as safely as the ordinary consumer would expect when used in an intended and reasonably foreseeable manner, and second, whether, on balance, the benefits of the challenged design outweighed the risk of danger inherent in the design. In making the latter determination, the jury may consider these factors: "the gravity of the danger posed by the challenged design, the likelihood that such danger would occur, the mechanical feasibility of a safer alternative design, the financial cost of an improved design, and the adverse consequences to the product and to the consumer that would result from an alternative design.''

Defendants assert that neither of these tests is applicable to a prescription drug like DES. As to the "consumer expectation" standard, they claim, the "consumer" is not the plaintiff but the physician who prescribes the drug, and it is to him that the manufacturer's warnings are directed. A physician appreciates the fact that all prescription drugs involve inherent risks, known and unknown, and he does not expect that the drug is without such risks. We agree that the "consumer expectation" aspect of the Barker test is inappropriate to prescription drugs. While the "ordinary consumer" may have a reasonable expectation that a product such as a machine he purchases will operate safely when used as intended, a patient's expectations regarding the effects of such a drug are those related to him by his physician, to whom the manufacturer directs the warnings regarding the drug's properties. The manufacturer cannot be held liable if it has provided appropriate warnings and the doctor fails in his duty to transmit these warnings to the patient or if the patient relies on inaccurate information from others regarding side effects of the drug.

The second test, which calls for the balancing of risks and benefits, is inapposite to prescription drugs, according to defendants, because it contemplates that a safer alternative design is feasible. * * *

We agree with defendants that Barker contemplates a safer alternative design is possible, but we seriously doubt their claim that a drug like DES cannot be "redesigned" to make it safer. For example, plaintiff might be able to demonstrate at trial that a particular component of DES rendered it unsafe as a miscarriage preventative and that removal of that component would not have affected the efficacy of the drug. Even if the resulting product, without the damaging component, would bear a name other than DES, it would do no violence to semantics to view it as a "redesign" of DES.

* * *

Of course, the fact that a drug with dangerous side effects may be characterized as containing a defect in design does not necessarily mean that its producer is to be held strictly liable for the defect. The determination of that issue depends on whether the public interest would be served by the imposition of such liability. As we have seen, the fundamental reasons underlying the imposition of strict liability are to deter manufacturers from marketing products that are unsafe, and to spread the cost of injury from the plaintiff to the consuming public, which will pay a higher price for the product to reflect the increased expense of insurance to the manufacturer resulting from its greater exposure to liability.

These reasons could justify application of the doctrine to the manufacturers of prescription drugs. It is indisputable, as plaintiff contends, that the risk of injury from such drugs is unavoidable, that a consumer may be helpless to protect himself from serious harm caused by them, and that, like other products, the cost of insuring against strict liability can be passed on by the producer to the consumer who buys the item. Moreover, as we observe below, in some cases additional testing of drugs before they are marketed might reveal dangerous side effects, resulting in a safer product.

But there is an important distinction between prescription drugs and other products such as construction machinery * * * Moreover, unlike other important medical products (wheelchairs, for example), harm to some users from prescription drugs is unavoidable. Because of these distinctions, the broader public interest in the availability of drugs at an affordable price must be considered in deciding the appropriate standard of liability for injuries resulting from their use.

Perhaps a drug might be made safer if it was withheld from the market until scientific skill and knowledge advanced to the point at which additional dangerous side effects would be revealed. But in most cases such a delay in marketing new drugs—added to the delay required to obtain approval for release of the product from the [FDA]—would not serve the public welfare. Public policy favors the development and marketing of beneficial new drugs, even though some risks, perhaps serious ones, might accompany their introduction, because drugs can save lives and reduce pain and suffering.

If drug manufacturers were subject to strict liability, they might be reluctant to undertake research programs to develop some pharmaceuticals that would prove beneficial or to distribute others that are available to be marketed, because of the fear of large adverse monetary judgments. Further, the additional expense of insuring against such liability—assuming insurance would be available—and of research programs to reveal possible dangers not detectable by available scientific methods could place the cost of medication beyond the reach of those who need it most.

* * *

The possibility that the cost of insurance and of defending against lawsuits will diminish the availability and increase the price of pharmaceuticals is far from theoretical. Defendants cite a host of examples of products which have greatly increased in price or have been withdrawn or withheld from the market because of the fear that their producers would be held liable for large judgments.

* * *

There is no doubt that, from the public's standpoint, these are unfortunate consequences. And they occurred even though almost all jurisdictions follow the negligence standard of comment k. It is not unreasonable to conclude in these circumstances that the imposition of a harsher test for liability would not further the public interest in the development and availability of these important products.

We decline to hold, therefore, that a drug manufacturer's liability for injuries caused by the defective design of a prescription drug should be measured by the standard set forth in Barker.

* * *

Notes and Questions

1. *Brown* applies comment k to *all* prescription drugs as a class without requiring a case by case determination of whether the conditions described in comment k should apply to a particular drug. The court justifies this blanket immunity from strict liability on the basis that failure to provide it would retard the development, introduction and availability of new drugs. Do you agree? How does one test the validity of such a proposition?

2. Some courts have held that comment k should be applied on a case-by-case adjudication. For example, in Hill v. Searle Laboratories, 884 F.2d 1064 (8th Cir.1989), a case involving the CU–7 intrauterine device, the Eighth Circuit found that Arkansas would adopt comment k, but would treat it as a qualified affirmative defense with the burden on the defendant to establish that the drug involved was incapable of being made safe and filled an exceptional social need, which it concluded the CU–7 did not:

> The drafters of comment k did not intend to grant all manufacturers of prescription drugs a blanket exception to strict liability. Such an exception was proposed at the American Law Institute meeting where section 402A and comment k were adopted, but this proposal was defeated. 38 ALI Proc. 19, 90–98 (1961). The language of comment k suggests that only exceptional products, albeit such exceptional products are more likely to be found in the field of prescription drug products, should be excluded from the strict liability provisions. But more importantly, the example given, the vaccine for the Pasteur treatment of rabies—suggests that only special products, those with exceptional social need, fall within the gamut of comment k.

* * *

With which court do you agree, *Brown* or *Hill* ? A significant number of those decisions, such as *Hill*, that have treated comment k as a limited affirmative defense have involved contraceptive devices. See, e.g., Kociemba v. G.D. Searle & Co., 680 F.Supp. 1293, 1301 (D.Minn.1988); Wheelahan v. G.D. Searle & Co., 814 F.2d 655 (4th Cir.1987); Coursen v. A.H. Robins & Co., 764 F.2d 1329, 1337 (9th Cir.1985). Should manufacturers of such devices be treated less favorably than manufacturers of other prescription drugs?

3. Restatement (Third) of Torts: Products Liability § 6 describes rules for liability for manufacturers and sellers of defective prescription drugs. In essence, the Restatement rules (a) provide for liability for drugs that contain (i) a manufacturing defect; (ii) a design defect; or (iii) a defect due to inadequate warnings or instructions. Section 6 preserves the established rule that under ordinary circumstances a drug manufacturer satisfies its warning obligations by conveying cautionary information to the appropriate health care constituency, most often the prescribing physician. Importantly, it

suggests that in some instances, for example mass immunization programs in which there may not be the more typical physician-patient consultation, the manufacturer may be required to take steps to make warnings or instructions directly accessible to the patient community. Lastly, the Products Liability Restatement provides that a pharmacist or other retail seller may incur liability for injury caused by (i) a manufacturing defect in the product; or (ii) failure to exercise reasonable care.

The pertinent parts of § 6 read as follows:

(c) A prescription drug or medical device is not reasonably safe due to defective design if the foreseeable risks of harm posed * * * are sufficiently great in relation to its foreseeable risks and therapeutic benefits that reasonable health-care providers, knowing of such foreseeable risks and therapeutic benefits, would not prescribe the drug or medical device for any class of patients.

(d) A prescription drug or medical device is not reasonably safe due to inadequate instructions or warnings if reasonable instructions or warnings regarding foreseeable risks of harm are not provided to:

> (1) prescribing physicians and other health-care providers who are in a position to reduce the risks of harm in accordance with the instructions or warnings; or(2) the patient when the manufacturer knows or has reason to know that health-care providers will not be in a position to reduce the risks of harm in accordance with the instructions or warnings.

(e) A retail seller or other distributor of a prescription drug or medical device is subject to liability for harm caused by the drug or device if:

> (1) at the time of the sale or other distribution the drug or medical device contains a manufacturing defect * * * ; or

> (2) at or before the time of sale or other distribution of the drug or medical device the retail seller or other distributor fails to exercise reasonable care and such failure causes harm to persons.

4. Comment k does not, even when applied as in *Brown*, create a safe harbor from all liability. In two locations within comment k the protection afforded is explicitly qualified: "such a product, properly prepared, and accompanied by proper directions and warnings, is not defective nor is it unreasonably dangerous ... The seller of such products, again with the qualification that they are properly prepared and marketed, and proper warnings given, where the situation calls for it, is not to be held strictly liable ... " Thus, a manufacturer may be held liable for failure to provide sufficient information about the risks attending use of the product or the means of avoiding or reducing those risks; the liability, however, is not strict: the product seller is liable only if it fails to warn of dangers of which it knew or should have known. There is no liability for failing to warn about the unknown or unknowable risks. The comment k test essentially amounts to a negligence standard.

5. While the court in *Brown* declines to apply strict liability for defective formulation to prescription drugs, it does point out that in its view such a defect theory could conceptually apply; that is, a drug might have an alternative safer design or formulation that could create a standard for

measuring the defectiveness of the formulation present in the drug. What about a manufacturer's *negligence* in formulating a drug? Does the opinion preclude a plaintiff from advancing such a theory? Does comment k? Or, as a practical matter, does the court's conclusion that a risk/utility evaluation under Barker v. Lull Engineering Co. is inappropriate in a pharmaceuticals case effectively bar plaintiffs from winning on a theory of defective formulation?

b. Biological Products: Special Problems of AIDS–Contaminated Blood Products

McKEE v. MILES LABORATORIES

United States District Court, Eastern District of Kentucky, 1987.
675 F.Supp. 1060, affirmed 866 F.2d 219 (6th Cir.1989).

SILER, J.

This matter is before the Court on the motion by defendant Miles Laboratories, Inc. and its division, Cutter Laboratories, for summary judgment. * * *

This action arose from the circumstances surrounding the blood transfusion of plaintiff's decedent, David Allen McKee. David McKee suffered from Hemophilia A, which meant he lacked a protein necessary for the normal coagulation of his blood. That missing protein is called Factor VIII. A method used by pharmaceutical companies for the treatment of hemophiliacs involved producing Factor VIII by combining (or pooling) plasma collected from thousands of individuals all over the United States. The Factor VIII is precipitated out of the combined plasma and then it is lyophilized (or freeze dried). David McKee used defendant's concentrated Factor VIII Product by the pooled lyophilized method. As a result of its use he contracted acquired immune deficiency syndrome ("AIDS"). Decedent was so diagnosed as having AIDS in October 1983 and subsequently died in 1984. His Administratrix and wife, Stella Mae McKee, brought this action for damages as representative of his estate and on her own behalf.

Defendants move for summary judgment as to plaintiff's strict liability claims, contending that these claims are barred by Kentucky's Blood Shield statute, K.R.S. 139.125. Defendants also move for summary judgment as to the merits of the case, contending that at the time plaintiff's decedent contracted AIDS there was no test which would have revealed the presence of this dreaded disease. In opposition to the motion for summary judgment, plaintiff argues that there is a genuine issue of material fact as to whether an alternative testing method was available in 1983 when decedent contracted AIDS. Plaintiff also asserts that Kentucky's blood shield statute did not bar product liability claims and that, in any event, the statute is not applicable to this situation, but, if applicable, then unconstitutional.

The two central issues before the Court are: (1) whether strict liability applies to defendant's conduct; and (2) whether there existed, at the time plaintiff's decedent contracted the disease, a plausible alternative testing for determining the AIDS virus.

* * *

The relevant statute in question provides:

Procurement, processing or distribution of blood or human tissue deemed service and not sale.

The procurement, processing, distribution or use of whole blood, plasma, blood products, blood derivatives and other human tissues such as corneas, bones or organs for the purpose of injecting, transfusing or transplanting any of them into the human body is declared to be, for all purposes, the rendition of a service by every person participating therein and, whether or not any remuneration is paid therefor, is declared not to be a sale of such whole blood, plasma, blood products, blood derivatives or other tissues, for any purpose, subsequent to enactment of this section.

K.R.S. 139.125.

[The Court is guided] by defendants' authority under Coffee v. Cutter Biological and Miles Laboratories, Inc., 809 F.2d 191 (2d Cir. 1987). In that case the Court analyzed a blood shield statute similar to Kentucky's blood shield statute. Based upon the analysis of that opinion and the plain language of the statute, this Court concludes that Kentucky's blood shield statute was intended to preclude the assertion of product liability claims arising out the sale of blood components. The plain and unambiguous words of the statute clearly state that supplying blood or blood derivatives is to be considered a service by every person participating therein. Only four jurisdictions in the nation have not legislatively barred the application of products liability theories to blood and blood products. Kentucky is not [one] of those four states. Because transactions involving blood and blood components are to be considered services, as opposed to sales, they are outside the purview of Kentucky's product liability statute. K.R.S. 411.300; 411.320; 411.340[.]

* * * [B]lood shield statutes in other states uniformly have been interpreted as barring strict liability claims. To permit the plaintiff to circumvent the exemption of blood and blood derivatives by pursuing claims under the product liability statute would defeat the obvious legislative intent of K.R.S. 139.125. Consequently, plaintiff's claims against defendants arising under strict liability should be dismissed.

The Court now turns its attention to the second issue, that is, whether at the time plaintiff's decedent contracted the AIDS virus a plausible alternative testing method existed to detect its presence within the blood derivatives. In reaching this answer, the Court is guided by the well-reasoned decision in Kozup v. Georgetown University, 663 F.Supp. 1048 (D.D.C.1987), which analyzed existing methods available for the testing of AIDS during the early 1980s. Kozup involved a newborn receiving a blood transfusion for hypovolemia, a condition associated with premature birth, in January 1983. The child received three transfusions which were contaminated with the virus now known to transmit AIDS. The contaminated blood was supplied by the American Red Cross, which received it from an individual in 1982, and was administered by the Georgetown University Hospital. The child subsequently died from complications related to the AIDS infection.

In its analysis, the District Court reviewed the medical chronology of the AIDS virus to determine exactly what was known about AIDS by the scientific and medical communities and when. As in the present case, much of what the plaintiffs claimed in Kozup turned on allegations that defendants knew or should have known certain facts related to AIDS. This Court needs not rehash the same chronology medical history of AIDS which the Kozup Court so methodically composed. It is suffice to conclude that it was not until 1984 that the medical community reached a consensus as to the proposition that AIDS was transmittable by blood. In April, 1984, scientists identified the virus HTLV–III as the cause of AIDS. By May, 1985, an enzyme-linked immunosorbent assay (ELISA) test was made available, which screens for the antibodies sensitive to HTVL–III. Once it was available, the Center for Disease Control issued guidelines for implementing the ELISA test. This laboratory test has proven 98.6 percent effective in detecting exposure to AIDS. When coupled with a second test, the Western Blot Analysis, the rate of detection for exposure to AIDS rises to 100 percent. However, there is still no test for presence for the virus itself, nor is there a cure for the disease. As no recent breakthrough has been cited to the Court for the diagnosis, testing or treatment of AIDS, it can rely upon the Court's analysis and conclusions in Kozup.

As in Kozup, plaintiff alleges negligence as a basis for recovery from defendant. In short, plaintiff alleges that Cutter was negligent in failing to take measures designed to protect her husband from being infected with AIDS. Specifically, plaintiff contends that alternatives existed for the testing of the AIDS virus in defendant's product, citing the procedure of heat treatment. However, a review of the medical chronology set forth in Kozup reveals this contention inaccurate. As of 1983, no pharmaceutical company, blood bank, hospital or federal health care regulator in the United States took special AIDS-related measures in connection with transfusions. Doctors diagnosed plaintiff's decedent with AIDS in the Fall of 1983 before any specialized measures existed. Furthermore, plaintiff can point to no organization, government entity or medical association within the United States which advocated the use of plaintiff's alternative testing as a means of screening defendant's product for AIDS. Instead, plaintiff offers testimony of an expert whose current opinion is that pharmaceutical companies should have used a heat treating method to exclude viruses such as AIDS. This expert cannot alone create a standard of care or a prima facie case of negligence, where he is entirely in opposition to the standard prevailing in 1982–83. His opinion cannot be permitted to supplant the standard of care as established by the conduct of the pharmaceutical community which plaintiff's expert criticizes. * * *

It is clear that in order to prevail on the theory of negligence, plaintiff must show that defendant, Cutter Laboratories, violated a standard of care. That standard is established by looking to the conduct of the industry or profession in similar circumstances as of that date. Ulrich v. Kasco Abrasives Co., 532 S.W.2d 197 (Ky.1976). The standard of care for pharmaceutical companies at the time of decedent's transfusions did not require defendant to screen or perform plaintiff's suggested alternative testing to eliminate the risk of AIDS contamination. Consequently, no negligence occurred as defendants met the standard of care as then existed within the industry.

As stated in Kozup, this Court is mindful of the terrible personal tragedy that David McKee's struggle with AIDS must have been for the McKee family, especially in light of the recent breakthroughs in AIDS research. However, because plaintiff fails to make out a prima facie case of negligence, summary judgment for defendant on the issue of negligence is proper as well. An appropriate Order shall be entered.

Notes and Questions

1. Most states have enacted statutes that expressly shield manufacturers or suppliers of blood products from strict liability. For example, prior to 1986, Maryland's statute was limited to serum hepatitis, but was later broadened to treat the supplying of blood products as the rendering of a service, and not the sale of a product, thereby requiring proof of negligence to establish liability.

In Doe v. Miles Laboratories, 675 F.Supp. 1466, 1479–80 (D.Md.1987), affirmed 927 F.2d 187 (4th Cir.1991), the plaintiff contracted AIDS from a blood transfusion in 1983 when the statute was confined to hepatitis. The court, therefore, was faced with a purely common law question of whether strict liability rules should apply to blood products contaminated with AIDS virus, at a time when the risk was allegedly unknown, unknowable, and beyond the state of scientific art. The court held that comment k should not apply because the comment relates only to drugs involving a "reasonable danger," which AIDS contaminated blood exceeds, especially considering the needs of hemophiliacs for blood products and the inevitably fatal nature of the disease for those who develop it. The court rejected the state of the art defense stating: "The fact that the virus was undetectable prior to 1985 is not a mitigating factor. The best view is to consider blood containing undetectable diseases to be a defective product and therefore that strict liability is applicable ... The arguments in favor of strict liability apply persuasively to blood and blood products as they do to any other product."

Do you agree with the court's conclusion? See Kozup v. Georgetown University, 663 F.Supp. 1048 (D.D.C.1987), reversed on other grounds 851 F.2d 437 (D.C.Cir.1988) (discussing the developments in AIDS research and relied upon by the court in *McKee*); Roberts v. Suburban Hospital Assn., 73 Md.App. 1, 532 A.2d 1081, 1086 n. 3 (1987) (involving AIDS, listing the 48 states that have blood shield statutes; only New Jersey, Vermont, and the District of Columbia did not at that time).

2. On liability for transfused blood containing the HIV virus, consider Hoemke v. New York Blood Center, 912 F.2d 550 (2d Cir.1990), which held that a blood center could not be held negligent for failing to screen out gay male donors in 1981, before AIDS had been discovered to be blood-borne disease, or for not having administered alanine aminotransferase (ALT) test on its blood supply. But see Moore v. Armour Pharmaceutical Co., [Not Reported in F.Supp.], Prod. Liab. Rep.(CCH) ¶ 12,665 (M.D. Fla.1990) (rejecting Armour's argument that it was not obligated to warn hemophiliacs that they could contract HIV virus through blood products until medical community reached a consensus that the disease was transmittable by blood products).

3. Another related issue that has arisen in contaminated blood products litigation is whether the standard of care is to be measured against a professional standard—such as that applicable to physicians and hospitals—or against that of the ordinary reasonable person. For a defendant such as blood bank, the advantage of the professional standard is that there can be no finding of negligence if its practices conformed to the industry standard in terms of screening and blood gathering procedures. In United Blood Services v. Quintana, 827 P.2d 509 (Colo.1992), the Colorado Supreme Court found a middle ground, concluding that while the professional standard of care was applicable to blood product suppliers, a plaintiff would be permitted to challenge that standard. Specifically, a plaintiff could overcome the rebuttable presumption that adherence to the standard of care adopted by profession is due care by offering expert testimony that the profession's standard is "unreasonably deficient by not incorporating readily available practices and procedures more protective of the harm suffered by the plaintiff."

4. What of actions brought against governmental blood providers, such as the armed forces? The effect of the discretionary function exemption to the Federal Tort Claims Act (FTCA), 28 U.S.C.A. § 2671 et seq., was considered by the federal trial court in C.R.S. by D.B.S v. United States, 820 F.Supp. 449 (D.Minn.1993), a suit brought by a serviceman who contracted the AIDS virus following a blood transfusion administered at a military hospital. The court held that the armed forces' adherence to FDA and American Association of Blood Banks screening and recipient notification guidelines rather than development of their own, was within the discretionary function exemption to the FTCA. Compare Andrulonis v. United States, 924 F.2d 1210 (2d Cir.1991), cert. granted and judgment vacated 502 U.S. 801, 112 S.Ct. 39, 116 L.Ed.2d 18 (1991), previous decision reinstated 952 F.2d 652 (2d Cir.1991), cert. denied 505 U.S. 1204, 112 S.Ct. 2992, 120 L.Ed.2d 869 (1992) (discretionary function exemption of the FTCA did not apply because decision of a government scientist not to warn a laboratory worker of dangerous laboratory conditions "did not lend itself to policy balancing, [nor] is there any indication that [the scientist] considered the policy implications or the pros and cons of allowing the experiment to proceed.").

5. The potentially harsh operation of a statute of repose is revealed in Bradway v. American Nat. Red Cross, 992 F.2d 298 (11th Cir.1993), an action brought by a patient against a blood bank, and alleging that she had contracted AIDS during a transfusion administered following surgery. Under

Georgia's five-year statute of repose governing medical malpractice actions, the court held that her cause of action accrued upon the blood bank's actions or omissions that caused contaminated blood to be released to the hospital, rather than at the later time when plaintiff became infected with the virus. Adoption of the earlier accrual date, the court held, necessitated dismissal of plaintiff's claim as untimely. See Chapter 12 for further consideration of the statutes of limitation and repose problems in contaminated blood products litigation.

6. Should strict liability apply only to some products—those possibly most dangerous—such as asbestos and tobacco? Or, alternatively, should it apply to all products, except those of the greatest social need such as prescription drugs as *Brown* held? Or apply to all products and some prescription drugs, but not to the most beneficial within that class, as *Feldman* held? Who should decide whether a product is entitled to "special" treatment—either placed in the strict liability class or placed in the protected class?

7. *L–Tryptophan.* In the early 1990s, hundreds of lawsuits were pending in federal and state courts arising out of the use of L-tryptophan, an amino acid supplement used to treat insomnia, depression and premenstrual syndrome. The FDA recalled L-tryptophan products in March 1990 and in April announced that its use was linked to eosinophilia-myalgia syndrome (EMS), a rare blood disorder which produces muscle and joint pain, hair loss, swelling and numbness of hands and feet, walking difficulties, rashes, fever, and shortness of breath. The FDA also announced that the outbreak of EMS was linked to a single manufacturer, Showa Denko KK, a Japanese producer of the raw product. While Showa Denko is a defendant in most of the litigation, other defendants include its American subsidiary and wholesalers, distributors, retailers, and packagers. The Center for Disease Control stated that as of November 15, 1990, there were 1,539 reported cases of EMS, including 27 deaths. The investigation by the CDC and FDA has found that the L-tryptophan amino acid tablets were contaminated with a bacteria used in an "untested" and "experimental" generic manufacturing process.

In Hill by Hill v. Showa Denko, K.K., 188 W.Va. 654, 425 S.E.2d 609 (1992), cert. denied 508 U.S. 908, 113 S.Ct. 2338, 124 L.Ed.2d 249 (1993), the West Virginia Supreme Court of Appeals affirmed a lower court's assertion of personal jurisdiction over the Japanese manufacturing parent of L–Tryptophan, whose wholly-owned subsidiary, the parent's sole U.S. distributor, upon a showing, inter alia, that the subsidiary had solicited business in West Virginia.

What theories of liability would be asserted in these cases? Will comment k possibly be available as a defense or qualified defense? Why or why not? What factors would influence the potential liability of U.S. firms involved in the distribution of the product? Will class actions be appropriate? How about consolidated trials? What are the likely common questions of fact or law in these cases? What factual and legal questions will necessitate individual resolution?

c. Medical Devices

HEGNA v. E.I. DU PONT DE NEMOURS AND COMPANY

United States District Court, District of Minnesota, 1993.
825 F.Supp. 880.

DOTY, J.

This matter is before the court on defendant E.I. DuPont de Nemours and Company's ("DuPont") motion for summary judgment on plaintiff Marilyn Hegna's ("Hegna") negligence and strict liability claims. In the alternative, DuPont requests that the court reconsider its prior ruling on Hegna's negligence and strict liability claims in light of the more fully developed factual record now before the court. Based on a review of the file, record and proceedings herein, the court grants DuPont's request for reconsideration and determines that summary judgment in favor of DuPont on Hegna's negligence and strict liability claims is appropriate.

BACKGROUND

* * *

The present action arises from alleged defects in implants ("TMJ implants") that Hegna received during surgery on her temporomandibular joints ("TMJ"). Vitek, Inc. ("Vitek") made the implants out of Proplast, a porous and fibrous compound made in an eight-step process in which polytetraflouroethylene ("PTFE") is mixed with other materials. Vitek purchased its PTFE from DuPont.

Hegna alleges that her implants disintegrated, that PTFE particles from the disintegrated implants caused her injury and that Dupont is liable for those injuries. Hegna claims that DuPont knew of studies questioning the propriety of using PTFE in medical implants and that Vitek was using PTFE to make the TMJ implants. Hegna thus claims that DuPont had a duty to warn her or her physician of the risks involved in using PTFE-based implants, that DuPont failed to provide any warning and that if DuPont had provided a warning, she could have avoided her injuries. * * *

DuPont previously moved for summary judgment on Hegna's negligence and strict liability claims. DuPont argued that Hegna's negligence claim fails because it merely supplied Vitek with raw materials and played no role in the design, manufacture or sale of the TMJ implants. DuPont argued that it was a bulk supplier and, as such, had no legal duty either to ascertain whether Vitek's specialized use of PTFE was safe or to warn Hegna or her physician of any potential dangers associated with the use of PTFE in implants. In the alternative, DuPont argued that even if it had a duty to warn as a bulk supplier, it satisfied that duty by warning Vitek that PTFE was not made for medical purposes, that it had conducted no tests to determine the efficacy of using PTFE for medical purposes and that Vitek would have to rely on its own medical and legal judgment if it chose to use PTFE to make implants. With respect to the strict liability claim, DuPont argued that Hegna's claim fails because Vitek's Proplast manufacturing process altered the chemistry, composition and mechanical properties of the raw PTFE.

The court denied DuPont's motion for summary judgment on Hegna's negligence claim. The court, relying in part on Forest v. E.I. DuPont de Nemours & Co., 791 F.Supp. 1460 (D.Nev.1992) and Hill v. Wilmington Chem. Corp., 156 N.W.2d 898 (Minn.1968), determined that DuPont, as a bulk supplier, had a duty to warn at least Vitek of the possible dangers of using PTFE to make TMJ implants and that material fact disputes concerning the sufficiency of DuPont's warning precluded summary judgment. * * *

* * *

The court also denied DuPont's motion for summary judgment on Hegna's strict liability claim. In making that determination, the court noted that: [t]he distinction between strict liability and negligence in ... failure to warn cases is that in strict liability, knowledge of the condition of the product and the risks involved in that condition will be imputed to the manufacturer, whereas in negligence these elements must be proven. The court concluded that: "[i]f Hegna is unable to support her negligence claim at trial by presenting sufficient evidence of DuPont's knowledge, the court will then determine whether such knowledge should be imputed to DuPont."

DuPont now asks the court to reconsider its prior ruling and grant its motion for summary judgment. DuPont renews its argument that as a bulk supplier to Vitek it had no duty to warn Hegna or her physician and had no duty to assure the safety of Vitek's specialized use of PTFE. * * * In the alternative, DuPont raises two new arguments in support of its summary judgment motion. First, DuPont contends that Hegna's claims are preempted by 21 U.S.C. § 360k of the Medical Device Amendments. Second, DuPont contends that the applicable statute of limitations bars Hegna's strict liability claim.

DISCUSSION

* * *

1. Hegna's Negligence Claim

In its previous order, the court found that under Minnesota law, DuPont, as a bulk supplier, had a duty to at least warn Vitek of the potential danger of using PTFE to make TMJ implants. Hegna, 806 F.Supp. at 826 ("The court thus concludes that if faced with the present situation, a Minnesota court would find that DuPont had a duty to warn at least Vitek of the possible dangers of using PTFE for jaw implants.").

The court adopted the test set forth in Forest, 791 F.Supp. 1460, another case involving DuPont's liability for alleged injuries stemming from disintegrated TMJ implants, to determine whether DuPont discharged its duty to warn.

The relevant question in bulk supplier cases is whether the bulk supplier was objectively reasonable in relying on a knowledgeable intermediary to provide a warning to ultimate users. This involves proof of two elements: 1) that the bulk supplier was reasonable in believing that the intermediary knew of the dangers associated with the bulk product, and 2) that the bulk supplier was reasonable in relying on the intermediary to warn the ultimate user of such dangers.... [F]or [d]efendant DuPont to succeed with its bulk supplier doctrine defense in the instant case, it will have to show that it reasonably relied upon Vitek's knowledge of the risks involved with using PTFE in medical implants and that it also reasonably relied upon Vitek to warn implant patients of those dangers. To do this, DuPont must show that it took some reasonable, affirmative steps to ascertain that Vitek was a knowledgeable intermediary. Such steps must rise above the level of a mere disclaimer but need not go so far as to have required DuPont to second-guess Vitek's actions in carrying-out its own duty to warn.

The factual record before the court has been supplemented since DuPont filed its previous summary judgment motion. It is now undisputed that Vitek knew both the properties of DuPont's PTFE and the scientific community's concerns regarding the use of PTFE-based materials to make implants such as the TMJ implant. Moreover, it is undisputed that DuPont informed Vitek of its concerns regarding the use of PTFE-based materials to make implants, that it had little overall knowledge concerning the efficacy of using PTFE-based materials to make implants, that it performed no testing to determine whether use of PTFE in implants is appropriate and that Vitek would have to rely on its own medical and legal judgment if it chose to use PTFE to make implants. Finally, it is undisputed that the FDA regulated the sale of the TMJ implants. Applying the standard set forth above to the supplemented factual record now before it, the court finds that DuPont reasonably believed that Vitek knew of the dangers associated with using PTFE-based materials to make implants and that DuPont reasonably relied on Vitek to warn the ultimate users of such dangers. Accordingly, the court concludes that, as a matter of law, DuPont discharged its duty to warn. Hegna cannot support one of the essential elements of her negligence claim and the court concludes that summary judgment in favor of DuPont on the negligence claim is appropriate.

2. *Hegna's Strict Liability Claim*

The court finds that its ruling with respect to Hegna's negligence claim is applicable to Hegna's strict liability claim because the limited distinction between negligent failure to warn and strict liability failure to warn claims is not outcome determinative in this case. In Minnesota, "[t]he distinction between strict liability and negligence in ... failure to warn cases is that in strict liability, knowledge of the condition of the product and the risks involved in that condition will be imputed to the manufacturer, whereas in negligence these elements must be proven." Bilotta [v. Kelley Co., Inc., 346 N.W.2d 616, 622 (Minn.1984)].

It is undisputed that DuPont had knowledge of the risks involved with using PTFE-based materials to make implants. Even with that knowledge, DuPont nevertheless satisfied its duty to warn and, therefore, Hegna cannot support one of the elements of her strict liability claim. Accordingly, the court concludes that summary judgment in favor of DuPont on Hegna's strict liability claim is appropriate. Because it concludes that DuPont, as a bulk supplier, satisfied its duty to warn and, therefore, Hegna can maintain no negligence or strict liability claim against DuPont, the court determines that it need not consider DuPont's other bases for summary judgment.

* * *

Notes and Questions

1. In the principal case, the court notes, at footnote 4: "DuPont also argued that it had no duty to warn, because the [FDA] approved the use of PTFE for TMJ implants and regulated their sale. In addition, DuPont claimed that Vitek was obligated under federal law and FDA regulations to both develop appropriate warnings and ensure that Hegna's physician received those warnings. Based on those arguments, DuPont argued that it would be superfluous to impose on it a second duty to warn. The court rejected those arguments[.]" On what rationale would the court reject DuPont's assertions?

4. CHEMICALS

a. Liability Standards for Warnings

WERCKENTHEIN v. BUCHER PETROCHEMICAL COMPANY

Appellate Court of Illinois, 1993.
248 Ill.App.3d 282, 188 Ill.Dec. 332, 618 N.E.2d 902.

DiVito, J.

Plaintiff Charles Werckenthein (plaintiff) filed this negligence and strict liability action against, among others, defendants Bucher Petroleum Chemical Company; PPG Industries, Inc.; Shell Oil Company; Sun Refining and Marketing Company; Dow Chemical Company; and Technical Petroleum (collectively, defendants), which supplied chemical products in bulk to his employer. He claimed that he had been injured as a result of their failure to warn him adequately of the dangers arising from his quality control analysis of the chemicals. Plaintiff's wife, Grace, added a count for loss of consortium; she was subsequently declared his guardian. The circuit court granted partial summary judgment for defendants on certain claims as untimely, and it later granted defendants summary judgment on the remaining claims against them. Plaintiff and his wife appeal both orders, asserting that the circuit court incorrectly determined that some claims were time-barred and that the circuit court erred in finding that as a matter of law, defendants had no duty to warn against using a particular testing procedure. We affirm.

In his complaint, plaintiff alleged that among his duties as chief chemist for Ashland was a routine company procedure requiring him to sniff, evaluate, and record the odors of the chemicals defendants supplied to his employer. He contended that as a result of the exposure from this procedure, he suffered a number of health problems, including cancers and fibrillation that resulted in a stroke. Although the exposure occurred between February 1969 and March 1983, plaintiff and his wife further alleged that they neither knew nor had reason to know of the causal link between his injuries and defendants' conduct until consultation with medical experts in industrial injuries, which did not occur until April 1986. Plaintiff filed his complaint shortly after this consultation.

* * *

[The court's discussion of the statute of limitations issue is deleted.]

Defendants then moved jointly for summary judgment on the remaining claims against them. They raised five independent grounds: (1) as bulk suppliers, their duty to warn extended only to their purchaser, Ashland, not to plaintiff; (2) Ashland was a sophisticated user and as such, needed no warning and could be relied upon to warn and protect its employees; (3) even if they did owe plaintiff a duty to warn, he had received the warnings and they were adequate; (4) the dangerous properties of the chemicals were obvious and well-known to both Ashland and plaintiff; and (5) even if the warnings were inadequate, their inadequacy was not the cause of plaintiff's injuries. In support of their motion, defendants attached a number of documents, including material safety data sheets (MSDS's) for the chemicals in question and an affidavit from Ashland's Director of Health and Safety since 1978. In that affidavit, Dr. Toeniskoetter stated that his department maintained a library with these sheets and other information on the safe handling of chemicals and that Ashland's policy was to make the MSDS's available to employees. Also attached were portions of depositions from two of plaintiff's former assistants and an article by plaintiff about printing solvents, which stressed the need for ventilation during use. In addition, through discovery, defendants obtained from plaintiff's home library many of the challenged warnings, indicating his awareness of the chemical's properties.

Plaintiff replied that (1) the bulk supplier and sophisticated user doctrines did not apply in Illinois; (2) whether warnings were given to him and the sufficiency thereof were fact questions precluding summary judgment; and (3) he had presented enough facts to support a reasonable inference that exposure to defendants' chemicals had caused his injuries. In his supporting affidavit, he explained that he or his assistant tested a sample from every bulk delivery during his tenure, that a 55–gallon drum of waste chemicals was kept open at all times in a storeroom adjacent to the lab, that the lab was inadequately ventilated, that he was not given any breathing apparatus, and that he was told that use of a fume hood was generally unnecessary. He commented in his deposition, however, that "we never inhaled over the TLV [threshold limit value] in sniff testing the samples." According to the other attached documents, defendants' representatives never reviewed the lab's procedures for quality control testing. In addition, an affidavit from plaintiff's assistant challenges Dr. Toeniskoetter's on a number of grounds: the assistant had never seen or heard of Dr. Toeniskoetter or his department; he had never been told of the TLV's of the chemicals he worked with and had not even heard the term "Threshold Limit Value" until he left Ashland; no MSDS's were kept on hand or made accessible to him; and few of Ashland's high-ranking employees had any knowledge of the products at issue, much less of their effects on health. In a 1982 memo, a manager commented that the vapor level in the laboratory had never been measured, commenting that "this might be in order sometime in the future."

At an interim hearing, the court asked for supplemental submissions on the issue of industry custom and practice for testing for odor by briefly inhaling the chemicals directly from an open container (the sniff test). The court wondered whether, if testing in the industry was performed in violation of the warnings given, manufacturers who knew this should have a duty to give express warnings against such testing methods. It then framed the issue for summary judgment as follows: if the industry custom was to test without exceeding TLV's (threshold limit values), the warnings defendants gave were adequate as a matter of law; if not, defendants would have had a duty to warn against the dangerous testing technique because they knew or should have known that quality control staff would misuse the products. Defendants' documents showed that the American Society for Testing and Materials (ASTM) recommended that testing be done by dipping filter paper into the chemical and then smelling the filter paper; plaintiff's expert opined that the only way to test for bulk odor was through direct inhalation, which he described as an "extremely dangerous" test albeit "widely used in industry." He opined that six minutes of this type of testing would be equivalent to six hours of deliberate solvent abuse, such as sniffing paint thinner.

The court granted summary judgment for defendants. * * *

* * *

III.

For injuries caused by defective products, a plaintiff may have four theories of recovery available: express warranty, implied warranty, negligence, and strict liability. Negligence, of course, concerns injuries arising from a defendant's breach of the duty of reasonable care; strict liability addresses injuries resulting from a product that was in an unreasonably dangerous condition when it left a defendant's control. The two theories are not identical, however: strict liability for failure to warn requires evidence of the industry's knowledge of the product's dangerous propensity, and it turns on the nature of the product and the adequacy of the warning; negligence focuses on the particular defendant's knowledge and conduct. * * *[3] Plaintiff grounded his complaint in both theories of recovery, alleging that defendants' breach of their duty to warn him against directly sniffing the chemicals while testing them caused his fibrillation and resultant stroke. For the purposes of this appeal, we assume without deciding that defendants had a duty to warn plaintiff as well as Ashland, so we address only whether defendants demonstrated as a matter of law that their warnings were not so inadequate as to render the chemicals "unreasonably dangerous."

The purpose of warnings is to reduce the risk of harm. This may be accomplished either by shifting or by reducing the risk of injury. Thus, if warnings are adequate, users proceed at their own risk. Examples of inadequate warnings include those that do not specify the risk, are inconsistent with use of the product, provide no reason for the warning, or do not reach the user. Adequacy of warnings generally is a question of fact. Accordingly, it is an issue inappropriate for summary judgment unless the movant demonstrates conclusively that there remains no triable question.

Here, the circuit court determined that defendants' warnings were adequate as a matter of law, reasoning that "because there was a safe method of doing this type of odor test, * * * the defendants were under [no] duty to warn of Ashland's particular method of doing this test." Plaintiff contends that the adequacy of these warnings is a question of fact not suitable for summary judgment and that, in particular, the warnings on the MSDS's or on the specifications sheet accompanying each shipment should have included quality control testing instructions, not just general warnings against exceeding TLV's and improper ventilation.

We cannot agree. Defendants' submissions made plain that dire consequences would flow from prolonged or intensive exposure to these products. For example, one document initialed by plaintiff in March 1979 contained the following safety rules for handlers of chlorinated solvents:

> "Always wear protective garments and use safety equipment when exposure to chlorinated solvents cannot be avoided.

* * *

3. Some jurisdictions view these two causes of action as identical for all practical purposes. (Note, Failures to Warn and the Sophisticated User Defense, 74 Va.L.Rev. 579, 583; Forest v. E.I. Du Pont de Nemours & Co. (D.Nev.1992), 791 F.Supp. 1460, 1463.) Not so Illinois. Hunt v. Blasius (1978), 74 Ill.2d 203, 210, 23 Ill.Dec. 574, 578, 384 N.E.2d 368, 372 ("The elements of a cause of action in strict products liability, of course, differ markedly from their counterparts in negligence.").

Do not use solvents in open containers unless ventilation is adequate to draw the vapors away from the work area.

* * *

Do not tolerate a continuing strong or objectionable solvent odor. It is an indication of excessive vapor in the air."

The document also warned that "[r]epeated and prolonged (chronic) exposure to organic solvents at or above levels producing beginning anesthetic effects, such as dizziness or light-headedness, should be considered a health hazard." In Illinois, manufacturers are entitled to assume that such warnings, if communicated, will be heeded. Furthermore, the standard testing procedure in the industry, as demonstrated by the ASTM recommendations, was to conduct the tests in a different, safer manner, which plaintiff elected not to follow. As to the alleged lack of warning against plaintiff's injury, the document further states that "concentrations of chlorinated solvents that produce 'drunkenness' or unconsciousness may sensitize the heart to [certain drugs]. This high exposure may result in cardiac arrhythmia, including ventricular fibrillation (a particular and serious kind of irregular heartbeat)." We also note that plaintiff presented no facts demonstrating that his injuries were caused by defendants' failure to warn him not to inhale the chemicals directly rather than by the chemicals themselves. Indeed, plaintiff himself said during his deposition that "the sniff test was not the problem."

In sum, defendants did not breach their duty, if any, to warn plaintiff, and their product was not unreasonably dangerous because the warnings did not need to include specific cautions against plaintiff's testing procedure to be adequate as a matter of law. Consequently, although adequacy of warnings is generally a fact question reserved for the jury, under the circumstances here the circuit court correctly held that defendants were entitled to summary judgment.

Affirmed.

Notes and Questions

1. The Material Safety Data Sheets (MSDS) which the court referred to are federally-mandated communications that require employers and suppliers to describe the toxic properties of chemicals and the means necessary to eliminate risks of injury. See Chapter 9 for a fuller discussion of MSDS and other requirements under the Occupational Safety & Health Act. What if the evidence in *Bucher* revealed that the defendants knew that plaintiff's employer was permitting employees to conduct sniff tests rather than following the prescribed procedure?

2. With *Bucher* compare Dougherty v. Hooker Chemical Corp., 540 F.2d 174 (3d Cir.1976), where evidence showed that workers used defendant's industrial solvent, trichloroethylene, which posed a latent, potentially lethal hazard; that no warnings of this risk were communicated by the employer, or by the manufacturer, to the workers who were being exposed; and that there was no reasonable basis on which the manufacturer could

rely upon the employer-purchaser to give "appropriate information to the employees of all the hazards of working with [the product]." In determining whether a manufacturer of a toxic product had a duty to provide warnings to persons other than the immediate purchaser, the court in *Dougherty* called for balancing of these considerations: "the dangerous nature of the product, the form in which the product is used, the intensity and the form of the warnings given, and the likelihood that the particular warning will be adequately communicated to those who will foreseeably use the product. * * * "How would the court in *Dougherty* have considered and decided *Bucher* ?

3. Should improper packaging that leads to the injurious dispersal of a chemical create a claim in products liability? Consider Thrasher v. B & B Chemical Co., 2 F.3d 995 (10th Cir.1993), the appeal from a grant of summary judgment for a manufacturer of paint stripper in a suit brought by an airline employee. Plaintiff suffered physical injury when paint thinner erupted from a valve in its container. The manufacturer of the paint thinner brought in the manufacturer of the drum as a third party defendant.

How might the following facts affect your answer:

(a) Neither the valve nor the drum could be located, but plaintiff testified that in his six months working as a paint stripper for the airline he only saw thinner barrels stenciled "B & B," and no invoices produced by the airline showed thinner other than that produced by "B & B" were purchased during the six months of plaintiff's employment.

(b) Testimony suggested that the barrel might have been improperly stored in sunlight, which could create abnormally high pressure.

4. In Herman v. Sunshine Chemical Specialties, Inc., 133 N.J. 329, 627 A.2d 1081 (1993), the New Jersey Supreme Court confirmed the availability, upon proper proof, of punitive damages in a chemical personal injury failure to warn case. In that case, plaintiff, an independent contractor who conducted demonstrations of the efficacy of defendant's product, developed "occupational asthma" from incidental inhalation of defendant's "Sun–Clean" all-purpose cleaner, which contained a caustic, sodium-hydroxide. The product's label stated that the product contained no caustics and contained no warnings against breathing its vapors. The court further endorsed the approach, adopted in most jurisdictions, of permitting jury consideration of the defendant's wealth in the course of weighing punitive damages.

5. Chemical contamination cases may lose the benefit of longer limitations periods under the theory of continuing nuisance or continuing injury where the contamination has abated, and thus be governed by the limitations period for ordinary torts. E.g., Montana Pole and Treating Plant v. I. F. Laucks & Co., 993 F.2d 676 (9th Cir.1993), in which the claims by operators of a wood treatment facility against the manufacturers of the preservative pentachlorophenol ("penta") were found barred under the state's two-year limitations period. A theory of continuing nuisance would not operate to toll the prescriptive period, the court held, as the injury had been abated upon cessation of plaintiff's operations two years before.

6. In Chapter 9 we examine the workers' compensation bar to employee claims against employers, and the limited exceptions to that bar, includ-

ing the intentional misconduct exception. Should there exist an intentional tort exception that would permit a manufacturer to sue an employer where the manufacturer claims that the products liability suit it must now defend against, brought by an injured employee, was caused by the employer's fraudulent misrepresentation? Consider the following two treatments:

a. In Belik v. Advance Process Supply Co., 822 F.Supp. 1184 (E.D.Pa. 1993), the trial court disallowed a manufacturing defendant's third-party claim against plaintiff's employer in which the third-party plaintiff claimed that the employee's injury from exposure to toxic chemicals was caused by the manufacturer's fraudulent misrepresentation. Acknowledging that the exclusivity of Pennsylvania workers' compensation law had countenanced a narrow exception permitting employee suits upon a showing of an employer's intentional misconduct, the court held that the narrow exception should not be enlarged to permit an intentional tort rationale for manufacturer claims against employers.

b. In Dole v. Dow Chemical Co., 30 N.Y.2d 143, 331 N.Y.S.2d 382, 282 N.E.2d 288 (1972), the underlying injury was the death of an employee who, at the direction of his employer, used the manufacturer's hazardous fumigant on a storage bin, in which he was overcome by fumes. The employer countered the manufacturer's action in indemnification with the defense that the manufacturer's failure to warn constituted active negligence, barring indemnification. On appeal, the New York Court of Appeals held that the relative liabilities of employer and manufacturer were properly apportionable according to their respective degrees of fault.

b. Bulk Suppliers of Chemicals: The Sophisticated User Defense

Hegna and *Bucher* establish that in evaluating the bulk supplier's informational obligation, the court may properly take into account the purchaser's superior knowledge of the end uses of the product and the hazards posed to those who will come into contact with it. The issue requires resolution of whether the bulk seller for resale discharges its duty by conveying adequate information to the distributor intermediary. It also extends to the question of what circumstances represent adequate assurance to the initial seller that the intermediary is likely to pass along such product information to the latter's customers or employees.

The question has been treated in actions on claims involving chemicals and natural gas, with a resolution that can be stated generally as providing that for products sold in bulk, the wholesaler discharges its duty to warn by conveying adequate warning to the immediate purchaser. If, on the other hand, the products sold by the bulk seller are already packaged, "ordinary prudence may require the manufacturer to put his warning on the package where it is available to all who handle it." Jones v. Hittle Service, Inc., 219 Kan. 627, 549 P.2d 1383 (1976).

SWAN v. I.P., INC.

Supreme Court of Mississippi, 1993.
613 So.2d 846 (en banc).

HAWKINS, C.J.:

Nancy Swan, a former teacher at Long Beach Junior High School, filed this action on January 7, 1986, in the Circuit Court of Harrison County, First Judicial District, alleging injury as a result of exposure to fumes and spray of polyurethane roofing materials being used to re-roof Long Beach Junior High School in October, 1985. Initially named as defendants were I.P., Inc. (I.P.), the manufacturer of the polyurethane foam used during the roofing project, and Miri, Inc. (Miri), the local polyurethane roofing contractor which applied the roofing materials to the school. In her First Amended Complaint, Swan added Carboline Company (Carboline), the manufacturer of the polyurethane coating used during the roofing project, as a defendant. In her Second Amended Complaint, Swan added as a defendant James C. English, the president of Miri, alleging that at all material times he was engaged in a joint venture with Miri. Swan's allegations against I.P. and Carboline were based on negligence, strict liability and breach of warranty. Her allegations against Miri and English were based solely on negligence.

On January 10, 1989, one week prior to trial, the trial court granted summary judgment in favor of I.P., Carboline and English. The next day Miri filed its motion for summary judgment and the trial court granted summary judgment in favor of Miri on October 11, 1989. The trial court denied Swan's motion to reconsider, and Swan now appeals. * * *

We reverse [.]

FACTS

On August 21, 1985, the Long Beach Municipal Separate School District entered into a contract with Miri, Inc. for the reroofing of the Long Beach schools. [Swan alleges that James C. English was also a party to the contract.] The roofing system consisted of a sprayed polyurethane foam, manufactured by I.P., which provided insulation, and a polyurethane coating, manufactured by Carboline, which created the necessary waterproofing for the roof. The polyurethane foam manufactured by I.P. is known by the trade name "Isofoam SS-0658" and contains the toxic ingredient methylene diphenyl isocyanate, or MDI. The color of the foam is beige when it is sprayed and it turns yellow as it begins to harden. The coating manufactured by Carboline is known by the trade name "Chem–Elast 2819S" and contains the toxic ingredient toluene diisocyanate, or TDI. The color of the coating is light gray.

Miri began working on the roof of Long Beach Junior High in early October, 1985. * * * Swan alleged that she was first exposed to the chemicals around noon on October 8, 1985, when she was accompanying her class to the cafeteria. She saw a yellow mist coming from the roof of a nearby building and she was soon in the middle of the mist, which had a strong, nauseating odor. She continued walking with the children to the cafeteria where she left them for the remainder of the lunch period, while she went to the teachers' lounge and to the women's restroom. In the restroom she observed that Miri's workers had removed the turbine on the roof and had sprayed the foam into the restroom. She left because the odor of the foam was too strong. * * *

Shortly after Swan arrived at her classroom the next morning, she noticed that Miri's workers were spraying foam on the roof of the building which contained her classroom. The fumes from the foam were strong and nauseating. She opened the windows for approximately ten minutes which only made the smell worse. * * * According to her, the spraying continued on her building all day except for one hour at lunch. During the lunch period, Swan and her class again had to walk through a cloud of spray on the way to the cafeteria. In addition to the nausea, the fumes also caused Swan's eyes to sting and burn. She opened her windows again that afternoon for about three hours because of the heat.

Other teachers and students complained to the school's administration about the physical effects of the spraying, and that afternoon the subject was discussed at a faculty meeting. Marlin Roger Ladner, the principal, told the teachers that from what he had read in a letter written by the architect who was handling the roofing project and other information he had received, the spray was not dangerous and would only cause mild irritation of the eyes. Ladner instructed the teachers to keep their classroom windows closed. * * *

Swan testified that her physical condition worsened that night. She experienced "[b]urning, sharp pains" in her chest and shoulders and her eyes continued to burn and sting. She also discovered that she was suddenly extremely hoarse and unable to project her voice. She testified that her throat hurt when she spoke. She also experienced frequent, painful headaches. * * *

Spraying operations continued on October 10, 1985. Miri's employees were spraying the roof of a building adjacent to her classroom and at times the mist drifted into Swan's classroom. She opened the windows several times because her students complained about the heat. When she took her students to the cafeteria during lunch period, they had to walk through a cloud of the spray and the particles got on Swan. Swan testified that water blisters developed on her arm either that afternoon or on Friday, October 11. After October 10 Miri no longer conducted spraying operations during school hours.

In addition to the physical problems described above, Swan testified that after her exposure to the spray, she often had problems maintaining her balance while walking. The right side of her body also became extremely weak, particularly her right arm and leg, and she suffered memory loss.

Two physicians by deposition testified that Swan's exposure to the chemical had caused serious throat and lung problems, and permanent brain damage.

* * *

In its study entitled "Criteria for a Recommended Standard— Occupational Exposure to Diisocyanates", The National Institute of Occupational Safety and Health (NIOSH) found that exposure to TDI and MDI can cause irritation to the respiratory tract and reduced pulmonary function which can lead to a condition resembling asthma or chronic bronchitis. Diisocyanates are also skin irritants and can cause irritation to the eyes. NIOSH also noted that studies have indicated that exposure to TDI can have neurological effects. I.P.'s material data safety sheet for its foam stated that with overexposure, it was an irritant to the eyes and respiratory tract and may cause headaches, nausea, coughing, shortness of breath, chest pains and respiratory distress. Similarly, Carboline's material data safety sheet lists several effects of overexposure including respiratory tract irritation, headaches, dizziness and nausea.

In its study, NIOSH recommended establishment of a threshold level value, or acceptable concentration level, of exposure to isocyanates for employees at five parts per billion for a ten-hour work shift. NIOSH also defined this level as 35 micrograms per cubic meter for TDI and 50 micrograms per cubic meter for MDI. NIOSH recommended a ceiling limit of twenty parts per billion (or .02 parts per million) for a ten-minute period which should never be exceeded. Frank Livingston, I.P.'s designee, testified that I.P. had conducted studies which measured the concentration of MDI when sprayed in confined areas and in these studies, the concentration had never exceeded .02 parts per million. John Montle, Carboline's technical representative, testified that if Carboline 2819–S is sprayed outdoors, the level of the isocyanate in the vapor could exceed the threshold limit value in the immediate area between the spray gun and the surface of the roof. However, according to Montle, the probability of the level of isocyanate in the vapor exceeding the threshold level even a "few feet away" from the immediate area being sprayed is extremely low. The defendants produced several experts who specialized in isocyanate chemistry who also testified that the concentration of the isocyanate once it leaves the nozzle spray would be below the threshold limit value. Dr. Frisch testified that isocyanates are very reactive chemicals, and when the spray hits the surface of the roof, the isocyanates in the foam react immediately and form the polyurethane, leaving only trace amounts of isocyanates behind. The reaction process in the coating is slower, however. The isocyanates in any overspray would immediately react with the moisture in the air to form the harmless material polyurea.

In his first deposition, English stated that he had not been informed by either I.P. or Carboline prior to the spraying operations of any hazard associated with the inhalation of either the foam or coating. In his second deposition, English testified that sometime after October 8, 1985, he had seen a brochure which I.P. provided Dr. Bob Ferguson, the superintendent of the Long Beach schools, which described the foam and its physical properties. According to English, he had not been provided any information directly from I.P. concerning possible hazards of the foam. Also, his second deposition, English said that Carboline did provide him with a technical data sheet for the coating sometime before October 8, 1985. He also had seen a Carboline brochure or catalog entitled "Chem–Elast Lasts" at some time but he was not sure when. Robert English, James English's son who was Miri's foreman and one of its principal sprayers, testified that to his knowledge, Miri had not received any documents from either I.P. or Carboline setting forth any hazards associated with the use of the foam and coating.

Frank E. Livingston testified that I.P. did not send Miri, James English or the Long Beach school system any material data safety sheets for the foam or any other warnings at any time prior to Swan's exposure. The material data safety sheets were sent to Long Beach Junior High School afterwards. In 1984, I.P. distributed copies of the Upjohn Technical Bulletin (recognized as the most complete compilation of information on polyurethane products and their safe application) to its distributors, including North Brothers, Inc. of Atlanta, whose Jackson office distributed the foam to Miri. Livingston had no knowledge as to whether the Upjohn Bulletin was ever distributed to Miri. John Montle and Van Rusling, Carboline's sales representative for the Gulf Coast, testified that Carboline provided material data safety sheets for its polyurethane coating to its customers upon request. Neither knew whether Miri ever requested a material data safety sheet.

James English testified that he and the other sprayers wore respirators when spraying the foam. He and Robert English both testified that before they began spraying on the roofs, they always instructed the school administration to make an announcement to the teachers instructing them to close the windows. If the teachers did not close the windows one of the Englishes or another employee of Miri would close the windows themselves. They also placed rope barricades around their work areas, although this was mainly done for the purpose of keeping the children away from the equipment. According to James English, representatives of both I.P. and Carboline visited the job site while the work was in progress and witnessed Miri's spraying procedures. None of the representatives expressed any concern about these procedures to Miri.

LAW

The Court Erred in Granting Summary Judgment in Favor of Defendants I.P. and Carboline.

* * *

The trial court granted summary judgment in favor of I.P. and Carboline based on the "learned intermediary" defense to products liability actions which provides that a manufacturer's duty to warn may be discharged by providing information to a third person upon whom it can reasonably rely to communicate the information to the ultimate users of the product or those who will be exposed to its hazardous effects. * * *

Swan's claims against I.P. and Carboline are based on negligent failure to warn and strict liability. [After quoting Restatement (Second) of Torts § 402A, the court continues:]

Lack of an adequate warning is a defect which makes a product unreasonably dangerous for strict liability purposes. This Court has extended this duty to bystanders, holding that the duty imposed by § 402A "exists in favor of anyone who may reasonably be expected to be in the vicinity of the product's probable use and to be endangered by it if it is defective." Coca Cola Bottling Co., Inc. v. Reeves, 486 So.2d 374, 378 (Miss.1986).

I.P. and Carboline contend that they had no duty to warn Miri or Swan about any possible hazards associated with their products because Miri was an experienced, knowledgeable applicator of these products and is therefore charged with knowledge of the properties of the products. This argument stems from § 388 of the Restatement (Second) of Torts and comment "k" under § 388. This section provides:

> One who supplies directly or through a third person a chattel for another to use is subject to liability to those whom the supplier should expect to use the chattel with the consent of the other or to be endangered by its probable use, for physical harm caused by the use of the chattel in the manner for which and by a person for whose use it is supplied, if the supplier (a) knows or has reason to know that the chattel is or is likely to be dangerous for the use for which it is supplied, and (b) has no reason to believe that those for whose use the chattel is supplied will realize its dangerous condition, and (c) fails to exercise reasonable care to inform them of its dangerous condition or of the facts which make it likely to be dangerous.

Comment "k" to § 388 provides in part:

> k. When warning of defects unnecessary. One who supplies a chattel to others to use for any purpose is under a duty to exercise reasonable care to inform them of its dangerous character in so far as it is known to him, or of facts which to his knowledge make it likely to be dangerous, if, but only if, he has no reason to expect that those for whose use the chattel is supplied will discover its condition and realize the danger involved. . . .

The learned intermediary theory developed in cases involving prescription drugs. * * * This Court has applied the learned intermediary theory in prescription drug cases. Generally, the cases discussing the learned intermediary theory which do not involve prescription drugs involve products which have injured employees on the job and the manufacturer's reliance on the employer to warn the employee of the dangers of the product. I.P. and Carboline rely on several cases. In Martinez v. Dixie Carriers, Inc., 529 F.2d 457 (5th Cir.1976), the widow of a worker, who died when he was overcome by noxious fumes while cleaning the tank of a barge which had been carrying a petrochemical mixture, filed suit against the owner of the barge and the manufacturer of the mixture alleging inadequate warning. The manufacturer had placed a warning card on the main deck of the barge which set out the hazards associated with the chemicals. The court held that the manufacturer was not liable for negligent failure to warn or strict liability. The court noted that the manufacturer marketed the chemical mixture only to industrial users and not to the general public, and the manufacturer could reasonably anticipate that only professionals familiar with the precautions necessary for the safe handling of the chemicals would come into contact with the chemicals. The card placed on the barge was an adequate warning to the limited class of professionals, of which the plaintiff's husband was a member, who were experienced in the stripping and cleaning of chemical storage tanks.

In Adams v. Union Carbide Corp., 737 F.2d 1453 (6th Cir.1984), the plaintiff, an employee of General Motors, filed suit against Union Carbide alleging that she suffered respiratory problems as a result of Union Carbide's failure to adequately warn the employees of General Motors of the hazards associated with toluene diisocyanate (TDI), which Union Carbide manufactured and supplied to General Motors for use in the automotive assembly process. Union Carbide had prepared a manual for General Motors which addressed the hazards associated with exposure to TDI and also included information on the safe use and handling of TDI and a chemical safety data sheet. Officials from Union Carbide and General Motors had also met to discuss the handling of TDI to minimize personnel exposure. The trial court granted summary judgment in favor of Union Carbide, and the Sixth Circuit affirmed. The court relied on Comment "n" to Restatement (Second) of Torts § 388 which states that the manufacturer's duty to warn may be discharged by providing information of the dangerous propensities of the product to a third person upon whom it can reasonably rely to communicate the information to the ultimate users of the product or those who will be exposed to its hazardous effects. The court held that the fact that General Motors repeatedly updated its information about TDI from Union Carbide, along with the fact that General Motors itself had a duty to its employees to provide them with a safe place to work, supported the conclusion that it was reasonable for Union Carbide to rely upon General Motors to convey the information about TDI to its employees.

In Smith v. Walter C. Best, Inc., 927 F.2d 736 (3d Cir.1990), the plaintiff was injured as a result of his inhalation of silica dust contained in sand supplied by various parties to his employer. He claimed that the suppliers had a duty to warn him directly about the hazards of the dust. The court affirmed the trial court's entry of summary judgment in favor of the suppliers, finding that the plaintiff's employer was a knowledgeable industrial purchaser of silica sand familiar with its dangers. The court analyzed whether it was reasonable for the suppliers of the sand to rely on the plaintiff's employer to warn its employees about the hazards of the sand under the factors set out in Comment "n" to § 388 of the Restatement: (1) the dangerous condition of the product; (2) the purpose for which the product is used; (3) the form of any warnings given; (4) the reliability of the third party as a conduit of necessary information about the product; (5) the magnitude of the risk involved; and (6) the burdens imposed on the supplier by requiring that he directly warn all users. The court held that it was reasonable for the sand suppliers to rely on the plaintiff's employer to warn the plaintiff of the dangers. The court listed several facts which led it to this conclusion: (1) common medical knowledge of the hazards; (2) there were various statutes and regulations governing silica; (3) the employer was a member of a non-profit foundation which provided information to its members relative to occupational diseases, including silicosis, and their prevention; and (4) the duty of the employer to provide its employees a safe working environment. The court therefore held that the suppliers did not have a duty to warn the plaintiff directly of any hazards associated with the sand.

In its ruling on the motion for summary judgment, the trial court referred to Helene Curtis Industries, Inc. v. Pruitt, 385 F.2d 841 (5th Cir.1967). In Helene Curtis, the plaintiff's scalp and ears were burned by a mixture of two bleaching products purchased from a beauty parlor and applied to the plaintiff's hair by a friend. The plaintiff alleged that she was not adequately warned. The label on the Helene Curtis product stated: "FOR PROFESSIONAL USE ONLY—NOT FOR PUBLIC SALE." It also warned against mixing the product with any products other than one recommended by Helene Curtis. The 5th Circuit Court held that Helene Curtis was not liable, and that the warning was sufficient because it need only be reasonably calculated to reach and be understood by the person likely to use the product, the professional beautician. The sale of the product by the beauty parlor to the plaintiff's friend was an intervening cause of the plaintiff's injuries, as was the mixing of the two bleaching products by the plaintiff's friend.

These cases are distinguishable. Unlike Helene Curtis, the polyurethane foam and coating were applied by an intended, professional user. In Martinez, the manufacturer of the chemicals placed a warning on the barge and it was unlikely that anyone but professional tank cleaners would come into contact with the chemicals. Swan received no warnings concerning the hazards associated with the chemicals and it is not certain that Miri received warnings from the manufacturers. Also, the likelihood that someone not knowledgeable about the hazards of the chemicals would come into contact with the chemicals was more likely in this case because the chemicals were being sprayed at a school. In Adams and Smith, the plaintiffs' employers had knowledge of the hazards associated with TDI and the silica dust. Here, although James English and Miri had much experience spraying polyurethane foam and coating, they both testified that they were not aware of any hazards associated with the spraying.

In other cases, courts have held that the presence of an intermediary did not relieve the manufacturer of its duty to warn. In Borel v. Fibreboard Paper Products Corp., 493 F.2d 1076 (5th Cir.1973), an insulation worker brought an action against the manufacturers of insulation which contained asbestos. The court rejected the manufacturers' argument that it was the responsibility of the insulation contractors to warn the insulation workers of the risk of harm. The court noted that under the Restatement, a seller may be liable to the ultimate user or consumer for failure to give adequate warnings. The seller's warning must be reasonably calculated to reach such persons and the presence of an intermediary party will not by itself relieve the seller of this duty.

In Hall v. Ashland Oil Co., 625 F.Supp. 1515 (D.Conn.1986), a widow brought suit against a manufacturer of benzene who sold benzene to her deceased husband's employer. The manufacturer filed a motion for summary judgment based on the learned intermediary theory, arguing that when a product is sold in bulk to an industrial user for use by its employees, the supplier's duty to warn extends only to the employer as a learned intermediary. Further, that a supplier's duty to warn an industrial purchaser is excused where the purchaser is held to know of the risks independently. The court held that even if the learned intermediary theory were to be applied to cases involving the sale of chemicals in the industrial workplace, that theory alone would not relieve the supplier of a duty to warn. The court noted that the prescription drug cases which apply the learned intermediary theory merely shift the direction that such a warning must take, by requiring the manufacturer to provide an adequate warning to the intermediary. The court held that the facts were disputed as to whether the manufacturer supplied any warnings to the deceased's employer and as to whether the deceased's employer could be considered knowledgeable of the health risks associated with benzene.

In Adkins v. GAF Corp., 923 F.2d 1225 (6th Cir.1991), the supplier contended that § 388 of the Restatement relieved it of its duty to warn since it sold the asbestos to a "sophisticated user," the plaintiff's employer, which had full knowledge of the hazards associated with the use of asbestos and which could be relied upon to take the appropriate precautions. The court stated that the pivotal inquiry in determining whether this defense is available is a fact-specific evaluation of the reasonableness of the supplier's reliance on the intermediary to provide the warning. In a similar case, the Fourth Circuit stated that Comment "n" to § 388 of the Restatement clearly focuses on what the product manufacturer knew and the reasonableness of its reliance on the intermediary to and during the time the plaintiff was exposed. Willis v. Raymark Industries, Inc., 905 F.2d 793, 797 (4th Cir.1990)[.] In Little v. Liquid Air Corp., 952 F.2d 841 (5th Cir.1992), the Court of Appeals held that * * * (t)he bulk seller may rely on an informed distributor to pass information concerning the dangers of the product to the consumer. However, the bulk seller's reliance upon the intermediate distributor must be reasonable, and it fulfills its duty to the ultimate consumer only if it ascertains (1) that the distributor to which it sells is adequately trained, (2) that the distributor is familiar with the properties of the product and the safe methods of handling it, and (3) that the distributor is capable of passing this knowledge to the consumer.

I.P. and Carboline contend that because they sold the foam and coating to Miri, a professional applicator chargeable with knowledge of the properties of the products, they had no duty to warn. Miri and James English indeed are experienced applicators of polyurethane roofing products. Miri's primary business was insulation and polyurethane roofing and the company had been involved in this business since 1977. * * *

* * *

The learned intermediary defense does not relieve the manufacturer of its duty to warn, however, unless the manufacturer's reliance on the intermediary is reasonable. Material issues of fact exist in this case as to whether I.P.'s and Carboline's reliance on Miri was reasonable. From this record we do not know whether James and Robert English, the principal sprayers of the foam and coating, had knowledge of the hazards associated with the foam and coating. James English testified that had he known of any hazards associated with the products, he would not have sprayed them while school was in session. Robert English testified that at the time the foam and coating were sprayed on the roof of the school, he had no knowledge of any hazards associated with the foam or the coating.

From this record we cannot know whether it was reasonable for I.P. and Carboline to assume that Miri was knowledgeable about the hazards because the facts are in dispute as to whether I.P. and Carboline ever sent Miri any information concerning the chemical properties of the products and the hazards associated with them.

Frank E. Livingston testified that I.P. did not send Miri, James English or the Long Beach school system any material data safety sheets for the foam or any other warnings at any time prior to Swan's alleged exposure.

Also, because the evidence was insufficient to conclude that Miri was a sophisticated user, the learned intermediary doctrine still required I.P. and Carboline to furnish information and warnings to Miri. The trial court recognized this in its ruling: "[T]his manufacturer is not required to go further than to furnish information to the applicator or the professional who is going to use the product itself." Because of these disputed material issues of fact, the trial court erred in granting summary judgment in favor of I.P. and Carboline.

* * *

Notes and Questions

1. In cases where the bulk supplier asserts a sophisticated or knowledgeable user defense, should it make any difference whether the plaintiffs are proceeding under § 402A or under a negligence theory?

2. Many of the decisions discussed in *Swan* focused on the reasonableness of the supplier's reliance on the employer to furnish necessary warnings and instructions. Consider how the following factors might influence a court or jury in deciding the reasonableness question: (1) identification of the actual users would require monitoring of the employer's workforce; (2) the manner in which the products are actually delivered to the purchaser—i.e., unpackaged railroad car lots, barrels, or small containers; (3) the manner in which the product is maintained or stored by the purchaser; (4) who is in the best position to provide training, housekeeping measures, and warnings on a continuous and systematic basis; (5) the possible confusion arising from having different suppliers of the same or similar products; and (6) the ability of a supplier to exert pressure on a customer to insist that certain procedures be followed.

3. How does the fact that many states' laws and the federal Occupational Safety and Health Act, discussed in Chapter 9, require employers to provide a safe working environment bear on the sophisticated user defense?

4. In addition to the decisions referred to in *Swan*, other decisions have also addressed the bulk supplier—sophisticated user issue. See Goodbar v. Whitehead Bros., 591 F.Supp. 552 (W.D.Va.1984), affirmed sub nom. Beale v. Hardy, 769 F.2d 213 (4th Cir.1985); Higgins v. E.I. DuPont de Nemours & Co., 671 F.Supp. 1055 (D.Md.1987).

c. *Foreseeable Users and Uses*

HIGH v. WESTINGHOUSE ELECTRIC CORP.

Supreme Court of Florida, 1992.
610 So.2d 1259.

OVERTON, J.

We have for review [an appellate affirmance of] the trial court summary judgment, holding that Westinghouse, as the manufacturer of electrical transformers, is not liable to an employee of a scrap metal salvage business for injuries allegedly sustained from a hazardous fluid that was released in dismantling transformers in the scrapping process. * * * While we approve the district court's decision on the question of strict liability, we find that there remains an issue of fact on the question of negligence. Consequently, we quash in part the decision of the district court of appeal and remand this case for further proceedings.

The relevant facts in the record are as follows. Westinghouse manufactured electrical transformers and sold them to Florida Power and Light Company (FPL). From 1967 to 1983, FPL sold its electrical transformers for junk to Pepper's Steel and Alloys (Pepper's), a scrap metal salvage business. To manufacture the electrical transformers sold to FPL, Westinghouse purchased products from Monsanto, a manufacturer of polychlorinated biphenyls (PCBs). In a January 15, 1972, letter and indemnification agreement from Westinghouse to Monsanto, Westinghouse acknowledged that Monsanto had notified Westinghouse that the PCBs used in its products tended to persist in the environment; that care was required in their handling, possession, use, and disposition; and that tolerance limits had been or were being established for PCBs in various food products.[2] In 1976, Westinghouse wrote a letter to its utility company customers, including FPL, disclosing the potential existence of PCBs in their transformers. In that letter, Westinghouse informed them that some oil-filled transformers had been contaminated with PCBs in the manufacturing process. Westinghouse's letter suggested that when performing repairs, routine maintenance, or disposal, all oil-filled transformers should be checked for the presence of PCBs.[3]

Studies of humans exposed to PCBs have shown numerous adverse effects, including but not limited to chloracne and other epidermal disorders, digestive disturbances, jaundice, impotence, throat and respiratory irritations, and severe headaches. It is undisputed that none of the junk transformers that FPL sold to Pepper's contained any labels, markings, or warnings of any kind[.] * * *

Willie J. High was the main truck driver for Pepper's from 1965 to 1983. As part of his duties, he picked up aluminum wire, cable, and other scrap metal. He also picked up transformers from FPL in Miami and other cities around Florida. * * * During this process, he came into contact with the PCB-contaminated transformer oil.

* * * [O]n July 9, 1983, High brought this action under strict liability and negligence theories.

The trial court granted Westinghouse's motion for summary judgment, holding as a matter of law that the ultimate disposal of the transformer was not foreseeable to the manufacturer as a reasonably intended "use." On appeal, the district court of appeal, in a split decision, affirmed. In explaining why strict liability under section 402A of the Restatement (Second) of Torts (1965) is not applicable, the district court stated: "The dismantling and recycling of products after they have been destroyed have been held to be product uses not reasonably foreseeable to manufacturers. . . .

. . . Westinghouse's transformers were destroyed prior to the alleged injuries. While the transformers were sealed and intact there was no harm. Rather, the alleged damage occurred after the contents of the devices were exposed through the dismantling process. * * *

2. In the letter and indemnity agreement, Westinghouse agreed to indemnify and hold harmless Monsanto from Westinghouse's use of PCBs purchased from Monsanto. * * *

3. The pertinent portion of the letter read as follows: "In addition, when performing repair, routine maintenance or disposal, oil-filled transformers should be checked for the presence of PCBs. We also suggest that you check your own transformer oil storage and handling systems for possible presence of PCBs."

Here, the determination of no liability is based upon a substantial change in the product from the time it left the manufacturer's control to the time of the subject incident[.]" * * *

The district court concluded that the actual products supplied by Westinghouse were the electrical transformers, not the contaminated dielectric fluid. As a matter of law, the unsealing, stripping, and dumping of the contents of Westinghouse's product in order to salvage junk components were not reasonably foreseeable "uses" of the product nor was Willie High an intended "user" within the meaning of section 402A.

There are two questions we must address. The first is whether strict liability applies under section 402A of the Restatement (Second) of Torts for injuries that occur in dismantling an item. The second is whether the manufacturer, Westinghouse, in this instance was negligent in failing to timely warn of dangerous contents in its product that could cause injuries in its alteration and dismantling.

While these are questions of first impression in this state, other courts have addressed similar issues. In Kalik v. Allis–Chalmers Corp., 658 F.Supp. 631 (W.D.Pa.1987), the owners of a scrap metal business that had been contaminated by PCBs sued the manufacturers and suppliers of the products containing the PCBs to recover cleanup costs and damages incurred under [CERCLA]. In that case, the scrap metal business had purchased junk electrical components as scrap. The electrical components contained, as they did in this instance, PCBs. During the course of dismantling, handling, and storing the junk electrical components, PCB-contaminated oil leaked or spilled onto the site. A furnace used in dismantling and processing the components caused PCBs in the components to allegedly produce dioxins, which also polluted the site. Plaintiff's damage claims were based upon a negligent failure to warn and strict liability in tort. The United States District Court in Pennsylvania considered whether plaintiff's use of the product was reasonably foreseeable to the manufacturer. Although the court agreed that this was ordinarily a question of fact, it held as a matter of law that the recycling of a product after it had been destroyed and the destruction of a product were not reasonably foreseeable uses to the manufacturer. * * * [Similarly], in Johnson v. Murph Metals, Inc., 562 F.Supp. 246 (N.D.Tex. 1983), a United States District Court in Texas granted a summary judgment and held that fumes and particulates from smelting lead from scrap batteries were not created from a "use" of the batteries. In that case, the employees of various lead-smelting companies who had sued certain automotive battery manufacturers stipulated that their injuries did not result from working with intact batteries or from the destruction of batteries to obtain the lead for smelting. The lead fumes and dust that allegedly injured them were created only after the lead was extracted from the destroyed batteries and used in the smelting process. "In determining that the plaintiffs were not 'users' of defendants' products, the court held that 'the defendants' product had ceased to exist."

With regard to the first question and the applicability of strict liability under section 402A of the Restatement (Second) of Torts, we find that strict liability is not applicable. [In Florida] for strict liability to apply to the manufacturer, the transformers in this instance must have been used for the purpose intended. In the instant case, High's injury resulted from dismantling the transformers and coming into contact with the PCBs as a result of this process. We agree with the district court that section 402A does not apply because of the substantial alteration of the product when High came into contact with the contaminated oil. Secondly, section 402A applies to intended uses of products for which they were produced. When an injury occurs under those circumstances, the manufacturer is strictly liable. We find, under the circumstances in the instant case, that dismantling a product is not an intended use as prescribed by section 402A. Therefore, we find, under these facts, that strict liability does not apply.

The second question we must address concerns liability based on negligence. We find that a manufacturer has a duty to warn of dangerous contents in its product which could damage or injure even when the product is not used for its intended purpose. This issue, which is not directly addressed by the district court of appeal, is whether Westinghouse was negligent in warning FPL of the possible danger of PCB contamination.

We find that Westinghouse had a duty to timely notify the entity to whom it sold the electrical transformers, FPL in the instant case, once it was advised of the PCB contamination. The record reflects that Monsanto, the PCB manufacturer, notified Westinghouse sometime between 1970 and 1972, of the dangerous toxic propensities of PCBs used by Westinghouse. We find that Westinghouse's November 22, 1976, letter to its utility customers, including FPL, relaying PCB information was adequate notice. However, whether or not the letter was timely is a question of fact that has not been resolved by this record. As stated earlier, Monsanto informed Westinghouse sometime between 1970 and 1972 of the dangers regarding PCB contamination, and in 1976, Westinghouse informed FPL that some products were contaminated. If Westinghouse knew or should have known from its early 1970s communications with Monsanto that some mineral oil transformers contained PCBs, then it is clear from the record that Westinghouse delayed in warning FPL of the contamination of these transformers. Although we hold that Westinghouse's letter to FPL was adequate notice, we find that Westinghouse had a duty to timely notify FPL so that FPL could timely notify Pepper's of the possible danger that could occur in dismantling the transformers so that it could proceed in the prescribed manner. If this notice was not timely, then the next question is whether the lack of timely notice by Westinghouse was the proximate cause of High's injury. Given the circumstances, we find the knowledge by Westinghouse of the PCB contamination in its transformers and the timeliness of Westinghouse's notice to FPL of that contamination are issues of fact that must be resolved in this case and are not proper for summary judgment.

For the reasons expressed, we approve in part and quash in part the decision of the district court of appeal and remand for further proceedings consistent with this opinion.

It is so ordered.

The partial concurrences and dissents of Barkett, J. and Kogan, J. are omitted.

Notes and Questions

1. In a partial concurrence and partial dissent, Justice Barkett wrote:

[I] agree with the majority's disposition of the duty-to-warn issue but also find the case presents a valid claim for strict liability.

The majority is correct in stating that section 402A of the Restatement (Second) of Torts "applies to intended uses of products for which they were produced." The majority's deficiency, however, is in failing to define "intended uses." The prevailing view recognizes that an "intended use" includes unintended uses of a product if they were reasonably foreseeable by the defendant. See, e.g., Bloxom v. Bloxom, 512 So.2d 839, 843 (La.1987) (" 'Normal use' is a term of art that includes all intended uses, as well as all foreseeable uses and misuses of the product."); J.I. Case Co. v. McCartin–McAuliffe Plumbing, [516 N.E.2d 260, 266 (Ill.1987)] ("Misuse is the use of a product 'for a purpose neither intended nor "foreseeable" (objectively reasonable) by the defendant' and may defeat a cause of action."); see also M. Stuart Madden, Products Liability § 13.9, at 20 (1988) (and cases cited therein) ("[A] use of the product for a purpose, or in a manner neither intended nor reasonably foreseeable will bar recovery. However, some abnormal, or unintended uses will not constitute a legal misuse of the product, if they are reasonably foreseeable.").

As the majority apparently recognizes, foreseeability is usually a jury question. Neither the majority opinion nor the cases cited therein explain why * * * the manufacturer would not have reasonably foreseen that its product would be dismantled.

Are Justice Barkett's additional observations more readily harmonized with the principle of actor liability for foreseeable harm than is the conclusion reached by the majority?

5. AGRICULTURAL CHEMICALS: USE OF EXPRESS WARRANTY THEORY

CIBA–GEIGY CORPORATION v. ALTER

Supreme Court of Arkansas, 1992.
309 Ark. 426, 834 S.W.2d 136.

NEWBERN, J.

John Alter sustained severe injury to his corn crop allegedly as the result of his use of Dual 8E, a herbicide manufactured by Ciba–Geigy, Inc. Alter sued Ciba–Geigy asserting theories of strict liability, negligence, breach of warranty, misrepresentation, and breach of a settlement contract. The jury returned a general verdict of $100,410.51 in Alter's favor. Ciba–Geigy argues the Trial Court abused its discretion by refusing to bifurcate the trial, separating the breach of settlement contract claim from the remaining claims. Ciba–Geigy contends the failure to bifurcate resulted in inadmissible evidence of settlement negotiations coming before the jury. We agree and reverse and remand on this point. Other issues which may arise on retrial will also be addressed. Dual is a herbicide registered with the [EPA], and it is widely used by farmers to control weeds and grass. The herbicide was advertised as giving farmers longer control over weeds and grass for a lower price than competitive products. It was "the longer lasting grass herbicide." The advertising materials which were distributed to farmers by Ciba–Geigy also stated, "Crop injury? You don't have to worry when you use Dual. Gives you peace of mind. That's worth a lot." Dual was accompanied by a "label," consisting of several printed pages, which contained the following language at page five:

> Conditions of Sale and Warranty[:] CIBA–GEIGY warrants that this product conforms to the chemical description on the label and is reasonably fit for the purposes referred to in the Directions for Use subject to the inherent risks referred to above. CIBA–GEIGY makes no other express or implied warranty of fitness or merchantability or any other express or implied warranty. In no case shall CIBA–GEIGY or the Seller be liable for consequential, special, or indirect damages resulting from the use or handling of this product.

> Directions for Use[:] FAILURE TO FOLLOW ALL PRECAUTIONS ON THIS LABEL MAY RESULT IN POOR WEED CONTROL, CROP INJURY, OR ILLEGAL RESIDUES.

The following warning is found in the label in a box at page six:

> Precaution: Injury may occur following the use of Dual BE under abnormally high soil moisture conditions during early development of the crop.

In early 1985, Ron Wulfkuhle and John McLeod, two Ciba–Geigy sales representatives, met with several Arkansas County farmers to promote the use of Dual. Alter was present at the meeting. Alter testified the salesmen told him Dual would control weeds longer at a cheaper price than other herbicides. They also said Dual was safe and would not injure a corn crop. Although Wulfkuhle knew that Dual could damage a corn crop if the crop received heavy moisture after planting, he did not tell Alter about that possibility. Hazards associated with Dual use were not mentioned. Alter testified he generally read the labels accompanying herbicides, but he could not recall whether he read the precautionary language on the Dual label. Alter did not read the Dual advertising materials, but purchased Dual in reliance on the representations made by the salesmen. He began planting his 997.8 acre corn crop on March 19th. A week and a half later Alter applied Dual to the crop. Midway through the Dual application, a heavy rain fell.

Alter noticed severe injury to his corn crop in early May. The greatest injury occurred in the field referred to as Pittman #3. Some corn was simply not coming up, and other plants looked twisted and "buggywhipped." The crops treated with Dual nearest the time of the rainfall were severely injured, but those treated with Dual after the rainfall were not injured.

Alter immediately reported the problem to his herbicide supplier, Martin Gilbert. Gilbert then called Wulfkuhle who came to the Alter farm. Wulfkuhle determined the percentages of injury of the crop in the various fields. He noticed that some fields were 100% injured, and there were others with less than 2% crop injury. Wulfkuhle admitted the damage looked like it had been caused by Dual. Wulfkuhle told Alter to replant his crop and that Ciba–Geigy would pay him $25.00 an acre for replanting costs. Alter replanted 139 acres. On May 30th, Alter's counsel sent a letter to Ciba–Geigy's main office in Greensboro, North Carolina. Counsel informed Ciba–Geigy of the injury to Alter's crop and demanded compensation for loss of crop yield resulting from the Dual application, as well as replanting costs.

* * *

Harper Grimes, a former trouble shooter for Ciba–Geigy, testified that Dual caused the damage in Alter's field. He stated Dual frequently caused damage when the soil was extremely wet or when a substantial rain occurred in a short period of time during or just after application. The critical point for Dual damage was from the time of germination. Grimes did not believe that the precautionary language on the Dual label adequately informed farmers about the risks of rainfall. The warning should have been placed in two locations, and it should have described the conditions of danger more adequately.

Dr. Everett Cowlett, director of technical services for Ciba–Geigy, stated there was a potential for crop injury resulting from Dual use when high moisture conditions occurred within seven days to a month after the seed was planted. Dr. Cowlett admitted a farmer could not determine whether it was safe to apply Dual after planting. The farmer will not know whether there will be an abnormally high moisture condition within seven days to a month after planting. For this reason, Ciba–Geigy put the precautionary language on the label. Dr. Cowlett further stated that the Dual label was approved by the EPA. Dr. Edward Higgins, an employee of the agricultural division at Ciba–Geigy, stated Dual was safe to use on corn. He stated Ciba–Geigy had conducted several studies and tests on Dual. The tests showed that the type of crop damage Alter experienced occurred in only one-tenth of one percent of cases.

Dr. Higgins said the warnings on the Dual label were adequate, and they were like those commonly used in the herbicide industry. Placing the warnings in two places on the label would be burdensome.

The jury returned a general verdict in Alter's favor for $100,410.51 in compensatory damages and no punitive damages.

* * *

I. BIFURCATION

[In this part of the court's opinion, it examines defendant's claim that the trial court abused its discretion in declining to bifurcate defendant's breach of settlement contract claim from plaintiff's claims in strict liability, negligence, breach of warranty and misrepresentation. Holding that failure to bifurcate had resulted in prejudice to defendant, the court reversed and ordered a retrial. It thereupon stated its expectations as to the issues and legal standards upon retrial.]

II. ISSUES ON RETRIAL

A. FIFRA preemption

[In this part of its opinion, entered before the Supreme Court's decision in Cipollone v. Liggett Group, the court concludes that FIFRA neither expressly nor impliedly preempts plaintiff's common law claims in tort or warranty.]

* * *

C. Breach of warranty

Ciba–Geigy also asserts a directed verdict should have been granted in its favor on the breach of express and implied warranty claims because the Dual label effectively disclaimed all warranties, and the label prohibited recovery for consequential damages in the form of lost profits.

To exclude the implied warranty of merchantability, the disclaimer must mention merchantability and be conspicuous. Ark. Code Ann. § 4–2–316(2) (Repl.1991). To exclude the implied warranty of fitness, the exclusion must be in writing and conspicuous. § 4–2–316(2). Words or conduct relevant to the creation of an express warranty and words or conduct tending to negate or limit the warranty shall be construed wherever reasonable as consistent with each other; but negation or limitation is inoperative to the extent that such construction is unreasonable. § 4–2–316(1). Consequential damages may be limited or excluded unless the limitation or exclusion is unconscionable, or the limited remedy fails of its essential purpose. Ark.Code Ann. § 4–2–719(2) and (3) (Repl.1991).

1. Disclaimer of warranties

We do not decide the question, but we note a factual issue with respect to the implied warranties claim. The language on the Ciba–Geigy label could have been effective to disclaim all implied warranties under § 4–2–316(2). The disclaimer was in bold type on page five of the label and clearly mentioned merchantability. The Uniform Commercial Code defines "conspicuous" as being "written in that a reasonable person against whom it is to operate ought to have noticed it. Language in the body of a form is conspicuous if it is in larger or other contrasting type or color." Ark.Code Ann. § 4–12–201(10) (Repl.1991)[.]

The next question is whether Ciba–Geigy's express warranties and the disclaimer of all express warranties can be reasonably construed as consistent with each other under § 4–2–316(1). If they cannot, the disclaimer is ineffective. First to be examined is the nature of the express warranties Ciba–Geigy made to Alter. "Any affirmation of fact or promise made by the seller to the buyer which relates to the goods and becomes part of the basis of the bargain creates an express warranty that the goods shall conform to the affirmation or promise." Ark.Code Ann. § 4–2–313(1)(a) (Repl.1991). An affirmation of the seller's opinion or commendation does not create an express warranty. Ark.Code Ann. § 4–2–313(2) (Repl.1991).

The advertising materials distributed to farmers by Ciba–Geigy contained an express warranty that a farmer need not worry about crop injury when using Dual. Alter, however, did not recall reading any of the advertising materials. An affirmation of fact must be part of the basis of the parties, bargain to be an express warranty. See Currier v. Spencer, 299 Ark. 182, 772 S.W.2d 309 (1989). When a buyer is not influenced by the statement in making his or her purchase, the statement is not a basis of the bargain. See generally American Law of Warranties § 2:7 (1991). Clearly, Alter was not influenced by the advertising materials when purchasing Dual, and hence they were not a basis of the bargain.

There was testimony that Wulfkuhle and McLeod told Alter during the sales meeting that Dual was safe and would not injure a corn crop. The question is whether this was a mere statement of opinion. In the misrepresentation context, we indicated "an opinion is merely an assertion of one man's belief as to a fact." Grendell v. Kiehl, 291 Ark. 228, 723 S.W.2d 830 (1987), citing Prosser & Keeton on Torts (5th Ed.),Ch. 19 § 109 (1984). There are no set criteria to help ascertain opinion from affirmation of fact, and the determination must be made on a case-by-case basis. Williston on Sales, § 17–6 (4th ed.1974).

The evidence before the Trial Court supported the conclusion that Ciba–Geigy's statements that Dual was safe and would not injure a corn crop were affirmations of fact and not mere opinions or commendations. The jury had sufficient evidence to conclude the statements were not "sales puffing" and constituted specific express warranties that the goods would conform to the affirmations. See, e.g., Pritchard v. Liggett & Myers Tobacco Co., 295 F.2d 292 (3d Cir.1961) (if a manufacturer assures the public that his product is safe when in fact it is harmful, he can "no doubt" be held liable for breach of warranty)[;] American Law of Warranties § 2:57 (1991) (a statement that a product is safe is generally an absolute undertaking that it is so). Again, we do not decide the issue, but we note that if the evidence is the same on retrial, a jury could conclude the disclaimer ineffective.

2. *Limitation of remedies*

A seller of goods may limit the buyer's remedies for breach of warranty pursuant to Ark.Code Ann. § 4–2–719(1)(a) (Repl.1991). A limitation of remedies provision restricts the remedies available to the buyer once a breach of warranty is established. An otherwise valid limitation of remedy is avoided by the buyer if the limitation fails of its essential purpose, or is unconscionable. § 4–2–719(3).

The "failure of essential purpose" exception is most commonly applied when the buyer's remedy is exclusively limited to repair or replacement of defective goods, and the seller is unable to repair or replace the goods to conform to the warranty. In this case, we are not dealing with a seller who failed to correct a defect after being asked to do so by the buyer, and the failure of essential purpose exception is not applicable. See Hill v. BASF Wyandotte Corp., 696 F.2d 287 (4th Cir. 1982). Ciba–Geigy has not limited or substituted Alter's remedy to repair or replacement of the defective goods and has only limited its liability for consequential damages.

While we cannot definitely resolve the issue, some comment on whether the limitation on consequential damages was unconscionable and unenforceable under § 4–2–719(3) is appropriate. Unconscionability must be determined in light of general commercial background, commercial needs in the trade or the particular case, the relative bargaining positions of the parties, and other circumstances existing when the contract was made. The commentary to § 4–2–719 states "it is of the very essence of a sales contract that at least minimum adequate remedies be available."

In Dessert Seed Co. v. Drew Farmers Supply, 248 Ark. 858, 454 S.W.2d 307 (1970), we held a limitation of liability clause unreasonable, unconscionable, and against public policy when negligence of the seller was clearly established, and the buyer was unable to discover the defect in the goods. See also Latimer v. William Mueller & Son, Inc., 149 Mich.App. 620, 386 N.W.2d 618 (1986) (limitation of remedy unconscionable when the defect could not be discovered); Majors v. Kalo Laboratories, Inc., 407 F.Supp. 20 (M.D.Ala.1975) (limitation of remedy unconscionable when a latent defect is involved). Because other evidence might be presented on this issue on retrial, we cannot pass on the unconscionability question on this appeal.

D. *Punitive damages*

Ciba–Geigy argues that, although no liability for punitive damages was imposed, the issue of punitive damages and evidence of financial condition should not have been submitted to the jury. Ciba–Geigy fails to mention that the jury was instructed on the tort of deceit. Although we do not know the basis of the general verdict in this case, punitive damages are available in cases of misrepresentation or deceit. Stein v. Lukas, 308 Ark. 74, 823 S.W.2d 832 (1992); Thomas Auto Co. v. Craft, 297 Ark. 492, 763 S.W.2d 651 (1989). If there is substantial evidence to show deliberate misrepresentation or deceit the issue of punitive damages may be submitted to the jury.

* * *

Reversed and remanded.

Notes and Questions

1. The manufacturer of agricultural chemicals may be required to take into account the fact that a sizeable proportion of the agricultural workforce speaks English as a second language. Some decisions suggest a manufacturer's duty to present warnings that go beyond English description to include as well international symbols of risk and means of avoidance. For example, in Hubbard–Hall Chemical Co. v. Silverman, 340 F.2d 402 (1st Cir.1965), the court held that the manufacturer of a pesticide might properly prepare warnings including international symbols of toxicity, such as the skull and crossbones, where the evidence showed that the product was applied by semi-English literate farm employees.

2. While a thorough discussion of the law governing liability under an express warranty theory is beyond the scope of this casebook, certain points should be recognized when considering the possible application of UCC § 2–313 to toxic product claims. First, the absence of manufacturer-buyer privity is not a bar to recovery, so that the express warranty runs directly to the ultimate purchaser of the product. See UCC § 2–318. Alternatives A, B and C ("Third Party Beneficiaries of Warranties—Express or Implied.") Second, the breach of an express warranty requires no showing of fault—that is, liability is strict, and the plaintiff need not establish negligence or intent on the part of the seller. Accordingly, the defendant need not be aware of the toxic characteristic of the product, nor have acted unreasonably in failing to learn or warn of it, so long as it warranted that it was not toxic.

Third, it is not necessary to prove the presence of a defective or unreasonably dangerous condition as it is under § 402A. The nonconformance of the product to the warranty constitutes the breach of the warranty and supports a finding of liability. E.g., Venie v. South Central Enterprises, 401 S.W.2d 495 (Mo.App.1966) (manufacturer's statements to the buyer that 2,4,5–t, a hormone herbicide, was "perfectly safe for strawberries" was actionable in breach of express warranty when, following application of the product in a normal manner, it killed not only the target weeds but the strawberries as well).

Fourth, state of the art is not a defense. Thus, even if the manufacturer made the product as safe as was possible under the state of the art existing at the time the warranty was made, it is not excused from liability so long as the warranty that the product would perform as represented was breached. Accordingly, even if it was not scientifically possible to make the product as safe as warranted, the manufacturer is liable.

Fifth, a general representation that a product is "safe" is ordinarily sufficient to support an express warranty action when the plaintiff or the plaintiff's property is injured or damaged by use of the product. E.g., Drayton v. Jiffee Chemical Corp., 395 F.Supp. 1081 (N.D.Ohio 1975), modified on other grounds 571 F.2d 352 (6th Cir.1978) (advertising claims that a particularly caustic drain cleaner was safe for household use held to be express warranty).

3. Another reason that dependence on express warranty theory is common is cases such as *Alter* is because of the economic loss doctrine. If a plaintiff suffers only an economic loss such as the costs of repair or replacement and consequential damages including lost profits—negligence and strict products liability are not ordinarily available because of the absence of personal injury or property damage. In other words, where a toxic product has not produced any safety-related harm, a plaintiff may have to rely on contractual warranties as a basis for compensation for economic losses.

4. *Note on Misrepresentation and Fraud.* While an action under UCC §§ 2–313, 2–314 or 2–315 may implicate seller misrepresentations, or fraud, plaintiffs may also evaluate potential separate claims in misrepresentation or fraud. Such claims may enjoy congruence with claims in warranty, but are not dependent upon them, *i.e.*, a seller's silence, while not constituting a statement of material fact for warranty purposes, may constitute a misrepresentation.

A.   Strict Liability for Innocent Misrepresentation Under Restatement (Second) of Torts § 402B

The Restatement (Second) recitation of strict liability for innocent misrepresentation provides:

Section 402B: Misrepresentation by Seller of Chattels to Consumers

One engaged in the business of selling chattels who, by advertising, labels, or otherwise, makes to the public a misrepresentation of a material fact concerning the character or quality of a chattel sold by him is subject to liability for physical harm to a consumer of the chattel caused by justifiable reliance upon the misrepresentation, even though

(a) it is not made fraudulently or negligently, and

(b) the consumer has not bought the chattel from or entered into any contractual relation with the seller.

This section derives from the outgrowth of the legal principles governing fraudulent and negligent misrepresentations, most of which involved non-product cases. While it is beyond the purpose of this book to address liability rules for fraud and negligent misrepresentation, a defendant in a toxic product case could be held liable under those theories, which require more stringent tests than those under § 402B. But a plaintiff proving fraud or negligent misrepresentation does have an advantage which may be relevant: he can recover not only for physical harm, but also for economic damages alone which are generally unrecoverable in product cases grounded in strict liability and negligence theory. A plaintiff seeking to recover only intangible economic losses must usually have to rely on its contractual and UCC remedies, unless an action for fraud or negligent misrepresentation can be established.

B. *Negligent Misrepresentation and Fraud*

Many of the rules governing innocent misrepresentation under § 402B are transplanted from the fraud and negligent misrepresentation torts. See generally, Michael Green, Strict Liability under Sections 402A and 402B: A Decade of Litigation, 54 Tex.L.Rev. 1185 (1976).

2. Fraud

To establish an action for fraud, the plaintiff must prove these elements:

(a) Defendant made a false representation;

(b) of an existing material fact;

(c) defendant knew the statement was false, or had no knowledge of its truth or falsity, or acted recklessly as to its truth or falsity;

(d) defendant intended the plaintiff to rely on the statement;

(e) the plaintiff did rely on the statement and the reliance was justifiable; and

(f) the plaintiff suffered damage.

To prove fraud, the plaintiff must essentially prove that the defendant intentionally or recklessly deceived him; in negligent misrepresentation, he must prove that the defendant negligently deceived him. Under § 402B no such proof of intentional or negligent deception is necessary: the liability is *strict*.

Allegations of fraud formed a basis for the suit brought by the City of New York against a lead-based paint trade association in New York v. Lead Industries Association, Inc., 190 A.D.2d 173, 597 N.Y.S.2d 698 (1993). In that suit, the New York appellate court affirmed the trial court's denial of defendants' motion to dismiss, and explained:

> According to the complaint, defendants have known for years, from their own privately financed studies, that lead-based interior house paint presented a health threat, putting children particularly at risk. Despite their decision not to use such paint on toys and childrens' furniture, they nevertheless not only continued to manufacture lead-based paint for interior surfaces, but also concealed their knowledge of the hazard, suppressed its dissemination, and lobbied against governmental regulation that would have required appropriate warnings to the public. Indeed, well into the 1950s, having known of the hazard for three decades, defendants continued to advertise and promote their lead-based product as appropriate for uses which might result in exposure to young children through inhalation, ingestion or absorption. Armed with such knowledge, which was clearly superior to that of the consuming public, defendants' actions cannot be protected as mere statements of opinion in an action for fraud and misrepresentation.

The scope of liability for fraud is generally broader than for negligence— under fraud it extends to anyone whom the defendant had "reason to know" might rely, and under negligence extends to only those foreseeable persons within a class defendant actually knew would rely. See Restatement (Second) of Torts § 552. The recoverable damages are also broader for fraud under § 549, with the plaintiff having the option of choosing between the out-of-pocket measure of damages or the benefit-of-the-bargain measure plus consequential economic losses, whereas under negligent misrepresentation in § 552B the plaintiff must settle for out-of-pocket losses and consequential economic losses.

The requirement that the defendant make a false representation of a material fact is the same under fraudulent, negligent or innocent misrepresentation. The representation must relate to a *material* fact. The usual test of materiality is whether the information would be regarded as important to a reasonable person in making a choice of action. Therefore, trivial or unimportant false statements are not actionable. In the toxic torts area, courts should properly regard as material any information about the safety, risks, or the harmful effects of the product. Any fact or risk sufficiently material to create an obligation to warn of it under § 402A would also be material if the defendant misrepresented that fact or risk under § 402B. Further, a statement would be material if it significantly affects the manner in which the plaintiff uses the product, thereby increasing its danger.

According to comment j of § 402B, liability will not be found "where the misrepresentation is not known, or there is indifference to it, and it does not influence the purchase or subsequent conduct." The representation need not, however, be the "sole inducement to purchase or to use the chattel, and it is sufficient that it has been a substantial factor in that inducement." In most product cases involving toxic products one would expect that the plaintiff's alleged reliance would relate to some representation about the safe use of the product or the absence of harmful effects, which might be one factor in inducing a consumer to purchase or use the product.

A plaintiff who is aware of the falsity of the representation is generally precluded from recovery. Moreover, some courts have held that if a reasonably prudent person would have been aware of the facts or would have investigated further, the plaintiff will be deemed to have knowledge of those facts which such an investigation would reveal and cannot recover for the misrepresentation.

Problem

In 1986, before Dr. James and Rhonda Conant moved into their newly constructed Pomeroy, South Hampshire home, the builder contracted with pesticide applicator Swat Terminating Co. ("Swat") to pre-treat the home for insects and termites. In 1987, soon after the family moved in, Swat applied 400 gallons of Chemco's Gold Crest C–100 termiticide to the basement walls and soil around the home. The chlordane-based product was applied through holes drilled into concrete blocks. Standard practice required that the holes be filled in afterward, but this did not occur.

Consequently, chlordane seeped into the living areas, and emitted toxic fumes throughout the house. The Conants and their three children began to experience illnesses, including headaches, nausea, and diarrhea. The couple's 15–month–old baby has been hospitalized and the family cat died. In November 1990, after an autopsy showed chlordane in the cat's liver, the family left the house.

The plaintiffs sued Chemco and Swat for personal injuries and property damage. They maintain that the house has been rendered uninhabitable, and the family's exposure to chlordane over a three-year period left them with severe permanent illnesses, including blood irregularities, liver problems, and immune system dysfunction.

There is evidence that Chemco's Gold Crest C–100 used by Swat carried labels on the canisters that stated that "independent studies reveal no evidence of any long-term latent health effects." Chemco maintains that these labels were intended solely as information to professional applicators, not for consumers.

After Swat settled with the plaintiffs, Chemco moved to dismiss all claims. The claims against Chemco, based on § 402A of the Restatement (Second) of Torts, contend that Chemco's Gold Crest C–100 was unreasonably dangerous to consumers and property. Specifically, plaintiffs contend that the product was unreasonably dangerous under the consumer expectation test of § 402A comment (i) and, alternatively, under a risk-utility test for design defect. In addition, they assert an informational defect related to the failure of the labels to inform consumers of the risks of short-term and long-term exposure. Finally, they assert express warranty claims predicated on the contents of the label.

A 1990 EPA study revealed that the use of chlordane-based termiticides on subterranean termites does create low-level risks of adverse health effects to those exposed, especially headaches, watery eyes, nausea, and similar symptomology. Additionally, the EPA recommended chemical alternatives to the ingredients in Gold Crest C–100 and other manufacturers' products, but those alternatives were not generally available in 1986 and 1987.

The county Board of Revisers lowered the appraised value of the Conants' property from $136,600 to $22,680. The arrived-at value was based on the land beneath the house, the pool, and the garage. The home itself was found to have no value because of the contamination.

Evaluate the plaintiffs' claims under § 402A and express warranty theory.

Chapter Eight

CAUSATION

Introduction

This Chapter deals with the broad topic of causation, which consists of several discrete elements, each of which is treated separately, but which are closely related: (1) Was the harm suffered by the plaintiff— usually a disease or illness which occurs generally in the population as integral to a background risk—caused by the exposure to the toxic substance? This raises the traditional question of cause-in-fact that is the focus of the basic torts course, but puts the inquiry into a different setting. (2) While some people may have experienced a harm caused by the defendant, is this plaintiff among that class of people? This is referred to in the literature as the indeterminate plaintiff or plaintiff identification problem. (3) Is the defendant the one who is responsible for the substance that produced the alleged harm—did the defendant cause the harm plaintiff allegedly suffered? This is the question that cases such as *Sindell v. Abbott Laboratories* wrestle with, which is often labeled the indeterminate defendant or indeterminate source problem.

A. CAUSATION: DID THE TOXIC SUBSTANCE CAUSE PLAINTIFF'S HARM?

1. INTRODUCTORY PRINCIPLES

KATIE BONNER v. ISP TECHNOLOGIES, INC.

United States Court of Appeals, Eighth Circuit, 2001.
259 F.3d 924.

WOLLMAN, Chief Judge.

ISP Technologies, Inc. (ISP) appeals the judgment entered by the district court [Cc] on a jury verdict against it for damages sustained by Katie Bonner. We affirm.

Taking the facts in the light most favorable to the verdict, Katie Bonner was twice exposed to FoamFlush, an organic solvent manufactured by ISP, during her employment on an assembly line in a urethane filter production plant. In March of 1995, the solvent partially dissolved a neoprene hose near Bonner's work station and sprayed over her in a dense mist. In July of 1995, FoamFlush vapors were released from a drum near her work station. Foamflush was used in the plant to clean urethane byproducts from manufacturing equipment. The product was marketed as a "drop-in" replacement for methylene chloride, a carcinogenic solvent, that could be used with systems designed for methylene chloride. FoamFlush contains 57% gamma-butyrolactone (BLO) and three other chemical compounds in smaller quantities. In the human body, BLO metabolizes into gamma-hydroxybutric acid (GHB). Bonner's work station was poorly ventilated at the time of the first exposure, and her protective gear was limited to gloves and goggles.

Bonner alleged three distinct permanent injuries: (1) psychological problems resulting from both her initial exposure and her health problems, (2) cognitive impairment and personality disorders caused by damage to her brain, and (3) Parkinsonian symptoms caused by damage to her brain. At trial, Bonner presented expert witness testimony tending to show that her exposure to FoamFlush caused all three injuries. The case was tried twice in the district court, and Bonner prevailed both times. After the first trial, the district court granted ISP's motion for a new trial because one of Bonner's experts had given testimony that went beyond the scope of his deposition. This appeal is from the second jury verdict, which awarded Bonner $2.2 million for her personal injuries.

II.

ISP argues that the court should have excluded expert witness testimony, that Bonner's evidence was insufficient to support the jury verdict, that the court improperly refused to give two of ISP's proposed jury instructions, and that the court should have granted ISP's motion for a new trial because of the excessiveness of the verdict.

ISP contends that the district court erred in admitting testimony of Dr. Terry Martinez, a pharmacologist and toxicologist, and of Dr. Raymond Singer, a neuropsychologist and neurotoxicologist. It further contends that, because Bonner could not show causation without their testimony, it is entitled to judgment as a matter of law.

To prove causation in a toxic tort case, a plaintiff must show both that the alleged toxin is capable of causing injuries like that suffered by the plaintiff in human beings subjected to the same level of exposure as the plaintiff, and that the toxin was the cause of the plaintiff's injury. See Wright v. Willamette Indus., Inc., 91 F.3d 1105, 1106 (8th Cir.1996). In other words, the plaintiff must put forth sufficient evidence for a jury to conclude that the product was capable of causing her injuries, and that it did. We have held, however, that "[t]he first several victims of a new toxic tort should not be barred from having their day in court simply because the medical literature, which will eventually show the connection between the victims' condition and the toxic substance, has not yet been completed." Turner v. Iowa Fire Equip. Co., 229 F.3d 1202,

1208–09 (8th Cir.2000). Bonner did not "need to produce" a mathematically precise table equating levels of exposure with levels of harm "in order to show" that she was exposed to a toxic level of FoamFlush, "but only 'evidence from which a reasonable person could conclude' " that her exposure probably caused her injuries. Bednar v. Bassett Furniture Mfg. Co., 147 F.3d 737, 740 (8th Cir.1998) (quoting Wright, 91 F.3d at 1107).

"If scientific, technical, or other specialized knowledge will assist the trier of fact to understand the evidence or to determine a fact in issue, a witness qualified as an expert by knowledge, skill, experience, training, or education, may testify thereto in the form of an opinion or otherwise." Fed.R.Evid. 702. We review under an abuse of discretion standard a district court's ruling admitting expert witness testimony under Rule 702. General Electric Co. v. Joiner, 522 U.S. 136, 141–42, 118 S.Ct. 512, 139 L.Ed.2d 508 (1997). In Daubert v. Merrell Dow Pharmaceuticals, Inc., 509 U.S. 579, 113 S.Ct. 2786 (1993), the Supreme Court detailed the Rule 702 standard for admission of scientific evidence. [Cc] Although Daubert offers four general criteria for assessing the reliability of scientific evidence, it also emphasizes that "[t]he inquiry envisioned by Rule 702 is ... a flexible one. Its overarching subject is the scientific validity—and thus the evidentiary relevance and reliability—of the principles that underlie a proposed submission. The focus, of course, must be solely on principles and methodology, not on the conclusions that they generate." 509 U.S. at 594–95, 113 S.Ct. 2786. The district court performs a gatekeeping function with respect to scientific evidence, ensuring that evidence submitted to the jury meets Rule 702's criteria for relevance and reliability. Id. at 590–91, 113 S.Ct. 2786. The rule's concern with "scientific knowledge" is a reliability requirement, while the requirement that the evidence "assist the trier of fact to understand the evidence or determine a fact in issue" is a relevance requirement. Id.

* * *

Note

No issue is more difficult in environmental tort litigation than resolving the question of whether the exposure to the toxic substance was the cause in fact of the plaintiff's harm. The special problems of causation in environmental torts are summarized by Professor Ora Fred Harris in his influential article, Toxic Tort Litigation and the Causation Element: Is There Any Hope of Reconciliation, 40 S.W.L.J. 909, 911–912 (1986):

> Causation problems are greatly compounded when applied to the field of toxic or hazardous exposure injury. A common, generally accurate, evaluation of humankind's understanding of the behavior of hazardous or toxic wastes and the effect of exposure on humans points to a vast amount of scientific uncertainty. This uncertainty is understandable given that many of these issues are at the very frontiers of science. Thus, a plaintiff attempting to establish that exposure to a particular substance has in fact caused his or her injury may face a dubious court or jury because of the lack of scientific certainty. Moreover, because this

"new" tort injury can have a latency period of up to as many as twenty to thirty years, it may be, as a practical matter, virtually impossible to establish the requisite causal relationship between an exposure that may have taken place many decades ago and a recently manifested injury now claimed to be the consequence of that exposure. Not only does this long latency period stymie the toxic or hazardous exposure victim's ability to isolate the alleged substance that precipitated the injury, it also diminishes the chances of identifying the responsible parties. These two requirements are critical if an injured plaintiff is to establish causation successfully in a toxic tort case. * * *

a. Problems With Causation Terminology

But what is meant by "cause" in the context of toxic torts? How does "cause" in law relate to the meaning of "cause" in science?

Causation in science finds its origins in Newtonian physics, with its emphasis on the laws of motion and acceleration, and a simplistic vision of mechanistic cause and effect—objects or particles changing direction following collisions with other objects or particles. Professor Troyen Brennan identifies this characterization of causation as "corpuscularian," and as requiring the presence of "causal chains." Troyen Brennan, Causal Chains and Statistical Links: The Role of Scientific Uncertainty in Hazardous–Substance Litigation, 75 Cornell L. Rev. 469 (1988). This mechanistic model of cause and effect has dominated the discourse on legal cause-in-fact, and has worked reasonably well in resolving causation in sporadic accident and intentional tort cases for hundreds of years. With toxic torts, however, new wrinkles arise because the mechanistic or corpuscularian model does not conform to the evolutions in science toward deeper dependence on probabilistic and statistical evidence to establish causal relationships. Brennan continues his analysis by relating tort law's dependency on mechanistic causation to the corrective justice rationale for tort liability, and how that model is strained by toxic tort litigation:

> In summary, legal notions of causation reflect a complex interplay of several concepts. But for causation or cause in fact, which reflects commonly held assumptions about causation as well as certain moral and political notions of responsibility, tends to dominate the disposition of tort claims. Moreover, this rendition of but for causation coincides neatly with that of corpuscularian science. Probabilistic linkage is distinguished from but for cause, but has a nebulous role in Anglo–American legal reasoning. Probabilistic causal notions correspond to the causal notions that modern science employs in that they are based on probabilistic evidence rather than simply deductively derived causal chains. * * *

From this discussion of competing notions of causation in law and science emerges a hypothesis that explains why courts have so much trouble with causation issues in toxic tort litigation. The scientific association between a toxic substance and injury to a person relies on probabilistic evidence: epidemiological studies and statistical associations. Philosophers of science readily accept such evidence and, indeed, acknowledge that probabilistic reasoning dominates much of physics and medicine. In corpuscularian writing, probabilistic evidence is second best, if acceptable at all, and corpuscularian notions of causation coincide with but for concepts of causation in tort law. Both rely heavily on causal chain analyses and individual actions. Corrective justice aspects of tort law assume the existence of traceable causal chains leading from actor to harm. As a result, tort law tends to induce a corpuscularian approach to scientific evidence. Litigants bringing scientific issues to court are expected to show causes in fact or but for causes, with minimal support from the policies of proximate cause.

A corpuscularian judge would not want to deal with probabilistic notions, as he would regard these as inferior methods of reasoning. Rather than accept probabilistic statements, a corpuscularian judge would delay a decision until deductive, mechanistic, but for causes are available. Nor would a corpuscularian judge welcome uncertainty in a scientific issue—uncertainty will be overcome according to positivism, and it is best to wait until this occurs. In addition, tort law's corrective justice aspects would not permit uncertainty in the causal assignment of responsibility.

In this regard, common law courts are neither unscientific nor ignorant. Rather, they cling to conceptions of individual responsibility that coincide neatly with eighteenth century science's notions of causation. Thus, it is not enough simply to say that courts should adopt probabilistic reasoning. They must be instructed. But given the importance of the moral concept of individual responsibility in tort law, we can expect courts to accommodate only so much probabilistic reasoning.

Unfortunately, toxic substance injury cases cannot produce mechanistic, deductively-derived causal evidence, and a corpuscularian judge cannot process the available probabilistic evidence. Thus, the causation problem in toxic tort litigation could result from an epistemological quandary. Judges, using but for causation when analyzing tort claims, may slip into corpuscularian reasoning about scientific evidence, even when that evidence is primarily probabilistic.

1. Why do corrective justice and notions of individual accountability require a mechanistic or causal chains treatment of cause-in-fact? Would the same be true if tort law's rationale rests or should rest on deterrence and efficiency considerations? Are there other reasons why science has moved inexorably toward probabilistic evidence while legal institutions have been more hesitant to do so?

2. On the philosophy of cause and effect, many writers have had influence over the centuries. For example, John Stuart Mill in 1862 defined the concept in these words: "The cause, then, philosophically

speaking, is the sum total of the conditions positive and negative taken together; the whole of the contingencies of every description, which being realized, the consequent invariably follows." John Stuart Mill, 3 A System of Logic, Ratiocinative and Inductive, ch. V, § 3, ch. VIII, §§ 1–4 in 7 The Collected Works of J.S. Mill (J. Robson, ed. 1973). It is interesting that Mill's definition is empirical because it does not require an understanding of how or why the relationship exists; only that if certain conditions do exist, then certain consequences follow. Understanding the mechanisms or instrumentalities that may explain these relationships among conditions and consequences is not a necessary part of the analysis. David Hume likewise observed that "we are never able, in a single instance, to discover any power or necessary connection, any quality which binds the effect to the cause, and renders the one the infallible consequence of the other. We only find that one does actually, in fact, follow the other." David Hume, 1 Treatise on Human Nature, Pt. III, §§ 14–15 (Selby–Bigge Rev. ed., P. Nidditch 1978); see also T. Beauchamp & A. Rosenberg, The Problem of Causation 284–300 (1981).

3. Based on the writings of Hume and Mill and others, it appears that the effort in law and science to define "cause" is not to identify a single, exclusive and unitary cause, but rather to identify or isolate some of the "contingencies" or "conditions" which are part of the causal web. Dr. Kenneth Rothman, one of the nation's leading epidemiologists, has described this same idea of a constellation of causes producing a disease. He notes that while "a cause which inevitably produces the effect is sufficient, * * * most causes that are of interest in the health field are components of sufficient causes, but are not sufficient in themselves." Kenneth J. Rothman, Causes, 104 Am.J.Epidem. 587, 588 (1976); see also Kenneth J. Rothman, Modern Epidemiology 11–12 (1986).

b. The Dual Causation Question

In determining whether a plaintiff can establish that the toxic substance and exposure to it was the cause in fact of the harm suffered, the inquiry can be analyzed as two separate inquiries: (1) Was the toxic substance *capable* of causing the *kind* of harm of which the plaintiff complains? This is a generic question since it focuses not on the particulars of the plaintiff's experience regarding the extent and duration of exposure, but on the general questions about propensities of the chemical agents to cause the kind of harm plaintiff alleges. The Bendectin cases set forth below address largely this question, which rely heavily upon epidemiological and other scientific studies and that are not dependent on the particulars of plaintiff's case. (2) Was *this plaintiff's* harm actually caused by the exposure to the defendant's chemical rather than being attributable to some other source? The answer to this question typically focuses on the testimony of medical doctors who have examined the plaintiff or his medical records, or conducted other tests specifically relating to the plaintiff.

In Sterling v. Velsicol Chemical Corp., 855 F.2d 1188 (6th Cir.1988) (set forth in Chapter 5), the Sixth Circuit considered the claims of various resident groups for enhanced risk of cancer, cancerphobia, and immune system dysfunction arising from defendant's hazardous waste which had contaminated plaintiffs' water supply. The trial court had certified a class action and had relied on the proofs of five representative plaintiffs to establish causation for the class. The Sixth Circuit's discussion of causation is extremely important because the court recognized that these causation-in-fact issues must usually be divided into two discrete analyses:

> [T]he [trial] court, as is appropriate in this type of mass tort class action litigation, divided its causation analysis into two parts. It was first established that Velsicol was responsible for the contamination and that the particular contaminants were capable of producing injuries of the types allegedly suffered by the plaintiffs. Up to this point in the proceedings, the five representative plaintiffs were acting primarily in their representative capacity to the class as a whole. This enabled the court to determine a kind of generic causation—whether the combination of the chemical contaminants and the plaintiffs' exposure to them had the capacity to cause the harm alleged. This still left the matter of individual proximate cause to be determined. Although such generic and individual causation may appear to be inextricably intertwined, the procedural device of the class action permitted the court initially to assess the defendant's potential liability for its conduct without regard to the individual components of each plaintiff's injuries. However, from this point forward, it became the responsibility of each individual plaintiff to show that his or her specific injuries or damages were proximately caused by ingestion or otherwise using the contaminated water. We cannot emphasize this point strongly enough because generalized proofs will not suffice to prove individual damages. The main problem on review stems from a failure to differentiate between the general and the particular. This is an understandably easy trap to fall into in mass tort litigation. Although many common issues of fact and law will be capable of resolution on a group basis, individual particularized damages still must be proved on an individual basis.

> Where the damages involve bodily injuries, it must be shown to a reasonable medical certainty that the contaminated water was the cause of the injury. * * * This standard implicates the qualifications of the witnesses testifying, the acceptance of the scientific community of their theories, and the degree of certainty as to their conclusions. This is particularly true when dealing with injuries or diseases of a type that may be the product of a variety of causes and inflict society at random, often with no known specific origin. * * *

It is important to recognize the relationship between the legal question to be resolved and the propriety of applying class action procedures: aggregative approaches work effectively in resolving the generic causation question but are of lesser utility in answering the individual causation question. (Chapter 13 contains a fuller discussion of these issues). The court identified the appropriate standard as that of a "reasonable medical certainty," which requires more than speculation or conjecture based on probability, likelihood, an educated guess, or an opinion that something is "more likely than not."

What do you think of the test of a "reasonable medical certainty" for determining whether the plaintiff's illness or disease was caused by exposure to the toxic substance? How high is a reasonable medical certainty? Is it like proof beyond a reasonable doubt?

In *Sterling* the court reviewed the causation evidence in each of the five individual cases point by point. It rejected as insufficient testimony regarding one plaintiff's kidney cancer:

> Plaintiff's testifying physician, Dr. Rhamy, stated that while "it's more likely it was caused by the chemicals, * * * [it] is difficult to determine." Dr. Rhamy further stated that "[n]o one knows what causes cancer of the kidney." Dr. Rhamy's conclusions that Wilbanks' environmental exposure to carbon tetrachloride was a "reasonable cause" for his kidney cancer and a statement by another testifying physician, Dr. Rodericks, that Wilbank's cancer was "consistent" with the exposure do not constitute sufficient medical proof of causation.

Why is the testimony of Dr. Rhamy deficient? The court also rejected such testimony as "most probably secondary to chemical exposure;" "probably due to exposure to toxic chemicals;" "most probable cause;" and "most likely reason." Four of the five cases were remanded for recalculation of damages to account for the exclusion of those items for which the court found there was insufficient proof of causation.

For another opinion discussing the nature of the dual causation inquiry, but rejecting the "reasonable medical certainty" standard in favor of the more typical "more probable than not" test, see Earl v. Cryovac, A Division of W.R. Grace & Co., 115 Idaho 1087, 772 P.2d 725 (1989), in which the court reversed a summary judgment for the defendant where a meatpacker had alleged that his obstructive pulmonary disease was caused by exposure to chemicals in defendant's plastic film used to wrap meat products.

This Chapter seeks to address the causation in fact question in some depth. Because environmental torts necessarily involve subtle and complex scientific and medical questions, this Chapter explores the subjects of toxicology and epidemiology in sufficient depth (it is hoped) to permit the student to intelligently assess what rules of causality courts are in fact applying to these questions and to evaluate for yourself what standards should be applied. These questions also require an examination of evidentiary issues and consideration of the standards for admissibility of scientific evidence, which have evolved in the last decade.

c. *Early Use of Probabilistic Evidence*

One early case to raise difficult issues of causality is Stubbs v. City of Rochester, 226 N.Y. 516, 124 N.E. 137 (1919) in which the New York

Court of Appeals addressed the causation-in-fact question between a contaminated city water supply and the plaintiff's typhoid fever. The City had two water systems, one called the Holley Water System which contained sewage from the Genesee River, and the other the Hemlock Water System, which provided drinking water to the residents in sections of the City. After complaints were received in June of 1910 the city health officers tested the water at several homes and discovered a "serious condition of contamination," whereupon the City notified the public not to drink the water without boiling it. An investigation lasting several months revealed the source of the contamination to be discharges from the Holley System into the Hemlock System because of a malfunctioning check valve between the two.

The plaintiff contended that the City was negligent in permitting poisonous and polluted water from the Genesee River to flow into the Holley System pipes and into the Hemlock Water System, contaminating the water and making it dangerous to the life and health of city residents. The plaintiff recovered a judgment at the trial court which the appellate division had reversed. The court framed the issue as whether the "plaintiff produced evidence from which inference might reasonably be drawn that the cause of his illness was due to the use of contaminated water furnished by the defendant." The defendant contended that plaintiff's evidence was deficient because (1) it failed to establish that he contracted typhoid fever by drinking contaminated water, and (2) it was incumbent on plaintiff to establish that his illness was not due to any other cause to which typhoid fever may be attributed. The expert testimony revealed *eight* other possible causes including impure raw fruits and vegetables, infected milk, certain flies, contact with an infected person, and other known and unknown causes. The court's discussion is instructive:

> * * * [T]he source of contamination having been discovered, the doctor made an investigation as to the reported cases of typhoid fever in the city in the months of August, September, and October, for the purpose of determining the number of cases, where the cases came from, what gave rise to it, and he stated that in his opinion the outbreak of typhoid was due to polluted water, contaminated as he discovered afterwards by sewage. In answer to a hypothetical question embracing generally the facts asserted by plaintiff the witness testified that he had an opinion as to the cause of the infection of plaintiff, and such opinion was that it was due to contaminated water.

> Dr. Dodge, of the faculty of the University of Rochester, a professor of biology, also bacteriologist of the city of Rochester, about October 1st made an analysis of samples of water taken from No. 58 Warehouse street, and from the Holley system, corner of Oak and Platt streets. The analysis of the water from Warehouse street disclosed the number of bacteria to be 880 cubic centimeter. The analysis of the Holley water disclosed 4,000 bacteria cubic centimeter. An analysis of the Hemlock water at the University disclosed

approximately 150 to 200. While his examination did not disclose any colon bacillus, it did disclose some evidence of the same. Dr. Brady, the physician who attended the plaintiff, and Dr. Culkin both testified that in their opinion the plaintiff contracted typhoid fever from drinking polluted water.

Plaintiff called a witness who resided on Brown street, about two minutes' walk from the bridge, and proved by her that she drank water from the Hemlock mains in the fall of 1910 and was ill with typhoid fever. Thereupon counsel for defendant stipulated that 57 witnesses which the plaintiff proposed to call will testify that they drank water from the Hemlock taps in the vicinity of the district west of the Genesee river and north of Allen street in the summer and fall of 1910, and during said summer and fall suffered from typhoid fever, that in view of the stipulation such witnesses need not be called by plaintiff, and the stipulation shall have the same force and effect as though the witnesses had been called and testified to the facts.

* * *

A table of statistics as to typhoid fever in the city of Rochester for the years 1901–1910, inclusive, was produced by the health officer and received in evidence. That exhibit was the subject of comment in the opinion of Justice Foote upon the first appeal. The fact is evident from a perusal of his opinion that upon the first trial plaintiff did not undertake to establish the number of cases of typhoid fever in the district where the water was contaminated as compared with the total number of cases in the city in 1910, which evidence was supplied upon this trial. The statistics disclose that the number of typhoid cases in the city in 1910 was 223, an excess of 50 cases of any year of the nine years preceding. Recalling that complaints as to water commenced in the summer of 1910, and as shown by the evidence that typhoid fever does not develop until two or three weeks after the bacilli have been taken into the system, in connection with the fact that the source of contamination was not discovered until October, the statistics disclose that of the 223 cases of typhoid in the city in the year 1910, 180 cases appear during the months of August, September, October, and November as against 43 cases during the remaining eight months, 35 of which were prior to August and 8 in the month of December, two months after the source of contamination of the water was discovered.

The evidence on the trial discloses that at least 58 witnesses, residents of the district, drank the contaminated water and suffered from typhoid fever in addition to plaintiff; thus one-third of the 180 cases during the months stated were shown to exist in that district.

Counsel for respondent asserts that there was a failure of proof on the part of plaintiff, in that he did not establish that he contracted disease by drinking contaminated water, and in support of his argument cites a rule of law that when there are several possible causes of injury for one or more of which a defendant is not responsible, plaintiff cannot recover without proving that the injury was sustained wholly or in part by a cause for which defendant was responsible. He submits that it was essential for plaintiff to eliminate all other of seven causes from which the disease might have been contracted. If the argument should prevail and the rule of law stated is not subject to any limitation, the present case illustrates the impossibility of a recovery in any case based upon like facts. One cause of the disease is stated by counsel to be "personal contact with typhoid carriers or other persons suffering with the disease, whereby bacilli are received and accidentally transferred by the hands or some other portion of the person or clothes to the mouth." Concededly a person is affected with typhoid some weeks before the disease develops. The plaintiff here resided three miles distant from his place of employment, and traveled to and from his work upon the street car. To prove the time when he was attacked with typhoid, then find every individual who traveled on the same car with him, and establish by each one of them that he or she was free from the disease even to his or her clothing is impossible. Again, the evidence disclosed that typhoid fever was caused by sources unknown to medical science. If the word of the rule stated is to prevail plaintiff would be required to eliminate sources which had not yet been determined or ascertained. I do not believe the rule stated to be as inflexible as claimed for. If two or more possible causes exist, for only one of which a defendant may be liable, and a party injured established facts from which it can be said with reasonable certainty that the direct cause of the injury was the one for which the defendant was liable, the party has complied with the spirit of the rule.

The plaintiff was employed in the immediate locality where the water was contaminated. He drank the water daily. The consumption of contaminated water is a very frequent cause of typhoid fever. In the locality there were a large number of cases of typhoid fever, and near to 60 individuals who drank the water and had suffered from typhoid fever in that neighborhood appeared as witnesses on behalf of plaintiff. The plaintiff gave evidence of his habits, his home surroundings, and his method of living, and the medical testimony indicated that his illness was caused by drinking contaminated water. Without reiteration of the facts disclosed on the trial I do not believe that the case on the part of plaintiff was so lacking in proof as matter of law that his complaint should be dismissed. On the contrary, the most favorable inferences deducible from the plaintiff were such as would justify a submission of the facts to a jury as to the reasonable inferences to be drawn therefrom, and a verdict rendered thereon for either party would rest, not in conjecture, but upon reasonable possibilities.

Notes and Questions

1. The opinion is remarkable for the sophistication it brings to the complex causation question over 70 years ago. The court employed a "reasonable certainty" test of causation. Do you think the evidence satisfied that standard of proof? Or did the court simply rule that there existed sufficient evidence to justify submitting the question to the jury, that is, the evidence of causation was not insufficient as a matter of law? What about the burden of eliminating other possible causes for the plaintiff's typhoid—how strongly must plaintiff's evidence exclude those other potential causes?

2. The role of expert witnesses was pervasive. Plaintiff obtained a favorable opinion from Dr. Goler, the health officer of the City, that the typhoid was caused by the contaminated water, and two other physicians similarly concluded that the typhoid was attributable to the contaminated water. The parties' use of statistical evidence was significant in demonstrating the substantial increase in the incidence of typhoid in 1910 over prior years, and the concentration of cases in the four months during which the contamination was discovered.

In a recent article, Professor Walker has reanalyzed the data from *Stubbs*, added population data and applied contemporary epidemiological methodologies to arrive at a relative risk of 2.5, meaning that for Stubbs and other persons similarly situated, the risk of contracting typhoid was two and one-half times greater for those who ingested the contaminated water than for those who did not. In this next section we explore those principles of epidemiology which enable such a comparison to be made and to draw causal inferences. Intuitively, should a 2½ times greater incidence suffice to establish causation in a toxic tort case? See Vern R. Walker, The Concept of Baseline Risk in Tort Litigation, 80 Ky. L.J. 631 (1992).

2. THE SCIENTIFIC METHOD: TOXICOLOGY AND EPIDEMIOLOGY

Because toxic and environmental harms involve complex and often elusive questions of science and medicine, it is necessary to develop some understanding of the basic concepts of toxicology and epidemiology. The outcome of many cases which are considered in this Chapter are, to a considerable extent, controlled by the quality of the scientific evidence which the parties introduce to the fact finder.

GERALD W. BOSTON, A MASS EXPOSURE MODEL OF TOXIC CAUSATION: THE CONTENT OF SCIENTIFIC PROOF AND THE REGULATORY EXPERIENCE
18 Colum. J. Envtl. L. 181, 213–25, 231–40 (1993).

B. Toxicology and Risk

Toxicology and toxicologists are primarily concerned with the capacity of chemicals or environmental agents to produce harmful effects in living organisms. Toxicologists study the interactions between chemicals and biological systems, attempt to identify the mechanism of action and attempt to assess quantitatively the relationship between doses of chemicals and responses in living systems.

* * *

For the most part, toxicologists conduct investigations of toxicity using exposed living animals, typically rats and mice (in vivo studies), or by studying cultures or treating isolated tissues or cells (in vitro and short term studies). The objectives of these studies are two-fold: (1) to examine the nature of the adverse effects produced by the chemical agent, and (2) to assess the probability and cause of their occurrence. The primary method by which the toxicologist accomplishes both tasks is the development and use of dose-response relationships or gradients.

All chemicals are toxic at some dose. An expression that captures this idea is that "there are no harmless substances—there are only harmless ways of using substances." This statement serves to emphasize the second basic function of toxicology, risk assessment, which is an evaluation of the conditions under which an adverse effect can be produced or is likely to have occurred.

* * *

To answer the questions of what level of exposure is sufficient to produce harm and what is the expected harm for that level of exposure necessitates development of dose-response relationships. Toxicologists state that a response exhibits a dose-response relationship when a consistent, mathematical relationship describes the proportion of individuals responding for a given dosage interval for a given exposure period. For example, the risk of contracting lung cancer from exposure to asbestos particles increases one percent for each fiber per cubic centimeter year of exposure.

* * *

C. Toxicologic Studies

The principal types of toxicologic studies are: (1) short term screening assays (such as in vitro laboratory experiments that examine bacteria or cells); (2) animal bioassays that involve exposure of groups of animals, usually rodents, to the chemical under investigation to test for the onset of various adverse effects; and (3) epidemiologic studies that compare populations of exposed and non-exposed humans in order to draw inferences respecting possible causal associations. * * *

1. Short Term Assays

Short term in vitro (i.e., test-tube) tests are used to identify various kinds of toxins by examining the biochemical effects of substances on cells, bacteria, organs, or embryos. For example, * * * [i]n vitro testing for teratogens involves transplanting animal fetal cells, organs, or embryos into a medium where they are subjected to the chemical under investigation in order to examine the effects on the transplanted tissues. Another form of toxicity study is the examination and comparison of the molecular structures of the agent under investigation with that of known toxins. It is believed that if the structures are similar, then the toxic effects produced may also be similar.

All of these forms of short term and in vitro assays focus on the biochemical mechanisms. They examine the smallest building blocks of life and subject them to intensive investigation and experimentation in hopes of developing data useful in understanding the cellular mechanics of the disease process in humans. Yet, despite their increasing sophistication, the value of such tests in establishing causal relationships in humans is problematic. * * *

2. Animal Toxicity Studies

a. Basic Objectives

The intermediate step in the hierarchy of toxicological evidence in support of causal relationships between a chemical and human pathology is animal toxicity studies. * * * As with all toxicity studies, the objective is to identify the nature of the adverse health effect produced by a chemical agent and the range of doses over which such effects are observed. * * * The beginning point for toxicity animal studies is to investigate the acute, single-dose toxicity of a chemical. * * * Toxicologists determine the lethal properties of a chemical and estimate its dose, which is defined as that dose which on average is lethal for fifty percent of the animals tested. * * *

Once acute toxicity data is arrived at, subchronic and chronic studies may be undertaken, which involve repeated or continuous exposures for several weeks or months or the full lifetime of the animal. These studies identify the specific organs or body systems that may be damaged and the conditions of exposure and dose that are required to produce such an effect and the exposure level at which no adverse effects are observed. * * *

* * *

b. Designs of Toxicity Animal Studies

Rats and mice are the favorite species among toxicologists because of cost and handling considerations as well as a greater understanding of their genetic background and disease susceptibility. Moreover, because their lifespans are short, toxicologists can perform lifetime studies within a reasonable period. * * *

Two important considerations in test design involve the magnitude of the doses administered and the duration of exposure. Beginning with the LD_{50} dose, investigators study the effects of lower doses administered over longer periods of time. * * * The selection of the dose range is controversial because the * * * doses administered are proportionally much higher than the levels to which humans are exposed. However, such high doses are essential because of the relatively short life spans of the bioassay tests and the practical limit on the number of animals that can be tested. * * *

c. Interpretation of Animal Studies

The single largest purpose for undertaking animal bioassays is to enable regulatory agencies to determine what substances to regulate and to set permissible exposure levels, including possibly zero, for such substances. * * *

d. Extrapolative Models

Critical to the risk assessment process is the selection of an extrapolative model that takes data from the bioassays and predicts the level of risk in humans. * * * Risk assessments must extrapolate from results in high-dosage animal tests to low-dose animal risks and then to long-term human hazards at significantly lower doses.[159] Scientists have developed a number of competing extrapolative models during the past two decades, but none has achieved general acceptance. * * *

* * *

III. EPIDEMIOLOGY

A. Introduction

Epidemiology is the study of the distribution and determinants of disease in human populations. Epidemiologists test biological inferences

---

159. The graph in Section III illustrates the problem of extrapolating from animal data at the top ranges of the dose level to human exposures at lower dose levels.

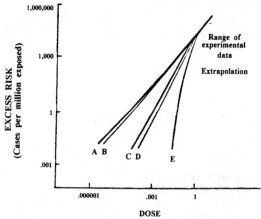

Figure 3A. Low-dose extrapolation for a carcinogen under several mathematical models: A, B, C, D, and E.
[G12423]

Logically, these are the two distinct routes to follow in the extrapolation, since there are logically two distinct dose-response curves involved. One can extrapolate from high dose to low dose using the animal dose-response curve, and then extrapolate to humans, or extrapolate to humans at high doses and then use a human dose-response curve to extrapolate to low doses. See Alan Rosenthal et al., Legislating Acceptable Cancer Risk from Exposure to Toxic Chemicals, 19 Ecology L.Q. 269, 282 (1992).

by combining the disciplines of statistics (biostatistics more precisely), sociology, and demography; they look for unusual incidences of human disease and endeavor to identify those factors which distinguish the affected population group from other groups. Epidemiologic studies can be either experimental or observational. In experimental studies one group is deliberately exposed to a carefully controlled amount of a chemical and compared to another equivalent but non-exposed group, as in the case of clinical trials of pharmaceutical products. However, society's ethical and practical constraints would not accept taking a putative carcinogen and experimentally subjecting it to one group of persons in order to assess whether they contracted cancer. Therefore, in the context of pollutants and the kinds of toxic substances involved in most toxic tort litigation, observational studies are the norm. These studies are made possible because of "unplanned experiments" in which certain persons have already been exposed to a chemical agent (e.g., persons voluntarily choosing to smoke cigarettes; or non-smoking persons choosing to live with persons who smoke), while others have not been so exposed, enabling investigators to compare the incidence of a particular disease among the two groups.

B. Study Designs and Objectives

1. Types of Study Designs

There are at least five kinds of epidemiological studies, although only the last two are the focus of much of this article. * * *

* * *

4. Case-control studies compare individuals with the disease (cases) to persons who do not have the disease (controls) in an attempt to retrospectively determine commonalities within the diseased group which may reveal a relationship to an exposure to a chemical agent. For example, if an investigator were interested in whether exposure to environmental tobacco smoke ("ETS") may be related to lung cancer in non-smokers, she could take non-smokers who contract the disease (cases) and compare them to those non-smokers without lung cancer (controls) in terms of whether they had lived with a smoking spouse. One would expect that if there is an association between lung cancer and exposure to environmental tobacco smoke, a greater proportion of cases than of controls would have a history of exposure to ETS. This one example reveals a number of potential problems that affect the validity of the association. First, it is essential to obtain accurate information about past exposures—i.e., were the cases actually exposed to ETS? When and for how long? Where did the exposures take place? And did the cases actually smoke themselves (were they ex-smokers or never-smokers)? Second is the problem of recall bias respecting past exposures in which it is possible that those with the disease (cases)

are more likely to recall exposures than those without the disease (controls). Third, in selecting the control group care must be taken to assure that persons exposed are not artificially excluded; that is, the cases and controls should be comparable in all respects except their disease status. If there are some exposed persons in the cases but none in the controls, it will likely increase the proportion of cases with the exposure and yield misleading proportional data.

The case-control study methodology is reflected diagrammatically as follows:

CASE–CONTROL (RETROSPECTIVE) STUDY

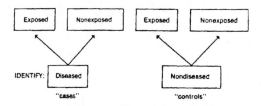

Viewed retrospectively, this study will compare the ratio of cases that were exposed to the ratio of controls that were exposed, and if exposure is a factor in the disease, the study should show a higher ratio of exposure status among cases than controls.

5. The cohort or follow-up study is regarded as the most powerful of the observational types in terms of its ability to identify causal associations. These studies begin with a group of exposed persons and compare them to a group of individuals who were not exposed and tracks them prospectively to determine the incidence over time within the two groups of a specific disease being investigated. In a prospective study, the objective is to determine if the risk of developing the disease is greater in exposed individuals than in non-exposed individuals. The cohort study alleviates one of the major problems of the case-control study—that of memory bias—because the exposure is the starting point for constructing the study.

The cohort study can be represented diagrammatically as follows:

DESIGN OF A PROSPECTIVE STUDY

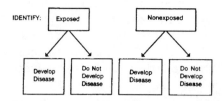

2. *Measurement of Risks*

The cohort study enables the investigator to calculate the comparative rates of disease within the exposed and non-exposed groups and to compare those two rates. This comparison of rates is the relative risk: The risk in the exposed population relative to the risk in the non-exposed population and may be expressed as:

Relative Risk (RR) = $\dfrac{R_1}{R_2}$,

where R_1 = the risk of disease in the exposed population and R_2 = the risk of disease in a non-exposed population.

If the relative risk equals one (i.e., the numerator is the same as the denominator), the risk in the exposed group is the same as the risk in the nonexposed group, and there is no suggestion of any association between the factor and the disease in question. If the relative risk is greater than one, the risk in the exposed group is greater than in the non-exposed group, and there is a positive association between the exposure and the disease. Conversely, if the relative risk is less than one, then the risk in exposed individuals is less than the risk in non-exposed individuals, suggesting a protective effect. A study of workers exposed to asbestos in connection with their employment by asbestos product manufacturers revealed that they were dying from lung cancer at a rate of 64 per 100,000 per year, whereas in the general population of males during the same period and at the same ages the death rate from lung cancer was only 31 per 100,000 per year. The relative risk for this study would be expressed as: RR = $\dfrac{64}{31}$ = 2.06.

In epidemiology the probability of causation is determined by the attributable risk ("AR"), which is defined as the difference between the risk in the exposed and the risk in the non-exposed, and is expressed as: AR = $\dfrac{P(RR - 1)}{P(RR - 1) + 1}$,

where P = proportion exposed in the study group and R = relative risk of the study group. If the entire group is exposed, P = 1 and AR = $\dfrac{RR - 1}{RR}$.

Based on the above study on asbestos workers the AR = $\dfrac{2.06 - 1.00}{2.06}$, or 51% which means that the probability that a given case of lung cancer in the exposed group was attributable to the asbestos exposure would be about even, or 51 percent. This percent is sometimes referred to as the etiologic probability or etiologic fraction.

Of course, not all cases of lung cancer are caused by asbestos exposure; that is, lung cancer has many causes, some known, such as smoking, and some unknown. Therefore within the exposed group there will be "background" cases of lung cancer which are not attributable to the exposure to asbestos. Additionally, the relative risks will vary according to occupational groups because of the different exposure levels and duration of the exposure to asbestos. Finally, note that if the RR for a certain exposure is 1 or less, the corresponding AR is 0; no etiologic probability can be attributed to that exposure and the cancer (or other disease) is simply a background case.

3. Criteria for Determining Causal Relationships

Epidemiological evidence which reveals that exposure to a chemical creates a relative risk greater than one does not end the inquiry into causality. The enhanced relative risk reveals only an association between two factors—the exposure and the disease. The association is not necessarily a causal relationship because other factors may be at work. For example, one major study revealed an association between coffee consumption and the development of pancreatic cancer. How should such an association be interpreted? Does coffee drinking actually cause pancreatic cancer or is coffee consumption associated with an increased risk of pancreatic cancer because of confounding by smoking? Smoking is known to increase the risk of pancreatic cancer and people who smoke often drink coffee. Thus, the association could be causal or could be explained by the association of smoking with both coffee drinking and pancreatic cancer.

To determine if an association is causal, epidemiologists have developed criteria that treat the statistical association as the starting point of the analysis. Because the associational data alone do not permit biological inferences, scientists apply additional, more particularistic, analytic and biologic tests before reaching a conclusion respecting a causal relationship. * * *

The criteria are:

1. *The strength of the association.* The greater the relative risk, the more likely it is that the association is causal. For example, Hill observed that the mortality rates for lung cancer among heavy cigarette smokers (those who smoked more than one pack per day) ranged from twenty to thirty times the normal rates of lung cancer across a large number of epidemiologic studies. The stronger the relative risks, the less likely it is that the association is explainable by confounding factors, bias, or other factors. On the other hand, smaller relative risks may be explainable on the basis of other factors, although the smallness of the risk does not rule out causal relationships.

2. *Consistency.* The presence of repeatedly consistent observations made in different populations over differing observation periods, utilizing different study designs and under different circumstances implies that the associations are causal. The chance that all

of the associations are the result of error or fallacy is simply too remote. Again, however, inconsistent associations across studies do not rule out a causal relationship, since differing study methodologies might produce varying relative risks.

3. *Specificity.* This criterion refers to the correspondence of exposure to a specific disease. Is the exposure associated with a specific disease and vice versa? Is the association restricted to specific workers and to a specific disease (specific cancer site or specific histological type)? The argument for a causal relationship is weakened if the relationship is nonspecific. However, this criterion has been de-emphasized in recent years because many causes have multiple effects and many diseases have multiple causes. For example, cigarette smoking can cause malignancies other than lung cancer and some lung cancer patients never smoke. In short, the presence of specificity adds to the cogency of the inference of a causal relationship, but its absence does not preclude such an inference.

4. *Temporality.* This seemingly simple criterion refers to the requirement that exposure to the causal factor must precede disease in order to support a causal association. This criterion is particularly important for chronic diseases with long latency periods (time between onset of exposure and diagnosis) and for study factors which change over time.

5. *Biologic gradient (dose-response relationship).* A dose-response relationship refers to the severity or frequency of disease increasing with the level or duration of exposure. If the association reveals such a dose-response relationship or biologic gradient, the argument for causal association becomes very persuasive. For example, the observation that lung cancer risk increases with the amount of cigarettes smoked lends great support to the argument that smoking is a causal factor of lung cancer. A dose-response relationship allows a simple and intuitive explanation, and obviously enhances the causal interpretation. Unfortunately, in many epidemiological studies, precise exposure data are absent, making it difficult or impossible to calculate dose-response relationships. The existence of a dose-response curve does not invariably suggest causality because there may be a confounding factor that also yields a separate gradient.

6. *Biologic plausibility.* This criterion looks to how compatible is the association with the biologic knowledge then known, including information from animal studies, pharmacokinetics, genotoxicity, and in vitro studies. However, given the constant flux in the state of knowledge respecting biology with new theories frequently advanced, rejected, and modified to fit new evidence, too much reliance on consistency with existing knowledge would run counter to more basic exploratory and creative scientific principles.

7. *Coherence.* This criterion, closely related to plausibility, considers whether the associational data seriously conflicts with the natural history and biology of the disease. For example, do animal studies, histopathological studies, or other evidence cohere with the epidemiologic findings? However, the absence of coherent information, as distinguished from the presence of conflicting evidence, should not be taken as proof that the association is not causal.

For further study on these topics, the following sources are suggested: Daivd. L. Faigman, et al., Science in the Law: Standards, Statistics and Research Issues (2002); U.S. Environmental Protection Agency, Guidelines for Carcinogen Assessment, 51 Fed. Reg. 33,992 (1986); James Huff, et al., Scientific Concepts: Value and Significance of Chemical Carcinogenesis Studies, 31 Annals Rev. of Pharm. & Toxic. 621 (1991); Ellen K. Silbergeld, The Role of Toxicology in Causation: A Scientific Perspective, 1 Courts, Health Science and the Law 374 (1991); Elements of Toxicology and Chemical Risk Assessment, Handbook for Nonscientists, Attorneys and Decisionmakers (Environ 1986); Ernest Hodgson & Patricia Levi, Modern Toxicology (1987); Michael A. Kamrin, Toxicology (1988).

3. STANDARDS OF ADMISSIBILITY OF SCIENTIFIC EVIDENCE

Because toxic tort cases necessarily implicate the scientific principles described above, a critical and controversial concern in the litigated cases is the admissibility of the expert opinions offered by the parties to establish the ultimate factual issue of causation. Whether an expert's opinion is admissible is governed by several sections of the Federal Rules of Evidence or state evidentiary counterparts. Rule 104(a) authorizes the trial court to make preliminary determinations "concerning the qualifications of a person to be a witness" and the "admissibility of evidence." The Rules of Evidence 401, 402 and 403 are also pertinent in determining the admissibility of expert testimony. Rule 401 defines "relevant evidence," Rule 402 declares that "all relevant evidence is admissible, except as otherwise provided by the Constitution, by Act of Congress or by these rules," and Rule 403 allows the exclusion of relevant evidence when "its probative value is substantially outweighed by the danger of unfair prejudice, confusion of issues or misleading the jury * * *" Finally, Rules 702 and 703 directly address the admissibility of expert testimony:

Rule 702—Testimony by Experts

If scientific, technical, or other specialized knowledge will assist the trier of fact to understand the evidence or to determine a fact in issue, a witness qualified as an expert by knowledge, skill, experience, training, or education, may testify thereto in the form of an opinion or otherwise.

Rule 703—Bases of Opinion Testimony by Experts

The facts or data in the particular case upon which an expert bases an opinion or inference may be those perceived by or made known to the expert at or before the hearing. If of a type reasonably relied upon by experts in the particular field in forming opinions or inferences upon the subject, the facts or data need not be admissible in evidence.

The credentials or qualifications of the proposed expert are relevant under Rule 702. The party calling the expert must satisfy the requirement by showing that the expert is qualified based on his or her knowledge, skill, experience, training, or education. Rule 702 does not require any specific degree, certification, or membership in particular societies or associations. Generally, the courts take a flexible and liberal attitude toward the sufficiency of the proposed experts' qualifications. See The National Institute for Trial Advocacy, Evidence: Text, Rules, Problems and Illustrations 250–52 (2d ed., rev. 1989) (hereafter NITA) for a description of the governing principles.

Courts in toxic tort cases have demonstrated considerable flexibility in allowing experts to render opinions as to the cause of plaintiff's injury, even though they were not medical doctors. For example, in Rubanick v. Witco Chemical Corp., 125 N.J. 421, 593 A.2d 733 (1991), the New Jersey Supreme Court held that an expert who possessed a doctorate in biochemistry, was a primary cancer researcher at the Sloan–Kettering Cancer Institute, and had published numerous articles on colon cancer, could testify that plaintiff's workplace exposure to PCBs had caused his colon cancer. Similarly, in Shilling v. Mobile Analytical Services, Inc., 65 Ohio St.3d 252, 602 N.E.2d 1154 (1992), the Ohio Supreme Court held that a Ph.D. specializing in neurotoxicology was qualified to render an opinion that the ingestion of gasoline injured the plaintiff's brain and nervous system.

The critical objective of Rule 702 is to enable expert testimony where it will assist the court and jury to understand the evidence introduced or to determine a fact, such as causation, in issue. In order for such expert testimony to be of assistance to the court or jury it must be predicated on a sufficiently reliable body of scientific, technical or other specialized knowledge. NITA identifies six factors which influence the reliability of the evidence derived from a scientific principle:

(1) the validity of the underlying scientific principle; (2) the validity of the technique or process that applies the principle; (3) the condition of any instrumentation used in the process; (4) adherence to proper procedures; (5) the qualifications of the person who performs the test; and (6) the qualifications of the person who interprets the results.

The test articulated in Frye v. United States, 293 Fed. 1013, 1014 (D.C.Cir.1923) has been applied by many courts to determine the validity of the scientific principle and the technique applying it, measured by whether they "have gained general acceptance in the particular field in which [they] belong." The student is aware of the considerable diversity of views regarding the *Frye* standard. See Charles T. McCormick, Evidence § 203 at 608 (3d ed. 1984); United States v. Gould, 741 F.2d 45, 49 (4th Cir.1984); Graham C. Lilly, Introduction to the Law of Evidence 494–95 (2d ed. 1987). See the thorough discussion of the *Frye* standard, a rationale for its rejection, and related evidentiary issues in United States v. Downing, 753 F.2d 1224, 1232–1243 (3d Cir.1985). On this topic generally, which has stimulated considerable law review comment, see Paul C. Giannelli & Edmund J. Imwinkelried, Scientific Evidence ch.1 (1986 & Supp. 1991).

In Daubert v. Merrell Dow Pharmaceuticals, Inc., 509 U.S. 579, 113 S.Ct. 2786, 125 L.Ed.2d 469 (1993), the Supreme Court unanimously laid the *Frye* test to rest and articulated a set of standards for federal courts to apply in determining the admissibility of expert testimony.

DAUBERT v. MERRELL DOW PHARMACEUTICALS, INC.

Supreme Court of the United States, 1993.
509 U.S. 579, 113 S.Ct. 2786, 125 L.Ed.2d 469.

JUSTICE BLACKMUN delivered the opinion of the Court.

In this case we are called upon to determine the standard for admitting expert scientific testimony in a federal trial.

I

Petitioners Jason Daubert and Eric Schuller are minor children born with serious birth defects. They and their parents sued respondent in California state court, alleging that the birth defects had been caused by the mothers' ingestion of Bendectin, a prescription anti-nausea drug marketed by respondent. Respondent removed the suits to federal court on diversity grounds.

After extensive discovery, respondent moved for summary judgment, contending that Bendectin does not cause birth defects in humans and that petitioners would be unable to come forward with any admissible evidence that it does. In support of its motion, respondent submitted an affidavit of Steven H. Lamm, physician and epidemiologist, who is a well-credentialed expert on the risks from exposure to various chemical substances. Doctor Lamm stated that he had reviewed all the literature on Bendectin and human birth defects—more than 30 published studies involving over 130,000 patients. No study had found Bendectin to be a human teratogen (i.e., a substance capable of causing malformations in fetuses). On the basis of this review, Doctor Lamm concluded that maternal use of Bendectin during the first trimester of pregnancy has not been shown to be a risk factor for human birth defects.

Petitioners did not (and do not) contest this characterization of the published record regarding Bendectin. Instead, they responded to respondent's motion with the testimony of eight experts of their own, each of whom also possessed impressive credentials. These experts had concluded that Bendectin can cause birth defects. Their conclusions were based upon "in vitro" (test tube) and "in vivo" (live) animal studies that found a link between Bendectin and malformations; pharmacological studies of the chemical structure of Bendectin that purported to show similarities between the structure of the drug and that of other substances known to cause birth defects; and the "reanalysis" of previously published epidemiological (human statistical) studies.

The District Court granted respondent's motion for summary judgment. The court stated that scientific evidence is admissible only if the principle upon which it is based is " 'sufficiently established to have general acceptance in the field to which it belongs.' " The court concluded that petitioners' evidence did not meet this standard. Given the vast body of epidemiological data concerning Bendectin, the court held, expert opinion which is not based on epidemiological evidence is not admissible to establish causation. Thus, the animal-cell studies, live-animal studies, and chemical-structure analyses on which petitioners had relied could not raise by themselves a reasonably disputable jury issue regarding causation. Petitioners' epidemiological analyses, based as they were on recalculations of data in previously published studies that had found no causal link between the drug and birth defects, were ruled to be inadmissible because they had not been published or subjected to peer review.

The United States Court of Appeals for the Ninth Circuit affirmed. 951 F.2d 1128 (1991). Citing Frye v. United States, 293 F. 1013, 1014 (1923), the court stated that expert opinion based on a scientific technique is inadmissible unless the technique is "generally accepted" as reliable in the relevant scientific community.

* * *

We granted certiorari, 506 U.S. 914, 113 S.Ct. 320, 121 L.Ed.2d 240 (1992), in light of sharp divisions among the courts regarding the proper standard for the admission of expert testimony.

II

A

In the 70 years since its formulation in the Frye case, the "general acceptance" test has been the dominant standard for determining the admissibility of novel scientific evidence at trial. Although under increasing attack of late, the rule continues to be followed by a majority of courts, including the Ninth Circuit.

The Frye test has its origin in a short and citation-free 1923 decision concerning the admissibility of evidence derived from a systolic blood pressure deception test, a crude precursor to the polygraph machine. In what has become a famous (perhaps infamous) passage, the then Court of Appeals for the District of Columbia described the device and its operation and declared: "Just when a scientific principle or discovery crosses the line between the experimental and demonstrable stages is difficult to define. Somewhere in this twilight zone the evidential force of the principle must be recognized, and while courts will go a long way in admitting expert testimony deduced from a well-recognized scientific principle or discovery, the thing from which the deduction is made must be sufficiently established to have gained general acceptance in the particular field in which it belongs." 293 F. at 1014. Because the deception test had "not yet gained such standing and scientific recognition among physiological and psychological authorities as would justify the courts in admitting expert testimony deduced from the discovery, development, and experiments thus far made," evidence of its results was ruled inadmissible.

The merits of the Frye test have been much debated, and scholarship on its proper scope and application is legion.[160] Petitioners' primary attack, however, is not on the content but on the continuing authority of the rule. They contend that the Frye test was superseded by the adoption of the Federal Rules of Evidence. We agree.

We interpret the legislatively-enacted Federal Rules of Evidence as we would any statute. * * *

Frye, of course, predated the Rules by half a century. In United States v. Abel, 469 U.S. 45, 105 S.Ct. 465, 83 L.Ed.2d 450 (1984), we considered the pertinence of background common law in interpreting the Rules of Evidence. We noted that the Rules occupy the field, 105 S.Ct. at 467, but, quoting Professor Cleary, the Reporter explained that the common law nevertheless could serve as an aid to their application: "In principle, under the Federal Rules no common law of evidence remains. 'All relevant evidence is admissible, except as otherwise provided * * *.' In reality, of course, the body of common law knowledge continues to exist, though in the somewhat altered form of a source of guidance in the exercise of delegated powers." 105 S.Ct. at 469.

Here there is a specific Rule that speaks to the contested issue. Rule 702, governing expert testimony, provides: "If scientific, technical, or other specialized knowledge will assist the trier of fact to understand the evidence or to determine a fact in issue, a witness qualified as an expert by knowledge, skill, experience, training, or education, may testify thereto in the form of an opinion or otherwise." Nothing in the text of this Rule establishes "general acceptance" as an absolute prerequisite to admissibility. Nor does respondent present any clear indication that Rule 702 or the Rules as a whole were intended to incorporate a "general acceptance" standard. The drafting history makes no mention of Frye, and a rigid "general acceptance" requirement would be at odds with the

---

160. See, e.g., Green, Expert Witnesses and Sufficiency of Evidence in Toxic Substances Litigation: The Legacy of Agent Orange and Bendectin Litigation, 86 Nw. U.L.Rev. 643 (1992) (hereinafter Green); [other citations omitted].

"liberal thrust" of the Federal Rules and their "general approach of relaxing the traditional barriers to 'opinion' testimony." Given the Rules' permissive backdrop and their inclusion of a specific rule on expert testimony that does not mention "general acceptance," the assertion that the Rules somehow assimilated Frye is unconvincing. Frye made "general acceptance" the exclusive test for admitting expert scientific testimony. That austere standard, absent from and incompatible with the Federal Rules of Evidence, should not be applied in federal trials.

B

That the Frye test was displaced by the Rules of Evidence does not mean, however, that the Rules themselves place no limits on the admissibility of purportedly scientific evidence. Nor is the trial judge disabled from screening such evidence. To the contrary, under the Rules the trial judge must ensure that any and all scientific testimony or evidence admitted is not only relevant, but reliable.

The primary locus of this obligation is Rule 702, which clearly contemplates some degree of regulation of the subjects and theories about which an expert may testify. "If scientific, technical, or other specialized knowledge will assist the trier of fact to understand the evidence or to determine a fact in issue" an expert "may testify thereto." The subject of an expert's testimony must be "scientific * * * knowledge." The adjective "scientific" implies a grounding in the methods and procedures of science. Similarly, the word "knowledge" connotes more than subjective belief or unsupported speculation. The term "applies to any body of known facts or to any body of ideas inferred from such facts or accepted as truths on good grounds." Webster's Third New International Dictionary 1252 (1986). Of course, it would be unreasonable to conclude that the subject of scientific testimony must be "known" to a certainty; arguably, there are no certainties in science. See, e.g., Brief for Nicolaas Bloembergen et al. as Amici Curiae 9 ("Indeed, scientists do not assert that they know what is immutably 'true'—they are committed to searching for new, temporary theories to explain, as best they can, phenomena"); Brief for American Association for the Advancement of Science and the National Academy of Sciences as Amici Curiae 7–8 ("Science is not an encyclopedic body of knowledge about the universe. Instead, it represents a *process* for proposing and refining theoretical explanations about the world that are subject to further testing and refinement") (emphasis in original). But, in order to qualify as "scientific knowledge," an inference or assertion must be derived by the scientific method. Proposed testimony must be supported by appropriate validation—i.e., "good grounds," based on what is known. In short, the requirement that an expert's testimony pertain to "scientific knowledge" establishes a standard of evidentiary reliability.

Rule 702 further requires that the evidence or testimony "assist the trier of fact to understand the evidence or to determine a fact in issue." This condition goes primarily to relevance. "Expert testimony which does not relate to any issue in the case is not relevant and, ergo, non-helpful." 3 Weinstein & Berger ¶ 702[02], p. 702–18. See also United States v. Downing, 753 F.2d 1224, 1242 (C.A.3 1985) ("An additional consideration under Rule 702—and another aspect of relevancy—is whether expert testimony proffered in the case is sufficiently tied to the facts of the case that it will aid the jury in resolving a factual dispute").

C

Faced with a proffer of expert scientific testimony, then, the trial judge must determine at the outset, pursuant to Rule 104(a), whether the expert is proposing to testify to (1) scientific knowledge that (2) will assist the trier of fact to understand or determine a fact in issue. This entails a preliminary assessment of whether the reasoning or methodology underlying the testimony is scientifically valid and of whether that reasoning or methodology properly can be applied to the facts in issue. We are confident that federal judges possess the capacity to undertake this review. Many factors will bear on the inquiry, and we do not presume to set out a definitive checklist or test. But some general observations are appropriate.

Ordinarily, a key question to be answered in determining whether a theory or technique is scientific knowledge that will assist the trier of fact will be whether it can be (and has been) tested. "Scientific methodology today is based on generating hypotheses and testing them to see if they can be falsified; indeed, this methodology is what distinguishes science from other fields of human inquiry." Green, at 645. See also C. Hempel, Philosophy of Natural Science 49 (1966) ("[T]he statements constituting a scientific explanation must be capable of empirical test"); K. Popper, Conjectures and Refutations: The Growth of Scientific Knowledge 37 (5th ed. 1989) ("[T]he criterion of the scientific status of a theory is its falsifiability, or refutability, or testability").

Another pertinent consideration is whether the theory or technique has been subjected to peer review and publication. Publication (which is but one element of peer review) is not a sine qua non of admissibility; it does not necessarily correlate with reliability and in some instances well-grounded but innovative theories will not have been published. Some propositions, moreover, are too particular, too new, or of too limited interest to be published. But submission to the scrutiny of the scientific community is a component of "good science," in part because it increases the likelihood that substantive flaws in methodology will be detected. The fact of publication (or lack thereof) in a peer-reviewed journal thus will be a relevant, though not dispositive, consideration in assessing the scientific validity of a particular technique or methodology on which an opinion is premised.

Additionally, in the case of a particular scientific technique, the court ordinarily should consider the known or potential rate of error, see, e.g., United States v. Smith, 869 F.2d 348, 353–354 (C.A.7 1989) (surveying studies of the error rate of spectrographic voice identification technique), and the existence and maintenance of standards controlling the technique's operation.

Finally, "general acceptance" can yet have a bearing on the inquiry. A "reliability assessment does not require, although it does permit, explicit identification of a relevant scientific community and an express determination of a particular degree of acceptance within that community." United States v. Downing, 753 F.2d, at 1238. Widespread acceptance can be an important factor in ruling particular evidence admissible, and "a known technique that has been able to attract only minimal support within the community," Downing, supra, at 1238, may properly be viewed with skepticism.

The inquiry envisioned by Rule 702 is, we emphasize, a flexible one. Its overarching subject is the scientific validity—and thus the evidentiary relevance and reliability—of the principles that underlie a proposed submission. The focus, of course, must be solely on principles and methodology, not on the conclusions that they generate.

Throughout, a judge assessing a proffer of expert scientific testimony under Rule 702 should also be mindful of other applicable rules. Rule 703 provides that expert opinions based on otherwise inadmissible hearsay are to be admitted only if the facts or data are "of a type reasonably relied upon by experts in the particular field in forming opinions or inferences upon the subject." Rule 706 allows the court at its discretion to procure the assistance of an expert of its own choosing. Finally, Rule 403 permits the exclusion of relevant evidence "if its probative value is substantially outweighed by the danger of unfair prejudice, confusion of the issues, or misleading the jury * * *." Judge Weinstein has explained: "Expert evidence can be both powerful and quite misleading because of the difficulty in evaluating it. Because of this risk, the judge in weighing possible prejudice against probative force under Rule 403 of the present rules exercises more control over experts than over lay witnesses." Weinstein, 138 F.R.D., at 632.

Accordingly, the judgment of the Court of Appeals is vacated and the case is remanded for further proceedings consistent with this opinion.

It is so ordered.

The opinion of CHIEF JUSTICE REHNQUIST, with whom JUSTICE STEVENS joins, concurring in part and dissenting in part, is omitted.

Notes and Questions

1. Deleted in the editing of Justice Blackmun's opinion were extensive citations to scientific and legal articles bearing on the nature of scientific proof and the scientific method. Students interested in these topics should consult the opinion for a virtual bibliography of relevant materials.

2. Based on Justice Blackmun's description of the qualifications and methodology of plaintiffs' experts, how is the trial court likely to rule on the admissibility issue on remand?

Problem

Plaintiff seeks damages for a condition or disease allegedly caused by defendant's drug or chemical. The disease, like cancer, provides no physical evidence of the inducing agent and the etiology of the illness is unknown. All relevant epidemiological studies to date conclude that there is no "statistically significant" link between exposure to defendant's product and the type of illness or injury suffered by plaintiff. The current scientific consensus is that it is impossible to conclude that a cause-and-effect relationship exists. Nevertheless, plaintiff's qualified expert is prepared to testify that it is more probable than not that causation exists. Her opinion is based upon chemical structure activity analysis, animal studies, in vivo and in vitro, and the patient's history. She has reached this conclusion by relying upon these sources, which would be considered by many scientists. However, most would find this data inadequate to support a finding of causation in the absence of positive epidemiological studies. Plaintiff's expert has either rejected the epidemiological data as a basis for her opinion or has reinterpreted the data underlying these negative studies to reach a contrary conclusion. Based on *Daubert*, can this opinion be admitted?

3. Justice Blackmun states that scientific evidence must "not only [be] relevant, but reliable," and declares that reliability is part of "scientific * * * knowledge" that is allowed under Rule 702 because "scientific knowledge" must be "derived by the scientific method" and "supported by appropriate validation." The term "reliable" does not appear in the text of Rule 702; from what source does Justice Blackmun derive his requirement of reliability?

Interestingly, a proposed amendment to Rule 702 of the Federal Rules of Evidence would have required that "testimony providing scientific * * * information, in the form of an opinion or otherwise, may be received if (1) [it] is *reasonably reliable* and will, if credited, *substantially* assist the trier of fact * * * and (2) the witness is qualified as an expert. * * * " Jud. Conf. of the U.S., Comm. on Rules of Prac. and Proc., Preliminary Draft of Proposed Amendments to the Federal Rules of Civil Procedure 83 (Law. Co-op., Aug. 15, 1991). The proposed committee notes indicated that while the revisions are intended to tighten the admissibility standards for expert testimony, the language was not intended to resolve the debate over the "general acceptance" test set forth in *Frye*. Assuming the desirability of such an amendment, does *Daubert* eliminate the need for it?

4. Did the Court offer sufficient guidance to the district court judges as to the considerations that should bear on whether the "reasoning or methodology underlying the testimony is scientifically valid"? What does the Court mean when it states that the theory or technique should be testable or falsifiable? Were you surprised that the Court gave importance to the peer review and publication process? It was the Ninth Circuit's emphasis on a requirement for peer review that drew an avalanche of criticism, much of it from the scientific community. What matters respecting peer review: that the expert's theory has been reviewed or that it has been reviewed *favorably* ? What does the Court mean by the consideration of the "known or

potential rate of error" of a particular scientific technique? What does that mean in the sciences of epidemiology and toxicology?

Finally, were you surprised that the Court resuscitated the "general acceptance" standard as part of the reliability calculus? The Court relies heavily on the Third Circuit's opinion in United States v. Downing, 753 F.2d 1224 (3d Cir.1985), which had rejected *Frye*, but allowed some inquiry into the "degree of acceptance within" the scientific community.

5. How would you characterize the role of district court judges in assessing admissibility after *Daubert*?—a strict scrutiny or "hard look" approach, moderate scrutiny, or deferential? What does the Court mean when it states that the "focus * * * must be solely on the principles and methodology, not on the conclusions that they generate"? Under the *Frye* test, the trial court would assess the proposed expert testimony against the consensus of the relevant scientific community; the former could be presented by affidavit, whereas the latter could be determined largely through judicial notice and the use of learned treatises under Rule 803(18). By contrast, *Daubert* will require district judges to make findings on a number of issues, and to weigh those findings in order to reach their ultimate conclusions. How demanding is this procedure likely to be on federal district judges? If you are plaintiff's counsel, what kind of record must you be prepared to offer to address the *Daubert* reliability criteria? What will defense counsel likely offer?

6. What standard of review will courts of appeal apply to district court admissibility determinations? Although evidentiary rulings are generally reviewed for abuse of discretion, district court determinations of general acceptance generally have been reviewed de novo because that conclusion does not vary according to the circumstances of each case, and because virtually all the materials needed to reach that conclusion are equally available to the courts of appeals. Will appellate courts under the *Daubert* multi-factor balancing test use the abuse of discretion standard? Consider these possibilities: In one case, a federal district judge determines that a proffered scientific technique or theory is testable but not peer-reviewed, with a low rate of error but not generally accepted across its scientific field— in other words, two positive findings against two negative ones. On balance, the judge concludes that the testimony is admissible. Assuming none of the underlying findings is clearly erroneous, is the judge's striking of the balance going to be disturbed on appeal?

In case two, another district judge in the same district, in an identical case, makes the same underlying findings, but concludes on balance that the evidence should not be admitted. Would that conclusion be an abuse of that judge's discretion, even if the affirmance of the first judge's decision had resulted in a published opinion?

7. In a portion of the opinion that was deleted, Justice Blackmun states that a trial court also retains the authority to direct a verdict when it concludes that a party has failed to offer sufficient evidence to reach a jury on causation or to grant summary judgment based on the insufficiency of plaintiff's evidence. In the next section we will focus on that aspect of the causation inquiry.

8. In Rubanick v. Witco Chemical Corp., 125 N.J. 421, 593 A.2d 733 (1991), the New Jersey Supreme Court, under state evidentiary rules similar to the Federal Rules, also overturned the *Frye* standard specifically for toxic tort cases. After discussing the special causation problems which plaintiffs encounter in toxics cases and the "undeniable indications that persons do suffer grave and lethal injury as a result of the wrongful and tortious exposure to toxic substances," it stated a new test:

> Accordingly, we hold that in toxic-tort litigation, a scientific theory of causation that has not yet reached general acceptance may be found to be sufficiently reliable if it is based on a sound, adequately-founded scientific methodology involving data and information of the type reasonably relied on by experts in the scientific field.

Is there a difference between the scientific *method* (referred to in *Daubert*) and scientific "methodology" (also referred to in *Daubert*)? The answer is clarified in *Rubanick* itself when the court unequivocally rejected the scientific method as a standard of admissibility, stating that "the scientific method fails to address or accommodate the needs and goals of the tort system." Is this true? Does the "methodology" standard include not only the types of data and information relied upon, but also embrace the reasoning process of getting from the data to the conclusions?

9. Justice Alan B. Handler, who authored the opinion in *Rubanick*, authored an article entitled, The Judicial Pursuit of Knowledge: Truth and/or Justice, 41 Rutgers L. Rev. 1 (1988), in which he recognized the important role which scientific evidence and theory play in civil and criminal litigation. He advocates an enhanced judicial role in scientific fact-finding and recommends that such enhanced participation occur in certain classes of cases, including "those where critically relevant scientific knowledge is controversial and experts are polarized, yet the decisional result hangs in the balance; or where there are serious litigational imbalances that realistically will impugn the integrity and soundness of the final determination; or where the public importance of the case eclipses the private interests of the individual litigants, implicating significant concerns of public policy." Was *Rubanick* such a case? Did the opinion reflect Handler's position?

4. SUFFICIENCY OF THE SCIENTIFIC EVIDENCE: NATURE AND QUANTUM OF PROOF

a. *Minimalist Requirements*

We turn now to the issue first raised in *Stubbs* at this Chapter's beginning: How much evidence of causation is enough? A closely related, indeed inseparable, issue is what *kind* of evidence must the plaintiff offer? Often the question turns on whether epidemiological studies supporting the causal association is indispensably necessary or merely desirable. The opinion which has come to stand most starkly for the proposition that supportive epidemiological studies are not an essential component of a plaintiff's prima facie case is Ferebee v. Chevron Chemical Company, 736 F.2d 1529 (D.C.Cir.1984). In *Ferebee* the plaintiff's decedent, an agricultural worker for the United States Department of

Agriculture, alleged that he had contracted pulmonary fibrosis, from which he ultimately died, as a result of long-term dermal exposure to dilute solutions of paraquat, an herbicide distributed by defendant. The jury had rendered a verdict for the plaintiff and on appeal defendant argued that plaintiff's experts' opinions were insufficient, standing alone, to make out a submissible case on causation. Plaintiff offered two pulmonary experts who testified, based on their examination of the decedent and medical studies which they reviewed, that dermal absorption of paraquat could cause pulmonary abnormalities and that, in this case, did cause the decedent's. The court first declared that the issue of weighing the experts' conflicting opinions is appropriate for jury determination, especially in cases such as this. It continued:

> [A] cause-effect relationship need not be clearly established by animal or epidemiological studies before a doctor can testify that, in his opinion, such a relationship exists. As long as the basic methodology employed to reach such a conclusion is sound, such as use of tissue samples, standard tests, and patient examination, products liability law does not preclude recovery until a "statistically significant" number of people have been injured or until science has had the time and resources to complete sophisticated laboratory studies of the chemical. In a courtroom, the test for allowing a plaintiff to recover in a tort suit of this type is not scientific certainty but legal sufficiency; if reasonable jurors could conclude from the expert testimony that paraquat more likely than not caused Ferebee's injury, the fact that another jury might reach the opposite conclusion or that science would require more evidence before conclusively considering the causation question resolved is irrelevant. That Ferebee's case may have been the first of its exact type, or that his doctors may have been the first alert enough to recognize such a case, does not mean that the testimony of those doctors, who are concededly well qualified in their fields, should not have been admitted.

Notes and Questions

1. The court in *Ferebee* seems to be applying a "willing testifier" standard for the admissibility and reliability of expert testimony in emerging areas of scientific knowledge—if an expert is willing to testify and meets the qualification requirement of Rule 702—they are the only criteria which must be satisfied before a jury is permitted to weigh the credibility and persuasiveness of the testimony. Do you agree with this standard? Federal Rule of Evidence 702 quoted earlier sets forth the requirement that the expert testimony be able to "assist the trier of fact;" is that what Judge Mikva is expressing in his "willing testifier" rule? Is the underlying premise of such a rule that courts are institutions established for resolution of disputes, not arbiters of scientific truth? Can courts ever be expected to seek to resolve the question of whether novel scientific theories are valid? Would the experts' opinions be admissible after *Daubert* ?

2.   Why did the court refuse to place reliance on epidemiological studies? Does the court make any minimum requirements on the nature of the proof necessary to make out a submissible case?

3.   Wells v. Ortho Pharmaceutical Corp., 615 F.Supp. 262 (N.D.Ga. 1985), affirmed 788 F.2d 741 (11th Cir.1986) (reducing plaintiff's verdict from $5.1 million to $4.7 million), cert. denied 479 U.S. 950, 107 S.Ct. 437, 93 L.Ed.2d 386 (1986), demonstrates a reliance on the *Ferebee* reasoning. In *Wells*, the parents of a child born with multiple birth defects brought a products liability action on behalf of the child against the manufacturer of a spermicide used by the child's mother before and after conception. The trial court, which tried the case without a jury, began its opinion by declaring what its scientific demands were:

> The Court emphasizes, however, that plaintiffs' ultimate burden was not to produce an unassailable scientific study which proves that spermicides have caused birth defects in rats, rabbits, or members of a large group health plan, but rather to show from *all* the evidence presented, to a reasonable degree of medical certainty, that the spermicide caused some or all of *Katie Well's* birth defects (emphasis in original).

Then, the court placed minimal weight on defendant's evidence showing that no statistical association had been shown to exist between use of the product and the kind of injury suffered. The court noted simply that "[a]lthough the studies on which defendant relied failed to detect an association between spermicides and birth defects, some of the defendants' own experts testified that these studies do not rule out all possibility that spermicides can cause birth defects." Does this indicate that negative epidemiological studies will not be persuasive in disproving generic causation? Is the court ignoring that the burden of proof is on the plaintiff?

Second, the court relied on testimony concerning "mechanisms" or theories to demonstrate causation. Specifically, experts testified about an amniotic-band syndrome and vascular-disruption hypotheses to explain the plaintiff's injury. This testimony influenced the court largely because it was based on examination of the plaintiff. The court pointed out that it was concerned only with "this plaintiff's injury." The court's opinion asserts that when epidemiological evidence shows no association between the product and the disease, but hypothesized " 'mechanisms' of causation" appear to support an association, a fact finder may find causation.

On appeal, Ortho Pharmaceutical argued that the trial court had failed to consider adequately the epidemiological evidence of no association. The Circuit Court rejected this argument, and after quoting *Ferebee*, continued: "As the D.C. Circuit noted in *Ferebee*, a distinction exists between legal sufficiency and scientific certainty."

The decision in *Wells* was roundly criticized by the medical community. In an article in the New England Journal of Medicine, two physicians from the National Institute of Child Health and Human Development noted that *Wells* took the medical community by surprise, because the overwhelming body of evidence indicates that spermicides are not teratogenic. James L. Mills & Duane Alexander, Teratogens and "Litogens," 315 New. Eng. J. Med. 1234, 1235 (1986). They further wrote that plaintiff had won "despite testimony citing the considerable medical evidence that spermicides do not cause birth defects," and despite the United States Food and Drug Administration's decision that warnings about birth defects were not warranted. Should the civil justice system care about these criticisms?

4. Brennan criticizes the *Ferebee* and *Wells* decisions. (Troyen Brennan, Causal Chains and Statistical Links: The Role of Scientific Uncertainty in Hazardous Substance Litigation, 73 Cornell L. Rev. 469, 497–499 (1988)) on the grounds that the court reversed the scientific method by finding an association even though the epidemiological evidence failed to show an association.

Some state courts have also concluded that supportive epidemiological evidence should not be required in order to reach a jury on the issue of causation. See Bloomquist v. Wapello County, 500 N.W.2d 1 (Iowa 1993) (relying on *Ferebee*, and concluding that "we reject the reasoning of *Brock*", set forth in the next section).

b. *Intermediate Standard of Sufficiency*

The facts of Bonner v. ISP Technologies, Inc., 259 F.3d 924 (8th Cir.2001), a toxic exposure case, were introduced at section A.1. to this chapter. This post-Daubert decision interprets a trial court's gatekeeper function in the middle registers. The Eighth Circuit emphasizes three points: (1) the plaintiff need not produce expert epidemiological evidence; (2) the proper focus of the trial court should be on the orthodoxy of the expert's scientific methodology, and not his conclusions; and (3) an expert's causation conclusion that is novel in the field should not be excluded solely on that basis. The court turns to the evidence adduced at trial with this analysis:

KATTIE BONNER v. ISP TECHNOLOGIES, INC.

United States Court of Appeals, Eighth Circuit, 2001
259 F.3d 924

* * *

Although the district court's gatekeeping function includes an analysis of the reliability of scientific evidence, neither Rule 702 nor Daubert requires that an expert opinion resolve an ultimate issue of fact to a scientific absolute in order to be admissible. Compare Turner, 229 F.3d at 1208 (differential diagnosis admissible when it identifies "the most probable cause" of a condition) with Glastetter v. Novartis Pharm. Corp., 252 F.3d 986, 989 (8th Cir.2001) (per curiam) (no abuse of discretion in exclusion of differential diagnosis that is "scientifically invalid"). The only question relevant to the admissibility of the scientific evidence is whether it is sufficiently reliable and relevant to assist the jury's determination of a disputed issue. Daubert, 509 U.S. at 594–95. As a general rule, the factual basis of an expert opinion goes to the credibility of the testimony, not the admissibility, and it is up to the opposing party to examine the factual basis for the opinion in cross-examination. Only if the expert's opinion is so fundamentally unsupported that it can offer no assistance to the jury must such testimony be excluded. Hose v. Chicago Northwestern Transp. Co., 70 F.3d 968, 974 (8th Cir.1996)[.] "Although it is common that medical experts often disagree on diagnosis and causation, questions of conflicting evidence must be left for the jury's determination." Hose, 70 F.3d at 976.

In a pre-trial motion, ISP sought to preclude the admission of Dr. Martinez's opinion that Bonner suffered from permanent and progressive Parkinsonian-type tremors because her exposure to FoamFlush damaged the dopaminergic receptors in her brain, as well as Dr. Singer's opinion that Bonner suffers from permanent organic brain dysfunction consistent with exposure to FoamFlush. The district court precluded Dr. Martinez from testifying that Bonner's permanent Parkinsonian symptoms were caused by FoamFlush exposure, but permitted him to testify that Bonner's acute symptoms were caused by FoamFlush. Dr. Singer was permitted to testify that Bonner suffers from organic brain dysfunction and personality disorders consistent with exposure to a toxic level of FoamFlush.

Dr. Martinez

Dr. Martinez testified at trial that the symptoms Bonner suffered immediately after her exposure to FoamFlush (nausea, headache, tiredness, respiratory problems, trembling, and skin irritation) were caused by that exposure. Dr. Martinez based his testimony on (1) the temporal connection between Bonner's exposure and acute symptoms; (2) animal studies of the effects of BLO; (3) studies of chemicals with similar structures; (4) his study of the mechanism of GHB and the way it acts on nerve pathways; and (5) Bonner's medical records. ISP contends that the testimony should have been excluded as irrelevant because of Bonner's claim of permanent injuries and as prejudicial because the jury may have drawn an impermissible inference that if FoamFlush could cause temporary injuries similar to Bonner's permanent injuries, it could also be the cause of her permanent injuries. We do not agree, for whether or not such an inference would in fact have been impermissible, Bonner's acute symptoms were relevant both to Dr. Martinez's analysis of whether and to what extent she was exposed to BLO and to Dr. Singer's analysis of her exposure level. ISP also argues that Dr. Martinez's opinion should have been excluded as unreliable because there was no epidemiological support for his conclusion that inhalation of FoamFlush could cause the short-term symptoms Bonner described. It argues that the sources Dr. Martinez relied on involve exposure through ingestion, rather than inhalation, of BLO, and do not describe symptoms like those manifested by Bonner after BLO exposure; that Dr. Martinez never determined the quantity of BLO to which Bonner was exposed; and that he failed to rule out other possible causes of her symptoms. In addition, it contends that the fact that Dr. Martinez had designed but not yet tested his theory evidences its unreliability.

As set forth above, our review of the district court's admission of Martinez's testimony is for abuse of discretion. General Electric, 522 U.S. at 141–42. In this case, the district court carefully reviewed Dr. Martinez's methodology and concluded that it was sufficiently reliable to allow him to testify to his opinion that FoamFlush caused Bonner's acute symptoms, but not his opinion that it caused her permanent symptoms. In comparing Martinez's conclusions on the causation of Bonner's acute and permanent symptoms, the court noted that Martinez had relied on substantially the same scientific bases for both conclusions, but that his conclusion as to the acute symptoms was more reliable because the temporal connection was a more reliable indicator of a causal relationship with respect to Bonner's acute symptoms than to her permanent symptoms. Dr. Martinez testified that he followed the same procedures with Bonner that he would have followed had he seen her as a patient suspected of having suffered a toxic exposure rather than in preparation for litigation. The consumer information provided by ISP describes inhalation symptoms as ranging from no symptoms to "pallor, nausea, anesthetic or narcotic effects," while Bonner described nausea, headache, tiredness, respiratory problems, skin irritation, and trembling.

Under some circumstances, a strong temporal connection is powerful evidence of causation. See Heller, 167 F.3d at 154 ("if a person were doused with chemical X and immediately thereafter developed symptom Y, the need for published literature showing a correlation between the two may be lessened"). We recognize, as did the district court, that Dr. Martinez considered case reports, which this court held in Turner are not "generally considered reliable evidence of causation," 229 F.3d at 1209 n. 5, among other factual bases in forming his opinion. The district court considered this shortcoming in Dr. Martinez's testimony, but determined that the immediacy of Bonner's acute symptoms to her exposure made Dr. Martinez's opinion on causation reliable enough to pass Rule 702 muster.

ISP's contentions notwithstanding, it was not necessary that Bonner's experts quantify the amount of FoamFlush to which she was exposed in order to demonstrate that she was exposed to a toxic level of BLO. See Wright, 91 F.3d at 1106. It is sufficient for a plaintiff to prove that she was exposed to a quantity of the toxin that "exceeded safe levels." Bednar, 147 F.3d at 740. Bonner presented witnesses who testified that her exposure to FoamFlush was of a duration and of a volume sufficient to support a conclusion that she inhaled and/or absorbed through her skin at least a quarter of a teaspoon of FoamFlush when she was sprayed with it. Dr. Martinez's conclusion that Bonner suffered a more severe acute reaction than those previously documented may have been novel; nonetheless, the district court conducted a thoughtful and thorough inquiry into its validity, and we find nothing in the record to suggest that it was the result of methodology so unreliable as to render its admission an abuse of discretion. See Glastetter, 252 F.3d at 992.

Dr. Singer

ISP argues that the district court abused its discretion when it permitted Dr. Singer to testify that FoamFlush caused Bonner permanent injury. Dr. Singer testified that, as a result of her exposure to FoamFlush, Bonner suffered permanent organic brain dysfunction manifesting itself in Parkinsonian physical symptoms, cognitive impairments, and personality disorders. Dr. Singer stated that he followed normal procedures for evaluating patients who might be suffering from toxic exposure. He testified that ingested doses of GHB, BLO's metabolite, as small as a quarter of a teaspoon can have toxic effects, and that inhalation is a more potent exposure mechanism than is ingestion. ISP contends that Dr. Singer's opinion that FoamFlush could cause injuries like Bonner's was unreliable, pointing to a number of alleged infirmities. The testimony, it argues, should have been excluded because Dr. Singer's theory was developed for litigation, was not subjected to peer review, has not appeared in scientific literature, and is not supported by epidemiological studies. Moreover, ISP contends, the text relied on by Dr. Singer notes that not all organic solvents have similar toxic effects. Additionally, Dr. Singer was unable to offer a threshold exposure amount for injury to occur, failed to determine how much FoamFlush Bonner was exposed to, failed to rule out other possible causes of her injury, and failed to follow established guidelines for diagnosing brain injury.

Our role is not to determine whether Dr. Singer's opinion was correct; that was for the jury to decide. [Cc] Nor is it our task to duplicate the district court's analysis of the scientific validity of expert testimony, for the gatekeeping function is reserved to the district court. General Electric, 522 U.S. at 142–143, 118 S.Ct. 512. We perform only the comparatively narrow analysis of whether the district court's determination that the opinion was sufficiently grounded in "good science" to assist the jury constituted an abuse of that court's discretion. See National Bank of Commerce, 191 F.3d at 862–63. ISP's attacks on Dr. Singer's testimony indicate no more than that his conclusion is not yet established as fact in the scientific community. ISP has not indicated that any scientific theory or studies indicate that BLO is incapable of causing permanent damage. See Hose, 70 F.3d at 976. ISP presented its own experts to rebut Dr. Singer's testimony. The district court conducted an exacting review of the science involved and correctly concluded that, because Dr. Singer's methodology was scientifically valid, the scientific questions were best addressed by allowing each side to present its experts and then submitting their opinions to the jury.

ISP contends on appeal that Dr. Singer was not qualified to offer opinions about the impact of FoamFlush on Bonner because he has no degree in toxicology and has done no formal academic work in toxicology. This argument was not presented to the district court, whose pre-trial order noted that "[t]he credentials of the experts are not questioned." Accordingly, we decline to consider this argument. See Hogan v. Apfel, 239 F.3d 958, 961 n. 3 (8th Cir.2001).

ISP's sufficiency of the evidence argument is based on the premise that the expert testimony should have been excluded, and that without it, Bonner did not meet her burden of proof on causation, thus entitling ISP to judgment as a matter of law. Because the district court did not abuse its discretion in admitting the expert witnesses' testimony, it thus did not err in denying the post-trial motion for judgment as a matter of law.

We have reviewed ISP's other contentions, and we conclude that the evidence was sufficient to support the verdict and that the district court did not abuse its discretion regarding the proffered jury instructions. ISP's final contention is that the district court abused its discretion when it denied ISP's motion for a new trial based on an excessive verdict. A verdict should be set aside as excessive only when it is so excessive that it shocks the conscience. Drotzmanns, Inc. v. McGraw–Hill, Inc., 500 F.2d 830, 835 (8th Cir.1974). In reviewing the district court's decision, we give great deference to its judgment, because the district court has the benefit of hearing the testimony and observing the demeanor of the witnesses throughout the trial. Sanford v. Crittenden Mem'l Hosp., 141 F.3d 882, 884 (8th Cir.1998). In this case, the jury heard evidence that Bonner's past and future earnings losses were expected to total some $600,000, and that she could be expected to suffer from disabling physical and psychological problems for the remainder of her twenty-five year life expectancy. In light of this evidence, we agree with the district court's determination that an award of $2.2 million does not shock the conscience.

The judgment is affirmed.

c. Rigorous Standards of Sufficiency: The Bendectin Litigation

BROCK v. MERRELL DOW PHARMACEUTICALS, INC.

United States Court of Appeals, Fifth Circuit, 1989.
874 F.2d 307.

GARZA, J.

Mr. & Mrs. Floyd Brock filed suit in federal district court on behalf of their minor child, Rachel Brock, to recover damages for birth defects that allegedly resulted from Mrs. Brock's ingestion during her pregnancy of the anti-nausea drug Bendectin, which is manufactured by Merrell–Dow Pharmaceuticals, Inc. ("Merrell–Dow"). The Brocks obtained a jury verdict in the amount of $550,000 against Merrell–Dow, representing $240,000 in compensatory damages and $310,000 in punitive damages. Merrell–Dow appeals that verdict here, arguing that the Brocks did not present sufficient evidence to allow the jury to conclude that Bendectin caused Rachel Brock's birth defect. After reviewing the record and decisions of other courts confronted with similar suits regarding Bendectin, we hold that Merrell–Dow was entitled to judgment notwithstanding the verdict, and the judgment in favor of the Brocks is therefore reversed and the case will be dismissed.

BACKGROUND

Mrs. Brock conceived Rachel Brock on or around July 2, 1981. On July 28, 1981, Mrs. Brock began to experience morning sickness, and she began to take Bendectin, a prescription drug manufactured by Defendant, Merrell–Dow. Rachel Brock was born on March 19, 1982 with a limb reduction defect known as Poland's Syndrome, which is recognized by a shortening or absence of fingers with a decrease in the corresponding pectoralis muscle on one side.

Mr. and Mrs. Brock filed a diversity suit against Merrell–Dow on behalf of their daughter in the U.S. District Court for the Eastern District of Texas. The complaint alleged theories of improper inspection, design defect, and failure to warn. Causation was a hotly contested issue, with both sides presenting expert testimony and studies regarding the possible teratogenicity[161] of Bendectin. At the end of trial, Merrell–Dow moved for a directed verdict, arguing that there was no credible evidence tending to show that Bendectin causes birth defects. Merrell–Dow's motion was denied, and the issue of whether Bendectin caused Rachel Brock's birth defect was given to the jury. The jury found for the Brocks, and awarded both compensatory and punitive damages. Merrell–Dow then moved for judgment notwithstanding the verdict, and that motion was denied. Merrell–Dow here appeals the denial of its motions for directed verdict and for judgment notwithstanding the verdict.

STANDARD FOR DETERMINING SUFFICIENCY OF THE EVIDENCE

The standard for granting a judgment notwithstanding the verdict is the same as that governing rulings on directed verdicts: judgment notwithstanding the verdict is proper only when there can be only one reasonable conclusion drawn from the evidence. * * * Viewing the evidence in the light most favorable to the party against whom the motion is made, the court must give that party the benefit of all reasonable inferences from the evidence.

These general and abstract formulations lose much of their usefulness, however, when we attempt to apply them to the concrete factual situation at hand. One certainly might infer from the evidence in the case that Bendectin causes birth defects, and further that Bendectin caused Rachel Brock's limb reduction defect—in fact, the jury concluded that this very thing occurred. However, the court must determine whether this is a reasonable inference to be drawn from the evidence presented, and the formulae provide us with little guidance as to what constitutes a reasonable, as opposed to unreasonable, inference that a jury could draw from the evidence. Ultimately, the "correctness" of our decision that there was insufficient evidence presented by plaintiff on the issue of whether Bendectin caused Rachel Brock's limb reduction defect to enable a jury to draw a reasonable inference may be just a matter of opinion, but hopefully the reasoning below will persuade others of the insights of our perspective.

The first problem is that there is often no consensus in the medical community regarding whether a given substance is teratogenic; this is the case with Bendectin. Moreover, while we now recognize some of the many factors which can cause birth defects, medical science is now

---

161. A teratogen is a substance that causes birth defects.

unable, and will undoubtedly remain unable for the foreseeable future, to trace a known birth defect back to its precipitating cause. The second problem, in addition to the problem of unknowability, is that juries are asked to resolve these questions, upon which even our brightest medical minds disagree, in order to resolve the case at hand and decide whether the plaintiff is entitled to recovery, and in so doing must necessarily resort to speculation.

Under the traditional approach to scientific evidence, courts would not peer beneath the reasoning of medical experts to question their reasoning. Confronted, as we now are, with difficult medical questions, courts must critically evaluate the reasoning process by which the experts connect data to their conclusions in order for courts to consistently and rationally resolve the disputes before them. Moreover, in mass torts the same issue is often presented over and over to juries in different cases, and the juries often split both ways on the issue. The effect of this is to create a state of uncertainty among manufacturers contemplating the research and development of new, and potentially lifesaving drugs. Appellate courts, if they take the lead in resolving those questions upon which juries will go both ways, can reduce some of the uncertainty which can tend to produce a sub-optimal amount of new drug development.

We are not without precedent in our approach to this problem. The case before us parallels in many respects the recently conducted Agent Orange Litigation. In those cases, plaintiffs attempted to prove that exposure to Agent Orange, a defoliant used during the Vietnam War, had caused them adverse health effects. Judge Weinstein granted summary judgment against opt-out plaintiffs on the basis that they had been unable to prove that exposure to low levels of dioxin caused their health problems. Although plaintiffs had provided the affidavits of experts indicating that exposure to Agent Orange had caused their health problems, the court attacked the reasoning of the experts and found it to be inadequate.

Courts have not always been so willing to analyze the reasoning employed by experts to reach their conclusions. [The court describes *Ferebee*].

The District of Columbia Circuit retreated from this approach recently when it considered, in a Bendectin case, the very same issue we are addressing here. In Richardson by Richardson v. Richardson–Merrell, Inc., 857 F.2d 823 (D.C.Cir.1988), the D.C. Circuit affirmed the lower court's grant of judgment notwithstanding the verdict to defendant. In its discussion of its approach to resolving the conflicting expert testimony in favor of defendant, the court opined that "[e]xpert witnesses are indispensible in a case such as this. But that is not to say that the court's hands are inexorably tied, or that it must accept uncritically any sort of opinion espoused by an expert merely because his credentials render him qualified to testify." The court then proceeded to look behind the conclusion of plaintiff's expert and found his reasoning inadequate.

In distinguishing *Ferebee*, the court narrowly interpreted the case to apply only where the causation issue is novel and "stands at the frontier of current medical and epidemilogical inquiry." The Bendectin cases are different, opined the D.C. Circuit, in that there is a wealth of published epidemiological data, none of which has concluded that the drug is teratogenic. Thus, in *Richardson,* the court affirmed its willingness to look behind the conclusions of experts, at least in cases which are not at the frontier of epidemiological inquiry. We too, have chosen to take the same approach as the *Richardson* court, and in the next section we will present our analysis of the reasoning employed by the expert witnesses in this case.

SUFFICIENCY OF THE EVIDENCE PRESENTED

Undoubtedly, the most useful and conclusive type of evidence in a case such as this is epidemiological studies. Epidemiology attempts to define a relationship between a disease and a factor suspected of causing it—in this case, ingestion of Bendectin during pregnancy. To define that relationship, the epidemiologist examines the general population, comparing the incidence of the disease among those people exposed to the factor in question to those not exposed. The epidemiologist then uses statistical methods and reasoning to allow her to draw a biological inference between the factor being studied and the disease's etiology.

One difficulty with epidemiologic studies is that often several factors can cause the same disease. Birth defects are known to be caused by mercury, nicotine, alcohol, radiation, and viruses, among other factors. When epidemiologists compare the birth defect rates for women who took Bendectin during pregnancy against those who did not take Bendectin during pregnancy, there is a chance that the distribution of the other causal factors may not be even between the two groups. Usually, the larger the size of the sample, the more likely that random chance will lead to an even distribution of these factors among the two comparison groups, unless there is a dependence between some of the other factors and the factor being studied. For example, there would be a dependence between variables if women who took Bendectin during pregnancy were more or less likely to smoke than women who did not take Bendectin. Another source of error in epidemiological studies is selective recall—i.e., women who have children with birth defects may be more likely to remember taking Bendectin during pregnancy than those women with normal children. Fortunately, we do not have to resolve any of the above questions, since the studies presented to us incorporate the possibility of these factors by use of a confidence interval. The purpose of our mentioning these sources of error is to provide some background regarding the importance of confidence intervals.

In this case, the parties described the results of epidemiologic studies in terms of two numbers: a relative risk and a confidence interval. The relative risk is a number which describes the increased or decreased incidence of the disease in question in the population exposed to the factor as compared to the control population not exposed to the factor. In this case, the relative risk describes the increased or decreased incidence of birth defects in the group of women who took Bendectin versus women who did not take Bendectin. A relative risk of 1.0 means that the incidence of birth defects in the two groups were the same. A relative risk greater than 1.0 means that there were more birth defects in the group of women who took Bendectin.

Just because an epidemiological study concludes that a relative risk is greater than 1.0 does not establish that the factor caused the disease. If the confidence interval is so great that it includes the number 1.0, then the study will be said to show no statistically significant association between the factor and the disease. For example, if a study concluded that the relative risk for Bendectin was 1.30, which is consistent with a 30% elevated risk of harm, but the confidence interval was from 0.95 to 1.82, then no statistically significant conclusions could be drawn from this study because the relative risk, when adjusted by the confidence interval, includes 1.0. Again, it is important to remember that the confidence interval attempts to express mathematically the magnitude of possible error, due to the above mentioned sources as well as others, and therefore a study with a relative risk of greater than 1.0 must always be considered in light of its confidence interval before one can draw conclusions from it.

The Brocks relied on a reanalysis conducted by Dr. Jay Glasser of the previously conducted Heinonen study. The Heinonen study, which was conducted by Professor O.P. Heinonen under the auspices of the U.S. National Institute of Neurological and Communicative Disorders, was based on over 50,000 pregnancy records collected in the United States. Dr. Heinonen, in analyzing these records, found that approximately 1,000 women had taken Bendectin during the first four months of their pregnancies. 63 of those women had infants with malformations as opposed to 3,200 out of 49,000 who had not taken Bendectin. This yielded a relative risk of 0.97 with confidence limits from 0.75 to 1.26. Therefore, this study does not support the proposition that Bendectin causes birth defects.

The Heinonen study considered as birth defects all malformations, of which limb reduction defects of the type experienced by Rachel Brock are a subset. Dr. Glasser's reanalysis of the data used in the Heinonen study only considered limb reduction defects. That study found a relative risk of 1.49. However, Dr. Glasser admits that the confidence interval was from 0.17 to 3; this renders the study statistically insignificant. The plaintiffs did not offer one statistically significant (one whose confidence interval did not include 1.0) study that concludes that Bendectin is a human teratogen. No published epidemiological study has found a statistically significant increased risk between exposure to Bendectin and birth defects. One of plaintiff's experts, Dr. Snodgrass, conceded that he was not aware of any such studies. Transcript at 198–99. Nor have any such studies been presented to the other two federal appeals courts which have considered this matter.

Although we find Dr. Glasser's results inconclusive due to the fact that the confidence intervals include 1.0, we further note that Dr. Glasser has not published his study or conclusions for the purposes of peer review. While we do not hold that this failure, in and of itself, renders his conclusions inadmissible, courts must nonetheless be especially skeptical of medical and other scientific evidence that has not been subjected to thorough peer review. Clearly, "the examination of a scientific study by a cadre of lawyers is not the same as its examination by others trained in the field of science or medicine."

We find, in this case, the lack of *conclusive* epidemiological proof to be fatal to the Brock's case. While we do not hold that epidemiologic proof is a necessary element in all toxic tort cases, it is certainly a very important element. This is especially true when the only other evidence is in the form of animal studies of questionable applicability to humans.
* * *

The Brocks have also introduced animal studies in order to prove that Bendectin is a teratogen.

* * *

We need not address at length the animal studies presented by plaintiffs below, except to note several of the more important studies and their methodological flaws. The plaintiffs presented an in vitro study conducted by Drs. Hassell and Horigan. This study used cells cut from the limbs of mice and chickens which were then exposed to various test compounds, including Bendectin. According to plaintiff's experts, limb bud cells which normally form in six days were reduced if those cells were exposed to Bendectin; these limb bud cells ultimately form the arms and legs. However, Dr. Hassell himself cautioned that the body may break down doxylamine, the active ingredient in Bendectin, into a metabolic product which may differ from the pure test compound. Thus, human limb bud cells in a fetus may not be exposed to doxylamine, but rather the metabolic product of doxylamine. Moreover, extrapolation of these findings to humans cannot be done without knowing the dosage level and the corresponding drug level in the bloodstream of the mother. Taking the concept of metabolic products one step further, the plaintiff introduced the testimony of Drs. Snodgrass and Newman, who hypothesized that the human body breaks down doxylamine into less complex molecules called metabolites. These metabolites, some of which are negatively charged, are attracted to the relatively alkaline embryotic fluids, and ultimately bond with the cells in the embryo, producing tissue damage. However, both experts admitted that different species of animals metabolize chemicals differently, and that there are no studies which show that doxylamine is broken down by humans into toxic metabolites. Thus, we must view the limb bud tests as quite speculative.

* * *

Dr. McBride, another expert called by plaintiffs, conducted research in Australia, exposing white rabbits and marmosets to high doses of doxylamine—up to 500 times the normal human dose. Thirteen of 18 of the rabbits died due to either the toxic effects of doxylamine or the improper insertion of gavage tubes which were used to administer the doxylamine to the rabbits. Of the marmosets, all four which were given high doses of doxylamine (500 times the human dosage) aborted their fetuses, and it was impossible to tell if those fetuses were malformed since the aborted fetus is generally eaten by the mother. Dr. McBride hypothesized that the abortions were the result of the teratogenic effect of doxylamine, rather than the high dosage. However, the fifth marmoset was given a lesser dose (100 times the human dosage), and two of the three fetuses later examined lacked a hind leg. On the basis of this, Dr. McBride concluded that doxylamine is a teratogen. He hypothesized that Bendectin, an anticholinergic drug, reduces the amount of acetylcholine, a neurotransmitter released by nerve cells, in the embryo. If the amount of acetylcholine in the embryo is diminished, the trophic effect on body growth is interfered with. Essentially, Dr. McBride speculated that the development of body tissue depends on the initial development of the nervous system. He cited another hypothesis, that of Professor Alexander Karczman, as supporting his theory of the anticholinergic action of doxylamine. However, the theory regarding the effects of doxylamine on acetylcholine, the nervous system and, ultimately, tissue development is nothing more than unproven medical speculation lacking any sort of consensus. Assuredly, one day in the future, medical science may have a clearer understanding of the mechanics of tissue development in the fetus. However, that is not the case today, and speculation unconfirmed by epidemiologic proof cannot form the basis for causation in a court of law.

In light of the evidence presented, we are convinced that the Brocks did not present sufficient evidence regarding causation to allow a trier of fact to make a reasonable inference that Bendectin caused Rachel Brock's limb reduction defect. We expect that our decision here will have a precedential effect on other cases pending in this circuit which allege Bendectin as the cause of birth defects. Hopefully, our decision will have the effect of encouraging district judges faced with medical and epidemiologic proof in subsequent toxic tort cases to be especially vigilant in scrutinizing the basis, reasoning, and *conclusiveness* of studies presented by both sides. However, we do not wish this case to stand as a bar to future Bendectin cases in the event that new and *conclusive* studies emerge which would give a jury a firmer basis on which to determine the issue of causation.

Reversed.

Notes and Questions

1. The subsequent history of *Brock* is fascinating. On a motion for rehearing en banc, the same panel, treating it as a motion for rehearing by the panel, modified its opinion in two respects. See 884 F.2d 166 (5th Cir.1989). The *underscored* language in the last paragraph of the opinion

and on the prior page originally appeared as "the lack of *conclusive* epidemiological proof," but was modified to read "statistically significant epidemiological proof." What is the importance of the court's replacing references to "conclusive epidemiological proof," with "statistically significant epidemiological proof?"

2. The Fifth Circuit then considered a rehearing en banc, with the court deciding 8 to 6 to deny the rehearing. 884 F.2d 167 (5th Cir.1989). Judge Reavley in his dissent from the denial of the rehearing makes the following statement:

> Six highly qualified and experienced experts testified that Bendectin is a human teratogen, i.e. capable of causing human birth defects. Three of them testified to the opinion that Bendectin was a cause of Rachel Brock's deformation. Their opinions of causation were not the product of faulty syllogisms but were predicated upon medical study and research and upon their explanation of the process by which the doxylamine element in Bendectin can interfere with the development of nerve cells in an embryo. The panel picks at details in the testimony lacking expert consensus, but its characterization of this voluminous expert proof as "speculation" could just as well doom virtually all expert testimony. The panel reaches its climax with the novel declaration that only epidemiological studies can prove causal relation between Bendectin and birth defects, and it enters into the debate with Dr. Glasser on the statistical significance of the Heinonen study. In the absence of expert consensus must we now always await populations studies before a jury verdict may be based upon medical opinion? So says the panel, at least for Bendectin cases. This, despite the testimony here that case reports and laboratory research reveal teratogens and that no epidemiological study has ever discovered a teratogen.

Judge Reavley also commented that the holding calls into question the "Seventh Amendment right to trial by jury." What is the Seventh Amendment argument? Does *Brock* survive *Daubert*? Apparently so, because Justice Blackmun cited it with approval for the proposition that trial judges retain the power to dispose of cases on the basis of the insufficiency of the plaintiff's evidence.

3. Michael Green, Expert Witnesses and Sufficiency of Evidence in Toxic Substances Litigation: The Legacy of Agent Orange and Bendectin Litigation, 86 Nw. L. Rev. 643, 680–82 (1992) offers the following criticism of *Brock*, and its requirement for statistically significant epidemiological studies:

> For most potentially toxic substances, there will not be a solid body of epidemiological evidence on which to rely. Epidemiology is expensive and time consuming, even ethically proscribed in certain contexts. There are thousands upon thousands of synthetic agents being used in the United States that might pose toxic risks, yet only a tiny fraction have been the subject of any epidemiologic inquiry. * * * Imposing a burden of production that includes an epidemiologic threshold will screen out all of these cases, but at a cost of precluding more refined attempts, based on animal studies, structure analysis, available knowledge about biologi-

cal mechanisms and related evidence, to make an assessment of whether there exists a causal relationship.

Toxic causation must be assessed with due regard for the available evidence. Where the epidemiologic record is substantial, reliable, and consistent, the saliency of animal studies or other evidence of toxicity is quite low. However, when epidemiologic evidence is lacking, thin, of questionable validity and ultimately inconclusive, dismissing other toxicological evidence is unjustifiable. The point is that plaintiffs should be required to prove causation by a preponderance of the *available evidence*, not by some predetermined standard that may require nonexistent studies. This means that in every case involving an alleged toxic agent for which a mature epidemiologic record does not exist, analysis of the sufficiency of plaintiff's evidence would begin by considering the universe of available evidence of toxicity. * * * No doubt, opening the courthouse doors to plaintiffs entering with such thin and attenuated evidence and rendering a decision on such a record is discomfiting and unfortunate. But the reality is that stronger and better evidence is unavailable through no fault of anyone and a decision based on the preponderance of the available evidence, rather than imposing an evidentiary threshold, would seem in keeping with the role of the civil justice system.

Even in those instances where a modicum of epidemiologic evidence exists, serious judicial scrutiny of the sort advocated and employed by Judge Weinstein [in the *Agent Orange* litigation discussed below] would require an appreciation for methodological errors and inadequacies in those studies, an ability to assess the validity of a reanalysis of those studies, an understanding of the biological record on mechanisms associated with the disease in question, and a firm grounding in the concept of relative risk, statistical significance and confidence intervals, and their relationship to the preponderance of the evidence standard. One must doubt that a judge will have sufficient expertise to make or review those judgments, especially when ruling on a motion for summary judgment without the benefit of a full hearing to explain these matters.

The *Brock* decision, in ascribing wondrous powers to the concept of statistical significance, contributes to doubts that these matters are ones that reasonably can be mastered by generalist judges. Statistical significance addresses only random error due to the sampling inherent in any epidemiologic study. It cannot and does not speak to systematic error, which requires an informed review of the methodology employed in conducting the study. Moreover, statistical significance is merely an instrument for assisting in evaluating a study, not a truth serum that can be simplistically prescribed. (emphasis in original).

Do you agree with Professor Green's arguments? Is his "preponderance of the *available* evidence" consistent with "role of the civil justice system"? How does he consider plaintiff's burden of proving that defendant did in fact cause the injury? For a contrary view, that requiring statistically significant supportive studies is appropriate, see Bert Black, A Unified Theory of Scientific Evidence, 56 Ford. L. Rev. 595 (1988).

4. *Statistical Significance and Hypothesis Testing. Brock* contained only a cursory reference to the principles of hypothesis testing, by which scientists attempt to "disprove" the null hypothesis that no relationship exists between the chemical studied and the effect observed. Albert Einstein observed that "no amount of experimentation can ever prove me right; a single experiment can prove me wrong." In DeLuca v. Merrell Dow Pharmaceuticals, Inc., 911 F.2d 941 (3d Cir.1990), another Bendectin case, the court describes hypothesis testing and the role of statistical significance in greater detail:

> * * * Epidemiological studies do not provide direct evidence that a particular plaintiff was injured by exposure to a substance. Such studies have the potential, however, of generating circumstantial evidence of cause and effect through a process known as hypothesis testing, a process which "amounts to an attempt to falsify the null hypothesis and by exclusion accept the alternative." K.J. Rothman, Modern Epidemiology 116 (1986) ("Rothman"). The null hypothesis is the hypothesis that there is no association between two studied variables, id.; in this case the key null hypothesis would be that there is no association between Bendectin exposure and an increase in limb reduction defects. The important alternative hypothesis in this case is that Bendectin use is associated with an increased incidence of limb reduction defects.

> * * *

> Epidemiological studies, of necessity, look to the experience of sample groups as indicative of the experience of a far larger population. Epidemiologists recognize, however, that the experience of the sample groups may vary from that of the larger population by chance. Thus, a showing of increased risk for birth defects among women using Bendectin in a particular study does not automatically prove that Bendectin use creates a higher risk of having a child with birth defects because the discrepancy between the exposed and unexposed groups could be the product of chance resulting from the use of only a small sample of the relevant populations. As a result of the acknowledged risk of this so-called "sampling error," researchers typically have rejected the associations suggested by epidemiological data unless those associations survive the rigors of "significance testing." This practice has also found favor in the legal context. A number of judicial opinions, discussed infra, have found Bendectin plaintiffs' causation evidence inadmissible because every published epidemiological study of the relationship of Bendectin exposure to the incidence of birth defects has concluded that there is not a "statistically significant" relationship between these two events.

> Significance testing has a "P value" focus; the P value "indicates the probability, assuming the null hypothesis is true, that the observed data will depart from the absence of association to the extent that they actually do, or to a greater extent, by actual chance." Rothman, supra, at 116. If P is less than .05 (or 5%) a study's finding of a relationship supportive of the alternative hypothesis is considered statistically significant, if P is greater than 5% the relationship is rejected as insignificant. Accordingly, the results of a particular study are reported as simply "significant" or "not significant" or as P<.05 or P>.05.

Use of a .05 P value to determine whether to accept or reject the null hypothesis necessarily enhances one of two types of possible error. Type one error is when the null hypothesis is rejected when it is in fact true. Type two error is when the null hypothesis is in fact false but is not rejected. Rothman notes that at .05, the null hypothesis will "be rejected about 5 per cent of the time when it is true," a relatively small risk of type one error. Unfortunately, the relationship between type one error and type two error is not simple; however, one study in the context of an employment discrimination case concluded that when the risk of type one error equalled 5%, the risk of type two error was 50%. Cohen, Confidence in Probability: Burdens of Persuasion in a World of Imperfect Knowledge, 60 N.Y.U.L.Rev. 329, 411 & n. 116 (1985) (citing Dawson, Investigation of Fact—The Role of the Statistician, 11 Forum 896, 907–08 (1976)). Type one error may be viewed here as the risk of concluding that Bendectin is a teratogen when it is not. Type two error is the risk of concluding that Bendectin is not a teratogen, when it in fact is.

Rothman contends that there is nothing magical or inherently important about .05 significance; rather this is just a common value on the tables scholars use to calculate significance. Rothman, supra, at 117; see also Cohen, supra, at 412 (noting that the .05 level of significance used in the social and physical sciences is a conservative and arbitrary value choice not necessarily valuable in the legal setting). He stresses that the data in a certain study may indicate a strong relationship between two variables but still not be "statistically significant" and that the level of significance which should be required depends on the type of decision being made and the relative values placed on avoiding the two types of risk.

* * *

A confidence interval is a way of graphically representing the probability that the relative risk figure or any other relationship between two studied variables is the actual relationship. The interval is a range of sets of possible values for the true parameter that is consistent with the observed data within specified limits. Rothman, supra, at 119. A 95% confidence interval is constructed with enough width so that one can be confident that it is only 5% likely that the relative risk attained would have occurred if the true parameter, i.e., the actual unknown relationship between the two studied variables, were outside the confidence interval. If a 95% confidence interval thus contains "1", or the null hypothesis, then a researcher cannot say that the results are "statistically significant," that is, that the null hypothesis has been disproved at a .05 level of significance. Kaye, Is Proof of Statistical Significance Relevant? [61 Wash.L.Rev.] at 1348.

The result of a study should be reported, in Rothman's view, by reference to the confidence intervals at various confidence levels, e.g., 90%, 95%, 99%. The inclusion of confidence intervals of a variety of levels reflects Rothman's view that the predominating choice of a 95% confidence level is but an arbitrarily selected convention of his discipline. More importantly, however, Rothman insists that the precise locations of the boundaries of the confidence intervals, the all important focus of "significance testing," are far less important than their size and location. According to Rothman, statistical theory suggests that it is "much more likely that the [true] parameter [i.e., the true relationship between the studied variables] is located centrally within an interval than it is that the parameter is located near the limits of the interval." Rothman, supra, at 124. As such, the primary focus should not be on the ends of an interval but rather on the "approximate position of the interval as a whole on its scale of measurement * * *." Id.

The court in *DeLuca* remanded the case for the district court to reevaluate its ruling on the admissibility of plaintiffs' expert's testimony, including whether significance testing "should be a threshold requirement" for any study purporting to find that Bendectin is a teratogen, and observing that "the root issue it poses is what risk of what type of error the judicial system is willing to tolerate."[162] The relationship between type I and II errors and hypothesis testing is demonstrated in the following tables where type I error and the probability of committing it is designated by the Greek letter ¥ (alpha); type II error and its probability is designated by the Greek letter β (beta).

FOUR POSSIBLE RESULTS OF AN HYPOTHESIS TEST

State of Reality as to Causation	Decision	
	H_0 Acceptable	H_0 Rejected
If H_0 is true	Correct decision. Probability = $1-\alpha$ = confidence level	Type I error. Probability = α
If H_0 is false	Type II error. Probability = β	Correct decision. Probability = $1-\beta$

How would you describe the meaning of type I error in a civil tort case? How does it relate to the plaintiff's burden of proof? What does type II error mean? Are the concerns in civil cases equivalent to those in criminal cases?

In remanding the case, the court in *DeLuca* pointed out that even if plaintiffs' expert's testimony is admitted, summary judgment might nevertheless be appropriate if the *only* evidence plaintiffs offered established a

---

162. This reference to type I and type II error in *DeLuca* is best illustrated by an example from the criminal law, where the jury is being asked to decide between H, the null hypothesis that the defendant is innocent, and the alternative H, that the defendant is guilty. A type I error results if an innocent person is convicted, while a type II error results if a guilty person is acquitted. The jury instruction that "guilt must be proved beyond a reasonable doubt" means that type II is kept very small.

The reciprocal nature of the type I and type II errors is shown by efforts to reduce type I error by use of the exclusionary rule preventing the admission of unfairly prejudicial evidence. This reduces the probability that an innocent person will be convicted but increases the likelihood that a guilty person will go free. The only way type I can be reduced without increasing type II errors is to obtain more evidence (i.e., a larger sample), which makes the distributions more accurate. What are the comparable statements in a civil trial?

relative risk of 2.0 or less, and noted also that statistical significance "may appropriately play some role in deciding" the sufficiency of the evidence. *DeLuca*'s suggestion (in applying New Jersey tort law) that a relative risk greater than 2.0 is essential has been undercut by the New Jersey Supreme Court in Landrigan v. Celotex Corp., 127 N.J. 404, 605 A.2d 1079 (1992).

5. For another Bendectin decision that adopts the insufficiency of the evidence rationale in dismissing plaintiff's claim, see Turpin v. Merrell Dow Pharmaceuticals, 959 F.2d 1349 (6th Cir.1992). In *Turpin,* the court expressed concern with special problems of inconsistency in the mass tort setting:

> For a judicial system founded on the premise that justice and consistency are related ideas, the inconsistent results reached by courts and juries nationwide on the question of causation in Bendectin birth defect cases are of serious concern.

The court stressed the duty of courts to inspect the reasoning of qualified scientific experts before permitting a case to reach the jury and declared flatly that whether Bendectin causes birth defects is "not capable of being proved to the requisite degree of legal probability based on the scientific evidence currently available." It described the inconsistency of outcomes as resulting from two factors: (1) the difficulty of scientists, judges, lawyers, and jurors in knowing what inferences to draw from toxicologic and epidemiologic evidence; and (2) the uncertainty of judges in knowing how far to intrude into the underlying reasoning and methodology adopted by experts. Choosing to pursue a "hard look" doctrine and perform a "close judicial analysis * * * of technical and specialized" proofs, the court exhaustively reviewed a "sampling" of six of the thirty-five epidemiological studies which have failed to find a statistically significant association between Bendectin and birth defects. In a balanced analysis, it identified a number of grounds for attacking the validity of the studies offered by defendant, observing that "Merrell Dow overstates the persuasive power of these statistical studies." Nevertheless, in examining the plaintiff's proofs, the court found that the animal and in vitro studies, while "capable" of showing Bendectin as a "possible" teratogen, failed to meet the plaintiffs' burden of proof:

> The decisive weakness in the plaintiffs' animal studies is that the factual and theoretical bases articulated for the scientific opinions stated will not support a finding that Bendectin more probably than not caused the birth defects here. * * * Here, except for Dr. Palmer's testimony discussed below, the plaintiffs' experts stop short of testifying that Bendectin more probably than not caused the birth defects in babies. They stop short because they have no factual or theoretical basis for a stronger hypothesis. They testify that the animal studies show that Bendectin is "capable of causing," "could cause" or its effects are "consistent with causing" birth defects, not that it probably causes birth defects in general or that it did in this case. In short, they testify to a possibility rather than a probability.

6. *Animal Studies.* What of animal studies referred to in the above cases? Other courts have also questioned the efficacy of relying on animal studies to prove causation. See, e.g., Lynch v. Merrell–National Labs., 830 F.2d 1190 (1st Cir.1987) (animal bioassays "do not have the capability of

proving causation in human beings in the absence of confirmatory epidemiological data"). There exists a vigorous debate within the scientific community as to the efficacy of such studies in serving to predict the effects of
chemicals on humans. Dr. Ellen Silbergeld has described the refusal of some
courts to consider animal studies in determining the potential of toxic
chemicals on human health as the equivalent of placing creationism over
Darwinism. She argues that toxicological studies of animals are indispensable because of the paucity of direct data of chemicals on humans, the
thousands of untested chemicals entering our environment, the importance
of prevention of damage to human health, and the ethical and practical
limitations on obtaining causation data from human research:

> Because of the essentiality of toxicology in understanding and prevent-
> ing human disease, it is unreasonable and inefficient to exclude toxicolo-
> gy from legal decision making. It would separate causation as under-
> stood in medicine from causation as understood in law. The rejection of
> any and all toxicological data from legal decision making merely because
> it is derived from nonhuman organisms is scientifically unreasonable
> because of two powerful concepts in biology, Darwinism and cell theo-
> ry.... To refuse to consider toxicology would be to consider rational the
> decision by a mother to allow her child to drink a substance that had
> just killed her cat on the grounds that no human had yet been harmed
> by it.

She points out further that "excluding toxicology [in making judicial decisions on human causality] has the effect of removing much of the scientifically relevant and useful information from consideration by a court." See
Ellen K. Silbergeld, The Role of Toxicology in Causation: A Scientific
Perspective, 1 Courts, Health Science and the Law 374 (1991); see also, for
similar statements, James Huff et al., Scientific Concepts: Value and Significance of Chemical Carcinogenesis Studies, 31 Ann. Rev. Pharm. Toxicol. 621,
622 (1991). For a view that animal studies are of limited utility in identifying
human carcinogens, see Bruce Ames & Lois Swirsky Gold, Too Many Rodent
Carcinogens: Mitogenesis Increases Mutagenesis, 249 Sci. 970 (1990); C.
Jelleff Carr & Albert C. Kolbye, A Critique of the Use of the Maximum
Tolerated Dose in Bioassays to Assess Cancer Risk from Chemicals, 14 Reg.
Toxicol. & Pharmacol. 78 (1991).

7.   Finally, perhaps the most ringing endorsement of treating supportive epidemiology as an indispensable element of a plaintiff's causation
evidence comes from Judge Weinstein in In re Agent Orange Product
Liability Litigation, 611 F.Supp. 1223, 1231 (E.D.N.Y.1985), where he dismisses a veteran's suit:

> A number of sound epidemiological studies have been conducted on
> the health effects of exposure to Agent Orange. These are the only
> useful studies having any bearing on causation.

> All the other data supplied by the parties rests on surmise and
> inapposite extrapolations from animal studies and industrial accidents.
> It is hypothesized that, predicated on this experience, adverse effects of
> Agent Orange on plaintiffs might at some time in the future be shown to
> some degree of probability.

The available relevant studies have addressed the direct effects of exposure on servicepersons and the indirect effects of exposure on spouses and children of servicepersons. No acceptable study to date of Vietnam veterans and their families concludes that there is a causal connection between exposure to Agent Orange and the serious adverse health effects claimed by plaintiffs.

Has Judge Weinstein overstated the case for epidemiology? How relevant is it that epidemiological studies of Vietnam servicepersons revealed no higher incidences of certain diseases associated with exposure to dioxin?

8. *Some Literature.* There are a number of articles that deal specifically with the role of epidemiological proof in environmental tort litigation which were cited or quoted in the above opinions. See, e.g., Bert Black, A Unified Theory of Scientific Evidence, 56 Fordham L. Rev. 595 (1988); Bert Black and David E. Lilienfeld, Epidemiological Proof in Toxic Tort Litigation, 52 Fordham L. Rev. 732 (1984); Susan R. Poulter, Science and Toxic Torts: Is There a Rational Solution to the Problem of Causation?, 7 High Tech. L. J. 1 (1993); Phantom Risk: Scientific Inference and the Law (Kenneth R. Foster, David E. Bernstein & Peter W. Huber eds. 1993). Michael Dore, A Commentary on the Use of Epidemiological Evidence in Demonstrating Cause-in-Fact, 7 Harv. Envtl. L. Rev. 429 (1983); Khristine L. Hall & Ellen K. Sibergeld, Reappraising Epidemiology: A Response to Mr. Dore, 7 Harv. Envtl. L. Rev. 441 (1983); Daniel S. Farber, Toxic Causation, 71 Minn. L. Rev. 1219 (1987); Troyen Brennan, Helping Courts With Toxic Torts: Some Proposals Regarding Alternative Methods for Presenting and Assessing Scientific Evidence in Common Law Courts, 51 U. Pitt. L. Rev. 1 (1989).

On the application of statistical evidence to litigation more generally, including topics such as statistical significance, standard deviations, "P" values and confidence intervals, see Neil B. Cohen, Conceptualizing Proof and Calculating Probabilities: A Response to Professor Kaye, 73 Cornell L. Rev. 78 (1987); David H. Kaye, Apples and Oranges: Confidence Coefficients and Burdens of Persuasion, 73 Cornell L. Rev. 54 (1987); D. Barnes & J. Conley, Statistical Evidence in Litigation (1986 & 1991 Supp.); Neil B. Cohen, Confidence in Probability: Burdens of Persuasion in a World of Imperfect Knowledge, 60 N.Y.U. L. Rev. 329 (1985); David H. Kaye, Is Proof of Statistical Significance Relevant? 61 Wash. L. Rev. 1833 (1986); 1 Steven M. Crafton, Quantitative Methods for Lawyers (1992).

Problem

A jury awarded Willie Earl Davis $676,000 in damages in a case alleging that his rare kidney disease resulted from exposure to solvents aboard defendants' oil rigs. At issue in the post-trial motion is a jury award to the former oil rig worker, who claimed he contracted Goodpasture's Syndrome from workplace exposure to hydrocarbon solvents aboard rigs owned and operated by Odeco Inc. Davis, a roustabout employed by Odeco, worked aboard 13 different offshore oil rigs between 1980 and 1990. His duties included spray-painting drilling vessels with solvent-based paints. The jury found Odeco liable under the Jones Act for negligence and negligence per se, determining that unseaworthy conditions on seven of the eleven Odeco vessels caused Davis' illness.

Evidence at trial showed the following: Davis began spitting up blood in November 1989, but had no other symptoms of illness. A diagnostic test at the time revealed excess protein and blood in his urine. In February 1990, Davis collapsed while working aboard another oil rig. He was diagnosed to be suffering from respiratory failure attributable to declining kidney function, with the illness diagnosed as Goodpasture's Syndrome, a rare autoimmune disease of the kidneys in which membrane inflammation is accompanied by pulmonary hemorrhaging. There have only been about 500 reported cases since the disease was first diagnosed in 1919.

Davis was discharged from the hospital in March 1990, but suffers permanent kidney damage and residual scarring of the lungs. At trial, Davis contended that Odeco failed "to institute adequate safety measures" to protect workers from hydrocarbon exposure, and failed to comply with regulations, pursuant to a state occupational safety statute, requiring the company to implement and enforce a comprehensive respiratory protection program for employees. Plaintiff's causation experts testified that seven of eight epidemiologic studies on the association between hydrocarbons and Goodpasture's Syndrome "revealed a statistically significant increased risk of contracting the disease" among individuals exposed to hydrocarbons. Those studies showed a relative risk elevation of between 1.09 and 1.47.

Defense causation experts testified that the association between the hydrocarbons and the illness was insufficient to establish a causal relationship. They also testified that the lack of any confirmatory animal data on the alleged relationship further strained the validity of the epidemiologic studies. The defense contended that Davis was the first employee in the company's 39–year history to allege he had the disease. Furthermore, the defense contended, the causes of Goodpasture's Syndrome are primarily hereditary. The defense maintains additionally that Davis' prior work at an auto body repair shop and his cigarette smoking—1 1/2 packs per day for ten years— also could have been a significant contributing cause of the illness.

Based on this record, the defense counsel has filed a motion for a judgment n.o.v. You are the law clerk for the trial judge who has received the motion. How would you rule on the motion? Prepare a memorandum setting forth your ruling and rationale.

d. Note on Exposure as an Element of Causation

1. In proving that substance X caused plaintiff's harm, the plaintiff must prove that he or she was sufficiently exposed to the toxic substance that its harmful characteristics had the opportunity to produce the injuries which plaintiff alleges. In cases involving the nuisance-type model—one landowner discharging a harmful substance and other landowners, usually residential, suffering some type of illness which they attribute to the discharge—proof of actual exposure to the toxic substance can often prove difficult, as the following case illustrates.

2. *Exposure in Nuisance–Model Cases*: A decision that demonstrates the difficulties plaintiffs may experience in proving exposure as integral to the causation question even where their injuries are uncon-

tested and defendants' contamination unquestioned, is Renaud v. Martin Marietta Corp., 749 F.Supp. 1545 (D.Colo.1990), affirmed, 972 F.2d 304 (10th Cir.1992). In granting defendants' motion for summary judgment the court stated: "[P]roof that Martin committed reprehensible acts coupled with evidence of injury is not enough to prevail on a tort claim. * * * Plaintiffs must prove that the reprehensible acts caused, or increased the likelihood of, the alleged injuries."

In *Renaud*, the plaintiffs were residents of an area that drew its water supply from a water treatment plant, one of whose sources was contaminated by defendant's missile operations. Plaintiff's evidence on causation consisted of experts' postulations that waste water containing a concentration of hydrazines and other contaminants had been discharged by Martin Marietta into a creek on a regular basis over an 11–year period and that these contaminants in smaller percentages arrived at the water treatment plant and were thereafter delivered in measurable quantities to the residents' neighborhood. This 11–year postulation by plaintiffs was extrapolated back by their experts from a single water sample, taken from Martin's waste water pond in 1985, two years *after* plaintiffs had received their water from the water treatment plant. The trial court concluded that an 11–year fate and transport model, supported by only a single data point, would not suffice to support a jury finding that contaminated water from Martin's plant had probably reached plaintiffs' taps over critical periods at levels sufficient to cause their injuries. The Tenth Circuit concurred that the trial court's refusal to infer exposure on the basis of a single water sample taken from defendant's pond was correct.

To overcome the nearly insurmountable difficulties in proving directly that they had been exposed to sufficient quantities of hydrazines to cause their injuries, the district court had stated that plaintiffs could also have offered circumstantial evidence in the form of epidemiological studies. The idea is that if an epidemiologic study of the residents living in a community reflects a significantly higher incidence of particular disease over the expected rates occurring in the general population, then it is possible to infer that they were exposed to the toxic chemicals. Plaintiffs argued that they should not be required to introduce epidemiologic evidence. However, this placed them in an untenable position because they needed such studies to serve as circumstantial evidence of exposure. Indeed, they sought to criticize the one study that had been performed showing a twofold higher rate of childhood cancer because the expert who performed it found it to be inconclusive due to the small sample involved. Finally, plaintiffs did not attempt their own epidemiological study because they thought it would be "futile," hence destroying any opportunity of circumstantially establishing exposure and causation.

It is important to understand that epidemiology would not be used here to establish a causal association between chemical hydrazines and cancer, which was not a seriously contested issue in the case; but rather to show a sufficiently greater incidence of cancer above expected rates to create circumstantial evidence that the residents of the area were in fact exposed to hydrazines.

Renaud stands as cogent evidence that nuisance model cases are extremely difficult for plaintiffs because of the multi-layered causation steps that must be overcome. *Renaud* illustrates that plaintiffs must be able to demonstrate actual exposure and dose at levels sufficient to cause the kinds of injuries alleged, and that such proof may be extremely difficult to develop.

How should plaintiffs go about proving exposure in nuisance model cases long after the alleged exposure occurred? In many cases the release of an exposure to toxic substances is documented by governmental agencies at the time it is occurring, making proof of this element more manageable. In Chapter 10 we consider The Agency for Toxic Substances and Disease Registry, created by the Comprehensive Environmental Response, Compensation and Liability Act, 42 U.S.C.A § 9601 et seq., which is designed to help address this very problem where hazardous waste sites are involved. See Ammons v. Wysong & Miles Co., 110 N.C.App. 739, 431 S.E.2d 524 (1993) (plaintiffs' strict liability action dismissed because they could not prove contaminants in their wells had migrated from leaks in nearby chemical storage tanks); Berry v. Armstrong Rubber Co., 780 F.Supp. 1097 (S.D.Miss.1991); Amorello v. Monsanto Corp., 186 Mich.App. 324, 463 N.W.2d 487 (1990).

3. *The Frequency, Regularity and Proximity Test.* In asbestos litigation, a frequently contested issue has been whether the plaintiff was actually and significantly exposed to the defendants' asbestos-containing products in the workplace. The courts developed a three-pronged "frequency, regularity and proximity" test, first articulated in Lohrmann v. Pittsburgh Corning Corp., 782 F.2d 1156 (4th Cir.1986), which requires that the plaintiff offer "evidence of exposure to a specific product on a regular basis over some extended period of time in proximity to where plaintiff actually worked." For example, in Fiffick v. GAF Corp., 412 Pa.Super. 261, 603 A.2d 208 (1992), the defendant Owens–Corning Fiberglass (OCF) manufactured Kaylo insulation. After 1972, OCF stopped using asbestos in the production of Kaylo. From 1947 until 1985, Fiffick worked at a steel plant where Kaylo was allegedly used. He sued OCF, among others, alleging that he had suffered injury from workplace exposure to airborne asbestos fibers. During discovery, plaintiff was unable to demonstrate how often he was exposed to Kaylo before the late 1970s. The trial court entered summary judgment in favor of OCF.

The Superior Court affirmed, holding that proof of frequent, regular work at a site near a defendant's asbestos-containing product is necessary to defeat a summary judgment motion on a claim alleging workplace exposure to asbestos. The court rejected plaintiff's argument that a jury could infer his exposure to Kaylo before 1972 based on expert testimony that asbestos fibers drift after they are released into the air. Although fiber drift testimony is valuable in meeting the proximity prong of the frequency-regularity-proximity test, it does not show how often a particular product was used or how often a worker was present where fibers may have drifted. Such evidence must be produced first in order to lay a proper foundation for introduction of expert testimony on fiber drift. Here, plaintiff had failed to show when, where, and how frequently asbestos-containing Kaylo had been used or that he had worked near it.

In contrast, in Slaughter v. Southern Talc Co., 949 F.2d 167 (5th Cir.1991), several hundred tire plant workers sued Owens–Corning Fiberglass Corporation (OCF), alleging workplace exposure to Kaylo. The trial court granted OCF summary judgment on the ground that plaintiffs had presented no eyewitness testimony that they had worked near Kaylo insulation.

The Fifth Circuit Court of Appeals reversed, acknowledging that the appropriate test for a minimum showing of exposure in asbestos cases is the "frequency-regularity-proximity test." However, it found sufficient, evidence showing that (1) Kaylo had been delivered to the plant, (2) Kaylo had been installed all over pipes in the plant, and (3) all plaintiffs had worked near the plant's insulated pipes. Thus, if a jury believed plaintiffs' circumstantial evidence, it could reasonably infer sufficient proximity to OCF's asbestos product to establish causation. See also, applying this theory, Blair v. Eagle–Picher Industries, 962 F.2d 1492 (10th Cir.1992); Robertson v. Allied Signal, Inc., 914 F.2d 360 (3d Cir.1990) (fiber drift may satisfy the proximity requirement, but not the regularity and frequency requirements); Thacker v. UNR Industries, 151 Ill.2d 343, 177 Ill.Dec. 379, 603 N.E.2d 449 (1992) (upholding a verdict against Manville which had supplied 3 percent of the asbestos material used at the plant, concluding that 3 percent of total dust was not insignificant as a matter of law, in light of medical evidence indicating that even a slight exposure could cause cancer, and in light of the total volume of asbestos at the UNR plant). Should expert testimony be required to show that asbestos fibers could have drifted from one section of a plant to the area where plaintiff worked regularly? How best can a defendant rebut the fiber drift hypothesis? Will evidence that plaintiff worked at job sites where other employees handled asbestos-containing insulation products be sufficient? See Augustine v. A.C. & S., Inc., 971 F.2d 129 (8th Cir.1992).

B. PLAINTIFF INDETERMINACY

In many respects, the question of whether the substance was capable of producing plaintiff's injury and whether we can differentiate the plaintiff from the background population that would have otherwise contracted the disease are closely related. Nevertheless, the focus of the Bendectin litigation was less on differentiating plaintiffs from all of the children suffering birth defects and more on whether the drug was or was not a teratogen. In this section our focus is on how the courts perform the function of differentiating between background cases of the disease and those attributable to the toxic exposure and what devices courts might use to facilitate the process and yet preserve the basic goals of tort liability rules. The first approach, as to which *Allen v. United States* is the paradigm, seeks to solve the indeterminate plaintiff problem by combining three evidentiary forms: (1) burden shifting; (2) strong probabilistic proof; and (3) an overlay of relevant particularistic or anecdotal proof. The second approach, described in the *Agent Orange* litigation, rejects the possibility of individualized proof and relies solely on classwide proportional causation proofs.

1. INDIVIDUALIZED MODEL: *ALLEN v. UNITED STATES*

Allen v. United States, 588 F.Supp. 247 (D.Utah 1984), reversed on other grounds 816 F.2d 1417 (10th Cir.1987), cert. denied 484 U.S. 1004, 108 S.Ct. 694, 98 L.Ed.2d 647 (1988) was an action brought against the United States government under the Federal Tort Claims Act (FTCA) by approximately 1200 named plaintiffs, alleging some 500 deaths and injuries as a result of radioactive fallout from open air atomic bomb tests held in Nevada in the 1950s and early 1960s. The district court selected twenty-four "bellwether" claims and held a full trial on those claims to develop a framework for managing the remainder of the claims. The court entered final judgment in favor of the government on fourteen of the claims, against the government on nine, and left one unresolved. Portions of the court's opinion (the entire opinion is 230 pages) address the complex questions of causation raised by the court's determination of whether the ionized radiation from the nuclear tests was the cause in fact of the variety of physical injuries and illnesses, including death, suffered by the twenty-four selected individual plaintiffs.

First, relevant for our purposes, was the court's description of what it meant by the statement that "radiation causes cancer": "We simply mean that a population exposed to a certain dose of radiation will show a greater incidence of cancer than the same population would have shown in the absence of the added radiation." Second, the court pointed out several reasons why causation is more problematic in these mass exposure cases, including the long latency periods, the possible involvement of "intervening causes," and the "non-specific nature" of the injury. Relying on J. Gofman, Radiation and Human Health (1981), Judge Jenkins found that radiation-induced cancer cannot be distinguished from cancer in the same organs attributable to natural, unknown, or "spontaneous" causes or sources. To overcome these difficulties, the court seeks to establish "exclusive factual connections"; for example, that the defendant engaged in particular risk-creating conduct by the manner in which it conducted the tests and its failure to provide either warnings to or monitoring of exposed persons and that the plaintiffs' injuries are consistent with the kind of harm that one would predict and observe as one of the risks created. The court adopted this test of establishing the necessary legal connection:

> Where the defendant who negligently creates a radiological hazard which puts an identifiable population group at increased

risk, a member of that group at risk develops a biological condition which is consistent with having been caused by the hazard to which he has been negligently subjected, such consistency having been demonstrated by substantial, appropriate, persuasive, and connecting factors, a fact finder may reasonably conclude that the hazard caused the condition absent persuasive proof to the contrary offered by the defendant.

How would you interpret this test? Does it mean that once the plaintiff establishes generic causation by the appropriate factors, the burden shifts to the defendant to disprove individual causation? Among the connecting factors it included: (1) the probability that the plaintiff was exposed to ionizing radiation from the Nevada Test Site (NTS) at rates in excess of the natural background radiation; (2) that the plaintiff's injury is of the type consistent with those known to be caused by radiation exposure; and (3) that the plaintiff resided in proximity to the NTS during the relevant period.

In addition, the court identified other relevant factors such as the time and extent of exposure, radiation sensitive factors such as age, sensitivity of certain organs or tissues to radiation, estimation of doses of radiation, consistency between latency period and known cancer etiology, and statistical incidence of the injury greater than that which would be expected in the population group. Further, the court applied a "substantial factor" test of causation, relying upon Restatement (Second) of Torts § 433 and treated its legal connecting factors approach as satisfying a substantial factor causation test. With such a test the plaintiff need not conclusively eliminate all other possible causes of the harm.

In a section entitled "problems with mathematical proof," Judge Jenkins rejected a reliance solely on statistical proof, even if such proof suggests that a particular plaintiff's disease is more likely than not to have been caused by the defendant's conduct, criticizing such an approach as reincarnating the "but for" test, which he explicitly rejected.

Judge Jenkins then explored the dose-response relationships between exposure to ionized radiation and the kind of plaintiffs' injuries, finding the following factors relevant: (1) type of radiation; (2) type of cancer; (3) personal variables of the individual exposed—age, sex, and physical characteristics; and (4) interactions with other stimuli and environmental factors. Unlike some chemical agents, medical scientists have not established any "safe" or threshold level of exposure for radiation; therefore cases could not simply be dismissed on the basis that the plaintiff's dose of the chemical or agent was below that threshold level. Despite the application of a substantial factor test, the consideration of multiple factors, the refusal to rely solely on statistical proof, and an obvious distaste for the government's role in conducting the tests without adequate precautions to the affected populations, it denied recovery to the majority of the twenty-four claimants.

The court treated each claimant individually and the reasons given for rejecting their claims varied; some claimants did not suffer the type of cancer which was shown to be caused by radiation exposure; one did not die from a provable cancer at all. Indeed, the rejection of ten of the fourteen claimants denied recovery were largely attributable to their inability to show an increased incidence of their specific type of cancers in the exposed population above the background level based on population studies.

For example, one man was denied recovery because the evidence showed an increase of stomach cancer among women from radiation exposure, but not among men; and the existence of a strong correlation among men between stomach cancer and other factors, such as diet and age, which contraindicated radiation as the cause. In contrast, the evidence supporting recovery for one woman, Peggy Orton, seemed overwhelming—a 240 to 340 percent increase in childhood leukemia in certain counties and age groups, a consistent latency period, and close proximity to the testing site.

Notes and Questions

1. What judicial support exists for the court's burden shifting in this case? Are the defendant identification cases such as Summers v. Tice, 33 Cal.2d 80, 199 P.2d 1 (1948) (the two hunters case), and Sindell v. Abbott Laboratories, 26 Cal.3d 588, 163 Cal.Rptr. 132, 607 P.2d 924 (1980) relevant? The court also relied upon Haft v. Lone Palm Hotel, 3 Cal.3d 756, 91 Cal.Rptr. 745, 478 P.2d 465 (1970), in which a father and son drowned at a motel where defendant, contrary to local ordinance, failed to provide a lifeguard or warnings; the California Supreme Court shifted the burden to defendant on the ground that the reason the causes of death were unknown was precisely because of defendant's negligence in not having a lifeguard present. Can you analogize the motel to the United States government in *Allen* ?

2. In determining that the government's testing program was a substantial factor in several of the leukemia cases, the court did not make any finding with respect to the degree of radiation exposure suffered by each of the plaintiffs. There was little evidence on this subject and, not surprisingly, a wide divergence in expert opinion. In Peggy Orton's case, for example, plaintiffs' expert testified that the absorbed dose of her bone marrow was 14.1 rads, while the government expert estimated 0.5 rads. Differences of this magnitude are important. The radioepidemiologic tables prepared by a National Institute of Health Ad Hoc Working Group estimated that the likelihood of developing leukemia by age 13 for a female exposed at age 0 is 4.6% for 1 rad, 34% for 10 rads, and 90% for 100 rads.

The Orphan Drug Act, 21 U.S.C.A. § 360ee, directed the U.S. Department of Health and Human Resources to construct radioepidemiologic tables to show the probabilities that various dosages of radiation caused various types of cancer. See Report of the National Institutes of Health Ad Hoc Working Group to Develop Radioepidemiologic Tables, NIH Pub. No. 85–2748 (1985). The tables include a recommendation that where the government's "assigned share" of the risk is more than 50% full recovery be allowed; where the assigned share is between 10–50% recovery be proportional; and where less than 10% there be no recovery.

3. The case is additionally noteworthy because the indeterminate causation problems did not overwhelm the court. Judge Jenkins held a three-month trial at which both sides introduced a significant volume of testimonial and documentary evidence, much of it highly sophisticated, which he was able to comprehend, digest and apply. Apparently the Judge did not alter his calendar significantly or even employ special masters. See Howard Ball, The Problems and Prospects of Fashioning a Remedy for Radiation Injury Plaintiffs in Federal District Court: Examining Allen v. United States, 1985 Utah L. Rev. 267, 302 n.147; see also Robert L. Rabin, Environmental Liability and the Tort System, 24 Houston L. Rev. 36–39 (1987). Would a jury have been as capable of resolving the causation questions? How would a jury trial have altered the nature of the evidence? The length of trial? Professor Rabin is critical of the decision and finds that it "engenders deep pessimism about the efficacy of tort [law] for multi-party cases," because of the long delay in reaching dispositive results. Of course, that is not peculiar to such cases and even no-fault systems, such as workers' compensation, involve long periods between injury and recovery (or denial).

4. The district court's rulings were reversed by the Court of Appeals, Allen v. United States, 816 F.2d 1417 (10th Cir.1987), cert. denied 484 U.S. 1004, 108 S.Ct. 694, 98 L.Ed.2d 647 (1988), on the grounds that the Atomic Energy Commission, in planning, conducting and monitoring the open air atomic bomb tests held in Nevada was engaged in policy judgments and discretionary-decisional activities exempting the government from liability under the FTCA, 28 U.S.C.A. §§ 1346(b), 2680(a). The Court of Appeals did not consider the causation issues which were the focus of the district court opinion. The story of the "downwinders," the medical controversy surrounding the issue of causation, and legal battle for compensation is chronicled in H. Bull, Justice Downwind (1986).

For the conflicting statistical studies at issue in the *Allen* case, compare Lyon, et al., Childhood Leukemias Associated with Fallout from Nuclear Testing, 300 New Eng. J. Med. 397 (1979) (concluding that the data show an excess of leukemia) with Land, et al., Childhood Leukemia and Fallout from the Nevada Nuclear Tests, 223 Science 139 (1984) (concluding that the data are not sufficient to support the finding of such an excess). See also Hamilton, Alternative Interpretations of Statistics on Health Effects of Low–Level Radiation (with comments and rejoinder), 37 The Am. Statistician 442 (1983).

5. *Legislative Remedy.* The victims of the Nevada nuclear testing were later provided a legislative solution. Congress has enacted the Radiation Exposure Compensation Act of 1990 at 42 U.S.C.A. § 2210 et seq., which offers compensation to those exposed to radiation from nuclear testing and from uranium mining. The Act establishes a trust fund of $100 million and specifies an individual's recovery of $50,000 if the disease is one specified by the Act, (e.g., childhood leukemia, female breast cancer), the exposure occurred at prescribed ages, the claimants resided in a specified area, and other requirements are satisfied, such as not being a heavy smoker.

2. THE COLLECTIVE MODEL: *AGENT ORANGE*

In contrast to *Allen*, in the Agent Orange settlement opinion, In re Agent Orange Product Liability Litigation, 597 F.Supp. 740 (E.D.N.Y. 1984), affirmed 818 F.2d 145 (2d Cir.1987),cert. denied sub nom. Pinkney v. Dow Chemical Co., 484 U.S. 1004, 108 S.Ct. 695, 98 L.Ed.2d 648 (1988), Judge Weinstein eschewed any attempt to make individualized determinations of causality and instead opted for a collective, proportional basis of liability. In approving a $180 million settlement which he was instrumental in crafting, he emphasized the need to view the indeterminate plaintiff problem in the aggregate rather than individually. He pointed out that the DES and asbestos litigation largely involved injuries that did not occur generally at background levels, so that the indeterminate plaintiff problem was not substantial. Further, even in *Allen*, he stated, the cancers attributable to ionized radiation did have some unusual characteristics that served to help differentiate among plaintiffs. Here, however, no such factors were present. Moreover, if plaintiffs were viewed individually, no single plaintiff could overcome the more probable than not standard and all would be denied recovery. His analysis and proposed solution continue:

IN RE AGENT ORANGE PRODUCT
LIABILITY LITIGATION

United States District Court, Eastern District of New York, 1984.
597 F.Supp. 740.

* * *

(a) APPLICATION OF THE PREPONDERANCE RULE TO MASS EXPOSURE CASES

Conventional application of the "weak" version of the preponderance rule would dictate that, if the toxic substance caused the incidence of the injury to rise more than 100% above the "background" level, each plaintiff exposed to the substance could recover if he or she is suffering from that type of injury. If, however, to put it in somewhat graphic, albeit artificial terms, the incidence rose only 100% or less, no plaintiff could recover—i.e., the probability of specific causation would not be more than 50%.

Where a plaintiff's injuries result from a series of unrelated sporadic accidents, this "all-or-nothing" rule is justifiably rationalized on the ground that it is the fairest and most efficient result. In mass exposure cases, however, this all-or-nothing rule results in either a tortious defendant being relieved of all liability or overcompensation to many plaintiffs and a crushing liability on the defendant. These results are especially troublesome because, unlike the sporadic accident cases, it may be possible to ascertain with a fair degree of assurance that the defendant did cause damage, and, albeit with somewhat less certainty, the total amount of that damage.

* * *

Under the traditional application of the preponderance rule, whether individual plaintiffs recover will depend on where the probability percentage line is drawn despite the fact that a reasonable trier would conclude that a large proportion of the plaintiffs were injured by the defendant and a large number were not. Even if the statistical increase attributed to the substance in question is just a few percentage points, if statistical theory supports a finding of correlation there is no reason why the industry as a whole should not pay for the damages it probably caused.

A simple hypothetical will illustrate why too heavy a burden should not be placed on plaintiffs by requiring a high percentage or incidence of a disease to be attributable to a particular product. Let us assume that there are 10 manufacturers and a population of 10 million persons exposed to their product. Assume that among this population 1,000 cancers of a certain type could be expected, but that 1,100 exist, and that this increase is "statistically significant," permitting a reasonable conclusion that 100 cancers are due to the product of the manufacturers. In the absence of other evidence, it might be argued that as to any one of the 1100 there is only a chance of about 9% ($^{100}/_{1100}$) that the product caused the cancer. Under traditional tort principles no plaintiff could recover.

(b) Inadequacy of Individualized Solutions

Any attempt to resolve the problem on a plaintiff-by-plaintiff basis cannot be fully satisfactory. The solution that would most readily suggest itself is a burden shifting approach, analogous to that used in the indeterminate defendant situation already discussed. *Allen v. United States* provides a good example of how burden-shifting would be applied in an indeterminate plaintiff case. A plaintiff must show that the defendant, in that case the United States, negligently put "an identifiable population group" of which he was a member at "increased risk" and that his injury is

> consistent with having been caused by the hazard to which he has been negligently subjected, such consistency having been demonstrated by substantial, appropriate, persuasive and connecting factors. * * *

Allen, 588 F.Supp. at 415. At that point, the burden shifts to the defendant which will be held liable unless it can offer "persuasive proof" of noncausation. *Id.*

Generally courts have shifted the burden to the defendant to prove that it was not responsible for plaintiff's injury only in sporadic accident cases where it was certain that one of a very limited number of defendants injured the plaintiff, *see, e.g., Summers v. Tice,* 33 Cal.2d 80, 199 P.2d 1 (1948); *Ybarra v. Spangard,* 25 Cal.2d 486, 154 P.2d 687 (1944), or in mass exposure cases where general causation was certain and liability was apportioned in accordance with some market-share theory.

Shifting the burden of proof in such cases will, at least theoretically, not result in crushing liability for the defendant either because the litigation only involves a sporadic accident, as in *Summers* and *Ybarra,* or because the defendant will only be held liable for the amount of damage it caused based on market share—although * * *, there may be practical problems in defining market share. By contrast, shifting the burden of proof in the indeterminate plaintiff situation could result in liability far out of proportion to damage caused. It is not helpful in most situations to say that the defendant will not be liable for "those harms which [he] can reasonably prove were *not* in fact a consequence of his risk-creating, negligent conduct," *Allen,* 588 F.Supp. at 415, since, were such individualized proof available, there would have been no need to shift the burden.

(3) Possible Solution in Class Action

Since the problem results from a plaintiff-by-plaintiff method of adjudication, one solution is to try all plaintiffs' claims together in a class action thereby arriving at a single, class-wide determination of the total harm to the community of plaintiffs. Given the necessarily heavy reliance on statistical evidence in mass exposure cases, such a determination seems feasible. The defendant would then be liable to each exposed plaintiff for a pro rata share of that plaintiff's injuries.

This approach can be illustrated using the hypothetical given above. Suppose all 1,100 of those who were exposed to the harmful substance and who developed the cancer in the example join in a class action against all 10 manufacturers. Let us say that damages average $1,000,000 per cancer. A recovery of $100,000,000 (100 × $1,000,000) in favor of the class would be allowed with the percentage of the award to be paid by each manufacturer depending on the toxicity of its product. For example, if a company produced only 20% of the substance in question but, because of the greater toxicity of its product, likely caused 60% of the harm, it would contribute 60% of the total amount. If accurate records are available on the composition of each defendant's product, that analysis should be possible.

Since no plaintiff can show that his or her cancer was caused by any one of the defendants, they should divide the $100,000,000 by 1,100, giving each a recovery of about $90,000. While any plaintiff might feel that his or her recovery denigrated the degree of harm, the alternative of receiving nothing is far worse. The latter is, of course, the necessary result in any plaintiff's individual suit. Moreover, the deterrent effect of this result on producers would be significant.

* * *

Notes and Questions

1. *Preponderance of the Evidence and Particularistic Proof.* Judge Weinstein makes clear the recurrent problem in mass exposure cases—that

it is extremely difficult for individual plaintiffs to establish causation under what he calls the "strong version" of the preponderance of the evidence rule because two conditions must exist: epidemiological studies which show that the add-on risk is 100% above the background risk (i.e., the relative risk must exceed 2.0) *and* "particularistic" proof which supports causation. Which version of the preponderance rule do you favor in sporadic accident cases, the weak version, which dispenses with the requirement of particularistic proof and allows recovery solely on the basis of probabilistic evidence, or the strong version? Which do you favor in mass exposure cases? What might justify the difference?

What kind of "particularistic" proof might exist in mass exposure cases like *Agent Orange* connecting plaintiff's injuries to the defendant's wrongful conduct and serve to distinguish plaintiffs from the "background" population? Are they precisely the same kinds of proof Judge Jenkins concentrated upon in *Allen*, such as the details of exposure and data on the dose-response relationships? Other factors could include any unique characteristics of the disease or plaintiff's condition that is medically remarkable; or the absence of other common causes (e.g. a non-smoker, no family history of the disease, little or no alcohol consumption) that would often be present for others suffering the disease. But how should a court address these particularistic proofs where there exist hundreds or thousands of plaintiffs? One approach, applied in some asbestos litigation, is described in Chapter 13.

2.   Consider the following statement:

In mass tort cases, the problem of reliance on "bare" statistics for an affirmative case is likely to be more hypothetical than real. When there is a causal mechanism that produces a strong statistical association, the epidemiologic data will generally be incorporated into a body of professional opinion that relies on a variety of biological as well as statistical evidence. To require such other evidence in a legal context is not unreasonable; epidemiologists themselves would generally insist on it before drawing a causal inference from the data. Michael O. Finkelstein & Bruce Levin, Statistics for Lawyers 21 (1990).

Would the approach suggested by these two authors undercut that promoted by Judge Weinstein?

3.   *Multiple Studies*. Most complex cases will not involve a single reliable study that reveals a statistically significant increase in the relative risk that is accepted by all of the parties and the court. In *Agent Orange* none of the epidemiological studies of Vietnam veterans showed any increase in any identifiable serious illness that was attributable to exposure to Agent Orange. In fact, in *Agent Orange* there were epidemiological studies performed of workers involved in industrial accidents that exposed them to large concentrations of dioxin that did reveal positive associations between dioxin and certain diseases. Why weren't these admissible? What if there are two epidemiological studies with differing results—one showing a positive correlation between a disease and the toxic substance and the other showing no correlation? How does the fact finder decide which is "correct" or "more likely than not" to be correct?

4.   *"Signature" Diseases*. Judge Weinstein pointed out that the indeterminate plaintiff problem is especially intractable in cases where the disease

is one that occurs generally in the population. But that is not always true. Some diseases are rare and are manifested *only* in persons exposed to a particular toxic substance. Professor Brennan describes these diseases in Troyen Brennan, Helping Courts With Toxic Torts: Some Proposals Regarding Alternative Methods for Presenting and Assessing Scientific Evidence in Common Law Courts, 51 U. Pitt. L. Rev. 1, 21, 22 (1989)

Judge Weinstein seems to suggest that some of the cancers in *Allen* were "signature" diseases, or at least ones rarely occurring in the absence of ionizing radiation. Is that true?

5. Judge Weinstein's commitment to rejecting individualized solutions was demonstrated in his dismissal of claims brought by "opt-out" plaintiffs. See In re Agent Orange Product Liability Litigation, 611 F.Supp. 1223 (E.D.N.Y.1985), affirmed 818 F.2d 187 (2d Cir.1987), cert. denied sub. nom.; Lombardi v. Dow Chemical Co., 487 U.S. 1234, 108 S.Ct. 2898, 101 L.Ed.2d 932 (1988); Lilley v. Dow Chemical Co., 611 F.Supp. 1267 (E.D.N.Y.1985). He granted defendants' summary judgment motions because of plaintiff's reliance on expert opinions that were not founded on epidemiological studies, but on animal studies and industrial accidents. In addition, his treatment of the individual plaintiffs was greatly influenced by his commitment to achieve a classwide settlement of the controversy and his refusal to differentiate among individual plaintiffs in any manner that might undermine the class-wide settlement.

More recently, Judge Weinstein would later preclude individual lawsuits against the Agent Orange manufacturers when he dismissed actions brought by thirty-seven Texas veterans and their families. See Ryan v. Dow Chemical Co., 781 F.Supp. 902 (E.D.N.Y.1991), affirmed 996 F.2d 1425 (2d Cir.1993). Judge Weinstein rejected the plaintiffs' arguments that they were not class members because their injuries did not manifest themselves until after the opt-out deadline for the $180 million settlement. The plaintiffs contended their claims should have been treated as an ordinary toxic tort action in the Texas court where they were filed. In contrast, he did remand to Texas courts two suits brought by Vietnam *civilians* who were not members of the class. Ivy v. Diamond Shamrock Chemicals Co., 781 F.Supp. 934 (E.D.N.Y. 1992).

6. *Proportionality proposals.* Professor Rosenberg, whose article was frequently quoted by Judge Weinstein, recommends the application of proportionality rules, rather than preponderance rules (even the weak version), as producing fairer outcomes in a system where corrective justice principles should predominate, compatible with goals of deterrence and compensation.

The emergence of proportional causation as a doctrine has gained respectability among a wide cross-section of scholars and is endorsed in 2 Reporters' Study, "Enterprise Responsibility for Personal Injury: Approaches to Legal and Institutional Change" (American Law Institute 1991). Chapter 12 of the Reporters' Study entitled "Standards of Environmental Liability" contains a number of proposals for improving the adjudication of toxic tort claims, including the adoption of proportionate compensation. The following is from pages 369–75:

IV. Proportionate Compensation

* * *

Consider a group of 1,000 people in an area surrounding an industrial plant that uses several carcinogens in its manufacturing process. When one of the chemicals escapes from a holding tank, all 1,000 neighbors are exposed. The escaped substance can cause hepatic carcinoma, or liver cancer. Suppose that 20 individuals out of the original 1,000 would have been expected to develop liver cancer in the absence of any exposure, but that 42 individuals rather than 20 actually develop hepatic cancer. This means that 22 out of the 40 cancers are attributable to the exposure, and an attributable fraction of 53 percent (22/40) would be applicable to each individual case. For each individual it is more probable than not that the cancer is a result of exposure to the hazardous substances. Under current rules all of the plaintiffs with hepatic cancer could prove that their disease is more probably than not the result of exposure to the hazardous substance.

In most environmental injury tort actions, however, exposure levels are usually relatively low; as a result, the increased risks are relatively small. Suppose that exposure to the substance leaking from the plant increased the risk of hepatic cancer by a factor of 1.5. This means that 30 individuals develop liver cancer. Since only 20 such cancers would be expected, the attributable fraction is 33 percent (10/30). None of these plaintiffs would be able to prove that their disease was caused more probably than not by exposure to the substance. * * *

One way to avoid these problems would be to provide compensation on the basis of attributable fractions of causation. The use of proportionate compensation based on the attributable fraction of disease would lower both the burden of proof on plaintiffs and the threshold for bringing environmental injury tort cases. Plaintiffs would be compensated for that fraction of their damages from a particular disease which is attributable to the environmental exposure in question. For example, in the cases cited above each of the individuals afflicted with hepatic cancer would receive some compensation. The compensation would, however, be only a portion of the total damages suffered, calculated using the attributable fraction derived from epidemiological evidence. In the first example each person afflicted with hepatic carcinoma would receive 53 percent of his or her damages as an award. In the second example the proportionate compensation would be 33 percent.

* * *

In the version in which it is sometimes proposed, probabilistic causation and proportionate liability are subject to this criticism, because liability would be imposed whenever the probability of future harm can be quantified. In such a setting liability would be imposed ex ante—that is, before the occurrence of injury. We believe that this legal step is premature at best.

Instead, we advocate only ex post use of probabilistic causation and proportionate liability. We propose that a trier of fact assess the probability of causation and impose proportionate liability only after epidemiological evidence has matured and the actual victims of disease are known. Probabilistic causation would then be used only to overcome the problems associated with indeterminate attribution, not the problems that arise when a party is put at risk of disease. Ours is a more conservative use of proportionate liability and is highly dependent on the use of medical monitoring during the latency period (see below).

We would further limit the scope of our proposal by cautioning against across-the-board use of attributable fractions of any and every size. Many exposures to environmental toxins will cause only slight increases in the risk of disease, sometimes on the order of 2 or 3 percent. If large enough groups of plaintiffs were exposed to such toxins, it could make economic sense for plaintiffs' attorneys to file claims if proportionate compensation were available. This would vastly expand the scope of environmental tort litigation, causing a great deal of legal and economic disruption. A major theme of this Report is the need to increase the predictability of litigation and to facilitate insurance for environmental liability. Allowing litigation no matter how low the attributable fraction would frustrate these efforts. This is not to say that society should attempt to eliminate these exposures. Efforts to eliminate environmental hazards that create a small risk to any single individual but nonetheless create a large disease burden for society should fall mainly within the purview of state and federal environmental regulation.

As a result, we must propose some threshold for the use of attributable fractions and proportionate compensation. The twin demands of fairness to defendants and a commitment to some economic liability require that the threshold represent a substantial increase above the background risk of disease. An attributable fraction of roughly 20 percent would, we believe, accomplish this goal. On the other hand, such a threshold would significantly lower the barrier now set by the "more probable than not" standard.

In summary a proportionate compensation scheme could operate in the following manner. The exposed population would be certified as a class. The class would include all individuals with a disease potentially associated with the exposure. A science panel or a court-appointed expert would estimate the attributable fraction of each disease at various levels of exposure. Once the attributable fractions dropped below 20 percent, the assumption would be that there was no causation of injury. For exposures causing an attributable fraction greater than 20 percent, each individual harmed would receive a fraction of his or her total damages, equal to the attributable fraction. To create symmetry and fairness, any injuries that involved an attributable fraction greater than 80 percent would be compensated at a level of 100 percent. In this way proportionate compensation based on attributable fractions drawn from epidemiological data would both create rational awards to environmental tort litigants and lower the threshold for bringing such cases.

———

The Reporters' Study, the conclusions of which were neither approved nor disapproved by its sponsor, The American Law Institute, also advocated extensive use of class actions as integral to the application of proportional liability, and greater availability of the medical monitoring remedy.

C. DID THE DEFENDANT CAUSE PLAINTIFF'S HARM: THE INDETERMINATE DEFENDANT PROBLEM

1. SOME DEVICES TO OVERCOME DEFENDANT INDETERMINACY

Environmental tort litigation often reveals causal indeterminacy on both sides of the caption: indeterminate plaintiffs and indeterminate defendants. A cardinal tenet of traditional tort law liability rules is that the plaintiff must prove that the defendant's conduct was a producing cause of the harm suffered. In the conventional sporadic accident case identifying the responsible defendant is usually not difficult because of the availability of physical or direct evidence that implicates a particular defendant. In toxic and environmental harm cases, however, the chemical agent or polluting source often does not come branded or trademarked with the defendant's name. While defendant or source indeterminacy arose occasionally in products liability cases and accident cases, the frequency and difficulty of source indeterminacy in environmental and toxic torts creates new demands on the courts to develop rules that continue to fulfill the objectives of tort law.

To date, the judicial response to this problem of source indeterminacy has been the creation of mechanisms to ease the plaintiff's burden, most commonly the shifting of the burden of proof to establish noncausation on the shoulders of the defendant. Much of the law in this area has developed in the DES cases. Their origin is found in a simple hunting accident.

a. *Alternative Liability*

The modern origin of the burden-shifting approach to tortfeasor indeterminacy is found in Summers v. Tice, 33 Cal.2d 80, 199 P.2d 1 (1948), an accident case with an unusual twist. The plaintiff was shot in the eye and in the lip from either of two guns fired by two negligent hunters, but the plaintiff could not prove which one fired the shot that struck his eye by a preponderance of the evidence because it was equally likely that each was the source of that bullet. The California Supreme Court, instilled with a corrective justice view of the situation and the dilemma faced by the plaintiff, held that the burden of proof as to which defendant caused his injury was shifted to the defendants for each to exculpate himself and to apportion damages, with the practical effect of making the defendants jointly and severally liable. See 2 M. Stuart Madden, Products Liability 2d § 15.2 at 88, 89 (1988) for a fuller description of the decision.

The alternative liability theory of *Summers* has considerable appeal to plaintiffs because of the ameliorative impact it has on the onus of causation. However, its principal limitations are that courts are reluctant to apply it in the absence of clear evidence that all or at least one of the defendants are at fault and all of the possible responsible parties are defendants before the court. See Restatement (Second) of Torts § 433B(3) (all actors' conduct must be negligent). What impediments do you see to applying alternative liability in toxic tort cases? For a modified version of alternative liability in the Agent Orange cases, see In re Agent Orange Prod. Liab. Litig., 597 F.Supp. 740, 826–32 (E.D.N.Y. 1984); for a decision declining to apply the alternative liability theory in the lead-based paint litigation, see Hurt v. Philadelphia Housing Authority, 806 F.Supp. 515 (E.D.Pa.1992).

b. Concert of Action Theory

Concert of action theory posits that a group of actors jointly carried on an activity in a consciously parallel manner, similar to two drivers engaging in a race on city streets. The idea is that they have implicitly agreed to follow a similar pattern of conduct, usually in research, manufacturing or marketing methods, that justifies treating them as jointly and severally liable, and allowing a plaintiff to sue one of the group and hold it liable for all of the damages suffered. While the theory is obviously attractive to plaintiffs, it is of minimal utility in toxic or environmental harm litigation because rarely can a plaintiff establish, by sufficient evidence, the presence of consciously parallel behavior together with proof of an implicit agreement. One opinion of the New York Court of Appeals utilized the theory in an early DES case, Bichler v. Eli Lilly & Co., 55 N.Y.2d 571, 450 N.Y.S.2d 776, 436 N.E.2d 182 (1982), but has been since rejected, in favor of a market share liability mechanism. Hymowitz v. Eli Lilly & Co., 73 N.Y.2d 487, 541 N.Y.S.2d 941, 539 N.E.2d 1069 (1989).

c. Enterprise or Industry–Wide Liability

Courts have occasionally used the novel approach of enterprise liability in an effort to help plaintiffs meet the causation burden of proof. The pioneer case in this area is Hall v. E.I. Du Pont De Nemours & Co., 345 F.Supp. 353 (E.D.N.Y.1972). In *Hall*, some exploding blasting caps injured a group of children, who sued several manufacturers of the blasting caps but could not identify the manufacturer of the blasting caps that actually caused them harm. As a consequence, the plaintiffs sued a limited number of defendants who manufactured blasting caps and their trade association, relying on "substantially similar industry-imposed safety standards," where the defendants had jointly rejected certain safety measures and had jointly lobbied against labeling regulation. Under the enterprise liability theory espoused in *Hall*, the industry-wide standard caused the injury by "joint or group control of risk," so that each defendant that used the standard contributed to and was liable for the plaintiffs' injuries. Enterprise liability thus is a hybrid theory combining elements of alternative liability and concert of action. See 2 M. Stuart Madden, Products Liability 2d § 15.3 at 93, 94 (1988). To date, the courts have not specifically embraced enterprise liability in an environmental tort case.

d. Market Share Liability

The seminal decision to apply a market share liability theory was Sindell v. Abbott Laboratories, 26 Cal.3d 588, 163 Cal.Rptr. 132, 607 P.2d 924 (1980), cert. denied 449 U.S. 912, 101 S.Ct. 285, 66 L.Ed.2d 140 (1980). The plaintiffs in these DES cases are often unable to identify which producer of the generic drug made the DES which their mothers ingested during pregnancy to minimize risks of miscarriages for several reasons: (1) the passage of many years since the ingestion of the drug (plaintiffs' exposure to the toxic substance in utero); (2) the long latency period before the adverse effects on the female children of the mothers were manifested; (3) the destruction or loss of marketing and manufacturing records of the producers; and (4) the significant number of firms producing the drug (several hundred companies produced or distributed DES in the United States between 1947 and 1962).

Assuming that the plaintiffs could prove negligence or the necessary elements of strict products liability, the court held that if the plaintiff could successfully sue firms which, in the aggregate represented a "substantial share" of the market for DES, the burden would shift to each named defendant to exculpate itself, i.e. to prove that it could not have caused plaintiff's harm because it did not market the kind of DES that her mother took, or did not market DES during the year(s) or in the location where it was purchased. For those defendants failing to carry that burden, each would be held liable for a percentage of plaintiff's damages corresponding to its market share. In a later decision, Brown v. Superior Court (Abbott Laboratories), 44 Cal.3d 1049, 245 Cal.Rptr. 412, 751 P.2d 470 (1988), the California Supreme Court determined that liability would be proportionate only.

There are two principal rationales for applying market share liability. The first, adopted in *Sindell*, is that a firm's share of the market (say 20%) represents the probability that it *actually caused* the individual plaintiff's harm, and imposing liability for 20% of the damages represents a judgment that it should be liable to that extent for the chance that it did in fact cause her damages. Indeed, in mass tort cases if courts in all states followed the identical approach, the theory goes, a manufacturer's damages under the market share analysis will converge with the actual harm it caused to all plaintiffs.

A second rationale, merging concepts of risk contribution with those of market share, was adopted in Hymowitz v. Eli Lilly & Co., 73 N.Y.2d 487, 541 N.Y.S.2d 941, 539 N.E.2d 1069 (1989), decided nine years after *Sindell*. In *Hymowitz* the court found the administrative difficulties engendered by local markets required a different approach. The New York Court of Appeals described the reasoning and structure of its modified market share liability as follows:

Consequently, for essentially practical reasons, we adopt a market share theory using a national market. We are aware that the adoption of a national market will likely result in a disproportion between the liability of individual manufacturers and the actual injuries each manufacturer caused in this State. Thus our market share theory cannot be founded upon the belief that, over the run of cases, liability will approximate causation in this State (see Sindell v. Abbott Labs). Nor does the use of a national market provide a reasonable link between liability and the risk created by a defendant to a particular plaintiff. Instead, we choose to apportion liability so as to correspond to the over-all culpability of each defendant, measured by the amount of risk of injury each defendant created to the public-at-large. Use of a national market is a fair method, we believe, of apportioning defendants' liabilities according to their total culpability in marketing DES for use during pregnancy. Under the circumstances, this is an equitable way to provide plaintiffs with the relief they deserve, while also rationally distributing the responsibility for plaintiffs' injuries among defendants.

To be sure, a defendant cannot be held liable if it did not participate in the marketing of DES for pregnancy use; if a DES producer satisfies its burden of proof of showing that it was not a member of the market of DES sold for pregnancy use, disallowing exculpation would be unfair and unjust. Nevertheless, because liability here is based on the over-all risk produced, and not causation in a single case, there should be no exculpation of a defendant who, although a member of the market producing DES for pregnancy use, appears not to have caused a particular plaintiff's injury. It is merely a windfall for a producer to escape liability solely because it manufactured a more identifiable pill, or sold only to certain drugstores. These fortuities in no way diminish the culpability of a defendant for marketing the product, which is the basis of liability here.

Finally, we hold that the liability of DES producers is several only, and should not be inflated when all participants in the market are not before the court in a particular case. * * *

Which rationale, Sindell or Hymowitz, do you find more convincing from a fairness perspective? From a deterrence standpoint?

Notes and Questions

1. *Limits of Decision.* The court in Hymowitz was concerned that its opinion not be read overly broad to extend to non-comparable circumstances. For example, it described the DES situation as a "singular case, [1] with manufacturers acting in a parallel manner, [2] to produce an identical, generically marketed product, [3] which causes injury many years later

* * * '' Can you think of any other circumstances where these three factors exist? Asbestos? Cigarettes? Lead paint? What do you think of the court's reasoning? Does it seem more consistent and more readily justiciable than local market share liability or individual risk contribution?

2.   a.   Following its decision in *Hymowitz*, the New York Court of Appeals has answered three questions about the scope of its risk contribution market share theory. First, in Enright v. Eli Lilly & Co., 77 N.Y.2d 377, 568 N.Y.S.2d 550, 570 N.E.2d 198 (1991), the court refused to extend liability of DES manufacturers to third generation plaintiffs, whose grandmothers consumed DES and whose mothers are the "DES daughters" typically suing in these cases for injuries to their reproductive systems. Drawing on an earlier medical malpractice decision that refused to extend a physician's duty to a child who was not yet conceived at the time of his negligence, the court declined to extend a DES manufacturer's duty to such children, observing that DES claimants were not "a favored class for whose benefit all traditional limitations on tort liability must give way," and citing the need to "confine liability within manageable limits," and the prospect of overdeterrence of the development of beneficial drugs.

b.   Second, in Anderson v. Eli Lilly & Co., 79 N.Y.2d 797, 580 N.Y.S.2d 168, 588 N.E.2d 66 (1991), it held that a plaintiff-husband, whose wife suffered from DES-related injuries, could not recover for loss of consortium because the tortious conduct and resultant injuries occurred prior to the marriage.

c.   Finally, in In the Matter of DES Market Share Litigation, 79 N.Y.2d 299, 582 N.Y.S.2d 377, 591 N.E.2d 226 (1992), the court held that the plaintiffs in the DES litigation are entitled to a jury trial on the issue of the respective market shares of the defendants, rejecting the view of defendants that *Hymowitz* established an equitable proceeding to which no jury trial rights attached.

d.   In perhaps the most extraordinary fallout of the *Hymowitz* decision, the federal district court in New York held that manufacturers of DES that had never sold their product in New York State are subject to the personal jurisdiction of the court under New York's long arm statute. Ashley v. Abbott Laboratories, 789 F.Supp. 552 (E.D.N.Y.1992). In that action Judge Weinstein held that jurisdiction could be exercised over such manufacturers that did not sell DES in New York and were not present in that state by virtue of the manufacturers' engagement in the national DES industry, on the rationale that the producers had marketed a generic drug in one part of the country that produced economic and trade consequences in other parts, including New York.

3.   Market share has received a mixed reaction in the courts, a number of which have refused to adopt the doctrine. See, e.g., Mulcahy v. Eli Lilly & Co., 386 N.W.2d 67 (Iowa 1986); Senn v. Merrell–Dow Pharmaceuticals, Inc., 305 Or. 256, 751 P.2d 215 (1988); Tidler v. Eli Lilly & Co., 851 F.2d 418 (D.C.Cir.1988); Smith v. Eli Lilly & Co., 137 Ill.2d 222, 148 Ill.Dec. 22, 560 N.E.2d 324 (1990). However, several decisions while rejecting certain aspects of the *Sindell* market share approach, provide plaintiffs with somewhat similar "solutions" to the defendant identification problems in the DES cases. See, e.g., Abel v. Eli Lilly & Co., 418 Mich. 311, 343 N.W.2d 164

(1984), cert. denied 469 U.S. 833, 105 S.Ct. 123, 83 L.Ed.2d 65 (1984) (concerted action, or modified alternative liability); Martin v. Abbott Laboratories, 102 Wash.2d 581, 689 P.2d 368 (1984) (modified market share); and Collins v. Eli Lilly Co., 116 Wis.2d 166, 342 N.W.2d 37 (1984), cert. denied, 469 U.S. 826, 105 S.Ct. 107, 83 L.Ed.2d 51 (1984) (individual risk contribution applying comparative fault statute). Conley v. Boyle Drug Co., 570 So.2d 275 (Fla.1990) applies an actual causation rationale, adopting an intensively local market definition including, where possible, identification of individual pharmacies. *Conley* further stated a rule that would require a showing of due diligence by plaintiffs to identify the actual producer, impose proportionate liability, and assign equal market shares to non-exculpating defendants who failed to establish their actual share.

4. Should a plaintiff seeking to utilize a market share (or similar) theory in a DES case be required to make a genuine effort first to identify the manufacturer that supplied her mother's DES? Compare Abel v. Eli Lilly & Co., 418 Mich. 311, 343 N.W.2d 164 (1984) (yes), with McCormack v. Abbott Laboratories, 617 F.Supp. 1521 (D.Mass.1985) (no).

If the plaintiff does have some, but not conclusive, identification evidence, should she be entitled to have both the individual and the market share claims submitted to the jury?

If a plaintiff establishes that a particular defendant's relevant market share was 51% (or higher), should she be entitled to recover 100% of her damages from the defendant on the grounds that it is more likely than not that the defendant was the cause-in-fact of her harm?

5. In Smith v. Eli Lilly & Co., 137 Ill.2d 222, 148 Ill.Dec. 22, 560 N.E.2d 324 (1990), the Illinois Supreme Court declined to adopt market share liability in a DES case, concluding (1) that the *Sindell-Hymowitz* line of cases resulted in overdeterrence of useful activity that would be deterred by excessive liability; (2) that because reliable market share data is rarely available, the courts would be imprudently bogged down in an almost "futile endeavor" that would "create a tremendous cost in terms of workload on the court system and litigants"; (3) that the inconsistency of verdicts in different cases when juries would apportion damages based on market share data that may be different or unavailable; (4) that the likelihood that the defendant who actually sold the product to the plaintiff would not be before the court, so none of the remaining defendants actually caused the harm, and imposing liability would be unfair and too speculative; (5) that market share liability might result in plaintiffs who cannot identify the manufacturer of the DES receiving a larger recovery than those who can, because the latter group of plaintiffs' recoveries will be dependent on the continued existence and solvency of that firm, whereas the former will be able to turn to many companies, some of whom are certain to remain viable and solvent.

Which of the rationales offered seems most persuasive? Does the *Hymowitz* approach solve the administrative-related concerns? The Illinois Supreme Court quoted heavily from an article by Professor Fischer. See David A. Fischer, Products Liability—An Analysis of Market Share Liability, 34 Vand. L. Rev. 1623, 1657 (1981) ("The legal fees and administrative costs arising from litigation of this magnitude easily could rival the cost of the plaintiff's judgment").

6.   a. *Vaccines*. Plaintiffs have pursued the application of market share liability with minimal success in areas other than DES cases. The plaintiff in Shackil v. Lederle Laboratories, 116 N.J. 155, 561 A.2d 511 (1989) became severely retarded as a result of diphtheria, pertussis and tetanus (DPT) vaccine. Unable to identify the specific manufacturer, plaintiff sued a number of manufacturers who potentially could have produced the vaccine she was given and argued for adoption of a market share liability theory. The court determined that (1) to adopt market share liability in a DPT case "would frustrate overarching public-policy and public-health considerations by threatening the continued availability of needed drugs and impairing the prospects of the development of safer vaccines"; (2) that another remedy was available to the plaintiff under the National Childhood Vaccine Injury Compensation Act of 1986, 42 U.S.C.A. § 300aa–1 et seq. (1993); and (3) that the absence of a generically identical product produced a major distinction between the vaccine in *Shackil* and DES because the DPT vaccine contained a defective batch, but was not generically defective. Accord, Senn v. Merrell–Dow Pharmaceuticals, Inc., 305 Or. 256, 751 P.2d 215 (1988); Chapman v. American Cyanamid Co., 861 F.2d 1515 (11th Cir.1988) (child died after receiving a DPT vaccine; parents could not proceed against three manufacturers on an alternative liability theory); Griffin v. Tenneco Resins, Inc., 648 F.Supp. 964 (W.D.N.C.1986) (court determined that producers of dyes could not be held liable based on market share theory); but see Morris v. Parke, Davis & Co., 667 F.Supp. 1332 (C.D.Cal.1987) (applying market share liability against manufacturers of DPT based on allegations of industry-wide manufacturing defects).

b.   *Asbestos Litigation*. In asbestos cases, most courts hold that market share liability should not be recognized. See Goldman v. Johns–Manville Sales Corp., 33 Ohio St.3d 40, 514 N.E.2d 691 (1987) in which the Ohio Supreme Court rejected its application in an action against suppliers and manufacturers of products containing asbestos. The court reasoned that market share liability is inappropriate "where it cannot be shown that all the products to which the injured party was exposed are completely fungible." Moreover, the court held that the risk the manufacturer created is not accurately reflected in its market share because many products contain different degrees of asbestos, and the largest asbestos supplier, Johns–Manville, was not amenable to suit.

Accord, Case v. Fibreboard Corp., 743 P.2d 1062, 1067 (Okl.1987) ("the public policy favoring recovery on the part of an innocent plaintiff does not justify the abrogation of the rights of a potential defendant to have a causative link proven between the defendant's specific tortious acts and the plaintiff's injuries"); Nutt v. A.C. & S. Co., 517 A.2d 690, 694 (Del.Super.1986) (rejecting market share liability and recognizing that such a change in tort law should be left to the legislature); Celotex Corp. v. Copeland, 471 So.2d 533 (Fla.1985), reversing 447 So.2d 908 (Fla.App.1984) rejecting application of market share theory on the facts before it because plaintiff was able to identify some of the specific products, and their manufacturers, to which he had been exposed, and because asbestos products contain a divergence of toxicity depending on several factors, including friability (the extent to which the fibers are released from the product into the air), the specific type (among six) of asbestos fiber used in the product, and the amount of asbestos used in the product.

2. MARKET SHARE AT THE BOUNDARIES: FACTOR VIII AND LEAD PAINT

a. Factor VIII and Contaminated Blood Products

One product line that has resulted in several opinions considering the application and scope of market share principles is blood products. Several recent opinions have considered whether producers of Factor VIII, an anti-coagulant taken by hemophiliacs, may be subjected to market share analysis when an HIV-contaminated batch of the product results in the transmission of HIV and the recipient plaintiffs are incapable of identifying the producer of the Factor VIII which was infected. Prior to the decision of the Florida Supreme Court in Conley v. Boyle Drug Co., 570 So.2d 275 (Fla.1990), a Florida federal district court refused to apply a market share liability theory to three brothers who alleged that they contracted the AIDS virus from contaminated blood products and were unable to identify the manufacturer of the product which was the source of the virus. Ray v. Cutter Laboratories, 744 F.Supp. 1124 (M.D.Fla.1990). See also Poole v. Alpha Therapeutic Corp., 696 F.Supp. 351 (N.D.Ill.1988). The following decision points in the other direction.

SMITH v. CUTTER BIOLOGICAL, INC.

Supreme Court of Hawaii, 1991.
72 Hawaii 416, 823 P.2d 717.

Lum, C.J.

This court has accepted a request to address certified questions from the Ninth Circuit Court of Appeals. Smith v. Cutter Biological, Inc., 911 F.2d 374 (9th Cir.1990).

I.

Certified Questions of Law

1. Does Hawaii's Blood Shield Law, Haw.Rev.Stat. § 327–51, preclude Smith from bringing a strict liability claim? 2. Does Hawaii's Blood Shield Law, Haw.Rev.Stat. § 327–51, preclude Smith from bringing a negligence claim? 3. Would Hawaii allow recovery in this case when the identity of the actual tortfeasor cannot be proven? If Hawaii would allow recovery, what theory (i.e. burden-shifting, enterprise liability, market share or other) would the Hawaii Supreme Court adopt? In considering our response to the questions, we note that the issue as to questions two and three concerns the causation factor in negligence. The instant problem is that the plaintiff cannot identify which particular defendant caused his injury.

Our consideration of the issues is limited to the facts as stated in this record. Procedurally, this case reached the Ninth Circuit Court on a summary judgment motion. The order granting summary judgment did not rule on duty and breach as to the manufacturers; summary judgment was granted on the basis that plaintiff failed to prove causation.

The other elements of negligence, i.e., duty, breach and damages, are not at issue here. We note that at least two courts have determined, in cases similar to the instant action, that there was no breach of duty. Jones v. Miles Laboratories, Inc., 887 F.2d 1576 (11th Cir.1989); McKee v. Cutter Laboratories, Inc., 866 F.2d 219 (6th Cir.1989). However, those cases are distinguishable. We do not render an opinion as to whether appellant here will overcome the obstacles met by plaintiffs in those cases; the duty and breach issue here has not only not been decided, it is not before this court on the certified questions. Therefore, we do not deal with the viability of those questions.

Our conclusions deal only with this case—as it comes to us. Therefore, on our reading of the record as it stands, the relevant statutes, and the relevant case law, we answer "yes" to question one, and "no" to question two. Our answer to question three is "yes," using the alternative market share theory of recovery, as defined herein.

II.

Appellant is a hemophiliac who has tested HIV-positive with the AIDS virus. He claims that his exposure to the AIDS virus occurred in 1983 or 1984, through injections of the Antihemophilic Factor Concentrate (Factor VIII or AHF). Factor VIII, is a blood protein which enables the blood to properly coagulate when a hemophiliac suffers a bleeding episode. The original source of the Factor VIII is through blood donors.

* * * Upon appellant's first being tested for HIV antibodies in 1986, the results were positive.

* * *

III.

The first question asks whether the Hawaii Blood Shield Law precludes a strict liability claim. The blood shield statute reads as follows: *Exemption from strict liability.* No physician, surgeon, hospital, blood bank, tissue bank, or other person or entity who donates, obtains, prepares, transplants, injects, transfuses, or otherwise transfers, or who assists or participates in obtaining, preparing, transplanting, injecting, transfusing, or otherwise transferring any tissue, organ, blood or component thereof, from one or more persons, living or dead, to another person, shall be liable as a result of any such activity, save and except that each such person or entity shall remain liable for the person's or *its own negligence* or wilful misconduct. Hawaii Revised Statutes (HRS) § 327–51 (1985) (emphasis added). The answer to this question then depends on whether Factor VIII can be categorized as a "blood component." Appellant argues that the legislature was merely referring to blood or blood plasma for the definition of blood component. The legislative history does not appear to us to be that narrow. * * *

* * *

Therefore, we believe that Factor VIII is a component prepared from blood. With that finding, we answer the first question in the affirmative; Hawaii's blood shield statute precludes a strict liability claim.

IV.

The second question is tied to the third question. It requires that this court decide what the Hawaii blood shield statute means by the phrase "its own negligence." Appellees argument is that the phrase bars a lawsuit where the tortfeasor cannot be positively identified. In other words, the question is virtually identical to the first query in the third certified question. The distinction is, in the first instance, whether the legislature, by means of the blood shield statute, allows a claim against an unidentified tortfeasor, and in the second instance, whether this court would allow such an action based on the general development of Hawaii tort law. If "its own negligence" literally means the negligence must be of that particular defendant and have caused the damage to the plaintiff, then there would be no room to consider any of the various multi-tortfeasor theories of liability.

Looking at the legislative history behind the blood shield statute, we note that it merely states that excluding strict liability does not "affect remedies based upon other legal theories, such as negligence or willful misconduct." Sen.Conf.Comm.Rep. No. 773, in 1971 Senate Journal, at 1135. The wording on which appellees rely so heavily, "own negligence," is conspicuously absent from the history. Lacking that wording, or any other wording giving such an indication, we believe that the legislature has not spoken on this issue. We believe a lacuna exists, and we are free to use our own determination to explain pertinent words in the blood shield statute. Therefore, the second question is answered in the negative.

V.

The final question posed to this court comes in two parts. The first part asks whether this court would allow recovery in negligence when the actual tortfeasor cannot be proven. We concluded, in Part IV, that the Hawaii blood shield statute does not mandate specific identification of the tortfeasor. We now consider whether general Hawaii tort law would allow the action.

The reason this case is before this court is because the legislature has not fully legislated in the field of torts. When the occasion arises for which there is no specific rule to apply, "we are free to fashion an appropriate rule of law."

Appellees take issue with applying theories which were developed, in a large part, for remedies in the field of diethylstilbestrol (DES) drug litigation and the inherent problems associated with those actions. Their strongest argument against using these theories is the lack of comparison of DES to Factor VIII as a fungible product. DES was produced by more than 200 different companies, some of which are defunct, but the identical formula was used universally in a highly regulated industry. With Factor VIII, there are only a handful of manufacturers, and although the product is fungible insofar as it can be used interchangeably, it does not have the constant quality of DES. The reason is obvious—the donor source of the plasma is not a constant. Therefore, Factor VIII is only harmful if the donor was infected; DES is inherently harmful. As we see that the lack of screening of donors and failure to warn are the breaches alleged, appellee's argument for not using DES theories is not convincing. We find consideration of the theories discussed in the DES cases to be helpful, as we strive to find an equitable and fair solution to the case at bar.

* * *

Our initial reference is to the reasoning of the Supreme Court of California, in Sindell v. Abbott Laboratories, 607 P.2d 924, cert. denied, 449 U.S. 912 (1980). We subscribe to the policy reasons propounded in Sindell * * * for by-passing the identification requirement.

In addition, we note that tort law is a continually expanding field. As discussed in the American Law Institute Enterprise Responsibility for Personal Injuries—Reporter's Study (1991) (ALI Study), the field of torts has now expanded to include personal injury actions described in three tiers of actions. * * * [T]he third tier includes "mass" torts where toxic exposure to many plaintiffs may, many years later, cause cancer or other illness. It is this final tier with which this case deals. It necessitates considering how to fairly deal with the plight of plaintiffs unable to identify, for no fault of their own, the person or entity who should bear the liability for their injury.

No longer can we apply traditional rules of negligence, such as those used in individual and low level negligence to mass tort cases, especially here, where we are dealing with a pharmaceutical industry that dispenses drugs on a wide scale that could cause massive injuries to the public, and where fungibility makes the strict requirements difficult to meet. The problem calls for adopting new rules of causation, for otherwise innocent plaintiffs would be left without a remedy. * * *

The policies in Sindell convince us that it is appropriate to consider a negligence action where the actual tortfeasor cannot be proven. Therefore, although inherent in the proof of negligence is proof of causation, we believe that this state is amenable to consideration of group theories of liability.

VI.

The second part of the third certified question asks what theory or theories this court might adopt where the tortfeasor cannot be proven. There are several theories which have evolved in the last several years. The genesis of these theories comes from Sindell v. Abbott Laboratories,

607 P.2d 924 (Cal.1980). The theories are generally described as: alternative liability, concert of action, enterprise or industry-wide liability, and market share liability. In the evolution of the DES cases, the market share theory has undergone various modifications, to suit the policies and needs of the particular courts.

* * *

D. MARKET SHARE LIABILITY & ITS PROGENY

This theory has been most susceptible to variations and refinements, especially in DES litigation, but also in line with the law of the state in which it has been applied. It was first defined in Sindell, 607 P.2d 924 (1980). * * * We expand on those policies to acknowledge that defendants may bear the loss by passing that cost of doing business on to consumers. In addition, we feel that equity and fairness calls for using the market share approach. Another justification is that where many drugs can be lethal, and it is difficult for the consumer to identify the source of the product, the burden should shift. The concept itself meets the objectives of tort law, both by providing plaintiffs a remedy, but also by deterring defendants from negligent acts.

* * * We feel that this basic theory, with modifications and distinctions to suit the policies of this state, discussed infra, provides an appropriate modem for appellant's case. The relevant considerations are: 1. defining the market, 2. identification and joint and several liability, and finally 3. exculpatory allowances.

1. *Defining the Market*

Criticisms of Sindell include the need for a definition of "substantial share" of the market, in order not to distort the share of liability. Martin v. Abbott Laboratories, 689 P.2d 368, 381 (1984). The Martin court adopted a narrow definition of the market, that being the plaintiff's particular geographic market. * * *

Another court has specifically adopted the national market as the best option. Hymowitz v. Eli Lilly and Co., 73 N.Y.2d 487, 511, 539 N.E.2d 1069, 1077 (1989). Several premises supported this holding: 1. it was difficult to reliably determine any market smaller than the national one, 2. it avoided the need to establish separate matrices as to market share, and 3. it avoided an unfair burden on litigants. The national market was intended to "apportion liability so as to correspond to the over-all culpability of each defendant, measured by the amount of risk of injury each defendant created to the public-at-large." This provides equitable relief for plaintiffs, and a rational distribution of responsibility among defendants. It also avoids a windfall escape to the producer who happens to sell only to certain distributors. The culpability, therefore, is for marketing the product.

As we are faced here with a minimal number of manufacturers of the product, we believe that culpability for marketing the product is a better policy. Should the issue arise under different circumstances at some point, we may find it appropriate to narrow the definition. For this case, however, we believe the national market is the more equitable consideration.

2.   *Identification and Joint and Several Liability*

Courts differ on their requirements of an assertive effort on the part of plaintiffs to identify the actual manufacturer of the specific product which caused the harm. We take another approach to this concern. Whereas manufacturers here argue that appellant should have kept a log of which manufacturer's product he was using, we fail to see how such failure affects the viability of appellant's suit in view of our adoption of the theory of market share liability.

Plaintiffs should use due diligence to join all manufacturers, but failure to do so is not a defense. Failure to do so may affect the percentage of recovery, discussed infra. However, manufacturers are permitted to implead other manufacturers. But, in this case, all manufacturers are joined, so the issue is not before us. However, we note in passing that the conditions of the Martin court, which would allow plaintiffs to initiate suit against only one defendant, and of Sindell, which would require plaintiffs to join a "substantial" number of defendants, are immaterial as long as plaintiffs realize their recovery will depend on joining as many manufacturers as they can; plaintiffs will endeavor to join all manufacturers.

We have already discussed our feeling that this action should not be subject to joint liability. * * * Therefore, we advocate several liability.

We define the rules of distribution as to market share for this case as was done in Martin, that is: "The defendants that are unable to exculpate themselves from potential liability are designated members of the plaintiffs' * * * market[ ] * * *. These defendants are initially presumed to have equal shares of the market and are liable for only the percentage of plaintiff's judgment that represents their presumptive share of the market. These defendants are entitled to rebut this presumption and thereby reduce their potential liability by establishing their respective market share of [Factor VIII] in the ... market." Martin, 689 P.2d 368, 383 (1984). As to several liability, we adopt the theory that a particular defendant is only liable for its market share. Defendants failing to establish their proportionate share of the market will be liable for the difference in the judgment to 100 percent of the market. However, should plaintiff fail to name all members of the market, the plaintiff will not recover 100 percent of the judgment if the named defendants prove an aggregate share of less than 100 percent.

3.   *Exculpatory Allowances*

As a result of our determination that a national market is appropriate, as long as defendant is actually one of the producers of Factor VIII, there is little to justify exculpation of defendant. However, the exception would occur where defendant could prove that it had no product on the market at the time of the injury. As far as the defendants in this suit are concerned, it appears that none of them would be able to escape liability on that basis.

VII.

In conclusion, we will recognize the basic market share theory of multi-tortfeasor liability, as defined herein. Acknowledging that this could open a Pandora's box of questions, we believe that we have defined at least a starting point as to appropriately responding to the certified questions. However, as we are deciding issues in a virtual factual vacuum, we recognize that our opinion is limited to the facts presented to us, and we reserve the right to modify or amend our answers to these questions.

MOON, J. concurring and dissenting.

I concur in the majority's decision that Hawaii's blood shield statute precludes plaintiff's claim for strict liability. I also concur in the majority's opinion to the extent that it rejects the alternative liability, concert of action, and enterprise liability theories of causation. However, as to the majority's decision to adopt the market share theory of liability, I respectfully dissent.

* * *

I. STATUTORY CONSTRUCTION

* * * Eliminating causation as an element of proof and shifting the burden to the defendant is not only a radical departure from traditional negligence law, but is inconsistent with Hawaii's blood shield statute.

* * *

The statute is plain and unambiguous. It protects manufacturers of blood products from all liability, with one exception: "save and except that each * * * entity shall remain liable for * * * *its own negligence* * * * "(emphasis added). In other words, the statute requires proof of all elements of a negligence action, including causation.

* * *

Hawaii's blood shield statute is similar to blood statutes enacted in virtually all states. Even in the absence of legislative history, the underlying purpose of such statutes is obvious. * * * These statutes reflect a legislative judgment that to require providers to serve as insurers of the safety of these materials might impose such an overwhelming burden as to discourage the gathering and distribution of blood.

In 1988, the American Medical Association reported that "in the pharmaceutical industry, meaningful product liability insurance has all but disappeared." A.M.A., Report of the Board of Trustees on Impact of Product Liability on the Development of New Medical Technologies 2 (1988). This lack of insurance is largely due to the development of non-identification theories of liability.

The application of the market share liability theory may result in liability being placed on defendants bearing no responsibility for the defective product and may create unpredictable costs to innocent parties. In enacting HRS § 327–51, the Hawaii legislature unquestionably sought to guard against the risk of adversely affecting the supply of blood and blood components. However, the majority's decision imposes that very risk and may not only jeopardize the supply of blood products which protect the "health * * * of the people of Hawaii," but may also "restrict the availability of important scientific knowledge and skills."

II. DES CASE LAW

The primary authority cited by the majority in support of its position is the DES case of Sindell v. Abbott Laboratories, * * * The court determined that two essential factual elements, fungibility and the inability to identify specific producers, must be present in order for the market share liability theory to be appropriate. Both elements are glaringly absent in the Factor VIII case before us.

A. Fungibility

* * *

Unlike DES, Factor VIII is not a generic, fungible drug. Each processor prepares its Factor VIII concentrate by its own proprietary processes using plasma collected from its own sources. Each firm's Factor VIII concentrate is clearly distinguishable by brand name, package color, lot number, and number of units of Factor VIII per vial; each firm's Factor VIII concentrate is separately licensed by the Food and Drug Administration. There is no evidence that all Factor VIII products caused or were equally capable of causing HIV infection. Thus, the risk posed by the different brands of Factor VIII is not identical.

The majority here admits that Factor VIII is not fungible, that is, it does not pose the same risk of harm to users because, as the majority states, "[t]he reason is obvious—the donor source of the plasma is not constant. Therefore, Factor VIII is only harmful if the donor was infected; DES is inherently harmful." However, having conceded that Factor VIII is not fungible, the majority disregards the fungibility requirement, which under Sindell renders market share inapplicable.

* * *

B. Inability to Identify Specific Producers

The second prerequisite of applying market share liability is that the product "cannot be traced to any specific producer." Sindell, 607 P.2d at 936. * * * Here, the majority dilutes the second prerequisite by merely requiring a showing that "it is difficult for the consumer to identify the source of the product * * *." Difficulty in identifying a wrongdoer is clearly an insufficient and unreasonable basis to distort Hawaii's tort law and adopt the market share liability theory.

Unlike the DES situation, this is not a case where product identification, and thus proof of causation, is impossible because a generation has lapsed between exposure and injury. * * * Here, the period of time from plaintiff's claimed exposure to the HIV virus, between 1983 and 1984, to the time he tested positive for HIV antibodies, in 1986, was no more than two to three years. Also, unlike the DES plaintiffs who were in utero and could not identify the source of DES used by their mothers, plaintiff here could have identified the Factor VIII he used. Unfortunately, through no fault of the defendant processors, plaintiff failed to observe and record the name and lot numbers of the Factor VIII he used and the dates he used them.

As noted by defendant Armour Pharmaceutical Company (Armour) in its answering brief, most hospitals and pharmacies maintain records of therapeutic materials purchased and dispensed. The fact that the particular pharmacy where Smith received his Factor VIII did not keep such records long enough or in a form appropriate to meet Smith's litigation requirements is not an inherent circumstance of all AIDS cases involving hemophiliacs which would justify a new rule of law.

Based on the foregoing discussion, I submit that the majority's reliance on DES cases to support its decision to adopt the market share theory of liability is misplaced.

* * *

Notes and Questions

1. With whom do you agree—the majority or the dissent—on the propriety of applying market share liability to Factor VIII? On what basis did the majority avoid the generic defect or fungibility problem? What is the role of the generic product requirement as originally described in the DES cases? Is Factor VIII more like DES or asbestos in terms of its similarity? Should plaintiffs in these cases argue that what is generic is that all firms employed similar screening procedures to obtain their blood products and therefore whether a particular firm's batch is tainted is a fortuity?

2. How about the inability to identify the tortfeasor requirement—should plaintiffs or defendants bear that burden on these facts? Are the DES cases distinguishable? As a matter of fairness, which so strongly motivated the courts in *Sindell* and *Hymowitz*, who can better maintain the records of what product and lots a particular hemophiliac purchased? Which way does the fact that the industry is comprised of only four firms cut? One of the decisions referred to in *Smith* was Ray v. Cutter Laboratories, 754 F.Supp. 193 (M.D.Fla.1991), decided after *Conley*, which also held that Florida's version of market share liability could be applied to Factor VIII.

Problem

Harrison H. Schmidt and Ellen Schmidt purchased a parcel of land in 1961, in the town of Salmon, which they owned outright until 1976. In 1972, after highway improvements had resulted in their parcel facing a busy intersection, the Schmidts began operating a gasoline service station at that location. In 1975 the Schmidts decided to lease the gas station to Mayfair and Martha Gooding. The Goodings maintained the lease and operated the station until 1979.

The station ceased operations in 1979. However, the Schmidts sold the underlying title in 1976 to Fal Allen, who owned it until 1978, and who sold it to Maurice and Katia Kraft who owned the property until 1980. In 1980 the Krafts sold the property to Roger Ressmeyer.

Thus, diagrammatically, the title to and operation of the property appear as follows:

	Owners
	Schmidts
1961–1976	Schmidts
1978	Allen
1980	Krafts
	Ressmeyer

	Operators
1972–1975	Schmidts
1979	Goodings

In 1980, the Salmon Fire Department informed Ressmeyer that the underground gasoline tanks had to be removed to comply with the Uniform Fire Code. When the tanks were removed, the soil was tested for contamination and substantial deposits of hydrocarbons were discovered. Ressmeyer retained an expert who is of the opinion that between 30,000 to 40,000 gallons of gasoline contamination had occurred. Roger Ressmeyer is required to clean up the property before he can resell it and has expended $350,000 in that effort. In 1983 Ressmeyer sues all prior owners and operators for recovery of his losses. The plaintiff maintains that he never used the gasoline station and that the tanks were empty when he purchased the land. However, defendants have one witness who will testify that she saw plaintiff place a gasoline hose from the site in his car a few years ago.

As defendants, the Krafts assert that the gasoline pumps and tanks on the property had been abandoned and were no longer in use at the time they sold the property to Ressmeyer. In Ressmeyer's tort action against the defendants he moves for summary judgment on the ground that there is no genuine issue of material fact in dispute as to the contamination occurring during defendants' ownership and operation of the site. Defendants also move for summary judgment on the grounds that plaintiff must identify which defendant(s) was (were) the cause of the contamination, and has failed to offer any proof to show how or when any particular defendant was responsible for the contamination.

As the law clerk to the trial judge presented with these cross motions for summary judgment, prepare a memorandum addressing how the motions should be resolved. Please address how the question of causal responsibility should be managed at trial if the motions are denied.

b. Lead Paint Pigments

The last Section addressing the scope of market share liability involve allegations that manufacturers of lead pigments incorporated into indoor paints applied in apartments and other buildings are liable on various products liability theories to occupants suffering injuries as a result of lead exposure and consumption. Here too the plaintiffs are unable to identify the manufacturers of the pigment that they ingested and have sought to rely on market share theory to overcome that difficulty. In Santiago v. Sherwin–Williams Co., 782 F.Supp. 186 (D.Mass.1992), affirmed 3 F.3d 546 (1st Cir.1993), the United States District Court in Massachusetts rejected application of the theory. Because the court was bound by Massachusetts law, it relied on Payton v. Abbott Labs, 386 Mass. 540, 437 N.E.2d 171 (1982) in which the Massachusetts Supreme Judicial Court had rejected the theory on the facts of that case. In *Payton* the court had stated that two purposes are served by requiring defendant and product identification: "it separates wrongdoers from innocent actors, and also ensures that wrongdoers are held liable only for the harm that they have caused." It then applied those principles in declining to apply the theory to the pigment manufacturers:

A. *Absence of a Unique Injury*

In DES cases, the market share theory succeeded in separating wrongdoers from innocent actors, because DES plaintiffs suffered from a signature DES injury—a rare form of cancer, adenocarcinoma, that was directly attributable to exposure to DES. * * * In contrast, defendants here assert that heredity, social and environmental factors, or lead in other products, could have caused, or at least contributed to, Santiago's injuries. In other words, defendants argue that Santiago does not suffer from a signature lead paint injury.

Santiago claims that lead poisoning retarded her "educational, social, vocational and intellectual development." Plaintiff's injury is manifested by "difficulties in spelling/language arts, in organization, in requiring extra time and effort to check her work, and with frustration in learning to type." Defendants counter that none of the deficits associated with Santiago "can ever be attributed solely or primarily to lead," and that such "injuries" have been "strongly associated in the vast literature on childhood development with a large variety of factors including heredity, child-rearing techniques, mental and physical health of the parents, and other factors in the social and educational setting in which children develop." * * *

Moreover, even if all of Santiago's injuries could be attributed to lead poisoning, she cannot prove that defendant's lead pigment was the cause of her lead poisoning. Defendants have shown that lead is widespread in many different forms, and that more than 90 percent of lead used in this country during the relevant period was contained in products other than paint. They further show that the air and water in and around Santiago's home during the relevant period may have contained lead that contributed to her blood levels. In addition, the City of Boston identified Santiago's neighborhood in Dorchester as a "hot spot" in soil lead contamination requiring attention by the Environmental Protection Agency. Defendants' expert asserts, as well, that vehicular traffic is a major source of elevated soil lead levels.

* * *

Defendants have produced evidence to show that factors other than lead pigment in paint were adequate producing causes of Santiago's injuries. The jury in this case, therefore, could only speculate as to the degree to which, if at all, the defendants' conduct caused her harm.

B. *Defendant's Market Share*

Market share liability holds defendants responsible only to the extent that their product has contributed to the risk of injury to the public. Presumably, defendants can calculate this risk by determining the percentage of the market that their product occupied during the relevant period. If factors significantly skewing this calculation exist, then Massachusetts would not apply market share, because of the danger that defendants could be held liable for harm "exceeding their responsibility."

1. Scope of the Market

In *Payton*, the SJC indicated that, in order to hold defendants liable, each had to have been "actively in the DES market during all or a substantial part of the relevant period of time in which the mothers of the plaintiffs ingested DES." There, the market was limited to the year in which the named plaintiff's mother ingested DES. Here, the market spans five decades. Santiago contends that the house was first painted around 1917, and that the walls inside the house contain five layers of paint, with the last layer having been applied between 1955 and 1969.

Defendants show that, by 1954, three of the five defendants had ceased producing white lead pigments. In addition, defendant Glidden did not begin producing white lead pigment until 1924, and it stopped in the late 1950's. Defendant Sherwin–Williams has shown, moreover, that by the mid–1930's its lead pigment was used primarily for commercial and industrial applications. Finally, defendants contend that, given the fifty-four year window here, there is insufficient data to establish to what degree each defendant's product was used in lead-based paint.

* * *

This court concludes that there is insufficient evidence that would warrant a jury in finding that all the defendants, or any of them, actively participated in the lead pigment market for lead based paint during the fifty-four year period involved here.

2. Defendants as Bulk Suppliers

Of particular significance as well is the fact that defendants here supplied lead pigment in bulk to paint manufacturers. They are not being sued as manufacturers or marketers of the allegedly offending paint. They, therefore, could not control all of the risks that their products may have presented to the public.

* * *

No court has applied market share theory to a defendant that supplies an ingredient for a product packaged and sold by others. The facts of this case do not warrant a different result.

* * *

Notes and Questions

1. How convincing is the court's analysis? What about the "signature injury" point that at least in DES cases there was no question that plaintiffs' injuries were caused by the DES, and not some other toxic exposure? In other words in lead paint cases plaintiffs have not satisfied the causation in fact issue addressed in the first portion of this chapter. How about the Factor VIII cases—could plaintiffs have contracted AIDS from other sources? Who should bear the burden on this issue?

2. How would a court define the market in these lead pigment cases? Would records be more likely available than in the DES cases? Would national market definitions help? How would you account for the fact that defendants' product was incorporated into another product—paints?

3. In a later opinion, the same court declined to apply a concert of action theory on these facts and held that Massachusetts did not recognize enterprise theory. Santiago v. Sherwin–Williams Co., 794 F.Supp. 29 (D.Mass.1992), affirmed 3 F.3d 546 (1st Cir.1993).

In Swartzbauer v. Lead Industries Association, 794 F.Supp. 142 (E.D.Pa. 1992), a class action on behalf of house painters, the court rejected the whole array of alternative liability theories. It found that the plaintiffs did not sufficiently allege a conspiracy among the industry trade association, paint and pigment manufacturers. It rejected enterprise theory because Pennsylvania courts had not yet accepted the theory. Third, it rejected market share and alternative liability theories because plaintiffs could identify some of the paint and pigment manufacturers of the products to which they were exposed. Accord Hurt v. Philadelphia Housing Authority, 806 F.Supp. 515 (E.D.Pa.1992).

Most recently, the Third Circuit affirmed the dismissal of a class action brought by the City of Philadelphia and its public housing authority to recover the costs of abatement, concluding that none of the plaintiffs' theories to circumvent the defendant identification causation requirement were recognized by Pennsylvania courts or were applicable on these facts. See City of Philadelphia v. Lead Industries Association, 994 F.2d 112 (3d Cir.1993). But see New York v. Lead Industries Association, 190 A.D.2d 173, 597 N.Y.S.2d 698 (1993) (complaint stated cause of action based on concert of action and fraud).

c. Note on Lead Paint and Causation

While the major lead paint litigation against the pigment manufacturers may have fallen on the defendant identification prong of causation, lead paint litigation also presents the extremely difficult questions of linking plaintiff's injuries to the lead exposure. As we saw in *Santiago*, the court actually used that point to buttress its rejection of market share liability. Lead has been recognized as poisonous for millennia, as evidenced by Hippocrates' diagnosis of a metal extractor as suffering from lead poisoning. However, not until the 1970s did the U.S. government take strong action against lead paint, banning it in government-controlled buildings accessible to children and banning the sale of lead-based paint; and banning lead in gasoline in the 1970s. For children, the most vulnerable population group, the exposure to lead is typically caused by ingestion of paint chips or the consumption of the lead chalk or dust. See Hearings Before the U.S. Senate Subcomm. on Toxic Substances, Environmental Oversight, Research and Development, March 8 and 9, 1990 (statements of Kathryn Mahalley, Ph.D., National Institutes of Health; Dr. Ellen K. Silbergeld).

The Centers for Disease Control has published extensive data on the exposure levels that represent a "level of concern." See CDC, Preventing Lead Poisoning in Young Children (Oct. 1991). Typically measured in micrograms per deciliter (μg/dL), the federally-defined threshold of "level of concern" has been lowered from 60 μg/dL to 15 μg/dL in 1991. By comparison, the average lead level in children under two years of age is 4.2 to 5.2 μg/dL and has been declining in recent years largely because of the ban on leaded gasoline. As noted in *Santiago*, a primary problem with lead poisoning is that it produces asymptomatic effects: cognitive difficulties by blocking neuroreceptors in the brain. Acute encephalopathy, usually associated with blood levels of 100 μg/dL, is the most serious condition, producing coma, seizures, ataxia, loss of coordination, vomiting, altered states of consciousness, and loss of recently acquired skills. Less severe symptoms, including decreases in play activity, anorexia, lethargy, abdominal pain and constipation are associated with levels as low as 50 μg/dL.

While there exists little dispute among medical scientists regarding the adverse effects of high blood levels, there is, unsurprisingly, considerable divergence of opinion respecting the effect of low-level lead exposures in children's learning skills and cognitive development. One study, by Dr. Herbert Needleman, suggests that exposed children are: (1) seven times more likely to drop out of high school; (2) six times more likely to have a reading disability; and (3) more likely to have decreased hand-eye coordination, reaction time, and finger tapping. See, e.g., Needleman, et al., The Long–Term Effects of Exposure to Low Doses of Lead in Childhood: An 11–Year Follow–Up Report, 322 New Eng. J. Med. 83 (1990). Another study, of children living near a lead smelter in Australia, is cited for the proposition that three to four IQ points are lost for every 10 μg/dL of exposure over 10 μg/dL.

As indicated, this research is hotly contested. Some scientists believe that the human research to date has not adequately controlled for the myriad of factors known to affect child development. Other researchers point out that the vast majority of children who sustain lead poisoning are from underprivileged socio-economic backgrounds and question whether the presence of such factors may provide an explanation for observed IQ variances and learning problems in the studied population. See, e.g., Ernhart, et al., Subclinical Lead Level & Developmental Deficit: Reanalysis of Data, 18 J. of Learning Disabilities 475 (1985). The debate includes hypotheses that children who are likely to eat paint chips are those already hyperactive, impulsive, or intellectually slower, which is what causes them to eat more paint, or are children of less attentive parents, which makes the children more likely to engage in thumb-sucking or other behaviors that may elevate blood lead levels. See, e.g., Ruff & Bijur, The Effects of Low to Moderate Lead Levels on Neurobehavioral Functioning in Children: Toward a Conceptual Model, 10:2 Developmental & Behavioral Pediatrics 103–09 (1989).

Moreover, as was stressed in the material on epidemiology earlier in this Chapter, causal inferences are undermined by the absence of proper controls for confounding social, economic, nutritional, familial and physical factors which may influence the cognitive and behavioral effects being investigated. Further, the study results have not been consistent regarding the presence of a specific pattern of cognitive deficits associated with lead poisoning. Faust & Brown, Moderately Elevated Blood Lead Levels: Effects on Neuropsychologic Functioning in Children, 80:5 Pediatrics 623–29 (1987). See studies collected in David A. Carter, Lead Poisoning Litigation: Causes of Action, Defenses and Challenging Causation, 7 Toxics L. Rptr. 1539, 1542 (5/26/93).

Assuming plaintiffs' counsel can sufficiently establish generic causation, what theories of liability are most promising in the lead paint cases? What about premises liability actions against landlords or property owners? What difficulties will such theories face? Would a private nuisance theory work in premises cases?

What defenses would be likely asserted in lead paint litigation? How about the bar of statutes of limitations? What about the landlord's lack of notice respecting the problem? How about exculpatory clauses in the tenants' leases? How will plaintiffs sufficiently eliminate other possible sources of lead—leaded gasoline (still available for older vehicles), plumbing fixtures, dust and soil, and industrial emissions? How will plaintiffs sufficiently establish that other factors did not cause or explain the cognitive or behavioral conditions, such as heredity, parental behavior, other health problems, poor nutrition, and other toxins?

D. APPORTIONMENT OF THE HARM OR DAMAGE

1. APPORTIONMENT BETWEEN PLAINTIFF AND DEFENDANT

Closely related to the issue of causal indeterminacy is the issue of the apportionment of damages. In some environmental tort cases—as in other tort cases—the harm which the plaintiff experienced can be attributable to both the defendant's activity and that of the plaintiff, as the *Dafler* case below demonstrates. The problem is to apportion that harm for which the defendant should be responsible and respond in damages, and that portion of the harm for which the plaintiff must accept responsibility.

DAFLER v. RAYMARK INDUSTRIES, INC.

Superior Court of New Jersey, Appellate Division, 1992.
259 N.J.Super. 17, 611 A.2d 136.

The opinion of the court was delivered by
KING, J.

I

This appeal and cross-appeal are taken from a verdict in plaintiff's favor and a jury's apportionment of responsibility between plaintiff and defendant in an asbestos product liability case. The case presents a question of first impression in this State concerning apportionment of damages for lung cancer between an asbestos producer and a cigarette smoker. The jury found that plaintiff contributed 70% to his lung cancer by cigarette smoking and that defendant Keene Corporation (Keene) contributed 30% to plaintiff's lung cancer by its asbestos products used in shipbuilding. The damage verdict for lung cancer was molded to reflect this apportionment. We conclude that both the apportionment by the jury and the general verdict in plaintiff's favor find reasonable factual support in the record and we affirm.

II

This is the procedural background. On October 10, 1986 plaintiff sued 11 defendants, all manufacturers or distributors of asbestos products. At the jury trial in May 1991 the only remaining defendant was Keene. Plaintiff claimed that he developed asbestosis and lung cancer as a result of occupational exposure to asbestos during his six-year employment at the New York Shipyard in Camden, from 1939 to 1945.

On May 21, 1991 the jury returned liability and damage verdicts in plaintiff's favor. The jury found unanimously that "asbestos exposure was a substantial contributing cause of Mr. Dafler's lung cancer." The jury found Keene, through its predecessors, a substantial contributing cause and 95% responsible. The jury found Garlock, Inc., a defendant who had settled for $2,500 before trial, 5% responsible. The monetary awards were: for asbestosis, $60,000; for lung cancer, $140,000—an aggregate of $200,000. * * *

* * *

Both plaintiff and Keene appeal. In this appeal plaintiff raises these claims of error: (1) there was insufficient evidence to allow the jury to apportion damages for plaintiff's lung cancer; (2) the judge improperly influenced the jury's apportionment decision. * * *

III

These are the facts presented at trial. Plaintiff, Frank Dafler, age 70, worked as a shipfitter at the New York Shipyard in Camden from 1939 to 1945. During the World War II era New York Shipyard was one of the world's busiest ship building facilities, employing 36,000 men. During this period plaintiff worked on 12 to 13 ships. * * *

Dafler spent all of his time at the Shipyard working on board these ships. He spent about 70% of his time working in engine rooms and boiler rooms in very close proximity to the pipefitters who used asbestos and asbestos-containing products to cover the numerous pipes housed in those areas. Dafler himself did not work with asbestos, but he said it was all around him. The pipefitters and pipe coverers worked continuously, cutting and cementing pipes. No masks were used or provided. He did recall that the pipefitters' use of asbestos made the air very dusty. There was no ventilation in the boiler or engine rooms during construction.

* * *

The plaintiff began experiencing shortness of breath in the 1970s. In 1984 he went to the hospital for breathing problems. The diagnosis in 1984 was asbestosis. He then decreased the time that he worked between 1984 and 1989 because of his breathing problem. In 1984 he began seeing Dr. Agia, a pulmonary specialist, twice a year for x-rays and pulmonary function tests. In 1989 the doctors found a cancerous tumor in plaintiff's lung and surgery ensued. Plaintiff said that he smoked cigarettes for almost 45 years, since age 18. He had a pack-a-day habit until his diagnosis of asbestosis in 1984 when he quit.

The plaintiff presented two medical experts: Dr. Guidice, a pulmonary specialist, and Dr. Stone, a pathologist. * * *

The experts also testified on the epidemiological aspects of asbestosis and cigarette smoking. Dr. Guidice explained that there is a "base line" relative risk of 11 cases of lung cancer per 100,000 persons in the general population per year. This "base line" is for people in the general population who do not smoke and are not exposed to asbestos. The relative risk of lung cancer with industrial exposure to asbestos, like plaintiff's occupational exposure, increases five-fold (5:1), or to 55 cases per 100,000 of population per year. The relative risk with cigarette smoking increases ten-fold (10:1), or to 110 cases per 100,000 of population per year. The relative risk of exposure to asbestos plus cigarette smoking is not additive, i.e., 10 + 5 or 15–fold, but becomes what Dr. Guidice described as "multiplicative or synergistic," or 50 times (50:1) the "base line," i.e., 550 cases per 100,000 of population per year.

Dr. Guidice could not apportion the causation of plaintiff's lung cancer between his asbestosis and his long-term cigarette smoking. He said when asked about apportionment: "No, and I don't know anybody that's able to do that. That's not possible. This relationship is synergistic and multiplicative between those two cancer causing agents. It's not possible to distinguish which contribution is caused by asbestos and which is caused by cigarette smoking." He conceded that the major cause of lung cancer in the United States is cigarette smoking.

Dr. Stone essentially agreed with Dr. Guidice on the epidemiological data. He thought the relative risk for cigarette smoking alone was about 10 to 12:1 above the "base line," the relative risk for asbestosis alone was about 6 to 7:1 above the "base line." He said that "the lung cancer was caused by the synergistic interaction of his cigarette smoking and asbestos exposure." He also agreed that cigarette smoking was by far the greatest cause of all lung cancers in the United States. He did not attempt to apportion responsibility, saying that "both were significant contributory causes." Both doctors agreed that the relative risk of smoking was twice as great as the relative risk for asbestos with respect to cancer.

As noted, the defendant's expert, Dr. DeMopolous, completely discounted any role for asbestos in causing the plaintiff's lung cancer. He emphasized the role of cigarette smoking as solely causative in this case and in lung cancer in general. * * * He recognized the theoretical synergistic effect of two causative factors but denied any role for asbestos in plaintiff's lung cancer. Dr. DeMopolous did not speak to apportionment.

The jury seemed to have apportioned the damages for plaintiff's lung cancer according to the relative risk factors for asbestos (5:1 or 30%) and cigarette smoking (10:1 or 70%), roughly one-third to two-thirds. The judge molded the jury's monetary verdict on the lung cancer aspect, $140,000, accordingly.

IV

Plaintiff's principal claim on this appeal is that the judge erred in submitting the issue of apportionment to the jury in the first place. Plaintiff contends that there was insufficient evidence in the record to provide any basis for apportionment. Judge Weinberg thought this case presented enough evidence to justify allowing the issue to go to the jury. * * * Although the issue is novel in this jurisdiction, we agree with the trial judge and affirm on this point.

Plaintiff asserts that the lung cancer was an indivisible harm with indivisible damages, that the defendant failed to meet its burden of showing that there was a reasonable basis for apportionment, and that the percentages found by the jury, 30%–70%, were against the weight of the evidence. Defendant Keene contends that the use of apportionment in this case was consistent with the evidence and the development of the law in this State.

Apportionment of damages among multiple causes is a well-recognized tort principle. The Restatement (Second) of Torts § 433A, at 434 (1965), regarding apportionment of harm to causes, states: "(1) Damages for harm are to be apportioned among two or more causes where (a) there are distinct harms, or (b) there is a reasonable basis for determining the contribution of each cause to a single harm. (2) Damages for any other harm cannot be apportioned among two or more causes." Comment (a) to the Restatement indicates that "[t]he rules stated apply also where one of the causes in question is the conduct of the plaintiff himself, whether it be negligent or innocent." Restatement (Second) of Torts § 433A, Comment (a), at 435. Prosser and Keeton, Law of Torts § 52, at 345 (5th ed. 1984), states the problem this way: "Once it is determined that the defendant's conduct has been a cause of some damage suffered by the plaintiff, a further question may arise as to the portion of the total damage sustained which may properly be assigned to the defendant, as distinguished from other causes. The question is primarily not one of the fact of causation, but of the feasibility and practical convenience of splitting up the total harm into separate parts which may be attributed to each of two or more causes. * * *" The Restatement and Prosser both recognize that the concern in apportioning responsibility is more practical than theoretical: is there "a reasonable basis for determining the contribution of each cause to a single harm?" Restatement, supra, § 433A(1)(b) at 434. Here the single harm to the plaintiff was his lung cancer. The two causes were his six-year occupational exposure to asbestos and his 45–year cigarette smoking habit. The trial judge had to determine, as a matter of law in the first instance, whether the harm was capable of apportionment. See Martin v. Owens–Corning Fiberglas Corp., 528 A.2d 947, 949 (Pa.1987). The burden of proving that the harm is capable of apportionment is on the party seeking it, here defendant Keene. Restatement, supra, § 433B(2), at 441.

Several state and federal courts have considered the apportionment issue in similar occupational asbestos-smoking cases. The Pennsylvania Supreme Court addressed the apportionment issue in Martin v. Owens–Corning Fiberglas Corp., supra. The plaintiff, a former insulation worker, brought suit against various asbestos manufacturers seeking damages for asbestosis and lung impairment. Plaintiff worked with asbestos for about 39 years, and smoked for about 37 years. At trial, plaintiff's experts testified that his lung impairment was due to the combined effect of emphysema, caused by cigarette smoking, and asbestosis, from occupational asbestos exposure. They said that it was impossible to apportion the lung impairment between the two causes. Defendant's expert testified that the lung impairment was caused solely by plaintiff's cigarette smoking. The question presented on appeal was whether the trial judge erred in instructing the jury that it could apportion damages between the asbestos exposure and smoking. There were no epidemiological data or relative risk factors before the jury in Martin.

A plurality of the Pennsylvania Supreme Court applied § 433A of the Restatement and held that it was error for the trial judge to instruct the jury on apportionment since the evidence failed to establish a reasonable basis on which to apportion. The court commented: "The jury," although presented with a great deal of testimony concerning appellant's history and physical condition, was provided no guidance in determining the relative contributions of asbestos exposure and cigarette smoking to appellant's disability. In fact, two experts testified that such a determination was not possible.

* * *

Here, the jury cannot be expected to draw conclusions which medical experts, relying on the same evidence, could not draw. The causes of disability in this case do not lend themselves to separation by lay-persons on any reasonable basis. Thus, common sense and common experience possessed by a jury do not serve as substitutes for expert guidance, and it follows that any apportionment by the jury in this case was a result of speculation and conjecture and hence, improper. "Rough approximation" is no substitute for "justice."

In his concurring opinion, Justice McDermott said that he would limit the holding of the three-judge plurality to a single proposition, that "under the facts and circumstances of this case there was not enough evidence to submit the issue of apportionment to the jury." Thus, the Pennsylvania Supreme Court did not rule out apportionment in cases where the evidence in fact supports a reasonable basis upon which to divide the harm.

In strong, separate dissents, both Chief Justice Nix, joined by Justice Zappala, and Justice Hutchinson criticized the plurality for overstepping its bounds and usurping the jury's fact-finding function. They emphasized that a jury should be allowed to make "rough approximations" where there is a reasonable basis to apportion, especially where the plaintiff's own conduct is a substantial factor in bringing about the harm. Justice Hutchinson, in his dissent, made these thoughtful comments in expressing his view that the jury should enjoy considerable latitude and employ common sense in its apportionment task: "I am at a loss to imagine what additional testimony would satisfy the majority. Requiring the experts to speak in terms of numerical percentages introduces a false precision into the evidence. Mathematical exactitude is not found in the real world of medicine. We should not mislead lay jurors by requiring experts to falsely imply its existence. Honest, but more flexible, words such as "substantial factor," "major contribution" or "significant cause" are more suitable to the proper jury function of justly and fairly resolving uncertainties. It is unfair and unjust to place on appellee the whole burden of supporting appellant for a disability his own experts admit he himself substantially caused.''

* * *

Some other jurisdictions have permitted apportionment in these cases. In Brisboy v. Fibreboard Corp., 418 N.W.2d 650 (Mich.1988), the Supreme Court of Michigan upheld a jury finding that plaintiff's smoking contributed 55% to his lung cancer while 45% was attributable to his asbestos exposure, apparently without the benefit of epidemiological testimony. See Jenkins v. Halstead Indus., 706 S.W.2d 191 (1986) (92% of worker's chronic obstructive pulmonary disease apportioned to lifelong cigarette smoking in workers' compensation case). See also Gideon v. Johns–Manville Sales Corp., 761 F.2d 1129, 1138–1140 (5th Cir.1985) (under Texas law, determination is for the jury); Fulgium v. Armstrong World Indus., Inc., 645 F.Supp. 761, 763 (W.D.La.1986) (apportionment allowed under Louisiana law); Champagne v. Raybestos–Manhattan, Inc., 562 A.2d 1100, 1118 (Conn.1989) (plaintiff's smoking found 75% contributory to his lung cancer, citing Michigan's Brisboy v. Fibreboard Corp., supra); Hao v. Owens–Illinois, Inc., 69 Haw. 231, 738 P.2d 416 (1987) (51% smoking; 49% asbestos exposure ratio of apportionment affirmed).

No New Jersey cases have specifically addressed the issue of apportionment of civil law damages in an asbestos-exposure cigarette smoking context. * * * However, the concept of apportionment of damages is not alien to this jurisdiction. The theory of § 433A of the Restatement (Second) of Torts has been applied in varied circumstances. See Scafidi v. Seiler, 574 A.2d 398 (N.J.1990) ("increased risk" and "lost chance" concepts in medical malpractice); Waterson v. General Motors Corp., 544 A.2d 357 (N.J.1988) (automobile "crashworthiness" case); Fosgate v. Corona, 66 N.J. 268, 330 A.2d 355 (1974) (medical malpractice aggravating tuberculosis)[.] These cases involve pre-existing or concurrent injuries; apportionment was limited to instances of distinct injuries or to circumstances when a reasonable basis existed to determine the contribution of each cause. The burden with respect to proof of apportionment rested, of course, with the party seeking it. Restatement (Second) of Torts § 433B(2).

* * *

As we well know, apportionment is also consistent with the principles of the Comparative Negligence Act, N.J.S.A. 2A:15–5.1 to–5.3, and the Contribution Among Tortfeasors Act, N.J.S.A. 2A:53A–1 to–5. See also Feldman v. Lederle Lab., 608 A.2d 356 (App.Div.1992) (apportionment of damages for incremental injury approved).

We conclude that there was ample basis in the record of this trial to submit the issue of apportionment to the jury. The extant legal precedent supports rational efforts to apportion responsibility in such circumstances rather than require one party to absorb the entire burden. The jury obviously accepted the epidemiological testimony based on relative risk factors, the smoking history over 45 years, and the substantial occupational exposure over six years. The synergistically resultant disease, lung cancer, was produced by a relative risk factor of 10:1 contributed by plaintiff and 5:1 contributed by defendant. The jury probably shaded the apportionment slightly in defendant's favor, 70% instead of two-thirds, because of the strong emphasis on cigarette smoking as the greatly predominant overall cause of lung cancer in this country.

The result was rational and fair. We can ask no more. This is fairer than requiring defendant to shoulder the entire causative burden where its contribution in fact was not likely even close to 100%. Or fairer, for certain, than no recovery at all for plaintiff who, while a victim of the disease of asbestosis which probably led in part to the lung cancer, confronts a reluctant jury which might not want to saddle a defendant with a 100% verdict in the circumstances of a particular case.

We conclude that our Supreme Court's recent decision in Landrigan v. Celotex Corp., 605 A.2d 1079 (N.J.1992), a colon cancer asbestos claim, supports the result we reach in relying on the epidemiological data for apportionment. This discipline of epidemiology "studies the relationship between a disease and a factor suspected of causing the disease, using statistical methods * * *." The Supreme Court recognized that "proof of causation in toxic-tort cases depends largely on inferences derived from statistics about groups," and conceded that plaintiffs in toxic-tort cases "may be compelled to resort to more general evidence, such as that provided by epidemiological studies."

* * *

Affirmed.

Notes and Questions

1.   Do you agree with the court's analysis? The Restatement (Second) of Torts § 433A quoted by the court is the primary authority relied upon to justify apportionment in these cases, and requires only a "reasonable basis" for the apportionment. If no apportionment can be made, what is the effect? As the court also observed, Restatement § 433B also places the burden of proving apportionment on the party seeking it—here the defendant Keene. Once the plaintiff succeeds in demonstrating that a defendant's tortious conduct is *a* cause of the harm, the burden shifts to the defendant to limit its liability. See § 433B(2).

2.   Were you impressed by the sophistication of the experts' testimony on relative risks? Did plaintiff undermine his case by having his experts provide the numerical basis for making the apportionment? Why didn't Dr. Guidice's statement that it is "not possible" to apportion causes of lung cancer preclude the jury findings on apportionment? What was the strategy of defendant's expert in testifying that cigarette smoking was the sole cause? Why didn't defendant's expert explicitly support the relative risk analysis of plaintiffs' experts?

3. In Martin v. Owens–Corning Fiberglas Corp., 515 Pa. 377, 528 A.2d 947 (1987), quoted and distinguished by the court in *Dafler*, the Pennsylvania Supreme Court refused to allow apportionment on comparable facts except the experts offered no epidemiological data demonstrating the relative risks of asbestos exposure and smoking. The experts in *Martin* testified identically to Dr. Guidice—both asbestos exposure and smoking were "contributory causes," but "it is not possible to apportion them." Why the different outcome? The dissenting opinions in *Martin* criticize the majority for demanding precise percentages before apportionment would be permissible, because "mathematical exactitude is not found in the real world of medicine." Do the relative risks provide mathematical exactitude?

4. As stated in *Dafler*, medical studies demonstrate the synergistic effect of smoking and asbestos exposure in causing lung cancer. One important study found that the relative risk (ratio of occurrence of disease in exposed group to occurrence in general population) of lung cancer for nonsmoking insulation industry workers exposed to asbestos was 5.17; for smokers not exposed to asbestos—10.85; but for exposed smokers—and for exposed heavy smokers—87.36. See Surgeon General of the United States, The Health Consequences of Smoking: Cancer and Chronic Lung Disease in the Workplace 213–20 (1986); United States Dep't of Labor, Disability Compensation for Asbestos–Associated Disease in the United States 335 (1981).

5. *Comparative Fault*. In comparative fault jurisdictions, juries may be required to apportion damages if they find that the plaintiff's smoking constituted contributory fault. In Brisboy v. Fibreboard Corp., 429 Mich. 540, 418 N.W.2d 650 (1988), cited in *Dafler*, the court upheld a jury's finding that decedent's smoking was contributorily negligent and that the smoking contributed 55 percent to his lung cancer. Addressing the quality of evidence on the apportionment question, the court stated: "We reject plaintiff's claim that there is no rational basis for the jury's apportionment of fault and note that juries are frequently called upon to make such judgments." See also Hao v. Owens–Illinois, Inc., 69 Hawaii 231, 738 P.2d 416 (1987) (applying pure comparative fault to apportion plaintiff's negligence in smoking and defendant's responsibility for providing asbestos products).

6. An interesting contrast to *Dafler* is found in Acosta v. Babcock & Wilcox, 961 F.2d 533 (5th Cir.1992). In *Acosta*, the jury rendered a verdict for defendant, which the appeals court reversed because the jury instruction improperly barred three plaintiffs from arguing that cigarette smoking and workplace exposure to asbestos may have combined to cause plaintiffs' cancer. The court held that the instruction by a federal trial court wrongly required the plaintiffs to prove that "but for" workplace exposure to asbestos, the long-term smokers would not have developed lung cancer. The court said it was medically impossible "to determine whether cigarettes alone or asbestos alone" caused the workers' cancer and remanded the cases for a new trial. One of the plaintiffs' medical experts testified that asbestos exposure was a "substantial contributing factor" to a worker's interstitial fibrosis and asbestosis. The expert also testified that smoking could have played a part in the development of the cancer. Another plaintiffs' expert contended that asbestos exposure was a causal factor of the cancer and that the two causes multiplied the risks.

The trial judge instructed the jury that the law recognizes that there may be more than one cause of an injury, but "each may be the cause, so long as it can reasonably be said that, except for asbestos exposure, the injury complained of would not have occurred." The appeals court explained:

> The testimony of the plaintiffs' witnesses was to the effect that the asbestos exposure "played a substantial part in bringing about or actually causing the injury." That the jury was not informed that this testimony could have been sufficient to establish legal causation * * * constitutes reversible error. In today's world of carcinogens, a conscientious jury would be hard pressed to state unequivocally that a person would not get cancer absent exposure to asbestos.

Would apportionment be possible in this case? If not, what will the defendants' liability be in the event the jury finds that asbestos was a contributing cause of the cancer? Should defendant use different tactics for its experts' testimony?

7. In several asbestos cases, defendants have sought to introduce plaintiffs' smoking history in order to demonstrate that plaintiffs would not have heeded any warnings on asbestos products even if they had been provided, and hence the defendants' failure to warn of the dangers of asbestos exposure was not the cause of their injuries. In other words, if plaintiffs ignored the warnings on cigarette packages, which contributed to lung cancer, they would have been unlikely to heed any warnings on asbestos containers. See Owens–Corning Fiberglas Corp. v. Watson, 243 Va. 128, 413 S.E.2d 630 (1992) (evidence that plaintiff did not heed warnings on cigarette carton was properly excluded by trial court; fact that plaintiff disregarded warnings on cigarette packages, without more, was not probative of whether he would have heeded any warnings that might have been affixed to packages of insulation products); Owens–Illinois v. Armstrong, 326 Md. 107, 604 A.2d 47 (1992) (same).

8. See Lewis A. Kornhauser & Richard L. Revesz, Sharing Damages Among Multiple Tortfeasors, 98 Yale L.J. 831 (1989); Mario J. Rizzo & Frank S. Arnold, Causal Apportionment in the Law of Torts: An Economic Theory, 80 Colum. L. Rev. 1399 (1980); William M. Landes & Richard A. Posner, Joint and Multiple Tortfeasors: An Economic Analysis, 9 J. Legal Stud. 517 (1980). Rizzo and Arnold's proposal and methodology are criticized in David Kaye & Michael Aickin, A Comment on Causal Apportionment, 13 J. Legal Stud. 191 (1984), and in Mark Kelman, The Necessary Myth of Objective Causation Judgments in Liberal Political Theory, 63 Chi.–Kent L. Rev. 579, 611–17 (1987).

2. APPORTIONMENT OR JOINT AND SEVERAL LIABILITY AMONG TORTFEASORS

If the plaintiff is entirely innocent—without fault and without having made any contribution to the injury—how should the courts allocate the harm among two or more defendants? The decision that follows answers that question in the nuisance setting.

MICHIE v. GREAT LAKES STEEL DIVISION

United States Court of Appeals, Sixth Circuit, 1974.
495 F.2d 213.

EDWARDS, C.J.

This is an interlocutory appeal from a District Judge's denial of a motion to dismiss filed by three corporations which are defendants-appellants herein. The District Court certified that the appeal presented a controlling issue of law and this court granted leave to appeal under 28 U.S.C. § 1292(b) (1970).

Appellants' motion to dismiss was based upon the contention that each plaintiff individually had failed to meet the requirement of a $10,000 amount in controversy for diversity jurisdiction set forth in 28 U.S.C. § 1332 (1970).

The facts in this matter, as alleged in the pleadings, are somewhat unique. Thirty-seven persons, members of thirteen families residing near LaSalle, Ontario, Canada, have filed a complaint against three corporations which operate seven plants in the United States immediately across the Detroit River from Canada. Plaintiffs claim that pollutants emitted by plants of defendants are noxious in character and that their discharge in the ambient air violates various municipal and state ordinances and laws. They assert that the discharges represent a nuisance and that the pollutants are carried by air currents onto their premises in Canada, thereby damaging their persons and property. Each plaintiff individually claims damages ranging from $11,000 to $35,000 from all three corporate defendants jointly and severally. There is, however, no assertion of joint action or conspiracy on the part of defendants.

* * *

We believe the principal question presented by this appeal may be phrased thus: Under the law of the State of Michigan, may multiple defendants, whose independent actions of allegedly discharging pollutants into the ambient air thereby allegedly create a nuisance be jointly and severally liable to multiple plaintiffs for numerous individual injuries which plaintiffs claim to have sustained as a result of said actions, where said pollutants mix in the air so that their separate effects in creating the individual injuries are impossible to analyze.

Appellants argue that the law applicable is that of the State of Michigan and that Michigan law does not allow for joint and several liability on the part of persons charged with maintaining a nuisance. They cite and rely on an old Michigan case. Robinson v. Baugh, 31 Mich. 290 (1875). They also quote and rely upon Restatement of Torts (First) 881:

"Where two or more persons, each acting independently, create or maintain a situation which is a tortious invasion of a landowner's interest in the use and enjoyment of land by interfering with his quiet, light, air or flowing water, each is liable only for such proportion of the harm caused to the land or of the loss of enjoyment of it by the owner as his contribution to the harm bears to the total harm."

* * *

Appellees rely strongly upon the opinion of the District Judge in denying the motion to dismiss:

"This court is of the view that this is not the state of the law in Michigan with respect to air pollution. In the absence of any Michigan cases on point, analogous Michigan cases in the automobile negligence area involving questions of joint liability after the simultaneous impact of vehicles and resultant injuries, are instructive."

In Watts v. Smith, 375 Mich. 120, 134 N.W.2d 194, the Michigan Supreme Court said:

"Although it is not always definitely so stated the rule seems to have become generally established that, although there is no concert of action between tort feasors, if the cumulative effects of their acts is a single indivisible injury which it cannot certainly be said would have resulted but for the concurrence of such acts, the actors are to be held liable as joint tort feasors."

In Maddux v. Donaldson, 362 Mich. 425, 108 N.W.2d 33, the Michigan Supreme Court * * * indicated that

" * * * it is clear that there is a manifest unfairness in 'putting on the injured party the impossible burden of proving the specific shares of harm done by each * * *. Such results are simply the law's callous dullness to innocent sufferers. One would think that the obvious meanness of letting wrongdoers go scot free in such cases would cause the courts to think twice and to suspect some fallacy in their rule of law.' "

Plaintiffs contend that the Maddux, id., and Watts, supra, language applies here since there is no possibility of dividing the injuries herein alleged to have occurred and that it is impossible to judge which of the alleged tortfeasors caused what harm.

It is the opinion of this court that the rule of Maddux, supra, and Landers, supra, cited therein is the better, and applicable rule in this air pollution case.

On this point we affirm the decision of the District Judge. This complaint appears to have been filed under the diversity jurisdiction of the federal courts. All parties have agreed that Michigan law alone controls.

Like most jurisdictions, Michigan has had great difficulty with the problems posed in tort cases by multiple causes for single or indivisible injuries. Compare Watts v. Smith, 375 Mich. 120, 134 N.W.2d 194 (1965); Maddux v. Donaldson, 362 Mich. 425, 108 N.W.2d 33 (1961).

* * *

We believe that the issue was decided in the lengthy consideration given by the Michigan court in the Maddux case. There Justice Talbot Smith in an opinion for the court majority held:

It is our conclusion that if there is competent testimony, adduced either by plaintiff or defendant, that the injuries are factually and medically separable, and that the liability for all such injuries and damages, or parts thereof, may be allocated with reasonable certainty to the impacts in turn, the jury will be instructed accordingly and mere difficulty in so doing will not relieve the triers of the facts of this responsibility. This merely follows the general rule that "where the independent concurring acts have caused distinct and separate injuries to the plaintiff, or where some reasonable means of apportioning the damages is evident, the courts generally will not hold the tort-feasors jointly and severally liable."

But if, on the other hand, the triers of the facts conclude that they cannot reasonably make the division of liability between the tortfeasors, this is the point where the road of authority divides. Much ancient authority, not in truth precedent, would say that the case is now over, and that plaintiff shall take nothing. Some modern courts, as well, hold that his is merely the case of the marauding dogs and the helpless sheep relitigated in the setting of a modern highway. The conclusion is erroneous. Such precedents are not apt. When the triers of the facts decide that they cannot make a division of injuries we have, by their own finding, nothing more or less than an indivisible injury, and the precedents as to indivisible injuries will control. * * * Maddux v. Donaldson, 362 Mich. 425, 432–433, 108 N.W.2d 33, 36 (1961).

* * *

* * * [A]ppellants call our attention to what appears to be a contrary rule applicable to nuisance cases referred to in the Maddux opinion. Restatement of Torts (First) 881.

In the latest Restatement, however, both the old and the newer rule are recognized and as the Michigan court held in Maddux, the question of whether liability of alleged polluters is joint or several is left to the trier of the facts. Where the injury itself is indivisible, the judge or jury must determine whether or not it is practicable to apportion the harm among the tortfeasors. If not, the entire liability may be imposed upon one (or several) tortfeasors subject, of course, to subsequent right of contribution among the joint offenders.

* * *

Assuming plaintiffs in this case prove injury and liability as to several tort-feasors, the net effect of Michigan's new rule is to shift the burden of proof as to which one was responsible and to what degree from the injured party to the wrongdoers.

* * *

Since our instant case has not been tried, we do not speculate about what the facts may show, either as to injury or liability. But it is obvious from the briefs that appellant corporations intend to make the defense that if there was injury, other corporations, persons and instrumentalities contributed to the pollution of the ambient air so as to make it impossible to prove whose emissions did what damage to plaintiffs' persons or homes. Like the District Judge, we see a close analogy between this situation and the Maddux case. We believe the Michigan Supreme Court would do so likewise.

* * *

As modified, the judgment of the District Court is affirmed.

Notes and Questions

1. Would the rule of the *Michie* case apply to most nuisance cases where there are multiple tortfeasors, each making some contribution to the total harm suffered by the plaintiffs? The synergistic nature of many toxic chemical agents could be relevant to such cases because it is the combined impact of the chemicals which caused the harm to the nearby residents and there would not appear to exist any feasible means for the plaintiff to apportion the damages or apportion the causation. In Chapter 10 we consider this same question in allocating the harm among potentially responsible parties in suits brought under the Comprehensive Environmental Response, Compensation and Liability Act.

2. Is the situation of the successive (and simultaneous) automobile collisions relied on in *Michie* analogous to the air or water pollution or waste site disposal situation?

3. *Michie* indicates the attitude of many of the more recent decisions in finding the defendants each liable for the total damage. Two different legal means are used to accomplish this result: (a) to find that the injury is indivisible and therefore not apportionable as a matter of substantive law, and (b) to hold that the burden of proof is upon the defendants to show factual basis for apportionment, with the result that apportionment is unavailable as a practical matter. Illustrations of the first approach are Holtz v. Holder, 101 Ariz. 247, 418 P.2d 584 (1966) (chain collision); Ruud v. Grimm, 252 Iowa 1266, 110 N.W.2d 321 (1961) (same); Landers v. East Texas Salt Water Disposal Co., 151 Tex. 251, 248 S.W.2d 731 (1952) (pollution). Illustrations of the second approach are Murphy v. Taxicabs of Louisville, 330 S.W.2d 395 (Ky.1959) (chain collision); Maddux v. Donaldson, 362 Mich. 425, 108 N.W.2d 33 (1961) (same); Phillips Petroleum Co. v. Hardee, 189 F.2d 205 (5th Cir.1951) (pollution); see Restatement (Second) of Torts § 433B(2). Is there any significant difference between these two ideas?

4. Suppose twenty-six defendants discharge waste into a stream; no one of them discharges enough to pollute the stream, but the combined

discharge does pollute it. Is the plaintiff entitled to damages, and if so, how much from each defendant? Does it make any difference that the defendants, although not acting in concert, each knows what the others are doing? See Woodland v. Portneuf Marsh Valley Irr. Co., 26 Idaho 789, 146 P. 1106 (1915); Sloggy v. Dilworth, 38 Minn. 179, 36 N.W. 451 (1888).

Two defendants independently pollute a stream by discharging oil into it. The oil on the surface catches fire, and the fire burns the plaintiff's barn. Can the damages be apportioned? Northup v. Eakes, 72 Okl. 66, 178 P. 266 (1918); Phillips Petroleum Co. v. Vandergriff, 190 Okl. 280, 122 P.2d 1020 (1942).

5. In apportioning the damages among joint tortfeasors the courts have taken a variety of approaches. Some courts have relied upon the comparative fault statutes and allocated liability based on each defendant's share of fault, as determined by the jury. See, e.g., Taylor v. Celotex Corp., 393 Pa.Super. 566, 574 A.2d 1084 (1990) (applying New Jersey law, allocated according to each defendant's causal fault under New Jersey Comparative Negligence Act, 2A:15–5.1); Rocco v. Johns–Manville Corp., 754 F.2d 110 (3d Cir.1985) (applying Pennsylvania Joint Tortfeasors Act, which is based on the Uniform Contribution Among Tortfeasors Act, each defendant is assigned a pro-rata share, one-ninth in this case).

6. *Effect of Comparative Fault on Joint and Several Liability.* Some states, as part of their enactment of comparative fault systems, have modified or abolished joint and several liability. For example, the New Jersey Comparative Negligence Act, N.J.S.A. 2A:15–1.1 et seq., altered joint and several liability so that only defendants determined to be 60% or more responsible for damages would be liable for the total amount of an award. A defendant found to be more than 20% but less than 60% responsible for the damages would be liable for the entire amount of economic loss, but only for that percentage of non-economic loss directly attributable to his fault. A defendant found to be responsible for 20% or less of any damages would be liable only for the percentage of the award directly attributable to his fault.

Consequently, defendants found only 1% responsible can no longer be held liable for the entire amount of an award. This demonstration is significant in toxic tort and environmental claims, where the value of damages can be enormous. The statute, however, contains an exception for environmental tort actions: "With regard to environmental tort actions the party so recovering may recover the full amount of the damage award from any party determined to be liable." N.J.S.A. 2A:15–5.3(d). An "environmental tort action" is defined as "a civil action seeking damages for personal injuries or death where the cause of the damages is the negligent manufacture, use, disposal, handling, storage or treatment of hazardous or toxic substances." N.J.S.A. 2A:15–5.3(i). New Jersey's Product Liability Act, N.J.S.A. 2A:58C–1 et seq., enacted at the same time as the Comparative Negligence Act, similarly exempted environmental tort actions. In that act, an "environmental tort action" is defined as "a civil action seeking damages for harm where the cause of the harm is exposure to toxic chemicals or substances, but * * * not * * * actions involving drugs or products intended for personal consumption or use." N.J.S.A. 2A:58C–1(b)(4).

In Stevenson v. Keene Corp., 254 N.J.Super. 310, 603 A.2d 521 (1992), affirmed 131 N.J. 393, 620 A.2d 1047 (1993), the appellate division held that asbestos cases did constitute "environmental tort actions" and hence the defendants were not entitled to the abolition of joint and several liability. The court emphasized that asbestos was regulated by a variety of state and federal environmental statutes. The New Jersey Supreme Court in a per curiam affirmance observed, however, that the "environmental tort action exception" should not be enlarged to include every conceivable injury involving a toxic product.

In Tragarz v. Keene Corp., 980 F.2d 411 (7th Cir.1992), the Seventh Circuit interpreted the Illinois exception to its elimination of joint and several liability (Ill.—S.H.A. 735 ILCS 5/2–1117; and 5/2–1118) which provides:

> notwithstanding the provisions of Section 2–1117 in any action in which the trier of fact determines that the injury or damage for which recovery is sought was caused by an act involving the discharge into the environment of any pollutant, including any waste, hazardous substance, irritant, or contaminant, including, but not limited to smoke, vapor, soot, fumes, acids, alkalis, asbestos, toxic or corrosive chemicals * * * any defendants found liable shall be jointly and severally liable for such damage.

The court held that the discharge of asbestos fibers into the internal environment of a building constituted "the discharge into the environment of any pollutant."

Other courts have reached similar conclusions. See, e.g., Sofie v. Fibreboard Corp., 112 Wash.2d 636, 771 P.2d 711 (1989), amended 780 P.2d 260 (Wash.1989) (as amended holding that Wash. Rev. Code Ann. 4.22.070 providing exception for "hazardous waste or substances" encompassed asbestos litigation).

What is the rationale for creating environmental tort exceptions, allowing joint and several liability to apply to such cases?

Problem

Buy–Products, Inc. operated a chemical research plant on Main and Third streets in Anytown, State from 1945 to 1979, when the plant was closed. Buy–Products' operations focused on research related to potential commercial uses or recycling of chemical by-products and wastes. These chemicals were purchased from other chemical manufacturers.

Although successful in part, Buy–Products could not find commercial uses for all of the chemical by-products and wastes which were shipped to its plant. From 1945 to 1968, unusable materials were dumped into several unlined open pits located near the back of the plant property. These pits were within ten yards of the Chem Creek which ran through the back of the property and through several surrounding neighborhoods.

When Buy–Products stopped pouring materials into the pits in 1968, it leveled a small storage building which had served as a transfer center for the disposal of chemicals. Several leaking barrels were left within the building rubble. In 1978, the pits were dug up and covered over with top soil. For a short period of time until the plant closed, Buy–Products poured some of its wastes into a sewer grate located near the plant entrance.

In 1979, the State Department of the Environment (DE) began its initial investigation of the site. The DE discovered that wastes from metal degreasing operations and byproducts from pesticide manufacture were the main source of material dumped into the pits. Of particular concern to DE were the relatively high concentrations of trichlorethylene and polychlorinated dibenzodioxins, which included 2, 3, 7, 8 tetrachlorodibenzodioxin (TCDD). Experts have estimated that 10,000 gallons of these wastes and byproducts were dumped into the pits over a 40–year period.

The DE also learned that byproducts from pesticide manufacture had been mixed with other chemicals and then spread over the plant property in the 1940s and 1950s for dust control. Periodically, the plant grounds would be plowed by bulldozers and the soil would be stored in a pile near the creek. Subsequently, this soil was sold to a developer and was used for landscaping the lawns of surrounding homes. Preliminary sampling by DE in 1985 indicated very localized "hot spots" of TCDD contamination in some yards, up to 20 ppb (parts per billion). All identified hot spots were excavated down to 12 inches and removed. Some residents refused DE access to their yards.

In 1987, DE, while digging up the property, discovered three leaking underground storage tanks containing gasoline. These tanks were all located on the western edge of the plant property. The gasoline had been used in the operation of Buy–Products' chemical trucking operation. It is believed that more than 500 gallons of gasoline had leaked into the soil over 15 years.

The Pure Water Aquifer, which is 100 feet below the surface, runs directly below the Buy–Products plant site and provides well water for some of the Anytown residents. Other Anytown residents receive municipal water from the Sparkle Reservoir five miles to the north. There is also a shallow aquifer 20 feet below the surface which is not used for drinking water. Trichloroethylene and other compounds at high levels (up to 1,000 ppm) have been found in the shallow aquifer. The Anytown sewer system runs through the plant property and down Main Street. When the storage building was leveled in 1968, local residents noted a strange odor, and releases of dust which settled on their houses and yards.

Main Street is an east/west street located on the south border of the site. Third Street forms the eastern border of the plant. Chem Creek runs along the northern boundary. The Jones family resides on the corner of Main and Fourth Streets on the western border of the property. The Smith family resides on Fourth Street on the western border of the plant along Chem Creek. The Lowe family resides across Fourth Street from the Smith family, and Mrs. High resides across Main Street from the plant entrance.

The following is known with regard to each family member:

Mr. Fred Jones: 60 years old; steel worker; moved into new home in 1954; Smoker; Mother had breast cancer; in 1990, was diagnosed with acute myelogenous leukemia; Of all plaintiffs, the Joneses live closest to site.

Mrs. Ethel Jones: 58 years old; Town Librarian; moved into new home in 1954; non-smoker; no history of cancer; frequently complained of "gasoline" odors in basement; doctor diagnoses immune system dysfunction manifested in frequent illnesses.

Ms. Judy Jones: daughter; born 1958; as child, waded in Chem Creek; now lives on Seventh Street; insurance broker; complains of frequent headaches and anxiety.

Mr. Sam Smith: 58 years old; steel worker; moved into new home in 1954; non-smoker; notes yard soil is discolored in areas and nothing grows.

Mrs. Shirley Smith: 57 years old; school teacher who left job because of claimed illness; non-smoker; had vegetable garden along west fence line of Buy–Products plant from 1955–1980; reveals elevated blood levels of TCDD.

Mr. Steve Smith: son; born 1956; had frequent skin rashes which have now ceased; married with one child; lives on Tenth Street; school teacher; as child, swam in Chem Creek.

Mr. John Lowe: 50 years old; banker; moved into home in 1989; non-smoker; recent tests indicate some liver dysfunction, but no overt disease.

Mrs. Jane Lowe: 50 years old; not employed; non-smoker.

Mrs. High: 68 years old; moved into home 1945; husband was plant foreman for Buy–Products from 1945–1975 and he died of a heart attack in 1975.

Ms. Lee High: daughter; born 1953

You are a private attorney in Anytown. You are visited by Sam Smith, who provides to you the above information. Speaking on behalf of his family, the Jones and the Lowes, he asks you to advise him of any potential legal claims the family members might pursue, individually or collectively. Please advise him, providing him as well with your evaluation of the likely legal responses of any parties against whom liability may be sought. In particular you are concerned respecting the possible causation problems which these clients may encounter in establishing the relationship between their injuries and the exposures.

Chapter Nine

WORKPLACE INJURIES AND TOXIC SUBSTANCES: INTERSECTION OF WORKERS' COMPENSATION AND TORT LIABILITY

A. INTRODUCTION TO THE WORKERS' COMPENSATION SYSTEM

1. A BRIEF HISTORY

Many of the cases in earlier chapters illustrate that employees may suffer physical harm or emotional distress as a result of exposure to toxic substances or chemicals in the workplace. The decisions we have previously considered are actions by the injured employee usually against third party product manufacturers, not against the employer. The rights and remedies which an employee may have against the employer are generally governed by workers' compensation and occupational disease statutes, whereas the rights against a third party manufacturer are governed by common law tort rules.

Under the law of virtually every state, an employee who is injured in a work-related capacity is barred from instituting a tort suit against her employer, provided that the employee is entitled to seek workers' compensation benefits from the employer's insurer. At the same time, the employee is not barred from suing a third party who causes or contributes to the injury. Workers' compensation protection does not affect the action against the third party, but the employer (or its carrier) usually is subrogated to the extent of benefits paid. Prior to the widespread enactment of the workers' compensation systems, an injured employee could institute a tort suit against her employer, but substantial obstacles hampered the injured employee's success in such common law actions. The employee had to establish the employer's negligence, a difficult task in most industrial accidents, and the employer was allowed to assert the defenses of contributory negligence, assumption of the risk, or the fellow servant doctrine—Dean Prosser's "unholy trinity." Prosser & Keeton on Torts § 80 at 569 (5th ed. 1984).

By the early twentieth century, workers' compensation statutes began to sweep the country. Almost universally these statutes provide for recovery of determinate amounts from the employer upon proof that the injury was one "arising out of and in the course of employment," without regard to fault. Thus, negligence of the employer or its agents, or of the injured employee, is irrelevant. At the same time, all workers' compensation statutes bar the injured employee from suing his employer in most cases, even when the employer would otherwise have been liable under common law doctrine. This exclusive remedy provision constitutes the core political trade-off. The employee receives defined compensation under a strict liability regime without the need to invest time, cost and uncertainty of litigation. The employer, in turn, is afforded immunity from tort suits. Third parties, such as product manufacturers, were not included in the trade-off barring the injured employee's common law suit.

As courts and juries in tort cases moved much more rapidly to increase the dollar amounts awarded than did legislatures and administrative boards in control of the workers' compensation system, injured workers and their lawyers found an increasing incentive to avoid the exclusive remedy provision and the accompanying damage limitation. While product liability suits are often available in workplace injuries, as the asbestos litigation demonstrates vividly, often the employee's injury did not involve the use of a product manufactured by a third party. Therefore, injured workers have sought to find gaps in the exclusivity bar that would free them to sue their employers in a tort suit.

The quest for tort liability against employers is also stimulated by the tremendous variation among state systems in the dollar amounts awarded for a given injury or disability. For example, an employee who loses a hand in Kansas receives benefits computed at 150 weeks, see Kan. Stat. Ann. 44–510d(11), while in Wisconsin, the loss of a hand is computed at 400 weeks, Wis. Stat. Ann. 102.52(3). An employee in Tennessee who loses an eye receives compensation computed at 100 weeks, Tenn. Code Ann. § 50–6–207(3)(A)(ii)(q), but in Maryland, receives 250 weeks, Md. Code Art. 101, § 36(3)(b) (1990).

2. ISSUE PRECLUSION

One issue bearing on the relationship between tort actions and workers' compensation claims is whether an adverse finding in a compensation proceeding will be given collateral estoppel effect in a subsequent tort suit against a third party, such as a product manufacturer or supplier. For example, if the compensation board determines that the claimant's injury or disease was not causally linked to her employment, will a court be bound by that adverse factual finding in a subsequent tort suit?

While the decisions are split, the weight of authority seems to answer the inquiry affirmatively, holding that the requirements for issue preclusion may be satisfied by the prior proceeding. In Grant v. GAF Corp., 415 Pa.Super. 137, 608 A.2d 1047 (1992), three widows brought wrongful death actions against various manufacturers of asbestos products, alleging that the decedents had developed asbestosis and carcinoma from workplace exposure to asbestos products. Prior to filing the civil action the plaintiffs had filed for workers' compensation/occupational disease benefits under Pennsylvania law. A workers' compensation referee determined that each "decedent's cancer and subsequent death were not a result of any occupational exposure," and that the widows had not met their "burden of proving that Decedent's lifetime disability or death [were] occupationally related." Those determinations were upheld on appeal. After reviewing the four essentials of issue preclusion: (1) the issue decided in the prior action was identical with the one presented in the later action; (2) there was a final judgment on the merits; (3) the party against whom the plea is asserted was a party or in privity with a party to the prior adjudication; and (4) the party against whom the plea is asserted has had a full and fair opportunity to litigate the issue in question in a prior action, the court held:

> The preclusive effect of this determination in a subsequent tort action is clear; the element of causation is necessary to recovery in a tort action against the defendants/manufacturers. * * * The issue of causation, injury as a result of exposure in the workplace, was decided adversely to the plaintiffs in the workmen's compensation proceeding and thus recovery in a subsequent tort action is precluded.

> * * *

> * * * Here, the referees' findings that the decedents' carcinoma was not related to occupational exposure were determined on appeal to be supported by sufficient competent evidence. The doctrine of collateral estoppel is not unavailable simply because administrative procedures are involved; where the agency is acting in a judicial capacity and resolves disputed issues of fact which the parties had an opportunity to litigate, the courts will not hesitate to apply preclusion principles.

See also Miller v. Pool and Canfield, Inc., 800 S.W.2d 120 (Mo.App.1990) (recognizing the applicability of issue preclusion, but refusing to apply it because the compensation determination was not a final judgment); Smith v. LTV Steel Co., 1992 WL 316324 (Ohio App. 1992); Hansen v. Estate of Harvey, 119 Idaho 333, 806 P.2d 426 (1991). But see Walker v. Kerr–McGee Chem. Corp., 793 F.Supp. 688 (N.D.Miss.1992) (refusing to apply issue preclusion because under Mississippi law strict mutuality is required between the parties in the two actions).

One of the casebook authors has offered these observations on dissimilarities between workers' compensation proceedings and ordinary civil trials. M. Stuart Madden, Issue Preclusion in Products Liability, 11 Pace L. Rev. 87, 131–133 (1990):

> Although workers' compensation boards are court-like "in legal effect," to accomplish the principal goal of compensation, administrative procedures in workers' compensation make substantial accommodations to economy and celerity. The jurisdiction of the workers' compensation tribunal is limited to findings of fact and conclusions of law pertaining to whether the claim arose "out of and in the course of employment." Explicit limitations are placed upon the appellate review of board findings of fact. In the proceedings themselves, a "rule of informality" obtains, and thus, compared with proceedings before courts of general jurisdiction, workers' compensation boards employ generally relaxed rules of notice and pleading.

> Hearsay and even incompetent evidence is admissible, and indeed, the rules of evidence are so relaxed that workers' compensation findings are more likely to be reversed for failure to admit evidence than for denying admission to evidence. Employee claimants frequently appear on their own behalf, without counsel.

> The specialized role of workers' compensation as a compensation system administered by agencies in a quasi-judicial capacity should disable any issue preclusive effect of such judgments in later tort actions against the manufacturer or other third parties. Agency findings and appellate affirmations that an injury was, or was not, sustained in the course of employment, merit conclusive effect, as ceding to compensation panels finality in deciding this issue is integral to the bargained-for exchange between employee and employer to forego tort remedies in return for expedited compensation for work-related injuries. However, grave fairness questions arise from giving preclusive effect to any other holdings a board may consider within its ancillary jurisdiction. In deciding the work-relatedness of an injury, for example, a board may have to reach conclusions on issues such as identification of the product or instrumentality causing claimant's injury, or the claimant's incautious conduct short of intentional misconduct. It does not, however, follow that findings on such ancillary matters should be accorded preclusive effect in later tort actions, for given the primary purpose, the limited parties, and the informality of workers' compensation proceedings, it would be quite unlikely for a claimant to anticipate and assert or defend fact issues solely because of the potential relevance of such issues in a later tort action against third parties.

In light of these considerations, what would you advise a client who may have sustained a work-related toxic injury or disease but who also has a potential tort claim against a third party? What are the strategic considerations which you must evaluate? What do you tell your client about the odds of risking an adverse impact on a tort suit?

B. AVOIDING THE EXCLUSIVITY BAR

Unsurprisingly, the efforts to avoid the exclusivity bar have yielded some success as the courts and some legislatures have engrafted exceptions to the basic employer immunity from tort suit.

1. THE INTENTIONAL TORT EXCEPTION TO EXCLUSIVITY

A major and expanding exception to the workers' compensation exclusivity provisions barring the employee's suit for tort liability is the intentional tort exception. Essentially, a recent line of cases has held that if an employee can establish that the employer committed an intentional tort, the employee can sue the employer directly and recover tort damages. In the landmark case of Blankenship v. Cincinnati Milacron Chemicals, Inc., 69 Ohio St.2d 608, 433 N.E.2d 572 (1982), cert. denied 459 U.S. 857, 103 S.Ct. 127, 74 L.Ed.2d 110 (1982), the Ohio Supreme Court held that employees could sue their employers for exposure to toxic chemicals under narrowly defined circumstances.

In *Blankenship*, eight employees alleged that they were exposed to fumes and noxious chemicals within the scope of their employment which rendered them "sick, poisoned, and chemically intoxicated, causing them pain, discomfort, and emotional distress * * * causing suffering and permanent disability." They further alleged that knowing that such conditions existed, the employer failed to take any corrective action, failed to warn employees of the dangers that existed, and failed to report the conditions to various state and federal agencies. The Ohio workers' compensation statute provided:

> Employers * * * shall not be liable to respond in damages at common law or by statute for any injury, or occupational disease, or bodily condition, received or contracted by any employee in the course of or arising out of his employment * * * whether or not such injury, occupational disease [or] bodily condition * * * is [otherwise] compensable under the Revised Code.

The court, in recognizing the intentional tort exception, reasoned:

> [W]here an employee asserts in his complaint a claim for damages based on an intentional tort, " * * * the substance of the claim is not an 'injury * * * received or contracted by any employee in the course of or arising out of his employment' within the meaning of R.C. 4123.74 * * *." No reasonable individual would equate intentional and unintentional conduct in terms of the degree of risk which faces an employee nor would such individual contemplate the risk of an intentional tort as a natural risk of employment. Since an employer's intentional conduct does not arise out of employment, R.C. 4123.74 does not bestow upon employers immunity from civil liability for their intentional torts and an employee may resort to a civil suit for damages.

* * *

* * * [T]he protection afforded by the Act has always been for negligent acts and not for intentional tortious conduct. Indeed, workers' compensation acts were designed to improve the plight of the injured worker, and to hold that intentional torts are covered under the Act would be tantamount to encouraging such conduct, and this clearly cannot be reconciled with the motivating spirit and purpose of the Act.

It must also be remembered that the compensation scheme was specifically designed to provide less than full compensation for injured employees. Damages such as pain and suffering and loss of services on the part of a spouse are unavailable remedies to the injured employee. Punitive damages cannot be obtained. Yet, these damages are available to individuals who have been injured by intentional tortious conduct of third parties, and there is no legitimate reason why an employer should be able to escape from such damages simply because he committed an intentional tort against his employee.

In addition, one of the avowed purposes of the Act is to promote a safe and injury-free work environment. Affording an employer immunity for his intentional behavior would not promote such an environment, for an employer could commit intentional acts with impunity with the knowledge that, at the very most, his workers' compensation premiums may rise slightly.

Moreover, as this court noted, workers' compensation " * * * is founded upon the principle of insurance * * *." An insurance policy does not protect the policyholder from the consequences of his intentional tortious act. Indeed, it would be against public policy to permit insurance against the intentional tort.

Notes and Questions

1. Which, if any, of the court's rationales do you find most convincing? Is the court correct that failure to recognize an intentional tort exception would "be tantamount to encouraging such conduct"? How about the concern with denying employees damages for pain and suffering and punitive damages? Employees injured by negligent or reckless acts are denied such damages under the Act. Is it unfair to deny such kinds of recovery to those intentionally injured?

2. The Ohio Supreme Court in subsequent decisions has broadened the intentional tort exception to embrace egregious negligence and, more surprisingly, has held that the employee's filing for and receiving a workers' compensation benefit does not preclude a separate tort action and, most surprisingly, the employer receives no set-off against the tort judgment for the amount of benefits awarded. See Jones v. VIP Development Co., 15 Ohio St.3d 90, 472 N.E.2d 1046 (1984). Finally, when the Ohio legislature sought to bring some rationality to this scheme, the Ohio Supreme Court struck down the statutory amendments as unconstitutional. See Brady v. Safety–Kleen Corp., 61 Ohio St.3d 624, 576 N.E.2d 722 (1991). For a criticism of the

Ohio court's actions, see 2A Arthur Larson, Workmen's Compensation Law § 68.15 at 13–15 (1990) & Supp. at 13–16 (1993).

3. A majority of states maintain that employers' intentional torts are outside the exclusive coverage of the workers' compensation system. States have recognized such an exception by judicial, as well as legislative, action and have imposed varying standards to satisfy the "intentional tort" exception. For a listing of states recognizing the intentional tort exception, see 2A A. Larson, id., § 68.13 at 13–10 (1990) & Supp. (1993).

2. JUDICIAL RATIONALES FOR CREATING THE EXCEPTION

In addition to rationales catalogued in *Blankenship*, others have been offered to justify the intentional tort exception.

a. The "Non-accident" Rationale

One theory applied by many courts is that an employer is prevented from claiming its own intentional acts were "accidental" because the employer should be estopped from relying on the limited accident-based recovery once its conduct is intentional and blameworthy. See, e.g., Stewart v. McLellan's Stores Co., 194 S.C. 50, 9 S.E.2d 35 (1940); Readinger v. Gottschall, 201 Pa.Super. 134, 191 A.2d 694, 696 (1963); National Can Corp. v. Jovanovich, 503 N.E.2d 1224 (Ind.App.1987).

b. Larson's Approach to the Accident Exception

Larson suggests that viewing whether an incident is an "accident" should be determined from the viewpoint of the person seeking protection under the exclusive remedy of the act. 2A Larson § 68.12, at 13–9. Difficulty arose because courts, by viewing the affair from the viewpoint of the victim, found deliberate assaults to be "accidents" under the acts. Larson recommends that when the employer is pleading the exclusive remedy provision as a defense to a tort suit, whether the incident is considered an accident would be determined from its perspective.

c. The "Severed" Relationship Rationale

Another theory advanced by some courts is that the employment relationship is "severed" by an employer's act of violence. Although this theory is criticized as being fictitious, it has been accepted and followed by several courts. See, e.g., Sontag v. Orbit Valve Co., 283 Ark. 191, 672 S.W.2d 50, 51 (1984) ("Whenever an employee is injured by the willful and malicious acts of the employer he may treat the acts of the employer as a breach of the employer-employee relationship and seek full damages in a common law action.").

3. THE "INTENTIONAL" TORT STANDARD USED BY STATES

Courts recognizing the intentional tort exception have developed different standards relating to the employer's state of mind.

a. *The Majority Rule: Deliberate Intent to Cause Injury*

As a rule, "the common law liability of the employer cannot be stretched to include * * * injuries caused by gross, wanton, wilful, deliberate, intentional, reckless, culpable or malicious negligence, or other misconduct of the employer short of genuine intent to cause injury." 2A Larson § 68.13, at 13–4. Most states limit the recovery under the intentional tort exception by implementing the "true intentional tort" or "actual, specific, and deliberate" intent standard. Under this view, the employer must have intended the specific injury as well as the act. See, e.g., National Can Corp. v. Jovanovich, 503 N.E.2d 1224 (Ind.App.1987) ("In light of the quid pro quo underlying * * * Indiana's Workmen's Compensation Act, we believe a stringent standard of specific intent is necessary to avoid the workmen's compensation scheme from being 'swallowed up' by a glut of common law suits outside the Act.").

b. *"Substantial Certainty" Test of Intent*

A few states utilize the broader Restatement (Second) of Torts definition of "intent." Restatement (Second) of Torts § 8A (1965); "The word 'intent' is used * * * to denote that the actor desires to cause consequences of his act, or that he believes that the consequences are substantially certain to result from it." Under this definition, the employer must have only intended the act that caused the injury, with knowledge that the injury was substantially certain to follow. See, e.g., Beauchamp v. Dow Chem. Co., 427 Mich. 1, 398 N.W.2d 882 (1986) (superseded by statute); Woodson v. Rowland, 329 N.C. 330, 407 S.E.2d 222 (1991).

c. *Wilful, Wanton or Reckless Test*

At least one state has applied a lesser standard of "wilful, wanton or reckless" conduct for the intentional act exception. Under this view the employer must have a subjective awareness of a substantial risk of bodily injury resulting from the activity. See Mandolidis v. Elkins Indus., Inc., 161 W.Va. 695, 246 S.E.2d 907 (1978). See Note, Workers' Compensation: Expanding the Intentional Tort Exception to Include Willful, Wanton, and Reckless Employer Misconduct, 58 Notre Dame L. Rev. 890 (1983).

d. *Legislative Standards of Intent*

Most state legislatures which have addressed the issue have opted for the narrow "true" intentional tort standard. See, e.g., Or. Rev. Stat.

656.156(2) ("If injury or death results to a worker from the deliberate intention of the employer of the worker to produce such injury or death"); Wash. Rev. Code Ann. 51.24.020 ("If injury results to a worker from the deliberate intention of his or her employer to produce such injury"); but see Ariz. Rev. Stat. § 23–1022(A) ("if the injury is caused by the employer's willful misconduct, * * * and the act causing the injury is the personal act of the employer * * * and the act indicates a willful disregard of the life, limb or bodily safety of employees").

After the Michigan Supreme Court had adopted the Restatement's substantial certainty test of intent in Beauchamp v. Dow Chemical Co., 427 Mich. 1, 398 N.W.2d 882 (1986), a case involving a chemist's exposures to dioxin, the legislature overruled the decision by expressly recognizing an intentional tort exception but adopting a "specific intent" test:

> An intentional tort shall exist only when an employee is injured as a result of a deliberate act of the employer and the employer specifically intended an injury. An employer shall be deemed to have intended to injure if the employer had actual knowledge that an injury was certain to occur and willfully disregarded that knowledge. The issue of whether an act was an intentional tort shall be a question of law for the court.

M.C.L.A. § 418.131(1).

What is the principal motivation for legislatures in defining "intentional tort" narrowly?

4. TOXIC EXPOSURE CASES

DAN J. OROS v. HULL & ASSOC., INC.

United States District Court, N.D. Ohio, Western Division, 2004.
302 F.Supp.2d 839.

ORDER

CARR, District Judge.

This is an employer intentional tort case in which the plaintiff, Dan Oros, accuses his former employer, defendant Hull & Associates ("Hull"), of intentionally causing him to be exposed to toxic waste during his employment. This court has jurisdiction pursuant to 28 U.S.C. §§ 1332 and 1441.

Pending is defendant's motion for summary judgment. For the following reasons, that motion will be denied in part and granted in part.

BACKGROUND

Plaintiff began employment with defendant in January, 2000. He was hired while still a graduate student at the University of Toledo, and worked part-time until March, 2000, when he became a full-time hydrogeologist.

On Friday, April 25, 2000, Bill Petruzzi, Hull's office manager, asked plaintiff to work over that coming weekend to supervise a waste removal project at a site in Toledo, Ohio. Plaintiff was referred to William Burkett, a senior project manager at Hull. Burkett, in charge of the project, had earlier that day discovered that the site Hull was excavating for the project contained several drums of some type of waste. These drums needed to be removed from the site over the weekend so that construction could continue on the site as planned.

Hull was to supervise the removal and remediation of the drums at the site. A company called Genesis Contracting, Inc. ("Genesis"), was to perform the removal and remediation, and plaintiff's responsibilities were to observe the excavation of the drums and document the weekend's activities. Plaintiff would be the only Hull employee present at the site that weekend.

Burkett was in charge of ensuring that plaintiff had all necessary safety equipment for the weekend's work. Plaintiff claims that when he asked Burkett whether any personal protective equipment would be needed for the project, Burkett said no and told plaintiff to "stay upwind" from the excavation. (Doc. 51, at 6). Plaintiff further claims that Burkett did not advise him that "he might be coming in contact with hazardous material." (Id. at 8–9).

Plaintiff alleges that Burkett failed to advise plaintiff to use any safety equipment at the site despite Burkett's personal knowledge that the site had once been an unregulated municipal waste dump and that several unknown and likely toxic chemicals had been discovered at the site. Plaintiff alleges that Burkett designated the site a "hot zone" on that Friday, August 25, 2000. This signified that no personnel should enter the site unless required to perform a specific task. (Id. at 6).

When plaintiff arrived at the site Saturday morning, August 26, 2000, Genesis had already begun excavation, and plaintiff found an upwind location from which to observe the activities. Sometime that morning, a Genesis worker struck and punctured a drum while excavating, and plaintiff smelled something akin to "paint-thinner." (Doc. 51 exh. 1, at 4). Later that morning, a Genesis employee gave plaintiff a respirator, but plaintiff claims that the respirator was too big and did not fit his face properly. According to plaintiff's brief, a respirators must be fitted with proper filters to be effective. It is not clear what, if any, filter was in place in the respirator plaintiff used. Because the chemicals present at the site had not been tested at that time, however, no one could have known which filter was appropriate for use in plaintiff's respirator. Plaintiff alleges that he mentioned the smell and the respirator he received from Genesis to Burkett during a phone call that day, but that Burkett simply told him to stay upwind and "use caution." (Id. at 5).

Plaintiff alleges that he suffered injuries from exposure to toxic fumes on the project site on August 26, 2000. Plaintiff asserts claims for: 1) employer intentional tort; 2) dual capacity; 3) ultrahazardous activity;

and 4) negligence. Defendant asserts that summary judgment is appropriate on all claims both because plaintiff has failed to establish a prima facie intentional tort case and because defendant is immune from tort actions under Ohio Rev.Code § 3746.24.

STANDARD OF REVIEW

[The court's recitation of the standards for granting summary judgment is omitted]

DISCUSSION

A. Employer Intentional Tort Claim

Because Ohio's workers' compensation program grants employers immunity from employee lawsuits except in cases where the employer has committed an intentional tort, plaintiff must establish that defendant committed an intentional tort to maintain his claim. Brady v. Safety–Kleen Corp., 61 Ohio St.3d 624, 631, 576 N.E.2d 722 (1991) (citing Jones v. VIP Dev. Co., 15 Ohio St.3d 90, 472 N.E.2d 1046 (1984) ("receipt of workers' compensation benefits does not preclude an employee or his representative from pursuing a common-law action for damages against his employer for an intentional tort.")).

To maintain an intentional tort action against his or her employer, a plaintiff must show:

1) knowledge by the employer of the existence of a dangerous process, procedure, instrumentality or condition within its business operation;

2) knowledge by the employer that if the employee is subjected by his employment to such dangerous process, procedure, instrumentality or condition, then harm to the employee will be a substantial certainty; and

3) that the employer, under such circumstances, and with such knowledge, did act to require the employee to continue to perform the dangerous task.

Fyffe v. Jeno's, Inc., 59 Ohio St.3d 115, 570 N.E.2d 1108 (1991) (syllabus); see also Johnson v. BP Chemicals, Inc., 85 Ohio St.3d 298, 707 N.E.2d 1107 (1999) (holding unconstitutional Ohio legislation superseding the decision in Fyffe).

* * * The employee must present "proof beyond that required to prove negligence and beyond that to prove recklessness." Fyffe, 59 Ohio St.3d at 115, 570 N.E.2d 1108. Intent means that "the employer knows that injuries to employees are certain or substantially certain to result from the process, procedure or condition." Id. If this is the case, and the employer still proceeds, "he is treated by the law as if he had in fact desired to produce the result.... [M]ere knowledge and appreciation of a risk—something short of substantial certainty—is not intent." Id.

1. Whether Defendant Knew of the Existence of Dangerous Conditions

Plaintiff's allegations, if credited by the jury, establish that defendant knew that the City of Toledo had once used the project site as an unregulated municipal dump and that deposits of toxic and harmful solid waste were to be found at the site. Moreover, a jury could find that Burkett, Hull's project manager, knew that harmful chemicals had been detected at the site the day before plaintiff was sent there to observe and document the removal and remediation activities. Therefore, a jury could find that plaintiff has established that defendant had knowledge of the existence of a dangerous condition at the site.

2. Whether Defendant Knew That if Plaintiff was Exposed to the Dangerous Conditions, Harm was Substantially Certain to Occur

Plaintiff does not deny that defendant required all its employees, including plaintiff, to participate in training sessions designed to familiarize employees with personal protective equipment. Defendant's general policy favored use of safety equipment when necessary and required plaintiff to understand how to use such equipment.

Defendant claims that its actions in the instant case were consistent with its safety policies and that it did not know plaintiff would need protective equipment. Defendant's account of the facts, however, is not material to this analysis. Plaintiff alleges, and I believe a jury could find, that defendant knew toxic waste chemicals were present at the project site, but did not provide plaintiff with appropriate protective equipment or warn plaintiff that protective equipment would be necessary.

The question, then, is whether defendant's alleged failure to provide protective equipment made plaintiff's injuries substantially certain to occur when he arrived at the project site without a respirator or other equipment. A finding of intent for the purposes of this claim, of course, requires more than that defendant knew of the risk and reacted recklessly or negligently to that risk. To prevail, plaintiff must convince the jury that defendant's actions so disregarded plaintiff's safety as to warrant treatment by the law as though defendant "desired to produce the result." Fyffe, 59 Ohio St.3d at syllabus, ¶ 1.

If the jury credits plaintiff's evidence, it could find that defendant knew that plaintiff's injuries were substantially certain to occur, given defendant's alleged knowledge of the dangerous conditions at the project site and the defendant's acknowledged awareness of the risks associated with exposure to toxic chemicals without proper protective equipment.

I conclude, therefore, that a jury could find that defendant's actions gave rise to a substantial certainty that plaintiff would be harmed by the known dangerous conditions at the project site.

3. Whether Defendant Acted to Require Plaintiff to Work in Dangerous Conditions

Defendant alleges that plaintiff had a choice about whether to work over the weekend at the project site at issue. If true, however, this fact does not vitiate defendant's liability for intentional tort under the third of the Fyffe factors. Regardless of whether plaintiff could have chosen not to work over the weekend at the project site, he was not able to make an informed decision about whether to work in dangerous conditions because the defendant did not inform him about the likely presence of such conditions. Plaintiff alleges that when he asked Burkett whether he would need protective equipment, Burkett answered no, without telling the plaintiff that toxic chemicals had been discovered at the site or that the site had once been a municipal dump at which toxic waste had been disposed.

If the jury credits plaintiff's evidence, it could find that defendant acted to require plaintiff to work in known dangerous conditions. Plaintiff alleges that he did not know he was going to be exposed to harmful chemicals, and that defendant sent him to work at the site without informing him of the risks he was undertaking and without providing him with basic equipment that would have protected him from harm.

Defendant also argues that plaintiff could have returned to Hull to obtain a proper respirator once he detected fumes at the project site, but failed to do so, and therefore cannot claim that he was required to be exposed to the dangerous conditions. The allegation that plaintiff failed to take action to reduce the effects of the harm to which he was exposed, however, does not negate the acts plaintiff alleges defendant took when it sent plaintiff to the project site. Plaintiff's allegations suffice to raise a genuine issue of material fact as to whether defendant required plaintiff to be present at a site where dangerous conditions were known to be present and where harm to plaintiff was substantially certain.

Thus, defendant' motion for summary judgment on the employer intentional tort claim will be denied.

B. Dual Capacity Claim

Plaintiff claims that defendant is also liable to him for his injuries from toxic fumes at the project site because defendant failed to protect him, as a member of the general public, from harm caused by its project. Plaintiff alleges that defendant is liable to plaintiff, therefore, under the "dual-capacity" doctrine adopted by the Ohio Supreme Court as an exception to employers' immunity from tort lawsuits under the worker's compensation system.

Under the dual-capacity doctrine, " 'an employer normally shielded from tort liability by the exclusive remedy principle may become liable in tort to his own employee if he occupies, in addition to his capacity as employer, a second capacity that confers on him obligations independent of those imposed on him as employer.' " Freese v. Consolidated Rail Corp., 4 Ohio St.3d 5, 8, 445 N.E.2d 1110 (1983) (quoting 2 Larson's Workmen's Compensation Law, § 72.80 (Desk Ed.1982)).

The dual-capacity doctrine was first adopted in Ohio in Guy v. Arthur H. Thomas Co., 55 Ohio St.2d 183, 378 N.E.2d 488 (1978). In Guy, the plaintiff, a laboratory technician, filed an action to recover from her employer, a hospital. The plaintiff, who contracted mercury poisoning in the course of her employment, alleged that she had been injured by the medical malpractice of the defendant hospital while confined there as a patient for treatment. Id. at 184–85, 378 N.E.2d 488.

In reaching its decision that the employer acted in a dual capacity, the Ohio Supreme Court held that "the decisive test of dual-capacity is not how separate the employer's second function is from the first, but whether the second function generates obligations unrelated to those flowing from the first, that of an employer." Id. at 188, 378 N.E.2d 488 (citing 2A Larson's Workmen's Compensation Law, § 72.80 at 14–117 (1976)). Thus, because the defendant hospital had obligations toward the plaintiff unrelated to and independent of those imposed upon it as an employer, the court determined that plaintiff's action was not barred by worker's compensation laws. Guy, 55 Ohio St.2d at 186, 378 N.E.2d 488.

Subsequently, in Freese, the Ohio Supreme Court reiterated the test articulated in Guy:

> Whatever the test applied to determine the status of the party claimed to owe an obligation, be it based upon a consideration of whether there exists an unrelated or independent relationship of the parties other than employer and employee, or based upon a test of whether the employment relationship is incidental or predominant, the same result may be reached. In either approach, what must be determined is whether the employer stepped out of his role as such, and had assumed another hat or cloak.

Freese, 4 Ohio St.3d at 10–11, 445 N.E.2d 1110.

The Ohio Supreme Court has acknowledged that an employer can play two roles— employer and manufacturer, for example—but both roles can be interrelated. Schump v. Firestone Tire and Rubber Co., 44 Ohio St.3d 148, 152, 541 N.E.2d 1040 (1989). Therefore, an employer could produce a product both for the general public and for its own use. In that case, the employer is liable to an employee under the dual-capacity doctrine only when the employee's use of the employer's product occurs outside the employment relationship. See id. at 152–53, 541 N.E.2d 1040 (employer manufactured tires for public consumption and its own company use; when employee was injured as a result of tires furnished to plaintiff solely as an employee, the dual-capacity doctrine did not apply).

In this instant case, plaintiff is alleging that defendant owed him a duty not as an employee but as a member of the general public. Plaintiff seems to argue that the fumes at the project site were so harmful that he would have been harmed had he been on the site as an employee or as a public passer-by. Plaintiff, however, has not denied the fact that he was present at the site solely because he was an employee of defendant assigned to work there that day. Defendant's relationship to plaintiff on that day was as his employer. While it may be true that passers-by could have been harmed by the fumes plaintiff alleges injured him, that supposition is not at issue for the purposes of this dual-capacity claim.

Defendant also contends that an employer may not be held liable as an owner/occupier of land under a dual-capacity theory. See Freese, 4 Ohio St.3d at 11, 445 N.E.2d 1110 ("[A] complying employer is not obligated to his employee as the owner or occupier of land, whether the cause of action is based on the common law obligations of landowners or on safe-place-to-work statutes or so-called structural work acts."). Plaintiff cannot maintain his claim based on defendant's alleged occupation of the project site.

Plaintiff argues in his response to the motion for summary judgment that the defendant, as an intentional tortfeasor, is also liable to plaintiff under the dual-capacity doctrine because an intentional tort is not an act committed within the normal scope of the employment relationship. This argument is unsupported by law or fact. If well-taken (as I find it is not), this contention would make the dual-capacity doctrine redundant in all employer intentional tort cases.

Thus, defendant's motion for summary judgment as to the dual-capacity claim will be granted.

C. *Ultrahazardous Activity and Negligence Claims*

Defendant claims immunity from plaintiff's ultrahazardous activity and negligence claims under the auspices of Ohio Rev.Code § 3746.01 et seq., Ohio's "Voluntary Action Program" statutes. These statutes provide a statutory scheme that encourages landowners and developers to redevelop polluted land.

Defendant alleges that because its conduct in the instant case was undertaken while performing voluntary actions as defined by § 3746.01(O) [Cc] of the voluntary action program statutes, it is immune from tort liability under § 3746.24(B) [Cc]. [Revised Code] § 3746.01(O) provides that:

"[v]oluntary action" means a series of measures that may be undertaken to identify and address potential sources of contamination of property by hazardous substances or petroleum and to establish that the property complies with applicable standards. "Voluntary action" may include, without limitation, a phase I property assessment ..., a phase II property assessment ..., a sampling plan, a remedial plan, or remedial activities followed by the issuance of a no further action letter.... Revised Code § 3746.24 provides immunity from tort actions for persons involved in the implementation of a [voluntary action program plan.] Therefore, defendant argues, summary judgment should be granted as to both of plaintiff's tort claims. Plaintiff argues that defendant is not immune because its actions in the instant case were not properly undertaken pursuant to a "voluntary action" plan as defined by the statute.

Defendant contracted with the City of Toledo in 1997, and again in 1999, to provide contractor oversight and project support for the remediation of hazardous substances for a large project that included the property at issue in the instant case. It appears from the record that defendant's contract with the City of Toledo was made pursuant to a O.R.C. § 3746.01 et seq. for remediation of property in accordance with an agreement between the City and DaimlerChrysler Corp. The City retained the defendant in 1997 to provide Phase I and Phase II environmental assessment work in accordance with a voluntary action program. (Doc. 41 exh. B, at 1–4). Defendant's 1999 contract with the City provided for a continuation of the work performed under the first contract. [Cc] (Doc. 41 exh. C, at 1–2, 6–8).

Defendant claims, and plaintiff does not dispute, that defendant's work at the project site in question was undertaken pursuant to its 1999 contract with the City of Toledo. It appears, therefore, that defendant performed its operations pursuant to a voluntary action program plan as defined by § 3746.01 et seq.

Section 3746.24 immunizes a contractor, like the defendant, from a "tort action resulting from the presence of hazardous substances or petroleum at, or the release of hazardous substances from, a property where a voluntary action is being or has been conducted under this chapter and rules adopted under it." Ohio Rev.Code § 3746.24(B). Defendant, therefore, is protected from tort actions arising from its actions undertaken pursuant to its contract with the City of Toledo. This immunity, however, does not apply when "an action or omission of the person ... constitutes willful or wanton misconduct r intentionally tortious conduct." Id.

Defendant does not suggest that § 3746.24 provides immunity against plaintiff's employer intentional tort claim. Even if defendant made such suggestion, that the "intentionally tortious conduct" exception in the statute abrogates immunity for the intentional tort claim. Thus, § 3746.24 does not protect defendant against plaintiff's intentional tort claim.

Defendant is correct, though, that § 3746.24 provides defendant immunity from plaintiff's negligence and ultrahazardous activity claims. A negligence claim requires a breach of a duty to provide some standard of care, and clearly requires a standard of care lower than "willful or wanton misconduct or intentionally tortious conduct."

Ultrahazardous activities are "lawful activities ... so dangerous that they are permitted only when the actor insures the public against the harmful propensities of them." Uland v. S.E. Johnson Cos., 1998 WL 123086 at *5 (Ohio App.1998) (citing Taylor v. City of Cincinnati, 143 Ohio St. 426, 434–35, 55 N.E.2d 724 (1944)). To determine whether a defendant's conduct constitutes ultrahazardous activity, a court considers the existence of a high degree of risk of harm, the likelihood that great harm will occur, the inability to eliminate the risk of harm through the exercise of ordinary care, how common or uncommon the activity is, whether the activity is appropriately conducted in the location where it is found, and the extent to which the activity's value outweighs the dangerous nature of the activity. Abraham v. BP Exploration & Oil, Inc.,

149 Ohio App.3d 471, 478, 778 N.E.2d 48 (2002) (citing Crawford v. Nat'l Lead Co., 784 F.Supp. 439 (S.D.Ohio 1989)).

* * *

I conclude that the tort immunity granted to contractors like defendant by § 3746.24 applies to protect defendant against plaintiff's ultrahazardous activity claim. Section 3746.24 provides broad protection against tort actions resulting from the presence or release of hazardous substances at the site being redeveloped under the voluntary action program. The purpose of the statute—to encourage redevelopment of polluted sites—would be controverted by a holding allowing an ultrahazardous activity claim to go forward against a contractor working to remediate the site in accordance with a voluntary action plan.

Thus, defendant's motion for summary judgment as to plaintiff's ultrahazardous activity and negligence claims will be granted.

* * * For now, I defer determination of plaintiff's demand for and defendant's opposition to a punitive damage claim. That issue may be raised at the close of trial, once the evidence is in. The instant motion for summary judgment as to that issue will be denied, without prejudice.

CONCLUSION

In light of the foregoing, it is

ORDERED THAT

1) Defendant's motion for summary judgment as to the employer intentional tort be, and hereby is, denied;

2) Defendant's motion for summary judgment as to the dual capacity claim be, and hereby is, granted;

3) Defendant's motion for summary judgment as to plaintiff's ultrahazardous activity and negligence claims be, and hereby is, granted;

4) Defendant's motion for summary judgment as to plaintiff's request for punitive damages be, and hereby is, denied, without prejudice.

So ordered.

Note

1. For examples of decisions applying the intentional tort exception in toxic exposure cases, see Gulden v. Crown Zellerbach Corp., 890 F.2d 195 (9th Cir.1989), where an employer had required employees to clean up spilled PCBs on their hands and knees for five days, with PCB levels in which they were in contact were 500 times greater than EPA allowable levels. The district court granted the defendant's motion for summary judgment based on the Oregon workers' compensation scheme's exclusive remedy provision. The court of appeals reversed and remanded, holding that "a jury could conclude that the intention to injure—in this case, to expose [plaintiffs] Gulden and Steele to toxic levels of PCB—was deliberate where

the employer had an opportunity to weigh the consequences and to make a conscious choice among possible courses of action." To be contrasted is Lantz v. National Semiconductor Corp., 775 P.2d 937 (Utah App.1989), where a former employee sued his supervisor and employer for injuries received from toxic fumes after the supervisor denied him permission to evacuate the work area following a chemical spill. The Utah Supreme Court left stand the trial court's dismissal, finding that the plaintiff failed to establish that the supervisor had actual, deliberate intent to injure the employee, so the employer was immune from any tort action.

Also illustrative is Acevedo v. Consolidated Edison Co. of New York, 189 A.D.2d 497, 596 N.Y.S.2d 68 (1993), holding that New York's workers' compensation act barred claims brought by utility workers who contended that they were intentionally exposed to friable asbestos when they were assigned to clean up debris from an explosion of asbestos-insulated steam pipes. The workers claimed that their employer had fraudulently concealed the danger of the asbestos. Relying upon the workers' compensation statute, the court also rejected their nuisance and medical monitoring claims, even though damages for such claims are not available in workers' compensation. The court explained: "[the] exclusive reach [of the Act] does not depend on compensability."

5. DECEIT EXCEPTION

A few courts have recognized what might be termed a "deceit" exception to the bar. For example, in O'Brien v. Ottawa Silica Co., 656 F.Supp. 610, 611–12 (E.D.Mich.1987), the federal district court, applying Michigan law, relieved a worker from the operation of the exclusivity doctrine when evidence showed that his employer was aware that its employees were suffering from asbestos-related disease but concealed that information. This withholding of specific medical information regarding the worker's personal health condition, the court concluded, constituted sufficient intentional fraud to fall outside of the exclusivity doctrine. Similarly, a Florida appellate court held that an employer's alleged deceit in exposing employees to toxic substances without warnings or appropriate safety measures constituted intentional conduct that brought the action outside the state workers' compensation scheme. Cunningham v. Anchor Hocking Corp., 558 So.2d 93 (Fla.App.1990).

However, a New Mexico decision, Johnson Controls World Services v. Barnes, 115 N.M. 116, 847 P.2d 761 (App.1993), explicitly rejected such an exception as part of the broader intentional tort exception. In *Johnson Controls*, the plaintiff was directed to remove underground storage tanks that his employer had allegedly falsely represented were "properly and completely drained of hazardous liquid." He further alleged that he was splashed with toxic liquid which caused him injury, and that the employer had "deliberately and intentionally failed to warn him of the dangers involved." In rejecting plaintiff's attempt to assert a tort claim, the court first stated a test of intent that required "an actual intent * * * to injure the worker," rather than the "substantial certainty" test of the Restatement. It continued:

Plaintiff also argues that since the allegations of his complaint alleged that Johnson engaged in fraudulent conduct, these acts rendered its conduct so egregious that it knew the injury that resulted was substantially certain to occur. Plaintiff reasons that his allegations of fraud distinguish this case from factual situations existing in earlier decisions of both our Supreme Court and this Court, and necessitate an expanded interpretation of the common-law exception to our exclusivity statute. We think the answer to this argument is governed by the plain language of Section 52–1–9. The words "accidentally sustained," as used in Section 52–1–9, refer to injury or death arising from an unintended or unexpected event.

Additionally, the inquiry is not whether the employer had an intent to deceive or misrepresent the facts, see § 52–1–9 (all injuries "accidentally" sustained are subject to the exclusivity provision of the Act), but rather whether the employer had an intent to injure the worker. An injury may unintentionally result even though an employer set the stage for the injury by deceiving or misrepresenting facts to the worker.

The majority of jurisdictions that have considered the question appear to agree that a mere showing of misrepresentation or deceit is insufficient to defeat the exclusivity provisions of their respective worker's compensation statutes. See generally Larson, supra, § 68.32(a). Instead, the intent issue should involve two steps. First, did the employer intend to commit the alleged act? Second, do the circumstances support a reasonable inference that the employer directly intended to harm the worker? The latter question involves the "true intent" requirement discussed above. Under this analysis, fraudulent misrepresentation, like any other act by the employer, may or may not remove an action from the exclusivity provision of the Act.

Applying this two-step analysis to the complaint, * * * [p]laintiff has satisfied the first prong of the test. We therefore look to Plaintiff's description of the incident to see whether it was an "accident" or whether it may be characterized as a deliberate consequence of Johnson's behavior. The complaint states that Plaintiff picked up a pipe with the trackhoe and the pipe "flew up, hit the trackhoe and sprayed a gasoline-benzene liquid all over [Plaintiff]." Based on this description of how Plaintiff was injured, we do not believe that it is reasonable to infer that Johnson truly intended this series of events to occur. Therefore, even if we assume as true Plaintiff's allegation that Johnson's conduct fraudulently misrepresented the hazard to Plaintiff, the facts do not show that Johnson's conduct was equivalent to a "left jab to the chin."

Notes and Questions

a. What explains the real resistance to enlargement of the exception to embrace substantially certain injuries or fraudulent concealment? Why do legislatures nearly unanimously reject anything other than a true intentional tort standard?

b. The decisions creating exceptions to the exclusivity provision of workers' compensation are roundly denounced by Professor Epstein. See Richard A. Epstein, The Historical Origins and Economic Structure of Workers' Compensation Law, 16 Ga. L. Rev. 775 (1982). For a different perspective, see Robert L. Rabin, The Historical Development of the Fault Principle: A Reinterpretation, 15 Ga. L. Rev. 925 (1981). Epstein argues that the workers' compensation system represents a voluntary bargain between employers and employees intended by both to substitute for a tort system that was perceived as unfair and cumbersome. For Epstein, "workers' compensation rules are in most instances a closer approximation to the consensual ideal than the negligence rules to which they are opposed." Moreover, the fact that the employer (but not the employee) knows that injury is likely to occur as a by-product of productive activity in the workplace does not justify breaching the exclusivity provision of the workers' compensation bargain. Epstein concludes that had the workers' compensation systems developed contractually by voluntary means, rather than statutorily, it would be inconceivable that exceptions to exclusivity such as *Blankenship* and *Johns–Manville Products* would have resulted. For a different analysis on the historical development of workers' compensation and tort laws, see Gary T. Schwartz, Tort Law and the Economy in Nineteenth Century America: A Reinterpretation, 90 Yale L.J. 1717, 1769 nn. 389–390 (1980).

6. ACTIONS BY SPOUSES OR CHILDREN AGAINST EMPLOY-ERS

In some instances a spouse or child may sustain an injury as a result of events which the other spouse or parent experienced in the workplace. See Jean Macchiaroli Eggen, Toxic Reproductive and Genetic Hazards in the Workplace: Challenging the Myths of the Tort and Workers' Compensation Systems, 60 Ford. L. Rev. 843, 878–79 (1992), for a thorough discussion of the cases.

a. Claims by Spouses

Claims by spouses arising out of the workers' occupational exposure generally fall into two categories: (1) those that are derivative, exemplified by suits for loss of consortium; and (2) those suits for spouses' direct personal injuries. Loss-of-consortium claims typically are barred by the workers' compensation exclusivity doctrine. However, as described by Eggen, the direct injury claim may be sustainable:

> In contrast, when spouses suffer independent injuries arising from the breach of an independent duty owed to the spouse by the employer, the exclusivity doctrine may be circumvented. To bring a personal injury action, however, a spouse must distinguish between the original injury to the worker and the independent injury to the spouse. * * *

* * *

One federal appellate case may shed some light on future judicial analysis of this problem. In Woerth v. United States [714 F.2d 648, 649 (6th Cir.1983)], the spouse of a federal employee contracted hepatitis from the employee. The employee, a nurse at a Veteran's Administration hospital, had contracted the disease in the course of her employment. When the spouse commenced an action against the United States pursuant to the Federal Tort Claims Act [28 U.S.C.A. §§ 2671–2680], the government argued that the action was barred by the exclusivity provision of the Federal Employee's Compensation Act [5 U.S.C.A. § 8116(c) ("FECA")], a federal scheme analogous to state workers' compensation statutes. The district court concluded that the FECA exclusivity provision barred the spouse's action because the employee was subject to the FECA provisions.

The United States Court of Appeals for the Sixth Circuit reversed, distinguishing the independent injury suffered by Mr. Woerth from the loss-of-consortium claims that typically would be barred by the FECA exclusivity provision. The court stated:

> The proper inquiry * * * is whether the claim is "with respect to the injury or death of an employee." While Woerth's hepatitis may derive from his wife as a matter of proximate cause, his cause of action does not. His right to recover for the negligence of the United States is based upon his own personal injury, not a right of "husband and wife." The fact that the disease was transmitted through his spouse does not place Woerth in a position different from that of any other unrelated, but similarly injured tort victim.

Accordingly, the court readily recognized that the spouse could maintain this action for personal injuries regardless of the fact that his immediate exposure was through the employee who was covered by FECA. This simple approach opts to draw the exclusivity line along the traditional boundary between derivative claims and individual claims rather than construct a more complicated distinction related to proximate cause.

b. Claims by Children

Children also may suffer a variety of injuries from either parent's exposure to workplace toxins. Like spouses, children bringing tort actions for injuries against a parent's employer must make the threshold showing of an independent injury.

One court has limited a child to the parent's workers' compensation benefits. In Bell v. Macy's California, 212 Cal.App.3d 1442, 261 Cal.Rptr. 447, 453 (1989), the injuries to a pregnant worker's fetus resulting in the death of the offspring at approximately two years of age were deemed to be covered by the California workers' compensation statute. However, the child recovered no benefits because the California workers' compensation statute failed to provide any actual compensation for the child's medical and other expenses. It held that the injury to the fetus "was derived from the compensable injury" to the worker and, therefore, was collateral to the covered injury. The court reasoned:

> * * * [W]ere the fetus of a pregnant worker to retain a separate tort cause of action for injury to it, the employer would face a serious risk. * * * The range of common workplace injury that could result in injury or death to a fetus needs little exposition. Trips and falls, car accidents, explosions, fires, and other unfortunate but not unheard-of incidents of employment all may cause serious injury or death to the unborn as well as its parent. Less obvious are cases of subtle poisoning by exposure to toxic substances, genetic damage caused by radiation, and the other numerous and cautionary byproducts of the Industrial Revolution.

The court expressed concern that allowing liability could lead to the unacceptable result that employers would exclude women from the workplace to avoid the liability from such accidents and exposures.

Why do courts, such as the California court in *Bell v. Macy's California*, opt for an analysis that limits the employer's exposure by treating the child's action as within the compensation system? Do the same considerations that have resulted in confining the intentional tort exception within narrow limits also explain the judicial reluctance to allow spouses and children to sue the employer in a tort action? Can you identify any policy justifications for treating the two situations differently?

7. FETAL PROTECTION POLICIES

In International Union, United Auto. Workers v. Johnson Controls, Inc., 499 U.S. 187, 111 S.Ct. 1196, 113 L.Ed.2d 158 (1991), a class action was brought challenging an employer's policy of barring all women, except those whose infertility was medically documented, from holding jobs involving actual or potential exposure to lead at defendant's battery manufacturing plant because of its concern that the exposure created a risk of harm to any fetus carried by a female employee. The Supreme Court held that the employer's fetal protection policy violated the anti-sex discrimination provisions of the Civil Rights Act of 1964 and the Pregnancy Discrimination Act, 42 U.S.C.A. § 2001 et seq., § 703 of Title VII. Although the Court acknowledged the concern of the employer that it could be subjected to tort liability for prenatal injuries suffered by the children whose mothers may choose to work in the lead-exposed job positions, it discounted the potential tort liability exposure:

> According to Johnson Controls, however, the company complies with the lead standard developed by OSHA and warns its female employees about the damaging effects of lead. It is worth noting that OSHA gave the problem of lead lengthy consideration and concluded that "there is no basis whatsoever for the claim that women of childbear-

ing age should be excluded from the workplace in order to protect the fetus or the course of pregnancy." 43 Fed. Reg. 52952, 52966 (1978). Instead, OSHA established a series of mandatory protections which, taken together, "should effectively minimize any risk to the fetus and newborn child." Without negligence, it would be difficult for a court to find liability on the part of the employer. If, under general tort principles, Title VII bans sex-specific fetal-protection policies, the employer fully informs the woman of the risk, and the employer has not acted negligently, the basis for holding an employer liable seems remote at best.

Justice White, in a concurring opinion, was not so sanguine about the remoteness of the tort liability:

> The Court dismisses the possibility of tort liability by no more than speculating. * * * Such speculation will be small comfort to employers. First, it is far from clear that compliance with Title VII will pre-empt state tort liability, and the Court offers no support for that proposition. Second, although warnings may preclude claims by injured *employees*, they will not preclude claims by injured children because the general rule is that parents cannot waive causes of action on behalf of their children, and the parents' negligence will not be imputed to the children. Finally, although state tort liability for prenatal injuries generally requires negligence, it will be difficult for employers to determine in advance what will constitute negligence. Compliance with OSHA standards, for example, has been held not to be a defense to state tort or criminal liability. * * * Moreover, it is possible that employers will be held strictly liable, if, for example, their manufacturing process is considered "abnormally dangerous." See Restatement (Second) of Torts § 869, comment b (1979). (White, J., concurring) (emphasis in original)

Who, in your opinion, has the better of the argument on the prospects for tort liability? What effect will state courts in tort suits likely give to the employer's defense that it complied with OSHA regulations? Would a court, federal or state, conclude that OSHA preempts state tort actions? Recall the material in Chapter Six on preemption, and the Supreme Court's holding in Cipollone v. Liggett Group, Inc.

8. TAKE–HOME TOXICS

Congress has recognized the problem of workers in industrial settings inadvertently tracking toxic chemicals from the workplace to their homes and contaminating family members. The Fire Administration Authorization Act of 1992, as amended with the Workers' Family Protection Act, 29 U.S.C.A. § 671(a) et seq., calls for the National Institute for Occupational Safety and Health as the lead agency to work with OSHA, the Environmental Protection Agency, the Agency for Toxic Substances and Disease Registry, and the Department of Energy in order to gather information and share data with experts in professions ranging from medicine to industrial hygiene to develop a strategy to combat the problem. The Act does not grant authority to federal agencies to issue regulations.

9. AGGRAVATION OF INJURY EXCEPTION

An aggravation of injury exception has been applied in a few states. In Johns–Manville Products Corp. v. Contra Costa Superior Court, 27 Cal.3d 465, 165 Cal.Rptr. 858, 612 P.2d 948 (1980), the California Supreme Court allowed a tort action brought by a worker against his employer on the basis of asbestos exposure in the workplace. The gravamen of the suit was that the employer had knowingly concealed the hazards of the occupational exposure from the worker, thus causing an aggravation of the physical condition of the employee. While the court refused to recognize a broad fraudulent concealment or deceit exception as it related to the employee's initially contracting the disease, it recognized a narrower exception for the aggravation of injury. Addressing the legal system's concerns that recognition of such an exception would invite a flood of litigation, the court stated:

> We conclude the policy of exclusivity of workers' compensation as a remedy for injuries in the employment [setting] would not be seriously undermined [by this exception], since we cannot believe that many employers will aggravate the effects of an industrial injury by not only deliberately concealing the existence but also its connection with the employment. Nor can we believe that the Legislature in enacting the workers' compensation law intended to insulate such flagrant conduct from tort liability.

The decision places the burden of showing how much harm was caused by the initial contraction of the disease, rather than by its subsequent aggravation, upon the defendant, as the problem of apportionment emanated from the defendant's wrongful acts. The holding led to the amendment of the California workers' compensation statute that includes an express exception to exclusivity for aggravation of injury, but limits the tort recovery to damages for aggravation only. See West's Ann. Cal. Lab. Code § 3682(2). Accord, Millison v. E.I. du Pont de Nemours & Co., 101 N.J. 161, 501 A.2d 505 (1985); Martin v. Lancaster Battery Co., Inc., 530 Pa. 11, 606 A.2d 444 (1992).

C. OCCUPATIONAL DISEASE ACTS

1. INTRODUCTION

Some states have enacted statutes which specifically address employers' liability for occupational diseases contracted by employees as a result of exposure to harmful substances in the workplace environment. Concerns with asbestos-related diseases were a major impetus for such legislation, which generally contain the same exclusivity provisions as the workers' compensation acts. 2A A. Larson, Workmen's Compensation Law § 41.00 at 7–94 (1992) summarizes the state of the law:

> All states now provide general compensation coverage for occupational diseases. For the purpose of defining the affirmative inclusion of diseases within this term, the older definition distinguishing occupational disease from accident has been largely abandoned, with its stress on gradualness and on prevalence of the disease in the particular industry. Jurisdictions having general coverage of occupational disease now usually define the term to include any disease arising out of exposure to harmful conditions of the employment, when those conditions are present in a peculiar or increased degree by comparison with employment generally. Thus, even a disease which is rare and which is due to the claimant's individual allergy or weakness combining with employment conditions will usually be held to be an occupational disease if the increased exposure occasioned by employment in fact brought on the disease.

2. JUDICIAL APPLICATION OF OCCUPATIONAL DISEASE ACTS

The following decision, Palmer v. Del Webb's High Sierra, 108 Nev. 673, 838 P.2d 435 (1992), places the Occupational Disease Acts in the contemporary context of environmental tobacco smoke (ETS). Before turning to the majority opinion, which does not recite the facts, the following description is drawn from a separate concurrence:

> For over twenty years, Palmer was employed at Del Webb's High Sierra Casino ("High Sierra") as a "pit boss." His job required that he supervise gaming tables from an area in the casino referred to as the "pit." The pit area had noticeably high levels of secondhand tobacco smoke. During most of Palmer's years at High Sierra, the casino encouraged smoking by providing free cigarettes and numerous ashtrays. * * *

> In Spring 1988, at the age of fifty-eight, Palmer experienced coughing and breathing problems. He curtailed his outdoor activities but continued working until August 1, 1988, when, following doctors' orders, he took a medical leave of absence. Although Palmer was not a smoker, several doctors diagnosed him as suffering from reactive airways disease, severe bronchitis and asthma. They concluded that Palmer's condition was caused by, or substantially aggravated by, the smoke-filled environment at High Sierra. His doctors ordered that he not return to work unless he could do so in a smoke-free environment.

* * *

[Despite uncontested medical testimony connecting Palmer's condition with his exposure to ETS, High Sierra and a hearings officer both denied his claim because he did not suffer a compensable occupational disease because lung diseases, under the Nevada Act, were restricted to firemen and police officers.]

The appeals officer reversed the decision of the hearings officer, finding that: "The evidence presented by testimony and by documents establish[es] a direct causal connection between Palmer's work in an enclosed area containing smoke in the air he breathed and his occupational disease of chronic pulmonary dysfunction. * * * His employment is the proximate cause of his occupational disease since he was not exposed to [secondhand tobacco] smoke in a greater amount than other workers. His chronic pulmonary disorder is incidental to the character of being a pit boss in a gaming establishment since he was required to be in a smokey area in order to perform his job duties."

The district court reversed the decision of the appeals officer, summarily concluding that the disease was not incidental to the character of the business.

The Nevada Occupational Disease Act (NODA) which is the subject of *Palmer* provided:

1. An occupational disease defined in this chapter shall be deemed to arise out of and in the course of the employment if:

(a) There is a direct causal connection between the conditions under which the work is performed and the occupational disease;

(b) It can be seen to have followed as a natural incident of the work as a result of the exposure occasioned by the nature of the employment;

(c) It can be fairly traced to the employment as the proximate cause; and

(d) It does not come from a hazard to which workmen would have been equally exposed outside of the employment.

2. The disease must be incidental to the character of the business and not independent of the relation of the employer and employee.

3. The disease need not have been foreseen or expected, but after its contraction must appear to have had its origin in a risk connected with the employment, and to have flowed from that source as a natural consequence.

PALMER v. DEL WEBB'S HIGH SIERRA

Supreme Court of Nevada, 1992.
108 Nev. 673, 838 P.2d 435.

SPRINGER, J.:

The issue in this case is whether a worker who claims to suffer from a disease caused by inhaling tobacco smoke exhaled by others in the work place is eligible for compensation under the Nevada Occupational Disease Act (NODA). Appellant Palmer filed a claim for occupational disease compensation, claiming that his lung disease was caused by environmental tobacco smoke present at his place of employment. The trial court, in reversing an appeals officers' adjudication in favor of Palmer, ruled that "[u]ntil such time as the Legislature so decides, the claim must fail." We agree with the trial court that until the legislature so decides, occupational disease claims based on inhalation of environmental smoke in the work place must fail. Specifically, we agree that environmental smoke, although usually present in a casino, is not uniquely "incidental to the character" of that business. Further, we conclude that secondary smoke is a hazard to which workers, as a class, may be "equally exposed outside of the employment." Therefore, we affirm the judgment of the trial court.

In reading the occupational disease statute one learns that an occupational disease must arise out of the employment, that is to say, it must be related to the nature of the employment at hand. The definitional statute, NRS 617.440, requires an occupational disease to be an incident of the employment and not merely an accidental consequence that is not related to the nature of the employment. Specifically, NRS 617.440(1) provides that the disease must be a *"natural incident of the work as a result of the exposure occasioned by the nature* of the employment." [court's emphasis]

What this language means is that the disease must arise out of job conditions, specifically, the "nature of the employment." With regard to this requirement, that the disease-causing conditions must be "incidental to the character of the business," it is apparent that the legislature intended that there must be a connection between the kind of job and the kind of disease. Mere causation is not enough. One could easily say that going to work caused a person to develop ulcers; but the "nature of the employment" is, in most cases, not inherently ulcerogenic; and ulcers are not in all probability a "natural incident of the work" claimed to be the cause of the disease.

We are, then, talking about a special kind of cause, "work-related" cause; and where, as appears to be the case here, disease is not related to the nature of the job, the disease cannot properly be called "occupational." It is apparent to us that despite its common presence in bars and casinos, environmental tobacco smoke is not incidental to the character of these businesses, is not a natural incident of these businesses.

The trial court disallowed Palmer's claim, stating that it "must fail under NRS 617.440(2)." We agree with this conclusion. Under NRS 617.440(2), an occupational "disease must be incidental to the character of the business and not independent of the relation of the employer and employee." Again, contracting the disease must be part of the actual job. Unless the disease is a part of the job, unless it is "incidental" to the character of the business, a disease cannot be said to have the necessary "direct causal relation" to the employment. NRS 617.440(1)(a). To illustrate: breathing in coal dust is certainly incidental to the character of coal mining work. Whereas coal dust, the cause of "black lung" disease, is certainly incidental to the character of coal mining (mining coal necessarily creates coal dust), tobacco smoke is not part of the nature or character of a bar or casino business. Tobacco smoke is not a "natural incident" of Palmer's employment nor is exposure to smoke "occasioned by the nature of the employment." NRS 617.440(1)(b). It is probably true that more environmental smoke is associated with the casino and bar businesses than with other businesses; still, the amount and density of such tobacco smoke is highly inconstant and may range from none to quite dense, depending on the particular bar or casino and depending on the air filtration systems and other variables that vary from business to business.

Of course, any individual business establishment might be shown to have an excessive amount of secondary smoke in the work place. Until fairly recently, many office environments were so filled with smoke that they were virtually intolerable to nonsmokers. Still, there is nothing in the "nature" of office work that would make stale tobacco smoke a "natural incident of the work." A nonsmoker unfortunate enough to contract some disease because of the excessive smoke rather clearly would not be entitled to compensation, because "environmental smoke disease" is not an occupational disease of office work. The legislature, of course, is free to declare that any person who contracts some secondary smoke-related disease at work is eligible for occupational disease compensation. The courts, we believe, do not have this power.

What we must not lose sight of is the reality that occupational disease coverage is designed to protect those who suffer illness because of the special nature of their occupation, those who suffer from an occupational disease. That is why words like "natural incident" of the employment and "occasioned by the nature of the employment" are used in NRS 617.440. In NRS 617.450, the statutory schedule of occupational diseases, we find further indication of the legislature's intention that occupational diseases be incidental to the character of the business and occasioned by the nature of the employment. The diseases listed in the statute are quite job-specific and are closely related to the nature of the particular occupation, diseases such as "brass and zinc poisoning" or "chrome ulceration of the skin or nasal passages." In addition, NRS 617.450 provides a description of the specific processes by which the listed diseases are contracted. The statutory purpose is clearly to provide protection for people who have diseases that are related to their particular jobs. If the disease is not related to the character of the particular business and not proximately caused by the "conditions under which the work is performed," it is not an occupational disease.

* * *

Based on the statutory provisions and on our case law, we hold as a matter of law that diseases claimed to be caused by environmental tobacco smoke present in the work place are not covered by the Nevada

Occupational Disease Act. We therefore affirm the judgment of the trial court.

Notes and Questions

1.   Is the court correct that environmental tobacco smoke (ETS) is not related to the nature of the job as a "pit boss"? What might be the court's unstated rationale for rejecting this claim? In a separate concurring opinion one justice concluded that the exposure to ETS was work-related, but that the Nevada Occupational Disease Act covered only those diseases specifically listed in the statute, and diseases from exposure to ETS were not listed. The majority opinion, by implication, concludes that nonlisted diseases and exposures may be covered if they satisfy the rigorous "nature of the employment" test. Another justice separately opined that had the legislature sought to limit coverage to the twenty-two tested diseases, that "the results of such a scheme would be unfair, discriminatory, and most probably lacking in a rational basis." Does this mean the Act is unconstitutional?

2.   Some jurisdictions, unlike Nevada, list specific diseases, but include a savings clause to capture non-listed conditions. See Idaho Code § 72–438 (Supp. 1991) ("Recognizing that additional toxic or harmful substances or matter are continually being discovered and used or misused, the above enumerated occupational diseases [the scheduled diseases] are not to be taken as exclusive. * * * "); Ohio Rev. Code § 4123.68 (Anderson 1991) ("A disease which meets the definition of an occupational disease is compensable pursuant to Chapter 4123 of the Revised Code though it is not specifically listed in this section.").

3.   Other jurisdictions do not list specific diseases, but contain instead generalized descriptions of the diseases covered by their respective acts. See, e.g., N.Y.—McKinney's Work. Comp. Law § 2(15) (occupational disease defined as "a disease resulting from the nature of employment and contracted therein"); R.I. Gen. Laws § 28–34–1(3) (1993) (occupational disease means "a disease which is due to causes and conditions which are characteristic of and peculiar to a particular trade, occupation, process or employment"); Utah Code Ann. 35–2–107 (Supp. 1991) (a compensable occupational disease "is defined as any disease or illness which arises out of and in the course of employment").

3.   DISTINGUISHING DISEASES INCIDENT TO ONE'S EMPLOYMENT FROM THE ORDINARY DISEASES OF LIFE

a.   All jurisdictions' statutes attempt to differentiate between the so-called "ordinary diseases of life" and occupational diseases. If you were drafting a statute, how might you attempt to make the distinction? Virginia's Code § 65.1–46.1 provides in part:

> An ordinary disease of life to which the general public is exposed outside of the employment may be treated as an occupational disease for purposes of this Act if it is established by clear and convincing evidence, to a reasonable medical certainty, that it arose out of and in the course of employment as provided in § 65.46 with respect to

occupational diseases and did not result from causes outside of the employment. * * *

Is this a sensible approach to the problem? How about alcoholism? Can an employee maintain that the disease of alcoholism resulted from stress in the workplace or other workplace conditions? See Pierce v. General Motors Corp., 443 Mich. 137, 504 N.W.2d 648 (1993) (court declines to extend workers' compensation benefits to cover diseases of addiction).

b. A Connecticut case illustrates how some courts attempt to address the occupational disease problem. In Hansen v. Gordon, 221 Conn. 29, 602 A.2d 560 (1992), plaintiff worked as a dental hygienist. In 1984 she began to wear a mask and gloves because of increased awareness of communicable diseases, and received precautionary vaccinations against hepatitis. In 1986 claimant's husband was diagnosed as having hepatitis B (HBV). Claimant was tested, and it was determined that she was a carrier. She ceased employment with her employer because she posed a threat to the patients. The commissioner determined that it was more likely than not that claimant's condition arose out of and in the course of her employment. Defendant contended, however, that claimant had not established that HBV was an occupational disease because diseases which occur broadly within the general public cannot be characterized as occupational. The Connecticut Supreme Court disagreed. References in case law that the disease must be a "natural" incident of the employment cannot be construed so as to hold the disease must be peculiar or unique to the employment. Moreover, the facts fulfilled all the requirements of an occupational disease because dental hygienists are at increased risk because of their contact with blood and other secretions.

4. INTENTIONAL TORT EXCEPTION IN OCCUPATIONAL DISEASES

Courts have been extremely reluctant to extend the intentional tort exception as applied in injury cases to the contracting of occupational diseases. For example, in Barber v. Pittsburgh Corning Corp., 521 Pa. 29, 555 A.2d 766 (Pa.1989), the Pennsylvania Supreme Court considered whether employees could maintain a tort action outside the exclusivity of the ODA where they alleged exposure to asbestos dust in a defendant's thermal insulation manufacturing plant. Plaintiffs alleged that the employer knew of the danger of asbestos and did nothing to protect the workers from the danger; allowed levels of asbestos dust to exceed safe levels; failed to implement controls to reduce airborne levels of asbestos dust; failed to warn employees of the health hazards created by exposure to the asbestos; and that defendant knew to a substantial certainty that harm would result to its employees. The court held that it would not recognize an intentional tort exception to the ODA, relying on the statutory language of the Pennsylvania ODA which stated that the exclusivity agreement "shall operate as a surrender by the parties thereto of their rights to any form or amount of compensation or damages for any disability or death resulting from occupational disease * * * other than as provided in [this Act]." Holding that this language "operates as a forfeiture by the employee of any and all common law causes of action," it refused to even recognize an intentional tort exception.

Why might occupational diseases be less susceptible to an intentional tort exclusion than are workplace injuries? See Buford v. American Telephone & Telegraph Co., 881 F.2d 432 (7th Cir.1989).

5. A NOTE ON ENVIRONMENTAL TOBACCO SMOKE

The facts in *Palmer* are not unique. No doubt millions of American workers have been subjected to ETS in the workplaces and many may have experienced resulting injury or aggravation of pre-existing conditions. Until recently, there has been some debate respecting whether ETS can be established as the cause (or "a" cause) of various conditions, including lung cancer. That debate, however, seems to have reached a scientific resolution as evidenced by an EPA report, Office of Health and Environmental Assessment, Respiratory Health Effects of Passive Smoking: Lung Cancer and Other Disorders (December 1992) (the Report), which concludes:

> Based on the assessment of all the evidence considered in * * * this report and in accordance with the EPA *Guidelines* and the causality criteria above for interpretation of human data, this report concludes that ETS is a Group A human carcinogen, the EPA classification "used only when there is sufficient evidence from epidemiologic studies to support a causal association between exposure to the agents and cancer."

The Report estimates that approximately 3,000 lung cancer deaths per year among nonsmokers (never-smokers and former smokers) of both sexes are attributable to ETS in the United States. It points out that while smoking is responsible for more than one of every six deaths in the United States, smokers are not the only ones exposed to tobacco smoke. Moreover, an excess cancer risk is biologically plausible because sidestream smoke emitted from a smoldering cigarette between puffs (the main component of ETS) contains virtually all of the same carcinogenic compounds (known or suspected human and animal carcinogens) that have been identified in the mainstream smoke (MS) inhaled by smokers. The Report reviewed thirty epidemiologic studies of effects from normally occurring environmental levels of ETS. It continues:

> Because there is widespread exposure and it is difficult to construct a truly unexposed subgroup of the general population, these studies attempt to compare individuals with higher ETS exposure to those with lower exposures. Typically, female never-smokers who are married to a smoker are compared with female never-smokers who are married to a nonsmoker. * * * Use of the female never-smoker

studies provides the largest, most homogeneous database for analysis to determine whether an ETS effect on lung cancer is present.

* * *

Results from all of the analyses described above strongly support a causal association between lung cancer ETS exposure. The overall proportion (9/30) of individual studies found to show an association between lung cancer and spousal ETS exposure at all levels combined is unlikely to occur by chance [less than one chance in 10,000]. When the analysis focuses on higher levels of spousal exposure, every one of the 17 studies with exposure-level data shows increased risk in the highest exposure group; 9 of these are significant at the $p < 0.05$ level, * * * another result highly unlikely to occur by chance [one chance in 1,000,000]. Similarly, the proportion (10/14); showing a statistically significant exposure-response trend is highly supportive of a causal association.

The Report's conclusions rest on a variety of separate indicia of causation:

[a] Biological plausibility. * * *

[b] Supporting evidence from animal bioassays and genotoxicity experiments. * * *

[c] Consistency of response. Four of the cohort studies and 20 of the 26 case-control studies observed a higher risk of lung cancer among the female never-smokers classified as ever exposed to any level of spousal ETS. Furthermore, every one of the 17 studies with response categorized by exposure level demonstrated increased risk for the highest exposure group. * * * Evaluation of the total study evidence from several perspectives leads to the conclusion that the observed association between ETS exposure and increased lung cancer occurrence is not attributable to chance.

[d] Broad-based evidence. These 30 studies provide data from 8 different countries, employ a wide variety of study designs and protocols, and are conducted by many different research teams. * * * No alternative explanatory variables for the observed association between ETS and lung cancer have been indicated that would be broadly applicable across studies.

[e] Upward trend in exposure-response. Both of the largest of the cohort studies * * * demonstrate a strong exposure-related statistical association between passive smoking and lung cancer. * * *

* * *

[f] Effects remain after adjustment for potential upward bias. Current and ex-smokers may be misreported as never-smokers, thus inflating the apparent cancer risk for ETS exposure. The evidence remains statistically significant and conclusive, howev-

er, after adjustments for smoker misclassification. For the United States, the summary estimate of relative risk from nine case-control plus two cohort studies is 1.19 (90% confidence interval [C.I.] = 1.04, 1.35; p < 0.05) after adjustment for smoker misclassification. For Greece, 2.00 (1.42, 2.83), Hong Kong, 1.61 (1.25, 2.06), and Japan, 1.44 (1.13, 1.85), the estimated relative risks are higher than those of the United States and more highly significant after adjusting for the potential bias.

[g] Strong associations for highest exposure groups. Examining the groups with the highest exposure levels increases the ability to detect an effect, if it exists. * * * The overall pooled estimate of [relative risk of] 1.81 for the highest exposure groups is highly statistically significant (90% C.I. = 1.60, 2.05). For the United States, the overall pooled estimate of 1.38 (seven studies, corrected for smoker misclassification bias) is also highly statistically significant (90% C.I. = 1.13, 1.70; p = 0.005).

The EPA Report has stimulated considerable response. The cigarette manufacturers filed suit against the EPA seeking to have the Report declared "null and void." The suit contends that EPA went beyond its statutory authority in preparing its risk assessment, failed to follow its own guidelines for conducting such cancer-risk studies, and made numerous mistakes in its assessment, which were compounded by "data manipulations." It also alleged that the EPA resorted to "manipulating and cherry picking" the data to "falsely disparage" cigarettes. The tobacco groups want the court to declare that EPA's classification of ETS as a Group A carcinogen and the ETS Risk Assessment violate the due process guarantee of the U.S. Constitution. See Flue–Cured Tobacco Cooperative Stabilization Corp. v. Environmental Protection Agency, 4 F.Supp.2d 435 (M.D.N.C. 1998).

Note and Questions

Consider whether a personal injury toxic tort action could be maintained on the basis of exposure to ETS. Might products liability attorneys who have been unsuccessful in suits on behalf of smokers be more successful on behalf of nonsmokers who suffer injury as a result of exposure to ETS? A major difference between an ETS claim brought by a nonsmoker and the many claims that have been litigated by smokers is that this new class of potential plaintiffs has not voluntarily chosen to expose themselves to the well-recognized dangers of smoking, and thus may represent a more sympathetic group to jurors and courts. What do you foresee as the primary problem facing plaintiffs in such suits? What about the effect of living in a home where the plaintiff's spouse or other family member smoked? Given the kinds of relative risks identified above, and assuming no other impediments to a tort suit, will they be sufficient to satisfy the requirements of causation as described in Chapter 8? What other particularistic evidence might a plaintiff offer to supplement the epidemiological studies?

6. EMPLOYEES' ACTIONS FOR RELIEF

a. *Injunctive Relief*

One method by which employees may seek relief from environmental tobacco smoke is through an injunction requiring an employer to provide employees with a smoke-free work environment. As an injunction provides equitable relief, rather than monetary relief, any court with equitable powers can grant an order requiring an employer to provide a smoke-free working environment. If monetary relief is requested, then the plaintiff must seek relief through the workers' compensation system.

Two cases in which state courts have granted injunctions requiring employers to ban smoking in work areas are relatively old: Shimp v. New Jersey Bell Telephone Co., 145 N.J.Super. 516, 368 A.2d 408 (1976) and Smith v. Western Electric Co., 643 S.W.2d 10 (Mo.App.1982). In *Shimp*, the plaintiff, who was allergic to ETS, worked in an area where the employer permitted employees to smoke. After a grievance procedure and requests to her employer failed to eliminate the employee's exposure to her co-workers' tobacco smoke, the employee requested an injunction requiring the employer to institute a no-smoking policy in the work areas. In granting the injunction, the court recognized that an employer is under an affirmative duty to provide a safe work area for its employees. After taking judicial notice of the "toxic nature of cigarette smoke and its well-known association with emphysema, lung cancer and heart disease," the court pointed out that cigarette smoke is not a necessary by-product of any business or manufacturing process, and that plaintiff, therefore, had not voluntarily assumed the risk of exposure to ETS in pursuing her career.

b. *Claims Based on Workers' Compensation Acts*

A few decisions have granted compensation benefits to employees asserting claims under workers' compensation acts. In Johannesen v. New York City Dept. of Housing Preservation & Development, 154 A.D.2d 753, 546 N.Y.S.2d 40 (1989), an employee worked in an office in which co-workers smoked. As a result of exposure to ETS over a period of years, the compensation claim alleged, the employee suffered from bronchial asthma. The administrative law judge granted benefits after finding that the "claimant had suffered from a compensable *occupational disease*." The Workers' Compensation Board rescinded that decision, but granted benefits by determining that the "claimant had sustained an *accidental injury* as a result of the repeated trauma of exposure to cigarette smoke." The New York Appellate Division affirmed the Board's decision, stating that the "Board could properly find that the concentration of smoke at claimant's work station constituted an unusual environmental hazard."

Which is the better argument: that injury from ETS is an "occupational disease" or that it is an "accidental injury?" See also Schober v.

Mountain Bell Telephone, 96 N.M. 376, 630 P.2d 1231 (App.1980) (collapse in workplace from ETS is an accident). In contrast, see Ate Fixture Fab v. Wagner, 559 So.2d 635 (Fla.App.1990), where the state compensation board awarded claimant "permanent total disability benefits for acceleration and aggravation of obstructive lung disease due to inhalation" of ETS, only to be reversed by the Florida Court of Appeals which remanded for further evidence on causation between the worker's condition and the exposure to ETS. Cf. Mack v. County of Rockland, 71 N.Y.2d 1008, 530 N.Y.S.2d 98, 525 N.E.2d 744 (1988), in which the court rejected a claim of aggravation of a pre-existing eye disorder from exposure to ETS on the basis of its conclusion that the claimant's injury was not an occupational disease under New York's Workers' Compensation Act.

c.   *Claims Based on Negligence*

A final theory of liability that has appeared in the cases is predicated on the employer's negligence, where the facts permitted the employee to circumvent the exclusivity provisions of the workers' compensation system. In McCarthy v. Department of Social & Health Services, 110 Wash.2d 812, 759 P.2d 351 (1988), an employee complained to her employer regarding the adverse health consequences of exposure to ETS in the office, but the employer took no remedial action. The employee developed chronic obstructive pulmonary disease with diminished pulmonary function which she claimed was a result of sensitivity to ETS. The employee's workers' compensation benefit claim was denied because the Board concluded that her pulmonary lung disease was not the result of an industrial injury and did not constitute an occupational disease within the Washington Industrial Insurance Act. Because she was denied her workers' compensation claim she filed a civil tort suit alleging that the employer had negligently failed to provide her a tobacco smoke-free working environment. On appeal, the Supreme Court of Washington first determined that denying a remedy for exposure to ETS through the Industrial Insurance Act, without allowing for a common law remedy, would disrupt the quid pro quo relationship between the employer and the employee that is the basis of the workers' compensation system. As a result, the court held that the employee could sustain a common law negligence action because the Workers' Compensation Board found that the employee's injury was not within the scope of the Industrial Insurance Act.

Second, the court stated that because the "hazardous nature of cigarette smoke to non-smokers is well established, * * * [the] employer's common law duty to provide a safe workplace includes the duty to provide a work environment reasonably free of tobacco smoke pollution." Moreover, the employer's failure to protect this employee from tobacco smoke, after receiving notice by the employee, could be a breach of the employer's common law duty. As a result, the court determined that the facts supported a prima facie case of negligence and remanded the case for trial.

What problems do you foresee from decisions such as *McCarthy*? Does denial of a workers' compensation claim on its merits form the basis of a negligence action? Must the denial be jurisdictional in order to avoid the exclusivity bar? How would you argue the reverse, i.e., that permitting the common law claim disrupts the quid pro quo relationship between, the employer and employee that is the basis of the workers compensation system?

d. Miscellaneous Contexts

That the impact of passive smoke can no longer be doubted is attested to by the variety of settings, outside of tort law, in which claims are brought based on exposure to passive smoke. Compare Hinman v. Yakima School District, 69 Wash.App. 445, 850 P.2d 536 (1993) (an asthmatic teacher's exposure to passive smoke due to her classroom's proximity to the smoking-permissive teachers' lounge, and not reassigning her until she was hospitalized, stated a cause of action under state's law requiring employers to provide reasonable accommodations to handicapped workers), with Helm v. Helm, 1993 WL 21983 (Tenn.App.1993) (father who smoked and exposed his child to passive smoke not denied custody on that ground). In Helling v. McKinney, 509 U.S. 25, 113 S.Ct. 2475, 125 L.Ed.2d 22 (1993), the Supreme Court held that prisoners have a constitutional right not to be exposed to cellmates' cigarette smoke if such exposure creates an extreme health risk. In addition to proving an "unreasonable" health risk, a prisoner would have to show that "society considers the risk so grave that it violates contemporary standards of decency to expose anyone unwillingly to such a risk." Moreover, the court stated, the prisoner would have to show that prison officials were "deliberately indifferent" to the health risk.

D. OCCUPATIONAL SAFETY AND HEALTH REQUIREMENTS

The relationship between toxic tort litigation and the workplace would be incomplete if it did not include some appreciation of one federal regulatory program that has considerable relevance in this field. The Occupational Safety and Health Administration (OSHA) administers the Occupational Safety and Health Act, 29 U.S.C.A. §§ 651–678 (OSH Act or Act), and the regulations promulgated pursuant to that statute. The Act contains a general duty clause which requires employers to provide "a place of employment which [is] free from recognized hazards that are causing or are likely to cause death or serious physical harm to his employees." 29 U.S.C.A. § 654(a)(1). In addition, certain rules and standards have been promulgated for regulating specific hazards in the workplace.

1. TOXIC AND HAZARDOUS SUBSTANCES

For most industrial facilities, the number one OSHA concern is workers' contact with toxic and hazardous substances. The Code of Federal Regulations has 25 separate standards for such substances, which include asbestos, coal tar pitch, vinyl chloride, arsenic, lead, benzene, cotton dust, and formaldehyde. See 29 C.F.R. §§ 1910.1001–1910.1101, which specify in great detail requirements concerning exposure levels, training requirements, warning signs, and medical surveillance.

OSHA also has issued permissible exposure limits for 376 air contaminants. See the tables at 29 C.F.R. § 1900.1000; "Air Contaminants–Permissible Exposure Limits," OSHA Pub. No. 3112. Employees who work in proximity to these toxic substances must use engineering controls and personal protection equipment to assure that the level of air contamination is within the permissible exposure limit. The regulations also provide short-term exposure limits, ceiling limits, and skin protection designations.

OSHA's promulgation of substance-specific health standards which establish the permissible exposure limits ("PELs") reflect the maximum amount of contaminants to which workers may be exposed over a given time period. After promulgating 425 initial PELs in 1971, by 1988 OSHA had issued only 24 new or updated substance-specific standards. In 1988 OSHA proposed over 400 new or revised PELs in one generic rulemaking. 54 Fed. Reg. 2332–2983 (Jan. 19, 1989). In AFL–CIO v. OSHA, 965 F.2d 962 (11th Cir.1992), the court of appeals held that OSHA's procedures in adopting these standards failed to comply with the Act. Specifically, the Act requires in § 3(8) (29 U.S.C.A. § 652(8)) that OSHA establish that the standards are "reasonably necessary or appropriate to provide safe or healthful employment or places of employment." The Supreme Court in Industrial Union Dept., AFL–CIO v. American Petroleum Inst., 448 U.S. 607, 100 S.Ct. 2844, 65 L.Ed.2d 1010 (1980) had previously interpreted this provision to require that before promulgating any permanent health standard, OSHA must make a threshold finding that a significant risk of material health impairment exists at the current levels of exposure to the toxic substance in question "and that a new, lower standard is therefore 'reasonably necessary or appropriate to provide safe or healthful employment and places of employment.'" Thus, OSHA is entitled to regulate only those risks which present a "significant" risk of "material" health impairment. Moreover, OSHA ultimately bears the burden of proving by substantial evidence that such a risk exists and that the proposed standard is necessary; and must provide at least an estimate of the actual risk associated with a particular toxic substance and explain why that risk is significant. Because OSHA had failed to estimate the risk that workers would contract various adverse health effects associated with each of the over 400 substances, the court held that the rulemaking was defective.

2. OSHA RECORDKEEPING REQUIREMENTS

Most employers are governed by OSHA's general recordkeeping rules. See 29 U.S.C.A. § 657(c). OSHA has been vigorously enforcing its injury reporting requirements, imposing a $10,000 fine per misrecorded or non-reported injury. The Budget Reconciliation Act of 1990 increased the maximum fine to $70,000 for each incorrectly recorded injury.

Except for certain exempt industries where the risk of physical injury is slight (e.g., banking), all employers (with 10 or more employees) must keep records of workplace injury. An employer must maintain a log and summary of all occupational illnesses, fatalities, and any workplace injury which causes a loss of a work-day, work restrictions, transfers to another job, loss of consciousness, or requires medical treatment, and complete this recordation within six working days of the injury. 29 C.F.R. §§ 1904.2, 1904.4; OSHA Forms Nos. 200, 101. A summary of occupational injuries and illnesses must be posted annually, and the records must be retained for five years and be available to employees. 29 C.F.R. §§ 1904.5, 1904.6.

An employer must maintain, for workers exposed to toxic substances or harmful physical agents, any medical records, exposure records, and analyses of such records which the employer has created. Moreover, given the long latency of many diseases, these records must be retained for thirty years after the employee leaves the workplace. 29 C.F.R. § 1910.20.

All occupational diseases must be recorded and placed into the following categories: occupational skin diseases or disorders, dust diseases of the lungs (pneumoconiosis), respiratory conditions due to toxic agents, poisoning, disorders due to physical agents, and disorders associated with repetitive trauma.

3. HAZARDOUS CHEMICALS

The hazard communication standard was written to ensure two goals: (1) that the hazards of all chemicals produced or imported by chemical manufacturers or importers are evaluated; and (2) that information concerning chemical hazards is transmitted to affected employers and employees. 29 C.F.R. § 1910.1200(a)(1). The key to compliance with the requirements of the standard is maintenance of a complete set of Material Safety Data Sheets (MSDS), a written hazardous communication program, and mandated training programs for all affected workers.

The standard requires that certain information and training be given to employees who handle any chemical "which is a physical hazard or health hazard." 29 C.F.R. § 1910.1200(c). Manufacturers and importers must provide MSDS for all hazardous chemicals. Employers can rely on the manufacturer's hazard determination and the manufacturer's Material Safety Data Sheets which it prepared. 29 C.F.R. § 1910.1200(d), and 1910.1200(g). In any event, the employer must obtain MSDS for all hazardous chemicals his "employees may be exposed [to] under normal conditions of use or in a foreseeable emergency." 29 C.F.R. §§ 1910.1200(b)(2), 1910.1200(g).

In accordance with 29 C.F.R. § 1910.1200(e), all employers must develop and implement a written hazard communication program which includes the following:

(1) A list of hazardous chemicals known to be present in the workplace;

(2) The methods the employer will use to inform employees [and exposed independent contractors] of the hazards associated with such chemicals; and

(3) The procedures to be followed with respect to labeling, MSDS and employee information and training.

Employers must ensure that each container of hazardous chemicals in the workplace is labeled, tagged, or marked with the identity of the hazardous chemicals contained therein and appropriate hazard warnings.

Information and training on hazardous chemicals in the employer's workplace must be provided to employees. They must be informed of the OSHA requirements, any operations in their work area where hazardous chemicals are present, and the location and availability of the written hazard communication program. 29 C.F.R. § 1910.1200(h).

4. THE ROLE OF NON–COMPLIANCE AND COMPLIANCE

OSHA and its regulations only govern the employer-employee relationship. Its jurisdiction is limited to the control of how employers treat their workers. Thus, OSHA cannot directly control environmental exposure to toxic substances. However, the standards set by OSHA are generally recognized as the minimum acceptable for reasonable conduct; hence, failure to meet the OSHA standards can indirectly result in non-statutory toxic tort liability based on a breach of the standard of reasonableness.

For example, an agricultural worker injured by exposure to toxins subject to OSHA standards was able to successfully argue that his employer's violation of various OSHA regulations constituted negligence per se. Sanchez v. Galey, 112 Idaho 609, 733 P.2d 1234 (1986). Accord, Dixon v. International Harvester Co., 754 F.2d 573, 581 (5th Cir.1985); Teal v. E.I. DuPont de Nemours & Co., 728 F.2d 799 (6th Cir.1984). However, the converse is not true—if an employer complies with all of the OSHA requirements, it will not necessarily escape liability. In egregious situations, the injured employee may be allowed to sue outside the workers' compensation system, and even criminal responsibility can attach based on willful and wanton disregard for a worker's safety.

In Pedraza v. Shell Oil Co., 942 F.2d 48 (1st Cir.1991), the plaintiff commenced a civil action alleging that he developed respiratory ailments from workplace exposure to Epichlorohydrin ("ECH"), a toxic chemical manufactured by the defendant Shell. The district court dismissed the action on the ground that the OSH Act preempted state tort law. Section 18 of the OSH Act, 29 U.S.C.A. § 667(a), provides that:

> (a) Nothing in this Act shall prevent any State agency or court from asserting jurisdiction under State law over any occupational safety or health issue with respect to which no standard is in effect under section 655 of this title.

> (b) Any State which, at any time, desires to assume responsibility for development and enforcement therein of occupational safety and health standards relating to any occupational safety or health issue with respect to which a Federal standard has been promulgated under section 655 of this title shall submit a State plan for the development of such standards and their enforcement.

Shell contended that the Act preempted all the state-created rights since the adjudication of private rights arising under state law would result in the imposition of "prospective normative constraints on the manufacture and distribution of ECH." The court observed that substantial authority exists for the view that this section preempts the unapproved establishment of state standards and regulatory schemes in competition with OSHA, but that there is no authority for the view that OSHA preempts provisions of state law of the sort relied upon by Pedraza.

It continued:

> We are aware of no case which holds that OSHA preempts state tort law. Rather, most courts have been concerned with how OSHA affects tort actions, not with whether it preempts state tort law. Thus, every court faced with the issue has held that OSHA creates no private right of action. We have embraced the majority view that the regulations promulgated under OSHA prescribe standards of care relevant in common law negligence actions.

> While we discern in OSHA's language, structure and context a clear congressional signal that section 18 preempts unapproved assertions of state jurisdiction in the development and enforcement of standards relating to occupational health and safety issues in competition with federal standards, we find no warrant whatever for an interpretation which would preempt enforcement in the workplace of private rights and remedies traditionally afforded by state laws of general application. Connecticut's accustomed maintenance of judicial fora for the enforcement of private rights in the workplace, under State laws of general application, seems to us a function far less prophylactic than reactive; less normative than compensatory; and less an arrogation of regulatory jurisdiction over an "occupational safety or health issue" than a neutral forum for the orderly adjustment of private disputes between, among others, the users and suppliers of toxic substances.

Additionally, the court drew on § 4(b)(4) of the Act which contains a savings clause explicitly stating that OSH Act shall not "affect any workmen's compensation law or affect in any other manner the common law or statutory rights, duties, or liabilities of any employers and employees * * * "

As a matter of fairness, should compliance with OSHA regulations constitute a defense to a toxic tort action based on an exposure entirely legal under applicable federal law?

Are the Hazard Communication Standard and related OSHA requirements likely to prove more advantageous to plaintiffs or to defendants? For a discussion of that question, see Michael D. Green, When Toxic Worlds Collide: Regulatory and Common Law Prescriptions for Risk Communication, 13 Harv. Envtl. L. Rev. 209 (1989).

Chapter Ten

CERCLA: LIABILITY AND COMPEN-SATION FOR CLEANING UP HAZARDOUS SUBSTANCES

A. OVERVIEW OF CERCLA

1. INTRODUCTION

The Comprehensive Environmental Response, Compensation and Liability Act of 1980 ("CERCLA"), 42 U.S.C. § 9601 et seq., is broadly concerned with the cleanup of hazardous substances that may be present in the environment. Its principal focus, however, is on the removal of hazardous waste and the remediation of waste sites. The term "waste sites" is an extremely broad concept that embraces everything from a traditional landfill to an abandoned railroad yard to a currently operating factory. Unlike most of the other major environmental statutes, its objective is not largely regulatory in the sense of command and control regulations although CERCLA does contain some regulatory provisions. It is designed instead to establish rules of liability upon certain classes of actors for the necessary costs of undertaking cleanups, and to establish measures of compensation of those who have in fact undertaken the cleanups of sites where hazardous substances have been released or are threatened to be released. Because CERCLA concentrates on liability and compensation, it becomes complementary to the law of toxic torts. As you review these materials, compare and contrast how the theories of liability and compensable interests described in the earlier chapters are similar to or different than the liability and compensation principles governing CERCLA litigation.

CERCLA was enacted as a last-minute compromise in the closing days of the Carter Administration in December 1980. Although the legislative history of CERCLA (which is also known as the "Superfund" Act because of the fund created to pay for some of the cleanups) is not a paragon of clarity, it is nonetheless clear that one of Congress' primary objectives was "assuring that those responsible for any damage, environmental harm, or injury from chemical poison bear the costs of their actions." See S. Rep. No. 848 at 13, to S. 1480, 96th Cong., 2d Sess. (1980). The objective of providing toxic tort compensation (such as for personal injury or emotional distress or medical monitoring damages) contained in earlier versions of the bill was deleted as part of last-minute compromises, in exchange for the establishment of a study group, known as the Section 301 Study Group, to examine toxic tort laws and determine if a *federal tort compensation* system was justified. CERCLA § 301(e).

Congress concluded that the states, including state common law tort liability principles, were unable to respond adequately to the distinctly national problem of mitigating the consequences of hazardous substance releases, and that a uniformly administered federal program that imposed a single liability standard would be more effective than a patchwork of differing state laws. Congress had previously enacted the Resource Conservation and Recovery Act (RCRA) of 1976, which established a prospective "cradle-to-grave" system for tracking hazardous wastes from their generation, through their transport, storage, and treatment, and to their disposal at permitted facilities. See 42 U.S.C. §§ 6901–6987. RCRA, however, did not give the EPA or the states the tools to address the retrospective problem of cleaning up abandoned hazardous waste sites, and hence, CERCLA was designed to focus on remediating the harm already visited on the environment.

CERCLA created the Hazardous Substances Response Trust Fund, the "Superfund," a $1.6 billion fund with a life span of five years, to cover the costs of government responses at hazardous waste sites. In 1986, Congress passed the Superfund Amendments and Reauthorization Act (SARA), which replenished the fund with $8.5 billion and addressed many of the problems identified since 1980 in securing prompt and effective cleanups of hazardous substances. In order to preserve the Superfund's resources, liable parties are required to reimburse the fund for the government's cleanup expenditures and private parties are encouraged to initiate and pay for cleanups that the fund otherwise would finance.

The central objective of CERCLA is to place ultimate responsibility for cleaning up sites of hazardous wastes upon the parties that were responsible for placing them at the sites. These parties are called "potentially responsible parties" (or PRPs). CERCLA addresses both short-term or emergency responses to spills or discharges of hazardous substances (so-called "removal costs"), and permanent responses to long-term releases of hazardous substances into the environment (known as "remedial" costs). See CERCLA § 104. CERCLA also authorizes the Attorney General to institute an action for abatement or other immediate relief when there exists "an imminent and substantial endangerment to the public health or welfare or the environment because of the actual or threatened release of a hazardous substance." CERCLA § 106(a).

Because of the thousands of hazardous sites existing throughout the country, the EPA is required to establish a National Contingency Plan which includes "criteria for determining priorities among releases or threatened releases throughout the United States for the purpose of taking remedial action." CERCLA § 105(a). The most significant component of the EPA's power to force remediation of waste sites is contained in CERCLA § 106 which empowers the agency to issue administrative orders or seek a court order requiring a responsible party to undertake response activities. Moreover, under § 106, the recipient of the administrative order may not challenge its issuance or its terms unless and until the EPA initiates an enforcement proceeding in federal court (§ 113(h), no pre-enforcement review), at which time the PRP may be subject to civil penalties of $25,000 per day (CERCLA § 106(b)(1)) and treble damages of the EPA's expended remediation costs unless the potentially responsible party (PRP) can affirmatively establish that it had "sufficient cause" for not complying with the order (CERCLA § 107(c)(3)). See Solid State Circuits, Inc. v. U.S. EPA, 812 F.2d 383 (8th Cir.1987) for a thorough treatment of the EPA's power under CERCLA § 106.

CERCLA §§ 102 and 103 require certain parties to give notice of a release of hazardous substances. Section 103 requires that any person in charge of a vessel or facility notify the National Response Center (33 U.S.C. § 1251 et seq.) as soon as the person has knowledge of any release of a hazardous substance equal to or greater than the reportable quantity (RQ) for that substance. A reportable quantity is the amount of a hazardous substance which must be reported, if released. EPA establishes RQs pursuant to § 102 of CERCLA. EPA has promulgated regulations listing the hazardous substances and specifying the reportable quantities for each. See, 40 C.F.R. § 302.

2. PRINCIPAL STATUTORY PROVISIONS

The basic principles of liability are set forth in CERCLA § 107, 42 U.S.C. § 9607:

Liability (a) * * * Notwithstanding any other provision or rule of law, and subject only to the defenses set forth in subsection (B) of this section–

(1) the owner and operator of a vessel or a facility,

(2) any person who at the time of disposal of any hazardous substance owned or operated any facility at which such hazardous substances were disposed of,

(3) any person who by contract, agreement, or otherwise arranged for disposal or treatment, or arranged with a transporter for transport for disposal or treatment, of hazardous substances owned or possessed by such person, by any other party or entity, at any facility or incineration vessel owned or operated by another party or entity and containing such hazardous substances, and

(4) any person who accepts or accepted any hazardous substances for transport to disposal or treatment facilities, incineration vessels or sites selected by such person, from which there is a

release, or a threatened release which causes the incurrence of response costs, of a hazardous substance, shall be liable for–

(A) all costs of removal or remedial action incurred by the United States Government or a State or an Indian tribe not inconsistent with the national contingency plan;

(B) any other necessary costs of response incurred by any other person consistent with the national contingency plan;

(C) damages for injury to, destruction of, or loss of natural resources, including the reasonable costs of assessing such injury, destruction, or loss resulting from such a release; and

(D) the costs of any health assessment or health effects study carried out under section 9604(I) of this title. * * *

(b) *Defenses*. There shall be no liability under subsection (a) of this section for a person otherwise liable who can establish by a preponderance of the evidence that the release or threat of release of a hazardous substance and the damages resulting therefrom were caused solely by–

(1) an act of God;

(2) an act of war;

(3) an act or omission of a third party other than an employee or agent of the defendant, or one whose act or omission occurs in connection with a contractual relationship, existing directly or indirectly, with the defendant * * *, if the defendant establishes by a preponderance of the evidence that (a) he exercised due care with respect to the hazardous substance, in light of all relevant facts and circumstances, and (b) he took precautions against foreseeable acts or omissions of any such third party and the consequences that could foreseeably result from such acts or omissions; or

(4) any combination of the foregoing paragraphs * * *.

Thus, the statute specifies the classes of persons who may be held liable (potentially responsible parties, or PRPs), given the congressional intent to allocate the financial burden of cleaning up contaminated sites broadly among parties who may be responsible for causing contamination. Potentially responsible parties include (1) the current owner or operator of the site; (2) any person who owned or operated the site at the time hazardous substances were disposed of; (3) any person who arranged to have waste taken to the site for disposal or treatment, usually referred to as generators or arrangers; and (4) any person who transported waste for disposal or treatment to a site it selected.

B. GOVERNMENT ACTIONS

While the focus of this Chapter is on private actions under CERCLA, the elements of a government action must first be understood because the government action often precedes private litigation and influences the liability and damage phase of the private actions.

1. RELEASE OR THREATENED RELEASE

In addition to establishing that a defendant satisfies one of the categories of PRPs, the government must also prove that there was a "release or threatened release * * * of a hazardous substance." 42 U.S.C. § 9607(a)(4). CERCLA § 101(22) defines release as "any spilling, leaking, pumping, pouring, emitting, emptying, discharging, injecting, escaping, leaching, dumping, or disposing into the environment (including the abandonment or discarding of barrels, containers, and other closed receptacles containing any hazardous substance or pollutant or contaminant)." As noted above, CERCLA requires that a person responsible for a release provide notification to the National Response Center if it meets or exceeds the reportable quantity.

But a release "into the environment" has some limitations. Thus, "environment" is defined as "navigable waters * * * , any other surface water, ground water, drinking water supply, land surface or subsurface strata, or ambient air * * *." 42 U.S.C. § 9601(8). When these in pari materia provisions of CERCLA are read together, it becomes clear that CERCLA requires reporting whenever a hazardous substance is *released from a facility, such as a tank or a lagoon, into the environment*, such as the ground or the air.

But in The Fertilizer Institute v. EPA, 935 F.2d 1303 (D.C. Cir. 1991), the Court of Appeals struck down an EPA rule that triggered CERCLA's notification requirement whenever a hazardous substance is placed into an "unenclosed containment structure." The court stated that the EPA defined an unenclosed containment structure as "any surface impoundment, lagoon, tank, or other holding device that has an open side with the contained materials directly exposed to the ambient environment." According to this interpretation, therefore, "the placement of an RQ of a hazardous substance in an unenclosed structure would constitute a 'release' regardless of whether an RQ of the substance actually volatizes into the air or migrates into surrounding water or soil." The court held that the EPA's interpretation of CERCLA's reporting requirement cannot be reconciled with CERCLA's express terms.

In New York v. Shore Realty Corp., 759 F.2d 1032 (2d Cir.1985), the Second Circuit held that "leaking tanks and pipelines," "continuing leaching and seepage," and "leaking drums" of hazardous materials all constituted releases. However, more than the act of disposal is required to constitute a release; there must be some evidence that the waste has affected or come into contact with the environment. When a contaminant is found near a disposal site, one may conclude that a release has occurred even though no proof exists that the particular contaminant actually flowed from the site. See United States v. Wade, 577 F.Supp. 1326 (E.D.Pa.1983). In addition, the Ninth Circuit has held that a plaintiff need not allege the particular manner in which a release, or threatened release, occurred in order to make out a prima facie case. Ascon Properties, Inc. v. Mobil Oil Co., 866 F.2d 1149 (9th Cir.1989).

In most of the decisions we consider in this chapter the question of whether a release occurred is not even contested. But in A & W Smelter & Refiners v. Clinton, 146 F.3d 1107 (9th Cir.1998), the court rejected EPA's effort to declare that an "abandonment" of ore-bearing drums that contained lead constituted a release; the EPA gave defendant 3 days within which to remove the drums and totally ignored defendant's intention to use the contents.

What constitutes a threatened release is more problematic. In *Shore Realty,* supra, the Second Circuit stated that "corroding and deteriorating tanks, [the defendant's] lack of expertise in handling hazardous waste, and even the failure to license the facility, amount to a threat of release." This language suggests that the harm from a threatened release need not be imminent. *Shore Realty* at 1045.

2. HAZARDOUS SUBSTANCE

a. *No Threshold Minimum*

To trigger liability under § 107 of CERCLA, the release or threatened release must involve a "hazardous substance." The statute defines "hazardous substance" in CERCLA § 101(14) primarily by reference to designations made in other environmental statutes, such as § 3001 of the Solid Waste Disposal Act, 42 U.S.C.A. § 6921, § 1321(b)(2)(A) of the Federal Water Pollution Control Act, 33 U.S.C.A. § 1321(b)(2)(A) and hazardous air pollutants, under the Clean Air Act, § 112. For a list of some of these substances, see 40 C.F.R. § 302.4 (1992); 40 C.F.R. § 401.15 (1989).

The one contested issue here is not whether a substance meets the definition of "hazardous," but whether CERCLA should be interpreted to require some *minimum threshold or quantity* of that substance before liability is triggered. Here the courts are unanimous in holding that no such minimum is required. See, e.g., U.S. v. Alcan Aluminum Corp., 990 F.2d 711, 720 (2d Cir.1993); B.F. Goodrich v. Murtha, 958 F.2d 1192, 1199–1201 (2d Cir.1992). That recognition was begrudging in A & W Smelter & Refiners v. Clinton, 146 F.3d 1107 (9th Cir.1998).

In *A & W Smelter* because the ore processed by defendant contained lead, EPA labeled it a hazardous substance. While not disputing that some level of concentration of lead is hazardous, A & W asked the Ninth Circuit to read a minimum level requirement into CERCLA. The court appeared sympathetic to A & W's argument, stating:

> Read as the EPA suggests, CERCLA seems to give the agency carte blanche to hold liable anyone who disposes of just about anything. Drop an old nickel that actually contains nickel? A CERCLA violation. Throw out an old lemon? It's full of citric acid, another hazardous substance.

However, the court found that CERCLA left it little choice but to agree with the EPA, noting that CERCLA refers simply to "any substance" designated under one of the various regulations, and the regulations in turn give no minimum levels. Also important, the court disagreed with the Fifth Circuit's attempt to impose a minimum level requirement "through the back door" by focusing on CERCLA's language which defines a liable person as one responsible for a release which "causes" incurrence of response costs. Amoco Oil Co. v. Borden, Inc., 889 F.2d 664, 669 (5th Cir.1989). The Fifth Circuit had held that a release "causes" EPA's response only if it poses a serious enough threat to justify the response; otherwise, the response is caused by the agency's overzealousness. The Ninth Circuit in *A & W Smelter* found this read too much into the word "causes."

In B.F. Goodrich Co. v. Murtha, 958 F.2d 1192, 1200 (2d Cir.1992), the court starkly stated the governing rule: "[I]t is plain that the definition does not depend on the concentration of the substance present. Thus, the concentration of hazardous substances in municipal solid waste—regardless of how low a percentage—is not relevant in deciding whether CERCLA liability is incurred."

Why do you think Congress might have made no quantitative minimum? Is it likely that the term "hazardous substance" implies that Congress preferred a no threshold rule? Or that it never considered the issue?

b. Useful Product or Waste

Another issue that has emerged in this area is whether the defendant has really just sold a "useful" product, rather than arranged for the disposal (§ 9607) of a hazardous substance contained in that "product."

In Pneumo Abex Corp. v. High Point, Thomasville & Denton Railroad Co., 142 F.3d 769 (4th Cir.1998), four factors were identified by the Fourth Circuit in making the distinction between a sale of a useful product and a disposal of a hazardous substance. The court looked to "the intent" of the parties to the contract as to whether the materials were to be reused entirely or reclaimed and then reused, the value of the materials sold, the usefulness of the materials in the condition in which they were sold, and the state of the product at the time of transferral (was the hazardous material contained or leaking/loose). *Id.* at 775. The court found that the transaction at issue, selling used railroad car wheel parts containing hazardous constituents to a foundry that melted them down to make new parts, did not amount to an "arrangement for disposal" under CERCLA.

In A & W Smelter and Refiners, Inc. v. Clinton, 146 F.3d 1107 (9th Cir.1998), the Ninth Circuit remanded the case for a factual determination of whether ore containing gold, silver and small amounts of lead was a useful product or waste, the difference being whether the material is the producer's "principal business product" or a by-product "that the producer intends to get rid of." In dicta, the court seemed to cast doubt on the validity of the "mixture rule" stating that "adding waste to an otherwise useful product may make it all waste (e.g., adding a small quantity of lead to a carton of milk) or it may only decrease its usefulness (e.g., adding a small quantity of lead to a bar of gold). It all depends on the materials and their relative quantity." *Id.* at 1113.

In an extensive review of the application of the "useful product" defense, the court in United States v. Pesses, 1998 WL 937235 (W.D.Pa. 1998), reiterated earlier decisions that "if a transaction involves the sale of a new useful product containing a hazardous substance, as opposed to the sale of a substance merely to get rid of it, CERCLA liability may not attach." In this decision, the court distinguished between those who sell "useful products" and brokers who resell materials (albeit for profit) that cannot be used for their original intended purpose and contain hazardous substances.

What reasons explain the emergence of this defense, which is not expressly set forth in the statute? What abuses is the government attempting to prevent in sometimes contending that the sale of a product or material constitutes disposal of a hazardous substance?

c. *Exclusions and Underground Storage Tanks*

The definition of hazardous substance is noteworthy for its exclusions, which include petroleum, petroleum derivatives and natural gas. For cases interpreting these provisions, see Eagle–Picher Indus. v. U.S. EPA, 759 F.2d 922 (D.C.Cir.1985); United States v. Union Gas Co., 586 F.Supp. 1522 (E.D.Pa.1984), aff'd 792 F.2d 372 (3d Cir.1986), vacated and remanded on other grounds 479 U.S. 1025, 107 S.Ct. 865, 93 L.Ed.2d 821 (1987).

Why might Congress have excluded petroleum products from CERCLA's jurisdiction? It has been stated that the legislative purpose behind the petroleum exclusion is simply that Congress did not intend appropriated Superfund moneys to be spent to clean up oil spills, and other releases strictly of oil. It also has been noted that, in enacting subsequent legislation establishing a program specifically addressing leaking gasoline from underground storage tanks, Congress recognized that such problems were not covered by CERCLA. See RCRA, 42 U.S.C. § 6991 et seq. RCRA was amended in 1984 to explicitly include a separate title, Title IX, "Regulation of Underground Storage Tanks." It has been noted that the purpose of the petroleum exclusion is to remove from CERCLA jurisdiction spills only of oil, not releases of hazardous substances with oil. Bear in mind that many of the decisions in Chapters 2, 3 and 4 involved leaking underground storage tanks, illustrating the pervasiveness of the Leaking Underground Storage Tank (LUST) problem.

To address these problems, Congress directed the EPA in 1984 to establish regulatory programs to prevent, detect, and clean up releases from UST systems containing petroleum or hazardous substances in

RCRA. Consequently, the EPA developed UST regulations which it promulgated in 1988. See 40 C.F.R. § 280. Although the EPA's regulations authorize states to take the lead role in implementing and enforcing these regulations (most states have developed their own administrative procedures and set statewide cleanup levels), the EPA set a national deadline of Dec. 22, 1998, for upgrading, replacing, or closing all substandard UST systems. 40 C.F.R. § 280.21(a). On Dec. 22, 1998, the deadline expired after UST owners and operators had a full 10 years to comply with the regulations. Thus, beginning on Dec. 23, 1998, UST owners and operators who are out of compliance are subject to fines of $10,000 per day for every day their UST systems are not in compliance. RCRA, 42 U.S.C. § 6991e(d).

3. FACILITY

The next question is where must the waste be located in order for liability to attach? Not surprisingly, the courts have interpreted the statutory language very broadly. See CERCLA § 101(9); New York v. Shore Realty Corp., 759 F.2d 1032, 1043 n. 15 (2d Cir.1985) ("CERCLA defines the term 'facility' broadly to include any property at which hazardous substances have come to be located"); Amland Properties Corp. v. Aluminum Co. of America, 711 F.Supp. 784 (D.N.J.1989) (facility includes enclosed manufacturing plants and warehouses); United States v. Mottolo, 695 F.Supp. 615, 622 (D.N.H.1988) ("a 'facility' is essentially any site where a hazardous substance is located").

The statute contains an exclusion from "facility" for "consumer products in consumer use." This provision helps define the overall scope of CERCLA by excluding consumer or household use of consumer products. Westfarm Associates Ltd. Partnership v. Washington Suburban Sanitary Comm., 66 F.3d 669 (4th Cir.1995) (publicly owned treatment works are a facility). These outcomes are understandable given the definition of "facility" under CERCLA. 42 U.S.C. § 9601(9).

A "facility" is defined under CERCLA as:

(A) any building, structure, installation, equipment, pipe or pipeline (including any pipe into a sewer or publicly owned treatment works), well, pit, pond, lagoon, impoundment, ditch, landfill, storage container, motor vehicle, rolling stock, or aircraft, or (B) any site or area where a hazardous substance has been deposited, stored, disposed of, or placed, or otherwise come to be located; but does not include any consumer product in consumer use or any vessel.

See What Constitutes "Facility" Within the Meaning of § 101(9) of CERCLA, 147 ALR Fed. 469 (1998).

The breadth of "facility" is vividly demonstrated in Uniroyal Chemical Co., Inc. v. Deltech Corp., 160 F.3d 238, 241 (5th Cir.1998). Despite defendants' efforts to characterize a tanker truck and the hazardous, though not waste, chemicals it carried as a "consumer product in consumer use," the Fifth Circuit ruled that CERCLA did apply to the transporting truck and its owner, the leasing company, and operator, the transporting company. The court held specifically that CERCLA does not "apply only to disposals at inactive or abandoned waste sites" and reversed the district court's holding that the rupture of the truck and the resulting release fell within the "consumer product" exception to the "facility" element of CERCLA.

At the other end of the spectrum, at least in terms of size of the "facility," the Sixth Circuit Court of Appeals held that a fifteen-acre area was properly designated as a "facility" because the entire area was operated together, the court rejecting defendant township's argument that several acres should be excluded because they contained only non-hazardous waste. United States v. Township of Brighton, 153 F.3d 307 (6th Cir.1998).

4. NATIONAL PRIORITIES LIST

Not every release of a hazardous substance poses the same risk to human health or the environment. The National Priorities List, known as the NPL, is the method by which the EPA classifies sites. CERCLA requires the EPA to develop criteria for determining priorities among the various releases or threatened releases throughout the nation. These criteria are based on risks to the public health, welfare, or the environment, taking into account a variety of factors including the size of the population at risk, the hazard potential of the facility's hazardous substances, the potential for contamination of drinking water supplies, the toxicity of the substances, location of potential receptors, exposure pathways, threats to the food chain and threats to the ambient air. See 42 U.S.C. § 9605(a)(8)(A). Applying these criteria, the EPA scores and ranks the various sites for possible listing on the NPL.

EPA's decision to list a site on the NPL is considered an action pursuant to the Administrative Procedures Act and subject to notice and public comment. CERCLA affords a party 90 days in which to challenge a listing. 42 U.S.C. § 9613(a). A failure to challenge acts as a bar to any subsequent challenge.

5. DAMAGES RECOVERABLE BY THE GOVERNMENT

What damages may be recovered by the government under CERCLA? CERCLA § 107(a)(3)(A) permits the recovery of "all costs of removal or remedial action incurred by the U.S. Government * * * not inconsistent with the national contingency plan." For government actions "all costs of removal or remediation action" affords compensation to the EPA for virtually all expenses in any way related to its efforts to secure cleanup of the area. The double negative "not inconsistent" with the national contingency plan (NCP) also has the practical effect of placing the burden on the defendant of proving such inconsistency.

A clue to the meaning of "response costs" as used in CERCLA § 107(a)(4)(B) comes from CERCLA's definition of the terms "respond" and "response." CERCLA § 101(25) states: "The terms 'respond' or 'response' mean remove, removal, remedy, and remedial action; all such terms (including the terms 'removal' and 'remedial action') include enforcement activities related thereto." In short, "response costs," means at a minimum all of the costs relating to the cleanup of the site.

A significant amount of litigation has addressed the issue of whether "response costs" include costs of investigating or monitoring a site as a prelude to or as part of actual cleanup operations. These costs generally involve determining the existence of the environmental problem, conducting tests and chemical analyses, and drilling or monitoring wells to determine the nature and extent of the problem. A majority of cases have held that these costs are recoverable. See, New York v. General Electric Co., 592 F.Supp. 291, 298 (N.D.N.Y.1984) ("removal" action is defined under CERCLA § 101(23) to embrace "such actions as may be necessary to monitor, assess and evaluate the release or threat of release of hazardous substances.") See also Cadillac Fairview/California, Inc. v. Dow Chemical Co., 840 F.2d 691 (9th Cir.1988) (testing and security expenditures available under CERCLA § 101(23)); Wickland Oil Terminals v. Asarco, Inc., 792 F.2d 887, 892 (9th Cir.1986) (testing expenses considered "cost of response.").

How about oversight costs? In 1993 the Third Circuit in United States v. Rohm and Haas Co., 2 F.3d 1265 (3d Cir.1993), found that oversight costs were *not* recoverable. The court explained that the Third Circuit adopted a standard of review under which "only a clear congressional statement will be sufficient for us to impose an agency's costs on a regulated private party," and that CERCLA contained no such "explicit imprimatur" for recovery of oversight costs.

"Mixed treatment" of the recoverability of oversight costs has followed in the wake of the *Rohm and Haas* decision. Three district court opinions have allowed for the recovery of *state* oversight costs and one court has "directly rejected" the *Rohm and Haas* decision. In that case, United States v. Lowe, 864 F.Supp. 628 (S.D.Tex.1994), the court held that the private party litigants responsible for hazardous waste pollution at a Superfund site were obliged to pay the direct costs of the cleanup and "a proportionate share of the oversight costs attributable to that site." The court there found oversight costs were directly authorized by CERCLA §§ 107(a) and 101(23) as "an activity necessary to 'monitor, assess, and evaluate' an actual or threatened release of hazardous material or necessary 'to prevent, minimize, or mitigate' a threat to the public health or welfare." The Texas court also found that it would be incongruous to find that EPA could recover costs of overseeing contractors acting on behalf of PRPs.

Another district court concurred, finding that "the Third Circuit's approach in *Rohm and Haas*" should be rejected in favor of the traditional standard of statutory construction. "Ordinarily, a federal agency's interpretation of an ambiguous statutory provision is given deference, when that interpretation is not unreasonable," the court said. In United

States v. Ekotek, Inc., 1995 WL 580079 (D.Utah 1995), the District of Utah held that EPA could recover its costs of overseeing the PRP cleanup of a refinery and hazardous waste site in Utah. Rejecting the rationale of the Third Circuit's decision in *Rohm and Haas*, the court found that under the traditional standard of statutory construction (giving deference to reasonable agency interpretations of ambiguous provisions), CERCLA "is properly understood to authorize the recovery of oversight costs." In so ruling, added that allowing the Agency to recover its oversight costs is consistent with CERCLA's general policy of compelling private party cleanups.

6. THE GOVERNMENT ACTION: STRICT, RETROACTIVE AND JOINT AND SEVERAL LIABILITY RULES

a. Strict Liability. CERCLA is virtually silent on the standard of liability that applies to cost recovery actions under § 107(a)(1), but the courts have interpreted the statute as a sharp departure from the requirements of common law tort litigation. "The traditional elements of tort culpability * * * simply are absent from CERCLA." United States v. Monsanto Co., 858 F.2d 160, 168 (4th Cir.1988), cert. denied 490 U.S. 1106, 109 S.Ct. 3156, 104 L.Ed.2d 1019 (1989). Section 101(32) defines liability to mean the standard of liability applicable to the oil spill liability provisions of the Clean Water Act, 33 U.S.C. § 1321, and the courts have uniformly agreed that this reference reveals Congress' intention to impose strict liability. E.g., Dedham Water Co. v. Cumberland Farms Dairy, Inc., 889 F.2d at 1150; New York v. Shore Realty Corp., 759 F.2d 1032, 1042 (2d Cir.1985) ("Congress intended that responsible parties be held strictly liable, even though an explicit provisions for strict liability was not included in the compromise * * * ."). For our purposes the point is that the fact that a PRP may not have been negligent, may have complied with industry practice, or even then-applicable laws, is irrelevant–they provide no defense to liability.

In enacting the SARA amendments in 1986, Congress reaffirmed its intention that courts impose a strict liability standard on PRPs under CERCLA. See H.R. Rep. No. 253, Admin. News 2835, 2856. Why not apply a negligence standard? A nuisance standard?

b. Retroactive Liability. CERCLA has staunch supporters and equally tenacious detractors. Its supporters assert that CERCLA is justified because it imposes the costs of remediation on those responsible for the creation of hazardous waste sites. The statute's detractors complain that CERCLA imposes liability without fault and that liability is joint and several. However, perhaps the most offensive part of the liability scheme is its retroactive application years after the act of disposal took place. Courts have construed CERCLA to impose liability for conduct that was not only legal at the time, but often took place at the direction of the very government plaintiff-agencies seeking recovery of remediation costs. U.S. v. South Carolina Recycling and Disposal, Inc., 653 F.Supp. 984, aff'd sub nom. U.S. v. Monsanto, 858 F.2d 160 (4th

Cir.1988), cert. denied 490 U.S. 1106, 109 S.Ct. 3156, 104 L.Ed.2d 1019 (1989). These agencies are typically immune from counterclaims pursuant to the doctrine of sovereign immunity. U.S. v. New Castle County, 727 F.Supp. 854 (D.Del.1989); New York v. City of Johnstown, 701 F.Supp. 33 (N.D.N.Y.1988); CPC Intern., Inc. v. Aerojet–General Corp., 731 F.Supp. 783, 20 ELR 20712 (W.D.Mich.1989) ("mere regulatory activities will not subject a state agency to liability") (citing United States v. Dart Indus., Inc., 847 F.2d 144, 18 ELR 21084 (4th Cir.1988)); Hassayampa Steering Comm. v. Arizona, 21 ELR 20549 (D.Ariz.1990) (state agency assistance in the development of landfill design, in determining the nature of the wastes to be disposed of, and periodic on-site inspections insufficient to impose liability).

    c. Retroactive Liability & Constitutional Concerns. Early in CERCLA's history, defendants attacked the retroactive aspect of the liability scheme. While the U.S. Supreme Court has failed to address the issue, a number of lower courts have consistently concluded that CERCLA is both properly construed to apply retroactively and constitutional (particularly with regard to the Takings and Due Process Clauses) when applied retroactively. See, e.g., United States v. Olin Corp., 107 F.3d 1506 (11th Cir.1997) (U.S. Commerce Clause-based challenge); United States v. Northeastern Pharm. & Chem. Co., 810 F.2d 726 (8th Cir. 1986), cert. denied, 484 U.S. 848, 108 S.Ct. 146, 98 L.Ed.2d 102 (1987) (hereinafter cited as NEPACCO) (retroactive application of CERCLA achieves a legitimate purpose in a rational manner, and accordingly does not violate due process or takings constitutional restraints); United States v. Alcan Aluminum Corp., 49 F.Supp.2d 96 (N.D.N.Y.1999) (retroactive application of CERCLA is not unconstitutional); United States v. Vertac Chem. Corp., 33 F.Supp.2d 769 (E.D.Ark.1998).

    It was the district court opinion in United States v. Olin Corp., 927 F.Supp. 1502, 1513 (S.D.Ala.1996), rev'd, 107 F.3d 1506 (11th Cir.1997), that triggered a flood of commentary and no doubt higher blood pressure readings among EPA personnel and the Department of Justice. In *Olin,* the district court relied heavily on United States v. Lopez, 514 U.S. 549, 115 S.Ct. 1624, 131 L.Ed.2d 626 (1995) to support its commerce clause violation conclusion:

> "Nothing shows that the alluvial aquifer carries water across state lines or into any river or other transportation source that would take it across any state lines, nor is there any indication of transport of contaminants through the air across state lines," the court wrote.

> The court declaimed "a duty to examine a consent decree not only to determine whether its factual and legal determinations are reasonable, but also to ensure that the decree does not violate the Constitution, a federal statute or the controlling jurisprudence."

927 F.Supp. at 1507. As to retroactivity the court found no language in CERCLA explicitly stating it is retroactive, and virtually no legislative history to overcome the presumption against retroactivity. Further, the fines, punitive damages in the form of treble damages, meant that

CERCLA retroactively poses the very nearly same ex post facto danger relied on in Landgraf v. USI Film Products, 511 U.S. 244, 114 S.Ct. 1483, 128 L.Ed.2d 229 (1994).

It is beyond our goal here to explore this issue because of its depth and complexity. Suffice it to say that subsequent decisions have sustained the Act on both commerce clause grounds and in finding that "Congress clearly intended retroactive liability for response costs incurred as a result of acts committed before CERCLA's enactment." Nevada v. United States, 925 F.Supp. 691 (D.Nev.1996).

d. Joint and Several Liability or Divisibility of the Harm. One issue of extreme importance in CERCLA litigation is whether the government or private plaintiff can hold all PRPs jointly and severally liable as, for example, where the plaintiff settles with one of three defendants, and can be assured of a full recovery of all remaining response costs from the nonsettling defendant. As one commentator has explained:

> The factual context in which most CERCLA liability cases arise makes the issue of joint and several liability particularly potent. CERCLA sites seldom contain a single hazardous waste deposited by a sole defendant. In most instances, sites contain hazardous substances deposited by a number of parties over substantial periods of time. It is almost always impossible to determine precisely which parties deposited which substances and at what times. The records of generators and transporters indicating the type and quantity of wastes sent to a site are often inaccurate, incomplete, or nonexistent. Moreover, many substances, when mixed, can interact synergistically to greatly amplify the resulting harm, thus making it difficult, if not impossible, to scientifically assign the harms attributable to each contributor at a multi-polluter site. The EPA has considerably increased the stakes in CERCLA cleanup actions by taking the firm stance that when hazardous substances are commingled, joint and several liability must necessarily and automatically be imposed upon the parties responsible for the substances—a stance that at least some courts have adopted.

> CERCLA's response to these factual uncertainties is the imposition of legal uncertainty upon defendants—that is, the imposition of joint and several liability. Although such a standard eases the government's task by relieving it of difficult burdens of proof, joint and several liability is potentially disastrous for defendants. First, the costs of cleaning up environmental contamination are extremely high. Second, defendants who voluntarily settle cleanup claims with the EPA may be insulated from contribution suits by nonsettling defendants. The threat of joint and several liability for massive cleanup costs, coupled with an inability to seek contribution from settling defendants, creates a powerful incentive for defendants to settle early and dissuades them from contesting liability. Even a small contribution to a hazardous waste site can result in a defendant being held jointly liable for millions of dollars of cleanup costs.

Oswald, New Directions in Joint and Several Liability Under CERCLA, 28 U.C. Davis L. Rev. 299, 301 (1995). Three recent decisions by the Second, Third, and Fifth Circuit Courts of Appeal–United States v. Alcan Aluminum Corp. (Alcan I), 990 F.2d 711 (2d Cir.1993); United States v. Alcan Aluminum Corp. (Alcan II), 964 F.2d 252 (3d Cir.1992); and In re Bell Petroleum Services, Inc. (Bell), 3 F.3d 889 (5th Cir.1993)–have re-examined CERCLA's joint and several liability standard.

We now examine the *Bell Petroleum* opinion.

IN THE MATTER OF BELL PETROLEUM
SERVICES, INC.

United States Court of Appeals, Fifth Circuit, 1993.
3 F.3d 889.

E.   GRADY JOLLY, CIRCUIT JUDGE

The Environmental Protection Agency (EPA) seeks to recover its response costs under the Comprehensive Environmental Response, Compensation and Liability Act (CERCLA) because of a discharge of chromium waste that contaminated a local water supply. Sequa Corporation appeals from the imposition of joint and several liability, challenges the EPA's decision to provide an alternate water supply system to the area in which the groundwater was contaminated by the chromium discharge, and contests the calculation of prejudgment interest and the application of the proceeds of the EPA's settlement with its co-defendants. We REVERSE the portion of the judgment imposing joint and several liability, and REMAND for further proceedings. Our review of the administrative record has convinced us that the EPA's decision to provide an alternate water supply was arbitrary and capricious; accordingly, we REVERSE the portion of the district court's judgment allowing the EPA to recover the costs of designing and constructing that system, and REMAND for deletion of those amounts and recalculating prejudgment interest.

In 1978, a citizen in the Odessa, Texas area complained about discolored drinking water. The Texas Water Commission conducted an investigation. It ultimately focused on a chrome-plating shop that was operated successively from 1971 through 1977 by John Leigh, Western Pollution Control Corporation (hereinafter referred to as Bell), and Woolley Tool Division of Chromalloy American Corporation (which later merged with Sequa). * * * The investigation showed that during the chrome-plating process, finished parts were rinsed, and the rinse water was pumped out of the building onto the ground.

In 1984, the EPA designated a 24–block area north of the facility as a Superfund site—"Odessa Chromium I." It authorized a response action pursuant to its authority under CERCLA § 104, 42 U.S.C. § 9604, and entered into a cooperative agreement with the State of Texas. The State was to perform a remedial investigation, feasibility study, and remedial design work for the site, with the EPA reimbursing the State for ninety percent of the costs. The remedial investigation revealed that the Trinity Aquifer, the only source of groundwater in the area, contained elevated concentrations of chromium.

A "focused" feasibility study (FFS) was undertaken to evaluate the need to provide an alternative water supply pending completion of the remaining portion of the feasibility study and implementation of final remedial action. The FFS concluded that the City of Odessa's water system should be extended to provide service in the Odessa Chromium I area. On September 8, 1986, the EPA Regional Administrator issued a Record of Decision (ROD), finding that city water service should be extended to the site. Pursuant to the cooperative agreement, the State, through its contractor, designed and constructed the system, which was completed in 1988.

II

In December 1988, the EPA filed a CERCLA cost-recovery action against Bell, Sequa, and John Leigh. * * * The EPA sought to recover direct and indirect costs it incurred in studying, designing, and constructing the alternate water supply system.

In July 1989, the district court entered a case management order providing that the case would be decided in three phases: Phase I–liability, Phase II–recoverability of the EPA's response costs, and Phase III–"responsibility." * * * In its memorandum opinion, it stated that the relative culpability of the parties and the "divisibility of liability" issues would be decided during Phase III. Although the district court ruled that CERCLA did not require the EPA to prove causation, it held an evidentiary hearing and made alternative findings and conclusions addressing causation, holding that "Leigh, Bell and Sequa caused the contamination." In March 1990, the district court granted the EPA's motion for clarification of the September 1989 summary judgment, holding that its previous opinion had provided that the defendants were jointly and severally liable. It also entered a declaratory judgment as to the defendants' liability for future response costs.

* * *

[I]n the Phase II proceeding on recoverability of response costs * * * the district court held that the defendants had not met their burden of proving that the EPA's decision to implement an alternate water supply was arbitrary and capricious, and held that they were liable for the EPA's direct and indirect response costs, plus prejudgment interest from the date such costs were incurred.

On March 2, 1990, the EPA sought approval of a proposed consent decree, in which it settled its claims against Bell for all costs, past and future, for $1,000,000. Sequa objected to the settlement, contending that Bell was not being required to pay its fair share. The district court granted Sequa's request for a hearing on the fairness of the proposed consent decree, and entered an order providing that a Phase III hearing regarding apportionment of liability was to be conducted before it ruled on the motion for entry of a consent decree.* * * After the Phase II hearing * * * the district court * * * approved the consent decree. It held that the evidence at the Phase I and Phase III hearings demonstrated that there was no method of dividing the liability among the defendants which would rise to any level above mere speculation, because each of the proposed apportionment methods involved a significant assumption factor, inasmuch as records had been lost, and because each of the apportionment methods differed significantly. In the alternative, it concluded that, based on equitable factors, responsibility should be divided as follows: Bell–35%; Sequa–35%; and Leigh–30%.

The district court entered an order approving another consent decree, pursuant to which the EPA settled its claims against Leigh for past and future costs—for $100,000.

In sum, the district court held that Sequa is jointly and severally liable for $1,866,904.19, including the costs of studying, designing, and constructing the alternate water supply system. In addition, Sequa is jointly and severally liable for all future costs incurred by the EPA in studying, designing, and implementing a permanent remedy.

* * *

IV

JOINT AND SEVERAL LIABILITY

Since CERCLA's enactment, the federal courts have struggled to resolve the complicated, often confusing, questions posed by the concept of joint and several liability, and its application under a statute whose provisions are silent with respect to the scope of liability, but whose legislative history is clear that common law principles of joint and several liability may affect liability. The issue is one of first impression in this court.

A

COMMON LAW: THE RESTATEMENT OF TORTS

Although joint and several liability is commonly imposed in CERCLA cases, it is not mandatory in all such cases. United States v. Monsanto Co., 858 F.2d at 171. Instead, Congress intended that the federal courts determine the scope of liability in CERCLA cases under traditional and evolving common law principles, guided by the Restatement (Second) of Torts. * * *

Section 433 of the Restatement provides that:

(1) Damages for harm are to be apportioned among two or more causes where

(a) there are distinct harms, or

(b) there is a reasonable basis for determining the contribution of each cause to a single harm.

(2) Damages for any other harm cannot be apportioned among two or more causes.

Restatement (Second) of Torts § 433A.

The nature of the harm is the key factor in determining whether apportionment is appropriate. Distinct harms—e.g., where two defendants independently shoot the plaintiff at the same time, one wounding him in the arm and the other wounding him in the leg—are regarded as separate injuries. Although some of the elements of damages (such as lost wages or pain and suffering) may be difficult to apportion, "it is still possible, as a logical, reasonable, and practical matter, * * * to make a rough estimate which will fairly apportion such subsidiary elements of damages." Id., comment *b* on subsection (1).

The Restatement also discusses "successive" harms, such as when "two defendants, independently operating the same plant, pollute a stream over successive periods of time." Id., comment c on subsection (1). Apportionment is appropriate, because "it is clear that each has caused a separate amount of harm, limited in time, and that neither has any responsibility for the harm caused by the other." Id.

The final situation discussed by the Restatement in which apportionment is available involves a single harm that is "divisible"—perhaps the most difficult type of harm to conceptualize. Such harm, "while not so clearly marked out as severable into distinct parts, [is] still capable of division upon a reasonable and rational basis, and of fair apportionment among the causes responsible. * * * Where such apportionment can be made without injustice to any of the parties, the court may require it to be made." Id., comment d on subsection (1). * * *

* * *

In sum, the nature of the harm is the determining factor with respect to whether apportionment is appropriate. Ultimately, the decision whether to impose joint and several liability turns on whether there is a reasonable and just method for determining the amount of harm that was caused by each defendant (or, in some cases, by an innocent cause or by the fault of the plaintiff). The question whether the harm to the plaintiff is capable of apportionment among two or more causes is a question of law. Restatement (Second) of Torts, § 434(1)(b). Once it has been determined that the harm is capable of being apportioned among the various causes of it, the actual apportionment of damages is a question of fact. Id., § 434(2)(b) & comment *d*.

Section 433B of the Restatement sets forth the burdens of proof. As a general rule, the plaintiff must prove that the defendant's tortious conduct caused the harm. Id., § 433B(1), which sets forth the burdens of proof with respect to apportionment, does apply and provides as follows:

> Where the tortious conduct of two or more actors has combined to bring about harm to the plaintiff, and one or more of the actors seeks to limit his liability on the ground that the harm is capable of

apportionment among them, the burden of proof as to the apportionment is upon each such actor.

As explained in the comment, this rule applies only to "a proved wrongdoer who has in fact caused harm to the plaintiff." Id., comment d on subsection (2). Thus, the rule stated in subsection (2) will not permit a defendant to escape liability altogether, but only to limit its liability, if it can meet its burden of proving the amount of the harm that it caused. If it is unable to do so, it is liable for the full amount of the harm. According to the Restatement, the typical case to which this rule applies "is the pollution of a stream by a number of factories which discharge impurities into it." Id., comment c on subsection (2).

Comment *e* notes that there is a possibility that the rule stated in subsection (2) may cause disproportionate harm to defendants where each of a large number of them contributes a relatively small and insignificant part to the total harm. For example, "if a hundred factories each contribute a relatively small, but still uncertain, amount of pollution to a stream, to hold each of them liable for the entire damage because he cannot show the amount of his contribution may perhaps be unjust." Id., comment e on subsection (2). The comment, however, expresses no conclusion with respect to the applicability of this illustration, noting that such a case had not arisen.

CERCLA is a strict liability statute, one of the purposes of which is to shift the cost of cleaning up environmental harm from the taxpayers to the parties who benefitted from the disposal of the wastes that caused the harm. See, e.g., U.S. v. Chem–Dyne Corp., 572 F.Supp. 802, 805–06 (S.D.Ohio 1983). "The improper disposal or release of hazardous substances is an enormous and complex problem of national magnitude involving uniquely federal interests." Id. at 808. Often, liability is imposed upon entities for conduct predating the enactment of CERCLA, and even for conduct that was not illegal, unethical, or immoral at the time it occurred. We recognize the importance of keeping these facts in mind when attempting to develop a uniform federal common law for CERCLA cases. We also recognize, however, that CERCLA, as a strict liability statute that will not listen to pleas of "no fault," can be terribly unfair in certain instances in which parties may be required to pay huge amounts for damages to which their acts did not contribute. Congress recognized such possibilities and left it to the courts to fashion some rules that will, in appropriate instances, ameliorate this harshness. Accordingly, Congress has suggested, and we agree, that common-law principles of tort liability set forth in the Restatement provide sound guidance. In applying those principles to this CERCLA case, we think that it will be helpful to examine briefly some of the relevant CERCLA jurisprudence.

B

The Jurisprudence

The first published case to address the scope of liability under CERCLA is United States v. Chem–Dyne Corp., 572 F.Supp. 802

(S.D.Ohio 1983), which was cited approvingly in the legislative history of the SARA amendments to CERCLA. In that case, 24 defendants, who allegedly generated or transported hazardous substances located at Chem–Dyne's treatment facility, sought "an early determination" that they were not jointly and severally liable for the EPA's response costs. * * *

The court described the nature of the "fairly complex factual determination" involved in deciding whether the defendants were jointly and severally liable.

* * *

The court concluded that the defendants had not met their burden of demonstrating the divisibility of the harm and the degree to which each was responsible, and denied their motion for summary judgment. Id.

United States v. Ottati & Goss, Inc., 630 F.Supp. 1361 (D.N.H.1985), was a cost recovery action against operators and former operators of drum reconditioning businesses, property owners, and generators of wastes contained in the drums that were sent to the site for reconditioning. The evidence showed that chemical substances leaked or spilled from drums and were mixed together. Although the generators satisfied their burden of proving approximately how many drums each brought to the site, the court nevertheless imposed joint and several liability, because "the exact amount or quantity of deleterious chemicals or other noxious matter [could not] be pinpointed as to each defendant [, and] [t]he resulting proportionate harm to surface and groundwater [could not] be proportioned with any degree of accuracy as to each individual defendant."

* * *

On the other hand, the Third Circuit reversed a summary judgment in favor of the EPA, and remanded the case for further factual development on the scope of liability, in United States v. Alcan Aluminum Corp. (Alcan-Butler), 964 F.2d 252, 255 (3d Cir.1992). This case involved the Butler Tunnel Site, a network of approximately five square miles of underground mines, tunnels, caverns, pools, and waterways, drained by the Butler Tunnel into the Susquehanna River in Pennsylvania. During the 1970s, millions of gallons of liquid wastes containing hazardous substances were disposed of through a borehole that led directly into the mine workings. In 1985, 100,000 gallons of contaminated water were released from the site into the river.

The government filed a cost-recovery action against 20 defendants; all but Alcan settled. The district court granted summary judgment for the government, holding that Alcan was jointly and severally liable for the response costs. The Third Circuit held that the "intensely factual nature of the 'divisibility' issue" highlighted the district court's error in granting summary judgment without conducting a hearing. It remanded the case in order to give Alcan the opportunity to limit or avoid liability by attempting to prove its personal contribution to the harm to the Susquehanna River. Thus, under the Third Circuit's approach, Alcan could escape liability altogether if it could prove that its "emulsion did not or could not, when mixed with other hazardous wastes, contribute to the release and the resultant response costs." Id. at 270.

The Third Circuit noted that the analysis involved in apportioning several liability is similar to that involved in apportioning damages among jointly and severally liable defendants in an action for contribution, because both focus on what harm was caused by the defendant. Id. at 270 n.29. However, it stated that the issue of joint and several liability should be resolved at the initial liability stage, rather than at the contribution stage. It noted that drastic consequences could result from delaying that determination, because "a defendant could easily be strong-armed into settling where other defendants have settled in order to avoid being held liable for the remainder of the response costs." Id. It also noted that contribution would not be available from settling defendants, pursuant to CERCLA § 113(f)(2). Id.

The Second Circuit essentially adopted the Third Circuit's approach to joint and several liability in another case involving Alcan, United States v. Alcan Aluminum Corp. (Alcan–PAS), 990 F.2d 711 (2d Cir. 1993). * * *

* * *

A "moderate" approach to joint and several liability was adopted in United States v. A & F Materials Co., Inc., 578 F.Supp. 1249 (S.D.Ill. 1984). That case involved a disposal site at which over 7,000,000 gallons of waste were deposited. The court concluded that a rigid application of the Restatement approach to joint and several liability was inappropriate. Under the Restatement approach, a defendant who could not prove its contribution to the harm would be jointly and severally liable. The court thought that such a result would be inconsistent with congressional intent, because Congress was "concerned about the issue of fairness, and joint and several liability is extremely harsh and unfair if it is imposed on a defendant who contributed only a small amount of waste to a site."

The court concluded that six factors delineated in an unsuccessful amendment to CERCLA proposed by then Representative Al Gore could be used to "soften" the modern common law approach to joint and several liability in appropriate circumstances. Under this "moderate" approach, a court has the power to impose joint and several liability upon a defendant who cannot prove its contribution to an injury, but it also has the discretion to apportion damages in such a situation according to the "Gore factors":

> (i) the ability of the parties to demonstrate that their contribution of a discharge[,] release or disposal of a hazardous waste can be distinguished;

> (ii) the amount of the hazardous waste involved;

(iii) the degree of toxicity of the hazardous waste involved;

(iv) the degree of involvement by the parties in the generation, transportation, treatment, storage, or disposal of the hazardous waste;

(v) the degree of care exercised by the parties with respect to the hazardous waste concerned, taking into account the characteristics of such hazardous waste; and

(vi) the degree of cooperation by the parties with Federal, State, or local officials to prevent any harm to the public health or the environment.

The court stated that its moderate approach would promote fairness by allowing courts to be sensitive to the inherent unfairness of imposing joint and several liability on minor contributors, and to make rational distinctions based on such factors as the amount and toxicity of a particular defendant's contribution to a waste site.

* * *

The A&F moderate approach, to the extent it is inconsistent with the Chem–Dyne approach to joint and several liability, was rejected in United States v. South Carolina Recycling and Disposal, Inc., 653 F.Supp. 984 (D.S.C.1984) aff'd in part and vacated in part, United States v. Monsanto Co., 858 F.2d 160 (4th Cir.1988). That case involved a site at which there were "thousands of corroded, leaking drums * * * not segregated by source or waste type. Unknown, incompatible materials commingled to cause fires, fumes, and explosions." 653 F.Supp. at 994. The district court concluded that the harm was indivisible, because all of the substances at the site contributed synergistically, and it was impossible to ascertain the degree or relative contribution of each substance. Id. The court rejected volume as a basis for apportionment, finding that it "is not an accurate predictor of the risk associated with the waste because the toxicity or migratory potential of a particular hazardous substance generally varies independently of the volume."

* * *

To summarize, our review of the jurisprudence leads us to conclude that there are three distinct, although closely-related approaches to the issue of joint and several liability. The first is the "Chem–Dyne approach," which relies almost exclusively on the principles of the Restatement (Second) of Torts. Under that approach, a defendant who seeks to avoid the imposition of joint and several liability is required to prove the amount of harm it caused.

The second approach, the "Alcan approach," is adopted by the Second and Third Circuits. Although that approach also relies on the Restatement, it recognizes that, under the unique statutory liability scheme of CERCLA, the plaintiff's common law burden of proving causation has been eliminated. Under the Restatement, the plaintiff must first prove that the defendant's conduct was a substantial factor in causing the harm; the defendant may limit its liability by proving its contribution to the harm. In contrast, the Alcan approach suggests that a defendant may escape liability altogether if it can prove that its waste, even when mixed with other wastes at the site, did not cause the incurrence of response costs.

The third approach is the "moderate" approach taken in A & F. Under that approach, the court applies the principles of the Restatement in determining whether there is a reasonable basis for apportionment. If there is not, the court may impose joint and several liability; the court, however, retains the discretion to refuse to impose joint and several liability where such a result would be inequitable.

Although these approaches are not entirely uniform, certain basic principles emerge. First, joint and several liability is not mandated under CERCLA; Congress intended that the federal courts impose joint and several liability only in appropriate cases, applying common-law principles. Second, all of the cases rely on the Restatement in resolving the issues of joint and several liability. The major differences among the cases concern the timing of the resolution of the divisibility question, whether equitable factors should be considered, and whether a defendant can avoid liability for all, or only some portion, of the damages. Third, even where commingled wastes of unknown toxicity, migratory potential, and synergistic effect are present, defendants are allowed an opportunity to attempt to prove that there is a reasonable basis for apportionment (although they rarely succeed); where such factors are not present, volume may be a reasonable means of apportioning liability.

With respect to the timing of the "divisibility" inquiry, we believe that an early resolution is preferable. We agree with the Second Circuit, however, that this is a matter best left to the sound discretion of the district court. We also agree with the majority view that equitable factors, such as those listed in the Gore amendment, are more appropriately considered in actions for contribution among jointly and severally liable parties, than in making the initial determination of whether to impose joint and several liability. We therefore conclude that the Chem–Dyne approach is an appropriate framework for resolving issues of joint and several liability in CERCLA cases. Although we express no opinion with respect to the Alcan approach, because it is not necessary with respect to the issues we are faced with in this case, we nevertheless recognize that the Restatement principles must be adapted, where necessary, to implement congressional intent with respect to liability under the unique statutory scheme of CERCLA.

* * *

C

APPLICATION OF JOINT & SEVERAL LIABILITY

* * *

First, we conclude that the district court erred in determining that there is no reasonable basis for apportionment.

* * *

In the district court, the EPA contended that there was no reasonable basis for apportionment, because the harm to the Trinity Aquifer was a single harm, and that single harm is the equivalent of an indivisible harm, thus mandating the imposition of joint and several liability. Apparently now recognizing the lack of support for that position, the EPA on appeal acknowledges that apportionment is available, at least theoretically, when there is a reasonable basis for determining the contribution of each cause to a single harm. It asserts, however, the Sequa failed to meet its burden of proof on that issue.* * *

Essentially, the question whether there is a reasonable basis for apportionment depends on whether there is sufficient evidence from which the court can determine the amount of harm caused by each defendant. If the expert testimony and other evidence establishes a factual basis for making a reasonable estimate that will fairly apportion liability, joint and several liability should not be imposed in the absence of exceptional circumstances. The fact that apportionment may be difficult, because each defendant's exact contribution to the harm cannot be proved to an absolute certainty, or the fact that it will require weighing the evidence and making credibility determinations, are inadequate grounds upon which to impose joint and several liability.

Our review of the record convinces us that Sequa met its burden of proving that, as a matter of law, there is a reasonable basis for apportionment. This case is closely analogous to the Restatement's illustrations in which apportionment of liability is appropriate. For example, where cattle owned by two or more defendants destroy the plaintiff's crops, the damages are apportioned according to the number of cattle owned by each defendant, based on the reasonable assumption that the respective harm done is proportionate to that number. Thus, the Restatement suggests that apportionment is appropriate even though the evidence does not establish with certainty the specific amount of harm caused by each defendant's cattle, and even though there is a possibility that only one of the defendant's cattle caused all of the harm, while the other defendant's cattle idly stood by. Likewise, pollution of a stream by two or more factories may be treated as divisible in terms of degree, and apportioned among the defendant on the basis of evidence of the respective quantities of pollution discharged by each.

* * *

Even though it is not possible to determine with absolute certainty the exact amount of chromium each defendant introduced into the groundwater, there is sufficient evidence from which a reasonable and rational approximation of each defendant's individual contribution to the contamination can be made. The evidence demonstrates that Leigh owned the real property at the site from 1967 through 1981, and conducted chrome-plating activities there in 1971 and 1972. In 1972, Bell purchased the assets of the shop and leased the property from Leigh. It continued to conduct similar, but more extensive, chrome-plating activities there until mid–1976. In August 1976, Sequa purchased the assets from Bell, leased the property from Leigh, and conducted similar chrome-plating activities at the site until late 1977. In response to the EPA's motion for summary judgment, Sequa introduced evidence regarding chrome flake purchases during each operator's tenure. It also introduced evidence with respect to the value of the chrome-plating done by each, as well as summaries of sales. Given the number of years that had passed since the activities were conducted, the records of these activities were not complete. However, there was testimony from various witnesses regarding the rinsing and wastewater disposal practices of each defendant, and the amount of chrome-plating activity conducted by each.

During the Phase III hearing, Sequa introduced expert testimony regarding a volumetric approach to apportionment. The first expert, Henderson, calculated the total amount of chromium that had been introduced into the environment by Leigh, Bell, and Sequa, collectively and individually. The second expert, Mooney, calculated the amount of chromium that would have been introduced into the environment by each operator on the basis of electrical usage records.

In addition to rejecting apportionment because of competing theories, the district court also rejected volume as a basis for apportionment, because there was no method of dividing the liability among the defendants which would rise to any level of fairness above mere speculation. It stated that each of the proposed apportionment methods involved significant assumption factors, because records had been lost and because the theories differed significantly.

The existence of competing theories of apportionment is an insufficient reason to reject all of those theories. It is true, as the district court noted, that the records of chrome-plating activity were incomplete. However, under the facts and circumstances of this case, and in the light of the other evidence that is available, that factor may be taken into account in apportioning Sequa's share of the liability. Finally, the fact that Sequa's experts relied on certain assumptions in forming their opinions is not fatal to Sequa's ability to prove that there is a reasonable basis for apportionment. Expert opinions frequently include assumptions. If those assumptions are well-founded and reasonable, and not inconsistent with the facts as established by other competent evidence, they may be sufficiently reliable to support a conclusion that a reasonable basis for apportionment exists.

In sum, we conclude that the district court erred in imposing joint and several liability, because Sequa met its burden of proving that there is a reasonable basis for apportioning liability among the defendants on a volumetric basis. We therefore remand the case to the district court for apportionment. * * *

REVERSED in part, VACATED in part, and REMANDED.

Notes and Questions

Bell Petroleum represents a new wrinkle to CERCLA litigation when combined with two other decisions involving Alcan, cited above and discussed below. But in contrast to these decisions, the typical government-initiated case usually has yielded considerable success to the EPA. We now turn to a leading decision that illustrates what in the 1980s and early 1990s was the predictable outcome—the government wins, and in the process reinforced important principles of CERCLA jurisprudence. We examine United States v. Monsanto Co., 858 F.2d 160 (4th Cir.1988), cert. denied, 490 U.S. 1106, 109 S.Ct. 3156, 104 L.Ed.2d 1019 (1989).

7. THE "TYPICAL" GOVERNMENT ACTION: UNITED STATES v. MONSANTO

One of the major decisions which has spelled out the scope of liability to the EPA or the United States is United States v. Monsanto Co., 858 F.2d 160 (4th Cir.1988), cert. denied 490 U.S. 1106, 109 S.Ct. 3156, 104 L.Ed.2d 1019 (1989). In these so-called Tier One actions, the government is suing one or more of the potentially responsible parties identified in CERCLA § 107 to recover for the response costs that it has or will incur in connection with the property.

In *Monsanto* Seidenberg and Hutchinson entered a lease in 1972 for a four-acre tract of land they owned with the Columbia Organic Chemical Company (COCC), a chemical manufacturing corporation, under a verbal, month-to-month arrangement. Thereafter, COCC expanded its business to include the brokering and recycling of chemical waste generated by third parties and used the site as a waste storage and disposal facility for its new operations. In 1976, COCC's principals incorporated South Carolina Recycling and Disposal Inc. (SCRDI), for the purpose of assuming COCC's waste-handling business, and the site-owners began accepting lease payments from SCRDI.

SCRDI contracted with numerous off-site waste producers for the transport, recycling, and disposal of their chemical and other wastes, including Monsanto, Allied Chemical and EM Industries (the nonsettling generators). Between 1976 and 1980, SCRDI haphazardly deposited more than 7,000 fifty-five gallon drums of chemical waste on the site. Over time, many of the drums rusted and deteriorated, permitting hazardous substances to leak from the decaying drums and ooze into the ground. The substances commingled with incompatible chemicals that had escaped from other containers, generating noxious fumes, fires, and explosions. After several fires and explosions occurred at the site, and after expending approximately $1.8 million in a partial cleanup, the United States sued all of the identified owners and operators of the site and generators of waste at the site, most of whom settled with the EPA.

The district court granted the government's motion for summary judgment on liability against the owners and nonsettling generators.

First, the Fourth Circuit held, consistent with various district court holdings, that CERCLA § 107(a) "established a strict liability scheme." The court's holdings and rationale are set forth in these excerpts from its opinion, beginning with the liability of the two owners of the site:

> In light of the strict liability imposed by section 107(a), we cannot agree with the site-owners' contention that they are not within the class of owners Congress intended to hold liable. The traditional elements of tort culpability on which the site-owners rely simply are absent from the statute. The plain language of section 107(a)(2) extends liability to owners of waste facilities regardless of their degree of participation in the subsequent disposal of hazardous waste.
>
> Under section 107(a)(2), *any* person who owned a facility at a time when hazardous substances were deposited there may be held liable for all costs of removal or remedial action if a release or threatened release of a hazardous substance occurs. The site-owners do not dispute their ownership of the Bluff Road facility, or the fact that releases occurred there during their period of ownership. Under these circumstances, all the prerequisites to section 107(a) liability have been satisfied. (emphasis added.).

Id. at 168.

The court also rejected the owners' affirmative defenses under CERCLA § 107(b)(3), which permit exculpation only upon proof of a complete absence of causation based on the actions of third parties not in a "contractual relationship," together with a showing that the defendants "took precautions" against the foreseeable actions of such parties:

> First, the site-owners could not establish the absence of a direct or indirect contractual relationship necessary to maintain the affirmative defense. They concede they entered into a lease agreement with COCC. They accepted rent from COCC, and after SCRDI was incorporated, they accepted rent from SCRDI. Second, the site-owners presented no evidence that they took precautionary action against the foreseeable conduct of COCC or SCRDI.

Id. at 169.

Next the Fourth Circuit considered the more complicated liability status of the three generator defendants:

> The generator defendants first contend that the district court misinterpreted section 107(a)(3) because it failed to read into a statute a requirement that the governments prove a nexus between the waste they sent to the site and the resulting environmental harm. They maintain that the statutory phrase "containing such hazardous substances" requires proof that the specific substances they generated and sent to the site were present at the facility at the time of release. * * *
>
> Reduced of surplus language, sections 107(a)(3) and (4) impose liability on off-site waste generators who:

arranged for disposal * * * of hazardous substances * * * at
any facility * * * *containing such hazardous substances* * * *
from which there is a release * * * of a hazardous substance.

In our view, the plain meaning of the adjective "such" in the
phrase "containing such hazardous substances" is "[a]like, similar,
of the same kind." Black's Law Dictionary 1284 (5th ed. 1979). As
used in the statute, the phrase "such hazardous substances" de-
notes hazardous substances alike, similar, or of a like kind to those
that were present in a generator defendant's waste or that could
have been produced by the mixture of the defendant's waste with
other waste present at the site. It does not mean that the plaintiff
must trace the ownership of each generic chemical compound found
at a site. Absent proof that a generator defendant's specific waste
remained at a facility at the time of release, a showing of chemical
similarity between hazardous substances is sufficient.

The overall structure of CERCLA's liability provisions also
militates against the generator defendants' "proof of ownership"
argument. * * * As the statute provides—"[n]otwithstanding any
other provision of rule of law"—liability under Section 107(a) is
"subject *only* to the defenses set forth" in section 107(b). Each of
the three defenses established in section 107(b) "carves out from
liability an exception based on causation." Congress, has, therefore,
allocated the burden of disproving causation to the defendant who
profited from the generation and inexpensive disposal of hazardous
waste. We decline to interpret the statute in a way that would
neutralize the force of Congress' intent.

Id. at 170. The court also concluded that defendants had failed to
establish that all of their waste had been removed from the site prior to
the commencement of cleanup operations.

Finally, the court rejected defendants' arguments that the district
court had erroneously held them jointly and severally liable because
their respective responsibilities were "divisible":

The [trial] court concluded that joint and several liability was
appropriate because the environmental harm at Bluff Road was
"indivisible" and the appellants had "failed to meet their burden of
proving otherwise." We agree with its conclusion.

While CERCLA does not mandate the imposition of joint and
several liability, it permits it in cases of indivisible harm. In each
case, the court must consider traditional and evolving principles of
federal common law, which Congress has left to the courts to supply
interstitially.

Under common law rules, when two or more persons act independently to cause a single harm for which there is a reasonable
basis of apportionment according to the contribution of each, each is
held liable only for the portion of harm that he causes. When such
persons cause a single and indivisible harm, however, they are held

liable jointly and severally for the entire harm. Restatement (Second) of Torts § 433A (1965). We think these principles, as reflected in the Restatement (Second) of Torts, represent the correct and uniform federal rules applicable to CERCLA cases.

* * *

Placing their arguments into the Restatement framework, the generator defendants concede that the environmental damage at Bluff Road constituted a "single harm," but contend that there was a reasonable basis for apportioning the harm. They observe that each of the off-site generators with whom SCRDI contracted sent a potentially identifiable volume of waste to the Bluff Road site, and they maintain that liability should have been apportioned according to the volume they deposited as compared to the total volume disposed of there by all parties. In light of the conditions at Bluff Road, we cannot accept this method as a basis for apportionment.

The generator defendants bore the burden of establishing a reasonable basis for apportioning liability among responsible parties. To meet this burden, the generator defendants had to establish that the environmental harm at Bluff Road was divisible among responsible parties. They presented no evidence, however, showing a relationship between waste volume, the release of hazardous substances, and the harm at the site. Further, in light of the commingling of hazardous substances, the district court could not have reasonably apportioned liability without some evidence disclosing the individual and interactive qualities of the substances deposited there. Common sense counsels that a million gallons of certain substances could be mixed together without significant consequences, whereas a few pints of others improperly mixed could result in disastrous consequences. Under other circumstances proportionate volumes of hazardous substances may well be probative of contributory harm. In this case, however, volume could not establish the effective contribution of each waste generator to the harm at the Bluff Road site.

Id. at 172. Finally, the *Monsanto* court held that the district court acted within its discretion in refusing to apportion liability among all the defendants pursuant to the contribution provisions of CERCLA § 113(f), and instead choosing to defer the contribution action until "the plaintiff has been made whole." Judge Widener dissented on that aspect of the court's holding, arguing that once any defendant to the government's action requests it, the court must incorporate the contribution phases into the main action.

Notes and Questions

1. *Strict Liability*. As *Monsanto* makes clear, the courts have uniformly interpreted CERCLA as providing for a strict liability standard, despite the congressional silence on this critical point. CERCLA's legislative history suggests that Congress intended to leave to the judiciary the task of

developing the appropriate liability standard rather than requiring the courts to impose a potentially inflexible or inequitable standard. Moreover, CERCLA § 101, the definition section, states that liability under CERCLA "shall be construed to be the standard of liability which obtains under § 311 of the Federal Water Pollution Control Act." Although the FWPCA is similarly silent on the liability standard, Congress was aware that courts had interpreted it to be a strict liability standard. In enacting the SARA amendments in 1986, Congress reaffirmed its intention that courts impose a strict liability standard on PRPs under CERCLA. See H.R. Rep. No. 253, 99th Cong., 2d Sess., pt. 1, at 74 (1986), reprinted in U.S.C.C.A.N. 2835, 2856 (1986). Why not apply a negligence standard? A nuisance standard?

2. *Joint and Several Liability*. Congress also chose to delete from the final legislation any reference to joint and several liability contained in earlier versions. Nonetheless, as *Monsanto* illustrates, the courts have generally interpreted CERCLA as inviting the application of a joint and several liability rule. See United States v. Chem–Dyne Corp., 572 F.Supp. 802 (S.D.Ohio 1983); O'Neil v. Picillo, 883 F.2d 176 (1st Cir.1989), cert. denied 493 U.S. 1071, 110 S.Ct. 1115, 107 L.Ed.2d 1022 (1990); New York v. Shore Realty Corp., 759 F.2d 1032 (2d Cir.1985).

3. *Causation*. As *Monsanto* demonstrates, the requirement of a causal link between the actions of the PRPs and the incurrence of response costs by the government is not a rigorous test. The original version of the legislation in the House of Representatives contained a causation requirement imposing liability upon "any person who caused or contributed to the release or threatened release" of a hazardous substance. The House Report was explained:

> [T]he usual common law principles of causation, including those of proximate causation, should govern the determination of whether a defendant "caused or contributed" to a release or threatened release. * * * Thus, for instance, the mere act of generation or transportation of hazardous waste or the mere existence of a generator's or transporter's waste in a site with respect to which cleanup costs are incurred would not, in and of itself, result in liability. * * * [F]or liability to attach under this section, the plaintiff must demonstrate a causal or contributory nexus between the acts of the defendant and the conditions which necessitated response action.

H.R. Rep. No. 1016, 96th Cong., 2d Sess., pt. 1, at 33–34, reprinted in 1980 U.S.C.C.A.N. 6119, 6136–37. See New York v. Shore Realty Corp., 759 F.2d 1032, 1044 (2d Cir.1985). However, the final version deleted that explicit requirement and instead contains no express causation requirement. Why would Congress have preferred silence on the important issue of causation?

8. DIVISIBILITY OF HARM: THE ALCAN OPINIONS

Despite the stringent holdings in *Monsanto* on causation and joint and several liability, a few more recent cases have suggested that occasionally responsible parties may be able to limit their liability. In two opinions, both as a result of Alcan Aluminum's determination to fight liability, the Second and Third Circuit Courts of Appeal have recognized a narrow channel through which a PRP must sail to avoid joint liability for the full costs of remediation. United States v. Alcan Aluminum Corp., 964 F.2d 252 (3d Cir.1992) (referred to as *Alcan-Butler*); United States v. Alcan Aluminum Corp., 990 F.2d 711 (2d Cir.1993).

In the Second Circuit's *Alcan* opinion, defendant argued that trace amounts of hazardous substances such as the amounts in "breakfast cereal" and "nearly everything else on which life depends" should not be a basis of CERCLA liability. However, the court rejected that argument because of its concern that "each potential defendant in a multi-defendant CERCLA case would be able to escape liability simply by relying on the low concentration of hazardous substances in its wastes, and the government would be left to absorb the cleanup costs." Moreover, the court noted that "the statute on its face applies to 'any' hazardous substance, and it does not impose quantitative requirements." As to the causation requirement, it held:

> The plain meaning of [CERCLA § 107(a)] dictates that the government need only prove: (1) there was a release or threatened release, which (2) caused incurrence of response costs, and (3) that the defendant generated hazardous waste at the clean-up site. What is not required is that the government show that a specific defendant's waste caused incurrence of cleanup costs.

However, the court then recognized that a defendant could escape joint and several liability by demonstrating the divisibility of harm:

> Based on these common law principles, *Alcan* may escape liability for response costs if it either succeeds in proving that its oil emulsion, when mixed with other hazardous wastes, did not contribute to the release and the clean-up costs that followed, or contributed at most to only a divisible portion of the harm. See *Alcan-Butler*, 964 F.2d at 270. *Alcan* as the polluter bears the ultimate burden of establishing a reasonable basis for apportioning liability. The government has no burden of proof with respect to what caused the release of hazardous waste and triggered response costs. It is the defendant that bears that burden. To defeat the government's motion for summary judgment on the issue of divisibility, *Alcan* need only show that there are genuine issues of material fact regarding a reasonable basis for apportionment of liability. As other courts have noted, apportionment itself is an intensely factual determination.

> In so ruling we candidly admit that causation is being brought back into the case—through the backdoor, after being denied entry at the front door—at the apportionment stage. We hasten to add nonetheless that causation—with the burden on defendant—is reintroduced only to permit a defendant to escape payment where its pollutants did not contribute more than background contamination and also cannot concentrate. To state this standard in other words, we adopt a special exception to the usual absence of a causation

requirement, but the exception is applicable only to claims, like *Alcan's*, where background levels are not exceeded. And, we recognize this limited exception only in the absence of any EPA thresholds. (emphasis added.)

Contrary to the government's position, commingling is not synonymous with indivisible harm, and Alcan should have the opportunity to show that the harm caused at [the site] was capable of reasonable apportionment. *It may present evidence relevant to establishing divisibility of harm, such as, proof* disclosing the relative toxicity, migratory potential, degree of migration, and synergistic capacities of the hazardous substances at the site. (emphasis added.)

Alcan declares that the response actions at [the site] were attributable to substances such as PCB's, nitro benzene, phenol, dichlonoethone, toluene, and benzene. It contends that no soil contamination due to heavy metals was found there, and insists that the metallic constituents of its oil emulsion are insoluble compounds, submitting an affidavit supporting this theory of divisibility. The government submitted a declaration stating that metal contaminants like those found in Alcan's waste emulsion were present in environmental media at [the site], that the commingling of metallic and organic hazardous substances resulted in indivisible harm, and that though some forms of lead, cadmium and chromium are insoluble, they may chemically react with other substances and become water-soluble. These differing contentions supported by expert affidavits raise sufficient questions of fact to preclude the granting of summary judgment on the divisibility issue.

Finally, the court disagreed with the Third Circuit on the timing of the divisibility determination. In *Alcan-Butler* the Third Circuit held that the divisibility inquiry is one "best resolved at the initial liability phase" because it involves "relative degrees of liability." See *Alcan-Butler*, 964 F.2d at 270, n.29. The Second Circuit, while stating that "we prefer this common sense approach," concluded that the "statutory dictates of CERCLA" were to the contrary:

Consequently, the language of CERCLA and SARA and their legislative histories appear to demonstrate the following chronology: liability is fixed first and immediately for enforcement purposes; litigation later to sort out what contribution is owed and by whom as a result of the remediation effort. But we do not rule that this chronology be followed or that the *Alcan-Butler* approach of deciding divisibility at the initial liability phase of the case is the best way for the district court to proceed. Instead, the choice as to when to address divisibility and apportionment are questions best left to the sound discretion of the trial court in the handling of an individual case.

Notes and Questions

1. *Burden of Proof and Timing.* How much benefit do you suppose Alcan will derive from the court's recognition of an affirmative defense? How often will defendants to a government action be able to sustain the rigorous burden which the Second Circuit placed on those seeking to avoid joint and several liability? Is the court correct on the timing of the divisibility issue? On the timing issue, what in fact *did* the court hold? Why would defendants prefer the *Alcan-Butler* chronology? Is the court confusing the contribution action, which is concerned with apportionment, with the divisibility issue, which goes to the heart of the initial proceeding with the government?

2. *All or Nothing?* Some important issues were not touched upon in this decision. For example, how does a remaining PRP such as Alcan attack the government's tendency to leave everyone who does not settle with the remainder of the costs? Will a showing of the level of contribution to the release or response costs be an "all or nothing" proposition that results in either total vindication or total responsibility or can such a judicial skirmish result in diminished levels of responsibility? Some courts have allowed "remainder" PRPs to attack the share of costs levied by the government, while other courts have allowed disproportionate allocations as the price for not settling.

3. *Background: Above or Below.* What does the court's reference to concentrations above background mean? Is it the typical background levels found in soil and water? Would this approach bar its use by any PRP whose substances are not naturally occurring? Is the measurement to be taken at the disposal site? In the neighborhood of the generator? In the area surrounding the site, but not at the site itself? Further, when can it be determined that pollutants have "concentrated"?

In *Alcan-Butler*, the Third Circuit did not include language linking the affirmative defense to situations where hazardous substances are at levels below background levels. Under *Alcan-Butler* so long as the defendant's substances "did not or could not, when mixed with other hazardous substances, contribute to the release and the resultant response costs, [the defendant] should not be responsible for any response costs." 964 F.2d at 270. How significant is this difference?

4. *Causation: More on Monsanto.* Before turning to the principal topic generated by *Bell Petroleum*, a brief discussion of the role of causation and the plaintiff's burden in respect thereto is essential. Must the government actually prove that it was a particular defendant's waste that caused the environmental harm and the incurrence of response costs? Tort law would most certainly demand such proofs. Consider this quotation from U.S. v. Monsanto Co., 858 F.2d 160 (4th Cir.1988). In *Monsanto,* generator-defendants' waste had been deposited at a site in 2000 drums and allowed to leak and ooze onto the ground, commingling with chemicals from other generators, creating fumes, fires and explosions, all resulting in an expensive government-initiated cleanup. Defendants argued that the government had to prove that each of its wastes had actually leaked, and contributed to the harm and the cleanup costs. In other words, the government had to trace the

waste and costs to each defendant, to "fingerprint" each as a cause. The Fourth Circuit rejected that contention, as we saw earlier in the quotation from the opinion:

> The generator defendants first contend that the district court misinterpreted section 107(a)(3) because it failed to read into the statute a requirement that the governments prove a nexus between the waste they sent to the site and the resulting environmental harm. They maintain that the statutory phrase "containing such hazardous substances" requires proof that the specific substances they generated and sent to the site were present at the facility at the time of release. * * *

> In our view, the plain meaning of the adjective "such" in the phrase "containing such hazardous substances" is "[a]like, similar, of the like kind." Black's Law Dictionary 1284 (5th ed. 1979). As used in the statute, the phrase "such hazardous substances" denotes hazardous substances alike, similar, or of a like kind to those that were present in a generator defendant's waste or that could have been produced by the mixture of the defendant's waste with other waste present at the site. Absent proof that a generator defendant's specific waste remained at a facility at the time of release, a showing of chemical similarity between hazardous substances is sufficient.

Id. at 170. The court also concluded that defendants had failed to establish that all of their waste had been removed from the site prior to the commencement of cleanup operations.

The *Monsanto* view is reiterated in many decisions. See, e.g., Amoco Oil Co. v. Borden, Inc., 889 F.2d 664 (5th Cir.1989) (in Amoco, the court noted that, "in cases involving multiple sources of contamination, a plaintiff need not prove a specific causal link between costs incurred and an individual generator's waste." Id. at 670 n. 8.); United States v. Alcan Aluminum Corp. (*Alcan PAS*), 990 F.2d 711, 721 (2d Cir.1993) (the government is not required to "show that a specific defendant's waste caused incurrence of clean-up costs"); United States v. Alcan Aluminum Corp. (*Alcan–Butler*), 964 F.2d 252, 266 (3d Cir.1992) ("the Government must simply prove that the defendant's hazardous substances were deposited at the site from which there was a release and that the release caused the incurrence of response costs"); United States v. Monsanto Co., 858 F.2d 160, 170 (4th Cir.1988) (liability is subject only to the causation-based affirmative defenses set forth in CERCLA § 107(b); "Congress has, therefore, allocated the burden of disproving causation to the defendant who profited from the generation and inexpensive disposal of hazardous waste.")

Does the language of the statute support these interpretations? The legislative history reveals that an earlier version of the bill contained an explicit causation requirement imposing liability only upon "any person who caused or contributed to the release" of a hazardous substance:

> [T]he usual common law principles of causation, including those of proximate causation, should govern the determination of whether a defendant "caused or contributed" to a release or threatened release * * * Thus, for instance, the mere act of generation or transportation of hazardous waste or the mere existence of a generator's or transporter's waste in a site with respect to which cleanup costs are incurred would

not, in and of itself, result in liability. * * * [F]or liability to attach under this section, the plaintiff must demonstrate a causal or contributory nexus between the acts of the defendant and the conditions which necessitated response action.

H.R. Rep. No. 1016, 96th Cong., 2d Sess., pt. 1, at 33–34, reprinted in 1980 U.S.C.C.A.N. 6119, 6136–37. See New York v. Shore Realty Corp., 759 F.2d 1032, 1044 (2d Cir.1985).

However, the final version deleted that explicit requirement and instead contains no express causation requirement. Why would Congress have preferred silence?

5. *More on the Government's Burden of Proof.* Perhaps the most explicit statement of the government's burden on causation is that contained in United States v. Alcan Aluminum Corp., 990 F.2d 711 (2d Cir.1993) (Alcan. PAS) (an opinion often cited for its unfavorable view to the government on divisibility versus joint and several liability, to be discussed below).

In the Second Circuit's *Alcan* opinion, defendant argued that trace amounts of hazardous substances such as the amounts in "breakfast cereal" and "nearly everything else on which life depends" should not be a basis of CERCLA liability. However, the court rejected that argument because of its concern that "each potential defendant in a multi-defendant CERCLA case would be able to escape liability simply by relying on the low concentration of hazardous substances in its wastes, and the government would be left to absorb the cleanup costs." Moreover, the court noted that "the statute on its face applies to 'any' hazardous substance, and it does not impose quantitative requirements." As to the causation requirement, it held:

> The plain meaning of [CERCLA § 107(a)] dictates that the government need only prove: (1) there was a release or threatened release, which (2) caused incurrence of response costs, and (3) that the defendant generated hazardous waste at the clean-up site. What is not required is that the government show that a specific defendant's waste caused incurrence of cleanup costs.

Id. at 721.

6. In 1999 the Restatement (Third) of Torts: Apportionment was adopted by the American Law Institute. Restatement (Second) of Torts § 433A, which had a conspicuous role in *Bell Petroleum* and the *Alcan* decisions, has been replaced by a new section 50 which reads:

§ 50. Apportionment of Liability When Damages Can Be Divided by Causation

(a) When damages for an injury can be divided by causation, the factfinder first divides them into their indivisible component parts. The factfinder then separately apportions liability for each indivisible component part under Topics 1 through 4.

(b) Damages can be divided by causation when there is a reasonable basis for the factfinder to determine:

(1) that any legally culpable conduct of a party or other relevant person to whom the factfinder assigns a percentage of

responsibility was a legal cause of less than the entire damages for which the plaintiff seeks recovery and

>   (2) the amount of damages separately caused by that conduct.

Otherwise, the damages are indivisible and thus the injury is indivisible. Liability for an indivisible injury is apportioned under Topics 1 through 4.

Assuming § 50 was in effect at the time *Bell Petroleum* was decided, how might it have affected the outcomes? What is the significant difference between old § 433A and new § 50?

C. PARTIES LIABLE UNDER CERCLA

As was observed above, the categories of parties that may be liable as PRPs include the present and past owners and operators of the site, generators of wastes that are deposited at the site, and transporters of the waste.

1. CURRENT OWNERS AND OPERATORS

CERCLA's focus on the status of parties, and not on their actual conduct or activities at a site, is reflected in the decisions interpreting what constitutes an "owner" or "operator." In United States v. Stringfellow, 661 F.Supp. 1053, 1063 (C.D.Cal.1987), the court imposed liability on the current owner of a waste disposal site, finding that proof of ownership of the facility is sufficient, and noting that CERCLA § 107(a)(1) "does not require that the present owner [of a facility] contribute to the release." See also Ecodyne Corp. v. Shah, 718 F.Supp. 1454, 1457 (N.D.Cal.1989).

Note

Early Authority re: Current Owners. For another early and influential interpretation of § 107(a)(1) liability, see State of New York v. Shore Realty Corp., 759 F.2d 1032 (2d Cir.1985) which involved a land developer who acquired through wholly-owned corporation property which he knew contained thousands of gallons and drums of hazardous waste stored at the site by prior tenant. The tenants were covered persons under § 107(a)(1) despite their non-participation in the transport or generation of waste on the premises. As noted by the court:

> Leo Grande incorporated Shore solely for the purpose of purchasing the Shore Road property. All corporate decisions and actions were made, directed, and controlled by him. By contract dated July 14, 1983, Shore agreed to purchase the 3.2 acre site, a small peninsula surrounded on three sides by the waters of Hempstead Harbor and Mott Cove, for condominium development. Five large tanks in a field in the center of the site hold most of some 700,000 gallons of hazardous chemicals located there, though there are six smaller tanks both above and below

ground containing hazardous waste, as well as some empty tanks, on the property. The tanks are connected by pipe to a tank truck loading rack and dockage facilities for loading by barge. Four roll-on/roll-off containers and one tank truck trailer hold additional waste. And before June 15, 1984, one of the two dilapidated masonry warehouses on the site contained over 400 drums of chemicals and contaminated solids, many of which were corroded and leaking.

It is beyond dispute that the tanks and drums contain "hazardous substances" within the meaning to CERCLA. 42 U.S.C. § 9601(14). * * * These substances are present at the site in various combinations, some of which may cause the toxic effect to be synergistic.

The purchase agreement provided that it could be voided by Shore without penalty if after conducting an environmental study Shore had decided not to proceed.* * * the period after Shore closed on the property and when Shore evicted the tenants. Shore was aware of the nature of the tenants' activities before the closing and could readily have foreseen that they would continue to dump hazardous waste at the site. In light of this knowledge, we cannot say that the releases and threats of release resulting of these activities were "caused solely" by the tenants or that Shore "took precautions against" these "foreseeable acts or omissions."

The stringency of liability on current owners and operators is also illustrated by a ruling in Uniroyal Chem. Co. v. Deltech Corp., 160 F.3d 238 (5th Cir.1998), where the Fifth Circuit Court of Appeals held that ownership at the time of disposal is not required in a private cost recovery action against a facility's present owner and operator. Here, a tanker truck ruptured, releasing an industrial chemical. In response to state requests, the receiving facility cleaned up the spill. It then sued the trucking company and another industrial facility, among others, to recover cleanup costs under CERCLA. The trial court granted defendants summary judgment.

Reversing, the Fifth Circuit noted that CERCLA was enacted as a broad remedial measure intended to assure that responsible parties bear the costs of any damage, environmental harm, or chemical poison injury. The court noted that CERCLA provides for private actions to recover costs associated with the cleanup of environmental threats. A prima facie case for such an action requires a plaintiff to show, among other factors, that (1) the defendant is a "responsible person" and (2) the site is a "facility." The court also noted Congress had rejected several narrower environmental bills in favor of CERCLA, a more expansive statute that addresses releases of hazardous substances generally, not just disposal at toxic waste sites. Based on the statutory scheme, legislative history, implementing regulations, and enforcing agency's policies, the court held disposal is not a requirement for owner and operator liability under CERCLA, and, thus, defendants are responsible persons under the statute.

2. LIABILITY OF CORPORATIONS AND AFFILIATED FIRMS AND PERSONS: DIRECT AND DERIVATIVE LIABILITY AND PARENT CORPORATIONS

CERCLA has been applied by some courts to permit the imposition on parent companies of liability as "operators" or "owners" under circumstances departing from the traditional rules. A few courts have applied a "capacity to control" test of parental liability. See, e.g., United States v. Northeastern Pharmaceutical & Chemical Co., 579 F.Supp. 823 (W.D.Mo.1984), reversed in part on other grounds and affirmed in part 810 F.2d 726 (8th Cir.1986), cert. denied 484 U.S. 848, 108 S.Ct. 146, 98 L.Ed.2d 102 (1987) (those who have the capacity and power to control the pollution-causing activities, to discover discharges when they occur, and to prevent and abate damage, are uniquely qualified to answer for their actions that result in CERCLA cleanup costs): Idaho v. Bunker Hill Co., 635 F.Supp. 665, 670–71 (D.Idaho 1986) (invoked the "capacity to control" test and found sufficient the "capacity, if not total reserved authority" of a parent corporation "to make decisions and implement actions and mechanisms to prevent and abate" hazardous substance contamination). Other courts have applied a narrower test, epitomized by United States v. Kayser–Roth Corp., 910 F.2d 24 (1st Cir.1990), cert. denied 498 U.S. 1084, 111 S.Ct. 957, 112 L.Ed.2d 1045 (1991) (imposing "operator" liability on the basis of the parent entity's actual participation in, or control of, the management of the facility that released the hazardous substances).

Not all courts have accepted these expansive approaches to liability of parent corporations. See Joslyn Manufacturing Co. v. T.L. James & Co., 893 F.2d 80 (5th Cir.1990), cert. denied 498 U.S. 1108, 111 S.Ct. 1017, 112 L.Ed.2d 1098 (1991), where the Fifth Circuit held that CERCLA does not impose liability on parent corporations. It noted that "CERCLA does not define 'owners' or 'operators' as including the parent company of offending wholly-owned subsidiaries." Moreover, the legislative history revealed that where Congress was silent it expected traditional and evolving principles of common law would govern. Further, in another definition section of CERCLA § 101(20)(A)(iii), Congress had expressly incorporated a control concept in the definition, but failed to do so in the definition of "owner" or "operator."

UNITED STATES v. BESTFOODS ET AL.

Supreme Court of the United States, 1998.
524 U.S. 51, 118 S.Ct. 1876, 141 L.Ed.2d 43.

JUSTICE SOUTER delivered the opinion of the Court.

The United States brought this action for the costs of cleaning up industrial waste generated by a chemical plant. The issue before us, under the Comprehensive Environmental Response, Compensation, and Liability Act of 1980 (CERCLA), 94 Stat. 2767, as amended, 42 U.S.C. § 9601 et seq., is whether a parent corporation that actively participated in, and exercised control over, the operations of a subsidiary may, without more, be held liable as an operator of a polluting facility owned or operated by the subsidiary. We answer no, unless the corporate veil may be pierced. But a corporate parent that actively participated in, and exercised control over, the operations of the facility itself may be held directly liable in its own right as an operator of the facility.

I

In 1980, CERCLA was enacted in response to the serious environmental and health risks posed by industrial pollution. See Exxon Corp. v. Hunt, 475 U.S. 355, 358–359, 106 S.Ct. 1103, 1107–1108, 89 L.Ed.2d 364 (1986). "As its name implies, CERCLA is a comprehensive statute that grants the President broad power to command government agencies and private parties to clean up hazardous waste sites." Key Tronic Corp. v. United States, 511 U.S. 809, 814, 114 S.Ct. 1960, 1964, 128 L.Ed.2d 797 (1994). If it satisfies certain statutory conditions, the United States may, for instance, use the "Hazardous Substance Superfund" to finance cleanup efforts, see 42 U.S.C. §§ 9601(11), 9604; 26 U.S.C. § 9507, which it may then replenish by suits brought under § 107 of the Act against, among others, "any person who at the time of disposal of any hazardous substance owned or operated any facility." 42 U.S.C. § 9607(a)(2). So, those actually "responsible for any damage, environmental harm, or injury from chemical poisons [may be tagged with] the cost of their actions," S.Rep. No. 96–848, pp. 6119, 13, U.S.Code Cong. & Admin.News 1980, p. 6119 (1980). The term "person" is defined in CERCLA to include corporations and other business organizations, see 42 U.S.C. § 9601(21), and the term "facility" enjoys a broad and detailed definition as well, see § 9601(9).[2] The phrase "owner or operator" is defined only by tautology, however, as "any person owning or operating" a facility, § 9601(20)(A)(ii), and it is this bit of circularity that prompts our review. Cf. Exxon Corp. v. Hunt, supra, at 363, 106 S.Ct., at 1109 (CERCLA, "unfortunately, is not a model of legislative draftsmanship").

II

In 1957, Ott Chemical Co. (Ott I) began manufacturing chemicals at a plant near Muskegon, Michigan, and its intentional and unintentional dumping of hazardous substances significantly polluted the soil and ground water at the site. In 1965, respondent CPC International Inc.[3] incorporated a wholly owned subsidiary to buy Ott I's assets in exchange for CPC stock. The new company, also dubbed Ott Chemical Co. (Ott II), continued chemical manufacturing at the site, and continued to pollute

---

2. "The term 'facility' means (A) any building, structure, installation, equipment, pipe or pipeline (including any pipe into a sewer or publicly owned treatment works), well, pit, pond, lagoon, impoundment, ditch, landfill, storage container, motor vehicle, rolling stock, or aircraft, or (B) any site or area where a hazardous substance has been deposited, stored, disposed of, or placed, or otherwise come to be located; but does not include any consumer product in consumer use or any vessel."

3. CPC has recently changed its name to Bestfoods. Consistently with the briefs and the opinions below, we use the name CPC herein.

its surroundings. CPC kept the managers of Ott I, including its founder, president, and principal shareholder, Arnold Ott, on board as officers of Ott II. Arnold Ott and several other Ott II officers and directors were also given positions at CPC, and they performed duties for both corporations.

In 1972, CPC sold Ott II to Story Chemical Company, which operated the Muskegon plant until its bankruptcy in 1977. Shortly thereafter, when respondent Michigan Department of Natural Resources (MDNR) examined the site for environmental damage, it found the land littered with thousands of leaking and even exploding drums of waste, and the soil and water saturated with noxious chemicals. MDNR sought a buyer for the property who would be willing to contribute toward its cleanup, and after extensive negotiations, respondent Aerojet–General Corp. arranged for transfer of the site from the Story bankruptcy trustee in 1977. Aerojet created a wholly owned California subsidiary, Cordova Chemical Company (Cordova/California), to purchase the property, and Cordova/California in turn created a wholly owned Michigan subsidiary, Cordova Chemical Company of Michigan (Cordova/Michigan), which manufactured chemicals at the site until 1986.

By 1981, the federal Environmental Protection Agency had undertaken to see the site cleaned up, and its long-term remedial plan called for expenditures well into the tens of millions of dollars. To recover some of that money, the United States filed this action under § 107 in 1989, naming five defendants as responsible parties: CPC, Aerojet, Cordova/California, Cordova/Michigan, and Arnold Ott. (By that time, Ott I and Ott II were defunct.) After the parties (and MDNR) had launched a flurry of contribution claims, counterclaims, and cross-claims, the District Court consolidated the cases for trial in three phases: liability, remedy, and insurance coverage. So far, only the first phase has been completed; in 1991, the District Court held a 15–day bench trial on the issue of liability. Because the parties stipulated that the Muskegon plant was a "facility" within the meaning of 42 U.S.C. § 9601(9), that hazardous substances had been released at the facility, and that the United States had incurred reimbursable response costs to clean up the site, the trial focused on the issues of whether CPC and Aerojet, as the parent corporations of Ott II and the Cordova companies, had "owned or operated" the facility within the meaning of § 107(a)(2).

The District Court said that operator liability may attach to a parent corporation both directly, when the parent itself operates the facility, and indirectly, when the corporate veil can be pierced under state law. See CPC Int'l, Inc. v. Aerojet–General Corp., 777 F.Supp. 549, 572 (W.D.Mich.1991). The court explained that, while CERCLA imposes direct liability in situations in which the corporate veil cannot be pierced under traditional concepts of corporate law, "the statute and its legislative history do not suggest that CERCLA rejects entirely the crucial limits to liability that are inherent to corporate law." Id., at 573. As the District Court put it, "a parent corporation is directly liable under section 107(a)(2) as an operator only when it has exerted power or influence over its subsidiary by actively participating in and exercising control over the subsidiary's business during a period of disposal of hazardous waste. A parent's actual participation in and control over a subsidiary's functions and decision-making creates 'operator' liability under CERCLA; a parent's mere oversight of a subsidiary's business in a manner appropriate and consistent with the investment relationship between a parent and its wholly owned subsidiary does not." Ibid.

Applying that test to the facts of this case, the District Court held both CPC and Aerojet liable under § 107(a)(2) as operators. As to CPC, the court found it particularly telling that CPC selected Ott II's board of directors and populated its executive ranks with CPC officials, and that a CPC official, G.R.D. Williams, played a significant role in shaping Ott II's environmental compliance policy.

After a divided panel of the Court of Appeals for the Sixth Circuit reversed in part, United States v. Cordova/Michigan, 59 F.3d 584, that court granted rehearing en banc and vacated the panel decision, 67 F.3d 586 (1995). This time, 7 judges to 6, the court again reversed the District Court in part. 113 F.3d 572 (1997). The majority remarked on the possibility that a parent company might be held directly liable as an operator of a facility owned by its subsidiary: "At least conceivably, a parent might independently operate the facility in the stead of its subsidiary; or, as a sort of joint venturer, actually operate the facility alongside its subsidiary." Id., at 579. But the court refused to go any further and rejected the District Court's analysis with the explanation:

"that where a parent corporation is sought to be held liable as an operator pursuant to 42 U.S.C. § 9607(a)(2) based upon the extent of its control of its subsidiary which owns the facility, the parent will be liable only when the requirements necessary to pierce the corporate veil [under state law] are met. In other words, ... whether the parent will be liable as an operator depends upon whether the degree to which it controls its subsidiary and the extent and manner of its involvement with the facility, amount to the abuse of the corporate form that will warrant piercing the corporate veil and disregarding the separate corporate entities of the parent and subsidiary." Id., at 580.

Applying Michigan veil-piercing law, the Court of Appeals decided that neither CPC nor Aerojet was liable for controlling the actions of its subsidiaries, since the parent and subsidiary corporations maintained separate personalities and the parents did not utilize the subsidiary corporate form to perpetrate fraud or subvert justice.

We granted certiorari, 118 S.Ct. 621, 139 L.Ed.2d 506 (1997), to resolve a conflict among the Circuits over the extent to which parent corporations may be held liable under CERCLA for operating facilities ostensibly under the control of their subsidiaries. We now vacate and remand.

III

It is a general principle of corporate law deeply "ingrained in our economic and legal systems" that a parent corporation (so-called because of control through ownership of another corporation's stock) is not liable for the acts of its subsidiaries. * * * 1 W. Fletcher, Cyclopedia of Law of Private Corporations § 33, p. 568 (rev. ed. 1990) ("Neither does the mere fact that there exists a parent-subsidiary relationship between two corporations make the one liable for the torts of its affiliate"); Horton, Liability of Corporation for Torts of Subsidiary, 7 A.L.R.3d 1343, 1349 (1966) ("Ordinarily, a corporation which chooses to facilitate the operation of its business by employment of another corporation as a subsidiary will not be penalized by a judicial determination of liability for the legal obligations of the subsidiary"); cf. Anderson v. Abbott, 321 U.S. 349, 362, 64 S.Ct. 531, 537, 88 L.Ed. 793 (1944) ("Limited liability is the rule, not the exception"); Burnet v. Clark, 287 U.S. 410, 415, 53 S.Ct. 207, 208, 77 L.Ed. 397 (1932) ("A corporation and its stockholders are generally to be treated as separate entities"). Thus it is hornbook law that "the exercise of the 'control' which stock ownership gives to the stockholders * * * will not create liability beyond the assets of the subsidiary. That 'control' includes the election of directors, the making of by-laws * * * and the doing of all other acts incident to the legal status of stockholders. Nor will a duplication of some or all of the directors or executive officers be fatal." Douglas 196 (footnotes omitted). Although this respect for corporate distinctions when the subsidiary is a polluter has been severely criticized in the literature, see, e.g., Note, Liability of Parent Corporations for Hazardous Waste Cleanup and Damages, 99 Harv.L.Rev. 986 (1986), nothing in CERCLA purports to reject this bedrock principle, and against this venerable common-law backdrop, the congressional silence is audible. * * * *The Government has indeed made no claim that a corporate parent is liable as an owner or an operator under § 107 simply because its subsidiary is subject to liability for owning or operating a polluting facility.*

But there is an equally fundamental principle of corporate law, applicable to the parent-subsidiary relationship as well as generally, that the corporate veil may be pierced and the shareholder held liable for the corporation's conduct when, inter alia, the corporate form would otherwise be misused to accomplish certain wrongful purposes, most notably fraud, on the shareholder's behalf. Nothing in CERCLA purports to rewrite this well-settled rule, either. CERCLA is thus like many another congressional enactment in giving no indication "that the entire corpus of state corporation law is to be replaced simply because a plaintiff's cause of action is based upon a federal statute," and the failure of the statute to speak to a matter as fundamental as the liability implications of corporate ownership demands application of the rule that "[i]n order to abrogate a common-law principle, the statute must speak directly to the question addressed by the common law," United States v. Texas, 507 U.S. 529, 534, 113 S.Ct. 1631, 1634, 123 L.Ed.2d 245 (1993). The Court of Appeals was accordingly correct in holding that when (but only when) the corporate veil may be pierced, may a parent corporation be charged with derivative CERCLA liability for its subsidiary's actions.

IV

A

If the act rested liability entirely on ownership of a polluting facility, this opinion might end here; but CERCLA liability may turn on operation as well as ownership, and nothing in the statute's terms bars a parent corporation from direct liability for its own actions in operating a facility owned by its subsidiary. As Justice (then-Professor) Douglas noted almost 70 years ago, derivative liability cases are to be distinguished from those in which "the alleged wrong can seemingly be traced to the parent through the conduit of its own personnel and management" and "the parent is directly a participant in the wrong complained of." Douglas 207, 208. In such instances, the parent is directly liable for its own actions. See H. Henn & J. Alexander, Laws of Corporations 347 (3d ed. 1983) (hereinafter Henn & Alexander) ("Apart from corporation law principles, a shareholder, whether a natural person or a corporation, may be liable on the ground that such shareholder's activity resulted in the liability"). The fact that a corporate subsidiary happens to own a polluting facility operated by its parent does nothing, then, to displace the rule that the parent "corporation is [itself] responsible for the wrongs committed by its agents in the course of its business," Mine Workers v. Coronado Coal Co., 259 U.S. 344, 395, 42 S.Ct. 570, 577, 66 L.Ed. 975 (1922), and whereas the rules of veil-piercing limit derivative liability for the actions of another corporation, CERCLA's "operator" provision is concerned primarily with direct liability for one's own actions. See, e.g., Sidney S. Arst Co. v. Pipefitters Welfare Ed. Fund, 25 F.3d 417, 420 (C.A.7 1994) ("the direct, personal liability provided by CERCLA is distinct from the derivative liability that results from piercing the corporate veil") (internal quotation marks omitted). It is this direct liability that is properly seen as being at issue here.

Under the plain language of the statute, any person who operates a polluting facility is directly liable for the costs of cleaning up the pollution. See 42 U.S.C. § 9607(a)(2). This is so regardless of whether that person is the facility's owner, the owner's parent corporation or business partner, or even a saboteur who sneaks into the facility at night to discharge its poisons out of malice. If any such act of operating a corporate subsidiary's facility is done on behalf of a parent corporation, the existence of the parent-subsidiary relationship under state corporate law is simply irrelevant to the issue of direct liability. * * * United States v. Kayser–Roth Corp., 910 F.2d 24, 26 (C.A.1 1990) ("a person who is an operator of a facility is not protected from liability by the legal structure of ownership").

This much is easy to say; the difficulty comes in defining actions sufficient to constitute direct parental "operation." Here of course we may again rue the uselessness of CERCLA's definition of a facility's "operator" as "any person * * * operating" the facility, 42 U.S.C. § 9601(20)(A)(ii), which leaves us to do the best we can to give the term its "ordinary or natural meaning." Bailey v. United States, 516 U.S. 137, 145, 116 S.Ct. 501, 506, 133 L.Ed.2d 472 (1995). * * * In a mechanical sense, to "operate" ordinarily means "[t]o control the functioning of; run: operate a sewing machine." American Heritage Dictionary 1268 (3d ed. 1992); see also Webster's New International Dictionary 1707 (2d ed. 1958) ("to work; as, to operate a machine"). And in the organizational sense more obviously intended by CERCLA, the word ordinarily means "[t]o conduct the affairs of; manage: operate a business." American Heritage Dictionary, supra, at 1268; see also Webster's New International Dictionary, supra, at 1707 ("to manage"). So, under CERCLA, an operator is simply someone who directs the workings of, manages, or conducts the affairs of a facility. To sharpen the definition for purposes of CERCLA's concern with environmental contamination, an operator must manage, direct, or conduct operations specifically related to pollution, that is, operations having to do with the leakage or disposal of hazardous waste, or decisions about compliance with environmental regulations.

B

With this understanding, we are satisfied that the Court of Appeals correctly rejected the District Court's analysis of direct liability. But we also think that the appeals court erred in limiting direct liability under the statute to a parent's sole or joint venture operation, so as to eliminate any possible finding that CPC is liable as an operator on the facts of this case.

1

By emphasizing that "CPC is directly liable under section 107(a)(2) as an operator because CPC actively participated in and exerted significant control over Ott II's business and decision-making," 777 F.Supp., at 574, the District Court applied the "actual control" test of whether the parent "actually operated the business of its subsidiary," id., at 573, as several Circuits have employed it, see, e.g., United States v. Kayser–Roth Corp., supra, at 27 (operator liability "requires active involvement in the affairs of the subsidiary"); Jacksonville Elec. Auth. v. Bernuth Corp., 996 F.2d 1107, 1110 (C.A.11 1993) (parent is liable if it "actually exercised control over, or was otherwise intimately involved in the operations of, the [subsidiary] corporation immediately responsible for the operation of the facility").

The well-taken objection to the actual control test, however, is its fusion of direct and indirect liability; the test is administered by asking a question about the relationship between the two corporations (an issue going to indirect liability) instead of a question about the parent's interaction with the subsidiary's facility (the source of any direct liability). If, however, direct liability for the parent's operation of the facility is to be kept distinct from derivative liability for the subsidiary's own operation, the focus of the inquiry must necessarily be different under the two tests. "The question is not whether the parent operates the subsidiary, but rather whether it operates the facility, and that operation is evidenced by participation in the activities of the facility, not the subsidiary. Control of the subsidiary, if extensive enough, gives rise to indirect liability under piercing doctrine, not direct liability under the statutory language." Oswald 269; see also Schiavone v. Pearce, 79 F.3d 248, 254 (C.A.2 1996) ("Any liabilities [the parent] may have as an operator, then, stem directly from its control over the plant"). The District Court was therefore mistaken to rest its analysis on CPC's relationship with Ott II, premising liability on little more than "CPC's 100–percent ownership of Ott II" and "CPC's active participation in, and at times majority control over, Ott II's board of directors." 777 F.Supp., at 575. The analysis should instead have rested on the relationship between CPC and the Muskegon facility itself.

In addition to (and perhaps as a reflection of) the erroneous focus on the relationship between CPC and Ott II, even those findings of the District Court that might be taken to speak to the extent of CPC's activity at the facility itself are flawed, for the District Court wrongly assumed that the actions of the joint officers and directors are necessarily attributable to CPC. The District Court emphasized the facts that CPC placed its own high-level officials on Ott II's board of directors and in key management positions at Ott II, and that those individuals made major policy decisions and conducted day-to-day operations at the facility: "Although Ott II corporate officers set the day-to-day operating policies for the company without any need to obtain formal approval from CPC, CPC actively participated in this decision-making because high-ranking CPC officers served in Ott II management positions." Id., at 559; see also id., at 575 (relying on "CPC's involvement in major decision-making and day-to-day operations through CPC officials who served within Ott II management, including the positions of president and chief executive officer," and on "the conduct of CPC officials with respect to Ott II affairs, particularly Arnold Ott"); id., at 558 ("CPC actively participated in, and at times controlled, the policy-making decisions of its subsidiary through its representation on the Ott II board of directors"); id., at 559 ("CPC also actively participated in and exercised control over day-to-day decision-making at Ott II through representation in the highest levels of the subsidiary's management").

In imposing direct liability on these grounds, the District Court failed to recognize that "it is entirely appropriate for directors of a parent corporation to serve as directors of its subsidiary, and that fact alone may not serve to expose the parent corporation to liability for its subsidiary's acts." American Protein Corp. v. AB Volvo, 844 F.2d 56, 57(C.A.2), cert. denied, 488 U.S. 852, 109 S.Ct. 136, 102 L.Ed.2d 109 (1988); see also Kingston Dry Dock Co. v. Lake Champlain Transp. Co.,

31 F.2d 265, 267 (C.A.2 1929) (L. Hand, J.) ("Control through the ownership of shares does not fuse the corporations, even when the directors are common to each"); Henn & Alexander 355 (noting that it is "normal" for a parent and subsidiary to "have identical directors and officers").

This recognition that the corporate personalities remain distinct has its corollary in the "well established principle [of corporate law] that directors and officers holding positions with a parent and its subsidiary can and do 'change hats' to represent the two corporations separately, despite their common ownership." Lusk v. Foxmeyer Health Corp., 129 F.3d 773, 779 (C.A.5 1997). Since courts generally presume "that the directors are wearing their 'subsidiary hats' and not their 'parent hats' when acting for the subsidiary," P. Blumberg, Law of Corporate Groups: Procedural Problems in the Law of Parent and Subsidiary Corporations § 1.02.1, at 12 (1983); see, e.g., United States v. Jon–T Chemicals, Inc., 768 F.2d 686, 691 (C.A.5 1985), cert. denied, 475 U.S. 1014, 106 S.Ct. 1194, 89 L.Ed.2d 309 (1986), it cannot be enough to establish liability here that dual officers and directors made policy decisions and supervised activities at the facility. The Government would have to show that, despite the general presumption to the contrary, the officers and directors were acting in their capacities as CPC officers and directors, and not as Ott II officers and directors, when they committed those acts. The District Court made no such inquiry here, however, disregarding entirely this time-honored common law rule.

In sum, the District Court's focus on the relationship between parent and subsidiary (rather than parent and facility), combined with its automatic attribution of the actions of dual officers and directors to the corporate parent, erroneously, even if unintentionally, treated CERCLA as though it displaced or fundamentally altered common law standards of limited liability. Indeed, if the evidence of common corporate personnel acting at management and directorial levels were enough to support a finding of a parent corporation's direct operator liability under CERCLA, then the possibility of resort to veil piercing to establish indirect, derivative liability for the subsidiary's violations would be academic. There would in essence be a relaxed, CERCLA-specific rule of derivative liability that would banish traditional standards and expectations from the law of CERCLA liability. But, as we have said, such a rule does not arise from congressional silence, and CERCLA's silence is dispositive.

2

We accordingly agree with the Court of Appeals that a participation-and-control test looking to the parent's supervision over the subsidiary, especially one that assumes that dual officers always act on behalf of the parent, cannot be used to identify operation of a facility resulting in direct parental liability. Nonetheless, a return to the ordinary meaning of the word "operate" in the organizational sense will indicate why we think that the Sixth Circuit stopped short when it confined its examples of direct parental operation to exclusive or joint ventures, and declined to find at least the possibility of direct operation by CPC in this case.

In our inquiry into the meaning Congress presumably had in mind when it used the verb "to operate," we recognized that the statute obviously meant something more than mere mechanical activation of pumps and valves, and must be read to contemplate "operation" as including the exercise of direction over the facility's activities. The Court of Appeals recognized this by indicating that a parent can be held directly liable when the parent operates the facility in the stead of its subsidiary or alongside the subsidiary in some sort of a joint venture. We anticipated a further possibility above, however, when we observed that a dual officer or director might depart so far from the norms of parental influence exercised through dual officeholding as to serve the parent, even when ostensibly acting on behalf of the subsidiary in operating the facility. * * * Yet another possibility, suggested by the facts of this case, is that an agent of the parent with no hat to wear but the parent's hat might manage or direct activities at the facility.

Identifying such an occurrence calls for line drawing yet again, since the acts of direct operation that give rise to parental liability must necessarily be distinguished from the interference that stems from the normal relationship between parent and subsidiary. Again norms of corporate behavior (undisturbed by any CERCLA provision) are crucial reference points. Just as we may look to such norms in identifying the limits of the presumption that a dual officeholder acts in his ostensible capacity, so here we may refer to them in distinguishing a parental officer's oversight of a subsidiary from such an officer's control over the operation of the subsidiary's facility. * * * The critical question is whether, in degree and detail, actions directed to the facility by an agent of the parent alone are eccentric under accepted norms of parental oversight of a subsidiary's facility.

There is, in fact, some evidence that CPC engaged in just this type and degree of activity at the Muskegon plant. The District Court's opinion speaks of an agent of CPC alone who played a conspicuous part in dealing with the toxic risks emanating from the operation of the plant. G.R.D. Williams worked only for CPC; he was not an employee, officer, or director of Ott II, * * * and thus, his actions were of necessity taken only on behalf of CPC. The District Court found that "CPC became directly involved in environmental and regulatory matters through the work of * * * Williams, CPC's governmental and environmental affairs director. Williams * * * became heavily involved in environmental issues at Ott II." He "actively participated in and exerted control over a variety of Ott II environmental matters," ibid., and he "issued directives regarding Ott II's responses to regulatory inquiries."

We think that these findings are enough to raise an issue of CPC's operation of the facility through Williams's actions, though we would draw no ultimate conclusion from these findings at this point. * * * The trial court offered little in the way of concrete detail for its conclusions about Williams's role in Ott II's environmental affairs, and the parties vigorously dispute the extent of Williams's involvement. Prudence thus counsels us to remand, on the theory of direct operation set out here, for reevaluation of Williams's role, and of the role of any other CPC agent who might be said to have had a part in operating the Muskegon facility.

V

The judgment of the Court of Appeals for the Sixth Circuit is vacated, and the case is remanded with instructions to return it to the District Court for further proceedings consistent with this opinion. It is so ordered.

Notes and Questions

1. *Back to Bedrock Corporate–Law Principles.* Over the past several years, the issue of liability of parent corporations and of individuals, including corporate officers, directors and shareholders, under CERCLA has generated inconsistency in the courts and confusion among businesses subject to that statutory regime. In a unanimous decision, the Supreme Court has provided some much-needed clarification of the involvement a corporate parent must have with a subsidiary's operations before CERCLA liability can be imposed. The decision in *Bestfoods* makes clear that the "bedrock principle" of limited liability long ingrained in the law of corporations has not been eradicated by CERCLA. It is, therefore, now settled that a "person"—whether a corporation or an individual—owning stock in a corporation cannot be held liable under CERCLA simply by virtue of that stock ownership. Moreover, the *Bestfoods* rationale strongly implies that neither limited partners nor corporate officers and directors should be held liable simply by virtue of their status as such.

These notes examine the *Bestfoods* decision and its potential impact on the liability of individuals and parent entities in environmental cases and the steps individuals can take to minimize their risk. While *Bestfoods* suggests that the corporate or other limited-liability form will rarely be ignored, this does not mean that those individuals who actively and directly participate in a facility's operation can avoid the risk of liability.

See, George Weiner v. Lara Bernstein Matthews, *Parent Corporation and Individual Liability Under CERCLA After Bestfoods*, 37 Chemical Waste Litig. Rep. 519 (March 1999).

2. *Pre-Bestfoods World.* Of course, as we have seen, CERCLA provides no meaningful guidance into the meaning of "owner" and "operator," the critical classification of PRP's under § 9607(a). But courts have shown great ingenuity in filling the definitional gap by expressing different analytical tests for determining when an individual could be held liable as an owner or operator under CERCLA. All the differing standards applied highly fact-specific analyses that often yielded inconsistent results and offered little comfort for officers, directors and shareholders seeking predictability with respect to the liability that might attach to their efforts on behalf of corporations.

Further, the various tests sometimes confused the issues of derivative and direct liability. Under traditional corporate law principles, a shareholder can be held derivatively liable where the circumstances warrant piercing the corporate veil, such as when the corporate form would otherwise be misused to accomplish wrongful purposes, including fraud. See, e.g., *Bestfoods*, 118 S.Ct. at 1884. Under CERCLA, a number of courts had held that derivative liability could arise in the context of "owner" liability without resort to the corporate veil-piercing doctrine. See, e.g., Riverside Market Development Corp. v. International Building Products, Inc., 931 F.2d 327 (5th Cir.), cert. denied, 502 U.S. 1004, 112 S.Ct. 636, 116 L.Ed.2d 654 (1991); Analytical Measurements, Inc. v. Keuffel & Esser Co., 843 F.Supp. 920 (D.N.J.1993). At the same time, a number of courts ruled that direct liability could still be imposed on a parent corporation, whenever that parent had or could have exercised control over a subsidiary or its facility. In those cases, the controlling entity was deemed an "operator."

A minority of jurisdictions, including the Fifth and Sixth Circuits, ruled that a corporate shareholder could be held liable under CERCLA as either an owner or operator only if circumstances warranted piercing the corporate veil. See, e.g., Joslyn Manufacturing Co. v. T.L. James & Co., 893 F.2d 80, 82–83 (5th Cir.1990), cert. denied, 498 U.S. 1108, 111 S.Ct. 1017, 112 L.Ed.2d 1098 (1991); United States v. Cordova Chemical Co., 113 F.3d 572, 580 (6th Cir.1997), vacated and remanded, 524 U.S. 51, 118 S.Ct. 1876, 141 L.Ed.2d 43 (1998). A few jurisdictions, most notably the Fourth Circuit, which we saw above in the *Nurad* decision, adopted a "capacity-to-control" test that allowed imposition of operator liability on those shareholders who were in a position to control the operations of a corporation, regardless of whether that control was ever exercised. See, e.g., Nurad, Inc. v. William E. Hooper & Sons Co., 966 F.2d 837 (4th Cir.), cert. denied, 506 U.S. 940, 113 S.Ct. 377, 121 L.Ed.2d 288 (1992); United States v. Carolina Transformer Co., 978 F.2d 832, 837 (4th Cir.1992). Under this expansive interpretation, a corporate parent could almost always be held liable for environmental contamination at a subsidiary's facility.

The majority of federal courts, including the First, Second, Third and Eleventh Circuits, had adopted an *"actual control"* test, under which operator liability was imposed on shareholders who actively participated in and exercised control over the corporation's business during a period of hazardous waste disposal. See United States v. Kayser–Roth Corp., 724 F.Supp. 15 (D.R.I.1989), aff'd, 910 F.2d 24 (1st Cir.1990), cert. denied. 498 U.S. 1084, 111 S.Ct. 957, 112 L.Ed.2d 1045 (1991); Schiavone v. Pearce, 79 F.3d 248, 254–55 (2d Cir.1996); Lansford–Coaldale Joint Water Authority v. Tonolli Corp., 4 F.3d 1209, 1220–25 (3d Cir.1993); Jacksonville Electric Authority v. Bernuth Corp., 996 F.2d 1107, 1110 (11th Cir.1993). It should be noted that the actual control test had been applied most commonly in the context of a parent-subsidiary relationship. Where applied by the lower courts, this analysis focused on the relationship between the parent and the subsidiary's operations generally, rather than the relationship between the parent and the contaminated facility at issue which the Supreme Court in *Bestfoods* made the operative inquiry. See, 37 CWLR at 520 (March 1999).

3. *Pre-Bestfoods Directors' and Officers' Liability.* Corporate law has traditionally protected individual directors and officers from the imposition

of personal liability absent the active, personal involvement of the individual in the tortious activity of the corporation. 3A W. Fletcher, Cyclopedia of The Law of Private Corporations § 1137 (rev. perm. ed. 1986). Before CERCLA, this general rule was interpreted to require either a showing of "direct personal involvement" in the activity causing the plaintiff's injury or evidence that the individual was "the guiding spirit" behind the corporation's tortious conduct. Escude Cruz v. Ortho Pharmaceutical Corp., 619 F.2d 902, 907 (1st Cir.1980); Marks v. Polaroid Corp., 237 F.2d 428 (1st Cir.1956), cert. denied, 352 U.S. 1005, 77 S.Ct. 564, 1 L.Ed.2d 550 (1957). As in the shareholder liability context, however, courts applying CERCLA's operator liability provisions to officers and directors often adopted inconsistent, and sometimes wide-reaching, liability standards.

Many court have held officers or directors liable based on facts establishing personal participation in or direct supervision of the disposal activity that resulted in the hazardous substance release. See, e.g., FMC Corp. v. Aero Industries, Inc., 998 F.2d 842 (10th Cir.1993). Three federal circuits, the Fifth, Seventh, and Eighth, have explicitly suggested that operator liability can be imposed on officers and directors only where there was direct personal involvement in the hazardous waste disposal at issue. See Riverside Market Development Corp. v. International Building Products, Inc., 931 F.2d 327 (5th Cir.1991); Sidney S. Arst Co. v. Pipefitters Welfare Educational Fund, 25 F.3d 417 (7th Cir.1994); United States v. Gurley, 43 F.3d 1188 (8th Cir.1994), cert. denied, 516 U.S. 817, 116 S.Ct. 73, 133 L.Ed.2d 33 (1995). These decisions stated that the personal involvement must be with the activity leading to the contamination, rather than with the operations of the facility generally. *Arst*, 25 F.3d at 421–22 (rejecting notion that "general corporate authority" or "serv[ing] generally in a supervisory capacity" could justify imposition of liability on corporate officers or directors). But see United States v. TIC Inv. Corp., 68 F.3d 1082 (8th Cir.1995), cert. denied, 519 U.S. 808, 117 S.Ct. 50, 136 L.Ed.2d 14 (1996) (retreating from *Gurley* and stating in dicta that "[i]t is sufficient for the person to have exercised authority or control over the operations of the *facility* * * *") (emphasis added.)

A minority of jurisdictions, on the other hand, applied the "capacity to control" test developed in shareholder liability cases to officer and director liability. See, e.g., Idaho v. Bunker Hill Co., 635 F.Supp. 665 (D.Idaho 1986); United States v. Northeastern Pharmaceutical & Chemical Co. (NEPACCO), 579 F.Supp. 823 (W.D. Mo.1984), aff'd, 810 F.2d 726 (8th Cir.1986), cert. denied, 484 U.S. 848, 108 S.Ct. 146, 98 L.Ed.2d 102 (1987). Even more than in the shareholder context, this standard imposes liability based almost solely on the status of the individual. For example, one court stated that the factors to be examined to determine operator liability include whether the individual holds the position of officer or director, especially where there is a coexisting management position; distribution of power within the corporation, including position in the corporate hierarchy and percentage of shares owned. Kelley v. ARCO Industries Corp., 723 F.Supp. 1214, 1219 (W.D.Mich.1989). Several lower courts applied the "actual control" test adopted by a majority of jurisdictions in the shareholder context to officer and director liability.

See, e.g., New York v. Shore Realty Corp., 759 F.2d 1032 (2d Cir.1985); Levin Metals Corp. v. Parr–Richmond Terminal Co., 781 F.Supp. 1454 (N.D.Cal.1991); Vermont v. Staco, Inc., 684 F.Supp. 822 (D.Vt.1988). As in the shareholder decisions, liability was imposed on those individuals who actively participated in and exercised control over the corporation's business. Unlike the officer and director cases applying the traditional test, these cases focused on control over the corporation generally.

In contrast with the issue of corporate shareholder or officer and director liability, few cases have examined the circumstances under which limited partners could be held directly or indirectly liable for contamination at facilities owned or operated by the partnership. The Eleventh Circuit, however, squarely addressed this issue in Redwing Carriers, Inc. v. Saraland Apts., 94 F.3d 1489 (11th Cir.1996).

In *Redwing*, the court applied state partnership law to determine whether a limited partner could be held indirectly liable under CERCLA as an owner of a facility to which the partnership held title. Noting that under Alabama law the partnership rather than the individual partners holds title, the court refused to impose owner liability on the limited partner. The court adopted the "actual control" test applied by a majority of courts to determine shareholder liability and focused on the limited partner's control over the partnership and the facility generally, not the control over the disposal of hazardous substances.

4. *Bestfoods and Beyond: What Are the "Rules?"* In *Bestfoods*, Justice Souter sought to clarify the circumstances in which a shareholder will be held liable as an operator under CERCLA for the acts of the corporation. The precise question before the court was whether the principle of limited liability fundamental to the corporate form had somehow been relaxed by Congress in crafting CERCLA.

First and foremost, Justice Souter rejected a "relaxed, CERCLA-specific rule of derivative liability," concluding that Congress did not rewrite the well-settled rule of limited liability of shareholders. *Bestfoods*, 118 S.Ct. at 1880–81. At the same time, the court stated that the failure by Congress to set aside the limited liability concept did not necessarily mean that a corporation's parent (or its principal shareholders) could always avoid liability. First, the corporate veil may be pierced. Second, CERCLA liability can still be imposed directly upon such persons for their own actions. In this respect, the Court noted that CERCLA's plain language renders any person who "operates" a polluting facility directly liable for the costs of cleaning up the pollution, and that this rule applied even if that person is the parent corporation of the facility's owner. Id. at 1885–86.

The impact of the *Bestfoods* decision is that corporate shareholders will normally be insulated from CERCLA liability unless one of the two following circumstances can be demonstrated:

a. The shareholder may be liable if it played an active, operational role concerning waste handling at the subject facility.

The opinion explained that the lower courts previously considering the owner/operator liability issue had improperly tended to focus on the general relationship existing between parent and subsidiary. In so doing, the lower courts often had blurred the distinction between direct and derivative liability and had held a parent liable for the acts of a subsidiary based solely upon stock ownership or the existence of common officers and directors. That sort of analysis, however, often failed to consider the question whether, stock ownership and common management aside, a corporate parent has played any role in environmental matters at the facility under review. Moreover, many courts had incorrectly presumed that the acts of dual officers and directors were taken on behalf of the subsidiary, rather than on behalf of the parent.

Departing from the various tests imposed by lower courts to determine when a shareholder may be held directly liable as an operator, the Court fashioned a narrower version of the "actual control" test adopted by the majority of federal circuits. Justice Souter's analysis focused on the actual control exercised by the parent over the subsidiary's polluting facility, rather than over the operations of the subsidiary generally. Building upon the definition of the term "operator," the Court said that in the CERCLA context an operator must manage, direct, or conduct operations specifically related to pollution, that is, operations having to do with the leakage or disposal of hazardous waste, or decisions about compliance with environmental regulations. Id. at 1887. Thus, contrary to the actual-control and capacity-to-control tests devised by the lower courts, a shareholder must participate directly in the environmental activities at issue to be deemed an operator under CERCLA.

The Court recognized that the acts of direct operation that give rise to parental liability must necessarily be distinguished from the interference.

As Weiner & Matthews explain:

> The critical question, in the Court's view, is whether "actions directed to the facility by an agent of the parent alone are eccentric" under accepted corporate norms, id., noting that a parent's management team often exercises general oversight over a subsidiary's actions that is consistent with monitoring of investments but is not the sort of control needed to impute CERCLA liability to the parent. Criticizing the analysis employed by the lower courts, Justice Souter rejected the supposition that dual officers and directors are always acting on behalf of the parent. He instead indicated that only when the actions of dual officers and directors are plainly contrary to the interests of the subsidiary, and of benefit to the parent, should those officers and directors be deemed to be acting for the parent. In such instances, the imputation of CERCLA liability on the parent would be appropriate.

> Again, to demonstrate such conduct, a claimant must show that the shareholder "managed, directed, or conducted operations that specifically related to * * * the leakage or disposal of hazardous waste, or decisions about compliance with environmental regulations." Id. Noting the dictionary definition of "operate," the *Bestfoods* Court concluded that under CERCLA an operator is simply someone who directs the workings of, manages, or conducts the affairs of a facility. If a shareholder does not play an active role in a facility's operation, but instead limits its involvement to the sort of general oversight that is consistent with that of an investor, then direct liability will not attach.

When the question is one of a controlling shareholder's liability for the acts of the corporation, the types of actions consistent with "normal supervision" include (1) supervising the corporation's finances; (2) approving the corporation's capital expenditures; and (3) formulating general policies and procedures. On the other hand, direct liability may be imposed on controlling shareholders where: (1) an agent or employee of the shareholder with no position in the corporation directs the operations of the corporation's facility involving hazardous substances or environmental compliance; (2) the shareholder itself actually operates the corporation's facility, such as when the shareholder is a lessee of the site; or (3) where the shareholder and the corporation operate the facility in a joint venture relationship.

37 Chem. Waste Litig. Rep. at 522 (1999).

b. *Absent any proof of direct involvement in operation of a facility, the shareholder may be liable if there exist extraordinary circumstances warranting piercing of the corporate veil.*

As discussed below, proving that a shareholder is derivatively liable under this standard may be very difficult, particularly when the shareholder is an individual. Generally speaking, the corporate veil may be pierced and the shareholder held personally liable for the corporation's conduct only when the corporate form would otherwise be misused to accomplish certain wrongful purposes, most notably fraud, on the shareholder's behalf. Absent proof of such misuse, the protective corporate veil usually cannot be pierced. Id. at 1885.

Unfortunately for shareholders seeking guidance as to how to protect themselves against the risk of CERCLA liability, corporate veil-piercing claims are decided on a case-by-case basis. The doctrine is thus subject to inconsistent application, and the split among the circuit courts as to whether state law or a federal common law applies was not resolved by the Supreme Court in *Bestfoods*. See 118 S.Ct. at 1885 n.9.

5. *Veil Piercing Factors.* At present, the main distinction among certain state laws and the federal common law is whether the corporate veil will be pierced in the absence of fraud or wrongdoing. Piercing of the corporate veil has been limited almost exclusively to cases involving controlling shareholders of closely held corporations and corporate groups (*i.e.*, parent-subsidiary relationships). Generally, to determine whether a corporation is an instrumentality or alter-ego, courts examine what has been termed a "laundry list" of factors. The factors relevant to individual shareholders include: (1) financing of the corporation by the shareholder, including payment of salaries; (2) the shareholder's use of the corporation's property and assets as its own; (3) extensive or pervasive control over the corporation's decisions and operations by the controlling shareholder; (4) observance of formal legal requirements by the corporation, including commencement of business without the issuance of shares, lack of shareholders or directors meetings, and lack of signing of consents; (5) intermingling of the corporation's properties or accounts with those of the shareholders; (6) siphoning of funds from the corporation; (7) absence of corporate records; (8) presence of non-functioning officers and directors; (9) undercapitalization of the corpora-

tion for the purposes for which it was organized; and (10) commercial reasonableness of contracts between the shareholder and the corporation.

No single factor on this list is determinative, and the presence of several typically will be necessary before liability will be imposed. Two of the most common factors justifying piercing are undercapitalization or the siphoning (or improper diversion) of corporate funds by the dominant shareholder. Even under the most expansive interpretation of federal common law, however, the existence of common officers, directors, or shareholders taken alone should not result in the imposition of shareholder liability.

Weiner & Matthews, Parent Corporation and Individual Liability After Bestfoods, 37 C.W.L.R. at 522–523 (1999).

6. *Subsequent Application of Bestfoods.* An Illinois district court's decision in Browning–Ferris Industries of Illinois, Inc. v. Ter Maat, 13 F. Supp.2d 756 (N.D.Ill.1998) aff'd, 195 F.3d 953 (7th Cir.1999), found the *Bestfoods* test to be appropriate for resolving operator claims against affiliates and shareholders. In Ter Maat, Browning–Ferris Industries sued the main shareholder and tracking affiliate of a defunct landfill operator for response costs on both direct and derivative theories of liability. Id. at 763. Although recognizing that the claims before it did not involve parent-corporation liability, the court noted the "share[d] officers and directors" in finding "the language of *Bestfoods* equally applicable here." Id.

A recent Michigan district court decision in Datron, Inc. v. CRA Holdings, 42 F.Supp.2d 736 (W.D.Mich.1999), applies the *Bestfoods* test to a direct liability claim. In this case, a purchaser of the stock of two former wholly-owned subsidiaries of another company sued the former parent to recover response costs being incurred in connection with the subsidiaries' facilities. The defendant moved to dismiss the CERCLA claims on the grounds that it was not the operator of the facilities in question because its subsidiaries were operated as independent businesses that made all decisions regarding compliance, and waste decisions were made at the plant level.

Datron countered that the parent's conduct in the operations of the subsidiaries' facilities exceeded the accepted norms of corporate behavior because: (1) the parent's corporate policies referred to the subsidiaries, (2) the parent's corporate safety director conducted semi-annual Occupational Safety and Health Administration inspections of the plants, (3) the parent's corporate policies required all employees to comply with the Resource Conservation and Recovery Act, (4) there were dual officers, and (5) the parent required the subsidiaries to obtain credit approval for any credit arrangements outside of the normal accounts. For one of the facilities in question, Datron argued that operator liability was appropriate because the parent assisted in obtaining insurance for the facility, hired a lawyer to defend the facility against an environmental claim and assisted in obtaining an easement for a drainage ditch.

The court found these activities were within the normal oversight by a parent of its subsidiaries. Although there was some direct involvement by the parent in hiring an attorney for the environmental matter, that aid came at the subsidiary's request and related to a problem caused by decisions that the plant-level employees had made. The circumstances were largely the same in obtaining of the drainage easement, which the court noted was not involved in transporting wastes but only water from the roof. The remaining patchwork of allegations was handled in summary fashion as the court found them all to be common activities for a parent corporation.

This decision demonstrates the real impact of *Bestfoods* on the scope of direct parent liability under CERCLA. The court's focus was facility-specific and the allegations had to be brought down to the plant level. There were no allegations regarding the parent's control of the subsidiary's boardroom at all. Second, the *Bestfoods* presumption that dual status employees are working for the subsidiary will defeat the mere allegation of that fact as warranting direct liability. Merely saying that the parent had dual status officers will simply not pass muster under the new *Bestfoods* test.

7. *Shareholders.* As to shareholder liability, some courts apply analyses similar to the corporate parent cases. See Donahey v. Bogle, 987 F.2d 1250 (6th Cir.1993) (holding that a sole shareholder of a corporation is a responsible party "as a matter of law" under CERCLA where the evidence showed that he "had the authority to prevent the contamination of the property of the corporation.") See also Kelley v. Thomas Solvent Co., 727 F.Supp. 1532 (W.D.Mich.1989); Riverside Market Development Corp. v. International Building Prods. Inc., 931 F.2d 327 (5th Cir.1991), cert. denied 502 U.S. 1004, 112 S.Ct. 636, 116 L.Ed.2d 654 (1991) (majority shareholder not an owner under facts of that case); United States v. Northeastern Pharmaceutical & Chemical Co., 810 F.2d 726 (8th Cir.1986) (shareholder and officer liable under § 107(a)(3) because he arranged personally for the disposal of hazardous waste).

Should courts take a different approach to shareholders than to parents and subsidiary relationships? How about officers or directors? At least two courts have adopted a "prevention test" that imposes operator liability on an officer if the individual officer "could have prevented or significantly abated" the waste activity. Kelley v. ARCO Industries Corp., 723 F.Supp. 1214, 1217 (W.D.Mich.1989); Quadion Corp. v. Mache, 738 F.Supp. 270 (N.D.Ill.1990). What incentives does such a rule create?

See Frank H. Easterbrook & Daniel R. Fischel, Limited Liability and the Corporation, 52 U. Chi. L. Rev. 89 (1985) (arguing in favor of strict preservation of corporate identities); Lynda J. Oswald, Strict Liability of Individuals under CERCLA, 20 B. C. Envtl. Aff. L. Rev. 579 (1993).

3. ADVISING YOUR CLIENT

Assume you are legal counsel to a corporation that has established subsidiaries that carry out most of the responsibility for the waste disposal needs of the affiliated companies. After *Bestfoods*, what advice do you give respecting the structure and operation of the corporate relationships?

a. *Is Liability Less Likely After Bestfoods for Parent Entities?* After *Bestfoods*, will it be more difficult to hold parent corporations liable under CERCLA for contamination at their subsidiary's sites? Much of the evidence upon which the government has traditionally relied in suing parent corporations is insufficient to establish CERCLA liability after *Bestfoods*. In the past, the government has built many of its cases against parent corporations by showing that the same individuals were officers or directors of both the parent and the subsidiary, that the parent established general policies and practices for the subsidiary to follow, and that the parent's approval was necessary before the subsidiary could make substantial expenditures. Now this evidence will be viewed as indications of a normal parent-subsidiary relationship, and without additional facts, not proof of CERCLA liability. To hold a parent company liable, the government or other plaintiff will have to either meet the common law standards of piercing the corporate veil or show that the parent directly controlled environmental activities at the subsidiary's site. Future cases will determine exactly what type of proof will be sufficient for liability, but the focus of proof will be on the relationship between the parent and the site, not the parent and the subsidiary.

b. Personnel Choices. After *Bestfoods*, may a parent corporation rely on its own environmental management staff to supervise its subsidiary's compliance without risk of Superfund liability? The *Bestfoods* decision implies that a parent company may risk CERCLA liability if it assigns its own environmental affairs manager to supervise its subsidiary's compliance, unless that manager also holds a position in the subsidiary. Does this suggest that a parent company should make sure that its subsidiary has its own environmental management staff, even if that staff includes individuals who hold dual positions with the parent and the subsidiary?

c. Measuring Bestfoods Against Prior Decisions. In a practical sense, however, it is difficult to tell what the impact of the *Bestfoods* decision is likely to be when viewed against the backdrop of existing case law. For example, in one of the leading cases applying the actual control test, U.S. v. Kayser–Roth Corp., 910 F.2d 24, 27 (1st Cir.1990), the First Circuit imposed operator liability in a factual context where:

> Kayser–Roth [the parent corporation] exercised pervasive control over Stamina Mills [the subsidiary] through, among other things: 1) its total monetary control including collection of accounts payable; 2) its restriction on Stamina Mills' financial budget; 3) its directive that subsidiary—governmental contact, including environmental matters, be funneled directly through Kayser–Roth; * * * and finally, its placement of Kayser–Roth personnel in almost all Stamina Mills' director and officer positions, as a means of totally ensuring that Kayser–Roth corporate policy was exactly implemented and precisely carried out.

Kayser's control included environmental matters. It is not clear whether these facts would justify direct liability under the actual control test established by the Court in *Bestfoods*. Moreover, whether these facts rise to the level of a breach of norms of corporate behavior may require some opinion testimony on this point. These norms are unspecified and unexplained. As a result, although the *Bestfoods* decision appears to narrow the scope of parent liability in theory, its practical impact may merely be to change how these cases are pled and presented. Only time will tell whether this new standard really narrows the scope of operator liability for parent corporations.

If you were deciding *Kayser-Roth* today, how would you decide the *Bestfoods* issues?

d. Choice of Law. Finally, it is important to note that the Supreme Court has left the question of the source of the veil-piercing rules for another day: "[T]here is significant disagreement among courts and commentators over whether, in enforcing CERCLA's indirect liability, courts should borrow state law, or instead apply a federal common law of veil piercing * * * the question is not presented in this case, and we do not address it further." 118 S.Ct. at 1886 n.9. The Court's discussion of this issue notes cases citing rationales of uniformity and consistency with federal statutory policy for adopting a federal common-law rule. Other Supreme Court decisions appear to indicate a reluctance to use federal common-law rules unless absolutely necessary. See, e.g., O'Melveny & Myers v. Federal Deposit Ins. Corp., 512 U.S. 79, 114 S.Ct. 2048, 129 L.Ed.2d 67 (1994).

One district court's opinion is, perhaps, illustrative. In AT & T Global Information Solutions Co. v. Union Tank Car Co., 29 F.Supp. 2d 857 (S.D.Ohio 1998), the court resolved the choice-of-law question left open in *Bestfoods* by reliance on an earlier Sixth Circuit decision, Donahey v. Bogle, 129 F.3d 838 (6th Cir.1997), vacated on other grounds, 524 U.S. 924, 118 S.Ct. 2317, 141 L.Ed.2d 692 (1998), requiring "that trial courts must look to *state corporation law when attempting to pierce the corporate veil in CERCLA cases*" (emphasis added). Applying Ohio law, the district court relied on a state Supreme Court decision which held that the fraud requirement in veil-piercing cases "no longer reflects the realities of modern corporate life," Belvedere Condominium Unit Owners' Ass'n v. R.E. Roark Cos., 67 Ohio St.3d 274, 286–87, 617 N.E.2d 1075, 1085–86 (1993), which in turn prompted the lower Ohio courts to substitute a standard that "allows a corporate veil to be pierced when inequitable or unfair consequences had resulted." Given CERCLA's purpose "of ensuring 'that those responsible for any damage, environmental harm, or injury from chemical poisons bear the costs of their actions,'" the court had no difficulty finding that it would be "inequitable and unfair" not to pierce the corporate veil of a long-defunct subsidiary to reach not its parent but its "grandparent" corporate entity.

We should pay attention to the Ninth Circuit's ruling in Atchison, Topeka and Santa Fe Railway Co. v. Brown & Bryant, Inc., 159 F.3d 358 (9th Cir.1997), in which the court held it would not apply the continuity of enterprise theory to determine a successor corporation's liability for Superfund contamination. The decision is important because it answers in the negative a question left open by the U.S. Supreme Court in *Bestfoods,* namely, whether federal common law should be used to determine corporate liability under CERCLA. The Ninth Circuit found no evidence that applying state corporation law would frustrate the Superfund law's objectives of cleaning up hazardous waste sites and imposing the costs on those responsible for the contamination. No state provides a haven for liable companies and there is no reason to think states will alter their existing successor liability rules in a race to attract corporate business, the court found. Other federal appeals courts disagree, however. In ruling for the defendant under California law in *Atchison*, the Ninth Circuit said it would have reached the same result under federal common law because it would not accept the "substantial continuation" exception to the traditional rule of no liability for asset purchasers.

Accordingly, parties should be careful when drafting agreements concerning the sale and purchase of an entity to ensure that it properly and clearly reflects how the parties intend to address environmental liabilities. Moreover, entities considering dissolution should consider and take into account the ramifications of potential CERCLA liability remaining long after the entity is "dead and buried."

e. Other Open Questions. For a thorough analysis of *Bestfoods* and the issues it does not resolve, see Lueia Ann Silecchia, Pinning the Blame & Piercing the Veil in the Mists of Metaphor: The Supreme Court's New Standards for CERCLA Liability of Parent Companies and Proposal for Legislative Reform, 67 Fordham L. Rev. 115, 173–174 (1998). She comments:

> The three problems left unresolved by the court's opinion [in *Bestfoods*] should come as no surprise. These problems are: (1) whether state or federal law should govern indirect liability via veil-piercing; (2) how "operator" should be defined for purposes of assessing direct liability; and (3) how the definition of "operator" may be best applied. They represent complexities that have long plagued the lower courts as they attempted to grapple with this issue. The fact that the Supreme Court itself was unable or unwilling to resolve these questions argues well for the need for a legislative solution. A Congressional solution is needed because only legislation will be able to address the problem with the level of detail necessary to eliminate the confusion that arises from piecemeal judicial pronouncements on these intricate questions. Allocating liability requires full discussion of practical and financial issues, not merely legal implications. These are fact intensive, empirically studied issues which are better handled by the legislature than by the courts. This is particularly true in a highly politicized area such as this which involves a reworking of the traditional common law rule on limited liability. Thus, although the Supreme Court's ruling goes a great distance in clarifying some of the underlying issues under the current CERCLA scheme, there remains much work for Congress in addressing three problems that endure after *Bestfoods*.

4. LIABILITY OF SUCCESSOR ENTITIES

With the merger-acquisition fever of the last decade, moving unabated into 2000 and beyond, the issue of successor liability for environmental liabilities, especially CERCLA liabilities, has assumed considerable importance in transactional negotiations and agreements, when the successor entities have acquired the equity or assets of an entity that, but for the acquisition, would have been a PRP under CERCLA.

a. *Recognition of Successor Liability Under CERCLA.* While there are a number of corporation law principles like veil piercing that are generally accepted in every state, on the issue of successor liability state-law rules differ, sometimes dramatically. In part because of these differences and a perceived need for uniformity in the application of CERCLA, the federal courts have developed a more expansive basis for successor liability—the "substantial continuity" doctrine—than found in the common law rules of most states—which adhere to the traditional "mere continuity" theory. Unlike the stricter traditional rule, the substantial continuity doctrine allows successor liability even though there is no exact identity of ownership interests between the purchasing and selling entities.

The Third Circuit was the first federal appeals court to hold that a successor corporation could have CERCLA liability. Smith Land & Improvement Corp. v. Celotex Corp., 851 F.2d 86 (3d Cir.1988), cert. denied, 488 U.S. 1029, 109 S.Ct. 837, 102 L.Ed.2d 969 (1989). Since then every other federal circuit court to have addressed the issue has agreed. See, Atchison, Topeka & Santa Fe Ry. Co. v. Brown & Bryant, 132 F.3d 1295 (9th Cir.1997), amended and replaced by 159 F.3d 358 (9th Cir. 1997); Anspec Co. v. Johnson Controls, Inc., 922 F.2d 1240 (6th Cir. 1991); United States v. Carolina Transformer Co., 978 F.2d 832 (4th Cir.1992); United States v. Mexico Feed and Seed Co., 980 F.2d 478 (8th Cir.1992); John S. Boyd Co. v. Boston Gas Co., 992 F.2d 401 (1st Cir.1993); B.F. Goodrich v. Betkoski, 99 F.3d 505 (2d Cir.1996).

At least one court has reasoned that successor liability is such a well understood principle of corporate law that Congress would have explicitly had to exclude successor corporations from the list of liable entities in order to insulate them from CERCLA liability. United States v. Mexico Feed and Seed Co., 980 F.2d 478, 486 (8th Cir.1992). Other courts have relied on statutory construction, noting that Congress has defined the words "company or association" whenever they appear in the United States Code to include "successors and assigns." 1 U.S.C. § 5. Virtually all courts have recognized that successor corporations should bear CERCLA liability in order to promote the remedial aims of the statute. See, e.g., Smith Land & Improvement Corp. v. Celotex Corp., 851 F.2d 86, 91–92:

> Congressional intent supports the conclusion that, when choosing between the taxpayers or a successor corporation, the successor

should bear the cost. Benefits from use of the pollutants as well as savings resulting from the failure to use non-hazardous disposal methods inured to the original corporation, its successors, and their respective stockholders and accrued only indirectly, if at all, to the general public.

b. Commonality Between the Federal Rule and the State Law Rule. But, if the CERCLA liability of corporate successors is now beyond dispute, the extensive footnote in *Bestfoods*, 118 S.Ct. at 1885 n.9, indicates that the Court has not decided whether federal common law or state law should be used in determining that liability. While much of the law defining corporate successors is virtually the same under federal common or state law, there are a few significant differences.

Both federal and state common law recognize that a purchaser of corporate assets is not liable for the acts of the seller unless certain exceptions apply. Both state and federal common law share four of these exceptions: (1) if the purchaser expressly or impliedly agrees to assume the liabilities; (2) if the transaction can be said to be a *de facto* merger or consolidation; (3) if the purchaser is a "mere continuation" of the seller; or (4) if the transaction is an effort fraudulently to escape liability. Federal courts, however, have developed a further exception, which broadens the "mere continuation" doctrine and allows for successor liability when there is "substantial continuity" in the business or "continuity of the enterprise." See, e.g., United States v. Carolina Transformer Co., 978 F.2d 832 (4th Cir.1992). The "substantial continuity" doctrine is the rule in only a few states. See, e.g., Kelly v. Kercher Machine Works, Inc., 910 F.Supp. 30 (D.N.H.1995) (New Hampshire law); State of New York v. N. Storonske Cooperage Co., 174 B.R. 366, 387 n. 38. (N.D.N.Y.1994) (noting that the New York Court of Appeals has not definitely rejected the substantial continuity theory); City Management Corp. v. U.S. Chemical Co., 43 F.3d 244, 252 (6th Cir.1994) (interpreting substantial continuity doctrine under Michigan law to apply only to products liability cases).[1]

c. The "Mere Continuation" Test. The traditional "mere continuation" theory recognized by most states requires an identity between the ownership interests of the selling and purchasing entities, so that it can be said "the purchasing corporation maintains the same or similar management and ownership [as the selling corporation] but wears a 'new hat.'" Fletcher, Cyclopedia of the Law of Private Corporations, § 7124.10 (perm. Ed. 1990). Thus, the traditional common law rule requires an identity of stock, stockholders, officers and directors between

---

1. A few jurisdictions have adopted a so-called "product-line" exception, which in most CERCLA fact patterns would be inapplicable. But see, Leo v. Kerr–McGee Chemical Corp., 37 F.3d 96, 102–03 (3d Cir.1994) (Atkins, J., concurring) (dictum that New Jersey Supreme Court would apply the product line exception in an environmental tort action because the same policy reasons underlying that exception exist). Under this minority strain, the injury must have occurred as a result of the continuation of manufacturing the same product, and there must be no available remedy against the original manufacturer. See also United States v. Western Processing Co., 751 F.Supp. 902 (W.D.Wash.1990).

the purchasing and selling corporations. As the Fourth Circuit has articulated it,

> [under] the 'mere continuation' exception * * * a corporation is not to be considered the continuation of a predecessor unless, after the transfer of assets, only one corporation remains, and there is an identity of stock, stockholders, and directors between the two corporations.

United States v. Carolina Transformer Co., 978 F.2d 832, 838 (4th Cir.1992). The inquiry focuses on whether the purchaser continues the *corporate entity* of the seller, not on whether the purchaser simply continues the same business operations. North Shore Gas Co. v. Salomon, Inc., 152 F.3d 642, 654 (7th Cir.1998).

d. The Substantial Continuity Test. By contrast, the substantial continuity rule, recognized by only a handful of states, requires only a substantial continuation of the corporate enterprise. This doctrine considers a number of factors including:

> an identity of stock, stockholders, and officers, but not determinatively. It also considers whether the purchasers retained the same facilities, same employees, same name, same production facilities in the same location, same supervisory personnel; and produced the same product; maintained a continuity of assets; continued the same general business operations; and held itself out to the public as a continuation of the previous enterprise.

Mexico Feed and Seed, 980 F.2d at 488 n.10. Most, but not all courts, have also interpreted the doctrine to require knowledge by the purchaser of the potential liability. Compare, Allied Corp. v. Acme Solvents Reclaiming, Inc., 812 F.Supp. 124, 129 (N.D.Ill.1993) (knowledge required) with Gould, Inc. v. A & M Battery and Tire Service, 950 F.Supp. 653, 659 (M.D.Pa.1997) (knowledge by asset purchaser not required).

For additional scholarly commentary on the issue of successor liability in the environmental context, see Clarke, Successor Liability Under CERCLA: A Federal Common Law Approach, 58 Geo. Wash. L. Rev. 1300 (1990); Note, CERCLA, Successor Liability, and the Federal Common Law: Responding to an Uncertain Legal Standard, 68 Tex. L. Rev. 1237 (1990); Semeraro, Toward an Optimal System of Successor Liability for Hazardous Waste Cleanup, 6 Stan. Envtl. L.J. 226 (1986–87).

e. Confusion As to the Better Rule: Federal or State. The issue is much more than an academic one because the choice of state or federal law as the rule of decision will often be dispositive on the question of liability. In United States v. Distler, the district court originally applied the federal common law "substantial continuity" doctrine to hold that a corporate asset purchaser formed by key employees of the selling company was liable as a successor. United States v. Distler, 741 F.Supp. 637 (W.D.Ky.1990). After the Sixth Circuit's decision in Anspec Co. v. Johnson Controls, 922 F.2d 1240 (6th Cir.1991), the district court reconsidered and vacated its earlier decision. The district court reasoned that Ohio–the state of incorporation of both the seller and purchaser–did not recognize successor liability under the "substantial continuity" theory but only under the "mere continuity" theory, and the facts did not show the necessary identity of ownership between the seller and purchaser. United States v. Distler, 865 F.Supp. 398 (W.D.Ky.1991).

Prior to *Bestfoods*, most circuit courts had resorted to federal common law on the ground that national uniformity was crucial in construing CERCLA and that, without a uniform rule, parties could frustrate the goals of CERCLA by tailoring their transactions under state laws that unduly limited successor liability. *Louisiana-Pacific*, supra, 909 F.2d at 1263 n.2. Only a few circuits have applied state law as the rule of decision for successor liability under CERCLA. See Anspec Co. v. Johnson Controls, Inc., 922 F.2d 1240 (6th Cir.1991). The Seventh Circuit recently discussed the issue but, taking its cue from *Bestfoods*, reserved deciding the choice-of-law issue because it had not been raised by the parties. See North Shore Gas Co. v. Salomon, Inc., 152 F.3d 642, 651 (7th Cir.1998). United States v. Davis, 1998 WL 166222 (D.R.I.1998) (recognizing the unresolved "issue of whether federal courts have the power to create federal rules of decision such as the substantial continuity test"). The Ninth Circuit has grappled with this issue without clearly resolving it. In Atchison, Topeka and Santa Fe Railway Co. v. Brown & Bryant, Inc., 159 F.3d 358 (9th Cir.1997), the court retreated from its earlier decision (at 132 F.3d 1295), which had expressly adopted state law as the appropriate rule of decision. Although it continued to criticize the rationales used to support application of a federal common law, the court's amended decision stopped short of embracing state law.

f. What Considerations Support a Federal Common Law Rule? Although it expressly left the question open in *Bestfoods*, the Supreme Court's recent decisions strongly suggest that state law should furnish the appropriate standard for determining successor liability under CERCLA. In United States v. Kimbell Foods, Inc., 440 U.S. 715, 99 S.Ct. 1448, 59 L.Ed.2d 711 (1979), the Court set forth a three-part test to determine whether federal common law was appropriate. The test requires a court to consider:

(1) whether the issue required a national uniform body of law;

(2) whether application of state law would frustrate specific objectives of the federal programs; and

(3) whether application of a federal rule would disrupt commercial relationships predicated on state law.

Kimball Foods, 440 U.S. at 728–29. Most courts have focused on factors (1) and (2) to justify application of the federal "substantial continuity" doctrine. See, e.g., Kleen Laundry & Dry Cleaning v. Total Waste Management, 867 F.Supp. 1136, 1141 (D.N.H.1994). Factor (3) has been given little if any consideration. The Supreme Court's latest pronouncements, however, should compel re-examination of this element in evaluating whether federal common law is appropriate.

In O'Melveny & Myers v. FDIC, 512 U.S. 79, 114 S.Ct. 2048, 129 L.Ed.2d 67 (1994), the Court refused to create a special federal common law rule on imputation of a corporate officer's fraudulent conduct to a savings and loan institution that had been taken over by the FDIC. The Court emphasized that "cases in which judicial creation of a special federal rule would be justified * * * are * * * 'few and restricted'." 512 U.S. at 87.

Given the Supreme Court's ambivalence on the issue in *Bestfoods* and its prior holdings in *Kimbell Foods* and *O'Melveny & Myers*, how would you predict that the Court would rule if squarely faced with the question?

How would you respond to this court's concerns:

> In United States v. Mexico Feed & Seed Co., [980 F.2d 478 (8th Cir.1992)], the Eighth Circuit adopted the doctrine of substantial continuity, but reversed the trial court's finding of successor liability under it. Although the court agreed that "Congress could not have intended that those corporations be enabled to evade their responsibility by dying paper deaths, only to rise phoenix-like from the ashes, transformed, but free of their former liabilities," *Id.* at 488, it found that "[t]he cases imposing 'substantial continuation' successorship have correctly focused on preventing those responsible for the wastes from evading liability through the structure of subsequent transactions." The court refused to impose successor liability. The court also noted that since the principal of the selling corporation was himself liable under CERCLA, "the very concern animating the doctrine of corporate successor liability—that the corporate veil thwart plaintiffs in actions against corporations which have sold their assets and distributed the proceeds—is not present".

Id. at 490.

> *g. What Considerations Support Applying State Law?* Those courts that have selected state law as the touchstone of liability have noted that state law is largely uniform on issues of successor liability and that there is no reason to think that states will unreasonably restrict successor liability rules in a "race to the bottom" to attract corporate business. *Atchison, Topeka & Santa Fe Ry. Co. v. Brown & Bryant, Inc.,* 132 F.3d 1295 (9th Cir.1997), amended by 159 F.3d 358 (9th Cir.1997). Moreover, "[t]he formation of corporations, and the dissolution and continuing liability of corporations are traditional matters of state law." *Id.* at 1300. By itself the non-uniformity of state common law successor liability theories does not necessarily indicate a conflict, much less a significant conflict, with CERCLA. As the Ninth Circuit noted in *Atchison,* where there is evidence of collusion or a fraudulent intent to evade cleanup responsibility, *every state recognizes that successor liability may be imposed.* Thus, there may not be any real need for a federal common law exception to ensure that successor corporations do not unfairly evade their obligations. *Atchison, Topeka & Santa Fe Ry.,* 132 F.3d at 1301–02. Finally, to the extent that state law principles furnish the generally-

recognized bases for commercial transactions, selecting those principles as the rule of decision is most consistent with the expectations of the parties. See Redwing Carriers, Inc. v. Saraland Apts., 94 F.3d 1489, 1502 (11th Cir.1996) (liability of limited partners under CERCLA should be decided by state law rather than by federal common law rules).

h. Choice of Law. But if state law should apply, *which state's law* is it that ought to govern, given the interstate nature of many acquisition transactions? For a list of relevant choice-of-law rules for such transactions, see Restatement (Second) Conflicts of Law §§ 301 and 302 (1980). See, Vincent Gentile, Should State or Federal Common Law Determine Successor Liability under CERCLA, 38 Chem. Waste Litig. Rep. 870 (Nov. 1999).

i. Purchasing Knowledge as Relevant? What role should a purchaser's knowledge of the seller's potential environmental liability have on the successor liability question? Is there a due diligence duty on purchasers? If actual knowledge increases the likelihood of CERCLA liability on purchasers, what incentives does such a rule create? See Allen Kezsbon & Alan Goldman, Corporate Successor Liability for CERCLA Cleanup Costs: Recent Developments, 7 Toxics L. Rptr. 1156 (1993) (drawing a distinction between the objective and subjective approaches to successor liability and criticizing the subjective knowledge test). See, Michael D. Green, Successors and CERCLA: The Imperfect Analogy to Products Liability and an Alternative Proposal, 87 Nw. L. Rev. 897 (1993).

j. Examples of Outcomes. In Waste Management, Inc. v. Aerospace America, Inc., 156 F.3d 1234 (6th Cir.1998), the Sixth Circuit held that successor liability should apply to a new owner where the language of an asset purchase agreement specifically indemnified prior owners for liabilities "known or unknown" as of 1981 and where a subsequent 1988 asset purchase agreement provided generally for assumption of liabilities, but did not refer specifically to CERCLA.

In United States v. Davis, 1 F.Supp. 2d 125 (D.R.I.1998), the court held that corporate successor liability should not apply where the predecessor still exists and is fully capable of providing relief, or where the successor did not have the opportunity to protect itself through an indemnification clause in an asset purchase agreement or a lower price. Noting that this holding did not preclude successor liability in CERCLA cases, the court held that where the successor corporation is only liable because of the activities of a predecessor, the successor should not be held responsible if the predecessor is a viable company that can provide a remedy.

In North Shore Gas Co. v. Salomon, Inc., 152 F.3d 642 (7th Cir. 1998), the Seventh Circuit held that the doctrine of corporate successor liability should apply to impose responsibility for CERCLA response costs where continuity of ownership and control was shown through retention of controlling stock, identity of officers and directors between the selling and purchasing corporations, and control of officers and directors by controlling stockholders, as well as evidence of a "single business enterprise."

5. LENDERS AS OWNERS

a. *Judicial Division*

Not surprisingly, the government has looked to lenders as a source of resources to fund cleanups. When lenders make loans to owners or operators of facilities and the borrower encounters financial difficulties, the lender may attempt to salvage its commitment by exercising some influence over the operations of the debtor's business. CERCLA § 101(20) does create a limited exemption for lenders by defining "owner" as "not includ[ing] a person, who, without participation in the management of a vessel or facility, holds indicia of ownership primarily to protect his security interest in the vessel or facility."

In 1990, two courts of appeal reached arguably conflicting conclusions with respect to the liability of lenders. In United States v. Fleet Factors Corp., 901 F.2d 1550 (11th Cir.1990), the court held:

> [A] secured creditor may incur section 9607(a)(2) liability, without being an operator, by participating in the financial management of a facility to a degree indicating *a capacity to influence the corporation's treatment of hazardous wastes*. It is *not necessary for the secured creditor actually to involve itself* in the day-to-day operations of the facility in order to be liable. * * * (emphasis added).

Shortly after the decision in *Fleet Factors*, the Ninth Circuit in In re Bergsoe Metal Corp., 910 F.2d 668 (9th Cir.1990), held that "[i]t is clear from the statute that, whatever the precise parameters of 'participation,' there must be *some* actual management of the facility before a secured creditor will fall outside the exception," while "[h]ere there was none."

b. *EPA Lender Rule*

In 1992 the EPA promulgated a final rule on lender liability that was designed to broaden lenders' exemptions from liability beyond the holding in *Fleet Factors*. 40 C.F.R. § 300.1100 "Security Interest Exception" (April 29, 1992). The rule sets forth various actions by the holder of a security interest that will constitute "participation in management," and thereby lose the exemption from CERCLA liability. See Ashland Oil, Inc. v. Sonford Products Corp., 810 F.Supp. 1057 (D.Minn.1993) (finding lender qualified for "safe harbor" from CERCLA liability and new EPA lender liability rule was consistent with the statutory language and entitled to deference).

When the U.S. Court of Appeals for the Eleventh Circuit suggested in 1990 in *Fleet Factors* that banks could forfeit their immunity from CERCLA liability if they had the mere capacity to control their borrower's operation, pressure grew for legislation to amend the secured creditor exemption. Fearing that such amendments could open the door to an evisceration of CERCLA, EPA promulgated its lender liability rule in 1992. 57 Fed. Reg. 18344 (April 29, 1992), codified at 40 C.F.R. § 300.100. This rule expressly rejected the *Fleet Factors* decision, saying lenders are not liable if they exercise financial oversight over a borrower's operations but could become liable if they control operations of the business. The rule also said financial institutions could engage in common "workout" practices without losing their exemption from liability and set forth a non-exclusive list of permissible workout activities. Finally, EPA indicated that lenders could foreclose on contaminated property and remain insulated from liability if they tried to resell the property in an expeditious manner. The agency created a bright-line test lenders could follow that would automatically establish that the lender was foreclosing to protect its security interest and therefore was protected by the exemption.

In 1994, however, the U.S. Court of Appeals for the District of Columbia ruled that the rule exceeded EPA's authority and vacated the regulation. Kelley v. EPA, 15 F.3d 1100 (D.C.Cir.1994). Lenders were then faced with the prospect of having their liability resolved on a case-by-case basis.

c. *Congress Enacts CERCLA Lender Amendment*

(i) *Redefinition of Owner*

In 1996 Congress stepped into the breach, creating lender liability limits, within the definition of "owner," at CERCLA § 107(20)(G)(iv). The amendments add a new section entitled "Exclusion of Lenders Not Participants in Management" to the end of the definition of owner or operator appearing in § 101(20). This new section restates the original secured creditor's exemption and then adds a number of definitions.

Instead of referring to the term "holder" that appears in the EPA lender liability rule, the amendments contain a detailed definition of "lender," which includes nine different classifications of "lenders." Also new is the definition of security interest, which includes "a right under a mortgage, deed or trust, assignment, judgment lien, pledge, security agreement, factoring agreement, or lease and any other right accruing to a person to secure the repayment of money, the performance of a duty, or any other obligation by a non-affiliated person." *Id.* at § 107(20)(G)(ii).

(ii) *Operational Versus Financial or Administrative Control*

The amendments also distinguish between operational control of a borrower and financial or administrative oversight. They define "operational function" to refer to functions "such as [those] of a facility or plant manager, operations manager, chief operating officer, or chief executive officer," while "financial or administrative function" includes functions like those of "a credit manager, accounts payable officer, accounts receivable officer, personnel manager, controller, or chief financial officer, or a similar function." These two definitions track the examples set forth in the EPA lender liability rule. *Id.* at § 107(20)(G)(iv).

A new term that did not appear in the agency's lender liability rule is the definition of "extension of credit." This term encompasses lease-back transactions where "the lessor does not initially select the leased vessel or facility and does not during the lease term control the daily operations or maintenance of the vessel or facility" or where the transaction "conforms with regulations issued by the appropriate federal banking agency or appropriate state bank supervisor." § 107(20)(G)(i).

(iii) Foreclosure Definition

The lender liability amendments also added a definition of "foreclosure." This term refers to acquiring a facility or vessel through the following means:

- Purchase at sale under a judgment or decree, power of sale, or non-judicial foreclosure sale;

- A deed in lieu of foreclosure, or similar conveyance from a trustee;

- Repossession;

- Conveyance pursuant to a previous extension of credit, including the termination of the lease agreement; or

- Any other formal or informal means in which a person acquires title to or possession of a vessel or facility for subsequent disposition in order to protect its security interest.

§ 107(20)(G)(iii).

(iv) Participation in Management

The lender liability amendments expressly state that "participation in management" requires actual participation in the management or operational affairs of a facility and does not include merely having the capacity to influence, or the unexercised right to control facility operations. Thus, Congress rejected the language contained in the *Fleet Factors* decision and also confirmed that the mere presence of clauses in a financing agreement giving a lender the right to take certain actions such as responding to violations of law or releases of hazardous substances will not expose the lender to liability. § 107(20)(F)(i).

Congress also adopted a two-prong test where a lender will be considered participating in management if, while the borrower is still in possession of the facility that is encumbered by the security interest, the lender:

- Exercises decision-making control over environmental compliance for the facility so that it has undertaken responsibility for hazardous substance handling or disposal practices, or,

- Exercises control or responsibility for the overall management of the facility (including day-to-day decision-making for environmental compliance), or over substantially all of the operational functions of the facility other than environmental compliance.

To provide further guidance to lenders, the lender liability amendments contain a list of nine categories of actions that do not constitute participation in management. See, § 107(20)(F)(ii). However, it is unclear what value these examples provide because the statute indicates that these actions will not rise to participation in management so long as they do not fail the two-prong test.

(v) Foreclosure

The lender liability amendments allow financial institutions to foreclose, re-lease (in the case of a sale/leaseback transaction), or sell its collateral so long as the lender attempts to divest itself of the facility or vessel "at the earliest practicable, commercially reasonable terms, taking into account market conditions and legal and regulatory requirements." § 107(20)(E)(ii).

D. PRIVATE COST RECOVERY ACTIONS

1. WHAT ARE PRIVATE COST RECOVERY ACTIONS?

Private cost recovery actions are indispensable to the achievement of CERCLA's objectives of obtaining efficient and effective cleanups of contaminated sites and distributing the costs of such cleanups among responsible parties. The material above, as illustrated by the *Monsanto* and *Alcan Aluminum* cases, demonstrates that frequently the United States and state governments will institute actions against a few or only one party, often the current site owner. In order to undertake remedial action, the involvement of the current owner is indispensable even though the owner is not necessarily a responsible party within CERCLA § 107(a). However, because the cleanups of real property contaminated by hazardous waste can be quite costly, owners of such property face difficult choices about how to remedy that contamination in the most cost-effective manner. As part of their strategy to recover the costs associated with cleanup, many landowners institute private cost recovery actions under the provisions of CERCLA to help them obtain contribution or a total shifting of those costs from a variety of parties who were responsible for the contamination.

CERCLA § 107(a)(4)(B) provides that "any other necessary costs of response incurred by *any other person* consistent with the national contingency plan" may be recovered from those who qualify as PRPs. It is also equally clear that no prior government action or approval is necessary before such an action can be maintained. See 40 C.F.R. § 300.71(a)(3); Cadillac Fairview/Calif., Inc. v. Dow Chem. Co., 840 F.2d 691 (9th Cir.1988). To protect against reimbursing inadequate or ill-conceived cleanups, the court in *Cadillac Fairview* identified two safeguards: (1) the party undertaking the response action must prove that the costs it incurred were "necessary," and (2) it incurred those costs in a manner "consistent with the National Contingency Plan." These cost recovery actions commonly arise in three situations:

a. Where innocent current owners of contaminated property are held liable to a state or federal government for all costs of cleaning up hazardous waste and, to avoid the cost and uncertainty of litigating the issue of liability, choose instead to clean up the property themselves and then sue other potentially responsible parties under CERCLA or state and common law theories of liability;

b. Where a property owner may be under no immediate threat of liability or enforcement order from any governmental entity, but finds the presence of contamination incompatible with its intended use of the property, and chooses to voluntarily clean up the contamination and then sue any PRPs to recover the full cost of the cleanup;

c. Where owners of adjacent property that is not itself contaminated but which is adversely affected by threatened releases of hazardous substances from nearby property attempt to clean up the threatened pollution to abate or avoid damage to their property.

2. PLAINTIFF'S PRIMA FACIE CASE

In the private cost recovery suit the plaintiff must prove the five elements required in all CERCLA actions: (1) the site in question must be a "facility"; (2) the defendant is a liable party under CERCLA § 107(a); (3) there is a release or threatened release; (4) of a hazardous substance has occurred; (5) which has caused the plaintiff to incur response costs. In many cases, these elements may be fairly easy to establish.

But CERCLA § 107(a)(4)(B) also states that private plaintiffs may only recover the "necessary costs of response incurred * * * consistent with the national contingency plan." The NCP is a document that sets forth procedures and standards for waste site cleanups and is designed to ensure that cleanups proceed in a consistent and orderly fashion. The EPA revised the NCP in 1990. See 40 C.F.R. § 300 (1990). How the requirement of "consistency" with the NCP fits into the plaintiff's prima facie case or whose burden it is to prove or disprove such consistency is a matter of considerable importance and difficulty.

One of the factors that influences the requirements of compliance with the NCP is whether the cleanup performed on the property is characterized as a "remedial" action, which results in the application of stringent standards, or as a "removal" action, where the NCP only prescribes minimal requirements.

In general, courts characterizing a cleanup was a removal action often find that plaintiff's costs are consistent with the NCP. See, e.g., General Electric v. Litton Business Systems, Inc., 715 F.Supp. 949 (W.D.Mo.1989), aff'd 920 F.2d 1415 (8th Cir.1990). On the other hand, courts characterizing a cleanup as a remedial action are less inclined to find that cleanup costs incurred are consistent with the NCP. See, e.g., Amland Properties Corp. v. Aluminum Co. of America, 711 F.Supp. 784 (D.N.J.1989); Gussin Enterprises, Inc. v. Rockola, 1993 WL 114643 (N.D.Ill.1993).

3. COMPLIANCE WITH THE NCP

a. General Rule

General Electric Co. v. Litton Industrial Automation Systems, Inc., 920 F.2d 1415 (8th Cir.1990), cert. denied 499 U.S. 937, 111 S.Ct. 1390, 113 L.Ed.2d 446 (1991), is a leading case on consistency with the NCP. From 1959 to 1962, during the occupancy of the company taken over by defendant Litton, improper disposal of cyanide-based electroplating wastes and other pollutants had occurred on the parcel. In the early 1980s, GE, which later acquired the property, and the Missouri Department of Natural Resources (MDNR) investigated the site and decided that no cleanup was necessary. In 1984, GE sold the site to a commercial real estate developer. Shortly thereafter, the MDNR changed its position on the need for a cleanup, and, threatened with CERCLA lawsuits by both its vendee and MDNR, GE agreed to clean up the site. GE then brought a cost recovery action against Litton under CERCLA § 107, which defended on the ground that the cleanup was not consistent with the NCP.

In reviewing the critical finding that the costs incurred were consistent with the NCP despite having omitted some detailed requirements mentioned in the NCP, the Eighth Circuit Court of Appeals wrote:

> We are satisfied that the thorough evaluation that was performed here is consistent with the NCP, specifically with 40 CFR § 300.65(b)(2). The site evaluation does not have to comply strictly with the letter of the NCP, *but only must be consistent with its requirements*. It is not necessary that every factor mentioned by the NCP be dealt with explicitly; thus, for instance, a failure to consider explicitly the weather conditions factor is not fatal to an evaluation's consistency with the NCP. (emphasis in original.)

Id. at 1420. The 1990 revisions of the NCP generally relax the standard of the NCP compliance by permitting private parties to recover their cleanup costs based upon a dual showing that they have (1) substantially complied with the requirements of the NCP and (2) performed a CERCLA-quality cleanup. See, 40 C.F.R. § 300.700(C)(3).

b. *State Claims Cannot Circumvent the NCP*

Not surprisingly, the party who has incurred environmental cleanup costs cannot use state tort law to recover costs of a remediation that did not conform to the superfund law's National Contingency Plan, a federal appeals court ruled in PMC, Inc. v. Sherwin–Williams Co., 151 F.3d 610 (7th Cir.1998). Provisions in CERCLA preserving state causes of action were not intended to allow a party responsible for cleanup to avoid the requirement for NCP compliance. The court ruled plaintiff PMC Inc. may not use the Illinois Contribution Act to recover costs it incurred cleaning up property it purchased from defendant Sherwin–Williams Co. The court said PMC did not submit its cleanup plan for public notice and comment, as the NCP required.

Although PMC conceded that it also dumped hazardous wastes at the site, the trial court found that all cleanup costs should be allocated to Sherwin–Williams. However, PMC could not be awarded any relief under CERCLA § 113 for the costs it already incurred, because it did not submit its cleanup plan for public comment, the district court said. Instead, the district court allowed PMC's claim for all past cleanup costs under the Illinois Contribution Act, reasoning that CERCLA's savings clause, which provides that CERCLA will not "affect or modify in any way the obligations or liabilities of any person under other * * * State law," allows such recovery. See, 42 U.S.C. § 9614(a).

The appeals court reversed, saying the trial court ruling would allow a party to avoid CERCLA's requirement of NCP compliance. CERCLA's savings clause was intended to protect tort victims, the court said, not tortfeasors: "The purpose of CERCLA's savings clause is to preserve to victims of toxic wastes the other remedies they may have under federal or state law. * * * That PMC may have rights against other, more culpable responsible parties does not change PMC into the victim of a tort; it is merely the less guilty of two tortfeasors." 151 F.3d at 618.

Congress intended that the sanction for NCP noncompliance is that a party incurring cleanup costs gets no recovery, the court said. A savings clause is intended to avoid the implication that the federal statute is the exclusive remedy for injury caused by the release of hazardous substances; it is not intended to allow a party to avoid the sanction imposed in the federal statute, the appeals court concluded. The court also affirmed the district court's order that Sherwin–Williams perform future cleanup at the site. The ruling did not affect the district court's allocation to Sherwin–Williams of all site-assessment costs, for which there is no public comment requirement.

A federal district court has also granted summary judgment to a prior landowner, dismissing all claims by current owners because the cleanup undertaken by plaintiffs was not consistent with the NCP because the plaintiffs provided no opportunity for public comment on the proposed cleanup. Estes v. Scotsman Group, Inc., 16 F.Supp. 2d 983 (C.D.Ill.1998).

c. *Is Compliance with State–Ordered Cleanups Sufficient?*

But what if a private party complies with a state agency ordered cleanup? Is that sufficient to ipso facto satisfy the NCP compliance requirement? No, held the Tenth Circuit in Public Service Co. of Colorado v. Gates Rubber Co., 175 F.3d 1177 (10th Cir.1999). PSCO, an owner of contaminated property listed on EPA's liability information system, retained two environmental consultants to investigate and clean-up the site. Subsequently, PSCO entered into an Order of Consent on September 20, 1993, which cataloged the work the Colorado Department of Health (CDH) expected PSCO to perform. It required PSCO to submit monthly progress reports and a final report documenting all soil removal activities. PSCO completed the cleanup in 1996.

In June 1993, PSCO notified the defendants of the subject case of their potential liability for a proportionate share of the $9 million expended to clean up the site. When the defendants balked, PSCO filed the underlying action seeking cost-recovery under CERCLA, 42 U.S.C. 9607(a), for contribution, 42 U.S.C. 9613(f), for declaratory judgment that defendants are liable for any future necessary response costs consistent with the NCP, 28 U.S.C. 2201, 42 U.S.C. 9613(g)(2), and under several state law causes of action.

The Tenth Circuit Court of Appeals, reviewing the district court's ruling de novo, found that both of PSCO's CERCLA claims, for response costs and for contribution, required compliance with the NCP. PSCO unsuccessfully sought to bootstrap itself to the presumption that a state may recover "all costs not inconsistent with the national contingency plan," rather than comply with the requirement for private parties in which it must prove its response action was consistent with the NCP. PSCO contended its cleanup, geared to less stringent requirements of a removal action, was generated by CDH's Consent Order and should be presumed to be consistent with the NCP.

PSCO next contended that its CDH-mandated cleanup must be deemed consistent with the NCP because of the state's intensive involvement and comprehensive oversight in the cleanup. It urged in effect the District Court erroneously applied a strict compliance standard rejecting its work because the documents did not bear the precise labels of the NCP requirements and that the district court devalued its effort to involve the surrounding community when, in fact, "the CDH did function as *parens patriae*." The Court of Appeals found that neither the record nor precedent supported PSCO's position. The record disclosed that PSCO undertook the site cleanup without reference to the NCP. Its predominating remedial concern was financial and to defuse or minimize any public scrutiny of the effort. Neither PSCO nor CDH developed an alternative course of action touching on "project scoping, data collection, risk assessment, treatability studies, and analysis of alternatives" as required under the NCP. The Consent Order was also silent on any requirement to inform the public about the site and its cleanup, nor did

PSCO do anything else to fulfill the NCP's community relations obligations. The court commented specifically on the NCP's community relations obligations, which it concluded PSCO did nothing to fulfill:

> Indeed, PSCO's only effort to involve the public was to place signs in English on the fence erected to contain the Site. The signs read "Any Question About Site Activities, please call 294–8488." This effort to inform the predominantly Hispanic community neighboring the Site or to solicit their comments wants substance.

175 F.3d at 1185. Accordingly, the Court of Appeals found that PSCO failed to set forth any facts permitting it to find a triable issue on the consistency of its cleanup with the NCP and therefore affirmed the district court's order granting the defendants summary judgment.

d. *Moral of the Story on the NCP Compliance*

1. *Actions taken pursuant to an EPA Consent Decree or Order.* One of the few bright line rules that emerge from the NCP-related case law is that actions taken by private parties pursuant to a court-approved Consent Decree with the EPA or an EPA Order are presumed to be consistent with the NCP. Bancamerica Commercial Corp. v. Trinity Indus., Inc., 900 F.Supp. 1427 (D.Kan.1995) (presumes NCP compliance for action taken pursuant to an EPA order). This rule makes sense because the existence of an EPA order or consent decree should normally eliminate the need for court concern that private parties are conducting self-serving and unnecessary cleanups.

The NCP itself creates a presumption that private party costs incurred in complying with an EPA cleanup mandate are consistent with the NCP. 40 C.F.R. § 300.700(C)(3)(i).

2. *Public participation.* Another bright line rule is that failure to provide some opportunity for public participation in selecting remedial actions will constitute a failure to comply with the NCP. This rule is sometimes easier to state than to apply because the "opportunity" for public comment can be provided in a variety of ways, including public meetings conducted by state or local agencies.

The requirement that the public must be given an opportunity to comment on remedy selection is clearly set forth in the 1990 NCP. Section 300.71 of the 1990 NCP provides that a private party conducting remedial activities must:

> provide[ ] for an opportunity for *appropriate* public comment concerning the selection of a remedial action consistent with 300.67.

40 C.F.R. § 300.71.

Section 300.67 provides:

> [F]easibility studies that outline alternative remedial measures must be provided to the public for review and comment for a period of not less than 21 calendar days. Such review and comment shall precede selection of the remedial response. * * *

40 C.F.R. § 300.67.

The lack of *any* opportunity for public comment is considered a material and substantial departure from the NCP. Many courts have so held, including various federal courts of appeal. See, e.g., Sherwin–Williams Co. v. City of Hamtramck, 840 F.Supp. 470, 476–78 (E.D.Mich. 1993); Channel Master Satellite Sys., Inc. v. JFD Elec. Corp., 748 F.Supp. 373, 389–90 (E.D.N.C.1990); County Line Inv. Co. v. Tinney, 933 F.2d 1508, 1514–15 (10th Cir.1991).

4. PROOF OF COMPLIANCE AS AFFECTING LIABILITY OR DAMAGES

One major judicial disagreement revolves around whether a showing of consistency with the NCP goes to the issue of liability, or whether liability can be determined independently of compliance with the NCP, with consistency bearing only on the amount of damages eligible for recovery.

One line of cases holds that consistency with the NCP is an element of a private plaintiff's prima facie case on liability. Artesian Water Company v. Government of New Castle County, 659 F.Supp. 1269 (D.Del.1987), aff'd 851 F.2d 643 (3d Cir.1988), so held, noting that the NCP plays a central role in the CERCLA scheme in that it establishes a standard against which response actions are judged appropriate or inappropriate in the first instance, not merely a limit on the amount of damages recoverable from liable parties. In any event, a failure to comply with the NCP will bar recovery of response costs. Carroll v. Litton Systems, Inc., 47 F.3d 1164 (4th Cir.1995), cert. denied, 516 U.S. 816, 116 S.Ct. 70, 133 L.Ed.2d 31 (1995).

In Amland Properties Corporation v. Aluminum Company of America, 711 F.Supp. 784 (D.N.J.1989), the district court stated that "the weight of recent authority in cases * * * of private party recovery actions holds that response costs incurred consistent with the NCP is an element of a CERCLA plaintiff's case on liability." In *Amland*, the determination of consistency was made after a full record had been developed. Accordingly, the *Amland* court stated it must address consistency with the NCP in order to determine whether a plaintiff is entitled to recover *any* of its response costs and to avoid the risk of a pointless trial at some later date. Accord, Ambrogi v. Gould, Inc., 750 F.Supp. 1233 (M.D.Pa.1990).

Another line of cases has differed with the above rationale and permitted a ruling on liability independent of a ruling on the specific amount of costs that a party may recover. In T & E Industries, Inc. v. Safety Light Corp., 680 F.Supp. 696, 709 (D.N.J.1988), the district court held that a plaintiff may establish liability under CERCLA § 107 by establishing that a "covered person" caused a "release" or "threatened release" of a "hazardous substance" from a "facility" which caused the plaintiff to incur "response costs." The court held that if undisputed facts establish each of these elements, the plaintiff is entitled to a summary judgment declaring the defendant liable. With regard to costs, the decision held:

> While the determination of whether such costs were "necessary" and "consistent" with the National Contingency Plan does not preclude this Court from entering summary judgment as to specific amounts of the costs, the question of amount can be dealt with at a later date. For now, it is clear that certain items which T&E seeks to recover are included within the meaning of response costs under CERCLA.

What are the strategic consequences of how the courts treat the issue of NCP compliance affecting damages or liability? Which rule is more likely to expedite cleanups? If a plaintiff fails to establish NCP consistency, could a common law tort theory rescue the case? Which of the basic theories considered in Chapters 2, 3 and 4 is most likely to offer assistance?

5. RECOVERY OF ATTORNEYS' FEES

In Alyeska Pipeline Service Co. v. Wilderness Society, 421 U.S. 240, 247, 95 S.Ct. 1612, 1616, 44 L.Ed.2d 141 (1975), the Supreme Court held that under the "American Rule" litigants must pay their own costs and "the prevailing litigant is ordinarily not entitled to collect a reasonable attorney's fee from the loser." In Runyon v. McCrary, 427 U.S. 160, 96 S.Ct. 2586, 49 L.Ed.2d 415 (1976), the Court stated that without explicit congressional authorization, attorneys' fees are not recoverable as a cost of litigation under federal statutes. With these principles in mind, the courts were initially divided on whether attorneys' fees are recoverable as a "necessary cost of response" under CERCLA § 107(a)(4)(B).

In General Electric Co. v. Litton Industrial Automation Systems, Inc., 920 F.2d 1415 (8th Cir.1990), cert. denied 499 U.S. 937, 111 S.Ct. 1390, 113 L.Ed.2d 446 (1991) (the same opinion in which the court adopted a liberal view of NCP consistency), the Eighth Circuit determined that the statutory language in CERCLA was explicit enough to permit GE to recover attorneys' fees in a private cost recovery action. The court looked for guidance in CERCLA § 107(a)(4)(B) which allows private parties to recover "necessary costs of response * * * consistent with the national contingency plan." "Response" is defined in § 101(25) as "remove, removal, remedy, and remedial action; all such terms (including the terms 'removal' and 'remedial action') *include enforcement activities thereto*." The court determined that a private party cost recovery action "such as this one is an enforcement activity within the meaning of the statute." The court's rationale focused on creating incentives for prompt, voluntary cleanups of contaminated property given that litigation costs could easily approach or even exceed the response costs, thereby serving as a disincentive to clean the site.

On the other side of the ledger, the Sixth Circuit in Donahey v. Bogle, 987 F.2d 1250 (6th Cir.1993) and two Eighth Circuit decisions, Gopher Oil Co. v. Union Oil Co. of California, 955 F.2d 519 (8th Cir.1992) and United States v. Mexico Feed & Seed Co., 980 F.2d 478 (8th Cir.1992), have followed *Litton.*

In Stanton Road Associates v. Lohrey Enterprises, 984 F.2d 1015 (9th Cir.1993), the Ninth Circuit's response to the Eighth Circuit was quite direct: "We are unpersuaded by the Eighth Circuit's explanation of its holding." The words "enforcement activities" used in CERCLA § 101(25) "do not explicitly authorize the payment of attorney fees," because "Congress has repeatedly demonstrated that it knows how to express its intention to create an exception to the American Rule." For example, in § 310(f) of CERCLA, Congress authorized courts "to award costs of litigation (including reasonable attorneys' fees and expert witness fees to the prevailing party or the substantially prevailing party whenever the court determines such an award is appropriate in citizen suit actions.").

The Ninth Circuit also disagreed that "necessary costs of response" is explicit enough to authorize the awarding of attorneys' fees. Rather than reading attorneys' fees out of § 107(a)(4) of CERCLA, which the Eighth Circuit said it feared doing, the Ninth Circuit felt that under *Alyeska* and *Runyon* it could not justify reading attorneys' fees into the statute. Finally, it rejected the public policy argument that Congress must have intended for private litigants to recover attorneys' fees to effectuate the rapid cleanup policy supposedly underlying CERCLA because *Alyeska* specifically rejected such an approach.

In the following decision the Supreme Court answered this important question.

KEY TRONIC CORPORATION v. UNITED STATES ET AL.

United States Supreme Court, 1994.
511 U.S. 809, 114 S.Ct. 1960, 128 L.Ed.2d 797.

JUSTICE STEVENS delivered the opinion of the Court.

Petitioner Key Tronic Corporation, one of several parties responsible for contaminating a landfill, brought this action to recover a share of its cleanup costs from other responsible parties. The question presented is whether attorney's fees are "necessary costs of response" within the meaning of § 107(a)(4)(B) of the Comprehensive Environmental Response, Compensation, and Liability Act of 1980 (CERCLA), as amended by the Superfund Amendments and Reauthorization Act of 1986 (SARA), 100 Stat. 1613, and therefore recoverable in such an action.

I

During the 1970's Key Tronic and other parties, including the United States Air Force, disposed of liquid chemicals at the Colbert

Landfill in eastern Washington State. In 1980 the Washington Department of Ecology (WDOE) determined that the water supply in the surrounding area had been contaminated by these chemicals. Various lawsuits ensued, including formal proceedings against Key Tronic, the Air Force, and other parties.

Two of those proceedings were settled. In one settlement with WDOE and the Environmental Protection Agency (EPA), Key Tronic agreed to contribute $4.2 million to an EPA cleanup fund. In the other, the Air Force agreed to pay the EPA $1.45 million. The EPA subsequently released the Air Force from further liability pursuant to CERCLA § 122(g)(5), 42 U.S.C. § 9622(g)(5) which provides that a party that has resolved its liability to the United States shall not be liable for contribution claims regarding matters addressed in the settlement.

Key Tronic thereafter brought this action against the United States and other parties seeking to recover part of its $4.2 million commitment to the EPA in a contribution claim under CERCLA § 113(f), 42 U.S.C. § 9613(f), and seeking an additional $1.2 million for response costs that it incurred before the settlements in a cost recovery claim under CERCLA § 107(a)(4)(B), 42 U.S.C. § 9607(a)(4)(B). The $1.2 million included attorney's fees for three types of legal services: (1) the identification of other potentially responsible parties (PRP's), including the Air Force, that were liable for the cleanup; (2) preparation and negotiation of its agreement with the EPA; and (3) the prosecution of this litigation.

The District Court dismissed Key Tronic's $4.2 million contribution claim against the Air Force when Key Tronic conceded that § 122(g)(5) precluded it from recovering any part of the consent decree obligation. Key Tronic's claim for $1.2 million of additional response costs could be pursued under CERCLA § 107(a)(4)(B), 42 U.S.C. § 9607 the court held, because it related to matters not covered by the Air Force's settlement with the EPA. 766 F. Supp. 865, 868 (E.D.Wash.1991). Section 107(a) provides that responsible parties are liable for "any * * * necessary costs of response incurred by any other person consistent with the national contingency plan." 42 U.S.C. § 9607(a)(4)(B). CERCLA's definitional section 101(25), as amended by SARA, provides that "response" or "respond" "means remove, removal, remedy, and remedial action" and that "all such terms (including the terms 'removal' and 'remedial action') include enforcement activities related thereto." 42 U.S.C. § 9601(25). Construing § 107 and § 101(25) "liberally to achieve the overall objectives of the statute," 766 F. 2d, at 872, the District Court concluded that a private party may incur enforcement costs and that such costs include attorney's fees for bringing a cost recovery action under § 107. The court went on to decide that attorney's fees encompassed within Key Tronic's PRP search costs also were recoverable as an enforcement activity under CERCLA, and that the costs Key Tronic's attorneys incurred in negotiating the agreement with the EPA were recoverable as necessary response costs under § 107.

The Court of Appeals reversed. 984 F. 2d 1025, 1028 (C.A.9 1993). Relying on its decision in *Stanton Road Associates* v. *Lohrey Enterprises*, 984 F. 2d 1015 (C.A.9 1993), which prohibited a litigant in a private response cost recovery action from obtaining attorney's fees from a party responsible for the pollution, the court held that the District Court lacked authority to award attorney's fees in this case. The court concluded that *Stanton Road* likewise precluded an award of attorney's fees for Key Tronic's search for other responsible parties and for negotiating the consent decree. "Because Congress has not explicitly authorized private litigants to recover their legal expenses incurred in a private cost recovery action," the District Court's award of attorney's fees could not stand. 984 F. 2d, at 1028. Judge Canby dissented, reasoning that Congress' 1986 amendment of the definition of "response" meant to authorize the recovery of attorney's fees even in private litigants' cost recovery actions.

Other courts addressing this question have differed over the extent to which attorney's fees are a necessary cost of response under CERCLA. See *General Electric Co.* v. *Litton Industrial Automation Systems, Inc.*, 920 F. 2d 1415 (C.A.8 1990) (fees recoverable); *Donahey* v. *Bogle*, 987 F. 2d 1250, 1256 (C.A.6 1993) (same); *Juniper Development Group* v. *Kahn*, 993 F. 2d 915, 933 (C.A.1 1993) (litigation fees not recoverable); *FMC Corp.* v. *Aero Industries, Inc.*, 998 F. 2d 842 (C.A.10 1993) (only nonlitigation fees may be recoverable). We granted certiorari to resolve the conflict.

As its name implies, CERCLA is a comprehensive statute that grants the President broad power to command government agencies and private parties to clean up hazardous waste sites. Sections 104 and 106 provide the framework for federal abatement and enforcement actions that the President, the EPA as his delegated agent, or the Attorney General initiates. 42 U.S.C. §§ 9604 9606. These actions typically require private parties to incur substantial costs in removing hazardous wastes and responding to hazardous conditions. Section 107 sets forth the scope of the liabilities that may be imposed on private parties and the defenses that they may assert. 42 U.S.C. § 9607.

Our cases establish that attorney's fees generally are not a recoverable cost of litigation "absent explicit congressional authorization." *Runyon* v. *McCrary*, 427 U.S. 160, 185 (1976) (citing *Alyeska Pipeline Service Co.* v. *Wilderness Society*, 421 U.S. 240, 247 (1975)). Recognition of the availability of attorney's fees therefore requires a determination that "Congress intended to set aside this longstanding American rule of law." *Runyon*, 427 U. S., at 185–186. Neither CERCLA § 107, the liabilities and defenses provision, nor § 113, which authorizes contribution claims, expressly mentions the recovery of attorney's fees. The absence of specific reference to attorney's fees is not dispositive if the statute otherwise evinces an intent to provide for such fees. The Eighth Circuit, for example, found "a sufficient degree of explicitness" in CERCLA's references to "necessary costs of response" and "enforcement activities" to warrant the award of attorney's fees and expenses. Mere "generalized commands," however, will not suffice to authorize such fees. *Id.*, at 186.

The three components of Key Tronic's claim for attorney's fees raise somewhat different issues. We first consider whether the fees for prosecuting this action against the Air Force are recoverable under CERCLA. That depends, again, upon whether the "enforcement activities" included in § 101(25)'s definition of "response" encompass a private party's action to recover cleanup costs from other potentially responsible parties such that the attorney's fees associated with that action are then "necessary costs of response" within § 107(a)(4)(B).

The 1986 SARA amendments to CERCLA are the genesis of the term "enforcement activities"; we begin, therefore, by considering the statutory basis for the claim in the original CERCLA enactment and the SARA amendments' effect on it. In its original form CERCLA contained no express provision authorizing a private party that had incurred cleanup costs to seek contribution from other potentially responsible parties. In numerous cases, however, district courts interpreted the statute—particularly the § 107 provisions outlining the liabilities and defenses of persons against whom the Government may assert claims— to impliedly authorize such a cause of action.

The 1986 SARA amendments included a provision—CERCLA § 113(f)—that expressly created a cause of action for contribution. See 42 U.S.C. § 9613(f). Other SARA provisions, moreover, appeared to endorse the judicial decisions recognizing a cause of action under § 107 by presupposing that such an action existed. An amendment to § 107 itself, for example, refers to "amounts recoverable in an action under this section." 42 U.S.C. § 9607(a)(4)(D). The new contribution section also contains a reference to a "civil action * * * under section 107(a)." 42 U.S.C. § 9613(f)(1). Thus the statute now expressly authorizes a cause of action for contribution in § 113 and impliedly authorizes a similar and somewhat overlapping remedy in § 107.

As we have said, neither § 107 nor § 113 expressly calls for the recovery of attorney's fees by the prevailing party. In contrast, two SARA amendments contain explicit authority for the award of attorney's fees. A new provision authorizing private citizens to bring suit to enforce the statute, ... expressly authorizes the award of "reasonable attorney and expert witness fees" to the prevailing party. 42 U.S.C. § 9659(f). And an amendment to the section authorizing the Attorney General to bring abatement actions provides that a person erroneously ordered to pay response costs may in some circumstances recover counsel fees from the Government. See 42 U.S.C. § 9606(b)(2)(E). Since its enactment CERCLA also has expressly authorized the recovery of fees in actions brought by employees claiming discriminatory treatment based on their disclosure of statutory violations. See 42 U.S.C. § 9610(c) ("aggregate amount of all costs and expenses (including the attorney's fees)" is recoverable).

Judicial decisions, rather than explicit statutory text, also resolved an issue that arose frequently under the original version of CERCLA—that is, whether the award in a government enforcement action seeking to recover cleanup costs could encompass its litigation expenses, including attorney's fees. Here, too, District Courts generally agreed that such fees were recoverable. Congress arguably endorsed these holdings, as well, in the SARA amendment redefining the term "response" to include related "enforcement activities." Key Tronic contends that a private action under § 107 is one of the enforcement activities covered by that definition and that fees should therefore be available in private litigation as well as in government actions.

For three reasons, we are unpersuaded. First, although § 107 unquestionably provides a cause of action for private parties to seek recovery of cleanup costs, that cause of action is not explicitly set out in the text of the statute. To conclude that a provision that only impliedly authorizes suit nonetheless provides for attorney's fees with the clarity required by *Alyeska* would be unusual if not unprecedented. Indeed, none of our cases has authorized fee awards to prevailing parties in such circumstances.

Second, Congress included two express provisions for fee awards in the SARA amendments without including a similar provision in either § 113, which expressly authorizes contribution claims, or in § 107, which impliedly authorizes private parties to recover cleanup costs from other PRP's. These omissions strongly suggest a deliberate decision not to authorize such awards.

Third, we believe it would stretch the plain terms of the phrase "enforcement activities" too far to construe it as encompassing the kind of private cost recovery action at issue in this case. Though we offer no comment on the extent to which that phrase forms the basis for the Government's recovery of attorney's fees through § 107, the term "enforcement activity" is not sufficiently explicit to embody a private action under § 107 to recover cleanup costs. Given our adherence to a general practice of not awarding fees to a prevailing party absent explicit statutory authority, *Alyeska Pipeline Service Co.* v. *Wilderness Society*, 421 U. S., at 262, we conclude that CERCLA § 107 does not provide for the award of private litigants' attorney's fees associated with bringing a cost recovery action.

The conclusion we reach with respect to litigation related fees does not signify that all payments that happen to be made to a lawyer are unrecoverable expenses under CERCLA. On the contrary, some lawyers' work that is closely tied to the actual cleanup may constitute a necessary cost of response in and of itself under the terms of § 107(a)(4)(B). The component of Key Tronic's claim that covers the work performed in identifying other potentially responsible parties falls in this category. Unlike the litigation services at issue in *Alyeska*, these efforts might well be performed by engineers, chemists, private investigators or other professionals who are not lawyers. As the Tenth Circuit observed, the

American rule set out in *Alyeska* does not govern such fees "because they are not incurred in pursuing litigation." *FMC Corp.* v. *Aero Industries, Inc.*, 998 F. 2d 842, 847 (1993).

The District Court in this case recognized the role Key Tronic's search for other responsible parties played in uncovering the Air Force's disposal of wastes at the site and in prompting the EPA to initiate its enforcement action against the Air Force. 766 F. Supp., at 872, n. 4. Tracking down other responsible solvent polluters increases the probability that a cleanup will be effective and get paid for. Key Tronic is therefore quite right to claim that such efforts significantly benefited the entire cleanup effort and served a statutory purpose apart from the reallocation of costs. These kinds of activities are recoverable costs of response clearly distinguishable from litigation expenses.

This reasoning does not extend, however, to the legal services performed in connection with the negotiations between Key Tronic and the EPA that culminated in the consent decree. Studies that Key Tronic's counsel prepared or supervised during those negotiations may indeed have aided the EPA and may also have affected the ultimate scope and form of the cleanup. We nevertheless view such work as primarily protecting Key Tronic's interests as a defendant in the proceedings that established the extent of its liability. As such, these services do not constitute "necessary costs of response" and are not recoverable under CERCLA.

The judgment of the Court of Appeals is affirmed in part and reversed in part, and the case is remanded for further proceedings consistent with this opinion.

It is so ordered.

JUSTICE SCALIA, with whom JUSTICE BLACKMUN and JUSTICE THOMAS join, dissenting in part.

Notes and Questions

1. Do you agree with Justice Stevens' arguments for rejecting the recoverability of attorneys' fees related to the litigation process itself? How important is the exception which the opinion carves out for attorneys' fees associated with the plaintiff's activities in identifying other PRPs?

2. *What About Reliance on State Law?* The cases have held–post-*Key Tronic*–that if state statutory law allows the prevailing party in a CERCLA-like action recovery of attorneys' fees, *Key Tronic* does not preclude such a result. Control Data Corp. v. S.C.S.C. Corp., 53 F.3d 930 (8th Cir.1995).

3. *Government Recovery of Fees?* In *Key Tronic*, the Supreme Court left open the question of whether the EPA might be able to recover its fees, limiting its holding to private plaintiffs. Subsequent opinions, focusing on the "enforcement activities" language have held that the EPA can recover reasonable attorneys' fees. B.F. Goodrich v. Betkoski, 99 F.3d 505 (2d Cir.1996). In United States v. Chapman, 146 F.3d 1166 (9th Cir.1998), the court reasoned that recovery of government attorneys' fees is also supported

by sound policy. CERCLA "is remedial legislation that should be construed liberally to carry out its purpose." In this case, Chapman was given the opportunity to clean up his property, and EPA intervened only after he had refused to do so. When he refused to pay for the EPA action, this court action became necessary. Awarding attorneys fees "can act as a powerful deterrent to other parties responsible for the cleanup of hazardous materials." The award can encourage parties to take their own remedial action and "might even encourage responsible parties not to pollute and contaminate property in the first place."

Chapman argued that the EPA could collect only those attorneys' fees that the court deemed reasonable, not necessarily its actual fees. The request for $400,000 in attorneys' fees was unreasonable, he claimed, when the response action only cost $34,000. The court agreed that some reasonableness requirement was necessary and remanded the matter to the district court. That court was to "provide a concise but clear explanation of its reasons for the fee award." Its determination was to be based on the standards set by the Supreme Court in a civil rights action, Hensley v. Eckerhart, 461 U.S. 424, 103 S.Ct. 1933, 76 L.Ed.2d 40 (1983).

6. CAUSATION IN PRIVATE COST RECOVERY ACTIONS

a. What Kind of Test to Apply

Does the private party suing to recover its costs secure the same advantages of watered-down causation standards, strict, and joint and several liability? In Dedham Water Co. v. Cumberland Farms Dairy, Inc., 889 F.2d 1146, 1150, 1154 (1st Cir.1989), the court phrased the causation issue as follows:

> The central question on appeal is whether, under CERCLA, the plaintiff must prove that a hazardous substance released by the defendant's facility physically migrated onto the plaintiff's property, causing contamination of the well field, or whether it is sufficient for the plaintiff to prove that there were releases or threatened releases of a hazardous substance from defendant's facility which caused the plaintiff reasonably to incur response costs, regardless of whether physical migration actually occurred.

The court answered the inquiry:

> CERCLA states: "the owner and operator * * * of a facility * * * from which there is a release or a threatened release of a hazardous substance, which causes the incurrence of response costs, shall be liable * * *." 42 U.S.C.A. § 9607(a). A literal reading of the statute imposes liability if releases or threatened releases from defendant's facility cause the plaintiff to incur response costs; it does *not* say that liability is imposed only if the defendant causes actual contamination of the plaintiff's property.
>
> To our knowledge, every court that has addressed this issue, with the exception of the district court in the instant case, has held that it is not necessary to prove actual contamination of plaintiff's

property by defendant's waste in order to establish liability under CERCLA. There is nothing in the statute, its legislative history, or the case law, which requires proof that the defendant's hazardous waste actually have migrated to plaintiff's property, causing contamination of plaintiff's property, before CERCLA liability is triggered. Nor is there anything in the statute suggesting that a "two-site" case be treated differently than a one-site case, where the issue is whether a release or threat of release caused "response costs." (emphasis in original.)

On remand, Dedham Water Co. v. Cumberland Farms Dairy, Inc., 770 F.Supp. 41 (D.Mass.1991), the district court held that plaintiffs' expenditure of funds for building and operating a water treatment plant was not related to any perceived threat of contamination of plaintiffs' well field by the defendant's facility, and thus that the plaintiffs could not recover from the defendant for those costs. The court concluded that from the record in this case, "the response for which the plaintiffs seek reimbursement was not related to the 'potential threat.'" Although the court said that the defendant appeared to be "a blatant polluter" and that it "would be gratifying to exact reimbursement from the defendant for the benefit of the plaintiffs," it concluded that "[a]s long as causation is a necessary element of liability * * * I cannot do so on this record." Are you surprised by this outcome? The court of appeals affirmed, 972 F.2d 453 (1st Cir.1992).

In cases such as *Dedham Water* the site of the release is different from the site on which response costs are incurred. The courts have shown more diversity in developing causation standards in these two-site cases. The Third Circuit discussed the causation question in Artesian Water Co. v. Government of New Castle County, 659 F.Supp. 1269 (D.Del.1987), aff'd 851 F.2d 643 (3d Cir.1988), where a water company sought recovery for its response costs in monitoring and evaluating the impact on its wells of leachate from an adjacent landfill. Applying a substantial factor rule of causation, the court found the plaintiff entitled to relief. The court stated first that CERCLA's strict liability scheme requires that a plaintiff demonstrate a causal connection between the defendant's released substance and the response costs incurred. However, the court rejected a "but-for" causation test because more than two causes had acted concurrently to bring about the harm, including pollutants from another landfill, saltwater intrusion, and the state's aquifer management policy. The court ruled that if the release or threatened release of contaminants from the defendant's site is a substantial factor in causing a plaintiff to incur response costs, then the court will hold the defendant liable under CERCLA.

Does *Dedham Water* adopt a substantial factor test of causation? The district court had required that defendant's hazardous substances have actually migrated to and contaminated plaintiff's property; in other words, the critical issue was "whether contaminants from the Cumberland Farms site ever reached the groundwater and thereafter found their way to WL–3." What, if anything, is objectionable respecting the district court's test? What disadvantages and advantages do you see in applying watered-down causation standards in private cost recovery actions? Is the substantial factor test of *Artesian Water* a logical approach? Later we examine in some detail causation standards in contribution actions where you will see considerable evolution toward more, not less, rigorous tests of causation.

b. Special Problems of Two–Site Cases

These two-site, passive migration cases present interesting issues of divisibility and causation as illustrated by Dent v. Beazer Materials & Services, Inc., 133 F.3d 914 (4th Cir.1998). In *Dent* the site consisted of two tracts, one consisting of 45 acres (Koppers' property, Beazer's predecessor), where for 50 years wood-treating chemicals had been disposed of (5 to 7 million gallons worth); and a second tract of 57 acres (Dent property) which was utilized for about 18 years by Agrico and later Conoco for a fertilizer manufacturing plant subsequently acquired by Dent. An EPA investigation revealed that the creosote released from the Koppers property for 50 years had resulted in some migration of those chemicals by passive subsurface migration to the Dent property and from there to the Ashley River. After the EPA commenced its investigation and remediation process, Dent sued Beazer, Agrico, and Conoco for cost recovery for past and future response costs incurred or to be incurred, pursuant to § 107(a), and defendants predictably counterclaimed for contribution against Dent and each other.

The district court explained Beazer's counterclaims against Conoco and Agrico stating that Conoco and Agrico were liable persons not only with respect to the release of hazardous substances from their fertilizer operations on the Dent property, but also with respect to the hazardous wood-treating substances released on the Koppers property that had found their way by subsurface migration onto the Dent property. The district court rejected Beazer's contention that Conoco and Agrico should be held jointly and severally liable with it for all past response costs incurred as a result of the release of hazardous substances on both properties comprising the Superfund site. The district court first assumed that Conoco and Agrico were potentially liable persons by virtue of the release of fertilizer constituents on the Dent property during their respective periods of ownership of that property. But, applying relevant divisibility and apportionment principles, see *Monsanto*, 858 F.2d at 171, it then held that those parties should not be held jointly liable with Beazer for all response costs incurred in remediation of the entire site.

The court of appeals adopted the district court's analysis respecting divisibility and causation:

> First, the [district] court found that any harms to the site caused by wood-treating chemicals were sufficiently distinguishable by scientific testing procedures from any caused by fertilizer constituents to permit reasonable apportionment of related response costs and other damages between the persons respectively responsible for release of

the two types. It then held that because no harm caused by wood-treating chemicals could be fairly attributed to Conoco and Agrico, they could only be severally liable, under property apportionment principles, for any harm and resulting response costs caused by fertilizer constituents for whose release they were responsible. And, it then found that the only hazardous fertilizer substance identified on the site was lead, and that it was not present in sufficient quantities to require any remediation. On the basis of these findings, the district court concluded that under relevant apportionment principles, all liability for response costs incurred at the site should be apportioned to Beazer and none to Conoco or Agrico. 133 F.3d at 914 [Table] [1998 WL 24977*6]. It correctly ruled as a matter of law on the undisputed facts before it that no harm caused by wood-treating constituents could fairly be attributed to Conoco and Agrico. No wood-treating constituents were released by those parties during their prior ownerships of the Dent property and they could not be held to have released those constituents simply because, unbeknownst to them and beyond any means of their control, the substances were leaching onto their property from their release point on the Koppers property by subsurface migration. Strict liability could not, therefore, be imposed upon them for the release of those constituents under any of the relevant "liable person" provisions of § 107(a)(1)-(4). *Id.* [Table], [1998 WL 24977 *6].

The Fourth Circuit cited as authority for its affirmance United States v. Rohm & Haas Co., 2 F.3d 1265, 1280 (3d Cir.1993) (recognizing that upon proof that a hazardous substance found on a site could not be "fairly attributable" to a party sued under § 107(a), the party's properly "apportioned share would be zero"); United States v. Alcan Aluminum Corp., 964 F.2d 252, 270 (3d Cir.1992) (holding that potentially liable party could avoid all liability by proving its released hazardous substances did not contribute to response costs.) But *Alcan* recognized the conflict with Nurad, Inc. v. William E. Hooper & Sons Co., 966 F.2d 837, 845 (4th Cir.1992) (former property owner liable for leakage of hazardous substance into soil of own property notwithstanding participation merely passive), cert. denied, 506 U.S. 940, 113 S.Ct. 377, 121 L.Ed.2d 288 (1992).

And finally, it concluded that the fertilizer constituents for whose disposal Conoco and Agrico were responsible parties "had *caused no harm* requiring remediation * * * because the quantities of lead [the only hazardous substance identified therein] were too low to require CERCLA remediation, and indeed evidence was that efforts to remove the quantities of lead involved would be environmentally counter-productive." 133 F.3d 914 (Table), 1998 WL 24977 *6.

E. STATUTORY DEFENSES
TO CERCLA LIABILITY

Given the incredible advantages accruing to governmental and private plaintiffs under the liability scheme of CERCLA one might have expected the emergence, either legislatively or judicially, of major affirmative defenses to liability. Just as § 107(a) lists the categories of responsible parties, § 107(b) sets forth the three statutory defenses. The language of § 107(b) is as follows:

> There shall be no liability under subsection (a) of this section for a person otherwise liable who can establish by a preponderance of the evidence that the release or threat of release of a hazardous substance and the damages resulting therefrom were caused solely by:
>
> > (1) an act of God;
> >
> > (2) an act of war;
> >
> > (3) an act or omission of a third party other than an employee or agent of the defendant, or than one whose act or omission occurs in connection with a contractual relationship, existing directly or indirectly, with the defendant * * * , if the defendant establishes by a preponderance of the evidence that (a) he exercised due care with respect to the hazardous substance concerned, taking into consideration the characteristics of such hazardous substance, in light of all relevant facts and circumstances, and (b) he took precautions against foreseeable acts or omissions of any such third party and the consequences that could foreseeably result from such acts or omissions; or
> >
> > (4) any combination of the foregoing paragraphs.

In addition, the 1986 amendments provided a fourth statutory defense, known as the innocent landowner defense, which is a variation of the third-party defense. This section addresses first the third-party defense set forth in § 107(b)(3), and then the innocent landowner defense created by a combination of §§ 101(35) and 107(b)(3).

1. THIRD–PARTY DEFENSE

What do you suppose Congress had in mind when it included § 107(b)(3)? The midnight marauder who secretly dumps barrels of substances on property that, it turns out, is owned by defendant?

It is important for the student to realize that these affirmative defenses essentially shift the burden of proof on causation to the defendant to establish that the release *"was caused solely by"* an act or actions of a third party. Two major issues that have emerged are first, whether the "contractual relationship" that bars reliance on the defense must itself relate in some way to the hazardous substances and, second, how to apply the "due care" requirements. As to the relationship between the contractual relationship and the release, the leading decision, Westwood Pharmaceuticals, Inc. v. National Fuel Gas Distribution Corp., 964 F.2d 85, 87 (2d Cir.1992), reasons as follows:

> The site which is the subject matter of this action was purchased in 1925 by Iroquois. Iroquois conducted gas manufacturing and storage operations on the land through 1951. For several years

thereafter, it continued to use the site for gas compression and storage. During these operations Iroquois placed or used various underground pipes and structures at the site. In 1968, Iroquois demolished certain structures on the northeast portion of the site, but left other structures on the site standing.

Iroquois sold the site to Westwood in 1972 for $60,100. Westwood demolished the remaining structures on the site and constructed a warehouse on the southern portion of the site. During these construction activities and associated soil testing, Westwood discovered various subsurface contaminants.

In the instant action Westwood seeks to recover the response costs—the costs of cleaning up the contaminants—for which it claims National Fuel is liable.

The district court held that National Fuel had raised a triable issue of fact by contending that, under the "third-party defense" of CERCLA § 107(b)(3), it was not liable on Westwood's CERCLA claims. National Fuel did not dispute the fact that its 1972 sales contract with Westwood was a "contractual relationship," since CERCLA § 101(35)(A) provides that "[t]he term 'contractual relationship', for the purpose of section 9607(b)(3) 'includes,' but is not limited to, land contracts, deeds or other instruments transferring title or possession * * *." National Fuel asserted, however, that Westwood's construction activities were not undertaken by Westwood. Furthermore, National Fuel asserted that, if in fact it placed hazardous substances at the site, it exercised due care with respect to such substances and took precautions against the foreseeable acts or omissions of third persons. Specifically, National Fuel asserted that any such substances that were not eventually removed from the premises for off-site use or disposal were left inside secure subsurface receptacles. Moreover, National Fuel asserted that the structural integrity of these subsurface receptacles left at the site would not have been breached and therefore hazardous substances would not have escaped but for the unforeseeable construction activities of Westwood.

The district court held that the phrase *"in connection with"* in § 107(b)(3) requires that there be some relationship between the disposal/releasing activity and the contract with the defendant for a defendant to be barred from raising the third-party defense. The court denied Westwood's motion for summary judgment stating that to hold otherwise would render the language "in connection with" superfluous, a result generally at odds with accepted principles of statutory construction. The court of appeals agreed:

To summarize:

We hold that the district court correctly held that the phrase "in connection with a contractual relationship" in CERCLA § 107(b)(3) requires more than the mere existence of a contractual relationship between the owner of land on which hazardous substances are or have been disposed of and a third party whose act or omission was the sole cause of the release or threatened release of such hazardous substances into the environment, for the landowner to be barred from raising the third-party defense provided for in that section. In order for the landowner to be barred from raising the third-party defense under such circumstances, the contract between the landowner and the third party must either relate to the hazardous substances or allow the landowner to exert some element of control over the third party's activities.

964 F.2d at 92–93.

Notes and Questions

1. *Who is Covered by the Defense?* Should the reasoning and holding of *Westwood Pharmaceuticals* extend to landowners who conduct no activities at the site, but lease it to others, and a release occurs as a result of the tenants' activities? Prior to the Second Circuit's decision, the Fourth Circuit held that the existence of the contractual relationship between landowner and tenant/lessee precludes the availability of the third-party defense. See, e.g., United States v. Monsanto Co., 858 F.2d 160, 169 (4th Cir.1988), cert. denied, 490 U.S. 1106, 109 S.Ct. 3156, 104 L.Ed.2d 1019 (1989), discussed earlier. The exclusion for persons in a contractual relationship precludes employees and independent contractors such as transporters from invoking the third-party defense. United States v. Ward, 618 F.Supp. 884 (E.D.N.C. 1985); United States v. Conservation Chem. Co., 619 F.Supp. 162 (W.D.Mo. 1985). Lessors are similarly precluded from invoking the defense. United States v. Northernaire Plating Co., 670 F.Supp. 742 (W.D.Mich.1987), aff'd. sub. nom., United States v. R.W. Meyer, Inc., 889 F.2d 1497 (6th Cir.1989).

2. *Caused Solely By.* In addition to proving the absence of a contractual relationship, a defendant seeking to prevail on the third-party defense must also prove that the release was caused *solely* by the third party. Courts have rigorously applied the "caused solely" element of the defense, requiring that the defendant prove "the complete absence of causation" on its part. *Monsanto*, 858 F.2d at 168. In Lincoln Properties, Ltd. v. Higgins, 823 F.Supp. 1528, 1542 (E.D.Cal.1992), the court held that the requirement that the release be "caused solely by" the unrelated third party "incorporates the concept of proximate or legal cause. If the defendant's release was not foreseeable, and if its conduct—including acts as well as omissions—was 'so indirect and insubstantial' in the chain of events leading to the release, then the defendant's conduct was not the proximate cause of the release and the third party defense may be available." Under this standard, a county was not responsible for the release into the soil and groundwater of PCE introduced into the county's leaking sewer lines by dry cleaners. But see Westfarm Associates Ltd. Partnership v. Washington Suburban Sanitary Comm'n, 66 F.3d 669 (4th Cir.1995) (sewer commission liable because "it had the power to abate the foreseeable release of PCE, yet failed to exercise that power.").

3. In several cases, the fate of PRP's asserted third-party defense has turned on whether it exercised the requisite "due care" with respect to the hazardous substances involved. The following case is as generous as any,

from the perspective of parties asserting the third-party defense, in finding due care.

STATE OF NEW YORK v. LASHINS ARCADE CO.

United States Court of Appeals, Second Circuit, 1996.
91 F.3d 353.

MAHONEY, CIRCUIT JUDGE.

Plaintiffs-appellants-cross-appellees the State of New York and Thomas C. Jorling, as trustee of the State of New York's natural resources (collectively "New York"), appeal from a final judgment entered June 20, 1995 in the United States District Court for the Southern District of New York, Charles L. Brieant, Judge, that granted summary judgment to defendants-appellees-cross-appellants Lashins Arcade Company and Lashins Arcade Corporation (collectively "Lashins") and denied New York's motion for summary judgment in this action brought under § 107(a) of * * * CERCLA, 42 U.S.C. § 9607(a), the common law of public nuisance, and § 841 of the New York Real Property Actions and Proceedings Law (which provides for a statutory action for nuisance), and for unjust enrichment and restitution. The complaint sought, *inter alia*, damages for costs New York incurred investigating and cleaning up the release of tetrachloroethene, or perchloroethylene ("PCE"), and its breakdown compounds, trichloroethene ("TCE"), 1,2–dichloroethene ("DCE"), and vinyl chloride, into the groundwater in the vicinity of the Bedford Village Shopping Arcade (the "Arcade") in Westchester County, New York. PCE is a chemical used as a solvent in dry cleaning operations.

The district court awarded Lashins summary judgment based upon the third-party defense provided by § 107(b)(3) of CERCLA, and dismissed the action "as against the Lashins defendants." *New York v. Lashins Arcade Co.*, 856 F. Supp. 153, 158 (S.D.N.Y.1994). * * *

On this appeal, New York contests * * * the dismissal of its claims against Lashins. * * *

We affirm the judgment of the district court.

BACKGROUND

This appeal involves the release of hazardous substances at the Arcade, which resulted in groundwater contamination in the area. The Arcade, a 6,800 square foot one-story building housing six retail stores, was built in 1955, and was owned by Holbrook B. Cushman until his death in 1966. The property was then held in trust by Cushman's widow, Beatrice Cushman, and the Bank of New York until 1972. Cushman leased a store in the Arcade to Astrologo from about 1958 to 1963, where Astrologo operated a dry cleaning business. The store was next leased to defendant Rocco Tripodi (with whom defendant Bedford Village Cleaners, Inc. is affiliated) in 1963, who maintained the dry cleaning business at the Arcade until 1971. During this period, Tripodi dumped powdered wastes from his dry cleaning machines, which contained the volatile organic compound ("VOC") PCE, on the ground outside the Arcade behind his store. In December 1971, Tripodi moved his dry cleaning business out of the Arcade, and no other dry cleaning establishment has operated there since that time. In November 1972, the trust sold the Arcade to Miriam Baygell, who owned the property until her death in 1977, when it was inherited by her husband, Milton Baygell.

In 1978, the Westchester County Department of Health (the "WCDOH") conducted a countywide survey regarding possible groundwater contamination by VOCs. The survey found elevated VOC levels in * * * Bedford Village. Further sampling of private wells in Bedford Village conducted by the WCDOH in 1979 revealed groundwater contamination in an area southeast of the Arcade. These samples contained high concentrations of PCE and its breakdown compounds, TCE and DCE. The WCDOH issued "boil water" notices to affected homeowners.

In 1982, the New York State Department of Environmental Conservation (the "NYSDEC") authorized state funds for an investigation and remediation of the groundwater problem at the Arcade and the nearby Hunting Ridge Shopping Mall pursuant to § 27–1301 *et seq.* of the New York Environmental Conservation Law.* * * The investigations conducted from 1982 to 1986 revealed fluctuating levels of VOC contamination in the wells adjacent to the Arcade. A "Phase I" investigation, completed in June 1983 by the Wehran Engineering Company ("Wehran"), reported that the highest level of contamination in the Arcade was found in the area formerly occupied by the dry cleaning establishment.

Following the Phase I investigation, the "Bedford Village Wells" site was listed on the New York State Registry of Inactive Hazardous Waste Disposal Sites (the "Registry"). The Registry is published annually by the NYSDEC pursuant to § 27–1305(1) of the New York Environmental Conservation Law, which requires the NYSDEC annually to "transmit a report to the legislature and the governor identifying every inactive hazardous waste disposal site in the state known to the [NYSDEC]." *Id.* (McKinney 1996 Supp.). The registered sites are prioritized based upon "the relative need for action at each site to remedy environmental and health problems resulting from the presence of hazardous wastes at such sites." N.Y. Envtl. Conserv. Law § 27–1305(4)(b) (McKinney 1996 Supp.). In the 1983 Registry, the Bedford Village Wells site was designated as a Class "2a" site, based in part upon information that disposition of dry cleaning solvents had probably occurred at the Arcade. Class "2a" sites are those that are suspected to be hazardous waste disposal sites, but which require further investigation to confirm the presence of hazardous wastes. This site was described as including the Arcade, the Hunting Ridge Shopping Mall, an Exxon gasoline station, the Bedford Theater Building, and an apartment building adjacent to the theater. In December 1987, the Arcade was separated from the Hunting Ridge Shopping Mall, and each was thereafter designated as a separate site in the Registry.

[By letter dated October 12, 1983 and addressed to Miriam Baygell (who by that time was deceased), the NYSDEC advised that it intended to conduct a Phase II investigation of the Bedford Village Wells, and also stated that Ms. Baygell had the right to conduct such an investigation herself.* * * In any event, Wehran conducted the Phase II fieldwork for the NYSDEC commencing in 1984, and reported its final conclusions in June 1985. During this period, the WCDOH requested in a letter to Milton Baygell dated March 6, 1984 that he install a granular activated carbon ("GAC") filter in the well supplying the Arcade with water to remedy the VOC problem; Baygell installed the GAC filter in May 1985.]

The final Phase II Report concluded that VOC contamination persisted at the Arcade site. * * * As a result of these findings, the Bedford Village Wells Site was reclassified from Class "2a" to Class "2" in the 1986 Registry, defined as a "[s]ignificant threat to the public health or environment—action required." N.Y. Envtl. Conserv. Law § 27–1305(4) (b)(2) (McKinney 1984). Milton Baygell was informed about the reclassification in a certified letter for which he signed a receipt on June 20, 1986.

In 1986, the United States Environmental Protection Agency (the "EPA") joined with the WCDOH to investigate the Arcade. Their joint surveys confirmed that VOCs persisted in three private wells at the Bedford Village Wells site, and low VOC concentrations also appeared east and southeast of the Arcade in water supplies that had previously been uncontaminated. In view of this problem, the NYSDEC requested and obtained approval from the EPA for a Remedial Investigation/Feasibility Study ("RI/FS") of the entire Bedford Village Wells site. * * *

Meanwhile, in January 1987, Milton Baygell entered into negotiations with Lashins for the sale of the Arcade after a real estate broker contacted Lashins about the property. In the course of these negotiations, Baygell's attorney, wrote Lashins' attorney, * * * to inform him that "there are chemicals in the ground being treated by ultra violet and activated carbon machines situated in the rear of the building to clean the water. Chemicals have to be replaced approximately every 8–9 months." *Lashins Arcade Co.*, 856 F. Supp. at 156. Prior to executing the contract of sale, Lashins contacted the Arcade's water service contractor, Environmental Recovery Co., who advised Lashins that the well on the premises had a water filter, but assured Lashins that the filter was "routine" and had been installed in response to an area-wide groundwater contamination problem, and that the suspected source of the contamination was a nearby Exxon gas station.

In addition, Lashins states that it contacted the Town of Bedford prior to purchasing the Shopping Arcade to determine whether there were any violations or other present or past problems with the property, and was assured that there were none. Lashins further asserts that it interviewed the Arcade's tenants, all of whom spoke enthusiastically about the property. New York contends, however, that Lashins made no inquiry concerning the groundwater contamination (other than the discussion with Environmental Recovery Co.) prior to purchasing the Arcade. In any event, Lashins executed a contract of sale with Baygell on April 6, 1987, and the transaction closed on June 26, 1987.

Lashins claims that at the time of the closing, it was unaware that the NYSDEC was conducting an administrative proceeding involving the Arcade, or that it had contracted with a firm to conduct the RI/FS concerning the Bedford Village Wells site. Baygell did not transmit any NYSDEC notices to Lashins, no public notice was issued, and the Arcade tenants, the Town of Bedford, and the local bank were allegedly unaware of the situation.

Lashins was first informed that the NYSDEC was conducting a formal investigation of the Arcade by letter dated August 13, 1987. That letter advised Lashins of the impending RI/FS requested by the NYS-DEC, and stated that NYSDEC representatives intended to enter the Arcade property "for the purpose of drilling, installing and operating groundwater monitoring wells and taking samples of soil, septage, surface water, and groundwater."

New York also informed Milton Baygell of the RI/FS by letter dated September 18, 1987.

* * *

After purchasing the Arcade, Lashins maintained the existing GAC filter and took water samples which were analyzed by a laboratory for VOC contamination on a semi-annual basis. It also instructed all tenants to avoid discharging any hazardous substances into the waste and septic systems, subsequently incorporated this requirement into the tenant leases, and conducted periodic inspections of the tenants' premises to assure compliance with this obligation.

The RI/FS was completed in February 1990. It concluded, *inter alia,* that the contamination in the affected wells,

"although unconfirmed, most probably originated from a former dry cleaning establishment located in the Shopping Arcade."

* * * The extent of significant ground water contamination appeared to be limited to the area of and immediately contiguous to the Shopping Arcade.

* * *

The NYSDEC issued a Record of Decision on March 30, 1990 setting forth its plan to abate and remedy the actual and threatened release of hazardous substances from the Arcade. Three remedial measures were suggested: (1) installation of GAC filters (which were already in place) for the affected homes and businesses; (2) a new source of water supply; and (3) re-charge of the contaminated ground water by a "pump and treat" system.

* * *

New York filed this action on December 7, 1992, *id.*, alleging violations of § 9607(a) and state law by Lashins and its codefendants as previously described. In October 1993, Lashins and New York filed opposing motions for summary judgment on the issue of Lashins' liability under CERCLA as a current owner of the Arcade. The district court granted summary judgment for Lashins and dismissed the action with respect to Lashins on May 12, 1994.

The district court concluded that all elements for strict liability as to Lashins under § 9607(a), were satisfied in this case, see *Lashins Arcade Co.*, 856 F. Supp. at 157, but that Lashins was entitled to summary judgment on its affirmative defense under § 9607(b)(3), see *Lashins Arcade Co.*, 856 F. Supp. at 157–58. In so ruling, the court noted that "Lashins had no direct or indirect contractual relationship with either of the third party dry cleaners who released the VOCs, or with the owners of the Shopping Arcade at the time the dry cleaners operated and when the pollution occurred," and that Lashins had done "everything that could reasonably have been done to avoid or correct the pollution."

As previously noted, consent decrees subsequently ensued with respect to Lashins' codefendants. Final judgment was accordingly entered on June 20, 1995. This appeal followed.

DISCUSSION

* * *

As an initial matter, there is no dispute that New York has established a prima facie case against Lashins under § 9607(a), for recovery of expenses incurred investigating and cleaning up the release of PCE at the Arcade.

Since Lashins is a current owner of the Shopping Arcade, it is a potentially responsible defendant under § 9607(a)(1), notwithstanding the fact that it did not own the Arcade at the time of disposal of the hazardous substances.* * * Thus, Lashins may be held strictly liable for New York's response costs unless it can satisfy one of CERCLA's affirmative defenses. We now turn to Lashins' claim that it may avoid such liability under the third-party defense of § 9607(b)(3).

Section 9607(b)(3), provides an affirmative defense for a party who can establish that the offending "release * * * of a hazardous substance and the damages resulting therefrom were caused solely by * * * an act or omission of a third party," provided that: (1) the third party is not "one whose act or omission occurs in connection with a contractual relationship, existing directly or indirectly, with the defendant," (2) the defendant "took precautions against foreseeable acts or omissions of any such third party and the consequences that could foreseeably result from such acts or omissions," and (3) the defendant "exercised due care with respect to the hazardous substance concerned, taking into consideration the characteristics of such hazardous substance, in light of all relevant facts and circumstances."

The offending release here was clearly caused by third parties (Tripodi, Bedford Village Cleaners, Inc., Astrologo, and (New York contends) Milton Baygell). Although paragraphs (1)-(3) of § 9607(b) speak exclusively in the singular, referring to events and damages "caused solely by—(1) *an* act of God; (2) *an* act of war; [or] (3) *an* act or omission of a third party," § 9607(b) (emphasis added), paragraph (4) of § 9607(b) refers to "any combination of the foregoing paragraphs." We read paragraph (4) as allowing consideration of multiple causes within, as well as among, the several preceding paragraphs. Thus, in our view, damage that resulted from an earthquake and a subsequent flood would fall within paragraph (1) of § 9607(b), and damages caused by a number of acts by a single third party (as typically occurs when pollution is caused by a course of conduct), or a number of acts by several third parties (as in this case), would fall within paragraph (3) * * *.

In this case, the only one of the allegedly offending third parties with whom Lashins had a contractual relationship was Milton Baygell. Further, Baygell's allegedly offending conduct did not "occur in connection with a contractual relationship * * * with [Lashins]" within the meaning of § 9607(b)(3), and therefore Lashins may not be disqualified from the protection afforded by § 9607(b)(3) because of its contractual relationship with Baygell.

This conclusion is mandated by * * * *Westwood Pharmaceuticals, Inc. v. National Fuel Gas Distribution Corp.*, 964 F.2d 85 (2d Cir.1992).

* * *

In *Westwood*, the seller of the contaminated site sought exoneration from the buyer's conduct, whereas in this case the buyer seeks exoneration from the seller's activities, but this is surely an immaterial distinction in terms of the *Westwood* rationale. See *id.* at 89 ("[A] landowner is precluded from raising the third-party defense only if the contract between the landowner and the third party somehow is connected with the handling of hazardous substances."). The straightforward sale of the Arcade by Baygell to Lashins clearly did not "relate to hazardous substances" or vest Lashins with authority "to exert some element of control over [Baygell's] activities" within the contemplation of our ruling in *Westwood*.

The second requirement for the successful assertion of a third-party defense demands that the defendant shall have taken adequate precautions against actions by the third party that would lead to a release of hazardous waste. Given that the last release in the instant case happened more than fifteen years before Lashins' purchase of the Arcade, there was obviously nothing Lashins could have done to prevent actions leading to a release.

Thus, the resolution of this appeal turns upon the validity of the district court's ruling that Lashins was entitled to summary judgment on the question whether Lashins "exercised due care with respect to the hazardous substance concerned * * * in the light of all relevant facts and circumstances" within the meaning of § 9607(b)(3). This requirement is not defined in the statute. CERCLA's legislative history, however, provides some guidance: "[T]he defendant must demonstrate that he took all precautions with respect to the particular waste that a similarly situated reasonable and prudent person would have taken in light of all relevant facts and circumstances." H.R. Rep. No. 1016, 96th Cong., 2d Sess., pt. 1, at 34 (1980), *reprinted in* 1980 U.S.C.C.A.N. 6119, 6137. Further, "due care 'would include those steps necessary to protect the public from a health or environmental threat.' " *United States v. A & N Cleaners & Launderers, Inc.*, 854 F. Supp. 229, 238 (S.D.N.Y.1994) (quoting H.R. Rep. No. 253, 99th Cong., 2d Sess. 187 (1986)); see also *Kerr-McGee Chem. Corp.*, 14 F.3d at 325 & n.3 (due care not established when no affirmative measures taken to control site); *Lincoln Properties v. Higgins*, 823 F. Supp. 1528, 1543–44 (E.D.Cal.1992) (due care exercised where defendant removed contaminated wells).

Against this background, New York contends that Lashins inadequately investigated the contamination problem before buying the Arcade despite being notified about it, and after its purchase "did *nothing* to contain, control or clean up the pollution except to continue to maintain a filter on its own property." New York points to cases such as *A & N Cleaners* and *Kerr-McGee Chemical Corp.* where § 9607(a) liability was imposed because the defendant did not take active measures to address a hazardous waste problem, and adds that *Kerr-McGee Chemical Corp.* and *United States v. DiBiase Salem Realty Trust*, 1993 WL 729662 (D.Mass. Nov.19, 1993), establish that the "due care" standard does not permit a landowner to remain passive simply because public environmental authorities are addressing a hazardous waste situation.

We are not persuaded by New York's arguments, nor by the authorities that New York cites to us. The pertinent language of § 9607(b)(3) focuses the "due care" inquiry upon "all relevant facts and circumstances" of the case at hand. In this case, the RI/FS * * * had been commissioned six months before Lashins purchased the Arcade, and before Lashins had even learned that the Arcade was for sale. It would have been pointless to require Lashins to commission a parallel investigation once it acquired the Arcade and became more fully aware of the environmental problem. Pressed at oral argument as to what Lashins might appropriately have been required to do at that juncture, New York contended that Lashins was obligated to pay some or all of the cost of the RI/FS undertaken at the behest of the EPA and the NYSDEC.

This is surely an anomalous proposal. Response costs are assessed when there is liability under § 9607(a). It is counterintuitive to suppose that a defendant is required to pay some or all of those response costs in order to establish the affirmative defense provided by § 9607(b)(3) to liability under § 9607(a), thereby rendering the affirmative defense partly or entirely academic.

Nor do we discern any policy reasons for imposing such a rule. We agree with *HRW Systems, Inc. v. Washington Gas Light Co.*, 823 F. Supp. 318 (D.Md.1993), that the "due care" mandate of § 9607(b)(3) does not "impose a duty on a purchaser of land to investigate prior to purchase, in order to determine whether there is pollution on the land caused by someone with whom the purchaser is not in contractual privity." *Id.* at 349. No claim is made that Lashins' purchase of the Arcade deprived New York of any remedy available to it against any predecessor owners or operators under § 9607(a); consent decrees were in fact entered against Tripodi and Astrologo. It is surely the policy of CERCLA to impose liability upon parties responsible for pollution, * * * rather than the general taxpaying public, but this policy does not mandate precluding a "due care" defense by imposing a rule that is tantamount to absolute liability for ownership of a site containing hazardous waste.

Finally, the cases cited by New York do not require the negation of Lashins' "due care" defense. None involved a defendant who played no role in the events that led to the hazardous waste problem and came on the scene after public authorities were well along in a program of investigation and remediation. *Kerr-McGee Chemical Corp.* involved a landowner who was aware of the environmental problem and made no attempt to address it after preliminary investigative efforts by federal and state authorities provided notice of the contamination. *See* 14 F.3d at 325 & n.3. In *A & N Cleaners*, the defendant landowners' sublessee (who subsequently became a lessee) was operating the offending dry cleaning establishment throughout the entire period of the defendants' ownership. *See* 854 F. Supp. at 232.

* * *

In sum, we perceive no basis for reversal of the district court's award of summary judgment to Lashins on the basis that Lashins satisfied its obligation to "exercise[] due care" with respect to the Arcade within the meaning of § 9607(b)(3). In so ruling, we proclaim no broad rule of exemption from the liability imposed by § 9607(a). Rather, mindful of the mandate of § 9607(b)(3) that the "due care" inquiry focus upon "all relevant facts and circumstances" of the case presented for decision, we conclude that Lashins' "due care" obligation did not require it to go beyond the measures that it took to address the contamination problem at the Arcade, and to supplant, duplicate, or underwrite the RI/FS previously commissioned by the EPA and NYDESC to address pollution that ensued from activities which occurred more than fifteen years before Lashins purchased the Arcade.

The judgment of the district court is affirmed.

Notes and Questions

1. *Limits on the Defense.* An owner who knows about the harmful consequences of disposal practices undertaken by third parties in a contrac-

tual relationship and fails to take precautions to prevent a release or foreseeable adverse consequences arising under a release is likely to be unable to rely upon this defense. United States v. Glidden Co., 3 F.Supp 2d 823 (N.D.Ohio 1997); United States v. Tyson, 17 Envtl. L. Rep. (ELI) 20527 (E.D.Pa.1986). Willful ignorance also may preclude successful resort to the defense, as may failure to inspect property annually, inquire into past uses, do test borings, or check government records before acquisition. E.g., United States v. A & N Cleaners & Launderers, Inc., 854 F.Supp. 229, 243–44 (S.D.N.Y.1994). One court described the consequences of a purchaser's failure to make appropriate inquiries as follows:

> Given the commercial/industrial setting of the Site, the high duty of inquiry attached to commercial transactions, the relative ease with which the contamination at the Site could have been discovered prior to purchase, the collective real estate experience of the [partners that owned the property], and the disparity between the purchase price and the appraised value of the Site before contamination, it was incumbent upon the [party invoking the defense] to investigate possible contamination at the Site; he or his partners could readily have discovered the contamination with reasonable inquiry prior to its acquisition. Yet even after discovering the contamination, neither he nor his partners took any steps to abate it, to notify the appropriate regulatory authorities or adjoining landowners of the contamination, or to secure the Site or restrict access to it. In sum, the [party] failed to exercise due care or take appropriate precautionary measures with respect to contamination at the Site. His failure to do so precludes his assertion of the innocent landowner defense or third-party defense.

Foster v. United States, 922 F.Supp. 642, 655 (D.D.C.1996). For other cases in which the defense failed as a result of the PRP's failure to demonstrate due care or adequate precautions, see Kerr–McGee Chem. Corp. v. Lefton Iron & Metal Co., 14 F.3d 321, 325 (7th Cir.1994); United States v. A & N Cleaners & Launderers, Inc., 854 F.Supp. 229 (S.D.N.Y.1994). But cf. Redwing Carriers, Inc. v. Saraland Apartments, 94 F.3d 1489, 1508 (11th Cir.1996) (general partners exercised due care in initiating plan to remove contaminants). For other cases in which the defense failed, see Acme Printing Ink Co. v. Menard, Inc., 870 F.Supp. 1465 (E.D.Wis.1994) (PRP should have known that hazardous substances may have been disposed of at the site).

2. *What of Criminal and Intentional Acts of Third Parties?* In Carter–Jones Lumber Co. v. Dixie Distributing Co., 166 F.3d 840, 847 (6th Cir. 1999), the Sixth Circuit Court of Appeals summarily rejected the defense:

> Reviewed either for clear error or de novo, the district court's determination that the third party defense is inapplicable here is correct. Because the third party alleged to have been the sole cause of the release was the employee of Henderson, the person with whom Dixie was said to have arranged for disposal, the third party defense is unavailable. It may indeed be true that the acts of Henderson's employee were intentional and criminal, but the acts and the consequences were not unforeseeable, as required by the statutory defense, see 42 U.S.C. § 9607(b)(3).

3. *Due Care Arguments. Lashins Arcade* does not stand alone in sustaining the third-party defense in the face of inadequate due care arguments by plaintiffs. For example, another decision upholding the assertion of the third-party defense is Redwing Carriers, Inc. v. Saraland Apartments, 94 F.3d 1489 (11th Cir.1996). Redwing Carriers operated a trucking terminal at the site in question from 1961 to 1972; its activities contaminated the site with hazardous substances that combined to form a black-tar-like substance. The property changed hands twice in 1971, and in 1973 it was acquired by Saraland Apartments, Ltd., which built an apartment complex on the site. Saraland Apartments, Ltd., first became aware of tar seepage at the site in 1977. In 1984, after tar seepage was also noted by HUD and by residents of the apartment complex, a group of investors bought out the original partners in Saraland Apartments, Ltd. Robert Coit and Roar Company became the limited partners. In 1985 and 1990, Redwing entered into two administrative orders by consent with the EPA requiring it to investigate and clean up the site. Redwing sued, among others, the general partners. The Eleventh Circuit upheld their third-party defense.

Coit and Roar have satisfied all the elements of this defense. The general partners never had a direct or indirect contractual relationship with either Redwing or Meador Contracting Company—the only two parties whose conduct potentially caused the release or threat of release of hazardous substances at the Saraland Site. Redwing closed its trucking terminal on the property in 1972. Approximately two years later, Meador graded and filled the property while building the apartment complex. Coit and Roar had no contact with these parties when they purchased their partnership interest in Saraland Limited in 1984–12 years after Redwing last buried toxic substances on the site. It is plain that the environmental damage to this property was done long before Coit and Roar ever became partners in Saraland Limited.

The record indicates that since 1984, the general partners have exercised due care towards hazardous substances contaminating the property. A HUD report identified tar seeps on the property in August 1984, and three months later Coit approved a maintenance plan to remove the seeps. In April and May of 1985, the EPA conducted its preliminary investigation of the Site. Two months later, the EPA entered into its first consent order with Redwing requiring Redwing to, among other things, periodically remove tar-like material from the surface of the property. Thus, less than a year after Coit and Roar became general partners, a program was in place to remedy the tar seeps on the property.

Meanwhile, Coit and Roar have demonstrated they did nothing to exacerbate conditions at the Site. Redwing has identified only two events after 1984–the repaving of the parking lot and the maintenance work on the gas line–that allegedly increased the amount of contaminated soil on the property. As general partners, Coit and Roar approved these projects. Nothing suggests, however, that in repaving the parking lot and repairing the gas line, workers disturbed contaminated soil or otherwise disposed of hazardous substances on the Site. The record supports the general partners' position that they have taken all necessary precautions in addressing a toxic waste problem created almost entirely by Redwing.

Id. at 1508. The court noted, however, that the general partners might still face liability if the partnership is found liable on remand for some portion of cleanup costs related to the construction work it undertook (building the apartment complex). *Id.* at 1508–09.

But see Westfarm Associates Ltd. Partnership v. Washington Suburban Sanitary Comm., 66 F.3d 669 (4th Cir.1995), cert. denied, 517 U.S. 1103, 116 S.Ct. 1318, 134 L.Ed.2d 471 (1996), holding dry cleaning association failed to satisfy defense because of willful blindness in recognizing and preventing and inspecting facility that used PCE and poured the substance into the sewer. See Craig Johnston, Current Landowner Liability Under CERCLA: Restoring Need for Due Diligence, 9 Fordham Envtl. L.J. 401 (1998) (excellent analysis of due diligence obligation of purchaser).

4. *What of the Act of God Defense?* United States v. Alcan Aluminum Corp., 892 F.Supp. 648 (M.D.Pa.1995), aff'd 96 F.3d 1434 (3d Cir.1996) (Table), illustrates the limited availability of § 107 defenses in general and the act of God defense in particular:

> First, no reasonable factfinder could conclude that Hurricane Gloria was the sole cause of the release and resulting response costs. Two million gallons of hazardous wastes were not dumped into the borehole by an act of God, and were it not for the unlawful disposal of this hazardous waste Hurricane Gloria would not have flushed 100,000 gallons of this chemical soup into the Susquehanna River. Second, the effects of Hurricane Gloria could "have been prevented or avoided by the exercise of due care or foresight." 42 U.S.C. § 9601(1). Clearly, exercise of due care or foresight would have militated against dumping hazardous wastes into mine workings that inevitably lead to such a significant natural resource as the Susquehanna River. Finally, as the Court in [United States v. Stringfellow, 661 F.Supp. 1053, 1061 (C.D.Cal.1987)] recognized, heavy rainfall is "not the kind of 'exceptional' natural phenomenon to which the act of God exception applies." Accordingly, it is appropriate to enter judgment in favor of the Government on Alcan's act of God defense.

892 F.Supp. at 658. For other cases rejecting the Act of God defense, see United States v. M/V Santa Clara I, 887 F.Supp. 825 (D.S.C.1995) (inclement weather); United States v. Amtreco, Inc., 809 F.Supp. 959 (M.D.Ga.1992) (flood that occurred after cleanup began).

5. *Third-Party Defense and Passive Migration.* One interesting decision considered the third-party defense when upriver landowners had deposited PCBs into a navigable river and a downriver riparian owner sought to assert the defense. In Kalamazoo River Study Group v. Rockwell International, 3 F.Supp. 2d 799 (W.D.Mich.1998), aff'd., 171 F.3d 1065 (6th Cir.1999), the court reasoned as follows:

> Plaintiff has asserted that Menasha, Pharmacia & Upjohn and Rock–Tenn are all liable for response costs simply on the basis that they own riparian land bordering on the Kalamazoo River, and PCBs have been found in sediments in the river bed adjacent to their properties.

The three defendants currently before this Court have all raised the third-party defense. CERCLA provides that persons who are responsible under § 107(a) may nevertheless escape liability if they can show that the release of the hazardous substance was caused solely by an act or omission of a third party. 42 U.S.C. § 9607(b)(3).

To establish a third-party defense the defendant must show:

1. that a third party was the sole cause of the release or threatened release of a hazardous substance;

2. that the act or omission of the third party causing the release did not occur in the context of a direct or indirect contractual relationship between the defendant and the third party; and

3. that the defendant took due care and precautions to prevent the foreseeable acts or omissions of the third party causing the release or threatened release.

* * *

Plaintiff contends that Defendants are not entitled to the third-party defense because they cannot establish that the contamination of the riparian property was caused solely by other parties, and because they cannot establish that they acted with reasonable care and took precautions against the foreseeable acts or omissions of third parties.

There are, however, some common legal issues regarding reasonable care and precautions that require some discussion at this time.

Plaintiff [a group of upstream firms that deposited PCBs into the river] takes the position that even if the PCBs in the river bed were released solely by plaintiff's members and migrated down the river, defendants would not be entitled to the third-party defense unless they could show that they took some affirmative action to clean up the hazardous substance or prevent its spread in order to be entitled to the third-party defense * * *.

Section 9607(b)(3) requires that the defendant establish that it exercised "due care with respect to the hazardous substance concerned, taking into consideration the characteristics of such hazardous substance, in light of all relevant facts and circumstances." 42 U.S.C. § 9607(b)(3).

* * * Defendants contend that the degree of care to be exercised by one asserting the third-party defense must be considered in light of the defendants' riparian position and the fact that this is a passive migration case. The public has unlimited access to the navigable waters, and the riparian owner has no right to control access to the property. The migration of hazardous materials downriver is not isolated to easily identifiable locations or time periods, but is rather spread throughout the river bed over a long-period of time.

The Court believes that riparian owners should not be required to take affirmative action to clean up the hazardous substance migrating down the river bed or prevent its spread in order to be entitled to the third-party defense. If that were the case, each and every property owner on the Kalamazoo River would be liable for the cost of the cleanup of Plaintiff's members' PCB contamination for having failed to prevent Plaintiff's members from contaminating their riparian property. CERCLA liability does not extend this far. Rather than placing an affirmative duty on riparian owners to cleanup or prevent the spread of contamination, the Court holds that the degree of care required for riparian owners who assert the third-party defense in passive migration cases is met if the riparian owner has not facilitated or encouraged the migration or spread of the hazardous substance and has not exacerbated the conditions at the Site.

3 F.Supp. 2d at 806–807. Does *Westwood Pharmaceuticals* help those seeking to assert the defense? How? What is the effect of the *Westwood* court's requirement that the contractual relationship relate to the hazardous substances? See 964 F.2d at 85.

Consider the following analysis of *Westwood* and the contractual relationship issue:

> The conclusion that the release must be related to the contractual relationship makes sense in most contexts. For example, with regard to an innocent seller, if the release occurs after one sells the property, there is no rational way to hold the seller responsible. The requirement also makes sense in the case of release by a tenant because one can exercise some control over a tenant's actions. The *Westwood* court failed, however, to make clear how an ordinary purchase and sale agreement is related to hazardous substances, when the buyer is unaware of the presence of the hazardous substances.

> In its simplest terms, the unanswered question is how a contract that makes no reference to hazardous substances, between two parties who may both be unaware of the presence of hazardous substances on the property, can be a contract that relates to hazardous substances. There is no doubt that under CERCLA Section 101(35) that such an agreement is related to hazardous substances for liability purposes, unless the appropriate inquiry is made. It cannot be that the transfer of property containing hazardous substances is always a contract related to hazardous substances. That would have prevented the defense in *Lashins*.

> Some courts have suggested that the goal of the "contractual relationship" requirement is to treat persons who benefited financially from the release of hazardous substances as responsible parties. * * * Based on that theory, a purchaser who gets a discounted price because of possible contamination may have responsibility because it benefits financially from any cleanup. However, if the price does not take contamination into account, there would seem to be no reason to treat that sales contract as related to the release of hazardous substances.

> This is a question the courts will have to deal with as the case law tests whether the reasoning of *Westwood* is consistent with the rest of the superfund law.

Aaron Gershonowitz, When Is a Superfund Property Owner Innocent Enough to Establish the Current Landowner Defense?, Toxics Law Rep. (BNA) 215–222 (1996). See also *Westwood* and *Lashins*. These cases do, however, provide some hope to those in the real estate industry who view the superfund law as "a black hole that indiscriminately devours all who come near it." J. Anderson, The Hazardous Waste Land, 13 Va. Envir. L. J. 1, 6–7 (1993).

2. INNOCENT LANDOWNER DEFENSE

a. Background

The innocent landowner defense is a hybrid form of the third-party defense: the idea is that some current owners of contaminated property who would clearly otherwise fall within the PRP categories of § 9607(a) may be "innocent" or "fault-free" to an extent that justifies exonerating them from CERCLA liability. But, as we have already seen, innocence, as a general matter, is not a defense. The superfund law does, however, provide a defense based on a form of innocence in the third-party defense. In CERCLA's early years, many purchasers who had nothing to do with causing the release of hazardous substances could not establish this defense because the documents by which they acquired the property (a purchase and sale agreement, for example) gave them a contractual relationship with someone who did have a role in the release of hazardous substances.

b. Congress' Attempt to Create a Defense for Purchasers

In response to the perceived inequity of denying purchasers the defense because of the sellers' actions, Congress added a provision in 1986 defining the term contractual relationship to exclude "land contracts, deeds and other instruments transferring title," if the defendant acquired the property after the disposal of hazardous substances, and, at the time the defendant acquired the property, he had no reason to know that any hazardous substance was disposed of on the property. The provision further provides that in order to establish that one had "no reason to know," the defendant must have undertaken "all appropriate inquiry consistent with good commercial and customary practice in an effort to minimize liability." 42 U.S.C. § 9601(35).

This so-called "innocent purchaser defense" quickly became the holy grail of most environmental due diligence. As applied by the courts, however, the defense is largely ineffective. The statute's definitional requirements for establishing an innocent purchaser defense based on innocence are: (1) that the release of hazardous substances was caused solely by a third party; (2) with whom the defendant did not have a contractual relationship; and (3) that the defendant exercised due care with regard to the hazardous substances and took precautions against the foreseeable acts of third parties. 42 U.S.C. § 9607(b)(3). Additionally, if one purchased the property from a responsible party, one can establish the lack of a contractual relationship element of the defense by establishing (1) that the release of hazardous substances occurred prior to the purchase; and (2) that there was no reason to know about the hazardous substances, after having engaged in "all appropriate inquiry * * * consistent with good commercial and customary practice."[2]

Congress explained its goal in enacting the defense in 1986 as follows:

> [Section 101(35)] is intended to clarify and confirm that under limited circumstances landowners who acquire property without knowing of any contamination at the site and without reason to know of any contamination * * * may have a defense to liability under section 107 and therefore should not be held liable for cleaning up the site if such persons satisfy the remaining requirements of section 107(b)(3). A person who acquires property through a land contract or deed or other instrument transferring title or possession that meets the requirements of this definition may assert that an act or omission of a third party should not be considered to have occurred in connection with a contractual relationship as identified in section 107(b) and therefore is not a bar to the defense.

H.R. Rep. No. 99–962, at 186–87 (1986), reprinted in 1986 U.S.C.C.A.N. 2835, 3279–80.

Based on the statutory elements, there are three primary reasons that a person claiming innocence might be found not innocent enough: (1) the release was not caused *solely* by others; (2) the release was caused solely by others, but defendant failed to exercise due care upon discovery of the release; and (3) defendant should have known about the release, but did not, because of inadequate pre-purchase inquiry.

2. Section 101(35) provides:

(35)(A) The term "contractual relationship", for the purpose of section 9607(b)(3) of this title, includes, but is not limited to, land contracts, deeds, or other instruments transferring title or possession, unless the real property on which the facility concerned is located was acquired by the defendant after the disposal or placement of the hazardous substance on, in, or at the facility, and one or more of the circumstances described in clause (i), (ii), or (iii) is also established by the defendant by a preponderance of the evidence:

(i) At the time the defendant acquired the facility the defendant *did not know and had no reason to know* that any hazardous substance which is the subject of the release or threatened release was disposed of on, in, or at the facility.

(ii) The defendant is a government entity ...

(iii) The defendant acquired the facility by inheritance or bequest.

In addition to establishing the foregoing, the defendant must establish that he has satisfied the requirements of section 9607(b)(3)(a) and (b) of this title.

(B) *To establish that the defendant had no reason to know*, as provided in clause (i) of subparagraph (A) of this paragraph, the defendant must have undertaken, at the time of acquisition, all appropriate inquiry into the previous ownership and uses of the property consistent with good commercial or customary practice in an effort to minimize liability. For purposes of the preceding sentence the court shall take into account any specialized knowledge or experience on the part of the defendant, the relationship of the purchase price to the value of the property if uncontaminated, commonly known or reasonably ascertainable information about the property, the obviousness of the presence or likely presence of contamination at the property and the ability to detect such contamination by appropriate inspection. (emphasis added.)

c. Caused "Solely By" Requirement

The defense applies only if the release was caused solely by a third party. Thus, an innocent purchaser who discovers a problem and inadvertently contributes to it, loses the defense. Permitting the problem to continue or failing to respond adequately can also destroy the defense. The use of the word "solely" also serves to encourage those who generate or dispose of hazardous wastes to mark and track their wastes properly. That is, by placing the burden on the defendant to prove that a release was not caused or contributed to by its actions, defendants are encouraged to fully document their activities. See, Violet v. Picillo, 648 F.Supp. 1283, 1294 (D.R.I.1986).

The need for an otherwise innocent purchaser to take all appropriate action after hazardous substances are discovered or risk being deemed partially responsible is illustrated by Shapiro v. Alexanderson, 741 F.Supp. 472, 478 (S.D.N.Y.1990). Shapiro was a purchaser who lost the defense largely because of his inaction after discovering the release. The court focused on the fact that it took Shapiro almost five (5) years after discovering the problem to properly respond. This delay contributed to the release and thus, the release was not caused solely by third parties.

Delivery of even the most minute quantity of waste to the site can prevent the release from being caused *solely* by third parties. In Louisiana–Pacific Corp. v. ASARCO, 735 F.Supp. 358, 363 (W.D.Wash.1990), the government brought suit against several parties who had deposited hazardous waste at a site. One of the defendants brought a third-party action against Louisiana–Pacific. Louisiana–Pacific's waste had been delivered to the site and was found to contain minute quantities of hazardous substances. The court concluded that even though the vast majority of the problem was caused by unrelated third parties, Louisiana–Pacific could not argue that the release of hazardous substances was caused *solely* by these third parties. Thus, courts have interpreted "solely" quite strictly so that any involvement, no matter how insignificant, can destroy the defense. Minute quantities of waste, the failure to quickly respond to an unforeseen problem, or the failure to take steps to prevent others from releasing hazardous substances may all prevent a third party from being the sole cause.

The innocent landowner defense potentially applies to three types of current property owners (and probably lessees): (1) non-governmental entities which intentionally acquired the site; (2) non-government entities which acquired it by inheritance or bequest; and (3) governmental entities which acquired the site by escheat or other involuntary transfer, or by means of eminent domain. All such entities must establish that the hazardous substances were placed at the site before they acquired it, § 101(35)(A), that they exercised due care regarding the hazardous substance concerned, and that they took precautions against foreseeable acts or omissions of third parties. § 107(b)(3)(A) and (B).

In addition, non-governmental entities which intentionally acquire a site must establish that, at the time of acquisition, they neither knew nor had reason to know of the disposal of hazardous substances at the property. § 101(35)(A)(i). The Act further specifies that, in order to prove such lack of knowledge or reason to know:

> * * * [T]he defendant must have undertaken, at the time of acquisition, all appropriate inquiry into the previous ownership and uses of the property consistent with good commercial or customary practice in an effort to minimize liability. For purposes of the preceding sentence the court shall take into account any specialized knowledge or experience on the part of the defendant, the relationship of the purchase price to the value of the property if contaminated, commonly known or reasonably ascertainable information about the property, the obviousness of the presence or likely presence of contamination at the property, and the ability to detect such contamination by appropriate inspection.

§ 101(35)(B). Initially, those seeking to invoke the innocent landowner defense were current property owners who acquired their CERCLA sites in the past, without knowing of the contamination, and now seek to invoke the defense to avoid CERCLA liability.

In at least one vigorously-litigated case where an already-contaminated site was purchased in 1969 without a site inspection, the court rejected the notion that the absence of an inspection automatically precludes proof of due diligence for purposes of the innocent landowner defense. United States v. Serafini, 706 F.Supp. 354 (M.D.Pa.1989). Ultimately, however, the government persuaded the court that it was not customary practice in Scranton, Pennsylvania, in 1969 to purchase property without viewing it, and the government defeated the attempt to invoke the defense. United States v. Serafini, 711 F.Supp. 197 (M.D.Pa. 1988), and United States v. Serafini, 791 F.Supp. 107 (M.D.Pa.1990).

The difficulty of applying the all appropriate inquiry test to transactions consummated years ago is illustrated in Juniper Development Group v. Kahn, 174 B.R. 148 (Bkrtcy.Mass.1994), where the court ruled that while a developer's actions and omissions in 1980 conformed to standards common in the industry, "it does not follow that the customary practices were either good or commercially reasonable" under CERCLA when examined in 1994.

d. Failure to Exercise Reasonable Care

The defense is available only if the person claiming to be innocent exercises reasonable care with regard to hazardous substances after they are discovered. As a practical matter, this means that an otherwise innocent landowner who discovers a problem and does not react appropriately loses his innocence. Failure to prevent additional releases may take the form either of failure to protect the property from third parties or failure to remove a source of contamination that is continuing to release hazardous substances. Idylwoods Associates v. Mader Capital, Inc., 915 F.Supp. 1290 (W.D.N.Y.1996) illustrates the first type. The buyer failed to put up new fencing after notice of continued dumping and therefore could not establish the "due care" element of the defense. *Id.* at 1301.

In *Shore Realty*, on the other hand, the failure to protect against third parties included the failure to remove leaking drums. The court found that the defendants were aware of the presence of these leaking drums and that the continued leaking and seeping constituted additional "releases." New York v. Shore Realty Corp., 759 F.2d 1032, 1045 (2d Cir. 1985).

Failure to test material found on-site can also constitute lack of due care. In Jersey City Redevelopment Authority v. PPG Industries, Inc., 866 F.2d 1411 (3d Cir.1988), defendants purchased property unaware that contaminated waste had been disposed of there, then, without testing the waste, removed it to another site. Moving the waste without testing it constituted failure to exercise due care with regard to hazardous waste, even though defendants did not recognize the waste as hazardous.

Additionally, failure to investigate the activities of others can constitute lack of due care. In United States v. A & N Cleaners and Launderers, Inc., 854 F.Supp. 229 (S.D.N.Y.1994), a property owner whose tenant was the source of the contamination was denied the defense because, for a period of almost 10 years after the owner had reason to suspect a source of contamination on his property, he did not ask the tenant any questions about disposal practices. Id. at 235. In explaining the extent of this duty to investigate, the court stated that had the property owner investigated and discovered that its tenant had improperly disposed of waste on the property "due care would have required that [the owner] take some steps to ascertain the nature of any environmental threats associated with this disposal." Id. at 243–44.

e. *Failure to Perform Appropriate Inquiry*

The "all appropriate inquiry" requirement has probably generated more comment than any other element of the defense. The greatest problem raised by this element of the defense is that the statute requires "appropriate inquiry" without giving any guidance on determining appropriateness. To the extent that the legislative history of the provision provides guidance, it indicates a shifting standard where more sophisticated purchasers will be held to a higher standard and the standard will change over time so that all defendants will be held to a higher standard as public awareness of environmental concerns grows. *Conference Report*, 1986 U.S. Code Cong. & Admin. News at 3280. Furthermore, at least one court rejected the notion that there is an affirmative duty to inquire into the existence of hazardous waste when one acquires an interest in property under any conceivable circumstance. See, United States v. Serafini, 706 F.Supp. 346 (M.D.Pa.1988).

In United States v. Pacific Hide and Fur Depot, Inc., 716 F.Supp. 1341 (D.Idaho 1989), the U.S. District Court for the District of Idaho rejected the government's argument that CERCLA required in every case such a preliminary inquiry into the existence of hazardous waste. The *Pacific Hide and Fur* court determined that transfer from a father to his three children in an inter-vivos trust was more like an inheritance than a private transaction, which permitted the defendants to successfully assert the innocent landowner defense. Importantly, the *Pacific Hide and Fur* court emphasized that private transactions and inheritances are to be treated differently with regard to the type and extent of inquiry that must be undertaken.

The court in *Pacific Hide and Fur* further emphasized that in determining what is a "reasonable" or "appropriate" inquiry in an inheritance situation, the five factors enumerated in 42 U.S.C. § 9601(35)(B) will be applied. Those five factors are (1) the knowledge and experience of the buyer, (2) the relationship of the purchase price to the value of the property when uncontaminated, (3) the information regarding the use of the property, (4) the obviousness of the presence of any contamination, and (5) the ability to detect the contamination. The *Pacific Hide and Fur* opinion implies that, even in the inheritance or bequest situation, the circumstances of the individual case may indicate that some inquiry must be done.

In response to this problem, several attempts to establish standards have been made. See HR 570 (1993), "[i]f Congress must shift the costs of ferreting out contamination from the general public to those involved in real estate transactions it should, at a minimum, define the scope of the required investigation." 139 Cong. Rec. H218 (Jan. 25, 1993). The legislation would have defined a Phase I Environmental Audit and provided that an audit that meets that definition is presumed to satisfy "all appropriate inquiry."

The ASTM (formerly the American Society for Testing and Materials) has published a standard for site assessments intended to satisfy the "all appropriate inquiry" standard. The ASTM standard has become quite popular and a site assessment satisfying that standard is now required by most lending institutions. But there appear to be no published court decisions addressing the adequacy of an ASTM site assessment. Why might parties and courts not have tested the ASTM standards? There are several possible reasons. First, the legislative history of the defense indicates that Congress intended the requirement to vary based on factors such as the nature of the transaction and the sophistication of the buyer. Congress's intent may mean, therefore, that "all appropriate inquiry" cannot be standardized.

Second, in those published opinions in which a site assessment was performed and the "all appropriate inquiry" requirement was not met, the courts have questioned the Phase II portion of the audit and not the Phase I. For example, in LaSalle National Trust v. Schaffner, 1993 WL 499742 (N.D.Ill.1993), the Phase I report noted that a laundry had used PCE and that there was staining in the concrete floor. The Phase II work, however, did not include additional sampling to see if there had been a release of PCE. Additionally, in Wickland Oil Terminals v. Asarco, Inc., 792 F.2d 887 (8th Cir.), the purchaser was aware of the presence of metal slag on the site and was informed by its consultant that this did not pose an environmental risk. In denying the innocent purchaser defense, the court reasoned that the purchaser's inquiry was inadequate because it failed to examine publicly available information that would have revealed a risk.

What to test for in Phase II and where to test will always be issues to be determined by the professional judgment of the consultant on a site-by-site basis, not by a standard. Thus, the Phase I standard can satisfy the appropriate inquiry requirement *only if it reveals no areas of potential concern*.

A third possible reason that the standard has not helped establish the defense may be that the standard serves a more important goal. The chief goal of environmental due diligence should not be to have a defense when disaster strikes. It should be to prevent disaster from striking. That is, environmental due diligence should be designed to uncover whatever significant problems exist so that they can be dealt with in the transaction, or if they cannot, the buyer can avoid the problem by avoiding the transaction and leaving the seller to address the contamination itself. It could be that the ASTM Standard has not helped anyone achieve the innocent purchaser defense because it has helped prospective purchasers make better informed decisions regarding whether to purchase in the first place.

f. Successful Invocations of the Defense

The earliest cases seemed to indicate that no one is really innocent. For example, by the end of 1991, there were only two published decisions upholding the defense. See, Topol & Snow, Superfund Law & Procedure, Section 5.6 (West 1992). One, United States v. Pacific Hide & Fur Depot, Inc., 716 F.Supp. 1341 (D.Idaho 1989), involved people who obtained their interest in contaminated property by inheritance. The court, not surprisingly, concluded that one does not need to engage in due diligence before inheriting. The other, International Clinical Laboratories, Inc. v. Stevens, 20 Envtl. L. Rep. 20560, 1990 WL 43971 (E.D.N.Y.1990), provided no discussion of what environmental inquiry was performed or discussion of the requirements for the defense. It merely concluded that the requirements had been met. The unusual procedural context of this case made it particularly likely that some defense would be found. The suit, brought by the generator of the waste who had released the hazardous substances, sought contribution from a subsequent purchaser of the property.

See also New York v. Lashins Arcade Co., 91 F.3d 353 (2d Cir.1996) aff'd, 856 F.Supp. 153 (E.D.N.Y.1994), in which a property owner was found to be innocent. The facts are set forth in the opinion earlier in this chapter.

F. ALLOCATING THE CLEAN–UP COSTS: CONTRIBUTION ACTIONS AND OTHER DEVICES

The mere passive leaking or migration of waste does not constitute "disposal" of a hazardous substance in the context of an innocent landowner defense, a federal appeals court ruled in U.S. v. 150 Acres of Land, 204 F.3d 698 (6th Cir.2000).

The Court of Appeals for the Sixth Circuit reversed a district court decision granting summary judgment against the landholders, reasoning that the lower court had blurred the distinction between "disposal" and "release" of hazardous waste.

The district court determined that the "release" was not solely caused by a third party and that the defendants were responsible for the on-going "disposal" of hazardous substances, which continued after they acquired the property. Based on this reasoning, the lower court granted the government's summary judgment motion, thereby perfecting a lien on the property.

But the appellate court reversed, stressing that "disposal" requires "human intervention." According to the court, "in the absence of any evidence that there was human activity involved in whatever movement of hazardous substances occurred since the [defendants] have owned it" the defendants have not "disposed" of hazardous substances on the property.

The appellate court stressed that under the language of the statute, any person who owned or operated a facility at the time of the "disposal" of a hazardous substance is liable for all removal or remedial costs. If the owner establishes that the disposal occurred before he acquired the property, he can then assert an innocent landowner defense.

Do you understand the relationship between "disposal," "passive migration," and the "innocent landowner defense"? The decision is significant because a passive definition of "disposal" would make it impossible for a potentially responsible party to prove an innocent landowner defense. Without requiring "an active element," the government would only need to show that the contamination moved one micron following an owner's acquisition of property to show that the owner had disposed of a substance, thereby defeating the defense.

1. STANDARDS FOR OBTAINING CONTRIBUTION

The contribution action is brought by one or more PRPs against other PRPs for the purpose of distributing the costs of cleanup among many parties. It is this area of CERCLA law that is most influenced by the law of torts, and particularly where nuisance and strict liability tort actions are often involved. Under tort law, the right of contribution enables one joint tortfeasor that has paid more than its fair share in resolving a tort claim to sue other joint tortfeasors to recover the amount that it has paid in excess of that fair share. This principle helps to soften the harsh effects of joint and several liability by allowing the contribution plaintiff to recoup some of the losses it incurred in paying the original plaintiff (either the government or a private cost recovery plaintiff). Thus, even though the harm was indivisible for purposes of a government or private cost recovery action, nevertheless the damages may be allocable among many PRPs for contribution purposes.

Under CERCLA, an action for contribution usually arises in one of three situations: (1) the EPA has sued fewer than all the PRPs at a site under CERCLA § 106 or 107(a), and those "named" parties seek contribution against the other, unnamed PRPs at the site; (2) a PRP that has financed the cleanup at a site has brought a cost recovery action under CERCLA § 107(a)(4)(B) against fewer than all of the other PRPs at the site, and those named parties bring actions for contribution against the unnamed PRPs at the site, as well as counter-claims for contribution against the PRP originally seeking to recover its costs; or (3) a PRP brings an action to recover its response costs from another PRP at a site. This last situation is not technically a contribution action, but rather a cost recovery action, discussed above. A PRP's liability in a contribution action is not joint and several; rather it is proportionate liability only, which differentiates it from the cost recovery action which may result in the imposition of joint and several liability.

a. *Contribution Summarized*

While contribution principles have not changed radically in recent years, a new Restatement (Third) of Torts: Apportionment (1999) [which replaces the Restatement (Second) of Torts § 886A] defines in the black-letter rule the law:

> § 33.   Contribution

>> (a) When two or more persons are or may be liable for the same harm and one of them discharges the liability of another by settlement or discharge of judgment, the person discharging the liability is entitled to recover contribution from the other, unless the other previously had a valid settlement and release from the plaintiff.

>> (b) A person entitled to recover contribution may recover no more than the amount paid to the plaintiff in excess of the person's comparative share of responsibility.

* * *

The "comparative share of responsibility" simply means the percentage of fault assigned under a pure system of comparative fault, which the ALI recommends in a separate section of the Restatement (Third) of Apportionment § 10 (1999). Thus, a person seeking contribution must extinguish the liability of the person against whom contribution is sought for that portion of liability, either by settlement with the plaintiff or by satisfaction of judgment. See § 33, and comments thereto. This last point is important. The courts acknowledge that a contribution plaintiff has to share in liability with contribution defendants but no judgment of liability is required; a settlement is sufficient recognition of that liability, as a contrary rule would unduly discourage settlement, especially of CERCLA claims. See, United States v. Compaction Systems Corp., 88 F. Supp.2d 339 (D.N.J.1999).

The Restatement (Third) recognizes that, unlike CERCLA, many states no longer apply joint and several liability because of tort reform revisions enacted since the mid–1980s. Therefore, it states that in jurisdictions that continue to employ joint and several liability, a person who otherwise is entitled to contribution is entitled to recover the percentage share of liability of the person against whom contribution is sought plus that person's proportionate share of any other person's comparative share of liability. § 33, comment *g*.

Further, a person seeking contribution must prove that the person against whom contribution is sought would have been liable to the plaintiff in an amount and share equal to or greater than the amount of contribution. The person seeking contribution has the burden to prove the plaintiff's cause of action, and the person against whom contribution is sought has the burden of proving defenses. § 33 comment *j*.

Comment *b* of § 33 and Reporters' Notes explain the Uniform Contribution Among Tortfeasors Act, the Uniform Comparative Fault Act and state statutory variations which have authorized contribution in some jurisdictions since 1935, and today in all jurisdictions.

b. *Private Cost Recovery Actions under § 107 Versus Contribution Actions under § 113*

(i) Pre–SARA Developments

Probably no issue has produced more written opinions and controversy in the last decade than the issue of what remedial section of CERCLA a PRP must rely upon in seeking recoupment from other PRPs for all or a portion of the cleanup costs it incurred at a site. We have explored already the private cost recovery response action under § 107 which essentially places the PRP in the shoes of the governmental plaintiff; we now turn to whether a separate section of CERCLA explicitly covering contribution rights, § 9613(f), is the sole and proper remedial mechanism in suits by one PRP against other PRPs.

As we have seen, § 107(a)(4)(A) and (B) clearly provide causes of action for those who have undertaken a cleanup of a contaminated site as § 107(d)(4)(B) provides that "any other person" may recover "any other necessary costs of response" from PRPs. Recall that "response" is defined by the terms "remove, removal, remedy, and remedial action" 42 U.S.C. § 9601(25), i.e., essentially meaning to cleanup contamination. Therefore, a § 107 cost recovery action would seem to exist for the purpose of allowing parties who have undertaken a cleanup to shift the cost thereof to others. But § 107 does not explicitly allow a party who has been *held liable* for a cleanup to force others to share a portion of that liability. Pre–SARA jurisprudence supports this interpretation of § 107(a). As we have seen, pre-SARA litigation held that one PRP who voluntarily cleaned up a site in conformity with the NCP could bring a cost recovery action pursuant to § 107(a)(4)(B). But as enacted in 1980 CERCLA contained no explicit provision by which a party held liable to the government or to the EPA could maintain an action against other PRPs for contribution.

Nonetheless, many courts found an implied right of contribution available under CERCLA. Some courts supported this implied right of contribution by looking to § 107(e)(2) which preserves any other cause of action a potentially responsible party has against any other person. See, e.g., Wehner v. Syntex Agribusiness, Inc., 616 F.Supp. 27, 31 (E.D.Mo. 1985) (implying a contribution right under CERCLA § 107(e)(2) and noting that "the Justice Department has interpreted § 9607(e)(2) as allowing for contribution among joint tortfeasors"); U.S. v. Conservation Chem. Co., 619 F.Supp. 162, 228 (W.D.Mo.1985) (same). Other courts determined that they had the authority to fashion a federal common law of contribution either through Congress's implication of such authority in the legislative history of CERCLA or through the need to protect the significant federal interests of promoting settlement and preserving Superfund resources. See, e.g., United States v. New Castle County, 642 F.Supp. 1258, 1266 (D.Del.1986) (looking to federal common law and concluding that CERCLA's legislative history "is replete with Congressional support for a judicially created right to contribution").

(ii) Congress Enacts Explicit Contribution Remedy

Congress conclusively established the availability of contribution in CERCLA through the 1986 Superfund Amendments and Reauthorization Act (SARA), Pub. L. No. 99–499, 100 Stat 1613 (1986). Congress enacted an explicit contribution action provision in 1986 in CERCLA § 113(f), 42 U.S.C. § 9613 (f)(1), which provides:

> (1) *Contribution.* Any person may seek contribution from any other person who is liable or potentially liable under section 9607(a) of this title, during or following any civil action under section 9606 of this title or under section 9607(a) of this title. Such claims shall be brought in accordance with this section and the Federal Rules of Civil Procedure, and shall be governed by Federal law. In resolving contribution claims, the court may allocate response costs among liable parties using such equitable factors as the court determines are appropriate. Nothing in this subsection shall diminish the right of any person to bring an action for contribution in the absence of a civil action under section 9606 of this title or section 9607 of this title.

But why is the issue of whether § 107 or § 113(f) is the proper statutory mechanism important? First is the question of the nature of the liability–joint and several or several or proportionate only? Section 107 actions have permitted joint and several liability; but what about actions for contribution? How are "orphan shares" to be treated? At almost any large hazardous waste site, there are many tons of hazardous wastes which cannot be traceable to a known generator or transporter, or the party that would otherwise qualify as a "responsible party" under CERCLA might be defunct, bankrupt, uninsured, or otherwise lack resources to bear its "ideal measure of responsibility." The portion of the costs which cannot be allocated to any individual defendant are called "orphan shares."

Secondly, Congress enacted different statutes of limitation (6 years for § 107 claims, but 3 years for contribution claims under § 113(f). See, 42 U.S.C. § 9613(g)(2)-(3) (1999)). Third, we have seen that § 107 actions have minimal causation requirements and infuse a hard-edged strict liability; will these principles apply with equal force to a contribution action based on "equitable factors"? What implications on the critical issue of whether PRPs can now avail themselves of § 107 can we infer from the enactment of § 113(f) expressly authorizing contribution claims?

The Senate Report to § 113(f) explained that the new provision "clarifies and confirms the right of a person held jointly and severally liable under CERCLA to seek contribution from other potentially liable parties." S. Rep. No. 99-11, at 44 (1985). The later Conference Report likewise explained that "parties found liable under sections 104, 106 and 107 of CERCLA have a right of contribution which would allow them to sue other liable or potentially liable persons." H.R. Rep. No. 99–962, at 221 (1986). These legislative statements imply two things. First, originally CERCLA did not provide an express remedy for those against whom liability had been imposed and therefore a contribution provision had to be adopted to fill this gap in the law. Second, parties held liable were not seeking "cost recovery" from other parties but were seeking "contribution." Thus, it would appear that § 107(a) cost recovery actions and the new § 113(f) contribution actions serve different purposes.

(iii) Continuing Confusion

The Supreme Court's decision in Key Tronic Corp. v. United States, 511 U.S. 809, 114 S.Ct. 1960, 128 L.Ed.2d 797 (1994), which we considered earlier in this chapter on the issue of attorneys' fees, provides some guidance in resolving this debate but also raises some questions. The Supreme Court, in deciding whether attorneys' fees are recoverable in a claim brought by a PRP, stated:

> The 1986 [SARA] amendments included a provision–CERCLA § 113(f)–that expressly created a cause of action for contribution. See 42 U.S.C. § 9613(f). Other SARA provisions, moreover, appeared

to endorse the judicial decisions recognizing a cause of action under § 107 by presupposing that such an action existed. An amendment to § 107 itself, for example, refers to "amounts recoverable in an action under this section." 42 U.S.C. § 9607(a)(4)(D). The new contribution section also contains a reference to a "civil action * * * under section 107(a)." 42 U.S.C. 9613(f)(1). Thus the statute now expressly authorizes a cause of action for contribution in § 113 *and impliedly authorizes a similar and somewhat overlapping remedy in § 107.* Id. at 1965 (emphasis added).

Although this language clearly suggests that responsible parties still have a claim under § 107, it does not define that claim. One possible interpretation that reconciles the Supreme Court's statement, the statutory language, and traditional concepts of contribution is that one who is discharging a liability by performing a compelled cleanup may have an implied "contribution" claim under § 107; whereas one who is discharging a liability through a compelled payment of money to the party who is conducting a cleanup has a "contribution" claim under § 113. Until the Supreme Court decides whether § 113 is the exclusive remedy for jointly liable parties, strong arguments can be made that a responsible party has a "contribution claim" under CERCLA § 113 and a "somewhat overlapping" and "similar" remedy in § 107.

Based on this language and the purposes of CERCLA, some courts have found that potentially responsible parties may sue other potentially responsible parties under § 107(a) to recover costs of cleanup. See, e.g., Amcast Industrial Corporation v. Detrex Corporation, 2 F.3d 746, 748 (7th Cir.1993), cert. denied, 510 U.S. 1044, 114 S.Ct. 691, 126 L.Ed.2d 658 (1994) (upholding an admittedly liable party's claim under section 107(a), stating "[t]he statute is clear that whoever (like [plaintiff]) incurs costs in cleaning up a contaminated site can seek to recover them from any responsible person, and if the responsible person believes as [defendant] does that his contribution to the mess was trivial and wants the point established promptly he can counterclaim for as large a percentage of the costs as he thinks he can prove was due to the plaintiff's own conduct"); In re Dant & Russell, Inc., 951 F.2d 246, 248 (9th Cir.1991) (upholding a section 107 claim by one responsible party against another responsible party, stating it is "well-settled that § 9607(a)(1–4)(B) permits a private party to recover from a responsible party response costs it incurs itself in conducting cleanup pursuant to CERCLA"; but holding further that such a claim is *subject to equitable apportionment* under section 113); Bethlehem Iron Works, Inc. v. Lewis Industries, Inc. 891 F.Supp. 221, 225 (E.D.Pa.1995) ("[a]n examination of the text of sections 107 and 113 gives no indication that PRPs are prohibited from bringing claims pursuant to section 107").

Alternatively, other courts, now a majority, have held that any claim by a PRP against another PRP for recoupment of costs is one for contribution and governed exclusively by § 113(f). See, e.g., United Technologies Corp. v. Browning–Ferris Indust., 33 F.3d 96, 99 (1st Cir.1994) (stating that "contribution is a standard legal term * * *

[that] refers to a 'claim by and between jointly and severally liable parties for an appropriate division of the payment one of them has been compelled to make' " and restricting liable parties to a section 113 claim in a case where the plaintiff was subject to government CERCLA consent decree) (quoting Akzo Coatings, Inc. v. Aigner Corp., 30 F.3d 761, 764 (7th Cir.1994)); Akzo Coatings, Inc. v. Aigner Corp., 30 F.3d 761, 764 (7th Cir.1994) (holding that plaintiff's claim was "a quintessential claim for contribution" and exclusively governed by section 113 in a case where the plaintiff was subject to an EPA unilateral administrative order); United States v. Colorado & Eastern RR Co., 50 F.3d 1530 (10th Cir.1995) (restricting plaintiff's third-party claims in a government enforcement action to claims governed by section 113).

One authority has summarized the stakes in this debate:

Given the tremendous risks and costs involved in conducting cleanups of hazardous waste sites, the differences of these interpretations are significant. CERCLA § 107(a) imposes joint and several liability and permits the plaintiffs to recover the full amount of their response costs (consistent with the NCP) subject to a contribution counter-claim. However, under section 113, if liability is considered several only, the plaintiff may be able to recover only the amount for which it proves each defendant is responsible. Proving each defendant's share of the liability may present daunting evidentiary problems, particularly where contaminating activities date back for a long period of time. These evidentiary problems compound the risk, for example, that parties conducting the cleanup and seeking contribution under section 113 will be stuck with the "orphan shares" of liability attributable to parties that are unknown or insolvent. See United States v. Atlas Minerals & Chems., Inc., 1995 WL 510304 (E.D.Pa.1995) ("In this situation, a PRP which is otherwise amenable to cleaning up may be discouraged from doing so if it knows that, where the harm is indivisible, its only recourse for reimbursement is contribution from the solvent PRP's). A prohibition against joint and several liability would leave the willing PRP holding the bag for the insolvent companies." (quoting Allied Corp. v. Acme Solvents Reclaiming, Inc., 691 F.Supp. 1100, 1118 (N.D.Ill.1988)).

Additionally, the interaction between section 107(a) claims and section 113(f) contribution will "define the contours of the actions and * * * importantly, establish the burden of proof to be borne by each party." Under section 107(a), once their liability has been established, defendants will have the burdens of demonstrating entitlement to allocation and then each contribution defendant's equitable portion of the total liability. In contrast, if section 113 is the exclusive remedy for responsible parties, plaintiffs may have the burdens of proving the defendant's liability as well as their own liability and establishing the equitable portion of all parties.

Hernandez, Cost Recovery or Contribution?: Resolving the Controversy Over CERCLA Claims Brought by Potentially–Responsible Parties, 21 Harv. Envt'l L. Rev. 105–106 (1997).

For further discussion of these issues, see Ridgway M. Hall Jr., et al., Superfund Response Cost Allocation: The Law, the Science, and the Practice, 49 Bus. Law. 1489, 1502–04 (1994); Jerome M. Organ, Superfund and the Settlement Decision: Reflections on the Relationship Between Equity and Efficiency, 62 Geo. Wash. L. Rev. 1043 (1994); William D. Araiza, Text, Purpose and Facts: The Relationship Between CERCLA Sections 107 and 113, 72 Notre Dame L. Rev. 193, 200, 247–50 (1996).

Finally, there are some limitations in the application of a § 113(f) contribution claim. According to the language of § 113, a CERCLA contribution action is predicated upon the liability or potential liability of the contribution defendant as defined by § 107(a). Additionally, although a party may state a claim for contribution under § 113 during any civil action under § 106 or § 107(a), a party cannot receive actual payment in contribution until CERCLA liability is established. In addition, recovery under a contribution claim is subject to the wide discretion authorized by the language of § 113 which states: "[i]n resolving contribution claims, the court may *allocate response costs among liable parties using such equitable factors as the court determines are appropriate.*" 42 U.S.C. § 113(f)(1). Indeed, by the statutory language, allocation itself is available only in the court's discretion. As a result, the recovery under a CERCLA contribution claim may vary markedly from case to case. We turn now to one of the many opinions holding that § 113(f) is the exclusive remedial provision among PRPs.

NEW CASTLE COUNTY ET AL. v. HALLIBURTON NUS CORP.

United States Court of Appeals, Third Circuit, 1997.
111 F.3d 1116.

Mansmann, Circuit Judge.

We must decide whether a person who is potentially responsible for the clean-up of a hazardous waste site under the Comprehensive Environmental Response, Compensation, and Liability Act (CERCLA), 42 U.S.C. § 9601 et seq., may bring a cost recovery claim against other potentially responsible persons under CERCLA section 107(a)(4)(B), id. § 9607(a)(4)(B), separate from a contribution claim under section 113(f) of the Superfund Amendments and Reauthorization Act (SARA), id. § 9613(f). We conclude that a potentially responsible person may not bring a section 107 cost recovery claim against another potentially responsible person, and we will therefore affirm the judgment of the district court.

I.

This appeal arises from efforts to clean up the Tybouts Corner Landfill, a hazardous substance site located in Delaware. In 1980, the United States filed suit against New Castle County, the owner and operator of the landfill, and against the predecessor of Rhone–Poulenc, Inc., who arranged for the disposal of hazardous substances at the landfill. The case was originally brought under the Resource Conservation and Recovery Act, 42 U.S.C. § 6901 et seq., but the complaint was amended in 1984 to add counts under CERCLA. The CERCLA counts sought to have the defendants conduct remedial action and reimburse the EPA for its response costs. The amended complaint also added as a defendant the predecessor of Zeneca, Inc., an arranger for disposal at the landfill.

On April 19, 1989, the EPA entered into a series of consent decrees with New Castle County, Rhone–Poulenc and Zeneca (collectively "New Castle") and others, requiring them to finance and implement remedial action at the landfill. Prior to entry of the consent decrees, the EPA contracted with Halliburton NUS Corporation ("NUS") to perform a Remedial Investigation/Feasibility Study to determine appropriate response actions. As part of that determination, NUS installed several monitoring wells in areas where refuse had been placed during the landfill's operation. One of the wells, TY–311, was installed to assess the "Merchantville Formation," a clay strata separating a shallow formation containing groundwater impacted by landfill material and a formation containing groundwater used by New Castle County as drinking water. NUS reported that the Merchantville Formation was missing in the vicinity of TY–311.

According to New Castle, NUS improperly constructed well TY–311 such that (1) NUS' conclusion about the missing formation was incorrect and (2) NUS' construction of the well improperly opened a "window" between the two groundwater formations. New Castle learned of these alleged mistakes on the part of NUS in a report dated October 28, 1991. On October 26, 1993, New Castle filed this lawsuit against NUS. In Count II, New Castle asserted that NUS was liable under CERCLA section 107(a)(4)(B) for all or part of the response costs incurred by New Castle in connection with the landfill.

NUS moved for summary judgment as to Count II on the ground that it actually constituted a claim for contribution under CERCLA section 113(f)(1), and that the claim was therefore time-barred under section 113's three-year statute of limitations (unlike a section 107 cost recovery action, which is generally governed by a six-year statute of limitations).

The district court held that Count II constituted a claim for contribution under section 113. New Castle County v. Halliburton NUS Corp., 903 F.Supp. 771, 780 (D.Del.1995). The court also determined that New Castle's cause of action accrued on the date of the consent decrees. Id. at 777.

The district court further concluded that the limitations period on New Castle's contribution action was not equitably tolled and thus expired three years after the consent decrees were entered. The court dismissed Count II with prejudice. * * *

II.

CERCLA and SARA together create two different kinds of legal actions by which parties can recoup some or all of the costs associated with clean-ups: section 107 cost recovery actions, see 42 U.S.C. § 9607(a), and section 113 contribution actions, see id. § 9613(f)(1).

Section 107 of CERCLA provides that certain enumerated parties—"potentially responsible persons"—

> shall be liable for * * * all costs of removal or remedial action incurred by the United States Government * * * ; [and] any other necessary costs of response incurred by any other person consistent with the national contingency plan.* * *

Id. § 9607(a). Cost recovery actions are generally subject to a six-year statute of limitations. Id. § 9613(g)(2).

Section 113 of SARA provides that "[a]ny person may seek contribution from any other person who is liable or potentially liable under [section 107], during or following any civil action under [section 107]." Id. § 9613(f)(1). "No action for contribution for any response costs or damages may be commenced more than 3 years after * * * the date of * * * entry of a judicially approved settlement with respect to such costs or damages." Id. § 9613(g)(3).

The primary question in this appeal is whether New Castle's action against NUS is a cost recovery action or a contribution action. If it is a cost recovery action, it is timely; if it is a contribution action and we do not apply the discovery rule or equitable tolling, the action is not timely.* * *

Every court of appeals that has examined this issue has come to the same conclusion: a section 107 action brought for recovery of costs may be brought only by innocent parties that have undertaken clean-ups. An action brought by a potentially responsible person is by necessity a section 113 action for contribution. See Redwing Carriers, Inc. v. Saraland Apartments, 94 F.3d 1489, 1496 (11th Cir.1996); United States v. Colorado & Eastern R.R. Co., 50 F.3d 1530, 1536 (10th Cir.1995); United Technologies Corp. v. Browning–Ferris Indus., Inc., 33 F.3d 96, 99 (1st Cir.1994); Akzo Coatings, Inc. v. Aigner Corp., 30 F.3d 761, 764 (7th Cir.1994); see also Amoco Oil Co. v. Borden, Inc., 889 F.2d 664, 672 (5th Cir.1989). We agree with the conclusion reached by our sister courts.

A section 107 cost recovery action imposes strict liability on potentially responsible persons for costs associated with hazardous waste clean-up and site remediation. United States v. Alcan Aluminum Corp., 964 F.2d 252, 259 (3d Cir.1992); see also United States v. CDMG Realty Co., 96 F.3d 706, 712 (3d Cir.1996); Colorado & Eastern, 50 F.3d at 1535 ("it is now well settled that § 107 imposes strict liability on [potentially responsible persons]");

In general, a section 107 cost recovery action also imposes joint and several liability on potentially responsible persons. Alcan Aluminum, 964 F.2d at 268; see also Rumpke of Indiana, Inc. v. Cummins Engine Co.,

Inc., 107 F.3d 1235, 1240 (7th Cir.1997); Colorado & Eastern, 50 F.3d at 1535 ("It is also well settled that § 107 imposes joint and several liability on [potentially responsible persons] regardless of fault."); United Technologies, 33 F.3d at 100 (recognizing "presumed existence of joint and several liability"); United States v. Rohm & Haas Co., 2 F.3d 1265, 1280 (3d Cir.1993).

* * *

If New Castle is correct, a potentially responsible person found liable under section 107 could bring a section 107 action against another potentially responsible person and could recoup all of its expenditures regardless of fault. This strains logic. "[I]t is sensible to assume that Congress intended only innocent parties—not parties who were themselves liable—to be permitted to recoup the whole of their expenditures." United Technologies, 33 F.3d at 100.

In contrast, the term "contribution" is a standard legal term that refers to a claim "by and between jointly and severally liable parties for an appropriate division of the payment one of them has been compelled to make." Id. at 99 (quoting Akzo Coatings, 30 F.3d at 764). To resolve contribution claims, section 113 provides that "the court may allocate response costs among liable parties using such equitable factors as the court determines are appropriate." 42 U.S.C. § 9613(f)(1);

In other words, while a potentially responsible person should not be permitted to recover all of its costs from another potentially responsible person, the person should be able to recoup that portion of its expenditures which exceeds its fair share of the overall liability. Section 113 provides potentially responsible persons with the appropriate vehicle for such recovery. See CDMG Realty, 96 F.3d at 712 (individual liable under section 107 may seek contribution from other parties pursuant to section 113); * * *

Thus, section 113 does not in itself create any new liabilities; rather, it confirms the right of a potentially responsible person under section 107 to obtain contribution from other potentially responsible persons.

Our analysis finds support in the background and legislative history of SARA. Prior to the passage of SARA (and before the existence of section 113), it was not clear whether a potentially responsible person under section 107 could recover from other potentially responsible persons that portion of its clean-up costs that exceeded its fair share. * * *

Congress codified this right when it created section 113. A principal goal of section 113 was to "clarif[y] and confirm[ ] the right of a person held jointly and severally liable under CERCLA to seek contribution from other potentially liable parties, when the person believes that it has assumed a share of the cleanup or cost that may be greater than its equitable share under the circumstances." H.R.Rep. No. 99–253(I), at 79 (1985), reprinted in 1986 U.S.C.C.A.N. 2835, 2861; H.R. Conf. Rep. No. 99–962, at 221 (1986), reprinted in 1986 U.S.C.C.A.N. 3276, 3314.

Thus, prior to the passage of SARA and section 113, section 107 potentially responsible persons were required to rely upon an uncertain common law right of contribution. It was only upon passage of section 113 that these persons had a clear, statutory right to seek an equitable division of clean-up costs. The history and language of section 113 lend support to our conclusion that it, and not section 107, is the appropriate mechanism for obtaining a fair allocation of responsibility between two or more potentially responsible persons.

New Castle observes that section 107 provides that a potentially responsible person shall be liable for costs incurred by "any * * * person," 42 U.S.C., § 9607(a)(4)(B), and that the section is not expressly limited to innocent parties. In Akzo Coatings, the Court of Appeals for the Seventh Circuit recognized that while section 107 permits recovery by any person, the "person" must experience an injury of the type giving rise to a claim under section 107 to obtain relief under that section. 30 F.3d at 764. Since section 107 was designed to enable innocent persons who incur expenses cleaning up a site to recover their costs from potentially responsible persons, a potentially responsible person does not experience section 107 injury and cannot obtain section 107 relief. Instead, a claim by a potentially responsible person is "a quintessential claim for contribution." Id. Section 113(f)(1) confirms this fact, permitting a party to seek contribution from "any other" party potentially liable under section 107.

Likewise, the appellants in United Technologies v. Browning–Ferris, 33 F.3d 96 (1st Cir.1994), observed that section 107 states that responsible parties shall be liable to "any other person." 33 F.3d at 101. The appellants contended that the court should not limit section 107 "person[s]" to innocent parties. The Court of Appeals for the First Circuit rejected this argument, finding that such a reading would enable section 107 to swallow section 113, thus nullifying the three-year statute of limitations associated with actions for contribution. Id.; see also Colorado & Eastern, 50 F.3d at 1536 (if potentially responsible persons were permitted to recover from other potentially responsible persons under section 107, section 113 would be rendered meaningless).

New Castle argues that potentially responsible persons should have the choice to proceed under either section 107 or section 113. We disagree. Allowing a potentially responsible person to choose between section 107 (with a six-year statute of limitations and joint and several liability) and section 113 (with a three-year statute of limitations and apportioned liability based upon equitable considerations) would render section 113 a nullity. Potentially responsible persons would quickly abandon section 113 in favor of the substantially more generous provisions of section 107. We will not read section 107 so broadly that section 113 ceases to have any meaningful application. * * *

At oral argument, New Castle suggested that allowing it to sue under section 107 would not render section 113 a nullity. New Castle contended that section 113 would remain viable for nonsettling potentially responsible persons who seek to apportion prospective liability among each other. While New Castle is correct that section 113 is an appropriate vehicle for nonsettling parties to apportion potential liability, section 113 may also be used by settling parties seeking to obtain contribution. Section 113 provides that any person may seek contribution *"during or following"* any civil action under section 107. 42 U.S.C. § 9613(f)(1) (emphasis supplied). The use of the phrase "during or following" implies that section 113 may be used by both nonsettling and settling parties seeking to obtain contribution from other potentially responsible persons. In addition, section 113(f)(3) states that a person who has "resolved its liability to the United States" may seek contribution from non-settling potentially responsible persons. 42 U.S.C. § 9613(f)(3)(B). Clearly, section 113 is available to consent decree signatories such as New Castle. If we adopt New Castle's interpretation of section 107, however, the provisions of section 113 relating to settling persons will be of no effect.

Who, then, may bring a cost recovery action under section 107? While section 107 historically has been used by governments to recover costs incurred in the clean-up of hazardous sites, it is possible that a private person may be permitted to recover costs under section 107. See Rumpke of Indiana v. Cummins Engine Co., 107 F.3d 1235, 1239–42 (7th Cir.1997) (noting that landowner may bring section 107 action if party seeking relief is itself not responsible for having caused any hazardous materials to be spilled onto property); United Technologies, 33 F.3d at 99 n. 8 (suggesting, without deciding, that potentially responsible person who initiates clean-up without government prodding might be permitted to bring section 107 action); Akzo Coatings, 30 F.3d at 764 (hinting that private landowner forced to clean up hazardous materials that third party spilled onto its property or that migrated there from adjacent lands might pursue section 107 claim).

We do not decide under what circumstances a private individual may rely on section 107, or whether we endorse any of the exceptions for "innocent" landowners suggested by our sister courts. It is sufficient that we decide that a potentially responsible person under section 107(a), who is not entitled to any of the defenses enumerated under section 107(b), may not bring a section 107 action against another potentially responsible person.

Where both parties are "non-innocent" responsible persons, our sister courts have unanimously held that any action to reapportion costs between the parties is an action for contribution. See, e.g., Colorado & Eastern, 50 F.3d at 1536 ("any claim that would reapportion costs between these [potentially responsible persons] is the quintessential claim for contribution"); United Technologies, 33 F.3d at 101 (since plaintiffs admitted that they were liable parties, court concluded that claim must be one for contribution under section 113); see also Rumpke of Indiana, 107 F.3d at 1240 ("when two parties who both injured the property have a dispute about who pays how much ... the statute directs them to § 113(f) and only to § 113(f)"). We agree.

While it is possible that a private person may, under certain circumstances, bring a section 107 action, New Castle is not that person. At oral argument, New Castle conceded that it is a potentially responsible person under section 107(a). New Castle is therefore not permitted, under any scenario, to pursue a section 107 cost recovery action against other potentially responsible persons.

III.

The district court properly characterized Count II of the complaint as a claim for contribution under section 113 of SARA, a claim that is governed by a three-year statute of limitations. 42 U.S.C. § 9613(g)(3). The district court determined that the limitations period began to run on April 19, 1989, the date of the consent decrees. See id. (limitations period begins to run from date of judicially approved settlement). New Castle did not file this lawsuit until October 26, 1993. It therefore appears that the limitations period expired and that the district court properly dismissed New Castle's contribution claim with prejudice.

Notes and Questions

1. *The Split in Authority.* Without doubt, the holding in *New Castle* respecting the primacy of § 113 contribution over § 107 cost recovery when the plaintiff is a PRP has emerged as the majority view in this important debate. Accord, all holding that § 113 is the exclusive mechanism among PRPs, see, e.g., Bedford Affiliates v. Sills, 156 F.3d 416 (2d Cir.1998); Centerior Service Co. v. Acme Scrap Iron & Metal Corp., 153 F.3d 344 (6th Cir.1998); Pneumo Abex v. High Point, Thomasville & Denton R.R., 142 F.3d 769 (4th Cir.), cert. denied, 525 U.S. 963, 119 S.Ct. 407, 142 L.Ed.2d 330 (1998); Sun Co. v. Browning–Ferris Inc., 124 F.3d 1187 (10th Cir.1997), cert. denied, 522 U.S. 1113, 118 S.Ct. 1045, 140 L.Ed.2d 110 (1998); Carter–Jones Lumber Co. v. Dixie Distributing Co., 166 F.3d 840 (6th Cir.1999) (by implication).

But a few decisions continue to adhere to the view that a PRP can assert a § 107 cost-recovery action against other PRPs. See, e.g., Laidlaw Waste Systems, Inc. v. Mallinckrodt, Inc., 925 F.Supp. 624, 629–31 (E.D.Mo.1996), where the court disagreed with the holdings of the circuit courts of appeals and found that its own Eighth Circuit in Control Data Corp. v. S.C.S.C. Corp., 53 F.3d 930 (8th Cir.1995) (reproduced below) did not resolve the issue.

More significantly, in AM Int'l v. Datacard Corp., 106 F.3d 1342 (7th Cir.1997), the Seventh Circuit held that a company that bought property knowing it was already contaminated could maintain recovery claims under § 107(a), and was not limited to § 113 contribution in its action against the former site owner. The court explained that its decision was consistent with its ruling in Akzo Coatings, Inc. v. Aigner Corp., 30 F.3d 761 (7th Cir.1994), in which it stated that although cost recovery actions between PRPs "should ordinarily be addressed as claims for contribution" under § 113, "if a landowner faces liability solely because a third party spilled or allowed hazardous waste to migrate onto its property, the landowner may directly sue for its response costs."

The court disagreed with AMI that the district court erred in its ruling that Datacard could pursue response costs under CERCLA § 107(a)(4)(B). The court acknowledged that it held in Akzo Coatings, Inc. v. Aigner Corp., 30 F.3d 761 (7th Cir.1994), that cost recovery actions between PRPs "should ordinarily be addressed as claims for contribution" under § 113. However, the court said, in *Akzo* it noted that "if a landowner faces liability solely because a third party spilled or allowed hazardous waste to migrate onto its property, the landowner may directly sue for its response costs." Even if Datacard bought the property at a reduced rate because of the contamination, the court said, it did not take part in the manufacture of Blankrola and "faces liability merely due to its status as landowner," and as a result qualified for the *Akzo* "innocent" party exception.

Another detailed opinion is Pinal Creek Group v. Newmont Mining Corp., 118 F.3d 1298 (9th Cir.1997) cert. denied 524 U.S. 937, 118 S.Ct. 2340, 141 L.Ed.2d 711 (1998). Plaintiff consisted of three mining companies who engaged in a voluntary cleanup of the Pinal Drainage Basin hazardous waste site. The plaintiff, admitting that it was a PRP, sued other PRPs "for the totality of the cleanup costs and to impose joint and several liability on defendant-PRPs for that amount." The court's analysis in part reads as follows:

> The Newmont PRPs [Defendants] counter that, even if the Pinal Group is free to assert a claim under § 107, their liability to the Pinal Group would be for contribution under the combined effect of §§ 107 and 113. Accordingly, the Newmont PRPs argue that the liability of each of them would be several, and not joint, and would extend only to each party's own equitable share of the costs incurred by the Pinal Group. We agree.

> Because all PRPs are liable under the statute, a claim by one PRP against another PRP necessarily is for contribution. A PRP's contribution liability will correspond to that party's equitable share of the total liability and will not be joint and several. CERCLA simply does not provide PRPs who incur cleanup costs with a claim for the joint and several recovery of those costs from other PRPs. As discussed below, our holding today is mandated by the text, structure, and legislative history of §§ 107 and 113, as well as by precedent.

> * * *

> The text of § 107 leads to the conclusion that only a claim for contribution lies between PRPs. Under the literal language of § 107, the Pinal Group, as a PRP, is partly responsible for its cleanup costs and, as "any other person" under § 107, can also hold other PRPs liable for a portion of those same costs. This duality is best implemented by permitting a PRP who has incurred cleanup costs to assert only a contribution claim against other PRPs. Viewed in that way, the Pinal Group is responsible only for that portion of the liability which it equitably should bear anyway, while being entitled to hold other PRPs severally liable for each of their, respective, equitable shares of the total costs.

That is the essence of a claim for contribution which, albeit implicitly, is imbedded in the text of § 107.

* * *

Together, §§ 107 and 113 provide and regulate a PRP's right to claim contribution from other PRPs. Key Tronic, 511 U.S. at 814–18, 114 S.Ct. at 1965–66 (remedies in §§ 107 and 113 described as "similar and somewhat overlapping"). The contours and mechanics of this right are now governed by § 113. Put another way, *while* § 107 *created the right of contribution, the "machinery" of* § 113 *governs and regulates such actions, providing the details and explicit recognition that were missing from the text of* § 107.

118 F.3d at 1301–02 (emphasis added).

This last point respecting the relationship between § 107 and § 113 is made by one court as follows:

Section 113(f), however, does not create the right of contribution– rather the source of a contribution claim is section 107(a). Under CERCLA's scheme, section 107 governs liability, while section 113(f) creates a mechanism for apportioning that liability among responsible parties.

United States v. ASARCO, Inc., 814 F.Supp. 951, 956 (D.Colo.1993).

In rejecting the joint and several approach advocated by plaintiff in *Pinal Group*, the Ninth Circuit reasoned:

As is the case traditionally in contribution actions between tortfeasors, CERCLA's claim for contribution creates several-only liability among PRPs. Accordingly, the Pinal Group is foreclosed from imposing joint and several liability on any of the Newmont PRPs, even with respect to any amount that may exceed the Pinal Group's own equitable share of the cleanup costs. A contrary approach is not supported by CERCLA's text, is inconsistent with the traditional doctrine of contribution, entails a significant risk of producing unfair results, and runs the risk of creating procedural chaos.

The "joint and several" approach would be contrary to the statutory scheme created by CERCLA. If a group of defendant-PRPs is held jointly and severally liable for the total response costs incurred by a claimant-PRP, reduced by the amount of claimant-PRP's own share, those defendant-PRPs would end up absorbing all of the cost attributable to "orphan shares"—those shares attributable to PRPs who either are insolvent or cannot be located or identified. There is no statutory support for such a rule, which would immunize the claimant-PRP from the risk of orphan-share liability and would restrict substantially the ability of courts to apportion costs equitably pursuant to § 113(f). Immunizing PRPs who have directly paid for cleanup operations from the risk of sharing the cost associated with orphan shares would undermine the ability of courts to allocate costs between all PRPs "using such equitable factors as the court determines are appropriate." 42 U.S.C. § 9613(f)(1). Under § 113(f)(1), the cost of orphan shares is distributed equitably among all PRPs, just as cleanup costs are.

118 F.3d at 1303. But does the voluntary PRP gain nothing from its initiative? In *Pinal Group* the court pointed to one possible benefit:

> Of course, in equitably allocating responsibility between PRPs, courts are free to consider, together with other relevant factors, the fact that a PRP has itself engaged in cleanup efforts and the circumstances surrounding those efforts. 41 U.S.C. § 9613(f)(1); H.R. Rep. No. 99–253, pt. 3, at 19 (1985), reprinted in 1986 U.S.C.C.A.N. 3038, 3042 (in apportioning costs, courts may consider "the degree of cooperation of the parties with government officials to prevent any harm to public health or the environment"); Central Me. Power Co. v. F.J. O'Connor Co., 838 F.Supp. 641, 646–47 (D.Me.1993) ("degree of cooperation with government officials to prevent any harm to * * * the environment" is a "very important" factor "in the contribution analysis").

118 F.3d at 1303 n.4.

Pinal Creek has an interesting post script. The Pinal Creek Group petitioned the Supreme Court for review on the grounds that the federal circuits had developed varying and conflicting interpretations of the interrelationship between CERCLA §§ 107 and 113. Newmont Mining [Defendants] opposed the petition, arguing that the Ninth Circuit's ruling turned on the question of whether a PRP may assert a claim against a fellow PRP for joint and several liability, not whether such a claim is grounded in § 107 or 113. The Supreme Court invited the U.S. Solicitor General to submit a brief presenting the government's position on the issue. The Solicitor General urged the high court to decline review. The Solicitor General argued to the Court that, contrary to the assertions presented by Pinal Creek Group:

> every court of appeals that has addressed the question presented has held, as did the court below, that a responsible private party seeking recovery of response costs under CERCLA from another jointly responsible party may sue only for contribution.

(Brief for the United States as Amicus Curiae on Petition for a Writ of Certiorari to the United States Court of Appeals for the Ninth Circuit at 6, 10, Pinal Creek Group v. Newmont Mining Corporation, et al., 118 F.3d 1298, 1301 (9th Cir.1997)). In addition, the Solicitor General stated, "the court of appeals decision is correct [on the merits]." *Id.* The Supreme Court, possibly agreeing as to the absence of conflict among the Courts of Appeal, denied the petition, 524 U.S. 937, 118 S.Ct. 2340, 141 L.Ed.2d 711 (1998).

2. *"Working PRPs."* A few courts have sought to carve out another distinction between so-called "working PRPs" who actually conduct cleanup operations, and PRPs seeking to recoup reimbursed costs paid to the earlier government plaintiff, typically the EPA. In United Technologies Corp. v. Browning–Ferris Industries, 33 F.3d 96 (1st Cir.1994) the court explained that the working PRP asserted a claim to apportion costs between all PRPs. However, to avoid the effect of § 113, the working PRP asserted that its claim was not really a "contribution" claim controlled by § 113, but rather a "cost recovery" claim under § 107 which, as such, was not subject to the limiting provisions of § 113.

> A "working PRP" is a convenient label for a PRP that actually conducts cleanup operations, as opposed to one that reimburses a third party for the cost of the latter's cleanup efforts. The First Circuit has referred to

costs incurred by a non-working PRP as "reimbursed costs" and to costs incurred by a working PRP as "first instance costs." *United Tech.*, 33 F.3d at 97.

Similarly, in United Technologies, 33 F.3d at 101–03, the First Circuit rejected a working PRP's attempt to avoid the shorter three-year statute of limitations that applies to contribution actions. 42 U.S.C. 9613(g). The PRP in United Technologies argued that only claims seeking apportionment of reimbursed costs are "contribution" claims subject to the shorter period of § 113(g)(3) and that, since its claim sought apportionment of first-instance costs, it really was asserting a cost recovery action subject to the longer limitation period of § 113(g)(2). As did the Seventh and Tenth Circuits, the First Circuit rejected this artificial distinction between working and non-working PRPs and applied the three-year statute of limitations to the working PRP's claim. United Tech., 33 F.3d at 101–03.

Rejecting the "working" and "non-working" PRPs distinction see, also, Akzo Coatings, Inc. v. Aigner Corp., 30 F.3d 761, 764 (7th Cir.1994); U.S. v. Colorado & Eastern R.R. Co., 50 F.3d 1530 (10th Cir.1995).

3. *Policy Arguments.* What about the policy argument that PRPs need the clout of § 107 in order to promote rapid voluntary cleanups, a goal sacrificed by the more fact-intensive contribution process? In *Pinal Group* the court rejected that proposition:

> In any event, we are not convinced that the policy of promoting rapid voluntary cleanups would be undermined to any significant degree by our holding. As discussed above, courts may take into account the degree of cooperation shown by a PRP when equitably allocating liability among PRPs under § 113(f)(1). * * * In addition, other incentives exist for PRPs to conduct cleanup operations promptly. For example, a PRP who (like the Pinal Group) conducts business at a contaminated site would, by engaging in cleanup operations itself, protect its on-going operations and be better able to control its cleanup costs, than if it waited for the government to intervene.

118 F.3d at 1304–1305.

4. Finally, what of this argument? That working PRPs must be allowed to maintain cost recovery actions under § 107 for the totality of its costs, because it would not qualify for a contribution action under § 113:

> The Pinal Group asserts it would not be entitled to assert a contribution claim under § 113(f) against the Newmont PRPs because it has not incurred any liability which would trigger such an action. Specifically, it contends that the requisite liability only attaches if the government incurs response costs, arguing that before then, no liability exists under § 107(a), and that the Pinal Group's status as a PRP, by itself, does not give rise to a claim for contribution.

> We reject this argument because it is wrong as well as internally inconsistent. As the Newmont PRPs have conceded, the Pinal Group is entitled to assert a contribution claim here. Although it is true that PRP status, by itself, does not generate liability, the Pinal Group ignores the "necessary costs of response incurred by [it] consistent with the national contingency plan." 42 U.S.C. § 9607(a). Prior to its expenditure, the

Pinal Group was not yet liable because no one, not the government, not any other PRPs or any non-PRP private parties, had yet incurred any costs under § 107.

However, once the Pinal Group undertook those "necessary costs of response," it, along with all PRPs associated with the Pinal Creek site, became partly responsible for those costs. This resulted in a situation where all PRPs, including the Pinal Group, bear some responsibility for those cleanup costs. Under § 107, the Pinal Group's responsibility for its own equitable share of the cleanup costs is generated independently of any liability that might arise from response costs incurred by the government. Cf. United Tech., 33 F.3d at 99 n. 8 (suggesting that "a PRP who spontaneously initiates a cleanup without governmental prodding might be able to pursue an implied right of action for contribution").

118 F.3d at 1305–1306.

Until or unless the Supreme Court enters the fray, it appears that for now PRPs are mostly limited to contribution actions against other PRPs, and do not have standing to assert a cost recovery action under § 107.

5. *More on "Innocence."* Pursuing the "innocence" idea a bit further, what of the party that cleans up a waste site in response to an EPA administrative order, and never itself contributed to the waste at the site? There is authority that such a plaintiff could avail itself of a § 107 cost recovery action. In Sun Company v. Browning–Ferris, Inc., 124 F.3d 1187 (10th Cir.1997), plaintiffs responded to a § 106 order to remediate the site, but never was a party to a § 107 action instituted by the government. The court rejected the § 107 standing:

The fact that Plaintiffs incurred cleanup costs by complying with a unilateral administrative order, without forcing the government to take them to court, does not change their status as jointly and severally liable parties. They concede that they generated wastes containing hazardous substances that were transported to the Site. Thus, Plaintiffs' claim is still by and between jointly and severally liable parties, seeking the equitable apportionment of a payment which Plaintiffs have been compelled to make, and is still a claim for contribution.

We express no opinion on whether PRPs who assert their innocence with regard to any waste at a site may be able to recover all of their costs from other PRPs in an action under § 107. See Redwing Carriers, Inc. v. Saraland Apts., 94 F.3d 1489, 1496 (11th Cir.1996); United Technologies v. Browning–Ferris Indus., Inc., 33 F.3d 96, 99–100 (1st Cir.1994), cert. denied, 513 U.S. 1183, 115 S.Ct. 1176, 130 L.Ed.2d 1128 (1995); Akzo Coatings, Inc. v. Aigner Corp., 30 F.3d 761, 764 (7th Cir.1994), after remand, 134 F.3d at 1190 n. 1.

It is thus clear that "because § 113(f) incorporates the liability provisions of 107, * * * a § 113(f) action for contribution is an action under § 107." Bancamerica Commercial, 100 F.3d at 801. While a § 113 contribution action is not a "cost recovery" action under § 107 as that action has been defined, because it does not impose strict, joint and several liability on the defendant PRPs, it is an action for recovery of the costs referred to in § 107. Under CERCLA's statutory scheme, therefore, a PRP's contribution action seeks to recover costs referred in to § 107 from PRPs whose liability is defined by § 107, but is governed by the equitable apportionment principles established in § 113(f).

Id. These issues are complicated by the abstruse statutes of limitation provisions governing § 113(f) contribution actions, which we intentionally do not explore with respect for the students' mental health.

At least one article makes an impassioned plea for more aggressive application of the due diligence test as integral to the innocent landowner and third party defenses as it relates to the § 107 versus § 113 issue. See, Craig Johnston, Current Landowner Liability Under CERCLA: Restoring the Need for Due Diligence, 9 Fordham Envtl. L.J. 401 (1998), the author summarizes why a finding of due diligence is so critical to defenses under CERCLA:

> The Seventh Circuit's decisions in AMI [AM International, Inc. v. Datacard Corp., 106 F.3d 1342 (7th Cir.1997)] and Rumpke [Rumpke of Indiana v. Cummins Engine Co., 107 F.3d 1235 (7th Cir.1997)] are not as troubling as either the Lashins [New York v. Lashins Arcade Co., 91 F.3d 353 (2d Cir.1996)] or Alcan/Rohm & Haas lines of cases, but they may still be problematic. Again, these cases addressed whether landowners which have played no direct role in causing contamination may pursue cost-recovery claims under section 107(a)(4) or, alternatively, whether they are limited to contribution claims under section 113(f). The court allowed both landowners to pursue cost-recovery claims. In *Rumpke*, the court appeared to indicate that this claim would be based on principles of joint and several liability.

> If these cases stand for the proposition that any landowners who did not actively contribute to contamination are entitled to full recovery as a matter of law in their actions against other PRPs, even where they do not meet the requirements of the innocent landowner defense, they are inconsistent with Congress's view of the "responsibility" that non-diligent landowners bear under CERCLA. Again, Congress considered those who have acquired contaminated property without having performed adequate investigations to be liability-worthy under CERCLA. The statute decrees that if they have not performed the appropriate investigations, they are to be treated as if they "had reason to know" of the relevant contamination. Their having proceeded with the purchase in the face of this constructive knowledge makes them "responsible" in the CERCLA sense of the term.

> The Second Circuit recently rejected the *AMI/Rumpke* analysis in a closely related context for this very same reason. In Bedford [Bedford Affiliates v. Sills, 156 F.3d 416 (2d Cir.1998)], the defendant landlord cited *Rumpke* in arguing that it should be allowed to go forward with a section 107(a)(4) cost recovery claim against its subtenant because the landlord was limited to a contribution claim, the court held, "[a] potentially responsible person under section 107(a) that is not entitled to any of the defenses enumerated under section 107(b), like Bedford, cannot maintain a section 107(a) action against another potentially responsible person." Elsewhere, the court explained its rationale in the

following terms: "One of the questions plaintiff raises is whether it, as a party 'innocent' of causing a hazardous spill, should completely escape liability for the costs of the cleanup." The answer is "no." To be innocent in a CERCLA response cost suit, one must be innocent in the eyes of the law. To be ignorant of the contaminated condition on one's property may be a generic form of innocence, but not the kind that will escape liability under the statute.

Once one recognizes that non-diligent landowners are not "blameless" in the eyes of CERCLA, the next question involves the type of claim they should have against other PRPs. But this question answers itself. As the *Bedford* court and others have recognized, Congress created section 113(f) for the express purpose of allocating liability among jointly and severally liable parties. Therefore, it only makes sense for courts to look to this provision. This should be true regardless of whether the landowner cleaned up the site at the behest of EPA or a State, thus giving rise to a prototypical contribution claim under section 113(f) (as was the case in *Bedford*), or whether the landowner may have cleaned up the site on its own initiative, thus possibly giving rise to an implied contribution claim under section 107(a)(4)(B).

9 Fordham Envtl. L.J. 465–467. We have yet to consider the contribution protection provisions of § 113(f)(2). Pursuant to § 113(f)(2), PRPs who settle with the EPA receive contribution protection to the extent of matters covered in the settlement. Thus, under CERCLA, settlement with the government is a defense to § 113 contribution claims, but not to § 107 cost recovery claims. If PRPs could proceed against other PRPs under § 107, settling PRPs would arguably have no contribution protection. Thus, allowing PRPs to maintain § 107 cost recovery claims would not only nullify the statute of limitations for contribution actions in § 113, it would also nullify the settlement and finality provision of § 113(f)(2), rendering that provision illusory. This topic is addressed later in this chapter in more detail. But taking a crack at some problems at this juncture seems timely.

Problems

The following problems are taken from Michael Hernandez, Cost Recovery or Contribution? Resolving the Controversy over CERCLA Claims Brought by Potentially Responsible Parties, 21 Harv. Envt'l L. Rev. 83, 114, 116, 120 (1997) (reprinted with permission).

PART A

"Site X" is a facility as defined by section 101(9) contaminated with hazardous substances as defined by section 101(14). There are four PRPs. "A" has owned and operated Site X during the entire time that hazardous substances have been released there. "B," an insolvent corporation, generated some of the hazardous substances. "C," a solvent corporation, generated the remaining hazardous substances. "D," a solvent company, delivered all of the hazardous waste generated by B and C to the site. The harm is indivisible, and the four PRPs share equal responsibility for the contamination, i.e., each PRP is responsible for 25% of the entire liability. The entire cleanup will cost $1 million.

Assume that the EPA cleans up Site X in a manner consistent with the NCP. The EPA either files a cost recovery action against C and D and C and D are held jointly and severally liable by final judgment or a consent decree, or the EPA simply settles with C and D without filing an action. C and D are obligated to pay more than their proportionate share of liability and thus want to sue A.

How would you characterize the claims of C and D against A? Why? How much can C and D each recover? How is B's share to be handled?

PART B

Continue to apply the basic facts from Part A. Assume A voluntarily cleans up Site X in a manner consistent with the NCP. It is irrelevant whether A receives input from the state or the EPA on how to conduct the cleanup. A is under no compulsion to clean up Site X; there is no state law requiring A to do so, and neither the state nor the EPA has initiated any action against any PRP. How would you decide the appropriate remedy here? Why or why not might it be different than Part A? Hint: Why is this *not* a "quintessential claim for contribution"? What is the core problem respecting the application of § 113(f).

PART C

Again apply the basic facts from Part A. Assume A cleans up Site X because it has a legal duty to do so. There are a number of reasons why A may have this duty. A may be subject to a section 106(a) administrative or judicial order. State law may require A to clean up the site, or A may have entered into a consent decree that obligates A to clean up Site X.

Now what remedy does A pursue against C and D? Why?

6. *Proposals for a Consistent Rule.* Some commentators have advocated a resolution of the § 107 versus § 113 debate by applying what they regard as a more consistent approach. Space doesn't permit describing all of these alternative approaches. The student is encouraged to read some of these articles cited in this section.

First, Professor Stephen Ferrey has advocated a "muscular" application of joint and several liability. Steven Ferrey, "Allocation and Uncertainty in the Age of Superfund: A Critique of the Redistribution of CERCLA Liability," 3 N.Y.U. Envt'l L. J. 36 (1994). Where a private party settles with EPA and thereby obtains global contribution protection under CERCLA § 113(f)(2), the settling PRP may use its settlement as both a "shield" and a "sword" and proceed against nonsettling PRPs under § 107(a). In a subsequent § 107(a) action, it is theoretically possible for a settling party to shift 100 percent of the liability to nonsettling PRPs under "entire" liability. Total shifting of liability to recalcitrant PRPs depends upon the court's employing a strict interpretation of joint and several liability and treating contribution protection as absolute.

Ferrey believes that a total shift of all cleanup costs to nonsettling PRPs would encourage earlier settlements and faster remedial action. Under this scenario, the conventional approach of many PRPs—hiding from identification and not volunteering to clean up—would likely be changed. If the settling PRPs can shift all their response costs, there is considerable incentive for PRPs to voluntarily step forward, negotiate an early settlement with EPA, and file a § 107(a) suit. Ferrey's proposal may promote swifter cleanups. Arguably, however, fundamental fairness will be achieved only if the nonsettlors actually were responsible for a substantial portion of the site's conditions. The proposed rule could unfairly shift cleanup costs to low level or minor PRPs, especially small volume generators. In other words, Ferrey's proposal could result in "mom and pop" operations having to pick up the entire cleanup cost. Since many low level PRPs are judgment-proof, Ferrey's "trickle down" proposal may be viewed as either impractical or unfair.

For other articles, see, Steven B. Russo, "Contribution Under CERCLA: Judicial Treatment After SARA," 14 Colum. J. of Envt'l L. 267 (1989); Jerome M. Organ, "Superfund and the Settlement Decision: Reflection on the Relationship Between Equity and Efficiency," 62 Geo. Wash. L. Rev. 1043 (1994).

Finally, Michael Hernandez' article, which we have quoted above, makes this simplified proposal to reconcile the 113 versus 107 issue. In his paper, Hernandez suggests a possible solution to the confusion surrounding cost recovery. He suggests that a PRP that voluntarily remediates a site should be able to file a cost recovery action against other PRPs and thereby be eligible to obtain joint and several judgment against them. This would create an incentive for parties to voluntarily clean up sites known to be contaminated. Also, he suggests that the court require these defendant PRPs to be responsible for any "orphan shares." Again, this would create an incentive for voluntary cleanups.

If a PRP does not remediate the site, but only wishes to share any liability imposed on it, he suggests the action be limited to contribution only, and the plaintiff will be proportionately responsible for any orphan shares. Furthermore, he says, if the PRP is legally forced to clean up a site, for example by the EPA, before it files a claim, the PRP can choose between bringing a cost recovery or a contribution claim. In this case, however, whether the party decides to pursue cost recovery or contribution, it would be required to pay for a portion of any left over orphan shares.

Hernandez does not believe that the courts would be imposing their will on the law by putting his plan in action. He believes that a common law reading of CERCLA would bring anyone to the same conclusion. Under common law, "If you incur costs, you have a right to seek cost recovery," he says. Where the contribution-only thinkers go wrong is when they interpret Sec. 113(f). Often, courts have said that if a party voluntarily cleans up a site, it has no right to seek cost recovery because it is not an "innocent" party. Hernandez notes that the word "potential" in potentially responsible parties does not imply automatic guilt. It means that a party might be responsible for the contamination, or it might not. Whether or not the party is responsible has yet to be established, so that party should be at least potentially able [to] recover all of its costs.

The main point of Hernandez's argument is that under his plan, parties would have an incentive to clean up hazardous sites before legal actions take place.

See Hernandez Cost Recovery or Contribution? Resolving the Controversy over CERCLA Claims Brought by Potentially Responsible Parties, 21 Harv. Envt'l L. Rev. 83 (1997). See also Frank Celia, Cost Recovery or Contribution under CERCLA: Untangling the Web of Caselaw and Suggesting How to End the Confusion, 19 Haz. Waste Litig. Rep. 1–7 (1998).

2. THE ALLOCATION PROCESS IN CONTRIBUTION ACTIONS

a. Introduction

Having resolved the threshold question that PRPs in virtually all situations can only seek to distribute or reallocate the costs of cleanup by virtue of § 113 contribution actions, the next set of issues relates to what considerations bear on how in fact will those costs be reallocated among all PRPs who are parties to the action.

Although CERCLA § 113 provides courts wide discretion in allocating costs of remediation, the statute does not provide express guidance on how the courts are to allocate the costs and the EPA has provided no significant guidance. See United States v. R.W. Meyer, 932 F.2d 568, 572 (6th Cir.1991) (stating the Congress's use of the phrase "such equitable factors as the court determines are appropriate" broadens the trial court's scope of discretion even further than the traditional "large degree of discretion"). In the absence of explicit statutory or agency guidance regarding what factors are relevant when allocating remediation costs, courts and parties have grappled with, fashioned and advocated differing methods of allocating such costs among the responsible parties.

Legislative history makes it clear that the apportionment is to be determined according to the facts of each case. See H.R. 253 (III), 99th Cong., 2d Sess. 19 (1985), reprinted in 1986 U.S.C.C.A.N. 3038, 3041–3042 ("The committee emphasizes that courts are to resolve claims for apportionment on a case-by-case basis pursuant to [f]ederal common law, taking relevant equitable considerations into account."). However, the starting point for many courts in allocating costs under § 113 is the so-called "Gore Factors." See Environmental Transp. Sys. v. ENSCO, Inc., 969 F.2d 503, 509 (7th Cir.1992) (stating Gore factors are "possible considerations when making an equitable allocation decision"); United States v. A & F Materials Co., Inc., 578 F.Supp. 1249, 1256 (S.D.Ill. 1984). See also H.R. Rep. No. 253, 99th Cong., 1st Session 19 (1985), reprinted in 1986 U.S.C.C.A.N. at 3042 (legislative history of § 9613(f) cites these criteria as factors a court may consider when deciding whether and how much to grant apportionment in a contribution action).

As private CERCLA actions play an increasingly prominent role, courts are being called upon more frequently to allocate liability among two or more PRPs. Because the contribution provision directs courts to "allocate response costs among liable parties using such equitable factors as the court determines are appropriate," § 113(f)(1), it is difficult to generalize about allocation decisions. The following sampling of two appellate court decisions concern the allocation of CERCLA liability among PRPs.

b.   *Elements of the Contribution Action*

Just as in § 107 cost-recovery actions, contribution actions have well-defined elements for the prima facie case, apart from evidence respecting the equitable allocation of the response costs. In Bedford Affiliates v. Sills, 156 F.3d 416 (2d Cir.1998), the court of appeals explained:

> Turning to CERCLA § 113(f)(1), Sills [the defendant operator] contends that Bedford [property owner] is not entitled to recover because it failed to establish a prima facie cause of action. The elements of an action under § 113(f)(1) are the same as those under § 107(a). See CERCLA § 113(f)(1), 42 U.S.C. § 9613(f)(1) ("Any person may seek contribution from any other person who is liable or potentially liable under [CERCLA § 107(a)(1)]."). Hence, to establish a prima facie cause of action for contribution, a private party must show
>
> (1) Defendant fits within one of the four classes of responsible parties outlined in § 107(a).
>
> (2) The site is a facility.
>
> (3) There is a release or threatened release of hazardous substances at the facility.
>
> (4) The plaintiff incurred costs responding to the release or threatened release.
>
> (5) The costs and response actions conform to the * * * (National Contingency Plan).

Accord, B.F. Goodrich v. Murtha, 958 F.2d 1192, 1198 (2d Cir.1992); B.F. Goodrich v. Betkoski, 99 F.3d 505, 514 (2d Cir.1996), cert. denied, 524 U.S. 926, 118 S.Ct. 2318, 141 L.Ed.2d 694 (1998). Add to the necessity of compliance with the NCP, the court of appeals in *Bedford Affiliates* held that the plaintiff-property owner's failure to provide any opportunity for public comment prior to initiating cleanup of the property did not preclude recovery of response costs in the contribution action on grounds that cleanup did not comply with the NCP because the state environmental agency was substantially involved in the formulation and execution of the preliminary remediation plan, and such involvement was an effective substitute for public comment.

Although not stated expressly in the list of elements in *Bedford Affiliates*, recall that § 107(a) authorizes recovery only for "necessary" costs of response. For example, in Bethlehem Iron Works, Inc. v. Lewis Industries, 1996 WL 557592 (E.D.Pa.1996), the district court held that a contribution action failed because of plaintiff's failure to prove "necessity" and to prove compliance with the NCP. The court found that, despite their evidence that the site was contaminated, the plaintiffs had not proved that their response costs were "necessary" where they had not shown that conditions there posed a threat to public health or the environment–for example, no risk assessment study was conducted, and no toxicological assessment was done that would identify chemicals of concern and their toxicity. On the other hand, the court found that Johnston Industries had demonstrated at trial that the site *did not* pose an imminent or substantial threat to public health or the environment. In order to show that costs are necessary under CERCLA, the court explained, citing G.J. Leasing Co. v. Union Electric Co., 854 F.Supp. 539 (S.D.Ill.1994), aff'd, 54 F.3d 379 (7th Cir.1995) and In re Bell Petroleum Services, Inc., 3 F.3d 889 (5th Cir.1993), plaintiffs must demonstrate that they responded to an actual and real threat to public health or the environment, and that the costs were necessary to address that threat.

Secondly, the court applied the 1990 NCP with respect to the groundwater treatment program and the soil bioremediation, and the 1985 NCP with respect to the other, earlier response actions, including excavation and consolidation of soil, blast sand and refuse material, inventory and disposal of drums and containers, excavation or disposal of storage tanks, and miscellaneous cleanup activities. However, in determining whether the plaintiffs had satisfied the requirements of the two NCPs, the court applied throughout the less stringent "substantial compliance" test under the 1990 NCP.

The court next determined that the groundwater treatment program and bioremediation and beneficial use programs were remedial actions, while the excavation, consolidation and disposal of soil, blast sand, drums and containers were removal actions. The distinction is significant, the court explained, because removal actions need comply with "relatively simple" NCP requirements, while remedial actions are subject to more detailed substantive and procedural provisions.

The court found that the bioremediation and beneficial use programs were not consistent with the NCP because the plaintiffs did not provide any opportunity for public comment regarding the selection of those actions, as required by 40 C.F.R. § 300.700(C)(6). "Courts have consistently held that the failure to provide an opportunity for public comment renders the response action inconsistent with the NCP and precludes recovery of costs," the court said, citing a number of cases. The court rejected the plaintiffs' claim that notifying the local government and communicating with state agencies about the response action served as a substitute for public comment.

The objective in describing these decisions is to clarify for students that the contribution action still demands proof of some heavy evidentiary burdens–indeed just as onerous as in a § 107(a) action. And, of course, the contribution-plaintiff has the burden of proving the equitable shares of each defendant-PRP–a task that often can be daunting.

The following decision in United States v. R.W. Meyer, Inc., 932 F.2d 568 (6th Cir.1991) demonstrates many of the considerations that may influence the apportionment of liability in contribution actions under CERCLA § 113(f).

UNITED STATES v. R. W. MEYER, INC.

United States Court of Appeals, Sixth Circuit, 1991.
932 F.2d 568.

BERTELSMAN, D.J.

This appeal involved the construction of the provisions of the Comprehensive Environmental Response, Compensation, and Liability Act (CERCLA) governing contribution actions among responsible parties following a cleanup of a hazardous waste site and an Immediate Removal Action by the Environmental Protection Agency (EPA). 42 U.S.C. §§ 9607, 9613(f)(1).

BACKGROUND

The facts and background necessary to place this opinion in context were well stated by Chief Judge Hillman in his unpublished opinion awarding contribution, as follows: "This matter stems from a suit brought by the United States against Northernaire Plating Company ('Northernaire') for recovery of its costs in conducting an 'Immediate Removal Action' pursuant to CERCLA. Northernaire owned and operated a metal electroplating business in Cadillac, Michigan. Beginning in 1972, it operated under a 10–year lease on property owned by R.W. Meyer, Inc. ('Meyer'). Northernaire continued operations until mid–1981 when its assets were sold to Toplocker Enterprises, Inc. ('Toplocker'). From July of 1975 until this sale, Willard S. Garwood was the president and sole shareholder of Northernaire. He personally oversaw and managed the day-to-day operations of the company. Acting upon inspection reports from the Michigan Department of Natural Resources ('MDNR'), the United States Environmental Protection Agency ('EPA') conducted an Immediate Removal Action at the Northernaire site from July 5 until August 3, 1983. Cleanup of the site required neutralization of caustic acids, bulking and shipment of liquid acids, neutralization of caustic and acid sludges, excavation and removal of a contaminated sewer line, and decontamination of the inside of the building. All of the hazardous substances found at the site were chemicals and by-products of metal electro-plating operations. In an earlier opinion and order this court found the defendants Garwood, Northernaire, and Meyer jointly and severally liable to plaintiff for the costs of the Immediate Removal Action under Section 107(a) of CERCLA. 42 U.S.C. § 9607(a). The court awarded plaintiff $268,818.25 plus prejudgment interest. The court later determined the prejudgment interest. Each defendant, (Northernaire and Garwood moving together) has brought cross-claims for contribution against the other. Currently before the court are the summary judgment motions on these cross-claims." CERCLA specifically allows actions for contribution among parties who have been held jointly and severally liable: [court quotes § 113(f)].

Apparently, the parties allowed the building to degenerate into a true environmental disaster area. As this court observed in the former appeal: " * * * State tests on samples of the soil, sludge, and drum contents disclosed the presence of significant amounts of caustic and corrosive materials. During their examination of the site, EPA and MDNR officials observed drums and tanks housing cyanide littered among disarray outside the facility. Based on their observations outside the building, the officials determined that Northernaire had discharged its electroplating waste into a 'catch' basin and that the waste had seeped into the ground from the bottom of the basin. The waste then entered a pipe that drained into a sewer line that discharged into the sewage treatment plant for the city of Cadillac." Meyer, 889 F.2d at 1498–99.

In the former appeal, this court affirmed the decision of the trial court finding that the damage to the site had been "indivisible" and imposing joint and several liability on the present parties to reimburse the EPA for the removal costs for the cleanup of the building.

* * * In this subsequent contribution action, the trial court held that two-thirds of the liability should be borne by Northernaire and its principal shareholder, each contributing one-third each. But the court held that the remaining one-third ($114,274.41) should be borne by the appellant property owner.

The appellant attacks this apportionment, arguing strenuously that its responsibility should be limited to an amount apportioned according to the degree that the sewer line mentioned in the above quote contributed to the cleanup costs. Applying this approach, the appellant generously offers to pay $1,709.03. Appellees accept the trial court's apportionment.

* * *

ANALYSIS

The trial court held that it was within its discretion to apply certain factors found in the legislative history of CERCLA in making its contribution apportionment. Although these factors were originally intended as criteria for deciding whether a party could establish a right to an apportionment of several liability in the EPA's initial removal action, the trial court found "these criteria useful in determining the proportionate share each party is entitled to in contribution from the other."

The criteria mentioned are: (1) the ability of the parties to demonstrate that their contribution to a discharge release or disposal of a hazardous waste can be distinguished; (2) the amount of the hazardous waste involved; (3) the degree of toxicity of the hazardous waste involved; (4) the degree of involvement by the parties in the generation, transportation, treatment, storage, or disposal of the hazardous waste;

(5) the degree of care exercised by the parties with respect to the hazardous waste concerned, taking into account the characteristics of such hazardous waste; and (6) the degree of cooperation by the parties with Federal, State, or local officials to prevent any harm to the public health or the environment.

The trial court recognized that the lessee was the primary actor in allowing this site to become contaminated. (Appellant argued that the lessee was the only actor.) The trial court found, however, that in addition to constructing the defective sewer line which contributed to the contamination, appellant bore significant responsibility "simply by virtue of being the landowner." The trial court observed further that appellant "neither assisted nor cooperated with the EPA officials during their investigation and eventual cleanup of the * * * site."

Chief Judge Hillman concluded, "As it is well within the province of this court, I have balanced each of the defendants' behavior with respect to the equitable guidelines discussed." As a result of the balancing, he made the apportionment described above. The trial judge was well within the broad discretion afforded by the statute in making the apportionment he did. Congress intended to invest the district courts with this discretion in making CERCLA contribution allocations when it provided, "the court may allocate response costs among the liable parties using such equitable factors as the *court determines are appropriate*." 42 U.S.C. § 9613(f)(1) (emphasis added).

Essentially, appellant argues here that a narrow, technical construction must be given to the term "contribution," so that, as in common law contribution, contribution under the statute is limited to the percentage a party's improper conduct causally contributed to the toxicity of the site in a physical sense. This argument is without merit. On the contrary, by using the term "equitable factors" Congress intended to invoke the tradition of equity under which the court must construct a flexible decree balancing all the equities in the light of the totality of the circumstances.

* * *

[U]nder § 9613(f)(1) the court may consider any factor it deems in the interest of justice in allocating contribution recovery. Certainly, the several factors listed by the trial court are appropriate, but as it recognized, it was not limited to them. No exhaustive list of criteria need or should be formulated. However, in addition to the criteria listed above, the court may consider the state of mind of the parties, their economic status, any contracts between them bearing on the subject, any traditional equitable defenses as mitigating factors and any other factors deemed appropriate to balance the equities in the totality of the circumstances.

Therefore, the trial court quite properly considered here not only the appellant's contribution to the toxic slough described above in a technical causative sense, but also its moral contribution as the owner of the site. Review of the trial court's equitable balancing process is limited to a review for "abuse of discretion." This is in accord with the principle of equity that the chancellor has broad discretion to frame a decree.

This case, even though it involves over $300,000, is but a pimple on the elephantine carcass of the CERCLA litigation now making its way through the court system. Some of these cases involve millions or even billions of dollars in cleanup costs and hundreds or even thousands of potentially responsible parties.

I do not believe Congress intended to require meticulous findings of the precise causative contribution each of several hundred parties made to a hazardous site. In many cases, this would be literally impossible. Rather, by the expansive language used in § 9613(f)(1) Congress intended the court to deal with these situations by creative means, considering all the equities and balancing them in the interests of justice. * * *

Although such an approach "cannot be applied with mathematical precision," it is the fairest and most workable approach for apportioning CERCLA liability. Such an approach furthers the legislative intent of encouraging the prompt cleanup of hazardous sites by those equitably responsible. The parties actually performing the cleanup can look for reimbursement from other potentially responsible parties without fear that their contribution actions will be bogged down by the impossibility of making meticulous factual determinations as to the causal contribution of each party. Chief Judge Hillman was well within the equitable discretion afforded him by Congress in the way he handled this CERCLA contribution action.

Affirmed.

Notes and Questions

1. *Meyer* is atypical in terms of the small number of parties and the relatively simple facts. For prior history in the *Meyer* case, see United States v. Northernaire Plating Co., 670 F.Supp. 742 (W.D.Mich.1987), affirmed sub nom. United States v. R.W. Meyer, Inc., 889 F.2d 1497 (6th Cir.1989), cert. denied 494 U.S. 1057, 110 S.Ct. 1527, 108 L.Ed.2d 767 (1990). Judge Guy in *Meyer* wrote a concurring opinion joined in by the third member of the panel. In it he concluded that the trial court had erroneously found that defects in the sewer line had contributed to Northernaire's inability to remove hazardous waste from the building because it was the city's revocation of Northernaire's permit, not Meyer's faulty sewer line, that contributed to its failure to properly dispose of its wastes. Nevertheless, he agreed with the trial court's allocation because Meyer was not in reality an "absentee" landlord but had involved itself in assuring that Northernaire could undertake its operations. Judge Guy also relied on Restatement (Second) of Torts § 886A, which provides that "no tortfeasor can be required to make contribution beyond his own equitable share of the liability." Finding that the facts revealed "that Meyer was instrumental in efforts to bring Northernaire to Cadillac, was fully aware of the nature of the manufacturing to be conducted on the site, built the building that housed the

facility and failed to construct or maintain an adequate sewer line," he concluded that Meyer's relative culpability justified the trial court's allocation. How much would you, as judge, have allocated to Meyer?

2. *R.W. Meyer* is not unusual in allocating a considerable share of the cleanup costs to a landowner who had no active role in causing the contamination. In United States v. DiBiase, 45 F.3d 541 (1st Cir.1995), the EPA entered into a settlement with a sewerage district that had deposited sewage sludge at the site in question. The settlement required the sewerage district to pay 85% of the cleanup costs, implicitly leaving DiBiase, the current owner–who did not participate in the settlement and instead fought for judicial rejection thereof–with the remaining 15%. DiBiase acquired the site without knowing that the prior owner had given permission to the sewerage district to deposit its waste there. When DiBiase learned of the practice, he demanded that the sewerage authority cease the dumping, which it did. Thereafter, although DiBiase placed gates on the entrances to the property, he did not maintain them, and other, unknown parties intermittently dumped substances at the site. The EPA and the sewerage district obtained district court approval of their settlement for the cleanup of the site, and the First Circuit rejected DiBiase's arguments challenging the settlement on appeal:

> In the first place, appellant does not cite–and we have been unable to locate–any CERCLA case in which a demonstrably *liable* party has been held entitled to safe passage in a global settlement. * * *

> Second, * * * we regard appellant's argument as a surreptitious attempt to relitigate his "innocent landowner" defense * * * rejected by the district court * * *.

> In the third place, the allocation proposed by EPA and ratified by Judge Mazzone does not strike us as either substantially disproportionate or manifestly unfair. To be sure, SESD [the sewerage authority] played a leading role in the contamination of the Site and appellant, who came on the scene later, played an appreciably less prominent role. But, an actor in a bit part is not to be confused with a mere spectator, whose only involvement is to lounge in the audience and watch events unfold. * * * despite being warned of a potentially dangerous condition, he twiddled his thumbs; he failed to safeguard the Site, thus permitting third parties to dump at will and exacerbate an already parlous situation; fiddled while the earthen berms deteriorated; and turned a blind eye to evolving public health and safety concerns. Allocating 15% of the historic removal costs as appellant's share seems commensurate with these shortcomings and with the quantum of comparative fault fairly ascribable to him.

> Fourth, appellant's concept—which seems to be that liable parties should go [without liability] in environmental cases if other parties are considerably more culpable—runs at cross-purposes with CERCLA's policy of encouraging settlements as opposed to endless court battles.

Id. at 545–546.

3.   MORE ON APPROACHES TO ALLOCATING COSTS

Meyer illustrates that there are various methods which a court might adopt for allocating response costs that satisfy the statutory requirement of applying "equitable factors." The following represent some of the major alternatives:

a.   Per Capita

This approach is the simplest and requires only the division of cleanup costs by the number of PRPs, with each paying an equal share. This method finds support in the Uniform Contribution Among Tortfeasors Act § 2, 12 U.L.A. 87 (1975) (UCATA) which was adopted in 1955, before most states enacted comparative fault statutes. Does this approach fulfill Congress's objectives under CERCLA § 113(f)? To date virtually no court has adopted this approach because it ignores the nature of hazardous substances released or the harm to the environment therefrom or the parties' conduct or blameworthiness. In what factual circumstances might the per capita approach be fair or "equitable"?

b.   Comparative Fault

This method requires a court to distribute liability among PRPs in accordance with each PRP's relative degree of fault in causing harm at the site. This method is reflected in the 1977 Uniform Comparative Fault Act §§ 1–10, 12 U.L.A. 39 (Supp. 1990) (UCFA). While this approach has obvious appeal from the perspective of fairness, it places an administrative burden on courts because of the necessity of examining each party's conduct. The UCFA scheme is not limited to negligence or reckless conduct, but also includes as "fault" acts or omissions which subject a party to strict liability. UCFA § 1(b), 12 U.L.A. 41. If a PRP is insolvent or absent from the action, the UCFA requires that its share be redistributed among all of the remaining PRPs according to their degrees of fault, rather than requiring the contribution plaintiff to bear all of that loss.

The comparative fault approach has been given extra momentum by Restatement (Third) of Torts: Apportionment § 33 (1999), quoted earlier, that uses "comparative responsibility" as the means for determining whether a party has paid more or less than its pro-rata share. The UCATA employs the term "pro-rata share," which is now defined as "comparative share of responsibility." Although the 1955 version of the UCATA § 2 explicitly provided that in "determining pro-rata shares of tortfeasors in the entire liability their relative *shares of fault shall not be considered* . . . and principles of equity applicable to contribution generally shall apply" (emphasis added), the explosion of comparative fault into 46 states since 1955 has changed that approach. The overwhelming majority of jurisdictions calculate each person's share according to percentages of responsibility. See, Restatement (Third) of Torts: Apportionment of Liability § 33, Reporters' Notes e (1999) (listing all states with statutory or judicial citations).

In Browning–Ferris Industries, Inc. v. Ter Maat, 13 F. Supp. 2d 756 (N.D.Ill.1998), aff'd in part, 195 F.3d 953 (7th Cir.1999), the court manifest its belief that the truest measure for assessing liability is to "consider the conduct of the parties as it relates to their respective categories of owner, operator, generator, and transporter." Liability should be based primarily on relative degrees of fault. The factors bearing on fault included: "(1) how much waste was contributed; (2) the type and nature of the waste; (3) compliance with regulatory schemes; (4) operation of the landfill, including closure and post-closure activities; and (5) cooperation and involvement in cleaning up the site."

c. Comparative Causation

This method allocates damages by looking to the amount and characteristics of hazardous substances each party has contributed to the site. Under this approach the court must analyze largely technical and scientific information on volume, toxicity, interaction among chemical substances, and the like. Recall that in *Monsanto*, the Fourth Circuit observed how difficult and unnecessary it was for the district court to attempt to make an allocation on that basis. However, § 122(e)(3) of CERCLA, which relates to settlement procedures does provide some support for use of this methodology. Specifically § 122(e)(3) lists ten factors as relevant in making preliminary non-binding assessment of responsibility: (1) volume of hazardous substance; (2) toxicity of each; (3) cooperation with governmental authorities; (4) mobility of the substances, (5) strength of evidence; (6) ability to pay; (7) litigative risks; (8) public interest considerations; (9) precedential value; and (10) inequities and aggravating factors.

d. Gore Amendment

Quoted in *Meyer*, this proposed amendment to CERCLA sponsored by then Representative Albert Gore (D. Tenn.) would have required the application of six criteria in determining the divisibility of response costs: (1) a PRP's ability to demonstrate that its contribution to the harm at a site can be distinguished from that of other PRPs; (2) the amount of hazardous waste attributable to the PRP; (3) the toxicity of that waste; (4) the PRP's involvement in the generation, transportation, treatment, storage, or disposal of the waste; (5) the degree of care that the PRP exercised with respect to the waste; and (6) the extent to which the PRP cooperated with government officials in preventing further harm. The Gore Amendment approach combines the comparative causation method (three technical factors that look only to the characteristics of the waste) with the comparative fault method (three conduct factors that look to the defendant's fault). There is no question that the Gore factors have emerged as the dominant allocation methodology.

e. Other Relevant Factors

What other factors did *Meyer* add to the mix? What other factors might be appropriate? Despite the fact that Congress did not enact the Amendment, it has received considerable acknowledgment in judicial opinions as evidenced by *Meyer*. Consistent with *Meyer*, the courts have repeatedly held that they are not bound to any particular set of factors, nor must they apply any particular test in allocating response costs. In Environmental Transp. Systems, Inc. v. ENSCO, Inc., 969 F.2d 503 (7th Cir.1992), the court stated that the "Gore factors are neither an exhaustive nor exclusive list," and pointed out that they had been originally proposed as elements bearing on divisibility of harm so as to defeat joint and several liability to the government, not for the purpose of allocating costs among those determined to be jointly and severally liable. The court in *ENSCO* also explicitly rejected applying a pro rata test in favor of a case-by-case approach that would "weigh and consider relevant factors, including fault, in order to effectuate Congress's intent." Nevertheless, it observed that "there may be cases in which a pro rata apportionment in a contribution action is appropriate."

Other examples of equitable factors identified by courts in interpreting § 113(f) include: B.F. Goodrich Co. v. Murtha, 958 F.2d 1192 (2d Cir.1992) (court may consider array of factors including *financial resources of the parties involved*); CPC Int'l, Inc. v. Aerojet–General Corp., 777 F.Supp. 549 (W.D.Mich.1991) (listing responsible party's degree of involvement in disposal of hazardous waste, amount of hazardous waste involved, and degree of care exercised by the parties); Weyerhaeuser Co. v. Koppers Co., 771 F.Supp. 1420, 1426 (D.Md.1991) (indicating as important factors the benefits received by the parties from contaminating activities and the knowledge and/or acquiescence of the parties in the contaminating activities). For further exploration of these issues of allocation, see Note, Contribution Under CERCLA, 14 Colum. J. Envtl. L. 267 (1989) (quoted in *Meyer*); Ellen J. Garber, Federal Common Law of Contribution Under the 1986 CERCLA Amendments, 14 Ecology L.W. 365 (1987); Elizabeth F. Mason, Note, Contribution Protection and Non–Settlor Liability Under CERCLA, 19 B.C. Envtl. Aff. L. Rev. 73 (1991); see Mandelbaum, Toward a Superfund Cost Allocation Principle, 3 Envtl. Lawyer 117 (1996). See also Wise, Maniatis & Koch, Allocating CERCLA Liabilities: The Applications and Limitations of Economics, 12 Toxics L. Rep. (BNA) 830 (1997); Hall, Harris & Riensdorf, Superfund Response Cost Allocations: The Law, the Science, and the Practice, 49 Bus. Lawyer 1489 (1994); Singh & Hinerman, Superfund Cost Allocation: Equitable Techniques and Principles, 9 Toxics L. Rep. (BNA) 531 (1994); Butler, et al, Allocating Superfund Costs: Cleaning Up the Controversy, 23 Envtl. L. Rep. 10,133 (1993).

CONTROL DATA CORPORATION v. S.C.S.C. CORP.

United States Court of Appeals, Eighth Circuit, 1995.
53 F.3d 930.

RICHARD S. ARNOLD, CHIEF JUDGE.

Control Data Corporation brought this suit under the Comprehensive Environmental Response, Compensation, and Liability Act of 1980 (CERCLA), 42 U.S.C. § 9601 et seq., and the Minnesota Environmental Response and Liability Act (MERLA), Minn.Stat. § 115B.01 et seq. Following a bench trial, the District Court found the Schloff defendants—S.C.S.C. Corp., Schloff Chemical, and Irvin and Ruth Schloff— liable under CERCLA and allocated responsibility for 33 1/3% of Control Data's response costs, as defined by CERCLA, to those defendants. Alternatively, the District Court found S.C.S.C. Corp. and Schloff Chemical liable under MERLA and allocated responsibility for 33 1/3% of Control Data's removal costs, as defined by MERLA, to those defendants. The District Court held that Irvin and Ruth Schloff were not liable under MERLA.

The Schloff defendants appeal. We affirm the judgment of the District Court finding the Schloff defendants liable under CERCLA and allocating 33 1/3% of Control Data's response costs to them. We also affirm the District Court's decision to award Control Data 33 1/3% of its attorneys' fees under MERLA, but reverse that part of the District Court's judgment awarding attorneys' fees under CERCLA.

I. FACTUAL BACKGROUND

Control Data owns and operates a printed-circuit-board facility on Meadowbrook Road in St. Louis Park, Minnesota. Across Meadowbrook Road and Minnehaha Creek, the Schloff defendants owned and operated a dry-cleaning supply business, Schloff Chemical, from 1975 until 1989. Irvin Schloff was president of Schloff Chemical from 1963 to 1989, and exercised day-to-day control over its operations until 1985, when a General Manager was hired. Ruth Schloff has been the record owner of the real property where Schloff Chemical was located since 1974. S.C.S.C. Corp. is the current corporate incarnation of Schloff Chemical.

In 1987, Control Data discovered a leak in its sewer line. Fearing contamination, Control Data initiated an investigation, and, indeed, discovered the presence of volatile organic compounds in the groundwater underlying the Control Data site. Principal among these contaminants were 1,1,1 trichloroethane (TCE) and its degradation substances and tetrachloroethylene (PERC) and its degradation substances. A degradation substance is what a chemical becomes when it begins to break down. PERC and TCE degrade into many of the same substances.

After confirming that groundwater contamination existed, Control Data reported its findings to the Minnesota Pollution Control Agency (MPCA) and began cooperating with that agency in an effort to clean up the site. Control Data has admitted that it is the source of the TCE and its degradation substances. TCE has been spilled, or "released" in CERCLA terminology, many times by Control Data. But Control Data denied ever using, much less releasing, PERC, a circumstance which led the MPCA to search for other sources for the PERC contamination. It turns out that Schloff Chemical was that source.

Schloff Chemical released PERC several times between 1975 and 1989. The PERC released by Schloff Chemical formed a "plume," or discernible body of contaminants, that has migrated beneath Minnehaha Creek and joined with the TCE plume, created by Control Data's releases, on the Control Data site. It is now impossible to discern [or distinguish] one plume from the other.

In April of 1988, Control Data entered into a consent decree with the MPCA that required it to investigate, monitor, and clean up the contamination. Pursuant to this agreement, Control Data has installed a remediation system which removes both the TCE and the PERC contaminants concurrently. This cleanup is ongoing and will proceed for an undetermined period of time.

Control Data brought this lawsuit in order to recover a portion of the costs it incurred as a result of the PERC contamination on its site. The District Court found that the Schloff defendants were all liable under CERCLA because they were responsible for releasing hazardous substances into the environment, and that release had caused Control Data to incur response costs. *Important to the District Court's reasoning was its finding that PERC is more toxic and more difficult to clean up than TCE.* Since the remediation system was designed and constructed around the need to clean up PERC, the release of PERC created additional response costs.

This greater level of toxicity was also central in the District Court's allocation of liability. Though the Schloff defendants were responsible for only 10% of the contamination on the site, the District Court allocated 33 1/3% of the cost of cleanup to them. It did so because PERC is more toxic, and thus more harmful and difficult to remove, than TCE.

* * *

Finally, the District Court awarded Control Data 33 1/3% of its attorneys' fees and litigation expenses under both CERCLA and MERLA. The Supreme Court of the United States has since held that attorneys' fees are not response costs under CERCLA in most instances, and thus are not recoverable. Key Tronic v. United States, 114 S.Ct. 1960, 1967, 128 L.Ed.2d 797 (1994). MERLA, however, specifically allows prevailing parties to recover attorneys' fees and litigation expenses.

In this appeal, the Schloff defendants challenge the District Court's ruling on several grounds. * * * [T]hey argue that the District Court erroneously allocated 33 1/3% of the response costs to them. They initially dispute the finding that PERC is more toxic than TCE. They also question whether toxicity is a measure which may be used to increase allocation beyond the volume of pollution chargeable to a defendant. Finally, they argue that the award of attorneys' fees is erroneous.

Control Data cross-appeals the District Court's award of 33 1/3% of its attorneys' fees instead of 100%. It argues that the Schloff defendants should be responsible for all of its litigation expenses because, but for the Schloff defendants' refusal to contribute their fair share to the cleanup, it would have had no litigation expenses at all.

II. CERCLA FRAMEWORK

We begin our discussion, as we must, with the language of the statute. Recovery of response costs by a private party under CERCLA is a two-step process. Initially, a plaintiff must prove that the defendant is liable under CERCLA. Once that is accomplished, the defendant's share of liability is apportioned in an equitable manner.

CERCLA liability is established under 42 U.S.C. § 9607(a) (CERCLA § 107(a)).

* * *

Thus, in order to prove liability, a plaintiff must show that a defendant is within one of the four classes of covered persons enumerated in subsections (1) through (4); that a release or threatened release from a facility has occurred; that the plaintiff incurred response costs as a result; and that the costs were necessary and consistent with the national contingency plan. 42 U.S.C. § 9607; see United States v. Aceto Agricultural Chemicals Corp., 872 F.2d 1373, 1378–79 (8th Cir.1989).

A problematic portion of this calculus is the causation element. At the outset, we note that CERCLA does not require the plaintiff to prove that the defendant caused actual harm to the environment at the liability stage. Alcan Aluminum, 964 F.2d at 264–66. Harm to the environment is material only when allocating responsibility, as we discuss infra. Instead, CERCLA focuses on whether the defendant's release or threatened release caused harm to the plaintiff in the form of response costs. General Electric Co. v. Litton Industrial Automation Systems, Inc., 920 F.2d 1415, 1417 (8th Cir.1990), cert. denied, 499 U.S. 937, 111 S.Ct. 1390, 113 L.Ed.2d 446 (1991). If so, and if the other elements are established, the defendant is liable under CERCLA.

Once liability is established, the focus shifts to allocation. Here, the question is what portion of the plaintiff's response costs will the defendant be responsible for? Allocation is a contribution claim controlled by 42 U.S.C. § 9613(f) (CERCLA § 113(f)). [The court quotes § 113(f).]

Courts have considered various factors in resolving contribution claims, see Nagle, CERCLA, Causation, and Responsibility, 78 Minn. L.Rev. 1493, 1522–23, n. 135 (1994), but the "Gore factors," so called after one of the sponsors of CERCLA, are the most widely used. The Gore factors are:

1.　the ability of the parties to demonstrate that their contribution to a discharge, release, or disposal of a hazardous waste can be distinguished;

2.　the amount of hazardous waste involved;

3.　the degree of toxicity of the hazardous waste;

4.　the degree of involvement by the parties in the generation, transportation, treatment, storage, or disposal of the hazardous waste;

5.　the degree of care exercised by the parties with respect to the hazardous waste concerned, taking into account the characteristics of such hazardous waste; and

6.　the degree of cooperation by the parties with Federal, State, or local officials to prevent any harm to the public health or the environment.

Id. at 1522 n. 133. A primary focus of these factors is the harm that each party causes the environment. Id. at 1522. Those parties who can show that their contribution to the harm is relatively small in terms of amount of waste, toxicity of the waste, involvement with the waste, and care, stand in a better position to be allocated a smaller portion of response costs.

One primary goal of this private cost-recovery framework is to "encourage timely cleanup of hazardous waste sites," Litton Industrial, 920 F.2d at 1418. See also United States v. Mexico Feed & Seed Co., 980 F.2d 478, 486 (8th Cir.1992). Thus, this Court has consistently held that CERCLA is a strict-liability statute, imposing liability without regard to degree of care or motivation for the plaintiff's actions in initiating a cleanup. Litton Industrial, 920 F.2d at 1418. At the same time, CERCLA seeks "to place the cost of that response on those responsible for creating or maintaining the hazardous condition." Mexico Feed & Seed, 980 F.2d at 486. Therefore, in the allocation phase, harm to the environment and care on the part of the parties plays a more substantial role. Cf. Farmland Industries, 987 F.2d at 1342 n. 6.

III.　The Schloff Defendants' CERCLA Liability

The Schloff defendants argue that they should not be liable under CERCLA for that portion of the response costs which are attributable to the investigation of contamination on the Control Data site. They do not, however, challenge the District Court's determination that they are liable for a share of the cleanup costs. Simply put, the Schloff defendants argue that Control Data's release was the sole cause of the investigation. Thus, because the Schloff defendants' releases had nothing to do with initiating the investigation, they cannot be held liable. In order to accept the Schloff defendants' argument, we would have to hold that CERCLA imposes upon a plaintiff the requirement to prove that each type of response cost was separately caused by the defendant's release.

CERCLA simply cannot be read this strictly. First, the language of the statute precludes this holding. Under CERCLA, if a responsible party, as defined by subsections (1) through (4), releases hazardous materials into the environment, and that release "causes the incurrence of response costs," then the party is liable. 42 U.S.C. § 9607(a). The question then becomes, liable for what? CERCLA's answer is that the party is liable for "any other necessary cost of response incurred by any other person consistent with the national contingency plan." 42 U.S.C. § 9607(a)(4)(B) . Thus, a plain reading of the statute leads us to the conclusion that once a party is liable, it is liable for its share, as determined by Section 9613(f), of "any" and all response costs, not just those costs "caused" by its release.

Second, the policy underlying CERCLA's private cost-recovery scheme precludes us from accepting the Schloff defendants' interpretation. As we noted previously, CERCLA's dual goals are to encourage quick response and to place the cost of that response on those responsible for the hazardous condition. Control Data quickly and efficiently responded to a perceived threat to the environment when it discovered its own release, thus fulfilling the first goal. In doing so, it discovered a second polluter, the Schloff defendants, who, in a perfect world according to CERCLA, should have reacted to their own releases much earlier. By not reacting and allowing the PERC plume to migrate, they became partially responsible for the hazardous condition of the Control Data site. Holding the Schloff defendants liable for a share of the costs of the investigation which uncovered their responsibility thus satisfies the second goal of CERCLA.

Under the Schloff defendants' interpretation, these goals would be frustrated. Control Data would have been better served simply to repair its own leak and do nothing about the contamination. Then, if another neighbor experienced a release which led to the discovery of the Control Data contamination, that third party would be liable for the entire cost of investigation. This result would offend CERCLA's goals. It would provide a disincentive for polluters to act quickly and aggressively to remedy the harm they have done in hopes that someone else will stumble upon their creation and be forced to bear the burden rightfully belonging to the original polluter.

Finally, the Supreme Court's most recent CERCLA decision convinces us that the Schloff defendants' argument must fail. In Key Tronic Corp. v. United States, 511 U.S. 809, 114 S.Ct. 1960, 128 L.Ed.2d 797 (1994), Key Tronic and others, including the United States Air Force, dumped hazardous chemicals into a landfill in Spokane County, Washington. When the resulting contamination was found in the surrounding groundwater supply, Key Tronic, on its own initiative, responded. See Key Tronic Corp. v. United States, 766 F.Supp. 865, 867 (E.D.Wash. 1991), rev'd, 984 F.2d 1025 (9th Cir.1993), aff'd in part and rev'd in part, 511 U.S. 809, 114 S.Ct. 1960, 128 L.Ed.2d 797 (1994). Part of this response was Key Tronic's effort to identify other responsible parties. This effort resulted in an Environmental Protection Agency enforcement action against the Air Force. Key Tronic, 114 S.Ct. at 1967. The Supreme Court held that the costs attributable to this search, though paid to attorneys, were "recoverable costs of response clearly distinguishable from litigation expenses," which are not recoverable under CERCLA. Ibid. (footnote omitted).

The reasoning of the Supreme Court is particularly applicable to the case before us. "Tracking down other responsible solvent polluters increases the probability that a cleanup will be effective and get paid for. Key Tronic is therefore quite right to claim that such efforts significantly benefitted the entire cleanup effort apart ... from the reallocation of costs." Key Tronic, 114 S.Ct. at 1967. Likewise, Control Data's efforts to identify all of the contaminants on its property "significantly benefitted" the entire effort. Without that effort, the full extent of the contamination, including contamination restricted to the Schloff site not at issue in this case, might not have been discovered and remedied. Perhaps it is fortuitous for Control Data that it happened on to the Schloff defendants' contamination, just as it was fortuitous for Key Tronic to happen on to the Air Force's. Both circumstances are more fortuitous, however, for the environment, which is the primary and decisive factor under CERCLA. We must affirm the judgment of the District Court imposing liability on the Schloff defendants for all response costs, including the costs of investigation.

Irvin Schloff also argues that the District Court erred in holding him individually liable as an "operator" of a "facility." 42 U.S.C. § 9607(a)(1), (2). We disagree. The District Court found Mr. Schloff liable as an operator, not merely because of his position as a corporate officer, but because of his control of the operations of Schloff Chemical, including the delivery, storage, handling, and transportation of PERC.

Irvin Schloff supervised the day-to-day operations of Schloff Chemical between 1963 and 1985. He remained as president with authority over those operations from 1985 until 1989. Included in those operations was the delivery, storage, handling, and transportation of dry-cleaning chemicals, including PERC. These findings are supported by ample evidence. Indeed, Mr. Schloff does not seriously challenge them. Rather, his dispute focuses on the legal conclusion drawn from these facts, that he is an "operator" under CERCLA.

* * *

It is so ordered.

Notes and Questions

1. *Generators of Waste.* Generally, the scheme for allocating costs among generators of wastes pivots upon a determination of the parties' contribution to the waste generated or disposed of at a site. See William N. Hedeman, et al, Superfund Transaction Costs: A Critical Perspective on the Superfund Liability Scheme, 21 Envt'l L. Rep. (ELI) 10413, 10428 (July 1991) (liability of generators "is often allocated based on a volumetric share

of total waste disposed''); United States v. Ottati & Goss, 1986 WL 10266 (D.N.H.) (approving an allocation of the costs based solely upon the number of drums of waste sent to the site). Additionally, some courts have recognized the importance of taking the characteristics of waste into account when allocating costs. For instance, in United States v. Stringfellow, 1993 WL 565393 (C.D.Cal.), the court advised that when determining liability, particularly among a group of generators, the court should consider the "volume, toxicity, migratory potential, etc.," of the waste. In addition, the court in United States v. Monsanto Co., 858 F.2d 160, 172 (4th Cir.1988) observed that "[c]ommon sense counsels that a million gallons of certain substances could be mixed together without significant consequences, whereas a few pints of others improperly mixed could result in disastrous consequences." Yet, the inherent scientific complexity of proving the principal or incremental effect of a specific waste's particular characteristic and the costs of determining and proving the effects of particular wastes may discourage courts and parties from using the more comprehensive scientific analysis of the waste at a particular site.

2. *Toxicity.* Do you agree with the court's conclusion in *Control Data* that the toxicity of the hazardous substances deposited at the site is relevant to the allocations of response costs? What evidence should bear on the issue of the relative toxicity? In Chapter 8 we examine in detail the science of toxicology and epidemiology. Note that toxicity alone is not the sole inquiry in *Control Data*: The ability to remove the hazardous substance from the ground or groundwater obviously bear very directly on the amount of response costs incurred in remediation or removal.

But another court of appeals has taken issue with the desirability of using toxicity as part of the allocation formula. In Akzo Nobel Coatings, Inc. v. Aigner Corp., 197 F.3d 302 (7th Cir.1999), the district court relied first on volume of wastes and then on divisibility of wastes, and finally toxicity of wastes in arriving at percentages of responsibility for each of the parties. Judge Easterbrook, for the Seventh Circuit, wrote that toxicity could play a role in apportioning costs, but was not a logically necessary element, writing:

> Suppose that Aigner's wastes were twice as toxic as Akzo's but equally costly (pound for pound or gallon for gallon) to remove from the ground, and no more dangerous to strangers after the cleanup had been completed. Then there would be no sound reason to measure contribution by toxicity rather than by the expense of doing the work. Even the word "toxic" may mislead; sometimes that word means deadly (cyanide is more toxic than polychlorinated biphenyls in this sense), but sometimes it means "hard to purge from other substances" (PCBs are more toxic than cyanide in this sense). Substances that are very poisonous may be simple to eliminate or dilute to a harmless level; substances that cling tenaciously to dirt, water, and living tissues may be very costly to clean up, not only because it is hard to get rid of them but because their toxicity leads to buildup over the years in exposed humans, so that the environmentally safe level is lower than that for acutely poisonous substances. Akzo has not disentangled these different meanings of toxic or demonstrated that the residuals in its solvents are less costly to clean up.

Id. at 305. Over and above the complex toxicity determination, a court also had to ask "how each party's wastes affected the total cost of cleanup." They may have added different marginal costs to the overall effort. It was significant to the Seventh Circuit that Akzo's contribution did not exceed "the cost that would have been necessary to clean up the pollutants attributable to its solvents if it had been Fisher–Calo's sole customer." The district court's decision to give each gallon equal weight was within its discretion.

3. *Different Classes of PRPs.* The analysis for allocating costs between a generator and a site owner can differ from the analysis applied to allocations between generators. See Weyerhaeuser Co. v. Koppers Co., 771 F.Supp. 1420, 1425 (D.Md.1991) ("contribution-to-harm analysis may not be applicable in apportioning liability among different classes of defendants though it can be quite useful in distinguishing between defendants of the same class"). The factors courts may consider most important when allocating costs between the generator of wastes and the owner of the site are the owner's knowledge of the generator's activities and the benefits the owner received from those activities. Other factors noted in *Meyer* are the circumstances of the conveyance and the contract of conveyance, the state of mind of the parties, their economic status, and any mitigating equitable factors. See United States v. R.W. Meyer, Inc., 932 F.2d 568 (6th Cir.1991); FMC Corp. v. Northern Pump Co., 668 F.Supp. 1285 (D.Minn.1987). For instance, in Weyerhaeuser Co. v. Koppers Co., 771 F.Supp. 1420, 1426 (D.Md.1991), the court found that, although the plant operator was the sole source of contamination, the property owner was responsible for part of the cleanup costs because it knew of the operator's activities, acquiesced to the activity, and received benefit from the activity. The court therefore allocated 75% of the costs to the operator and 25% of the costs to the land owner. Id. In addition, the court in South Florida Water Management District v. Montalvo, 1989 WL 260215 (S.D.Fla.), held that though the operator of the facility on the property was the sole source of contamination and the landowner received no benefit (and, in fact, suffered damages because of the contamination), the landowner was required to pay 25% of the costs of remediation because of the landowner's knowledge and acquiescence to the operator's activity. *Id.* at *7.

In Bedford Affiliates v. Sills, 156 F.3d 416 (2d Cir.1998), an owner versus operator case, the Second Circuit, after a careful review of the record evidence, affirmed the district court's allocation pursuant to § 113(f)(1). First, it held that allocation of 95% of the liability for environmental cleanup of property to a sublessee which operated a dry cleaning business on the property was not an abuse of discretion, in CERCLA contribution action brought by property owner, absent evidence that parties which operated dry cleaning facility during other time periods caused contamination. Second, allocation of 5% of liability for cleanup of the property to the property owner was not an abuse of discretion, in owner's CERCLA contribution action against former lessees and sublessee, even if the owner did not contribute to hazardous conditions at site and cooperated with state agency in effectuating cleanup, in view of the owner's ownership status during period of contamination and the owner's failure to begin cleanup for three years after learning of contamination.

4. *Other Relevant Factors: Benefit Derived.* Given the opinions in *Meyer, Control Data* and the many notes, are there factors you might want to add to the calculus? What if the landowner derives a substantial benefit in the form of contamination-free property? How might that fact affect the allocation of costs? For example, how much a court will attribute to a landowner appears in Ellman v. Woo, 22 Envtl. L. Rep. 20875, 1991 WL 274838 (E.D.Pa.). In *Ellman* the landowner purchased the property knowing it was contaminated. *Id.* at *1. The owner then sued the generator of the waste for reimbursement of the costs. However, the court found that ongoing remediation would also remediate contamination for which the generator was not responsible and allow the landowner to receive the benefit of contamination-free land at the expense of only one liable party. *Id.* at *8. Therefore, the court held that since the landowner was receiving the benefit of remediation of all the contamination at the site, the landowner should bear some of the costs of that remediation. *Id.*

Also, the court in BCW Associates v. Occidental Chemical Corporation, 1988 WL 102641 (E.D.Pa.), held the lessee of the contaminated land, the lessor of the contaminated land, and the generator of the contamination equally liable for the costs of remediation. The court held all parties equally liable, although the generator was the sole source of contamination, because the lessee received benefit from a cleaner and safer work environment, and the landowner received the increased value of contamination-free land.

5. *Generators Versus Operators.* When allocating costs between waste generators and the operator of a waste disposal site, courts may focus on the last three Gore factors. Specifically, courts will look at the parties' degree of involvement, degree of care, and degree of cooperation with the government to clean up the site. For example, in United States v. Tyson, 1989 WL 159256 (E.D.Pa.), the court held the operator of the disposal site liable to the generators for 50% of the response costs because the operator was an active participant in the activity that caused the damage, failed to show it exercised due care or employed reasonable precautions, and refused to cooperate with government officials in cleaning up the site.

6. *Further Thoughts on Allocation and Burden of Proof.* The major problem with the Gore factors or any other list or collection of equitable considerations is that they are factually-intensive and case-specific, and therefore provide little pre-litigation predictability as to a party's ultimate share of responsibility that a court may assign among many PRPs. And this fluidity is buttressed by the broad discretion afforded district courts, coupled with a clearly erroneous standard of review. But whatever vagueness may inhere in the allocation process, it is not unconstitutionally vague in violation of due process norms under the Fifth Amendment. See, Carter–Jones Lumber Co. v. Dixie Distributing Co., 166 F.3d 840, 847 (6th Cir.1999).

For a scholarly and exhaustive analysis of the equitable factors see Judge Robert Keeton's opinion in Acushnet Co. v. Coaters Inc., 948 F.Supp. 128 (D.Mass.1996), *aff'd* Acushnet Co. v. Mohasco Corp., 191 F.3d 69 (1st Cir.1999) (which is reproduced below in this chapter).

Judge Keeton, who was influential in drafting the Restatement (Second) of Torts, explains the burden of proof in contribution actions:

The "equitable factors" mandate is appropriately interpreted as at least authorizing, if not mandating for this case, making comparisons between plaintiffs in a contribution action and defendants whom they allege to be potentially responsible parties, by considering evidence before the court (and jury, if one is used) for the purpose of determining whether the nature and extent of their respective ties to the hazards to persons property, and the environment make it fair and reasonable to order that a defendant, or defendants grouped together for good reason, reimburse the plaintiffs in some amount or some share of "contribution", allocated on an equitable basis reasoned from evidence concerning all the "equitable factors" for the application of which in this case some evidentiary basis exists.

Eleven. It is a fundamental principle of the legal system that courts are to leave harms and losses where they find them unless some good reason appears for shifting a loss from one party (or set of parties) to another party (or set of parties).

Twelve. Since, at least in the First Circuit, [where] the primary relief sought by plaintiffs against each defendant in a contribution action is an order that the defendant pay to plaintiffs an equitably determined share in partial reimbursement, *plaintiffs must proffer evidence sufficient to support a finding that hazardous substances traceable to that defendant were (in nature, quantity, and durability) sufficient to invoke an exception to point Eleven.*

A corollary of keypoint Twelve bears emphasis. Plaintiffs must show reasons for court intervention that outweigh the public interest against recognizing causes of action the enforcement costs of which exceed the added resources that would be tapped for waste-site remediation. They must make at least a prima-facie showing that equitable allocation may occur without placing on the defendant a burden proportionally inequitable to the burden remaining on plaintiffs after collection of contribution. The plaintiffs' assertion that this prima-facie showing has been made must be supported by the evidence before the court at the close of plaintiffs' case.

948 F.Supp. at 135–136.

One authority shared this observation respecting the process:

Despite these cases, there is an absence of maturity and marked trends in the developing allocation case law. Accordingly, when allocating costs of remediation, the parties must consider all factors in light of the particular facts and circumstances of the parties' case. The argument successfully used in the past have ranged from as complex as using scientific arguments regarding the exact effect on a particular type of remediation of a specific waste deposited at a specific time to as simple as pointing a finger at the other parties as "the bad guys." Nonetheless, taking an approach that at least initially looks to the liability categories of parties involved in the matter will provide some guidance in determining which factors the court may consider persuasive. In CERCLA allocation, *there is no rigid certainty, and all the skills required of trial lawyers involved in other types of equitable and damages claims must be relied on to develop factual and legal arguments supporting a particular allocation method.*

Nicholas J. Wallwork, Spreading the Costs of Environmental Cleanup: Contribution Claims under CERCLA, 175, 185 (1998). An economic analysis on allocation issues, see Kenneth T. Wise, et al., Allocating CERCLA Liabilities: The applications and Limitations of Economics, 11 Toxics L. Rep. (BNA) 830 (1997).

4. CONTRIBUTION AND CAUSATION

A considerable amount of material has already been dedicated to the issue of causation in government-initiated suits and in private response cost recovery actions–most of it to demonstrate the *absence* of any rigorous causation element in actions brought pursuant to § 9607. The issue we now address is whether in contribution suits brought pursuant to § 113(f)—by far the most "tort-like" of CERCLA's liability provisions—courts have continued the minimalist approach to causation or have invoked a more "tort-like" cause-in-fact standard.

As you review the materials that follow, be sure to isolate precisely the causation standards in contribution action versus the § 107 actions. What might justify the differences you find? Also be sure to notice the overlap between the question addressed early in this chapter that no threshold amounts of hazardous substances are necessary to trigger § 107(a) liability so long as response costs were incurred, and the related issue of whether a contribution-plaintiff must prove some significance threshold of environmental harm before liability attaches.

There is certainly no question that in the past few years, courts in contribution actions under § 9613(f) have shown greater willingness to incorporate a more demanding "tort-like" test of causation than in suits brought pursuant to § 9607(a). What explains this difference in judicial attitude? As you read the following cases bear in mind that § 9613(f) requires that the court, in allocating costs among responsible parties, apply such "equitable factors" as the court determines appropriate. Equity, of course is a broad and discretionary concept that authorizes recognition of factors that may be inadmissible or irrelevant to the government-initiated action under § 9607(a).

ACUSHNET COMPANY v. MOHASCO CORPORATION

United States Court of Appeals, First Circuit, 1999.
191 F.3d 69.

BOWNES, SENIOR CIRCUIT JUDGE.

This appeal stems from the contamination and subsequent clean up of an area popularly known as Sullivan's Ledge, located in New Bedford, Massachusetts. Plaintiffs-appellants, collectively known as the Sullivan's Ledge Group, are thirteen corporations which received notices from the

U.S. Environmental Protection Agency ("EPA") advising that the government considered them responsible for the pollution of Sullivan's Ledge under the Comprehensive Environmental Response, Compensation, and Liability Act of 1980 ("CERCLA"). In the early 1990's, the group entered into consent decrees with EPA in which it agreed to perform remediation at the site.

Invoking § 9613(f) of CERCLA, the Sullivan's Ledge Group thereafter filed the present action in federal court seeking contribution from several parties not targeted by the EPA, including defendants-appellees: Mohasco Corporation; Monogram Industries Inc. and Nortek Inc., doing business as American Flexible Coduit ("AFC"); New England Telephone & Telegraph Company ("NETT"); and Ottaway Newspapers, Inc.

The district court dismissed these contribution claims, granting NETT's motion for summary judgment before trial, and entering judgment as a matter of law for Mohasco, AFC, and Ottaway at the close of plaintiffs' case-in-chief. We affirm, but on somewhat different grounds than the district court. As we understand it, the district court ruled principally that the defendants deposited so little waste at the site that it could not reasonably be said that they caused plaintiffs to incur response costs. To the extent that the court's ruling may be interpreted to incorporate into CERCLA a causation standard that would require a polluter's waste to meet a minimum quantitative threshold, we disagree. Nevertheless, we conclude that the record was insufficient to permit a meaningful equitable allocation of remediation costs against any of these defendants under § 9613(f).

I.

Once a pristine and picturesque area well-suited for swimming, hiking, and impromptu gatherings by local residents, over the years Sullivan's Ledge became little more than an industrial dumping ground for scrap rubber, waste oils, gas, combustion ash, and old telephone poles. Sullivan's Ledge was the source of smoke dense enough periodically to obscure the visibility of drivers on nearby roads; residents in the surrounding region commonly blamed the pollution for diminished air quality. The sludge became so toxic, the refuse so thick, and the stench so overwhelming, that city officials closed down the area in the 1970's.

Eventually, the EPA identified a number of business entities, or their successors-in-interest, which it believed were legally responsible for the decades-long pollution at the site. In 1991 and 1992, after lengthy negotiations, members of the Sullivan's Ledge Group entered into two separate consent decrees with the United States. The decrees required them to implement a remediation plan and, to some extent, shoulder the costs of restoring the contaminated site to its non-hazardous state, without foreclosing their right to seek contribution from any other responsible parties. They duly commenced clean up efforts in compliance with the consent decrees, and, in turn, brought this contribution action to recover some portion of the realized and anticipated costs.

Plaintiffs accused NETT of dumping the butts of old telephone poles that had been treated with liquid creosote chock-full of Polycyclic Aromatic Hydrocarbons ("PAHs"). They alleged that Nortek and Monogram d/b/a AFC, a manufacturer of conduit and lead-based cable, generated and discarded scrap cable containing lead, copper, and zinc. According to the complaint, New Bedford Rayon, the predecessor-in-interest to Mohasco, deposited waste from the manufacture of rayon filament thread containing, inter alia, sodium hydroxide, copper, and sulfuric acid. In rounding out the cast of defendants, plaintiffs alleged that The New Bedford Standard Times, the predecessor to Ottaway, generated and disposed of ink sludge bursting with sulfuric acid, nitric acids, and various metals.

In due course, NETT moved for summary judgment. Although NETT conceded for purposes of the motion that it had discarded utility pole butts containing PAHs at the site, NETT argued that its waste added so few PAHs to the mix compared to the overall quantity of PAHs found at Sullivan's Ledge that NETT could not fairly be said to have contributed to the environmental harm or "caused" any of the remediation expenses.

The district court granted the motion during a hearing on June 11, 1996, (followed by a more extensive opinion issued July 24), ruling that NETT had proffered "uncontradicted expert testimony asserting that NETT did not cause, and, in fact, could not have caused the plaintiffs to incur any 'response costs.' " Acushnet Co. v. Coaters Inc., 937 F.Supp. 988, 992 (D.Mass.1996) ("Acushnet I"). Specifically, the district court stated that this scientific evidence showed that the creosote-treated pole butts could not have leached PAHs into the soil in an amount greater than pre-existing background PAH levels and that other sources provided the overwhelming proportion of PAH found at Sullivan's Ledge. Because, according to the court, plaintiffs failed to adduce any evidence directly challenging this expert testimony, the court found no triable issue of fact as to causation and entered summary judgment in favor of NETT.

The remaining defendants proceeded to trial. Upon the completion of plaintiffs' case-in-chief, the district court entertained dispositive motions. Mohasco, AFC, and Ottaway moved for judgment as a matter of law, arguing in substance that the environmental harm at Sullivan's Ledge was divisible and that the evidence was insufficient to permit a finding that the material the defendants dumped at the site caused any response costs. Ottaway also argued that plaintiffs had failed to establish that its wastes had actually been transported to Sullivan's Ledge....

[T]he court determined that, viewed in the light most favorable to plaintiffs, the case against each of the three defendants suffered "primarily from insufficiency of the evidence." It found that "the evidence the plaintiffs proffered against these three defendants * * * is so dramatically below any conceivable appropriate formulation of the [applicable legal] standard, that the outcome of judgment for these defendants at this time is clear without resolving just where those guidelines will ultimately leave the formulation.''

The court explained that, at most, plaintiffs had succeeded in showing that two cubic yards of solid cable waste was attributable to AFC, comprising no more than a fraction of the lead and zinc found at Sullivan's Ledge:

Looking at AFC as perhaps plaintiffs' best shot among the three, * * * at best, * * * a jury could not find that on an equitable basis, consistent with the Gore factors and with precedent[s] interpreting the statute, AFC would not be responsible for more than one in 500,000th—one in 500,000 share, and that would translate * * * into one hundred dollars. That demonstrates that we're so far below anything that could be classified as an equitable standard of determining shares of legal accountability, that anybody that low, any entity that low, ought to be kept out.* * *

For this reason, it concluded that the evidence at trial against AFC ''fails every version one might conceive of an 'equitable factors' test.'' Acushnet Co. v. Coaters, Inc., 948 F.Supp. 128, 139 (D.Mass.1996) (''Acushnet II'').

As for Mohasco, the court found plaintiffs' evidence against Mohasco even weaker than that against AFC. Not only was Mohasco's apparent share of the hazardous waste far smaller than plaintiffs' contribution, plaintiffs' own witnesses conceded that the types of hazardous substances attributable to Mohasco would not ''persist in the environment,'' and ''would not have even reached the site because of chemical reactions with other materials.'' Id.

In dismissing Ottaway from the litigation, the court said little other than that the case against Ottaway was ''obviously weaker than plaintiffs' case against * * * either of these [other] two defendants.''

Lest there be any doubt, the trial judge reiterated that the Sullivan's Ledge Group's claims against these three defendants failed ''on two independent grounds'': first, the evidence was insufficient to bring AFC, Mohasco, and Ottaway within the group for which ''the calculus of appropriate proportional shares'' of liability for response costs could be made ''and, secondly, on grounds of a lack of showing of causal connection with respect to remediation costs.'' See also Acushnet II, 948 F.Supp. at 139.

The district court entered judgment accordingly. Plaintiffs now appeal from each of the court's rulings.

II.

CERCLA, as we have said on other occasions, sketches the contours of a strict liability regime. See, e.g., Millipore Corp. v. Travelers Indem. Co., 115 F.3d 21, 24 (1st Cir.1997). Broad categories of persons are swept within its ambit, including the current owner and operator of a vessel or facility; the owner or operator of a facility at the time hazardous waste was disposed of; any person who arranged for the transportation of hazardous substances for disposal or treatment; and anyone who accepted hazardous waste for transportation. See 42 U.S.C. § 9607(a)(1)-(4). There are a few affirmative defenses available, see § 9607(b), but they are generally difficult to satisfy (they include showing that the release or threat of release was caused solely by an act of God or an act of war). By and large, a person who falls within one of the four categories[defined in § 9607(a) is exposed to CERCLA liability.

While CERCLA casts the widest possible net over responsible parties, there are some limits to its reach. The courts of appeals have generally recognized that "although joint and several liability is commonly imposed in CERCLA cases, it is not mandatory in all such cases." In re Bell Petroleum Servs., Inc., 3 F.3d 889, 895 (5th Cir.1993) (discussing import of deletion of joint and several liability language from final version of bill); see United States v. Alcan Aluminum Corp., 964 F.2d 252, 268 (3d Cir.1992) ("Alcan I").

In O'Neil v. Picillo, 883 F.2d 176 (1st Cir.1989), we embraced the Restatement (Second) of Torts approach in construing the statute, stating that a defendant may avoid joint and several liability if the defendant demonstrates that the harm is divisible. In that event, damages should be apportioned according to the harm to the environment caused by that particular tortfeasor. Id. at 178–79; accord Dent v. Beazer Materials and Servs., 156 F.3d 523, 529 (4th Cir.1998); United States v. Township of Brighton, 153 F.3d 307, 317–18 (6th Cir.1998); United States v. Alcan Aluminum Corp., 990 F.2d 711, 722 (2d Cir.1993) ("Alcan II"); Alcan I, 964 F.2d at 268–70. See generally Restatement (Second) of Torts § 433A (1965).

A responsible party, in turn, may bring an action for contribution under § 9613(f) to recover a portion of costs from "any other person who is liable or potentially liable under § 9607(a)." The standard for contribution liability is the same as that under § 9607(a), see Prisco v. A & D Carting Corp., 168 F.3d 593, 603 (2d Cir.1999), but in resolving contribution claims, a court may, in its discretion, "allocate response costs among liable parties using such equitable factors as the court determines are appropriate." § 9613(f)(1).

A plaintiff seeking contribution must prove that:

1.   The defendant must fall within one of four categories of covered persons. 42 U.S.C. § 9607(a).

2.   There must have been a "release or threatened release" of a hazardous substance from defendant's facility. 42 U.S.C. § 9607(a)(4); § 9601(14), (22).

3.   The release or threatened release must "cause[ ] the incurrence of response costs" by the plaintiff. 42 U.S.C. § 9607(a)(4).

4.   The plaintiff's costs must be "necessary costs of response * * * consistent with the national contingency plan." 42 U.S.C. § 9607(a)(4)(B); § 9601(23)-(25).

* * *

Generators whose waste has been deposited in the facility from which there has been a release are presumptively responsible for the response costs, subject to the opportunity to prove (i) that the harm was solely caused by someone (or something) else (see § 9607(b)) or (ii) that the harm they caused is divisible (see O'Neil, 883 F.2d at 179), and subject further to the equitable allocation of relative shares of responsibility in an action for contribution (see § 9613(f)(1)).

The parties do not dispute that Sullivan's Ledge is a "facility" or that each of the defendants was a responsible person within the meaning of § 9607(a). Instead, they hotly contest the correct legal standard by which one could be said to have "caused" plaintiffs to incur remediation expenditures, and whether the record was adequate to allow any meaningful award of response costs.

III.

The Sullivan's Ledge Group mounts a three-fold attack on the district court's reasoning in resolving the respective motions. Its arguments on appeal are broad-brushed in nature, focusing almost entirely on the legal meaning of "causation" and CERCLA's underlying policy goals. First, plaintiffs insist that reading any causal element into CERCLA is inconsistent with the principle of strict liability. Second, they contend that doing so would run counter to the remedial purpose of CERCLA because, among other things, it will let smaller polluters off the hook and discourage responsible parties from entering into consent agreements with the government. Third, to the extent the district court may have considered equitable factors in ruling in favor of Mohasco, Ottaway, and AFC, plaintiffs claim that the court did so without providing a "full and fair allocation trial" within the meaning of section 9613(f).

Defendants-appellees, for their part, contend that it makes sense to say that a de minimis polluter has not caused a responsible party to incur clean up costs; and that, in all events, plaintiffs' contribution claims against them founder for a more fundamental reason: the record did not permit a finding that each should bear a meaningful share of the costs associated with restoring Sullivan's Ledge. In their view, these fatal weaknesses in the plaintiffs' case justified judgment as a matter of law in their favor.

* * *

We affirm the district court's handling of NETT's summary judgment motion, albeit based on a slightly different rationale than the court's own. Although the court initially framed it in terms of causation (erroneously, we believe), a finding of no liability on the part of NETT is nevertheless justified under the principle of equitable allocation under § 9613(f).

We have strong reservations about interpreting the statute's causation element to require that a defendant be responsible for a minimum quantity of hazardous waste before liability may be imposed. The text of the statute does not support such a construction—CERCLA itself does not expressly distinguish between releases (or threats of releases) by the quantity of hazardous waste attributable to a particular party. At least on its face, any reasonable danger of release, however insignificant, would seem to give rise to liability. On this point, the courts of appeals are in unison. See, e.g., A & W Smelter and Refiners, Inc. v. Clinton, 146 F.3d 1107, 1110 (9th Cir.1998); Alcan II, 990 F.2d at 720; Alcan I, 964 F.2d at 260–63; Amoco Oil Co. v. Borden, Inc., 889 F.2d 664, 669 (5th Cir.1989); see also 42 U.S.C. § 9601(14) (defining "hazardous substance" without mentioning minimum levels); § 9607(a) (employing broad "any person" language).

To read a quantitative threshold into the language "causes the incurrence of response costs" would cast the plaintiff in the impossible role of tracing chemical waste to particular sources in particular amounts, a task that is often technologically infeasible due to the fluctuating quantity and varied nature of the pollution at a site over the course of many years.

Moreover, it would be extremely difficult, if not impossible, to articulate a workable numerical threshold in defining causation. How low would a polluter's contribution to the mix have to be before a judge could find, with equanimity, that the polluter was not a but-for "cause" of the clean up efforts? Less than 0.5% or 1%? We do not see how such a line, based on the quantity or concentration of the hazardous substance at issue, can be drawn on a principled basis in defining causation. To even begin down that path, we feel, is to invite endless confusion.

Our own decisions provide no basis for such an approach. * * * And we have never discussed CERCLA causation in quantitative terms. To satisfy the causal element, it is usually enough to show that a defendant was a responsible party within the meaning of 9607(a); that clean up efforts were undertaken because of the presence of one or more hazardous substances identified in CERCLA; and that reasonable costs were expended during the operation. To the extent that the district court held that some minimal quantity of hazardous waste must be involved before a defendant may be held to have "caused" the expenditure of response costs, it was mistaken. See O'Neil, 883 F.2d at 179 n. 4 (expressly rejecting, in a related context, the argument that one must demonstrate that defendant was a "substantial" cause of the contamination before CERCLA liability attaches).

This does not mean, however, that the de minimis polluter must necessarily be held liable for all response costs. The approach taken by the Second Circuit is instructive. In Alcan II, 990 F.2d 711 (2d Cir.1993), the Second Circuit reaffirmed the Restatement (Second) of Torts approach to fleshing out the scope of CERCLA liability, holding that where environmental harms are divisible, a defendant may be held responsible only for his proportional share of the response costs. In extending the principle a half-step, the Second Circuit went on to say that:

[A defendant] may escape any liability for response costs if it either succeeds in proving that its [waste], when mixed with other hazardous wastes, did not contribute to the release and cleanup costs that followed, or contributed at most to only a divisible portion of the harm. Id. at 722. The court emphasized that this particular defense was limited to situations where a defendant's "pollutants did not contribute more than background contamination and also cannot concentrate." Id. It acknowledged that causation was, in some sense, "being brought back into the case—through the backdoor, after being denied entry at the frontdoor— at the apportionment stage." Id. Nevertheless, the court concluded that a defendant who successfully meets its burden can "avoid liability or contribution." Id. at 725. The Alcan II panel took great pains to leave questions of liability, including the divisibility of environmental harm, and equitable apportionment of clean up expenses, to the sound discretion of the trial judge to be handled in the manner and order he or she deems best. Id. at 723. We think the Second Circuit had it right.

We therefore hold that a defendant may avoid joint and several liability for response costs in a contribution action under § 9613(f) if it demonstrates that its share of hazardous waste deposited at the site constitutes no more than background amounts of such substances in the environment and cannot concentrate with other wastes to produce higher amounts. This rule is not based on CERCLA's causation requirement, but is logically derived from § 9613(f)'s express authorization that a court take equity into account when fixing each defendant's fair share of response costs. We caution, however, that not every de minimis polluter will elude liability in this way. As always, an equitable determination must be justified by the record.

There are several reasons why, after all is said and done, an otherwise responsible party may be liable for only a fraction of the total response costs or escape liability altogether. In the first place, § 9613(f) expressly contemplates that courts will take equity into account in resolving contribution claims. We have in the past suggested that while a defendant in a direct EPA enforcement action invoking the divisibility of harm defense bears an "especially heavy burden," a defendant in a contribution proceeding seeking to limit his liability has a "less demanding burden of proof" by virtue of the equitable considerations that come immediately into play. In re Hemingway Transp., Inc., 993 F.2d 915, 921 n. 4 (1st Cir.1993); see also O'Neil, 883 F.2d at 183 (stating that a defendant's burden is "reduced" in a contribution action). A court, in evaluating contribution claims under § 9613(f), is "free to allocate responsibility according to any combination of equitable factors it deems appropriate." O'Neil, 883 F.2d at 183. Accord FMC Corp. v. Aero Indus., Inc., 998 F.2d 842, 846–47 (10th Cir.1993); Environmental Transp. Sys., Inc. v. ENSCO, Inc., 969 F.2d 503, 509 (7th Cir.1992). In an appropriate set of circumstances, a tortfeasor's fair share of the response costs may even be zero. * * *

In the second place, there is nothing to suggest that Congress intended to impose far-reaching liability on every party who is responsible for only trace levels of waste. Several courts, albeit taking different paths to a similar result, have rejected the notion that CERCLA liability "attaches upon release of *any* quantity of a hazardous substance." Licciardi v. Murphy Oil USA, 111 F.3d 396, 398 (5th Cir.1997) (quoting Amoco Oil, 889 F.2d at 670) (emphasis in original); see e.g., PMC, 151 F.3d at 616; Gopher Oil Co. v. Union Oil Co. of Cal., 955 F.2d 519, 527 (8th Cir.1992).

Third, allowing a CERCLA defendant to prevail on issues of fair apportionment, even at the summary judgment stage, is consistent with Congress's intent that joint and several liability not be imposed mechanically in all cases. Permitting a result that is tantamount to a no-liability finding is in keeping with the legislative goal that clean up efforts begin in a speedy fashion and that litigation over the details of actual responsibility follow. In fact, to require an inconsequential polluter to litigate until the bitter end, we believe, would run counter to Congress's mandate that CERCLA actions be resolved as fairly and efficiently as possible. On the whole, the costs and inherent unfairness in saddling a party who has contributed only trace amounts of hazardous waste with joint and several liability for all costs incurred outweigh the public interest in requiring full contribution from de minimis polluters.

Plaintiffs complain that any consideration of causation is at odds with CERCLA's objectives and would discourage responsible parties from entering into consent decrees. Because we ground the quantum inquiry solidly in § 9613(f), we are satisfied their prophesy will not come to pass. The ultimate failure of a contribution claim because someone did only a negligible amount of harm does not impede enforcement by the EPA or frustrate any of CERCLA's objectives.

A.

Relying on favorable case law from the Second and Third Circuits, NETT attempted to prove that it contributed only trace amounts of hazardous waste to Sullivan's Ledge. * * *

In its motion for summary judgment, NETT contended that "it is beyond material dispute that no wastes disposed of by [NETT] * * *, even when considered with wastes disposed by other persons, could have contributed to the environmental harm at the Site or to the incurrence of response costs" and therefore "such wastes cannot be the basis for the imposition of any liability" upon it. * * *

It offered extensive expert evidence to the effect that the concentration of PAHs from NETT telephone poles, if in fact such poles were left at the site, was negligible. In a series of reports, Dr. John Tewhey estimated that some 335,000 pounds of PAHs were disposed of at Sullivan's Ledge, confirmed that the Sullivan's Ledge Group was responsible for most of this pollution, and stated that PAHs from telephone pole butts could have added no more than negligible amounts to existing PAHs in the surrounding region. He stated that PAH levels in soil samples from areas near where utility poles were located revealed the same amount of PAH found in many popular foods.

We have already rejected the district court's reasoning inasmuch as it may have been rooted in a theory of causation that required some quantitative threshold. But even if NETT may be said to have caused plaintiffs to incur response costs, plaintiffs failed to rebut NETT's evidence showing that it should bear no more than a de minimis share of the remediation expenditures under § 9613(f). NETT essentially offered evidence tending to show that its equitable share would amount to zero; plaintiffs gave only a non-responsive rejoinder, mostly by insisting (wrongly) that causation is irrelevant.

Questions of causation and appropriate equitable allocation of response costs involve quintessential issues of fact. But we see nothing especially onerous about requiring the Sullivan's Ledge Group to come forward with admissible evidence where a defendant has fairly raised the issues. All that need be done to survive that stage is to submit admissible evidence sufficient to point up a factual dispute. It is no different than asking a plaintiff to proffer some evidence as to damages where a defendant has claimed in summary judgment papers that the plaintiff has, in fact, suffered no compensable harm. Given the Sullivan's Ledge Group's failure to meet its burden in this regard, the trial court properly entered judgment for NETT.

We turn now to the district court's rulings in favor of AFC, Mohasco, and Ottaway.

B.

* * *

We affirm the judgment on the basis that the evidence was inadequate to permit a rational factfinder to make a quantifiable allocation of response costs to AFC, Mohasco, or Ottaway under § 9613(f).

While no precise allocations were made in this case, a trial court's perspective is nevertheless instructive as to the equitable considerations most relevant to the dispute at hand. Here, the court found the respective quantities of hazardous materials attributable to each defendant, the toxicity of the respective wastes, and their durability to be highly relevant to fixing an equitable share. Within this general framework, the court assessed the Sullivan's Ledge Group's evidence and found it inadequate. We agree.

Plaintiffs' evidence at trial tended to show that AFC was responsible for hazardous waste at Sullivan's Ledge on a scale "thousands of times less than the remaining contribution of others"; that, in terms of sheer mass, the two cubic yards of solid waste attributable to AFC constituted an insignificant amount of pollution when compared to over one million cubic yards of waste found at Sullivan's Ledge; that the remediation plan was largely driven by the presence of hazardous substances other than copper and zinc; and that the materials attributable to AFC was not as toxic as the other substances discovered at the site, namely, PAHs, Volatile Organic Compounds, and Polychlorinated Biphenyls. Taking at face value plaintiffs' own estimates of the costs of remediation, AFC's share of response costs, in the most generous formulation, would amount to no more than 1/500,000 of $50 million amounting to less than $100.

Two main factors underlay the trial court's ruling in favor of Mohasco: (1) Plaintiffs' evidence against Mohasco was far weaker than that against AFC; and (2) undisputed scientific testimony by plaintiffs' own experts that hazardous substances attributed to Mohasco "would not persist in the environment."

As for Ottaway, beyond the small amount of material attributable to its predecessor-in-interest, The New Bedford Standard Times, plaintiffs' evidence actually linking The New Bedford Standard Times to the ink waste at Sullivan's Ledge was thin at best.

* * *

They first suggest that equitable determinations played no role in the court's decision and therefore provide an inadequate ground for affirmance. Even a cursory examination of the record puts this argument to rest. The court repeatedly referred to the equitable factors it found most salient, and discussed the weight of the evidence as to each of these factors. While the judge was not making specific allocations, it is plain to us he was holding that, in light of the equitable factors he would apply should he make explicit findings, plaintiffs' evidence showed too little pollution to justify compelling defendants to take on any meaningful share of the response costs. We read him to say that if he had to make an allocation for AFC, Mohasco, and Ottaway, the evidence dictated that each of their shares for response costs would be zero. The court's reasoning is therefore sufficiently transparent as to provide a basis for affirmance.

* * *

Affirmed. Costs awarded to defendants-appellees.

Notes and Questions

1. *Searching for a Middle Ground.* The First Circuit was unprepared to take the larger leap of affirming the district court's ruling that some threshold of hazardous substances had to be released as a prerequisite to any liability. What reasons does the court offer for refusing to require that a contribution-defendant be responsible for a minimum quantity of hazardous waste before liability may be imposed? Is the best argument textual (not found within the language of § 107 or § 113) or practical (the tracing problem and difficulty in articulating a workable threshold)? If you were making this decision and wanted to establish some threshold, how might you express it? Recall your torts course and language of causation such as "substantial factor."

2. *Access Order Reviewability.* The Tenth Circuit Court of Appeals in Aztec Minerals Corp. v. E.P.A., 198 F.3d 257 (10th Cir.1999), affirmed a

holding that the courts lacked jurisdiction to review an owner's challenge to an EPA access order prior to the completion of site cleanup under § 113(h). Plaintiffs argued that they were not challenging the cleanup itself but objecting only to provisions of the order that restricted their access to the site during the EPA investigation and that restricted their ability to transfer the site. The court held that these provisions were integral to the EPA effort and protection of health and the environment and hence not subject to challenge.

Section 113(h) of CERCLA [42 U.S.C. § 9613(h)] clearly bars challenges to EPA removal and remedial activities until such activities are completed. The plaintiffs claimed that they were not challenging such activities but complained only about portions of the access order that restricted their own access to and transfer of the property. The court disagreed, writing that "[u]nrestricted access to a site at which there has been a release or threatened release of a hazardous substance and/or unrestricted conveyances of any or all interests in such a site would significantly interfere with, and impede, the EPA's response activities at that site." Hence, the access order's limitations were necessary to protect public health and the environment, and judicial review was precluded by § 113(h). That section bars the court from hearing even constitutional claims. Allegations of irreparable harm were deemed irrelevant, and the court affirmed the dismissal of the claims.

3. *Divisibility and Burden of Proof.* How would you state the court's holding? How does the issue of divisibility of the harm which we considered earlier enter into the contribution action? What does the *Acushnet* court mean when it states that in a "contribution action" a defendant's burden of proof is less than in a government action? Why should that be true? How does the "equitable factors" language of § 113(f) alter the burden of proof?

Can the quotation that "Congress [never] intended to impose far reaching liability on every party who is responsible for only trace levels of waste," be reconciled with the no minimum level of hazardous substances rule encountered earlier? In other words, how does the fair apportionment process allow thresholds into the merits of the case?

What is a contribution-plaintiff's burden of proof in establishing that a defendant should be assessed some portion of response costs? How does the volume of waste, the toxicity thereof, and the durability in the environment enter the calculation process?

Clearly *Acushnet* is unusual in the sense that one defendant, AFC, accounted for one cubic yard of solid waste out of over *one million* cubic yards of total waste, amounting to 1/500,000 of $50 million, or $100.

4. *Lower Court Opinions in Acushnet.* In three district court opinions, Judge Keeton, developed his conception of the appropriate causation test in these contribution actions.

In Acushnet Co. v. Coaters Inc. ("Acushnet I"), 937 F.Supp. 988 (D.Mass.1996), PRPs who entered into a consent decree with the EPA regarding a waste dump in New Bedford known as Sullivan's Ledge brought a contribution action against other nonsettling PRPs. The plaintiffs sought cost recovery from defendant New England Telephone & Telegraph Co. ("NETT") which had disposed of utility pole butts contaminated with PAHs (polycyclic aromatic hydrocarbons) at the site, even though the evidence showed that the pole butts would not leach PAHs to the site at levels above background levels. Id. at 990. The court rejected the contention that *"any hazardous substance in any quantity will open the floodgates of liability, and will do so even if the hazardous substance disposed of by the party is not causing any harm, is not threatening to cause any harm, and is not any part of the reason a response is needed and costs of the response are incurred."* Id. at 993 (emphasis added). The court granted summary judgment to NETT because of the insufficiency of plaintiffs' proffered evidence to support a finding of a causal connection between the sparse quantity of allegedly hazardous substances traceable to NETT, and plaintiffs' incurring costs for which they sought contribution.

In a second opinion regarding Sullivan's Ledge the court granted judgment as a matter of law to three more defendants based upon the insufficiency of the evidence, and developed what it described as the "threshold-of-significance standard" for application in contribution actions under § 113. Achusnet Co. v. Coaters, Inc. ("Acushnet II"), 948 F.Supp. 128, 134–38 (D.Mass.1996). See also Acushnet Co. v. Coaters, Inc. ("Acushnet III"), 972 F.Supp. 41, 49 (D.Mass.1997) ("a settling party may claim reimbursement of a share of remediation costs against a nonsettling party upon satisfaction of a threshold-of-significance standard").

According to the *Acushnet II* court, § 113(f) authorizes an equitable approach to determining liability in a contribution action:

> The "equitable factors" mandate is appropriately interpreted as at least authorizing, if not mandating for this case, making comparisons between plaintiffs in a contribution action and defendants whom they allege to be potentially responsible parties, by considering evidence before the court * * * for the purpose of determining whether the nature and extent of their respective ties to the hazards to persons, property, and the environment make it fair and reasonable to order that a defendant * * * reimburse the plaintiffs in some amount or some share of "contribution", allocated on an equitable basis reasoned from evidence concerning all the "equitable factors" for the application of which in this case some evidentiary basis exists.

Acushnet II, 948 F. Supp. At 135–136. According to *Acushnet*, plaintiffs must proffer evidence sufficient to support a finding that hazardous substances traceable to the defendant are in nature, quantity, and durability sufficient to invoke an exception to the fundamental principle of the legal system that courts are to leave harms and losses where they find them unless some good reason appears for shifting a loss from one party to another party. Id. at 136. "In other words, plaintiffs must proffer sufficient evidence as to a particular defendant to satisfy *a minimum standard of significance of that defendant's responsibility as a source of one or more hazardous substances deposited at the site."* Id. (emphasis added). This standard demands more than would a de minimis or scintilla standard.

Judge Keeton may be the first judge to articulate expressly a standard along the lines of a "minimum standard of significance" test as a causation threshold for contribution actions.

The authority that keeps recurring in the *Acushnet* opinions, and other cases is the statement quoted with approval from the Third Circuit's decisions in United States v. Alcan Aluminum Corp., 964 F.2d 252 (3d Cir.1992):

> [I]f [the defendant] proves that the emulsion did not or could not, *when mixed with other hazardous wastes,* contribute to the release and the resultant response costs, then [the defendant] should not be responsible for *any* response costs. In this sense, our result thus injects causation into the equation but, as we have already pointed out, places the burden of proof on the defendant instead of the plaintiff.

But the inquiries are intensely factual. In *Acushnet* for example, the defendant, New England Telephone and Telegraph Company (NETT) had demonstrated by uncontradicted expert affidavit that:

> * * * PAHs used in creosote-treated utility pole butts could not have leached into the surrounding soil to create a level of PAHs in the soil greater than the pre-existing background levels of PAHs already in the soil. Therefore, NETT asserts that the elevated levels of PAHs in the soil at the Site must have been caused by waste other than the utility pole butts. NETT's expert testified that even if NETT disposed of creosote-treated utility pole butts at the Site, the butts could not have contributed to any response costs incurred by the Plaintiffs. The response costs that have been incurred (or as to which there is any evidentiary basis for determining that an actionable risk exists for incurring future response costs) have been (and will be) required, not because of PAH levels to which NETT contributed in any way, but because of contamination as to which there is no proffer of evidence that NETT contributed in any way.

972 F.Supp. at 992–993. How often will a contribution-defendant be able to proffer such evidence to defeat liability?

5. *Rejection of Plaintiffs' Other Arguments in Acushnet.* The court noted that the method of analysis is "to characterize the issue as one of defining the scope and limits of liability consistently with manifestations in sources of authority * * * regarding the public policies underlying the applicable substantive-law rules." The Sullivan's Ledge Group's argument was that it need only prove with respect to NETT:

> (1) that the [defendant] generator disposed of waste material; (2) at a facility which contains hazardous substances of the type found in the defendant's waste; (3) [and that] there is a release or threatened release of that *or any* hazardous substance; (4) which triggers the incurrence of response costs.

That argument, the Group claimed, was premised on the text of CERCLA, caselaw, and traditional principles of strict liability under tort law.

The court first disagreed with the Group that § 107's text was silent on causation. That argument "defeats itself by purporting to prove too much," the court said, adding: "there are many requirements in CERCLA that, without a doubt, exist yet are not stated in the plain language of § 107." Furthermore, the court noted, the text of response costs that are *caused* by a "release or a threatened release"; i.e., the text "include[s] a causation requirement as to one form of limitation on the scope of liability."

Neither did the court agree that CERCLA's structure supported the Group's causation argument. That argument was based on the Second Circuit decision in State of New York v. Shore Realty Corp., 759 F.2d 1032 (2d Cir.1985), in which that court said that interpreting § 107(a) as including a causation requirement made the § 107(b) defenses "superfluous." The Massachusetts court said that "the relationship between § 107(a) and § 107(b) is sufficiently complex that § 107(b) need not necessarily be interpreted as impliedly negating the inference that § 107(a) regarding what may be called affirmative defenses rather than elements of the prima facie theory of strict liability."

Illustrating its point, the court pointed out that "[t]he exceptions listed in § 107(b) explicitly carve out from the *scope* of liability that might otherwise exist under § 107, any responsibility for parts of a practically indivisible harm if the party otherwise liable, and perhaps jointly liable, for some harm nevertheless makes the showing that another part of the harm was 'solely caused' in one of the designated ways, and also meets other requirements (e.g., 'he exercised due care')." If the strict liability in the statute did not encompass some causation, the court noted, then the implication of § 107(b) would be that in the absence of proving an affirmative defense, "a defendant would, prima facie, be subject to liability for not exercising due care over waste that had been produced by another and disposed of by another. * * * The defendant would also be required to 'take into consideration the characteristics' of the waste over which it had no control, and take precautions with respect to that waste of which it may well have had no knowledge and no reasonable way of obtaining knowledge." *Id.* at 995.

The court found that interpreting CERCLA to make NETT liable "produces a result not explained on any reasoned ground—a kind of result that a court, respectful of legislation, should not interpret the legislation as mandating without any apparent supporting reason." The court explained:

> In order for NETT to meet the requirements of § 107(b)(3) as Plaintiffs propose to read it, NETT would have had to police which entities were dumping waste into the Site and control every action taken at the Site to ensure that proper precautions were being taken. The record before me would not support a finding that NETT does now or ever did have the authority to police which actors would be permitted to interpretation of CERCLA as having established a regime of strict liability under which ordinarily a defendant will be held liable for any pollution caused by its waste, even if that defendant took every possible precaution to prevent its waste from causing pollution. The scope of this liability, however, is both defined and limited in ways consistent with common-law precedents regarding other forms of strict liability.

Id. at 1000. That interpretation was supported by § 107(b) defenses, the court noted, commenting: "it is possible that by including the exceptions in § 107(b), Congress may have merely been choosing which of the various common-law formulations [of strict liability and causation] should apply to the CERCLA regulatory scheme." Thus, Judge Keeton, probably more than any jurist in CERCLA jurisprudence, really comes to grips with the complexities and consequences of causation. No more qualified jurist could be found–

one of Judge Keeton's most influential books is Keeton, Legal Causation in Tort Law (1963).

It remains to be seen how influential his opinion and reasoning will be on other federal courts. Clearly the First Circuit in *Acushnet* as we have seen was not prepared to accept all of Keeton's reasoning.

For an excellent analysis of the causation issues in contribution actions, see, Aaron Cooper, Understanding Causation and Threshold of Release in CERCLA Liability: The Difference Between Single-and Multi–Polluter Contexts, 52 Vand. L. Rev. 1449 (1999).

6. *Other Opinions and Threshold Standards.* In Kalamazoo River Study Group v. Rockwell International, 3 F.Supp. 2d 799 (W.D.Mich.1998), aff'd 171 F.3d 1065 (6th Cir.1999), in an action brought by PRPs against other potentially responsible parties, alleging that they had contributed PCB contamination to the Kalamazoo River, after quoting Judge Keeton in *Acushnet*, the district court reasoned:

> The Court is aware of no Sixth Circuit case law on the subject of causation under CERCLA. However, in United States v. Cordova Chemical Co., 113 F.3d 572 (6th Cir.), cert. granted, 522 U.S. 1024, 118 S.Ct. 621, 139 L.Ed.2d 506 (1997) [In *Bestfoods*, included earlier, and reversed on unrelated grounds] the Sixth Circuit instructed as follows:

>> Thus, while the liability provisions concerning facility operators should be construed so that financial responsibility for clean-up operations falls upon those entities that contributed to the environmental problem, the widest net possible ought not be cast in order to snare those who are either innocently or tangentially tied to the facility at issue. * * *

>> * * * [W]e adhere to the tenet that liability attaches only to those parties who are culpable in the sense that they, by some realistic measure, helped create the harmful conditions.

Id. at 578.

> This Court recognizes that in [*Bestfoods*] the Sixth Circuit was addressing the issue of whether a parent corporation could be held liable for the acts of its subsidiary, which contributed to the contamination at a particular site. The *Bestfoods* court was not concerned with the significance of a particular release. This Court believes that the essence of the Sixth Circuit's statement in *Bestfoods* is applicable in this case as well. The Court's concern with culpability and "realistic measure" *supports application of a test in a contribution action that asks whether a particular defendant's responsibility was of sufficient significance to justify the response costs.*

> In reviewing the cross-motions for summary judgment, this Court will apply the threshold of significance standard: is the evidence of defendant's release of sufficient significance to justify holding defendant liable for response costs?

3 F.Supp. 2d at 806–807. Later in the *KRSG* district court opinion the court denied summary judgment as to one defendant precisely because its significance standard was ostensibly met by plaintiff's evidence:

The Court is satisfied that the evidence, viewed in the light most favorable to KRSG, is sufficient to support a reasonable inference that Rock–Tenn has been releasing PCBs on a regular basis for the last ten years. There is at least a question of fact as to whether PCBs are being resuspended and discharged by Rock–Tenn on a regular basis to the Kalamazoo river. Although the time period of Rock–Tenn's ownership of the facility is relatively short, and the total quantity of PCBs allegedly released appears to be very small compared to the releases by Plaintiff's members, *this Court cannot say, as a matter of law, that the evidence fails to meet the threshold of significance.* In contrast to Upjohn's situation, the alleged releases in this case are not attributed to sporadic cleaning activities. They are attributed to daily wastewater treatment practices. Moreover, a high concentration of PCBs has been detected in the lagoons, and Rock–Tenn's release is directly to the River.

* * *

There are issues of fact for trial that preclude the entry of summary judgment for either Rock–Tenn or KRSG at this time. The question of the sufficiency of the evidence against Rock–Tenn must be reserved for trial. It is worth noting, however, that even if the liability of Rock–Tenn is established at trial, the damages attributable to Rock–Tenn during the allocation phase may very well prove to be de minimis in comparison to the well-documented and extensive liability of Plaintiff's members.

Id. at 814. Earlier in the *KRSG* opinion the court also noted that: "These equitable contribution principles permit the court to consider whether or to what degree the defendant caused the response costs in a § 113(f) contribution action." The Sixth Circuit affirmed the district court in *KRSG*, but without ever referring to the threshold of significance standard; instead the court found no sufficient evidence that plaintiff raised a material issue of dispute over whether defendants contributed *any PCBs to the site*, relying extensively on the testimony of the parties' experts. Kalamazoo River Study Group v. Rockwell International Corp., 171 F.3d 1065 (6th Cir.1999).

Two Fifth Circuit opinions also appear to demand a strong causal nexus between the defendant's release and the incurrence of response costs. For example, in Amoco Oil Co. v. Borden, Inc., 889 F.2d 664, 670 (5th Cir.1989), the Fifth Circuit did not base liability on the release of a minimum quantity of hazardous substances, but did require a release sufficient to justify response costs.

The question of whether a release has caused the incurrence of response costs should rest upon a factual inquiry into the circumstances of a case and the relevant factual inquiry should focus on whether the particular hazard justified any response actions.

Id. at 670. Then in Licciardi v. Murphy Oil U.S.A., Inc., 111 F.3d 396 (5th Cir.1997), where the plaintiffs had shown no breach of any regulatory standard, the finding of hazardous substances "above background levels" was held to be insufficient to support a finding that the release caused response costs. "As we explained in Amoco, responsible parties are not liable unless there is evidence that they 'posed [a] threat to the public or the environment.'" *Licciardi*, 111 F.3d at 399. "While *Amoco* allows a CERCLA plaintiff to prove that response costs were caused by a release without resort to an applicable legal standard of justification, bare proof that there was a release is not enough." *Id.*

See also Farmland Industries, Inc. v. Morrison–Quirk Grain Corp., 987 F.2d 1335 (8th Cir.1993) (stating that causation standard in § 113(f) action is more rigorous than in a government or private action pursuant to § 9607(a)).

7. *Source of Contamination As a Causal Issue.* In United States v. Dico, Inc. 136 F.3d 572, 578 (8th Cir.1998), the Eighth Circuit Court of Appeals held that summary judgment in an action to recover cleanup costs was inappropriate where the company had raised fact questions regarding whether or not it was the source of groundwater contamination. Here, the EPA discovered the Des Moines, Iowa, public water supply was contaminated with trichloroethylene (TCE). Dico, Inc.'s land was included in the designated cleanup site because Dico had used TCE in industrial degreasing operations. The EPA later sued Dico under § 9607(a) for recovery of costs the agency had incurred in cleaning up the site. The trial court granted the EPA summary judgment.

Vacating in part, the Eighth Circuit noted that for liability to attach under § 9607(a), defendant must have been an owner or operator of the facility at the time the contaminant was released and *there must be a causal nexus between the release and the incurrence of cleanup costs.*

Examining to the causal nexus, the court found that defendant had raised a fact question concerning the origin of the groundwater contamination. The only evidence that defendant had caused the contamination was that the highest TCE concentrations had been found below its property. Defendant had submitted evidence, however, that the EPA's soil tests of the area failed to establish a continuous line of contamination from the soil surface to the groundwater. Assessing the credibility of this testimony and evaluating its weight is the job of the fact finder, not of the trial court on a summary judgment motion, the court said. Although not a contribution action under § 113(f), the causal principle raised in *Dico* would undoubtedly be applicable to private party actions as well as government-initiated claims for response costs. And, of course, the factual question is driven by the science of hydrogeology.

8. *Alternative Liability and Burden Shifting.* In New Jersey Turnpike Authority v. PPG Industries, 197 F.3d 96 (3d Cir.1999), the New Jersey Turnpike Authority (NJTA) sued several processors that had plants located near the eastern spur of the New Jersey Turnpike (which had been divided into many sites for CERCLA purposes) for contribution under CERCLA and the New Jersey Spill Act, N.J.S.A. § 58:1–.23.11(g)(c)(1), for disposing of chromate ore processing residue (COPR) which had contaminated the sites over a period from 1950 to 1977. The plaintiff alleged that given the difficulty it faced in proving causation that a theory of alternative liability should be applied to shift the burden of proof to defendants to disprove causation. The Turnpike had admitted it could not produce direct evidence to prove CERCLA liability, and that it had instead urged the Court to apply an alternative liability doctrine, whereby the "burden would shift to the

Generator Defendants to prove that COPR originating from their plants was not the source of the COPR detected on each site in question."

The Third Circuit's analysis proceeded as follows:

First, we find that the Turnpike has misconstrued the nature of the proof required of a plaintiff under CERCLA. * * * We * * * agree with the District Court in this matter that in order to fulfill CERCLA's "causation" requirements, the Turnpike must offer some proof that Allied, PPG, and Occidental deposited, or caused the disposal of, COPR at each of the sites at issue in this case. * * * Some courts, in describing this evidentiary burden, have termed it a "nexus" requirement.

* * *

The Turnpike argues that it produced sufficient evidence to survive summary judgment apart from the application of an alternative liability theory, but it also argues that the District Court erred by failing to shift the burden of proof to Allied, PPC, and Occidental via common law principles of alternative liability on the basis of the evidence that it produced of the appellees' COPR production and disposal. Although general tort law principles require a plaintiff to bear the burden of proving causation, see Restatement (Second) of Torts, § 433B(1) (1965), courts have fashioned exceptions to this rule in situations in which plaintiffs would be otherwise unable to recover, such as alternative liability, market share liability, and enterprise liability.

* * *

The application of an alternative liability theory does place certain requirements on a plaintiff before any burden shifting occurs. Some courts have set forth the following test for alternative liability: 1) all defendants must have acted tortiously; 2) the plaintiff must have been harmed by the conduct of at least one of the defendants, and therefore plaintiff must bring all possible defendants before the court; and 3) the plaintiff must be unable to identify which defendant caused the injury. * * * Alternative liability applies "only where it is proved that each of two or more actors has acted tortiously and that the harm has resulted from the conduct of some one of them. On these issues the plaintiff has still the burden of proof." Restatement (Second) of Torts, § 433B(3), cmt. *g.*

We find the Directives and the proffered expert report to be of little probative value, because they contain no evidence regarding the responsibility of these appellees for COPR deposits at the sites in question. *The Turnpike relies upon a collection of facts that could be summarized as "if it is there, it must be theirs."* The Turnpike urges that the conceded large scale production of CPR by the appellees, the need for its local disposal, the proximity of the appellees' production facilities to the sites at issue, and the use of this material as fill over the years, combine to create a question of material fact as to whether these appellees bear responsibility and must pay contributions to the Turnpike for depositing COPR at the sites in question. For example, the Turnpike argues that since sites 56, 131, and 201 are close to Occidental's former processing plant, it is liable for those sites, and since site 21 is close to PPG's plant,

PPG should be held accountable for the COPR contamination there. Although these facts might serve as corroboration if there were other proofs of the actual involvement of the appellees with disposal at the sites in question, *they provide no proof whatsoever that they did in fact dispose of their COPR at the sites in question.* The expert report commissioned by the Turnpike from Louis Beger and Associates is even less helpful, since it paints a generalized contamination scenario at the Turnpike locations, again lacking in a link to one or more of the appellees, and also lacking in certainty as to the precise nature of the contamination. The report * * * draws no conclusions as to which appellee is accountable for the contamination at a particular site. (emphasis added).

* * *

In sum, we find that the evidence produced by the Turnpike is insufficient to prove the nexus required for the Turnpike to recover from the appellees under either CERCLA or the Spill Act, *nor is this evidence sufficient to show that each of these appellees acted in a tortious manner within the meaning of these statutes toward these sites such that an alternative liability theory would be appropriate.* (emphasis added).

We note, further, that we also concur with the District Court's conclusion that the Turnpike may not be the innocent plaintiff that in fairness should be permitted to take advantage of alternative liability. As the District Court noted, *the Turnpike is a PRP in this case, and a joint tortfeasor; as such it may very well be inappropriate to utilize an alternative liability theory, which is meant to apply to wholly innocent plaintiffs,* to shift the burden of proof to its fellow tortfeasors in a contribution action.

We also note that the Turnpike clearly did not do all that it could to prove causation such that a burden shifting approach should be utilized in this matter. The Turnpike's lack of diligence clearly militates against a finding that alternative liability should be applied here. * * *

The Turnpike has, quite simply, not done enough. The Turnpike has, instead, asked us to rewrite the burdens that a litigant must meet under the CERCLA and the Spill Act, and the burden placed upon a plaintiff when alternative liability is applicable, to make up for the shortcomings in its proof. We will not do so. We will affirm the order of the District Court.

197 F.3d at 107–114.

9. *Issue Preclusion, Causation, and Prior Government Suits.* The causation question in private actions was considered in Farmland Industries, Inc. v. Morrison–Quirk Grain Corp., 987 F.2d 1335 (8th Cir.1993). In *Farmland*, the EPA had originally sued Morrison for response costs, in which action the district court found it to be a PRP as an owner during the time that a disposal of hazardous substances had occurred on the site, but had not made any determination that it had caused the contamination. Farmland and Morrison subsequently filed cross actions for indemnity or contribution for response costs already incurred and any future response costs. Morrison had owned and used the site for a grain storage and liquid

fumigant facility, which Farmland later acquired. Sometime during the Morrison's and Farmland's respective periods of ownership, 2500 gallons of the fumigants had been released. In its private cross action Farmland had sought an issue preclusion ruling on Morrison's liability based on the EPA's successful suit. The court of appeals rejected that argument by pointing out that liability in the government action is strict and does not depend on any showing of causation or fault, and therefore, the EPA's action did not determine that Morrison had caused the contamination at the site.

The court stated that the issue of whether Morrison should be liable to Farmland for any expenses incurred as a result of contamination at the subsite is inextricably linked to causation. The district court, however, had specifically refused to consider issues of causation in the EPA's suit, but had ruled that Morrison was a responsible party under CERCLA § 107. The court of appeals concluded that the jury instructions were erroneous because they incorrectly stated the law governing the allocation of costs between private parties. The trial court instructed the jury on Morrison's claim against Farmland by defining the elements in terms of the causation of "response costs," when the proper inquiry was the causation of the contamination at the site:

> Reading these instructions together, we are forced to conclude that the district court's instructions were, at least, incomplete. The second paragraph of this counterclaim instruction, read in conjunction with the previous case instruction, made it difficult, if not impossible, for the jury to find for Morrison. The court had already told the jury that as a matter of law Morrison "caused the United States to incur response costs," and that Morrison was "a person responsible" for those costs. Therefore, without further explanation of the CERCLA statutory scheme, the jury may have had difficulty concluding that Farmland was "the sole cause of the incurrence of response costs by Morrison–Quirk." Had the district court given more detailed instructions on the various facets of CERCLA liability, to the government under section 9607 and for liability to a third party under section 9613, these instructions might have been a harmless error. In the absence of further direction, these instructions tended to be confusing, and, therefore, could have resulted in prejudice to Morrison.

987 F.2d at 1342–1343. The court also found objectionable the trial court's use of the term "person responsible" without explaining that in CERCLA lexicon its meaning differs from common parlance.

5.   NOTE ON JOINT AND SEVERAL LIABILITY

a.   Revisiting the § 113(f) Versus § 107 Debate

The decisions that ruled that private PRPs are required to rely on § 113(f) contribution mechanisms rather than § 107(a) cost recovery provisions often used as one rational for so holding that § 107(a) affords the successful plaintiff the benefits of joint and several liability, whereas a contribution action pursuant to § 9613(f)(1) calls for several or proportionate liability only. The courts such as in *Pinal Creek* reasoned that a joint and several liability regime in § 113(f) proceedings would be inherently unfair because it would permit an admitted PRP to shift the entire liability to other PRPs, and avoid any liability for orphan shares, subject possibly to counterclaims for contribution asserted by the PRP defendants. But what about joint and several liability in contribution actions–are there circumstances where joint liability might be appropriate even in contribution claims?

As summarized in Sun Company, Inc. v. Browning–Ferris, Inc., 124 F.3d 1187 (10th Cir.1997), the nearly uniformly accepted rule is as follows:

> Together, §§ 107 and 113 allow "any person" who has incurred cleanup costs consistent with the National Contingency Plan to recover some or all of those costs from PRPs who were responsible for the waste. A government entity (Federal, State or Indian) or a party who did not contribute to the waste may recover all of its expenditures in a traditional § 107(a) "cost recovery" action against any PRP. Liability will be strict, *joint and several*. A PRP who contributed to the waste may recover from other PRPs a portion of the costs it expended in cleaning up the site in a contribution action under § 113(f). The liability of the other PRPs will be defined by § 107, but under *§ 113(f), that liability will be several, and the total cleanup costs—including responsibility for "orphan shares"—will be equitably apportioned among all the PRPs, with the court being able to consider any factors it deems relevant.* 124 F.3d at 1193.

Similar statements abound in other opinions, such as, Pinal Creek Group v. Newmont Mining Corp., 118 F.3d 1298, 1303 (9th Cir.1997), cert. denied, 524 U.S. 937, 118 S.Ct. 2340, 141 L.Ed.2d 711 (1998), quoted earlier. See, also, United States v. Colorado & Eastern R.R. Co., 50 F.3d 1530, 1535 (10th Cir.1995); Centerior Service Co. v. Acme Scrap Iron & Metal Corp., 153 F.3d 344, 348 (6th Cir.1998).

Recently, however, a few courts of appeal have challenged the proposition that contribution actions may only impose several or proportionate liability. As one commentator summarized regarding the problem of a several liability regime only:

> It is "well settled" that, absent proof of divisibility, CERCLA § 107 imposes joint and several liability. It is also quite clear in most cases that liability is only several in CERCLA § 113 contribution claims. Parties limited to contribution claims are, therefore, potentially at a distinct disadvantage. This is especially true in CERCLA litigation where, in most cases, many liable parties cannot be sued because of bankruptcy, dissolution or other similar circumstances. In the typical CERCLA case, a plaintiff limited to contribution faces the prospect of absorbing a significant "orphan share" of liability. As one court observed, "a prohibition against joint and several liability would leave the willing PRP holding the bag for the insolvent companies."

Steven DeGeorge, Seventh Circuit Further Confuses Availability and Significance of CERCLA § 107 Standing, 33 Chem. Waste Litig. Rep.

1107, 1110 (May 1997), quoting Allied Corp. v. Acme Solvents Reclaiming, Inc., 691 F.Supp. 1100, 1118 (N.D.Ill.1988).

But the quoted material is probably an overstatement, because contribution claims are equitable in nature, invoking "all the equitable powers of the District Court * * * for the proper and complete exercise of [its equitable] jurisdiction." A court's equitable authority is especially broad in CERCLA contribution suits, given that the statute authorizes allocation of response costs "using such equitable factors as the court determines are appropriate." Thus, even absent joint and several liability, courts have reached the same result by allocating orphan shares proportionately among solvent parties. Some courts, however, have refused to wield their equitable power in this fashion. The Middle District of Pennsylvania, for example, has imposed the entire orphan share on a liable plaintiff relegated to a § 113 contribution claim, finding that "it would be most inequitable to hold Defendants liable for any of the 'orphan shares.' * * * " Gould, Inc. v. A & M Battery and Tire Service, 901 F.Supp. 906, 913 (M.D.Pa.1995). At the other extreme, the Eastern District of Virginia has allowed a liable plaintiff to sue under § 107, and imposed all orphan share liability on defendants. Pneumo Abex Corp. v. Bessemer and Lake Erie R.R. Co., Inc., 921 F.Supp. 336, 348 (E.D.Va. 1996).

Also downplaying the "orphan share" problem is Stearns & Foster Bedding Co. v. Franklin Holding Corp., 947 F.Supp. 790 (D.N.J.1996) in which the court minimized the concerns that PRPs would be discouraged from conducting cleanups because, in the absence of § 107 joint and several liability, they bore the risk of unrecoverable "orphan shares" of liability, calling that risk a "statutory paper tiger", writing "Several courts have recognized that the powers provided by § 113(f)(1) allow district courts to allocate any 'orphan shares' among viable PRPs, with the result that each viable PRP's allocable share may include a portion of whatever 'orphan shares' there are.... The residual power granted to a district court in § 113 to apportion liability according to equitable principles more than adequately protects a PRP who undertakes a cleanup of another party's toxic legacy." 947 F.Supp. at 800–801.

b. Courts of Appeal Move to Joint and Several: Carter–Jones Lumber Co.

Carter–Jones Lumber Co. v. Dixie Ditributing Co., 166 F.3d 840 (6th Cir.1999) appears to be the first court of appeals to recognize that joint and several liability may be proper in some contribution actions under § 9613(f). The Sixth Circuit Court of Appeals affirmed a ruling holding the seller of PCB-contaminated transformers liable as an arranger in a CERCLA contribution action. The court found that circumstantial evidence sufficiently created an inference that the transaction was an arrangement for disposal and not the sale of a useful product. The sole shareholder, president and CEO of the company, Denune, was personally liable as an arranger because of his direct involvement in the transaction. The opinion reversed a ruling that the arranging company and its sole shareholder/officer were severally liable for shares of cleanup costs because they might properly be held jointly liable for each other's share of such costs.

Simplifying the facts, the district court found that Denune was personally liable for personally participating in the arrangements for disposal. He was president, CEO, and sole shareholder of Dixie, his company that had arranger liability under § 9607(a), and the district court apparently relied on his position in finding liability. Applying the Supreme Court's decision in *Bestfoods* to arranger as well as operator liability, the court held that Denune could be liable if he personally was "actively involved in the arrangements for disposal." As a shareholder, he could be liable only after piercing the corporate veil. The court affirmed the personal liability due to Denune's "intimate participation" in the disposal arrangements. But the district court held Denune and Dixie severally liable only.

Carter–Jones, the contribution-plaintiff, appealed the decision holding Dixie only severally liable for cleanup costs under § 113. The court found that the application of state law was "appropriate in resolving liability issues relating to corporations and officers," as implied by the Supreme Court in *Bestfoods*. In general, contribution liability is merely several, but "CERCLA's regulation of an environmental tort should not and does not relieve a corporation, its officers, or its owners of their bargained-for duties and liabilities as they do business in the corporate form." 166 F.3d at 848. CERCLA did not "alter state laws governing the liability of corporations vis-a-vis their officers and owners." Under this law, both Dixie and Denune should be jointly and severally liable for that portion of cleanup costs attributable to Denune. Denune would be liable for Dixie's share of cleanup costs, if the corporate veil were subject to piercing, a matter on which the lower court did not rule. The ruling that each of the defendant's liability was only several was reversed and remanded.

Interestingly, in *Carter-Jones* the court explicitly disavowed reliance on federal or CERCLA jurisprudence in reaching its conclusion, noting that, "It is not necessary, however, that we reach Carter–Jones's argument as to this court's ability to create joint and several liability in a CERCLA contribution case by using its equitable powers and the federal common law. Application of the law of Ohio corporations to CERCLA liability may well resolve the issue." 166 F.3d at 847.

c. *Seventh Circuit Adopts Broader Joint and Several Liability Recognition*

In the opinion that follows, Browning–Ferris Industries, Inc. v. Ter Maat, 195 F.3d 953 (7th Cir.1999), Chief Judge Richard Posner, one of tort law's most influential theoreticians in recent decades, especially for his intellectual leadership in expanding and popularizing the law and economics movement, applies his typical pedagogical style (recall he authored *Indiana Harbor Belt* in Chapter 4) in addressing the joint and several liability issue and a related *Bestfoods* issue regarding affiliated firms and a causation issue, which is deleted for inclusion in the next section.

BROWNING–FERRIS INDUSTRIES OF ILLINOIS, INC. v. RICHARD TER MAAT, ET AL.

United States Court of Appeals, Seventh Circuit, 1999.
195 F.3d 953.

POSNER, CHIEF JUDGE.

Browning–Ferris and several other companies have brought a suit for contribution under the Comprehensive Environmental Response, Compensation, and Liability Act (CERCLA—the Superfund statute). The suit is against Richard Ter Maat and two corporations of which he is (or was—one of the corporations has been sold) the president and principal shareholder; they are M.I.G. Investments, Inc. and AAA Disposal Systems, Inc.

Back in 1971 the owners of a landfill had leased it to a predecessor of Browning–Ferris, which operated it until the fall of 1975. Between then and 1988 it was operated by M.I.G. and AAA. In June of that year, after AAA was sold and Ter Maat moved to Florida, M.I.G. abandoned the landfill without covering it properly. For tax reasons, M.I.G. had been operated with very little capital, and it lacked funds for a proper cover. Two years after the abandonment, the EPA placed the site on the National Priorities List, the list of the toxic waste sites that the Superfund statute requires be cleaned up, see 42 U.S.C. § 9605(8)(B), 9616(d), (e), and shortly afterward Browning–Ferris and the other plaintiffs, which shared responsibility for some of the pollution at the site, agreed to clean it up.

Section 113(f)(1) of the Superfund law authorizes any person who incurs costs in cleaning up a toxic-waste site to "seek contribution from any other person who is liable or potentially liable under section 9607(a) of this title.* * * In resolving contribution claims, the court may allocate response costs among liable parties using such equitable factors as the court determines are appropriate." 42 U.S.C. § 9613(f)(1). Section 107(a)(1), 42 U.S.C. § 9607(a)(1), a part of the statutory provision to which section 113(f)(1) refers, includes in the set of potentially liable persons anyone who owned or operated a landfill when a hazardous substance was deposited in it, and this set is conceded to include both M.I.G. and AAA. The district judge held, however, that Ter Maat was not himself a potentially liable person, because he had done nothing that would subject him to liability on a "piercing the corporate veil" theory for the actions of the two corporations. * * *

Browning–Ferris and the other companies that have incurred clean-up costs at the site of the former landfill have appealed.

* * *

Two issues are relatively simple and we address them first. One is whether an individual can shield himself from liability for operating a hazardous-waste facility merely by being an officer or shareholder of a corporation that also operates the facility. The answer is no. The principle of limited liability shields a shareholder from liability for the debts (including debts arising from tortious conduct) of the corporation in which he owns shares (with the exception discussed later for "veil piercing" situations), but not for his personal debts, including debts arising from torts that he commits himself. In other words, the status of being a shareholder does not immunize a person for liability for his, as distinct from the corporation's, acts. * * * There is no liability shield at all for an officer. If he commits an act that is outside the scope of his official duties, his employer may not be liable; but he is whether or not the act was within that scope. E.g., Itofca, Inc. v. Hellhake, 8 F.3d 1202, 1204 (7th Cir.1993); Carter–Jones Lumber Co. v. Dixie Distributing Co., 166 F.3d 840, 846–47 (6th Cir.1999); United States v. Northeastern Pharmaceutical & Chemical Co., 810 F.2d 726, 744 (8th Cir.1986). Which is not to say, however, that the officer is automatically liable for the acts of the corporation; there is no doctrine of "superiors' liability," comparable to the doctrine of respondeat superior, that is, the employer's strict liability for torts of the employee committed within the scope of his employment.

So if Ter Maat operated the landfill personally, rather than merely directing the business of the corporations of which he was the president and which either formally, or jointly with him (as well as with each other), operated it, he is personally liable. United States v. Bestfoods, 524 U.S. § 51, 55 (1998). * * * The line between a personal act and an act that is purely an act of the corporation (or of some other employee) and so not imputed to the president or to other corporate officers is sometimes a fine one, but often it is clear on which side of the line a particular act falls. If an individual is hit by a negligently operated train, the railroad is liable in tort to him but the president of the railroad is not. Or rather, not usually; had the president been driving the train when it hit the plaintiff, or had been sitting beside the driver and ordered him to exceed the speed limit, he would be jointly liable with the railroad. If Ter Maat did not merely direct the general operations of M.I.G. and AAA, or specific operations unrelated to pollution, United States v. Bestfoods, supra, 524 U.S. at 66–67; United States v. Township of Brighton, 153 F.3d 307, 313–15 (6th Cir.1998), but supervised the day-to-day operations of the landfill—for example, negotiating waste-dumping contracts with the owners of the wastes or directing where the wastes were to be dumped or designing or directing measures for preventing toxic substances in the wastes from leeching into the ground and thence into the groundwater—then he would be deemed the operator, jointly with his companies, of the site itself. E.g., Control Data Corp. v. S.C.S.C. Corp., 53 F.3d 930, 937 (8th Cir.1995); * * * Unfortunately the district court did not consider this possibility, although urged to do so by the plaintiffs, and so a remand is necessary to determine Ter Maat's status.

It is also clear we think that CERCLA does not preclude the imposition of joint as distinct from several liability in a suit for contribution. This is, or at least should be considered, a case of first impression at the appellate level. Carter–Jones Lumber Co. v. Dixie Distributing Co., supra, 166 F.3d at 847–48, does hold that CERCLA permits joint liability in a contribution suit, *but on the unsatisfactory ground that state law so required, when it is plain that actions for CERCLA contribution are governed by federal law.* Section 113(f), 42 U.S.C. § 9613(f)(1), the CERCLA contribution provision, provides expressly that actions under it are to be governed by federal law, with the federal court to "allocate response costs among liable parties using such equitable factors as the court determines are appropriate." There is a savings provision in CERCLA, 42 U.S.C. § 9652(d), but the plaintiffs' claims in this case are based exclusively on the federal contribution provision, and not on state law.

* * *

[Here the court refers to authority holding or stating that liability is several only].

In traditional common law, when two or more persons inflict an indivisible injury each is fully liable for the injury. That is, the plaintiff can if he wants sue one of the tortfeasors for the entire damages and let the other go, and the one who is sued has no remedy against the one who got off scot-free. CERCLA modifies the traditional common law rule (as many other statutes do and as many state courts have done by modifying the common law) by allowing one liable party to sue another for contribution. It does not follow that if, as in this case, contribution is sought from more than one party, the defendants cannot be held jointly liable. It is up to the district judge, guided only by equitable considerations—a broad and loose standard, to decide, and it is easy to imagine cases, of which this may be one, where such considerations weigh heavily in favor of joint liability.

Suppose, to alter the facts for simplicity's sake, that Browning–Ferris had been made to clean up the entire site even though it had made only a small (say, 1 percent) contribution to its toxicity. Suppose M.I.G. and AAA were the bad actors jointly responsible for the other 99 percent. Suppose that for tax or other reasons M.I.G. had no assets. Under the view of the district court, even though M.I.G. and AAA had combined to inflict an indivisible injury (the contamination for which they were jointly responsible as joint operators), AAA would have to pay only 50 percent of the contamination for which it and M.I.G. were jointly liable, or 49.5 percent of the total clean-up cost (remember that we're assuming that the two corporations are jointly responsible for 99 percent of the total contamination), while Browning–Ferris would have to pay 50.5 percent of the total clean-up cost even though it was responsible for only 1 percent of that cost. * * * These are not our facts, but they show that a rule against ever holding contribution defendants jointly liable would be inconsistent with the statutory direction that the district court allocate liability equitably among the liable parties. * * * The judge did not make such an allocation, mistakenly believing himself constrained to allocate liability equally among joint polluters, and so this is another issue requiring further consideration on remand.

The next issue is whether the district judge allocated too large a share (40 percent) of responsibility for the cost of the clean up to Browning–Ferris relative to the defendants, who had operated the landfill for a lot longer time and had dumped a much larger quantity of wastes in it. The judge allocated as large a share as he did to Browning–Ferris because he found that it had operated the landfill poorly and had dumped particularly toxic wastes from a nearby Chrysler plant in violation of its operating permit, and the liquid character of the wastes had hastened their absorption into groundwater. Browning–Ferris argues both that these findings are erroneous and that, in any event, there is no evidence that the wastes from the Chrysler plant increased the cost of cleaning up the site and anyway the amount dumped in the landfill was not as great as the district judge found. From evidence that a considerable portion of the Chrysler wastes were dumped elsewhere, Browning–Ferris argues that defendants' expert had exaggerated the amount deposited in the landfill. Browning–Ferris may be correct on all these factual points, but we cannot say that the district court committed any clear errors in finding as it did, and that of course is our criterion.

* * *

It remains to consider two issues of derivative liability. If Ter Maat is deemed on remand to be personally liable as an operator of the landfill, and especially if the judge allocates 100 percent of the joint liability of M.I.G. and AAA to AAA, the solvent one of the pair (there is no suggestion that the change of ownership gets AAA off the liability hook), then Browning–Ferris and the other plaintiffs will be able to collect the amount of contribution to which they are entitled from the defendants. But these are big "ifs" (how big is for the district judge to decide, in the first instance, on remand). The judge may find that Ter Maat was not an operator and that AAA should not bear the entirety of its joint liability with M.I.G. In that event, it will become important whether Ter Maat and AAA are derivatively liable for the conduct of M.I.G., and as the issue is fully briefed we shall resolve it now and hope to head off a further appeal.

[Judge Posner then determined that the evidence was insufficient to pierce the corporate veil, so that Ter Maat could not be held personally liable for M.I.G.'s debt to plaintiff. He emphasized that veil piercing is especially questionable in situations where the debtor is "involuntary" and in no way relied upon what it believed was greater solvency of the corporation than existed. He repeated the argument that just because defendants engaged in hazardous enterprises they must have a sufficient "capital cushion" to pay any losses incurred by their activities. Finally, the evidence revealed no major corporate departures from the legal requirements for operating in the corporate form.]

Notes and Questions

1. *Split in Authority.* With the *Carter-Jones* and *Browning-Ferris v. Ter Maat* opinions we clearly have a split among the courts of appeals as to the availability of joint and several liability in contribution actions brought under § 113(f). Are *Carter-Jones* and *Ter Maat* distinguishable from most CERCLA cases such as *Pinal Creek*? If both cases had involved purely corporate parties without the complicating officer and shareholder issues (*Bestfoods* problems), would the courts ever had to even reach the issue of joint and several liability?

2. *Effect of Joint and Several Liability on the § 107 Versus § 113 Debate.* If we predict that courts will more routinely apply joint and several liability, what does that forbode about the ancillary debate over whether a PRP can only sue other PRPs for contribution pursuant to § 113(f)? Doesn't that remove one of the primary arguments developed earlier for courts opting for the § 113 solution over § 107 cost recovery? Might some courts now reconsider their earlier positions if joint liability were available under § 113? What distinctions remain if both remedies offer joint liability of defendant PRPs?

3. *Additional Authority.* At least one other court has followed *Carter-Jones* and *Ter Maat*. In United States v. Hunter, 70 F.Supp.2d 1100 (C.D.Cal.1999), the federal district court for the Central District of California granted the federal government's motion for partial summary judgment enabling it to seek joint and several liability for its cleanup costs at a disposal site, even though it was a PRP. Government agencies were PRPs who used the site for disposal. While a private party in this circumstance would be barred from bringing a § 107 action for joint and several liability, the court found that the government was different when acting in its enforcement capacity. This ruling was grounded in legislative history and in policy concerns.

The case involved the Casmalia Resources Hazardous Waste Management Facility, which had been operated from 1973–1989 as a treatment, storage, and disposal facility for hazardous wastes. The site contained over fifty surface impoundments and several waste landfills for hazardous substances. It accepted more than four billion pounds of hazardous waste. In 1989, the California Regional Water Quality Control Board (RWQCB) ordered the site to stop accepting waste. In 1992, EPA took steps to stabilize the site, at a cost of more than $13 million. The U.S. proceeded with a permanent remediation at the site.

The United States filed this action under § 107 against the owners and operators of the site. The government was pursuing a plan for cash-out at the site for the thousands of entities that may have disposed wastes there. The United States was allegedly a PRP at the site. The parties filed cross-motions for summary judgment on the issue of whether the U.S. could claim against the defendants for joint and several liability. Defendants cited a line of cases especially holding that potentially responsible parties could not sue under § 107 for joint and several liability but were limited to a remedy in contribution. Pinal Creek Group v. Newmont Mining Corp., 118 F.3d 1298 (9th Cir.1997). The United States argued that these opinions such as *Pinal Creek* should not apply to the federal government when it was acting in its enforcement capacity.

The court turned to the legislative history of the Superfund Amendments and Reauthorization Act of 1986, which created the formal statutory contribution authority. That record "indicates that Congress intended the government to have a unique role in enforcing CERCLA." It provided that governments were not liable under § 107 for their cleanup actions so long as they were conducted in a non-negligent manner. Congress clearly did not intend to change the general rule of joint and several liability at CERCLA sites.

In *Pinal Creek* the court expressed concern that a rule of joint and several liability would immunize the plaintiff PRP from the risk of orphan share liability and restrict a court's ability to apportion costs equitably. This concern did not apply when the government was the claimant. The defendants could still proceed against the government for contribution. Simply because the court might award the government full recovery did not mean that the defendants here had to assume the complete burden of orphan shares, as the court could apportion those costs among the solvent PRPs, including government agencies that were involved. The court stressed that the "relative shares of liability will be determined during the course of this litigation regardless of whether there is a prior imposition of joint and several liability."

The court held that the government could potentially impose joint and several liability on private parties, even when it was a PRP at the subject site. This was "in harmony with the overall policy aims of CERCLA." It did not rule on whether the defendants in this action should be subject to such joint and several liability. They have an opportunity, for example, to establish the divisibility of the harm. The court also indicated an intent to apportion costs in an equitable manner.

Do you agree with the court's reasoning?

4. *Orphan Shares Allocation.* Both *Carter-Jones* and *Ter Maat* in dicta implied that orphan shares were subject to allocation under § 113. That position is now well established by further district court support. For example, in United States v. Kramer, 953 F.Supp. 592 (D.N.J.1997) the federal District Court in New Jersey concluded that "orphan shares" in a contribution action may be allocated among all potentially responsible parties, rather than forcing only named defendants to bear the burden of amounts attributed to unidentified or insolvent parties.

The EPA and the State of New Jersey brought actions under CERCLA to recover over $100 million in response costs that it had incurred in cleaning up a Superfund site known as the Helen Kramer landfill. The government named 30 direct defendants as owners or operators of the landfill, or as generators and/or haulers of hazardous substances, contending that these 30 parties were responsible for reimbursing the state and federal governments for the $100 million cleanup. These 30 parties thereafter brought several hundred entities into the case as alleged generators or haulers of hazardous substances from which the named defendants sought contribution pursuant to § 113 of CERCLA.

The hundreds of third-party defendants argued that the court could not require them to bear the costs of any orphan shares. The court disagreed, stating that Congress provided district courts with broad discretion to consider and apply equitable factors in order to achieve a just and fair allocation among liable parties. The court noted that CERCLA § 113(f), under which the third parties had been sued, permits the court to allocate response costs "among liable parties." The court found that this phrase in no way precludes a finding that equity requires that response costs consisting of orphan shares be borne by third-party defendants as well as defendants named directly.

The court stated that the result sought by the third-party defendants might have the impact of hindering future CERCLA actions brought by the government. The court stated that such a rule would likely require the government to attempt, at the outset, to search out all liable parties and sue as many of these as possible. In the first instance, the court found that to take such a position would effectively undo a statutory scheme enacted by Congress that envisions a two-step process–the United States first securing full costs for recovery, and thereafter leaving the determination of exact shares to the parties who caused the harm. Additionally, the court stated that the government's transactional costs would be massive in size and complexity if they needed to determine at the outset all parties to be named.

Lastly, the court rejected the argument by the third-party defendants that assigning them orphan shares would violate the several liability provision afforded by CERCLA § 113(f). The court rejected this argument, stating that it failed to recognize that a third-party defendant does not have an assigned "share" of responsibility until the court has determined, through its power of equitable allocation, the respective liabilities of each party. The court acknowledged that, after orphan shares had been apportioned among the parties, the third-party defendants could not be forced to satisfy judgments against other parties that proved unrecoverable.

Accord, United States v. Maryland Sand, Gravel & Stone Co., 1994 WL 541069 (D.Md.), in which the court concluded that it would include the orphan shares when allocating the costs in the § 113(f) contribution action. "Equity and fairness dictate that the orphan shares should be equitably apportioned among all the solvent responsible parties," the court said. "Having been found liable under CERCLA for the recoverable response costs incurred by the government at the Maryland Sand, Gravel & Stone site, Metal Film will not be excluded from the apportionment."

6. LITERATURE

The applicability of alternative liability in the context of federal environmental statutes has been food for scholarly thought rather than the subject of much judicial opinion. See, e.g., John Copeland Nagle, CERCLA, Causation, and Responsibility, 78 Minn. L. Rev. 1493 (1994) (an especially excellent article); John W. Mill, Agricultural Chemical Contamination of Ground Water: An Econ. Analysis of Alternative

Liability Rules, 1991 U. Ill. L. Rev. 1135 (1991); Thomas C.L. Roberts, Allocation of Liability Under CERCLA: A "Carrot and Stick" Formula, 14 Ecology L.Q. 601, 616–23 (1987); James M. Olson, Essay, Shifting the Burden of Proof: How the Common Law Can Safeguard Nature and Promote an Earth Ethic, 20 Envtl. L. 891 (1990); Paul L. Dickman, Leaking Underground Storage Tanks: The Scope of Regulatory Burdens & Potential Remedies under RCRA and CERCLA, 21 N. Ky. L. Rev. 619 (1994). A few courts have recognized the applicability of alternative liability theories under the Resource Conservation and Recovery Act. See, e.g., Aurora National Bank v. Tri Star Marketing, 990 F.Supp. 1020 (N.D.Ill.1998); Zands v. Nelson, 797 F.Supp. 805, 812–13 (S.D.Cal.1992).

7. CAUSATION: FINAL THOUGHTS

Recall how early in this chapter courts seemed hell bent on extracting causation as a core issue in government and even in private cost recovery actions under § 9607. The foregoing material in this section clearly manifests a tectonic shift in emphasis.

Without doubt since the opinions of the Second and Third Circuits in United States v. Alcan Aluminum Corp., 990 F.2d 711 (2d Cir.1993), and 964 F.2d 252 (3d Cir.1992), buttressed by In re Bell Petroleum, 3 F.3d 889 (5th Cir.1993), the holy grail of parties defending CERCLA actions has been a successful causation defense. We have now seen in *Acushnet* (the district court opinions of Judge Keeton) and the First Circuit to a lesser extent, that in some cases, albeit not typical, proving causation can be a difficult hurdle for plaintiffs.

Consider the following observations made by a practitioner in the field:

The basic lesson of *Acushnet* for superfund practice is that it is worth a substantial investment of time and money to explore the causation issue. Not all defendants will benefit; not everyone has a "pole butt" defense. However, to the extent that the reasoning of *Acushnet* is applied widely, the decision cannot help but be relevant in many cases. If the facts of a case might support a causation argument, the following constitutes a short To Do List to maximize the probability of success:

    • Put the burden of proof on the plaintiff—It is appropriate to argue in the alternative and to assert both § 107(b) and the *Alcan* cases as affirmative defenses, but it is also important not to concede that the burden of proof on causation is on the defendant.

    • Think creatively about the causation issue—Although partial causation arguments are not discussed extensively in *Acushnet*, it is clear from the decision that many different kinds of causation arguments can be made. Depending upon the case, the following issues may be in play:

    • *De minimis volume.* The volume of hazardous substances disposed by the defendant was so small that it did not cause or contribute to response costs. This is essentially the argument made successfully by NETT in *Acushnet*.

- *Different hazardous substances.* A party that disposed of copper should certainly argue that it is not responsible for the cost of cleaning up benzene.

- *Different geographic areas.* Although not key to the decision in *Acushnet*, the court certainly indicated that a party will not be liable for cleaning up areas of a site where its wastes are not present.

- *Different media.* If a defendant's wastes are present in soil, but not ground water (or vice versa), it should certainly argue that it did not cause the costs incurred in responding to ground water contamination and cannot be liable for such costs under CERCLA.

- Obtain a highly qualified expert. Obviously, this is a truism. However, its importance cannot be overstated for these cases and a few additional thoughts are in order. First, it may be appropriate initially to obtain the best possible consultant to provide the necessary technical input. If that person would not necessarily make a good witness, a separate testifying expert could be retained once the validity of a causation argument has been determined. Secondly, it is helpful to retain the expert early enough in the litigation to provide useful advice during discovery.

CONCLUSION

The decision in *Acushnet*, if affirmed and if adopted in other circuits, may represent a return to more traditional modes of legal analysis of superfund issues, and away from reliance on simplistic expressions of the view that the remedial goals of the statute always justify an ever-expanding liability net, regardless of whether the actual language of the statute or applicable judicial precedent require imposition of liability. It may go some little way towards ensuring that fairness–a concept heretofore unknown in CERCLA liability determinations–is not totally absent from judicial analysis of CERCLA actions.

The injection of causation into CERCLA litigation means also that superfund attorneys now have both the opportunity and obligation to begin thinking again more like traditional tort litigators, to consider issues like burden of proof and the availability and persuasiveness of expert testimony. The traditional question of "who did what," which has largely been relevant in CERCLA thus far only at the allocation stage of contribution actions, must now be confronted directly, by both plaintiffs and defendants, at the liability stage.

Seth Jaffe, Winning a Causation Case Under CERCLA: An Analysis of Acushnet, Toxics Law Reporter (BNA) 536, 540 (1996).

8. RIGHTS TO A JURY TRIAL

While there is no guarantee of a right to a jury trial in a CERCLA cost recovery case, at least one court has held that there is a right to jury trial in contribution actions under CERCLA § 113(f). In United States v. Shaner, 23 Envtl. L. Rep. 20,236, 1992 WL 154618 (E.D.Pa.1992), the court stated that use of the term "equitable factors" in § 113(f) did not convert the action to one in equity because the essence of the contribution action is a tort action for damages. Accord, In re Acushnet River & New Bedford Harbor, 712 F.Supp. 994 (D.Mass.1989) (holding that jury trial rights exist for natural resource damage actions because they are legal in nature, but not for cost recovery actions because they seek restitution). Is it relevant that contribution actions under the Federal Tort Claims Act against the United States permit jury trials? See Globig v. Greene & Gust Co., 184 F.Supp. 530 (E.D.Wis.1960) (contribution actions are legal not equitable in nature, and rights to a jury trial attach to such actions). Why should parties to cost recovery actions not have a right to a jury trial, but parties in a contribution action have such rights?

Indeed, the authority seems to be moving against allowing jury trial rights in contribution actions. The one federal appeals court to have considered the issue is the Court of Appeals for the Third Circuit, which ruled in Hatco Corp. v. W.R. Grace & Co., 59 F.3d 400 (3d Cir.1995), that there is no such right. The Third Circuit held in *Hatco* that § 113 calls on courts to "resolve claims for apportionment on a case-by-case basis pursuant to Federal common law, taking relevant equitable considerations into account." Accord, CPI Plastics, Inc. v. USX Corp., 22 F.Supp. 2d 1373 (N.D.Ga.1995). A claim under § 113 of CERCLA is an equitable, rather than legal, claim, the court reasoned. The Seventh Amendment to the U.S. Constitution guarantees the right to a jury trial only in legal claims, it said, granting a motion by plaintiffs CPI Plastics Inc. and CPI Plastics LLC (CPI), to withdraw their jury demand.

9. EFFECT OF SETTLEMENT WITH THE GOVERNMENT

In 1986 Congress added settlement provisions expressly authorizing EPA to enter into settlement agreements with PRPs to clean up sites if it is in the public interest. If the EPA can obtain all or nearly all of the cleanup costs without resorting to protracted litigation it may expedite remedial actions and minimize transaction costs. CERCLA encourages private parties to settle in five ways: (1) by allocating response costs among the PRPs, which avoids joint and several liability; (2) making partial settlements available in some circumstances; (3) releasing settling parties by giving covenants not to sue; (4) creating protection from contribution actions; and (5) giving de minimis contributors favorable treatment.

To help achieve settlement, CERCLA § 122(e)(3) authorizes the EPA to prepare non-binding allocations of responsibility (NBARs) which allocate 100 percent of the response costs among PRPs. In making allocations, the EPA is not limited by so-called "indivisible" harm (which it advances in litigation) but rather is permitted to allocate costs among classes of PRPs by applying various factors including: volume, toxicity, mobility, strength of evidence, ability to pay, litigative risks, public interest considerations, precedential value, inequities, and aggravating factors. In addressing classes of PRPs, it allocates first among generators based on volume; it then adjusts those allocations based on the equitable criteria above; it then factors in transporter, owner and operator participation. For owners and generators, the EPA examines the length of time of ownership or operation and the degree of involvement and knowledge of the disposal of hazardous substances. Lastly, the EPA reallocates the shares of "orphans," insolvent or absent PRPs among the remaining solvent parties. See Daniel R. Hansen, CERCLA Cost Allocation and Nonparties' Responsibility: Who Bears the Orphan Shares, 91 J. Envtl. L. 37 (1992).

If a settlement is reached, the EPA may grant a release from present and future liability, if such a covenant not to sue is in the "public interest," a term defined in the statute. See CERCLA § 122(f)(4). However, releases are required to contain a "reopener" provision, except under "extraordinary circumstances." CERCLA § 122(f)(6)(A).

Of special relevance for our purposes is the effect which settlement with the government may have on a private party's exposure to future contribution actions.

a. *Effect of Settlement on Contribution: CERCLA's Provisions*

CERCLA's settlement provisions influence contribution in two ways: (1) those PRPs who settle are immune from contribution actions by nonsettling PRPs who litigate with the EPA and end up paying more than their "equitable" share of the cleanup costs; and (2) the amount which the settling PRPs pay will be applied to reduce the liability of the nonsettlors. These points are explicitly covered in CERCLA § 113(f)(2) which states:

> *A person who has resolved its liability to the United States or a State in an administrative or judicially approved settlement shall not be liable for claims for contribution regarding matters addressed in the settlement.* Such settlement does not discharge any of the other potentially liable persons unless its terms so provide, but it reduces the potential liability of the others by the amount of the settlement. (emphasis added).

In United States v. Cannons Engineering Corp., 899 F.2d 79 (1st Cir.1990), the court held that the language "amount of the settlement" requires only a dollar-for-dollar reduction. Is the language capable of any other interpretation? We consider this issue below in greater depth. Also see *Cannons Engineering* for a thorough discussion of settlement procedures.

The contribution protection provision of § 113(f)(2) comports clearly with the common law, as both the Uniform Contribution Among Tortfeasors' Act (UCATA) and Uniform Comparative Fault Act (UCFA) authorize a settlor to be shielded from later suits for contribution brought by a nonsettlor who eventually pays more than what it regards as its "fair" or "equitable" share. This too is the position adopted in the Restatement (Third) of Torts: Apportionment § 33 (1999), comment i, which reads in part: "*i. Contribution against a settlor.* A person who settles with the plaintiff before final judgment is not liable for contribution to others for the injury."

The Reporters' notes to comment *i* continues:

Comment i. Contribution against a settlor. Comment *i* protects a person who makes a good-faith settlement from contribution by other tortfeasors. A contrary rule would remove most of the incentive for a settlement. Settlement after final judgment or after a settlement between the plaintiff and the person seeking contribution has no purpose other than destroying contribution rights. Thus, it does not protect the settlor.

Comment i follows Section 4(b) of the 1955 version of the Uniform Contribution Among Tortfeasors Act: "[A release] discharges the tortfeasor to whom it is given from all liability for contribution to any other tortfeasor." It also follows the Uniform Comparative Fault Act.

Thus CERCLA § 113(f)(2) represents no departure from the near universal rule by encouraging settlements via the contribution protection provision.

But, as with most important CERCLA issues, given the potential stakes involved, the issue is not as clear-cut as it might appear. Once again the dichotomy between § 107(a) cost recovery actions and § 113(a) contribution actions has driven a wedge into a neat or harmonic system. On its face, § 113(f)(2) appears to limit the protection against future litigation to § 113 contribution claims, thus offering no protection against § 107 cost recovery claims. This has prompted some private plaintiffs to sue settling defendants for cost recovery under § 107, to circumvent the § 113(f)(2) contribution protection. As we have already seen above, most courts, using a variety of approaches, have rejected such claims. Indeed, even courts that allow liable parties to sue under § 107 generally draw the line where a plaintiff "brings a § 107 claim merely to circumvent contribution protection granted by the government to another party pursuant to Section 113(f)(2) * * * " In such cases, "CERCLA policy militates against allowing Section 107 standing." Pinal Creek Group v. Newmont Mining Corp., 926 F.Supp. 1400, 1409 (D.Ariz. 1996), aff'd, 118 F.3d 1298 (9th Cir.1997), cert. denied, 524 U.S. 937, 118 S.Ct. 2340, 141 L.Ed.2d 711 (1998).

You will recall that in *Halliburton* and *Pinal Creek* one rationale referred to by both courts for *not* permitting cost recovery actions between PRPs is that allowing § 107(a) cost recovery actions will undermine the efficacy of the contribution protection provisions.

But the Seventh Circuit in Akzo Coatings, Inc. v. Aigner, 30 F.3d 761 (7th Cir.1994), had recognized what is now referred to as the "Akzo" exception, allowing "innocent PRPS" (however defined) to maintain a § 107 cost recovery action against other PRPs, rather than being limited to § 113(a) contribution actions. The opinion that follows, Rumpke of Indiana v. Cummins Engine Co., 107 F.3d 1235 (7th Cir.1997), considers the intersection of the § 107 versus § 113 debate, described earlier in this chapter, with the contribution protection provisions of § 113(f). *Rumpke* also considers the related issue of whether an earlier consent decree related to the same "matters" as to which Rumpke, as plaintiff, is now seeking recoupment from a group of admitted PRPs.

RUMPKE OF INDIANA, INC. v. CUMMINS ENGINE COMPANY, INC., ET AL.

United States Court of Appeals, Seventh Circuit, 1997.
107 F.3d 1235.

DIANE P. WOOD, CIRCUIT JUDGE.

The net of potential liability under the Comprehensive Environmental Response, Compensation and Liability Act, better known as CERCLA, 42 U.S.C. §§ 9601 et seq., is wide indeed, reflecting the need both to clean up the nation's toxic waste sites and the practical imperative to find the necessary money for the job. The cleanup will be less likely to occur if potentially responsible parties do not come forward, yet the often astronomical sums needed to restore these sites can deter prompt remedial action. CERCLA protects parties who settle claims with the government from liability for contribution in suits relating to "matters addressed" in administratively or judicially settled consent decrees. See § 113(f)(2), 42 U.S.C. § 9613(f)(2). In this interlocutory appeal, certified pursuant to 28 U.S.C. § 1292(b), we have been asked to decide several questions relating to the breadth of one of those settlements. The central issue is whether a 1982 consent decree approved in United States v. Seymour Recycling Corp., 554 F.Supp. 1334 (S.D.Ind.1982), to which Cummins Engine Co. and its fellow appellants were parties (to which we refer as the "Cummins group"), stands in the way of the efforts of Rumpke of Indiana, Inc. ("Rumpke"), either to recover its costs of cleaning up a site arguably not covered by the Seymour decree under § 107(a) of the Act, 42 U.S.C. § 9607(a), or to obtain contribution from the Cummins group under § 113(f)(1) of the Act, 42 U.S.C. § 9613(f)(1). We agree with the district court that the Seymour decree did not encompass the matters Rumpke is now raising and we accordingly affirm its order.

I

The background facts are relatively straightforward. In 1984, Rumpke bought a 273–acre dump known as the Uniontown Landfill from George and Ethel Darlage. At that time, the Darlages informed Rumpke that the landfill had never accepted hazardous waste. For reasons undisclosed on this record, Rumpke did not conduct its own inspection of the land for environmental hazards prior to the sale. In light of where we are today, it is easy to predict what happened next. In 1990, to its professed surprise, Rumpke discovered that the Darlages' beliefs about the landfill had been quite wrong. In fact, a cocktail of hazardous wastes had been deposited at Uniontown for many years, and volatile organic compounds (VOCs) were migrating to surrounding areas. Looking into the matter, Rumpke determined that much of this material had come from the Seymour Recycling Corporation, which was located about ten miles away in Seymour, Indiana. For many years, Seymour had distilled for reuse acetones, alcohols, paint thinners, chlorinated solvents, and Freon materials, all of which had been discarded by various manufacturers. The distilling process yielded both reusable solvents and a toxic sludge. Seymour disposed of the sludge by shoveling it into 55–gallon drums, or on other occasions, incinerating it and storing the resulting ash in similar drums. Rumpke believed that some of those 55–gallon drums made their way to the Uniontown landfill. Because Seymour Recycling was by this time out of the picture, Rumpke brought this action against the manufacturers that used to send materials to Seymour Recycling for processing.

Rumpke's lawsuit opened a Pandora's Box of its own. Whatever one might say about the Uniontown site, it had become clear in the 1980's that the Seymour site was an environmental disaster area. Seymour Recycling had left some 60,000 drums and 98 bulk storage tanks, in various stages of decay, strewn about the site. By 1980, the drums and tanks were leaking, exploding, and sending clouds of toxic chemicals into the air over nearby residential areas. The United States responded with a complaint in May 1980, alleging violations of section 7003 of the Resource Conservation and Recovery Act (RCRA), 42 U.S.C. § 6973, and section 311 of the Clean Water Act, 33 U.S.C. § 1321. In 1982, the United States filed an amended complaint adding allegations under CERCLA, §§ 106 and 107, 42 U.S.C. §§ 9606 and 9607, which had been enacted in the meantime. The amended complaint added 24 new defendants who allegedly had transported hazardous wastes to the Seymour site for handling, storage, disposal, or treatment. At the same time, the State of Indiana and the County of Jackson moved to intervene in the action.

The amended complaint was accompanied by a proposed consent decree that was filed with the court, as required by § 122(d), 42 U.S.C. § 9622(d), which the court accepted in due course.... The decree resolved all obligations and responsibilities of the settling companies with respect to "the Seymour site." The companies paid agreed amounts into the Seymour Site Trust Fund, which was then available to trustees to perform the work described in an exhibit to the decree. It provided for penalties in the event the work was not performed satisfactorily; it gave the United States and the State the right to access and inspect the site at all times until the work was completed; and it contained various administrative provisions. The decree also promised, in section XII, that the United States, the State, and the local governments would not bring any more civil actions against the settling companies:

> * * * arising out of or related to the storage, treatment, handling, disposal, transportation or presence or actual or threatened release or discharge of any materials at, to, from or near the Seymour site, including any action with respect to surface cleanup and soil or groundwater cleanup at the Seymour site.

Our case arises because the defendants Rumpke wants to pursue— Cummins, Ford Motor Company, International Business Machines Corp., General Motors Corp., and Essex Group, Inc.—were among the Seymour settling parties.

II

After Rumpke filed its action with respect to the contaminated Uniontown site, the Cummins group moved for summary judgment against Rumpke's claims. They argued that Rumpke's suit was blocked by the language just quoted from the 1982 Seymour consent decree, by virtue of CERCLA § 113(f)(2), which reads as follows:

> A person who has resolved its liability to the United States or a State in an administrative or judicially approved settlement shall not be liable for claims for contribution regarding matters addressed in the settlement. Such settlement does not discharge any of the other potentially liable persons unless its terms so provide, but it reduces the potential liability of the others by the amount of the settlement.

The Cummins group reasoned that (1) the Rumpke suit presented "claims for contribution," and (2) the claims were "matters addressed in the settlement" by virtue of section XII of the decree. Specifically, with appropriate ellipses, they argued that section XII covered actions "arising out of * * * the * * * transportation * * * of any materials * * * from * * * the Seymour site." Rumpke's claim against them alleged that materials from the named manufacturers had been transported from the Seymour site to the Uniontown site; thus, they asserted, it fell squarely within the language of section XII and the claim was barred by § 113(f)(2).

In the order on interlocutory appeal, the district court did not dwell on the question whether the Rumpke suit presented claims for contribution, evidently for two reasons. First, it noted that Rumpke's suit was in part based on § 107(a) of the Act, which provides for private cost recovery, rather than contribution. It acknowledged that Akzo Coatings, Inc. v. Aigner Corp., 30 F.3d 761 (7th Cir.1994), held that claims by one potentially responsible party (PRP) (here, Rumpke as present landowner) against another (here, the Cummins group) must normally be brought as contribution claims under § 113(f)(1), but it noted that Akzo also recognized an exception to that rule. Under the exception, a landowner may bring a § 107 action to recover for its direct injuries "if the party seeking relief is itself not responsible for having caused any of the hazardous materials to be spilled onto the property." * * * The court found that it was factually uncertain whether Rumpke was entitled to invoke the Akzo exception, and it accordingly denied summary judgment for the Cummins group on that point. Second, the court knew that Rumpke's complaint also asserted, in Count II, an express claim for contribution under § 113(f)(1). Thus, recognizing that the case at least for Count II raised a contribution claim, the court's order proceeded immediately to the question whether the Seymour settlement resolved all potential liability of the Cummins group with respect to the Uniontown site.

Construing the language of the Seymour decree as a whole, the court found that it dealt only with the Seymour site. It noted that nothing else in the decree, apart from the excerpt from section XII quoted above, contained even a hint of an attempt to resolve future disputes caused by the trucking of waste from Seymour to other locations. CERCLA and the Superfund Amendments and Reauthorization Act of 1986 (SARA) (which added § 113 to CERCLA), anticipate site-specific remedial activity, which led the district court to conclude that "the settlement authority of the United States is limited to the individual facility." * * * Finally, the court concluded that the word "transportation" in section XII, on which the Cummins group relied so heavily, could be interpreted reasonably to mean either leaching from the Seymour site or any other transportation to contiguous sites. It accordingly granted Rumpke's cross-motion for summary judgment on the issue of the applicability of the 1982 consent decree to the problems at Uniontown.

In a supplemental order written in response * * * the district court [has] described the primary controlling question of law as follows: "whether Rumpke's action against Settlers is barred pursuant to the earlier consent decree with the United States." Encompassed within that question were several others: (1) whether the pertinent environmental statutes limit the settlement authority of the United States to individual facilities; (2) whether a settlement dealing with one facility (here, Seymour) may bar liability for waste disposed by or through that facility to another one (here, Uniontown); and (3) whether the consent decree itself is ambiguous, thus making a ruling on its effect as a matter of law inappropriate. The district court recognized that if it had erred on the effect of the 1982 Seymour decree, the litigation would be terminated for the Cummins group.

III

* * *

The central question that concerned the district court was whether the 1982 settlement protects the Cummins defendants from this suit, as a result of the protection afforded by § 113(f)(2). As we noted above, § 113(f)(2) is triggered when several circumstances are present: (1) a person must have resolved liability either to the United States or a State in an administrative or judicially approved settlement, (2) it must be facing "claims for contribution" in the present suit, and (3) those claims must encompass "matters addressed in the settlement." In our view, however, before addressing the specifics of § 113(f)(2), we must decide how Rumpke's § 107(a) theory affects the case.

A. CLAIMS FOR DIRECT COST RECOVERY AND CONTRIBUTION

Rumpke's suit against the Cummins group was based on both the cost recovery theory of § 107(a) and the contribution theory of § 113(f)(1). The district court, as noted above, did not find it necessary to decide definitively whether the § 107(a) theory was sustainable, because it believed that issues of fact needed to be resolved regarding the question whether Rumpke was the kind of innocent landowner entitled to bring a § 107(a) cost recovery action under our Akzo opinion. It did not discuss the differences between § 113(f)(1) and § 107(a) in the order we are reviewing. We believe, nonetheless, that we should reach the question whether this suit may proceed under § 107(a), or under § 113(f)(1), or both. If § 107(a) is unavailable as a matter of law to Rumpke, we have only the § 113(f)(1) arguments to consider, which in turn requires us to interpret the Seymour consent decree. On the other hand, if Rumpke is entitled to proceed under § 107(a), the contribution bar of § 113(f)(2) may not apply at all; if it does not, then the dispute about the scope of the Seymour decree might be beside the point. Either way, it appears to us that the proper basis for Rumpke's action is a question fairly comprehended within the order under review.

1. *Rumpke's § 107(a) claim.* Rumpke pointed out in both its brief and at oral argument that it is not subject to any administrative cleanup order from the Indiana Department of Environmental Management (IDEM), the federal Environmental Protection Agency (EPA), or any other public authority. Thus, Rumpke is not a party that is now or ever has been subject to a civil action under CERCLA § 106, 42 U.S.C. § 9606 (which authorizes the President to bring an action to require responsible parties to clean up sites threatening the environment). It is also undisputed that no party has ever brought a cost recovery action against Rumpke under § 107. Instead, Rumpke has stated that it "intends to act, consistent with the National Contingency Plan, to assure that the VOCs it has discovered outside of the waste disposal area of the Uniontown Landfill, but within the property boundaries of the Landfill, do not become a threat to health or the environment." Furthermore, like the district court, on this review from a grant of summary judgment, we assume that Rumpke did nothing to contribute to the presence of the hazardous substances. Its status as a PRP for CERCLA purposes is based solely on its ownership of the Uniontown site—ownership, we

assume at this stage, it acquired without knowledge of the presence of environmental hazards and after all the deposits had been made.

The question is whether our Akzo exception applies to Rumpke: may a landowner PRP bring a direct liability suit for cost recovery under § 107(a) against other PRPs (in this case "arrangers"), if it contributed nothing to the hazardous conditions at the site, or is the Akzo exception available only to a narrower group of parties, such as the landowner who discovers someone surreptitiously dumping wastes on its land? In this connection, it is useful to review our decision in Akzo in somewhat more detail. In that case, Akzo sued Aigner Corporation and a number of other companies seeking contribution for initial cleanup work it had performed at the Fisher–Calo site and the costs it had incurred in studying the long term cleanup of the site with other PRPs. Akzo itself had sent hazardous wastes to the site. 30 F.3d at 764. It argued nevertheless that it was entitled to bring a direct cost recovery action under § 107(a), because the language of § 107(a) broadly permits any "person" to seek recovery of appropriate cleanup costs. Id. at 764. We rejected that argument, noting that:

> * * * Akzo has experienced no injury of the kind that would typically give rise to a direct claim under section 107(a)—it is not, for example, a landowner forced to clean up hazardous materials that a third party spilled onto its property or that migrated there from adjacent lands. Instead, Akzo itself is a party liable in some measure for the contamination at the Fisher–Calo site, and the gist of Akzo's claim is that the costs it has incurred should be apportioned equitably amongst itself and the others responsible. * * * That is a quintessential claim for contribution.

Id. Both the majority and the dissenting judges agreed, therefore, that Akzo's claim was governed solely by the contribution action § 113(f). In other words, when two parties who both injured the property have a dispute about who pays how much—a derivative liability, apportionment dispute—the statute directs them to § 113(f) and only to § 113(f).

Decisions in this area have not been notable for their clarity. The other courts of appeals that have considered the problem have agreed with our conclusion that claims properly characterized as those for contribution may normally be brought only under § 113(f). [See, e.g., Redwing Carriers, Inc. v. Saraland Apartments, 94 F.3d 1489, 1496 (11th Cir.1996); United States v. Colorado & Eastern R.R. Co., 50 F.3d 1530, 1534–36 (10th Cir.1995); United Technologies Corp. v. Browning–Ferris Industries, 33 F.3d 96, 101–03 (1st Cir.1994), cert. denied, 513 U.S. 1183, 115 S.Ct. 1176, 130 L.Ed.2d 1128 (1995); Amoco Oil Co. v. Borden, Inc., 889 F.2d 664, 672 (5th Cir.1989).] These cases, like Akzo, all involved PRPs who themselves contributed to part of the problem. Also like Akzo, at least some of these courts have acknowledged that a class of cases might remain in which a PRP might sue under § 107(a). See Redwing Carriers, 94 F.3d at 1496; United Technologies, 33 F.3d at 99 n. 8.

As our Akzo decision implied, we see nothing in the language of § 107(a) that would make it unavailable to a party suing to recover for direct injury to its own land, under circumstances where it is not trying to apportion costs (i.e., where it is seeking to recover on a direct liability theory, rather than trying to divide up its own liability for someone else's injuries among other potentially responsible parties). [It is true that liability under § 107(a) is joint and several, and § 113(f) exists for the express purpose of allocating fault among PRPs. See Town of Munster, Ind. v. Sherwin–Williams, 27 F.3d 1268, 1272 n. 2 (7th Cir. 1994); Environmental Transp. Systems, Inc. v. ENSCO, Inc., 969 F.2d 503, 508 (7th Cir.1992). Nevertheless, one of two outcomes would follow from a landowner suit under § 107(a): either the facts would establish that the landowner was truly blameless, in which case the other PRPs would be entitled to bring a suit under § 113(f) within three years of the judgment to establish their liability among themselves, or the facts would show that the landowner was also partially responsible, in which case it would not be entitled to recover under its § 107(a) theory and only the § 113(f) claim would go forward. Neither one of those outcomes is inconsistent with the statutory scheme promoting allocation of liability.]

The statutes of limitations available for § 107(a) and § 113(f) actions also provide no reason for concern. * * *

The language of § 113(f) also suggests that Rumpke's § 107(a) suit is consistent with the statute as a whole. Section 113(f)(1) begins with the following sentence:

> Any person may seek contribution from any other person who is liable or potentially liable under section 9607(a) [§ 107(a)] of this title, during or following any civil action under section 9606 [§ 106] of this title or under section 9607(a) of this title.

Because neither a § 106 nor a § 107(a) proceeding has been concluded, Rumpke's action obviously does not "follow" such an action. Rumpke has brought its own § 107(a) action, in Count I of its complaint. If it turns out that Rumpke is not the innocent party it portrays itself to be, then Rumpke will not qualify for the Akzo exception. It would still be entitled to seek contribution for its expenses from the other PRPs, assuming it met the requirements of § 113(f)(1). (We acknowledge, as other courts have, that this seems to provide a disincentive for parties voluntarily to undertake cleanup operations, because a § 106 or § 107(a) action apparently must either be ongoing or already completed before § 113(f)(1) is available. This appears to be what the statute requires, however.)

If one were to read § 107(a) as implicitly denying standing to sue even to landowners like Rumpke who did not create the hazardous conditions, this would come perilously close to reading § 107(a) itself out of the statute. As one district court in New Jersey recognized, this position would "mean that Section 107(a) private party plaintiffs will be few and far between. Truly innocent private party plaintiffs would be limited to, for example, a neighbor of a contaminated site who has acted to stem threatened releases for which he is not responsible, see Akzo, 30 F.3d at 764, or a party who can claim one of the complete defenses set forth in 42 U.S.C. § 9607(b)." Stearns & Foster Bedding Co. v. Franklin Holding Corp., 947 F.Supp. 790, 801 (D.N.J.1996). Notwithstanding that observation, the New Jersey district court adopted the narrower approach to § 107(a), relying in part on a rather narrow reading of our Akzo opinion. We disagree, however, that Akzo requires such a result, or that it would be consistent with the broader purpose and structure of CERCLA. We conclude instead that landowners who allege that they did not pollute the site in any way may sue for their direct response costs under § 107(a). * * *

Rumpke, as a landowner seeking to recover for direct injury to its property inflicted by the Cummins group, was therefore entitled to sue under § 107(a). Unlike the plaintiff in Akzo, Rumpke alleges that it was not responsible for any of the waste at the Uniontown site. On the basis of the present record, we must regard it as a landowner on whose property others dumped hazardous materials, before Rumpke even owned the property. We see no distinction between this situation and a case where a landowner discovers that someone has been surreptitiously dumping hazardous materials on property it already owns, apart from the potentially more difficult question of fact about the landowner's own responsibility in the latter case.

Last, we must consider whether the contribution bar of § 113(f)(2) has any role to play in a direct cost recovery action under § 107(a). We conclude that it does not. The theory of a direct cost recovery action is that other parties must pay Rumpke for the cost of restoring the property. Contribution among the defendants could be of no possible benefit to a party entitled to recover its full direct costs, nor could the settlement carve-out feature of § 113(f)(2) be of any possible benefit to Rumpke as a Uniontown PRP. Cummins conceded at oral argument that its Seymour settlement will not and cannot reduce Rumpke's liability as a landowner of Uniontown by as much as a penny. This means that § 113(f)(2) has no role to play insofar as this is a direct liability action under § 107(a)(1).

2. Rumpke's § 113(f)(1) claim. If the facts show, contrary to Rumpke's protestations, that it was partially responsible for the mess at Uniontown, Akzo holds that it can proceed only under § 113(f)(1) in a suit for contribution. In that case, the scope of the settlement bar of § 113(f)(2) would become important. We therefore turn to the question whether the 1982 Seymour settlement addressed the Cummins defendants' liability for sites other than the Seymour site itself.

B.   MATTERS ADDRESSED IN THE SETTLEMENT

The starting point for our analysis of this question is, as we noted in Akzo, the language of the consent decree itself. We said there that "the 'matters addressed' by a consent decree must be assessed in a manner consistent with both the reasonable expectations of the signatories and the equitable apportionment of costs that Congress has envisioned." 30 F.3d at 766 (citation omitted). This does not mean that the language of the decree is subject to an ill-defined equitable trump card; the congressional intent was viewed instead as something like a canon of construction for the language of the decree. The Akzo majority was especially concerned about the potential for negotiated consent decrees to affect third-party rights, through the contribution bar of § 113(f)(2). The statute itself addresses this problem directly, by making the contribution bar applicable only for administrative and judicially approved settlements, rather than to every private settlement that might be negotiated. In keeping with this extra care, Akzo held that terms in a decree that are especially likely to affect third-party rights must be more explicit. Using this approach, the court concluded that the consent decree before it did not bar Akzo's claim, largely because "Akzo's work [stood] apart in kind, context, and time from the work envisioned in the consent decree * * * ." Id. at 767.

None of the factors found important in Akzo suggest that the 1982 Seymour decree addressed the settling parties' liability for waste from Seymour Recycling dumped at virtually any or every other spot on the globe, including the Uniontown landfill. Rumpke's Uniontown work is apart in "kind, context, and time" from the Seymour surface cleanup. The decree defined, very specifically, the parties' responsibilities for the Seymour Recycling site in Seymour, Indiana. For example, Exhibit B of the decree defined the decree's object as *"The Removal and Disposal of Drummed Hazardous Chemicals and Waste Materials Located at: Seymour Recycling Center[,] Seymour, Indiana."* Section VIII of the decree gave the United States, the State, and their authorized representatives *"access to the Seymour site at all times until such time as the Work is completed."* Section IX allowed the various governmental authorities *"access to the site for the sampling of wastes at the site * * *."* Section XII itself, on which the Cummins group has pinned its hopes, declared it to be the intention of the parties *"[t]o avoid litigation * * * in connection with the Seymour site * * *."* (emphasis added.)

Read as a whole, we do not find the decree to be ambiguous. The Cummins defendants read far too much into their ellipsis-ridden phrase "arising out of * * * the * * * transportation * * * of any materials * * * from * * * the Seymour site," when they claim that this covers all transshipments away from the site. If we are playing with ellipses, we could also say that the decree covers matters "arising out of the * * * transportation * * * of any materials * * * near the Seymour site," but even Cummins' lawyer agreed that it would be absurd to conclude that the Cummins group was protected even if any of its wastes had ever been "near" Seymour, perhaps passing on their way to Uniontown or other locales.

We agree with the district court that section XII of the consent decree makes both internal sense and fits in with the entirety of the settlement quite comfortably if the word "from" is understood to relate to more modest phenomena such as leaching and other similar leakage from the Seymour site itself. This assures us that none of the language is superfluous, as required by general contract principles. * * * The Cummins group is protected from liability for matters directly related to the Seymour site; the decree does not have the global reach they have urged here.

Because we find the decree clear on its face, it is neither necessary nor appropriate to consider the defendants' extrinsic evidence, including affidavits from the settling defendants' lawyer about what he really meant in approving the language of section XII. * * * Goluba v. School Dist. of Ripon, 45 F.3d 1035, 1038 (7th Cir.1995) (explicit terms of consent decree control unless terms are facially ambiguous). This decree settled the defendants' liability for the Seymour site, not others.

* * *

We therefore AFFIRM the district court's order denying summary judgment based on the 1982 consent decree to Cummins Engine and its co-defendants, and granting partial summary judgment on this issue to Rumpke.

Notes and Questions

1. *More Muddy Waters.* Thus, in Rumpke of Indiana, Inc. v. Cummins Engine Co., the Seventh Circuit muddied both the § 107 versus § 113 issue and the contribution protection question. The court considered "whether the contribution bar of § 113(f)(2) has any role to play in a direct cost recovery action under § 107(a)," concluding that it "does not." The court found that "contribution among the defendants could be of no possible benefit to a party entitled to recover its full direct costs, nor could the settlement carve-out feature of § 113(f)(2) be of any possible benefit to [the landowner]." "This means," the court concluded, "that § 113(f)(2) has no role to play insofar as this is a direct liability action under § 107(a)(1)." Id. at 1242.

This holding, in turn, forces reconsideration of the so-called "innocent PRP" exception to the now general rule that PRPs are limited to contribution claims, precluding claims for cost recovery under § 107(a). Obviously in circuits adopting the *Rumpke* analysis and recognizing an "innocence" exception, the incentive by a nonsettlor to sue under § 107 is enormous. The innocent PRP exception, sometimes called the *"Akzo"* exception, based on Akzo Coatings v. Aigner, 30 F.3d 761 (7th Cir.1994) (in dicta, since it held that barring "innocence" a PRP is limited to § 113(a) contribution), was reaffirmed in *Rumpke.*

In *Rumpke*, the Seventh Circuit considered whether the *Akzo* exception applies to any "landowner PRP" that "contributed nothing to the hazardous conditions at the site," or "only to a narrower group of parties, such as the landowner who discovers someone surreptitiously dumping wastes on its land?" As a threshold matter, one can maintain that it makes little sense to frame the issue in this way; there is no need for a judicially created "exception" for a "landowner who discovers someone surreptitiously dumping wastes on its land," because such a landowner should already qualify for CERCLA's third-party defense against liability.

2. *Matters Addressed in the Settlement.* As *Rumpke* makes clear the critical question in many contribution protection arguments will be interpreting the "matters" that the consent decree addressed, since the scope of the decree defines the boundaries of the protection.

One influential early decision is United States v. Union Gas Co., 743 F.Supp. 1144 (E.D.Pa.1990), where the district court, in a case involving complex facts, developed a four-point "test" for resolving the "matters addressed" question: 1) the particular hazardous substances involved in the prior settlement; 2) the location or site in question; 3) the time frame covered by the settlement; and 4) the cost of the cleanup. *Id.* at 1154. See also, Crown Cork & Seal Company, Inc. v. Dockery, 907 F.Supp. 147, 150–51 (M.D.N.C.1995) ("In determining whether a particular claim regards matters addressed in the settlement, a court should consider the particular hazardous substance at issue in the settlement, the location or site in question, the time frame covered by the settlement, and the cost of the cleanup.").

In Akzo Coatings, Inc. v. Aigner Corp., 30 F.3d 761 (7th Cir.1994), differing from the court in *Union Gas* which focused on the circumstances surrounding the drafting of a consent decree to define "matters addressed," the *Akzo* court tried first to rely on the explicit text of the settlement. In the *Akzo* decision, for example, the court acknowledged the usefulness of the list of four factors delineated in *Union Gas*, but held that the factors "should not be treated as an exhaustive list of appropriate considerations," for the relevance of each factor will vary. * * * Id. at 766. Instead, the court felt that Congress envisioned "a flexible approach to contribution issues," and set the language of the consent decree itself as the starting point for this flexible inquiry. *Id.* at 765.

Analyzing the language in Aigner's settlement, the court held that while Aigner successfully protected itself from government suit, the decree fell short of the explicit language necessary to carry that protection through against third parties.

> [T]he decree includes a covenant not to sue the settling defendant's for "covered matters," which include "any and all claims available to the United States * * * relating to the Facility, and any and all claims relating to the Facility available to the State under Indiana Code." * * * But the fact that the decree bestows comprehensive immunity from claims by the state and federal governments does not necessarily mean that Aigner enjoys the same immunity from claims brought by a Party in Akzo's position. * * * The government's agreement to seek nothing more from the parties to the decree does not signal an intent to preclude nonsettling parties from seeking contribution.

Id. at 765–66. Unable to make a clear determination based solely on the decree's plain language, the court turned to an examination of "the decree as a whole to decide whether its provisions encompass the type of activity for which Akzo seeks contribution." At this point, the endeavor focused on many of the same criteria as *Union Gas*, and the court found that "[b]ecause Akzo's work stands apart in kind, context, and time from the work envisioned by the consent decree, we conclude that it is not a 'matter addressed' by the decree." Id. at 767.

The majority opinion in *Akzo* continued:

The United States correctly observes that this should not be treated as an exhaustive list of appropriate considerations, for the relevance of each factor will vary with the facts of the case. Amicus Br. at 17 n.15. Ultimately, the "matters addressed" by a consent decree must be assessed in a manner *consistent with both the reasonable expectations of the signatories and the equitable apportionment of costs that Congress has envisioned.*

* * *

Because Akzo's work stands apart in kind, context, and time from the work envisioned by the consent decree, we conclude that it is not a "matter addressed" by the decree. Akzo as required to engage in "removal" work (42 U.S.C. § 9601(23))—that is, a short-term, limited effort to abate any immediate threat posed by the wastes present at the site. The consent decree, on the other hand, provides for the kind of long-term, "remedial" work (42 U.S.C. § 9601(24)) necessary to accomplish a complete clean-up of the site. This distinction is reflected in the two different orders implementing the work. The 1988 order unilaterally directed Akzo to undertake certain "emergency removal activities," including the extraction and disposal of leaking drums and other hazards from the Two–Line Road facility. In contrast, the 1992 consent decree embodies a negotiated settlement designed to implement a long-range remedial plan for the entire site, as outlined in the EPA's 1990 Record of Decision ("ROD"). Neither the decree nor the ROD purports to incorporate the 1988 order; on the contrary, the ROD explicitly assumes "that all drums, tanks, and containers on the Two–Line Road property requiring remedial action are being addressed" by that order. ROD Summary at 5. Indeed, by the time Aigner entered into the consent decree, Akzo's removal work had already been completed. Consequently, it comes as no surprise that this work was not addressed in the consent decree.

Akzo, 30 F.3d at 766. Judge Easterbrook, concurring in part and dissenting in part, authored a thoughtful opinion, which with the students' indulgence we quote from:

How then can it be that Akzo's claims are not "matters addressed in the settlement"? The majority answers: everything is subject to "equitable" adjustments. It plucks some language from § 113(f)(1) and uses this language as a warrant to disregard the scope of the settlement. Section 113(f)(1) gives a court leeway in fixing the amount of contribution; this task is unrelated to the scope of protection offered by the next subsection. Section 113(f)(2) serves a valuable purpose in promoting settlements. Risk that in the name of "equity" a court will disregard the actual language of the parties' bargain * * * will lead potentially responsible parties to fight harder to avoid liability (and to pay less in settlements, reserving the residue to meet contribution claims), undermining the function of § 113(f)(2).

There is a second element in the majority's argument. The consent decree and the covenant not to sue regulate only the settling parties' liability to the United States and to Indiana. *How, my colleagues ask, can language so limited extinguish claims by strangers? The answer is:*

Because § 113(f)(2) says so. "A person who has resolved its liability to the United States or a State in an administrative or judicially approved settlement shall not be liable for claims for contribution regarding matters addressed in the settlement." Nothing here about resolving liability to private parties; nothing here implying that the consent decree must contain a separate provision blotting out claims by private actors. Aigner fully resolved its liability to the United States. *By "resolv[ing]" its liability to the United States Aigner thereby obtained protection from private parties' claims for contribution.* (Easterbrook, concurring and dissenting.) (emphasis added).

Id. at 771.

Judge Easterbrook then offered, as Judge Posner often does, a hypothetical example to explain his interpretation of § 113(f)(2):

Section 113(f)(2) permits the EPA to negotiate global settlements–to promise that if certain firms perform projects A and B, they will not be liable for the costs of projects C and D, which other persons have undertaken. The EPA's ability to make such promises gives it a valuable bargaining chip. The agency may demand that polluters do more as a condition of discharging their full responsibility. Freedom from contribution may be the key to a settlement. Consider a simple illustration. Recycling Industries has two plants, East and West. Toxic substances seep from both plants. The EPA identifies two firms that sent toxic substances to Recycling Industries. PRP #1 spends $10 million to clean up the West plant. If the "matters addressed" under § 113(f)(2) are project-specific, PRP #2 would be a fool to agree. For it would spend $10 million to clean up the West plant and then be directed to pay $5 million in contribution to PRP #1 for cleaning up the East plant. Final position: PRP #1 pays $5 million, PRP #2 pays $15 million. (One cannot reply that the $5/$15 million division in this hypothetical is not "equitable" under § 113(f)(1) without abandoning the project-specific approach that the majority embraces.)

To avoid this, PRP #2 will litigate to the gills and sue PRP #1 for contribution as well. Each PRP, however, will be willing to do its share, and with less litigation, if the EPA can divide the tasks, assigning one plant to each firm and using § 113(f)(2) to preclude contribution. The majority replies that its interpretation permits this happy outcome; all the parties have to do is "negotiate a global settlement encompassing both East and West plants." But that is exactly what these parties did! Aigner and the EPA negotiated a "global settlement" covering the entire Fisher–Calo facility, and the majority says this is not enough. To drive the point home, my colleagues add that even the most explicit language is just a "factor" that does "not foreclose the fact-specific evaluation" it prefers. Woe unto the drafters, who think their agreement counts. (Easterbrook, concurring and dissenting.)

Id. at 772.

The analysis of Judge Easterbrook finds support both in the new Restatement (Third) of Torts: Apportionment § 33, and an admiralty decision of the United States Supreme Court in McDermott, Inc. v. AmClyde,

511 U.S. 202, 114 S.Ct. 1461, 128 L.Ed.2d 148 (1994), which is also referred to later, in which the Supreme Court made these observations:

> Admiralty law permits contribution–but not from defendants that have settled.
>
> > [A] right of contribution against the settling defendant is clearly inferior to [other options], because it discourages settlement and leads to unnecessary ancillary litigation. It discourages settlement, because settlement can only disadvantage the settling defendant. If a defendant makes a favorable settlement, in which it pays less than the amount a court later determines is its share of liability, the other defendant (or defendants) can sue the settling defendant for contribution. The settling defendant thereby loses the benefit of its favorable settlement. In addition, the claim for contribution burdens the courts with additional litigation. The plaintiff can mitigate the adverse effect on settlement by promising to indemnify the settling defendant against contribution, * * * This indemnity, while removing the disincentive to settlement, adds yet another potential burden on the courts, an indemnity action between the settling defendant and plaintiff.

McDermott, Inc. v. AmClyde, 511 U.S. 202, 114 S.Ct. 1461, 1467, 128 L.Ed.2d 148 (1994). The importance of this question of contribution protection and "matters addressed" is exemplified by the emergence of a substantial body of law within a few short years. See, e.g., United States v. Colorado & Eastern Railroad Co., 50 F.3d 1530 (10th Cir.1995); United States v. Alexander, 771 F.Supp. 830, 833 (S.D.Tex.1991) (nonsettlors barred from recovering from settling parties "for *any* type of contribution") vacated, 981 F.2d 250 (5th Cir.1993); see also United States v. Cannons Engineering Corp., 899 F.2d 79 (1st Cir.1990) ("Congress specifically provided that contribution actions could not be maintained against settlors."); United States v. SCA Services of Indiana, Inc., 827 F.Supp. 526, 533 (N.D.Ind.1993) ("nonsettlors are barred from making claims for contribution against the settlors").

Model Settlement Documents. The EPA has published a series of model consent decrees and administrative orders to reduce the time needed to negotiate and draft individual consent decrees, thereby reducing transaction costs and providing greater consistency and predictability. See EPA's Revised Model CERCLA RD/RA Consent Decree, 60 Fed. Reg. 38,817 (1995); The Model CERCLA Section 107 Consent Decree for Recovery of Past Response Costs, 60 Fed. Reg. 62,446 (1995). The Model CERCLA Section 122(h)(1) Agreement for Recovery of Past Response Costs, 60 Fed. Reg. 62,446 (1995), assists the EPA and the Justice Department when negotiating § 122(h) administrative agreements for recovery of past response costs. These last two models are not intended to be used to resolve claims for future work or payment of future response costs. See also Revised Model De Minimis Contributor Consent Decree and Administrative Order on Consent, 60 Fed. Reg. 62,849 (1995).

See, also, Transtech Industries, Inc. v. A & Z Septic Clean, 798 F.Supp. 1079 (D.N.J.1992), in which 221 contribution defendants had entered into a consent decree with the United States paying $4.9 million which covered the government's claims "for Past Response Costs and Past Response Actions and for any administrative costs and civil penalties which may have accrued prior to April 30, 1987 * * * *'' The court held that the plaintiff, who had paid $13 million to clean up the site, which included costs not accrued at the date in the decree, could maintain the contribution action under § 113(f) against the settling parties.

While nonsettlors lose their right to seek contribution, settling PRPs retain their contribution rights and may sue nonsettlors to distribute some of the damages they paid.

b. *Judicial Review of Settlements*

1. *Generally.* As we have already seen, settlements are not always approved by the courts precisely because they are found to unfairly allocate the costs of cleanups. For example, in New York v. SCA Services, 1993 WL 59407 (S.D.N.Y.), the court considered the government's request to enter a consent judgment settling CERCLA claims with third-party waste generators. The site also involved a transporter that had borne the bulk of the cleanup costs, and the court stressed that private parties would not accept such responsibility if they confronted the risk of such an unfair settlement. In reviewing the standards for approval of the consent judgment, the court reviewed the fairness of its terms, including fairness to nonsettling parties. The court found the settlement terms unfair, noting that the "settling third-party defendants comprise 20 out of the 24 known generators of hazardous waste materials disposed at the site, and over 90% of the hazardous waste materials."

While SCA bears a "major responsibility" for the site problems, the court continued, "it is also significant that the hazardous materials generated and disposed of by the settling third-party defendants would have been disposed of at some site and required response costs in that event." The consent judgment "does not come close to reflecting this division of responsibility for pollution at the site." The generators of more than 90% of the waste would be excused for less than one-third of the past costs of response, leaving the few nonsettling third-party defendants the remaining two thirds. Although SCA may seek contribution from the settling defendants for certain future RI/FS costs, this fact did not reduce the "gross inequity of the proposed settlement's distribution of past costs and [natural resource damage] liability."

Having now seen the critical importance of the provisions of a consent decree on the rights of *third parties* who are not signatories thereto, it should come as no surprise that nonsettlors may seek to intervene in or object to the terms of a decree before it is judicially approved. As you would expect here too a rather sizable body of law has emerged in the past few years, again given the incredibly high financial exposures and transaction costs, and the private party CERCLA litigation explosion.

2. *Right to Intervene to Challenge Proposed Settlement.* An example or two may illustrate the rationale which courts have proffered for rejecting

or approving a proposed decree between the EPA or a state and a settling PRP. But first is the issue of whether nonsettlors have standing to intervene, and second, the general review standards courts apply to determine if a particular decree or settlement should receive judicial imprimatur.

First, in United States v. Union Elec. Co., 64 F.3d 1152 (8th Cir.1995), the Eighth Circuit Court of Appeals held that a nonsettling PRP under CERCLA may intervene to oppose a consent decree the federal government has reached with settling PRPs. A group of nonsettling PRPs sought to intervene in a consent decree to preserve possible contribution claims against settling defendants. The trial court denied the intervention, finding that because they had not settled, the PRPs' interest was too speculative to warrant intervention as a matter of right. Reversing, the Eighth Circuit Court of Appeals said in order to intervene, a party must have a recognized interest in the litigation. The party's interest must be potentially impaired by the disposition and not adequately protected by the existing parties. The court held the possibility of the nonsettling parties' contribution rights being affected under the settlement created a "direct and immediate interest" in the litigation. Because the settling defendants did not share the same interest, they could not adequately represent the intervener. Thus, the court concluded, the nonsettling parties have a legally protectable interest under CERCLA sufficient to warrant intervention.

3. *Challenging the Substantive Fairness: A Few More Examples.* As to the review process, both procedural and substantive fairness are relevant to the review. The decisions in United States v. Cannons Engineering Corp., 899 F.2d 79 (1st Cir.1990) and United States v. Charles George Trucking, Inc., 34 F.3d 1081 (1st Cir.1994), confirm that courts will only overturn the district courts' action approving the consent decree where there had been "manifest abuse of discretion," i.e., "the lower court made a serious error of law or suffered a meaningful lapse of judgment." The district court, in turn, must let a settlement agreement stand if it finds that it is "reasonable, fair, and consistent with the purposes that CERCLA is intended to serve."

In United States v. DiBiase, 45 F.3d 541, 544 (1st Cir.1995), on appeal, DiBiase did not challenge his liability, but rather objected to the substantive fairness of the court's allocation of the removal costs. The court quoted from its description of the nature of "substantive fairness" in *Cannons*:

> Substantive fairness introduces into the equation concepts of corrective justice and accountability: a party should bear the cost of the harm for which it is legally responsible. The logic behind these concepts dictates that settlement terms must be based upon, and roughly correlated with, some acceptable measure of comparative fault, apportioning liability among settling parties according to rational (if necessarily imprecise) estimates of how much harm each PRP has done. * * *

Whatever formula or scheme EPA advances for measuring comparative fault and allocating liability should be upheld so long as the agency supplies a plausible explanation for it, welding some reasonable linkage between the factors it includes in its formula or scheme and the proportionate shares of settling PRPs.

"Viewing the SESD decree in this deferential perspective, we find EPA's rationale for the proposed allocation to be plausible, and also find the district court's endorsement of that rationale to be well within the parameters of fundamental fairness," the court concluded.

In *DiBiase*, the First Circuit upheld a CERCLA settlement allocating 85% of the costs of two emergency removal actions to a generator/transporter whose wastes contaminated a site and the remaining 15% to the landowner. Although the landowner owned the site only during one shipment of waste for disposal at "sludge pits" on the property–a shipment of which he was unaware until after the fact–the landowner had failed to qualify as an innocent landowner because he had taken no steps to prevent others from illegally dumping waste on his property and he had not maintained the site or taken measures to prevent releases of contamination there. The court found that the appellant landowner could not meet the "heavy burden" of convincing the appeals court that the district court had committed a "manifest abuse of discretion" in finding the proposed settlement to be "reasonable, fair, and consistent with the purposes that CERCLA is intended to serve."

In evaluating how important a particular court will view the specific facts surrounding a consent decree, settlors should be aware of certain themes that appear to apply regardless of what method a court uses to define "matters addressed." First, no definition of "matters addressed" will provide certainty in contribution protection where the settlement amount bears no relation to the settlor's proportion of total liability. In Kelley v. Wagner, 930 F.Supp. 293 (E.D.Mich.1996), Akzo Coatings, Inc. challenged a consent decree offered for entry between General Electric (GE) and the State of Michigan for the cleanup of a landfill site. The document defined "matters addressed" to include "all response costs incurred or to be incurred by the State, or any other party at or in connection with the Facility, including, but not limited to, all removal and remedial costs." To receive this broad protection, GE would pay the state $35,000, which equaled the share of the State's total response costs equivalent to GE's fraction of the site's waste.

Akzo argued that while this amount may have seemed fair from the perspective of State response costs, the settlement purported to grant GE freedom from liability for *all* response costs (including those of private parties and other PRPs), for which the State estimated GE's share approached $646,000. The court agreed and refused to approve the consent decree.

The figure for settlement falls far short of [GE's estimated responsibility]. I do not judge whether this is the "best" settlement possible, but the State and GE have failed to explain how they rationally arrived at a figure that does not appear to be "in the ballpark" of the State's own estimate of GE's liability.

Id. at 299. What risks do you see if you are counsel for Akzo and decide *not* to challenge the proposed decree? If you do challenge it, but unsuccessfully?

This case highlights a strategic issue faced by nonsettling PRPs. Such parties must determine whether to challenge the entry of the consent decree, seeking to have the scope of EPA's authority to preclude private parties from pursuing contribution claims interpreted narrowly. Such a challenge can be successful. If a challenge is mounted and the court rejects the interpretation offered by the nonsettlors, however, the decision may be considered *res judicata*. Conversely, if the nonsettlors do not challenge the entry of the decree, the settling party can claim that challenges to the scope of the contribution protection clause are waived.

4. *A Constitutional Challenge to a Consent Order.* Another interesting ruling is set forth in Waste Management of Pennsylvania v. York, 910 F.Supp. 1035 (M.D.Pa.1995), which involved a CERCLA administrative order by consent (AOC) between the EPA and the city of York, Pa., at the Old City of York Landfill Site. The city, joined by the EPA as an intervenor, argued that the AOC, combined with the superfund law's contribution protection provision,[3] insulated the city from response costs claims by Waste Management. Waste Management countered that the AOC did not, and could not, "address" its costs.

The court agreed with Waste Management. First, it held that CERCLA's statutory language restricts the "matters" that an AOC could "address" to "costs incurred by the United States Government". Nongovernment costs could not possibly be "matters addressed" in an administrative settlement. Second, the court noted that administrative settlements are not subject to judicial review for reasonableness and fairness. The court pointed out that judicial review "affords a PRP the opportunity to adjudicate the fairness of contribution protection in the context of a complete site remediation plan." *Id.* at 1040. Without judicial approval, the court held that it would be unfair to authorize an administrative order to prevent a private party claim.

Finally, the court focused on the fundamental unfairness of allowing a settlement of the government's costs to interfere with a private party claim: Clearly, Congress did not intend agreements between the govern-

---

3. Section 122(h) of CERCLA, 42 U.S.C. 9622(h), authorizes the EPA, in certain circumstances, to enter into administrative settlements for the United States' response costs. Section 122(h)(4), 42 U.S.C. 9622(h)(4), parallels the contribution language of § 113(f). It states that "[a] person who has resolved its liability to the United States under this subsection shall not be liable for claims for contribution regarding matters addressed in this settlement."

Section 122(h)(1). The court distinguished administrative settlements under § 122(h) from other settlements, such as de minimis settlements under § 122(g) and consent decrees to perform cleanups under § 122(d). Unlike an administrative settlement under § 122(h), the statutory language authorizing settlements under §§ 122(d) and 122(g) does not restrict either of these types of decrees to "costs incurred by the United States Government."

ment and private parties to foreclose all other private party claims against the settling parties. Such a result would be fundamentally unfair to nonsettling parties and would discourage such parties to engage in cleanup operations, contrary to one of CERCLA's primary goals.

The court added that *to foreclose all other private party claims against nonsettling parties "would implicate Fifth Amendment issues," in that "[t]he right to sue a party for contribution or to recover costs incurred may be viewed as a property right. Depriving a party of that right raises a question of whether there has been a taking of property without just compensation."* Id. at 1043 (emphasis added). The court found the constitutional concern to be greatest in circumstances in which a private party has incurred substantial costs that the AOC is threatening to extinguish. For these reasons, it allowed Waste Management to go forward with its response cost claim.

Of course, not all proposed settlements are disapproved; the vast majority pass whatever judicial review the district or appeals court gives to them. Thus, in Foamseal, Inc. v. Dow Chemical Co., 991 F.Supp. 883 (E.D.Mich.1998), the court approved a private settlement resolving cost recovery allocation, finding that the agreements roughly approximated the settlor's liability, taking into account factors including the reduction in transaction costs that will be realized from approval of the voluntary settlements.

In New York v. City of Johnstown, 1998 WL 167311 (N.D.N.Y.), the court approved a settlement under CERCLA despite objections by primary defendants that the EPA had offered unfair terms to third-party defendants that were not offered to first-party defendants. The court concluded that the settlement was consistent with CERCLA's policy, favoring settlement over protracted litigation, and was reasonable and fair in the context of the action.

In United States v. BASF Corp., 990 F.Supp. 907 (E.D.Mich.1998), aff'd 52 F.3d 326 (6th Cir.1995), the Sixth Circuit approved a past-costs settlement concerning the Metamora Landfill in Michigan over the objections of some nonsettling defendants that they would bear a disproportionate share of cleanup costs. Applying criteria developed in United States v. Cannons Engineering Corp., 899 F.2d 79 (1st Cir.1990), and other cases, the court found that the settlement was "fair, reasonable, and faithful to CERCLA's purposes." *Id.* at 94.

In United States v. Kramer, 19 F.Supp. 2d 273 (D.N.J.1998), the district court held that entry of a negotiated consent decree should be approved where the decree is fair and reasonable. Nonsettling defendants' objections that the settlement process was substantially flawed in allocating liability did not warrant rejection of the consent decree. The court emphasized that a presumption of validity will be applied where a settlement is the product of informed, arms-length bargaining by the EPA with defendants. This "presumption of validity" standard clarifies that whoever wishes to challenge a proposed decree or settlement bears a heavy burden of proof.

In United States v. Glens Falls Newspapers, Inc., 160 F.3d 853 (2d Cir.1998), the Second Circuit held that a newspaper and reporter were not entitled to access to CERCLA settlement negotiation information that was subject to a protective order and thus were not entitled to intervene in CERCLA litigation for purposes of vacating the protective order. The court explained that settlement discussions and documents did not carry a presumption of public access and public disclosure could impede the court's role in facilitating settlement of the case.

10.   DIVERSITY OF VIEWS ON NONSETTLOR LIABILITY

a.   *Framing the Issue*

As a result of contribution's equitable genesis, each joint tortfeasor is responsible only for its "equitable share" of the common liability. However, there are different methods to determine this equitable share. The simplest approach, the per capita approach, establishes each defendant's share by dividing the total amount paid to the plaintiff by the number of the defendants. The second common method, the proportionate or comparative fault approach, apportions contribution liability more equitably by holding each defendant responsible for an amount proportionate to each defendant's comparative fault. Notably, in determining these equitable shares of liability, the common liability is generally divided among only those parties involved in the action. The "orphan shares" of liability attributable to parties that are unknown or insolvent are equitably divided among the parties to the action.

The two prevalent approaches to determining the effect of a settlement or release on the contribution claims of nonsettling parties are exemplified by the Uniform Contribution Among Tortfeasors Act (UCATA) and the Uniform Comparative Fault Act (UCFA). Both acts abrogate the common law rule that the release of one tortfeasor releases all, both provide that a settlement and release of one joint tortfeasor will not discharge the liability of the other tortfeasor unless the agreement so provides. Moreover, under both acts, the settling tortfeasor is relieved of contribution liability to the nonsettling tortfeasors. However, the acts differ significantly in determining the effect the settlement has upon the plaintiff's claim against the nonsettling tortfeasors. The UCATA, which represents the *pro tanto* approach, credits the nonsettling parties with the dollar amount paid by the settling party. Alternatively, the UCFA, which represents the proportionate share rule, credits nonsettlors with the settlors' *equitable* share of the costs, regardless of the actual settlement amount.

Let's return again to the language of § 113(f)(2), which reads:

A person who has resolved its liability to the United States or a State in an administrative of judicially approved settlement shall not be liable for claims for contribution regarding matters addressed in the settlement. Such settlement does not discharge any of the other potentially liable persons unless its terms so provide, but it reduces the potential liability of the others by the amount of the settlement. 42 U.S.C. § 9613(f)(2) (West 1999).[4]

With the massive numbers of settlements among parties occurring at greater frequency, the issues referred to in § 113(f)(2) have become of paramount importance.

For an excellent analysis of these issues, see J. Pesnell, The Contribution Bar in CERCLA Settlements and Its Effect on the Liability of Nonsettlors, 58 St. Louis. L. Rev. 167 (1997).

b. The Uniform Contribution Among Tortfeasors Act and § 113(f)(2): Pro Tanto or Dollar Reduction Method

Courts examining the issue of settlements in the CERCLA context have reviewed the traditional debate associated with the two methods, the *pro tanto* and proportionate share (or relative fault) approaches, in determining the affect of a settlement on the nonsettling parties.

Under the UCATA approach, a settlement made in good faith between the claimant and the settling tortfeasor reduces the liability of the other tortfeasors to the claimant on a *pro tanto* or dollar-for-dollar basis—i.e., "to the extent of any amount stipulated by the release or the covenant, or in the amount of the consideration paid for it, whichever is the greater."[5] Consequently, the UCATA or *pro tanto* approach places the risk that the claimant may settle with a tortfeasor for less than that tortfeasor's pro rata share of the liability on the nonsettling tortfeasors. It the claimant and the settling tortfeasor agree in good faith to settle for an amount that is less than the settling tortfeasor's pro rata share of the liability, the other tortfeasors will be stuck with the tab for the remainder of the settling tortfeasor's share of the liability. Under the UCATA approach, they remain jointly and severally liable to the claim-

---

4. See 42 U.S.C. § 9613(f)(2) (West 1999). Language almost identical to 42 U.S.C. § 9613(f)(2) is also found in 42 U.S.C. § 9622, the section of CERCLA, as amended by SARA, that deals with settlements between the United States and PRPs. See *id.* § 9622(h)(4) ("A person who has resolved its liability to the United States under this subsection shall not be liable for claims for contribution regarding matters addressed in the settlement. Such settlement shall not discharge any of the other potentially liable persons unless its terms so provide, but it reduces the potential liability of the others by the amount of the settlement.").

In addition, 42 U.S.C. § 9622(g), which deals with de minimis settlements, contains language that is almost identical to that of 42 U.S.C. § 9622(h)(4), making it clear that the same scheme that applies to major party settlements with the United States under 42 U.S.C. § 9622(h) also applies to de min-

imis settlements under 42 U.S.C. § 9622(g). See *id.* § 9622(g)(5). The only difference between 42 U.S.C. § 9622(h)(4) and 42 U.S.C. § 9622(g)(5) is that 42 U.S.C. § 9622(h)(4) refers to "*persons*" who have resolved their liability to the United States, while 42 U.S.C. § 9622(g)(5) refers to "*parties*" who have resolved their liability to the United States. This distinction appears to be insignificant.

5. UCATA § 4, 12 U.L.A. 264 (1996) ("When a release or a covenant not to sue or not to enforce judgment is given in good faith to one of two or more persons liable in tort for the same injury or the same wrongful death: (a) It does not discharge any of the other tortfeasors from liability for the injury or wrongful death unless its terms so provide; but it reduces the claim against the others to the extent of any amount stipulated by the release or the covenant, or in the amount of the consideration paid for it, whichever is greater * * * .").

ant for the difference between the full amount of the common liability and the amount of the settlement. In personal injury litigation, plaintiffs' counsel prefer the *pro tanto* approach because it assures that so long as one solvent (insured) non-settlor is accountable he or she (the plaintiff) will recover 100% of her damage.

What happens if the claimant and settling tortfeasor agree to settle for an amount that turns out to be *greater* than the settlor's pro-rata or equitable share of the response costs? Who benefits in that circumstance? The claimant (i.e., the EPA) or the nonsettlors?

It is difficult at this juncture to declare that the *pro tanto* approach has carried the day in this important debate, but it has clearly garnered considerable support. For example, in United States v. Cannons Engineering Corp., 899 F.2d 79 (1st Cir.1990), the court asserts that the *pro tanto* reduction rule contained in § 113(f)(2) precludes any conclusion that the liability of nonsettling PRPs can be reduced by any other amounts, such as the total of the settling PRPs' equitable shares of the response costs at a site. See *Cannons Eng'g*, 899 F.2d at 92.

In addition, most of those courts have recognized that their interpretation of § 113(f)(2) might compel the nonsettlors to "absorb any shortfall" between the settlors' equitable shares of the response costs and the amounts paid by the settlors under the settlement. See, e.g., *Cannons Eng'g*, 899 F.2d at 91 ("The statute immunizes settling parties from liability for contribution and provides that only the amount of the settlement–not the pro rata share attributable to the settling party–shall be subtracted from the liability of the nonsettlors. This can prove to be a substantial benefit to settling PRPs–and a corresponding detriment to their more recalcitrant counterparts."); Kelley v. Thomas Solvent, 790 F.Supp. 731, 736 (W.D.Mich.1991) ("[T]he *amici*'s argument that the consent decree should contain a provision that would reduce their liability by the amount of the settlor's equitable shares, not by the amount of the settlement judgment is without statutory support and inconsistent with [C]ongress' intent to promote early settlement. According to the express terms of the statute, a settlement 'reduces the potential liability of the others by the amount of the *settlement.*' "); United States v. Rohm & Haas, 721 F.Supp. 666, 675 (D.N.J.1989); In re Acushnet River, 712 F.Supp. 1019, 1026–27 (D.Mass.1989) ("[I]f the settlor pays less than its proportionate share of liability, the nonsettlors, being jointly and severally liable, must make good the difference. In this respect, the words of the statute are clear: the potential liability of the others is reduced 'by the amount of the settlement,' not by the settlor's proportionate share of any damages ultimately determined to have been caused."); New York v. Exxon Corp., 697 F.Supp. 677, 681 n. 5, 683 (S.D.N.Y.1988).

The "Sticky Wicket". In fact, some of those courts have asserted, based upon the language of § 113(f)(2) alone, that Congress explicitly intended to create a disproportionate liability scheme that would allow the government and the PRPs settling with it to unilaterally shift much of the settlor's equitable shares of the response costs at a site to the nonsettlors. See, e.g., *Cannons Eng'g*, 899 F.2d at 91–92 ("Congress proposed that *all who choose not to settle confront the same sticky wicket of which appellants complain.*") (emphasis added); In re Acushnet River, 712 F.Supp. at 1026–27.

Another Court of Appeals in United States v. Colorado & Eastern Railroad Co., 50 F.3d 1530 (10th Cir.1995) weighed in on the side of the *pro tanto* option, stating that the plain language of CERCLA § 113(f)(2) provides that a settlement reduces the potential liability of nonsettlors by the amount of the settlement. The court found that the language of § 113(f)(2) "mandates the application" of the Uniform Contribution Among Joint Tortfeasors Act's *pro tanto* rule—i.e., that a nonsettlor is entitled to a credit of the actual dollar settlement regardless of the fault of the parties—rather than the "proportionate credit rule" set forth in the Uniform Comparative Fault Act, i.e, that contribution claims against nonsettlors are reduced by the percentage of the settling party's fault. Id., at 1535.

So there is no ambiguity on the point of disproportionate liability, see, United States v. GenCorp, Inc., 935 F.Supp. 928 (N.D.Ohio 1996), where the court, quoting in part from *Cannons Engineering* rejected an objection interposed by a nonsettlor to a proposed decree. The court stated that the objector had not shown that the result of its paying more than its fair share was in conflict "with Congress' judgment that nonsettlors bear the risk of increased liability in a government enforcement action." The court quoted United States v. Cannons Engineering Corp., 899 F.2d 79, 91–92 (1st Cir.1990) as follows:

> Congress explicitly created a statutory framework that left nonsettlors at risk of bearing a disproportionate amount of liability * * * Disproportionate liability, a technique which promotes early settlements and deters litigation for litigation's sake, is an integral part of the statutory plan * * * Congress purposed that all who choose not to settle confront the *same sticky wicket of which appellant complains.* (emphasis added).

Accord, United Technologies Corp. v. Browning–Ferris Industries, 33 F.3d 96, 103 (1st Cir.1994). (Because only the amount of the settlement, not the pro rata share attributable to the settling party, is subtracted from the aggregate liability of the nonsettling parties, see id., § 9613(f)(2) envisions that nonsettling parties may bear disproportionate liability. This paradigm is not a scrivener's accident. It "was designed to encourage settlement and provide PRPs a measure of finality in return for their willingness to settle.")

Finally, in two more district court opinions, in light of the "congressional purpose of minimizing litigation and encouraging settlement of CERCLA cases," the court in Atlantic Richfield Co. v. American Airlines, Inc., 836 F.Supp. 763 (N.D.Okla.1993), adopted the *pro tanto* approach. Id. at 770. The *Atlantic Richfield* court concluded that in the private cost recovery action "application of the *pro tanto* rule seems particularly appropriate, as opposed to unfair. The defendants who seek to apply the proportionate rule are obviously motivated by the desire to minimize their liability at the expense of the remediating plaintiff, and, perhaps, (having a keen appreciation of the time-value of money) to delay and unduly complicate the trial proceedings." Id. at 771. The *Atlantic Richfield* court concluded that imposing disproportionate liability on recalcitrant defendants in a private cost recovery action furthered the congressional intent behind CERCLA § 107(a). The *Atlantic Richfield* court further noted that, "[s]ince non-settling parties remain jointly and severally liable, they pay the balance owed to plaintiff regardless of whether any settling defendant has paid more or less than its proportionate share. The practical effect in a case where the total cost of the remediation has not been finally fixed is to increase the risk the longer a defendant stays in the suit, creating a strong incentive for earlier and/or universal settlement." Id.

Similarly, in discussing the policy of encouraging settlement, the district court held in Arizona v. Motorola, Inc., 139 F.R.D. 141, 145 (D.Ariz.1991):

> CERCLA was designed "to protect and preserve public health and the environment." That Congressional purpose is better served through settlements which provide funds to enhance environmental protection, rather than the expenditure of limited resources on protracted litigation. Without question, Congress passed the SARA amendments [which include contribution provisions] to encourage settlements for this very reason. * * * *[U]nder CERCLA, even "if the settlor pays less than its proportionate share of liability, the non-settlors, being jointly and severally liable, must make good the difference." * * * This risk of disproportionate liability encourages parties to resolve their liability early, lest they be found responsible for amounts not paid by settling defendants.*

The concept that CERCLA anticipates disproportionate allocation of contribution liability as a means of encouraging settlements adds a new dimension to the traditional debate between the *pro tanto* and proportionate share approaches.

See also, United States v. Rohm & Haas Co., 721 F.Supp. 666 (D.N.J.1989), the district court, in approving a partial settlement, concluded that Congress had purposefully incorporated UCATA § 4 into CERCLA, mandating that courts bar nonsettlors' claims for contribution and credit nonsettlors "with the amount of the settlement and nothing more," notwithstanding that nonsettlors would be stuck bearing more than their equitable share of the costs. In *Rohm & Haas*, the court also rejected application of the UCFA method of crediting nonsettlors a proportionate reduction because it found that Congress had expressly chosen language more closely tracking the UCATA. Moreover, it believed that the UCFA method would disserve CERCLA's goals of minimizing litigation and promoting voluntary settlements because it would compel the government to litigate with nonsettlors the issue of whether the settlors had paid their proportionate share. Do you understand why this would discourage settlements? What might be the consequence on the recovery of all cleanup costs *if a court later held that settling PRPs had paid less than their equitable shares*? Is the nonsettlor any worse off than it would be if the government had sued it initially and sought complete cleanup costs under the rule of joint and several liability? See Central Illinois Public Service Co. v. Industrial Oil Tank & Line Cleaning Service, 730 F.Supp. 1498 (W.D.Mo.1990) (suggesting that it is not); Allied Corp. v. Frola, 730 F.Supp. 626, 638 (D.N.J.1990) ("Since the nonsettlors remain jointly and severally liable, they must make good the balance regardless of whether the settlor pays less than its proportionate share of liability."). *Cannons Engineering* and the foregoing authorities hold what now ostensibly represents the majority view that CERCLA § 113(f)(2) reduces nonsettlors' liability by the dollar amount of the settlement.

c. Uniform Comparative Fault Act and § 113(f): Proportionate Reduction

1. *Generally.* Under the UCFA approach, a settlement between the government and PRPs reduces the potential liability of the nonsettlors by the settlors' equitable shares of the response costs at a site, whatever those equitable shares may be. See UCFA § 6, 12 U.L.A. 147 (1996). Section 113(f)(2) declares that settlements between the government and PRPs "reduce the potential liability of the others by the amount of the settlement." The language of that provision of § 113(f)(2) is not necessarily inconsistent with the UCFA approach, if the purpose of that provision is to ensure that the government does not receive a "windfall" when the amount of a settlement exceeds the settlors' equitable shares of the response costs at a site. If no provision of CERCLA limited the operation of the UCFA approach in situations where the amount of a settlement exceeds the settlors' equitable shares of the response costs at a site, the government could recover more than the total costs of responding to the releases of hazardous substances at a site. It could do so by settling with some of the PRPs for amounts which exceed their equitable shares of the response costs, and proceeding against the remaining PRPs for the full amounts of their equitable shares of the response costs. The UCFA approach would only reduce the liability of the nonsettlors by the settlors' equitable shares of the response costs at the site, even though the settlors had paid more than the sum of their equitable shares of the response costs in order to settle the claims against them. Section 113(f)(2) may have been intended to ensure that CERCLA operated in the manner intended—i.e., as a cost recovery statute–by preventing windfalls or double recoveries under the UCFA approach when the amount which the government receives in a settlement exceeds the sum of the settlors' equitable shares of the response costs at a site. It does so by ensuring that a settlement between the government and PRPs reduces the liability of the nonsettling PRPs, at a

minimum, by the amount of the settlement. See, Pesnell, 58 La. L. Rev. 167, 181.

A few courts have found these arguments persuasive.

Some courts have declined to adopt the UCATA-based *pro tanto* analysis and instead give the nonsettlors the benefit of a proportionate share reduction in their potential liability. Illustrating that approach is Allied Corp. v. ACME Solvent Reclaiming, Inc., 771 F.Supp. 219 (N.D.Ill. 1990), where the court ruled that when some defendants in a private CERCLA cost-recovery action settle their liability to the plaintiffs, they are entitled to protection from contribution claims of any other defendants, and that the liability of the nonsettling defendants is reduced by the equitable share of liability attributable to the settling defendants, as later determined at the trial of the nonsettlors, rather than by the dollar amount of the settlement. In so ruling, the court adopted the approach of the UCFA rather than that of the UCATA.

Although CERCLA § 113(f)(2) is modeled on the UCATA, the court said that this applied only to settlements with the federal or state government and *not to private party actions*. The court stressed that CERCLA's contribution protection provision "expressly applies to settlements with the federal or state government, and the statute *is silent as to its applicability to private party settlements*." (emphasis added.) It said that a uniform federal rule of contribution should be developed independently of state contribution and settlement law. The court chose to follow those cases that viewed the UCFA, rather than the UCATA, as being more consistent with CERCLA. Moreover, it observed that applying the comparative fault approach would eliminate the necessity of holding a separate hearing to determine the fairness of the initial settlement, since a nonsettling party will only be held liable for its equitable share, not the entire amount paid in the settlement.

Which approach do you find more persuasive—the UCATA *pro tanto* alternative or the UCFA *ACME Solvent* choice? Does it make sense to have one rule for government settlements and a different one for private settlements? Perhaps your answer depends on which of the two is more widely accepted in tort cases. Which better fosters CERCLA's goals as you conceive of them?

There have developed in the 1990s two powerful counter-currents that may accelerate the acceptance of the proportionate reduction alternative. First is an admiralty decision of the United States Supreme Court, McDermott, Inc. v. AmClyde, 511 U.S. 202, 114 S.Ct. 1461, 128 L.Ed.2d 148 (1994), where the Court ruled that the proportionate equitable share reduction approach of the UCFA will be applied to reduce nonsettlors' liability in maritime litigation,[6] not the *pro tanto* approach.

---

6. Section 6 of the Uniform Comparative Fault Act exemplifies the proportionate share rule:

A release, covenant not to sue, or similar agreement entered into by a claimant and a person liable discharges that person

The *McDermott* opinion continued by concluding that the proportionate share approach was more consistent with *Reliable Transfer*. *Pro tanto* allocation, however, was unlikely to reflect proportionate fault:

> Under the *pro tanto* approach, * * * a litigating defendant's liability will frequently differ from its equitable share, because a settlement with one defendant for less than its equitable share requires the nonsettling defendant to pay more than its share. Such deviations from the equitable apportionment of damages will be common, because settlements seldom reflect an entirely accurate prediction of the outcome of a trial.

Id. at 1467. Further, "the settlement figure is likely to be less than the settling defendant's equitable share * * * , because settlement reflects the uncertainty of 'trial' and a plaintiff would be willing to settle for a lower amount in order to build a 'war chest.' " Id.

Further, the Court found that in comparing the effects of the two alternatives on settlements, they were "ambiguous," and so too would their effects on "judicial economy be ambiguous," concluding that "Congestion in the courts cannot justify a legal rule that produces unjust results in litigation simply to encourage speedy out-of-court accommodations." Id. at 1469 n.23.

The second major development in the 1990s was the adoption of Restatement (Third) of Torts: Apportionment § 22 (1999), which, as quoted earlier, expressly adopts the proportionate reduction alternative.

Recall that § 113(f) of CERCLA calls for the federal courts to apply "*federal law*" in contribution actions and according to the legislative history of CERCLA to use the "*evolving common law*" of torts as a major interpretative tool in implementing this complex statute. Will these two sources of common law—the *McDermott* decision and the Restatement (Third) of Torts—influence the resolution of this issue in CERCLA cases? While it is too early to answer this inquiry, the Seventh Circuit Court of Appeals in Akzo Nobel Coatings v. Aigner Corp., 197 F.3d 302, 307–308 (7th Cir.1999) (a later appeal of the *Akzo* decision referred to earlier), holds that *McDermott* really treated the two alternatives as a "toss up" and "closely matched"; and the court holds that the *pro tanto* approach is preferable in CERCLA litigation:

> If as *McDermott* explained the choice between the pro tanto approach and claim reduction [proportionate reduction] is a toss-up, 511 U.S. at 217, then it is best to match the handling of settlements with the way intersecting principles of law work. For admiralty that meant claim reduction. For CERCLA the most closely related rule of law is § 113(f)(2), which reduced third-party claims by the actual

from all liability for contribution, but it does not discharge any other persons liable upon the same claim unless it so provides. However, the claim of the releasing person against other persons is *reduced by the amount of the released* *person's equitable share of the obligation,* determined in accordance with the provisions of Section 2 [of the Act].

Unif. Comparative Fault Act § 6, 12 U.L.A. 57 (1993) (emphasis added).

cash value of settlements reached with governmental bodies. Extending the pro tanto approach of § 113(f)(2) to claims under § 113(f)(1) enables the district court to avoid what could be a complex and unproductive inquiry into the responsibility of missing parties. The extended litigation between Akzo and Aigner well illustrates the difficulties of fixing responsibility for wastes sent years (if not decades) ago to a firm that did not keep good records and contaminated a wide area. Excluding only actual collections from third parties enables the court to conserve its resources.

Thus, as we move into a new decade of the 2000s, the diversity of views on the treatment of nonsettlor liability remains just that: a diversity, with no uniform rule having emerged. But if one acknowledges that the Restatement (Third) represents the essence of the "evolving common law," and no other single source carries equivalent authoritative weight, then one may predict that the UCFA—proportionate reductions alternatives—should emerge as the dominant choice under § 113(f).

For more literature on this topic, see, J. Wylie Donald, CERCLA and the Choice Between Pro Tanto and Proportionate Share Settlement Allocation & Looking to the Supreme Court for Guidance, 25 Envtl. L. Rep. 10293 (1995); Marc L. Frohman, Rethinking the Partial Settlement Credit Rule in Private Party CERCLA Actions: An Argument in Support of the Pro Tanto Credit Rule, 66 U. Colo. L. Rev. 711, 748–49 (1995); Lynette Boomgaarden and Charles Breer, Surveying the Superfund Settlement Dilemma, 27 Land & Water L. Rev. 83, 111–12 (1992); Joseph A. Fischer, All CERCLA Plaintiffs Are Not Created Equal: Private Parties, Settlements, and the UCATA, 30 Hous. L. Rev. 1979 (1994); Elizabeth F. Mason, Contribution, Contribution Protection, and Non–Settlor Liability Under CERCLA: Following Laskin's Lead, 19 B.C. Envtl. Aff. L. Rev. 73 (1991); Steven B. Russo, Contribution Under CERCLA: Judicial Treatment After SARA, 14 Colum. J. Envtl. L. 267 (1989); Superfund Settlements: The Failed Promise of the 1986 Amendments, 74 Va. L. Rev. 123 (1988); A Right of Contribution Under CERCLA: The Case for Federal Common Law, 71 Cornell L. Rev. 668 (1986).

2. *Settlement Criteria.* The courts evaluate the overall procedural and substantive fairness and reasonableness of the consent decrees that embody the settlements. See *Cannons Engineering* for a discussion of this process. Courts typically evaluate these decrees according to a set of criteria which include the following: (1) the relative costs and benefits of litigating the case: (2) the strength of the government's case against the settling PRPs; (3) the degree to which the bargain between the government and PRP negotiators was conducted in good faith, at arm's-length, and with candor and openness; (4) the rational relationship of the settlement amount to a plausible, if inaccurate, estimate of the settlors' volumetric contribution of wastes to the site; (5) the ability of the settlors to satisfy an even larger judgment; and (6) finally, the degree to which the settlement serves the public interest. See United States v.

Rohm & Haas, 721 F.Supp. 666 (D.N.J.1989); United States v. Acton Corp., 733 F.Supp. 869 (D.N.J.1990); In re Acushnet River & New Bedford Harbor, 712 F.Supp. 1019 (D.Mass.1989) (proposing settlement criteria); Kelley v. Thomas Solvent Co., 717 F.Supp. 507 (W.D.Mich. 1989) (proposing settlement criteria).

Although *Cannons Engineering* typifies the courts' deferential approach to CERCLA settlements, some settlements have failed to garner the judicial stamp of approval. In United States v. Montrose Chemical Corp., 50 F.3d 741 (9th Cir.1995), the Ninth Circuit held that the district court abused its discretion in approving a consent decree that lacked an estimate of projected natural resource damages at issue, and identified at least four separate inquiries that the district court should have undertaken:

> We * * * vacate the district court's approval of the consent decree and remand the matter for the district court to conduct an independent evaluation of the settlement with LACSD and the 150 local governmental agencies to determine whether it is "reasonable, fair, and consistent with the purposes that CERCLA is intended to serve." (citation omitted).

> In conducting that evaluation, [1] the court, in addition to considering any other relevant factors, should determine the proportional relationship between the $45.7 million to be paid by the settling defendants and the governments' current estimate of total potential damages. [2] The court should evaluate the fairness of that proportional relationship in light of the degree of liability attributable to the settling defendants.

> [3] Moreover, we believe that the nature of the liability of the various defendants is of considerable relevance in determining whether the settlement is fair, reasonable and consistent with the public interest. For example, if joint and several liability does not apply to the natural resources damages, the governments' ability to collect the totality of remaining damages from the non-settling defendants certainly would have an impact on the settlement's merits.

> * * *

> [4] We recognize that, in holding that the district court erred in approving the proposed consent decree, we tread relatively uncharted territory in the area of Superfund litigation. By so holding, however, we do not denigrate CERCLA's primary goal of encouraging early settlement. Nor do we vitiate the district courts' considerable discretion in approving such settlements. Deference, however, does not mean turning a blind eye to an empty record on a critical aspect of settlement evaluation. Where clear error occurs, we will reverse. Swaddling is not armor. Because we believe that the district court did not possess sufficient information to adequately determine

whether the LACSD consent decree was fair, reasonable, and consistent with CERCLA's objectives, we vacate and remand.

Id. at 747–48. Clearly *Cannons Engineering* and *Montrose Chemical* articulate standards useful in the judicial review of settlements. As noted, the appeals courts afford considerable deference to the district courts in fashioning and approving consent decrees and other settlements.

See also United States v. American Cyanimid, 31 F.Supp.2d 45 (D.R.I.1998) (the opinion contains an excellent discussion of public interest in settlement approval process, and concluding that the fact that other responsible parties remain in litigation from which EPA can pursue its costs [specifically 124 third-party defendants and 22 fourth-party defendants]. Although it may be easier for EPA to collect from UTC than from the remaining defendants, a court must consider the fairness of doing so) the court added:

> Finally, as EPA points out, the public's interest in being compensated for cleanup is matched by its interest in preventing a PRP from being saddled, unfairly, with liability for remediation costs that far exceed its fair share. Thus, even though CERCLA's harsh "joint and several liability" provisions permit collecting the entire amount of response costs from UTC, alone, fundamental fairness prohibits the imposition of liability that is totally disproportionate to UTC's share of responsibility.

Accord, United States v. National Railroad Passenger Corp. ("Amtrak"), 1999 WL 199659 (E.D.Pa.) (excellent analysis of procedural fairness, substantive fairness, and reasonableness of consent decree).

Once the EPA obtains a decree that covers recovery of all response costs, it can no longer force other PRPs into decrees that augment that recovery. See, United States v. Occidental Chemical Corp., 1998 WL 1032569 (M.D.Pa.1998).

Appropriately the EPA has no authority to order a potentially responsible party to participate in a remedial action when the agency already has a consent decree requiring another party to undertake the entire cleanup. The ruling could undercut EPA's ability to use its administrative and penalty powers to encourage—or coerce—PRPs to settle with "working PRPs," as those parties actively undertaking cleanup are often called. The U.S. District Court for the Middle District of Pennsylvania found the government's claim under CERCLA was fully satisfied by a financially assured remedy in a consent decree it entered with Ruetgers–Nease Corp. EPA was not entitled to a double recovery, and therefore had no authority to issue a unilateral administrative order requiring Occidental Chemical Corp. to perform identical response actions at the Centre County Kepone Site in College Township, Pa., the court ruled.

3. *Contribution Protection and Notice.* On the point also considered in *Cannons Engineering, Rohm & Haas,* and *ACME Solvent* respecting

contribution protection afforded to settling PRPs, the courts have held that the protection against future contribution action applies to later claims brought by nonsettling PRPs *even though the nonsettlors had no actual notice of the settlement.* In United States v. Serafini, 781 F.Supp. 336 (M.D.Pa.1992), the court ruled that the contribution protection accorded settling parties by CERCLA § 113(f) extends even to such claims brought by parties who had no actual notice of the settlement or of the fact that they might be potentially responsible parties. The court also held that the cross-claim plaintiffs' rights to due process and equal protection were not violated. But see, General Time Corp. v. Bulk Materials, Inc., 826 F.Supp. 471 (M.D.Ga.1993) (holding nonsettlor could pursue contribution action against settling PRP when it was given no notice or opportunity to comment on an administrative settlement).

It has also been held that the contribution protection afforded by CERCLA § 113(f) extends not only to contribution suits brought under CERCLA, but also to claims based on state law. See United States v. Alexander, 771 F.Supp. 830 (S.D.Tex.1991), vacated on other grounds, 981 F.2d 250 (5th Cir.1993). Thus, state law contribution claims based on nuisance, negligence or strict liability will be barred against any PRP that has entered a settlement agreement with the government. Would that bar personal injury claims? Why or why not? Go back to Chapter 5 remedies we considered: would it bar an emotional distress claim based on fear of future disease? How about a state-law medical monitoring claim?

4. *Effect of Private Partial Settlements.* Can a private party that has settled with a private plaintiff, but has not reimbursed all of the plaintiff's cleanup costs, maintain a contribution action against third parties? In Amland Properties Corp. v. Aluminum Co. of America, 808 F.Supp. 1187, 1198–1199 (D.N.J.1992), the court answered in the negative. It observed that CERCLA § 113(f)(3)(B) expressly authorizes those who settle their liability to the United States or a State to seek contribution from persons not party to the settlement "for some or all of a response action * * * or for some or all of the costs of such action * * *." Thus, when a settlement with the government precedes the contribution action, the settlor's right to contribution does not depend on whether it had extinguished all claims the government may have against other parties. However, the court said § 113(f)(1) is silent as to the settling party's right to seek contribution against defendants whose liability has not been extinguished. It continued:

> In contrast, Congress created a general right of contribution in private party actions but declined to include a provision which would secure that right for settlements of less than the entire action. This is particularly important in light of the fact that the great weight of common law and statutory authority prior to the Superfund amendments adhered to the requirement that a settling party must have at least extinguished the plaintiff's claims against the party from whom contribution is sought. See, e.g., Restatement (Second) of Torts § 886A(2) ("The right of contribution exists only in favor of a

tortfeasor who has discharged the entire claim for the harm by paying more than his equitable share of the common liability * * * ''); Uniform Contribution Among Tortfeasors Act § 1(d), 12 U.L.A. 63 (1975) ("A tortfeasor who enters into a settlement with a claimant is not entitled to recover contribution from another tortfeasor whose liability for the injury or wrongful death is not extinguished by the settlement nor in respect to any amount paid in a settlement which is in excess of what was reasonable."); Uniform Comparative Fault Act § 4(b), 12 U.L.A. 53 (Supp. 1992) ("Contribution is available to a person who enters a settlement with a claimant only (1) if the liability of the person against whom contribution is sought has been extinguished and (2) to the extent that the amount paid in settlement was reasonable.") The clear implication to be drawn is that Congress did not intend to alter these clear and ringing common-law principles of contribution in actions between private parties.

What rationale, apart from Congressional silence, might support the court's rule? Later in its opinion the court observed that allowing such contribution actions "could spawn even more litigation, as parties scramble to redistribute liability in any number of directions." Why might more litigation ensue? The one underlying rationale for the court's approach is that of prohibiting a party that has settled for no more than its appropriate equitable share of liability from seeking contribution from other parties who might yet be found to be liable to the original plaintiff, thereby exposing such third-party defendants to a disproportionate share of liability. See, also, United States v. Compaction Systems Corp., 88 F.Supp.2d 339 (D.N.J.1999) (court holds that no prior judgment against the contribution defendant and plaintiff is necessary; a settlement is sufficient recognition of defendant and the contribution plaintiff's shared liability).

What if the statute of limitations has already run against the third parties so that they could not be sued by the original plaintiff? In fact, in *Amland* that was true, but the court found it immaterial. Does the court's opinion conflict with the language of CERCLA § 113(f)(1), which allows "any person" to seek contribution from "any other person who is liable or potentially liable" under CERCLA § 107, "during or following" any CERCLA action under § 106 or § 107? If such a claim may be brought *during* the action against the original defendant, how could that defendant have already resolved the entire claim of the plaintiff, so as to have completely extinguished any liability that might exist on the part of the third-party defendants?

5. *Contribution in favor of a settlor.* A person who is otherwise entitled to contribution can recover contribution even though the person extinguished the liability of another by settlement rather than payment of judgment. A settlor need not prove that he would have been found liable to the plaintiff. A settlor must show only that the settlement was reasonable. United States v. Compaction Systems Corp., 88 F.Supp.2d 339 (D.N.J.1999). But see, Restatement (Third) of Torts: Apportionment

§ 22, comment h (1999); Reporters' Note § 22, comment *b*. (The person seeking contribution must extinguish the liability of the person against whom contribution is sought, citing UCATA § 1(d)).

G. INDEMNIFICATION AGREEMENTS

1. THE STATUTORY PROVISION

Indemnification provisions are often used in transactions involving the acquisition of property to address unknown environmental and other liabilities relating to the assets and business transferred. Two key issues are raised by CERCLA's statutory language and decisions concerning the enforceability of indemnification agreements. First, are indemnification agreements barred by the language of CERCLA § 107(e)? Second, if CERCLA does not bar such agreements, should they, nonetheless, be construed narrowly?

CERCLA § 107(e)(1) provides:

> No indemnification, hold harmless, or similar agreement or conveyance shall be effective to transfer from the owner or operator of any vessel or facility or from any person who may be liable for a release or threat of release under this section, to any other person the liability imposed under this section. Nothing in this subsection shall bar any agreement to insure, hold harmless, or indemnify a party to such agreement for any liability under this section.

2. ARE SUCH AGREEMENTS PERMITTED UNDER CERCLA?

A majority of federal courts interpret § 107(e) as allowing indemnity agreements. Thus, as a consequence, indemnity agreements have become an integral part of real estate transactions. For example, in Mardan Corp. v. C.G.C. Music, Ltd., 804 F.2d 1454, 1459 (9th Cir.1986), a seller sold real property on which it had manufactured musical instruments and deposited waste. As part of the sale the purchaser agreed to release the seller from undisclosed environmental liabilities. After the EPA brought an enforcement action against the purchaser (which had also deposited waste on the property), the purchaser sued the seller under § 107 of CERCLA for recovery of its cleanup costs. The court of appeals affirmed a summary judgment for the seller:

> Contractual arrangements apportioning CERCLA liabilities between private ''responsible parties'' are essentially tangential to the enforcement of CERCLA's liability provisions. Such agreements cannot alter or excuse the underlying liability, but can only change who ultimately pays that liability.

Since the *Mardan* decision, many federal courts to discuss the indemnity issue under CERCLA § 107 have accepted the *Mardan* rationale. See, e.g., Danella Southwest v. Southwestern Bell Telephone Co., 775 F.Supp. 1227 (E.D.Mo.1991); Versatile Metals, Inc. v. Union Corp.,

693 F.Supp. 1563 (E.D.Pa.1988). Thus, in AM International v. International Forging Equip. Corp., 982 F.2d 989, 994 (6th Cir.1993) the Court of Appeals for the Sixth Circuit joined the chorus of those courts holding that § 107(e) does not bar indemnification agreements:

> The underlying purpose of the statutory language under scrutiny is to ensure that responsible parties will pay for the cleanup and that they may not avoid liability to the government by transferring this liability to another. However, this purpose is not inconsistent with parties responsible for the cleanup transferring or allocating among themselves the cost associated with this liability, so long as they remain liable to the third party who can demand the cleanup. This is what is permitted by the second sentence—the shifting or allocation of the risk of the cost of liability between potentially responsible persons, without diluting CERCLA liability for the cleanup itself.

The Ninth Circuit reached the same conclusion in Jones–Hamilton Co. v. Beazer Materials & Services, Inc., 973 F.2d 688 (9th Cir.1992) and the Ninth in Truck Components, Inc. v. Beatrice Co., 143 F.3d 1057 (7th Cir.1998).

A majority of courts have now interpreted § 107(e) to authorize private contractual indemnity agreements among PRPs or sellers and buyers of property. See, e.g., Armotek Indus., Inc. v. Freedman, 790 F.Supp. 383, 386–87 (D.Conn.1992); C.P.C. Int'l v. Aerojet–Gen. Corp., 759 F.Supp. 1269, 1283 (W.D.Mich.1991); Niecko v. Emro Mktg. Co., 769 F.Supp. 973, 988 (E.D.Mich.1991), aff'd 973 F.2d 1296 (6th Cir.1992); Channel Master Satellite Sys. , Inc. v. JFD Elecs. Corp., 702 F.Supp. 1229, 1231 (E.D.N.C.1988); Southland Corp. v. Ashland Oil, Inc., 696 F.Supp. 994, 1000 (D.N.J.1988); Versatile Metals, Inc. v. Union Corp. 693 F.Supp. 1563, 1571 (E.D.Pa.1988); see also Lisl E. Miller, Comment, Indemnification Agreements Under CERCLA, 23 Envtl. L. 333, 333 n.5 (1993) ("[R]elease agreements may bar CERCLA claims even if the agreements predate the statute.") (quoting United States v. Monsanto Co., 858 F.2d 160 (4th Cir.1988), cert. denied, 490 U.S. 1106, 109 S.Ct. 3156, 104 L.Ed.2d 1019 (1989)); Ellis, Private Indemnity Agreements Under Section 107 of CERCLA, 22 Env't Rep. (BNA) 1953, 1954 (1991) (suggesting that Congress intended to prohibit avoidance of statutory liability, rather than disallow private allocation of costs). But see Joseph A. Sevack, Note, Passing the Big Bucks; Contractual Transfers of Liability Between Potentially Responsible Parties Under CERCLA, 75 Minn. L. Rev. 1571, 1575 (1991) (arguing for prohibition of contractual transfers of CERCLA liability).

Settling parties that have expressly agreed to indemnify other PRPs may try to escape their contractual liability by raising the contribution bar of § 113. The few courts that have directly addressed this argument, however, have rejected it, indicating that settlors should not be released from their indemnity agreements. See United States v. Cannons Eng'g Corp., 899 F.2d 79, 91–92 (1st Cir.1990) ("Although such immunity [via indemnification] creates a palpable risk of disproportionate liability

* * * [it] promotes early settlement and deters litigation."); United States v. Pretty Prods., Inc., 780 F.Supp. 1488, 1496 (S.D.Ohio 1991) ("[T]he parties * * * should have negotiated mutually acceptable indemnification provisions and included them in their contracts."); Central Ill. Pub. Serv. Co. v. Industrial Oil Tank & Line Cleaning Serv., 730 F.Supp. 1498, 1507 (W.D.Mo.1990) ("CERCLA * * * permits enforcement of an indemnity agreement."). These courts prohibited claims for *equitable* indemnity against settling parties, indicating a different result for *contractual* indemnification. Such a conclusion, based on a review of CERCLA's legislative history and public policy considerations, suggests that contractual indemnity does not fall within the meaning of "contribution" as set forth in § 113. Rather, public policy strongly favors freedom of contract with which courts are reluctant to interfere. But see United States v. Pretty Prods., 780 F.Supp. 1488, at 1496 n. 7 (S.D.Ohio 1991). ("Even if [the] claim for indemnification was based on a contractual provision, this Court would be skeptical of any attempt to make an end run around CERCLA's contribution immunity.")

In Smith Land & Improvement Corp. v. Celotex Corp., 851 F.2d 86 (3d Cir.1988), cert. denied 488 U.S. 1029, 109 S.Ct. 837, 102 L.Ed.2d 969 (1989), the court pointed out that indemnity agreements are recognized in contribution actions. CERCLA contemplates that the parties to a property transaction may negotiate an allocation of potential future cleanup liability. In other words, if a purchase and sale transaction includes an agreement by the seller to indemnify and hold harmless the buyer regarding any CERCLA liability that may arise as a result of pre-closing conditions at the property, and the EPA sues the buyer, the current owner, under § 107(a)(1) for cleanup costs covered by the indemnity, the buyer may not avoid liability to the EPA on the basis of the indemnity agreement. Any liability incurred by the buyer, however, may be transferred back to the seller by means of the indemnity agreement. The net effect of these provisions is to ensure that the EPA has maximum access to the widest range of assets to accomplish Superfund cleanups, leaving the private parties subject to the risks that the indemnity agreement will turn out not to be enforceable, or that the seller lacks sufficient assets to satisfy its obligations as a PRP to the EPA.

If the goal is to encourage cleanups which conclusion is more likely to foster that objective? In fact, permitting laws like CERCLA to override private agreements may arguably *discourage* cleanups, as new parties who might restore and rehabilitate sites in exchange for a limit on their liability would be deterred by the prospect of becoming liable without limit. Fortunately, these decisions have all been reversed or overruled, and all circuit courts that have addressed this issue have agreed that CERCLA does not override contractual allocation of liability. See, e.g., Joslyn Mfg. Co. v. Koppers Co., 40 F.3d 750, 754 (5th Cir.1994); Beazer East, Inc. v. Mead Corp., 34 F.3d 206, 211 (3d Cir.1994); John S. Boyd Co. v. Boston Gas Co., 992 F.2d 401, 405 (1st Cir.1993); United States v. Hardage, 985 F.2d 1427, 1434 (10th Cir.1993).

3.   HOW SHOULD SUCH AGREEMENTS BE CONSTRUED?

Most of the courts that have considered the application of indemnification have applied, either explicitly or implicitly, a rule that such arrangements can stand as a bar to CERCLA liability only in the presence of *clear language in the agreement* anticipating and requiring such a result. As stated by one commentator, Daniel R. Avery, Enforcing Environmental Indemnification Against a Settling Party Under CERCLA, 23 Seton Hall L. Rev. 872, 875 (1993), enforcement of an indemnification agreement is difficult. A court "will cast a very leery and critical eye towards any contractual language that purports to allocate environmental cleanup responsibility." Id.

a.   *Unknown Liabilities*

Judicial reluctance to release parties from hazardous waste liability is reflected in the Sixth Circuit's decision in *AM International*. In that case, plaintiff, AMI, which had leased a manufacturing facility, sold its assets "as is" to defendants in 1982, and in 1984 provided defendants a release of all claims "of every kind and description, known or unknown" in settlement of various outstanding disputes in return for a payment of $2 to $3 million. AMI later agreed to perform a cleanup of the facility and sued defendants for contribution. The Sixth Circuit held that even though the release was not barred under CERCLA, it may not be effective as to unanticipated environmental claims:

> Under Ohio case law, even where a release contains unambiguous language that purports to bar claims based on unknown future causes, the release will not be effective where evidence clearly indicates that, at the time they signed the release, *the parties had neither foreseen nor considered the specific cause which later gave rise to the claim.* (emphasis added).

Id. 982 F.2d at 991. The court stated further, "the fact that events causing the harm upon which liability is predicated has not occurred at the time of the signing of a release is strong evidence that the parties did not intend the release to bar such liability."

In interpreting release and indemnification agreements, courts have been reluctant to apply those agreements to CERCLA liability absent a finding that the agreement expressly provided for a release of such liabilities or, at a minimum, of "CERCLA-like" environmental liabilities. See Mobay Corp. v. Allied–Signal Inc., 761 F.Supp. 345 (D.N.J.1991); Southland Corp. v. Ashland Oil Inc., 696 F.Supp. 994 (D.N.J.1988). This is a particular concern in cases in which the agreement at issue was entered into before enactment of CERCLA and in the absence of knowledge of the potential for CERCLA-like liabilities. See Westwood Pharmaceuticals, Inc. v. National Fuel Gas Dist. Corp., 737 F.Supp. 1272 (W.D.N.Y.1990), aff'd, 964 F.2d 85 (2d Cir.1992); Wiegmann & Rose Int'l v. NL Industries, 735 F.Supp. 957 (N.D.Cal.1990).

b. *Effect of Pre–CERCLA Contracts on CERCLA Claims*

In the years since CERCLA's enactment, one issue that repeatedly arises in contractual litigation is whether and when pre-CERCLA agreements affect CERCLA claims. Most courts conclude that this federal law issue should be resolved by referring to state law. The law in most states is relatively similar, however, and these cases tend to cite one another, even though they purport to be resolving matters under their respective states' laws.

The result is a largely uniform rule: a contractual provision clearly *encompassing any and every possible liability, past, present, and future, will be read to encompass CERCLA liability, even though CERCLA postdated the contract*. Thus, courts have found CERCLA claims covered by indemnities or releases that referred to "all claims and obligations of any character or nature whatsoever," Rodenbeck v. Marathon Petroleum Co., 742 F.Supp. 1448, 1456–57 (N.D.Ind.1990); "all claims, demands or causes of action * * * which [the releasor] had, has or may have," FMC Corp. v. Northern Pump Co., 668 F.Supp. 1285, 1292 (D.Minn.1987), dismissed mem., 871 F.2d 1091 (8th Cir.1988); "and any other issues between them," Mardan Corp. v. CGC Music Ltd., 804 F.2d 1454, 1458–59 (9th Cir.1986); "all the * * * liabilities * * * of whatever kind, character and description * * * existing or arising after April 30, 1977," United States v. South Carolina Recycling & Disposal, Inc., 653 F.Supp. 984, 1011 (D.S.C.1984), aff'd sub nom., United States v. Monsanto, 858 F.2d 160 (4th Cir.1988), cert. denied 490 U.S. 1106, 109 S.Ct. 3156, 104 L.Ed.2d 1019 (1989) ("all liabilities, obligations and indebtedness * * * as they exist on the Closing Date or arise thereafter,"); Olin Corp. v. Consolidated Aluminum Corp., 5 F.3d 10, 15 (2d Cir.1993) ("all * * * liabilities * * * without any limitation * * * whether known or unknown * * * and whether existing on the date of this agreement or coming into existence hereafter,"); Harley–Davidson, Inc. v. Minstar, Inc., 41 F.3d 341, 344 (7th Cir.1994) (or "any claim, demand, action or cause of action or liability (whether or not now known, suspected or claimed), including any claim for contribution or indemnity, which any of the [parties] ever had, now has or hereafter may have * * *."); Lyncott Corp. v. Chemical Waste Management, Inc., 690 F.Supp. 1409, 1413 (E.D.Pa.1988); see also Olin Corp., 5 F.3d at 15–16; SmithKline Beecham Corp. v. Rohm & Haas Co., 854 F.Supp. 1201, 1206 (E.D.Pa. 1994).

Less sweeping provisions have still been held to include CERCLA liability when they referred to "CERCLA-type liability," see, e.g., Kerr–McGee Chem. Corp. v. Lefton Iron & Metal Co., 14 F.3d 321, 327 (7th Cir.1994) (pre-CERCLA agreement to indemnify against losses arising from "the maintenance of any action, claim or order concerning pollution or nuisance"); Armotek Indus. Inc. v. Freedman, 790 F.Supp. 383, 391–92 (D.Conn.1992) (pre-CERCLA representation referring to compliance with environmental laws); Mobay Corp. v. Allied–Signal, Inc., 761

F.Supp. 345, 358 (D.N.J.1991) (pre-CERCLA agreement mentioning that one party is assuming environmental-type liabilities may include CERCLA liability, or at least to liability arising out of noncompliance with applicable laws, if the release triggering CERCLA liability occurred in violation of law); Jones–Hamilton Co. v. Kop–Coat, Inc., 750 F.Supp. 1022, 1028 (N.D.Cal.1990). Note, however, that one need not violate any law to become liable under CERCLA. See Beazer East, Inc. v. Mead Corp., 34 F.3d 206, 217 (3d Cir.1994) (pre-CERCLA assumption of responsibility for compliance with specified environmental permits, licenses, or orders did not unambiguously assume liability for CERCLA response costs). On the other hand, language that refers only to enumerated types of liabilities, that has no reference to environmental matters, that creates no inferences about future-arising liabilities, and that does not indicate that consideration was paid for a release or indemnity, is generally insufficient to affect CERCLA claims. John S. Boyd Co. v. Boston Gas Co., 992 F.2d 401, 406–07 (1st Cir.1993); see also Mobay Corp. v. Allied–Signal, Inc., 761 F.Supp. at 355–58; Southland Corp. v. Ashland Oil, Inc., 696 F.Supp. 994, 1001–02 (D.N.J.1988); Jersey City Redev. Auth. v. PPG Indus., 1987 WL 54410 (D.N.J.1987), aff'd mem., 866 F.2d 1411 (3d Cir.1988). This result is often achieved in cases in which it can be shown that the party seeking to avoid liability had no knowledge of contamination or environmental problems at the time of contract. See, e.g., John S. Boyd Co. v. Boston Gas Co., 992 F.2d 401, 407 (1st Cir.1993).

In GNB Battery Technologies, Inc. v. Gould, Inc., 65 F.3d 615 (7th Cir.1995) the Seventh Circuit Court of Appeals held an assumption agreement clearly transferred all liabilities under CERCLA even though the agreement did not expressly mention the act. The court reasoned that an agreement need not specifically mention CERCLA to transfer liability under the act. Looking to the contract language, the court noted that the agreement (1) specifically provided for assumption of any and all obligations and liabilities of any nature incurred except as otherwise provided and (2) listed three specific exemptions. The court held the enumeration of certain exemptions indicates the parties intended to exclude only the situations they specifically itemized.

c. *Governing Law*

A second threshold issue raised in every case involving CERCLA or another federal statute is whether the contractual language at issue is to be interpreted according to a uniform federal rule or to state law. All courts agree that the issue is one of federal law, since they are addressing the possible surrender of a federal cause of action. The matter becomes more complex, however, as most courts then hold that they must look to state law to provide the *content* of that federal law, rather than forging a uniform federal rule. See *Beazer East*, 34 F.3d at 212–15 (discussing reasons for agreeing with "our sister courts of appeals [which] have uniformly selected state law"); see also *Harley-Davidson*,

41 F.3d at 344; *Joslyn*, 40 F.3d at 755; *Olin Corp.*, 5 F.3d at 15. These cases agree that there is no particular need for national uniformity, that the use of state law will not frustrate CERCLA's purpose, and that application of a uniform federal rule would disrupt commercial relationships based on state law. See, e.g., American Int'l Enters., Inc. v. FDIC, 3 F.3d 1263, 1268–69 (9th Cir.1993) (applying a three-factor analysis established by the U.S. Supreme Court in United States v. Kimbell Foods, Inc., 440 U.S. 715, 727–28, 99 S.Ct. 1448, 59 L.Ed.2d 711 (1979)). Only a few trial courts have bucked this trend by concluding that a uniform federal rule should govern the issue at stake, and some appellate courts have disagreed with those rulings. Hatco Corp. v. W.R. Grace & Co., 801 F.Supp. 1309, 1318 (D.N.J.1992), vacated, 59 F.3d 400, 400–05 (3d Cir.1995); Mobay Corp. v. Allied–Signal, Inc., 761 F.Supp. 345, 351–52 (D.N.J.1991); Wiegmann & Rose Int'l Corp. v. NL Indus., 735 F.Supp. 957, 961–62 (N.D.Cal.1990). In many cases, though, the issue has no practical effect, as courts have acknowledged that they would rule the same way whether federal or state law controlled. See, e.g., *Beazer East*, 34 F.3d at 215 n.4; Purolator Prods. Corp. v. Allied–Signal, Inc., 772 F.Supp. 124, 131 n. 3 (W.D.N.Y.1991). Resorting to state law does have at least two benefits. First, it allows parties to choose by use of a choice-of-law clause the law that will govern an incipient contract and to ascertain with reasonable confidence what law will govern an already existing contract. Second, the practical effect of referring to state law is to lessen the pressure on a court to make the polluter pay regardless of what the agreement in question said.

How narrowly should courts construe such indemnification agreements? If CERCLA is not interpreted to preclude the private allocations of cleanup expenses, what limitations should courts place on their enforcement? If an indemnity agreement is negotiated after CERCLA's enactment and with the explicit transference of CERCLA-like liabilities, how will the seller actually "pay" for its pollution? Should bargaining power be treated as a factor in enforcing indemnity agreements between liable parties? What if the language of the agreement mentions CERCLA-type liabilities, but in fact neither party was aware of any facts—i.e., the existence of contamination—that might trigger liability? See Thadeus Bereday, Contractual Transfers of Liability Under CERCLA Section 107(e)(1): For Enforcement of Private Risk Allocation in Real Property Transactions, 43 Case W. Res. L. Rev. 161 (1992); James Conrad, Jr., So Sue Me: Common Contractual Provisions and Allocating Environmental Liability, 26 Envt. Law Rep. 10219 (1996).

What of ambiguous language in the agreement? How should courts construe such language—against the drafter? In Toledo v. Beazer East, Inc., 103 F.3d 128 (Table) 1996 WL 683505*2 (6th Cir.), the Sixth Circuit held that courts should *not* construe ambiguous terms against the drafter without considering evidence of the parties' intent. The Court of Appeals said the trial court erroneously found a purchase agreement's indemnification clause assigned a seller's liability under CERCLA to the buyer. The appeals court found that the agreement's indemnification for "discharges * * * into" the environment did not necessarily contemplate discharges onto land and remanded to the district court to consider evidence regarding the term's meaning. The City of Toledo, Ohio, sued the former owners of a parcel previously used as a commercial benzene disposal facility to recover CERCLA cleanup costs. Former owners Beazer East Inc. and Interlake Co. cross-claimed, each arguing that the other party assumed the site's potential CERCLA liabilities in the purchase agreement signed when Interlake sold the property to Beazer in 1978. The district court found that Beazer's assumption of liability for discharging hazardous substances at the facility included Interlake's benzene disposal onto land.

The Sixth Circuit disagreed, finding the scope of "discharge * * * into" could not be determined within the four corners of the agreement. Under Ohio law, the court said, the question of contract ambiguity is a question of law for the court. A legal determination that contract language is ambiguous then raises a question of fact as to the parties' intent, the court said. The court found that the indemnity agreement did not fully define the "discharge" liability to be indemnified. Nor did the agreement reflect whether the parties intended the term to be synonymous with federal statutes' definitions of "disposal." The court therefore ordered the parties to present to the district court any extrinsic evidence of intent, including "the parties' awareness of environmental problems at the plant and the environmental regulatory horizon."

d. What Role for Sophistication of the Parties?

Consider the decision in Waste Management, Inc. v. Aerospace America, Inc., 156 F.3d 1234 (6th Cir.1998). Waste Management, Inc. ("WMI") sued 99 parties, including Questor Automotive Products, Inc. ("Questor") d/b/a/ Northern Tube Division, in 1994 seeking past and future response costs at the Hartley & Hartley landfill site located in Michigan. Questor filed a third-party complaint against AP Parts Manufacturing company ("AP Parts") for reimbursement of all costs associated with the site under a theory of indemnification. The indemnification arose under contract provisions from the 1981 sale of Northern Tube to AP Parts. Northern Tube was a manufacturer of exhaust pipes for trucks. According to the evidence, between the years of 1971–1978, Northern Tube disposed of 49,200 gallon equivalent units of hazardous waste, including waste oils and waste oil solvents generated through its manufacturing process, at the Hartley & Hartley landfill site.

In December 1981, Questor sold some of its assets, including the Northern Tube division, to AP Parts ("Old AP") pursuant to an Asset Purchase Agreement. Under the 1981 contract, Old AP agreed to indemnify Questor for all losses resulting from any liability or obligation assumed by Old AP. The liability assumed by Old AP included:

> All debts, liabilities, obligations, contracts, leases and commitments of seller ("Questor") relating to its AP Division as of September 30, 1981 *known* or *unknown*, disclosed or undisclosed to buyer

(Old AP), and whether of a contingent nature or otherwise, provided only that the same were incurred in the ordinary course of business of the AP Division * * *. (emphasis added.)

Seven years later, in 1988, Old AP sold some of its assets to AP Parts Acquisition Company, known as "New AP." The 1988 contract contained similar terms that, in essence, would hold New AP liable for all of Old AP's liabilities and obligations. The terms of both agreements essentially provided that liability followed the continued operation of the business.

Despite the fact that neither contract expressly provided for the assumption of CERCLA liability, the court determined that the contracts were unambiguous because the parties were sophisticated enough to be familiar with CERCLA. Another factor in the court's decision to uphold the indemnity provisions in the Purchase Agreements was that the contracts covered both "known and unknown" liabilities. The fact that CERCLA was enacted in 1980, one year *prior* to the execution of the 1981 contract, and because of the level of sophistication of the parties, the court believed they would have specifically excluded CERCLA liability had that been their intent. In fact, the 1988 Agreement had a specific exclusion dealing with liability associated with underground storage tanks. By 1988, New AP would have been aware of CERCLA issues and, had it been their intent, would have excluded that liability. The court held that the broad language of the contracts identifying "any and all liabilities whether known or unknown," was sufficient to cover liabilities incurred under CERCLA.

Other courts have followed this line of reasoning. In Purolator Products Corp. v. Allied–Signal, Inc., 772 F.Supp. 124 (W.D.N.Y.1991), the District Court for the Western District of New York stated:

> Although parties could not have been expected to have foreseen CERCLA before it was enacted, an agreement which is broad enough to encompass any and all claims, or which clearly refers to environmental liability has been held to cover CERCLA liability.

772 F.Supp. at 132. In Mardan Corp. v. CGC Music, Ltd., 804 F.2d 1454 (1986), the United States Court of Appeals for the Ninth Circuit held:

> Finally, CERCLA had been in existence for nearly a year at the time the settlement agreement and the release agreement were executed. In light of these undisputed facts, the District Court ruled that, "given the broad and unambiguous language of the general release involved in this case, it must be concluded that Mardan intended to give up all claims which it had or might someday have against CGA and MacMillan in exchange for approximately $995,000."

Mardan at 1461. The reasoning followed by these courts is that, if the parties to a transaction are sophisticated enough to know about potential environmental liabilities, and are sophisticated enough to be aware of

CERCLA, then broad indemnification clauses will cover potential CERC-LA liability.

One might question whether courts would come to the same conclusion if the parties were not "sophisticated companies." The *Mardan* court made general assumptions about the level of sophistication which cannot necessarily be made about all companies. The language the courts find broad enough, namely, "any and all liabilities, known and unknown" arguably encompasses any size company participating in the transaction.

Finally, with the *Waste Management* decision, Michigan has accepted the reasoning of other states and districts regarding encompassing CERCLA liability under broad indemnification agreements. Other cases have not transferred liability when the language was not broad enough to transfer unforeseen environmental cleanup liability to a former owner. In John S. Boyd Co. v. Boston Gas Co., 992 F.2d 401, 406 (1st Cir.1993), the court held that:

> To transfer CERCLA liability, the agreement must contain language broad enough to allow us to say that the parties intended to transfer either contingent, environmental liability, or all liability.

In *Boyd*, the contract language initially looked to be broad enough by requiring buyer to " * * * assume and take over all the duties and liabilities." The agreement, however, went on to list the obligations which included obligations to serve gas customers, honor contracts for the purchase and sale of new facilities, and to provide reserves to account for bad debt and depreciation on the gas plant. This language, the court held, does not show "the intent to transfer environmental liability in the requisite broad language." The restrictions, in essence, narrow the otherwise broad language of the contract. The *Boyd* case, unlike the *Waste Management* case, held that the language of the contract was not broad enough to evidence the parties' intent to transfer environmental liability.

e.   *Trace Amounts and Rationality*

In the following opinion a California court decides that some indemnification obligations may simply be unreasonable and, hence unenforceable as construed, because the clause appeared to be targeted at "phantom" concerns.

**SDC/PULLMAN PARTNERS v.
TOLO INCORPORATED**

Court of Appeal, California, Fourth District, 1998.
60 Cal.App.4th 37, 70 Cal.Rptr.2d 62.

Sills, Presiding Justice.

I.

This case centers on a toxic substance clause in a lease of land to an aerospace manufacturer. The former lessee, defendant Tolo Incorporated, manufactured fusion reactors, particle accelerator parts and radar antennas, among other things. Tolo occupied the property, which is just off the Costa Mesa Freeway, from the late 1960's to the mid 1990's. It began leasing the land from plaintiff SDC in 1985 after a sale-lease back deal. The lease was renewed in July 1989. It is that lease which contains the clause in question.

Quite remarkably—for an aerospace manufacturer—the land in question is not the subject of any cleanup actions on the part of any government entities, local, state or federal. Unlike some of Tolo's neighbors, the property has suffered no groundwater pollution; levels of toxic and hazardous substances in the soil have not been high enough to trigger any cleanup order. Perhaps the most remarkable fact to emerge from the trial exhibits is that in one sampling of soil from five feet beneath a fenced drum storage area near one of the buildings, some tetrachloroethene (PCE) was indeed found—but at a level, 5 parts per billion, which is only slightly above that found in chocolate sauce, which is 3.6 parts per billion. In the same vein, another expert report dryly opined, in a risk assessment of the soils at the Tolo site, that if a person contacted and "ingest[ed]" soil from the property 350 days a year for 30 years the additional risk of cancer would be 0.007 in one million.

The case comes to us after the trial judge directed a verdict for defendant Tolo. The plaintiff and drafter of the toxic substance clause, SDC/Pullman Partners, appeals from the ensuing judgment, arguing that the toxic substance clause in the lease obligated Tolo to clean up all toxic and hazardous substances at the property, and therefore the presence of detectable amounts of various chemicals, particularly in the Oakite Processing area of the facility, precluded the directed verdict. According to SDC, it makes no difference that the amounts of toxic or hazardous substances have not warranted governmental legal action; Tolo must still spend whatever is necessary to clean up even the trace amounts that do exist, and is in breach of its lease if it hasn't.

We disagree. The toxic substance clause here must be examined in light of the circumstances under which it was made and in light of principles articulated by our Supreme Court in the analogous cases of Brown v. Green (1994) 8 Cal.4th 812, 35 Cal.Rptr.2d 598, 884 P.2d 55 and Hadian v. Schwartz (1994) 8 Cal.4th 836, 35 Cal.Rptr.2d 589, 884 P.2d 46. When it is, it is clear that the mere presence of de minimis amounts of certain substances otherwise toxic in larger quantities does not trigger the clause's cleanup obligation.

II

As this case is fundamentally a dispute over a clause in a lease, we begin our analysis with the text itself, which, as the Hadian court said, is "presumptively controlling." (Hadian, supra, 8 Cal.4th at pp. 844–845, 35 Cal.Rptr.2d 589, 884 P.2d 46.) The toxic substance clause itself is a block of text arranged into one densely worded paragraph of over four hundred words. Rather than set forth the entire text all at once, we will exegete the language sentence by sentence.

The first sentence opens with the words, "except as provided below," and then sets out a blanket prohibition on the presence of any toxic material on the property without prior written permission. This thought is immediately followed by a requirement that if the tenant wants to use toxic substances, it must comply with all applicable laws and, further, show evidence of such compliance "reasonably" acceptable to the landlord. The next two sentences give the landlord the right to require a detailed explanation of the use of any toxic substances as well as obtain any copies of documents turned over to any governmental authorities regulating the use of toxic substances. Then follows a blanket and absolute prohibition on the storage of any toxic materials in an underground tank. The sixth sentence requires that the tenant obtain approval from the local fire department for the use of any toxic substances and that there be a label on the exterior of the premises as to what chemicals or toxic substances are "located within the premises."

The next sentence—one of the two mainly relied on by SDC here—states that if "any such wastes, substances or materials" are "found" on or under the property resulting from the tenant's use, the tenant will spend all necessary sums to "cause the same to be cleaned up"; at the same time the landlord is to be absolutely not liable for those cleanup costs. Then comes a requirement that the tenant be in "compliance" with all environmental laws, after which there is listed a compendium of environmental statutes.

The ninth sentence in the clause deals with the tenant's duties in the event that the tenant receives notice of violation of any environmental laws, which duties include immediately curing the "deficiency or complained of matter" and giving the landlord proof of that curing.

The penultimate sentence provides for the indemnification of the landlord by the tenant by reason of the tenant's failure to perform its obligations under the clause.

In the 1994 *Brown* and *Hadian* cases, our Supreme Court was confronted with the construction of certain lease clauses operationally similar to the toxic substance clause at issue here. Both cases involved "compliance with laws" clauses which regulated the tenant's use of the property, and which, ostensibly, could be read to require that the tenant bear the cost of expensive capital improvements mandated by a governmental agency. In *Brown* the question involved asbestos cleanup; in *Hadian* it was earthquake retrofitting. In reaching different results for each case (in *Brown*, the tenant had to pay, in *Hadian* it was the landlord) the high court emphasized that not only must there be "a close consideration * * * of the terms of the lease but of the circumstances surrounding its making." (*Brown*, supra, 8 Cal.4th at p. 825, 35 Cal. Rptr.2d 598, 884 P.2d 55.) In particular, the nature of the tenant's use of the property as contemplated by the parties is extremely important * * * as well as six judicially developed factors which serve as "clues" or indicators of the risks and burdens which the parties intended to establish. (See *Brown*, supra, 8 Cal.4th at p. 829, 35 Cal.Rptr.2d 598, 884 P.2d 55.)

* * *

In the present case, we affirm the trial court's judgment because the terms and circumstances of the toxic substance clause, confirmed by the policy expressed in the judicially developed factors used in *Brown* and *Hadian*, all point to the conclusion that the toxic substance clause was intended to protect the landlord against actual liability—or at least the realistic threat of actual liability—from the tenant's noncompliance with environmental law, not require the tenant to spend potentially enormous sums to extract trace and de minimis amounts of certain molecules to avoid purely speculative environmental liability.

III

If one thing is clear from the toxic substance clause here, particularly in light of the circumstances under which the lease was made, it is that the parties certainly intended that Tolo would be allowed to continue its normal, high-tech manufacturing operations, and would be allowed to use toxic materials incidental to those operations. Taken as a whole, the entire toxic substance clause here is devoted to conditioning and regulating Tolo's use of "toxic" materials, not blanketly prohibiting their use. Most of the sentences in the clause revolve around the need for precautions to be taken and Tolo's responsibilities if precautions are not. The only real ironclad prohibition is of toxic materials in underground storage tanks.

If there is any doubt from the text, the circumstances of the lease are dispositive. At the time the lease was made Tolo was engaged, as it had been for about 20 years, in the manufacture of parts for the aerospace industry. There is no way that such parts can be made without using toxic materials; radar antennas and such things, *if we may be forgiven for making the point facetiously, are not made of tofu and sprouts*. The idea therefore, which permeates SDC's brief, that in 1989 the parties were starting from ground zero and that Tolo was going to have to obtain written permission every time any toxic materials came onto Tolo's plant after 1989, even if such materials were part of its normal manufacturing processes, is untenable. SDC reads the first sentence in a way which would have frustrated the purpose of the lease, forcing Tolo to go out of business altogether.

SDC places great stress on the need for written permission, and asks what purpose could those words have if not to first establish a blanket prohibition on the use of toxic substances, subject to the written permission requirement. * * *

The argument, however, relies on a false dichotomy. The parties may have contemplated that Tolo should continue to do what it had been doing; they did not necessarily contemplate that Tolo could change its manufacturing operations and subject the landlord to a substantially increased risk of environmental liability without written permission. The company could not, for example, have converted its plant to the local equivalent of Lockheed's famous "Skunkworks," and manufactured, say, the (apparently very toxic) coating of stealth aircraft without first obtaining written permission. Even though such manufacturing per se might not necessarily violate any antipollution law, there certainly would be an increased risk of a spill on the property.

That leaves sentence number seven, with its statement that if "any" toxic wastes, substances or materials are "found" on or under the property resulting from the tenant's use, the tenant will spend all necessary sums to "cause the same to be cleaned up." If read in literal isolation, that is, apart from the balance of the clause and the circumstances under which the lease was made, and if one interprets the word "any" in an extreme and absolutist way, one can indeed conclude that Tolo was required to spend untold sums of money to eliminate every last vestige of any toxic substance "found" anywhere on the property.

But contract terms cannot be read in isolation. (Civ.Code, § 1641). They must be read as a consistent whole, so that some effect will be given to all clauses, consistent with the general intent and purpose of the instrument. (Civ.Code, § 1652). The words of a contract may be explained by reference to the circumstances under which the contract was made. (Civ. Code, § 1647). In fact, literal language of a contract does not control if it leads to absurdity (Civ.Code, § 1638) or if it is wholly inconsistent with the main intention of the parties (Civ.Code, § 1653). And if these rules are not enough, the language of a contract should be "interpreted most strongly" against the party who caused the uncertainty to exist (Civ.Code, § 1654), in this case SDC, as it is undisputed its in-house counsel wrote the document. In light of these rules, there are three reasons we reject the absolutist reading of "any" in the seventh sentence proffered by SDC.

First, such a reading is inconsistent with textual context. The balance of the toxic substance clause—important because the very first words of the opening line indicate that some use of toxics is being provided for—contradicts SDC's proffered interpretation. As we have already indicated, *most of the clause is predicated on the idea that Tolo would use toxic materials, but such use would have to be regulated to ensure that SDC incurred no legal liability under applicable environmental law because of that regulated use.* Sentence after sentence points the reader to applicable environmental law, the implication being that it would serve as a benchmark. [emphasis added by court].

Second, an absolutist reading of the seventh sentence is unreasonable under the circumstances of this lease. This is not a residential lease. Tolo's use of the property was already ongoing when SDC bought the property and became a landlord with a tenant already in place. SDC knew that Tolo was an aerospace manufacturer and could not conduct even the cleanest operations without some use of toxic substances. Obviously, in such circumstances, Tolo had to be cut a little slack as far as the containment of those substances was concerned. " '[S]afe,' " as the United States Supreme Court noted in *Industrial Union v. American Petrol. Inst.* (1980) 448 U.S. 607, 642, 100 S.Ct. 2844, 2864, 65 L.Ed.2d 1010, "is not the equivalent of 'risk-free.' " The "nature of the lessee's use of the property" (see *Brown*, supra, 8 Cal.4th at p. 823, 35 Cal. Rptr.2d 598, 884 P.2d 55) meant that at least a few molecules on the list of hazardous substances might escape into the environment and on to the ground.

Third, an absolutist reading of the seventh sentence is unreasonable from the standpoint of actual hazard or toxicity. The list of hazardous substances found in appendix A to section 302.4 of title 40 of the Code of Federal Regulations [pursuant to CERCLA] contains a number of common materials which are not "toxic" in de minimis or infinitesimal concentrations. The list contains zinc and chromium, for example, which one can obtain at health food or vitamin stores, and cadmium, which is contained in stainless steel cutlery. Nickel and silver are also listed, even though no one would ever think that collections of silver coins were "hazardous." Another example is acetone. Acetone is formed in the human liver when fats are metabolically broken down (see Stryer, Biochemistry (Freeman and Company, 3d ed. 1988) pp. 478–479 [discussing formation of ketone bodies in the liver from acetyl coenzyme if fat breakdown predominates]), as, for example, in exercise. And, as this very record shows, another listed hazardous substance, tetrachloroethene, naturally occurs in chocolate.

It would be ludicrous to hold that, say, a buried bag of silver coins constituted a "hazardous substance." Obviously, a rule of reason must be used in explicating what is hazardous. SDC, however, is unable to point to any health hazard. Indeed, the evidence is quite the contrary: If you can eat the soil 350 days a year for 30 years and incur an increased cancer risk of only 0.007 in one million you don't really have "any" "toxic" substances in any sane or intelligent sense at all.

IV

In addition to basic contract interpretation rules, our conclusion is confirmed by reference to the six judicially developed factors actually used in the context of compliance with laws clauses as explicated in *Brown* and *Hadian*. Those six factors are: (1) the relationship of the cost of curative action to the rent reserved; (2) the term for which the lease was made; (3) the relationship of the benefit to the lessee to that of the reversioner; (4) whether the curative action is structural or nonstructural in nature; (5) the degree to which the lessee's enjoyment of the premises will be interfered with while the curative action is being undertaken; and (6) the likelihood that the parties contemplated the application of the particular law or order involved.

* * *

Preliminarily, of course, we should note that the six factors were not developed to explicate toxic substance clauses, and do not readily lend themselves to rote, mechanical application to such clauses. * * * [T]he first factor (cost of curative action as a proportion of total rent received) reveals that the law disfavors the allocation of curative burdens in a grossly disproportional way. Yet the elimination of pollution is subject to the law of diminishing returns. The cost of eliminating every last molecule otherwise toxic in larger quantities is necessarily prohibitive.

The Supreme Court illustrated the importance of disproportionality by self-consciously contrasting the results it reached in *Brown* and *Hadian*.

* * *

The next four factors used in *Brown* and *Hadian* convey roughly the same idea: The shorter the term of the lease (2), the less likely it is that the parties contemplated the allocation of a relatively expensive burden on the tenant. The same idea courses through the relation between the benefit to the tenant and benefit to the landlord (3), the structural or nonstructural nature of the curative action (4), and degree of interference with the tenant's enjoyment of the premises (5). The harsher the burden on the tenant in relation to what it receives from the lease, the less likely the parties intended that the curative action be visited on the tenant.

The sixth *Brown* and *Hadian* factor—the contemplation of the specific application of the particular law—is especially relevant. If there is a drumbeat theme in this toxic substances clause here, it is reference to existing environmental laws and assurance of compliance with those laws. The enumerated environmental statutes were very much in the mind of the parties in entering into the lease agreement. Again, as we have noted above, the strong implication from the continual reference to compliance with applicable environmental statutes is that the actual application of such laws would serve as the trigger for the tenant's cleanup duties.

V

We must now confront the problem of the energumenical lengths to which the definition of "hazardous substance" under the federal environmental law known as CERCLA has been taken. It is true that as a matter of liability under CERCLA, some federal courts have held there is no "threshold concentration requirement." (U.S. v. Alcan Aluminum Corp. (3d Cir.1992) 964 F.2d 252, 259; accord: Amoco Oil Co. v. Borden, Inc. (5th Cir.1989) 889 F.2d 664, 669.) Unlike our approach above to the lease terms here, these federal courts have adopted an absolutist reading of what is "hazardous": If the substance is found in one of the designated categories set forth in 42 U.S.C. section 9601(14), it is hazardous, without regard to quantity. (E.g., Alcan Aluminum, supra, 964 F.2d at p. 260.) Thus we must ask, as SDC would have us ask, if "hazardous substance" is read without regard to quantity under CERCLA, why should it not be read without regard to quantity in the lease term here?

We are merely a state intermediate appellate court charged, in this appeal, with interpreting terms in a lease of real property under state contract law, and so the issue of how CERCLA should be interpreted is not before us. *If federal courts have insisted on reading a federal law without any reference to reason or common sense, that is their business.* However, our conclusion is not necessarily inconsistent with those federal decisions. There is a significant difference between liability in a CERCLA action and a private cleanup duty pursuant to a lease.

* * *

[The court discusses the *Alcan Aluminum* opinion].

The reason the Alcan Aluminum court then rejected the point about the absurdity of defining hazardous substances without regard to quantity was the possible cumulative effect of small amounts of waste to a larger whole by many contributors.

* * *

VI

We now come, if we may be forgiven the pun, to the real nitty gritty of the case. SDC is clearly afraid of any potential liability under CERCLA, and argues that the lease clause in the present case should be read in an absolute manner so as to give effect to the lease's evident purpose of protecting the landlord from potential CERCLA liability.

SDC's fear is not wholly unreasonable.

* * *

But while SDC's fears are not wholly unfounded, they are answered by the difference between actual CERCLA liability and speculative CERCLA liability. Using an absolutist definition of hazardous substance, there probably isn't a person in the United States—at least over age 10—who could not in theory be tagged for some sort of cleanup cost somewhere. Anyone who has ever painted anything, who ever put on or took off fingernail polish, who ever used an insecticide, drove a car, changed its oil or had oil changed, smoked a cigarette or changed the toner in a photocopy machine, or who has so much as thrown away a small battery into the trash, could be theoretically held liable for expensive cleanup costs. Yet to base an interpretation of a contract on such theoretical liability is self-evidently absurd. It would reify an unreasonable fear into an actuality.

* * *

In light of the circumstances under which the lease in the case before us was made and the clear contemplation of the parties that the property would continue to be used for aerospace manufacturing, we hold that only real CERCLA liability—or at least a "realistic threat" of it—can reasonably trigger a tenant's cleanup duty. Anything else merely perpetuates phantasms.

Of course, in the event that a government agency were to require SDC to spend sums to clean up the property, the indemnity clause would still be available to it to recover those sums from Tolo. Our decision here would certainly not be res judicata on the operation of the indemnity clause in the context of real CERCLA liability. Indeed, nothing in this opinion is meant to minimize SDC's right to recover costs from Tolo in such an eventuality.

VII

The trial judge's reading of the toxic substance clause was thus correct, and the directed verdict based on that reading was therefore correct as well. Since SDC could not show a breach of the lease, the balance of its causes of action which are predicated on the idea that Tolo polluted the property must fall as well.

* * *

The judgment is affirmed.

Notes and Questions

1. *Refreshing Candor.* The language in *SDC Pullman* and what we witnessed earlier in most of the government-initiated CERCLA cases is quite a contrast. Especially noteworthy is the idea that the toxic substances clause was to protect against "actual liability—or at least the realistic threat of actual liability—from the tenant's noncompliance with environmental law, not require the tenant to spend potentially enormous sums to extract *trace and de minimis amounts of certain molecules* to avoid purely speculative environmental liability." 70 Cal.Rptr.2d at 66 (emphasis added); later "if one interprets the word 'any' in an extreme and absolutist way, one can indeed conclude that Tolo was required to spend untold sums of money to eliminate every last vestige of any toxic substance 'found' anywhere on the property." Id. at 67. Additionally, the court uses the word *"unreasonable"* to characterize plaintiff's reading on several occasions, and insists on a rule of reason in construing such documents.

2. *Is Consistency Possible?* Is it possible to find that the opinions refusing to create any threshold of hazardous substances releases for prima facie CERCLA liability can be reconciled with *SDC Pullman*? Is there an important distinction between prima facie CERCLA liability under § 9607(a) and contractual liability under the lease in *SDC* that might justify the different outcomes? Quite clearly the *SDC* court is comfortable with facetious, "tongue-in-cheek" discussion one would not expect in a CERCLA opinion.

3. *State Law Factors.* The court lists and analyses the six factors the California Supreme Court developed to interpret "compliance with laws" clauses. Which of the so-called *Brown* and *Hadian* factors seems most relevant in this context? Why? Would or should these factors be relevant in all CERCLA indemnification cases?

4. *Causation Reprised.* Recall that in the *Acushnet* opinion of the First Circuit and Judge Keeton's opinions in the district court drew heavily on the same kind of argument as the *SDC* opinion in developing contribution-causation standards that avoided "absolutist" and "extreme" positions. So

too in *Kalamazoo River Study Group* the quest for a "threshold of significance" test was motivated by a fear of absurd results. Whether these opinions and others constitute a "new rationality" in CERCLA jurisprudence remains to be seen.

5. *Seller's Knowledge As Affecting Indemnification.* The Sixth Circuit held in White Consolidated Industries, Inc. v. Westinghouse Electric Corp., 179 F.3d 403 (6th Cir.1999), that the buyer of a TCE-contaminated facility assumed responsibility for environmental liabilities in the purchase agreement. The seller's failure to disclose to the buyer that there was a TCE spill at the facility was not a material breach of the purchase agreement.

The parties did not dispute that a large quantity of trichloroethylene spilled from a 2,000–gallon tank at the facility in 1970 and that Westinghouse did not disclose the spill to White. The court's decision turned in large part on whether Westinghouse had knowledge of any potential liability for this contamination when the contract between the parties was written in 1975. The seller could not have known at the time of sale that a prior spill of TCE could give rise to environmental remediation because CERCLA and the state waste statute did not exist at that time. In addition, the assumption of liabilities provision in the purchase agreement allocated to the buyer the risk of environmental liabilities after the expiration of a one-year indemnification period. Further, the seller did not fraudulently conceal a defect by not informing the buyer of the TCE spill. The seller had no knowledge at the time of contracting that the facility was contaminated from the TCE spill or that the spill would subject the buyer to liability.

The Sixth Circuit found the contract language unambiguously said White agreed to assume any unknown environmental liabilities at the Westinghouse properties. Furthermore, the court said, where an agreement is entered into by "sophisticated companies after arduous negotiations, we will give effect to the parties' * * * terms." 179 F.3d at 410. The court rejected an argument that the purchase agreement imposed a "constructive knowledge" standard on Westinghouse in that Westinghouse should have known that the TCE spill was a fact or condition that would give rise to liability at the time of contracting.

Westinghouse warranted that to the "best of its knowledge and belief" there were no facts or conditions that might give rise to liability in connection with the business or its assets. This contract language requires more than a mere showing that Westinghouse should have known by virtue of the spill alone that liability might result from the spill.

6. *Non-Indemnification Under State Law As Affecting CERCLA Indemnification.* The Eighth Circuit Court of Appeals held that an earlier Minnesota state court's denial of contractual indemnification for environmental liability under the state's cleanup law (Minnesota Environmental Response and Liability Act—MERLA) precluded an oil company from later asserting a CERCLA indemnify claim. Gopher Oil Co. v. Bunker, 84 F.3d 1047 (8th Cir.1996). The court said that the reasoning of the state court's opinion, although never mentioning CERCLA, applied equally to CERCLA indemnity claims.

"The district court held that the doctrine of collateral estoppel prohibits the relitigation of the indemnity claim because the state court judgment determined the claim adversely to Gopher Oil," the Eighth Circuit said. Although Gopher Oil "correctly asserts" that the Minnesota Court of Appeals was referring to MERLA, not CERCLA, when it determined that the environmental liabilities at issue were not contemplated by the indemnity agreement, the reasoning applied to liability under any later-enacted environmental law, the court said.

7. *What of an "As Is" Clause?* An "as is" clause in a real estate sales contract relieved the seller of liability for hazardous waste cleanup under the superfund law even though the sale predated the superfund statute, a federal district court in Tennessee ruled. Velsicol Chemical Corp. v. Reilly Industries Inc., 67 F.Supp. 2d 893, 900 (E.D.Tenn.1999). Applying state contract law, the U.S. District Court for the Eastern District of Tennessee said that Tennessee courts generally enforce "as is" clauses against the purchaser. According to the court's findings of fact, after extensive negotiations Smith included the "as is" clause that read:

> It is clearly understood by all parties that Seller makes no representations or warranties to the usability of the above described property under present or future Federal, State, or local air and water pollution laws, ordinances or regulations.

Before selling its coal tar distillation facility to Velsicol in 1975, Reilly and its predecessors had operated the Chattanooga, Tenn., plant for almost 60 years. Velsicol already owned a chemical plant on land neighboring the Reilly facility, which it had purchased in 1963. Protracted negotiations for the sale of the Reilly tract began in 1972 and were consummated in 1975.

The court found that Velsicol knew that the property it purchased from Reilly was contaminated, explaining, "Velsicol was an experienced, sophisticated chemical manufacturing company and was familiar not only with the then existing environmental laws but also anticipated that the future portended additional and more stringent environmental laws and regulations." Velsicol inspected the Reilly property prior to purchase, and Velsicol's plant manager testified that "you couldn't miss" seeing coal tar waste on the site during the inspection. When, in 1974, Velsicol was sued by a third party for releases of pollution from its site, it impleaded Reilly as a co-defendant.

Problem

In 1985 Carey Recycling Products (CRP) acquired some of the business assets of Western Metals Co. (Western), which related to buying and reselling scrap metals and used batteries. As part of the purchase CRP agreed to "assume all liabilities for or arising from claims related to the assets to be acquired, their condition and/or the processing of inventory from any and all sources whether related to events, conditions occurrences arising or accruing before or after closing and regardless of whether based on statute, regulatory or common law." Three years after the sale, Western was targeted as a potentially responsible party under Superfund for a battery recycling site in Richmond, Columbia. Western seeks indemnification from CRP. The latter refuses, and both parties have filed actions in United States District Court seeking declaratory judgments of non-liability.

CRP argues that the "processing of inventory" phrase only requires CRP to indemnify Western for acts done to prepare the inventory for sale.

Because the environmental liabilities at issue resulted from Western's sale of inventory to contaminated facilities, the express terms of the indemnification provision exclude such liabilities. CRP points out that the liability for which Western seeks indemnity does not stem from the sale of inventory, but rather from Western's arranging for the disposal of hazardous substances (i.e., inventory) at contaminated off-site facilities. Facts also show that CRP was eager to buy Western without much negotiation, and was confident that its knowledge of Western's operations would protect it from any unforeseen liabilities.

Who has the better of the argument? Should a court enforce an indemnification agreement on these facts? What considerations are most important in resolving that question?

Now many decades since its inception, CERCLA continues to show considerable vitality, if by "vitality" we mean capacity for change. The past and the future are summarized in these excerpts from Lemuel Srolovic and Pamela Esterman, Fold or Fight: The Changing Settlement Calculus in CERCLA Enforcement Actions, 9 Fordham Envtl. L.J. 469, 470, 473, 475, 476, 477, 479–480 (1998):

> In the 1980's and the early 1990's, the federal courts seemingly rejected all arguments against broad liability in government enforcement and cost recovery actions under CERCLA. The courts invoked the remedial goals of the Act in broad decisions expanding the reach of the statute. At the same time, the courts accorded a potentially responsible party ("PRP") targeted by the government with ample means to distribute the costs of hazardous substance remediation to other PRPs. This dynamic promoted settlements in government enforcement actions. The inevitable handful of PRPs selected by the government to remediate a site or reimburse the government's cleanup costs had powerful incentives to invest their resources in spreading the costs to other PRPs rather than fighting a losing battle against the government.

> As CERCLA enters its third decade, new trends are emerging that could significantly alter this dynamic. On the one hand, courts are curtailing the expansive reach of CERCLA liability and breathing new life into its limited defenses. This trend offers a PRP, who is targeted by the government, new weapons with which to defend itself. On the other hand, some courts are more frequently placing obstacles in the way of PRPs trying to shift costs to other PRPs on an equitable basis. For the PRP selected by government enforcers to clean up a contaminated site or to reimburse the government's expenditures under joint and several liability, these dual trends provide new incentives to fight the government as opposed to settling and shouldering the burden of allocating costs more broadly.

> To foster settlements and voluntary cleanups with private monies, the courts should continue to exercise their considerable power under CERCLA's contribution provision and fashion rules which promote the equitable distribution of CERCLA liability. Such an approach is consistent with curtailing the expansive reach of CERCLA and protects those

parties identified by the government from bearing responsibility for contamination by others.

* * *

A. *Bestfoods* and Corporate Parent Liability

During CERCLA's first fifteen years, the courts deciding Superfund cases rewrote traditional rules of liability to further CERCLA's broad remedial purposes. More recent appellate decisions, however, have limited the seemingly boundless expansion of CERCLA. This trend may be seen in the Supreme Court's decision in United States v. Bestfoods, the Court's first decision addressing the reach of CERCLA's liability provision, Section 107. The trend may also be seen in recent decisions curtailing liability from the passive migration of contaminants. Decisions breathing life into CERCLA's third-party defense are further examples of the recent judicial trend narrowing the scope of CERCLA liability.

The Supreme Court rejected the notion that Congress intended to establish some CERCLA-specific liability rule for corporations that would outrank traditional common law doctrine. For example, the Court refused to cast off the presumption that officers employed by both a parent and a subsidiary are serving the subsidiary when they act on behalf of the subsidiary. The Court explained: "There would in essence be a relaxed, CERCLA-specific rule of derivative liability that would banish traditional standards and expectations from the law of CERCLA liability." The *Bestfoods* rejection of CERCLA-specific rules of corporate parent liability is a major change in the way the statute has been interpreted by the courts.

B. Passive Migration

Courts have also contracted the scope of CERCLA liability in the passive migration arena. In the late 1980's and the early 1990's, the majority of courts that addressed this issue viewed passive migration of contaminants as a form of disposal under CERCLA. The Fourth Circuit in Nurad, Inc. v. William E. Hooper & Sons Co. held a former owner of property liable as an owner at the time of disposal because hazardous substances had leaked from underground storage tanks during its ownership. The former owner moved for summary judgment, arguing that it had not "actively dealt with hazardous substances at the site" and so was not an owner or operator at the time of the disposal. The District Court agreed and dismissed the claim. The Fourth Circuit reversed, reasoning that to read "disposal" to require "active participation would frustrate [CERCLA's] policy of encouraging 'voluntary private action to remedy environmental hazards.' "

More recently, courts have moved away from such a broad reading of "disposal." Under current decisions, passive migration of contamination does not give rise to CERCLA liability unless a party consciously acted to dispose of the waste in a manner that promoted its migration through the soil or water.

For example, in ABB Industrial Systems, Inc. v. Prime Technology, Inc. [120 F.3d 351 (2d Cir.1997)], the Second Circuit held that former owners and operators of a contaminated site were not liable under CERCLA for the passive migration of chemicals that were already in the ground at the site. The Second Circuit was persuaded by the Third Circuit's 1996 decision in United States v. CDMG Realty Co., [96 F.3d 706 (3d Cir.1996)], which found that CERCLA's definition of "disposal" was not so broad as to hold a prior owner or operator liable for the passive migration of contaminants from a landfill.

The Second Circuit agreed with the Third Circuit in *CDMG* that rejecting liability for passive migration of contaminants is consistent with CERCLA's goal "to force polluters to pay the cost associated with their pollution." That goal is not served if "a person [who] merely controlled a site on which hazardous chemicals have spread without that person's fault" is held liable as a polluter.

C.   The Third–Party Defense

In the 1980's and the early 1990's, the majority of courts rejected attempts made by various PRPs to invoke any defense to Superfund liability, including those premised on the CERCLA third-party defense. In New York v. Shore Realty Corp., [759 F.2d 1032 (2d Cir.1985)], the Second Circuit rejected a third-party defense to Superfund liability in a case involving the leakage of chemicals during the defendant's ownership of the site. The court concluded that the release was not caused "solely" by the acts or omissions of a third-party, and the defendant failed to take precautions against the foreseeable acts of others.

Yet recently, courts have been more receptive to the third-party defense. In New York v. Lashins Arcade Co., [91 F.3d 353 (2d Cir.1996)], the Second Circuit affirmed a district court's decision that a shopping center owner was not liable under CERCLA for contamination from a dry cleaner that leased space years before the site owner had acquired the property. The Second Circuit held that the shopping center owner was shielded from liability by the third-party defense.

The Second Circuit's acceptance of a third-party defense in *Lashins*, eleven years after rejecting the same defense in *Shore Realty*, is consistent with a judicial trend curtailing rather than expanding CERCLA's reach.

D.   The Growing Burden on Cost Shifting

At the same time that the courts are refusing to expand CERCLA liability, courts are also placing impediments on redistributing CERCLA liability through contribution. This latter trend appears in decisions analyzing whether under CERCLA a PRP can pursue a § 107 cost recovery action against other PRPs or whether a PRP is limited to a contribution claim under § 113 of CERCLA.

The distinction between §§ 107 and 113 raises several issues that affect the rights and liabilities of PRPs. The significance of making this distinction is most obvious where contribution is barred either because defendant-PRPs have received contribution protection as a result of settling with the government or because the three-year statute of limitations for contribution claims has expired.

Even though § 107 of CERCLA clearly authorizes private parties to bring actions to recover response costs, a question nonetheless arises when such a private party pursues a Section 107 action and is itself liable under that Section. May a PRP maintain a Section 107 "cost recovery" action or must a PRP proceed with a "contribution" action under § 113? While there is still a split of authority in the lower courts, "[e]very court of appeals that has examined this issue has come to the same conclusion: a § 107 action brought for recovery of costs may be brought only by innocent parties that have undertaken clean-ups," and a non-innocent PRP may only bring a § 113 action for contribution.

The United States Courts of Appeals for the First, Third, Seventh, Ninth, Tenth, and Eleventh Circuits have addressed this issue and have uniformly held that PRPs are limited to § 113 contribution actions. The Fifth and Eighth Circuits, while not directly addressing the issue, have taken the same position.

The unsettled nature of the relationship between §§ 107 and 113 creates impediments for the PRP seeking to shift CERCLA response costs to other PRPs. While those impediments flow indirectly from the divergence in judicial decisions and resulting uncertainty, two courts have placed direct impediments on contribution by fashioning a threshold burden of proof that a PRP must meet in order to shift a portion of cleanup costs to others. [The article summarizes the reasoning of those courts opting to make § 113 the exclusive remedy for PRPs, and then summarizes the district court opinions in *Acushnet* [937 F.Supp. 988 (D. Mass. 1996)] and *Kalamazoo River Study Group* [3 F.Supp. 2d 799 (W.D.Mich.1998)], which recognized a minimum standard of significance threshold to prove causation in a contribution action.]

If followed by other courts, this amorphous threshold burden would establish a significant impediment to shifting costs under CERCLA. Such a rule shifts the focus of contribution actions from determining shared responsibility to conducting cost-benefit analyses of litigation. Under this additional burden, the PRP contemplating cost shifting would face a powerful disincentive against pursuing any parties beyond those most obviously responsible.

E. Conclusion

As the federal courts develop rules governing shifting CERCLA costs among PRPs, they should consider the effects of those rules on the statutory goals of fostering settlements and using private rather than public monies to remediate contaminated sites. Restricting the ability to spread costs to others impedes rather than fosters those important CERCLA goals.

Chapter Eleven

INSURANCE

A. INTRODUCTION

While questions regarding the nature and scope of insurance coverage are important in all tort contexts, insurance issues occupy center stage in toxic tort and environmental remediation litigation. As this Chapter will reveal, such litigation, involving billions of dollars in claims, has produced a wealth of disputes between insureds and insurers, implicating virtually every major aspect of the insurance contract. This Chapter identifies the principal areas of controversy that are engendered by at least three major types of underlying litigation: (1) tort suits involving defective or dangerous toxic products resulting in bodily injury or property damage, of which asbestos is a primary example; (2) tort suits of the nuisance, trespass, or strict liability model involving the disposal of hazardous or toxic wastes or substances producing bodily injury or property damage; and (3) CERCLA actions, initiated by the government or a private party, involving the remediation of property that has been contaminated by release of hazardous wastes or substances.

When the insured becomes a defendant or party in one of these three genres of litigation, it seeks to shift all or part of the cost of defending the action and the payments of settlements or judgments to the insurer. This is typically done pursuant to comprehensive general liability (CGL) policies, which were renamed commercial general liability policies in the mid 1980s. These CGL policies were first introduced in the United States in the early 1940s, and have become the predominant source of insurance protection in three categories of coverage. The first category provides for the protection of the insured because of an injury or a loss suffered by a third party while an activity of the insured is in progress, and prior to the completion thereof, as the result of an act of negligence or an omission by the insured. Such an activity might be the disposal of hazardous waste as part of a manufacturing process. The second category, commonly referred to as "completed operations" coverage, deals with situations involving operations of the insured which have been completed, such as the installation of PCB-containing transformers or the construction of a landfill, and liability results thereafter either by reason of a defect in merchandise or improper workmanship. The third category is "products" coverage which pertains to products distributed in commerce where liability results from defects in the products causing bodily injury or property damage.

Early general liability policies used an accident-based insuring agreement whereby the insurer agreed to pay damages because of bodily injury or property damage "caused by an accident." In 1966, most insurers changed to an occurrence-based general liability form which read:

> [The insurer] hereby agrees to pay on behalf of the insured all sums which the insured shall become legally obligated to pay as damages because of (A.) bodily injury or (B.) property damage to which this insurance applies caused by an occurrence, and the [insurer] shall have the right and duty to defend any suit against the insured seeking damages on account of such bodily injury or property damage.

The typical grant of coverage provision was simplified in 1985 to read:

> [The insurer] hereby agrees to pay on behalf of the insured all sums which the insured shall become legally obligated to pay as damages because of bodily injury or property damage, to which the policy applies, caused by an occurrence.

As a general rule of insurance law, the insurer's duty to defend is broader than the duty to indemnify because the latter depends on the applicable law giving rise to a claim under the policy. The typical CGL policy provides that "the company shall have the right and duty to defend any suit against the insured seeking damages on account of bodily injury or property damage, even if any of the allegations of the suit are groundless, false or fraudulent * * *." Generally, courts determine the obligation of the insurer to defend by comparing the allegations of the underlying complaint with the terms of the insurance policy, and if any allegations (regardless of their frivolousness or falsity) are embraced by the coverage provided, the insurer must defend the action. Moreover, any ambiguity in the factual allegations of the complaint is resolved in favor of the duty to defend. Finally, it is immaterial that the underlying complaint also alleges matters that are outside of the policy's coverage, until such time as those allegations within the policy are stricken or eliminated. See generally Robert Keeton & Alan Widiss, Insurance Law § 9.1(b) (1988).

B. INSURANCE COVERAGE FOR ENVIRONMENTAL AND TOXIC TORTS

In these insurance coverage cases the insured is seeking to be indemnified against bodily injury or property damage claims brought by third parties arising out of its release or use of hazardous substances. Among the issues that have engendered considerable controversy among insureds and insurers is what constitutes an "occurrence" triggering coverage.

1. OCCURRENCE

The definition of what constitutes an "occurrence" has been the source of considerable dispute. Prior to 1966, the terms of the CGL policy typically required the insurer to respond to claims resulting from an "accident." In 1966 the policy language changed from "accident" to "occurrence," which typically is defined to mean:

> an accident, including a continuous or repeated exposure to conditions, which results, during the policy period, in bodily injury or property damage neither expected nor intended from the standpoint of the insured.

Although the language change broadened coverage to reach beyond the common understanding of the term "accident" to include continuous or repeated exposure to conditions, not all damages from long-term exposure to conditions or substances are recoverable under the CGL policy. This is so because by the terms of the "occurrence" definition, the damage must be "neither expected nor intended from the standpoint of the insured."

Insurers take the position that this issue can be resolved in their favor as a matter of law when the insured engages in an intentional act, such as the discharge of waste as a part of its business, i.e., where the discharge is known, routine, and repeated. In contrast, insureds argue that it is the *damage*, not the discharge, which must be expected or intended. They contend that they are covered in so far as they do not subjectively desire or know to a substantial certainty that damage will result from the discharge. The majority of courts have adopted the insureds' perspective, which focuses on the intent to cause damage.

a. *The General Rule*

In the asbestos case of United States Fidelity & Guaranty Co. v. Wilkin Insulation Co., 144 Ill.2d 64, 161 Ill.Dec. 280, 578 N.E.2d 926 (1991), the Supreme Court of Illinois rejected the insurers' argument that the alleged damage was expected or intended because the underlying complaints alleged that the insured intentionally installed asbestos-containing products in the buildings "with knowledge of the products' threat to human health." The court stated: "it is the contamination of the buildings and their contents that must be neither expected nor intended from the standpoint of the insured." Based on its review of the underlying complaints the court found no allegations that the insured expected or intended "to contaminate the buildings and the contents therein with toxic asbestos fibers." Thus, the court concluded that the

complaint alleged potential coverage for "property damage" caused by
an "occurrence" sufficient to trigger the insurers' duty to defend. See
also Village of Morrisville Water & Light Dept. v. U.S. Fidelity &
Guaranty Co., 775 F.Supp. 718 (D.Vt.1991), holding that where the
insured city sent hazardous PCB-laden materials to another's site where
the harm occurred, that intentional act did not negate coverage "because
Morrisville neither expected nor intended to damage the site."

In Olin Corporation v. Insurance Company of North America, 762
F.Supp. 548 (S.D.N.Y.1991), the district court denied the insurers' motion for summary judgment based on the argument that the insured
manufacturer expected or intended the damages that resulted from its
continuous release of DDT over a sixteen-year period. Although the court
acknowledged that strong evidence had been presented to show that Olin
should have known that damages would result from its release of DDT,
the court concluded that the evidence "permitted the inference that Olin
did not 'intend' to cause the damages" based on the standard of review
previously set forth by the Second Circuit. As explained by that court:

> In general, what makes injuries or damages expected or intended
> rather than accidental are the knowledge and intent of the insured.
> It is not enough that an insured was warned that damages might
> ensue from its actions, or that, once warned, an insured decided to
> take a calculated risk and proceed as before. Recovery will be barred
> only if it can be said that the damages were, in a broader sense,
> "intended" by the insured because the insured knew that the
> damages would flow directly and immediately from its intentional
> act. City of Johnstown v. Bankers Standard Ins. Co., 877 F.2d 1146,
> 1150 (2d Cir.1989).

b. Differing Views

Not all courts agree, with some entering a finding of no coverage
upon the lesser showing that the insured knew of the likelihood or the
substantial probability of the resultant harm. See American Mutual
Liability Ins. Co. v. Neville Chemical Co., 650 F.Supp. 929 (W.D.Pa.1987)
(where insured continued its disposal of hazardous wastes despite knowledge that it was contaminating nearby wells, court granted insurer's
motion for summary judgment because the insured knew or should have
known that there was a substantial probability that the contamination
would result); Independent Petrochemical Corp. v. Aetna Casualty &
Sur. Co., 654 F.Supp. 1334, 1360 (D.D.C.1986) (in case involving personal injury claims arising out of exposure to dioxin, court concluded that
there would be no coverage if facts show that insured "was aware of the
likely results of its acts in disposing of the waste materials"), affirmed in
part, rev'd in part, 944 F.2d 940 (D.C.Cir.1991); Jackson Township Mun.
Utils. Auth. v. Hartford Accident & Indem. Co., 186 N.J.Super. 156, 451
A.2d 990, 993–94 (1982) (where residents alleged personal injury and
property damage resulting from exposure to water contaminated by
insured's landfill operations, court stated that manufacturer "who dis-

charges * * * waste material knowingly, or who may have been expected to know, that it would pollute, will be excluded from coverage by the clause. The industry, for example, which is put on notice that its emissions are a potential hazard to the environment and who continues those emissions is an active polluter excluded from coverage by the clause.").

c. *Objective versus Subjective Test*

Another issue sometimes raised in determining whether an event was "expected or intended" is the state of mind and/or degree of foreseeability necessary to trigger this clause. The provision typically states that the event or damage must be expected or intended "from the standpoint of the insured." Insurers argue that the test for meeting this requirement is *objective*: if a reasonable insured should have foreseen the event/harm, it was "expected or intended." Insureds argue that the test is *subjective*: the insurer must prove that the event or injury was "subjectively foreseen as practically certain," *by the insured*.

Most courts reject a purely objective "reasonably foreseeable" test because such a test would deny coverage for simple negligence—a result which most courts find a reasonable insured would not expect. See, e.g., Queen City Farms, Inc. v. Central Nat'l Ins. Co. of Omaha, 64 Wash. App. 838, 827 P.2d 1024 (1992) (trial court erred by instructing the jury that the insured's expectation was to be determined on a reasonable person basis); Broderick Investment Co. v. The Hartford Accident & Indem. Co., 954 F.2d 601 (10th Cir.1992) (applying Colorado law) (jury properly instructed to apply subjective standards). At the opposite end of the spectrum, some courts go so far as to find that the test is wholly subjective, and/or an occurrence is not expected or intended unless the resultant injury is a "substantial certainty." See, e.g., City of Johnstown, New York v. Bankers Standard Ins. Co., 877 F.2d 1146, 1150 (2d Cir.1989); Honeycomb Systems Inc. v. Admiral Ins. Co., 567 F.Supp. 1400 (D.Me.1983). Other courts take the middle road, finding that the operative degree of expectation is "substantial probability"—higher than reasonable foreseeability, but lower than a more subjective, substantial certainty. See, e.g., New Castle County v. Hartford Accident and Indem. Co., 685 F.Supp. 1321, 1330, 1331 (D.Del.1988) and New Castle County v. Continental Casualty Co., 725 F.Supp. 800, 813 (D.Del.1989) (companion case). Cf. Allstate Ins. Co. v. Freeman, 432 Mich. 656, 443 N.W.2d 734, 743 (1989) (substantial probability test applied, but from subjective viewpoint of insured).

Application of the subjective test generally increases the burden on the insurer. However, in Diamond Shamrock Chemicals v. Aetna, 258 N.J.Super. 167, 609 A.2d 440 (1992), the insured still lost the battle of whether there had been an occurrence. The court affirmed the trial judge's finding that the insured subjectively knew the waste that it discharged would cause harm where the insurers proved that Diamond Shamrock knew that it was discharging a hazardous substance and that some employees had contracted skin diseases from contact with its product. Despite this knowledge, the insured purposefully discharged waste water containing contaminants onto the ground and into a nearby river. Furthermore, the insured rejected a process which would have lowered the level of dioxin in its product since it would have decreased production efficiency. Based on this evidence, the court found that Diamond Shamrock subjectively expected or intended the injury which occurred: "Diamond did know the nature of the chemicals it was handling, it did know that they were being continuously discharged into the environment, and it did know they were doing at least some harm. * * * [W]e cannot ignore reality by accepting the blithe assurance of Diamond that it did not intend to injure others. The evidence abounds the other way. * * * Instead we are convinced that subjective knowledge of harm was proven as a matter of fact."

Problem

Larco Inc., sought insurance coverage with respect to an action brought by the Columbia Department of Natural Resources ("CDNR") for remediation of chemical contamination at Larco's plant in Big Rapids, Columbia. The CDNR filed its action against Larco in 1990. The trial court granted Larco's motion for summary disposition on the issue of the duty to defend and issued an order requiring American Insurance Co. to indemnify plaintiff for 68% of the remediation costs.

On appeal, American Insurance argued that the trial court clearly erred in finding that the plaintiff had not "intended or expected" volatile organic compounds ("VOCs") to disperse into the groundwater.

The trial record consisted of testimony of numerous former Larco employees who testified that they intentionally dumped VOCs into the drains that led to an unlined seepage lagoon in back of the plant over a 15 year period from 1964 to 1979. Several of these former employees also testified that they had observed other Larco employees doing the same. One of the witnesses testified that he observed a Larco employee deliberately dump about 150 gallons of VOCs directly onto the bare ground behind the plant and another employee deliberately dump VOCs into the drains. Former Larco employees also testified that VOCs were used to mop the plant floor from at least 1964 to 1979, which mopping was often performed on and around the drains which led directly to the lagoon, and that some of the VOCs would invariably go into the drains and be washed into the lagoon. Larco's expert witness testified that during the manufacturing process, VOCs were discharged into the lagoon, and Larco's plant chemist testified that he knew as early as 1972 that VOCs should not be discharged into the unlined lagoon because they would degrade the environment. Nevertheless, Larco's corporate policy had been to require its employees to comply with environmental laws and regulations and notices were posted commencing in 1980 advising employees not to discard chemicals into the drains or on the ground. Further beginning in 1978 Larco had hired a reputable waste hauler to remove all VOCs created in the manufacturing process.

Based on this record, Larco argues that it did not know with substantial certainty that the acts of its employees would result in contamination of the groundwater, and that had it not "intended" or "expected" such contamination to result from its employees' activities.

As a law clerk for an appeals court judge, resolve the question of whether the actions of Larco and its employees constitute an exception to the definition of an occurrence within the standard CGL policy.

2. BODILY INJURY AND EMOTIONAL HARM

What constitutes "bodily injury" within the scope of CGL policies in the toxic tort context raises important coverage questions. The typical policy defines "bodily injury" as "bodily injury, sickness or disease sustained by any person which occurs during the policy period." While insureds generally will take the position that all toxic tort-related damages fall within the bodily injury definition, insurers oppose judicial expansion of the meaning of the term, arguing that the policy language is unambiguous and that its plain meaning is limited to physical injury alone.

A few courts that have addressed the issue of whether claims for emotional distress or mental anguish fall within the bodily injury definition have concluded that they do not. A California appellate court, reading the policy language in its "ordinary sense," held that the term "bodily injury" is unambiguous and, based on various dictionary definitions of the word "bodily," concluded that the term "does not reasonably encompass, and in fact suggests a contrast with, the purely mental, emotional and spiritual." Aim Ins. Co. v. Culcasi, 229 Cal.App.3d 209, 280 Cal.Rptr. 766, 772 (1991); accord Chatton v. National Union Fire Ins. Co., 10 Cal.App.4th 846, 13 Cal.Rptr.2d 318 (1992).

A few courts, however, have concluded that the term "bodily injury" should be construed in its broad sense to encompass claims for emotional distress. For example, the New York Court of Appeals in Lavanant v. General Accident Ins. Co., 79 N.Y.2d 623, 584 N.Y.S.2d 744, 595 N.E.2d 819 (1992) addressed the issue in the context of a ceiling collapse case and concluded that mental injury alone is recoverable. The underlying claimants did not allege any physical injury or property damage based on the insured building owner's alleged tortious acts. The policy at issue defined bodily injury as "bodily injury, sickness or disease." Finding the policy language ambiguous, the court observed that "[t]he categories 'sickness' and 'disease' in the insurer's definition not only enlarge the term 'bodily injury', but also, to the average reader, may include mental as well as physical sickness." Moreover, the insurer could have limited bodily injury by providing for "bodily sickness" or "bodily disease" but did not do so. The court also relied on its analysis of recent case law in New York that allowed recovery for pure emotional distress in other contexts. In light of that development, the court looked to the reasonable expectations of the insured and concluded that:

the reasonable expectation of property owners purchasing a comprehensive policy such as plaintiffs' would be that their liability for purely mental injury would fall within their insurance coverage.

See also Voorhees v. Preferred Mut. Ins. Co., 246 N.J.Super. 564, 588 A.2d 417, 422 (1991) ("mental anguish qualifies as 'bodily injury' at least to the extent that emotional distress alleged does not constitute 'parasitic' damages attached to an independent cause of action").

Still other courts have acknowledged the difficulty in distinguishing between physical and emotional injuries because "there is no bright line separating them." Keating v. National Union Fire Ins. Co., 754 F.Supp. 1431, 1438 (C.D.Cal.1990); See Abellon v. Hartford Ins. Co., 167 Cal. App.3d 21, 212 Cal.Rptr. 852, 855–57 (1985). How would you resolve the question of whether purely emotional distress should be embraced within the "bodily injury" category? What if a state only allows recovery for negligently inflicted distress if it is accompanied by objective physical manifestations? Should fear of future illness be treated differently than other forms of mental distress or anguish? See Techalloy Co. v. Reliance Ins. Co., 338 Pa.Super. 1, 487 A.2d 820 (1984) ("[A]t a minimum, personal injury encompasses allegations of exposure to a hazardous substance, increased risk of injury, anxiety, various internal disorders and tissue damage. * * * "). How should courts analyze claims for increased risk of future disease if that state's courts would recognize such a claim?

3. PROPERTY DAMAGE

In the asbestos context, much litigation has resulted from the costs of removing asbestos-containing materials from the interior of buildings because of the owners' concerns that such materials may pose a risk to the health of occupants. A leading decision that considers whether an insured, who must respond to such claims brought by building owners, can be indemnified under CGL policies on the basis of the property damage clause, is United States Fidelity & Guaranty Co. v. Wilkin Insulation Co., 144 Ill.2d 64, 161 Ill.Dec. 280, 578 N.E.2d 926 (1991). The Illinois Supreme Court's resolution of that issue follows:

> We have reviewed each of the nine underlying complaints pursuant to the liberal duty to defend standard set forth above. Each complaint alleges that asbestos-containing products were installed in the buildings. The complaints further allege that, upon deterioration of the asbestos-containing product itself or upon disturbance from an outside force, asbestos fibers are released into the air. These fibers are extremely durable and lasting. * * * [T]he buildings and their contents (e.g., carpets, upholstery, drapery, etc.) are virtually contaminated or impregnated with asbestos fibers, the presence of which poses a serious health hazard to the human occupants. Finally, under various theories of recovery, the underlying complaints seek damages in the form of the costs of inspecting their buildings and the contents therein for the presence of asbestos

fibers. The complaints further seek to recover from all defendants, including Wilkin, any costs associated with the containment, removal and/or replacement of the asbestos-containing products.

Turning to the definitions of property damage[,] * * * [t]he post–1973 standard form policy * * * defines property damage as:

> (1) physical injury to or destruction of tangible property, which occurs during the policy period, including the loss of use thereof at any time resulting therefrom.

All plaintiffs essentially argue that the underlying complaints do not allege physical injury to tangible property. Rather, plaintiffs contend that the presence of health-threatening, asbestos-containing products results only in intangible economic loss in the form of diminished market values of the buildings.

> This court, however, has already found that asbestos fiber contamination constitutes physical injury to tangible property, i.e., the buildings and their contents. (Board of Education v. A.C. & S., Inc., 546 N.E.2d 580 (Ill.1989)). In *Board of Education*, * * * this court found:

>> [I]t would be incongruous to argue there is no damage to other property when a harmful element exists throughout a building or an area of a building which by law must be corrected * * *. The view that asbestos fibers may contaminate a building sufficiently to allege damage to property has been recently adopted in a number of cases.

> * * *

>> The essence of the allegations [of the complaints] is that the buildings have been contaminated by asbestos to the point where corrective action, under the law, must be taken. Thus, the buildings have been damaged.

In the instant action, the underlying complaints allege that the buildings and the contents therein were contaminated by toxic asbestos fibers. Therefore, the underlying complaints allege physical injury to tangible property. Thus, we find that the underlying complaints allege potentially covered property damage.

Do you agree that property damage existed in these cases? What might motivate the court to find property damage in these asbestos removal cases? How does the threat of bodily injury bear on the resolution of this issue? Does the court sufficiently dispose of the economic loss argument?

A number of decisions that have considered the question have held that contamination of the environment constitutes "property damage" as that term is used in the CGL policies. See A.Y. McDonald Industries, Inc. v. Ins. Co. of North America, 475 N.W.2d 607 (Iowa 1991); Montrose Chem. Corp. of California v. Superior Court, 18 Cal.App.4th 1386, 10 Cal.Rptr.2d 687 (1992), affirmed 6 Cal.4th 287, 24 Cal.Rptr.2d 467, 861 P.2d 1153 (1993) (natural resource damages for injuries to land, water and wildlife sought by CERCLA complaint, as well as response costs, are forms of property damage); Hazen Paper Co. v. U.S. Fidelity & Guaranty Co., 407 Mass. 689, 555 N.E.2d 576 (1990) (contamination of soil and groundwater is "property damage"); Continental Ins. Cos. v. Northeastern Pharmaceutical & Chem. Co., 842 F.2d 977 (8th Cir.1988), cert. denied 488 U.S. 821, 109 S.Ct. 66, 102 L.Ed.2d 43 (1988).

4. TRIGGERS OF COVERAGE FOR BODILY INJURY

In determining whether a particular CGL policy will respond to a given claim requires an initial determination of whether the policy has been "triggered" by the occurrence of an event or loss within the period covered by the policy. Toxic tort and remediation cases present difficult issues of triggering because contamination may go undetected for long periods or diseases characterized by long latency periods may not manifest themselves until long after the defendant's conduct, whether it involved installation of a defective product or the disposal of hazardous substances.

Various theories on how to pinpoint the date or time of an occurrence are currently in debate, including: (1) exposure; (2) injury-in-fact; (3) manifestation or discovery; and (4) triple or continuous trigger. The trigger theory selected can have a significant impact on what policies may cover the loss. For example, over a twenty-five year period an insured might have various carriers, changing each year; if carriers learn, years later, of claims lodged against insureds for their activities undertaken years or decades earlier, one issue will be whether the policy's coverage had been triggered during the finite term of their coverage. As a general rule, carriers on the risk early, but who did not write insurance in the later years, will favor a manifestation theory. Conversely, those who wrote the later years' policies will favor an exposure theory. The respective theories are briefly described below:

a. Exposure

Under this theory, the trigger is the date of the first injurious exposure. The leading case adopting the exposure theory is Insurance Company of North America v. Forty–Eight Insulations, Inc., 633 F.2d 1212, 1217–22 (6th Cir.1980), modified on other grounds 657 F.2d 814 (6th Cir.1981) (en banc), cert. denied 454 U.S. 1109, 102 S.Ct. 686, 70 L.Ed.2d 650 (1981) (applying Illinois and New Jersey law). There, the court rejected the manifestation theory, noting that although keying the ripeness of a claim to the manifestation of diagnosable symptoms of disease may be appropriate for the purposes of statute of limitations questions and protecting the injured claimant, the same policy considerations are not present with regard to the coverage issue:

> A manifestation rule would deny coverage to the insured manufacturer. Moreover, it is the injury and not its discovery that makes the manufacturer liable in the underlying tort suit. As noted above, such

underlying liability should also trigger insurance coverage * * *. Statutes of limitations are meant to protect defendants against stale claims, not bar injured plaintiffs who have acted in good faith. Insurance contracts are meant to cover the insured.

In addition, the *Forty–Eight Insulations* court held that liability should be pro-rated among the various insurers on the risk during the exposure period.

Many other courts have adopted the exposure theory, as illustrated by Jackson Township Municipal Utilities Authority v. Hartford Accident & Indemnity Co., 186 N.J.Super. 156, 451 A.2d 990 (N.J.Super.1982) where it was alleged that the township was negligent in its design and maintenance of a hazardous waste site and residential plaintiffs were exposed to chemicals through ingestion and showering, causing sub-clinical injury and a risk of future disease. The court stated:

> The policy insures against an injury; sub-clinical body or tissue change caused by chemicals is an injury, even though nonobservable. This exposure theory is more easily and equitably applied to a groundwater contamination than manifestation, since plaintiffs here receive money damages for emotional distress, medical surveillance for potential disease, and not the disease itself. Since the disease may never manifest itself, it should be the sub-clinical injury which triggers coverage. Moreover, if we applied the manifestation theory, coverage would be triggered by the fortuitous event of disclosure of the condition, which may depend upon many factors unrelated to the contamination process.

In Lloyd E. Mitchell v. Maryland Casualty Co., 324 Md. 44, 595 A.2d 469 (1991), in a case where the insured was liable for asbestos-related bodily injuries, the Maryland Court of Appeals traced the nature of the asbestos-related diseases. In opting for the exposure theory, and rejecting the manifestation theory which would have resulted in no coverage, the court stressed that "the exposure to asbestos fibers and the inflammatory response of the body to those fibers constitute sub-clinical injuries and disease processes which would be detectable by a pathologist if he could examine the bodily tissue prior to the manifestation of the asbestos related disease." The insurer argued that microscopic subclinical alterations which produce no functional impairment are not bodily injury. The court concluded:

> Considering the plain meaning of the term "bodily injury," as used in the policy, and in light of the medical evidence concerning the development of asbestos-related diseases, we align ourselves with the overwhelming weight of authority in the country and conclude that "bodily injury" occurs when asbestos is inhaled and retained in the lungs. In this regard, for purposes of policy coverage, it is not important that [the experts] may disagree as to the time when the changes in the lungs may be classified as a disease. On the record developed in this case, we conclude that, at a minimum, coverage under the policy to provide a defense and indemnification

of the insured is triggered upon exposure to the insured's asbestos products during the policy period by a person who suffers bodily injury as a result of that exposure. Accordingly, we hold that the trial judge erred in adopting, as the sole trigger of coverage, the "manifestation" theory of coverage, namely, that coverage is not afforded until harm actually becomes manifest.

Would these results be unique to asbestos-related diseases?

b. Manifestation/Discovery

Under the manifestation theory, the occurrence is deemed to take place at the time when the illness or disease is reasonably capable of medical diagnosis i.e., when it manifests itself in diagnosable symptoms of disease. The manifestation theory was applied in an asbestos personal injury action in Eagle–Picher Industries, Inc. v. Liberty Mutual Insurance Co., 829 F.2d 227 (1st Cir.1987). There, the court affirmed the district court's ruling that coverage is triggered "when the asbestos-related disease becomes manifest, as measured by the date of actual diagnosis or, with respect to those cases in which no diagnosis was made prior to death, the date of death." The court concluded that the date of manifestation is when the disease is "reasonably capable of medical diagnosis." The court approved the district court's adoption of a six-year "rollback" theory under which the date of diagnosability is presumed to precede actual diagnosis by six years. The court further noted that the rollback presumption was rebuttable and could be overcome by the insurer's clear and convincing medical evidence that the asbestos-related disease was first reasonably capable of diagnosis at some time outside of the insurer's policy periods. See also Hartford Accident & Indem. Co. v. Aetna Life & Cas. Ins. Co., 98 N.J. 18, 483 A.2d 402 (1984) (ingestion of drug by child); American Motorists Ins. Co. v. E.R. Squibb & Sons, Inc., 95 Misc.2d 222, 406 N.Y.S.2d 658 (1978) (manifestation trigger theory applied in the DES context).

c. Injury-in-Fact

Another theory, although adopted by few courts, is that of injury-in-fact which comes close to the manifestation theory. This theory holds the insurer on the risk when bodily injury first occurs to be liable for coverage, without regard to when the victim may have been exposed or when the disease was first diagnosed. In Continental Casualty Company v. Rapid–American Corporation, 80 N.Y.2d 640, 593 N.Y.S.2d 966, 609 N.E.2d 506 (1993), the New York Court of Appeals impliedly adopted an injury-in-fact rule, describing it as "when the injury, sickness, disease or disability actually began," the "onset of disease, whether discovered or not."

In American Home Products Corporation v. Liberty Mutual Insurance Company, 748 F.2d 760, 764 (2d Cir.1984), another bodily injury asbestos case, the court, applying New York law, held that coverage is triggered when real personal injury first occurs. The Second Circuit affirmed a lower court decision that the trigger-of-coverage clause in a general liability policy unambiguously provides for coverage based upon "the occurrence during the policy period of an injury in fact. We reject only so much of the [lower] court's decision as holds that 'injury in fact' means an injury was 'diagnosable' or 'compensable' during the policy period."

d. Multiple or Continuous Trigger

Under the multiple or continuous trigger theory, any policies in effect from the time of initial exposure to the time of manifestation are on the risk in terms of the duty to defend and indemnify the insured. Because this theory maximizes coverage, it is generally the most favored by insureds. In the landmark case of Keene Corp. v. Insurance Co. of North America, 667 F.2d 1034 (D.C.Cir.1981), cert. denied 455 U.S. 1007, 102 S.Ct. 1645, 71 L.Ed.2d 875 (1982), the court held coverage in bodily injury continuous tort cases is triggered in a manner such that insurance policies in effect during the entire period from first exposure to disease onset had defense and indemnification duties. Coverage was triggered, *Keene* held, throughout the period from the injured person's first exposure to the insured's asbestos, through the period of residence *in situ* of the asbestos fibers, until the asbestos-related disease was diagnosed.

The Pennsylvania Supreme Court in J.H. France Refractories Company v. Allstate Insurance Company, 534 Pa. 29, 626 A.2d 502 (Pa.1993) adopted the multiple trigger approach whereby each insurance policy in force during the course of a continuous injury—from the first exposure to a toxic substance through manifestation of disease symptoms—is triggered and must indemnify the policyholder for any damages caused by the injury. The court said asbestos-related disease is a continuous injury because the fibers begin to harm human tissue upon first exposure, and then cause progressive harm. The court reversed a lower court ruling that held policyholders were required to share indemnity costs for periods of time they were uninsured, finding that such a pro rata apportionment would be inconsistent with the multiple-trigger theory.

Additionally, the court held that once the policy limits of a given insurer are exhausted, the policyholder is free to seek coverage from any of the remaining insurers. The court noted that the insurers are free to seek contribution from each other. Finally, a California appeals court adopted the continuous trigger rule in Armstrong World Industries, Inc. v. Aetna Cas. & Sur. Co., 20 Cal.App.4th 296, 26 Cal.Rptr.2d 35 (1993).

What benefit might *insurers* derive from the continuous trigger approach? Will it depend on how many different insurers wrote policies during the continuous period? How should damages be allocated among different insurers? Is it fair to let the insured select from which insurer it will seek indemnity?

5. TRIGGERS OF COVERAGE FOR PROPERTY DAMAGE

The trigger of coverage in continuing bodily injury cases is not, however, necessarily the trigger in continuing property damage cases. Although several property damage decisions have adopted a continuous trigger theory, controversy exists as to whether the continuous trigger approach is correct in property damage cases. For example, in United States Fidelity & Guaranty Co. v. Thomas Solvent Co., 683 F.Supp. 1139, 1163 (E.D.Mich.1988), a case involving property damage from industrial contamination, the court adopted a hybrid continuous trigger, observing:

> There is no reason why some variation of the "continuous trigger" theory should not be seen as applicable here—at least at this juncture where the facts are quite complex and the issue of precisely when the so-called "continuous occurrences" should be "fixed" is so hotly disputed. Such a "hybrid" continuous trigger theory would clearly require all the insurers to defend where the date upon which the "continuous" damage first occurred has not been settled and/or where continuing exposure (damage) is also alleged. Under such a theory every policy in effect at any time during the (continuous) injury process—from the initial exposure(s) until the last manifest development of bodily injury or property damage would be triggered for coverage.

Ray Industries, Inc. v. Liberty Mutual Insurance Co., 974 F.2d 754 (6th Cir.1992) also rejected uniform application of the manifestation rule. The insured in that case had disposed of some of its waste by trucking it to independently owned landfills. The insured was subsequently named as a potentially responsible party for the cleanup of one of these sites. The court found that, because the insured's waste was "constantly dumped" at the landfill between 1966 and 1979, the insured could look to every policy written during those years for coverage. The court specifically refrained, however, from establishing continuous trigger as a general rule in environmental pollution insurance cases.

What rule makes the most sense in these environmental contamination cases? Should the courts follow the continuous versus permanent nuisance or trespass theory that applied in the statutes of limitation context, using a manifestation or discovery trigger rule in cases of permanent damage, but a continuing trigger in continuing damage cases?

6. NUMBER OF OCCURRENCES

Because waste discharge may occur repeatedly or continuously, a question arises whether one or multiple occurrences have taken place. This distinction becomes important when there is a dollar limit for each occurrence, a deductible for each occurrence, or coverage is provided by more than one policy. See, e.g., Uniroyal Inc. v. Home Ins. Co., 707 F.Supp. 1368, 1382 (E.D.N.Y.1988). *Uniroyal* involved the spraying of

Agent Orange herbicide in Vietnam. The insurer argued that each of tens of thousands of sprayings was a separate occurrence, requiring a separate deductible. The insured argued (and the court found) that there had been only one occurrence with one deductible. The decision includes a thorough survey of the one/multiple occurrence case law.

Most courts determining this issue in a nonenvironmental context agree that the focus should be on the causal event or underlying circumstances, not the number of injuries or claims arising from the event or circumstances. On the other hand, a few courts have calculated the number of occurrences on the basis of *effects*, particularly when the cause has been interrupted.

Applying even the majority test, moreover, can be difficult and lead to apparently inconsistent results. For example, in Michigan Chemical Corp. v. American Home Assurance Co., 728 F.2d 374 (6th Cir.1984), the court found that various shipments of the allegedly defective goods constituted several occurrences; in contrast, separate shipments of Agent Orange were deemed one occurrence in *Uniroyal*, 707 F.Supp. at 1386. In *Uniroyal*, Judge Weinstein tried to reconcile the apparently disparate results in the case law by stating that courts are more likely to find multiple occurrences when there is a small number of events—as opposed to when hundreds or thousands of events are involved.

For an interesting case involving HIV-contaminated blood products, see American Red Cross v. Travelers Indem. Co., 816 F.Supp. 755 (D.D.C.1993), where the insured had been subjected to numerous claims by donees of its blood products. Travelers argued that all the claims combined constituted a single "occurrence," and therefore, fell within the $1 million "per occurrence" liability limit for the policies at issue. The parties agreed that the court should examine the circumstances underlying the claims, rather than the effect of each claimant's injury, to define a single occurrence. Under this analysis, a court asks if there was but one proximate, uninterrupted, and continuing cause that resulted in all of the injuries and damages.

The court held that the facts do not support the suggestion that the Red Cross engaged in a single, negligent practice that could be considered "one cause." Rather, the Red Cross made many decisions regarding its handling of the blood—whether to screen donors, test blood, and provide warnings to recipient hospitals. Therefore, each of these decisions independently may have affected whether bodily injury would result from a given transfusion. Moreover, negligence regarding screening, testing, or notification could not result in injury until a particular unit of contaminated blood was provided to a facility that would administer the transfusion. The court concluded that the proximate cause of the injuries was the distribution of the HIV-tainted blood and that each act of distribution constituted an "occurrence" for purposes of applying the $1 million per occurrence limit.

C. SPECIAL INSURANCE PROBLEMS OF ENVIRONMENTAL CLEANUPS

Most of the insurance questions focused on above arose out of toxic tort bodily injury or property damage claims. Here, in contrast, we focus on insurance problems that are directly related to governmental action, federal or state, pursuant to CERCLA or state-law counterparts. Typically, the insured is required to expend resources remediating a contaminated site, either voluntarily in anticipation of a government mandate that it do so, or in response to a letter or suit from the EPA making such a demand. The property contaminated can be insured's own or, as is required under nearly all CGL policies, that of third parties where the hazardous waste has caused environmental harm.

1. PAY "AS DAMAGES" AND "SUIT" CONTROVERSIES

The "as damages" controversy relates to property damage claims resulting from the release of hazardous substances on property owned by third parties. As noted above, the post–1966 language requires the insurer to pay on behalf of its insured "all sums which the insured shall become legally obligated to pay as damages * * *." Insurers have argued that the term "as damages" means legal damages only and does not include expenses connected with equitable remedies or statutorily-mandated environmental cleanup activities. The issue arises in connection with governmentally-mandated environmental remediation such as orders or actions brought under CERCLA.

Closely related is whether the administrative process pursued by the EPA or an equivalent state environmental agency against an insured qualifies as a "suit" against an insured within the meaning of the CGL policy in which the insurer agrees to indemnify against and defend "any *suit* against the insured seeking damages on account of bodily injury or property damage."

The following decision, Coakley v. Maine Bonding & Casualty Co., 136 N.H. 402, 618 A.2d 777 (1992) represents the trend and majority view on both issues.

COAKLEY v. MAINE BONDING AND CASUALTY COMPANY

Supreme Court of New Hampshire, 1992.
136 N.H. 402, 618 A.2d 777.

JOHNSON, J.

The central issue in this appeal is whether the defendants, Maine Bonding and Casualty Company (Maine Bonding) and St. Paul Fire and Marine Insurance Company (St. Paul), must indemnify the plaintiffs, Ronald C. Coakley and Coakley Landfill, Inc. (collectively, the Coakleys), for environmental "response" costs imposed or likely to be imposed by the United States Environmental Protection Agency (EPA) and the New Hampshire Department of Environmental Services (NHDES) pursuant to the Comprehensive Environmental Response, Compensation, and Liability Act, 42 U.S.C.A. §§ 9601 et seq. (CERCLA), and comparable State statutes (RSA chapter 147–B (1990 & Supp.1991)). The Superior Court granted the defendants' motion for summary judgment below, ruling that the word "damages," found in the granting clause of the defendants' comprehensive general liability policies, does not include these response costs. In addition, the court ruled that the EPA and NHDES demands concerning Coakley Landfill, contained in "notices of potential responsibility" and other letters, are not "suits," and that therefore the defendants are not bound to defend the Coakleys. The Coakleys appeal both rulings and we reverse.

Coakley Landfill, the focal point of this dispute, straddles the border of Greenland and North Hampton. For many years, it accepted municipal and industrial waste from the Portsmouth area, as well as incinerator residue from the Pease Air Force Base. In 1984, the Coakleys were forced to close the landfill after the NHDES discovered contaminants in the area's groundwater and in the wells of neighboring properties. The contamination also forced surrounding municipalities to extend water supply distribution lines to service the residents who had depended on the well-water.

In 1984, the environmental protection division of the State Attorney General's office notified Ronald Coakley that he was "potentially responsible" for the contamination at the Coakley Landfill and asked him to fund and help conduct a "Remedial Investigation/Feasibility Study" (RI/FS) of the site, at an expected cost of at least $500,000. The division warned that "EPA is prepared to initiate the RI/FS process whenever it appears that our cooperative effort will not succeed." It appears that the Coakleys chose not to heed this warning because the EPA eventually conducted an RI/FS itself. The cost of the RI/FS and other landfill-related investigations exceeded $1,225,000.

In September 1987, the EPA sent Ronald Coakley a "Request for Information" about the landfill. The letter stated that compliance with the request was mandatory, and subject to a $25,000 penalty for each day of noncompliance. The record does not disclose whether the Coakleys complied with this "request." * * *

[I]n February 1990, the EPA sent Coakley Landfill, Inc. a "Notice of Potential Liability." The notice warned that, under CERCLA, a potentially responsible party (PRP) could be obligated to (1) "implement relief actions deemed necessary by EPA to protect the public health, welfare or environment"; (2) pay "for all costs incurred by the government in responding to any release or threatened release at the [landfill]"; and (3) "pay damages for injury to, destruction of, or loss of natural resources." * * *

The "response activities" referenced in the EPA's PRP notice consist of "[d]esign and implementation of the Remedial Action selected and approved by EPA for the [landfill]" and "[o]peration, maintenance and monitoring necessary at the [landfill]." As of February 1990, the EPA's proposed "Remedial Action," or "Preferred Alternative," included "placing a cap over the landfill to minimize the migration of contaminants from the landfill" and "collection and treatment of groundwater to remove and prevent further migration of contaminants." This containment and cleanup plan, bearing an estimated cost of $20,200,000, represents a compromise between less expensive, less environmentally protective plans and more costly, more protective ones.

* * *

In the midst of all this agency activity, the Coakleys contacted two of their insurance carriers, Maine Bonding and St. Paul, and requested coverage for any costs they might be forced to bear in connection with the EPA and NHDES demands. The relevant portion of the carriers' comprehensive general liability policies, purchased by the Coakleys, reads as follows: "The Company will pay on behalf of the insured all sums which the insured shall become legally obligated to pay as damages because of A. bodily injury or B. property damage to which this insurance applies, caused by an occurrence, and the Company shall have the right and duty to defend any suit against the insured seeking damages on account of such bodily injury or property damage, even if any of the allegations of the suit are groundless, false or fraudulent, and may make such investigation and settlement of any claim or suit as it deems expedient * * *."

* * *

Maine Bonding and St. Paul each filed motions for summary judgment. St. Paul's motion was confined solely to the two main questions we address here on appeal—the interpretation of the words "damages" and "suit"—and explicitly reserved other, more fact-based coverage issues. The Coakleys objected to both motions on the grounds "that there are genuine issues of material fact as to whether [the carriers] must provide insurance coverage to [the Coakleys] under the terms of its insurance policies and, therefore, [the carriers are] not entitled to judgment as a matter of law." * * * Relying on Desrochers v. Casualty Co., 99 N.H. 129, 106 A.2d 196 (1954), and on dictionary definitions, the superior court granted the carriers' motions for summary judgment and denied the Coakleys' motions. This appeal followed.

The issues presented by the parties on appeal are narrow and limited: 1. Are response costs, including the costs of complying with an injunction and reimbursing the EPA for its expenditures, covered as "damages" by the carriers' insurance policies? 2. Are the EPA's and NHDES's demands "suits" for purposes of triggering the carriers' duty to defend the Coakleys? * * *

Preliminarily to the "damages" issue, we note that the parties and amici curiae have deluged the court with arguments, citations, references, and exhibits. No small forest fell to deliver their contentions to our steps. In particular, counsel have consumed reams of paper in an effort to focus our attention on the workings of the numerous other jurisdictions forced to interpret the term "damages" in the CERCLA context. Neither side of the issue appears to enjoy a clear majority, although state adjudicators evidently tend towards granting coverage. See AIU Ins. Co. v. FMC Corp., 51 Cal.3d 807, 274 Cal.Rptr. 820, 829–30, 799 P.2d 1253, 1262–63 (1990) (citing cases). We acknowledge that the issue before us is in many ways identical to the one decided by these foreign courts, but emphasize that, like those courts, we must decide our case on the basis of State law and State rules of construction. We therefore eschew a detailed survey of out-of-state decisions and instead center our inquiry on our own precedent, using the arguments of other courts only as occasional guides.

The "damages" issue presents a question of contract interpretation, and "[i]n general, the rules governing the construction and interpretation of written contracts apply with equal force to insurance policies. Thus, in interpreting contracts, the fundamental inquiry centers on determining the intent of the parties at the time of agreement. Any determination of intent is generally made by this court." Trombly v. Blue Cross/Blue Shield, 120 N.H. 764, 770, 423 A.2d 980, 984 (1980) (citations omitted). The burden of proof here is on the insurance carrier. RSA 491:22–a.

An insurance contract is interpreted according to state law, and where judicial precedent clearly defines a term at issue, we need look no further than that definition. Cf. 13 J. Appleman & J. Appleman, Insurance Law and Practice § 7404, at 339 (1976) (if policy terms have clear meaning by judicial decision, they are not ambiguous). If no such definition exists and the contract itself contains no explanation of the term, we construe the policy "in the light of what a more than casual reading of the policy would reveal to an ordinarily intelligent insured."

Where the policy's terms are unambiguous, the language "must be accorded its natural and ordinary meaning." Trombly, 423 A.2d at 984. But where the language is ambiguous, and one possible interpretation favors coverage, we resolve the ambiguity in favor of the insured. 423 A.2d at 985. * * *

The reasons for the ambiguity rule are two-fold. First, "it is the insurer who controls the language of the policy and, therefore, any resulting ambiguity should be resolved in favor of the insured." Trombly. Second, "since the object of the contract is to provide protection for the insured, the construction that best achieves this purpose should be adopted." Trombly. The one exception to the rule is that a term in a contract already clearly defined by judicial decision cannot be considered ambiguous. 13 Appleman, supra § 7404, at 339.

Armed with these standards of construction, we proceed with our analysis. We look first to the seminal case of Desrochers v. Casualty Co., 99 N.H. 129, 106 A.2d 196 (1954), as both parties argue that it dispositively defines "damages" in their favor. Desrochers involved an insurance policy with language similar to that at issue here. The underlying dispute arose when the plaintiffs blocked a town culvert, causing the neighboring property to flood. The neighbors sued the plaintiffs, and the plaintiffs were ordered to remove the obstruction and to pay $200 for injury to the flooded property. Although the plaintiffs' insurance carrier agreed to indemnify them for the $200, it refused to pay for the costs of complying with the injunction.

The court decided the case in favor of the insurance carrier, holding that the costs of complying with the injunction did not constitute "damages." "Damages," the court stated, "are recompense for injuries sustained." Desrochers. "They are remedial rather than preventive, and in the usual sense are pecuniary in nature. The expense of restoring the plaintiff's property to its former state will not remedy the injury previously done, nor will it be paid to the injured parties." Furthermore, the court reasoned, "the cost of removing the obstruction has no relation to the amount of damages which might result to adjoining premises if the obstruction should not be removed."

The court also rejected an argument that the injunction was a substitute for future damages, for which the plaintiffs would be liable every time the neighbors' land flooded. "The defendant's [insurance carrier's] liability under [the policy]," the court explained, "is limited to the payment of sums which the plaintiffs became legally obligated to pay while the policy was in effect * * *. Consequently the affirmative relief could not be a 'substitute' for any monetary damages for which the defendant was liable." Desrochers. Based in part on this policy limitation, the court denied coverage.

We find the Desrochers case, a pre-Trombly decision in which the question of ambiguity is never addressed, to be inconclusive authority for the issue before us. Desrochers' definition of "damages" as "recompense for injuries sustained" is far from clear in the context of CERCLA and RSA chapter 147–B response costs. See 13 Appleman, supra § 7404, at 339. Moreover, while some of the statements explaining that definition help the Coakleys' case, others hurt it. For example, the cost of cleaning up the contaminated groundwater is undoubtedly "remedial rather than preventive," Desrochers, as is reimbursement of that portion of the EPA's investigatory costs necessary to a cleanup. The same cannot be said, however, of the proposed containment cap, a predominantly preventive measure, and those investigatory costs related to the cap. Moreover, while reimbursement of response costs is directly "pecuniary in nature," Desrochers, an injunction is not.

In the Coakleys' favor, we note that neither insurance carrier has argued that a policy limitation such as the one used by the Desrochers court could be used here to dispel the argument that the injunction was a substitute for a future damages action. The substitution argument is persuasive here: an EPA injunction to clean up the groundwater is an alternative to a monetary damages action for injury to the groundwater, see 42 U.S.C.A. § 9607(a)(4) (Supp.1992); Desrochers, 106 A.2d at 198–

99, the measure of which would likely be the cost of cleaning up the contamination, see 42 U.S.C.A. § 9607(f)(1) (Supp.1992); Ohio v. United States Dept. of Interior, 880 F.2d 432, 446 (D.C.Cir.1989) (42 U.S.C.A. § 9607(f)(1) "carries in it an implicit assumption that restoration cost will serve as the basic measure of damages in many if not most CERCLA cases").

Similarly, the cost of cleaning up the contamination, including related investigatory costs, is directly related "to the amount of damages which might result" to the groundwater if the groundwater is not cleaned up. Desrochers, 106 A.2d at 199. The damage has already been done to the groundwater, and thus the cost of cleaning it up would likely be the same as the amount of "damages" which have resulted. See 42 U.S.C.A. § 9607(f)(1) (Supp.1992); Ohio v. United States Dept. of Interior, 880 F.2d at 446. The cost of constructing the preventive containment cap and related investigatory costs, however, are not related to the amount of "damages" which have resulted and thus do not easily fit into the Desrochers definition of "damages."

* * *

* * * State v. Charpentier "involve[d] the liability of a landowner * * * for the cost of cleaning a hazardous waste dump located on her property * * *." State v. Charpentier, 126 N.H. 56, 58, 489 A.2d 594, 596 (1985). We stated that "[t]he present action was brought by the State * * * to recover damages for the cost of cleaning up the Gilson Road dump site, which now contains large quantities of hazardous chemical wastes." Throughout the opinion, we referred to the action as one for "damages."

* * *

From the foregoing, it appears that, but for the non-pecuniary nature of an injunction, Desrochers and Charpentier would support coverage for the cost of cleaning up the contaminated groundwater and related investigations, although not for the cost of building the containment cap and its related investigations. See Desrochers, 106 A.2d at 198 ("damages" are "pecuniary in nature"; plaintiffs' injunction not "damages" in part because costs of compliance will not "be paid to the injured parties"). The Desrochers "pecuniary in nature" limitation apparently would allow coverage only if the EPA cleaned up the contaminated groundwater itself and demanded reimbursement from the Coakleys. If the Coakleys, and not the EPA, perform the cleanup, they would pay the costs of the cleanup directly to an engineering firm, instead of indirectly, through the federal and State governments.

We reject as specious this distinction between direct and indirect payment. It should make no difference in terms of insurance coverage whether the engineering firms hired to clean up the polluted groundwater receive their money from the Coakleys or from the federal or State government. Direct payment is in a "real sense equivalent" to indirect payment, see Desrochers, 106 A.2d at 199, because either way, the damage to the groundwater is repaired. Moreover, if we were to allow coverage only when the EPA performs the cleanup, we would encourage parties such as the Coakleys to ignore EPA cleanup demands and court injunctions, at an added cost to the environment, the insurance companies, and the public. See, e.g., AIU, 274 Cal.Rptr. at 845, 799 P.2d at 1278.

We disapprove the apparent distinction found in Desrochers between direct and indirect payment, and find that the case, along with Charpentier, otherwise supports coverage of remedial, though not preventive, response costs, including reimbursement of investigatory costs related to the cleanup. We acknowledge that Desrochers does not clearly define the terms at issue, however. Cf. 13 Appleman, supra § 7404, at 339. We therefore proceed for additional support to examine the insurance policies, which themselves contain no definition of "damages," for the term's plain and ordinary meaning. See Trombly, 423 A.2d at 984.

The insurance carriers, Maine Bonding and St. Paul, insist that the plain and ordinary meaning of the word "damages," as found in their insurance policies, includes neither injunctive relief nor restitution, such as reimbursement of the money spent on investigative costs. We disagree. As Maine Bonding argues in its brief, the distinctions among "legal damages," "injunctive relief," and "restitution" are alive and well in the legal field, and are probably still taught in remedies courses in most American law schools. The average insured, however, has not attended law school, much less a law school remedies class. To discover the plain and ordinary meaning of "damages" in the absence of a clear definition from Desrochers or the insurance policies, we turn not to the distillation of a law student after a semester's worth of course work, but to the word's plain and ordinary meaning as understood by a layperson of average intelligence. See Trombly, 423 A.2d at 984.

Webster's defines "damages" as "the estimated reparation in money for detriment or injury sustained: compensation or satisfaction imposed by law for a wrong or injury caused by a violation of a legal right." Webster's Third New International Dictionary 571 (unabridged ed. 1961) (Webster's). This definition is similar to the one found in Desrochers, 106 A.2d at 198 ("recompense for injuries sustained"), and is just as unhelpful in the CERCLA and RSA chapter 147–B context. The distinctions among injunctive relief, restitution, and traditional legal damages that the carriers insist are so obvious here elude us. * * *

* * * The first part of the dictionary definition of "damages," "reparation in money," excludes injunctive relief by its very terms, but the second part does not. Webster's, supra at 571. To the extent there is any conflict between the two or ambiguity, we must of course accept the interpretation that affords coverage. Consequently, we focus our attention on the second part of the definition—compensation or satisfaction imposed by law for a legal injury.

An EPA-ordered cleanup injunction, as well as reimbursement of related investigatory costs, easily fit this second part of the definition.

They both qualify as the discharge of a legal obligation, and they both make up, or make good, for the legal injury the Coakleys are accused of committing—the contamination of the groundwater. If an administrative order requires the Coakleys to both comply with such an injunction and reimburse the EPA for its investigatory costs, the order will be "compensation or satisfaction imposed by law."

It follows then that cleanup costs and reimbursement for related investigatory costs satisfy the plain and ordinary definition of "damages." If insurance carriers wish to limit coverage to non-injunctive, non-restitutionary costs, they are free to do so in plain, intelligible language.

On the other hand, containment costs, including related investigatory costs, do not fit the definition because they are not "compensation or satisfaction imposed by law for a wrong or injury caused by a violation of a legal right." The hazardous waste sought to be contained within the landfill has not yet injured the groundwater. The containment plan is thus essentially preventive and, as Desrochers explained, "damages" are "remedial rather than preventive," Desrochers, 106 A.2d at 198.

The carriers argue that our interpretation of "damages" in essence reads the word right out of the insurance policy, making it mere surplusage. Our resolution of the issue, they insist, makes an insurance carrier responsible for payment of all sums an insured is legally obligated to pay, not just those which the insured is obligated to pay as "damages." We disagree. Our determination does not strip the word "damages" of all meaning; to the contrary, it refines the definition to include only those costs which are remedial, not preventive. Moreover, we have already stated in the insurance context that "damages" may exclude interest. * * *

The carriers also contend that CERCLA itself distinguishes between "damages" and injunctive relief or restitution, thus supporting the argument that the word "damages" excludes the costs of complying with an injunction or reimbursing the EPA. See, e.g., 42 U.S.C.A. §§ 9607(i), 9613(a) (1983 & Supp.1992). We reject this contention for two reasons. First, assuming arguendo that the parties could have foreseen the passage of CERCLA, we cannot believe that any of them divined the wording of the statute at the time they signed the insurance policy. Second, we decide an insurance dispute on the basis of State law, and State rules of construction, not on the basis of federal law. CERCLA may be the immediate source of this controversy, but its use of the word "damages" has nothing to do with our interpretation of the word found in the insurance policies at issue here.

We next turn to the question whether Maine Bonding and St. Paul must defend the Coakleys against the actions of the EPA and NHDES. The carriers argue that there is no duty to defend because none of the agency actions to date initiated a "suit" within the meaning of the word as it appears in the insurance policies. There are no cases in New Hampshire in point, and therefore we turn to the language of the policy to determine its plain and ordinary meaning. As the carriers point out, while the policies do not define "suit," they do distinguish between "claim" and "suit," requiring a defense only in the case of a "suit." Therefore, their argument goes, a "suit" must be more than a "claim." We have no quarrel with this reasoning, but cannot agree that the agency actions here are necessarily merely "claims" and, thus, not subject to the defense requirement.

To determine the plain and ordinary meaning of the word "suit," as understood by a layperson of average intelligence, we look again to the dictionary. Webster's gives several definitions for the word, the two most relevant being: (1) "the attempt to gain an end by legal process: prosecution of a right before any tribunal"; and (2) "an action or process in a court for the recovery of a right or claim: a legal application to a court for justice." Webster's, supra at 2286. If the agency actions fit either of these definitions, then our ambiguity rule requires that we hold in favor of the Coakleys.

A close look at the EPA's PRP notice, as well as relevant portions of CERCLA, reveals an agency action that fits the first definition above. The PRP notice, like a civil complaint, alerted the Coakleys that the EPA had begun a legal process to conclusively and legally determine, subject only to review for abuse of discretion, see 42 U.S.C.A. §§ 9604(c)(4), 9613(j)(2), 9621 (Supp.1992), the appropriate "response activities" liable parties must perform or pay for to abate the pollution at Coakley Landfill. This determination is akin to the determination of "damages" in a tort suit.

While it is true that the PRP notice does not purport to establish the Coakleys' liability for the pollution, CERCLA liability is strict and has few exceptions. See 42 U.S.C.A. § 9607 (Supp.1992). The predominant question under CERCLA is not whether a PRP is liable, but rather for how much. One would not expect a traditional tort defendant to concede the "damages" portion of a case, and it likewise would be myopic to conclude that the Coakleys' rights are not substantially determined by the administrative process described in the PRP notice. See id. We therefore find that the EPA's action fits the first definition of "suit" listed above. As the process falls within one possible meaning of the word "suit," we interpret it as such and need not examine the second definition described above.

The NHDES administrative order, compelling Ronald Coakley to perform certain remedial tasks, also satisfies the "suit" requirement. It hardly needs saying that an administrative order manifests an "attempt to gain an end by legal process." Webster's, supra at 2286. Administrative proceedings are the equivalent of court proceedings for purposes of the "suit" requirement, see 7C J. Appleman, Insurance Law and Practice § 4682, at 25 (W. Berdal ed., 1979), and an administrative order quite obviously indicates that an administrative proceeding is under way.

* * *

For the foregoing reasons, we hold that remedial, "response" costs, imposed by the EPA under CERCLA and by the NHDES under RSA chapter 147–B (1990 & Supp.1991), including the costs of complying with a cleanup injunction and reimbursing the EPA for related investigatory costs, are "damages" for purposes of coverage under the carriers' comprehensive general liability and excess liability policies. Although it appears from the record before us that certain costs, such as the cost of constructing the containment cap, do not fall within the definition of "damages," while other costs do, we recognize that these issues were not directly argued or decided in the superior court. Given the procedural posture of this case, we do not here finally determine whether any particular cost constitutes "damages" as we have defined them in this opinion; we leave such disputes to be resolved in the first instance by the superior court. Further, we hold that the EPA's PRP notice and the NHDES's administrative order satisfied the policies' "suit" requirement. We remand for proceedings consistent with this opinion.

Reversed and remanded.

Opinion of BROCK, C.J., dissenting is omitted.

Notes and Questions

1. Many of the decisions which have held against the insured on the "as damages" question have relied upon *Desrochers*, which the New Hampshire Supreme Court has now distinguished. The leading decisions finding remediation costs are not covered come from two federal appellate courts interpreting state law: Continental Ins. Cos. v. Northeastern Pharmaceutical and Chemical Co., 842 F.2d 977 (8th Cir.1988), cert. denied 488 U.S. 821, 109 S.Ct. 66, 102 L.Ed.2d 43 (1988) ("*NEPACCO* "); Maryland Casualty Co. v. Armco, Inc., 643 F.Supp. 430, 434 (D.Md.1986), affirmed 822 F.2d 1348 (4th Cir.1987), cert. denied 484 U.S. 1008, 108 S.Ct. 703, 98 L.Ed.2d 654 (1988). The *Armco* decision has been repudiated by the Court of Appeals of Maryland, Bausch & Lomb v. Utica Mutual Ins. Co., 330 Md. 758, 625 A.2d 1021 (1993). What about the court's distinction between remediation costs, which are covered, and preventative or containment costs, which are not? Is that a logical basis upon which to allocate total costs associated with environmental cleanups?

2. A substantial and growing body of law supports the view taken in *Coakley* that cleanup costs are within the ambit of the CGL's policy "pay as damages" provision. The California Supreme Court unanimously held that government-ordered cleanup costs are "damages" covered by CGL insurance policies. AIU Insurance Co. v. Superior Court, 51 Cal.3d 807, 274 Cal.Rptr. 820, 799 P.2d 1253 (1990). The court ruled that policy language should be construed according to the mutual intentions of the parties and its plain and ordinary meaning, explicitly rejecting the holdings in *Armco* and *NEPACCO* and also agreed with *Coakley* that the costs of preventative actions were not covered. The earliest and most influential of the pro-insurance decisions was United States Aviex Co. v. Travelers Insurance Co., 125 Mich.App. 579, 336 N.W.2d 838 (1983).

3.   The decisions in *Armco* and *NEPACCO* involve federal courts interpreting *state* law; the construction of insurance contracts is governed by state law, not the federal law which controls in CERCLA cases. Although state supreme courts did not decide the "damages" issue during the 1980s, many would later do so. These state decisions stand in contrast to the more closely divided prior predictions of state law outcomes as they emerged from the federal circuits that have ruled on the question. Most of the state supreme courts to decide the damages issue have ruled in favor of policyholders. In addition to *Coakley* and *AIU*, see, e.g., A.Y. McDonald Ind., Inc. v. Insurance Co. of North America, 475 N.W.2d 607 (Iowa 1991); Boeing Co. v. Aetna Casualty & Surety Co., 113 Wash.2d 869, 784 P.2d 507 (1990) (en banc); Hazen Paper Co. v. U.S. Fidelity & Guaranty Co., 407 Mass. 689, 555 N.E.2d 576 (1990); Minnesota Mining & Mfg. Co. v. Travelers Indem. Co., 457 N.W.2d 175 (Minn.1990).

4.   See Stephen Mountainspring, Insurance Coverage of CERCLA Response Costs: The Limits of "Damages" in Comprehensive General Liability Policies, 16 Ecology L.Q. 755, 801 (1989), where the author supports the outcomes finding "damages" by focusing on market principles:

> In balancing the social usefulness of a strong insurance industry against the interests of insured parties in receiving the (unanticipated) benefits of their policies, the judicial view sees each insurance contract as an isolated transaction, and from this perspective, law and equity favor the insured. From a societal viewpoint, insurance companies are independent enterprises performing a valuable function. While we might think of insurance companies as free market entities, in reality because of extensive government regulation, coverage is assured even if the insurance company becomes bankrupt. As a societal issue, insurance coverage of CERCLA response cost claims should not be seen as an impediment to the industry's vitality. Rather, coverage will lead to more expensive insurance, to the bankruptcy of inefficient or unfortunate companies, and perhaps to some extent to the government subsidization of involuntary insurance guaranty associations. These phenomena are part of a free market, of evolution toward greater economic efficiency. Concerns that insurance industry vitality will be diminished are inconsistent with a free market viewpoint, even if it leads us to new vistas of self-insurance, risk retention mechanisms, or government insurance agencies. To this extent, the argument that the narrow definition of damages is necessary to maintain the position of the insurance industry is founded on specious premises, for it assumes a superior right of economic existence of insurance companies over other enterprises. Thus, in balancing the insured's interests against the insurer's on this issue, societal interests are best served by focusing on the insurance contract's legal implication per se, without additionally considering the impact on the social functions of the present insurance system.

Do you agree with the author?

5.   *What is a "Suit"?* The holding in *Coakley* on the "suit" issue also seems to be the emerging view favoring insureds. Should a PRP letter be

treated differently than a § 106 order?[1] Must the PRP letter contain an immediate threat of liability?

If the § 106 proceeding is adjudicatory, seeks damages, or affects the conduct of the insured, should the duty to defend be triggered? How about if the insured voluntarily agrees to participate in a remediation investigation and feasibility study?

If voluntary actions result in a determination of no "suit," does that encourage insureds to "fight" rather than settle? See Aetna Cas. & Sur. Co. v. Pintlar Corp., Gulf Resources & Chem. Co., 948 F.2d 1507 (9th Cir.1991), concluding that because a PRP's substantive rights and ultimate liability are affected from the start of the administrative process, and the ordinary person receiving such a notice would believe that it was the commencement of a suit, coverage was triggered.

2. SUDDEN AND ACCIDENTAL POLLUTION EXCLUSION

The insurance industry first inserted a pollution exclusion into the standard CGL policy in 1970. This exclusion is known as the "standard" or "sudden and accidental" exclusion and was used until 1985. The exclusion provides:

> This policy does not apply to bodily injury or property damage arising out of the discharge, dispersal, release or escape of smoke, vapors, soot, fumes, acids, alkalines, toxic chemicals, liquids or gases, waste materials, or other irritants, contaminants or pollutants into or upon land, the atmosphere or any water course or body of water; but this exclusion does not apply if such discharge, dispersal, release or escape is sudden and accidental.

This exclusion has given rise to at least three interpretative issues in toxic tort and remediation litigation: (1) whether the dispersal, release or escape of pollutants was "sudden and accidental"; (2) whether the substance released was a "pollutant" within the clause; and (3) whether the substance was released "into or upon land [or] the atmosphere."

a. *Sudden and Accidental Exception to the Pollution Exclusion*

Courts addressing the so-called sudden and accidental pollution exclusion have been required to determine whether the discharge, dispersal, release or escape is sudden and accidental, and therefore, not excluded from coverage. Most of the decisional law addressing this question has arisen in the context of environmental insurance coverage litigation involving property damage. The courts are split on the meaning of the "sudden and accidental" clause. Some courts, finding the clause to be clear and unambiguous, have concluded that for coverage to

---

1. A § 106 order is an administrative order issued by the EPA pursuant to CERCLA § 106, 42 U.S.C.A. § 9606, following an administrative proceeding and may require the policyholder to conduct a cleanup or require other remedial steps. Failure to comply may result in liability for EPA's costs of cleanup, plus treble damages.

exist, the discharge, dispersal or release must be both sudden, defined in the temporal sense meaning instantaneous or abrupt, and accidental, defined as unexpected and unintended. Thus, according to these courts, no coverage exists for gradual releases.

Other courts, finding the clause to be ambiguous because the term "sudden" is susceptible to more than one reasonable interpretation, have concluded that the "sudden and accidental" language is merely a restatement of the occurrence definition and means only "unexpected and unintended." Many early cases construed this exclusion to be co-extensive with the definition of "occurrence" so that, in practice, the exclusion excluded few pollution-related claims. This trend began with the New Jersey decision of Lansco v. Department of Environmental Protection, 138 N.J.Super. 275, 350 A.2d 520, 524 (1975), affirmed 145 N.J.Super. 433, 368 A.2d 363 (1976), cert. denied 73 N.J. 57, 372 A.2d 322 (1977).

An Illinois Supreme Court decision summarizes the logic of the interpretation favoring insureds. In Outboard Marine Corp. v. Liberty Mutual Insurance Co., 154 Ill.2d 90, 180 Ill.Dec. 691, 607 N.E.2d 1204 (1992), the court, in reversing a lower court, held that the pollution exclusion for costs of responding to pollution that is not "sudden and accidental" is ambiguous, and thus that coverage exists even for pollution that occurs in a gradual fashion. In that action, the EPA and the State of Illinois brought suit against Outboard Marine for the discharge of toxic PCBs into Lake Michigan during the period from 1959 until 1972. As to the issue of the pollution exclusion, the Illinois Supreme Court stated:

> We find that the term "sudden" as used in the pollution exclusion exception contained in these * * * policies is ambiguous * * *.
>
> Numerous dictionaries define "sudden" as happening unexpectedly, without notice or warning, or unforeseen. These same dictionaries also define "sudden" as abrupt, rapid, or swift. * * * Courts throughout the country are divided on the meaning of "sudden" within the instant context. * * * We conclude that the two definitions of "sudden" as set forth above are both reasonable interpretations of this term in the context in which it appears. Therefore, sudden is, at a minimum, ambiguous as used in these policies. In Illinois, ambiguities and doubts in insurance policies are resolved in favor of the insured, especially those that appear in exclusionary clauses. * * * Consequently, in this particular context, we construe "sudden" in favor of OMC and find it to mean unexpected or unintended. * * *
>
> In addition, * * * construing "sudden" to mean "abrupt" creates a contradiction within this particular clause and the policy as a whole.
>
> * * * The pollution exclusion retriggers coverage for toxic releases which are "sudden and accidental." The policy defines "accident" to include "continuous or repeated exposure to conditions."

* * * To construe "sudden" to mean "abrupt" results in a contradiction if one accepts the insurers' own definition of the term "accident." * * * Such a construction would result in the pollution exception clause retriggering coverage for toxic releases which are "abrupt" *and* gradual or "continuous and repeated" releases. Clearly, under such a construction this clause would be rendered absurd.

Other courts have interpreted "sudden" differently and have found that, for a release or discharge of hazardous waste to be sudden within the meaning of the pollution exclusion, it must occur abruptly or quickly or over a short period of time. They have given "sudden" a temporal meaning, rather than interpreting it as "unexpected" and found the term "sudden" to be unambiguous. See, e.g., Borg–Warner Corp. v. Insurance Co. of North America, 174 A.D.2d 24, 577 N.Y.S.2d 953 (1992); Technicon Electronics Corp. v. American Home Assurance Co., 141 A.D.2d 124, 533 N.Y.S.2d 91 (1988); Upjohn Co. v. New Hampshire Ins. Co., 438 Mich. 197, 476 N.W.2d 392, 397 (1991) ("The term 'sudden,' when considered in its plain and easily understood sense, is defined with a temporal element that joins together conceptually the immediate and unexpected; the common everyday understanding of the term 'sudden' is happening, coming, made or done quickly without warning or unexpectedly, abrupt; and 'accidental' means occurring unexpectedly and unintentionally, by chance."); Lumbermens Mut. Cas. Co. v. Belleville Indus., Inc., 407 Mass. 675, 555 N.E.2d 568 (1990). Dimmitt Chevrolet Inc. v. Southeastern Fidelity Ins. Corp., 636 So.2d 700 (Fla. 1993) (court holds 5 to 4 that the drafting history of the sudden and accidental exception is immaterial because the language is clear; while "sudden" standing alone could connote unexpected, when it is joined by the conjunctive with "accidental," it would be redundant to give it the same meaning).

Does the nearly even split in decisions itself constitute proof of the existence of ambiguity?

Several courts have focused on the drafting history of the sudden and accidental clause. The definition of "occurrence" was added in 1966 to include unexpected and unintended damage, and explicitly provided that occurrence includes "continuous or repeated exposure to conditions." The pollution exclusion was designed to re-emphasize that distinction by eliminating coverage for deliberate and intentional pollution, but continuing to cover damage from gradual, unintended, "accidental" pollution. See American Home Prods. Corp. v. Liberty Mut. Ins. Co., 565 F.Supp. 1485, 1500–03 (S.D.N.Y.1983), affirmed as modified 748 F.2d 760 (2d Cir.1984) (discussing drafting history and background of the standard CGL policy); Joy Technologies Inc. v. Liberty Mut. Ins. Co., 187 W.Va. 742, 421 S.E.2d 493 (1992). For example, the New Jersey Supreme Court has ruled that insurers are estopped from arguing that the qualified pollution exclusion clause bars costs for cleaning up gradual environmental contamination because the industry should not be rewarded for "misrepresentation and nondisclosure" to state regulatory authorities. Morton International, Inc. v. General Accident Ins. Co. of

America, 134 N.J. 1, 629 A.2d 831 (1993). The court found that the insurance industry "knowingly misstated [the exclusion's] intended effect" in 1970 when it sought to have state insurance regulators approve the new policy language. It concluded:

> We hold that notwithstanding the literal terms of the standard pollution-exclusion clause, that clause will be construed to provide coverage identical with that provided under the prior occurrence-based policy, except that the clause will be interpreted to preclude coverage in cases in which the *insured* intentionally discharges a known pollutant, irrespective of whether the resulting property damage was intended or expected. (emphasis in original).

See generally 10A Couch, Couch on Insurance 2d § 42:396 (rev. ed. 1983).

The exclusion has also been applied in toxic tort and product cases. See, for example, Techalloy Co. v. Reliance Ins. Co., 338 Pa.Super. 1, 487 A.2d 820, 827 (1984) in which the court found no duty to defend where the claimant's injuries resulted from exposure to toxic substances that the insured sporadically discharged over a 25–year period. The court concluded that the "allegations disclosing the circumstances and nature of the chemical discharge explicitly negate any potential for finding a sudden event in order to render the exclusion inapplicable."

Park–Ohio Industries Inc. v. The Home Indemnity Co., 975 F.2d 1215 (6th Cir.1992) held that the pollution exclusion could operate to bar coverage for injuries caused by allegedly defective products. In *Park–Ohio* the insured sought coverage for claims arising from the manufacture of induction furnaces, an allegedly defective product. The furnaces allegedly released rubber combustion products which were inhaled by workers and caused bodily injury. The insured argued that the pollution exclusion should not apply in products liability cases where the insured was not actively engaged in the discharge of the pollutants at issue or did not discharge the pollutants on its premises. The Sixth Circuit rejected these arguments: "The 'discharge' applies to any discharge, and there is nothing in the facts of this case which bring into question the meaning of 'the discharge' or who must make the discharge. In a sense, the pollution exclusion follows the product, as do all the terms of the policy."

Problem

In 1965, the Ciamarataro Brothers (the Brothers) established an open dump at the East Columbia landfill site in Tonka County. At that time, the Brothers believed the soil underlying a dump or landfill would act as a filter to prevent pollutants from migrating into and contaminating the groundwater. The landfill, as an open dump, received film and photo processing chemicals, oil filters containing waste oil, asphalt and solvents, paint, ink, liquid ether, foundry slag, asphalt tar, roofing materials, waste ash, kerosene, oil-soaked rags, cleaning solvents and dry cleaning solvents.

In 1970, because of the potential for causing groundwater problems, both the Columbia Pollution Control Agency (CPCA) and Tonka County adopted regulations prohibiting the acceptance of toxic and hazardous waste by landfills. Following promulgation of these regulations, the Brothers operated the East Columbia site as one of the state's first sanitary landfills. In 1974, East Columbia became a "modified sanitary" landfill, accepting only demolition fill, certain waste generated by companies involved in the construction industry, and municipal solid waste brought by individuals living in the area. The landfill is currently operated as a modified sanitary/demolition landfill.

In 1980, Tonka County hired an engineering firm to evaluate data collected from the testing of groundwater at four of the county's landfill sites. The firm's evaluation concluded that there existed extensive groundwater contamination at East Columbia. The CPCA notified the Brothers that they would be regarded as a potentially responsible party for purpose of studying and remediating the groundwater contamination. In 1985, the Brothers and the CPCA entered into a consent decree which made them responsible for all costs involved in the investigation and cleanup of groundwater contamination at East Columbia. The Brothers have instituted a declaratory judgment action against their insurers under policies which contain the standard pollution exclusion with the "sudden and accidental" exception to the exclusion. The Brothers maintain that the exception is satisfied because, by looking at individual releases, by each chemical, they are sudden, not gradual. The State of Columbia Supreme Court has previously held that "sudden" has a temporal meaning, implying "abrupt, quickly or over a short period of time."

The defendant insurers move for summary judgment on the grounds that no genuine factual issue exists as to the gradual nature of the contamination, and that they are therefore entitled to a judgment in their favor as a matter of law. An affidavit from one of the plaintiff's experts counters that there are, indeed, triable issues of fact, for it may be feasible to determine for many of the chemicals the proximity of the releases in time and space, the number of releases and the mechanism of the release, thus enabling a jury to determine if individual releases were "sudden." For the landfill's later period of operation commencing in 1974 during which the waste was limited to the sanitary landfill, another of plaintiffs' experts has given an affidavit stating that it is "normally possible to make an estimate of the timing of the discharge, at least for certain substances." The affidavit states further that the contamination that continues to the present time is caused by materials that were disposed of at the landfill over 20 years ago.

Based upon this record, can the insurers motion be granted?

b.   Does the Claim Involve Release of a "Pollutant" into the Atmosphere?

In Olin Corp. v. Insurance Co. of North America, 762 F.Supp. 548 (S.D.N.Y.1991), the court rejected the insured's argument that the exclusion did not apply because the alleged pollutant, DDT, was its own "product." The court concluded that "the same substance may be a useful product when employed for its intended purpose and yet still be a pollutant when inappropriately introduced into the environment." See also Weber v. IMT Ins. Co., 462 N.W.2d 283 (Iowa 1990) (hog manure "unambiguously constitutes waste" when it is spilled on the road).

However, numerous other decisions have declined to apply the exclusion in the toxic products setting. In Continental Casualty Co. v. Rapid–American Corp., 80 N.Y.2d 640, 593 N.Y.S.2d 966, 609 N.E.2d 506 (1993), the New York Court of Appeals held that the clause "is ambiguous with regard to whether the asbestos fibers at issue—fibers inhaled by persons working closely with or suffering long term exposure to asbestos products—were discharged into the 'atmosphere' as contemplated by the exclusion." It observed that the terms "discharge" and "dispersal" coupled with the three places of discharge—into or upon land, the atmosphere, and bodies of water—"support the conclusion that the clause was meant to deal with broadly dispersed environmental pollution * * * not the confined environs of the present complaints." Accord, U.S. Fidelity & Guaranty Co. v. Wilkin Insulation Co., 144 Ill.2d 64, 161 Ill.Dec. 280, 578 N.E.2d 926 (1991) (asbestos exposure); Atlantic Mut. Ins. Co. v. McFadden, 413 Mass. 90, 595 N.E.2d 762 (1992) (rejecting application of exclusion where underlying complaint alleged bodily injuries caused by exposure to lead paint because the term "pollutant" did not embrace such products, nor was the product dispersed into the atmosphere).

In a case involving injuries from inhalation of a sprayed insecticide, one federal trial court declined to apply the exclusion and drew a distinction between pollutants and products:

> [T]here is virtually no substance or chemical in existence that would not irritate or damage some person or property. The terms "irritant" or "contaminant," however, cannot be read in isolation, but must be construed as substances generally recognized as polluting the environment. In other words, a "pollutant" is not merely any substance that may cause harm to the "egg shell plaintiff," but rather it is a toxic or particularly harmful material which is recognized as such in industry or by governmental regulators.

Westchester Fire Ins. Co. v. City of Pittsburg, 768 F.Supp. 1463 (D.Kan. 1991). Which is the better interpretation of pollutant—to include otherwise useful products or to apply the *Westchester* analysis? See generally Seth A. Ribner, Modern Environmental Insurance Law: "Sudden and Accidental", 63 St. John's L. Rev. 755 (1989), which concluded:

> The contract analysis that judges perform in insurance coverage disputes is familiar and routine. However, in high-stakes, highly charged environmental coverage litigation, courts applying the same general principles often do not agree. At best, the disagreements reflect legitimate differences of opinion. At worst, as in New York and Illinois, competing courts ignore the precedents that supposedly bind them. One immediate result of all this was that in 1986 ISO (the Insurance Services Office) extensively revised the standard CGL

policy, which among other changes, includes a sweeping pollution exclusion that eliminates the "sudden and accidental" exception. However, because pollution damage frequently happens over long periods of time and is often not discovered until long after the pollution begins, pre–1986 policies will be litigated well into the next century. In the end, if things continue as they are, the process of case-by-case adjudication will yield a rough justice with insurers and industry each paying a share of the daunting tab for cleaning up the environment.

For the present, the disarray in the judiciary, which makes every case a potential winner, only encourages more litigation. But before they enter the fray both insurers and insureds should take pause. Only fools fight in a burning house.

3. ABSOLUTE POLLUTION EXCLUSION

In 1986 the insurance industry expanded the pollution exclusion as part of an overall revision of the CGL policy. The 1986 standard policy excludes from coverage:

(1) "Bodily injury" or "property damage" arising out of the actual, alleged or threatened discharge, dispersal, release or escape of pollutants:

    (a) At or from premises you own, rent or occupy;

    (b) At or from any site or location used by or for you or others for the handling, storage, disposal, processing or treatment of waste;

    (c) Which are at any time transported, handled, stored, treated, disposed of, or processed as waste by or for you or any person or organization for whom you may be legally responsible;

* * *

(2) Any loss, cost, or expense arising out of any governmental direction or request that you test for, monitor, clean up, remove, contain, treat, detoxify or neutralize pollutants.

Pollutants mean any solid, liquid, gaseous or thermal irritant or contaminant, including smoke, vapor, soot, fumes, acids, alkalis, chemicals and waste. Waste includes materials to be recycled, reconditioned or reclaimed.

In sum, the revised provision excludes coverage of injury or damage *arising from* an actual or threatened release of "pollutants" (a) at or from the policyholder's owned premises or site of ongoing operations using the pollutants, or (b) from the policyholder's "waste" (wherever it is located). The exclusion also precludes coverage of any expenses arising out of governmental requests to monitor or clean up "pollutants." Virtually every court which has addressed the meaning of the "absolute" pollution exclusion has held, on summary judgment, that the exclusion was clear and unambiguous, and thus, precluded insurance coverage. See, e.g., Smith v. Hughes Aircraft Co. Corp., 783 F.Supp. 1222 (D.Ariz. 1991); Ascon Properties, Inc. v. Illinois Union Ins. Co., 908 F.2d 976 (9th Cir.1990), opinion at 1990 WL 98860 (interpreting California law); E.I. du Pont de Nemours & Co. v. Admiral Ins. Co., 1990 WL 140100 (Del.Super.1990); Vantage Development Corp. v. American Envt. Technologies Corp., 251 N.J.Super. 516, 598 A.2d 948 (1991); Colonial Tanning Corp. v. Home Indem. Co., 780 F.Supp. 906 (N.D.N.Y.1991).

Despite the seeming clarity of the exclusion, one author has concluded that one may anticipate courts finding coverage. See generally Burke, Pollution Exclusion Clauses: The Agony, the Ecstasy, and the Irony for Insurance Companies, 17 N. Ky. L. Rev. 443, 471 (1990), where the writer states:

> The history of pollution insurance has been marked with attempts to provide coverage, and then repeated attempts to severely limit that coverage. The 1973 pollution exclusion succeeded somewhat in restricting pollution coverage, but not until after 13 years of judicial interpretation did its restrictions begin to have some effect. The irony for the insurance industry is that it had ditched the 1973 pollution exclusion by the time most courts had begun giving it at least some of the force and effect that the insurers had sought from the beginning.

> That effect, of course, had been mixed. Federal courts are much more likely to restrict coverage and a duty to defend under the 1973 pollution exclusion, but they also are following the majority rule of a fact-specific analysis of what the insured business intended or expected, or knew or should have known. The result has been cases almost evenly split regarding landfills, underground pipes and storage tanks, and pollution that was a continuous part of regular business practices. Coverage and a duty to defend are less likely to be granted for continuous industrial pollution, while insurers are more likely to lose cases involving leaks from underground tanks and pipes.

> Given the millions of dollars at stake in hundreds of pollution cases across the country, it is uncertain whether the courts will give a restrictive reading to the 1985 pollution exclusion. Ample evidence exists, however, to support the thesis that insurance companies and their clients will endure the same sorting-out period with the next exclusion as they had to experience with the old one. The new exclusion proscribes many types of coverage, but enough ambiguities exist to provide at least several instances of coverage that the insurers may never have intended.

What kinds of contamination-related injuries can you identify that would not be within the scope of the exclusion? See Pipefitters Welfare Educational Fund v. Westchester Fire Ins. Co., 976 F.2d 1037 (7th Cir.1992), where insured was sued in a toxic tort suit arising from PCB-laden oils that injured an employee of a scrap metal dealer who received electrical transformers from the insured. The court held that an insurer with an absolute pollution exclusion clause had no duty to defend or indemnify because the transfer of the transformer for scrap was "waste" and the discharge of eighty gallons of PCB oil onto land was "pollution."

4. PERSONAL INJURY ENDORSEMENT

In an attempt to avoid some of the limitations on coverage under the terms, conditions and exclusions of the CGL policy, insureds have sought new approaches to obtaining coverage for toxic tort and environmental claims. One approach has been to invoke an endorsement sometimes found in CGL policies known as the "personal injury and advertising liability" endorsement, which provides coverage for "damages because of personal injury or advertising injury." Personal injury typically is defined in the policy to mean:

(1) false arrest, detention, imprisonment, or malicious prosecution;

(2) wrongful entry or eviction or other invasion of the right of private occupancy;

(3) a publication or utterance

    (a) of a libel or slander or other defamatory or disparaging material, or

    (b) in violation of an individual's right of privacy.

It would seem at first reading that coverage for personal injury under the endorsement is precisely limited to damages resulting from one of the specifically enumerated torts. Nevertheless, in Pipefitters Welfare Educational Fund v. Westchester Fire Insurance Co., 976 F.2d 1037 (7th Cir.1992), the Seventh Circuit found a duty to defend under the personal injury endorsement in a case involving the release of PCBs. Evidence showed that a spill of eighty gallons of oil laden with PCBs took place while the claimant in the underlying action was preparing a transformer purchased from the insured for resale as scrap. The claimant alleged that the insured had disposed of the transformer unlawfully by failing to warn that it contained PCBs, and sought damages arising out of the spill, including cleanup costs, diminution of property value, imposition of a reclamation lien by the government and restricted access as a result of the government's actions.

In the coverage action, the insured argued that the underlying claim alleged a "wrongful entry or eviction or other invasion of the right to private occupancy" within the meaning of the personal injury endorsement. The insurer, on the other hand, argued that coverage under the endorsement is limited to conduct that is: (1) undertaken by one claiming an interest in property; and (2) intended to deprive the injured party of its right to privately occupy that property. The court observed that the term "other invasion of the right to private occupancy" has "less than a precise meaning" and encompassed the conduct alleged in the underlying claim.

The court found that the underlying claim did not allege an "eviction" because, by its plain and ordinary meaning, that term refers to the landlord/tenant context, but nevertheless, observed that the term "wrongful entry" is substantially similar to trespass. Moreover, "to commit a trespass, one need not intend to take possession of the encroached-upon premises, or to deprive occupants of their right to possess those premises." Thus, the court concluded that the underlying complaint "arguably alleges an 'other invasion' " sufficient to trigger the insurer's duty to defend.

See also Titan Holdings Syndicate v. City of Keene, 898 F.2d 265 (1st Cir.1990), where the underlying claim against the insured city alleged that as a result of the city's operation of a sewage treatment plant claimants were "continuously bombarded by and exposed to noxious, fetid and putrid odors, gases and particulates, to loud and disturbing noises during the night, and to unduly bright night lighting." In the coverage action, although the court agreed with the insured's argument that the pollution exclusion clause did not apply to coverage under the personal injury endorsement, it determined that, with one possible exception, the underlying claims did not fall within the scope of the personal injury coverage. The court stated: "[t]o come within the personal injury coverage, a suit must be based upon allegations of an offense to which the City might become liable." The court noted that New Hampshire law does not define the tort of "wrongful entry" as used in the personal injury endorsement and, thus, turned to the law on trespass. It concluded that the sewage plant's emissions did not reach the level of "intentional invasion" necessary to be actionable under New Hampshire law and, thus, did not constitute "wrongful entry" within the meaning of the personal injury endorsement.

However, the court then focused on a term contained in the personal injury endorsement of only one of the policies before it, which provided coverage for liability arising out of any "other invasion of the right of private occupancy." Because under New Hampshire law an invasion of the right of private occupancy need not involve a "physical invasion," the court concluded that the underlying allegations relating to the treatment plant's noxious odors, noise and light fell within the meaning of the personal injury endorsement and thus, triggered the insurer's duty to defend.

Can trespass and nuisance-like claims be reasonably interpreted as within the scope of the "right of occupancy" coverage? What might the insurers have intended in these clauses? See Columbia v. Continental Ins. Co., 189 A.D.2d 391, 595 N.Y.S.2d 988 (1993) (the wrongful entry, eviction or invasion of private occupancy was directed at liability for purposeful acts aimed at dispossession of real property by someone asserting an interest therein, not leachate contaminations, regardless of whether the legal theory is trespass or nuisance).

5. OWNED PROPERTY EXCLUSION

CGL policies are third party policies which provide coverage only for damages to such third parties, not for first party losses of the insured. This is reflected in the standard CGL's "owned property exclusion" which typically states:

This insurance does not apply to property damage to

(1) property owned or occupied by or rented to the insured.

(2) property used by the insured, or

(3) property in the care, custody or control of the insured or as to which the insured is for any purpose exercising physical control.

For example, a policyholder defending a CERCLA suit often seeks to recover from its insurer the costs of cleaning up its own property or the underlying groundwater. Policyholders often argue that these costs are covered despite the owned property exclusion because the cleanup prevents damages to the property of others or, under the common law, the policyholder does not "own" the groundwater.

Of the few that have considered the issue, the most significant case is the New Jersey Supreme Court opinion in State, Dept. of Environmental Protection v. Signo Trading Int'l, Inc., 130 N.J. 51, 612 A.2d 932 (1992). In a 4–3 decision, the court held that the owned property exclusion precludes coverage when there is only a "threat" of damage to the property of a third party, even if that threat is "imminent" and "immediate." Despite public policy which strongly favors a finding of coverage, the court stated the clear language of the policy must govern:

[T]hus, under its clear terms, the policy does not cover the costs of cleanup performed by or on behalf of an insured on its own property when those costs are incurred to alleviate damage to the insured's own property and not to the property of a third party.

In *Signo Trading*, a chemical fire occurred at the insured's warehouse. After the fire, the New Jersey Department of Environmental Protection and Energy discovered hazardous waste in the warehouse and filed suit to have the property cleaned. The issue presented was whether the imminent or immediate threat of damage to properties adjacent to the warehouse from the leaking hazardous wastes would be sufficient to trigger coverage under the policies despite the owned property exclusion. The trial court had previously found that while potential damages to adjacent properties were imminent, no actual damages to third parties had occurred.

The court rejected the holding of the appellate division in *Signo Trading* as well as the logic of another case, Summit Associates, Inc. v. Liberty Mutual Fire Insurance Co., 229 N.J.Super. 56, 550 A.2d 1235

(1988), which had held that an insured may recover the cost of measures intended to prevent future injury to a third party, if the threat of such injury appears to be "imminent" or "immediate." Instead, the court held that the "plain language" of the policy whose "definition of property damage does not encompass 'threatened harm' even if that threat is 'imminent' and 'immediate' " governed.

Do you agree with the majority here? The dissent argues that unless these costs are expended on the insured's property, damage to third parties will occur, and therefore, they are not within the exclusion.

In contrast, a Wisconsin appeals court in City of Edgerton v. General Casualty Co. of Wisconsin, 172 Wis.2d 518, 493 N.W.2d 768 (App.1992) held that the owned property exclusion would not bar coverage where there was ongoing groundwater contamination. The court concluded that "repairs to the site itself, when made as an element of a comprehensive cleanup and remediation plan designed to repair the environment, are not excluded from coverage by an owned-property exclusion." See also, United States Aviex Co. v. Travelers Ins. Co., 125 Mich.App. 579, 336 N.W.2d 838 (1983) (under Michigan law, groundwater was not "owned" by the surface landowner, and therefore, groundwater was outside the exclusion for property owned by the insured). But cleanup costs for soil contamination or exclusively on-site contamination may invite a different coverage result from groundwater contamination. See Western World Ins. Co. v. Dana, 765 F.Supp. 1011 (E.D.Cal.1991) (coverage for removal of hazardous materials from policyholder's soil before materials reached adjacent land or groundwater barred by owned property exclusion).

What do you think regarding the treatment of groundwater? How about an aquifer partially situated under the insured's land?

In an unusual twist, the Maryland Court of Appeals in Bausch & Lomb v. Utica Mutual Insurance Co., 330 Md. 758, 625 A.2d 1021 (1993) held that insured's cleanup of groundwater contamination was not covered because the state's interest in the groundwater did not constitute a property interest sufficient to make the insured's pollution a damage to a third party's property.

6. KNOWN RISK LIMITATION

Related but not identical to the "expected or intended" issue is the insurer's argument that an event or harm is not covered because it was a "known risk" at the time the insured entered into its CGL policy. It is generally accepted in insurance law that one cannot obtain insurance for a risk that has already transpired or for damage that was known prior to the effective date of an insurance contract. See, e.g., Appalachian Ins. Co. v. Liberty Mut. Ins. Co., 676 F.2d 56 (3d Cir.1982). In other words, once the risk of loss is a certainty, it is no longer an insurable interest.

Insurers argue that when a policy period commenced at a time when an insured already had been discharging waste for a considerable time, or worse, had known that a site was contaminated, the loss was already in progress, so that the "known risk" doctrine should apply and preclude coverage. In response, insureds argue that there is a difference between a "known risk" and a "known loss": insureds obtain insurance for known *risks*; only prior knowledge of actual *loss* should make the risk uninsurable. Consequently, they argue, it is not enough to show that the insured knew that a site was contaminated; instead the determinative fact is whether the insured knew that it was going to be liable for damage resulting from the discharge of toxic substances. See Outboard Marine Corp. v. Liberty Mut. Ins. Co., 154 Ill.2d 90, 180 Ill.Dec. 691, 607 N.E.2d 1204 (Ill.1992) in which the court held that proof that a policyholder knew it was discharging pollution did not make any resulting loss a "known risk" sufficient to defeat coverage. To preclude coverage, the court held that a carrier must show the policyholder also knew or should have known the pollution would lead to a loss or liability.

Some cases do hold that once an insured receives a notification from a governmental agency that it is responsible for contamination of property, it becomes a known loss and is uninsurable. For example, in Township of Gloucester v. Maryland Casualty Co., 668 F.Supp. 394, 403 (D.N.J.1987), Home Insurance Co. moved for summary judgment on the grounds that its coverage commenced after the New Jersey Department of Environmental Protection filed a complaint against the township. Sustaining the insurer's denial of coverage, the court stated:

> It is clear, based on the record before the court, that the township had actual knowledge of the occurrence prior to The Home's policy period. In the case of The Home policy, this is not a situation where the township could have reasonably expected that it "was free of the risk of becoming liable for injuries of which it could not have been aware prior to its purchase of insurance." * * * One cannot obtain insurance for a risk that the insured knows has already transpired.

If the insured obtains a policy without disclosing receipt of a PRP letter or receipt of other notice that it may be liable for cleanup costs, does that constitute fraud? See, e.g., Time Oil Co. v. Cigna Property & Casualty Ins. Co., 743 F.Supp. 1400 (W.D.Wash.1990) (discussing the duty of the insured to act in good faith and make disclosure to the insurer of information revealing a "substantial probability" that it would be liable).

What if the insured is named as a potentially responsible party by the EPA for remediating a site, then acquires insurance which disclosed the proceeding, and later is sued by private parties arising out of the migration of the wastes beyond the site? See Stonewall Ins. Co. v. City of Palos Verdes Estates, 18 Cal.App.4th 1234, 9 Cal.Rptr.2d 663 (1992), review granted and limited by 13 Cal.Rptr.2d 724, 840 P.2d 266 (1992). Should it make a difference whether the loss arises out of first party coverage i.e., the site is owned by the insured, or out of third party liability coverage?

Chapter Twelve

DEFENSES

A. INTRODUCTION

This Chapter brings together the defenses commonly asserted in toxic tort litigation. In prior Chapters we considered some issues that may be asserted by a defendant, such as the absence of proof of injury, uncertainty as to causation, superseding causes, and the bulk supplier/knowledgeable purchaser defense. Here the primary focus will be on statutes of limitation, statutes of repose, contributory negligence or fault, and assumption of the risk—most of which are affected by the plaintiff's conduct, be it action or the failure to act.

As we briefly mentioned in Chapter 1, toxic tort litigation presents special statutes of limitation problems which distinguish such cases from sporadic accident cases. The difficulties posed for plaintiffs derive from factors which have been explored in earlier chapters: (1) the long latency periods between exposure to a toxic substance and manifestation of the disease or condition which may have resulted from the exposure; (2) the uncertainty as to the causal relationships between the exposure and the harm suffered by the plaintiff; (3) the physiological evolution in the nature of the harm itself—for example, from a plaintiff developing pleural thickening at one stage in the exposure/manifestation process, to symptoms of asbestosis at a later stage, to finally developing lung cancer or mesothelioma at an even later stage; and (4) the problem of whether a plaintiff will be permitted to split her causes of action as her physical conditions evolve, or whether she must assert all her claims in one unitary proceeding.

Because of these time-based problems which a plaintiff may experience, some state legislatures have enacted special statutes reviving toxic tort claims that would have otherwise lapsed. Other states have enacted so-called "discovery" statutes of limitation. All of these discovery statutes prevent a plaintiff's cause of action from accruing until such time as a reasonable person would have discovered the injury, and some delaying accrual until both the injury and defendant's contribution to it could reasonably be discovered. Still other states have enacted statutes of repose which grant defendants immunity after a prescribed number of years from a particular event, such as the construction of a building or sale of a product.

Another important dichotomy respecting statutes of limitation is the influence which plaintiff's theory of the case has on the selection of the appropriate statute. Nuisance and trespass cases have special statute of limitation conundra rarely present in products liability, strict liability or negligence cases—that of the "continuing" versus permanent invasion, a distinction which has spawned a body of often abstruse opinions seeking to apply them. For that reason, we have divided the discussion between "land-based" theories of liability from product and occupational cases.

B. STATUTES OF LIMITATION FOR INJURY TO REAL PROPERTY

It can be extremely important in cases based on theories of nuisance, trespass, and strict liability to understand the special problems posed by statutes of limitation. As the cases below demonstrate, resolution of statutes of limitation issues will turn on whether the nuisance or trespass is characterized as "continuing" or "permanent." First, we consider Mangini v. Aerojet–General Corp., 230 Cal.App.3d 1125, 281 Cal.Rptr. 827 (1991). In *Mangini*, the plaintiffs were current landowners who were suing lessees of a prior owner of the property for contamination that occurred during the lessees' occupancy and as a result of their industrial uses of the land. The material below is the appellate court's determination of whether each of plaintiffs' claims can survive statutes of limitation challenges.

MANGINI v. AEROJET–GENERAL CORPORATION

California Court of Appeals, 1991.
230 Cal.App.3d 1125, 281 Cal.Rptr. 827.

SIMS, J.

* * *

Defendant leased the property in question from its former owners, the Cavitts, from 1960 to 1970. Plaintiffs acquired the property pursuant to an exchange of other real property from the executor and administrator of the Cavitts' estate, codefendant James H. Cavitt, in 1975.

Defendant's lease (attached to the complaint as an exhibit) provided, "The term of this lease is for a period of ten (10) years, commencing [in 1960] and ending [in 1970] * * *." The lease also stated, among other things, "Upon termination of this lease, Lessee shall surrender the premises in as good state and condition as when received by Lessee, reasonable use and wear thereof consistent with the business engaged in by Lessee * * * excepted." Despite this provision, defendant failed to remove millions of pounds of waste rocket fuel materials and other hazardous substances which it burned, buried, or otherwise disposed of on the property during the term of its lease, creating hazardous conditions which remain on the property.

Plaintiffs have been compelled by the Sacramento County Air Pollution Control District to undertake testing of the property and may be required under state and federal law to abate the hazardous conditions created by defendant.

Plaintiffs did not learn of the hazardous conditions until "recently."

* * *

III

PLAINTIFFS SHOULD BE ALLOWED TO AMEND THEIR COMPLAINT TO ALLEGE FACTS SHOWING CONTINUING NUISANCE AND TRESPASS

Defendant contends all of plaintiffs' counts are barred by the statute of limitations and that plaintiffs cannot escape this bar by any amendment to their complaint.

A. *A Claim for Damages for a Permanent Public Nuisance is Subject to the Three–Year Statute of Limitations in Code of Civil Procedure Section 338, Subdivision (b)*

Plaintiffs assert their count based upon public nuisance is not barred by the statute of limitations because in their view a claim based on public nuisance is never barred by the statute of limitations. This argument is not well taken.

Plaintiffs assert there is no statute of limitations running on their claim for public nuisance because section 3490 provides: "No lapse of time can legalize a public nuisance, amounting to an actual obstruction of public right."

Section 3490 has been construed to mean that the statute of limitations is no defense to an action brought by a public entity to abate a public nuisance. However, where private citizens have sued for damages for special injury based on public nuisance, our Supreme Court has characterized the nuisance as either "continuing" or "permanent" and has used the characterization to determine whether the suit is subject to the statute of limitations. * * *

Thus, for example, in Phillips v. City of Pasadena [162 P.2d 625 (Cal.1945)], plaintiff sued for damages for the unlawful obstruction of a public road. * * *

Addressing defendant's contention that plaintiff's claim was barred by the statute of limitations, the Phillips court concluded, "Where a nuisance is of such character that it will presumably continue indefinitely it is considered permanent, and the limitations period runs from the time the nuisance is created. On the other hand, if the nuisance may be discontinued at any time it is considered continuing in character. Every repetition of a continuing nuisance is a separate wrong for which the person may bring successive actions for damages until the nuisance is abated, even though an action based on the original wrong may be barred."

Our Supreme Court recently applied Phillips's rule in Baker v. Burbank–Glendale–Pasadena Airport Authority [705 P.2d 866 (Cal. 1985)]. There, plaintiffs sued for (among other things) nuisance caused by noise, smoke, and vibrations from flights over their homes. The trial court ruled the action was barred by the statute of limitations. In reversing the trial court, our Supreme Court framed the issue as whether the nuisance was permanent or continuing: "Two distinct classifications have emerged in nuisance law which determine the remedies available to injured parties and the applicable statute of limitations. On the one hand, permanent nuisances are of a type where 'by one act a permanent injury is done, [and] damages are assessed once for all.' " * * * In such cases, plaintiffs ordinarily are required to bring one action for all past, present and future damage within three years after the permanent nuisance is erected * * *. Damages are not dependent upon any subsequent use of the property but are complete when the nuisance comes into existence * * *.

"On the other hand, if a nuisance is a use which may be discontinued at any time, it is considered continuing in character and persons harmed by it may bring successive actions for damages until the nuisance is abated * * *. Recovery is limited, however, to actual injury suffered prior to commencement of each action. Prospective damages are unavailable."

* * * We therefore conclude the continuing/permanent nuisance distinction drawn by Phillips and Baker applies to private suits for damages based upon public nuisances.

* * *

Thus, where a private citizen sues for damages to real property caused by a public nuisance, and the nuisance is permanent, the three year statute of limitations in Code of Civil Procedure section 338, subdivision (b) (for trespass or injury to real property), begins to run when the permanent nuisance is created.

B. *Plaintiffs May Amend Their Complaint to Plead Facts Showing a Continuing Nuisance*

This leaves the question whether the nuisance alleged in the instant case is permanent or continuing. "In case of doubt as to the permanency of the injury the plaintiff may elect whether to treat a particular nuisance as permanent or continuing." Baker v. Burbank–Glendale–Pasadena Airport Authority, supra[.]

Defendant argues that plaintiffs' complaint manifests an election of permanent nuisance. Defendant points out that plaintiffs have alleged their property is "unusable and extremely difficult to market for an indefinite period of time" and there is "little likelihood that the Subject Property will ever be as valuable as it would have been if not contaminated." Moreover, defendant notes that plaintiffs seek to recover all diminution in the market value of their property by seeking an injunction that would make defendant buy the property from plaintiffs at its market value unaffected by contamination. This form of relief is incompatible with a claim based on injuries caused by continuing nuisance.

On the other hand, plaintiffs allege they can amend their complaint to allege facts showing a continuing nuisance, i.e., the contamination can be abated and defendant has entered into a federal consent decree agreeing to clean up the property. The question is whether these proposed averments sufficiently allege a continuing nuisance.

"The cases finding the nuisance complained of to be unquestionably permanent in nature have involved solid structures, such as a building encroaching upon the plaintiff's land, a steam railroad operating over plaintiff's land, or regrade of a street for a rail system."

"The classic example of a continuing nuisance is an ongoing * * * disturbance, caused by noise, vibration or foul odor [and] * * * the distinction to be drawn is between encroachments of a permanent nature erected upon one's lands, and a complaint made, not of the location of the offending structures, but of the continuing use of such structures." Baker v. Burbank–Glendale–Pasadena Airport Authority, supra.

Here, according to plaintiffs, no structures are involved and the nuisance consists of the offensive chemical pollution which can be abated. In the decisions of our Supreme Court, the crucial distinction between a permanent and continuing nuisance is whether the nuisance may be discontinued or abated. * * *

Plaintiffs' proposed pleading therefore meets the crucial test of a continuing nuisance: that the offensive condition is abatable.

We note plaintiffs' land may be subject to a continuing nuisance even though defendant's offensive conduct ended years ago. That is because the "continuing" nature of the nuisance refers to the continuing damage caused by the offensive condition, not to the acts causing the offensive condition to occur.

* * *

In cases of doubt respecting the permanency of an injury caused by a nuisance, courts are inclined to favor the right to successive actions. * * * Whether contamination by toxic waste is a permanent or continuing injury is ordinarily a question of fact turning on the nature and extent of the contamination. We therefore conclude plaintiffs should be allowed to amend their complaint to state their proposed facts so as to aver a theory of continuing nuisance and to seek damages caused them within three years of the date of filing the complaint.

C. Plaintiffs May Amend Their Complaint to Allege a Continuing Trespass

Historically, the application of the statute of limitations for trespass has been the same as for nuisance and has depended on whether the trespass has been continuing or permanent. As we have recounted, the crucial test of the permanency of a trespass or nuisance is whether the trespass or nuisance can be discontinued or abated. We have already seen how plaintiffs' proposed amendments to their complaint meet this test.

We note that plaintiffs' theory of continuing trespass is sanctioned by the Restatement (Second) of Torts, which states: "(b) Continuing trespass. The actor's failure to remove from land in the possession of another a thing which he has tortiously * * * placed on the land constitutes a continuing trespass for the entire time during which the thing is on the land and * * * confers on the possessor of the land an option to maintain a succession of actions based on a theory of continuing trespass or to treat the continuance of the thing on the land as an aggravation of the original trespass." (Id. at § 161, comm. b.)

We therefore conclude plaintiffs should be afforded the opportunity to amend their complaint clearly to allege facts that show a continuing trespass.

IV

PLAINTIFFS' COUNTS FOR NEGLIGENCE, NEGLIGENCE PER SE, AND STRICT LIABILITY ARE BARRED BY THE STATUTE OF LIMITATIONS

We have no occasion to determine whether plaintiffs' counts for negligence, negligence per se, or strict liability state facts sufficient to constitute a cause of action because, assuming they do, each is barred by the statute of limitations. The parties agree each of these counts is subject to the three-year statute of limitations. As we shall explain, plaintiffs had good reason to inquire about (and therefore learn about) these matters more than three years before their complaint was filed.

In the third count, the complaint avers defendant was negligent by selecting the subject property as a site for disposing of hazardous substance disposal, improper disposing of hazardous substances, failing to determine the nature and extent of the contamination, failing to contain or remedy the contamination, and failing to inform plaintiffs of the contamination.

The fourth count, for negligence per se, is premised on defendant's alleged violation of statutes and regulations by their discharge of hazardous waste on the property and into the waters of the state.

The sixth count, for strict liability, is premised on defendant's alleged use, disposal, storage and maintenance of hazardous substances on the subject property.

The traditional rule is that a statute of limitations begins to run upon the occurrence of the last element essential to the cause of action, even if the plaintiff is unaware of his cause of action. The harshness of that rule has been ameliorated in cases where it would be manifestly unjust to deprive a plaintiff of a cause of action before he is aware he has been injured. A cause of action under this discovery rule accrues when "'plaintiff either (1) actually discovered his injury and its negligent cause or (2) could have discovered injury and cause through the exercise of reasonable diligence.'" The limitations period begins once the plaintiff has notice or information of circumstances to put a reasonable person on inquiry. Subjective suspicion is not required. If a person becomes aware of facts which would make a reasonably prudent person suspicious, he or she has a duty to investigate further and is charged with knowledge of matters which would have been revealed by such an investigation.

* * *

Here, the complaint alleges that defendant released toxic substances on the property from 1960 to 1970. Plaintiffs acquired their interests in the property between 1975 and 1983. The lawsuit was filed on January 14, 1988, and alleges that plaintiffs did not learn of the hazardous conditions until "recently." The complaint fails to allege when plaintiffs made the discovery, the circumstances of the discovery and why, in the exercise of reasonable diligence, they could not have made the discovery sooner.

The question then becomes whether the defect can be cured by amendment.

Plaintiffs set forth the following additional facts which they intend to plead if allowed to do so:

"In late 1979, the Manginis were contacted by an investigator for the California Department of Justice, who informed the Manginis that he was conducting an investigation of [defendant's] hazardous waste disposal practices and was interviewing people who owned land near [defendant's] Sacramento facilities. The investigator asked the Manginis whether they had any knowledge of [defendant's] waste disposal practices in the area. The Manginis told him that they did not. He informed them that there was no reason for them to be concerned about any environmental problems on their property."

"On or about April 24, 1984, more than four years later, the Manginis received a letter from [defendant] asking for permission to inspect the property. For the next two years, [defendant] discussed with the Manginis its plans for inspecting and conducting tests on the property. Never during that period of time did [defendant] tell the Manginis anything about the nature of [defendant's] activities while it had leased the property." * * *

* * *

At some undisclosed time, defendant took soil samples and plaintiffs hired an independent laboratory. In January 1987, defendant gave plaintiffs its laboratory test results, which appeared to show chemical contamination in the soil, but told plaintiffs this was laboratory error. In April 1987, the Sacramento Air Pollution Control District informed plaintiffs their property was contaminated with hazardous substances. In mid–1987, plaintiffs retained an attorney and obtained [EPA] records, including 1979–1980 Department of Justice investigative reports.

Plaintiffs state, "Those reports disclosed for the first time to the Manginis the nature of [defendant's] activities while it had leased the property from 1960 to 1970. The reports showed that [defendant] had disposed of thousands of pounds of trichloroethylene (TCE), ammonium perchlorate rocket fuel and other chemical contaminants on the property. The reports also showed that the California Attorney General's Office and the EPA had filed lawsuits against [defendant] to compel it to clean up contamination on property which [defendant] owned or leased in the Sacramento area." Plaintiffs filed their complaint on January 14, 1988.

* * *

Thus, in 1984, more than three years before filing the complaint, plaintiffs knew the following facts: (1) the recorded lease gave notice that defendant had engaged in activities of a potentially hazardous nature on their land; (2) the Department of Justice investigated defendant's practices regarding disposal of hazardous waste in the area; and (3) defendant asked plaintiffs for permission to inspect their property.

Whether any of these three facts in isolation would be sufficient to impart notice is open to dispute. However, the combination of these facts together establish as a matter of law that, when defendant contacted plaintiffs in 1984, plaintiffs had sufficient information to put them on notice of the possibility that defendant had dumped hazardous waste on their land.

That defendant gave evasive, or even untruthful, reasons for the inspection did not relieve plaintiffs of their duty of inquiry once they had sufficient facts to suspect the cause of action. Indeed, the evasiveness gave further reason for suspicion.

Here, had plaintiffs investigated in a timely fashion, they would have discovered the Department of Justice reports, which they admittedly received shortly after requesting them from the EPA in 1987. Plaintiffs are charged with knowledge of the information in those reports.
* * *

We therefore conclude the statute of limitations on plaintiffs' claims for negligence, negligence per se, and strict liability began to run no later than April 24, 1984, when plaintiffs received defendant's letter asking to inspect the property. These claims, asserted in the complaint filed January 14, 1988, are barred by the three-year statute of limitations.

Notes and Questions

1. The distinction between permanent or continuing nuisances and trespasses, which sometimes are described as permanent or temporary for damage purposes, is well described in William H. Rodgers, Jr., Environmental Law § 2.9 at 29–30 (Supp. 1984):

Statutory limitation periods, adding the weight of legislative opinion to arguments for respecting the status quo, are of some importance in nuisance cases. The key distinction that emerges here is that insufferable one between a permanent and a temporary nuisance. With due respect for the obscurity of the differences, a permanent nuisance describes those continuous polluters with odds-on prospects of conducting business as usual in the years ahead. For these offenders, the expectation is that permanent damages will be recovered in a single lawsuit. The damage action accrues for limitation purposes when the first actionable injury occurs, which usually is when the polluting business commences operations.

The classical understanding of a temporary nuisance is the occasional invasion dependent upon contingencies such as wind and rain. The definition is usually extended to include all nuisances with prospects of being controlled, so that anything not a permanent nuisance is temporary. If the nuisance is temporary, the plaintiff is entitled to have it abated and may recover for all injury sustained during the statutory period.

The permanent/temporary nuisance classification has troubling features. As an abstract matter, there are obvious transaction costs in encouraging repeated lawsuits (by invoking the temporary category) and obvious risks of error in attempting to effectuate a final accounting of a social conflict with high uncertainties (by invoking the permanent category). Enhancing a money judgment if a nuisance is "uncontrollable" skews incentives for plaintiffs who are expected to be pressing for controls to the limits of technology. Giving defendants advantages for demonstrating that their spillovers are "uncontrollable" relieves them of the obligation to develop imaginative new abatement strategies.

Perhaps the best way out of this difficulty is to allow plaintiffs to make an election, typically after discovery, between the permanent or temporary characterization. Presumably in most cases the prospects of a "bigger" judgment for a permanent nuisance would be overcome by plaintiff's fears of no compensation for injuries not discovered or hopes that the future will bring some corrective technology or practice. * * *

2. For a comprehensive analysis of the permanent and temporary distinction, see Goldstein v. Potomac Electric Power Company, 285 Md. 673, 404 A.2d 1064 (1979), where the Maryland Court of Appeals held that plaintiffs' action for the diminution in value to their land was barred by a three-year statute because the injury occurred at the time the public utility's pollution commenced to invade plaintiffs' land and constituted a permanent nuisance. The court was influenced by the fact that it could not order the utility to cease operations, and hence, the nuisance was not abatable.

Some other examples of courts' treatment of this issue include: Atlas Chemical Industries v. Anderson, 524 S.W.2d 681 (Tex.1975) (longstanding air pollution is a permanent nuisance); Sundell v. Town of New London, 119 N.H. 839, 409 A.2d 1315 (1979) (longstanding water pollution is a temporary nuisance); Moy v. Bell, 46 Md.App. 364, 416 A.2d 289, 294 (1980) ("Recognizing * * * that any nuisance man creates, man can abate, it seems that the question * * * is not the possibility of abatement but rather its likelihood'').

For an extensive discussion of temporary versus permanent damages where defendant's salt plant damaged the aquifer, which in turn, harmed plaintiffs' agricultural operations and land values, see Miller v. Cudahy Company, 592 F.Supp. 976 (D.Kan.1984), affirmed 858 F.2d 1449 (10th Cir.1988). Defendants often argue that the nuisance *is permanent* so that all actions are time-barred. Rejecting this argument, see Haenchen v. Sand Products Co., 626 P.2d 332, 334 (Okl.App.1981); Cox v. Cambridge Square Towne Houses, Inc., 239 Ga. 127, 236 S.E.2d 73 (1977). See Annot., Statute of Limitations for Nuisance Based on Air Pollution, 19 A.L.R. 4th 442 (1979); Application of Statute of Limitations in Private Tort Actions Based on Injury to Persons or Property Caused by Underground Flow of Contaminants, 11 ALR 5th 438 (1993).

One likely inference of adopting the continuing nuisance analysis is that it undermines a defendant's argument that it has obtained prescriptive rights to pollute plaintiff's property. See Miller v. Cudahy Company, 592 F.Supp. 976 (D.Kan.1984), affirmed 858 F.2d 1449 (10th Cir.1988). This is especially so for public nuisances. See also Smallpage v. Turlock Irrigation District, 26 Cal.App.2d 538, 79 P.2d 752 (1938) (''One may not acquire an easement by prescription to maintain a public nuisance, and there can be no prescriptive right to pollute a stream to the detriment of the public''); and Strong v. Sullivan, 180 Cal. 331, 181 P. 59 (1919) (''No lapse of time can legalize a public nuisance * * * No right by prescription may be acquired to obstruct a sidewalk. Nor to maintain any other sort of nuisance.'').

3. Another recent California case, Capogeannis v. Superior Court (Spence), 12 Cal.App.4th 668, 15 Cal.Rptr.2d 796 (1993), sets forth a rationale for classifying most nuisances as continuing. In *Capogeannis*, plaintiffs, who acquired the property in 1984, sued the prior owner and one of its tenants for leaking underground storage tanks that had contaminated the property during the 1970s. Plaintiffs first learned of the tanks in 1986 and of the contamination in early 1987, but did not sue until December 1990. To overcome the three-year statute, plaintiffs offered affidavits of a registered geologist and an environmental assessor who opined that the contamination from the petroleum products was ''abatable through environmental remediation,'' whereas defendant's experts opined that the contamination would not be ''entirely abatable because there will always be some residual contamination regardless of the technology or combination of [remediation] technologies used.'' Finding for the plaintiffs on this issue, the court articulated the rationale for its holding:

> The Capogeannises do not quarrel with the defendants' two factual premises. They acknowledge in essence that they may be unable to prove the contamination can be wholly removed from the soil and groundwater. And although they assert (and the Spences' expert cannot deny) that they can reduce contamination to officially acceptable levels, it may be inferred from the record as a whole that the reduction will be a slow and uncertain process, in some measure dependent on variables such as climatic conditions.

But the Capogeannises assert, and we conclude as a matter of law, that the defendants' premises do not compel a conclusion that the nuisance was permanent. At the very least the question whether this was a permanent or continuing nuisance was so close or doubtful as to empower the Capogeannises to proceed on a theory of continuing nuisance.

Our conclusion is influenced primarily by policy considerations * * *. First and foremost, today's environmental awareness establishes beyond argument that there is simply no legitimate interest to be served by permitting this contamination to persist. Conversely, the well-documented tendency of such contamination to migrate, particularly in groundwater, strongly supports a conclusion that the contamination should be cleaned up as promptly and thoroughly as possible. Both considerations support application, in this case, of the courts' general preference for a finding of continuing nuisance (or, at least, of a question close enough to empower the Capogeannises to proceed upon that theory). Such a finding will tend to encourage private abatement, and perhaps monetary cooperation in abatement efforts, if only to limit successive lawsuits. On the other hand a finding that the nuisance is permanent would leave the Capogeannises with private recourse barred, and with no practical motivation to proceed promptly and efficiently beyond that provided by the enforcement practices of governmental agencies acting at public expense. * * * That in this case abatement efforts may take considerable time and may never be wholly successful should not be permitted to dictate a result that would lessen incentives to proceed as promptly and effectively as possible to abate the contamination.

4.   Do you agree with the court's rationales for construing the permanent/continuing distinction in a manner that facilitates the cleanup of properties? Why shouldn't plaintiffs be bound by whatever contractual or warranty rights that they may have against the prior owners? See also Arcade Water District v. United States, 940 F.2d 1265 (9th Cir.1991), applying continuing nuisance to contamination of wells caused by a military laundry that had closed thirteen years prior to suit.

Interestingly, after the appellate decisions in *Mangini* and *Capogeannis*, the court that tried *Mangini* on remand vacated a jury award of $13.2 million based on the continuing nuisance and trespass theories. The court concluded that the "jury's finding that the trespass and nuisance are abatable is contrary to the weight of the evidence," because the nature and extent of the contamination was not established, nor did the evidence support the technical feasibility of remediating the property, particularly in light of plaintiffs' expectation that the land be rendered useful for residential development considering its current use of grazing land for cattle.

Moreover, the court found that the $13.2 million award, which represented the "taint" placed on the entire 2400–acre parcel, even though the contamination was largely confined to 125 acres, was more consistent with a permanent nuisance, not a continuing one. While acknowledging that some federal cases allow nuisances to be classified as continuing for statutes of limitation purposes and permanent for assessing damages, it could find no support in California law for doing so. See Mangini v. Aerojet–General Corp., 12 Cal.4th 1087, 51 Cal.Rptr.2d 272, 912 P.2d 1220 (Cal.1996).

5.   The significance of the continuing nuisance doctrine is illustrated by the New York case of Jensen v. General Electric Co., 182 A.D.2d 903, 581 N.Y.S.2d 917 (1992), where a special statute of limitations had been enacted which provided:

> The three-year period within which an action to recover damages for * * * injury to property caused by the latent effects of exposure to any substance or combination of substances * * * upon or within property must be commenced shall be computed from the date of discovery of the injury by the plaintiff or from the date when through the exercise of reasonable diligence such injury should have been discovered by the plaintiff, whichever is earlier.

The court held that

> Although these causes of action do qualify as actions "to recover damages for * * * injury to property caused by the latent effects of exposure" to the toxic chemicals present on plaintiffs' property, being recurring wrongs they are not subject to any Statute of Limitations because they constantly accrue, thus giving rise to successive causes of action. As a consequence they are unaffected by the enactment of CPLR 214–c(2), which is aimed at providing "relief to injured New Yorkers whose claims would otherwise be dismissed for untimeliness simply because they were unaware of the latent injuries until after the limitation period had expired."

The Court of Appeals, 4–3, reversed the Appellate Division, 82 N.Y.2d 77, 603 N.Y.S.2d 420, 623 N.E.2d 547 (1993), stating that the 1986 law had an "all-encompassing sweep" and left "no room for judicial insertion of qualification or exceptions by interpretation." The court said with the passage of the 1986 law, the Legislature intended to alter the accrual date for "all property damage actions caused by all substances."

According to the opinion, "If no statute of limitations at all was to apply, as the Appellate Division found, then the provision for a three-year period from discovery of the act of wrongdoing would be rendered a theoretical and superfluous appendage to the state statute with no practical vitality."

In addition, the court said the result of exempting continuing trespass and nuisance claims in many cases would be to eliminate any repose, "even against parties who choose to sit interminably on known rights before bringing suit."

However, the majority preserved plaintiffs' actions for injunctive relief because the statute by its terms applied only to damages actions.

Why were the continuing damage approaches unavailable to the Manginis on the negligence and strict liability claims? What is the fundamental distinction between nuisances and negligence so far as applying statutes of limitation?

6.   As *Mangini* demonstrated, actions based on negligence or strict liability for abnormally dangerous activity are subjected to a firmer limitations period. The point is illustrated dramatically by yet another California

decision, CAMSI IV v. Hunter Technology Corp., 230 Cal.App.3d 1525, 282 Cal.Rptr. 80 (1991). Monsanto owned a parcel of land and conducted manufacturing operations from 1950 to 1983 and disposed of liquid and solid wastes. It leased a portion of the property to Hunter, which, until 1983, manufactured printed circuit boards. In its manufacturing process, Hunter discharged volatile organic chemicals (VOCs) and TCE. In 1983, Monsanto sold the parcel to third parties who sold it to KSP in October 1984. In 1985, KSP sold it to CAMSI IV, a partnership. In July 1985, the San Francisco Bay Regional Water Quality Control Board issued an order naming Monsanto and KSP as dischargers of TCE and VOCs on the land. In 1986, CAMSI IV sold an uncontaminated portion of the property. In 1987, the Regional Board issued a tentative cleanup order and in 1988 a final order naming Monsanto, Hunter, and CAMSI IV as parties responsible for the cleanup of the site.

The court held that for injury to real property the cause of action accrues with the last act causing the injury. The fact that CAMSI IV asserted that it didn't suffer any harm until it acquired the property didn't toll the statute:

> [I]t is apparent as an abstract proposition, and has been assumed in a number of cases, that for limitations purposes the harm implicit in a tortious injury to property is harm to the property itself, and thus to any owner of the property once the property has been injured and not necessarily to a particular owner. Thus once the sewer line has been improperly located on the property, or the lot preparation and foundation construction have been improperly done, or the encroaching buildings are constructed, the tort is complete and the statute of limitations (unless forestalled by the "discovery rule" or some other special doctrine) begins to run: An owner must bring its claim to court within the statutory period or the claim will be barred for that and all subsequent owners. Normally a subsequent owner will not be personally harmed by the tort until he or she becomes the owner, but no case has held that each new owner thus becomes entitled to a new statute of limitations against the tortfeasor. Such a rule would wholly disregard the repose function of statutes of limitations.

The court also held that CAMSI could not rely on the discovery rule because the court concluded that it should have discovered the contamination, and was put on notice of the problem, by the Regional Board's July 1985 order which it received more than three years before suit was filed.

Why do you suppose that plaintiff didn't allege a continuing nuisance count? If it had, would the outcome been different? Why is a subsequent owner of the property better off, for statutes of limitation purposes, relying on a nuisance theory rather than a strict liability or negligence theory? Recall that in most jurisdictions a nuisance theory would only extend to horizontally related parties and would not grant standing to those in a vertical relationship as to the same parcel of land. What is a buyer's best protection against acquiring property that is subsequently subjected to a government-mandated remediation order?

7. It is important to identify the relevant statutes of limitation that may be implicated by one set of facts. In the toxic tort field typical possibilities to investigate include statutes applicable to personal injury,

trespass to personal or real property, special statutes for products liability and special statutes for exposure to toxic substances.

C. STATUTES OF LIMITATION IN PRODUCT AND OCCUPATIONAL EXPOSURE CASES

Many toxic tort cases arise because a consumer or user of a product or an employee in a workplace has sustained injury as a result of exposure to a toxic substance. As a general rule, the date of accrual of a cause of action is either one of two dates: the date when all elements necessary to the tort are first completed; or the date when the plaintiff knew or should have known of the cause of action.

1. DATE OF THE INJURY

In the absence of judicial precedent to the contrary, the common law rule is that a cause of action accrues, and the statute of limitation begins to run, on the date of the injury to plaintiff. As interpreted originally, plaintiff's claim would be deemed to have arisen irrespective of whether the plaintiff knew or even could know of the nature or extent of his injuries. See, e.g., McWilliams v. Union Pac. Resources Co., 569 So.2d 702, 703–04 (Ala.1990) (citing Home Ins. Co. v. Stuart–McCorkle, Inc., 291 Ala. 601, 608, 285 So.2d 468, 473 (1973)). For causes of action based on negligence or strict liability, damage to the plaintiff is a necessary element of the cause of action. A few courts have extended this proposition to mean that a substantial injury is necessary, based on the principal of de minimis non curat lex. See, e.g., Cloud v. Olin Corp., 552 F.Supp. 528 (N.D.Ala.1982); Locke v. Johns–Manville Corp., 221 Va. 951, 275 S.E.2d 900, 905 (1981) (asbestos statute begins running from date cancer or lung impairment begins).

One familiar variation on this theme states that injury occurs on the date of last exposure to the offending substance. See, e.g., Meadows v. Union Carbide Corp., 710 F.Supp. 1163, 1166 (N.D.Ill.1989) (applying Illinois law). Such a rule is understandable if it is assumed that exposure equals injury. Under this view, each exposure to an offending substance creates an injury at that time. Thus, continuing exposures lead to continuing injuries, similar to the continuing nuisance rule discussed earlier, and plaintiff's claims concerning all of the exposures which occur within the statute of limitation will escape the bar. On the other hand, if all of the exposures take place outside of the limitation period, the cause of action will be held to be time-barred. When exposures take place both inside and outside of the limitation period, there is a split of authority as to whether the exposures outside of the limitation period will be time-barred. Compare *Cloud* (exposures outside limitation period are barred) with Chase v. Cassiar Mining Corp., 622 F.Supp. 1027 (N.D.N.Y.1985) (in personal injury action, plaintiff is not limited to damages caused by exposure to asbestos within the statute of limitation period and is instead entitled to recover for 25–year cumulative effect).

2. ACCRUAL BASED ON THE DISCOVERY RULE

Either as a result of judicial decision or statutory enactment, most jurisdictions have adopted a discovery rule for determining when a cause of action accrues. Under the discovery rule, a cause of action accrues on either of two dates: on the date that the plaintiff first knew or should have known of the injury *or* on the date when the plaintiff first knew or should have known of the injury *and* of the causal link to the defendant. One of the earliest recognitions of the fundamental fairness of adopting a discovery rule in a toxic tort case is found in Urie v. Thompson, 337 U.S. 163, 69 S.Ct. 1018, 93 L.Ed. 1282 (1949), in which the Supreme Court interpreted the Federal Employers' Liability Act to sustain a railroad employee's action for disability caused by the inhalation of silica dust. Urie became permanently disabled in 1940 and filed suit on November 25, 1941; FELA cases were subject to a three-year limitation period. Defendant railroad argued that because he had been exposed to silica dust since 1910, he must have contracted silicosis long before 1938, and hence, the action accrued before 1938. Alternatively, defendant argued that if each inhalation of silica dust was a separate tort, Urie was limited to that injury occasioned by his exposures between 1938 and when he last worked in 1940.

The Court rejected both arguments, and instead, adopted a discovery rule:

> [I]f we assume that Congress intended to include occupational diseases in the category of injuries compensable under the Federal Employers' Liability and Boiler Inspection Acts, such mechanical analysis of the "accrual" of petitioner's injury—whether breath by breath, or at one unrecorded moment in the progress of the disease—can only serve to thwart the congressional purpose.

> If Urie were held barred from prosecuting this action because he must be said, as a matter of law, to have contracted silicosis prior to November 25, 1938, it would be clear that the federal legislation afforded Urie only a delusive remedy. It would mean that at some past moment in time, unknown and inherently unknowable even in retrospect, Urie was charged with knowledge of the slow and tragic disintegration of his lungs; under this view Urie's failure to diagnose within the applicable statute of limitations a disease whose symptoms had not yet obtruded on his consciousness would constitute waiver of his right to compensation at the ultimate day of discovery and disability.

> Nor can we accept the theory that each intake of dusty breath is a fresh "cause of action." In the present case, for example, application of such a rule would, arguably, limit petitioner's damages to that aggravation of his progressive injury traceable to the last eighteen months of his employment. Moreover petitioner would have been wholly barred from suit had he left the railroad, or merely been

transferred to work involving no exposure to silica dust, more than three years before discovering the disease with which he was afflicted.

We do not think the humane legislative plan intended such consequences to attach to blameless ignorance. * * * There is no suggestion that Urie should have known he had silicosis at any earlier date. It follows that no specific date of contact with the substance can be charged with being the date of injury, inasmuch as the injurious consequences of the exposure are the product of a period of time rather than a point of time; consequently the afflicted employee can be held to be "injured" only when the accumulated effects of the deleterious substance manifest themselves * * *.

The following decision illustrates how the discovery rule has evolved and applies in close cases.

EVENSON v. OSMOSE WOOD PRESERVING COMPANY OF AMERICA, INC.

United States Court of Appeals, Seventh Circuit, 1990.
899 F.2d 701.

Wood, Jr., C.J.

This products liability action arises from injuries allegedly caused by the plaintiff's exposure to wood-treating chemicals. Gary E. Evenson appeals from the district court's grant of summary judgment for defendants Osmose Wood Preserving, Inc. ("Osmose"), Mineral Research & Development Corporation, Inc. ("Mineral Research"), and American Wood Preservers Institute ("American Wood"), on the ground that the district court erred in holding that the Indiana statute of limitations barred his action. [W]e reverse and remand.

I.   Factual Background

The defendants are parties to this suit because of their involvement with chromated copper arsenate ("CCA"). Osmose and Mineral Research manufacture a wood preservative that contains CCA. Osmose prepared a "Material Safety Data Sheet" and wrote the label used on CCA containers. American Wood represented the interests of the CCA industry before the federal [EPA] during that agency's regulatory investigation of the arsenic used in treating wood. Indiana Wood Preserving, Inc. ("Indiana Wood") purchased CCA from Osmose and Mineral Research to treat lumber. Indiana Wood then sold the treated lumber. Evenson worked at Indiana Wood as a wood treatment worker where he was exposed to CCA while carrying out his duties.

The events of this case are best understood chronologically: Late summer-early fall 1983: Dr. Dean Felker, Evenson's general practitioner, diagnoses hay fever, nasal polyps, asthma, and allergic rhinitis. Dr. Felker makes no causal diagnosis except to say that severe allergies are the usual cause of nasal polyps. He refers Evenson to Dr. Steven

Isenberg, an ear, nose, and throat specialist, for treatment of the nasal polyps in August 1983. April 1984: Dr. Steven Isenberg refers Evenson to Dr. Paul Isenberg, an asthma specialist. Dr. Paul Isenberg diagnoses Evenson as having an asthma triad (asthma, nasal polyps, and aspirin sensitivity) as well as certain other allergies. February 20, 1985: Because he is concerned that CCA may be causing his medical problems, Evenson asks Dr. Felker to run tests for CCA in his urine. March 20, 1985: The urine test is completed and shows normal levels of the chemicals that make up CCA. Because of the test results, Dr. Felker believes that CCA is not causing Evenson's symptoms. April 1985: For the second time, Dr. Steven Isenberg removes Evenson's nasal polyps. Evenson requests that the polyps be checked for CCA. Dr. Steven Isenberg sends out a sample for testing but never receives the results and is unable to identify the cause of the polyps. Evenson also asks Dr. Paul Isenberg if CCA might be related to his problems but receives no affirmative response. December 3, 1986: Evenson first speaks with attorney David McCrea, who is involved in other CCA litigation. January 1987: On McCrea's referral, Evenson sees Dr. Henry Peters, [who] tells Evenson that exposure to CCA for any length of time is extremely hazardous. March 13, 1987: Evenson files his complaint in state court. April 1987: Dr. Daniel Teitelbaum, examines Evenson after McCrea arranges an appointment. Dr. Teitelbaum confirms Evenson's suspicions that CCA is the cause of his injuries.

Evenson sought recovery on theories of strict liability in tort, negligence, wilful misconduct for failure to warn of the dangers associated with CCA exposure, and for fraudulent concealment of such dangers.

The district court granted the defendants' motions for summary judgment, holding that the two-year Indiana statute of limitations barred Evenson's product liability action as well as his fraudulent concealment and failure-to-warn claims. * * *

II. Discussion

In the context of a summary judgment motion based on the statute of limitations, we must find (1) that the statute of limitations has run and (2) there exists no genuine issue of material fact as to when the plaintiff's cause of action accrued. * * *

Indiana's applicable statute of limitations provides: "[A]ny product liability action in which the theory of liability is negligence or strict liability in tort must be commenced within two (2) years after the cause of action accrues * * *." Ind.Code § 33–1–1.5–5. Because chemicals and products are capable of causing injuries that often do not become evident until well after a plaintiff's last exposure to them, Indiana, like many other states, has adopted a discovery rule. Under this rule, the Indiana statute of limitations begins to run from the date that the plaintiff knew or should have discovered (1) that the plaintiff suffered an injury or impingement and (2) that the injury or impingement was caused by the product or act of another. Thus, the Indiana discovery rule has both an injury and a causation prong.

Evenson was aware that he was experiencing medical problems in the latter part of 1983, well over two years before he filed his complaint. The focus is therefore on the causation prong—when Evenson knew or should have discovered that his injuries were caused by his exposure to CCA.

The district court observed that the Indiana discovery rule emphasizes knowledge of a potential rather than an actual link. Citing Miller v. A.H. Robins Co., 766 F.2d 1102 (7th Cir.1985), the district court stated that the causation prong of the discovery rule "is satisfied if the plaintiff is informed of a 'possible causal connection' between the foreign substance and the injury of which he complains." Again relying on Miller, the district court noted that having a fair opportunity to investigate available sources of information does not require possessing irrefutable proof of causation. The district court believed it was enough that Evenson himself suspected that CCA may have been causing his injuries. The court therefore held that the statute of limitations began to run on February 20, 1985, when Evenson requested Dr. Felker to order tests that might substantiate Evenson's theory about CCA being a possible cause of his medical problems. Because Evenson did not file his complaint until March 13, 1987, the district court concluded that the statute of limitations barred his action.

The district court's conclusion was clearly reasonable. We would agree with the court's holding except we believe that the court, in applying the Indiana discovery rule, did not give sufficient weight to an unusual factor in this case. Evenson, despite his diligent efforts, received no indication anytime prior to the two-year period before he filed his complaint that his suspicion as to the cause of his injuries might be correct. * * *

Evenson, a mere layperson, only suspected that CCA was causing his medical problems. Although Evenson asked various doctors over the course of his continuous medical treatment if CCA could be the cause of his injuries, no doctor, prior to the two-year period before he filed his complaint, confirmed his suspicions that CCA might be the cause. Evenson, because of his suspicions, also requested appropriate tests to substantiate his theory; yet the urine test done under Dr. Felker's direction came back negative and Dr. Steven Isenberg never received the results of the tests done on the polyp sample following Evenson's second surgery.

On appeal, Evenson argues that a layperson's mere suspicion is not sufficient to trigger the statute of limitations under Indiana's discovery rule. He contends that information as to the probable, not possible, cause of the injury is required before the statute will begin to run. Evenson urges this court to construe the causation prong to require actually finding a doctor willing to testify, based on medical probability, that the defendant's product caused the injury. Evenson asserts that the statute began to run on December 3, 1986, because it was then that he first spoke with his attorney, David McCrea. McCrea knew Dr. Teitelbaum through other CCA litigation and was aware of Dr. Teitelbaum's belief that a causal link existed between CCA and the type of injuries exhibited by Evenson. Because he filed his complaint within two years of his first conversation with McCrea, Evenson argues his action is not time barred.

Although we agree locating a doctor willing to testify that a particular product is the probable cause of the plaintiff's injuries would trigger the statute of limitations, we disagree with Evenson that this is the only event capable of doing so. Defendants correctly point out that the cases cited by Evenson applying the Indiana discovery rule establish only that a medical diagnosis causally connecting a plaintiff's exposure to a product and his injuries is sufficient to start the statute running, not that such a diagnosis is necessary. At the same time, we disagree with defendants that a layperson's mere suspicion, even when coupled with the start of an investigation, automatically triggers the statute. Fed. R.Civ.P. 11 would arguably require sanctions against a party who files suit based on nothing more than the kind of suspicions Evenson had in the present case.

While we are aware of the value of bright lines in rules of procedure, it is futile to try to draw firm lines in the context of the discovery rule in these circumstances. We can be no more specific than to say that where knowledge of causation is at issue, a person knows or should have discovered the cause of his injury when he has or should have discovered some evidence that there was a reasonable possibility that his injury was caused by the act or product of another. A reasonable possibility, while less than a probability, requires more than the mere suspicion possessed by Evenson, a layperson without technical or medical knowledge. In applying this rule, district courts will necessarily be bound to a fact-specific inquiry.

In the present case, the evidence on the record does not show that as of February 20, 1985, Evenson had or should have discovered some evidence that there was a reasonable possibility that his CCA exposure was the cause of his injuries. Although Evenson himself suspected at this time that CCA was the culprit, his attempts to determine the actual cause were rebuffed by his doctors in whom he could place some reliance. What Evenson had on February 20, 1985, was not some evidence of a reasonable possibility that CCA was the cause but only a layman's mere suspicion to this effect.

Events short of a doctor's diagnosis can provide a plaintiff with evidence of a reasonable possibility that another's act or product caused his injuries. Nevertheless, there must be something more than a plaintiff's mere suspicion or speculation—a reasonable, not a mere, possibility is required to trigger the statute.

Evenson filed his complaint on March 13, 1987, and we have concluded that the statute had not begun to run as of February 20, 1985. Evenson's claim, therefore, will be barred by the two-year statute of limitations only if, between February 20, 1985 and March 13, 1985, Evenson knew or should have discovered some evidence that there was a reasonable possibility that CCA was the cause of his injuries. Although we ordinarily would remand to the district court to determine when the statute of limitations began to run, we need not burden the district court in this case. We have the complete record before us and our review of the record reveals that nothing happened during that critical three-week period to satisfy this test. We therefore conclude that Evenson's suit is not barred by Indiana's statute of limitations.

* * *

[The dissent of MANION, J. is omitted].

Notes and Questions

1. The court finds plaintiff's "mere suspicion" insufficient to trigger the statute. Do you agree with the court's adoption of the reasonable possibility test? What if plaintiff had not received negative or equivocal responses from his doctors? What if he never saw any doctors until after he visited the attorney? What if he knew several co-workers had confirmed diagnoses of CCA-related injuries similar to Evenson's injuries? Perhaps the court's most telling criticism of the mere suspicion test is the statement that suits filed on such a basis would "arguably require sanctions" under Rule 11 of the Federal Rules of Civil Procedure. Does this sound reasonable? In a dissenting opinion in *Evenson*, Judge Manion observes that plaintiff would obviously need an expert to testify as to causation at trial, but it is not essential to have a physician confirm plaintiff's belief in order to file suit, to establish accrual of the cause of action, or to avoid Rule 11 sanctions. With whom do you agree? One court has held that a special statute of limitation that it interpreted as triggering the running of the limitation period based on a "mere possibility" was unconstitutional under the right to a remedy and due process clauses of the Ohio Constitution. See Burgess v. Eli Lilly & Co., 66 Ohio St.3d 59, 609 N.E.2d 140 (1993).

2. *Community Knowledge.* Should a general knowledge in the community about the risks posed by certain toxic exposures be sufficient to satisfy the discovery rule? One court's treatment of this issue is found in Allen v. United States, 588 F.Supp. 247 (D.Utah 1984), reversed on other grounds 816 F.2d 1417 (10th Cir.1987), cert. denied 484 U.S. 1004, 108 S.Ct. 694, 98 L.Ed.2d 647 (1988), where the district court held that knowledge of the general hazards associated with radiation, and knowledge of the fact that defendant had been exploding nuclear devices, did not constitute discovery until plaintiff became aware of the precise risks of particular diseases. In Joseph v. Hess Oil, 867 F.2d 179, 184 (3d Cir.1989), in reversing the trial court's order for summary judgment, the appeals court noted that the plaintiff knew that he was sick and knew that exposure to asbestos, a substance with which he worked, could be harmful was not enough to demonstrate that the plaintiff knew or should have known that his injury was asbestos-related.

In order to prove when a plaintiff should have known of the injury and the causal link to defendant's product, the defendant frequently will attempt to demonstrate community awareness of the harm or potential for harm.

Defendant may adduce proof that a plaintiff knew of the hazard, for example, by showing that the plaintiff had actually read articles describing the harm and its cause. See O'Brien v. Eli Lilly & Co., 668 F.2d 704, 707–10 (3d Cir.1981) (accrual if and when the plaintiff actually read articles linking DES and her disease). In most instances, however, proving a general community awareness of the causal linkage and of the likelihood of injury may be the defendant's only way to pinpoint the accrual date. In Allen v. A.H. Robins Co., 752 F.2d 1365 (9th Cir.1985), the manufacturer of the Dalkon shield attempted to show that a statute of limitations began to run when defendant sent out over two hundred thousand "Dear Doctor" letters informing *doctors* of the medical risks associated with the Dalkon shield. The court rejected this argument, holding that such awareness in the medical community was insufficient to cause the statute of limitations to begin to run. The court commented that the plaintiff could not be considered to have been aware of the causal connection between the defendant's product and her ailment until she had watched a televised report on the subject by *60 Minutes.*

3. *Level of Medical Knowledge Required.* Consider the following testimony from the plaintiff on deposition:

> Plaintiff remembered that his family physician had informed him that he had "bad lungs" and should change jobs so that plaintiff's "lungs don't get worse." Plaintiff gave the following deposition testimony during examination by defense counsel:

> Q. "What did [the family physician] tell you about why you should quit?"

> A. "So it doesn't get worse."

> Q. "So what is 'it'?"

> A. "Whatever it is. My lungs don't get worse. I don't know which way he meant it." * * *

> Q. "[The family physician] told you at that time you had a lung problem from your work?"

> A. "Right. He didn't say from the work. He just says, 'You have a lung problem.' He must have meant from work, because he says 'You have worked with asbestos. It must be from work,' is what he told me."

> * * *

> Q. "Did [the family physician] describe your lung problem with any kind of word?"

> A. "Word, no, he just said, 'You have bad lungs,' that's all."

Reversing the trial court, an appeals court held that it was a jury question of whether the plaintiff possessed sufficient information to cause him to inquire further in order to determine whether a legal wrong had occurred from occupational exposure to asbestos. Martin v. A & M Insulation Co., 207 Ill.App.3d 706, 152 Ill.Dec. 688, 566 N.E.2d 375 (1990).

In contrast, in Weger v. Shell Oil Co., 966 F.2d 216 (7th Cir.1992), Weger was a sheet metal worker for fourteen years, until he was forced to leave his job in 1982 because of kidney problems. He sued defendants in 1986, alleging his kidney problems were caused by exposure to solvents produced by the defendants. In December 1982, he suffered renal failure, and he and his wife began to investigate the cause of his kidney problems. In November 1983, Marilyn Weger read an article in the *International Association of Machinists and Aerospace Workers Journal* on the long-term negative health effects of workplace exposure to solvents. Marilyn Weger wrote George Robinson, the article's author, stating, "I feel solvents are directly related to his [Mr. Weger's] medical problems." Robinson responded, advising the couple to seek medical advice and referring them to a specialist, Dr. Samuel Epstein. On January 12, 1984, Marilyn Weger wrote to Epstein, saying her husband was exposed to chemicals at work. The doctor replied July 30, 1984, recommending that the couple contact a lawyer. In August 1984, attorney Robert Douglas filed a workers' compensation claim on Weger's behalf. The claim stated, "As a result of exposure to chemicals, Petitioner has liver and kidney disease." On July 16, 1985, Dr. David Main examined Weger and reported to Douglas that it was not clear what caused Weger's illness.

In finding the action barred, according to the court, it was apparent that the Wegers understood that someone might be responsible for Roger Weger's kidney condition. As the court summarized: "Mrs. Weger expressed that belief in a letter to Robinson which he, in turn, confirmed. They were advised to contact a lawyer to pursue the matter and did so, showing that they possessed sufficient information that caused them to inquire further."

For another illustrative case about the level of medical knowledge sufficient to trigger the running of the statute of limitations, see University of Miami v. Bogorff, 583 So.2d 1000 (Fla.1991) (where plaintiff's 3–year–old son with leukemia received injection of defendant's drug and later developed quadriplegia, statute began to run when parents were aware of child's dramatically changed condition after last injection and had constructive knowledge of medical opinion that the drug may have contributed to the injuries).

4. *AIDS-Related Issues.* Suits filed by hemophiliacs against the suppliers of blood clotting agents for transmission of the HIV virus raise varied issues of when a claim was reasonably discoverable. In Doe v. Cutter Biological, 813 F.Supp. 1547 (M.D.Fla.1993), the plaintiff received a memorandum from the defendant, a blood bank in 1983 that enclosed a letter notifying that certain lot numbers of KOATE were being withdrawn because they contained plasma whose donor was diagnosed as having AIDS. Plaintiff actually returned six vials to the blood bank. In 1985, plaintiff tested positive for HIV, and his physician told him he had a 50/50 chance of developing AIDS. During this time, however, the National Hemophilia Information Foundation published pamphlets read by plaintiff stating that many hemophiliacs exposed to the HIV virus had not developed full-blown AIDS.

In 1988, Doe, after hearing about a suit brought by another family, spoke with a physician who worked with the Florida Hemophilia Association, who told him that the other family was wrong to sue, claiming that because, as the makers of the agents, they did everything possible to make their product safe, it would be "asinine" to sue because it would force the producers out of business. In 1989, the same physician consulted for Cutter on another case. In 1990, Doe developed AIDS and sued Cutter. Rejecting Doe's argument that he suffered no injury until he developed symptoms of AIDS in 1990, the court held the action was time-barred under a four-year statute. The court held that although the receipt of the tainted blood constituted injury, the statute wasn't triggered until 1985 when he tested positive for HIV and was informed that he had a 50/50 chance of developing AIDS, a disease he knew would result in death. The court also held that the physician's statements to Doe in 1988 did not constitute fraudulent concealment because Doe already knew he had a cause of action by 1985.

At least one court has held that a plaintiff is on notice that he was injured when the blood supplier recalled some of its factor concentrate in 1983. Doe v. American National Red Cross, 796 F.Supp. 395 (W.D.Wis.1992).

At least two state supreme courts have held that shorter statutes of limitation applicable to physicians and hospitals in some states do not apply to actions against blood product suppliers, which are governed by the longer general statutes. See Silva v. Southwest Florida Blood Bank, 601 So.2d 1184 (Fla.1992) (blood bank did not render diagnosis, treatment or care to hospital patients, and thus suits governed by the four-year negligence statute of limitations, not the shorter two-year statute for malpractice actions); Kaiser v. Memorial Blood Center of Minneapolis, Inc., 486 N.W.2d 762 (Minn.1992); contra Bradway v. American National Red Cross, 263 Ga. 19, 426 S.E.2d 849 (1993).

Problem

Diana Krause filed suit in 1987 against Feldman Laboratories, Inc. (Feldman), the manufacturer of a medication used to treat blood clots, Coumadin. Krause was treated with Coumadin in February 1981 for blood clots in her legs. The prescribing physician told Diana not to get pregnant and to stop taking Coumadin if she did. Additionally, the doctor wrote her a letter repeating his instructions to stop the medication if she became pregnant. Krause stated on deposition that she stopped using the drug as soon as she learned of her pregnancy in June or July of 1981. David P. Krause, Jr. was born prematurely on December 6, 1981. He had problems immediately, including birth trauma, blood clots, respiratory difficulties, and cerebral palsy.

In February 1985, Diana was treated again for blood clots and resumed taking Coumadin. While in the hospital for this course of treatment, she received and kept two Feldman pamphlets regarding Coumadin. She stated on deposition that she read the information but was not immediately concerned about the contents because she and her husband had no plans to conceive additional children. However, she said the pamphlets made her begin to think it was dangerous to take Coumadin during pregnancy. She further testified that when David was born, no one specifically told her the child's birth problems might have been caused by the child's exposure in utero to Coumadin. While David's medical records documented Coumadin-related malformities, she never had access to these records.

A trial court granted Feldman's motion for dismissal on grounds that the suit, filed in March 1987, was time-barred under the applicable two-year discovery rule statute of limitations. The court held that her doctor's directive that she stop using the drug Coumadin if she became pregnant, the fact she did stop the medication when she suspected pregnancy, her child's severe birth defects, and informational pamphlets she received during the second course of treatment several years after the birth all combined to put her on notice of injury and causation no later than February 1985.

In the trial court's view, the fact that neither the manufacturer nor the plaintiff's treating physician told her specifically that the drug caused her son's problems did not defeat the statute of limitations defense. The trial court emphasized that though the pamphlets Diana received during the 1984 or 1985 hospitalization might not be sufficient information by itself to put her on notice of the cause of her son's problems, the information "did not come to her in a vacuum." In combination with Diana's other experiences, the court held, the pamphlets were sufficient to trigger the limitations statute.

Plaintiff appeals the dismissal of her case, contending she did not know and could not reasonably have discovered that her son's problems were related to prenatal exposure to Coumadin more than two years before she filed suit. Specifically, she contends that no doctor ever told her that David's problems were caused by the drug, that she had no medical training that would have allowed her to come to this conclusion on her own, and that she did not have access to her son's medical records that could have indicated his condition was related to the drug. She emphasizes further that at the time of the pregnancy and birth, she was not given any warning information from Feldman concerning Coumadin.

These events occurred in the State of Southshire, where in Bales v. Gun, 85 S.S. 2d 146 (1981), the Southshire Supreme Court said the limitations period starts "when a person knows or reasonably should know of his or her injury and also knows or reasonably should know that it was wrongfully caused."

Decide the appeal. Will you affirm or reverse the trial court? Why? Prepare a brief opinion.

D. SUCCESSIVE ACTIONS AND STATUTES OF LIMITATION

Plaintiffs in toxic tort cases may face the problem that the toxic exposures produce multiple kinds of harm which are manifested at different points in time. This paradigm is illustrated by asbestos cases where the worker first may sustain damage in the form of pleural thickening of the lung walls, later experiences asbestosis, and still later may develop lung cancer or mesothelioma. If plaintiff sues for asbestosis, is he barred by the doctrine of claim preclusion (res judicata) if ten years later he sues for mesothelioma? If he waits to file suit until he develops mesothelioma, has the statute expired because his cause accrued when he learned of the asbestosis but chose not to sue? The tension between these two issues focuses on how the "cause of action" is defined for each purpose, and whether it is appropriate to make the definition turn on the purpose for which the inquiry is made. To enhance judicial efficiency and discourage piecemeal litigation, courts have adopted a broad "transactional" approach in determining if a second suit is barred by a judgment in the first. See Restatement (Second) of Judgments § 24(1) (1982); Nevada v. United States, 463 U.S. 110, 130 n. 12, 103 S.Ct. 2906, 2918 n. 12, 77 L.Ed.2d 509 (1983); Federated Department Stores v. Moitie, 452 U.S. 394, 101 S.Ct. 2424, 69 L.Ed.2d 103 (1981).

Some courts have held the second suit to be barred because of the importance placed on the policy reasons for the claim preclusion doctrine. See, e.g., Graffagnino v. Fibreboard Corp., 776 F.2d 1307, 1308 (5th Cir.1985) ("[E]xposure to asbestos can give rise to only a single cause of action for all injuries that are caused by that exposure, whether or not all the injuries have become manifest at the time the cause of action accrues."); Gideon v. Johns–Manville Sales Corp., 761 F.2d 1129, 1137 (5th Cir.1985) ("Gideon could not split his cause of action and recover damages for asbestosis, then later sue for damages caused by such other pulmonary disease as might develop, then still later sue for cancer should cancer appear."); Joyce v. A.C. & S., Inc., 785 F.2d 1200 (4th Cir.1986) (applying Virginia law).

In the statutes of limitation context, even if courts define the cause of action more narrowly in order to preserve a plaintiff's ability to sue for subsequently acquired harm, the tension and risk are not entirely eliminated. The case that follows attempts to resolve this difficulty.

WILSON v. JOHNS–MANVILLE
SALES CORPORATION

United States Court of Appeals, District of Columbia Circuit, 1982.
684 F.2d 111.

GINSBURG, J.

This case presents a novel and difficult legal issue in the context of the mounting volume of litigation relating to deaths or injuries caused by exposure to asbestos products. We are asked to decide whether manifestation of any asbestos-related disease (in this case, asbestosis) triggers the running of the statute of limitations on all separate, distinct, and later-manifested diseases (here, malignant mesothelioma, an extremely lethal form of cancer) engendered by the same asbestos exposure. We hold that time to commence litigation does not begin to run on a separate and distinct disease until that disease becomes manifest.

I. INTRODUCTION

A. *The Facts*

Beginning in 1941, Henry J. Wilson was steadily employed as an insulation worker at various construction sites in the metropolitan Washington, D.C. area. As an integral element of this employment, Wilson regularly handled and was otherwise exposed to asbestos and asbestos products.

On February 14, 1973, Wilson was x-rayed as part of his local union's routine program instituted to determine which workers, if any, had contracted asbestosis. Evaluation of these x-rays revealed that Wilson was indeed suffering from "mild asbestosis." Following his receipt of this diagnosis, Wilson began a new job, still in the insulation trade, but involving little, if any, exposure to asbestos.

Subsequent to 1973, Wilson's health rapidly deteriorated. He suffered two heart attacks in June 1974 and a collapsed lung in February 1975, and was hospitalized on each occasion. Because of these episodes and on the advice of his physician, Wilson retired.

Complaining of sharp pains in his chest, Wilson was again hospitalized in February 1978. On this occasion, Wilson was diagnosed as having mesothelioma, a cancer of the mesothelial cells with a poor prognosis for recovery. Wilson died on May 17, 1978.

B. The District Court Proceedings

On May 16, 1979, just short of one year after Wilson's death, his widow, Blannie S. Wilson ("Appellant"), instituted the instant diversity action. Named as defendants (collectively "Johns–Manville") were designers, manufacturers, and distributors of asbestos and asbestos products. * * * Appellant asserted that Johns–Manville's actions were the direct and proximate cause of her husband's pulmonary illnesses and death. * * *

After extensive discovery by the parties, Johns–Manville moved for summary judgment on both statutory counts. Johns–Manville asserted that Henry Wilson had one, and only one, indivisible cause of action for all past, present, and future injuries resulting from his exposure to asbestos products. This cause of action, Johns–Manville claimed, accrued, at the latest, when Wilson first knew or should have known that he was suffering from any asbestos-related disease, i.e., in February 1973, when Wilson was diagnosed as suffering from asbestosis. Therefore, Johns–Manville concluded, the applicable three-year statute of limitations barred the 1979 Survival action. Furthermore, Johns–Manville argued, Appellant's Wrongful Death action was also time-barred; as a wholly derivative claim, Johns–Manville maintained, a Wrongful Death action may not proceed unless the decedent at the time of his death could have initiated a timely action for personal injuries had he lived.

[T]he district court granted Johns–Manville's motion and dismissed Appellant's complaint with prejudice. This appeal followed.

II. ANALYSIS

The applicable statute of limitations, D.C.Code § 12–301(8), provides that a Survival claim "may not be brought after (3 years) from the time the right to maintain the action accrues." Appellant's Survival claim, therefore, is timely only if Henry Wilson had a right of action which "accrued" after May 17, 1976.

A. The Discovery Rule

The accrual date of a claim for relief based on a disease with a long incubation period, such as asbestosis or mesothelioma, is an issue on which judicial opinion is in flux. Some courts adhere to the traditional view that "'the cause of action accrues at the time of invasion of (plaintiff's) body.'" Steinhardt v. Johns–Manville Corp., 446 N.Y.S.2d 244, 246 (N.Y.1981). Other courts employ the "discovery" rule under which a "cause of action accrues when the plaintiff knows or through the exercise of due diligence should have known of the injury." See Burns v. Bell, 409 A.2d 614, 617 (D.C.App.1979). Johns–Manville points out that to date "the District of Columbia Court of Appeals has not extended the 'discovery' rule to cases beyond the area of professional malpractice." We are persuaded, however, that, if faced with the issue, the District of Columbia courts would apply the discovery rule to latent disease cases.

* * *

Johns–Manville principally argues, however, that even if the discovery rule is applicable to the instant case, Appellant's claim is nonetheless barred by the three-year limitations period. Henry Wilson, Johns–Manville urges most strenuously, had only one indivisible cause of action for asbestos-related injuries and that cause of action accrued five years before he "discovered" that he had cancer; it accrued in 1973 when Wilson "discovered" he was suffering from "mild asbestosis." We now turn to that central contention.

B. Distinct Illnesses as Separate Causes of Action

Johns–Manville focuses on the alleged wrongful conduct and asserts that once some harm is apparent, a claim accrues not only for harm then manifest, but for all harm that may eventuate in the future as a result of the same conduct. Johns–Manville's theory is that Henry Wilson's claim ripened no later than February 1973 when he was diagnosed as having "mild asbestosis." Within three years of that diagnosis, Johns–Manville reasons, Wilson could have instituted a personal injury action seeking damages, not only for asbestosis, but for consequences that might develop later, including separate and distinct illnesses such as mesothelioma[33] or another form of cancer. Had Wilson sued between 1973 and 1976, and then attempted to return to court after the February 1978 malignant mesothelioma diagnosis, he would have been blocked, Johns–Manville asserts, by the well-established rule that a claim or cause of action may not be split. See generally Restatement (Second) of Judgments §§ 24–26 (1982). It follows, Johns–Manville concludes, that Wilson's mesothelioma claim is similarly barred when, as occurred here, he simply sat on his right to sue and did not institute any tort action

---

33. Johns–Manville concedes that asbestosis and mesothelioma are separate and distinct diseases, and that mesothelioma is not a complication of the former. Johns– Manville does maintain that both diseases "had the same precise cause," i.e., "(Wilson's) years of exposure to asbestos."

between February 1973 and February 1976. In essence, Johns–Manville argues, Wilson did not have the option to waive tort recovery for asbestosis, and sue for a lethal cancer if and when such a condition developed. We disagree.

Preliminarily, we note that we need not and do not decide whether Johns–Manville's initial premise is correct, i.e., whether judgment on a claim for asbestosis pursued between 1973 and 1976 would have precluded a subsequent claim based on the 1978 mesothelioma diagnosis.[34] It suffices to point out that res judicata (claim preclusion) doctrine and policy would control the decision of that question. * * * This case requires us to focus, not on judgments and their preclusive effects, but on statutes of limitations and the policies they implicate in personal injury actions. We therefore consider below the appropriate delineation of the claim or cause of action in suit in the relevant context.

"Statutes of limitation find their justification in necessity and convenience rather than in logic. They represent expedients, rather than principles." Chase Securities Corp. v. Donaldson, 325 U.S. 304 (1945). Two considerations, particularly, motivate legislation placing time limitations on the commencement of litigation. The first, which may be designated evidentiary, relates to "the search for truth (which) may be seriously impaired by the loss of evidence, whether by death or disappearance of witnesses, fading memories, disappearance of documents, or otherwise." The second, repose, concerns the potential defendant's interests in security against stale claims and in planning for the future without the uncertainty inherent in potential liability.

In the case at hand, these considerations pull in opposite directions. Repose, beyond question, is best served by Johns–Manville's broad definition of the "cause of action" at stake. But in situations involving the risk of manifestation of a latent disease, unlike the mine run of litigation, the evidentiary consideration counsels narrower delineation of the dimensions of a claim. Key issues to be litigated in a latent disease case are the existence of the disease, its proximate cause, and the resultant damage. Evidence relating to these issues tends to develop, rather than disappear, as time passes.

Looking beyond repose and evidentiary considerations, we take into account the interests generally involved in personal injury and death cases: plaintiff's in obtaining at least adequate compensation, defendant's in paying no more than that. Integrating these two, the community seeks to advance, through the system of adjudication, relief that will sufficiently, but not excessively, compensate persons for injuries occasioned by the tortious acts of others. In latent disease cases, this community interest would be significantly undermined by a judge-made rule that upon manifestation of any harm, the injured party must then, if ever, sue for all harms the same exposure may (or may not) occasion some time in the future.

34. But cf. Restatement (Second) of Judgments, supra, § 26(1)(b) & comment b (court in first action may expressly reserve plaintiff's right to maintain second action).

The traditional American rule, adopted in the District of Columbia, is that recovery of damages based on future consequences may be had only if such consequences are "reasonably certain." Recovery of damages for speculative or conjectural future consequences is not permitted. To meet the "reasonably certain" standard, courts have generally required plaintiffs to prove that it is more likely than not (a greater than 50% chance) that the projected consequence will occur. If such proof is made, the alleged future effect may be treated as certain to happen and the injured party may be awarded full compensation for it; if the proof does not establish a greater than 50% chance, the injured party's award must be limited to damages for harm already manifest.

In view of the "reasonably certain" standard, it appears that Johns–Manville is urging for cases of this sort (in which cancer is diagnosed years after asbestosis becomes manifest) more than a time-bar; it is urging, in essence, that there can never be a recovery for cancer unless (1) a lawsuit is filed within three years of the asbestosis diagnosis, and (2) cancer becomes manifest during the course of that lawsuit. For it is altogether likely that had Wilson, upon receiving the "mild asbestosis" diagnosis, sought to recover for a cancer which might (or might not) develop, Johns–Manville would have argued forcibly that the probability of such a development was far less than 50%, and was therefore too speculative, conjectural, uncertain to support a damage award.

Concern for judicial economy also influences our decision. Upon diagnosis of an initial illness, such as asbestosis, the injured party may not need or desire judicial relief. Other sources, such as workers' compensation or private insurance, may provide adequate recompense for the initial ailment. If no further disease ensues, the injured party would have no cause to litigate. However, if such a person is told that another, more serious disease may manifest itself later on, and that a remedy in court will be barred unless an anticipatory action is filed currently, there will be a powerful incentive to go to court, for the consequence of a wait-and-see approach to the commencement of litigation may be too severe to risk. Moreover, a plaintiff's representative in such a case may be motivated to protract and delay once in court so that the full story of his client's condition will be known before the case is set for trial.

* * * With respect to the statute of limitations issue before us, we conclude that a potential defendant's interest in repose is counterbalanced and outweighed by other factors, including evidentiary considerations, securing fair compensation for serious harm, and deterring uneconomical anticipatory lawsuits. We therefore hold that the diagnosis of "mild asbestosis" received by Henry Wilson in February 1973 did not start the clock on his right to sue for the separate and distinct disease, mesothelioma, attributable to the same asbestos exposure, but not manifest until February 1978. Blannie Wilson's action, we decide, to the extent that it seeks recovery based on mesothelioma, from which her husband suffered and died, was timely filed.

* * *

It is so ordered.

Notes and Questions

1.   Although not the first case to reach the same holding, *Wilson* is the decision most frequently cited for the proposition that in toxic tort cases involving multiple stages of disease, each is a separate cause of action for statutes of limitation purposes. See also Pierce v. Johns–Manville Sales Corp., 296 Md. 656, 464 A.2d 1020 (1983); Wilber v. Owens–Corning Fiberglas Corp., 476 N.W.2d 74 (Iowa 1991); Marinari v. Asbestos Corp., Ltd., 417 Pa.Super. 440, 612 A.2d 1021 (1992); Miller v. Armstrong World Industries, Inc., 817 P.2d 111 (Colo.1991). Do these cases turn on the medical fact that each of the asbestos-related diseases is separate and independent? What if they were stages of a single disease process that always resulted in cancer?

2.   *Claim Preclusion.* The court declines to resolve the issue preclusion question of what happens if the plaintiff does file an earlier action for asbestosis or pleural thickening and then files a later action for cancer or mesothelioma. How would the court have resolved it if Wilson had instituted an earlier action for asbestosis? See Smith v. Bethlehem Steel Corp., 303 Md. 213, 492 A.2d 1286, 1296 (1985); Ayers v. Township of Jackson, 106 N.J. 557, 525 A.2d 287 (1987) (explicitly reserving plaintiffs' right to bring a second action for cancer should it develop after declining to recognize a cause of action for increased risk of future disease). The discussion in Chapter 5 on the availability of present compensation for future consequences necessarily implies some recognition of the claim or issue preclusion problem. Can you see why?

3.   *Filing Workers' Compensation Claims.* The decisions are split on whether the filing of a workers' compensation claim starts the running of the limitations period for a later-filed tort suit. In Welch v. Celotex Corp., 951 F.2d 1235 (11th Cir.1992), Welch, an insulator, began to experience shortness of breath and became concerned that he was developing an asbestos-related disease. He filed a workers' compensation claim against his employer in 1984. In 1987, Welch was diagnosed as having asbestosis and filed a tort action against several manufacturers and distributors of asbestos products. The trial court granted defendants' summary judgment on the ground that Georgia's two-year statute of limitations for personal injury actions had already run. The Eleventh Circuit reversed, stating that the limitations period does not begin to run until a plaintiff reasonably should have known the causal connection between the injury and a defendant's allegedly negligent conduct. In the court's view, while plaintiff may have known that asbestos had caused his injury when he filed his workers' compensation action, the filing did not show that plaintiff had reason to know that defendants' conduct had caused his injury. The court noted that the only evidence showing the extent of plaintiff's knowledge of defendants' conduct was that he had (1) worked with asbestos products for many years; and (2) given a sworn affidavit that he had been unaware of any wrongdoing by defendants until he consulted an attorney about the present action.

In Brown v. Dow Chemical Co., 875 F.2d 197 (8th Cir.1989), the court held that plaintiff's workers' compensation claim alleging that his sterility was caused by exposure to dibromochloropropane (DBCP) was sufficient to trigger the statute against his later filed tort action.

Should there be a presumption that a compensation claim demonstrates sufficient knowledge of injury and causation to start the limitations period? Given the knowledge of asbestos-related diseases, is it likely that the plaintiff in *Welch* did not know that the producers of the product were responsible? How about the lawyer who handled the compensation claim? What are some of the strategy considerations which might influence an employee in deciding whether or not to file a claim against his employer? How about issue preclusion (collateral estoppel) if a substantive issue, such as causation, is determined adversely to the claimant? In *Brown*, the court also held that the finding by the Compensation Commission that plaintiff did not establish by a preponderance of the evidence that exposure to DBCP had caused his sterility was entitled to preclusive effect in the tort action.

4. A proposal directed at the claim preclusion-statute of limitations tension appears in Note, Claim Preclusion in Modern Latent Disease Cases: A Proposal for Allowing Second Suits, 103 Harv. L. Rev. 1989 (1990). The Note argues that application of the claim preclusion rule ignores the unique situation of the victim of a double-harm toxic tort. If the development of the latent injury is unforeseeable to both the plaintiff and the court at the time of the first action, inclusion of a claim for that second injury—even an increased risk claim—is impossible. Even if epidemiological studies or other medical knowledge alert the plaintiff to the risk of a second disease, the court will reject the demand for immediate compensation unless the court determines that it is probable that the plaintiff will actually contract the second disease. The Note argues that a narrower definition of the cause of action—which separates the immediate disease or injury and the latent disease—would permit compensation for victims' later developing harm. The Note proposes a limited second suit, consisting of four components: (1) adoption of a definition of a cause of action consistent with the discovery rule; (2) elimination of pain and suffering damages from the second suit; (3) suspension of the collateral source rule in those jurisdictions where it would otherwise apply; and (4) an application of attorney's fee shifting:

A. *Definition of the Cause of Action*

* * * This Note does not propose allowing a plaintiff to bring a separate suit for each distinct disease, because that would virtually defeat all the beneficial effects of claim preclusion and would simply replace the problem currently plaguing plaintiffs with potentially greater problems for the legal system and defendants. Instead, courts should adopt an approach similar to the "entire controversy doctrine" currently in effect in New Jersey. Under this doctrine, the plaintiff must consolidate in a single suit all related claims, even if each claim can be supported by a separate cause of action. The unit of litigation is the "entire controversy" rather than its constituent claims or causes of action. Therefore, the "entire controversy" rule should be modified to exclude claims for unknown or speculative harms, thereby permitting plaintiffs to bring a second suit for those distinct harms that subsequently materialize.

B. *Pain and Suffering Damages*

Disallowing pain and suffering is a key element of the proposed intermediate solution. Eliminating pain and suffering damages in the second suit would preserve some measure of protection to defendants and would encourage settlement by making the amount of damages more predictable. Although pain and suffering damages may be warranted for many suits, they cannot be justified for the second suits allowed under this proposal on the basis of the tort system's two primary goals—deterrence and compensation. Deterring the tortfeasor justifies pain and suffering damages for the first suit but not the second, while simply compensating the plaintiff never justifies such damages.

* * *

C. *The Collateral Source Rule*

The collateral source rule allows plaintiffs to recover economic losses even when those losses are already covered by insurance. Although this rule often results in windfalls to plaintiffs, it is nevertheless generally allowed because it enhances the deterrence value of the suits. The deterrence factor in the second suits, however, is indeterminate and thus cannot support the collateral source rule. Therefore, under the proposal advanced here, courts should not apply the collateral source rule in the second suits.

After the simultaneous elimination of pain and suffering damages and the collateral source rule, pecuniary losses would be the only possible recovery. Because most people are covered by workers' compensation or some other form of first-party insurance and would thus receive compensation for their pecuniary losses through insurance awards, disallowing both the collateral source rule and pain and suffering damages would eliminate the incentive to sue for all plaintiffs except those few not covered by insurance. Thus, the proposed scheme would preclude the possibility of duplicative compensation and would minimize the incentive for lawyers to bring suits that are not necessary for compensatory purposes.

D. *Attorney Fee–Shifting*

The elimination of both pain and suffering damages and the collateral source rule from the second suits risks leaving plaintiffs no recovery from which to pay their lawyers. The second suits would only compensate plaintiffs for their pecuniary losses, and plaintiffs would be left to pay their lawyers out of their own pockets or out of awards that may not even cover the lawyer's bill. That outcome might inhibit even those few suits that plaintiffs could bring under the proposed exception to claim preclusion. * * * Under this arrangement, if the plaintiff wins, the defendant would pay the plaintiff's reasonable legal fees. This result makes sense intuitively and is economically justified, because the plaintiff's legal fees are both a loss that the defendant imposes on the plaintiff by committing the tort and a loss that is "economic"—the loss increases the plaintiff's marginal utility of money and can be replaced by a monetary payment. * * *

Note, Claim Preclusion in Modern Latent Disease Cases: A Proposal for Allowing Second Suits, 103 Harv. L. Rev. 1989, 1998, 1999, 2002–03 (1990). Copyright ©1990 by the Harvard Law Review Association. What do you think of this proposal? How might the plaintiffs' bar view it? The defense bar?

5. *Wrongful Death and Survival Actions.* Some courts hold that the limitations period is derivative of the decedent's claim had he or she lived to bring a personal injury action. For example, in Russell v. Ingersoll–Rand Co., 795 S.W.2d 243 (Tex.App.1990), the plaintiff's survivors brought an action against a company that supplied the decedent with equipment for his sandblasting career. In 1981 the decedent discovered that he had silicosis and commenced suit against several suppliers but not against the current defendant. Following his January 1988 death, the decedent's survivors brought suit in March 1988 against the current defendant, only to have the court grant summary judgment for the defendant, reasoning that had the decedent not perished, his action against the current defendant would have been time barred as the injury was discovered in 1981.

In other jurisdictions, however, a survivor's legal right to recover is considered independent from any claim that might have vested in the decedent prior to his death. Decisions following this rule hold that the statute of limitations for wrongful death actions begins to run upon the death of the decedent, not the time that the injury was discovered. Frongillo v. Grimmett, 163 Ariz. 369, 788 P.2d 102 (App.1989) (held: wrongful death action accrued on the date of the husband's death even though the statute of limitations on the husband's personal injury action had expired before his death).

The Georgia Supreme Court held that the discovery rule did not apply in wrongful death actions. Miles v. Ashland Chemical Co., 261 Ga. 726, 410 S.E.2d 290 (1991) (answering certified questions from the Court of Appeals for the Eleventh Circuit). Many states agree and refuse to apply the discovery rule in wrongful death or survival actions. See, e.g., Ayo v. Johns–Manville Sales Corp., 771 F.2d 902 (5th Cir.1985) (discovery rule unavailable in survival action); Trimper v. Porter–Hayden, 305 Md. 31, 501 A.2d 446 (1985) (discovery rule unavailable in wrongful death or survival action); Symbula v. Johns–Manville Corp., 514 Pa. 527, 526 A.2d 328 (1987) (discovery rule may not be employed to extend the time for filing wrongful death or survival action).

In *Miles*, three decedents, all of whom worked for the same firm, had died from cancer, two in 1984 and one in 1979. In 1987 plaintiffs learned that their decedent's deaths may have been caused by occupational exposure to methylene chloride and sued the manufacturers of a product containing that chemical. The Georgia statute provided for a two-year limitations period. The court acknowledged that if the cause of their injuries had been discovered during their lifetimes, they would have derived the benefit of the discovery rule, but because the wrongful death action accrues at death, not when an injury or cause is discovered, the actions were barred:

Under OCGA § 9–3–33, the defendants' liability extended two years from the date of death. To prolong the running of this period would be to subject the defendants to potentially infinite liability and is counter to the policy underlying statutes of limitation. We decline to extend the statute of limitation by adopting the discovery rule in wrongful death cases.

The dissent was harsh:

The majority opinion causes the wrongful death statutes to become a "delusive remedy" for those who cannot detect a causal link between the decedent's death and the tortfeasor's acts within two years of the decedent's death. See Urie v. Thompson, 337 U.S. 163, 69 S.Ct. 1018, 93 L.Ed. 1282 (1949). "We do not think the humane legislative plan intended such consequences to attach to blameless ignorance."

The legislature granted us the flexibility to punish wrongdoers and meet social and economic needs by allowing us to determine when an action "accrues." The Eleventh Circuit offered us the opportunity to use our flexibility; the majority of this Court prefers rigidity without rationale.

* * *

The majority's obdurate opinion fails to scrutinize the policy considerations that underlie the wrongful death statutes.

* * *

The majority opinion has brought the evolution of the wrongful death statutes to an abrupt halt; the ability to punish wrongdoers and meet the social and economic needs of our citizens has ended. * * *

The danger we face today comes in a far more furtive manner through toxins and carcinogens that do not instantly maim or kill, but that destroy life cell by cell, slowly, painfully, and as finally as any major physical trauma. The people who commit homicide with these toxins and carcinogens are just as culpable as those who commit homicide with exploding boilers. Our public policy requires that these people be punished and the survivors be compensated. Those goals can only be achieved by tolling the statutes until the causal link and the tortfeasor are discovered.

With whom do you agree? Is there a rational basis for not applying the discovery rule to extend wrongful death limitations statutes? The North Carolina Supreme Court has held that a wrongful death claim filed more than three years after diagnosis of a fatal disease, but within two years of death, is not barred. Dunn v. Pacific Employers Ins. Co., 332 N.C. 129, 418 S.E.2d 645 (1992).

6. *Federally–Mandated Statute of Limitation for Toxic Harms.* A provision of CERCLA § 309, as amended by SARA 42 U.S.C. § 9658, actually preempts state statutes of limitation for personal injury or property damage actions arising from exposure to hazardous substances when the state provisions are more restrictive than the federally mandated limitations periods. The federal statute creates a federally required commencement date which is defined as "The date the plaintiff knew (or reasonably should have

known) that the personal injury or property damage * * * were caused or contributed to by the hazardous substance or pollutant or contaminant concerned." CERCLA § 309(b)(4)(A). The federal statute governs whenever "the applicable limitations period for such action (as specified in the state statute of limitations or under common law) provides a commencement date which is earlier than the federally-required commencement date." CERCLA § 309(a)(1).

The language of the statute may be expansive enough to encompass products liability actions based on occupational exposure to toxic substances, as well as land-based trespass/ nuisance/strict liability suits. Section 9658 applies to actions meeting the following conditions: (1) "any action brought under state law for personal injury, or property damage"; (2) caused by exposure to any "hazardous substance, or pollutant or contaminant"; (3) which substances are "released into the environment"; (4) "from a facility." A toxic substance products liability claim would, by its very nature, satisfy the first condition. In regard to the second condition, the definition of "pollutant or contaminant" includes all agents that upon release into the environment cause "death, disease, cancer, and physiological malfunctions." See CERCLA § 101(33), 42 U.S.C.A. § 9601(33) (West 1994). Finally, the definition of "facility" in CERCLA § 101(9), 42 U.S.C.A. § 9601(9) includes any "building, structure, [or] installation * * * "and the definition of "environment" in CERCLA § 101(8), 42 U.S.C.A. § 9601(8) includes "any * * * land surface or subsurface strata, or ambient air within the United States." Thus, the nub of the interpretation question is whether the sale of a toxic product by a manufacturer or distributor constitutes a "release" of the toxin into the "environment." The definition of "facility" does contain an exception for "any consumer product in consumer use," which suggests that the federally-mandated statute of limitation provision would not apply to exposure to consumer toxic products. For a discussion of cases addressing the definition of "release," see Elizabeth Ann Glass, Superfund and SARA: Are There Any Defenses Left?, 12 Harv. Envtl. L. Rev. 385, 400–402 (1988).

At least some legislative history suggests that this limitation provision was primarily concerned with hazardous waste litigation, which would not encompass products liability claims. See Superfund § 301(e) Study Group, Injuries and Damages from Hazardous Wastes—Analysis and Improvement of Legal Remedies, Serial No. 97–12, 97th Cong. 2d Sess. 26027 (Comm. Print 1982). Two cases addressing this issue are Covalt v. Carey Canada Inc., 860 F.2d 1434 (7th Cir.1988), and Knox v. AC & S, Inc., 690 F.Supp. 752 (S.D.Ind.1988). Both courts agreed that although asbestos is a "hazardous substance" that came from a "facility," it was not "released into the environment." Hence, the applicable state statutes of limitation and repose were not preempted by CERCLA § 309.

For those states which have not adopted a discovery rule, this federal law now mandates that statutes of limitation not begin to run until the plaintiff knows or should have known that the injury or property damage was caused by the hazardous substance. Thus, the prerequisites for the running of the statute of limitations in all such actions are an awareness of the injury and a recognition of the causal connection between the injury and exposure to a hazardous substance.

Significantly, the statute appears broad enough to delay the commencement of the statutes of limitation in death cases until the administrator of the estate knows of the toxic agent's causal contribution to the decedent's disease. Even among those states that have adopted a discovery rule for injury cases, a number have refused to apply it to death cases, as noted above. The statute also contains a retroactivity provision which provides that the federally mandated discovery rule is applicable to all cases brought after December 11, 1980. This provision thus revives claims that would have been barred by existing state statute of limitations provisions. CERCLA § 309(b), 42 U.S.C.A. § 9658(b). See also Michael Green, When Toxic Worlds Collide: Regulatory and Common Law Prescriptions for Risk Communication, 13 Harv. Envtl. L. Rep. 209, 229–31 (1989). Regarding the constitutionality of this federal statute of limitations as applied to state law nuisance claims that would otherwise have been barred, the United States District Court in Bolin v. The Cessna Aircraft Co., 759 F.Supp. 692 (D.Kan.1991), upheld the law in the face of Tenth Amendment and Commerce Clause challenges.

E. STATUTES OF REPOSE

1. HOW THEY DIFFER FROM STATUTES OF LIMITATION

In contrast to statutes of limitation, which bar actions at a specified time period *after* the cause accrued, statutes of repose bar the institution of an action a specified number of years after a particular event, such as the date of first sale of a product or the date of improvements to real property. After that time, no action can be brought, even though the elements of a claim may not have all yet occurred and only occur years after the period has run. Thus, a cause of action may be extinguished before it ever accrues, with the repose conferring an immunity upon the defendant. The difference is illustrated by the fact that while fraudulent concealment can toll the running of a statute of limitations, it has no such effect upon the repose statute. See First United Methodist Church v. U.S. Gypsum Co., 882 F.2d 862, 866 (4th Cir.1989), cert. denied 493 U.S. 1070, 110 S.Ct. 1113, 107 L.Ed.2d 1020 (1990):

> Statutes of repose are based on considerations of the economic best interests of the public as a whole and are substantive grants of immunity based on a legislative balance of the respective rights of potential plaintiffs and defendants struck by determining a time limit beyond which liability no longer exists. * * * [A]s a general rule, a statute of limitations is tolled by a defendant's fraudulent concealment of a plaintiff's injury because it would be inequitable to allow a defendant to use a statute intended as a device of fairness to perpetrate a fraud. Conversely, a statute of repose is typically an absolute time limit beyond which liability no longer exists and is not tolled for any reason because to do so would upset the economic balance struck by the legislative body.

In other words, while statutes of limitation are procedural in nature, repose statutes are substantive because they confer a vested, substantive right on the defendant. See Menne v. Celotex Corp., 722 F.Supp. 662

(D.Kan.1989), where the court described the differences between limitations and repose in determining whether a statute was procedural or substantive.

A statute of repose does not have to specifically refer to toxic torts in order to be applicable. For example, if a manufacturer of asbestos or other allegedly toxic building material is sued in a state with a construction no-action statute, and the manufacturer supplied the material for use in the construction of an improvement to real property, the statute of repose may bar an action for personal injury or wrongful death. To utilize this defense, the manufacturer must demonstrate that it comes within the statute's protection, as a supplier of a good for use in construction. The wording of the particular statute involved is dispositive. The version in effect in Ohio reads as follows:

> No action to recover damages for any injury to property, real or personal, or for bodily injury or wrongful death, arising out of the defective and unsafe condition of an improvement to real property * * * shall be brought against any person performing services for or furnishing the design, planning, supervision of construction, or construction of such improvement to real property, more than ten years after the performance or furnishing of such services and construction.

Ohio Rev. Code Ann. § 2305.131 (Anderson 1989).

The Ohio Supreme Court found that "the statute * * * does not apply to any person who supplies materials, rather than services, to be used in the construction of an improvement to real property, as they may be liable for damages caused by defects in the materials under Section 402A of the Restatement (Second) of Torts (1965)." Sedar v. Knowlton Constr. Co., 49 Ohio St.3d 193, 551 N.E.2d 938, 942 (1990). Thus, asbestos manufacturers in Ohio would be unable to avail themselves of this statute of repose in suits premised on products liability. See also Eagles Court Condominium Unit Owners Ass'n v. Heatilator, Inc., 239 Va. 325, 389 S.E.2d 304 (1990) (interpreting Va. Code § 8.01–250 (1973) as applying only to manufacturers or suppliers of machinery or equipment).

However, the same is not true in all jurisdictions. In Maryland, a statute of repose simply bars any action based on injury caused by an improvement to real property after the period has run, without regard to the parties protected. Md. Code Ann., Cts. & Jud. Proc. § 5–108 (1989). The Fourth Circuit has interpreted the statute very broadly:

> This statute unequivocally states that "no cause of action for damages accrues" after the 20–year time limit. And, it is completely silent as to any limitation on the class of persons it protects. To remove manufacturers from the ambit of § 5–108(a) as First United suggests, would be flatly inconsistent with this language's plain mandate.

First United Methodist Church v. United States Gypsum Co., 882 F.2d 862, 865 (4th Cir.1989), cert. denied 493 U.S. 1070, 110 S.Ct. 1113, 107 L.Ed.2d 1020 (1990); accord McIntosh v. A & M Insulation Co., 244 Ill.App.3d 247, 185 Ill.Dec. 69, 614 N.E.2d 203 (1993) (Illinois statute of repose applies to latent disease claims).

2. CONSTITUTIONAL QUESTIONS

Federal constitutional attacks on statutes of repose have recently been brought in a number of jurisdictions, including Minnesota (Lourdes High School, Inc. v. Sheffield Brick & Tile Co., 870 F.2d 443 (8th Cir.1989)), Kansas (Tomlinson v. Celotex Corp., 244 Kan. 474, 770 P.2d 825 (1989), reversed on other grounds sub nom. Gilger v. Lee Constr., Inc., 249 Kan. 307, 820 P.2d 390 (1991)), South Carolina (Jenkins v. Meares, 302 S.C. 142, 394 S.E.2d 317 (1990), Hoffman v. Powell, 298 S.C. 338, 380 S.E.2d 821 (1989)), and Ohio (Sedar v. Knowlton Constr. Co., 49 Ohio St.3d 193, 551 N.E.2d 938 (1990)). In each of these cases, statutes of repose barring actions based on injuries caused by improvements to real property, wrongful death, or damage to real or personal property withstood constitutional challenge under the Fifth and Fourteenth Amendments. Each court noted that it was neither a due process violation nor a violation of the Equal Protection clause to hold that certain types of causes of action were time-barred before they ever actually arose.

Differing results have been reached when interpreting state constitutions. In Alabama, a state constitutional provision that "all courts shall be open; and that every person, for any injury done to him, in his lands, goods, person or reputation, shall have a remedy by due process of law; and right and justice shall be administered without sale, denial, or delay," was interpreted to mean that a statute of repose could not completely bar an action for personal injury before it ever arose. Instead, a limited period of time would have to be made available during which personal injury plaintiffs could bring an action. See Jackson v. Mannesmann Demag Corp., 435 So.2d 725 (Ala.1983) (invalidating statute of repose relating to improvements to real estate); see also Tucker v. Nichols, 431 So.2d 1263 (Ala.1983) (medical malpractice statute of repose upheld, with six months "saving provision").

The primary difference between federal and state constitutional attacks is that many state constitutions contain a "right to a remedy" clause similar to the Alabama constitution excerpted above, whereas no such provision is found in the United States Constitution. Nevertheless, a few courts which have recently considered the question have found statutes of repose to be consistent with such clauses. Sealey v. Hicks, 309 Or. 387, 788 P.2d 435 (1990), cert. denied, 498 U.S. 819, 111 S.Ct. 65, 112 L.Ed.2d 39 (1990); Sedar v. Knowlton Constr. Co., 49 Ohio St.3d 193, 551 N.E.2d 938 (1990); Rodarte v. Carrier Corp., 786 S.W.2d 94 (Tex.App.1990); Commonwealth v. Owens–Corning Fiberglas Corp., 238 Va. 595, 385 S.E.2d 865 (1989).

But see Perkins v. Northeastern Log Homes, 808 S.W.2d 809 (Ky. 1991), where the Kentucky Supreme Court held unconstitutional a seven-year statute of repose (although it was entitled a statute of limitations), which required tort actions involving real property to be filed within seven years of any improvement, on the grounds that it violated protections against legislative interference guaranteed by the Kentucky Constitution of 1891. The statute gave plaintiff only until 1982 to file suit, even though she did not realize until 1989 that pentachlorophenol in the log home kit she purchased in 1977 may have caused her disease, non-Hodgkins lymphoma.

F. REVIVAL STATUTES

Some states have enacted special statutes that are targeted at resuscitating claims that had previously expired because of the statute of limitations bar. For example, the New York legislature in 1986 enacted a statute to revise claims related to exposure to certain identified toxic substances—DES, asbestos, chlordane, and polyvinylchloride—for one year which had previously expired. In Hymowitz v. Eli Lilly & Co., 73 N.Y.2d 487, 541 N.Y.S.2d 941, 539 N.E.2d 1069 (1989), the New York Court of Appeals upheld the statute as not transgressing any constitutional right of the defendants because it did not create new substantive rights, but rather was a procedural device:

> The Federal Due Process Clause provides very little barrier to a State Legislature's revival of time-barred actions (see Chase Sec. Corp. v. Donaldson, 325 U.S. 304, 65 S.Ct. 1137, 89 L.Ed. 1628 (1945)). In *Chase*, the United States Supreme Court upheld the revival of a time-barred action, stating that Statutes of Limitation "represent a public policy about the privilege to litigate * * * the history of pleas of limitation show them to be good only by legislative grace and to be subject to a relatively large degree of legislative control. [T]he Legislature may constitutionally revive a personal cause of action where the circumstances are exceptional and are such as to satisfy the court that serious injustice would result to plaintiffs not guilty of any fault if the intention of the Legislature were not effectuated."

Thus, if revival statutes are viewed as retroactive modifications to the statute of limitations, they are deemed procedural, and hence, subject to legislative modification without violating vested rights of defendants. See also Independent School District No. 197 v. W.R. Grace & Co., 752 F.Supp. 286 (D.Minn.1990) (asbestos).

G. CONTRIBUTORY FAULT/ASSUMPTION OF THE RISK IN REAL PROPERTY ACTIONS

1. DEFENSES TO NUISANCE AND REAL PROPERTY ACTIONS

William H. Rodgers, Environmental Law § 2.9 at 31 (Supp. 1984) summarizes the defenses predicated on a plaintiff's conduct as it relates to nuisance cases:

> Plaintiff misconduct defenses are theoretically significant and practically confusing. Contributory negligence is not a defense in those nuisance cases where liability is strict, either on an intentional tort or abnormally dangerous activity theory. Contributory negligence is a defense where the nuisance rests upon negligence, which makes the choice of theory highly important in a practical way. The New York Court of Appeals recently adopted this negligence/contributory negligence model in a nuisance case of pollution exposure over time, despite a strong dissent that the case deserved a strict liability analysis. The conflict did present cause-in-fact doubts and involved two commercial establishments (an automobile servicing business complaining about damage to cars from a power plant), not the starkly non-reciprocal interactions of a power plant and a home owner. Despite this, it appears that the better analysis would be to call this an instance of strict liability, allowing as a defense a showing of bargained-for risk acceptance which would be called assumption of risk.

> For the record, however, it must be noted that assumption of risk is a defense essentially unrecognized in nuisance law. The defenses that can be called plaintiff misconduct or risk acceptance are described as either contributory negligence or discussed under the heading of coming to the nuisance.

2. CONTRIBUTORY NEGLIGENCE OR FAULT

The Restatement (Second) of Torts addresses the defenses of contributory fault and assumption of the risk. Section 840B makes the availability of the plaintiff's fault as a defense turn on the kind of conduct engaged in by the defendant which gave rise to the nuisance. Because § 822, discussed in Chapter 3, recognizes that negligent, reckless, intentional, and abnormally dangerous activity can be the basis for a nuisance, the availability of contributory fault is controlled by whether the nuisance is created by negligent conduct.

§ 840B. Contributory Negligence

(1) When a nuisance results from negligent conduct of the defendant, the contributory negligence of the plaintiff is a defense to the same extent as in other actions founded on negligence.

(2) When the harm is intentional or the result of recklessness, contributory negligence is not a defense.

(3) When the nuisance results from an abnormally dangerous condition or activity, contributory negligence is a defense only if the plaintiff has voluntarily and unreasonably subjected himself to the risk of harm.

Therefore, when negligent conduct creates the nuisance, contributory negligence of the plaintiff is available as a defense as fully and under the same rules and conditions as in any other case predicated on negligence. See § 840, comment d. If defendant's conduct is reckless, then plaintiff's fault must be contributory recklessness in order to constitute a defense; and if intentional, as in fact most nuisances are because the defendant knows that its conduct is causing a nuisance or is substantially certain to do so and continues its action in the face of such knowledge, then contributory fault is not a defense.

As the student learned in the first-year torts course, states have enacted or judicially adopted a potpourri of comparative fault approaches. The UCFA adopts a "pure" comparative fault system under which, conceptually at least, a 99 percent at-fault plaintiff still recovers 1 percent of its damages. In contrast to the "pure" comparative negligence rule is the "modified" rule under which the plaintiff who is less than 100 percent at fault may, because of his negligence, be precluded from recovering, depending upon whether the jurisdiction follows the "50 percent bar" or the "51 percent bar." For example, in Maine and Minnesota, which adopted the "50 percent bar," a plaintiff to whom is attributed less than 50 percent of the total fault may recover damages reduced by his share of the negligence. See Me. Rev. Stat. Ann. tit. 14 and Minn. Stat. Ann. § 604.01. The States of Hawaii and New Hampshire, for example, in adopting the "51 percent bar," allow the plaintiff to recover so long as his negligence does not exceed that of the others who have caused him harm. See Hawaii Rev. Stat. § 663–31 and also N.H. Rev. Stat. Ann. 507:7–a.

3. ASSUMPTION OF THE RISK

The Restatement (Second) of Torts § 840C provides that assumption of the risk is a defense to an action for nuisance to the same extent as in other tort actions. The burden rests with the defendant who must show (a) the plaintiff knew that the exposure was dangerous; (b) the plaintiff appreciated the nature or extent of the danger; and (c) the plaintiff voluntarily exposed himself to the danger. A mere showing of negligence in failing to discover risks associated with an exposure, for example, would not constitute an adequate defense. Professor Rodgers' statements to the contrary notwithstanding, assumption of the risk is asserted in nuisance-type cases. For example, in Cornell v. Exxon Corp., 162 A.D.2d 892, 558 N.Y.S.2d 647 (1990), plaintiffs, who relied upon a well on their property for drinking and other purposes, sued in nuisance, trespass, and negligence to recover for physical injuries suffered as a result of contamination traceable to defendants' underground storage tanks.

Following an investigation by the State Department of Transportation revealing that the water was contaminated with gasoline traced to underground storage tanks, DOT installed the first of several double charcoal filters on plaintiffs' well. The filters were routinely replaced through December 1982. At the time the initial filter was installed, DOT indicated to plaintiffs that the filter "should deal with [their] problem" and that "[i]t should filter out most of it." However, plaintiffs were also advised at that time not to drink the water. Although plaintiffs subsequently attempted to abstain from drinking the water, the record indicates that they continued to use it for bathing, cooking and cleaning purposes.

The appeals court held that assumption of the risk may be a complete bar to recovery if the evidence showed that plaintiffs had knowledge of the risk and voluntarily chose to encounter it. The court, in remanding for trial on the issue, commented:

> Here, there is an absence of evidence indicating that plaintiffs were instructed not to use the well water for purposes other than drinking or that they were aware, at that time, of the potential health risk. While there is evidence in the record that after the filters were installed plaintiffs were told not to drink the water, there is also evidence that they were told that the filters "should deal with [their] problem." Thus, factual questions are present requiring jury resolution.

What if plaintiffs were unequivocally instructed not to use the well water? What if they were so instructed, but replacement water was expensive or hard to obtain?

4. COMING TO THE NUISANCE

Closely related to assumption of the risk is the defense of coming to the nuisance, where the plaintiff has acquired or improved her property after a nuisance interfering with its use and enjoyment has come into existence. See Restatement (Second) of Torts § 840D. However, § 840D also states that proof of the defense does not bar an action but is "a factor to be considered in determining whether the nuisance is actionable." The principal policy considerations involved in assigning weight to the defendant's priority in time has been summarized as follows:

> In addressing this question, courts have considered two views which two views which lead in opposite directions. On the one hand, it seems inequitable for a plaintiff to be able to come into an area where the defendant has long operated and force the defendant out. This is especially so in light of the likelihood that the plaintiff obtained his interest in his own land at a price discounted to reflect any inconvenience caused by the defendant's operations. Granting such a plaintiff relief results in a windfall for the plaintiff at the defendant's expense.
>
> On the other hand, allowing this defense may effectively grant the defendant an easement free of charge with which it can burden

its neighbors' land. Plaintiffs could then argue that this too is inequitable, in that it amounts to a windfall for the defendant and might encourage people entering a low density area to impose the maximum burdens upon the surrounding area and thereby gain rights to continue doing so indefinitely.

The majority rule in this area is that each purchaser of land is entitled to use it in the same degree as any prior purchaser. Therefore, generally there is no coming to the nuisance defense.

See Ernest Getto & James Arnone, Nuisance Law in a Modern Industrial Setting: Confusion, Misinformation Can Be Dangerous, 6 Toxics L. Rptr. 1122–23 (Feb. 6, 1991).

A recent North Dakota decision, Rassier v. Houim, 488 N.W.2d 635 (N.D.1992), demonstrates that the doctrine still carries some weight. In *Rassier*, the plaintiff sued to abate a private nuisance created by a neighboring defendant's use of a wind generator in a residential area. Defendant erected a tower and installed a wind generator on his residential lot in 1986. In October 1988, Rassier and her family purchased the adjoining lot and moved a mobile home onto the lot. Two years later, in November 1990, she sued Houim, claiming that his wind generator was a private nuisance. After a bench trial, the trial court dismissed her claim.

In affirming the trial court, the Supreme Court emphasized that "the basic criterion of the whole law of private nuisance is reasonable conduct" and the plaintiff's coming to the nuisance bears directly on the reasonableness of the defendant's use of its own property and the reasonableness of the interference with plaintiff's use and enjoyment. It found that the trial court had engaged in a weighing of the circumstances.

Stating that the basis for denying plaintiff's claim was the fact that she "came to the nuisance," the Court observed that "anyone who comes to a nuisance has a heavy burden to establish liability." This holding was reached despite the fact that the generator was located only 40 feet from her house, that the noise levels as measured by the State Department of Public Health were between 50 and 69 decibels, that most communities (but not this one) had ordinances prohibiting noise exceeding 55 decibels, and that evidence that the noise was irritating, stressful, and interfered with plaintiffs' sleep. One justice dissented.

Most courts, however, have rejected the defense. See, for example, Patrick v. Sharon Steel Corp., 549 F.Supp. 1259, 1267 (N.D.W.Va.1982), where West Virginia residents sought damages from pollution from Sharon Steel's coke works. The coke works were in operation at the time plaintiffs moved into their residences, and Sharon argued that by such conduct they "assumed the risk of living near a nuisance." The court disagreed:

This argument is untenable. Sharon relies upon an outdated doctrine that has never been recognized in West Virginia and which has been rejected by the majority of jurisdictions in which it had been previously adopted. * * * Support for the majority view is found in the argument that the doctrine is out of place in modern society where people often have no real choice as to whether or not they will reside in an area adulterated by air pollution. In addition, the doctrine is contrary to public policy in the sense that it permits a defendant to condemn surrounding land to endure a perpetual nuisance simply because he was in the area first. Another reason given for rejecting the doctrine is that the owner of land subject to a nuisance will either have to bring suit before selling his land in order to attempt to receive the full value of the land or reconcile himself to accepting a depreciated price for the land since no purchaser would be willing to pay full value for land subject to a nuisance against which he is barred from bringing an action.

There are some courts, however, that take a contrary position. These cases have arisen in instances where a plaintiff knowingly and voluntarily chose to locate near a defendant in whose operations the public has an important interest. One such case is East St. Johns Shingle Co. v. City of Portland, 195 Or. 505, 246 P.2d 554 (1952). There the plaintiff, a shingle mill company, moved onto land knowing that the city was disposing of sewage in a slough running through the land. The court held that by knowingly locating near a nuisance in which the public has a substantial interest, the plaintiff was estopped from suing for damages from the nuisance. See also Powell v. Superior Portland Cement, 15 Wash.2d 14, 129 P.2d 536 (1942). The concept of "coming to the nuisance" which effectively barred equitable relief to persons who intentionally placed themselves in a position to be interfered with has also been rationalized by notions of protecting the reasonable investment expectations of the existing industry. See Fischer v. Atlantic Richfield, 774 F.Supp. 616, 619 (W.D.Okl.1989) (coming to nuisance doctrine applies only where the injury caused is permanent). See also Donald Wittman, First Come, First Served: An Economic Analysis of "Coming to the Nuisance," 9 J. Legal Stud. 557 (1980).

5. SALE OF PROPERTY DEFENSE

Another defense, rarely invoked, to nuisance liability is that asserted by a defendant who has disposed of the property causing the nuisance prior to the institution of suit. Restatement (Second) of Torts § 840A provides:

(1) A vendor or lessor of land upon which there is a condition involving a nuisance for which he would be subject to liability if he continued in possession remains subject to liability for the continuation of the nuisance after he transfers the land.

(2) If the vendor or lessor has created the condition or has actively concealed it from the vendee or lessee the liability stated in Subsection (1) continues until the vendee or lessee discovers the condition and has reasonable opportunity to abate it. Otherwise the

liability continues only until the vendee or lessee has had reasonable opportunity to discover the condition and abate it.

The rationale for continuing to impose liability on the seller of property who was responsible for creating the nuisance is straight forward: it would be unfair to allow those who had created tortious conditions to walk away from their liability by disposing of the property. However, if the buyer was aware of the condition or has sufficient opportunity to discover and abate the condition, then liability of the seller ends. Comment c to § 840A states that the best rationale for imposing continuing liability is that "his responsibility toward those outside of his land is such that he is not free to terminate his liability to them for the condition that he himself caused or concealed, by passing the land itself on to a third person. The effect of the rule is to require vendors and lessors in order to avoid liability to take reasonable steps to abate existing conditions involving any nuisance before they transfer the land." See also Restatement (Second) of Torts § 373 which supplies the same principles to dangerous conditions created on the land prior to sale which involves an unreasonable risk of harm to those outside the land.

In Fetter v. De Camp, 195 A.D.2d 771, 600 N.Y.S.2d 340 (1993) plaintiffs sued the former owner of a neighboring home, alleging that the defendants' repair of their septic system had caused the contamination of their water wells with fecal matter. Defendants moved for summary judgment on the grounds that any liability they may have had ended with their sale of the property, and alternatively, they had no actual or constructive knowledge of the defect in the septic system. The trial court denied the motion, but the appeals court reversed. First, the court observed that while the general rule under the Restatement (Second) of Torts § 372 terminated liability for conditions on land upon the transfer of the property, an exception is recognized under § 373. It continued:

> Because it is obvious that an improperly designed and installed septic system can present an unreasonable risk of harm to others, especially where the water source for the properties in the immediate area are private wells which draw from subterranean streams or percolating water, there can be little doubt that to the extent plaintiffs can prove that defendants' actions relative to the septic system were negligent or satisfied the requisite elements of a nuisance, they can recover against defendants.

However, the court said, "because of the often unknown course of subterranean streams or the channel of percolating water, the rule has evolved that for negligence liability to ensue in cases involving the pollution of underground waters, the plaintiff must demonstrate that the defendant failed to exercise due care in conducting the allegedly polluting activity or in installing the allegedly polluting device, and that he or she know or should have known that such conduct could result in the contamination of the plaintiff's well." Here, because plaintiffs offered no evidence to establish that the septic system was defective or that defendants knew or should have known of any defect, summary judgment was granted.

For another decision addressing the sale of property defense where a purchaser of a manufacturing site sued a former operator of the site for the costs of cleaning up the property, see Westwood Pharmaceuticals, Inc. v. National Fuel Gas Distribution Corp., 737 F.Supp. 1272 (W.D.N.Y.1990), affirmed, 964 F.2d 85 (2d Cir.1992).

CERCLA, which was considered in Chapter 10, will trump these Restatement rules in cases where remediation is undertaken in response to actual or possible governmental action.

H. PLAINTIFF'S CONDUCT AS A BAR IN TOXIC PRODUCTS CASES

The doctrine of assumption of risk acts to bar or reduce a plaintiff's recovery for any harm caused him due to a risk which he or she knowingly accepts. In toxic products cases the key issue is typically whether the proof demonstrates that a particular toxic risk was a known or appreciated risk. In cases brought under Restatement (Second) of Torts § 402A, governing strict products liability, two provisions are especially relevant. First, as noted in comment j, if directions or warnings are given which would keep a product from being unreasonably dangerous, "the seller may reasonably assume that [the warning] will be read and heeded; and a product bearing such a warning which is safe for use if it is followed, is not in a defective condition, nor is it unreasonably dangerous." Thus, if instructions are given as to the use of a potentially hazardous product which will minimize exposure to the risk, and the *specific danger* associated with the product is pointed out, a seller may avoid liability under § 402A. See Jackson v. Johns–Manville Sales Corp., 750 F.2d 1314, 1320 (5th Cir.1985) ("Because one of the purposes of the warning is to allow the user to make his own decision whether to expose himself to the risks of harm, a manufacturer fulfills its duty to warn * * * only if it warns of all dangers associated with its product of which it has actual or constructive knowledge."). On the other hand, if the precise toxic risk is not warned against, or if the warning provided is not calculated to reach the ultimate user, the doctrine of assumption of the risk will not function as a bar.

Secondly, comment n to § 402A explicitly recognizes assumption of the risk as a separate defense to strict liability:

> *n. Contributory negligence.* Since the liability with which this Section deals is not based upon negligence of the seller, but is strict liability, the rule applied to strict liability cases applies. Contributory negligence of the plaintiff is not a defense when such negligence consists merely in a failure to discover the defect in the product, or to guard against the possibility of its existence. On the other hand the form of contributory negligence which consists in voluntarily and unreasonably proceeding to encounter a known danger, and

commonly passes under the name assumption of the risk, is a defense under this Section as in other cases of strict liability. If the user or consumer discovers the defect and is aware of the danger, and nevertheless proceeds unreasonably to make use of the product and is injured by it, he is barred from recovery.

Additionally, § 496 repeats the same principle more broadly to embrace risks beyond those satisfying the narrower product requirements of § 402A:

> A plaintiff who voluntarily assumes a risk of harm arising from the negligent or reckless conduct of the defendant cannot recover for such harm.

Section 496C explains further:

> [A] plaintiff who fully understands a risk of harm to himself or his things caused by defendant's conduct or by the condition of defendant's land or chattels, and who nevertheless voluntarily chooses to enter or remain, or to permit his things to enter or to remain within the area of that risk, under circumstances that manifest his willingness to accept it, is not entitled to recover for harm within that risk.

Section 496D emphasizes that a plaintiff does not assume the risk "unless he then knows of the existence of the risk and appreciates its unreasonable character."

Assumption of the risk does not meet with general approval in the toxic tort or hazardous waste disposal situation, particularly where there are long latency periods associated with injuries or disease or deaths related to exposure. From the defense perspective, frequently, the defendant does not have access to sources of proof dating back to a person's first exposure to the hazardous substance, and therefore, the defense cannot counter plaintiff's claim that he was unaware of the risks associated with the toxic or hazardous substance when he was allegedly first exposed to it. Furthermore, in toxic tort cases where plaintiff's theory is generally defendant's failure to warn, it will, as a practical matter, be difficult for a defendant, who has allegedly failed to warn of the health hazards associated with the exposure, to convince court or jury that the plaintiff, nevertheless, knew of the alleged hazard and chose to encounter it voluntarily.

From the standpoint that the assumption of the risk defense can operate unfairly to bar a plaintiff's claim, some courts have declined to apply the doctrine in the employment relationship on the theory that exposure to a known danger in the course of one's job is not truly voluntary, or that the encounter with the danger was not unreasonable. See, e.g., Johnson v. Clark Equipment Co., 274 Or. 403, 547 P.2d 132 (1976) (design defect case); Cremeans v. Willmar Henderson Mfg. Co., 57 Ohio St.3d 145, 566 N.E.2d 1203 (1991). However, as was noted in Chapter 9 on the workplace, federal laws are increasingly requiring the disclosure of hazard-related information to employees whose jobs necessitate exposure to or use of toxic substances. Statutes such as the OSH

Act mandate that employees be provided training respecting the safe use of toxic materials and that employers post detailed information describing the health risks posed by and instructions for the safe use of toxic chemicals. See 29 C.F.R. § 1910.1200. An assumption of the risk defense might be implicated if the employee were to ignore the training and instructions and act in a manner that causes a harmful exposure. See James T. O'Reilly, Risks of Assumptions: Impact of Regulatory Label Warnings Upon Industrial Products Liability, 37 Cath. U. L. Rev. 85 (1987).

Chapter Thirteen

SPECIAL PROBLEMS IN TRIAL MANAGEMENT AND SETTLEMENT OF TOXICS LITIGATION

This Chapter addresses in a preliminary way a collection of issues that have emerged from the legal system's effort to manage the increasing volume and complexity of toxic tort litigation, especially that which is assigned the label "mass" tort. While there exists no uniform definition of what constitutes "mass" toxic tort litigation, it is clear that the phrase contemplates hundreds or thousands of claimants, all of whom were exposed to the same or similar toxic substances either simultaneously, as in an explosion at a chemical plant or a chemical spill precipitated by a tank car derailment, or by gradual, separately-occurring events, as in occupational exposure to asbestos, or consumption of a prescription drug, or ingestion of contaminated water by a community.

We first focus on the aggregative mechanisms that are available for the trial of mass tort litigation, with emphasis on class action devices, consolidation and multidistrict litigation procedures. Second, we consider some of the controls that trial courts have exercised to manage toxic tort cases more effectively and to protect the basic rights of the litigants, such as case management orders, protective orders, and special discovery orders. Third, we examine settlement procedures and look at least one creative approach to the resolution of a toxic tort dispute. And finally, because mass toxic torts often implicate challenging choice-of-law problems, we examine some of the proposals that have been advanced to federalize either the substantive tort law or the choice-of-law rules.

A. CLASS ACTIONS

One of the most profound and controversial developments in the law of federal civil procedure is the growth of the class action, spawned by the 1966 amendments to Rule 23 of the Federal Rules of Civil Procedure. A class action provides a means by which one or more may sue or be sued as representatives of a class without the necessity of joining every member of the group of persons interested in a matter. See generally 7B Charles A. Wright, Arthur Miller, & Mary K. Kane, Federal Practice and Procedure § 1785 (2d ed. 1986).

Class actions serve two essential purposes. First, a class action achieves judicial economy by avoiding multiple suits. See Crown, Cork & Seal Co. v. Parker, 462 U.S. 345, 103 S.Ct. 2392, 76 L.Ed.2d 628 (1983); American Pipe & Constr. Co. v. Utah, 414 U.S. 538, 553, 94 S.Ct. 756, 766, 38 L.Ed.2d 713 (1974); In re A.H. Robins Co., 880 F.2d 769 (4th Cir.1989); Jenkins v. Raymark Indus., Inc., 782 F.2d 468, 471 (5th Cir.1986). Second, a class action can protect the rights of those who for practical reasons—most frequently cost—would not press claims individually. See Kramer v. Scientific Control Corp., 534 F.2d 1085, 1091 (3d Cir.1976), cert. denied 429 U.S. 830, 97 S.Ct. 90, 50 L.Ed.2d 94 (1976).

Upon promulgation of the current rule, however, the Federal Rules of Civil Procedure Advisory Committee expressed a restrictive view of the applicability of Rule 23 class actions in mass tort litigation:

> A "mass accident" resulting in injuries to numerous persons is ordinarily not appropriate for a class action because of the likelihood that significant questions, not only of damages but of liability and defenses to liability, would be present, affecting the individuals in different ways. In these circumstances an action conducted nominally as a class action would degenerate in practice into multiple lawsuits separately tried.

Fed. R. Civ. P. 23(b)(3) Advisory Committee's Notes, reprinted in 39 F.R.D. 69, 103 (1966).

On the use of class actions generally, see Williams, Mass Tort Class Actions: Going, Going, Gone?, 98 F.R.D. 323, 329 (1983) (Judge Williams suggests there exists an "unarticulated antipathy and aversion that appellate courts display toward class action use in the mass tort context."); Linda S. Mullenix, Class Resolution of Mass Tort Cases: A Proposed Federal Procedure Act, 64 Tex. L. Rev. 1039 (1986). For an article debunking some of the myths about the individualized relationship between attorney and client which is often proffered as a reason for denying class certification, see Deborah Hensler, Resolving Mass Toxic Torts: Myths and Realities, 1989 U. Ill. L. Rev. 89.

There is, in fact, substantial authority suggesting that class actions as a viable and helpful procedure for handling mass tort claims and especially mass toxic tort cases. In In re School Asbestos Litigation, 789 F.2d 996, 1008 (3d Cir.1986), cert. denied 479 U.S. 915, 107 S.Ct. 318, 93 L.Ed.2d 291 (1986), the Court of Appeals for the Third Circuit stated:

> [T]here is a growing acceptance of the notion that some mass accident situations may be good candidates for class action treatment. * * * Determination of the liability issues in one suit may represent a substantial savings in time and resources. Even if the action thereafter "degenerates" into a series of individual damage

suits, the result nevertheless works an improvement over the situation in which the same separate suits require adjudication on liability using the same evidence over and over again.

The following Fed. R. Civ. Proc. 23(b)(3) "opt-out" second-hand smoke class action is illustrative:

DENNIS MULLEN, ET AL. v. TREASURE CHEST CASINO, LLC, ET AL.

United States Court of Appeals for the Fifth Circuit, 1999.
186 F.3d 620.

JUDGES: Garza, Benavides and Dennis Circuit Judges. Garza, Dissenting

Opinion by: Benavides

Treasure Chest Casino, LLC ("Treasure Chest") appeals from an interlocutory order of the district court certifying under Federal Rule of Civil Procedure 23(b)(3) a plaintiff class consisting of injured Treasure Chest employees. We affirm the district court's class certification.

I. BACKGROUND

The appellees, Dennis Mullen, Sheila Bachemin, and Margaret Phipps (collectively, the "Named Plaintiffs"), are former employees of the M/V Treasure Chest Casino (the "Casino"), a floating casino owned and operated out of Kenner, Louisiana by appellant Treasure Chest. Mullen was an assistant pit boss, Bachemin was a dealer, and Phipps was employed as a slot-floor person and dealer.

Each Named Plaintiff has suffered respiratory illness allegedly caused by the Casino's defective and/or improperly maintained air-conditioning and ventilating system. Each was diagnosed with asthma and bronchitis while employed aboard the Casino. Mullen and Bachemin, while aboard the Casino, suffered respiratory attacks requiring hospitalization. Kathleen McNamara, the Named Plaintiffs' physician, testified in a deposition that as many as half of the 300 Casino employees that she had treated suffered from similar respiratory problems. She attributed the Named Plaintiffs' and other crew members' maladies to extremely smoky conditions in the Casino.

In January 1996, the Named Plaintiffs filed suit against Treasure Chest,making Jones Act, unseaworthiness, and maintenance and cure claims. They sought Rule 23 certification of a class consisting of "all members of the crew of the M/V Treasure Chest Casino who have been stricken with occupational respiratory illness caused by or exacerbated by the defective ventilation system in place aboard the vessel."

The parties conducted pre-certification discovery that included deposing the Named Plaintiffs, Dr. McNamara, and two other physicians. The parties then briefed the district court, which heard arguments in July 1997.

On August 29, 1997, the district court certified the proposed class under Rule 23(b)(3). Under the court's plan, the liability issues common to all class members will be tried together in an initial trial phase. Those common issues include whether the employees of the Casino are seamen within the meaning of the Jones Act, whether the Casino is a vessel within the meaning of the Jones Act, whether the Casino was rendered unseaworthy by the air quality aboard, and whether Treasure Chest was negligent in relation to the Casino's ventilation system. If the class prevails on the common liability issues in phase one, the issues affecting only individual class members will be tried in a second phase in waves of approximately five class members at a time. These limited issues include causation, damages, and comparative negligence.

Treasure Chest sought to appeal the class certification order, and the district court certified the issue for interlocutory appeal under 28 U.S.C. § 1292(b). We granted Treasure Chest permission to appeal.

II. DISCUSSION

[The court lists the four prerequisites to class certification found in Rule 23(a) and the two additional requirements found in Rule 23(b)(3), citing Amchem Products, Inc. v. Windsor, 521 U.S. 591 (1997).]

"Common questions must 'predominate over any questions affecting only individual members'; and class resolution must be 'superior to other available methods for the fair and efficient adjudication of the controversy.' " [Fed. R. Civ. P. 23(b)(3)].

Treasure Chest argues on appeal that the district court erred in finding any of the Rule 23 requirements satisfied. [Cc] Before evaluating the six requirements seriatim, we note that the district court maintains great discretion in certifying and managing a class action. See Montelongo v. Meese, 803 F.2d 1341, 1351 (5th Cir.1986). We will reverse a district court's decision to certify a class only upon a showing that the court abused its discretion, see Jenkins v. Raymark Industries, 782 F.2d 468, 471–72 (5th Cir.1986), or that it applied incorrect legal standards in reaching its decision[.][Cc]

A. Numerosity

The [trial] court found that "the class is so numerous that joinder of all members is impracticable," Fed. R. Civ. P. 23(a)(1), referring to three factors. First, the class would likely consist of between 100 and 150 members. Second, owing to the transient nature of employment in the gambling business, it was likely that some of the putative class members were geographically dispersed and unavailable for joinder. Third, putative class members still employed by the Casino might be reluctant to file individually for fear of workplace retaliation. Treasure Chest challenges only the second of the district court's three reasons. It asserts that the district court's claim that class members would be geographically dispersed was unsupported by evidence. They reference the court's own comment that the "plaintiff has not introduced any specific evidence that there are potential class members that have moved out of the area.''

We find no abuse of discretion in the district court's finding of numerosity. Although the number of members in a proposed class is not determinative of whether joinder is impracticable, [Cc], the size of the class in this case—100 to 150 members—is within the range that generally satisfies the numerosity requirement. See 1 Newberg on Class Actions § 3.05, at 3–25 (3d ed. 1992) (suggesting that any class consisting of more than forty members "should raise a presumption that joinder is impracticable"); cf. Boykin v. Georgia–Pacific Corp., 706 F.2d 1384, 1386 (5th Cir.1983) (finding that numerosity requirement would not be met by a class with 20 members but was met by a class with 317 members).

Furthermore, the additional factors mentioned by the district court support its finding of numerosity. [Cc] Notwithstanding the lack of any direct evidence, the district court reasonably inferred from the nature of the putative class members' employment that some of them would be geographically dispersed. It also reasonably presumed that those potential class members still employed by Treasure Chest might be unwilling to sue individually or join a suit for fear of retaliation at their jobs. Based upon those considerations, it was within the district court's discretion to find that joinder of all 100 to 150 class members would be impracticable.

B.   Commonality

The district court found that "there are questions of law or fact common to the class," Fed. R. Civ. P. 23(a)(2), on the basis of the class members' identical theories of liability, their common claims under the Jones Act, and their uniform allegations of suffering injury from second-hand smoke. Treasure Chest challenges the district court's assertion that all plaintiffs' claims relate to second-hand smoke.

The district court did not abuse its discretion in finding commonality. The test for commonality is not demanding and is met "where there is at least one issue, the resolution of which will affect all or a significant number of the putative class members." [Cc] In this case, the putative class members will assert claims for negligence under the Jones Act and for operating an unseaworthy vessel. The common issues pertaining to these theories of liability—i.e., the class members' status as Jones Act seamen, the negligence of Treasure Chest, and the unseaworthiness of the Casino—are independently sufficient to establish commonality. It is therefore irrelevant whether the class members uniformly allege damages from second-hand smoke.

C.   Typicality

The district found the "the claims or defenses of the parties are typical of the claims or defenses of the class," Fed. R. Civ. P. 23(a)(3), because the Named Plaintiffs and the class members, by definition, all allege to have suffered occupation-related respiratory illness. Treasure

Chest contends that the Named Plaintiffs' claims are not typical of the class because a wide array of claims could fall under the "respiratory illness" category.

We find no abuse in the district court's finding of typicality. Like commonality, the test for typicality is not demanding. It "focuses on the similarity between the named plaintiffs' legal and remedial theories and the theories of those whom they purport to represent." [Cc] In this case, the Named plaintiffs' and the proposed class members' legal and remedial theories appear to be exactly the same. The class complaint indicates that they will all premise liability for the Casino's defective air ventilation system under the Jones Act and the doctrine of seaworthiness. Any variety in the illnesses the Named Plaintiffs and the class members suffered will not affect their legal or remedial theories, and thus does not defeat typicality.

D. Adequacy of Representation

The district court stated that "the representative parties will fairly and adequately protect the interests of the class," Fed. R. Civ. P. 23(a)(4), because the Named Plaintiffs' interests are identical to the interests of the proposed class and their attorneys have extensive experience litigating class actions and Jones Act cases. Treasure Chest argues on the appeal that the district court's finding was erroneous because the Named Plaintiffs and the class members have suffered from varied illnesses and have varying susceptibilities to respiratory ailments.

We find no abuse of discretion in the district court's finding. Differences between named plaintiffs and class members render the named plaintiffs inadequate representatives only if those differences create conflicts between the named plaintiffs' interests and the class members' interests. See Jenkins v. Raymark Industries, Inc., 782 F.2d 468, 472 (5th Cir.1986) (considering whether named plaintiffs have "an insufficient stake in the outcome or interests antagonistic to the unnamed members" in evaluating adequate representation requirement). The differences described by Treasure Chest may create variances in the ways that the Named Plaintiffs and class members will prove causation and damages. A class member who has never smoked, for example, may have less difficulty in proving that the conditions inside the Casino caused her asthma than will Bachemin, who has a history of smoking and whose claim may be subject to a defense of contributory negligence. Such a difference, however, does not affect the alignment of their interests. Nothing indicates that the class members will be inadequately represented by the Named Plaintiffs and their counsel.

E. Predominance

We see no abuse in the district court's finding that "the questions of law or fact common to the members of the class predominate over any questions affecting only individual members." Fed. R. Civ. P. 23(b)(3). [HN7] "In order to 'predominate,' common issues must constitute a significant part of the individual cases." Jenkins, 782 F.2d at 472. The district court held that the issues to be tried commonly—seamen status, vessel status, negligence, and seaworthiness—were significant in relation to the individual issues of causation, damages, and contributory negligence. Treasure Chest argues on appeal that the district court abused its discretion by failing to weigh the common against the individual issues and by improperly finding causation to be a common issue.

Treasure Chest's arguments are without merit. First, although the court's predominance inquiry was not lengthy, there is no indication that the court limited its inquiry to counting issues instead of weighing them. Second, explicit in the district court's decision is a finding that causation is a unique issue that will be resolved in the trial plan's second-phase individual trials.

Even examining the district court's predominance analysis more closely, we find no abuse. The common issues in this case, especially negligence and seaworthiness, are not only significant but also pivotal. They will undoubtedly require the parties to produce extensive evidence regarding the Casino's air ventilation system, as well as testimony concerning Treasure Chest's knowledge of, and response to, the Casino employees' respiratory problems and complaints. The phase-one jury will have the difficult task of determining whether the air quality aboard the Casino resulted from a negligent breach of Treasure Chest's duty to its employees or rendered the Casino unseaworthy. If Treasure Chest prevails on those two issues alone, they will prevail in the case.

Moreover, this case does not involve the type of individuated issues that have in the past led courts to find predominance lacking. For example, in [Amchem Products, Inc. v. Windsor, 521 U.S. 591 (1997)], the Supreme Court found that common issues did not predominate where the members of the plaintiff class were exposed to asbestos-containing products from different sources over different time periods, some of the class members were asymptomatic while others had developed illnesses, and the class members were from a variety of states requiring the application of a multitude of different legal standards. See [id.], (citing Georgine v. Amchem Products, Inc., 83 F.3d 610, 626 (3d Cir.1996)). Similarly, in Castano v. American Tobacco Co., 84 F.3d 734 (5th Cir.1996), this Court found that a putative class of addicted smokers did not meet the predominance requirement because there were complex choice-of-law issues and the case involved novel addiction-as-injury claims with no track record from which a court could determine which issues were "significant." See id. at 741–45. Here, by contrast, the putative class members are all symptomatic by definition and claim injury from the same defective ventilation system over the same general period of time. Because all of the claims are under federal law, there are no individual choice-of-law issues. And, because negligence and doctrine-of-seaworthiness claims are time-tested bases for liability, the district court could reasonably evaluate the significance of the common issues without first establishing a track record.

F. Superiority

We also find no abuse of discretion in the district court's finding that "a class action is superior to other available methods for the fair and efficient adjudication of the controversy." Fed. R. Civ. P. 23(b)(3). The district court based its superiority finding on the fact that the class litigation in this case would not present the degree of managerial complexities that prompted this Court to decertify the putative class in Castano. Specifically, the district court mentioned the lack of any complex choice-of-law or Erie problems, and that the class would consist of only hundreds, instead of millions, of members. The bifurcated-trial plan, the court found, would "promote judicial economy and avoid the wasteful, duplicative litigation which would inevitably result if these cases were tried individually." Treasure Chest argues that the district court abused its discretion by failing adequately to consider how a trial on the merits would be conducted. It contends that because the Named Plaintiffs describe somewhat different causes for their ailments, a phase-one judgment of negligence or unseaworthiness related solely to tobacco smoke would be inadequate insofar as it would preclude plaintiffs from recovering for ailments that were caused by sources other than tobacco smoke in the phase-two trials.

* * * [E]ven if the class does claim at trial that the Casino's ventilation system was defective in relation to more than tobacco smoke, we are confident that the district court can ably manage [*628] this case as a class action. Our precedent limits a negligent party's liability to injuries that are caused by the same condition that rendered the party negligent. See Gavagan v. United States, 955 F.2d 1016, 1020–21 (5th Cir.1992). The court can easily abide by this precedent by instructing the jury to answer special verdicts finding whether the Treasure Chest was negligent, or the Casino was unseaworthy, as to each alleged causal agent, i.e., tobacco smoke, dust mites, fungi, paint fumes, et cetera. The court can then properly limit the injuries for which the phase-two juries could find Treasure Chest liable. Thus, if the phase-one jury were to find that Treasure Chest was negligent as to tobacco smoke but not as to paint fumes, any class member whose injuries were found by a phase-two jury to be caused by paint fumes would be unable to recover. Even though rendering multiple special verdicts would complicate the task for the phase-one jury and the court, we would see no abuse in the district court's finding such a process superior to conducting duplicative individual trials.

We also agree with the district court that none of the superiority concerns raised by our decision in Castano requires a different result. There, many of the manageability problems stemmed from the million-person class membership, the complex choice-of-law issues, the novel addiction-as-injury cause of action, and the extensive subclassing requirements. As already discussed, none of those problems exist in this case. In fact, unlike the "Frankenstein's monster" feared in Castano, 84 F.3d at 745 n.19, this class is akin to other bifurcated class actions this Court has approved. See Watson v. Shell Oil Co., 979 F.2d 1014 (5th Cir.1992) (finding no abuse in the district court's certification of a bifurcated class action arising from an oil refinery explosion where liability and punitive damages would be resolved commonly and injury, causation, and actual damages would be resolved individually); Jenkins, 782 F.2d 468 (finding no abuse of discretion in district court's certification of a bifurcated class action where asbestos producers' "state of the art defense" as well as product identification, product defectiveness, negligence, and punitive damages would be resolved commonly and causation, actual damages, and comparative fault would tried individually); Hernandez v. Motor Vessel Skyward, 61 F.R.D. 558 (S.D. Fla.1973), aff'd, 507 F.2d 1278, 1279 (5th Cir.1975) (unpublished) (certifying bifurcated class action on behalf of 350 passengers who were fed contaminated food aboard cruise ship where negligence would be tried commonly and causation and damages would be tried individually).

In Castano, this Court expressed a concern that having one jury consider the defendant's conduct and another consider the plaintiffs' comparative negligence could create Seventh Amendment problems. See Castano, 84 F.3d at 750–51 (citing In re Rhone–Poulenc Rorer Inc., 51 F.3d 1293, 1303 (7th Cir.1995)). This does not change our view of the district court's superiority finding. Treasure Chest did not raise this issue to the district court nor has it been argued on appeal. We are reluctant to find that the district abused its discretion by failing to consider an issue that was not raised by the parties.

In any case, we would not find the risk of infringing upon the parties' Seventh Amendment rights significant in this case. The Seventh Amendment does not prohibit bifurcation of trials as long as the " 'the judge [does] not divide issues between separate trials in such a way that the same issue is reexamined by different juries.' " Cimino v. Raymark Industries, Inc., 151 F.3d 297, 320 n.50, (5th Cir.1998) (quoting Rhone–Poulenc, 51 F.3d at 1303); see Alabama v. Blue Bird Body Co., Inc., 573 F.2d 309, 318 (5th Cir.1978). In Castano, we were concerned that allowing a second jury to consider the plaintiffs' comparative negligence would invite that jury to reconsider the first jury's findings concerning the defendants' conduct. We believe that such a risk has been avoided here by leaving all issues of causation for the phase-two jury. When a jury considers the comparative negligence of a plaintiff, "the focus is upon causation. It is inevitable that a comparison of the conduct of plaintiffs and defendants ultimately be in terms of causation." Lewis v. Timco, Inc., 716 F.2d 1425, 1431 (5th Cir.1983) (en banc); see id. (permitting the use of comparative negligence in strict liability claims). Thus, in considering comparative negligence, the phase-two jury would not be reconsidering the first jury's findings of whether Treasure Chest's conduct was negligent or the Casino unseaworthy, but only the degree to which those conditions were the sole or contributing cause of the class member's injury. Because the first jury will not be considering any issues of causation, no Seventh Amendment implications affect our review of the district court's superiority finding.

III. CONCLUSION

For the foregoing reasons, we find that the district court did not abuse its discretion in certifying under Rule 23(b)(3) a class of all Casino employees stricken with occupation-related respiratory illnesses. AFFIRMED.

[Dissenting Opinions Omitted]

Notes and Questions

The prerequisites and rationale for class certification were briefly summarized in one influential toxic tort case involving personal injury and property damage claims brought against a chemical company which had disposed of hazardous waste at a site in proximity to plaintiffs' homes, Sterling v. Velsicol Chemical Corp., 855 F.2d 1188 (6th Cir.1988), affirming in part, reversing in part 647 F.Supp. 303 (W.D.Tenn.1986). In the appeal of that suit, the Sixth Circuit affirmed the district court's order to certify as a class all of their claims, despite the individual nature of the causation and damage issues:

> Velsicol argues that the district court improperly certified this case as a Fed.R.Civ.P. 23(b)(3) class action because common questions of law or fact did not predominate over individual questions. As to the requirements necessary for certification of a Rule 23(b)(3) class action, the district court held * * * that (1) the class was so large that joinder of all members was impractical (Rule 23(a)(1)); (2) there were questions of law or fact common to the class (Rule 23(a)(2)); (3) representative claims were typical of the claims of the class (Rule 23(a)(3)); and (4) the representative parties would fairly and adequately protect the interests of the class (Rule 23(a)(4)). The court further found that questions of law or fact common to the members of the class predominated over any questions affecting only individual members and that a class action would be superior to other available methods for the fair and efficient adjudication of the controversy (Rule 23(b)(3)).[7]
>
> The procedural device of a Rule 23(b)(3) class action was designed not solely as a means for assuring legal assistance in the vindication of small claims but, rather, to achieve the economies of time, effort, and expense. However, the problem of individualization of issues often is cited as a justification for denying class action treatment in mass tort accidents. While some courts have adopted this justification in refusing to certify such suits as class actions, numerous other courts have recognized the increasingly insistent need for a more efficient method of disposing of a large number of lawsuits arising out of a single disaster or a single course of conduct. In mass tort accidents, the factual and legal

---

7. In its September 29, 1986 order, the court stated in pertinent part: "Early on in this case, because of the sheer magnitude of this litigation, the claims of five representative plaintiffs, whose claims are fairly representative of the claims of the class as a whole, were selected for trial. It was decided all claims would be tried by the court in this phase of the trial and final judgment entered on all of the claims of the five representative plaintiffs * * *. This approach was adopted by the Court as the only reasonable way for the Trial Court to manage in an efficient way the complex factual and legal issues presented by this mind-boggling class action lawsuit."

issues of a defendant's liability do not differ dramatically from one plaintiff to the next. No matter how individualized the issue of damages may be, these issues may be reserved for individual treatment with the question of liability tried as a class action. Consequently, the mere fact that questions peculiar to each individual member of the class remain after the common questions of the defendant's liability have been resolved does not dictate the conclusion that a class action is impermissible.

The district court retains broad discretion in determining whether an action should be certified as a class action, and its decision, based upon the particular facts of the case, should not be overturned absent a showing of abuse of discretion. In complex, mass, toxic tort accidents, where no one set of operative facts establishes liability, no single proximate cause equally applies to each potential class member and each defendant, and individual issues outnumber common issues, the district court should properly question the appropriateness of a class action for resolving the controversy. However, where the defendant's liability can be determined on a class-wide basis because the cause of the disaster is a single course of conduct which is identical for each of the plaintiffs, a class action may be the best litigation solution for such a controversy.

In the instant case, each class member lived in the vicinity of the landfill and allegedly suffered damages as a result of ingesting or otherwise using the contaminated water. Almost identical evidence would be required to establish the level and duration of chemical contamination, the causal connection, if any, between the plaintiffs' consumption of the contaminated water and the type of injuries allegedly suffered, and the defendant's liability. The single major issue distinguishing the class members is the nature and amount of damages, if any, that each sustained. To this extent, a class action in the instant case avoided duplication of judicial effort and prevented separate actions from reaching inconsistent results with similar, if not identical, facts. The district court clearly did not abuse its discretion in certifying this action as a Rule 23(b)(3) class action. However, individual members of the class still will be required to submit evidence concerning their particularized damage claims in subsequent proceedings.

Notes and Questions

1. The conclusions reached in Sterling and Mullen have been accepted by other courts faced with the prospect of trying hundreds or thousands of individual cases. See, e.g., Watson v. Shell Oil Co., 979 F.2d 1014 (5th Cir.1992) (over 18,000 class members in mass tort litigation arising out of an explosion at an oil refinery); In re Agent Orange Product Liability Litigation, 506 F.Supp. 762 (E.D.N.Y.1980), modified 100 F.R.D. 718 (E.D.N.Y.1983), mandamus denied sub nom. In re Diamond Shamrock Chem. Co., 725 F.2d 858 (2d Cir.1984), cert. denied, 465 U.S. 1067, 104 S.Ct. 1417, 79 L.Ed.2d 743 (1984); Jenkins v. Raymark Indus., Inc., 782 F.2d 468, 473 (5th Cir. 1986) ("Courts have usually avoided class actions in the mass accident or tort setting. Because of differences between individual plaintiffs on issues of

liability and defenses of liability, as well as damages, it has been feared that separate trials would overshadow the common disposition for the class. The courts are now being forced to rethink the alternatives and priorities by the current volume of litigation and more frequent mass disasters."); accord In re A.H. Robins Co., 880 F.2d 709 (4th Cir.1989) ("Many courts are now abandoning their historical reluctance to certify mass tort class actions in light of what is often an overwhelming need to create an orderly, efficient means for adjudicating hundreds of thousands of related claims."). Moreover, where the defendant's assets are limited and the prospect exists that many later claimants will face empty coffers, class treatment is increasingly recognized as a viable means to equitably distribute those assets.

See also In re Jackson Lockdown/MCO Cases, 107 F.R.D. 703, 712 (E.D.Mich.1985) ("Where a limited fund exists in a particular litigation and the projected number of claims would exceed the amount of that fund, it is both equitable and reasonable that the mere fortuitousness of one party filing before another should not be the deciding factor in determining the availability of recompense.").

2. Observe that the court in Sterling employed class representatives whose causation and damages factual issues were thought to be typical of others in the class. In the asbestos litigation, discussed below, you will observe how some courts have utilized this procedure, coupled with statistical methods, to arrive at class-wide damages. What Constitutional concerns are triggered by using class representatives whose outcomes are applied to other class members?

3. Federal courts are not alone in utilizing class action procedures. See, e.g., Warner v. Waste Management, Inc., 36 Ohio St.3d 91, 521 N.E.2d 1091 (1988) (court affirms class certification with modifications to the definition of the class limited to all those "who live or owned real property within a five mile radius of the * * * hazardous waste site."); Lowe v. Sun Refining & Mktg. Co., 73 Ohio App.3d 563, 597 N.E.2d 1189 (1992) (number of residents and businesses in Sandusky River Watershed were indeterminate, precluding certification in action alleging negligence, nuisance, and strict liability, because the geographic parameters of class were imprecise; requirement that there be questions of law or fact common to class was satisfied; and common questions predominated over questions affecting individual members in action arising out of spill of toluene in creek). Some courts have concluded that the purported class was insufficiently defined and have refused certification on that basis. See, e.g., Daigle v. Shell Oil Co., 133 F.R.D. 600 (D.Colo.1990). For a view that class actions are of limited utility, see Marjorie H. Mintzer & Yasmin Daley–Duncan, Mass Tort Litigation: Why Class Action Suits Are Not the Answer, For the Def., Fall 1992, at 25.

B. OTHER AGGREGATIVE OR DISAGGREGATIVE PROCEDURES

1. CONSOLIDATION

Consolidation of individual actions against a single defendant or multiple defendants is a valuable procedural tool, especially in the context of mass toxic torts. Joint trials or hearings may prevent needless repetition of discovery and presentations of evidence. The text of Fed. R. Civ. P. 42(a) provides:

> When actions involving a common question of law or fact are pending before the court, it may order a joint hearing or trial of any or all the matters in issue in the actions; it may order all the actions consolidated; and it may make such orders concerning proceedings therein as may tend to avoid unnecessary costs or delay.

The term consolidation has been used to denote two different situations. 7B Charles A. Wright, Arthur Miller & Mary K. Kane, Federal Practice and Procedure § 2382 at 254 (2d ed. 1986). In the first situation, several actions are combined into one and each loses its separate identity, thereby returning a single judgment. In the second situation, several actions are tried together at the same trial, but each case retains its separate character as an individual cause of action and a separate judgment is entered for each case.

The chief prerequisite for consolidation is a common question of law or fact. A plaintiff is not entitled to have his action consolidated with another action pending in the same court, even though some of the same parties are involved, if the questions of law and fact in the two actions are not the same. The court is given broad discretion in deciding the existence of common issues of law or fact and in deciding the general propriety of consolidation. Additionally, the principal consideration for the court beyond common issues of law or fact is whether consolidation promotes convenience and judicial economy, and accordingly, the court may order consolidation without the consent of the parties. Further, Rule 42(a) is permissive, and a court is under little obligation to order consolidation. However, consolidation is impermissible if a party is aligned with another party with whom the first party has a conflicting interest in another portion of the consolidated cases. E.g., Dupont v. Southern Pac. Co., 366 F.2d 193 (5th Cir.1966) (consolidation of conflicting interests was reversible error), cert. denied 386 U.S. 958, 87 S.Ct. 1027, 18 L.Ed.2d 106 (1967).

In Malcolm v. National Gypsum Co., 995 F.2d 346 (2d Cir.1993), the Second Circuit held that a trial court had abused its discretion in consolidating 48 asbestos cases for trial. It noted that the goals of "convenience and economy must yield to a paramount concern for a fair and impartial trial." The court identified a number of criteria that district courts had applied as guidelines in determining the propriety of consolidation. In Malcolm, 48 plaintiffs had worked in 250 different work sites where they were exposed to asbestos, each for different periods of time, in a period ranging from the 1940s to the 1970s, and suffered from different diseases (asbestosis, lung cancer and mesothelioma), and some were deceased but others survived. The Court concluded that such factual divergences made consolidation unfair. Accord, Cain v. Armstrong World Industries, 785 F.Supp. 1448 (S.D.Ala.1992).

Individual suits may be consolidated in the pretrial stage, thereby enabling common discovery and pretrial conferences which can often prove economically and administratively desirable. 9B Charles A. Wright, Arthur Miller & Mary K. Kane, Federal Practice and Procedure § 2382 at 257 (2d ed. 1986).

2.   BIFURCATION OF CLAIMS AND ISSUES

Closely related to consolidation is the procedure of bifurcation or separating particular claims and issues. Judicial economy and prevention of jury confusion or prejudice provide the primary rationale for allowing separate trials of various issues or claims. Fed. R. Civ. P. 42(b) provides:

> Separate trials. The court, in furtherance of convenience or to avoid prejudice, or when separate trials will be conducive to expedition or economy, may order a separate trial of any claim, cross-claim, counterclaim, or third-party claim, or of any separate issue or of any number of claims, cross-claims, counterclaims, third-party claims, or issues, always preserving inviolate the right of trial by jury as declared by the Seventh Amendment to the Constitution or as given by a statute of the United States.

Bifurcation has proven to be an especially popular procedural device in toxic tort cases, usually involving the separation of the issue of liability from damages. Ordering bifurcation is discretionary with the trial court and will not be reversed in the absence of an abuse of discretion. See In re Bendectin Litig., 857 F.2d 290 (6th Cir.1988), cert. denied 488 U.S. 1006, 109 S.Ct. 788, 102 L.Ed.2d 779 (1989). Bifurcation may take several forms. In the first, the judge will sequence the presentation of evidence so that the weakest portion of a plaintiff's case (as determined perhaps at pretrial conference under Fed. R. Civ. P. 16) is heard first. If plaintiff is unable to make out a prima facie case on this essential element, the judge will direct a verdict or otherwise dismiss the complaint. In the second type of bifurcation, the jury is asked to return a verdict on the first essential issue or claim to be tried; if this verdict is favorable to the defendant and dispositive of other issues or claims to be tried, then the trial is terminated and the jury never hears evidence on the other issues or claims.

Given the critical importance and difficulty of the proof of the causation element of a plaintiff's case, it is not surprising that some courts have bifurcated causation and liability. In the Bendectin class action products liability litigation, Chief Judge Carl B. Rubin ordered the jury to return a verdict on the issue of whether Bendectin can cause birth defects. In re Bendectin Litig., M.D.L. No. 486, Doc. No. 1577 (S.D.Ohio April 12, 1984). See 624 F.Supp. 1212 (S.D.Ohio 1985). Under the terms of the order, if plaintiffs prevailed in this first phase, the jury would then be asked to decide whether the manufacturer was negligent in failing to test the drug adequately and warn users of potential side effects. If the plaintiffs were to prevail on the liability issue, they would pursue damages individually in the district courts in which their cases were filed originally. This resolution is an interesting synthesis of consolidation, bifurcation, and multidistrict consolidation under Rules 42(a) and (b) and 28 U.S.C.A. § 1407 (1976). However, the jury returned a verdict for defendants on the causation issue, which was affirmed. In re Bendectin Litig., M.D.L. No. 486, Doc. No. 3051 (S.D.Ohio March 12, 1985), modified 857 F.2d 290 (6th Cir.1988).

Which party is most likely to prefer bifurcation? Won't a defendant always prefer to isolate the damages issue from the question of liability? What types of prejudice might a defendant assert from the jury hearing the damages evidence before it renders a verdict on liability? Defendants are especially eager to obtain bifurcation of plaintiff's claim, if any, for punitive damages because in most jurisdictions evidence of defendant's wealth and income are relevant and admissible to enable the jury to assess the amount of the award. Simpson v. Pittsburgh Corning Corp., 901 F.2d 277 (2d Cir.1990) (describing bifurcation as the "preferred method" of trying punitive damages issues, but deferring to trial court's discretion in denying bifurcation in this case). See generally Gerald W. Boston, Punitive Damages in Tort Law §§ 32.14–32.18 (1993).

3. MULTIDISTRICT LITIGATION

The last of the devices that are available to assist courts in the management of mass toxic tort cases is the employment of multidistrict consolidations of cases pending in various federal districts. Section 1407 of the Judicial Code, 28 U.S.C.A. § 1407, authorizes the temporary transfer of multidistrict litigation to a single district for coordinated pretrial proceedings. The statute establishes a special Judicial Panel on Multidistrict Litigation to determine whether transfer is appropriate in a particular case and what district should be denominated the transferee forum. While the statute does not set forth any particular genre of litigation to which consolidated pretrial transfers should be applied, the House Report accompanying the legislation provides that products liability actions and "common disasters" litigation are contemplated by the Act. See 1968 U.S. Code Cong. & Admin. News 1898–1900. Section 1407 contains no explicit limitations on the designations of the transferee forum, as the Panel is permitted to transfer actions "to any district." 28 U.S.C.A. § 1407(A).

C. ASBESTOS LITIGATION: CLASSES, CONSOLIDATIONS, BIFURCATIONS AND MULTIDISTRICT LITIGATION

The asbestos litigation—by any numerical criterion one might apply—is the most significant mass tort litigation in the nation's history. As one author stated:

> The large number of claims, the severity of injuries, the financial stakes involved, the social issues raised by the past behavior of asbestos manufacturers, and the possibility that the available resources for compensation will be insufficient have led many observers to view asbestos litigation as a test of the civil justice system's ability to efficiently and equitably compensate injured parties while deterring future injurious behavior.

Deborah R. Hensler et al., Asbestos in the Courts: The Challenge of Mass Toxic Torts v (1985).

One of the earliest asbestos cases to apply an aggregative approach was Wilson v. Johns–Manville Sales Corp., 107 F.R.D. 250 (S.D.Tex. 1985), in which the federal district court consolidated 50 of 150 pending cases for a single trial on two issues: product defectiveness and punitive damages, both of which turned on the state of the art evidence—what the defendants knew or should have known respecting the dangers posed by exposure to asbestos and when they knew or should have known such knowledge and informed users of those risks. That same year, Judge Robert Parker in Jenkins v. Raymark Industries, Inc., 109 F.R.D. 269 (E.D.Tex.1985), affirmed, 782 F.2d 468 (5th Cir.1986) went beyond Wilson and considered whether to certify a class under Fed. R. Civ. P. 23(b)(1)(B). First, he found that a class consisting of 893 cases, with over 1000 plaintiffs, satisfied the Rule 23 requirements of numerosity, commonality, typicality, and adequate representation. Judge Parker granted plaintiffs' motion to certify the class under Rule 23(b)(3) relating to situations where the common questions of law and fact predominate over individual questions. The court concluded, as in Wilson, that the predominant common question was state of the art, which would be determinative of both underlying liability for failure to warn and punitive damages liability. The Fifth Circuit Court of Appeals affirmed Jenkins, 782 F.2d 468 (5th Cir.1986):

> [T]he decision at hand is driven in one direction by all the circumstances. Judge Parker's plan is clearly superior to the alternative of repeating, hundreds of times over, the litigation of the state of the art issues with, as that experienced judge says, "days of the same witnesses, exhibits and issues from trial to trial."
>
> This assumes plaintiffs win on the critical issues of the class trial. To the extent defendants win, the elimination of issues and docket will mean a far greater saving of judicial resources. Further-

more, attorneys' fees for all parties will be greatly reduced under this plan, not only because of the elimination of so much trial time but also because the fees collected from all members of the plaintiff class will be controlled by the judge. From our view it seems that the defendants enjoy all of the advantages, and the plaintiffs incur the disadvantages, of the class action—with one exception: the cases are to be brought to trial. That counsel for plaintiffs would urge the class action under these circumstances is significant support for the district judge's decision.

After Jenkins, Judge Parker sought to employ the class action mechanisms to get beyond the common issues of state of the art and gross negligence, which focused exclusively on the conduct and knowledge of the defendants, and sought to try the plaintiff-specific factual questions of causation and damages.

In In re Fibreboard Corporation, 893 F.2d 706 (5th Cir.1990), the Fifth Circuit, in the opinion that follows, held that Judge Parker had exceeded the authority granted in Rule 23 and implemented a procedure that raised constitutional and other concerns.

IN RE FIBREBOARD CORPORATION

United States Court of Appeals, Fifth Circuit, 1990.
893 F.2d 706.

Higginbotham, J.

Defendants Fibreboard Corporation and Pittsburgh Corning Corporation, joined by other defendants, petition for writ of mandamus, asking that we vacate pretrial orders consolidating 3,031 asbestos cases for trial entered by Judge Robert Parker, Eastern District of Texas.

In 1986 there were at least 5,000 asbestos-related cases pending in this circuit. We then observed that "because asbestos-related diseases will continue to manifest themselves for the next fifteen years, filings will continue at a steady rate until the year 2000."[8] Id. at 470. That observation is proving to be accurate. In Jenkins v. Raymark, we affirmed Judge Parker's certification of a class of some 900 asbestos claimants, persuaded that the requirements of Rule 23(b)(3) were met for the trial of certain common questions including the "state of the art" defense. After that order and certain settlements, approximately 3,031 asbestos personal injury cases accumulated in the Eastern District of Texas.

The petitions for mandamus attack the district court's effort to try these cases in a common trial.

The standard of review is familiar. We are to issue a writ of mandamus only "to remedy a clear usurpation of power or abuse of discretion" when "no other adequate means of obtaining relief is available." As we stated in In re Willy, 831 F.2d 545, 549 (5th Cir.1987):

---

8. See Jenkins v. Raymark Industries, Inc., 782 F.2d 468, 470 (5th Cir.1986).

"Mandamus cannot be used as a substitute for appeal even when hardship may result from delay or from an unnecessary trial. Mandamus is an extraordinary remedy that should be granted only in the clearest and most compelling cases. [M]andamus relief is ordinarily inappropriate when review is obtainable on direct appeal." After a brief look at the background of these cases, we will return to the question of whether petitioners have met this extraordinary burden.

I

On September 20, 1989, Professor Jack Ratliff of the University of Texas Law School filed his special master's report in Cimino v. Raymark. The special master concluded that it was "self-evident that the use of one-by-one individual trials is not an option in the asbestos cases." On October 26, the district court entered the first of the orders now at issue. The district court concluded that the trial of these cases in groups of 10 would take all of the Eastern District's trial time for the next three years, explaining that it was persuaded that "to apply traditional methodology to these cases is to admit failure of the federal court system to perform one of its vital roles in our society * * * an efficient, cost-effective dispute resolution process that is fair to the parties." The district court then consolidated 3,031 cases under Fed.R.Civ.P. 42(a) "for a single trial on the issues of state of the art and punitive damages and certified a class action under Rule 23(b)(3) for the remaining issues of exposure and actual damages." The consolidation and certification included all pending suits in the Beaumont Division of the Eastern District of Texas filed as of February 1, 1989, by insulation workers and construction workers, survivors of deceased workers, and household members of asbestos workers who were seeking money damages for asbestos-related injury, disease, or death

Phase I is to be a single consolidated trial proceeding under Rule 42(a). It will decide the state of the art and punitive damages issues. The district court explained that: "the jury will be asked to decide issues such as (a) which products, if any, were asbestos-containing insulation products capable of producing dust that contained asbestos fibers sufficient to cause harm in its application, use, or removal; (b) which of the Defendants' products, if any, were defective as marketed and unreasonably dangerous; (c) when each Defendant knew or should have known that insulators or construction workers and their household members were at risk of contracting an asbestos-related injury or disease from the application, use, or removal of asbestos-containing insulation products; and (d) whether each Defendant's marketing of a defective and unreasonably dangerous product constituted gross negligence. In answering issue (d), the Jury will hear evidence of punitive conduct including any conspiracy among the Defendants to conceal the dangers (if any) of asbestos. The wording of issues (c) and (d) will depend on the applicability of the 1987 Texas Tort Reform legislation to a particular class member's individual case." By its order of December 29, 1989, the district court explained that "the jury may be allowed to formulate a multiplier for each defendant for which the jury returns an affirmative finding on the issue of gross negligence."

The district court also described the proceedings for Phase II in its October 26 order. In Phase II the jury is to decide the percentage of plaintiffs exposed to each defendant's products, the percentage of claims barred by statutes of limitation, adequate warnings, and other affirmative defenses. The jury is to determine actual damages in a lump sum for each disease category for all plaintiffs in the class. Phase II will include a full trial of liability and damages for 11 class representatives and such evidence as the parties wish to offer from 30 illustrative plaintiffs. Defendants will choose 15 and plaintiffs will choose 15 illustrative plaintiffs, for a total of 41 plaintiffs. The jury will hear opinions of experts from plaintiffs and defendants regarding the total damage award. The basis for the jury's judgment is said to be the 41 cases plus the data supporting the calculation of the experts regarding total damages suffered by the remaining 2,990 class members.

Class members have answered questionnaires and are testifying in scheduled oral depositions now in progress. Petitioners attack the limits of discovery from the class members, but we will not reach this issue. It is sufficient to explain that defendants are allowed a total of 45 minutes to interrogate each class member in an oral deposition. These depositions will not be directly used at the trial in Phase II. Rather, the oral depositions, with the other discovery from class members, provide information for experts engaged to measure the damages suffered by the class.

II

Defendants find numerous flaws in the procedures set for Phase II of the trial. They argue with considerable force that such a trial would effectively deny defendants' rights to a jury under the Seventh Amendment, would work an impermissible change in the controlling substantive law of Texas, would deny procedural due process under the Fifth Amendment of the United States Constitution, and would effectively amend the rules of civil procedure contrary to the strictures of the enabling acts.

A

The contentions that due process would be denied, the purposes of Erie would be frustrated, and the Seventh Amendment circumvented are variations of a common concern of defendants. Defendants insist that one-to-one adversarial engagement or its proximate, the traditional trial, is secured by the seventh amendment and certainly contemplated by Article III of the Constitution itself. Defendants point out, and plaintiffs quickly concede, that under Phase II there will inevitably be individual class members whose recovery will be greater or lesser than it would have been if tried alone. Indeed, with the focus in Phase II upon the "total picture," with arrays of data that will attend the statistical presentation, persons who would have had their claims rejected may recover. Plaintiffs say that "such discontinuities" would be reflected in the overall omnibus figure. Stated another way, plaintiffs say that so long as their mode of proof enables the jury to decide the total liability of defendants with reasonable accuracy, the loss of one-to-one engagement infringes no right of defendants. Such unevenness, plaintiffs say, will be visited upon them, not the defendants.

With the procedures described at such a level of abstraction, it is difficult to describe concretely any deprivation of defendants' rights. Of course, there will be a jury, and each plaintiff will be present in a theoretical, if not practical, sense. Having said this, however, we are left with a profound disquiet. First, the assumption of plaintiffs' argument is that its proof of omnibus damages is in fact achievable; that statistical measures of representativeness and commonality will be sufficient for the jury to make informed judgments concerning damages. It is true that there is considerable judicial experience with such techniques, but it is also true we have remained cautious in their use. Indeed, as the district court stated in one massive Title VII case resting on math models: "[I]t has to judicial eyes a surrealistic cast, mirroring the techniques used in its trial. Excursions into the new and sometimes arcane corners of different disciplines is a familiar task of American trial lawyers and its generalist judges. But more is afoot here, and this court is uncomfortable with its implications. This concern has grown with the realization that the esoterics of econometrics and statistics which both parties have required this court to judge have a centripetal dynamic of their own. They push from the outside roles of tools for 'judicial' decisions toward the core of decision making itself. Stated more concretely: the precision-like mesh of numbers tends to make fits of social problems when I intuitively doubt such fits. I remain wary of the siren call of the numerical display * * *."[9]

This concern is particularly strong in this case, where there are such disparities among "class" members.

The plaintiffs' answers to interrogatories and the depositions already conducted have provided enough information to show that if, as plaintiffs contend, the representative plaintiffs accurately reflect the class, it is a diverse group. The plaintiffs' "class" consists of persons claiming different diseases, different exposure periods, and different occupations. The depositions of ten tentative class representatives indicate that their diseases break down into three categories: asbestosis (plural and pulmonary)—eight representatives; lung cancer—three representatives; and Mesothelioma—one representative. The class breaks down as follows:

9. Vuyanich v. Republic Nat. Bank of Dallas, 505 F.Supp. 224, 394 (N.D.Tex. 1980).

Disease	#	%
Pleural cases	907	37.2%
Asbestosis cases	1184	48.6%
Lung cancer cases	219	9.0%
Other cancer cases	92	3.8%
Mesothelioma cases	33	1.4%

In addition, plaintiffs' admissions of fact show the following disparities among class members. a. The class includes persons who do not have legal claims against Defendant ACandS, Inc. b. One or more members of the class may be barred from prosecuting claims against ACandS by virtue of their prior employment with ACandS. c. The severity and type of physical or mental injuries varies among class members. d. The nature and type of damage varies among class members. e. Not all of the Plaintiffs have been injured by the acts, omissions, conduct or fault of all of the Defendants. f. The dates of exposure to asbestos-containing products varies among class members. g. The types of products to which class members were exposed varies among class members. h. The dates that class members knew or should have known of their exposure to asbestos-containing products is not identical among class members.

We are also uncomfortable with the suggestion that a move from one-on-one "traditional" modes is little more than a move to modernity. Such traditional ways of proceeding reflect far more than habit. They reflect the very culture of the jury trial and the case and controversy requirement of Article III. It is suggested that the litigating unit is the class and, hence, we have the adversarial engagement or that all are present in a "consolidated" proceeding. But, this begs the very question of whether these 3,031 claimants are sufficiently situated for class treatment; it equally begs the question of whether they are actually before the court under Fed.R.Civ.Proc.Rules 23 and 42(b) in any more than a fictional sense. Ultimately, these concerns find expression in defendants' right to due process.

These concerns are little more than different ways of looking at a core problem. The core problem is that Phase II, while offering an innovative answer to an admitted crisis in the judicial system, is unfortunately beyond the scope of federal judicial authority. It infringes upon the dictates of Erie that we remain faithful to the law of Texas, and upon the separation of powers between the judicial and legislative branches.

Texas has made its policy choices in defining the duty owed by manufacturers and suppliers of products to consumers. These choices are reflected in the requirement that a plaintiff prove both causation and damage. In Texas, it is a "fundamental principle of traditional products liability law ... that the plaintiffs must prove that the defendant supplied the product which caused the injury."[10] These elements focus upon individuals, not groups. The same may be said, and with even greater confidence, of wage losses, pain and suffering, and other elements of compensation. These requirements of proof define the duty of the manufacturers.

10. Gaulding v. Celotex Corp., 772 S.W.2d 66, 68 (Tex.1989).

Plaintiffs say, of course, that these requirements will be met by the proposed procedures. This proof for 2,990 class members will be supplied by expert opinion regarding their similarity to 41 representative plaintiffs. Plaintiffs deny that they will be extrapolating a total universe from a sample. While we are skeptical of this assertion, plaintiffs' characterization is of little moment. The inescapable fact is that the individual claims of 2,990 persons will not be presented. Rather, the claim of a unit of 2,990 persons will be presented. Given the unevenness of the individual claims, this Phase II process inevitably restates the dimensions of tort liability. Under the proposed procedure, manufacturers and suppliers are exposed to liability not only in 41 cases actually tried with success to the jury, but in 2,990 additional cases whose claims are indexed to those tried.

Texas has made its policy choices in its substantive tort rules against the backdrop of a trial. Trials can vary greatly in their procedures, such as numbers of jurors, the method of jury instruction, and a large number of other ways. There is a point, however, where cumulative changes in procedure work a change in the very character of a trial. Significantly, changes in "procedure" involving the mode of proof may alter the liability of the defendants in fundamental ways. We do not suggest that procedure becomes substance whenever outcomes are changed. Rather, we suggest that changes in substantive duty can come dressed as a change in procedure. We are persuaded that Phase II would work such a change.

The basic changes in the dynamics of trial caused by the rules of evidence and procedure have been particularly noted with respect to the use of expert testimony. A contemplated "trial" of the 2,990 class members without discrete focus can be no more than the testimony of experts regarding their claims, as a group, compared to the claims actually tried to the jury. That procedure cannot focus upon such issues as individual causation, but ultimately must accept general causation as sufficient, contrary to Texas law. It is evident that these statistical estimates deal only with general causation, for "population-based probability estimates do not speak to a probability of causation in any one case; the estimate of relative risk is a property of the studied population, not of an individual's case." This type of procedure does not allow proof that a particular defendant's asbestos "really" caused a particular plaintiff's disease; the only "fact" that can be proved is that in most cases the defendant's asbestos would have been the cause. This is the inevitable consequence of treating discrete claims as fungible claims. Commonality among class members on issues of causation and damages can be achieved only by lifting the description of the claims to a level of generality that tears them from their substantively required moorings to actual causation and discrete injury. Procedures can be devised to implement such generalizations, but not without alteration of substantive principle.

We are told that Phase II is the only realistic way of trying these cases; that the difficulties faced by the courts as well as the rights of the class members to have their cases tried cry powerfully for innovation and judicial creativity. The arguments are compelling, but they are better addressed to the representative branches—Congress and the State Legislature. The Judicial Branch can offer the trial of lawsuits. It has no power or competence to do more. We are persuaded on reflection that the procedures here called for comprise something other than a trial within our authority. It is called a trial, but it is not.

The 2,990 class members cannot be certified for trial as proposed under Rule 23(b)(3), Fed.R.Civ.Pro.Rule 23(b)(3) requires that "the questions of law or fact common to the members of the class predominate over any questions affecting individual members." There are too many disparities among the various plaintiffs for their common concerns to predominate. The plaintiffs suffer from different diseases, some of which are more likely to have been caused by asbestos than others. The plaintiffs were exposed to asbestos in various manners and to varying degrees. The plaintiffs' lifestyles differed in material respects. To create the requisite commonality for trial, the discrete components of the class members' claims and the asbestos manufacturers' defenses must be submerged. The procedures for Phase II do precisely that, but, as we have explained, do so only by reworking the substantive duty owed by the manufacturers. At the least, the enabling acts prevent that reading.

Finally, it is questionable whether defendants' right to trial by jury is being faithfully honored, but we need not explore this issue. It is sufficient now to conclude that Phase II cannot go forward without changing Texas law and usurping legislative prerogatives, a step federal courts lack authority to take.

We admire the work of our colleague, Judge Robert Parker, and are sympathetic with the difficulties he faces. This grant of the petition for writ of mandamus should not be taken as a rebuke of an able judge, but rather as another chapter in an ongoing struggle with the problems presented by the phenomenon of mass torts. The petitions for writ of mandamus are granted.

Notes and Questions

1. Was causation or damages the more intractable problem according to Judge Higginbotham? Can causation ever be established on an aggregative or representative basis? Refer back to the material in Chapter 8 and the dual nature of the causation question. In Sterling v. Velsicol Chemical Corp., discussed supra, while the Sixth Circuit approved the certification of the class action, it also held that only the generic causation issue could be resolved on a class-wide basis—i.e., whether the kinds of harm suffered by plaintiffs could have been produced by exposure to the chemicals released, whereas the individual causation inquiry must be resolved on a plaintiff-by-plaintiff basis. If that is true, how can a class action ever resolve all of the elements of the plaintiffs' prima facie case? Was it Judge Parker's hope that resolution of the representative plaintiffs' causation elements (if favorable) would have resulted in some global settlement?

2. In Fibreboard isn't it "obvious" that most of the plaintiffs' injuries were caused by exposure to asbestos? For mesothelioma the relative risk for asbestos exposure is extremely high, meaning that few people ever contract that disease unless exposed to asbestos. Why not apply epidemiological data and the principle of proportionality discussed in Chapter 8 to arrive at a total value to the class for each disease category?

3. Is Texas' substantive tort law on causation unique? Was Judge Higginbotham concluding that the proportionality principle has no basis in Texas tort law? Is there any jurisdiction referred to in Chapters 5 or 8 that might find the approach advocated by Judge Parker acceptable?

4. What were the defendants' motivations for seeking a writ of mandamus? Wouldn't they save substantial litigation expenses under Judge Parker's proposed methods?

5. Of at least four separate rationales advanced by Judge Higginbotham to justify granting the writ of mandamus, which seemed the most persuasive? Why didn't he simply hold that the Phase II class failed to satisfy the requirements of Rule 23(b) that common questions predominate? Was the remainder of the opinion dicta? How compelling is the argument (which the court declined to reach) that defendants are denied their right to a jury trial guaranteed by the Seventh Amendment? Don't class actions under Rule 23 necessarily place some constraint on individual jury trials?

6. Judge Parker applied reverse bifurcation in Jenkins and Fibreboard by first trying common defenses and punitive damages before trying causation and compensatory damages. What is the rationale for applying reverse bifurcation?

7. Observe that Judge Parker sought to utilize both consolidation under Rule 42(a) for the common issues (defenses and punitive damages), as he had done successfully in Jenkins, and a class action under Rule 23(b) for the individual issues of causation and damages. Judge Higginbotham, in a deleted segment of the opinion, praised Judge Parker for his imaginative and innovative approaches and encouraged him to seek to find other techniques to manage these cases.

8. In Cimino v. Raymark Industries, 751 F.Supp. 649 (E.D.Tex.1990), Judge Parker sought to steer between the success of Jenkins and the failure of Fibreboard.

a. Judge Parker described the Phases of the trial as follows:

Phase I would involve trial of the common questions of product defectiveness under § 402A, adequacy of the warnings, the state of the art defense and punitive damages liability.

Phase II required a jury finding for each of nineteen worksites during certain time periods regarding which asbestos containing insulation products were used, which crafts were sufficiently exposed to asbestos fibers from those products for such exposure to be a producing cause of an asbestos-related injury or disease and an apportionment of causation among defendants, settling and non-settling.

In other words, the exposure questions to be submitted would be specific as to time, place, craft, and amounts of exposure.

He then described the stipulation to which the parties had agreed on Phase II pertaining to exposure and causation:

The Court first compiled a list of worksites, various locations consisting mostly of oil and chemical refineries, where the majority of the plaintiffs allegedly were occupationally exposed to asbestos in the course of their employment. The Court next compiled a list of job classifications, or crafts, which the plaintiffs worked in during their employment at the worksites. It was contemplated that any plaintiff whose work history did not include a threshold amount of time in any of the worksites would have the exposure issue tried in an individual mini-trial.

Prior to the Court drafting a verdict form for Phase II, the parties agreed to stipulate as to what the jury findings would have been had the Phase II been tried to a jury. The parties stipulated that the jury would have apportioned causation among the defendants in the amounts of 10% causation for each of the non-settling defendants and 13% causation for the settling defendant Johns–Manville Corporation.

The verdict form for Phase II would have been worksites. For each worksite there would have been two interrogatories. The first interrogatory would have asked whether or not each of the various crafts at a worksite was sufficiently exposed to asbestos for that exposure to be a producing cause of the disease of asbestosis during successive time periods. The second interrogatory then would have requested the jury to determine, for each craft and each time period answered affirmatively in the first interrogatory, the percentage of comparative causation, if any, that each defendant's products contributed to the exposure.

Why do you suppose the defendants agreed to stipulate causation on this basis? If there had not been agreement would this approach have satisfied the concerns of Judge Higginbotham? What central fact made Phase II a workable approach?

b. Phase III dealt with damages:

The 2,298 class members were divided into five disease categories based on the plaintiff's injury claims. The Court selected a random sample from each disease category as follows:

	SAMPLE SIZE	DISEASE CATEGORY POPULATION
Mesothelioma	15	32
Lung Cancer	25	186
Other Cancer	20	58
Asbestosis	50	1,050
Pleural Disease	50	972
TOTAL	160	2,228

The damage case of each trial sample class member randomly drawn was then submitted to a jury. Each plaintiff whose damage case was submitted to the jury is to be awarded his individual verdict for each disease category will constitute the damage award for each non-sample class member.

Plaintiffs have agreed to the procedure, thereby waiving their rights to individual damage determinations.

In addition, Phase III addressed any contributory fault by the representative plaintiffs, including smoking, if the evidence showed that a plaintiff had subjective knowledge of the synergistic relationship between the asbestos-related disease and smoking and appreciated the danger of continued smoking. These elements of contributory fault were also applied to the failure of a plaintiff to wear a respirator and the failure to follow a doctor's advice. In cases where there was no evidence of smoking constituting contributory fault, evidence of a plaintiff's smoking was allowed on the issue of damages to show quality of life and life expectancy.

The damage Phase depended on the application of statistical methods. Judge Parker described those methods and explained why they satisfied the defendants' constitutional rights:

> The Court finds no persuasive evidence why the average damage verdicts in each disease category should not be applied to the non-sample members. The averages are calculated after remittitur and take into consideration those cases where plaintiffs failed to prove the existence of an asbestos-related injury or disease resulting in a zero verdict. Individual members of a disease category who will receive an award that might be different from one they would have received had their individual case been decided by a jury have waived any objections, and the defendants cannot show that the total amount of damages would be greater under the Court's method compared to individual trials of these cases. Indeed, the millions of dollars saved in reduced transaction costs inure to defendants' benefit.

* * *

> The 160 damage cases tried with all the variables inherent in such cases produced a result to a 99% confidence level the average of which would be comparable to the average result if all cases were tried. If the existence of variables are the driving force behind defendants' due process argument, then due process has been served.

> However, a due process concern remains that is very troubling to the Court. It is apparent from the effort and time required to try these 160 cases, that unless this plan or some other procedure that permits damages to be adjudicated in the aggregate is approved, these cases cannot be tried. Defendants complain about the 1% likelihood that the result would be significantly different. However, plaintiffs are facing a 100% confidence level of being denied access to the courts. The Court will leave it to the academicians and legal scholars to debate whether our notion of due process has room for balancing these competing interests.

Judge Parker also held that these procedures satisfied any requirements set forth in the Fibreboard opinion. In your opinion, do they deny defendants any constitutional rights of due process? Any Seventh Amendment rights to jury trial? Any other rights? For an excellent discussion of the constitutional and practical propriety of the Cimino methodology, see Glen O. Robinson &

Kenneth S. Abraham, Collective Justice in Tort Law, 78 Va. L. Rev. 1481 (1992).

9. Judge Parker is not the only one applying aggregative mechanisms to resolve asbestos litigation. In one suit, the state circuit court in Baltimore, Maryland consolidated the suits brought by 8,550 plaintiffs. The court first submitted to a jury the common issues of state of the art and product defectiveness and then applied "mini-trials" on compensatory and punitive damages. See Abate v. AC & S, Inc., Md. Cir. Ct., Baltimore City, No. 89236704 (Dec. 12, 1992), 6 Toxics L. Rptr. 863 (12–23–92). The jury awarded $11.2 million in compensatory damages to three plaintiffs, and zero to three others; it also established punitive damage multipliers for each of six defendants, ranging from a low of .35 for each $1 of compensatory damages to a high of $2.50. The trial judge, fearing that the punitive awards would deplete the assets of defendants to pay future compensatory awards, held that all punitive awards made in the mini-trials would be delayed until all compensatory damages are paid.

10. In 1991, the Judicial Panel on Multi–District Litigation in In re Asbestos Products Liability Litigation, 771 F.Supp. 415 (Jud.Pan. Mult.Lit.1991) ordered the pretrial consolidation of 26,639 cases pending in 87 federal districts.

11. *Bankruptcy of Manville.* The asbestos litigation was further complicated by the 1982 bankruptcy filing of Johns–Manville Corporation, the largest of the asbestos producers. Johns–Manville, faced with claims from current and future victims of asbestos exposure estimated to total $2 billion, filed a voluntary petition in bankruptcy under chapter 11 on August 26, 1982. The reorganization proceeding involved both "present claimants," those who had developed an asbestos-related disease, and "future claimants," those who had been exposed to Manville asbestos but had not yet shown any signs of disease. After four years of negotiation, a Plan of Reorganization ("The Plan") was confirmed in 1986, In re Johns–Manville Corp., 68 B.R. 618 (Bkrtcy.N.Y.1986). The cornerstone of the plan was the Manville Personal Injury Settlement Trust ("The Trust"), a mechanism designed to satisfy the claims of all asbestos health claimants and which required all claimants to proceed only against the Trust, not against Manville. If a settlement could not be reached with the Trust, the claimant could elect mediation, binding arbitration, or traditional tort litigation in state or federal court, including trial by jury. The claimant could collect from the Trust the full amount of whatever compensatory damages are awarded, but punitive damages were prohibited. Another provision called for the settlement of claims against the Trust on a first in, first out basis.

The plan was approved by the Second Circuit. Kane v. Johns–Manville Corp., 843 F.2d 636 (2d Cir.1988). Pursuant to the Plan, the Trust received $909 million in cash, two bonds with an aggregate value of $1.8 billion, 24 million shares of Manville common stock, and 7.2 million shares of Manville convertible preferred stock, aggregating 80 percent of the stock of the reorganized Manville. See In re Joint Eastern & Southern Districts Asbestos Litigation, 120 B.R. 648, 652 (E.D.N.Y.1990). Despite this funding, it was apparent by 1990 that the liquidation of the claims of thousands of asbestos victims was substantially depleting the Trust's cash. By March 30, 1990, the

Trust had received more than 150,000 claims, 50 percent above the highest number estimated when the Plan was approved. The Trust had settled 22,386 of those claims at an average liquidated value of $42,000.

In 1990, Judge Jack Weinstein of the Eastern District of New York was given supervisory authority over the Plan because he was separately handling the trials of hundreds of asbestos cases pending in that court. Judge Weinstein appointed a special master in response to a motion by the Trust for a determination that its assets constituted a limited fund within the meaning of Fed. R. Civ. P. Rule 23(b)(1)(B). The Special Master's report concluded that the Trust was "deeply insolvent." In November 1990, beneficiaries under the Trust filed a class action on behalf of all beneficiaries which Judge Weinstein and Bankruptcy Judge Lifland certified. A proposed settlement reordered the priorities of the Trust by dividing all claimants into two levels: those most severely injured, which included cancer, other serious conditions, and death claims; and all others. In addition, it set payment levels ranging from a maximum of $350,000 for mesothelioma to $30,000 for pleural disease. Secondly, Level One would receive up to 45 percent of their claims in the first two years, but Level Two recipients would be deferred until the third year.

Some personal injury claimants and co-defendant manufacturers opposed the settlement. The health claimants challenged the accord on several fronts, arguing that it violated procedural due process, Rule 23 requirements, and violated the Bankruptcy Code. In In re Joint Eastern and Southern District Asbestos Litigation, 982 F.2d 721 (2d Cir.1992), the Second Circuit (2–1) overturned portions of the Plan.

The Second Circuit held that the orders and procedures embodied in Judge Weinstein's efforts to control the disposition of the Trust assets and dispose of pending asbestos claims were not authorized under Rule 23(b)(1)(B) (a limited fund class) and violated provisions of the Bankruptcy Code. The court concluded that combining co-defendant manufacturers (other than Manville) and all health claimants into a single class transgressed the requirements of Rule 23 that those with adverse interests cannot have the same representatives. Similarly, in the court's view, treating all health claimants as a class, when the Proposed Settlement would significantly alter priorities that existed under the original Manville Plan, was improper because consent to the settlement was given by representatives who purported to represent an undifferentiated class of claimants, rather than the interests of the subclasses whose rights were altered. Further, it held that the Plan was an impermissible modification of a confirmed and substantially consummated plan of reorganization without complying with all of the requirements of the Bankruptcy Code.

Six months later, in response to a motion for reconsideration, the Second Circuit reversed itself and held that separate subclasses of claimants were not necessary. 993 F.2d 7 (2d Cir.1993). For a scholarly proposal that would permit modifications of a mass tort debtor's Chapter 11 plan to ensure compensation for mass tort victims, see Comment, Modifications of a Chapter 11 Plan in the Mass Tort Context, 92 Col. L. Rev. 192 (1992).

D. JUDICIAL CASE MANAGEMENT

After a court has resolved the manner in which the litigation is to be structured—class action, consolidations, or individual trials—most courts in toxic tort cases use pretrial orders or other orders that organize the sequence of litigation milestones. Plaintiffs' counsel will typically prefer parallel track discovery procedures that permit each side to conduct depositions, request documents, and propound interrogatories. Defense counsel, on the other hand, will strongly prefer that plaintiffs be required to prepare their cases first. The defendants will, therefore, attempt to obtain a court order requiring the plaintiffs to disclose their experts and set forth individualized statements establishing a connection between the alleged toxic exposure and each plaintiff's medical complaints. Some courts are persuaded to follow this approach when convinced that it will save judicial resources and provide an opportunity for a prompt resolution of the entire case.

1. "LONE PINE" ORDERS

a. The expression "Lone Pine" order has become a term of art in toxic tort litigation and refers to orders that require plaintiffs to submit, at the pretrial stage, supporting proofs, including expert opinions, to establish causation and injury. The term derived from the case of Lore v. Lone Pine Corp., No. L–03306–85, slip op. (N.J. Sup. Ct., Law Div., Nov. 18, 1986). The case management order in that case, which ultimately resulted in the dismissal of plaintiff's action for failure to comply with its terms, read as follows:

> Order * * * that on or before June 1, 1987: (1) plaintiffs would provide the following documentation with respect to each claim for personal injuries: (a) facts of each individual plaintiff's exposure to alleged toxic substances at or from the Lone Pine landfill; (b) reports of treating physicians and medical or other experts, supporting each individual plaintiff's claim of injury and causation by substances from Lone Pine landfill; (2) plaintiffs would provide the following with respect to each individual plaintiff's claims for diminution of property value: (c) each individual plaintiff's address, including tax block and lot number, for the property alleged to have declined in value; (d) reports of real estate or other experts supporting each individual plaintiff's claim of diminution of property values, including the timing and degree of such diminution and the causation of same. These were considered to be the basic facts plaintiff must furnish in order to support their claim of injury and property damage.

Interrogatories to be propounded that would support a Lone Pine order would request the plaintiffs to list every chemical they were exposed to, to list every injury caused by the chemical, to list the name of every doctor who says the injury was caused by the chemical, and to list the evidence that they have that each defendant is responsible for the injury caused by the chemical.

b.   Illustrative of an order, but more comprehensive in its coverage, was that issued in Grant v. E.I. Du Pont De Nemours & Co., 1993 WL 146634 (E.D.N.C.), order aff'd, 1993 WL 146638 (E.D.N.C. 1993). U.S. Dist. Ct., E.D.N.C., Feb. 17, 1993. The litigation involved twelve separate civil actions brought against Du Pont by twenty-two residents who alleged that Du Pont had contaminated their homes and personally injured them through the release of certain chemicals into the air and groundwater. The total amount in controversy, including punitive damages claims of $500 million, exceeded $1.3 billion.

With some deletions, the court's order included the following provisions:

1.   Plaintiffs are to complete the scientific testing of their properties, including soil, groundwater, surface water, and air, by May 31, 1993. On or before June 15, 1993, Plaintiffs are to provide Du Pont with all testing results, analyses and other data, and file with the Court and provide Du Pont with the affidavit of a competent expert witness, specifying the nature, duration, and level of contamination of each Plaintiff's property. The expert's affidavit must specify each chemical substance by name, the date of testing, the level and concentration of the substance detected as of the testing date, the testing methodology, the detection limits of the methodology, the connection of the chemical to Kentec Inc. and Du Pont, and the path and route of the chemical from Kentec to the Plaintiff's property. The failure of any Plaintiff to comply with this paragraph may result in his or her action being dismissed.

2.   Du Pont shall have from July 1, 1993 through September 30, 1993 to complete its scientific testing of the properties, including soil, groundwater, surface water, and air, of all Plaintiffs who have demonstrated their interest in continuing in this litigation by their compliance with the preceding paragraph. The failure of any Plaintiff to cooperate with Du Pont's efforts to comply with this paragraph may result in his or her action being dismissed. * * * The failure of Du Pont to comply with this paragraph may result in its being precluded from introducing evidence on this issue at trial.

3.   Plaintiffs are to complete all appraisals of their properties by April 30, 1993. On or before May 15, 1993, Plaintiffs are to provide Du Pont with all such appraisals, and file with the Court and provide Du Pont with the affidavit of each qualified real estate appraiser, specifying the value of each Plaintiff's property, the comparables upon which such value is based, whether the property has been in any way impaired, and the reason for the impairment. * * * The failure of any Plaintiff to comply with this paragraph may result in his or her claims for injury to property being dismissed.

4.   Du Pont is to have from June 1, 1993 through July 31, 1993 to complete its appraisals of the properties of all Plaintiffs * * *

5. Plaintiffs are to have until July 31, 1993 to consult with competent expert witnesses and conduct scientific testing to determine the costs of cleaning up their properties or otherwise restoring the properties' value. On or before August 15, 1993, Plaintiffs are to provide Du Pont with all results, analyses, conclusions, and other data, and file with the Court and provide Du Pont with the affidavit of a competent expert witness specifying the actions each Plaintiff intends to conduct to clean up his property. The affidavit must specify a timetable for completion of the cleanup, an estimate of the costs of the cleanup, and the methodology for calculating the cleanup costs. The failure of any Plaintiff to comply with this paragraph may result in his or her claims for recovery of cleanup costs being dismissed.

6. [Sets forth Du Pont's obligations respecting the determination of clean up costs]

7. Plaintiffs are to have until May 31, 1993 to consult with and be examined by physicians, psychiatrists, psychologists, and any other health care providers regarding Plaintiffs' claims of potential future harm to their health, fear of harm to their health, stress, anxiety, or other emotional harm, or any other personal injury. On or before June 15, 1993, Plaintiffs are to provide Du Pont with all results, analyses and other data, and file with the Court and provide Du Pont with a physician's affidavit specifying the nature, duration, and amount of exposure (including blood levels) each Plaintiff has had to chemical contamination, when such exposure occurred, and the nature and extent of each such Plaintiff's personal injury. The physician's affidavit may be supplemented with the affidavits of other competent expert witnesses, but submission of such supplementary affidavits will not excuse the failure to submit the physician's affidavit, including the required contents, described in this paragraph. The physician's affidavit shall state his or her opinion, based on a reasonable degree of medical certainty, that the particular Plaintiff has suffered injuries as a result of exposure to chemicals from Kentec Inc.; shall specify any and every injury, illness or condition suffered by the Plaintiff that, in the opinion of the physician, caused each and every specific injury, illness, and condition listed; shall include differential diagnoses which rule out alternative possible causes of Plaintiffs' injuries; and shall state the scientific and medical bases for the physician's opinions. With regard to future personal injury, the affidavit shall state the physician's opinion, based upon a reasonable degree of medical certainty, that the particular Plaintiff is more likely than not to suffer a particular injury in the future; shall identify such specific injury; shall state the time at which such future injury shall manifest itself; and shall comply with the remaining requirements of this paragraph as if the injury currently existed. The failure of any Plaintiff to comply with this paragraph may result in his or her claims for personal injury being dismissed.

Notes and Questions

1. The effect of non-compliance with such orders is dismissal, which is recited in each paragraph. What is the justification for dismissals on that basis? Is that too drastic a sanction? Does it deprive plaintiffs of those protections that summary judgment procedures would afford? In Cottle v. Superior Court (Oxnard Shores Co.), 3 Cal.App.4th 1367, 5 Cal.Rptr.2d 882 (1992), a California appeals court, in affirming dismissal of plaintiff's claims for failing to comply with a series of case management orders, sustained orders (which were similar to those in *Lone Pine*) requiring "statements establishing a prima facie claim for personal injury or property damage" and excluding plaintiffs' causation evidence for failure to comply. The court first held that in complex litigation courts have broad inherent powers to control the management of such cases:

> The extent of the trial court's inherent managerial power in complex civil litigation has not yet been delineated by this state's reviewing courts. However, federal courts have long recognized that active and effective judicial management of such litigation is crucial. One federal court has explained, "Managerial power is not merely desirable. It is a critical necessity. * * * We face the hard necessity that, within proper limits, judges must be permitted to bring management power to bear upon massive and complex litigation to prevent it from monopolizing the services of the court to the exclusion of other litigants."

> In view of all these authorities, most of which were relied upon by the trial court, it is apparent that courts have the power to fashion a new procedure in a complex litigation case to manage and control the case before it. Although it is not possible to set forth precise guidelines as to when such an order can be issued or what other kinds of procedure can be used, we conclude that a court should consider the totality of the circumstances of the particular case in deciding how to manage a complex litigation case.

> We conclude that Judge Johnson properly used the court's inherent powers to manage the complex litigation case before her and hold that in a complex litigation case which has been assigned to a judge for all purposes, a court may order the exclusion of evidence if the plaintiffs are unable to establish a prima facie claim prior to the start of trial.

Second, the court held that the exclusion orders were valid, given the extensive, repeated opportunities afforded to plaintiffs to comply. Third, the court held that such orders did not deprive plaintiffs of any due process rights nor rights to a jury trial. Although plaintiffs had argued that the "cauldron of chemicals" present on their properties made precise exposure and causation testimony impossible, the court emphasized that the trial court indicated its willingness to accept "a synergistic cause and effect linkage between exposure and symptoms" which they had not provided. The dissenting opinion in Cottle argued that the judiciary lacks the kind of sweeping inherent powers relied upon by the majority and designation of the case as "complex" or "toxic tort" does not create special powers:

> [U]nder the authority of this section and similar provisions in the [California] Code of Civil Procedure (§ 128(a), § 177), courts have

devised various procedural rules to fairly and expeditiously handle litigation before them which presented procedural problems not otherwise covered in the statutes or rules.

However, appellate decisions construing these provisions indicate resort to a trial court's inherent authority to craft new rules of civil procedure is only a proper exercise of inherent powers when made necessary because of the absence of any statute or rule governing the situation. Thus, the rationale for devising new rules of procedure has historically been one of necessity. In other words, to fill a void in the statutory scheme, a court had a duty to create a new rule of procedure in the interests of justice and in order to exercise its jurisdiction. However, unlike the "procedure" employed in the case at bar, none of the judicially created procedures involved a ruling to decide the merits of a cause of action and, on that basis, to remove that cause of action from jury consideration.

In the instant case, there was not statutory void which required the court's "inherent power" to fill. To the contrary, the trial court's case management order was the substantial equivalent of a mechanism the Legislature has long provided—the motion for summary judgment. The Legislature, however, has surrounded this mechanism with procedural protections it considers essential to fairness and justice. These procedural protections were not afforded plaintiffs in this case.

Plaintiffs were ordered to present evidence of physical injury from exposure to the toxic substances through medical records, physician affidavits and the like. When the trial court deemed this evidence insufficient it terminated plaintiffs' causes of action, preventing them from being considered by the jury. As a consequence, the case management order in this case changed the legislatively established procedure of Code of Civil Procedure section 437c. Had the procedural guidelines for summary judgment been followed, the defendants would have had to have initiated the process and have supplied evidence causation could not be proved. Strictly construing these moving papers and liberally construing plaintiffs' documents in opposition to the motion, the court would have then decided whether there remained any triable issues of material fact as to causation. However, the trial court here did not employ the statutory provision for summary judgment with its built-in procedural safeguards. In its place the trial court substituted a bastardized process which had the purpose and effect of summary judgment but avoided the very procedures and protections the Legislature deemed essential.

The Legislature has provided a pretrial procedure for terminating a cause of action because the plaintiff has insufficient evidence to warrant a jury trial of the claim. That procedure is summary judgment. Consequently, trial courts lack "inherent power" to do the same thing under another name, especially one which omits vital procedural protections the Legislature guaranteed in its summary judgment statute. This attempt to grant the functional equivalent of a summary judgment in the guise of a case management order impinges on a litigant's constitutional right to have material issues of fact decided by a jury without affording the procedural protections the Legislature deemed essential before this drastic step would be allowed.

With whom do you agree: the majority or the dissenter? Do complex cases justify more extreme controls? What about plaintiffs' argument that they were denied a right to a jury trial? Doesn't a grant of a summary judgment motion have the same effect? While the Federal Rules of Civil Procedure authorize courts to issue pretrial and discovery orders, and to issue sanctions for non-compliance, the Rules do not explicitly refer to case management orders as such. Some federal courts have linked non-compliance with CMOs with the summary judgment procedure. See Serrano–Perez v. FMC Corp., 985 F.2d 625 (1st Cir.1993); Renaud v. Martin Marietta Corp., 749 F.Supp. 1545 (D.Colo.1990), affirmed, 972 F.2d 304 (10th Cir.1992). See also Atwood v. Warner Electric Brake & Clutch Co., 239 Ill.App.3d 81, 179 Ill.Dec. 18, 605 N.E.2d 1032 (1992) (requiring plaintiffs to certify their personal injury claims and causation; held: trial court possessed authority to bar non-certified claims, and use of partial summary judgment, rather than discovery sanctions, was permissible).

2. PROTECTIVE ORDERS

a. *Non-disclosure Orders*

Courts have issued a wide range of orders designed to protect a party or witness from disclosing information which courts find unnecessarily injurious to a person's legitimate interests. For example, in Eli Lilly & Co. v. Marshall (Hon. John), 850 S.W.2d 155 (Tex.1993), the Texas Supreme Court ruled that Eli Lilly did not have to disclose the identities of health care providers such as hospitals and physicians, which had reported adverse reactions in patients using the antidepressant drug Prozac. The decision arose in a products liability case filed against Lilly by the estate of Michael Hays Biffle, who committed suicide six days after he began using Prozac. The court ruled that the Texas District Court abused its discretion by ordering Lilly to disclose the provider names or face a default judgment on the Biffles' $25 million complaint without requiring the plaintiffs to show "particularized relevance and need" for the information. (See also dissenting opinion at 850 S.W.2d 164 (Tex.1993)).

Doctors voluntarily report adverse drug reactions to pharmaceutical companies, which are then required to provide the information to the Food and Drug Administration. The reports are available from the FDA, but only after the names of the patient and health care provider are redacted. The Texas Supreme Court stressed the public policy behind confidentiality because disclosure of provider names would jeopardize the voluntary reporting system because doctors would fear being pulled into litigation or violating physician/patient confidentiality. It stated:

> To the extent that Lilly has been ordered to act in a manner inconsistent with the public interest concerns manifested by federal law, and without due consideration having been given to those concerns, that order is erroneous as a matter of law.

b. Donor Identification

A frequently debated issue is whether the identities of blood donors, who may have transmitted the HIV or AIDS virus to recipients of blood products, may be subject to protective orders. In Irwin Memorial Blood Centers v. Falconer, 229 Cal.App.3d 151, 279 Cal.Rptr. 911 (1991), plaintiff had received blood products during her heart transplant therapy, and subsequently, tested positive for the AIDS antibody. The trial court issued discovery orders that would authorize a referee to conduct depositions of donors of defendant's blood products behind a screen. A California statute provides:

> To protect the privacy of individuals who are the subject of blood testing for antibodies to the probable causative agent of acquired immune deficiency syndrome (AIDS) * * * no person shall be compelled in any state, county, city or other local civil, criminal, administrative, legislative, or other proceedings to identify or provide identifying characteristics which would identify any individual who is the subject of a blood test to detect antibodies to the probable causative agent of AIDS.

The court held that the trial court's order violated the statute:

> Real parties contend that the orders challenged do not violate section 199.20 because the identity of the donor is completely protected, or can be completely protected if petitioner will cooperate in having the deposition at the blood bank and behind a screen. We cannot agree. The donor will be seen or heard during the deposition by at least the referee and the reporter. The appearance and the voice of a person are obviously identifying characteristics.
>
> More fundamentally, however, the production of the donor for deposition is in itself an identification within the meaning of the statute. * * * Until the time that the donor appears for deposition, the donor is a number unconnected to a person. Once the person is required to step forth, the connection between the number and the person is made. The donor has been identified. The extent to which that identification is made known to third parties will depend upon the care taken at the deposition but the identification in a civil proceeding has been made. This the statute prohibits.

Is the court's reading of the statute too restrictive? How should courts balance the privacy rights of donors and plaintiffs' right to develop their cases?

In contrast to Irwin Memorial Blood Centers, the Supreme Court of Louisiana in Most v. Tulane Medical Center, 576 So.2d 1387 (La.1991) held that the need of a patient at a medical center to discover the identity of the donor of blood which infected the patient with the HIV virus outweighed the privacy interests of the donor and public policy considerations favoring non-disclosure. The patient sought only the identity of the donor of one specific unit of blood, and sought to question the donor about the screening process he went through when donating blood, rather than the details of his personal life. Accord Stenger v. Lehigh Valley Hosp. Ctr., 530 Pa. 426, 609 A.2d 796 (1992); Doe v. Puget Sound Blood Center, 117 Wash.2d 772, 819 P.2d 370 (1991). The relevance of the donor's testimony was the respective plaintiffs argued, to establish whether the blood bank used reasonable care in screening donors by asking donors what questions were asked and what procedures were utilized in selecting the donor.

Some courts are inclined to reject, at least in part, the defendant's and donors' interests in favor of disclosure by permitting inquiry into the validity of their premises. In Watson v. Lowcountry Red Cross, 974 F.2d 482 (4th Cir.1992), the appeals court upheld a lower court order allowing the plaintiff to prepare confidential questions for approval by the defendant. The donor's identity, already known to the Red Cross, would be revealed only to the court and to the court-appointed lawyer. All answers were to be maintained in a sealed envelope marked "confidential," and the answers provided by the donor must have the signature redacted prior to filing. The donor's answers would exclude all references to identity.

The Fourth Circuit held that the district court did not abuse its discretion or violate the donor's privacy rights by ordering discovery. The court remarked that acceptance of defendant's position that even limited discovery would threaten the U.S. blood supply "would amount to a grant of virtual blanket immunity from donation-related liability." The court determined that "there is not one shred of tangible evidence in the nature of hard statistical data to substantiate an otherwise speculative claim that the blood supply will be jeopardized." The dissenting opinion said the public interest in maintaining a safe and adequate blood supply and the blood donor's privacy interest outweigh the plaintiff's interest in deposing the donor and that even the restricted discovery does not adequately protect these important interests.

How would you balance the interests of donors in preserving their privacy and the needs of plaintiffs to develop evidence supportive of their theory of the case?

c. Sanctions for Violation of Protective Orders

Plaintiffs and their counsel must be exceedingly careful not to violate a protective order preserving the confidentiality of a blood donor's identity. For example, in Coleman v. American Red Cross, 145 F.R.D. 422 (E.D.Mich.1993), the federal district judge dismissed plaintiffs' suit against the Red Cross after their attorney hired a private investigator to find out the name and location of the donor whose social security number had been inadvertently disclosed during discovery. Earlier in the case, the district court issued a protective order that was affirmed on appeal restricting the plaintiffs' access to the identity of the donor of the infected blood. After discovering the donor's name and address through a private investigator, plaintiffs' attorney conveyed this information to the plaintiffs and informed defense counsel they had learned the donor's name. The defendants filed an emergency motion for a second protective order.

Treating the question as a motion under Fed. R. Civ. P. 37, which authorizes sanctions for discovery abuse, the district court found four factors relevant to the motion: prejudice to the defendants, warning of probable dismissal for violation of the order, the parties' blameworthiness, and consideration of less drastic sanctions. The prejudice to defendants was based on evidence showing a 13 percent drop in blood donations after a 1992 Detroit Free Press article headlined "Pair Can Sue Donor of AIDS Blood":

> Plaintiffs' violation went to the very heart of the protective order: the perceived need to protect the privacy of the implicated donor and the Southeastern Michigan blood supply. * * * [A]ny party who has complied with a court order to produce is necessarily prejudiced when another party abuses this judicial process to discover protected information. If the case against defendants is not dismissed, plaintiffs will benefit substantially from the deliberate violation by being able to bring suit against both defendants and the donor. This court can find no excuse or mitigating circumstances to explain the flagrant disregard of the court's order and the bad faith and egregious conduct exemplified by plaintiffs and their counsel.

Turning to the parties' blameworthiness, the court observed that the flagrant and deliberate violation of plaintiffs' counsel is imputable to the clients. The court noted that the plaintiffs were not left without a remedy, for they could sue their attorney for malpractice based on his "inexcusable error in judgment." Finally, the court said, "no sanction less drastic than dismissal would suffice to cure the harm suffered by the defendants." Do you agree with the severity of this sanction? What about the court's comment—most unusual—that the clients sue their attorney for malpractice? Is that the best, or the only, remedy?

d. Gag Orders; Sealing of Documents

Orders that require the parties or their counsel not to discuss the case with the media or third parties have been issued in toxic tort litigation. In Davenport v. Garcia (Hon. Carolyn), 834 S.W.2d 4 (Tex. 1992), the Texas Supreme Court, relying on the Texas Constitution's free speech clause, overruled a gag order that had prohibited a guardian ad litem of children exposed to chemicals from a dump site from speaking in public about the case or in private to the children that she represented.

Orders sealing documents that defendants produced in discovery have been subject to challenge, especially after the case has been concluded. In In re Agent Orange Product Liability Litigation, 104 F.R.D. 559 (E.D.N.Y.1985), affirmed, 821 F.2d 139 (2d Cir.1987), a protective order was entered during the discovery and settlement phases of the case protecting some of defendants' documents against disclosure. The Second Circuit recognized that the settlement would not end the public debate about what should be done with respect to veterans exposed to phenoxy herbicides. The court found that the reasons for secrecy had changed since the pretrial phase of the case. The Agent Orange protective order was entered as a way to move the complex case to trial. But once it settled, other factors, such as the public interest in the underlying controversy, required that non-confidential discovery materials be available to the public.

The tobacco litigation has been a fertile source of controversy respecting the sealing of documents. In Public Citizen v. Liggett Group, Inc., 858 F.2d 775 (1st Cir.1988), the First Circuit agreed with arguments by Public Citizen and other health organizations that important public health concerns about tobacco products warranted disclosure of sealed data. In Haines v. Liggett Group Inc., 975 F.2d 81 (3d Cir.1992), the Third Circuit vacated an order of a district court judge that had reversed a magistrate's finding that 1500 documents were entitled to protection from disclosure based on the attorney-client privilege. Judge H. Lee Sarokin had ordered the disclosure because based on his review (and the review of materials in the *Cipollone* litigation, discussed in Chapter 6), the documents revealed that defendants and their research association, the Council for Tobacco Research, had concealed evidence on the health risks related to smoking. Judge Sarokin, in reversing the magistrate, found that the fraud exception to the attorney-client privilege vitiated their protection, and made this stinging rebuke of the industry:

> In light of the current controversy surrounding breast implants, one wonders when all industries will recognize their obligation to voluntarily disclose risks from the use of their products. All too often in the choice between the physical health of consumers and the financial well-being of businesses, concealment is chosen over disclosure, sales over safety, and money over morality. Who are these persons who knowingly and secretly decide to put the buying public at risk solely for the purpose of making profits and who believe that illness and death of consumers is an appropriate cost of their own prosperity! * * * As the following facts disclose, despite some rising pretenders, the tobacco industry may be the king of concealment and disinformation.

The defendants filed a writ of mandamus to the Third Circuit, which it granted. The Third Circuit held that the quoted statements and others justified removal of Judge Sarokin from trial of the case and reversed his order vacating the magistrate because he (1) considered the record in *Cipollone*, which the magistrate did not have before him; (2) incorrectly applied the Federal Magistrates Act, 28 U.S.C.A. § 636(b)(1)(A); and (3) had not "zealously protected" the attorney-client privilege.

e. State Statutes

In the last few years several states have enacted statutes or court rules that seek to limit a party's ability to seal court documents and to narrow the circumstances under which a trial court may grant protective orders for discovery materials after the litigation has settled or concluded. See Florida Sunshine in Litigation Act, West's Fla.Stat.Ann. ch. 69.081 (1992); Vernon's Ann.Tex.R.Civ.P., Rule 76a; Va. Code Ann. § 8.01–42.01 (Michie 1989) (banning unwarranted protective orders that prevent information sharing among attorneys in similar personal injury or wrongful death cases); N.C. Gen. Stat. § 132–12.2 (prohibiting confidential settlements in suits relating to duties of state officials and employees); Act of April 12, 1993, ch. 4.16 and 4.24, West's Rev.Code Wash.Ann. (adding sections similar to Florida's Sunshine in Litigation Act); N.Y. Ct. R. Rev. Part 216 (1991) (prohibiting sealing court records without a finding of good cause and consideration of public interest). For a thorough discussion of these subjects, see Arthur R. Miller, Confidentiality, Protective Orders, and Public Access to the Courts, 105 Harv. L.Rev. 428 (1991).

E.   SETTLEMENTS

It is well recognized that most lawsuits are resolved by a settlement between the parties, rather than by a dismissal or judgment for the plaintiffs. Toxic tort litigation is no different in this regard, but mass toxics cases present particularly difficult issues that may distinguish them from catastrophic mass accident cases.

1.   GENERAL STRATEGY

The following statement, authored by a defense counsel, summarizes some of the principal issues through the eyes of the defense:

> A defendant facing a toxic tort lawsuit is confronted with divergent choices for handling such litigation. On the one hand, there is a desire to pursue an aggressive defense all the way through to trial because the plaintiffs are not believed to be injured and to do otherwise would only encourage the filing of more cases. An aggressive defense dictates high transactional costs in the short run, but hopefully lower transactional costs over the long term.

> On the other hand, a defendant may seek to buy its way out as early as possible in order to reduce litigation costs at a particular toxic site. When to settle is a difficult question, the answer to which will vary from site to site.

> In approaching toxic tort litigation, it is difficult to prescribe a blueprint to be used for each and every toxic substance or site. The identity of the defendants, the identity of the toxic substance and the client's role changes with each site. However, a basic framework

for preparing and resolving your case in your client's best interests can be suggested.

The cost of a trial is significant, but it is only when plaintiffs know that you are willing to "go to the mat" that settlement demands plummet and new case filings decline. The trick is knowing which cases to settle and which to try because if you try the "wrong one" (and lose), then settlement demands and new filings will increase.

There are disadvantages to settlement. It fuels the plaintiffs' war chest against the non-settling defendants, thereby causing feelings of mistrust between your client and the non-settling defendants and enhancing a "soft touch" image among other plaintiffs' attorneys. Non-settling defendants may distrust such a defendant because it did not share in defense costs (thereby reducing their transactional costs) and became a "traitor" to the cause—the cause being to fight the battle through trial to dissuade the filing of meritless cases.

However, sometimes the plaintiffs have a good medical case, i.e., toxin did cause severe physical injury or death. These cases must be taken seriously in today's pro-environmental society and an early assessment of your client's liability should be made. If an opportunity for settlement presents itself, only an unsophisticated defendant would fail to realize that your client had made a "good deal."

Even in non-medically serious cases, if you can pay low value settlements to resolve a large volume of cases, then the resultant savings in transactional costs may be worth it. There is a cost/benefit analysis that must be considered at each site. This analysis can only be made after the facts as to medical causation, damages and liability have been fully developed.

For example, in a recent asbestos "single" case the jury awarded $2.5 million in compensatory damages and $4.5 million in punitive damages. In hindsight, the defendant is surely second guessing itself for not accepting the pretrial demand and settling the case; such a decision would have saved millions. At that point you can't afford to think about how settlement may appear to non-settling defendants. Experience shows that in toxic tort cases plaintiffs will often only settle with only one or two defendants. Thus it is not only sometimes wise to settle, but often becomes a race to settle.

Judging from experience in toxic tort litigation, it is difficult for a company to be both an "appeaser" (i.e., one who will pay money in virtually any case simply to keep litigation costs down) and a "fighter" (i.e., one who will aggressively litigate every case). In my experience, most plaintiffs' attorneys will not settle with a defendant at a low price early in the litigation unless the attorney is convinced that the settling defendant is a marginal or peripherally involved player.

It may therefore be difficult, if not impossible, for a defendant to buy its way out of cases cheaply unless and until the plaintiffs' attorney has identified a sufficient critical mass of "big players." Plaintiffs do not want to risk finding that an early settlement was grossly disproportionate to the settling party's actual liability.

N. Kathleen Strickland, Reducing Costs in Toxic Tort Litigation with Case Management and Defense Cooperation, 7 Toxics Law Reporter 1189–1190 (March 10, 1993) (reprinted with permission). How would you articulate the plaintiffs' viewpoint on each of the concerns that she identifies? Do plaintiffs actually share some of the same problems? For which party whom are transaction costs typically the greater barrier?

Federal courts have issued several rulings rejecting the use of class action devices to manage the trial or settlement of mass tort litigation. In 1997 the Supreme Court decided Amchem Products Inc. v. Windsor, 521 U.S. 591, 117 S.Ct. 2231, 138 L.Ed.2d 689 (1997), overturning the settlement reached by the parties and countenanced by the trial court. The Court held, in an opinion by Justice Ginsberg, that Rule 23 established class action requirements which must be enforced and met in each case, including those involving class action settlements. Thus, the rule limits judicial inventiveness, and that a proposed class has sufficient unity so that absent members can fairly be bound by decisions of class representatives is a crucial concern in both the trial and settlement contexts.

The district court had concluded that the predominance requirement was met because the class members shared the experiences of asbestos exposure and they had a common interest in receiving prompt and fair compensation for their claims. The Supreme Court rejected this conclusion, deciding that the common questions did not predominate over questions affecting only individual members. Further, as Rule 23 also requires that the class representatives fairly and adequately protect the interests of the class, the Court found that this requirement was not met due to the conflicts of interest between the named parties and the class they sought to represent. Named parties had diverse medical conditions, and their interests were neither aligned nor could the representatives represent the single giant class proposed. For those currently injured, a critical goal was generous, immediate payments. This is in conflict with the interest of exposure only plaintiffs which were interested in having an ample, inflation-protected fund for the future. In the Court's view, the settling parties had achieved a global compromise with no structural assurance of fair and adequate representation for the diverse groups and individuals affected.

The Supreme Court observed that it is sensible that a nationwide administrative claims processing regime would provide the most secure, fair and efficient means of compensating victims of asbestos exposure. However, Congress has not adopted such a solution and Rule 23 could not fill this void.

The Supreme Court opinion reversed a trend that had developed over the years that would allow certification of cases "for settlement," a trend premised upon the theory that the interest in resolving mass tort cases justified the expansive interpretation of the rules requiring similarity of claims in a class action. Justice Ginsberg wrote that a "sprawling" case involving claims which are not sufficiently similar created conflicting interests. These conflicts rendered the class plaintiffs inadequate representatives for the class. Justice Ginsberg issued a stern warning to those judges who would bend the federal rules to meet the exigencies of the situation in the interest of simplifying complex case management:

> [O]f overriding importance, courts must be mindful that the rule as now composed sets the requirements they are bound to enforce. Federal Rules take effect after an extensive deliberative process involving many reviewers: a Rules Advisory Committee, public commenters, the Judicial Conference, this Court, [and] the Congress. The text of a rule thus proposed and reviewed limits judicial inventiveness. Courts are not free to amend a rule outside the process Congress ordered, a process properly tuned to the instruction that rules of procedure "shall not abridge ... any substantive right."

* * *

> Federal courts, in any case, lack authority to substitute for Rule 23's certification criteria a standard never adopted—that if a settlement is "fair," then certification is proper. Applying to this case criteria the rulemakers set, we conclude that the Third Circuit's appraisal is essentially correct. Although that court should have acknowledged that settlement is a factor in the calculus, a remand is not warranted on that account. The Court of Appeals' opinion amply demonstrates why—with or without a settlement on the table—the sprawling class the District Court certified does not satisfy Rule 23's requirements.

The Supreme Court continued, focussing now upon the "commonality" requirement of Fed. R. Civ. P. 23(b)(3):

> The predominance requirement stated in Rule 23(b)(3), we hold, is not met by the factors on which the District Court relied. The benefits asbestos-exposed persons might gain from the establishment of a grand-scale compensation scheme is a matter fit for legislative consideration, but it is not pertinent to the predominance inquiry. That inquiry trains on the legal or factual questions that qualify each class member's case as a genuine controversy, questions that pre-exist any settlement.

> But it is not the mission of Rule 23(e) to assure the class cohesion that legitimizes representative action in the first place. If a common interest in a fair compromise could satisfy the predominance requirement of Rule 23(b)(3), that vital prescription would be stripped of any meaning in the settlement context.

The District Court also relied upon this commonality: "The members of the class have all been exposed to asbestos products supplied by the defendants. . . . " Even if Rule 23(a)'s commonality requirement may be satisfied by that shared experience, the predominance criterion is far more demanding. Given the greater number of questions peculiar to the several categories of class members, and to individuals within each category, and the significance of those uncommon questions, any overarching dispute about the health consequences of asbestos exposure cannot satisfy the Rule 23(b)(3) predominance standard.

* * *

That certification cannot be upheld, for it rests on a conception of Rule 23(b)(3)'s predominance requirement irreconcilable with the rule's design.

117 S. Ct. at 2248–50.

However, *Anchem Products* did not sound the death knell for all class action settlements. The Fifth Circuit appeals court upheld for the second time a $1.5 billion class settlement of future asbestos claims against Fibreboard Corp., finding its earlier ruling unaffected by the Supreme Court's *Amchem* decision to strike down a different asbestos class settlement. In re Asbestos Litigation: Flanagan v. Ahearn, 134 F.3d 668 (5th Cir.1998). 90 F.3d 963 (5th Cir.1996), vacated, 521 U.S. 1114, 117 S.Ct. 2503, 138 L.Ed.2d 1008 (1997).

In a terse, 2–1 opinion, the Court of Appeals found two controlling differences between the settlements. It reasoned that the Supreme Court disallowed the settlement in *Amchem* because common issues did not predominate over individual ones and the named parties did not fairly represent the class. But the Fifth Circuit stressed that the *Amchem* accord was certified under Fed. R. Civ. P. 23(b)(3), which requires proof of the predominance of common issues. The *Fibreboard* settlement had been certified as a limited fund under Fed. R. Civ. P. 23(b)(1)(B), which does not require a predominance showing. Second, unlike *Amchem*, the *Fibreboard* settlement contemplated no allocation or difference in awards according to the nature or severity of injury. In *Fibreboard*, all class members—those who had not sued the company by Aug. 27, 1993—were treated alike, with each individual proceeding through a claims resolution process.

In affirming its earlier decision, the Fifth Circuit stressed that after extensive analysis, the district court found the class satisfied the limited fund criteria of Rule 23(b)(1)(B) insofar as separate actions by class members would impair other class members' interests.

While acknowledging that *Amchem* held that a settlement class, like all federal class actions, cannot proceed unless the requirements of Rule 23(a) are met, regardless of whether the proposed settlement is deemed fair under Rule 23(e), the Fifth Circuit noted that its previous opinion upholding the class detailed how the settlement satisfies Rule 23(a): All members of the class, and all class representatives, shared common interests, which is to say, all suffered harm from asbestos exposure and sought equitable distribution of compensation from limited funds. "None of the uncommon questions, abounding in Amchem, exist in this case," the opinion concluded.

2. RELEASES OF FUTURE INJURIES

As we have seen, toxic exposure may produce immediate and manifested injuries or it may produce latent harms that are not manifested for many years, even decades. As a general practice, parties to a settlement execute a general release that settles all liabilities that arise from a particular occurrence. Such general releases, however, may not be binding in toxic tort settlements because releases purporting to discharge liability for unknown injuries often conflict with state statutory law imposing limitations on such releases.

In California, for example, Cal. Civil Code § 1542 provides that a "general release does not extend to claims which the creditor does not know or suspect to exist * * * at the time of executing the release, which if known by him would have materially affected his settlement. * * * Therefore, such statutory public policy will prevail over generalized releases of future injuries in the absence of a clear expression of the parties' intent." California courts have interpreted Civil Code § 1542 as precluding the application of a release to unknown claims in the absence of a showing, apart from the words of the release, of an intent to include such claims. See, e.g., Casey v. Proctor, 59 Cal.2d 97, 28 Cal.Rptr. 307, 378 P.2d 579 (1963).

Even though a release may set forth the statutory language evidencing plaintiffs' intent to waive rights to sue for future injuries, plaintiffs may nevertheless later argue mistake as to the nature and extent of the injuries which are the subject of the release. Therefore, an enforceable release agreement will require that plaintiffs know they are releasing all future injuries resulting from the alleged exposure, whether presently known or suspected, including cancer and death.

What steps would you take to insure that your client fully comprehends a release applying to latent injuries? Should you list all of those conditions for which there exist some epidemiological or toxicological evidence connecting them to the kind of exposure involved? How about future fear of cancer? What risks might such a list create? What steps should defense counsel take to insure that claims for future unknown injuries are released? How would the parties value the consideration for the release of future injuries? In an asbestos exposure case, if the plaintiff currently manifested asbestosis, how would you value the risk of lung cancer or mesothelioma? Defendant will not pay a settlement equivalent to the value of actually contracting cancer, so each party will be assuming some risk—plaintiff will be overcompensated if he never develops a further or more serious disease, but undercompensated if he does.

3. GREEN CARDS AND MEDICAL MONITORING

a. *General Approach*

One solution to the problems created by efforts to settle future and unknown injuries is to preserve explicitly the plaintiff's right to seek redress for subsequently-manifested injuries. Such a provision authorizing future claims should conditions warrant is called a "green card" and is becoming increasingly common in toxic tort litigation. Green card settlements typically require considerable specificity in identifying both the claims released by the settlement and those preserved for future assertion. A green card provision normally incorporates a waiver of the defendant's right to assert a statute of limitations defense as to the claims being preserved. The defendant will obviously prefer not to have a wholly open-ended exposure to liability and will seek provisions requiring plaintiff to assert a claim at the time of earliest manifestation of the condition.

Settlements involving the preservation of future claims are often accompanied by defendant's agreement to fund medical monitoring expenses for some specified period or until the preserved condition manifests itself. If the condition is one for which early detection and treatment are especially beneficial, both parties may reap some economic benefit from the monitoring program. What disagreement are the parties likely to have regarding the funding of monitoring expenses? Must the agreement identify precisely what kinds of tests and examinations are covered? Will negotiations over medical monitoring expenses be influenced by the state's recognition or non-recognition of monitoring costs as compensable damages?

A few examples of settlements involving monitoring may be suggestive of the variety of ways in which that remedy may be implemented.

b. *Three Mile Island*

In the Three Mile Island (TMI) litigation arising of the 1979 accident at a nuclear facility near Harrisburg, Pennsylvania, thousands of individual plaintiffs' actions were consolidated into three classes, two seeking economic losses and a third, Class III, requesting the costs of obtaining medical detection services for those residing within 25 miles of TMI. See In re Three Mile Island, 557 F.Supp. 96 (M.D.Pa.1982). The stipulation and agreement of settlement called for the creation of a $5 million Public Health Fund to finance studies of the long term health effects relating to the accident. The Fund would provide for:

> (b) funding of studies or analyses relating to the possible health related effects (and related studies and analyses) resulting from the TMI Accident and related events and approved, now or hereafter, by the TMI Advisory Board on Health Research Studies * * *

> (c) funding of public education programs involving the general public residing or working within twenty-five miles of TMI or the

medical community within or serving that region on the subjects of [cancer and cancer detection; evacuation procedures; or public education of any nature to reduce stress];

* * *

(e) funding general research into the effects of low level radiation on human health and related studies and analyses.

The results of the epidemiological studies performed pursuant to the settlement may be found in Hatch, et al., Cancer Near The Three Mile Island Nuclear Plant: Radiation Emissions, 132 Am. J. Epidemiol. 397 (1990). See also Three Mile Island Public Health Fund, 1989–1990 Annual Report (1991). What considerations might have resulted in a settlement providing for generalized epidemiological studies, but not including individual plaintiff medical monitoring?

c. *Fernald Litigation*

A comprehensive medical surveillance program resulted from the settlement of the Fernald Litigation which arose out of the release of uranium and other hazardous substances from National Lead's operation of U.S. Department of Energy's Feed Material Production Center in Fernald, Ohio. See, In re Fernald Litig., No. C–1–85–0149 (S.D.Ohio 1985), opinion and order approving settlement, 1989 WL 267039. The settlement is described in Amy B. Blumenberg, Medical Monitoring Funds: The Periodic Payment of Future Medical Surveillance Expenses in Toxic Exposure Litigation, 43 Hastings L. J. 661, 706–708 (1992):

> Plaintiffs sought an order requiring the defendants to establish a fund to pay the medical monitoring costs of all class members and to fund epidemiological studies to determine the adverse health effects of the radiation exposure. An advisory summary jury trial was conducted in 1989 to facilitate pretrial settlement. The summary jury returned a non-binding verdict in favor of the plaintiffs, awarding them a total of one hundred thirty-six million dollars, including eighty million dollars for a medical monitoring fund.
>
> Under the terms of a settlement agreement which the parties reached subsequent to the summary jury trial, the defendants agreed to pay a total of seventy-three million dollars to the plaintiff class. The court appointed three special masters, or trustees, to receive and manage all of the settlement proceeds that formed the Fernald Settlement Fund. The trustees were authorized to develop and administer a medical monitoring program to provide class members with medical examinations and to conduct epidemiological studies.
>
> Pursuant to a court-approved agreement between the Fernald Settlement Fund trustees and the University of Cincinnati, a pilot medical monitoring program was conducted in September and Octo-

ber 1990. Shortly after completion of the pilot program, the Fernald Medical Monitoring Program was fully implemented.

The Program provides uniform diagnostic examinations to Fernald Settlement Fund claimants at the Fernald Program Facility at Mercy Hospital, a Fernald area hospital. Child and adolescent medical examinations are provided pursuant to a contract with Children's Hospital Medical Center of Cincinnati. The Program director provides the Fernald Settlement Fund trustees with monthly reports and quarterly summaries. Because the health of thousands of Fernald area residents will be monitored at the same medical facility by the same staff and with the same procedures, the information gathered may paint a useful picture of the specific health consequences, if any, that result from the plaintiffs' exposure to uranium and other toxic substances.

As of June 1991, the trustees had received more that 5600 applications to participate in the Medical Monitoring Program. As of May 1991, 1175 class members had received medical examinations.

4. DISTRIBUTION OF SETTLEMENT FUNDS

As the material on the asbestos litigation illustrated, there are a variety of distribution formulae that have been applied. For example, the proposed agreement set forth in the asbestos section, supra, used a sliding scale of payments depending on which of certain conditions a claimant manifested.

In the Agent Orange litigation discussed in Chapter 8, Judge Jack B. Weinstein seduced a $180 million settlement from the producers of the herbicide to the Vietnam veterans. The plan called for awards in varying amounts up to $13,800, based on the severity of injuries. To qualify for payment, claimants needed to show only: (1) service in areas where the spraying of Agent Orange was conducted; (2) disability as defined in the Social Security Act; and (3) that their injuries were not accidental, traumatic, or self-inflicted. This type of settlement minimizes battles over the intractable causation issue by establishing criteria that do not require a claimant to offer even colorable evidence of causation. This approach has the principal advantage of lowering transactional costs by simplifying the administration of the settlement proceeds.

5. VALUE PROTECTION PROGRAMS

Many of the toxic tort cases described in this casebook resulted in claims that defendant's release of toxic substances has adversely affected the value of plaintiffs' property, especially in residential areas. Residential homeowners represent special settlement concerns because the value of their properties is typically their most important asset. Of course, property values are influenced by many variables, one of which is the fear that contamination of their properties poses a health risk to the occupants. But see the discussion in Chapter 3 of Adkins v. Thomas Solvent Co., 440 Mich. 293, 487 N.W.2d 715 (1992), where the Michigan Supreme Court held that plaintiffs who alleged diminution in property values could not maintain a nuisance action where the actual contamination of their properties had not occurred. Media publicity and governmental reports can have an extraordinary impact on a neighborhood's property values. One of the innovations that has evolved in recent years to settle toxic tort claims is the value protection program. The elements of such a program may include:

1. Guarantees against loss of property value.

2. Low interest mortgage subsidies.

3. Below–market financing for new buyers.

4. Grants and low interest home improvement loans.

5. Reimbursement of relocation expenses for residents choosing to move.

6. Temporary relocation costs.

Du Pont's Value Protection Programs

In 1990, Du Pont learned that lead and mercury were released from its Pompton Lakes Works facility in northern New Jersey into a creek which fed a flood plain in which over 100 homes with market values between $125,000 and $180,000 were situated. Pursuant to a New Jersey Spill Act Consent Order, Du Pont agreed to remediate the site and affected portions of the community within the flood plain. Du Pont was required to move heavy earth moving equipment and backhoes into the community and remove elevated levels of lead and mercury from homeowners' yards. After Du Pont signed an administrative consent order with the New Jersey Department of Environmental Protection that required it to conduct tests of the water quality in the Brook, it communicated to both the DEP and area residents that the soil in the flood plain was contaminated with metals. To address concerns for potential health consequences from the contamination, Du Pont undertook to test the fish in the Acid Brook and the vegetables in homeowners' gardens. Based upon the results of those tests, Du Pont announced, in conjunction with local public health officials and retained outside experts, that garden vegetables and fish did not create a pathway of exposure that could cause a health problem. The health advisory issued by Du Pont was issued jointly by Du Pont and local health officers.

Du Pont also followed a program of ringing doorbells and dealing with individual community members one on one. The results of soil and vegetable sampling and an analysis explaining the significance of these results were discussed with each individual family in terms of how these results affected that particular family. Du Pont then offered a Value Protection Program which was developed on the basis of discussions with homeowners and experts. Du Pont offered Level I benefits to 135 homeowners which included the following:

    1.   property value protection for three years;

    2.   guaranty of the appreciation rate of property for three years;

    3.   low interest mortgage financing of first or second mortgages or refinancing of existing mortgages, at approximately 3 percent below existing market rates;

    4.   a home improvement restoration benefit for each property for three years pursuant to which Du Pont would pay 75 percent of up to $6,000 of approved costs (25 percent of approved costs are paid by the homeowner. The maximum Du Pont payment is $4,500).

In addition, Du Pont offered benefits to Level I homeowners who left the neighborhood, including property value and appreciation protection, as well as payment of an additional incentive commission to the selling broker equal to 1.5 percent of the sale price at the time of closing and an interest-free bridge loan up to the value of the owner's equity in the affected neighborhood to purchase new property, and relocation expenses.

Level II benefits were offered to 49 homeowners who resided next to Level I beneficiaries but whose property revealed no contamination. They received no value guarantee, but were eligible for home improvement grants.

F. CHOICE–OF–LAW PROBLEMS

Mass tort cases generally, and mass toxic tort cases more particularly, generate complex choice-of-law issues. Judges and practitioners have recognized the problematic choice-of-law problems dogging their mass tort cases. Many of the cases considered in this casebook have involved multiple plaintiffs dispersed across state lines or even if all plaintiffs were situated in one state, defendants or defendants' activities implicating many jurisdictions, with the result that courts have struggled to determine which state's substantive tort law should govern the controversy. As the section on class actions and other aggregative approaches revealed, mass tort cases are often perceived as poor candidates for class treatment because common factual or legal questions may not predominate over individualized questions of causation and damages. The choice-of-law problems provide an additional dimension of difficulty for courts struggling to resolve the "common" versus "individualized" balancing, with the result that many courts have cited choice-of-law problems as a reason for denying class certification. See, e.g., Ikonen v. Hartz Mountain Corp., 122 F.R.D. 258, 265 (S.D.Cal.1988) (denying class certification after holding that the law of the states of the various plaintiffs would need to be separately analyzed and applied to each class member, creating a situation in which common issues of law and fact would not predominate over individual ones); Blake v. Chemlawn Serv. Corp., 1988 WL 6151 (E.D.Pa. 1988) (denying class certification, in part because "choice of law problems would be unmanageable"); Linda S. Mullenix, Class Resolution of the Mass–Tort Case: A Proposed Federal Procedure Act, 64 Texas L. Rev. 1039, 1057 (1986); David F. Boyle, Note, Mass Accident Class Actions, 60 Cal. L. Rev. 1615, 1622 (1972).

Under current law, a federal court exercising diversity jurisdiction will apply the conflicts rules of the forum state based on the Supreme Court's decision in Klaxon Co. v. Stentor Electric Manufacturing Co., 313 U.S. 487, 61 S.Ct. 1020, 85 L.Ed. 1477 (1941). Thus, depending on which of the alternative conflicts approaches the forum state adopts, the federal court analysis will vary from state to state. State courts have adopted four basic approaches to conflicts resolution:

1. LEX LOCI DELECTI: VESTED RIGHTS

A substantial number of jurisdictions apply the choice-of-law principle that looks to the place of the wrong—the state where the plaintiff's legal interest has been invaded as a result of defendant's tortious act. Restatement (First) of Conflicts of Law § 377 (1934) adopted the lex loci or vested rights approach, which offered a moderately simple, consistent, or predictable standard for resolving conflicts issues in tort litigation.

2. MOST SIGNIFICANT RELATIONSHIP

The Restatement (Second) of Conflicts of Law abandoned the vested rights approach in favor of a more complex balancing approach which seeks to identify which state has the "most significant relationship to the occurrence and the parties." Under this approach the courts are expected to examine four kinds of "contacts" by applying seven different principles. According to § 145, the four contacts to be examined are: (1) the place where the injury occurred; (2) the place where the conduct causing the injury occurred; (3) the places of domicile, residence, nationality, incorporation, and business of the parties; and (4) the place where the relationship, if any, between the parties is centered. Moreover, the Second Restatement in § 145(1) does not seek to determine the law to apply to the entire cause of action but rather is addressed to which state has the most significant relationship to "that issue." Hence it is possible for a court to conclude that one state's law is more significantly related to liability questions and another state's law more significantly related to the damages issues.

3. STRONGEST GOVERNMENTAL INTEREST

This approach looks less to the interests of the parties involved and more to the interests of the competing jurisdictions. This "interest analysis" as it is sometimes labeled necessitates the identification and analysis of the policies which underlie each state's law and a determination of whether those policies would result in the state's having an "interest" in seeing its substantive law applied to the controversy. Because the forum state will often possess a strong interest in applying its own law, this approach tends to favor the forum jurisdiction, in the absence of a compelling competing state's interest.

4. OTHER APPROACHES

Finally, at least one state has adopted what is known as the "better law" approach, derived from Professor Leflar's work on conflicts of law. Robert A. Leflar, American Conflicts of Law § 110 (1968); Zelinger v. State Sand & Gravel Co., 38 Wis.2d 98, 156 N.W.2d 466 (1968). This approach focuses on five separate concerns which emphasize judicial administration and the "better" rule of law: (1) predictability of results; (2) maintenance of interstate and international order; (3) simplification of the judicial task; (4) the advancement of the forum's governmental interest; and (5) the application of the better rule of law.

5. PROPOSALS FOR REFORM

Consequently, in dispersed mass tort cases the potential number of applicable state laws is extraordinary, given the interstate nature of many claims relating to Agent Orange, asbestos, DES, Bendectin, breast implants, lead paint, and others.

Faced with these difficulties in resolving mass tort litigation choice-of-law problems, it is not surprising that various proposals have surfaced that would attempt to simplify and unify their resolution. There are at least three basic models that reformers have advanced to manage choice-of-law rules in mass tort cases. See Linda S. Mullenix, Federalizing Choice of Law for Mass–Tort Litigation, 70 Tex. L. Rev. 1623 (1992) for a thoughtful description of the alternative approaches.

a. *Federal Substantive Law*

The first and most dramatic would be for Congress to enact, under its plenary commerce powers, federal substantive tort and products liability legislation that would embrace substantive legal standards, jurisdictional requisites, statutes of limitation, and damages. One of the provisions of CERCLA, 42 U.S.C.A. § 9651(e)(1) as enacted in 1980, called for the establishment of a study group to make recommendations as to the need for and content of a federal toxic tort compensation program. The study group was instructed to "determine the adequacy of existing common law and statutory remedies in providing legal redress for harm to man and the environment caused by the release of hazardous substances into the environment."

Section 9651(e)(3) specified in greater detail that among the issues which the study group should address were "the nature of barriers to recovery (particularly with respect to burdens of going forward and of proof and relevancy)," the "scope of evidentiary burdens placed on the plaintiff," including the impact of scientific uncertainty over causation regarding "carcinogens, mutagens and teratogens" and the effects of low doses of hazardous substances, and barriers to recovery posed by existing statutes of limitation. The internal workings of the study group are described by two members of the group in James R. Zazzali & Frank P. Grad, Hazardous Wastes: New Rights and Remedies? The Report and Recommendations of the Superfund Study Group, 13 Seton Hall L. Rev. 446 (1983).

The study group concluded that the recurring problems encountered by plaintiffs in recovering for physical harm to person or property primarily centered on the statutes of limitation problems, the joinder and combination of parties, and the proof of causation. See Zazzali & Grad, supra, at 454–458 for a fuller explanation of these problems.

The study group issued a two-tiered remedial proposal. The Tier One proposal called for a no-fault compensation system for personal injury resulting from hazardous waste, to be managed by the states but under a federal legislative program. This compensation plan, functioning analogously to a workers' compensation program, would provide full recovery for medical expenses and two-thirds recovery of lost earnings. Under Tier One, "[t]o establish a claim, the claimants must offer proof of exposure, proof of disease or injury, and proof of causation." However, proof of causation would be eased considerably by reliance on appropriate rebuttable presumptions:

> The first rebuttable presumption requires a showing that: (1) the defendant was engaged in a waste activity; (2) the claimant was exposed to such waste; and (3) the claimant suffered resulting injury. Upon proof that the claimant was exposed to waste and suffered injury which is known to result from such exposure, the rebuttable presumption then arises that the exposure proximately caused the death, injury, or disease, and that the source of such exposure was responsible.

In addition, an injured party could pursue a Tier Two tort remedy in state court, but states would be encouraged to adopt five unifying principles to govern such cases:

> (a) The unified adoption of a broad discovery rule, i.e., that the cause of action accrues from the time the plaintiff discovers or should have discovered the injury and its cause;

> (b) the adoption of liberal joinder rules to allow complex issues of causation and liability to be tried together, leaving individual damages to a separate trial if necessary;

> (c) substantive and procedural rules to shift the burden of damage apportionment to the defendants proven to have contributed to the risk or injury;

> (d) the adoption of the rule of joint and several liability; and

(e) application of strict liability which would focus on the nature of the hazardous waste activity and the magnitude of the risk of injury.

The Report, however, rejected use of Tier One rebuttable presumptions and class suits in a Tier Two personal injury claim.

Shortly after the issuance of the Study Group Report, two bills were introduced in Congress, each containing some of the recommendations contained in the report but also with substantial differences. Senator Mitchell (D–Maine) and Senator Stafford (R–Vermont) introduced the Environmental Poisoning Compensation Act, as an amendment to the Federal Insecticide, Fungicide and Rodenticide Act (FIFRA) (S.1486, 97th Cong., 1st Sess., 127 Cong. Rec. S 7694), which would create a private right of action but not include the Tier One compensation plan. Congressman LaFalce (D–New York) introduced a Toxic Victims Compensation Act, which would establish a compensation board similar to the Tier One recommendations. H.R. 7300, 97th Cong., 2d Sess., 128 Cong. Rec. H 8490 (Oct. 1, 1982). When CERCLA was amended in 1986 only the recommendation for a discovery rule was enacted, which is discussed in Chapter 12.

One of the most expansive administrative reform proposals, in the form of a model statute, is authored by Professor Trauberman, entitled Compensating Victims of Toxic Substances Pollutions: A Proposed Model Statute, contained in an article written in 1983. See Jeffrey Trauberman, Statutory Reform of "Toxic Torts": Relieving Legal, Scientific and Economic Burdens of the Chemical Victim, 7 Harv. Envtl. L. Rev. 177 (1983). See also Mullenix, supra, at 1631–33, bemoaning the lack of any serious substantive legislative effort.

b. Federal Common Law

What some have labeled as the first truly mass toxic tort case, In re Agent Orange Product Liability Litigation, 506 F.Supp. 737 (E.D.N.Y. 1979), reversed 635 F.2d 987 (2d Cir.1980), the federal district judge who initially was assigned the case held that federal common law should govern the controversy. Judge Pratt ruled that federal question subject matter jurisdiction applied because federal common law should apply to mass tort claims brought by Vietnam veterans and their families. The court identified three analytical factors in deciding whether to allow the common law tort theories to be governed by a uniform federal approach: "(1) the existence of a substantial federal interest in the outcome of [the] litigation; (2) the effect on this federal interest should state law be applied; and (3) the effect on state interests should state law be displaced by federal common law." Applying these considerations, the court found significant federal interests at stake in the litigation because of (1) the rights of soldiers to be compensated for their harms; (2) the potentially "broad questions about the conduct of military operations"; (3) the legal uncertainty engendered for both war veterans and contractors by the prospect of applying different state laws; and (4) the unfairness of according different legal treatment to litigants who, in all relevant respects, had similar claims. See earlier discussion of federal common law at Chapter 6.

The Court of Appeals for the Second Circuit reversed Judge Pratt. Judge Kearse held that there was no "identifiable federal policy at stake in this litigation that warrants the creation of federal common law rules." Therefore, the cases would be controlled by assorted state substantive law rules relating to statutes of limitation, products liability rules, causation standards, and damages.

As discussed by Professor Peter Schuck, the Second Circuit decision represents "a classic example of the perils of treating [a toxic tort dispute like] Agent Orange as a larger version of a conventional tort dispute. [This] approach, perfectly defensible in the ordinary case in which one or a few soldiers sue concerning a discrete incident, made no sense at all in a mass action going to the heart of a broad federal policy." Peter H. Schuck, Agent Orange on Trial: Mass Toxic Disasters in the Courts 67 (1986).

Five years later, the Fifth Circuit in Jackson v. Johns–Manville Sales Corp., 750 F.2d 1314 (5th Cir.1985), cert. denied 478 U.S. 1022, 106 S.Ct. 3339, 92 L.Ed.2d 743 (1986), in an en banc opinion, similarly rejected the position that the volume, nationwide distribution and complexity of asbestos litigation warranted the adoption of federal common law rules, rather than various state law rules under diversity requirements, to resolve these cases. While acknowledging the "unique nature" of asbestos litigation, the court rejected fashioning a federal common law in asbestos cases and concluded that "ensuring the availability of compensation for injured [asbestos] plaintiffs is predominantly a matter of state concern and, in the absence of congressional enactments, state law, both as to the extent of compensation available and punitive damages, must apply." Moreover, the court articulated a policy reason to support its condition, namely that if it were applied in asbestos cases, "there would be no principled means of restricting the application of federal common law to other matters, either in the context of asbestos litigation or in relation to similar legal problems."

Five judges on the court of appeals dissented from the Jackson en banc decision. The dissenters viewed the problems of mass toxic tort suits as a threat to the continued functioning of the federal judiciary. They observed: "[W]e confront a sequence of massive tort claims that has unparalleled geographic and financial dimensions. We confront cases where the application of divergent governing principles can destroy the rights of similarly situated claimants. We confront no less than a challenge to our purpose as courts." For an analysis of the broader area of federal common law, see generally Martha A. Field, Sources of Law: The Scope of Federal Common Law, 99 Harv. L. Rev. 881 (1986). See also Robert Blomquist, American Toxic Tort Law: An Historical Background 1979–1987, 10 Pace Envtl. L. Rev. 85, 88–89, 123–24 (1992), tracing the history and rejection of federal common law in toxic tort cases.

c. *Federalized Choice of Law*

The bulk of recent proposals focus on the adoption of a federalized choice-of-law approach. The House, in the Multiparty, Multijurisdiction Reform Act of 1991, H.R. 2450, 102d Cong., 2d Sess. (1991), proposed the creation of criteria that a federal judge would apply in determining which states' substantive law should govern the controversy. See also Multiparty, Multiforum Jurisdiction Act of 1990, H.R. 3406, 101st Cong., 2d Sess. (1990) (also providing for a federalized choice-of-law rule). This latter legislation was passed by the House of Representatives under a suspension of the rules by a two-thirds vote on June 5, 1990 and referred to the Senate Judiciary Committee on June 11, 1990. The legislation died in committee through inaction. Professor Mullenix critically describes this legislation:

> Reviewing each scholar's list of relevant preference factors for a federalized, mass-tort choice-of-law scheme tends to induce intellectual vertigo. The apotheosis of this process was epitomized by Congress's first draft version of its Multiparty, Multiforum Jurisdiction Act of 1991, which inadvertently parodied the worst excesses of conflicts law. In this version, Congress would have had a transferee federal judge in a consolidated mass-tort case determine the source of applicable federal law according to the following factors:
>
> > (1) the law that might have governed if the jurisdiction created * * * by this title did not exist;
> >
> > (2) the forums in which the claims were or might have been brought;
> >
> > (3) the location of the accident on which the action is based and the location of related transactions among the parties;
> >
> > (4) the place where the parties reside or do business;
> >
> > (5) the desirability of applying uniform law to some or all aspects of the action;
> >
> > (6) whether a change in applicable law in connection with removal or transfer of the action would cause unfairness;
> >
> > (7) the danger of creating unnecessary incentives for forum shopping;
> >
> > (8) the interest of any jurisdiction in having its law applied;
> >
> > (9) any reasonable expectation of a party or parties that the law of a particular jurisdiction would apply or not apply; and
> >
> > (10) any agreement or stipulation of the parties concerning the applicable law.
>
> Clearly, Congress had serious second thoughts about its federalized choice-of-law rules, because it went back to the drawing board

and reported new draft legislation six months later in November 1991. This version of the bill would have a transferee federal judge determine applicable law in consolidated mass-tort cases according to the following considerably pared-down list:

(1) the principal place of injury;

(2) the place of the conduct causing the injury;

(3) the principal places of business or domiciles of the parties;

(4) The danger of creating unnecessary incentives for forum shopping; and

(5) whether choice of law would be reasonably foreseeable to the parties.

Congress then instructs that "[t]he factors set forth in paragraphs (1) through (5) shall be evaluated according to their relative importance with respect to the particular actions."

Congress's revised approach is a highly distilled pastiche of conflicts concerns: territorialism, contacts, and Erie jurisprudence, with the policy value of foreseeability thrown in for good measure. It is a kind of essence of conflicts law. Congress's latest approach is, more importantly, a fascinating variation on Professor Juenger's proposed rules for mass tort cases (Friedrich K. Juenger, Mass Disasters and Conflicts of Law, 1989 U. Ill. L. Rev. 105, 121–22, 126), which would reduce the choice of law inquiry to what are essentially Congress's first three concerns. Professor Juenger said it first, though. Thus, Professor Juenger would resolve mass tort choice of law problems as follows:

In selecting the rule of decision applicable to any issue in a mass disaster case, the court will take into account the laws of the following jurisdictions:

(a) the place of the tortfeasor's conduct;

(b) the place of injury;

(c) the home state of each party.

As to each issue, the court shall select from the laws of these jurisdictions the most suitable rule of decision.

* * *

The problems with Congress's original ten-factor choice-of-law scheme are evident, and Congress abandoned that idea. Congress's revised five-factor scheme reflects an interesting conflicts triage, but why these factors made the short list can only be subject to speculation and forthcoming legislative history, if the legislators choose to enlighten the citizenry concerning their own conflicts preferences. But if Congress's proposed five-factor list is an improvement over its earlier version, then why is Professor Juenger's three-factor list not an even further improvement? And if Professor Juenger is conceptually correct in suggesting that his list merely embodies the old notion of federal common law, then why not simply go all the way and authorize federal common law?

Published originally in 70 Texas Law Review 1623, 1658–60 (1992). Copyright 1992 by the Texas Law Review Association. Reprinted by permission.

Professors Robert Sedler and Aaron Twerski prepared a thoughtful critique of the draft legislation as well as a Mass Torts Proposal of the American Bar Association. See Robert Sedler & Aaron Twerski, The Case Against All–Encompassing Federal Mass Tort Legislation: Sacrifice Without Gain, 73 Marq. L. Rev. 76 (1989).

Notes and Questions

1. The intuitive appeal for federal substantive law is considerable, particularly when one observes the tremendous judicial management problems engendered by the asbestos litigation catalogued earlier in this chapter. Why has Congress not enacted substantive law to govern mass tort controversies? What interest groups are likely to favor such legislation? What groups are likely to oppose it? Why might Congress be reluctant to federalize tort law? Are there any constitutional impediments?

The Section 301 Study Group recommendations never got beyond the introduction stage in Congress. Why? What is the "conservative" position on these issues—states' rights or pro-business? How might those views differ? What is the "liberal" position—federal government programs or consumer rights?

2. Why have the federal courts been so reluctant to find a sufficient federal interest in mass tort litigation to justify a federal common law? What federal or national interests can you identify that support a federal common law approach? What states' interests cut in the other direction? In Jackson, quoted earlier, the majority refers to the line-drawing problem—if we adopt federal common law in asbestos litigation there is no principled stopping point. How persuasive is this? Is the federal interest in the efficient operation and administration of justice in the federal judiciary a significant factor favoring national common law?

Judge Weinstein, who inherited the Agent Orange litigation from Judge Pratt, proposed a "national consensus law" to govern the litigation. In re Agent Orange Prod. Liab. Litig., 580 F.Supp. 690 (E.D.N.Y. 1984). Is that a workable compromise in mass tort litigation?

3. Are any equal protection problems implied by two plaintiffs injured by the same toxic exposure being subjected to differing states' laws, one recognizing fear of future illness, medical monitoring, and increased risks claims and the other rejecting such remedies? The Second Circuit in Agent Orange dismissed such concerns cavalierly: "The fact that application of state law may produce a variety of results is of no moment. It is the nature of a federal system that differing states will apply different rules of law." 635 F.2d 987, 994 (2d Cir.1980). Is that a satisfactory response to the question?

4. What is your assessment of the proposed federal legislation that would in effect create a statutory Restatement of Conflicts multiple-factor approach? Why hasn't this proposal generated more political support?

The American Bar Association also offered a Federal Mass Tort Jurisdiction Reform Act. See ABA Mass Tort Report (1989). The proposed Act, which is directed at mass toxic tort litigation, and cites the asbestos, Bendectin, Agent Orange, vaccine, and DES litigations, calls for the establishment of a federal judicial panel for mass tort litigation. Whenever at least 100 civil tort actions, claiming damages in excess of $50,000 arising from a single accident, or use of or exposure to the same product or substance, are pending in state or federal courts, the panel may declare the cases "mass tort litigation" and transfer some or all of the actions to a federal court authorized to resolve all issues, including liability and damages. The transferee court may decide which issues should be tried on a consolidated basis, and which issues it wishes to remand for individualized resolution. Acting pursuant to the interstate commerce clause, the legislation sets forth federal question jurisdiction as the grounds for asserting removal power over pending state and federal actions.

However, the ABA-proposed statute would not have adopted federal substantive law, nor did it call for the judicial creation of a federal common law for mass torts. Instead, it sought to empower federal courts to develop their own choice-of-law rules for mass tort cases. In calling for legislative overruling of Klaxon Co. v. Stentor Electric Manufacturing Co. in mass tort cases, the ABA proposal sought the application of the law of a single state to govern the mass tort claim. The only statutory guideline provided to the court was that it makes its determination "in light of reason and experience as to which State(s) rule(s) shall apply to some or all of the actions, parties or issues." Did this represent a better approach?

G. JUDICIAL MANAGEMENT OF SCIENTIFIC AND TECHNOLOGY ISSUES

In Chapter 8, the role of scientific and technological evidence was center stage in resolving seemingly intractable causation questions implicated in much toxic tort litigation. As the opinions in this casebook, especially those in the causation and remedies Chapters, demonstrate, the parties engage in an intensive struggle to obtain expert testimony sufficiently powerful to persuade judge and jury. Moreover, the fact finder's conclusions can have extraordinary impact upon plaintiffs, industries, and government.

A study entitled, "Science and Technology in Judicial Decision Making: Creating Opportunities and Meeting Challenges," A Report of the Carnegie Commission (1993) at 12–13, described the situation facing the judiciary:

> Recent developments in both law and science have conspired to bring increasingly complex scientific issues before the courts for resolution. In particular, the dramatic growth in toxic torts and environmental litigation has put new pressure on the legal system,

which is simultaneously being asked to adjudicate issues on the cutting edge of science and to develop theories of substantive law. This pressure is intense because of the large numbers of people that are involved and the profound social, economic, and public policy concerns that these new legal claims raise.

The growing prominence of science in the courtroom has exacerbated criticism of the courts' management and adjudication of S & T issues. Some allege that "junk science" is flooding the courtroom through the testimony of "experts," whose primary qualification is their willingness to testify in support of their client's position. As a result of these and similar concerns, there have been calls to remove certain categories of cases from the judicial system altogether. While some commentators believe that current legal procedures must be overhauled to deal with these abuses, others go even further in suggesting that the courts, dependent as they are on lay judges and juries, are incapable of properly resolving issues that turn on abstruse principles of epidemiology, toxicology, or statistics. Still others claim that the volume of litigation, as for instance in the cases arising from the use of asbestos, threatens the traditional model of individualized decision making. Given our judicial resources, it may be impossible to treat each case separately.

1. USE OF COURT–APPOINTED EXPERTS

Judges and juries are expected to evaluate complex technological evidence and scientific theories on the basis of the parties' diametrically opposed testimony. One increasingly employed means to assist the court (and often juries) is for the judge to appoint scientific experts who can perform a variety of functions. One study concluded that when experts had been appointed, it was either because of "a thorough disagreement among the parties' experts over interpretation of technical evidence, or when one or more of the parties failed to present expert testimony on a critical issue and the judge perceived an extraordinary need to protect minors or the public health." Joe S. Cecil & Thomas E. Willging, Defining a Role for Court Appointed Experts, Federal Judicial Center Directions, No. 4 at 9 (1992).

Interestingly, however, the same study found that while 87 percent of the federal judges surveyed thought appointment of experts were likely to be helpful in some cases, only 20 percent had ever appointed one under Rule 706 of the Federal Rules of Evidence. Rule 706, Court Appointed Experts, provides in part:

(a) Appointment. The court may on its own motion or on the motion of any party enter an order to show cause why expert witnesses should not be appointed, and may request the parties to submit nominations. The court may appoint any expert witnesses agreed upon by the parties, and may appoint expert witnesses of its own selection. * * * A witness so appointed shall advise the parties of his findings, if any; his deposition may be taken by any party; and he may be called to testify by the court or any party. He shall be subject to cross-examination by each party, including a party calling him as a witness.

Thus, the court-appointed expert can be used for testimonial purposes and be subject to cross-examination by the parties. In that sense, such experts are more aligned with the adversarial process. The objective of the Rule, as described in the Advisory Committee notes, is that the use of court-appointed experts will exert a "sobering effect" on the parties' experts. Moreover, Rule 706 allows the court to inform the jury that the expert is court-appointed which, according to the same study, found a strong correlation between those experts' testimony and the outcomes of the cases in which they testified. Cecil & Willging, supra, at 14.

In Cimino v. Raymark Industries, Inc., 751 F.Supp. 649 (E.D.Tex. 1990), Judge Robert Parker, whose innovative approaches in applying aggregative mechanisms in asbestos litigation are described earlier in this Chapter, appointed an expert in statistics and quantitative methods to determine if the damages phase of the trial, which involved determining category-wide damages from sample plaintiffs in each category, would yield accurate results sufficient to satisfy defendants' due process objections. The expert concluded, and the judge adopted as a finding, that the results would be within a 99 percent level of confidence.

Similarly, Renaud v. Martin Marietta Corp., 972 F.2d 304 (10th Cir.1992), affirming 749 F.Supp. 1545 (D.Colo.1990), illustrates the impact of a court-appointed expert. The federal district judge's expert critiqued the methodology of plaintiff's expert for determining the amount of toxic substances that had reached plaintiff's drinking water by relying on a single data point (water sample) to extrapolate contamination over a large geographic area for an eleven-year period. The court-appointed expert opined that plaintiff's expert's methodology was deficient and "inappropriate," resulting in summary judgment for defendants.

2. SPECIAL MASTERS

In addition, judges may appoint special masters pursuant to Federal Rule of Civil Procedure 53. Such masters can perform a variety of non-testimonial functions, including pretrial tasks such as investigating factual issues; examining and evaluating physical, documentary and oral evidence and issuing a report thereon; administering pretrial tests; and promoting or evaluating settlements. Unlike under Rule 706, the parties do not possess any discovery rights to the work product of the masters. See generally Wayne D. Brazil, Special Masters in Complex Cases: Extending the Judiciary or Reshaping Adjudication, 53 U. Chi. L. Rev. 394, 413–14 (1986); Linda S. Mullenix, Beyond Consolidation: Post–Aggregative Procedure in Asbestos Mass Tort Litigation, 32 Wm. & Mary L. Rev. 475, 547 (1991) ("Mass tort litigation repeatedly demonstrates that the parties need assistance in presenting technical testimony because their own experts are not always sufficient").

3. REASONS FOR UNDERUTILIZATION

Despite their utility, Cecil & Willging identify numerous reasons why judges are reluctant to appoint their own experts, observing that "judges acknowledged that relying only on parties' experts * * * may hinder a reasoned solution to the conflict, but found such concerns to be outweighed by the importance of maintaining the adversarial system and the control exercised by the parties in the presentation of evidence." Cecil & Willging at 8. The study revealed that each of these reasons plays some part in the underutilization of court-appointed experts:

(1) Lawyers' antipathy toward court-appointed experts because of their lack of control over and inability to conduct ex parte communications with such experts.

(2) The lack of an effective referral system from which courts can select an expert.

(3) Reputable scientists may be reluctant to serve as expert witnesses.

(4) The difficulty in structuring compensation even though Rule 706 and Rule 53 explicitly provide for the parties to bear the cost.

(5) The existence of ex parte communications between the judge and the expert causes the parties to object to appointment of such experts, especially Rule 53 masters, who bring knowledge and background to the task that may influence his or her conclusions.

4. RECOMMENDATIONS FOR CHANGE

The Carnegie Commission Report made some findings that were intuitive and interesting:

a. Federal judges have adequate authority under the present Federal Rules of Civil Procedure and of Evidence to manage S & T issues effectively, and the rules of many state judicial systems are modeled on the federal rules.

b. Increased attention to S & T issues at the pretrial stage makes cases more amenable to disposition by summary judgment, facilitates settlement, and leads to more focused, speedier trials.

c. Expert testimony can be made more comprehensible to jurors.

d. Judges and jurors may need information or assistance in handling S & T information that the parties cannot furnish because of insufficient expertise, mismatched resources, or excessive partisanship.

The Report made the following recommendations for addressing these problems (at 16–18):

a. Judges should take an active role in managing the presentation of science and technology issues in litigation whenever appropriate.

Many tools are available to state and federal judges to manage the presentation of S & T issues in litigation. The judicial reference manual and protocols, which are being developed by the Task Force in collaboration with the Federal Judicial Center, are two key elements of the effort to facilitate greater use of these tools.

The reference manual outlines the wide range of techniques that judges have used to manage S & T issues in litigation. It focuses on process and on the encouragement of judicial control. The manual presents judges with a range of options available to resolve a given issue and refers judges to S & T cases where those options have been used; it does not suggest substantive outcomes on contested science and technology issues.

Using the protocols, which are being developed jointly with members of the S & T community, will enable judges to identify and employ techniques that will permit quicker and more effective rulings on challenges to expert testimony, whether those challenges are based on the qualifications of experts, the validity of the theory on which the expert is relying, the reliability of the data underlying the theory, or the sufficiency of the expert's opinion to sustain a verdict.

* * *

b.   Scientific and technical issues should be integrated into traditional judicial education programs, "modules" should be developed that can be appended to existing programs, and intensive programs should be supported.

Judicial education programs play an important role in introducing judges to scientific methodology, which is an essential element in reducing misunderstandings about S & T evidence and in increasing judicial willingness to take an active role in managing that evidence. * * * These programs offer the greatest opportunity to give judges extensive, hands-on experience in dealing with the difficult S & T issues they may encounter in court.

c.   Institutional linkages between the judicial and scientific communities should be developed.

Sustained improvement of judicial decision making on matters of science and technology requires the establishment of institutional ties to encourage greater dialogue and cooperation between the judicial and scientific communities.

(i) The federal and state judiciaries should create S & T resource centers to provide judges with access to the collective experience of their colleagues in case management techniques for S & T issues and to educate judges on scientific methodology. Each resource center would also act as a clearinghouse for substantive scientific information compiled by the scientific community, monitor the impact of S & T issues on the courts, and serve as a bridge for cooperation with the scientific community. * * *

(ii) The scientific community should create a resource center as a counterpart to the proposed judicial S & T resource centers in order to facilitate cooperation among the professional societies and to explore the benefits of continued interaction between the judicial and scientific communities.

(iii) A judicial S & T education clearinghouse should be established to collect and distribute curricula and other materials on science education for judges.

d. An independent non-governmental Science and Justice Council of lawyers, scientists, and others outside the judiciary should be established to monitor changes that may have an impact on the ability of the courts to manage and adjudicate S & T issues; it should also initiate improvements in the courts' access to and understanding of S & T information, including judicial education and communication between the judicial and scientific communities.

Notes and Questions

1. Why might the parties' counsel resist court-appointed experts, apart from the reasons identified above (lack of control and ex parte communications with the court)? Do the materials raise questions respecting the efficacy of the adversarial system in dispensing justice? Do toxic and environmental tort cases raise scientific and technological issues absent from other major categories of litigation? Absent from other kinds of tort cases?

2. Which of the Carnegie Commission recommendations appear most feasible? Which are likely to engender the greatest opposition from trial lawyer associations—defense or plaintiff? How about the appointment of scientific panels to adumbrate or decide the scientific issues which are then only for use by courts? Could a federal judge appoint three experts and authorize them to reach "consensus" on scientific issues before the court?

Index

†